Five hundred copies
of this edition
of the

Connecticut State Register and Manual

were numbered and bound
in cloth.

Photo courtesy of T. Charles Erickson

Photo courtesy of Thomas Giroir

Connecticut's Katharine Hepburn

America is the birthplace of the "movies" and has nurtured the development of what can justifiably be described as an American art form. "Hollywood," as we casually refer to it, is a world that fascinates hundreds of millions and to many seems larger than life. It has an attraction to hyperbole, is accustomed to superlatives, and calls upon them with great frequency and ease.

It seems that every year or season brings us the biggest, boldest or greatest. But, even in such a world, a constellation of "stars," the star of Katharine Hepburn shines as bright as any in that sky. There is something about her that is enduring and eludes easy definition. Certainly there is talent, beauty and intelligence, but many others have possessed these qualities. There is strength and determination—confidence born of conviction, but even these qualities, as dramatic as they are, don't fully explain the esteemed place she holds with her audiences.

It began here. She was born in Hartford, second child of Dr. Thomas N. and Katharine Houghton Hepburn. She grew up on Hawthorn Street, where she began her acting career in a backyard "theater" that her father had built for her. Her mother, an active suffragist, brought her four year old daughter with her to meetings and lectures that advocated equal rights for women.

From there, the facts are widely known. She graduated from Bryn Mawr College; acted in summer stock theater; and achieved success on Broadway in 1932. She has starred in a series of films that continue to be adored and shown to this day, including *Little Women* (1933); *Stage Door* (1937); *Holiday* (1938); *Bringing Up Baby* (1938); *The Philadelphia Story* (1940), in which she recreated the role of Tracy Lord, another Broadway success of 1939; *Woman of the Year* (1942); *State of the Union* (1949); *The African*

Queen (1951); *Summertime* (1955). Throughout the years of success, she has always maintained a home in Connecticut and her affection for her native state has never faded.

Although we associate her with the movies, it cannot be forgotten that her early successes were on the stage. She has been in love with the theater for her whole life. She has breathed life into the words of playwrights from Shakespeare to Philip Barry and has even accepted the challenge of the Broadway musical, singing the role of Coco Channel in 1969.

Nominated 12 times, she has won four Academy Awards—more nominations and awards than any other actor. Her list of Oscar winning performances began with *Morning Glory* (1933) and continued with *Guess Who's Coming to Dinner* (1967), *The Lion in Winter* (1968) and *On Golden Pond* (1981). If there is a common thread running through her most powerful roles, it would be her portrayals of women possessed of true moral courage. The characters she brought to life in films such as *The African Queen, Guess Who's Coming to Dinner?,* and *On Golden Pond* are women who, when faced with a great challenge, find within themselves great reservoirs of strength and resourcefulness.

That strength is always a formidable force. Formidable in real life as well, Katharine Hepburn has been working in theater and film for almost seventy years, still performing in movies with great skill and devotion at the age of 87. She is, unquestionably, one of the most enduring actors in history.

She has been described as radiant, inspiring, and hardworking. But she also treasures a quiet life, avoids the spotlight of celebrity, and is generous in her support of fellow actors, knowing quite well the powerful effect that a few sincere words of encouragement from an accomplished professional can have on an uncertain young actor.

She is an artist, and perhaps that explains it best. We can, each of us, think of one of her films and remember a performance that dazzled us. As we watch her on the screen we cannot help but be caught up in what is happening before our eyes. The willing suspension of disbelief that is critical to the success of any artistic effort is made to appear effortless. We do not see a performance, we see life—perhaps the greatest tribute that we can pay her. That is the magic that all artists seek and so few find: to be able to capture that spark, that indescribable something that turns the ordinary or the studied into something charged with the truth, an experience that moves us and remains with us forever.

She is an individual whose signature attributes include intelligence and beauty, strength and determination, brashness and conviction, humility and kindness. She has that spark, that something, that we can only struggle to describe. The Connecticut State Register and Manual salutes an extraordinary artist whose artistry we will have the pleasure of enjoying for generations. She is our neighbor and friend. She is Connecticut's "local girl"—Katharine Hepburn.

Miles S. Rapoport
Secretary of the State

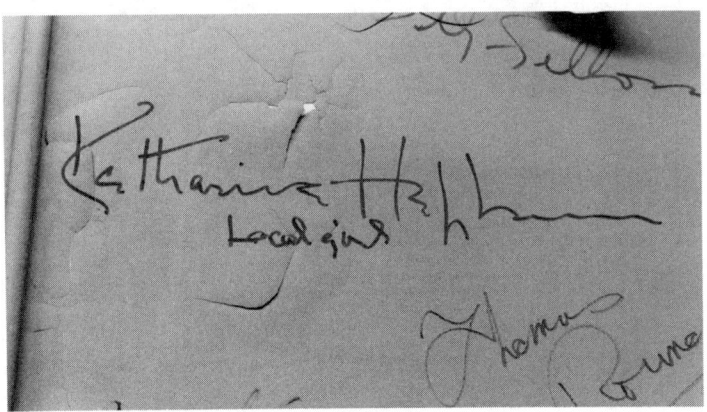

Photo courtesy of The Bushnell

Table of Contents

Section I—Historical

The Declaration of Independence 3
Constitution of the United States 8
Constitution of the State of Connecticut, 1965 26
The First Constitution of Connecticut 55
Charter of the Colony of Connecticut, 1662 60
Selected Dates in Connecticut's History 67

Historical Rosters:
    U.S. Presidents and Vice Presidents 70
    U.S. Senators from Connecticut 72
    U.S. Representatives in Congress from Connecticut 74
    Connecticut Elective State Officers 80
    Connecticut Chief Justices 95
    Presidents Pro Tempore of the Connecticut State Senate 97
    Speakers of the Connecticut House of Representatives 99

Section II—Biographies and Photographs

President of the United States 104
Connecticut Elective State Officers 106
United States Senators from Connecticut 118
United States Representatives from Connecticut 122
Leaders of the Connecticut General Assembly, 1997-98 134
Justices of the Connecticut Supreme Court 146
Judges of the Connecticut Appellate Court 150

Section III—State Government-Legislative

Joint Committee on Legislative Management	157
Auditors of Public Accounts	157
Legislative Commissioners' Office	157
Office of Legislative Research	157
Office of Fiscal Analysis	158
Office of Senate and House Clerks	158
Finance Advisory Committee	161
Members and Officers of the State Senate, 1997-98	162
Members and Officers of the House of Representatives, 1997-98	165
Alphabetical Roll of the Senate and House of Representatives, 1997-98	177
Legislative Committees, 1997	181
Sessions of the General Assembly Since 1884	188
Political Division of the Conn. General Assembly Since 1887	192
Officials and Their Duties	196
Enactment of Bills	199

Section IV—State Government-Executive and Administrative

Elective State Officers and Personnel	205
State Departments and Related Agencies, Boards and Commissions	214

Section V—State Government-Judicial

Supreme Court	301
Appellate Court	301
Superior Court	302
Chief Court Administrator, Office of	307
Administrative Services	307
Judicial Districts	311
Geographical Areas GA's	314
Juvenile Matters	318
Division of Public Defender Services	319

Practice of Law—Admission to the Bar 320
Probate Courts 321

Section VI—Counties

County Sheriffs 337
Composition of Counties 342

Section VII—Local Government

Dates of Town, City and Borough Elections 345
Cities and Boroughs in Connecticut with Date of Incorporation 346
Grand Lists, Tax Rates and Due Dates 347
Towns, Cities and Boroughs—Officers and Statistics 354
Regional Councils of Governments 597
Regional Planning Agencies 602
Regional and Municipal Transit Districts 606
Population of Connecticut by Counties 609
Population of Towns, 1800-1990 610
Post Offices in Connecticut (Towns, Villages and Districts
   with Post Office of Same Name) 613
Towns, Villages and Districts with no Post Office of Same Name .. 617
Distances to all Towns in Connecticut from Hartford 629
Connecticut Towns in the Order of their Establishment 631

Section VIII—Political

State Central Committees 643
Town Chairpersons and Vice Chairpersons 647

Election Statistics:
   Connecticut Congressional Districts 657
   Connecticut Senatorial Districts 663
   Connecticut Assembly Districts 669
   Towns as Districted for Election Purposes 678
   Electoral Votes for President, 1964-1996 682

Summary Vote for President, 1996 683
Vote for President, 1996 685
Vote for U.S. Representatives in Congress, 1996 689
Summary Vote for State Officers, 1994 694
Summary Vote for U.S. Senator, 1994 695
Vote for State Senators, 1996 696
Vote for State Representatives, 1994 705
Vote for State Representatives, Special Elections 729
Summary of Vote for Proposed Constitutional Amendment,
  November 5, 1996 730
Election Day Registration, Turnout, and Absentee Ballot
  Statistics, November 5, 1996 735
Registration and Party Enrollment as of October 22, 1996 741

Section IX—United States Government

U.S. Government—Executive and Judiciary 747
Members of 105th Congress, 1st Session 748
U.S. Courts Serving Connecticut 754
U.S. Departments and Agencies Serving Connecticut 757
U.S. and Territories 764

Section X—Miscellaneous

Historical Societies 769
General Museums 782
Public Libraries 791
Press of Connecticut 796
Radio Stations and TV Stations 807
Selected Facts about Connecticut 815
Legal Holidays in Connecticut 820
Medal of Honor Recipients 821
Illustrations and Descriptions of State Seal, State Flag
  and other Emblems 825

Index 841

State of Connecticut

REGISTER & MANUAL

1997

SECTION I

HISTORICAL

The Declaration of Independence

Constitution of the United States

Constitution of the
State of Connecticut, 1965

The First Constitution
of Connecticut

Charter of the
Colony of Connecticut, 1662

Selected Dates in
Connecticut's History

Historical Rosters

PREFACE TO THE
DECLARATION OF INDEPENDENCE

The Declaration of Independence is generally regarded as one of the most famous documents in the history of the world. On June 10, 1776, the Continental Congress appointed a committee, consisting of Thomas Jefferson, Benjamin Franklin, John Adams, Roger Sherman and Robert R. Livingston to draft a Declaration of Independence.

Jefferson wrote out a rough draft of the Declaration, which was carefully revised by the committee and presented to Congress for adoption. After some further slight revisions by that body, it was adopted on July 4, 1776, at Philadelphia.

The parchment with the original signatures was deposited with the Department of State when the government was organized in 1789.

The original Declaration of Independence was transferred from the Department of State, by direction of the late President Warren G. Harding, to the Library of Congress. In 1952, at the direction of Congress, it was transferred to the National Archives Building, Washington, D.C., where it rests today.

THE DECLARATION OF INDEPENDENCE

In Congress, July 4, 1776

THE UNANIMOUS DECLARATION
of the
THIRTEEN UNITED STATES OF AMERICA

When, in the course of human events, it becomes necessary for one people to dissolve the political bands which have connected them with another, and to assume, among the powers of the earth, the separate and equal station to which the laws of nature and of nature's God entitle them, a decent respect to the opinions of mankind requires that they should declare the causes which impel them to the separation.

We hold these truths to be self-evident, that all men are created equal, that they are endowed, by their Creator, with certain unalienable rights, that among these are life, liberty, and the pursuit of happiness.—That to secure these rights, governments are instituted among men, deriving their just powers from the consent of the governed, that whenever any form of government becomes destructive of these ends, it is the right of the people to alter or to abolish it, and to institute new government, laying its foundation on such principles, and organizing its powers in such form, as to them shall seem most likely to effect their safety and happiness. Prudence, indeed, will dictate, that governments long established, should not be changed for light and transient causes; and accordingly all experience hath shown, that mankind are more disposed to suffer, while evils are sufferable, than to right themselves by abolishing the forms to which they are accustomed. But when a long train of abuses and usurpations, pursuing invariably the same object, evinces a design to reduce them under absolute despotism, it is their right, it is their duty, to throw off such government, and to provide new guards for their future security. Such has been the patient sufferance of these Colonies; and such is now the necessity which constrains them to alter their former systems of government. The history of the present King of Great Britain is a history of repeated injuries and usurpations, all having in direct object the establishment of an absolute tyranny over these States. To prove this, let facts be submitted to a candid world.

He has refused his assent to laws, the most wholesome and necessary for the public good.

He has forbidden his governors to pass laws of immediate and pressing importance, unless suspended in their operations till his assent should be obtained; and when so suspended, he has utterly neglected to attend to them.

He has refused to pass other laws for the accommodation of large districts of people, unless those people would relinquish the right of representation in the legislature, a right inestimable to them, and formidable to tyrants only.

He has called together legislative bodies at places unusual, uncomfortable, and distant from the depository of their public records, for the sole purpose of fatiguing them into compliance with his measures.

He has dissolved representative houses repeatedly, for opposing with manly firmness his invasions on the rights of the people.

He has refused for a long time, after such dissolutions, to cause others to be elected; whereby the legislative powers, incapable of annihilation, have returned to the people at large for their exercise; the State remaining, in the meantime, exposed to all the dangers of invasion from without, and convulsions within.

He has endeavored to prevent the population of these States; for that purpose obstructing the laws for naturalization of foreigners; refusing to pass others to encourage their migrations hither, and raising the conditions of new appropriations of lands.

He has obstructed the administration of justice, by refusing his assent to laws for establishing judiciary powers.

He has made judges dependent on his will alone, for the tenure of their offices, and the amount and payment of their salaries.

He has erected a multitude of new offices, and sent hither swarms of officers to harass our people, and eat out their substance.

He has kept among us, in times of peace, standing armies, without the consent of our legislatures.

He has affected to render the military independent of and superior to the civil power.

He has combined with others to subject us to a jurisdiction foreign to our constitution, and unacknowledged by our laws; giving his assent to their acts of pretended legislation:

For quartering large bodies of armed troops among us:

For protecting them, by a mock trial, from punishment for any murders which they should commit on the inhabitants of these States:

For cutting off our trade with all parts of the world:

For imposing taxes on us without our consent:

For depriving us, in many cases, of the benefits of trial by jury:

For transporting us beyond seas to be tried for pretended offences:

For abolishing the free system of English laws in a neighboring province, establishing therein an arbitrary government, and enlarging its boundaries, so as to render it at once an example and fit instrument for introducing the same absolute rule into these Colonies:

For taking away our charters, abolishing our most valuable laws, and altering fundamentally the forms of our governments:

For suspending our own legislatures, and declaring themselves invested with power to legislate for us in all cases whatsoever.

He has abdicated government here, by declaring us out of his protection, and waging war against us.

He has plundered our seas, ravaged our coasts, burnt our towns, and destroyed the lives of our people.

He is, at this time, transporting large armies of foreign mercenaries to complete the works of death, desolation, and tyranny, already begun with circumstances of cruelty and perfidy, scarcely paralleled in the most barbarous ages, and totally unworthy the head of a civilized nation.

He has constrained our fellow-citizens, taken captive on the high seas, to bear arms against their country, to become the executioners of their friends and brethren, or to fall themselves by their hands.

He has excited domestic insurrections amongst us, and has endeavored to bring on the inhabitants of our frontiers, the merciless Indian savages, whose known rule of warfare is an undistinguished destruction of all ages, sexes, and conditions.

In every stage of these oppressions we have petitioned for redress in the most humble terms: our repeated petitions have been answered only by repeated injury. A prince, whose character is thus marked by every act which may define a tyrant, is unfit to be the ruler of a free people.

Nor have we been wanting in attentions to our British brethren. We have warned them, from time to time, of attempts by their legislature to extend an unwarrantable jurisdiction over us. We have reminded them of the circumstances of our emigration and settlement here. We have appealed to their native justice and magnanimity, and we have conjured them by the ties of our common kindred to disavow these usurpations, which would inevitably interrupt our connections and correspondence. They, too, have been deaf to the voice of justice and of consanguinity. We must, therefore, acquiesce in the necessity, which denounces our separation, and hold them, as we hold the rest of mankind, enemies in war, in peace friends.

We, therefore, the Representatives of the United States of America, in General Congress assembled, appealing to the Supreme Judge of the world for the rectitude of our intentions, do, in the name, and by the authority of the good people of these Colonies, solemnly publish and declare, that these United Colonies are, and of right ought to be, *free and independent States;* that they are absolved from all allegiance to the British crown, and that all political connection between them and the State of Great Britain is, and ought to be, totally dissolved; and that as *free and independent States* they have full power to levy war, conclude peace, contract alliances, establish commerce, and to do all other acts and things which *independent States* may of right do. And for the support of this declaration, with a firm reliance on the protection of Divine Providence, we mutually pledge to each other our lives, our fortunes, and our sacred honour.

JOHN HANCOCK.

New Hampshire,

Josiah Bartlett,
Wm. Whipple,
Matthew Thornton;

Massachusetts Bay,

Saml. Adams,
John Adams,
Robt. Treat Pain,
Elbridge Gerry;

Rhode Island etc.,

Step. Hopkins,
William Ellery;

Delaware

Caesar Rodney,
Geo. Read,
Tho. M'Kean;

Connecticut,

Roger Sherman,
Saml. Huntington,
Wm. Williams,
Oliver Wolcott;

Maryland,

Samuel Chase,
Wm. Paca,
Thos. Stone,
Charles Carroll,
of Carrolton;

New York,

Wm. Floyd,
Phil Livingston,
Frans. Lewis,
Lewis Morris;

New Jersey,

Richd. Stockton,
Jno. Witherspoon,
Fras. Hopkinson,
John Hart,
Abra. Clark;

Pennsylvania,

Robt. Morris,
Benjamin Rush,
Benja. Franklin,
John Morton,
Geo. Clymer,
Jas. Smith,
Geo. Taylor,
James Wilson,
Geo. Ross;

Virginia,

George Wythe,
Richard Henry Lee,
Thos. Jefferson,
Benja. Harrison,
Thos. Nelson, jr.,
Francis Lighfoot Lee,
Carter Braxton;

North Carolina,

Wm. Hooper,
Joseph Hewes,
John Penn;

South Carolina,

Edward Rutledge,
Thos. Heyward, junr.,
Thomas Lynch, junr.,
Arthur Middleton;

Georgia,

Button Gwinnett,
Lyman Hall,
Geo. Walton.

IN CONGRESS,
January 18, 1777.

Ordered

That an authenticated copy of the Declaration of independence, with the names of the Members of Congress subscribing the same, be sent to each of the United States, and that they be desired to have the same put on record.

JOHN HANCOCK,
President.

By Order of Congress,
Attest, CHAS. THOMSON,
    Secy.

A true copy,
JOHN HANCOCK,
  Presidt.

PREFACE TO THE
UNITED STATES CONSTITUTION

The United States Constitution is the oldest federal constitution in existence. It was so well framed that it has served as the basis for this government for two centuries. Only once has it been seriously endangered, this being during the Civil War. Many of its principles have been adopted by other countries.

The Constitution was the outgrowth of a convention of delegates from the different states that met in Philadelphia in May, 1787, Rhode Island not being represented. George Washington presided over the convention, which lasted from May to September.

The Constitution was then submitted to the then existing states for ratification, with a provision that it should become effective when ratified by nine states. New Hampshire was the ninth state to ratify, June 21, 1788, and the Constitution went into effect in 1789.

The states ratified the Constitution in the following order: Delaware, Dec. 7; Pennsylvania, Dec. 12, and New Jersey, Dec. 18, 1787; Georgia, Jan. 2; Connecticut, Jan. 9; Massachusetts, Feb. 6; Maryland, Apr. 28; South Carolina, May 23; New Hampshire, June 21; Virginia, June 25, and New York, July 26, 1788; North Carolina, Nov. 21, 1789, and Rhode Island, May 29, 1790.

*CONSTITUTION OF THE UNITED STATES OF AMERICA (PREAMBLE.)

WE THE PEOPLE OF THE UNITED STATES, in Order to form a more perfect Union, establish Justice, insure domestic Tranquility, provide for the common defence, promote the general Welfare, and secure the Blessings of Liberty to ourselves and our Posterity, do ordain and establish this Constitution for the United States of America.

ARTICLE I.

Section 1. All legislative Powers herein granted shall be vested in a Congress of the United States, which shall consist of a Senate and House of Representatives.

Section 2. The House of Representatives shall be composed of Members chosen every second Year by the People of the several States, and the Electors in each State shall have the Qualifications requisite for Electors of the most numerous Branch of the State Legislature.

No Person shall be a Representative who shall not have attained to the Age of twenty five Years, and been seven Years a Citizen of the United States, and who shall not, when elected be an Inhabitant of that State in which he shall be chosen.

Representatives and direct Taxes shall be apportioned among the several States which may be included within this Union, according to their respective Numbers, which shall be determined by adding to the whole Number of free Persons, including those bound to Service for a Term of Years, and excluding Indians not taxed, three fifths of all other Persons. The actual Enumeration shall be made within three Years after the first Meeting of the Congress of the United States, and within every subsequent Term of ten Years in such Manner as they shall by Law direct. The Number of Representatives shall not exceed one for every thirty Thousand, but each State shall have at Least one Representative; and until such enumeration shall be made, the State of New Hampshire shall be entitled to chuse three, Massachusetts eight, Rhode Island and Providence Plantations one, Connecticut five, New York six, New Jersey four, Pennsylvania eight, Delaware one, Maryland six, Virginia ten, North Carolina five, South Carolina five and Georgia three.

When vacancies happen in the Representation from any State, the Executive Authority thereof shall issue Writs of Election to fill such Vacancies.

The House of Representatives shall chuse their Speaker and other Officers; and shall have the sole Power of Impeachment.

Section 3. The Senate of the United States shall be composed of two Senators from each State, chosen by the Legislature thereof, for six Years; and each Senator shall have one Vote.

Immediately after they shall be assembled in Consequence of the first Election, they shall be divided as equally as may be into three Classes.

The Seats of the Senators of the first Class shall be vacated at the Expiration of the second Year, of the second Class at the Expiration of the fourth Year, and of the third Class at the Expiration of the sixth Year, so that one third may be chosen every second Year; and if Vacancies happen by Resignation, or otherwise, during the Recess of the Legislature of any State, the Executive thereof

---

*Connecticut ratified the Constitution Jan. 9, 1788, having been the fifth State to vote for ratification.

may make temporary Appointments until the next Meeting of the Legislature, which shall then fill such Vacancies.

No Person shall be a Senator who shall not have attained to the Age of thirty Years, and been nine Years a Citizen of the United States, and who shall not, when elected, be an Inhabitant of that State for which he shall be chosen.

The Vice President of the United States shall be President of the Senate, but shall have no Vote unless they be equally divided.

The Senate shall chuse their other Officers, and also a President pro tempore, in the Absence of the Vice President, or when he shall exercise the Office of President of the United States.

The Senate shall have the sole Power to try all Impeachments. When sitting for that Purpose they shall be on Oath or Affirmation. When the President of the United States is tried, the Chief Justice shall preside: And no Person shall be convicted without the Concurrence of two thirds of the Members present.

Judgment in Cases of Impeachment shall not extend further than to removal from Office, and disqualification to hold and enjoy any Office of honor, Trust or Profit under the United States: but the Party convicted shall nevertheless be liable and subject to Indictment, Trial, Judgment and Punishment, according to Law.

Section 4. The Times, Places and Manner of holding Elections for Senators and Representatives, shall be prescribed in each State by the Legislature thereof; but the Congress may at any time by Law make or alter such Regulations, except as to the Places of chusing Senators.

The Congress shall assemble at least once in every Year, and such Meetings shall be on the first Monday in December, unless they shall by Law appoint a different Day.

Section 5. Each House shall be the Judge of the Elections, Returns and Qualifications of its own Members, and a Majority of each shall constitute a Quorum to do Business; but a smaller Number may adjourn from day to day, and may be authorized to compel the Attendance of absent Members, in such Manner, and under such Penalties as each House may provide.

Each House may determine the Rules of its Proceedings, punish its Members for disorderly Behavior, and with the Concurrence of two thirds, expel a Member.

Each House shall keep a Journal of its Proceedings, and from time to time publish the same, excepting such Parts as may in their Judgment require Secrecy; and the Yeas and Nays of the Members of either House on any question shall, at the Desire of one fifth of those Present, be entered on the Journal.

Neither House, during the Session of Congress, shall without the Consent of the other, adjourn for more than three days, nor to any other Place than that in which the two Houses shall be sitting.

Section 6. The Senators and Representatives shall receive a Compensation for their Services, to be ascertained by Law, and paid out of the Treasury of the United States. They shall in all Cases, except Treason, Felony and Breach of the Peace, be privileged from Arrest during their Attendance at the Session of their respective Houses, and in going to and returning from the same; and for any Speech or Debate in either House, they shall not be questioned in any other Place.

No Senator or Representative shall, during the Time for which he was elected, be appointed to any civil Office under the Authority of the United States, which shall have been created, or the Emoluments whereof shall have been encreased during such time; and no Person holding any Office under the United States, shall be a Member of either House during his Continuance in Office.

Section 7. All Bills for raising Revenue shall originate in the House of Representatives; but the Senate may propose or concur with Amendments as on other Bills.

Every Bill which shall have passed the House of Representatives and the Senate, shall, before it becomes a Law, be presented to the President of the United States; If he approve he shall sign it, but if not, he shall return it, with his Objections to that House in which it shall have originated, who shall enter the Objections at large on their Journal, and proceed to reconsider it. If after such Reconsideration two-thirds of that House shall agree to pass the Bill, it shall be sent, together with the Objections to the other House, by which it shall likewise be reconsidered, and if approved by two-thirds of that House, it shall become a Law. But in all such Cases the Votes of both Houses shall be determined by yeas and nays, and the Names of the Persons voting for and against the Bill shall be entered on the Journal of each House respectively. If any Bill shall not be returned by the President within ten Days (Sundays excepted) after it shall have been presented to him, the Same shall be a Law, in like Manner as if he had signed it, unless the Congress by their Adjournment prevent its Return, in which Case it shall not be a law.

Every Order, Resolution, or Vote to which the Concurrence of the Senate and House of Representatives may be necessary (except on a question of Adjournment) shall be presented to the President of the United States; and before the Same shall take Effect, shall be approved by him, or being disapproved by him, shall be repassed by two-thirds of the Senate and House of Representatives, according to the Rules and Limitations prescribed in the Case of a Bill.

Section 8. The Congress shall have Power To lay and collect Taxes, Duties, Imposts and Excises, to pay the Debts and provide for the common Defence and general Welfare of the United States; but all Duties, Imposts and Excises shall be uniform throughout the United States;

To borrow Money on the credit of the United States;

To regulate Commerce with foreign Nations, and among the several States, and with the Indian Tribes;

To establish an uniform Rule of Naturalization and uniform Laws on the subject of Bankruptcies throughout the United States;

To coin Money, regulate the Value thereof, and of foreign Coin, and fix the Standard of Weights and Measures;

To provide for the Punishment of counterfeiting the Securities and current Coin of the United States;

To establish Post Offices and post Roads;

To promote the Progress of Science and useful Arts, by securing for limited Times to Authors and Inventors the exclusive Right to their respective Writings and Discoveries;

To constitute Tribunals inferior to the supreme Court;

To define and punish Piracies and Felonies committed on the high Seas, and Offences against the Law of Nations;

To declare War, grant Letters of Marque and Reprisal, and make Rules concerning Captures on Land and Water;

To raise and support Armies, but no Appropriation of Money to that Use shall be for a longer Term than two Years;

To provide and maintain a Navy;

To make Rules for the Government and Regulation to the land and naval Forces;

To provide for calling forth the Militia to execute the Laws of the Union, suppress Insurrections and repel Invasions;

To provide for organizing, arming, and disciplining, the Militia, and for governing such Part of them as may be employed in the Service of the United States, reserving to the States respectively, the Appointment of the Officers, and the Authority of Training the Militia according to the discipline prescribed by Congress;

To exercise exclusive Legislation in all Cases whatsoever, over such District (not exceeding ten Miles square) as may, by Cession of particular States, and the Acceptance of Congress, become the Seat of the Government of the United States, and to exercise like Authority over all Places purchased by the Consent of the Legislature of the State in which the Same shall be, for the Erection of Forts, Magazines, Arsenals, Dock-Yards and other needful Building;—And

To make all Laws which shall be necessary and proper for carrying into Execution the foregoing Powers, and all other Powers vested by this Constitution in the Government of the United States, or in any Department or Officer thereof.

Section 9. The Migration or Importation of such Persons as any of the States now existing shall think proper to admit, shall not be prohibited by the Congress prior to the Year one thousand eight hundred and eight, but a Tax or duty may be imposed on such Importation, not exceeding ten dollars for each Person.

The Privilege of the Writ of Habeas Corpus shall not be suspended, unless when in Cases of Rebellion or Invasion the public Safety may require it.

No bill of Attainder or ex post facto Law shall be passed.

No Capitation, or other direct Tax shall be laid, unless in Proportion to the Census or Enumeration herein before directed to be taken.

No Tax or Duty shall be laid on Articles exported from any State.

No Preference shall be given by any Regulation of Commerce or Revenue to the Ports of one State over those of another; nor shall Vessels bound to, or from, one State, be obliged to enter, clear, or pay Duties in another.

No Money shall be drawn from the Treasury, but in Consequence of Appropriations made by Law; and a regular Statement and Account of the Receipts and Expenditures of all public Money shall be published from time to time.

No Title of Nobility shall be granted by the United States: And no Person holding any office of Profit or Trust under them, shall, without the Consent of the Congress accept of any present, Emolument, Office, or Title, of any kind whatever, from any King, Prince, or foreign State.

Section 10. No State shall enter into any Treaty, Alliance, or Confederation; grant Letters of Marque and Reprisal; coin Money; emit Bills of Credit; make any Thing but gold and silver Coin a Tender in Payment of Debts; pass any Bill of Attainder, ex post facto Law, or Law impairing the Obligation of Contracts, or grant any Title of Nobility.

No State shall, without the Consent of the Congress, lay any Imposts or Duties on Imports or Exports, except what may be absolutely necessary for executing its inspection Laws; and the net Produce of All Duties and Imposts, laid by any State on Imports or Exports, shall be for the Use of the Treasury of the United States: and all such Laws shall be subject to the Revision and Controul of the Congress.

No State shall, without the Consent of Congress, lay any Duty of Tonnage, keep Troops, or Ships of War in time of Peace, enter into any Agreement or Compact with another State, or with a foreign Power, or engage in War, unless actually invaded, or in such imminent Danger as will not admit of delay.

ARTICLE II.

Section 1. The executive Power shall be vested in a President of the United States of America. He shall hold his Office during the Term of four Years, and, together with the Vice President, chosen for the same Term, be elected, as follows:

Each State shall appoint, in such Manner as the Legislature thereof may direct, a Number of Electors, equal to the whole Number of Senators and Representatives to which the State may be entitled in the Congress: but no Senator or Representative or Person holding an office of Trust or Profit under the United States, shall be appointed an Elector.

The Electors shall meet in their respective States, and vote by Ballot for two Persons, of whom one at least shall not be an Inhabitant of the same State with themselves. And they shall make a List of all the Persons voted for, and of the Number of Votes for each; which List they shall sign and certify, and transmit sealed to the Seat of the Government of the United States, directed to the President of the Senate. The President of the Senate shall, in the Presence of the Senate and House of Representatives, open all the Certificates, and the Votes shall then be counted. The Person having the greatest Number of Votes shall be the President, if such Number be a Majority of the whole Number of Electors appointed; and if there be more than one who have such Majority, and have an equal Number of Votes, then the House of Representatives shall immediately chuse by Ballot one of them for President; and if no Person have a Majority, then from the five highest on the list the said House shall in like Manner chuse the President. But in chusing the President, the Votes shall be taken by States, the Representation from each State having one Vote; a quorum for this Purpose shall consist of a Member or Members from two-thirds of the States, and a Majority of all the States shall be necessary to a Choice. In every Case, after the Choice of the President, the Person having the greatest Number of Votes of the Electors shall be the Vice President. But if there should remain two or more who have equal Votes, the Senate shall chuse from them by Ballot the Vice President.

The Congress may determine the Time of chusing the Electors, and the Day on which they shall give their Votes; which Day shall be the same throughout the United States.

No Person except a natural born Citizen, or a Citizen of the United States, at the time of the adoption of this Constitution, shall be eligible to the Office of President; neither shall any person be eligible to that Office who shall not have attained to the age of thirty five Years, and been fourteen Years a Resident within the United States.

In case of the Removal of the President from Office, or of his Death, Resignation, or Inability to discharge the Powers and Duties of the said Office, the Same shall devolve on the Vice President, and the Congress may by Law provide for the Case of Removal, Death, Resignation or Inability, both of the President and Vice President, declaring what Officer shall then act as President, and such Officer shall act accordingly, until the Disability be removed, or a President shall be elected.

The President shall, at stated Times, receive for his Services, a Compensation which shall neither be increased nor diminished during the Period for which he shall have been elected, and he shall not receive within that Period any other Emolument from the United States, or any of them.

Before he enter on the Execution of his Office, he shall take the following Oath or Affirmation:—"I do solemnly swear (or affirm) that I will faithfully execute the Office of President of the United States, and will to the best of my Ability, preserve, protect, and defend the Constitution of the United States."

Section 2. The President shall be Commander in Chief of the Army and Navy of the United States, and of the Militia of the several States, when called into the actual Service of the United States; he may require the Opinion, in writing, of the principal Officer in each of the executive Departments, upon any subject relating to the Duties of their respective Offices, and he shall have Power to grant Reprieves and Pardons for Offences against the United States, except in cases of Impeachment.

He shall have Power, by and with the Advice and Consent of the Senate, to make Treaties, provided two-thirds of the Senators present concur; and he shall nominate, and by and with the Advice and Consent of the Senate, shall appoint Ambassadors, other public Ministers and Consuls, Judges of the supreme Court, and all other Officers of the United States, whose Appointments are not herein otherwise provided for, and which shall be established by Law; but the Congress may by Law vest the Appointment of such inferior Officers, as they think proper, in the President alone, in the Courts of Law, or in the Heads of Departments.

The President shall have power to fill up all Vacancies that may happen during the Recess of the Senate, by granting Commissions which shall expire at the End of their next Session.

Section 3. He shall from time to time give to the Congress Information of the State of the Union, and recommend to their Consideration such Measures as he shall judge necessary and expedient; he may, on extraordinary Occasions, convene both Houses, or either of them, and in Case of Disagreement between them, with Respect to the Time of Adjournment, he may adjourn them to such Time as he shall think proper; he shall receive Ambassadors and other public Ministers; he shall take Care that the Laws be faithfully executed, and shall Commission all the Officers of the United States.

Section 4. The President, Vice President, and all civil Officers of the United States, shall be removed from Office on Impeachment for, and Conviction of, Treason, Bribery, or other high Crimes and Misdemeanors.

ARTICLE III.

Section 1. The judicial Power of the United States, shall be vested in one supreme Court, and in such inferior Courts as the Congress may from time to time ordain and establish. The Judges, both of the supreme and inferior Courts, shall hold their Offices during good Behavior, and shall, at stated Times, receive for their Services, a Compensation, which shall not be diminished during their Continuance in Office.

Section 2. The judicial Power shall extend to all Cases, in Law and Equity, arising under this Constitution, the Laws of the United States, and Treaties made, or which shall be made, under their Authority;—to all Cases affecting Ambassadors, other public Ministers and Consuls;—to all Cases of admiralty and maritime Jurisdiction;—to Controversies to which the United States shall be a party;—to Controversies between two or more States:—between a State and Citizens of another State;—between Citizens of different States;—between Citizens of the same State claiming Lands under Grants of different States, and between a State, or the Citizens thereof, and foreign States, Citizens or Subjects.

In all Cases affecting Ambassadors, other public Ministers and Consuls, and those in which a State shall be Party, the supreme Court shall have original jurisdiction. In all other Cases before mentioned, the Supreme Court shall have appellate Jurisdiction, both as to Law and Fact, with such Exceptions, and under such regulations as the Congress shall make.

The trial of all Crimes, except in Cases of Impeachment, shall be by Jury; and such Trial shall be held in the State where the said Crimes shall have been committed; but when not committed within any State, the Trial shall be at such Place or Places as the Congress may by Law have directed.

Section 3. Treason against the United States, shall consist only in levying War against them, or in adhering to their Enemies, giving them Aid and Comfort. No Person shall be convicted of Treason unless on the Testimony of two Witnesses to the same overt Act, or on Confession in open Court.

The Congress shall have Power to declare the Punishment of Treason, but no Attainder of Treason shall work Corruption of Blood, or Forfeiture except during the Life of the Person attainted.

ARTICLE IV.

Section 1. Full Faith and Credit shall be given in each State to the Public Acts, Records, and judicial Proceedings of every other State. And the Congress may by general Laws prescribe the Manner in which such Acts, Records and Proceedings shall be proved, and the Effect thereof.

Section 2. The Citizens of each State shall be entitled to all Privileges and Immunities of Citizens in the several States.

A Person charged in any State with Treason, Felony, or other Crime, who shall flee from Justice, and be found in another State, shall on Demand of the executive Authority of the State from which he fled, be delivered up, to be removed to the State having Jurisdiction of the Crime.

No Person held to Service or Labour in one State, under the Laws thereof, escaping into another, shall, in Consequence of any Law or Regulation therein, be discharged from such Service or Labour, but shall be delivered up on Claim of the Party to whom such Service or Labour may be due.

Section 3. New States may be admitted by the Congress into this Union; but no new State shall be formed or erected within the Jurisdiction of any other State; nor any State be formed by the Junction of two or more States, or Parts of States, without the Consent of the Legislatures of the States concerned as well as of the Congress.

The Congress shall have Power to dispose of and make all needful Rules and Regulations respecting the Territory or other Property belonging to the United States; and nothing in this Constitution shall be so construed as to Prejudice any Claims of the United States, or of any particular State.

Section 4. The United States shall guarantee to every State in this Union a Republican Form of Government, and shall protect each of them against Invasion; and on Application of the Legislature, or of the Executive (when the Legislature cannot be convened) against domestic Violence.

ARTICLE V.

The Congress, whenever two-thirds of both Houses shall deem it necessary, shall propose Amendments to this Constitution, or, on the Application of the Legislatures of two-thirds of the several States, shall call a Convention for proposing Amendments, which, in either Case, shall be valid to all Intents and Purposes, as Part of this Constitution, when ratified by the Legislatures of three-fourths of the several States, or by Conventions in three-fourths thereof, as the one or the other Mode of Ratification may be proposed by the Congress; Provided that no Amendment which may be made prior to the Year One thousand eight hundred and eight shall in any Manner affect the first and fourth Clauses in the Ninth Section of the first Article; and that no State, without its Consent, shall be deprived of its equal Suffrage in the Senate.

ARTICLE VI.

All debts contracted and Engagements entered into, before the Adoption of this Constitution, shall be as valid against the United States under this Constitution, as under the Confederation.

This Constitution, and the Laws of the United States which shall be made in Pursuance thereof; and all Treaties made, or which shall be made, under the Authority of the United States, shall be the supreme Law of the Land; and the Judges in every State shall be bound thereby, any Thing in the Constitution or Laws of any State to the Contrary notwithstanding.

The Senators and Representatives before mentioned, and the Members of the several State Legislatures, and all executive and judicial Officers, both of the United States and of the several States, shall be bound by Oath or Affirmation, to support this Constitution; but no religious Test shall ever be required as a Qualification to any Office or public Trust under the United States.

ARTICLE VII.

The Ratification of the Conventions of nine States, shall be sufficient for the Establishment of this Constitution between the States so ratifying the Same.

The Word "the," being interlined between the seventh and eighth Lines of the first Page, The Word "Thirty" being partly written on an Erazure in the fifteenth Line of the first Page, The Words "is tried" being interlined between the thirty second and thirty third Lines of the first Page and the Word "the" being interlined between the forty third and forty fourth lines of the second Page. Attest William Jackson Secretary

Done in Convention by the Unanimous Consent of the States present the Seventeenth Day of September in the Year of our Lord one thousand seven hundred and eighty seven and of the Independence of the United States of America the Twelfth In witness whereof We have hereunto subscribed our Names,

Go. WASHINGTON—Presidt.
and deputy from Virginia

New Hampshire	JOHN LANGDON, NICHOLAS GILMAN;
Massachusetts	NATHANIEL GORHAM, RUFUS KING;
Connecticut	WM. SAM^L. JOHNSON, ROGER SHERMAN;
New York	ALEXANDER HAMILTON;
New Jersey	WIL: LIVINGSTON, DAVID BREARLEY, WM. PATERSON, JONA: DAYTON;
Pennsylvania	B. FRANKLIN, THOMAS MIFFLIN, ROBT. MORRIS, GEO. CLYMER, THOS. FITZSIMONS, JARED INGERSOLL, JAMES WILSON, GOUV MORRIS;
Delaware	GEO: READ, GUNNING BEDFORD JUN, JOHN DICKINSON, RICHARD BASSETT, JACO: BROOM;
Maryland	JAMES MCHENRY, DAN OF S^T. THO^S. JENIFER, DAN^L CARROLL;
Virginia	JOHN BLAIR, JAMES MADISON JR.;
North Carolina	W^M. BLOUNT, RICH^D. DOBBS SPAIGHT, HU WILLIAMSON;

South Carolina	J. Rutledge, Charles Cotesworth Pinckney, Charles Pinckney, Pierce Butler;
Georgia	William Few, Abr Baldwin.

The orthography and punctuation both of the constitution and the several amendments, as printed in a copy furnished for the purpose by the Secretary of State of the United States, have been followed exactly in printing this work.

AMENDMENTS TO THE CONSTITUTION OF THE UNITED STATES

Articles

In addition to, and Amendment of the constitution of the united states of america,

Proposed by Congress, and ratified by the Legislatures of the several States, pursuant to the fifth Article of the Original Constitution.

ARTICLE I.†

Congress shall make no law respecting an establishment of religion, or prohibiting the free exercise thereof; or abridging the freedom of speech, or of the press; or the right of the people peaceably to assemble, and to petition the Government for a redress of grievances.

ARTICLE II.

A well regulated Militia, being necessary to the security of a free State, the right of the people to keep and bear Arms, shall not be infringed.

ARTICLE III.

No Soldier shall, in time of peace, be quartered in any house, without the consent of the Owner, nor in time of war, but in a manner to be prescribed by law.

ARTICLE IV.

The right of the people to be secure in their persons, houses, papers, and effects, against unreasonable searches and seizures, shall not be violated, and no Warrants shall issue, but upon probable cause, supported by oath or affirmation, and particularly describing the place to be searched, and the persons or things to be seized.

---

†The first ten Amendments were ratified December 15, 1791, and form what is known as the ''Bill of Rights.'' Ratified by this State April 19, 1939.

ARTICLE V.

No person shall be held to answer for a capital, or otherwise infamous crime, unless on a presentment or indictment of a Grand Jury, except in cases arising in the land or naval forces, or in the Militia, when in actual service in time of War or public danger; nor shall any person be subject for the same offence to be twice put in jeopardy of life or limb; nor shall be compelled in any criminal case to be a witness against himself, nor be deprived of life, liberty, or property, without due process of law; nor shall private property be taken for public use, without just compensation.

ARTICLE VI.

In all criminal prosecutions, the accused shall enjoy the right to a speedy and public trial, by an impartial jury of the State and district wherein the crime shall have been committed, which district shall have been previously ascertained by law, and to be informed of the nature and cause of the accusation; to be confronted with the witnesses against him; to have compulsory process for obtaining witnesses in his favor, and to have the Assistance of Counsel for his defence.

ARTICLE VII.[1]

In Suits at common law, where the value in controversy shall exceed twenty dollars, the right of trial by jury shall be preserved, and no fact tried by a jury, shall be otherwise re-examined in any Court of the United States, than according to the rules of the common law.

ARTICLE VIII.

Excessive bail shall not be required, nor excessive fines imposed, nor cruel and unusual punishments inflicted.

ARTICLE IX.

The enumeration in the Constitution, of certain rights, shall not be construed to deny or disparage others retained by the people.

ARTICLE X.

The powers not delegated to the United States by the Constitution, nor prohibited by it to the States, are reserved to the States respectively, or to the people.

ARTICLE XI.[2]

The Judicial power of the United States shall not be construed to extend to any suit in law or equity, commenced or prosecuted against one of the United States by Citizens of another State, or by Citizens or Subjects of any Foreign State.

---

[1]This applies only to United States courts.
[2]Ratified by this State May 15, 1794 (See House Journal 1794 and State Records 1794).

ARTICLE XII.[3]

The Electors shall meet in their respective states, and vote by ballot for President and Vice-President, one of whom, at least, shall not be an inhabitant of the same state with themselves; they shall name in their ballots the person voted for as President, and in distinct ballots the person voted for as Vice-President, and they shall make distinct lists of all persons voted for as President, and of all persons voted for as Vice-President, and of the number of votes for each, which lists they shall sign and certify, and transmit sealed to the seat of the government of the United States, directed to the President of the Senate;—The President of the Senate shall, in the presence of the Senate and House of Representatives, open all the certificates and the votes shall then be counted;—The person having the greatest number of votes for President, shall be the President, if such number be a majority of the whole number of Electors appointed; and if no person have such majority, then from the persons having the highest numbers not exceeding three on the list of those voted for as President, the House of Representatives shall choose immediately, by ballot, the President. But in choosing the President, the votes shall be taken by States, the representation from each state having one vote; a quorum for this purpose shall consist of a member or members from two-thirds of the states, and a majority of all the states shall be necessary to a choice. And if the House of Representatives shall not choose a President whenever the right of choice shall devolve upon them, before the fourth day of March next following, then the Vice-President shall act as President, as in the case of the death or other constitutional disability of the President.—The person having the greatest number of votes as Vice-President, shall be Vice-President, if such number be a majority of the whole number of Electors appointed, and if no person have a majority, then from the two highest numbers on the list, the Senate shall choose the Vice-President; a quorum for the purpose shall consist of two-thirds of the whole number of Senators, and a majority of the whole number shall be necessary to a choice. But no person constitutionally ineligible to the office of President shall be eligible to that of Vice-President of the United States.

ARTICLE XIII.[4]

Section 1. Neither slavery nor involuntary servitude, except as a punishment for crime whereof the party shall have been duly convicted, shall exist within the United States, or any place subject to their jurisdiction.

Section 2. Congress shall have power to enforce this article by appropriate legislation.

ARTICLE XIV.[5]

Section 1. All persons born or naturalized in the United States, and subject to the jurisdiction thereof, are citizens of the United States and of the State wherein they reside. No State shall make or enforce any law which shall abridge

---

[3]Proposed by Congress December 12, 1803. Not ratified by this State. Ratification announced by Secretary of State, September 25, 1804.

[4]Proposed by Congress February 1, 1865. Ratified by this State May 5, 1865. Ratification announced by Secretary of State, December 18, 1865.

[5]Proposed by Congress June 16, 1866. Ratified by this State June 30, 1866. Ratification announced by Secretary of State, July 28, 1868.

the privileges or immunities of citizens of the United States; nor shall any State deprive any person of life, liberty, or property, without due process of law; nor deny to any person within its jurisdiction the equal protection of the laws.

Section 2. Representatives shall be apportioned among the several States according to their respective numbers, counting the whole number of persons in each State, excluding Indians not taxed. But when the right to vote at any election for the choice of electors for President and Vice-President of the United States, Representatives in Congress, the Executive and Judicial officers of a State, or the members of the Legislature thereof, is denied to any of the male inhabitants of such State, being twenty-one years of age, and citizens of the United States, or in any way abridged, except for participation in rebellion, or other crime, the basis of representation therein shall be reduced in the proportion which the number of such male citizens shall bear to the whole number of male citizens twenty-one years of age in such State.

Section 3. No person shall be a Senator or Representative in Congress, or elector of President and Vice-President, or hold any office, civil or military, under the United States, or under any State, who, having previously taken an oath, as a member of Congress, or as an officer of the United States, or as a member of any State legislature, or as an executive or judicial officer of any State, to support the Constitution of the United States, shall have engaged in insurrection or rebellion against the same, or given aid or comfort to the enemies thereof. But Congress may by a vote of two-thirds of each House, remove such disability.

Section 4. The validity of the public debt of the United States, authorized by law, including debts incurred for payment of pensions and bounties for services in suppressing insurrection or rebellion, shall not be questioned. But neither the United States nor any State shall assume or pay any debt or obligation incurred in aid of insurrection or rebellion against the United States, or any claim for the loss or emancipation of any slave; but all such debts, obligations and claims shall be held illegal and void.

Section 5. The Congress shall have power to enforce, by appropriate legislation, the provisions of this article.

ARTICLE XV.[6]

Section 1. The right of citizens of the United States to vote shall not be denied or abridged by the United States or by any State on account of race, color, or previous condition of servitude.

Section 2. Congress shall have power to enforce this article by appropriate legislation.

ARTICLE XVI.[7]

The Congress shall have power to lay and collect taxes on incomes, from whatever source derived, without apportionment among the several States, and without regard to any census or enumeration.

---

[6]Proposed by Congress February 27, 1869. Ratified by this State May 19, 1869. Ratification announced by Secretary of State, March 30, 1870.
[7]Proposed by Congress July 12, 1909. Not ratified by this State. Ratification announced by the Secretary of State of the United States, February 25, 1913.

ARTICLE XVII.[8]

The Senate of the United States shall be composed of two Senators from each state, elected by the people thereof, for six years; and each Senator shall have one vote. The electors in each State shall have the qualifications requisite for electors of the most numerous branch of the State legislatures. When vacancies happen in the representation of any State in the Senate, the executive authority of such State shall issue writs of election to fill such vacancies: Provided, that the legislature of any State may empower the executive thereof to make temporary appointments until the people fill the vacancies by election as the legislature may direct. This amendment shall not be so construed as to affect the election or term of any Senator chosen before it becomes valid as part of the Constitution.

ARTICLE XVIII.[9]

Section 1. After one year from the ratification of this article the manufacture, sale, or transportation of intoxicating liquors within, the importation thereof, into, or the exportation thereof from the United States and all territory subject to the jurisdiction thereof for beverage purposes is hereby prohibited.

Section 2. The Congress and the several States shall have concurrent power to enforce this article by appropriate legislation.

Section 3. This article shall be inoperative unless it shall have been ratified as an amendment to the Constitution by the legislatures of the several States, as provided in the Constitution, within seven years from the date of the submission hereof to the States by the Congress.

ARTICLE XIX.[10]

Section 1. The right of citizens of the United States to vote shall not be denied or abridged by the United States or by any State on account of sex.

Section 2. Congress shall have power to enforce this article by appropriate legislation.

ARTICLE XX.[11]

Section 1. The terms of the President and Vice President shall end at noon on the 20th day of January, and the terms of Senators and Representatives at noon on the 3rd day of January, of the years in which such terms would have ended if this article had not been ratified; and the terms of their successors shall then begin.

Section 2. The Congress shall assemble at least once in every year, and such meeting shall begin at noon on the 3rd day of January, unless they shall by law appoint a different day.

---

[8] Proposed by Congress May 13, 1912. Ratified by this State April 15, 1913. Ratification announced by the Secretary of State of the United States, May 31, 1913.

[9] Proposed by Congress December 18, 1917. Ratification announced by the Acting Secretary of the United States, January 29, 1919. Became effective January 16, 1920. Not ratified by this State. Repealed by Article XXI effective December 5, 1933.

[10] Proposed by Congress June 4, 1919. Ratification announced by the Secretary of State of the United States, August 26, 1920. Ratified by this State September 14, 1920, and September 21, 1920.

[11] Proposed by Congress March 2, 1932. Ratification announced by the Secretary of State of the United States, February 6, 1933. Ratified by this State January 27, 1933.

Section 3. If, at the time fixed for the beginning of the term of the President, the President elect shall have died, the Vice President elect shall become President. If a President shall not have been chosen before the time fixed for the beginning of his term, or if the President elect shall have failed to qualify, then the Vice President elect shall act as President until a President shall have qualified; and the Congress may by law provide for the case wherein neither a President elect nor a Vice President elect shall have qualified, declaring who shall then act as President, or the manner in which one who is to act shall be selected, and such person shall act accordingly until a President or Vice President shall have qualified.

Section 4. The Congress may by law provide for the case of the death of any of the persons from whom the House of Representatives may choose a President whenever the right of choice shall have devolved upon them, and for the case of the death of any of the persons from whom the Senate may choose a Vice President whenever the right of choice shall have devolved upon them.

Section 5. Sections 1 and 2 shall take effect on the 15th day of October following the ratification of this article.

Section 6. This article shall be inoperative unless it shall have been ratified as an amendment to the Constitution by the legislatures of three-fourths of the several States within seven years from the date of its submission.

ARTICLE XXI.[12]

Section 1. The eighteenth article of amendment to the Constitution of the United States is hereby repealed.

Section 2. The transportation or importation into any State, Territory, or possession of the United States for delivery or use therein of intoxicating liquors, in violation of the laws thereof, is hereby prohibited.

Section 3. This article shall be inoperative unless it shall have been ratified as an amendment to the Constitution by conventions in the several States, as provided in the Constitution, within seven years from the date of the submission hereof to the States by the Congress.

ARTICLE XXII.[13]

Section 1. No person shall be elected to the office of the President more than twice, and no person who has held the office of President, or acted as President, for more than two years of a term to which some other person was elected President shall be elected to the office of the President more than once. But this Article shall not apply to any person holding the office of President when this Article was proposed by the Congress, and shall not prevent any person who may be holding the office of President, or acting as President, during the term within which this Article becomes operative from holding the office of President or acting as President during the remainder of such term.

---

[12]Proposed by Congress February 20, 1933. Ratified by this State July 11, 1933. Ratification announced by the Secretary of State of the United States, December 5, 1933.
[13]Proposed by Congress March 24, 1947. Ratified by this State May 21, 1947. Ratification announced by the Secretary of State of the United States, March 1, 1951.

Section 2. This article shall be inoperative unless it shall have been ratified as an amendment to the Constitution by the legislatures of three-fourths of the several States within seven years from the date of its submission to the States by the Congress.

ARTICLE XXIII.[14]

Section 1. The District constituting the seat of Government of the United States shall appoint in such manner as the Congress may direct: A number of electors of President and Vice President equal to the whole number of Senators and Representatives in Congress to which the District would be entitled if it were a State, but in no event more than the least populous State; they shall be in addition to those appointed by the States, but they shall be considered, for the purposes of the election of President and Vice President, to be electors appointed by a State; and they shall meet in the district and perform such duties as provided by the twelfth article of amendment.

Section 2. The Congress shall have power to enforce this article by appropriate legislation.

ARTICLE XXIV.[15]

Section 1. The right of citizens of the United States to vote in any primary or other election for President or Vice President, for electors for President or Vice President, or for Senator or Representative in Congress, shall not be denied or abridged by the United States or any State by reason of failure to pay any poll tax or other tax.

Section 2. The Congress shall have power to enforce this article by appropriate legislation.

ARTICLE XXV.[16]

Section 1. In case of the removal of the President from office or of his death or resignation, the Vice President shall become President.

Section 2. Whenever there is a vacancy in the office of the Vice President, the President shall nominate a Vice President who shall take office upon confirmation by a majority vote of both Houses of Congress.

Section 3. Whenever the President transmits to the President pro tempore of the Senate and the Speaker of the House of Representatives his written declaration that he is unable to discharge the powers and duties of his office, and until he transmits to them a written declaration to the contrary, such powers and duties shall be discharged by the Vice President as Acting President.

Section 4. Whenever the Vice President and a majority of either the principal officers of the executive departments or of such other body as Congress may by law provide, transmit to the President pro tempore of the Senate and the

---

[14]Proposed by Congress June 16, 1960. Ratified by this State March 9, 1961. Ratification announced by the Administrator of General Services of the United States, April 3, 1961.

[15]Proposed by Congress August 27, 1962. Ratified by this State March 20, 1963. Ratification announced by the Administrator of General Services of the United States, February 4, 1964. Became effective on January 23, 1964.

[16]Proposed by Congress January 6, 1965. Ratified by this State February 14, 1967. Ratification consummated February 10, 1967 and announced by the Administrator of General Services of the United States, February 23, 1967.

Speaker of the House of Representatives their written declaration that the President is unable to discharge the powers and duties of his office, the Vice President shall immediately assume the powers and duties of the office as Acting President.

Thereafter, when the President transmits to the President pro tempore of the Senate and the Speaker of the House of Representatives his written declaration that no inability exists, he shall resume the powers and duties of his office unless the Vice President and a majority of either the principal officers of the executive department or of such other body as Congress may by law provide, transmit within four days to the President pro tempore of the Senate and the Speaker of the House of Representatives their written declaration that the President is unable to discharge the powers and duties of his office. Thereupon Congress shall decide the issue, assembling within forty-eight hours for that purpose if not in session. If the Congress, within twenty-one days after receipt of the latter written declaration, or, if Congress is not in session, within twenty-one days after Congress is required to assemble, determines by two-thirds vote of both Houses that the President is unable to discharge the powers and duties of his office, the Vice President shall continue to discharge the same as Acting President; otherwise, the President shall resume the powers and duties of his office.

ARTICLE XXVI.[17]

Section 1. The right of citizens of the United States, who are eighteen years of age or older, to vote shall not be denied or abridged by the United States or by any State on account of age.

Section 2. The Congress shall have power to enforce this article by appropriate legislation.

ARTICLE XXVII.[18]

No law, varying the compensation for the services of the Senators and Representatives, shall take effect, until an election of Representatives shall have intervened.

---

[17]Proposed by Congress March 23, 1971. Ratified by this State March 23, 1971. Ratification consummated June 30, 1971 and announced by the Administrator of General Services of the United States, July 5, 1971.

[18]Proposed by Congress on September 25, 1789. Ratified in this state by House Joint Resolution No. 54, which was adopted by the House of Representatives on May 6, 1987, and by the Senate on May 13, 1987 and certified by the Archivist of the United States on May 18, 1992.

CONSTITUTION OF THE STATE OF CONNECTICUT

PREAMBLE.

The People of Connecticut acknowledging with gratitude, the good providence of God, in having permitted them to enjoy a free government; do, in order more effectually to define, secure, and perpetuate the liberties, rights and privileges which they have derived from their ancestors; hereby, after a careful consideration and revision, ordain and establish the following constitution and form of civil government.

ARTICLE FIRST.
DECLARATION OF RIGHTS

That the great and essential principles of liberty and free government may be recognized and established,

WE DECLARE:

SEC. 1. All men when they form a social compact, are equal in rights; and no man or set of men are entitled to exclusive public emoluments or privileges from the community.

SEC. 2. All political power is inherent in the people, and all free governments are founded on their authority, and instituted for their benefit; and they have at all times an undeniable and indefeasible right to alter their form of government in such manner as they may think expedient.

SEC. 3. The exercise and enjoyment of religious profession and worship, without discrimination, shall forever be free to all persons in the state; provided, that the right hereby declared and established, shall not be so construed as to excuse acts of licentiousness, or to justify practices inconsistent with the peace and safety of the state.

SEC. 4. Every citizen may freely speak, write and publish his sentiments on all subjects, being responsible for the abuse of that liberty.

SEC. 5. No law shall ever be passed to curtail or restrain the liberty of speech or of the press.

SEC. 6. In all prosecutions or indictments for libels, the truth may be given in evidence, and the jury shall have the right to determine the law and the facts, under the direction of the court.

SEC. 7. The people shall be secure in their persons, houses, papers and possessions from unreasonable searches or seizures; and no warrant to search any place, or to seize any person or things, shall issue without describing them as nearly as may be, nor without probable cause supported by oath or affirmation.

SEC. 8. In all criminal prosecutions, the accused shall have a right to be heard by himself and by counsel; to be informed of the nature and cause of the accusation; to be confronted by the witnesses against him; to have compulsory process to obtain witnesses in his behalf; to be released on bail upon sufficient security, except in capital offenses, where the proof is evident or the presumption great; and in all prosecutions by indictment or information, to a speedy, public trial by an impartial jury. No person shall be compelled to give evidence against himself, nor be deprived of life, liberty or property without due process of law, nor shall excessive bail be required nor excessive fines imposed. No person shall be held to answer for any crime, punishable by death or life imprisonment, unless on a presentment or an indictment of a grand jury, except in the armed forces, or in the militia when in actual service in time of war or public danger.

(Sec. 8 amended in 1982. See Art. XVII of Amendments to the Constitution of the State of Connecticut.)

SEC. 9. No person shall be arrested, detained or punished, except in cases clearly warranted by law.

SEC. 10. All courts shall be open, and every person, for an injury done to him in his person, property or reputation, shall have remedy by due course of law, and right and justice administered without sale, denial or delay.

SEC. 11. The property of no person shall be taken for public use, without just compensation therefor.

SEC. 12. The privileges of the writ of habeas corpus shall not be suspended, unless, when in case of rebellion or invasion, the public safety may require it; nor in any case, but by the legislature.

SEC. 13. No person shall be attainted of treason or felony, by the legislature.

SEC. 14. The citizens have a right, in a peaceable manner, to assemble for their common good, and to apply to those invested with the powers of government, for redress of grievances, or other proper purposes, by petition, address or remonstrance.

SEC. 15. Every citizen has a right to bear arms in defense of himself and the state.

SEC. 16. The military shall, in all cases, and at all times, be in strict subordination to the civil power.

SEC. 17. No soldier shall, in time of peace, be quartered in any house, without the consent of the owner; nor in time of war, but in a manner to be prescribed by law.

SEC. 18. No hereditary emoluments, privileges or honors, shall ever be granted, or conferred in this state.

SEC. 19. The right of trial by jury shall remain inviolate.

(Sec. 19 amended in 1972. See Art. IV of Amendments to the Constitution of the State of Connecticut.)

SEC. 20. No person shall be denied the equal protection of the law nor be subjected to segregation or discrimination in the exercise or enjoyment of his civil or political rights because of religion, race, color, ancestry or national origin.

(Sec. 20 amended in 1974. See Art. V of Amendments to the Constitution of the State of Connecticut.)
(Sec. 20 amended in 1984. See Art. XXI of the Amendments to the Constitution of the State of Connecticut.)

ARTICLE SECOND.*
OF THE DISTRIBUTION OF POWERS.

The powers of government shall be divided into three distinct departments, and each of them confided to a separate magistracy, to wit, those which are legislative, to one; those which are executive, to another; and those which are judicial, to another.

*(ARTICLE SECOND amended in 1982. See Art. XVIII of Amendments to the Constitution of the State of Connecticut.)

ARTICLE THIRD.
OF THE LEGISLATIVE DEPARTMENT.

SEC. 1. The legislative power of the state shall be vested in two distinct houses or branches; the one to be styled the senate, the other the house of representatives, and both together the general assembly. The style of their laws shall be: Be it enacted by the Senate and House of Representatives in General Assembly convened.

SEC. 2. There shall be a regular session of the general assembly to commence on the Wednesday following the first Monday of the January next succeeding the election of its members, and at such other times as the general assembly shall judge necessary; but the person administering the office of governor may, on special emergencies, convene the general assembly at any other time. All regular and special sessions of the general assembly shall be held at Hartford, but the person administering the office of governor may, in case of special emergency, convene the assembly at any other place in the state. The general assembly shall adjourn each regular session not later than the first Wednesday after the first Monday in June following its organization and shall adjourn each special session upon completion of its business. If any bill passed by any regular or special session or any appropriation item described in Section 16 of Article Fourth has been disapproved by the governor prior to its adjournment, and has not been reconsidered by the assembly, or is so disapproved after such adjournment, the secretary of the state shall reconvene the general assembly on the second Monday after the last day on which the governor is authorized to transmit or has transmitted every bill to the secretary with his objections pursuant to Section 15 of Article Fourth of this constitution, whichever occurs first; provided if such Monday falls on a legal holiday the general assembly shall be reconvened on the next following day. The reconvened session shall be for the sole purpose of reconsidering and, if the assembly so desires, repassing such bills. The general assembly shall adjourn sine die not later than three days following its reconvening.

(Sec. 2 amended in 1970. See Art. III of Amendments to the Constitution of the State of Connecticut.)

SEC. 3. The senate shall consist of not less than thirty and not more than fifty members, each of whom shall be an elector residing in the senatorial district from which he is elected. Each senatorial district shall be contiguous as to territory and shall elect no more than one senator.

(Sec. 3 amended in 1970. See Art. II, Sec. 1 of Amendments to the Constitution of the State of Connecticut.)

SEC. 4. The house of representatives shall consist of not less than one hundred twenty-five and not more than two hundred twenty-five members, each of whom shall be an elector residing in the assembly district from which he is elected. Each assembly district shall be contiguous as to territory and shall elect no more than one representative. For the purpose of forming assembly districts no town shall be divided except for the purpose of forming assembly districts wholly within the town.

(Sec. 4 amended in 1970. See Art. II, Sec. 2 of Amendments to the Constitution of the State of Connecticut.)

SEC. 5. The establishment of districts in the general assembly shall be consistent with federal constitutional standards.

(Sec. 5 amended in 1980. See Art. XVI, Sec. 1 of Amendments to the Constitution of the State of Connecticut.)

SEC. 6. a. The assembly and senatorial districts as now established by law shall continue until the regular session of the general assembly next after the completion of the next census of the United States. Such general assembly shall, upon roll call, by a yea vote of at least two-thirds of the membership of each house, enact such plan of districting as is necessary to preserve a proper apportionment of representation in accordance with the principles recited in this article. Thereafter the general assembly shall decennially at its next regular session following the completion of the census of the United States, upon roll call, by a yea vote of at least two-thirds of the membership of each house, enact such plan of districting as is necessary in accordance with the provisions of this article.

b. If the general assembly fails to enact a plan of districting by the first day of the April next following the completion of the decennial census of the United States, the governor shall forthwith appoint a commission consisting of the eight members designated by the president pro tempore of the senate, the speaker of the house of representatives, the minority leader of the senate and the minority leader of the house of representatives, each of whom shall designate two members of the commission, provided that there are members of no more than two political parties in either the senate or the house of representatives. In the event that there are members of more than two political parties in a house of the general assembly, all members of that house belonging to the parties other than that of the president pro tempore of the senate or the speaker of the house of representatives, as the case may be, shall select one of their number, who shall designate two members of the commission in lieu of the designation by the minority leader of that house.

c. The commission shall proceed to consider the alteration of districts in accordance with the principles recited in this article and it shall submit a plan of districting to the secretary of the state by the first day of the July next succeeding the appointment of its members. No plan shall be submitted to the secretary unless it is certified by at least six members of the commission. Upon receiving such plan the secretary shall publish the same forthwith, and, upon publication, such plan of districting shall have the full force of law.

d. If by the first day of the July next succeeding the appointment of its members the commission fails to submit a plan of districting, a board of three persons shall forthwith be empaneled. The speaker of the house of representatives and the minority leader of the house of representatives shall each designate, as one member of the board, a judge of the superior court of the state, provided that there are members of no more than two political parties in the house of representatives. In the event that there are members of more than two political parties in the house of representatives, all members belonging to the parties other than that of the speaker shall select one of their number, who shall then designate, as one member of the board, a judge of the superior court of the state, in lieu of the designation by the minority leader of the house of representatives. The two members of the board so designated shall select an elector of the state as the third member.

e. The board shall proceed to consider the alteration of districts in accordance with the principles recited in this article and shall, by the first day of the October next succeeding its selection, submit a plan of districting to the secretary. No plan shall be submitted to the secretary unless it is certified by at least two members of the board. Upon receiving such plan, the secretary shall publish the same forthwith, and, upon publication, such plan of districting shall have full force of law.

(Sec. 6, subsections a through e, amended in 1976. See Art. XII of Amendments to the Constitution of the State of Connecticut; amended in 1980. See Art. XVI, Sec. 2 of Amendments to the Constitution of the State of Connecticut.)

SEC. 7. The treasurer, secretary of the state, and comptroller shall canvass publicly the votes for senators and representatives. The person in each senatorial district having the greatest number of votes for senator shall be declared to be duly elected for such district, and the person in each assembly district having the greatest number of votes for representative shall be declared to be duly elected for such district. The general assembly shall provide by law the manner in which an equal and the greatest number of votes for two or more persons so voted for for senator or representative shall be resolved. The return of votes, and the result of the canvass, shall be submitted to the house of representatives and to the senate on the first day of the session of the general assembly. Each house shall be the final judge of the election returns and qualifications of its own members.

SEC. 8. A general election for members of the general assembly shall be held on the Tuesday after the first Monday of November, biennially, in the even-numbered years. The general assembly shall have power to enact laws regulating and prescribing the order and manner of voting for such members, for filling vacancies in either the house of representatives or the senate, and providing for the election of representatives or senators at some time subsequent to the Tuesday after the first Monday of November in all cases when it shall so happen that the electors in any district shall fail on that day to elect a representative or senator.

SEC. 9. At all elections for members of the general assembly the presiding officers in the several towns shall receive the votes of the electors, and count and declare them in open meeting. The presiding officers shall make and certify duplicate lists of the persons voted for, and of the number of votes for each. One list shall be delivered within three days to the town clerk, and within ten days after such meeting, the other shall be delivered under seal to the secretary of the state.

SEC. 10. The members of the general assembly shall hold their offices from the Wednesday following the first Monday of the January next succeeding their election until the Wednesday after the first Monday of the third January next succeeding their election, and until their successors are duly qualified.

SEC. 11. No member of the general assembly shall, during the term for which he is elected, hold or accept any appointive position or office in the judicial or executive department of the state government, or in the courts of the political subdivisions of the state, or in the government of any county. No member of congress, no person holding any office under the authority of the United States and no person holding any office in the judicial or executive department of the state government or in the government of any county shall be a member of the general assembly during his continuance in such office.

SEC. 12. The house of representatives, when assembled, shall choose a speaker, clerk and other officers. The senate shall choose a president pro tempore, clerk and other officers, except the president. A majority of each house shall constitute a quorum to do business; but a smaller number may adjourn from day to day, and compel the attendance of absent members in such manner and under such penalties as each house may prescribe.

SEC. 13. Each house shall determine the rules of its own proceedings, and punish members for disorderly conduct, and, with the consent of two-thirds, expel a member, but not a second time for the same cause; and shall have all other powers necessary for a branch of the legislature of a free and independent state.

SEC. 14. Each house shall keep a journal of its proceedings, and publish the same when required by one-fifth of its members, except such parts as in the judgment of a majority require secrecy. The yeas and nays of the members of either house shall, at the desire of one-fifth of those present, be entered on the journals.

SEC. 15. The senators and representatives shall, in all cases of civil process, be privileged from arrest, during any session of the general assembly, and for four days before the commencement and after the termination of any session thereof. And for any speech or debate in either house, they shall not be questioned in any other place.

SEC. 16. The debates of each house shall be public, except on such occasions as in the opinion of the house may require secrecy.

SEC. 17. The salary of the members of the general assembly and the transportation expenses of its members in the performance of their legislative duties shall be determined by law.

(Sec. 18 added in 1992. See Art. XXVIII of the Amendments to the Constitution of the State of Connecticut.)

ARTICLE FOURTH.
OF THE EXECUTIVE DEPARTMENT.

SEC. 1. A general election for governor, lieutenant-governor, secretary of the state, treasurer and comptroller shall be held on the Tuesday after the first Monday of November, 1966, and quadrennially thereafter.

(Sec. 1 amended in 1970. See Art. I of Amendments to the Constitution of the State of Connecticut.)

SEC. 2. Such officers shall hold their respective offices from the Wednesday following the first Monday of the January next succeeding their election until the Wednesday following the first Monday of the fifth January succeeding their election and until their successors are duly qualified.

SEC. 3. In the election of governor and lieutenant-governor, voting for such offices shall be as a unit. The name of no candidate for either office, nominated by a political party or by petition, shall appear on the voting machine ballot labels except in conjunction with the name of the candidate for the other office.

SEC. 4. At the meetings of the electors in the respective towns held quadrennially as herein provided for the election of state officers, the presiding officers shall receive the votes and shall count and declare the same in the presence of the electors. The presiding officers shall make and certify duplicate lists of the persons voted for, and of the number of votes for each. One list shall be delivered within three days to the town clerk, and within ten days after such meeting, the other shall be delivered under seal to the secretary of the state. The votes so delivered shall be counted, canvassed and declared by the treasurer, secretary, and comptroller, within the month of November. The vote for treasurer shall be counted, canvassed and declared by the secretary and comptroller only; the vote for secretary shall be counted, canvassed and declared by the treasurer and comptroller only; and the vote for comptroller shall be counted, canvassed and declared by the treasurer and secretary only. A fair list of the persons and number of votes given for each, together with the returns of the presiding officers, shall be, by the treasurer, secretary and comptroller, made and laid before the general assembly, then next to be held, on the first day of the session thereof. In the election of governor, lieutenant-governor, secretary, treasurer, comptroller and attorney general, the person found upon the count by the treasurer, secretary and comptroller in the manner herein provided, to be made and announced before December fifteenth of the year of the election, to have received the greatest number of votes for each of such offices, respectively, shall be elected thereto; provided, if the election of any of them shall be contested as provided by statute, and if such a contest shall proceed to final judgment, the person found by the court to have received the greatest number of votes shall be elected. If two or more persons shall be found upon the count of the treasurer, secretary and comptroller to have received an equal and the greatest number of votes for any of said offices, and the election is not contested, the general assembly on the second day of its session shall hold a joint convention of both houses, at which, without debate, a ballot shall be taken to choose such officer from those persons who received such a vote; and the balloting shall continue on that or subsequent days until one of such persons is chosen by a majority vote of those present and voting. The general assembly shall have power to enact laws regulating and prescribing the order and manner of voting for such officers. The general assembly shall by law prescribe the manner in which all questions concerning the election of a governor or lieutenant-governor shall be determined.

SEC. 5. The supreme executive power of the state shall be vested in the governor. No person who is not an elector of the state, and who has not arrived at the age of thirty years, shall be eligible.

SEC. 6. The lieutenant-governor shall possess the same qualifications as are herein prescribed for the governor.

SEC. 7. The compensations of the governor and lieutenant-governor shall be established by law, and shall not be varied so as to take effect until after an election, which shall next succeed the passage of the law establishing such compensations.

SEC. 8. The governor shall be captain general of the militia of the state, except when called into the service of the United States.

SEC. 9. He may require information in writing from the officers in the executive department, on any subject relating to the duties of their respective offices.

SEC. 10. The governor, in case of a disagreement between the two houses of the general assembly, respecting the time of adjournment, may adjourn them to such time as he shall think proper, not beyond the day of the next stated session.

SEC. 11. He shall, from time to time, give to the general assembly, information of the state of the government, and recommend to their consideration such measures as he shall deem expedient.

SEC. 12. He shall take care that the laws be faithfully executed.

SEC. 13. The governor shall have power to grant reprieves after conviction, in all cases except those of impeachment, until the end of the next session of the general assembly, and no longer.

SEC. 14. All commissions shall be in the name and by authority of the state of Connecticut; shall be sealed with the state seal, signed by the governor, and attested by the secretary of the state.

SEC. 15. Each bill which shall have passed both houses of the general assembly shall be presented to the governor. Bills may be presented to the governor after the adjournment of the general assembly, and the general assembly may prescribe the time and method of performing all ministerial acts necessary or incidental to the administration of this section. If the governor shall approve a bill, he shall sign and transmit it to the secretary of the state, but if he shall disapprove, he shall transmit it to the secretary with his objections, and the secretary shall thereupon return the bill with the governor's objections to the house in which it originated. After the objections shall have been entered on its journal, such house shall proceed to reconsider the bill. If, after such reconsideration, that house shall again pass it, but by the approval of at least two-thirds of its members, it shall be sent with the objections to the other house, which shall also reconsider it. If approved by at least two-thirds of the members of the second house, it shall be a law and be transmitted to the secretary; but in such case the votes of each house shall be determined by yeas and nays and the names of the members voting for and against the bill shall be entered on the journal of each house respectively. In case the governor shall not transmit the bill to the secretary, either with his approval or with his objections, within five calendar days, Sundays and legal holidays excepted, after the same shall have been presented to him, it shall be a law at the expiration of that period; except that, if the general assembly shall then have adjourned any regular or special session, the bill shall be a law unless the governor shall, within fifteen calendar days after the same has been presented to him, transmit it to the secretary with his objections, in which case it shall not be a law unless such bill is reconsidered and repassed by the general assembly by at least a two-thirds vote of the members of each house of the general assembly at the time of its reconvening.

(See Art. III of Amendments to the Constitution of the State of Connecticut.)

SEC. 16. The governor shall have power to disapprove of any item or items of any bill making appropriations of money embracing distinct items while at the same time approving the remainder of the bill, and the part or parts of the bill so approved shall become effective and the item or items of appropriations so disapproved shall not take effect unless the same are separately reconsidered and repassed in accordance with the rules and limitations prescribed for the passage of bills over the executive veto. In all cases in which the governor shall exercise the right of disapproval hereby conferred he shall append to the bill at the time of signing it a statement of the item or items disapproved, together with his reasons for such disapproval, and transmit the bill and such appended statement to the secretary of the state. If the general assembly be then in session he shall forthwith cause a copy of such statement to be delivered to the house in which the bill originated for reconsideration of the disapproved items in conformity with the rules prescribed for legislative action in respect to bills which have received executive disapproval.

SEC. 17. The lieutenant-governor shall by virtue of his office, be president of the senate, and have, when in committee of the whole, a right to debate, and when the senate is equally divided, to give the casting vote.

SEC. 18. In case of the death, resignation, refusal to serve or removal from office of the governor, the lieutenant-governor shall, upon taking the oath of office of governor, be governor of the state until another is chosen at the next regular election for governor and is duly qualified. In case of the inability of the governor to exercise the powers and perform the duties of his office, or in case of his impeachment or of his absence from the state, the lieutenant-governor shall exercise the powers and authority and perform the duties appertaining to the office of governor until the disability is removed or, if the governor has been impeached, he is acquitted or, if absent, he has returned.

(Sec. 18 amended in 1984. See Art. XXII of Amendments to the Constitution of the State of Connecticut.)

SEC. 19. If the lieutenant-governor succeeds to the office of governor, or if the lieutenant-governor dies, resigns, refuses to serve or is removed from office, the president pro tempore of the senate shall, upon taking the oath of office of lieutenant-governor, be lieutenant-governor of the state until another is chosen at the next regular election for lieutenant-governor and is duly qualified. Within fifteen days of the administration of such oath the senate, if the general assembly is in session, shall elect one of its members president pro tempore. In case of the inability of the lieutenant-governor to exercise the powers and perform the duties of his office or in case of his impeachment or absence from the state, the president pro tempore of the senate shall exercise the powers and authority and perform the duties appertaining to the office of lieutenant-governor until the disability is removed or, if the lieutenant-governor has been impeached, he is acquitted or, if absent, he has returned.

SEC. 20. If, while the general assembly is not in session, there is a vacancy in the office of president pro tempore of the senate, the secretary of the state shall within fifteen days convene the senate for the purpose of electing one of its members president pro tempore.

SEC. 21. If, at the time fixed for the beginning of the term of the governor, the governor-elect shall have died or shall have failed to qualify, the lieutenant-governor-elect, after taking the oath of office of lieutenant-governor, may qualify as governor, and, upon so qualifying, shall become governor. The general assembly may by law provide for the case in which neither the governor-elect nor the lieutenant-governor-elect shall have qualified, by declaring who shall, in such event, act as governor or the manner in which the person who is so to act shall be selected, and such person shall act accordingly until a governor or a lieutenant-governor shall have qualified.

SEC. 22. The treasurer shall receive all monies belonging to the state, and disburse the same only as he may be directed by law. He shall pay no warrant, or order for the disbursement of public money, until the same has been registered in the office of the comptroller.

SEC. 23. The secretary of the state shall have the safe keeping and custody of the public records and documents, and particularly of the acts, resolutions and orders of the general assembly, and record the same; and perform all such duties as shall be prescribed by law. He shall be the keeper of the seal of the state, which shall not be altered.

SEC. 24. The comptroller shall adjust and settle all public accounts and demands, except grants and orders of the general assembly. He shall prescribe the mode of keeping and rendering all public accounts. He shall, ex officio, be one of the auditors of the accounts of the treasurer. The general assembly may assign to him other duties in relation to his office, and to that of the treasurer, and shall prescribe the manner in which his duties shall be performed.

SEC. 25. Sheriffs shall be elected in the several counties, on the Tuesday after the first Monday of November, 1966, and quadrennially thereafter, for the term of four years, commencing on the first day of June following their election. They shall become bound with sufficient sureties to the treasurer of the state, for the faithful discharge of the duties of their office. They shall be removable by the general assembly. In case the sheriff of any county shall die or resign, or shall be removed from office by the general assembly, the governor may fill the vacancy occasioned thereby, until the same shall be filled by the general assembly.

SEC. 26. A statement of all receipts, payments, funds, and debts of the state, shall be published from time to time, in such manner and at such periods, as shall be prescribed by law.

(New Section added in 1984. See Art. XXIII of Amendments to the Constitution of Connecticut.)

ARTICLE FIFTH.*
OF THE JUDICIAL DEPARTMENT.

SEC. 1. The judicial power of the state shall be vested in a supreme court, a superior court, and such lower courts as the general assembly shall, from time to time, ordain and establish. The powers and jurisdiction of these courts shall be defined by law.

(Sec. 1 amended in 1982. See Art. XX. Sec. 1 of Amendments to the Constitution of the State of Connecticut.)

SEC. 2. The judges of the supreme court and of the superior court shall, upon nomination by the governor, be appointed by the general assembly in such manner as shall by law be prescribed. They shall hold their offices for the term of eight years, but may be removed by impeachment. The governor shall also remove them on the address of two-thirds of each house of the general assembly.

(See Art. XI of Amendments to the Constitution of the State of Connecticut.)
(Sec. 2 amended in 1982. See Art. XX, Sec. 2 of Amendments to the Constitution of the State of Connecticut.)

SEC. 3. Judges of the lower courts shall, upon nomination by the governor, be appointed by the general assembly in such manner as shall by law be prescribed, for terms of four years.

SEC. 4. Judges of probate shall be elected by the electors residing in their respective districts on the Tuesday after the first Monday of November, 1966, and quadrennially thereafter, and shall hold office for four years from and after the Wednesday after the first Monday of the next succeeding January.

SEC. 5. Justices of the peace for the several towns in the state shall be elected by the electors in such towns; and the time and manner of their election, the number for each town, the period for which they shall hold their offices and their jurisdiction shall be prescribed by law.

(Sec. 5 repealed in 1974. See Art. VIII, Sec. 1 of Amendments to the Constitution of the State of Connecticut.)

SEC. 6. No judge or justice of the peace shall be eligible to hold his office after he shall arrive at the age of seventy years, except that a chief justice or judge of the supreme court, a judge of the superior court, or a judge of the court of common pleas, who has attained the age of seventy years and has become a state referee may exercise, as shall be prescribed by law, the powers of the superior court or court of common pleas on matters referred to him as a state referee.

(Sec. 6 amended in 1974. See Art. VIII, Sec. 2 of Amendments to the Constitution of the State of Connecticut.)
*(Art. Fifth amended in 1976. See Art. XI of Amendments to the Constitution of the State of Connecticut.)

ARTICLE SIXTH.†
OF THE QUALIFICATIONS OF ELECTORS.

SEC. 1. Every citizen of the United States who has attained the age of twenty-one years, who has resided in the town in which he offers himself to be admitted to the privileges of an elector at least six months next preceding the time he so offers himself, who is able to read in the English language any article of the constitution or any section of the statutes of the state, and who sustains a good moral character, shall, on his taking such oath as may be prescribed by law, be an elector.

(Sec. 1. amended in 1976. See Art. IX of Amendments to the Constitution of the State of Connecticut. See Art. XXVI of Amendments to the Constitution of the United States of America.)

SEC. 2. The qualifications of electors as set forth in Section 1 of this article shall be decided at such times and in such manner as may be prescribed by law.

SEC. 3. The general assembly shall by law prescribe the offenses on conviction of which the privileges of an elector shall be forfeited and the conditions on which and methods by which such rights may be restored.

(Sec. 3 amended in 1974. See Art. VII of Amendments to the Constitution of the State of Connecticut.)

SEC. 4. Laws shall be made to support the privilege of free suffrage, prescribing the manner of regulating and conducting meetings of the electors, and prohibiting, under adequate penalties, all undue influence therein, from power, bribery, tumult and other improper conduct.

SEC. 5. In all elections of officers of the state, or members of the general assembly, the votes of the electors shall be by ballot, either written or printed, except that voting machines or other mechanical devices for voting may be used in all elections in the state, under such regulations as may be prescribed by law. The right of secret voting shall be preserved. At every election where candidates are listed by party designation and where voting machines or other mechanical devices are used, each elector shall be able at his option to vote for candidates for office under a single party designation by operating a straight ticket device, or to vote for candidates individually after first operating a straight ticket device, or to vote for candidates individually without first operating a straight ticket device.

(Sec. 5 amended in 1986. See Art. XXIV of Amendments to the Constitution of the State of Connecticut.)

SEC. 6. At all elections of officers of the state, or members of the general assembly, the electors shall be privileged from arrest, during their attendance upon, and going to, and returning from the same, on any civil process.

SEC. 7. The general assembly may provide by law for voting in the choice of any officer to be elected or upon any question to be voted on at an election by qualified voters of the state who are unable to appear at the polling place on the day of election because of absence from the city or town of which they are inhabitants or because of sickness, or physical disability or because the tenets of their religion forbid secular activity.

SEC. 8. The general assembly may provide by law for the admission as electors in absentia of members of the armed forces, the United States merchant marine, members of religious or welfare groups or agencies attached to and serving with the armed forces and civilian employees of the United States, and the spouses and dependents of such persons.

(Sec. 8 amended in 1992. See Art. XXVII of Amendments to the Constitution of the State of Connecticut.)

SEC. 9. Any person admitted as an elector in any town shall, if he removes to another town, have the privileges of an elector in such other town after residing therein for six months. The general assembly shall prescribe by law the manner in which evidence of the admission of an elector and of the duration of his current residence shall be furnished to the town to which he removes.

(Sec. 9 repealed in 1980. See Art. XIII of Amendments to the Constitution of the State of Connecticut.)

SEC. 10. Every elector shall be eligible to any office in the state, except in cases provided for in this constitution.

(Sec. 10 amended in 1970. See Art. II, Sec. 3 of Amendments to the Constitution of the State of Connecticut.)

†(Art. Sixth amended in 1976. See Art. X of Amendments to the Constitution of the State of Connecticut.)

ARTICLE SEVENTH.
OF RELIGION.

It being the right of all men to worship the Supreme Being, the Great Creator and Preserver of the Universe, and to render that worship in a mode consistent with the dictates of their consciences, no person shall by law be compelled to join or support, nor be classed or associated with, any congregation, church or religious association. No preference shall be given by law to any religious society or denomination in the state. Each shall have and enjoy the same and equal powers, rights and privileges, and may support and maintain the ministers or teachers of its society or denomination, and may build and repair houses for public worship.

ARTICLE EIGHTH.
OF EDUCATION.

SEC. 1. There shall always be free public elementary and secondary schools in the state. The general assembly shall implement this principle by appropriate legislation.

SEC. 2. The state shall maintain a system of higher education, including The University of Connecticut, which shall be dedicated to excellence in higher education. The general assembly shall determine the size, number, terms and method of appointment of the governing boards of The University of Connecticut and of such constituent units or coordinating bodies in the system as from time to time may be established.

SEC. 3. The charter of Yale College, as modified by agreement with the corporation thereof, in pursuance of an act of the general assembly, passed in May, 1792, is hereby confirmed.

SEC. 4. The fund, called the SCHOOL FUND, shall remain a perpetual fund, the interest of which shall be inviolably appropriated to the support and encouragement of the public schools throughout the state, and for the equal benefit of all the people thereof. The value and amount of said fund shall be ascertained in such manner as the general assembly may prescribe, published, and recorded in the comptroller's office; and no law shall ever be made, authorizing such fund to be diverted to any other use than the encouragement and support of public schools, among the several school societies, as justice and equity shall require.

ARTICLE NINTH.
OF IMPEACHMENTS.

SEC. 1. The house of representatives shall have the sole power of impeaching.

SEC. 2. All impeachments shall be tried by the senate. When sitting for that purpose, they shall be on oath or affirmation. No person shall be convicted without the concurrence of at least two-thirds of the members present. When the governor is impeached, the chief justice shall preside.

SEC. 3. The governor, and all other executive and judicial officers, shall be liable to impeachment; but judgments in such cases shall not extend further than to removal from office, and disqualification to hold any office of honor, trust or profit under the state. The party convicted, shall, nevertheless, be liable and subject to indictment, trial and punishment according to law.

SEC. 4. Treason against the state shall consist only in levying war against it, or adhering to its enemies, giving them aid and comfort. No person shall be convicted of treason, unless on the testimony of at least two witnesses to the same overt act, or on confession in open court. No conviction of treason, or attainder, shall work corruption of blood, or forfeiture.

ARTICLE TENTH.
OF HOME RULE.

SEC. 1. The general assembly shall by general law delegate such legislative authority as from time to time it deems appropriate to towns, cities and boroughs relative to the powers, organization, and form of government of such political subdivisions. The general assembly shall from time to time by general law determine the maximum terms of office of the various town, city and borough elective offices. After July 1, 1969, the general assembly shall enact no special legislation relative to the powers, organization, terms of elective offices or form of government of any single town, city or borough, except as to (a) borrowing power, (b) validating acts, and (c) formation, consolidation or dissolution of any town, city or borough, unless in the delegation of legislative authority by general law the general assembly shall have failed to prescribe the powers necessary to effect the purpose of such special legislation.

SEC. 2. The general assembly may prescribe the methods by which towns, cities and boroughs may establish regional governments and the methods by which towns, cities, boroughs and regional governments may enter into compacts. The general assembly shall prescribe the powers, organization, form, and method of dissolution of any government so established.

ARTICLE ELEVENTH.
GENERAL PROVISIONS.

SEC. 1. Members of the general assembly, and all officers, executive and judicial, shall, before they enter on the duties of their respective offices, take the following oath or affirmation, to wit:

You do solemnly swear (or affirm, as the case may be) that you will support the constitution of the United States, and the constitution of the state of Connecticut, so long as you continue a citizen thereof; and that you will faithfully discharge, according to law, the duties of the office of...........to the best of your abilities. So help you God.

SEC. 2. Neither the general assembly nor any county, city, borough, town or school district shall have power to pay or grant any extra compensation to any public officer, employee, agent or servant, or increase the compensation of any public officer or employee, to take effect during the continuance in office of any person whose salary might be increased thereby, or increase the pay or compensation of any public contractor above the amount specified in the contract.
(Sec. 2 amended in 1982. See Art. XIX of Amendments to the Constitution of the State of Connecticut.)

SEC. 3. In order to insure continuity in operation of state and local governments in a period of emergency resulting from disaster caused by enemy attack, the general assembly shall provide by law for the prompt and temporary succession to the powers and duties of all public offices, the incumbents of which may become unavailable for carrying on their powers and duties.

SEC. 4. Claims against the state shall be resolved in such manner as may be provided by law.

SEC. 5. The rights and duties of all corporations shall remain as if this constitution had not been adopted; with the exception of such regulations and restrictions as are contained in this constitution. All laws not contrary to, or inconsistent with, the provisions of this constitution shall remain in force, until they shall expire by their own limitation, or shall be altered or repealed by the general assembly, in pursuance of this constitution. The validity of all bonds, debts, contracts, as well of individuals as of bodies corporate, or the state, of all suits, actions, or rights of action, both in law and equity, shall continue as if no change had taken place. All officers filling any office by election or appointment shall continue to exercise the duties thereof, according to their respective commissions or appointments, until their offices shall have been abolished or their successors selected and qualified in accordance with this constitution or the laws enacted pursuant thereto.

ARTICLE TWELFTH.*
OF AMENDMENTS TO THE CONSTITUTION.

Amendments to this constitution may be proposed by any member of the senate or house of representatives. An amendment so proposed, approved upon roll call by a yea vote of at least a majority, but by less than three-fourths, of the total membership of each house, shall be published with the laws which may have been passed at the same session and be continued to the regular session of the general assembly elected at the general election to be held on the Tuesday after the first Monday of November in the next even-numbered year. An amendment so proposed, approved upon roll call by a yea vote of at least three-fourths of the total membership of each house, or any amendment which, having been continued from the previous general assembly, is again approved upon roll call by a yea vote of at least a majority of the total membership of each house, shall, by the secretary of the state, be transmitted to the town clerk in each town in the state, whose duty it shall be to present the same to the electors thereof for their consideration at the general election to be held on the Tuesday after the first Monday of November in the next even-numbered year. If it shall appear, in a manner to be provided by law, that a majority of the electors present and voting on such amendment at such election shall have approved such amendment, the same shall be valid, to all intents and purposes, as a part of this constitution. Electors voting by absentee ballot under the provisions of the statutes shall be considered to be present and voting.

*(Art. Twelfth amended in 1974. See Art. VI of Amendments to the Constitution of the State of Connecticut.)

ARTICLE THIRTEENTH.
OF CONSTITUTIONAL CONVENTIONS.

SEC. 1. The general assembly may, upon roll call, by a yea vote of at least two-thirds of the total membership of each house, provide for the convening of a constitutional convention to amend or revise the constitution of the state not earlier than ten years from the date of convening any prior convention.

SEC. 2. The question "Shall there be a Constitutional Convention to amend or revise the Constitution of the State?" shall be submitted to all the electors of the state at the general election held on the Tuesday after the first Monday in November in the even-numbered year next succeeding the expiration of a period of twenty years from the date of convening of the last convention called to revise or amend the constitution of the state, including the Constitutional Convention of 1965, or next succeeding the expiration of a period of twenty years from the date of submission of such a question to all electors of the state, whichever date shall last occur. If a majority of the electors voting on the question shall signify "yes", the general assembly shall provide for such convention as provided in Section 3 of this article.

Sec. 3. In providing for the convening of a constitutional convention to amend or revise the constitution of the state the general assembly shall, upon roll call, by a yea vote of at least two-thirds of the total membership of each house, prescribe by law the manner of selection of the membership of such convention, the date of convening of such convention, which shall be not later than one year from the date of the roll call vote under Section 1 of this article or one year from the date of the election under Section 2 of this article, as the case may be, and the date for final adjournment of such convention.

Sec. 4. Proposals of any constitutional convention to amend or revise the constitution of the state shall be submitted to all the electors of the state not later than two months after final adjournment of the convention, either as a whole or in such parts and with such alternatives as the convention may determine. Any proposal of the convention to amend or revise the constitution of the state submitted to such electors in accordance with this section and approved by a majority of such electors voting on the question shall be valid, to all intents and purposes, as a part of this constitution. Such proposals when so approved shall take effect thirty days after the date of the vote thereon unless otherwise provided in the proposal.

ARTICLE FOURTEENTH.
OF THE EFFECTIVE DATE OF THIS CONSTITUTION.

This proposed constitution, submitted by the Constitutional Convention of 1965, shall become the constitution of the state of Connecticut upon approval by the people and proclamation by the governor as provided by law.

Approved at referendum on December 14, 1965; proclaimed by the Governor as adopted on December 30, 1965.

AMENDMENTS TO THE CONSTITUTION
OF THE STATE OF CONNECTICUT

ARTICLE I.

Section 1 of article fourth of the constitution is amended to read as follows: A general election for governor, lieutenant-governor, secretary of the state, treasurer, comptroller and attorney general shall be held on the Tuesday after the first Monday of November, 1974, and quadrennially thereafter.
Adopted November 25, 1970.

ARTICLE II.

SEC. 1. Section 3 of article third of the constitution is amended to read as follows: The senate shall consist of not less than thirty and not more than fifty members, each of whom shall have attained the age of twenty-one years and be an elector residing in the senatorial district from which he is elected. Each senatorial district shall be contiguous as to territory and shall elect no more than one senator.
(Sec. 1 amended in 1980. See Art. XV of Amendments to the Constitution of the State of Connecticut.)

SEC. 2. Section 4 of said article third is amended to read as follows: The house of representatives shall consist of not less than one hundred twenty-five and not more than two hundred twenty-five members, each of whom shall have attained the age of twenty-one years and be an elector residing in the assembly district from which he is elected. Each assembly district shall be contiguous as to territory and shall elect no more than one representative. For the purpose of forming assembly districts no town shall be divided except for the purpose of forming assembly districts wholly within the town.
(Sec. 2 amended in 1980. See Art. XV of Amendments to the Constitution of the State of Connecticut.)

SEC. 3. Section 10 of article sixth of the constitution is amended to read as follows: Every elector who has attained the age of twenty-one years shall be eligible to any office in the state, but no person who has not attained the age of twenty-one shall be eligible therefor, except in cases provided for in this constitution.
Adopted November 25, 1970.
(Sec. 3 amended in 1980. See Art. XV of Amendments to the Constitution of the State of Connecticut.)

ARTICLE III.

Section 2 of article third of the constitution is amended to read as follows: There shall be a regular session of the general assembly on the Wednesday following the first Monday of January in the odd-numbered years and on the Wednesday following the first Monday of February in the even-numbered years, and at such other times as the general assembly shall judge necessary; but the person administering the office of governor may, on special emergencies, convene the general assembly at any other time. All regular and special sessions of the general assembly shall be held at Hartford, but the person administering the office of governor may, in case of special emergency, convene the assembly at any other place in the state. The general assembly shall adjourn each regular session in the odd-numbered years not later than the first Wednesday after the first Monday in June and in the even-numbered years not later than the first Wednesday after the first Monday in May and shall adjourn each special session upon completion of its business. If any bill passed by any regular or special session or any appropriation item described in Section 16 of Article Fourth has been disapproved by the governor prior to its adjournment, and has not been reconsidered by the assembly, or is so disapproved after such adjournment, the

secretary of the state shall reconvene the general assembly on the second Monday after the last day on which the governor is authorized to transmit or has transmitted every bill to the secretary with his objections pursuant to Section 15 of Article Fourth of this constitution, whichever occurs first; provided if such Monday falls on a legal holiday the general assembly shall be reconvened on the next following day. The reconvened session shall be for the sole purpose of reconsidering and, if the assembly so desires, repassing such bills. The general assembly shall adjourn sine die not later than three days following its reconvening. In the even year session the general assembly shall consider no business other than budgetary, revenue and financial matters, bills and resolutions raised by committees of the general assembly and those matters certified in writing by the speaker of the house of representatives and president pro tempore of the senate to be of an emergency nature.
Adopted November 25, 1970.

ARTICLE IV.

Section 19 of article first of the constitution is amended to read as follows: The right of trial by jury shall remain inviolate, the number of such jurors, which shall not be less than six, to be established by law; but no person shall, for a capital offense, be tried by a jury of less than twelve jurors without his consent. In all civil and criminal actions tried by a jury, the parties shall have the right to challenge jurors peremptorily, the number of such challenges to be established by law. The right to question each juror individually by counsel shall be inviolate.
Adopted December 22, 1972.

ARTICLE V.

Section 20 of article first of the constitution is amended to read as follows: No person shall be denied the equal protection of the law nor be subjected to segregation or discrimination in the exercise or enjoyment of his or her civil or political rights because of religion, race, color, ancestry, national origin or sex.
Adopted November 27, 1974.
(Amended in 1984. See Art. XXI of the Amendments to the Constitution of the State of Connecticut.)

ARTICLE VI.

Article Twelfth of the constitution is amended to read as follows: Amendments to this constitution may be proposed by any member of the senate or house of representatives. An amendment so proposed, approved upon roll call by a yea vote of at least a majority, but by less than three-fourths, of the total membership of each house, shall be published with the laws which may have been passed at the same session and be continued to the regular session of the general assembly elected at the next general election to be held on the Tuesday after the first Monday of November in an even-numbered year. An amendment so proposed, approved upon roll call by a yea vote of at least three-fourths of the total membership of each house, or any amendment which, having been continued from the previous general assembly, is again approved upon roll call by a yea vote of at least a majority of the total membership of each house, shall, by the secretary of the state, be transmitted to the town clerk in each town in the state, whose duty it shall be to present the same to the electors thereof for their consideration at the next general election to be held on the Tuesday after the first Monday of November in an even-numbered year. If it shall appear, in a manner to be provided by law, that a majority of the electors present and voting on such amendment at such election shall have approved such amendment, the

same shall be valid, to all intents and purposes, as a part of this constitution. Electors voting by absentee ballot under the provisions of the statutes shall be considered to be present and voting.
Adopted November 27, 1974.

ARTICLE VII.

Section 3 of article sixth of the constitution is amended to read as follows: The general assembly shall by law prescribe the offenses on conviction of which the right to be an elector and the privileges of an elector shall be forfeited and the conditions on which and methods by which such rights may be restored.
Adopted November 27, 1974.

ARTICLE VIII.

SEC. 1. Section 5 of article fifth of the constitution is repealed.

SEC. 2. Section 6 of said article fifth is amended to read as follows: No judge shall be eligible to hold his office after he shall arrive at the age of seventy years, except that a chief justice or judge of the supreme court, a judge of the superior court, or a judge of the court of common pleas, who has attained the age of seventy years and has become a state referee may exercise, as shall be prescribed by law, the powers of the superior court or court of common pleas on matters referred to him as a state referee.
Adopted November 27, 1974.

ARTICLE IX.

Section 1 of article sixth of the constitution is amended to read as follows: Every citizen of the United States who has attained the age of eighteen years, who is a bona fide resident of the town in which he seeks to be admitted as an elector and who takes such oath, if any, as may be prescribed by law, shall be qualified to be an elector.
Adopted November 24, 1976.

ARTICLE X.

Article sixth of the constitution is amended by adding the following section:

SEC. 11. Any citizen who will have attained the age of eighteen years on or before the day of a regular election may apply for admission as an elector within the period of four months prior to such election, at such times and in such manner as may be prescribed by law, and, if qualified, shall become an elector on the day of his or her eighteenth birthday.
Adopted November 24, 1976; amended in 1980. (See Art. XIV of Amendments to the Constitution of the State of Connecticut.)

ARTICLE XI.

Article fifth of the constitution is amended by adding a new section to read as follows:

SEC. 7. In addition to removal by impeachment and removal by the governor on the address of two-thirds of each house of the general assembly, judges of all courts, except those courts to which judges are elected, may, in such manner as shall by law be prescribed, be removed or suspended by the supreme court. The general assembly may establish a judicial review council which may also, in such manner as shall by law be prescribed, censure any such judge or suspend any such judge for a definite period not longer than one year.

Adopted November 24, 1976.

ARTICLE XII.

Section 6 of article third of the constitution is amended to read as follows:

SEC. 6. a. The assembly and senatorial districts as now established by law shall continue until the regular session of the general assembly next after the completion of the next census of the United States. On or before the fifteenth day of February next following the completion of the decennial census of the United States, the general assembly shall appoint a reapportionment committee consisting of four members of the senate, two who shall be designated by the president pro tempore of the senate and two who shall be designated by the minority leader of the senate, and four members of the house of representatives, two who shall be designated by the speaker of the house of representatives and two who shall be designated by the minority leader of the house of representatives, provided there are members of no more than two political parties in either the senate or the house of representatives. In the event that there are members of more than two political parties in a house of the general assembly, all members of that house belonging to the parties other than that of the president pro tempore of the senate or the speaker of the house of representatives, as the case may be, shall select one of their number, who shall designate two members of the commission in lieu of the designation by the minority leader of that house. Such committee shall advise the general assembly on matters of apportionment. Such general assembly shall, upon roll call, by a yea vote of at least two-thirds of the membership of each house, enact such plan of districting as is necessary to preserve a proper apportionment of representation in accordance with the principles recited in this article. Thereafter the general assembly shall decennially at its next regular session following the completion of the census of the United States, upon roll call, by a yea vote of at least two-thirds of the membership of each house, enact such plan of districting as is necessary in accordance with the provisions of this article.

b. If the general assembly fails to enact a plan of districting by the fifteenth day of the May next following the completion of the decennial census of the United States, the governor shall forthwith appoint a commission designated by the president pro tempore of the senate, the speaker of the house of representatives, the minority leader of the senate and the minority leader of the house of representatives, each of whom shall designate two members of the commission, provided that there are members of no more than two political parties in either the senate or the house of representatives. In the event that there are members of more than two political parties in a house of the general assembly, all members of that house belonging to the parties other than that of the president pro tempore of the senate or the speaker of the house of representatives, as the case may be, shall select one of their number, who shall designate two members of the commission in lieu of the designation by the minority leader of that house. The eight members of the commission so designated shall within fifteen days select an elector of the state as a ninth member.

c. The commission shall proceed to consider the alteration of districts in accordance with the principles recited in this article and it shall submit a plan of districting to the secretary of the state by the first day of the September next succeeding the appointment of its members. No plan shall be submitted to the secretary unless it is certified by at least five members of the commission. Upon receiving such plan the secretary shall publish the same forthwith, and, upon publication, such plan of districting shall have the full force of law. If the commission shall fail to submit such a plan by the first day of September, the secretary of the state shall forthwith so notify the chief justice of the supreme court.

d. Original jurisdiction is vested in the supreme court to be exercised on the petition of any registered voter whereby said court may compel the commission, by mandamus or otherwise, to perform its duty or to correct any error made in its plan of districting, or said court may take such other action to effectuate the purposes of this article, including the establishing of a plan of districting if the commission fails to file its plan of districting by the first day of September as said court may deem appropriate. Any such petition shall be filed within forty-five days of the date specified for any duty or within forty-five days after the filing of a plan of districting. The supreme court shall render its decision not later than sixty days following the filing of such petition or shall file its plan with the secretary of the state not later than the fifteenth day of December next following the completion of the decennial census of the United States. Upon receiving such plan the secretary shall publish the same forthwith, and, upon publication, such plan of districting shall have the full force of law.

Adopted November 24, 1976; amended in 1980. (See Art. XVI of Amendments to the Constitution of the State of Connecticut.)

ARTICLE XIII.

Section 9 of article sixth of the constitution is repealed.

Adopted November 26, 1980.

ARTICLE XIV.

Article tenth of the amendments to the constitution is amended to read as follows: Any citizen who will have attained the age of eighteen years on or before the day of a regular election may apply for admission as an elector at such times and in such manner as may be prescribed by law, and, if qualified, shall become an elector on the day of his or her eighteenth birthday.

Adopted November 26, 1980.

ARTICLE XV.

SEC. 1. Section 1 of article two of the amendments to the constitution is amended to read as follows: The senate shall consist of not less than thirty and not more than fifty members, each of whom shall have attained the age of eighteen years and be an elector residing in the senatorial district from which he is elected. Each senatorial district shall be contiguous as to territory and shall elect no more than one senator.

SEC. 2. Section 2 of article two of the amendments to the constitution is amended to read as follows: The house of representatives shall consist of not less than one hundred twenty-five and not more than two hundred twenty-five members, each of whom shall have attained the age of eighteen years and be an elector residing in the assembly district from which he is elected. Each assembly district shall be contiguous as to territory and shall elect no more than one representative. For the purpose of forming assembly districts no town shall be divided except for the purpose of forming assembly districts wholly within the town.

SEC. 3. Section 3 of article two of the amendments to the constitution is amended to read as follows: Every elector who has attained the age of eighteen

years shall be eligible to any office in the state, but no person who has not attained the age of eighteen shall be eligible therefor, except in cases provided for in this constitution.
Adopted November 26, 1980.

ARTICLE XVI.

SEC. 1. Section 5 of article third of the constitution is amended to read as follows: The establishment of congressional districts and of districts in the general assembly shall be consistent with federal constitutional standards.

SEC. 2. Article twelve of the amendments to the constitution is amended to read as follows:

a. The assembly and senatorial districts and congressional districts as now established by law shall continue until the regular session of the general assembly next after the completion of the taking of the next census of the United States. On or before the fifteenth day of February next following the year in which the decennial census of the United States is taken, the general assembly shall appoint a reapportionment committee consisting of four members of the senate, two who shall be designated by the president pro tempore of the senate and two who shall be designated by the minority leader of the senate, and four members of the house of representatives, two who shall be designated by the speaker of the house of representatives and two who shall be designated by the minority leader of the house of representatives, provided there are members of no more than two political parties in either the senate or the house of representatives. In the event that there are members of more than two political parties in a house of the general assembly, all members of that house belonging to the parties other than that of the president pro tempore of the senate or the speaker of the house of representatives, as the case may be, shall select one of their number, who shall designate two members of the committee in lieu of the designation by the minority leader of that house. Such committee shall advise the general assembly on matters of apportionment. Upon the filing of a report of such committee with the clerk of the house of representatives and the clerk of the senate, the speaker of the house of representatives and the president pro tempore of the senate shall, if the general assembly is not in regular session, convene the general assembly in special session for the sole purpose of adopting a plan of districting. Upon the request of the speaker of the house of representatives and the president pro tempore of the senate, the secretary of the state shall give notice of such special session by mailing a true copy of the call of such special session, by registered or certified mail, return receipt requested, to each member of the house of representatives and of the senate at his or her address as it appears upon the records of said secretary not less than ten nor more than fifteen days prior to the date of convening of such special session or by causing a true copy of the call to be delivered to each member by a sheriff, deputy sheriff, constable, state policeman or indifferent person at least twenty-four hours prior to the time of convening of such special session. Such general assembly shall, upon roll call, by a yea vote of at least two-thirds of the membership of each house, adopt such plan of districting as is necessary to preserve a proper apportionment of representation in accordance with the principles recited in this article. Thereafter the general assembly shall decennially at its next regular session or special session called for the purpose of adopting a plan of districting following the completion of the taking of the census of the United States, upon roll call, by a yea vote of at least two-thirds of the membership of each house, adopt such plan of districting as is necessary in accordance with the provisions of this article.

b. If the general assembly fails to adopt a plan of districting by the first day of the August next following the year in which the decennial census of the United States is taken, the governor shall forthwith appoint a commission designated by the president pro tempore of the senate, the speaker of the house of representatives, the minority leader of the senate and the minority leader of the house of representatives, each of whom shall designate two members of the commission, provided that there are members of no more than two political parties in either the senate or the house of representatives. In the event that there are members of more than two political parties in a house of the general assembly, all members of that house belonging to the parties other than that of the president pro tempore of the senate or the speaker of the house of representatives, as the case may be, shall select one of their number, who shall designate two members of the commission in lieu of the designation by the minority leader of that house. The eight members of the commission so designated shall within thirty days select an elector of the state as a ninth member.

c. The commission shall proceed to consider the alteration of districts in accordance with the principles recited in this article and it shall submit a plan of districting to the secretary of the state by the thirtieth day of the October next succeeding the appointment of its members. No plan shall be submitted to the secretary unless it is certified by at least five members of the commission. Upon receiving such plan the secretary shall publish the same forthwith, and, upon publication, such plan of districting shall have the full force of law. If the commission shall fail to submit such a plan by the thirtieth day of October, the secretary of the state shall forthwith so notify the chief justice of the supreme court.

d. Original jurisdiction is vested in the supreme court to be exercised on the petition of any registered voter whereby said court may compel the commission, by mandamus or otherwise, to perform its duty or to correct any error made in its plan of districting, or said court may take such other action to effectuate the purposes of this article, including the establishing of a plan of districting if the commission fails to file its plan of districting by the thirtieth day of October as said court may deem appropriate. Any such petition shall be filed within thirty days of the date specified for any duty or within thirty days after the filing of a plan of districting. The supreme court shall render its decision not later than forty-five days following the filing of such petition or shall file its plan with the secretary of the state not later than the fifteenth day of January next following the time for submission of a plan of districting by the commission. Upon receiving such plan the secretary shall publish the same forthwith, and, upon publication, such plan of districting shall have the full force of law.

Adopted November 26, 1980.

(Sec. 2 amended in 1990. See Art XXVI of Amendments to the Constitution of the State of Connecticut.)

ARTICLE XVII.

Section 8 of the article first of the constitution is amended to read as follows: In all criminal prosecutions, the accused shall have a right to be heard by himself and by counsel; to be informed of the nature and cause of the accusation; to be confronted by the witnesses against him; to have compulsory process to obtain witnesses in his behalf; to be released on bail upon sufficient security, except in capital offenses, where the proof is evident or the presumption great; and in all prosecutions by information, to a speedy, public trial by an impartial jury. No person shall be compelled to give evidence against himself, nor be deprived of life, liberty or property without due process of law, nor shall excessive bail be required nor excessive fines imposed. No person shall be held to answer for any crime, punishable by death or life imprisonment, unless upon probable cause shown at a hearing in accordance with procedures prescribed by law, except in the armed forces, or in the militia when in actual service in time of war or public danger.

Adopted November 24, 1982.

ARTICLE XVIII.

Article second of the constitution is amended to read as follows: The powers of government shall be divided into three distinct departments, and each of them confided to a separate magistracy, to wit, those which are legislative, to one; those which are executive, to another; and those which are judicial, to another. The legislative department may delegate regulatory authority to the executive department; except that any administrative regulation of any agency of the executive department may be disapproved by the general assembly or a committee thereof in such manner as shall by law be prescribed.

Adopted November 24, 1982.

ARTICLE XIX.

Section 2 of the article eleventh of the constitution is amended to read as follows: Except as provided in this section, neither the state nor any political subdivision of the state shall pay or grant to any elected official of the state or any political subdivision of the state, any compensation greater than the amount of compensation set at the beginning of such official's term of office for the office which such official holds or increase the pay or compensation of any public contractor above the amount specified in the contract. The provisions of this section shall not apply to elected officials in towns in which the legislative body is the town meeting. The compensation of an elected official of a political subdivision of the state whose term of office is four years or more may be increased once after such official has completed two years of his term by the legislative body of such political subdivision. The term "compensation" means, with respect to an elected official, such official's salary, exclusive of reimbursement for necessary expenses or any other benefit to which his office would entitle him.

Adopted November 24, 1982.

ARTICLE XX.

SEC. 1. Section 1 of article fifth of the constitution is amended to read as follows: The judicial power of the state shall be vested in a supreme court, an appellate court, a superior court, and such lower courts as the general assembly shall, from time to time, ordain and establish. The powers and jurisdiction of these courts shall be defined by law.

SEC. 2. Section 2 of article fifth of the constitution is amended to read as follows: The judges of the supreme court, of the appellate court and of the superior court shall, upon nomination by the governor, be appointed by the general assembly in such manner as shall by law be prescribed. They shall hold their offices for the term of eight years, but may be removed by impeachment.

The governor shall also remove them on the address of two-thirds of each house of the general assembly.

Adopted November 24, 1982.
(Sec. 2 amended in 1986. See Art. XXV of Amendments to the Constitution of the State of Connecticut.)

ARTICLE XXI.

Article fifth of the amendments to the constitution is amended to read as follows: No person shall be denied the equal protection of the law nor be subjected to segregation or discrimination in the exercise or enjoyment of his or her civil or political rights because of religion, race, color, ancestry, national origin, sex or physical or mental disability.

Adopted November 28, 1984.

ARTICLE XXII.

Section 18 of article fourth of the constitution is amended to read as follows:

a. In case of the death, resignation, refusal to serve or removal from office of the governor, the lieutenant-governor shall, upon taking the oath of office of governor, be governor of the State until another is chosen at the next regular election for governor and is duly qualified.

b. In case of the impeachment of the governor or of his absence from the State, the lieutenant-governor shall exercise the powers and authority and perform the duties appertaining to the office of governor until, if the governor has been impeached, he is acquitted or, if absent, he has returned.

c. Whenever the governor transmits to the lieutenant-governor his written declaration that he is unable to exercise the powers and perform the duties of his office, and until the governor transmits to the lieutenant-governor a written declaration to the contrary, the lieutenant-governor shall exercise the powers and authority and perform the duties appertaining to the office of governor as acting governor.

d. In the absence of a written declaration of incapacity by the governor, whenever the lieutenant-governor or a majority of the members of the Council on Gubernatorial Incapacity transmits to the Council on Gubernatorial Incapacity a written declaration that the governor is unable to exercise the powers and perform the duties of his office, the Council shall convene within forty-eight hours after the receipt of such written declaration to determine if the governor is unable to exercise the powers and perform the duties of his office. If the Council, within fourteen days after it is required to convene, determines by two-thirds vote that the governor is unable to exercise the powers and perform the duties of his office, it shall transmit a written declaration to that effect to the president pro tempore of the Senate and the speaker of the House of Representatives and to the lieutenant-governor and the lieutenant-governor, upon receipt of such declaration, shall exercise the powers and authority and discharge the duties appertaining to the office of the governor as acting governor; otherwise, the governor shall continue to exercise the powers and discharge the duties of his office. Upon receipt by the president pro tempore of the Senate and the speaker of the House of Representatives of such a written declaration from the Council, the General Assembly shall, in accordance with its rules, decide the issue, assembling within forty-eight hours for that purpose if not in session. If the General Assembly, within twenty-one days after receipt of the written declaration or, if the General Assembly is not in session, within twenty-one days after the General Assembly is required to assemble, determines by two-thirds vote of each house that the governor is unable to exercise the powers and discharge the duties of his office, the lieutenant-governor shall continue to exercise the powers and authority and perform the duties appertaining to the office of governor; otherwise, the governor shall resume the powers and duties of his office.

e. In the absence of a written declaration of incapacity by the governor and in an emergency, when the governor is unable to exercise the powers and perform the duties of his office and the business of the State requires the immediate exercise of those powers and performance of those duties, the lieutenant-governor shall transmit to the Council on Gubernatorial Incapacity a written declaration to that effect and thereupon shall exercise the powers and authority and discharge the duties appertaining to the office of governor as acting governor. The Council shall convene or the members of the Council shall otherwise communicate with each other collectively within twenty-four hours after the receipt of such written declaration to determine if the governor is unable to exercise the powers and perform the duties of his office. If the Council, within fourteen days after it is required to convene, determines by two-thirds vote that the governor is unable to exercise the powers and perform the duties of his office, it shall transmit a written declaration to that effect to the president pro tempore of the Senate and the speaker of the House of Representatives and to the lieutenant-governor and the lieutenant-governor shall continue to exercise the powers and authority and perform the duties appertaining to the office of governor as acting governor; otherwise, the governor shall resume the powers and duties of his office. Upon receipt by the president pro tempore of the Senate and the speaker of the House of Representatives of such a written declaration from the Council, the General Assembly shall, in accordance with its rules, decide the issue, assembling within forty-eight hours for that purpose if not in session. If the General Assembly, within twenty-one days after receipt of the written declaration or, if the General Assembly is not in session, within twenty-one days after the General Assembly is required to assemble, determines by two-thirds vote of each house that the governor is unable to exercise the powers and discharge the duties of his office, the lieutenant-governor shall continue to exercise the powers and authority and perform the duties appertaining to the office of governor; otherwise, the governor shall resume the powers and duties of his office.

f. Whenever the governor transmits to the president pro tempore of the Senate and the speaker of the House of Representatives his written declaration that no inability exists he shall resume the powers and duties of his office upon the determination by a majority vote of each house of the General Assembly, in accordance with its rules, that he is able to exercise the powers and perform the duties of his office.

g. There shall be a Council on Gubernatorial Incapacity, the membership, procedures and terms of office of the members of which the General Assembly shall establish by law.

h. The Supreme Court shall have original and exclusive jurisdiction to adjudicate disputes or questions arising under this section.
Adopted November 28, 1984.

ARTICLE XXIII.

Article fourth of the constitution is amended by adding a new section to read as follows: There shall be established within the executive department a division

of criminal justice which shall be in charge of the investigation and prosecution of all criminal matters. Said division shall include the chief state's attorney, who shall be its administrative head, and the state's attorneys for each judicial district, which districts shall be established by law. The prosecutorial power of the state shall be vested in a chief state's attorney and the state's attorney for each judicial district. The chief state's attorney shall be appointed as prescribed by law. There shall be a commission composed of the chief state's attorney and six members appointed by the governor and confirmed by the General Assembly, two of whom shall be judges of the Superior Court. Said commission shall appoint a state's attorney for each judicial district and such other attorneys as prescribed by law.
Adopted November 28, 1984.

ARTICLE XXIV.

Section 5 of article sixth of the constitution is amended to read as follows:

In all elections of officers of the state, or members of the general assembly, the votes of the electors shall be by ballot, either written or printed, except that voting machines or other mechanical devices for voting may be used in all elections in the state, under such regulations as may be prescribed by law. No voting machine or device used at any state or local election shall be equipped with a straight ticket device. The right of secret voting shall be preserved.
Adopted November 19, 1986.

ARTICLE XXV.

Section 2 of article twenty of the amendments to the constitution is amended to read as follows:

Judges of all courts, except those courts to which judges are elected, shall be nominated by the governor exclusively from candidates submitted by the judicial selection commission. The commission shall seek and recommend qualified candidates in such numbers as shall by law be prescribed. Judges so nominated shall be appointed by the general assembly in such manner as shall by law be prescribed. They shall hold their offices for the term of eight years, but may be removed by impeachment. The governor shall also remove them on the address of two-thirds of each house of the general assembly and the supreme court may also remove them as is provided by law.
Adopted November 19, 1986.

ARTICLE XXVI

Section 2 of article sixteen of the amendments to the constitution is amended to read as follows:

a. The assembly and senatorial districts and congressional districts as now established by law shall continue until the regular session of the general assembly next after the completion of the taking of the next census of the United States. On or before the fifteenth day of February next following the year in which the decennial census of the United States is taken, the general assembly shall appoint a reapportionment committee consisting of four members of the senate, two who shall be designated by the president pro tempore of the senate and two who shall be designated by the minority leader of the senate, and four members of the house of representatives, two who shall be designated by the speaker of the house of representatives and two who shall be designated by the minority leader of the house of representatives, provided there are members of no more than two political parties in either the senate or the house of representatives. In the event that there are members of more than two political parties in a house of the general assembly, all members of that house belonging to the parties other than that of the president pro tempore of the senate or the speaker of the house of representatives, as the case may be, shall select one of their number, who shall designate two members of the committee in lieu of the designation by the minority leader of that house. Such committee shall advise the general assembly on matters of apportionment. Upon the filing of a report of such committee with the clerk of the house of representatives and the clerk of the senate, the speaker of the house of representatives and the president pro tempore of the senate shall, if the general assembly is not in regular session, convene the general assembly in special session for the sole purpose of adopting a plan of districting. Upon the request of the speaker of the house of representatives and the president pro tempore of the senate, the secretary of the state shall give notice of such special session by mailing a true copy of the call of such special session, by registered or certified mail, return receipt requested, to each member of the house of representatives and of the senate at his or her address as it appears upon the records of said scretary not less than ten nor more than fifteen days prior to the date of convening of such special session or by causing a true copy of the call to be delivered to each member by a sheriff, deputy sheriff, constable, state policeman or indifferent person at least twenty-four hours prior to the time of convening of such special session. Such general assembly shall, upon roll call, by a yea vote of at least two-thirds of the membership of each house, adopt such plan of districting as is necessary to preserve a proper apportionment of representation in accordance with the principles recited in this article. Thereafter the general assembly shall decennially at its next regular session or special session called for the purpose of adopting a plan of districting following the completion of the taking of the census of the United States, upon roll call, by a yea vote of at least two-thirds of the membership of each house, adopt such plan of districting as is necessary in accordance with the provisions of this article.

b. If the general assembly fails to adopt a plan of districting by the fifteenth day of the September next following the year in which the decennial census of the United States is taken, the governor shall forthwith appoint a commission designated by the president pro tempore of the senate, the speaker of the house of representatives, the minority leader of the senate and the minority leader of the house of representatives, each of whom shall designate two members of the commission, provided that there are members of no more than two political parties in either the senate or the house of representatives. In the event that there are members of more than two political parties in a house of the general assembly, all members of that house belonging to the parties other than that of the president pro tempore of the senate or the speaker of the house of representatives, as the case may be, shall select one of their number, who shall designate two members of the commission in lieu of the designation by the minority leader of that house. The eight members of the commission so designated shall within thirty days select an elector of the state as a ninth member.

c. The commission shall proceed to consider the alteration of districts in accordance with the principles recited in this article and it shall submit a plan of districting to the secretary of the state by the thirtieth day of the November next succeeding the appointment of its members. No plan shall be submitted to the secretary unless it is certified by at least five members of the commission.

Upon receiving such plan the secretary shall publish the same forthwith, and, upon publication, such plan of districting shall have the full force of law. If the commission shall fail to submit such a plan by the thirtieth day of November, the secretary of the state shall forthwith so notify the chief justice of the supreme court.

d. Original jurisdiction is vested in the supreme court to be exercised on the petition of any registered voter whereby said court may compel the commission, by mandamus or otherwise, to perform its duty or to correct any error made in its plan of districting, or said court may take such other action to effectuate the purposes of this article, including the establishing of a plan of districting if the commission fails to file its plan of districting by the thirtieth day of November as said court may deem appropriate. Any such petition shall be filed within thirty days of the date specified for any duty or within thirty days after the filing of a plan of districting. The supreme court shall render its decision not later than forty-five days following the filing of such petition or shall file its plan with the secretary of the state not later than the fifteenth day of February next following the time for submission of a plan of districting by the commission. Upon receiving such plan the secretary shall publish the same forthwith, and, upon publication, such plan of districting shall have the full force of the law.
Adopted November 28, 1990.

ARTICLE XXVII.

Section 8 or article sixth of the constitution is amended to read as follows:

The general assembly may provide by law for the absentee admission of electors.
Adopted November 25, 1992.

ARTICLE XXVIII.

Article third of the constitution is amended by adding section 18 as follows:

Sec. 18 a. The amount of general budget expenditures authorized for any fiscal year shall not exceed the estimated amount of revenue for such fiscal year.

b. The General assembly shall not authorize an increase in general budget expenditures for any fiscal year above the amount of general budget expenditures authorized for the previous fiscal year by a percentage which exceeds the greater of the percentage increase in personal income or the percentage increase in inflation, unless the governor declares an emergency or the existence of extraordinary circumstances and at least three-fifths of the members of each house of the general assembly vote to exceed such limit for the purposes of such emergency or extraordinary circumstances. The general assembly shall by law define "increase in personal income", "increase in inflation" and "general budget expenditures" for the purposes of this section and may amend such definitions, from time to time, provided general budget expenditures shall not include expenditures for the payment of bonds, notes or other evidences of indebtedness. The enactment or amendment of such definitions shall require the vote of three-fifths of the members of each house of the general assembly.

c. Any unappropriated surplus shall be used to fund a budget reserve fund or for the reduction of bonded indebtedness; or for any other purpose authorized by at least three-fifths of the members of each house of the general assembly.
Adopted November 25, 1992.

ARTICLE XXIX.

Article seventeen of the amendments to the constitution is amended to read as follows:

a. In all Criminal prosecutions, the accused shall have a right to be heard by himself and by counsel; to be informed of the nature and cause of the accusation; to be confronted by the witnesses against him; to have compulsory process to obtain witnesses in his behalf; to be released on bail upon sufficient security, except in capital offenses, where the proof is evident or the presumption great; and in all prosecutions by information, to a speedy, public trial by an impartial jury. No person shall be compelled to give evidence against himself, nor be deprived of life, liberty or property without due process of law, nor shall excessive bail be required nor excessive fines imposed. No person shall be held to answer for any crime, punishable by death or life imprisonment, unless upon probable cause shown at a hearing in accordance with procedures prescribed by law, except in the armed forces, or in the militia when in actual service in time of war or public danger.

b. In all criminal prosecutions, a victim, as the General Assembly may define by law, shall have the following rights: (1) the right to be treated with fairness and respect throughout the criminal justice process; (2) the right to timely disposition of the case following arrest of the accused, provided no right of the accused is abridged; (3) the right to be reasonably protected from the accused throughout the criminal justice process; (4) the right to notification of court proceedings; (5) the right to attend the trial and all other court proceedings the accused has the right to attend, unless such person is to testify and the court determines that such person's testimony would be materially affected if such person hears other testimony; (6) the right to communicate with the prosecution; (7) the right to object to or support any plea agreement entered into by the accused and the prosecution and to make a statement to the court prior to the acceptance by the court of the plea of guilty or nolo contendere by the accused; (8) the right to make a statement to the court at sentencing; (9) the right to restitution which shall be enforceable in the same manner as any other cause of action or as otherwise provided by law; and (10) the right to information about the arrest, conviction, sentence, imprisonment and release of the accused. The General Assembly shall provide by law for the enforcement of this subsection. Nothing in this subsection or in any law enacted pursuant to this subsection shall be construed as creating a basis for vacating a conviction or ground for appellate relief in any criminal case.

HISTORICAL ANTECEDENTS

THE FIRST CONSTITUTION OF CONNECTICUT

*The "Fundamental Orders," 1638-9.

"Voted" January 14 1638 the Fundamental Orders were the beginning of Connecticut as a commonwealth. Their spirit was that of a sermon preached by the Rev. Thomas Hooker a short time before their adoption in the course of which he laid down the proposition "The foundation of authority is laid in the free consent of the people" and which he closed with the challenge: "As God has given us liberty let us take it." They recognized no allegiance on the part of the colonists to England but in effect set up an independent government. In the sense that they were intended to be a framework of government more permanent than the usual orders adopted by the General Court they were in essence a constitution. The historian John Fiske was justified in his statement that this instrument was "the first written constitution known to history that created a government and it marked the beginning of American democracy." While in 1662 the Fundamental Orders were in a sense superseded by the charter that document drawn up in the colony and taken to England by its representative was never regarded by the colonists as the source of their government but as a protection for and guaranty of the government they had already set up for themselves. So it was that for forty years after the independence of this nation Connecticut could still carry on its government under the charter. And so it is that this commonwealth has preserved a continuity of development beyond that of almost any other state or nation in the world.

By: William M. Maltbie

Forasmuch as it hath pleased the Almighty God by the wise disposition of his divine providence so to order and dispose of things that we the Inhabitants and Residents of Windsor, Hartford, and Wethersfield are now cohabiting and dwelling in and upon the River of Connectecotte and the lands thereunto adjoining; and well knowing where a people are gathered together the word of God requires that to maintain the peace and union of such a people there should be an orderly and decent Government established according to God, to order and dispose of the affairs of the people at all seasons as occasion shall require; do therefore associate and conjoin ourselves to be as one Public State or Commonwealth; and do for ourselves and our Successors and such as shall be adjoined to us at any time hereafter, enter into Combination and Confederation together, to maintain and preserve the liberty and purity of the Gospel of our Lord Jesus which

---

*The original "Fundamental Orders" of 1638-39 are on permanent exhibition at the Museum of Connecticut History, 231 Capitol Ave., Hartford.

we now profess, as also the discipline of the Churches, which according to the truth of the said Gospel is now practiced amongst us; as also in our Civil affairs to be guided and governed according to such Laws, Rules, Orders, and Decrees as shall be made, ordered, and decreed as followeth:—

1. It is Ordered, sentenced, and decreed, that there shall be yearly two General Assemblies or Courts, the one the second Thursday in April, the other the second Thursday in September following; the first shall be called the Court of Election, wherein shall be yearly chosen from time to time so many Magistrates and other public Officers as shall be found requisite: Whereof one to be chosen Governor for the year ensuing and until another be chosen, and no other Magistrate to be chosen for more than one year: provided always there be six chosen besides the Governor, which being chosen and sworn according to an Oath recorded for that purpose, shall have power to administer justice according to the Laws here established, and for want thereof, according to the rule of the Word of God; which choice shall be made by all that are admitted freemen and have taken the Oath of Fidelity, and do cohabit within this Jurisdiction (*Having been admitted Inhabitants by the major part of the Town wherein they live) or the major part of such as shall be then present.

2. It is Ordered, sentenced, and decreed, that the Election of the aforesaid Magistrates shall be on this manner: every person present and qualified for choice shall bring in (to the persons deputed to receive them) one single paper with the name of him written in it whom he desires to have Governor, and he that hath the greatest number of papers shall be Governor for that year. And the rest of the Magistrates or public officers to be chosen in this manner: the Secretary for the time being shall first read the names of all that are to be put to choice and then shall severally nominate them distinctly, and every one that would have the person nominated to be chosen shall bring in one single paper written upon, and he that would not have him chosen shall bring in a blank; and every one that hath more written papers than blanks shall be a Magistrate for that year; which papers shall be received and told by one or more that shall be then chosen by the court and sworn to be faithful therein; but in case there should not be six chosen as aforesaid, besides the Governor, out of those which are nominated, then he or they which have the most written papers shall be a Magistrate or Magistrates for the ensuing year, to make up the aforesaid number.

3. It is Ordered, sentenced, and decreed, that the Secretary shall not nominate any person, nor shall any person be chosen newly into the Magistracy which was not propounded in some General Court before, to be nominated the next Election; and to that end it shall be lawful for each of the Towns aforesaid by their deputies to nominate any two whom they conceive fit to be put to election; and the Court may add so many more as they judge requisite.

---

*This clause was interlined in a different handwriting, and is of a later date. It was adopted by the General Court of November, 1643.

4. It is Ordered, sentenced, and decreed, that no person be chosen Governor above once in two years, and that the Governor be always a member of some approved congregation, and formerly of the Magistracy within this Jurisdiction; and all the Magistrates, Freemen of this Commonwealth; and that no Magistrate or other public officer shall execute any part of his or their office before they are severally sworn, which shall be done in the face of the court if they be present, and in case of absence by some deputed for that purpose.

5. It is Ordered, sentenced, and decreed, that to the aforesaid Court of Election the several Towns shall send their deputies, and when the Elections are ended they may proceed in any public service as at other Courts. Also the other General Court in September shall be for making of laws, and any other public occasion, which concerns the good of the Commonwealth.

6. It is Ordered, sentenced, and decreed, that the Governor shall, either by himself or by the Secretary, send out summons to the Constables of every Town for the calling of these two standing Courts one month at least before their several times: And also if the Governor and the greatest part of the Magistrates see cause upon any special occasion to call a General Court, they may give order to the Secretary so to do within fourteen days' warning: And if urgent necessity so required, upon a shorter notice, giving sufficient grounds for it to the deputies when they meet, or else be questioned for the same; And if the Governor and major part of Magistrates shall either neglect or refuse to call the two General standing Courts or either of them, as also at other times when the occasions of the Commonwealth require, the Freemen thereof, or the major part of them, shall petition to them so to do; if then it be either denied or neglected, the said Freemen, or the major part of them, shall have power to give order to the Constables of the several Towns to do the same, and so may meet together, and choose to themselves a Moderator, and may proceed to do any act of power which any other General Courts may.

7. It is Ordered, sentenced, and decreed, that after there are warrants given out for any of the said General Courts, the Constable or Constables of each Town, shall forthwith give notice distinctly to the inhabitants of the same, in some public assembly or by going or sending from house to house, that at a place and time by him or them limited and set, they meet and assemble themselves together to elect and choose certain deputies to be at the General Court then following to agitate the affairs of the Commonwealth; which said deputies shall be chosen by all that are admitted Inhabitants in the several Towns and have taken the oath of fidelity; provided that none be chosen a Deputy for any General Court which is not a Freeman of this Commonwealth.

The aforesaid deputies shall be chosen in manner following: every person that is present and qualified as before expressed, shall bring the names of such, written in several papers, as they desire to have chosen for that employment, and these three or four, more or less, being the number agreed on to be chosen for that time, that have greatest number of papers written for them shall be deputies for that Court; whose names shall be endorsed on the back side of the warrant and returned into the Court, with the constable or constables' hand unto the same.

8. It is Ordered, sentenced, and decreed, that Windsor, Hartford, and Wethersfield shall have power, each Town, to send four of their Freemen as their deputies to every General Court; and Whatsoever other Town shall be hereafter added to this Jurisdiction, they shall send so many deputies as the Court shall judge meet, a reasonable proportion to the number of Freemen that are in the said Towns being to be attended therein; which deputies shall have the power of the whole Town to give their votes and allowance to all such laws and orders as may be for the public good, and unto which the said Towns are to be bound.

9. It is Ordered and decreed, that the deputies thus chosen shall have power and liberty to appoint a time and a place of meeting together before any General Court, to advise and consult of all such things as may concern the good of the public, as also to examine their own Elections, whether according to the order, and if they or the greatest part of them find any election to be illegal they may seclude such for present from their meeting, and return the same and their reasons to the Court; and if it prove true, the Court may fine the party or parties so intruding, and the Town, if they see cause, and give out a warrant to go to a new election in a legal way, either in part or in whole. Also the said deputies shall have power to fine any that shall be disorderly at their meetings, or for not coming in due time or place according to appointment; and they may return the said fines into the Court if it be refused to be paid, and the Treasurer to take notice of it, and to escheat or levy the same as he does other fines.

10. It is Ordered, sentenced, and decreed, that every General Court, except such as through neglect of the Governor and the greatest part of Magistrates the Freemen themselves do call, shall consist of the Governor, or some one chosen to moderate the Court, and four other Magistrates at least, with the major part of the deputies of the several Towns legally chosen; and in case the Freemen, or major part of them, through neglect or refusal of the Governor and major part of the Magistrates, shall call a Court, it shall consist of the major part of Freemen that are present or their deputies, with a Moderator chosen by them: In which said General Courts shall consist the supreme power of the Commonwealth, and they only shall have power to make laws or repeal them, to grant levies, to admit of Freemen, dispose of lands undisposed of, to several Towns or persons, and also shall have power to call either Court or Magistrate or any other person whatsoever into question for any misdemeanor, and may for just causes displace or deal otherwise according to the nature of the offense; and also may deal in any other matter that concerns the good of this Commonwealth, except election of Magistrates, which shall be done by the whole body of Freemen.

In which Court the Governor or Moderator shall have power to order the Court, to give liberty of speech, and silence unseasonable and disorderly speakings, to put all things to vote, and in case the vote be equal to have the casting voice. But none of these Courts shall be adjourned or dissolved without the consent of the major part of the Court.

11. It is Ordered, sentenced, and decreed, that when any General Court upon the occasions of the Commonwealth have agreed upon any sum, or sums of money to be levied upon the several Towns within this Jurisdiction, that a committee be chosen to set out and appoint what shall be the proportion of every Town to pay of the said levy, provided the committee be made up of an equal number out of each Town.

14th January 1638 the 11 Orders above said are voted.

*CHARTER OF THE COLONY OF CONNECTICUT, 1662

CHARLES THE SECOND, BY THE GRACE OF GOD, King of England, Scotland, France and Ireland, defender of the Faith, &c.; To all to whome theis presents shall come Greetings: WHEREAS, by the severall Navigacons, discoveryes and susscessfull Plantacons of diverse of our loving Subjects of this our Realme of England, Severall Lands, Islands, Places, Colonies and Plantacons have byn obtayned and setled in that parte of the Continent of America called New England, and thereby the Trade and Comerce there hath byn of late yeares much increased, AND WHEREAS, wee have byn informed by the humble Peticon of our Trusty and welbeloved John Winthrop, John Mason, Samuell Willis, Henry Clerke, Mathew Allen, John Tappen, Nathan Gold, Richard Treate, Richard Lord, Henry Woolicott, John Talcott, Daniell Clerke, John Ogden, Thomas Wells, Obedias Brewen, John Clerke, Anthony Haukins, John Deming and Mathew Camfeild, being Persons Principally interested in our Colony or Plantacon of Connecticut in New England, that the same Colony or the greatest parte thereof was purchased and obteyned for greate and valuable Consideracons, And some other part thereof gained by Conquest and with much difficulty, and att the onely endeavours, expence and Charge of them and their Associates, and those vnder whome they Clayme, Subdued and improved, and thereby become a considerable enlargement and addicon of our Dominions and interest there.—NOW KNOW YEA, that in consideracion thereof, and in regard the said Colony is remote from other the English Plantacons in the Places aforesaid, And to the end the Affaires and Business which shall from tyme to tyme happen or arise concerning the same may be duely Ordered and managed. WEE HAVE thought fitt, and att the humble Peticon of the Persons aforesaid, and are graciously pleased to Create and Make them a Body Pollitique and Corporate, with the powers and Priviliges herein after menconed; And Accordingly Our will and pleasure is, and of our especiall grace, certeine knowledge and meere mocon wee have Ordeyned, Constituted and Declared, And by theis presents, for vs, our heires and Successors, Doe Ordeine, Constitute and Declare That they, the said John Winthrop, John Mason, Samuell Willis, Henry Clerke, Mathew Allen, John Tappen, Nathan Gold, Richard Treate, Richard Lord, Henry Woollcot, John Talcot, Daniell Clerke, John Ogden, Thomas Wells, Obadiah Brewen, John Clerke, Anthony Hawkins, John Deming and Mathew Camfeild, and all such others as now are or hereafter shall bee Admitted and made free of the Company and Society of our Collony of Connecticut in America, shall from tyme to tyme and forever hereafter, bee one Body Corporate and Pollitique in fact and name, by the Name of Governour and Company of the English Collony of Connecticut in New England in America; And that by the same name they and their Successors shall and may have perpetuall Succession, and shall and mey bee Persons able and Capable in the law to Plead and bee Impleaded, to Answere and to be Answered vnto, to Defend and bee Defended in all and Singular, Suits, Causes, quarrelles, Matters, Accons

---

*The original Charter of the Colony of Connecticut, is on permanent exhibition at the Museum of Connecticut History, 231 Capitol Ave., Hartford.

and things of what kind or nature soever, And alsoe to have, take, possesse, acquire and purchase lands Tenements or hereditaments, or any goods or Chattells, and the same to, Lease, Graunt, Demise, Alien, bargaine, Sell and dispose of, as other our leige People of this our Realme of England, or any other Corporacon or Body Politique within the same may lawfully doe. AND FURTHER, that the said Governour and Company, and their Successors shall and may for ever hereafter have a Comon Seale to serve and vse for all Causes, matters, things and affaires, whatsoever of them and their Successors, and the same Seale to alter, change, breake and make new from tyme to tyme att their wills and pleasures, as they shall thinke fitt. And further, wee will and Ordeine, and by theis presents for vs, our heires and Successors Doe Declare and appoint, that for the better ordering and manageing of the affaires and businesse of the said Company and their Successors, there shall be one Governour, one Deputy Governour and Twelve Assistants to bee from tyme to tyme Constituted, Elected and Chosen out of the Freemen of the said Company for the tyme being, in such manner and forme as hereafter in these presents is expressed; which said Officers shall apply themselves to take care for the best disposeing and Ordering of the Generall business and affaires of and concerning the lands and hereditaments herein after menconed to bee graunted, and the Plantacon thereof and the Government of the People thereof. And for the better execucon of our Royall Pleasure herein, WEE DOE for vs, our heires and Successors, Assigne, name, Constitute and appoint the aforesaid John Winthrop to bee *the* first and present Governour of the said Company; And the said John Mason to bee *the* Deputy Governour; And the said Samuell Willis, Mathew Allen, Nathan Gold, Henry Clerke, Richard Treat, John Ogden, Thomas Tappen, John Talcott, Thomas Wells, Henry Woolcot, Richard Lord and Daniell Clerke to bee the Twelve present Assistants of the said Company; to contynue in the said severall Offices respectively, vntill the second Thursday which shall bee in the moneth of October now next comeing. AND further, wee will, and by theis presents for vs, our heires and Successors DOE Ordaine and Graunt that the Governour of the said Company for the tyme being, or, in his absence by occasion of sicknes, or otherwise by his leave or permission, the Deputy Governour for the tyme being, shall and may from tyme to tyme vpon all occasions give Order for the assembling of the said Company and calling them together to Consult and advise of the businesse and Affairs of the said Company, And that for ever hereafter Twice in every yeare, (That is to say,) on every Second Thursday in October and on every Second Thursday in May, or oftener, in Case it shall bee requisite, The Assistants and freemen of the said Company, or such of them, (not exceeding twoe Persons from each Place, Towne or Citty) whoe, shall bee from tyme to tyme therevnto Elected or deputed by the major parte of the freemen of the respective Townes, Cittyes and Places for which they shall bee soe elected or Deputed, shall have a generall meeting or Assembly, then and their to Consult and advise in and about the Affaires And businesse of the said Company; And that the Governour, or in his absence the Deputy Governour of the said Company for the tyme being, and such of the Assistants and freemen of the said Company as shall be soe Elected or Deputed and bee present att such meeting or Assembly, or the greatest number of them, whereof the Governour or Deputy Governour and Six of the Assistants, at least, to bee Seaven, shall be called the Generall Assembly, and shall have full power and authority to alter and change their dayes and tymes of meeting or Generall Assemblies for Electing the Governour, Deputy Governour and Assistants or other Officers or any other Courts, Assemblies or meetings, and to Choose, Nominate and appoint such and soe many other Persons as they shall thinke fitt and shall bee willing to accept the same, to bee free of the said Company and Body Politique, and them into the same to Admitt and to Elect, and Constitute such Officers as they shall thinke fitt and requisite for the Ordering, Manageing and disposeing of the Affaires of the said Governour and Company and their Successors. AND WEE DOE hereby for vs, our heires and Successors, Establish and Ordeine, that once in the yeare for ever hereafter, namely, the said Second Thursday in May, the Governour, Deputy Governour, and Assistants of the said Company and other Officers of the said Company, or such of them as the said Generall Assembly shall thinke fitt, shall bee in the said Generall Court and Assembly to be held from that day or tyme, newly Chosen for the yeare ensuing, by such greater parte of the said Company for the tyme being then and there present. And if the Governour, Deputy Governour and Assistants by these presents appointed, or such as hereafter bee newly Chosen into their Roomes, or any of them, or any other the Officers to bee appointed for the said Company shall dye or bee removed from his or their severall Offices or Places before the said Generall day of Eleccon, whome wee doe hereby Declare for any misdemeanour or default to bee removeable by the Governour, Assistants and Company, or such greater part of them in any of the said publique Courts to be Assembled as is aforesaid, That then and in every such Case itt shall and may bee lawfull to and for the Governour, Deputy Governour and Assistants and Company aforesaid, or such greater parte of them soe to bee Assembled as is aforesaid in any of their Assemblies, to proceede to a New Eleccon of one or more of their Company in the Roome or place, Roomes or Places of such Governour, Deputy Governour, Assistant or other Officer or Officers soe dyeing or removed, according to their discretions; and immediately vpon and after such Eleccon or Eleccons made of such Governour, Deputy Governour, Assistant or Assistants, or any other Officer of the said Company in manner and forme, Aforesaid, The Authority Office and Power before given to the former Governour, Deputy Governour or other Officer and Officers soe removed, in whose stead and Place new shall be chosen, shall as to him and them and every of them respectively cease and determine. PROVIDED, alsoe, and our will and pleasure is, That as well such as are by theis presents appointed to bee the present Governour, Deputy Governour and Assistants of the said Company as those that *shall* succeed them, and all other Officers to bee appointed and Chosen as aforesaid, shall, before they vndertake the Execucon of their said Offices and places respectively, take their severall and respective Corporall Oathes for the due and faithfull performance of their dutyes in their severall Offices and Places, before such Person or Persons as are by these Presents hereafter appoynted to take and receive the same; That is to say, the said John Winthrop, whoe is herein before nominated and appointed the present Governour of the said Company, shall take the said Oath before one or more of the Masters of our Court of Chancery for the tyme being, vnto which Master of Chancery WEE DOE, by theis presents, give full power and authority to administer the said Oath to the said John Winthrop accordingly. And the said John Mason, whoe is herein before nominated and appointed the present Deputy Governour of the said Company, shall take the said Oath before the said John Winthrop, or any twoe of the Assistants of the said Company, vnto whome WEE DOE by these presents, give full power and authority to Administer the said Oath to the said John Mason accordingly. And the said Samuell Willis, Henry Clerke, Mathew Allen, John Tappen, Nathan Gold, Richard Treate, Richard Lord, Henry Woolcott, John

Talcott, Daniell Clerke, John Ogden and Thomas Welles, whoe are herein before Nominated and appointed the present Assistants of the said Company, shall take the Oath before *the* said John Winthrop and John Mason, or one of them, to whome WEE DOE hereby give full power and authority to Administer the same accordingly. And our further will and pleasure, is that all and every Governour or Deputy Governour to bee Elected and Chosen by vertue of theis presents, shall take the said Oath before two or more of the Assistants of the said Company for the tyme being, vnto whom wee doe, by theis presents, give full power and authority to give and Administer the said Oath accordingly. And the said Assistants and every of them, and all and every other Officer or Officers to bee hereafter Chosen from tyme to tyme, to take the said Oath before the Governour or Deputy Governour for the tyme being, vnto which said Governour or Deputy Governour wee doe, by theis presents, give full power and authority to Administer the same accordingly. AND FURTHER, of our more amplegrace, certeine knowledge and meere mocon WEE HAVE given and Graunted, and by theis presents, for vs, our heires and Successors, DOE give and Graunt vnto the said Governour and Company of the English Colony of Connecticut in New England in America, and to every Inhabitant there, and to every Person and Persons Trading thither, And to every such Person and Persons as are or shall bee free of the said Collony, full power and authority from tyme to tyme and att all tymes hereafter, to take, Ship, Transport and Carry away, for and towards the Plantacon and defence of the said Collony such of our loveing Subjects and Strangers as shall or will willingly accompany them in and to their said Collony and Plantacon: (Except such Person and Persons as are or shall bee therein restrayned by vs, our heires and Successors:) And alsoe to Ship and Transport all and all manner of goods, Chattells, Merchandizes and other things whatsoever that are or shall be vsefull or necessary for the Inhabitants of the said Collony and may lawfully bee Transported thither; Neverthe lesse, not to bee discharged of payment to vs, our heires and Successors, of the Dutyes, Customes and Subsidies which are or ought to bee paid or payable for the same. AND FURTHER, Our will and pleasure is, and WEE DOE for vs, our heires and Successors, Ordeyne, Declare and Graunt vnto the said Governour and Company and their Successors, That all and every the Subjects of vs, our heires or Successors which shall goe to Inhabite within the said Colony, and every of their Children which shall happen to bee borne there or on the Sea in goeing thither or returneing from thence, shall have and enjoye all liberties and immunities of free and naturall Subjects within any the Dominions of vs, our heires or Successors, to all intents, Construccons and purposes whatsoever, as if they and every of them were borne within the Realme of England, AND WEE DOE authorize and impower the Governour, or in his absence the Deputy Governour for the tyme being, to appointe two or more of the said assistants att any of their Courts or Assemblyes to bee held as aforesaid, to have power and authority to Administer the Oath of Supremacy and obedience to all and every Person and Persons which shall att any tyme or tymes hereafter goe or passe into the said Colony of Connecticutt, vnto which said Assistants soe to bee appointed as aforesaid, WEE DOE, by these presents, give full power and authority to Administer the said Oath accordingly. AND WEE DOE FURTHER, of our especiall grace, certeine knowledge and meere mocon, give and Graunt vnto the said Governour and Company of the English Colony of Connecticutt in New England in America, and their Successors, that itt shall and may bee lawful to and for the Governour or Deputy Governour and such of the Assistants of the said Company for the tyme being as shall bee

Assembled in any of the Generall Courts aforesaid, or in any Courts to be especially Sumoned or Assembled for that purpose, or the greater parte of them, whereof the Governour or Deputy Governour and Six of the Assistants, to be all wayes Seaven, to Erect and make such Judicatories for the heareing and Determining of all Accons, Causes, matters and things happening within the said Colony or Plantacon and which shall bee in dispute and depending there, as they shall thinke fitt and convenient; And alsoe from tyme to tyme to Make, Ordaine and Establish All manner of wholesome and reasonable Lawes, Statutes, Ordinances, Direccons and Instruccons, not contrary to the laws of this Realme of England, as well for setling the formes and Ceremonies of Government and Magestracy fitt and necessary for the said Plantacon and the Inhabitants there as for naming and Stileing all sorts of Officers, both superior and inferior, which they shall find needfull for the Government and Plantacon of the said Colony, and the distinguishing and setting forth of the severall Dutyes, Powers and Lymitts of every such Office and Place, and the formes of such Oaths, not being contrary to the Laws and Statutes of this our Realme of England, to bee administered for the Execucon of the said severall Offices and Places; As alsoe for the disposeing and Ordering of the Eleccon of such of the said Officers as are to bee Annually Chosen, and of such others as shall succeed in case of death or removall, and Administering the said Oath to the new Elected Officers, and Graunting necessary Comissions, and for imposicon of lawfull Fines, Mulcts, Imprisonment or other Punishment vpon Offenders and Delinquents, according to the Course of other Corporacons within this our Kingdome of England, and the same Lawes, fines, Mulcts and Execucons to alter, change, revoke, adnull, release or Pardon, vnder their Comon Seale, As by the said Generall Assembly or the major part of them shall be thought fitt; And for the directing, ruleing and disposing of all other matters and things whereby our said people, Inhabitants there, may bee soe religiously, peaceably and civilly Governed as their good life and orderly Conversacon may wynn and invite the Natives of the Country to the knowledge and obedience of the onely true God and Saviour of mankind, and the Christian faith, which in our Royall intencons and the Adventurers free profession is the onely and principall end of this Plantacon; WILLING, Commanding and requireing, and by these presents, for vs, our heires and Successors, Ordaineing and appointeing. That all such Lawes, Statutes and Ordinances, Instruccons, Imposicons, and Direccons as shall bee soe made by the Governour, Deputy Governour, and Assistants, as aforesaid, and published in writeing vnder their Comon Seale, shall carefully and duely bee observed, kept, performed and putt in execucion, according to the true intent and meaning of the same. AND these our letters Patents, or the Duplicate or Exemplification thereof, shall bee to all and every such Officers, Superiors and inferiors, from tyme to tyme, for the Putting of the same Orders, Lawes, Statutes, Ordinances, Instruccons and Direccons in due Execucon, against vs, our heires and Successors, a sufficient warrant and discharge. AND WEE DOE FURTHER, for vs, our heires and Successors, give and Graunt vnto the said Governor and Company and their Successors, by these presents, That itt shall and may bee lawfull to and for the chiefe Comanders, Governours and Officers of the said Company for the tyme being whoe shall bee resident in the parts of New England hereafter menconed, and others inhabitating there by their leave, admittance, appointment or direccon, from tyme to tyme and att all tymes hereafter, for their speciall defence and safety, to Assemble, Martiall, Array, and putt in Warlike posture the Inhabitants of the said Colony, and to; Commissionate, Impower and authorize such Person or

Persons as they shall thinke fitt to lead and Conduct the said Inhabitants, and to encounter, expulse, repell and resist by force of Armes, as well by Sea as by land, And alsoe to kill, Slay and destroy, by all fitting wayes, enterprizes and meanes whatsoever, all and every such Person or Persons as shall at any tyme hereafter Attempt or enterprize the destruccon, Invasion, detriment or annoyance of the said Inhabitants or Plantacon, And to vse and exercise the law Martiall, in such Cases onely as occasion shall require, And to take or surprize by all wayes and meanes whatsoever, all and every such Person and Persons, with their Shipps, Armour, Ammunicon, and other goods of such as shall in such hostile manner invade or attempt the defeating of the said Plantacon or the hurt of the said Company and Inhabitants; and vpon just Causes to invade and destroy the Natives or other Enemyes of the said Colony. NEVERTHELESSE, Our Will and pleasure is, AND WEE DOE hereby Declare vnto all Christian Kings, Princes and States, That if any Persons which shall hereafter Bee of the said Company or Plantacon, or any other, by appointment of the said Governor and Company for the tyme being, shall at any tyme or tymes hereafter Robb or Spoile by Sea or by land, and doe any hurt, violence or unlawful hostility to any of the Subjects of vs, our heires or Successors, or any of the Subjects of any Prince or State beinge then in league with vs, our heires or Successors, vpon Complaint of such injury done to any such Prince or State, or their Subjects WEE, our heires and Successors, will make open Proclamacon within any parts of our Realme of England fitt for that purpose, That the Person or Persons committinge any such Robbery or Spoile, shall within the tyme lymitted by such Proclamacon, make full restitucon or satisfaccon of all such injuries done or committed, Soe as the said Prince or others soe complayneing may bee fully satisfied and contented. And if the said Person or Persons whoe shall commit any such Robbery or Spoile shall not make satisfaccon accordingly, within such tyme soe to bee limited, That then itt shall and may bee lawful for vs, our heires and Successors, to put such Person or Persons out of our Allegiance and Proteccon: And that it shall and may bee lawfull and free for all Princes or others to Prosecute with hostility such Offenders and every of them, their and every of their Procurers, ayders, Abettors and Councellors in that behalfe. PROVIDED, alsoe, and our expresse will and pleasure is, AND WEE DOE by these presents for vs, our heires and Successors, Ordeyne and appointe that these presents shall not in any manner hinder any of our loveing Subjects whatsoever to vse and exercise the Trade of Fishinge vpon the coast of New England in America, but they and every or any of them shall have full and free power and liberty to contynue and vse the said Trade of Fishing upon the said Coast, in any of the Seas therevnto adioyning, or any Armes of the Seas or Salt Water Rivers where they have byn accustomed to Fish, and to build and sett vpon the wast land belonging to the said Colony of Connecticutt, such Wharfes, Stages and workehouses as shall bee necessary for the Salting, dryeing and keeping of their Fish to bee taken or gotten vpon that Coast, any thinge in these presents conteyened to the contrary notwithstanding. AND KNOWE YEE FURTHER, That Wee, of our more abundant grace, certaine knowledge and meere mocon HAVE given, Graunted and Confirmed, And by theis presents for vs, our heires and Successors, DOE give, Graunt and Confirme vnto the said Governor and Company and their Successors, ALL that parte of our Dominions in Newe England in America bounded on the East by Norrogancett River, commonly called Norrogancett Bay, where the said River falleth into the Sea, and on the North by the lyne of the Massachusetts Plantacon, and on the South by the Sea, and in longitude as the lyne of the Massachusetts Colony, runinge from East to West, (that is to say,) from the Said Norrogancett Bay on the East to the South Sea on the West parte, with the Islands thervnto adioyneinge, Together with all firme lands, Soyles, Grounds, Havens, Ports, Rivers, Waters, Fishings, Mynes, Mynerals, Precious Stones, Quarries, and all and singular other Comodities, Iurisdiccons, Royalties, Priviledges, Francheses, Preheminences, and hereditaments whatsoever within the said Tract, Bounds, lands and Islands aforesaid, or to them or any of them belonging. TO HAVE AND TO HOLD the same vnto the said Governor and Company, their Successors and Assignes, for ever vpon Trust and for the vse and benefitt of themselves and their Associates, freemen of the said Colony, their heires and Assignes, TO BEE HOLDEN of vs, our heires and Successors, as of our Mannor of East Greenewich, in Free and Common Soccage, and not in Capite nor by Knights Service, YEILDING AND PAYINGE therefore to vs, our heires and Successors, onely the Fifth parte of all the Oare of Gold and Silver which from tyme to tyme and at all tymes hereafter shall bee there gotten, had or obteyned, in liew of all Services, Dutyes and Demaunds whatsoever, to bee to vs, our heires or Successors, therefore or thereout rendered, made or paid. AND LASTLY, Wee doe for vs, our heires, and Successors, Graunt to the said Governor and Company and their Successors, by these presents, that these our Letters Patent shall bee firme, good and effectuall in the lawe to all intents, Construccons and purposes whatsoever, accordinge to our true intent and meaneing herein before Declared, as shall be Construed, reputed and adiudged most favourable on the behalfe and for the best benefitt and behoofe of the said Governor and Company and their Successors, ALTHOUGH EXPRESSE MENCON of the true yearely value or certeinty of the premises, or of any of them, or of any other Guifts or Graunts by vs or by any of our Progenitors or Predecessors heretofore made to the said Governor and Company of the English Colony of Connecticut in New England in America aforesaid in theis presents is not made, or *any* Statute, Act, Ordinance, Provision, Proclamacon or Restriccon heretofore had, made. Enacted, Ordeyned or Provided, or any other matter, Cause or thinge whatsoever to the contrary thereof in any wise notwithstanding. IN WITNES whereof, we have caused these our Letters to be made Patent; WITNES our Selfe, att Westminister, the three and Twentieth day of Aprill, in the Fowerteenth yeare of our Reigne.

By writt of Privy Seale   HOWARD

SELECTED IMPORTANT DATES IN CONNECTICUT'S HISTORY

Prepared by the
Connecticut Historical Commission

1614—Adriaen Block, representing the Dutch, sails up the Connecticut River.
1633—The Dutch erect a fort, the House of (Good) Hope, on the future site of Hartford.
1633—John Oldham and others explore and trade along the Connecticut River. Plymouth Colony sends William Holmes to found a trading post at Windsor.
1634—Wethersfield founded by people from Massachusetts.
1635—Fort erected at Saybrook by Lion Gardiner.
1635—Group from Dorchester, Massachusetts join Windsor settlement.
1636—Thomas Hooker and company journey from Newtown (Cambridge), Massachusetts to found Hartford.
1637—Pequot War. Captain John Mason leads colonists to decisive victory.
1638—New Haven Colony established by John Davenport and Theophilus Eaton.
1639—Fundamental Orders of Connecticut adopted by Hartford, Wethersfield and Windsor; John Haynes chosen first governor.
1643—Connecticut joins in forming the New England Confederation.
1646—New London founded by John Winthrop, Jr.
1650—Code of laws drawn up by Roger Ludlow and adopted by legislature.
1662—John Winthrop, Jr. obtains a charter for Connecticut.
1665—Union of New Haven and Connecticut Colonies completed.
1665—The first division of any Connecticut town—Lyme's separation from Saybrook.
1675-76—Connecticut participates in King Philip's War which was fought in Rhode Island and Massachusetts.
1687—Andros assumes rule over Connecticut; Charter Oak episode occurs.
1689—Connecticut resumes government under charter.
1701—Collegiate School authorized by General Assembly.
1708—Saybrook Platform, providing more centralized control of Established Congregational Church, approved by General Assembly.
1717—New Haven State House erected on the Green.
1717—Collegiate School moves to New Haven; called Yale the next year.
1740—Manufacture of tinware begun at Berlin by Edward and William Pattison.
1740's—Height of religious "Great Awakening".
1745—Connecticut troops under Roger Wolcott help capture Louisburg.
1755—*Connecticut Gazette* of New Haven, the Colony's first newspaper, printed by James Parker at New Haven.
1763—Brick State House erected on New Haven Green.
1764—*Connecticut Courant* the oldest American newspaper in continuous existence to the present, launched at Hartford by Thomas Green.
1765—Sharp opposition to Stamp Act.
1766—Governor Thomas Fitch who supported Stamp Act defeated by William Pitkin.
1767—Thomas and Samuel Green launch newspaper which after many changes in name continues today as New Haven *Journal-Courier*.
1774—Connecticut officially extends jurisdiction over Susquehanna Company area in Northern Pennsylvania.
1774—Silas Deane, Eliphalet Dyer, and Roger Sherman represent Connecticut at First Continental Congress.
1775—Several thousand militia rush to Massachusetts in "Lexington Alarm."
1775—Connecticut men help plan and carry out seizure of Ft. Ticonderoga.
1775—Tapping Reeve begins legal instruction at Litchfield; out of this develops Litchfield Law School.
1775—First gun powder mill in Connecticut started in East Hartford.
1776—Samuel Huntington, Roger Sherman, William Williams and Oliver Wolcott sign the Declaration of Independence; large majority of Connecticut people under Governor Jonathan Trumbull support the Declaration.
1777—British troops under General Tryon raid Danbury.
1779—British troops under General Tryon raid New Haven, Fairfield and Norwalk.
1781—Benedict Arnold's attack upon New London and Groton involves massacre at Ft. Griswold.
1781—Washington and Rochambeau confer at Webb House in Wethersfield.
1783—Meeting of 10 Anglican clergy at Glebe House, Woodbury, leads to consecration of Bishop Samuel Seabury and beginning of Protestant Episcopal Church in United States.
1784—Earliest Connecticut cities incorporated—Hartford, Middletown, New Haven, New London and Norwich.
1784—Governor Trumbull retires from governorship.
1784—Connecticut relinquishes Westmoreland area to Pennsylvania.
1784—Act passed providing for emancipation of all Negroes at age of twenty-five.
1787—Oliver Ellsworth, William Samuel Johnson and Roger Sherman serve as Connecticut's representatives at Philadelphia Constitutional Convention.

1788—Convention at Hartford approves Federal Constitution by 128-40 vote.
1789—Oliver Ellsworth and William Samuel Johnson begin service as first United States Senators from Connecticut.
1792—First turnpike road company, New London to Norwich, incorporated.
1792—First banks established at Hartford, New London and New Haven.
1793-96—Old State House, Hartford, erected; designed by Charles Bulfinch.
1795—Connecticut Western Reserve lands (now Northeastern Ohio) sold for $1,200,000 and the proceeds were used to establish the School Fund.
1795—First insurance company incorporated as the Mutual Assurance Company of the City of Norwich.
1796—Thomas Hubbard starts *Courier* at Norwich. In 1860 paper merges with the *Morning Bulletin* and continues as Norwich *Bulletin* to present.
1799—Eli Whitney procures his first Federal musket contract; within next decade develops a system of interchangeable parts, applicable to many industries.
1802—Brass industry begun at Waterbury by Abel Porter and associates.
1806—First important English dictionary in United States published by Noah Webster.
1810—Hartford Fire Insurance Company incorporated.
1812—Joseph Barber starts *Columbian Register* at New Haven. In 1911 combined with New Haven *Register* and continues as *Register* to present.
1812-14—War of 1812 unpopular in Connecticut; new manufactures, especially textiles, boom.
1814—Hartford Convention held in Old State House.
1815—First steamboat voyage up the Connecticut River to Hartford.
1817—Federalists defeated by reformers in political revolution.
1817—Thomas Gallaudet found school for the deaf in Hartford.
1817—Hartford *Times* founded by Frederick D. Bolles and John M. Niles.
1818—New Constitution adopted by convention in Hartford and approved by voters; ends system of established church.
1821—Captain John Davis and Captain Amos Palmer leaders in Antarctic exploration.
1823—Washington College (now Trinity) founded in Hartford.
1827—"New" State House erected in New Haven; Ithiel Town, architect.
1828—Farmington Canal opened.
1831—Wesleyan University founded in Middletown.
1831—Mutual Insurance Company of Hartford founded.
1832—First Connecticut railroad incorporated as the Boston, Norwich and New London.
1835—Revolver patented by Colt.
1835—Music Vale Seminary, first American music school, founded at Salem by Oramel Whittlesey.
1838—Railroad completed between New Haven and Hartford.
1840's and 1850's—Peak of whaling from Connecticut ports and especially from New London.
1842—Wadsworth Atheneum, Hartford, first public art museum, established.
1843—Charles Goodyear develops vulcanizing process for rubber.
1843—Civil rights of Jews protected through act guaranteeing equal privileges with Christians in forming religious societies.
1844—Dr. Horace Wells uses anesthesia at Hartford.
1846—Connecticut Mutual Life Insurance Company, the first life insurance company, chartered in Connecticut.
1847—First American agricultural experiment station—at Yale.
1849—First teachers' college founded at New Britain (now Central Connecticut State University).
1851—Phoenix Mutual Life Insurance Company started (under another name) in Hartford.
1853—Aetna Life Insurance Company started in Hartford.
1860—Lincoln speaks in several Connecticut cities.
1861-65—Approximately 55,000 men serve in Union Army; William Buckingham wartime governor.
1864—Travelers Insurance issues its first policy.
1865—Connecticut General Life Insurance Company founded.
1868—Land at Groton given by Connecticut to U.S. Navy for a naval station; in February, 1917 converted into a submarine base.
1875—Hartford made sole capital city.
1877—First telephone exchange in world opened in New Haven.
1879—New Capitol building in Hartford completed; Richard Upjohn, architect.
1881—Storrs Agricultural College founded (became University of Connecticut in 1939).
1890—Disputed election causes Morgan Bulkeley to continue two extra years as governor (1891-93).
1897—Manufacture of automobiles begun by Pope Manufacturing Company of Hartford.
1900—First United States Navy submarine constructed by Electric Boat Co.
1901—First American state law regulating automobile speeds.
1902—Constitutional Convention held; proposed new constitution defeated in a statewide referendum.
1905—General Assembly adopted public accommodations act ordering full and equal service in all places of public accommodation.
1907—The first Boy Scout Troop in Connecticut (Troop 1) was established in East Hartford.
1910—U.S. Coast Guard Academy moves to New London.
1911—Connecticut College for Women founded at New London.
1917-18—Approximately 67,000 Connecticut men serve in World War I.

DATES IN CONNECTICUT HISTORY

1920—University of New Haven founded.
1927—University of Bridgeport founded.
1932—St. Joseph College founded in West Hartford.
1936—Floods cause enormous damage in Connecticut River Valley.
1938—Hurricane and floods produce heavy loss of life and property.
1938—First section of Merritt Parkway opened.
1939—First section of Wilbur Cross Parkway opened.
1941-45—Approximately 210,000 Connecticut men serve in World War II.
1943—General Assembly established Inter-Racial Commission, recognized as the nation's first statutory civil rights agency.
1947—Fair Employment Practices Act adopted outlawing job discrimination.
1950-52—Approximately 52,000 Connecticut men serve in Korean War.
1954—*Nautilus* world's first atomic-powered submarine, launched at Groton.
1955—Serious floods cause heavy damage and loss of life.
1955—Shakespeare Memorial Theater opened at Stratford.
1957—University of Hartford founded.
1957—Ground broken for first building in New Haven's Oak Street redevelopment area.
1958—129-mile Connecticut Turnpike opened.
1959—Assembly votes to abolish county government (effective 1960); also to abolish local justice courts and establish district courts.
1960—Ground broken for first building in Hartford's Front Street redevelopment area; now known as Constitution Plaza.
1961—New state circuit court system goes into effect.
1964—General Assembly creates six Congressional districts reasonably equal in population.
1964-75—Approximately 104,000 Connecticut men and women served in the armed forces during the Vietnam War era.
1965—Constitutional Convention held. New Constitution approved by voters.
1966—First elections held for reapportioned General Assembly under new Constitution.
1972—Under constitutional amendment adopted in 1970, General Assembly held first annual session since 1886.
1974—Ella Grasso, first woman elected Governor.
1978—Common pleas and juvenile courts become part of the superior court.
1982—Appellate Court created by Constitutional Amendment (Effective July 1, 1983.)
1990—Eunice S. Groark, first woman elected lieutenant governor.

PRESIDENTS OF THE UNITED STATES

Year of qualification	Name	State	Term of Office
1789	George Washington	Virginia	8 yrs.
1797	John Adams	Massachusetts	4 yrs.
1801	Thomas Jefferson	Virginia	8 yrs.
1809	James Madison	Virginia	8 yrs.
1817	James Monroe	Virginia	8 yrs.
1825	John Quincy Adams	Massachusetts	4 yrs.
1829	Andrew Jackson	Tennessee	8 yrs.
1837	Martin Van Buren	New York	4 yrs.
1841	Wm. H. Harrison[1]	Ohio	1 m.
1841	John Tyler	Virginia	3 yrs. 11 m.
1845	James Knox Polk	Tennessee	4 yrs.
1849	Zachary Taylor[2]	Louisiana	1 yr. 4 m. 5 d.
1850	Millard Fillmore	New York	2 yrs. 7 m. 26 d.
1853	Franklin Pierce	New Hampshire	4 yrs.
1857	James Buchanan	Pennsylvania	4 yrs.
1861	Abraham Lincoln[3]	Illinois	4 yrs. 1 m. 10 d.
1865	Andrew Johnson	Tennessee	3 yrs. 10 m. 20 d.
1869	Ulysses S. Grant	Illinois	8 yrs.
1877	Rutherford B. Hayes	Ohio	4 yrs.
1881	James A. Garfield[4]	Ohio	6 m. 15 d.
1881	Chester A. Arthur	New York	3 yrs. 5 m. 15 d.
1885	Grover Cleveland	New York	4 yrs.
1889	Benjamin Harrison	Indiana	4 yrs.
1893	Grover Cleveland	New York	4 yrs.
1897	William McKinley[5]	Ohio	4 yrs. 6 m. 9 d.
1901	Theodore Roosevelt	New York	7 yrs. 5 m. 21 d.
1909	William H. Taft	Ohio	4 yrs.
1913	Woodrow Wilson	New Jersey	8 yrs.
1921	Warren G. Harding[6]	Ohio	2 yrs. 4 m. 27 d.
1923	Calvin Coolidge	Massachusetts	5 yrs. 7 m. 4 d.
1929	Herbert C. Hoover	California	4 yrs.
1933	Franklin D. Roosevelt[7]	New York	12 yrs. 1 m. 8 d.
1945	Harry S. Truman	Missouri	7 yrs. 9 m. 9 d.
1953	Dwight D. Eisenhower	Pennsylvania	8 yrs.
1961	John F. Kennedy[8]	Massachusetts	2 yrs. 10 m. 2 d.
1963	Lyndon B. Johnson[9]	Texas	5 yrs. 1 m. 29 d.
1969	Richard M. Nixon[10]	New York	5 yrs. 6 m 20 d.
1974	Gerald R. Ford[11]	Michigan	2 yrs. 5 m. 11 d.
1977	Jimmy Carter	Georgia	4 yrs.
1981	Ronald Reagan	California	8 yrs.
1989	George Bush	Texas	4 yrs.
1993	William J. Clinton	Arkansas	

[1] Died in office, April 4, 1841, and was succeeded by Vice President Tyler.

[2] Died in office, July 9, 1850, and was succeeded by Vice President Fillmore.

[3] Assassinated April 14, 1865, and was succeeded by Vice President Johnson, April 15, 1865.

[4] Died September 19, 1881, from wounds by assassin, and was suceeded by Vice President Arthur.

[5] Died September 14, 1901, from wounds by assassin, and was succeeded by Vice President Roosevelt.

[6] Died in office, August 2, 1923, and was succeeded by Vice President Coolidge.

[7] Died in office, April 12, 1945, and was succeeded by Vice President Truman.

[8] Assassinated November 22, 1963, and was succeeded by Vice President Lyndon B. Johnson.

[9] Acceded to the Presidency November 22, 1963; elected President on November 3, 1964.

[10] Elected November 5, 1968, reelected November 7, 1972; resigned on August 9, 1974.

[11] Acceded to the Presidency August 9, 1974.

VICE PRESIDENTS OF THE UNITED STATES

Year of qualification	Name	State
1789	John Adams	Massachusetts
1797	Thomas Jefferson	Virginia
1801	Aaron Burr	New York
1805	George Clinton[1]	New York
1813	Elbridge Gerry[2]	Massachusetts
1817	Daniel D. Tompkins	New York
1825	John C. Calhoun[3]	South Carolina
1833	Martin Van Buren	New York
1837	Richard M. Johnson	Kentucky
1841	John Tyler[4]	Virginia
1845	George M. Dallas	Pennsylvania
1849	Millard Fillmore[5]	New York
1853	William R. King[1]	Alabama
1857	John C. Breckinridge	Kentucky
1861	Hannibal Hamlin	Maine
1865	Andrew Johnson[6]	Tennessee
1869	Schuyler Colfax	Indiana
1873	Henry Wilson[1]	Massachusetts
1877	William A. Wheeler	New York
1881	Chester A. Arthur[7]	New York
1885	Thomas A. Hendricks[1]	Indiana
1889	Levi P. Morton	New York
1893	Adlai E. Stevenson	Illinois
1897	Garret A. Hobart[1]	New Jersey
1901	Theodore Roosevelt[8]	New York
1905	Charles W. Fairbanks	Indiana
1909	James S. Sherman[1]	New York
1913	Thomas R. Marshall	Indiana
1921	Calvin Coolidge[9]	Massachusetts
1925	Charles G. Dawes	Illinois
1929	Charles Curtis	Kansas
1933	John N. Garner	Texas
1941	Henry A. Wallace	Iowa
1945	Harry S. Truman[10]	Missouri
1949	Alben W. Barkley	Kentucky
1953	Richard M. Nixon	California
1961	Lyndon B. Johnson[11]	Texas
1965	Hubert H. Humphrey	Minnesota
1969	Spiro T. Agnew[12]	Maryland
1973	Gerald R. Ford[13]	Michigan
1974	Nelson A. Rockefeller[14]	New York
1977	Walter F. Mondale	Minnesota
1981	George Bush	Texas
1989	Dan Quayle	Indiana
1993	Albert A. Gore	Tennessee

[1] Died in office.

[2] Died in office, Nov. 23, 1814.

[3] Resigned December 28, 1832, to become U.S. Senator.

[4] Became President by death of Harrison.

[5] Became President by death of Taylor.

[6] Became President by death of Lincoln.

[7] Became President by death of Garfield.

[8] Became President by death of McKinley.

[9] Became President by death of Harding.

[10] Became President by death of Roosevelt.

[11] Became President by death of John F. Kennedy, November 22, 1963.

[12] Elected November 5, 1968; reelected November 7, 1972; resigned October 10, 1973.

[13] First Vice President nominated by the President and confirmed by the Congress pursuant to the 25th amendment to the Constitution of the United States; took oath of office on December 6, 1973; succeeded to the Presidency on August 9, 1974 upon resignation of Richard M. Nixon.

[14] Nominated to be Vice President by President Ford on August 20, 1974; confirmed by the Senate on December 10, 1974; confirmed by the House and took oath of office on December 19, 1974.

UNITED STATES SENATORS FROM CONNECTICUT SINCE 1789

(Abbreviations for political parties denote the following: A, American; D, Democrat; F, Federalist; FS, Free Soil; NR, National Republican; O, No record; R, Republican; R*, Jeffersonian Republican; VBD, Van Buren Democrat; W, Whig.)

Name	Residence & Pol.	Term of Service
Oliver Ellsworth	Windsor, F	1789-96
William Samuel Johnson	Stratford, O	1789-91
Roger Sherman[1]	New Haven, O	1791-93
Stephen Mix Mitchell	Wethersfield, F	1793-95
Jonathan Trumbull	Lebanon, F	1795-96
Uriah Tracy[2]	Litchfield, F	1796-1807
James Hillhouse	New Haven, F	1796-1810
Chauncey Goodrich	Hartford, F	1807-13
Samuel W. Dana	Middletown, F	1810-21
David Daggett	New Haven, F	1813-19
James Lanman	Norwich, D	1819-25
Elijah Boardman[3]	New Milford, D	1821-23
Henry W. Edwards	New Haven, D	1823-27
Calvin Willey	Tolland, D	1825-31
Samuel A. Foot	Cheshire, W	1827-33
Gideon Tomlinson	Fairfield, R	1831-37
Nathan Smith[4]	New Haven, W	1833-35
John M. Niles	Hartford, D	1835-39, 43-49
Perry Smith	New Milford, D	1837-43
Thaddeus Betts[5]	Norwalk, W	1839-40
Jabez W. Huntington	Norwich, W	1840-47
Roger S. Baldwin	New Haven, W	1847-51
Truman Smith	Litchfield, W	1849-54
Isaac Toucey	Hartford, D	1852-57
Francis Gillett	Hartford, W	1854-55
LaFayette S. Foster	Norwich, R	1855-67
James Dixon	Hartford, R	1857-69
Orris S. Ferry[6]	Norwalk, R	1867-75
William A. Buckingham[7]	Norwich, R	1869-75
James E. English	New Haven, D	1875-76
William W. Eaton	Hartford, D	1875-81
William H. Barnum	Salisbury, D	1876-79

[1] Died in Office, July 23, 1793.
[2] Died in Office, July 19, 1807.
[3] Died in Office, October 8, 1823.
[4] Died in Office, December 6, 1835.
[5] Died in OfficeI, April 7, 1840.
[6] Died in Office, November 21, 1875.
[7] Died in Office, February 5, 1875.

UNITED STATES SENATORS FROM CONNECTICUT SINCE 1789

Name	Residence & Pol.	Term of Service
Orville H. Platt[8]	Meriden, R	1879-1905
Joseph R. Hawley	Hartford, R	1881-1905
Morgan G. Bulkeley	Hartford, R	1905-11
Frank B. Brandegee[9]	New London, R	1905-24
George P. McLean	Simsbury, R	1911-29
Hiram Bingham[10]	New Haven, R	1924-33
Frederic C. Walcott	Norfolk, R	1929-35
Augustine Lonergan	Hartford, D	1933-39
Francis T. Maloney[11]	Meriden, D	1935-45
John A. Danaher	Portland, R	1939-45
Brien McMahon[12]	Norwalk, D	1945-52
Thomas C. Hart[13]	Sharon, R	1945-46
Raymond E. Baldwin[14]	Stratford, R	1946-49
William Benton[15]	Fairfield, D	1949-53
William A. Purtell[16]	West Hartford, R	1952-59
Prescott Bush[17]	Greenwich, R	1952-63
Thomas J. Dodd	West Hartford, D	1959-71
Abraham A. Ribicoff	Hartford, D	1963-81
Lowell P. Weicker, Jr.	Greenwich, R	1971-88
Christopher J. Dodd	East Haddam, D	1981-
Joseph I. Lieberman	New Haven, D	1989-

[8]Died in Office, April 21, 1905.

[9]Died in Office, October 14, 1924.

[10]State election was held November 6, 1924. Hiram Bingham was elected Governor. On December 16th, he was elected U.S. Senator at a special election; he accepted the office after being inaugurated Governor, and resigned the Governorship.

[11]Died in Office, January 16, 1945, and was succeeded in office by Thomas C. Hart.

[12]Died in Office, July 28, 1952.

[13]Appointed February 8, 1945, to fill the vacancy caused by the death of Francis T. Maloney. Resigned November 5, 1946.

[14]Elected November 5, 1946, to fill the vacancy caused by the resignation of Thomas C. Hart and for the full term beginning January 3, 1947. Resigned to accept appointment as an Associate Justice of the Connecticut Supreme Court of Errors December 17, 1949.

[15]Appointed December 17, 1949 and elected November 7, 1950, to fill vacancy caused by the resignation of Raymond E. Baldwin.

[16]Appointed August 29, 1952, to fill the vacancy caused by the death of Brien McMahon, served until November 4, 1952. Elected for full term beginning January 3, 1953.

[17]Elected November 4, 1952, to fill the unexpired term of Brien McMahon.

REPRESENTATIVES IN CONGRESS FROM CONNECTICUT SINCE 1789

Prior to 1837 the Representatives from this state were elected by the people at large. The number at first, under the Constitution, was five and by later apportionments was changed in 1793 to seven, in 1823 to six, and in 1843 to four. From 1837 to 1843 they were elected one from each of the six districts into which the state was divided by an act of the General Assembly; from 1843 to 1911 they were elected, one from each of the four districts established by the General Assembly of 1842, as follows: District number one, consisting of the counties of Hartford and Tolland; district number two, the counties of New Haven and Middlesex; district number three, the counties of New London and Windham; district number four, the counties of Fairfield and Litchfield. A fifth representative, to which the state was entitled under the census of 1900, was chosen at large. At the session of 1911 the state was divided into five districts as follows: District No. 1, County of Hartford; District No. 2, Counties of Tolland, Windham, New London and Middlesex; District No. 3, Towns of Bethany, Branford, Cheshire, East Haven, Guilford, Hamden, Madison, Meriden, Milford, New Haven, North Branford, North Haven, Orange, Wallingford, West Haven and Woodbridge in County of New Haven; District No. 4, County of Fairfield; District No. 5, County of Litchfield and the Towns of Ansonia, Beacon Falls, Derby, Middlebury, Naugatuck, Oxford, Prospect, Seymour, Southbury, Waterbury and Wolcott in the County of New Haven. The 1921 session of the General Assembly enacted a law creating the office of Congressman-at-Large if a reapportionment stemming from the 1920 census gave Connecticut a sixth congressional seat. However, Congress did not reapportion until after the 1930 census and, at this time, the state received the sixth post of Congressman-at-Large. A 1931 act of the General Assembly stated this representative was to be "designated as 'Representative-at-Large.'" The State was divided into six districts by act of the General Assembly in Special Session, April 1964, abolishing the post of Representative-at-Large.

In instances where no districts are given, the elections were at large.

Name	Residence & Pol.	District	Congress	Term of Service
Allen, John	Litchfield, F		5	1797-99
Arnold, Samuel	Haddam, D	2	35	1857-59
Austin, Albert E.	Old Greenwich, R	4	76	1939-41
Bakewell, Charles M.	New Haven, R		73	1933-35
Baldwin, John	Windham, W		19,20	1825-29
Baldwin, Simeon	New Haven, F		8	1803-05
Ball, Thomas R.	Old Lyme, R	2	76	1939-41
Barber, Noyes	Groton, D		17-23	1821-35
Barnum, William H.	Salisbury, D	4	40-44	1867-77
Belcher, Nathan	New London, D	3	33	1853-55
Bishop, Wm. D.	Bridgeport, D	4	35	1857-59
Boardman, Wm. W.	New Haven, W	2	27	1841-43
Booth, Walter	Meriden, FS		31	1849-51
Bowles, Chester	Essex, D	2	86	1959-61
Brace, Jonathan	Hartford, F		5,6	1798-1801
Brandegee, Augustus	New London, R	3	38,39	1863-67
Brandegee, Frank B.[1]	New London, R	3	57-59	1902-05
Brockway, John H.	Ellington, W	6	26,27	1839-43
Buck, John R.	Hartford, R	1	47-49	1881-83 1885-87
Burnham, Alfred A.	Windham, R	3	36,37	1859-63
Burrows, Daniel	Groton, D		17	1821-23
Butler, Thomas B.	Norwalk, W	4	31	1849-51

[1] Elected to fill vacancy to March 4, 1903, and for the 58th and 59th sessions of Congress. Resigned in 1905 to become U.S. Senator, to fill vacancy caused by death of Senator Orville H. Platt.

REPRESENTATIVES IN CONGRESS FROM CONNECTICUT SINCE 1789

Name	Residence & Pol.	District	Congress	Term of Service
Catlin, George S.	Windham, D	3	28	1843-45
Chapman, Charles	Hartford, W	1	32	1851-53
Champion, Epaphroditus	East Haddam, F		10-14	1807-17
Citron, William M.	Middletown, D		74,75	1935-39
Clark, Ezra, Jr.	Hartford, R	1	34,35	1855-59
Cleveland, Chauncey F.	Hampton, D	3	31,32	1849-53
Coit, Joshua	New London, F		3-5	1793-98
Compton, Ranulf	Madison, R	3	78	1943-45
Cotter, William R.[2]	Hartford, D	1	92-97	1971-81
Cretella, Albert W.	North Haven, R	3	83-85	1953-59
Daddario, Emilio Q.	Hartford, D	1	86-91	1959-71
Dana, Samuel W.	Middletown, F		4-11	1796-1810
Davenport, James	Stamford, O		4,5	1796-97
Davenport, John	Stamford, F		6-14	1799-1817
Dean, Sidney	Thompson, R	3	34,35	1855-59
DeForest, Robert E.	Bridgeport, D	4	52,53	1891-95
DeLauro, Rosa	New Haven, D	3	102	1991-
Deming, Henry C.	Hartford, R	1	38,39	1863-67
DeNardis, Lawrence J.	Hamden, R	3	97	1981-83
Dixon, James	Hartford, W	1	29,30	1845-49
Dodd, Christopher J.	Norwich, D	2	94-96	1975-81
Dodd, Thomas J.	West Hartford, D	1	83,84	1953-57
Donovan, Jeremiah	Norwalk, D	4	63	1913-15
Downs, LeRoy D.	So. Norwalk, D	4	77	1941-43
Dwight, Theodore	Hartford, F		9	1806-07
Eaton, William W.	Hartford, D	1	48	1883-85
Edmond, William	Newtown, F		5,6	1797-1801
Edwards, Henry W.	New Haven, D		16,17	1819-23
Ellsworth, Wm. W.[3]	Hartford, W		21-23	1829-33
English, James E.	New Haven, D	2	37,38	1861-65
Fenn, E. Hart	Wethersfield, R	1	67-71	1921-31
Ferry, Orris S.	Norwalk, R	4	36	1859-61
Fitzgerald, William J.	Norwich, D	2	75-77	1937-39 / 1941-43
Foot, Samuel A.	Cheshire, W		16,18, 23	1819-21 / 1823-25 / 1833-35
Foote, Ellsworth B.	No. Branford, R	3	80	1947-49
Franks, Gary A.	Waterbury, R	5	102-104	1991-97
Freeman, Richard P.	New London, R	2	64-72	1915-33
French, Carlos	Seymour, D	2	50	1887-89
Geelan, James P.	New Haven, D	3	79	1945-47
Gejdenson, Sam	Bozrah, D	2	97-	1981-
Giaimo, Robert N.	North Haven, D	3	86-96	1959-81
Gilbert, Sylvester	Hebron, O		15	1818-19

[2] Died during term, September 8, 1981.
[3] Resigned 1833.

Name	Residence & Pol.	District	Congress	Term of Service
Glynn, James P.	Winsted, R	5	64-67 69-71	⎡1915-23 ⎣1925-31
Goddard, Calvin	Plainfield, F		7,8	1801-05
Goodrich, Chauncey	Hartford, F		4-6	1795-1801
Goodrich, Elizur	New Haven, F		6	1799-1801
Goss, Edward W.	Waterbury, R	5	71-73	1930-35
Grabowski, Bernard F.	Bristol, D	6	88,89	⎡1963-65 ⎣1965-67
Granger, Miles T.	North Canaan, D	4	50	1887-89
Grasso, Ella T.	Windsor Locks, D	6	92-93	1971-75
Griswold, Roger	Lyme, F		4-8	1795-1805
Haley, Elisha	Groton, D	3	24,25	1835-39
Hawley, Joseph R.	Hartford, R	1	43,46	⎡1873-75 ⎣1879-81
Henry, E. Stevens	Vernon, R	1	54-62	1895-1913
Higgins, Edwin W.[4]	Norwich, R	3	59-62	1905-13
Higgins, William L.	So. Coventry, R	2	73,74	1933-37
Hill, Ebenezer J.[5]	Norwalk, R		54-62, 64,65	⎡1895-1913 ⎣1915-17
		4		
Hillhouse, James	New Haven, F		2-5	1791-96
Holmes, Uriel	Litchfield, F		15	1817-18
Holt, Orrin	Willington, D	6	25	1837-39
Hotchkiss, Julius	Middletown, R	2	40	1867-69
Hubbard, John H.	Litchfield, R	4	38,39	1863-67
Hubbard, Richard D.	Hartford, R	1	40	1867-69
Hubbard, Samuel D.	Middletown, W	2	29,30	1845-49
Huntington, Benjamin	Norwich, O		1	1789-91
Huntington, Ebenezer	Norwich, W		11,15	⎡1810-11 ⎣1817-19
Huntington, Jabez W.	Litchfield, W		21-23	1829-35
Ingersoll, Colin M.	New Haven, D	2	32,33	1851-55
Ingersoll, Ralph I.	New Haven, D		19-22	1825-33
Ingham, Samuel	Saybrook, D	2	24,25	1835-39
Irwin, Donald J.	Norwalk, D	4	86, 89-90	⎡1959-61 ⎣1965-69
Jackson, Ebenezer, Jr.[4]	Middletown, W		24	1834-35
Johnson, Nancy L.	New Britain, R	6	98-	1983-
Judson, Andrew T.	Canterbury, D		24	1835-37
Kellogg, Stephen W.	Waterbury, R	2	41-43	1869-75
Kennedy, William	Naugatuck, D	5	63	1913-15
Kennelly, Barbara B.[6]	Hartford, D	1	97-	1982-
Kopplemann, Herman P.	Hartford, D	1	73-75, 77,79	⎡1933-39 1941-43 ⎣1945-47

---

[4]Elected to fill vacancy.

[5]Died during term.

[6]Elected January 12, 1982, to fill the vacancy created by the death of William R. Cotter. Took oath of office on January 25, 1982.

REPRESENTATIVES IN CONGRESS FROM CONNECTICUT SINCE 1789

Name	Residence & Pol.	District	Congress	Term of Service
Kowalski, Frank, Jr.	Meriden, D		86,87	1959-63
Landers, George M.	New Britain, D	1	44,45	1875-79
Law, Lyman	New London, F		12-14	1811-17
Learned, Amasa	New London, O		2,3	1791-95
Lilley, George L.	Waterbury, R		58-60	1903-09
Lodge, John Davis	Westport, R	4	80,81	1947-51
Lonergan, Augustine	Hartford, D	1	63, 65,66, 72	1913-15 1917-21 1931-33
Loomis, Dwight	Hartford, R	1	36,37	1859-63
Luce, Clare Boothe	Greenwich, R	4	78,79	1943-47
Maciora, Lucien J.	New Britain, D		77	1941-43
Mahan, Bryan F.	New London, D	2	63	1913-15
Maloney, Francis T.	Meriden, D	3	73	1933-35
Maloney, James H.	Danbury, D	5	105	1997-
May, Edwin H., Jr.	Wethersfield, R	1	85	1957-59
McGuire, John A.	Wallingford, D	3	81,82	1949-53
McKinney, Stewart B.[7]	Fairfield, R	4	92-100	1971-87
McWilliams, John D.	Norwich, R	2	78	1943-45
Merritt, Schuyler[8]	Stamford, R	4	65-71, 73,74	1917-31 1933-37
Merwin, Orange	New Milford, O		19,20	1825-29
Meskill, Thomas J.	New Britain, R	6	90,91	1967-71
Miles, Frederick	Salisbury, R	4	46,47, 51	1879-83 1889-91
Miller, William J.	Wethersfield, R	1	76,78, 80	1939-41 1943-45 1947-49
Miner, Phineas[8]	Litchfield, W		24	1834-35
Mitchell, Charles L.	New Haven, D	2	48,49	1883-87
Moffett, Anthony Toby	Farmington, D	6	94-97	1975-83
Monagan, John S.	Waterbury, D	5	86-92	1959-73
Monkiewicz, Boleslaus J.	New Britain, R		76,78	1939-41 1943-45
Morano, Albert P.	Greenwich, R	4	82-85	1951-59
Morrison, Bruce A.	Hamden, D	3	98-101	1983-91
Moseley, Jonathan O.	East Haddam, F		9-16	1805-21
Oakey, P. Davis	Hartford, R	1	64	1915-17
Osborne, Thomas B.	Fairfield, W	4	26,27	1839-43
O'Sullivan, Patrick B.	Derby, D	5	68	1923-25
Patterson, James T.	Watertown, R	5	80-85	1947-59
Perkins, Elias	New London, F		7	1801-03
Phelps, Elisha	Simsbury, D		16, 19,20	1819-21 1825-29
Phelps, James	Essex, D	2	44-47	1875-83
Phelps, Lancelot	Colebrook, D	5	24,25	1835-39

---

[7]Died during term, May 7, 1987.
[8]Elected to fill vacancy.

REPRESENTATIVES IN CONGRESS FROM CONNECTICUT SINCE 1789

Name	Residence & Pol.	District	Congress	Term of Service
Phillips, Alfred N., Jr.	Stamford, D	4	75	1937-39
Pigott, James P.	New Haven, D	2	53	1893-95
Pitkin, Timothy	Farmington, F		9-15	1805-19
Plant, David	Stratford, NR		20	1827-29
Pratt, James T.	Rocky Hill, D	1	33	1853-55
Ratchford, William R.	Danbury, D	5	96-98	1979-85
Reilly, Thomas L.	Meriden, D	d3	62,63	1911-15
Ribicoff, Abraham A.	Hartford, D	1	81,82	1949-53
Rockwell, John A.	Norwich, W	3	29,30	1845-49
Rowland, John G.	Waterbury, R	5	99-101	1985-91
Russ, John	Hartford, D		16,17	1819-23
Russell, Chas. A.[9]	Killingly, R	3	50-57	1887-1902
Ryter, Joseph F.	Hartford, D		79	1945-47
Sadlak, Antoni N.	Rockville, R		80-85	1947-59
Sarasin, Ronald A.	Beacon Falls, R	5	93-95	1973-79
St. Onge, William L.[10]	Putnam, D	2	88-91	1963-70
Seely-Brown, Horace, Jr.	Pomfret, R	2	80, 82-85, 87	1947-49, 1951-59, 1961-63
Seymour, Edward W.	Bridgeport, D	4	48,49	1883-87
Seymour, Origen S.	Litchfield, D	4	32,33	1851-55
Seymour, Thomas H.	Hartford, D	1	28	1843-45
Shanley, James A.	New Haven, D	3	74-77	1935-43
Shays, Christopher[11]	Stamford, R	4	100-	1987-
Sherman, Roger	New Haven, O		1	1789-91
Sherwood, Sam'l B.	Fairfield, F		15	1817-19
Sibal, Abner W.	Norwalk, R	4	87,88	1961-65
Simonds, Wm. E.	Canton, R	1	51	1889-91
Simons, Samuel	Bridgeport, D	4	28	1843-45
Smith, John Cotton	Sharon, F		6-9	1800-06
Smith, J. Joseph	Waterbury, D	5	74-77	1935-43
Smith, Nathaniel	Woodbury, F		4,5	1795-99
Smith, Truman	Litchfield, W	5	26,27,	1839-43
		4	29,30	1845-49
Sperry, Lewis	So. Windsor, D	1	52,53	1891-95
Sperry, Nehemiah D.	New Haven, R	2	54-61	1895-1911
Starkweather, Henry H.	New London, R	3	40-44	1867-77
Steele, Robert H.[12]	Vernon, R	2	91-93	1970-75
Sterling, Ansel	Sharon, O		17,18	1821-25
Stevens, James	Stamford, D		16	1819-21
Stewart, John	Chatham, D	2	28	1843-45

---

[9] Died during term.

[10] Died during term, May 1, 1970.

[11] Elected August 18, 1987, to fill vacancy caused by the death of Stewart B. McKinney. Took office on Sept. 9, 1987.

[12] Elected November 3, 1970, to fill the vacancy caused by death of William L. St. Onge and for the full term beginning January 3, 1971.

d District changed from Second to Third.

REPRESENTATIVES IN CONGRESS FROM CONNECTICUT SINCE 1789

Name	Residence & Pol.	District	Congress	Term of Service
Stoddard, Ebenezer	Woodstock, O		17,18	1821-25
Storrs, William L.	Middletown, W		21,22,	1829-33
		2	26	1839-41
Strong, Julius L.	Hartford, R	1	41,42	1869-73
Sturges, Jonathan	Fairfield, F		1,2	1789-93
Sturgis, Lewis B.	Fairfield, F		9-14	1805-17
Swift, Zephaniah	Windham, F		3,4	1793-97
Talbot, Joseph E.	Naugatuck, R	5	77-79	1942-47
Talmadge, Benjamin	Litchfield, F		7-14	1801-17
Terry, Nathaniel	Hartford, O		15	1817-19
Tierney, William L.	Greenwich, D	4	72	1931-33
Tilson, John Q.	New Haven, R	3	61,62,	1909-13
			64-72	1915-33
Tomlinson, Gideon	Fairfield, R		16-19	1819-27
Toucey, Isaac	Hartford, D	1	24,25	1835-39
Tracy, Uriah	Litchfield, F		3,4	1793-96
Trumbull, Jonathan	Lebanon, F		1-3	1789-95
Trumbull, Joseph[13]	Hartford, W	1	24-27	1834-43
Tweedy, Samuel	Danbury, W		23	1833-35
Vance, Robert J.	New Britain, D	1	50	1887-89
Wadsworth, Jeremiah	Hartford, F		1-3	1789-95
Wait, John T.	Norwich, R	3	45-49	1877-87
Waldo, Loren P.	Tolland, D	1	31	1849-51
Warner, Levi	Norwalk, D	4	45	1877-79
Warner, Samuel L.	Middletown, R	2	39	1865-67
Weicker, Lowell P., Jr.	Greenwich, R	4	91,92	1969-71
Welch, William W.	Norfolk, A	4	34	1855-57
Whitman, Lemuel	Farmington, D		18	1823-25
Whittlesey, Thos. T.	Danbury, VBD	4	25	1837-39
Wildman, Zalmon[14]	Danbury, D		24	1835
Wilcox, Washington F.	Saybrook, D	2	51,52	1889-93
Williams, Thomas S.	Hartford, O		15	1817-19
Williams, Thomas W.	New London, W	3	26,27	1839-43
Woodhouse, Chase Going	New London, D	2	79,81	1945-47
				1949-51
Woodruff, George C.	Litchfield, D	4	37	1861-63
Woodruff, John	New Haven, A	2	34,36	1855-57
				1859-61
Young, Ebenezer	Killingly, F		21-23	1829-35

[13]Elected for unexpired portion of term in 1834.
[14]Died at Washington, December 10, 1835.

GOVERNORS OF CONNECTICUT

The supreme executive power of the state is vested by the Constitution in the Governor. The Governor has the power to administer oaths, sign writs, issue processes, and to see that the laws of the state are faithfully executed. In case of emergency the Governor may convene the General Assembly in special session. The Governor is commander-in-chief of the militia of the state, has power to grant reprieves in all cases except impeachment, and has jurisdiction in the matter of requisitions from other states for criminals. The Governor has power to veto any bills passed by the General Assembly, but the veto may be overridden by at least a two-thirds majority vote of each house upon reconsideration. Any bill which is neither signed nor vetoed within five days after being presented to the Governor (Sundays and legal holidays excepted) during the session of the General Assembly, becomes a law, in like manner as if signed. After adjournment of the General Assembly the Governor is allowed fifteen calendar days after bills have been presented in which to act. In each odd-numbered year, the Governor must also present a biennial budget for the state to the General Assembly and has control over quarterly allotments granted after the budget has been acted on by the General Assembly. The Governor must from time to time give to the General Assembly information concerning the state and recommend such measures as deemed expedient. The Governor may adjourn the General Assembly in case of disagreement between the two houses to such time as the Governor thinks proper, but not beyond the day of the next stated session.

The Governor nominates to the General Assembly the Judges of the Supreme, Superior and Appellate Courts and the Chief Court Administrator; and appoints the members of several boards and commissions, at times with the consent of either House of the General Assembly, and appoints with the advice and consent of either House of the General Assembly, the Commissioner of the Department of Administrative Services, the Commissioner of the Department of Agriculture, the Commissioner of the Department of Banking, the Commissioner of the Department of Children and Families, the Commissioner of the Department of Consumer Protection, the Commissioner of the Department of Correction, the Commissioner of the Department of Economic and Community Development, the Commissioner of the Department of Environmental Protection, the Commissioner of the Board of Higher Education, the Commissioner of the Department of Housing, the Commissioner of the Department of Insurance, the Commissioner of the Department of Labor, the Commissioner of the Department of Mental Health, the Commissioner of the Department of Mental Retardation, the Commissioner of the Department of Motor Vehicles, the Secretary of the Office of Policy and Management, the Commissioner of the Department of Public Health and Addiction Services, the Commissioner of the Department of Public Safety, the Commissioner of the Department of Public Works, the Commissioner of the Department of Revenue Services, the Commissioner of the Department of Social Services, the Commissioner of the Department of Transportation, the Commissioner of the Department of Veterans' Affairs. The Governor appoints, with the consent of both houses, members of the State Board of Education, the New England Board of Higher Education, members of the Public Utilities Control Authority in the Department of Public Utility Control, and other boards and commissions. The Governor appoints directly the Board of Trustees of the University of Connecticut, Liquor Control Commissioners, and the members of various other boards and commissions. The Governor is *ex-officio* a member of the Conn. Agricultural Experiment Station, State Bond Commission, Expressway Bond Committee, Finance Advisory Committee, Commission on Intergovernmental Cooperation, Education Commission of the States, Board of Trustees of the University of Connecticut, and the Corporation of Yale University.

The Governor presided over the General Assembly before it was divided into two houses in 1698; from that date until the adoption of the Constitution of 1818 the Governor presided in the council or upper house, with a casting vote, but no veto power. At the present time the Lieutenant Governor presides over the Senate.

The Governor holds office for four years and receives an annual salary of $78,000. The Governor also is furnished a Governor's Residence located at 990 Prospect Avenue, Hartford 06106.

Abbreviations for political parties denote the following: A, American; ACP, A Connecticut Party; AD, American Democrat; AR, American Republican; D, Democrat; F, Federalist; FSA, Free Soil American; NR, National Republican; O, No record; R, Republican; R*, Jeffersonian Republican; U, Union; W, Whig. Prior to 1660, state law prohibited governors from serving successive terms.

Governor	Town & Pol.	Term of Service	Years of Service
John Haynes	Hartford, O	(1639, 41, 43, 45, 47, 49, 51, 53)	8 yrs.
Edward Hopkins	Hartford, O	(1640, 44, 46, 48, 50, 52, 54)	7 yrs.

GOVERNORS OF CONNECTICUT

Governor	Town & Pol.	Term of Service	Years of Service
George Wyllys	Hartford, O	1642	1 yr.
Thomas Welles	Hartford, O	1655, 58	2 yrs.
John Webster	Hartford, O	1656	1 yr.
John Winthrop	New London, O	1657, 59-76	18 yrs.
William Leete	Guilford, O	1676-83	7 yrs.
Robert Treat[1]	Milford, O	1683-98	15 yrs.
Fitz-John Winthrop	New London, O	1698-1707	9 yrs. 6 m.
Gurdon Saltonstall	New London, O	1708-24	17 yrs. 4 m.
Joseph Talcott[2]	Hartford, O	1724-41	16 yrs. 5 m.
Jonathan Law[3]	Milford, O	1741-50	9 yrs. 1 m.
Roger Wolcott	Windsor, O	1750-54	3 yrs. 6 m.
Thomas Fitch	Norwalk, O	1754-66	12 yrs.
William Pitkin[4]	Hartford, O	1766-69	3 yrs. 5 m.
Jonathan Trumbull	Lebanon, O	1769-84	14 yrs. 7 m.
Matthew Griswold	Lyme, F	1784-86	2 yrs.
Samuel Huntington[5]	Norwich, F	1786-96	9 yrs. 8 m.
Oliver Wolcott[6]	Litchfield, F	1796-97	1 yr. 11 m.
Jonathan Trumbull, 2nd[7]	Lebanon, F	1797-1809	11 yrs. 8 m.
John Treadwell	Farmington, F	1809-11	1 yr. 9 m.
Roger Griswold[8]	Lyme, F	1811-12	1 yr. 5 m.
John Cotton Smith	Sharon, F	1812-17	4 yrs. 7 m.
Oliver Wolcott, Jr.	Litchfield, R*	1817-27	10 yrs.
Gideon Tomlinson[9]	Fairfield, R*	1827-31	4 yrs.
John S. Peters	Hebron, NR	1831-33	2 yrs.
Henry W. Edwards	New Haven, D	1833-34	1 yr.
Samuel A. Foot	Cheshire, W	1834-35	1 yr.
Henry W. Edwards	New Haven, D	1835-38	3 yrs.
Wm. W. Ellsworth	Hartford, W	1838-42	4 yrs.
Chauncey F. Cleveland	Hampton, D	1842-44	2 yrs.

[1] Gov. Treat's term includes the period when Sir Edmund Andros as royal governor with *de facto* executive.

[2] Died in office October 11, 1741. The General Assembly, then being in session, elected Jonathan Law Governor.

[3] Died in office November 6, 1750. At a special session of November 21-22 the General Assembly elected Roger Wolcott Governor.

[4] Died October 1, 1769. At its October 1769 session of the General Assembly elected Jonathan Trumbull, Sr., Governor.

[5] Died January 5, 1796. At the regular May 1796 election the freemen failed to give any candidate a majority. The General Assembly then elected Oliver Wolcott, Governor.

[6] Died December 1, 1797. At the regular May 1798 election the freemen elected Jonathan Trumbull, Jr., Governor.

[7] Died August 7, 1809. At the regular October 1809 session the General Assembly elected John Treadwell Governor.

[8] Died October 25, 1812. At the regular October 1812 session the General Assembly refused to elect a Governor. At the regular May 1813 election the freemen elected John Cotton Smith Governor.

[9] Resigned to become United States Senator.

GOVERNORS OF CONNECTICUT

Governor	Town & Pol.	Term of Service	Years of Service
Roger S. Baldwin	New Haven, W	1844-46	2 yrs.
Isaac Toucey	Hartford, D	1846-47	1 yr.
Clark Bissell	Norwalk, W	1847-49	2 yrs.
Joseph Trumbull	Hartford, W	1849-50	1 yr.
Thomas H. Seymour	Hartford, D	1850-53	3 yrs. 1 m.
Charles H. Pond[10]	Milford, D	1853-54	11 m.
Henry Dutton	New Haven, W	1854-55	1 yr.
William T. Minor	Stamford, A	1855-57	2 yrs.
Alexander H. Holley	Salisbury, AR	1857-58	1 yr.
Wm. A. Buckingham	Norwich, R	1858-66	8 yrs.
Joseph R. Hawley	Hartford, R	1866-67	1 yr.
James E. English	New Haven, D	1867-69	2 yrs.
Marshall Jewell	Hartford, R	1869-70	2 yrs.
James E. English	New Haven, D	1870-71	1 yr.
Marshall Jewell	Hartford, R	1871-72	2 yrs.
Charles R. Ingersoll[11]	New Haven, D	1873-77	3 yrs. 9 m.
Richard D. Hubbard	Hartford, D	1877-79	2 yrs.
Charles B. Andrews	Litchfield, R	1879-81	2 yrs.
Hobart B. Bigelow	New Haven, R	1881-83	2 yrs.
Thomas M. Waller	New London, D	1883-85	2 yrs.
Henry B. Harrison	New Haven, R	1885-87	2 yrs.
Phineas C. Lounsbury	Ridgefield, R	1887-89	2 yrs.
Morgan G. Bulkeley	Hartford, R	1889-93	4 yrs.
Luzon B. Morris	New Haven, D	1893-95	2 yrs.
O. Vincent Coffin	Middletown, R	1895-97	2 yrs.
Lorrin A. Cooke	Winsted, R	1897-99	2 yrs.
George E. Lounsbury	Ridgefield, R	1899-1901	2 yrs.
George P. McLean	Simsbury, R	1901-03	2 yrs.
Abiram Chamberlain	Meriden, R	1903-05	2 yrs.
Henry Roberts	Hartford, R	1905-07	2 yrs.
Rollin S. Woodruff	New Haven, R	1907-09	2 yrs.
George L. Lilley[12]	Waterbury, R	1909	3 m. 15 d.
Frank B. Weeks	Middletown, R	1909-11	1 yr. 8 m. 15 d.
Simeon E. Baldwin	New Haven, D	1911-15	4 yrs.
Marcus H. Holcomb	Southington, R	1915-21	6 yrs.
Everett J. Lake	Hartford, R	1921-23	2 yrs.
Chas. A. Templeton	Waterbury, R	1923-25	2 yrs.
Hiram Bingham[13]	New Haven, R	1925	1 d.

[10]Governor Pond was elected Lieutenant-Governor in April, 1853, and became Governor by resignation of Governor Seymour on October 13, 1853, when the latter was appointed Minister to Russia.

[11]By Constitutional Amendment of 1875, the term for 1876-7 was made to expire January, 1877.

[12]Died in office, April 21, 1909, and Frank B. Weeks became Governor.

[13]Resigned January 8, 1925 to become United States Senator.

GOVERNORS OF CONNECTICUT

Governor	Town & Pol.	Term of Service	Years of Service
John H. Trumbull[14]	Plainville, R	1925-31	6 yrs.
Wilbur L. Cross	New Haven, D	1931-39	8 yrs.
Raymond E. Baldwin	Stratford, R	1939-41	2 yrs.
Robert A. Hurley	Bridgeport, D	1941-42	2 yrs.
Raymond E. Baldwin[15]	Stratford, R	1943-46	3 yrs. 11 m. 21 d.
Wilbert Snow[16]	Middletown, D	1946-47	13 d.
James L. McConaughy[17]	Cornwall, R	1947-48	1 yr. 2 m.
James C. Shannon	Bridgeport, R	1948-49	9 m. 29 d.
Chester Bowles	Essex, D	1949-51	2 yrs.
John Lodge	Westport, R	1951-55	4 yrs.
Abraham Ribicoff[18]	Hartford, D	1955-61	6 yrs. 16 d.
John Dempsey[19]	Putnam, D	'1961-71	9 yrs. 11 m. 15 d.
Thomas J. Meskill	New Britain, R	1971-75	4 yrs.
Ella T. Grasso[20]	Windsor Locks, D	1975-80	5 yrs. 11 m. 28 d.
William A. O'Neill[21]	East Hampton, D	1980-91	10 yrs. 10 d.
Lowell P. Weicker, Jr.	Greenwich, ACP	1991-95	3 yrs. 11 m. 26 d.
John G. Rowland	Waterbury, R	1995-	

[14] Succeeded Hiram Bingham.

[15] Resigned December 27, 1946 to become U.S. Senator.

[16] Became Governor December 27, 1946.

[17] Died in office, March 7, 1948 and James C. Shannon became Governor.

[18] Resigned January 21, 1961 to become Secretary of Health, Education and Welfare.

[19] Became Governor January 21, 1961, in succession to Abraham Ribicoff. Elected Governor for a full term beginning January 9, 1963; reelected November 8, 1966.

[20] Resigned December 31, 1980 because of ill health.

[21] Became Governor December 31, 1980 in succession to Ella T. Grasso. Elected Governor for a full term beginning January 5, 1983; reelected November 4, 1986.

DEPUTY OR LIEUTENANT GOVERNORS

Before the Constitution of 1818 the Deputy Governor presided in council, or the upper house of the General Assembly, in the absence of the Governor, but when the Governor was present the Deputy Governor had a voice in council. Until 1818 the Deputy Governor could exercise the office of a justice of the peace throughout the State, and could sign writs until 1879.

The Lieutenant Governor is president of the Senate, has a casting vote therein, and the right to debate when it is in Committee of the Whole. Under the Constitution, the Lieutenant Governor becomes Governor in case of the death, resignation, refusal to serve or removal from office of the Governor. If the Governor is impeached or absent from the state, the Lieutenant Governor "shall exercise the powers and authority and perform the duties appertaining to the office of Governor until, if the Governor has been impeached, he is acquitted, or if absent, he has returned."

The Constitution also provides that the Lieutenant Governor shall exercise the powers and perform the duties of Governor if the Governor informs the Lieutenant Governor in writing that he is unable to do so, "until the Governor transmits to the Lieutenant Governor a written declaration to the contrary."

The Constitution also establishes procedures, under a Council on Gubernatorial Incapacity, whereby the Lieutenant Governor may assume the powers and duties of the Governor in the absence of a written declaration of incapacity by the Governor until it is determined that the Governor is able to resume the powers and duties of his office.

The Lieutenant Governor is a member of the Finance Advisory Committee, the Commission on Intergovernmental Cooperation (ex-officio) and the Corporation of Yale University.

The Lieutenant Governor is elected for four years and receives an annual salary of $55,000.

Lieutenant Governor	Town & Pol.	Term of Service	Years of Service
Roger Ludlow	Windsor, O	1639, 42, 48	3 yrs.
John Haynes	Hartford, O	1640, 44, 46, 50, 52	5 yrs.
George Wyllys	Hartford, O	1641	1 yr.
Edward Hopkins	Hartford, O	1643, 45, 47, 49, 51, 53	6 yrs.
Thomas Welles	Hartford, O	1654, 56, 57, 59	4 yrs.
John Webster	Hartford, O	1655	1 yr.
John Winthrop	New London, O	1658-59	1 yr.
John Mason	Norwich, O	1660-69	9 yrs.
William Leete	Guilford, O	1669-76	7 yrs.
Robert Treat	Milford, O	1676-83	7 yrs.
James Bishop	New Haven, O	1683-92	9 yrs.
William Jones	New Haven, O	1692-98	6 yrs.
Robert Treat	Milford, O	1698-1708	10 yrs.
Nathan Gold	Fairfield, O	1708-24	16 yrs.
Joseph Talcott	Hartford, O	1724-25	1 yr.
Jonathan Law	Milford, O	1725-41	16 yrs. 5 m.
Roger Wolcott	Windsor, O	1741-50	9 yrs. 10 m.
Thomas Fitch	Norwalk, O	1750-54	3 yrs. 1 m.
William Pitkin	Hartford, O	1754-66	12 yrs.
Jonathan Trumbull, Sr.	Lebanon, O	1766-69	3 yrs. 5 m.
Matthew Griswold	Lyme, F	1769-84	15 yrs.
Samuel Huntington	Norwich, O	1784-86	2 yrs.
Oliver Wolcott	Litchfield, F	1786-96	9 yrs. 8 m.
Jonathan Trumbull, 2nd	Lebanon, F	1796-97	1 yr. 7 m.
John Treadwell[1]	Farmington, F	1797-1809	11 yrs. 5 m.

[1] Was appointed Governor by the General Assembly in October, 1809, Governor Trumbull having died August 7, 1809.

DEPUTY OR LIEUTENANT GOVERNORS

Lieutenant Governor	Town & Pol.	Term of Service	Years of Service
Roger Griswold[2]	Lyme, F	1809-11	1 yr. 7 m.
John Cotton Smith[3]	Sharon, F	1811-13	2 yrs.
Chauncey Goodrich[4]	Hartford, F	1813-15	2 yrs. 3 m.
Jonathan Ingersoll[5]	New Haven, R*	1816-23	6 yrs. 8 m.
David Plant	Stratford, O	1823-27	4 yrs.
John S. Peters	Hebron, NR	1827-31	4 yrs.
No election		1831-32	
Thaddeus Betts	Norwalk, O	1832-33	1 yr.
Ebenezer Stoddard	Woodstock, O	1833-34	1 yr.
Thaddeus Betts	Norwalk, O	1834-35	1 yr.
Ebenezer Stoddard	Woodstock, O	1835-38	3 yrs.
Charles Hawley	Stamford, O	1838-42	4 yrs.
William S. Holabird	Winsted, O	1842-44	2 yrs.
Reuben Booth	Danbury, O	1844-46	2 yrs.
Noyes Billings	New London, O	1846-47	1 yr.
Charles J. McCurdy	Lyme, O	1847-49	2 yrs.
Thomas Backus	Killingly, O	1849-50	1 yr.
Charles H. Pond	Milford, D	1850-51	1 yr.
Green Kendrick	Waterbury, W	1851-52	1 yr.
Charles H. Pond	Milford, D	1852-54	2 yrs.
Alexander H. Holley	Salisbury, W	1854-55	1 yr.
William Field	Pomfret, FSA	1855-56	1 yr.
Albert Day	Hartford, AR	1856-57	1 yr.
Alfred A. Burnham	Windham, R	1857-58	1 yr.
Julius Catlin	Hartford, R	1858-61	3 yrs.
Benjamin Douglas	Middletown, R	1861-62	1 yr.
Roger Averill	Danbury, U	1862-66	4 yrs.
Oliver F. Winchester	New Haven, R	1866-67	1 yr.
Ephraim H. Hyde	Stafford, D	1867-69	2 yrs.
Francis Wayland	New Haven, R	1869-70	1 yr.
Julius Hotchkiss	Middletown, D	1870-71	1 yr.
Morris Tyler	New Haven, R	1871-73	2 yrs.
George G. Sill	Hartford, R	1873-77	4 yrs.
Francis B. Loomis	New London, D	1877-79	2 yrs.
David Gallup	Plainfield, R	1879-81	2 yrs.
William H. Bulkeley	Hartford, R	1881-83	2 yrs.
George G. Summer	Hartford, D	1883-85	2 yrs.
Lorrin A. Cooke	Winsted, R	1885-87	2 yrs.
James L. Howard	Hartford, R	1887-89	2 yrs.
Samuel E. Merwin	New Haven, R	1889-93	4 yrs.
Ernest Cady	Hartford, D	1893-95	2 yrs.
Lorrin A. Cooke	Winsted, R	1895-97	2 yrs.
James D. Dewell	New Haven, R	1897-99	2 yrs
Lyman A. Mills	Middlefield, R	1899-1901	2 yrs
Edwin O. Keeler	Norwalk, R	1901-03	2 yrs.
Henry Roberts	Hartford, R	1903-05	2 yrs.
Rollin S. Woodruff	New Haven, R	1905-07	2 yrs.
Everett J. Lake	Hartford, R	1907-09	2 yrs.

---

[2]Was appointed by the General Assembly in October, 1809, in place of Lieutenant Governor Treadwell.

[3]Was Acting-Governor from time of Governor Griswold's death, October 25, 1812, until May, 1813.

[4]Died August 18, 1815, while in office.

[5]Died January 12, 1823.

DEPUTY OR LIEUTENANT GOVERNORS

Lieutenant Governor	Town & Pol.	Term of Service	Years of Service
Frank B. Weeks[6]	Middletown, R	1909	3 m. 15 d.
Dennis A. Blakeslee	New Haven, R	1911-13	2 yrs.
Lyman T. Tingier	Vernon, D	1913-15	2 yrs.
Clifford B. Wilson	Bridgeport, R	1915-21	6 yrs.
Charles A. Templeton	Waterbury, R	1921-23	2 yrs.
Hiram Bingham	New Haven, R	1923-25	2 yrs.
John H. Trumbull	Plainville, R	1925	1 d.
J. Edwin Brainard[7]	Branford, R	1925-29	4 yrs.
Ernest E. Rogers	New London, R	1929-31	2 yrs.
Samuel R. Spencer	Suffield, R	1931-33	2 yrs.
Roy C. Wilcox	Meriden, R	1933-35	2 yrs.
T. Frank Hayes	Waterbury, D	1935-39	4 yrs.
James L. McConaughy	Middletown, R	1939-41	2 yrs.
Odell Shepard	Hartford, D	1941-43	2 yrs.
William L. Hadden	West Haven, R	1943-45	2 yrs.
Wilbert Snow[8]	Middletown, D	1945-46	1 yr. 11 m. 25 d.
James C. Shannon[9]	Bridgeport, R	1947-48	1 yr. 2 m.
Robert E. Parsons[10]	Farmington, R	1948-49	9 m. 29 d.
William T. Carroll	Torrington, R	1949-51	2 yrs.
Edward N. Allen	Hartford, R	1951-55	4 yrs.
Charles W. Jewett	Lyme, R	1955-59	4 yrs.
John N. Dempsey[11]	Putnam, D	1959-61	2 yrs. 16 d.
Anthony J. Armentano[12]	Hartford, D	1961-63	1 yr. 11 m. 15 d.
Samuel J. Tedesco[13]	Bridgeport, D	1963-66	3 yrs. 6 d.
Fred J. Doocy[14]	South Windsor, D	1966-67	11 m. 19 d.
Attilio R. Frassinelli	Stafford, D	1967-71	4 yrs.
T. Clark Hull[15]	Danbury, R	1971-73	2 yrs. 4 m. 25 d.
Peter L. Cashman[16]	Lyme, R	1973-75	1 yr. 7 m. 1 d.
Robert K. Killian	Hartford, D	1975-79	4 yrs.
William A. O'Neill[17]	East Hampton, D	1979-80	1 yr. 11 m. 28 d.
Joseph J. Fauliso[18]	Hartford, D	1980-91	10 yrs. 8 d.
Eunice S. Groark	Hartford, ACP	1991-95	3 yrs. 11 m. 26 d.
M. Jodi Rell	Brookfield, R	1995-	

[6] Governor Weeks was elected Lieutenant Governor and became Governor on the death of Governor Lilley, taking the oath of office, April 22, 1909.

[7] Lieutenant Governor Brainard was chosen president pro-tem of the Senate and succeeded to the office of Lieutenant Governor, to fill vacancy caused by the resignation of Governor Trumbull, January 8, 1925.

[8] Became Governor December 27, 1946, when Governor Baldwin resigned to become U.S. Senator.

[9] Became Governor upon the death of Governor McConaughy. Took oath of office March 8, 1948.

[10] Became Lieutenant Governor when Lieutenant Governor Shannon became Governor. Term began March 8, 1948.

[11] Became Governor January 21, 1961 in succession to Abraham Ribicoff who resigned to become Secretary of Health, Education and Welfare.

[12] Was chosen president pro-tem of the Senate and succeeded to the office of Lieutenant Governor when John Dempsey became Governor, January 21, 1961.

[13] Resigned January 15, 1966 to become Judge of the Superior Court on August 13, 1966.

[14] Succeeded to the office of Lieutenant Governor by virtue of being president pro tempore of the Senate. Took oath of office on January 17, 1966.

[15] Resigned June 1, 1973 to become Judge of the Superior Court.

[16] Succeeded to the office of Lieutenant Governor by virtue of being president pro tempore of the Senate. Took oath of office on June 7, 1973.

[17] Became Governor December 31, 1980 in succession to Ella Grasso who resigned because of ill health.

[18] Succeeded to the office of Lieutenant Governor by virtue of being president pro tempore of the Senate. Took oath of office on December 31, 1980.

SECRETARIES OF THE STATE

The Office of the Secretary of the State was established by the Fundamental Orders of Connecticut adopted in 1639. Edward Hopkins was chosen as the first Secretary. The duties and responsibilities of the office have grown substantially since that time paralleling the growth of governmental activities in Connecticut. Today, there are more than fifty constitutional and statutory mandates affecting the office.

By virtue of the office, the Secretary of the State is the Commissioner of Elections. The office administers all state constitutional and statutory provisions, and federal requirements, relating to state elections, primaries, nominating procedures and the acquisition and exercise of voting rights and the campaign finance law. The Secretary is responsible for the issuance, receipt, tabulation and approval or disapproval of nominating petitions for all elective offices to be filled, lists of nominations, certificates of party endorsement and of primary eligibility, absentee ballots and sample ballot labels; the preparation and distribution of absentee voting forms; the sending of written opinions and the answering of telephone inquiries on questions of election law; and the prescribing of the forms, guides and pamphlets for the admission and enrollment of electors, the nomination of candidates and the conduct of elections and primaries; and the preparation, distribution and filing of campaign financing statements. Disclosure statements are received from both state and federal political and candidate committees. The Secretary of the State conducts conferences for local election officials, the Town Clerks and Registrars of Voters. The office trains moderators and voting machine mechanics and certifies their eligibility.

The Secretary of the State is keeper of the Seal of the State and is charged with the custody of public documents and formal records of the State, among the more important of which are the Acts, Resolutions and Orders of the General Assembly. The Secretary provides certified copies of official records, and affixes the Seal to all commissions issued by the State. The Secretary also calls the Senate to order and administers the official oath on the first day of the session in the odd-numbered years.

Under the provisions of the General Statutes, the Secretary is responsible for the administration of many aspects of the corporation, limited liability company and limited partnership laws including: the approval of all certificates of incorporation, organization and dissolution, as well as annual and biennial reports, providing information on file to the public.

The Secretary of the State receives and files certain commercial transactions where title is affected by a security interest as provided under the Uniform Commercial Code Act.

The 1963 Trademark Law requires all marks to be registered with the Secretary of the State.

Notaries Public are appointed at the discretion of the Secretary of the State. The Secretary also publishes the *Connecticut Notary Public Manual.*

Other duties of the Secretary include the registration of trading stamp companies; the filing of administrative regulations of state departments or agencies, which become effective on the date filed; the filing of updated compilations of ordinances and special acts of every city, town and borough in the state; and the annual filing of schedules of regular meetings of all state departments and commissions of the executive branch for the ensuing year.

The Secretary of the State supervises the publication of the Connecticut State Register and Manual, the Statement of Vote, the Public Acts from Passage, and individual volumes devoted to Election Laws, Voters Handbook, Moderators Handbook and Handbook for Admission of Electors, and distributes The Constitution of Connecticut and Its Historical Trilogy of Antecedents.

The office of the Secretary of the State is a revenue producing agency. These revenues are derived from corporation filing and franchise fees, notary public fees, uniform commercial code fees and from sales of publications and services.

The State Board of Accountancy became a part of the Office of the Secretary of the State on January 1, 1986. The Board's responsibility is to insure that the highest standards of integrity and professionalism are maintained by Connecticut's Certified Public Accountants and licensed Public Accountants. It evaluates the qualifications of applicants for the CPA exam, provides a written examination process, sets experience requirements, licenses eligible candidates, develops regulations, holds hearings and imposes disciplinary action.

The Secretary of the State is a member of the State Board of Canvassers.

Election to the Office of Secretary of the State is for a term of four years, at an annual salary of $50,000.

SECRETARIES OF THE STATE

Secretary of the State	Town & Pol.	Term of Service	Years of Service
Edward Hopkins	Hartford, O	1639-41	2 yrs.
Thomas Welles	Hartford, O	1641-48	7 yrs.
John Cullick	Hartford, O	1648-58	10 yrs.
Daniel Clark	Windsor, O	1658-64, 65-67	8 yrs.
John Allyn	Hartford, O	1664-65, 67-96	30 yrs.
Eleazer Kimberly	Glastonbury, O	1696-1709	13 yrs.
William Whiting	Hartford, O	1709	3 m.
Caleb Stanly	Hartford, O	1709-12	3 yrs.
Richard Lord	Hartford, O	1712	17 d.
Hezekiah Wyllys	Hartford, O	1712-35	23 yrs.
George Wyllys	Hartford, O	1735-96	61 yrs.
Samuel Wyllys	Hartford, O	1796-1810	14 yrs.
Thomas Day	Hartford, O	1810-35	25 yrs.
Royal R. Hinman	Southbury, O	1835-42	7 yrs.
Noah A. Phelps	Hartford, O	1842-44	2 yrs.
Daniel P. Tyler	Pomfret, O	1844-46	2 yrs.
Charles W. Bradley	Hartford, O	1846-47	1 yr.
John B. Robertson	New Haven, O	1847-49	2 yrs.
Roger H. Mills	N. Hartford, O	1849-50	1 yr.
Hiram Weed[1]	Danbury, D	1850	1 m.
John P. C. Mather	New London, D	1850-54	3 yrs. 11 m.
Oliver H. Perry	Fairfield, W	1854-55	1 yr.
Nehemiah D. Sperry	New Haven, A	1855-57	2 yrs.
Orville H. Platt	Meriden, AR	1857-58	1 yr.
John Boyd	Winchester, R	1858-61	3 yrs.
J. H. Trumbull	Hartford, R	1861-66	5 yrs.
Leverett E. Pease	Somers, U	1866-69	3 yrs.
Hiram Appleman	Groton, R	1869-70	1 yr.
Thomas M. Waller	New London, D	1870-71	1 yr.
Hiram Appleman[2]	Groton, R	1871-73	2 yrs.
D. W. Edgecomb	Fairfield, R	1873	12 d.
Marvin H. Sanger	Canterbury, D	1873-77	4 yrs.
Dwight Morris	Bridgeport, D	1877-79	2 yrs.
David Torrance	Derby, R	1879-81	2 yrs.
Charles E. Searls	Thompson, R	1881-83	2 yrs.
D. Ward Northrop	Middletown, D	1883-85	2 yrs.
Charles A. Russell	Killingly, R	1885-87	2 yrs.
Leverett M. Hubbard	Wallingford, R	1887-89	2 yrs.
R. Jay Walsh	Greenwich, R	1889-93	4 yrs.
John J. Phelan	Bridgeport, D	1893-95	2 yrs.
William C. Mowry	Norwich, R	1895-97	2 yrs.
Charles Phelps	Rockville, R	1897-99	2 yrs.

[1] Died in office, June 7, 1850, and John P. C. Mather was appointed by the General Assembly, June 21, 1850 to fill the vacancy.

[2] Resigned April 25, 1873, and D. W. Edgecomb was appointed to the vacancy by Governor Jewell.

SECRETARIES OF THE STATE

Secretary of the State	Town & Pol.	Term of Service	Years of Service
Huber Clark	Willimantic, R	1899-1901	2 yrs.
Charles G. R. Vinal	Middletown, R	1901-05	4 yrs.
Theodore Bodenwein	New London, R	1905-09	4 yrs.
Matthew H. Rogers	Bridgeport, R	1909-13	4 yrs.
Albert Phillips	Stamford, D	1913-15	2 yrs.
Charles D. Burnes	Greenwich, R	1915-17	2 yrs.
Frederick L. Perry	New Haven, R	1917-21	4 yrs.
Donald J. Warner	Salisbury, R	1921-23	2 yrs.
Francis A. Pallotti	Hartford, R	1923-29	6 yrs.
William L. Higgins	Coventry, R	1929-33	4 yrs.
John A. Danaher	Hartford, R	1933-35	2 yrs.
C. John Satti	New London, D	1935-39	4 yrs.
Sara B. Crawford	Westport, R	1939-41	2 yrs.
Chase G. Woodhouse	New London, D	1941-43	2 yrs.
Frances B. Redick	Newington, R	1943-45	2 yrs.
Charles J. Prestia	New Britain, D	1945-47	2 yrs.
Frances B. Redick	Newington, R	1947-49	2 yrs.
Winifred McDonald	Waterbury, D	1949-51	2 yrs.
Alice K. Leopold[3]	Weston, R	1951-53	2 yrs. 10 m. 27 d.
Charles B. Keats[4]	Bridgeport, R	1953-55	1 yr. 1 m. 4 d.
Mildred P. Allen	Hartford, R	1955-59	4 yrs.
Ella T. Grasso	Windsor Locks, D	1959-71	12 yrs.
Gloria Schaffer[5]	Woodbridge, D	1971-78	7 yrs. 8 m. 19 d.
Henry S. Cohn[6]	West Hartford, D	1978-79	3 m. 9 d.
Barbara B. Kennelly[7]	Hartford, D	1979-82	3 yrs. 22 d.
Maura L. Melley[8]	Wethersfield, D	1982-83	11 m. 8 d.
Julia H. Tashjian	Windsor, D	1983-91	8 yrs.
Pauline R. Kezer	Plainville, R	1991-95	4 yrs.
Miles S. Rapoport	West Hartford, D	1995-	

[3]Resigned November 30, 1953 to become Director of Women's Bureau, U.S. Labor Dept.

[4]Appointed December 1, 1953 by Governor John Lodge to fill the vacancy caused by the resignation of Alice K. Leopold.

[5]Resigned September 25, 1978 to become a member of the Federal Civil Aeronautics Board.

[6]Appointed Secretary of the State by Governor Ella Grasso effective September 25, 1978, to fill the vacancy caused by the resignation of Gloria Schaffer.

[7]Resigned January 25, 1982. Elected to the 97th Congress on January 12, 1982, to fill the vacancy caused by the death of William R. Cotter.

[8]Appointed Secretary of the State by Governor William A. O'Neill effective January 29, 1982, to fill the vacancy caused by the resignation of Barbara B. Kennelly.

TREASURERS

The State Treasurer receives all cash receipts of the State from the various departments and institutions. The Treasurer is custodian of and responsible for all State funds. The Treasurer has the responsibility for investing the monies and has custody of all securities of the various State pension, retirement and temporary funds. The Treasurer is the custodian of all deeds covering state-owned property. The Treasurer has the care and management of the School and the Agricultural College Funds. The Treasurer is a member of the State Board of Canvassers, Banking Commission, Finance Advisory Committee, various Bond Commissions, the Connecticut Development Authority, Connecticut Housing Authority, Connecticut Health and Education Facilities Authority and the Connecticut Housing Finance Authority.

The Treasurer appoints a Deputy State Treasurer who is responsible for the office in his absence. The State Treasurer is bonded for the amount of $100,000 for the care and management of the School Fund; $200,000 as State Treasurer. The State Treasurer makes a complete report annually to the Governor of the receipts and expenditures of the State for the fiscal year ending on the 30th day of June preceding. The Treasurer is elected for four years and receives an annual salary of $50,000.

Treasurer	Town & Pol.	Term of Service	Years of Service
Thomas Welles	Hartford, O	1639-41	2 yrs.
William Whiting	Hartford, O	1641-48	7 yrs.
Thomas Welles	Hartford, O	1648-52	4 yrs.
John Talcott, Sr.	Hartford, O	1652-60	8 yrs.
John Talcott, Jr.	Hartford, O	1660-76	16 yrs.
William Pitkin	Hartford, O	1676-79	3 yrs.
Joseph Whiting	Hartford, O	1679-1718	39 yrs.
John Whiting	Hartford, O	1718-50	32 yrs.
Nathaniel Stanly	Hartford, O	1750-56	6 yrs.
Joseph Talcott	Hartford, O	1756-69	13 yrs.
John Lawrence	Hartford, O	1769-89	20 yrs.
Jedediah Huntington	Norwich, O	1789-90	1 yr.
Peter Colt	New Haven, O	1790-94	4 yrs.
Andrew Kingsbury	Hartford, O	1794-1818	24 yrs.
Isaac Spencer	E. Haddam, O	1818-35	17 yrs.
Jeremiah Brown	Hartford, O	1835-38	3 yrs.
Hiram Ryder	Willington, O	1838-42	4 yrs.
Jabez L. White, Jr.	Bolton, O	1842-44	2 yrs.
Joseph B. Gilbert	Hartford, O	1844-46	2 yrs.
Alonzo W. Birge	Coventry, O	1846-47	1 yr.
Joseph B. Gilbert	Hartford, O	1847-49	2 yrs.
Henry D. Smith	Middletown, D	1849-51	2 yrs.
Thomas Clark	Coventry, W	1851-52	1 yr.
Edwin Stearns	Middletown, D	1852-54	2 yrs.
Daniel Camp	Middletown, W	1854-55	1 yr.
Arthur B. Calef	Middletown, AD	1855-56	1 yr.
Frederick P. Coe	Killingly, A	1856-57	1 yr.
Frederick S. Wildman	Danbury, R	1857-58	1 yr.
Lucius J. Hendee	Hebron, A	1858-61	3 yrs.
Ezra Dean	Woodstock, R	1861-62	1 yr.
Gabriel W. Coite	Middletown, U	1862-66	4 yrs.
Henry G. Taintor	Hampton, R	1866-67	1 yr.
Edward S. Moseley	Hampton, R	1867-69	2 yrs.
David P. Nichols	Danbury, R	1869-70	1 yr.
Charles M. Pond	Hartford, D	1870-71	1 yr.
David P. Nichols	Danbury, R	1871-73	2 yrs.
Wm. E. Raymond	New Canaan, R	1873-77	4 yrs.
Edwin A. Buck	Windham, D	1877-79	2 yrs.
Tallmadge Baker	S. Norwalk, R	1879-81	2 yrs.
David P. Nichols[1]	Danbury, R	1881-82	1 yr.
James D. Smith	Stamford, R	1882-83	1 yr.
Alfred R. Goodrich	Vernon, D	1883-85	2 yrs.

[1] Died January 2, 1882, and James D. Smith was appointed by the Governor to fill the vacancy.

TREASURERS

Treasurer	Town & Pol.	Term of Service	Years of Service
V. B. Chamberlain	New Britain, R	1885-87	2 yrs.
Alexander Warner	Ridgefield, R	1887-89	2 yrs.
E. Stevens Henry	Vernon, R	1889-93	4 yrs.
Marvin H. Sanger	Canterbury, D	1893-95	2 yrs.
George W. Hodge	Windsor, R	1895-97	2 yrs.
Charles W. Grosvenor	Pomfret, R	1897-99	2 yrs.
Charles S. Mersick	New Haven, R	1899-1901	2 yrs.
Henry H. Gallup	Norwich, R	1901-05	4 yrs.
James F. Walsh	Greenwich, R	1905-07	2 yrs.
Freeman F. Patten	Stafford, R	1907-11	4 yrs.
Costello Lippitt	Norwich, R	1911-13	2 yrs.
Edward S. Roberts	Canaan, D	1913-15	2 yrs.
F.S. Chamberlain	New Britain, R	1915-19	4 yrs.
G. Harold Gilpatric	Putnam, R	1919-24	5 yrs. 7 m. 10 d.
Anson T. McCook[2]	Hartford, R	1924	4 m. 21 d.
Ernest E. Rogers	New London, R	1925-29	4 yrs.
Samuel R. Spencer	Suffield, R	1929-31	2 yrs.
Roy C. Wilcox	Meriden, R	1931-33	2 yrs.
J. William Hope	Bridgeport, R	1933-35	2 yrs.
John S. Addis[3]	New Milford, R	1935-37	2 yrs. 8 m. 29 d.
Thomas Hewes[4]	Farmington, D	1937	1 m.
Guy B. Holt	W. Hartford, D	1937-39	1 yr. 2 m. 3 d.
Joseph E. Talbot	Naugatuck, R	1939-41	2 yrs.
Frank M. Anastasio	New Haven, R	1941-43	2 yrs.
Carl M. Sharpe	Abington, R	1943-45	2 yrs.
William T. Carroll	Torrington, D	1945-47	2 yrs.
Joseph A. Adorno	Middletown, R	1947-55	8 yrs.
John Ottaviano, Jr.	New Haven, R	1955-59	4 yrs.
John A. Speziale[5]	Torrington, D	1959-61	2 yrs. 10 m. 8 d.
Donald J. Irwin[6]	Norwalk, D	1961-63	1 yr. 1 m. 20 d.
Gerald A. Lamb[7]	Waterbury, D	1963-70	7 yrs. 1 m. 2 d.
John A. Iorio[8]	Waterbury, D	1970-71	10 m. 28 d.
Robert I. Berdon[9]	Branford, D	1971-73	2 yrs. 5 m. 22 d.
Alden A. Ives[10]	Glastonbury, R	1973-75	1 yr. 6 m. 6 d.
Henry E. Parker[11]	New Haven, D	1975-86	11 yrs. 26 d.
Joan R. Kemler[12]	West Hartford, D	1986-87	11 m. 5 d.
Francisco L. Borges[13]	Hartford, D	1987-93	6 yrs. 1m. 19 d.
Joseph M. Suggs, Jr.[14]	Bloomfield, D	1993-95	1 yr. 9 mo. 26 d.
Christopher B. Burnham	Stamford, R	1995-	

[2] Anson T. McCook was appointed to succeed G. Harold Gilpatric, who resigned August 16, 1924.

[3] Died September 29, 1937, and Thomas Hewes was appointed by the Governor to fill the vacancy.

[4] Resigned November 1, 1937, and Guy B. Holt was appointed by the Governor to fill the vacancy.

[5] Resigned November 15, 1961 to become a Judge of the Court of Common Pleas.

[6] Appointed November 20, 1961 by Governor Dempsey to fill the vacancy caused by the resignation of John A. Speziale.

[7] Resigned February 11, 1970 to become State Bank Commissioner.

[8] Appointed February 11, 1970 by Governor Dempsey to fill the vacancy caused by the resignation of Gerald A. Lamb.

[9] Resigned June 28, 1973 to become Judge of the Superior Court.

[10] Appointed June 29, 1973 by Governor Meskill to fill the vacancy caused by the resignation of Robert I. Berdon. Took oath of office on July 2, 1973.

[11] Resigned February 3, 1986 to accept a position in private industry.

[12] Appointed February 3, 1986 by Governor O'Neill to fill the vacancy caused by resignation of Henry E. Parker.

[13] Resigned effective March 1, 1993 to accept a position in private industry.

[14] Appointed March 3, 1993 by the General Assembly to fill the vacancy caused by the resignation of Francisco L. Borges. Took oath of office on March 9, 1993.

COMPTROLLERS

The Office of the State Comptroller was created in 1786 by an act of the General Assembly. The Constitutional Amendment of 1836 provided that the Comptroller be elected by the people in a manner similar to that of other State Officers. Since 1838, this method has been in effect.

Prior to the establishment of this office, orders on the Treasurer could be drawn by the Governor, or his assistants, or by justices of the peace for sums under 40 shillings. The Committee of the Pay-Table, which the Comptroller's Office replaced, was originally established to liquidate and adjust accounts of expenses incurred during the Revolutionary War.

The Comptroller prescribes the mode of keeping and rendering all public accounts. The Comptroller is required to adjust and settle all public accounts and demands excepting grants and orders of the General Assembly. The Comptroller also renders a monthly accounting of the State's financial condition.

The Comptroller is a member, *ex officio* of the following committees: The State Board of Canvassers, the State Bond Commission, the State Banking Commission, the State Insurance Purchasing Board, the Finance Advisory Committee, the State Employees' Group Insurance Commission, and the State Employees' Retirement Commission. The Comptroller administers the records of the Retirement Commission. The Comptroller is a member of the National Association of State Auditors, Treasurers, and Comptrollers. The Comptroller is also, *ex officio* one of the Auditors of the accounts of the Treasurer.

The Comptroller approves and records all obligations against the State. The Comptroller maintains all official accounting records and is responsible for the employee payrolls of all State agencies, departments, and institutions. The office administers all Retirement Systems other than Teachers' retirement. Additionally, by direction of the General Assembly, the Comptroller administers numerous miscellaneous appropriations of the State.

Elected for a term of four years, the Comptroller receives an annual salary of $50,000.

Comptroller	Town & Pol.	Term of Service	Years of Service
James Wadsworth	Durham, O	1786-88	2 yrs.
Oliver Wolcott	Litchfield, O	1788-90	2 yrs.
Ralph Pomeroy	Coventry, O	1790-91	1 yr.
Andrew Kingsbury	Hartford, O	1791-93	2 yrs.
John Porter	Lebanon, O	1793-1806	13 yrs.
Elisha Colt	Hartford, O	1806-19	13 yrs.
James Thomas	Hartford, O	1819-30	11 yrs.
Elisha Phelps	Simsbury, O	1830-34	4 yrs.
Roger Huntington	Norwich, O	1834-35	1 yr.
Gideon Welles	Hartford, D	1835-36	1 yr.
William Field	Pomfret, O	1836-38	2 yrs.
Henry Kilbourn	Hartford, O	1838-42	4 yrs.
Gideon Welles	Hartford, D	1842-44	2 yrs.
Abijah Carrington	New Haven, O	1844-46	2 yrs.
Mason Cleveland	Hampton, O	1846-47	1 yr.
Abijah Catlin	Harwinton, O	1847-50	3 yrs.
Rufus G. Pinney	Stafford, D	1850-54	4 yrs.
John Dunham	Norwich, W	1854-55	1 yr.
Alexander Merrell	New London, A	1855-56	1 yr.
Edward Prentis	New London, A	1856-57	1 yr.
Joseph G. Lamb	Norwich, AR	1857-58	1 yr.

COMPTROLLERS

Comptroller	Town & Pol.	Term of Service	Years of Service
William H. Buell	Clinton, R	1858-61	3 yrs.
Leman W. Cutler	Watertown, R	1861-66	5 yrs.
Robbins Battell	Norfolk, U	1866-67	1 yr.
Jesse Olney	Straford, D	1867-69	2 yrs.
James W. Manning	Putnam, R	1869-70	1 yr.
Seth S. Logan	Washington, D	1870-71	1 yr.
James W. Manning	Putnam, R	1871-73	2 yrs.
Alfred R. Goodrich	Vernon, D	1873-77	4 yrs.
Charles C. Hubbard	Middletown, D	1877-79	2 yrs.
Chauncey Howard	Coventry, R	1879-81	2 yrs.
Wheelock Batcheller	Winsted, R	1881-83	2 yrs.
Frank D. Sloat	New Haven, R	1883-85	2 yrs.
Luzerne I. Munson	Waterbury, R	1885-87	2 yrs.
Thomas Clark	N. Stonington, R	1887-89	2 yrs.
John B. Wright	Clinton, R	1889-91	2 yrs.
Nicholas Staub	New Milford, D	1891-95	4 yrs.
Benjamin P. Mead	New Canaan, R	1895-99	4 yrs.
Thompson S. Grant	Enfield, R	1899-1901	2 yrs.
Abiram Chamberlain	Meriden, R	1901-03	2 yrs.
William E. Seeley	Bridgeport, R	1903-05	2 yrs.
Asahel W. Mitchell	Woodbury, R	1905-07	2 yrs.
Thomas D. Bradstreet	Thomaston, R	1907-13	6 yrs.
Daniel P. Dunn	Windham, D	1913-15	2 yrs.
Morris C. Webster	Torrington, R	1915-21	6 yrs.
Harvey P. Bissell	Ridgefield, R	1921-23	2 yrs.
Frederick M. Salmon	Westport, R	1923-33	10 yrs.
Anson F. Keeler	Norwalk, R	1933-35	2 yrs.
Charles C. Swartz	Norwalk, D	1935-39	4 yrs.
Fred R. Zeller	Stonington, R	1939-41, 43-45, 47-49, 51-59	14 yrs.
John M. Dowe[1]	Killingly, D	1941-43, 45-46	3 yrs. 4 m.
Raymond S. Thatcher[2]	E. Hampton, D	1946-47, 49-51, 59-66	10 yrs. 2 m. 4 d.
James J. Casey[3]	Winchester, D	1966-67	5 m. 16 d.
Louis I. Gladstone	Bridgeport, D	1967-71	4 yrs.
Nathan G. Agostinelli	Manchester, R	1971-75	4 yrs.
J. Edward Caldwell	Bridgeport, D	1975-91	16 yrs. 1 d.
William E. Curry, Jr.	Farmington, D	1991-95	4 yrs.
Nancy S. Wyman	Tolland, D	1995-	

[1] Died in office May 15, 1946 and Raymond S. Thatcher was appointed by the General Assembly to fill the vacancy.

[2] Resigned July 19, 1966 to become a member of the Public Utilities Commission.

[3] Appointed by the Governor July 19, 1966 to fill the unexpired term of Raymond S. Thatcher.

ATTORNEYS GENERAL

The Attorney General is the chief legal officer of the State. The Attorney General has general supervision over all legal matters in which the state is an interested party, except those over which criminal prosecutors have direction.

The Attorney General represents the state government, its elected officers, and state boards, commissions and agencies in suits and other civil proceedings in which the state has an interest. The Attorney General also provides opinions to the agencies of state government, state officers and the General Assembly upon questions of law submitted to him by such parties. The Attorney General also acts as general counsel for state officials in matters pertaining to their official duties. The Attorney General has a role in screening regulations of state agencies, state contracts and extradition papers.

By virtue of this statutory responsibility to provide legal direction to state government, the Attorney General is in a critical position to insure that the duties of all segments of the government are being conducted in accordance with the law.

In addition to this role as counsel to government, the Attorney General possesses extensive common law powers that enable him to represent the public interest more generally.

The Attorney General is elected by the people to a term of four years, is committed by law to serving full-time, and must be an attorney-at-law who has been admitted to practice in Connecticut for at least ten years. The Attorney General receives an annual salary of $60,000.

Attorney General	Town & Pol.	Term of Service	Years of Service
Charles Phelps	Vernon, R	1899-1903	4 yrs.
William A. King	Windham, R	1903-07	4 yrs.
Marcus H. Holcomb	Southington, R	1907-10	3 yrs. 8 m. 9 d.
John H. Light[2]	Norwalk, R	1910-15	4 yrs. 3 m. 21 d.
George E. Hinman	Windham, R	1915-19	4 yrs.
Frank E. Healy	Windsor Locks, R	1919-27	8 yrs.
Benjamin W. Alling	New Britain, R	1927-31	4 yrs.
Warren B. Burrows	Groton, R	1931-35	4 yrs.
Edward J. Daly[3]	Hartford, D	1935-37	2 yrs. 9 m. 22 d.
Chas. J. McLaughlin[4]	W. Hartford, D	1937-38	1 yr. 2 m.
Dennis P. O'Connor[5]	Hartford, D	1938-39	1 m. 13 d.
Francis A. Pallotti[1]	Hartford, R	1939-45	6 yrs. 6 m.
William L. Hadden[6]	West Haven, R	1945-51	5 yrs. 6 m. 20 d.
George C. Conway[1]	Guilford, R	1951-53	2 yrs. 7 m. 20 d.
William L. Beers[7]	New Haven, R	1953-55	1 yr. 4 m. 11 d.
John J. Bracken	Hartford, R	1955-59	4 yrs.
Albert L. Coles[1]	Bridgeport, R	1959-63	4 yrs. 7 m. 22 d.
Harold M. Mulvey[8]	New Haven, D	1963-67	4 yrs. 2 m. 17 d.
Robert K. Killian[9]	Hartford, D	1967-75	7 yrs. 1 m. 22 d.
Carl R. Ajello	Ansonia, D	1975-83	8 yrs.
Joseph I. Lieberman[10]	New Haven, D	1983-89	6 yrs.
Clarine Nardi Riddle[11]	New Haven, D	1989-91	2 yrs.
Richard Blumenthal	Stamford, D	1991-	

[1]Resigned to become a judge of the Superior Court.
[2]Appointed September 15, 1910, by Governor Weeks, to fill the unexpired term of Marcus H. Holcomb. Elected for a full term of 4 years in November, 1910.
[3]Appointed a judge of the Superior Court, effective September 22, 1937.
[4]Appointed by the Governor, September 22, 1937, to fill the unexpired term of Edward J. Daly.
[5]Appointed by the Governor, November 21, 1938, to fill the unexpired term of Charles J. McLaughlin, who resigned to become Tax Commissioner.
[6]Appointed by the Governor, June 13, 1945, to fill the unexpired term of Francis A. Pallotti, who resigned to become a judge of the Superior Court.
[7]Appointed by the Governor, to fill the unexpired term of George C. Conway, who resigned to become a judge of the Superior Court, effective August 24, 1953.
[8]Appointed by the Governor, August 29, 1963, to fill the unexpired term of Albert L. Coles, who resigned to become a judge of the Superior Court; elected for a full term November 8, 1966; resigned November 16, 1967 to become a judge of the Superior Court, effective January 1, 1968.
[9]Appointed by the Governor, November 16, 1967, to fill the unexpired term of Harold M. Mulvey. Elected for a full term November 3, 1970.
[10]Resigned January 3, 1989 to become U.S. Senator.
[11]Appointed by the Governor to fill the unexpired term of Joseph I. Lieberman, effective January 3, 1989, as Deputy Attorney General serving as Acting Attorney General. Sworn in as Attorney General October 27, 1989.

CHIEF JUSTICES

The highest court in Connecticut was the General Assembly, until 1784, when it relinquished its functions as an appellate tribunal to the upper house, which, when sitting for these purposes, was designated as the Supreme Court of Errors. The presiding officer or Chief Judge was at first the Deputy Governor, and later the Governor. In 1807 the membership of this court was completely changed by substituting, under an Act of the preceding year, the Judges of the Superior Court, the Chief Judge of which became the presiding officer. The customary appellation was for some years, Chief Judge, but in the Constitution of 1818 the term Chief Justice was employed and confirmed a practice already established in that respect.

Chief Judge	Town	Term Beginning	Term Ending
Gurdon Saltonstall	New London	1711	1712
Nathan Gold	Fairfield	1712	1713
William Pitkin	Hartford	1713	1714
Nathan Gold	Fairfield	1714	1723
Peter Burr	Fairfield	1723	1725
Jonathan Law	Milford	1725	1741
Roger Wolcott	Windsor	1741	1750
Thomas Fitch	Norwalk	1750	1754
William Pitkin	Hartford	1754	1766
Jonathan Trumbull	Lebanon	1766	1769
Matthew Griswold	Lyme	1769	1784
Samuel Huntington	Norwich	1784	1785
Richard Law	New London	1785	1789
Eliphalet Dyer	Windham	1789	1793
Andrew Adams	Litchfield	1793	1798
Jesse Root	Hartford	1798	1807

THE FOLLOWING IS A LIST OF CHIEF JUSTICES SINCE THE PRESENT FORM OF ORGANIZATION WAS ADOPTED

Chief Judge	Town	Term Beginning	Term Ending
Stephen Mix Mitchell	Wethersfield	1807	1814
Tapping Reeve	Litchfield	1814	1815
Zephaniah Swift	Windham	1815	1819
Stephen Titus Hosmer	Middletown	1819	1833
David Daggett	New Haven	1833	1834
Thomas Scott Williams	Hartford	1834	1847
Samuel Church	Sharon	1847	1854
Henry Matson Waite	Lyme	1854	1857
William Lucius Storrs	Hartford	1857	1861
Joel Hinman	Waterbury	1861	1870
Thomas Belden Butler	Norwalk	1870	1873
Origen Storrs Seymour	Litchfield	1873	1874
John Duane Park	Norwich	1874	1889
Charles B. Andrews	Litchfield	1889	1901
David Torrance	Derby	1901	1907
Simeon E. Baldwin	New Haven	1907	1910

CHIEF JUSTICES

Chief Judge	Town	Term Beginning	Term Ending
Frederic B. Hall	Bridgeport	1910	1913
Samuel O. Prentice	Hartford	1913	1920
George W. Wheeler	Bridgeport	1920	1930
William M. Maltbie	Granby	1930	1950
Allyn L. Brown	Norwich	1950	1953
Ernest A. Inglis	Middletown	1953	1957
Patrick B. O'Sullivan[1]	Orange	1957	1957
Kenneth Wynne[2]	Woodbridge	1957	1958
Edward J. Daly[3]	Hartford	1958	1959
Raymond E. Baldwin[4]	Middletown	1959	1963
John Hamilton King[5]	Willimantic	1963	1970
Howard Wells Alcorn[6]	Suffield	1970	1971
Charles S. House[7]	Manchester	1971	1978
John P. Cotter[8]	West Hartford	1978	1981
Joseph W. Bogdanski[9]	Meriden	1981	1981
John A. Speziale[10]	Torrington	1981	1984
Ellen A. Peters[11]	West Hartford	1984	1996
Robert J. Callahan[12]	Norwalk	1996	

[1] Appointed Chief Justice effective April 16, 1957; retired by limitation of age on August 11, 1957.

[2] Appointed Chief Justice effective August 11, 1957 in succession to Patrick B. O'Sullivan.

[3] Appointed Chief Justice effective May 6, 1958 in succession to Kenneth Wynne, who retired by limitation of age on May 5, 1958.

[4] Appointed Chief Justice by the Governor, July 24, 1959 in succession to Edward J. Daly who died July 20, 1959.

[5] Appointed Chief Justice effective August 31, 1963 in succession to Raymond E. Baldwin, who retired by limitation of age on said date.

[6] Appointed Chief Justice effective April 21, 1970 in succession to John Hamilton King, who retired by limitation of age on said date.

[7] Appointed Chief Justice effective May 14, 1971 in succession to Howard Wells Alcorn, who retired by limitation of age on said date.

[8] Appointed Chief Justice effective April 24, 1978 in succession to Charles S. House, who retired by limitation of age on said date.

[9] Appointed Chief Justice effective March 2, 1981 in succession to John P. Cotter, who retired by limitation of age on said date.

[10] Appointed Chief Justice effective November 12, 1981 in succession to Joseph W. Bogdanski, who retired by limitation of age on said date.

[11] Appointed Chief Justice effective November 21, 1984 in succession to John A. Speziale, who retired on said date.

[12] Appointed Chief Justice effective September 1, 1996 in succession to Ellen A. Peters, who resigned.

PRESIDENTS PRO TEMPORE OF THE CONNECTICUT STATE SENATE SINCE 1845

Name	Town & Pol.	Term of Service
Aaron N. Skinner	New Haven, W	1845
Samuel Ingham	Saybrook, D	1846
Thomas C. Perkins	Hartford, W	1847
Thomas B. Butler	Norwalk, W	1848
Henry Dutton	New Haven, W	1849
Samuel Ingham	Saybrook, D	1850
Henry E. Peck	New Haven, W	1851
James T. Pratt	Rocky Hill, D	1852
Daniel B. Warner	East Haddam, D	1853
John Boyd	West Winsted, Free Soil Dem.	1854
James F. Babcock	New Haven, W	1855
Leman W. Cutler	Watertown, AR	1856
Ammi Giddings	Plymouth, U	1857
Elisha Carpenter	Killingly, R	1858
Thaddeus Welles	Glastonbury, R	1859
Joseph G. Lamb	Norwich, AR	1860
Andrew B. Mygatt	New Milford, R	1861
Hiram Goodwin	Hitchcockville, R (U)	1862
Gilbert W. Phillips	Putnam, R (U)	1863
John T. Adams	Norwich, U	1864
Orlando J. Hodge	Robertsville, U	1865
John T. Wait	Norwich, U	1866
Amos J. Gallup	Sterling, R	1867
Edwin H. Bugbec	Killingly, R	1868
David Gallup	Plainfield, R	1869
Edward Harland	Norwich, R	1870
Ezra Hall	Marlborough, R	1871
S. Storrs Cotton	Pomfret, R	1872
Allen Tenny	Norwich, R	1873
Luzon B. Morris	New Haven, D	1874
Caleb B. Bowers	New Haven, D	1875
Ephraim H. Hyde	Stafford, D	1876
Oliver Hoyt	Stamford, R	1877,78
Gilbert W. Phillips	Putnam, R (U)	1879
Lyman W. Coe	Torrington, R	1880,81
Robert Coit	New London, R	1882,83
Lorrin A. Cooke	Winsted, R	1884
Stiles T. Stanton	Stonington, R	1885,86
Robert J. Walsh	Greenwich, R	1887,88
John M. Hall	Willimantic, R	1889,90
David M. Read	Bridgeport, D	1891,92
Frederick W. Holden	Ansonia, D	1893,94

Name	Town & Pol.	Term of Service
John Ferris	So. Norwalk, R	1895,96
William Marigold	Bridgeport, R	1897,98
Edwin O. Keeler	Norwalk, R	1899,1900
Henry Roberts	Hartford, R	1901,02
Rollin S. Woodruff	New Haven, R	1903,04
Samuel Fessenden	Stamford, R	1905,06
Stiles Judson	Stratford, R	1907,08
Isaac W. Brooks	Torrington, R	1909,10
Frank C. Woodruff	Orange, R	1911,12
George Landers	New Britain, D	1913,14
Frederic A. Bartlett	Bridgeport, R	1915,16
Henry H. Lyman	Middlefield, R	1917,18
William H. Heald	Stafford Springs, R	1919,20
William H. Hall	So. Willington, R	1921,22
John H. Trumbull	Plainville, R	1923,24
Edwin Brainard	Branford, R	1925,26
Frederic C. Walcott	Norfolk, R	1927,28
Roy C. Wilcox	Meriden, R	1929,30
Albert E. Lavery	Fairfield, R	1931,32
David Goldstein	Bridgeport, D	1933,34
John F. Lynch	West Haven, R	1935,36
Joseph H. Lawlor	Waterbury, D	1937,38
Charles J. Arrigoni	Durham, R	1939,40
Joseph B. Downes	Norwich, D	1941,42
Frank H. Peet	Kent, R	1943,44
Samuel H. Malkan	New Haven, D	1945,46
Robert E. Parsons	Farmington, R	1947,48
Cornelius Mulvihill, Jr.	Bridgeport, D	1949,50
William Perry Barber	Putnam, D	1951,52
Oscar Peterson, Jr.	Stratford, R	1953,54
Patrick J. Ward	Hartford, D	1955,56
Theodore S. Ryan	Sharon, R	1957,58
Anthony Armentano	Hartford, D	1959-62
Fred J. Doocy[1]	Wapping, D	1963-1/16/66
Paul J. Falsey[2]	New Haven, D	1/26/66-1966
Charles T. Alfano	Suffield, D	1967-72
Peter L. Cashman[3]	Lyme, R	1973-6/7/73
Florence D. Finney[4]	Cos Cob, R	7/10/73-1974
Joseph J. Fauliso[5]	Hartford, D	1975-80
James J. Murphy, Jr.	Franklin, D	1981-84
Philip S. Robertson	Cheshire, R	1985-87
John B. Larson	East Hartford, D	1987-95
M. Adela Eads	Kent, R	1995-97
Kevin B. Sullivan	Hartford, D	1997-

[1] Succeeded to the office of Lieutenant Governor. Took oath of office January 17, 1966.

[2] Became President Pro Tempore when Fred Doocy became Lieutenant Governor.

[3] Succeeded to the office of Lieutenant Governor. Took oath of office June 7, 1973.

[4] Became President Pro Tempore when Peter L. Cashman became Lieutenant Governor.

[5] Succeeded to the office of Lieutenant Governor. Took oath of office December 31, 1980.

SPEAKERS OF THE HOUSE OF REPRESENTATIVES OF CONNECTICUT SINCE 1819

Name	Town & Pol.	Term of Service
David Plant	Stratford, O	1819,20
Elisha Phelps	Simsbury, O	1821
Seth P. Beers	Litchfield, O	1822,23
Ralph I. Ingersoll	New Haven, O	1824
Samuel A. Foot	Cheshire, R	1825,26
Ebenezer Young	Killingly, O	1827,28
Elisha Phelps	Simsbury, O	1829
Henry W. Edwards	New Haven, D	1830
Martin Welles	Wethersfield, O	1831,32
Samuel Ingham[2]	Saybrook, O	1833
Roger Huntington[1]	Norwich, O	1834
William L. Storrs	Middletown, O	1834
Samuel Ingham	Saybrook, O	1835
Chauncey F. Cleveland	Hampton, D	1835,36
Stillman K. Wightman	Middletown, O	1837
William W. Boardman	New Haven, W	1838,39
Charles J. McCurdy	Lyme, O	1840,41
Stillman K. Wightman	Middletown, O	1842
Noyes Billings	New London, O	1843
Charles J. McCurdy	Lyme, O	1844
William W. Boardman	New Haven, W	1845
Cyrus H. Beardslee	Monroe, D	1846
LaFayette S. Foster	Norwich, W	1847,48
John C. Lewis	Plymouth, F	1849
Origen S. Seymour	Litchfield, D	1850
Samuel Ingham	Saybrook, D	1851
Charles B. Phelps	Woodbury, D	1852
William W. Eaton	Hartford, D	1853
LaFayette S. Foster[3]	Norwich, W	1854
Green Kendrick	Waterbury, W	1854
Austin Baldwin	Middletown, A	1855
Green Kendrick	Waterbury, W	1856
Eliphalet A. Bulkeley	Hartford, U	1857
Alfred A. Burnham	Windham, R	1858
Oliver H. Perry	Fairfield, R	1859,60
Augustus Brandegee[4]	New London, R	1861
Henry C. Deming	Hartford, D	1861

[1]Resigned May 24, 1834, having been appointed Comptroller, and William L. Storrs was appointed to fill the vacancy.

[2]Resigned May 15, 1835, and Chauncey F. Cleveland was chosen to fill the vacancy.

[3]Resigned June 8, 1854, having been elected U.S. Senator, and Green Kendrick was chosen to fill the vacancy.

[4]At a special session held Oct. 9, 1861, the speaker, Mr. Brandegee, being detained from the House by illness, Mr. Deming was chosen speaker, *pro tempore*.

Name	Town & Pol.	Term of Service
Josiah M. Carter	Norwalk, R	1862
Chauncey F. Cleveland	Hampton, R	1863
John S. Rice	Farmington, U	1864
Eleazer K. Foster	New Haven, R	1865
David Gallup	Plainfield, U	1866
John T. Wait	Norwich, U	1867
Charles Ives	East Haven, R	1868
Orville H. Platt	Meriden, R	1869
LaFayette S. Foster[5]	Norwich, R	1870
Alfred A. Burnham	Windham, R	1870
Edwin H. Bugbee	Killingly, R	1871
Amos S. Treat	Woodbridge, R	1872
William W. Eaton	Hartford, D	1873
Tilton E. Doolittle	New Haven, D	1874
Charles Durand	Derby, R	1875
Thomas M. Waller	New London, D	1876
Lynde Harrison	Guilford, R	1877
Charles H. Briscoe	Enfield, R	1878
Dexter R. Wright	New Haven, R	1879
Dwight Marcy	Vernon, R	1880
William C. Case	Granby, R	1881
John M. Hall	Windham, R	1882
Charles H. Pine	Derby, R	1883
Henry B. Harrison	New Haven, R	1884
William Edgar Simonds	Canton, R	1885
John A. Tibbits	New London, R	1886
Heusted W. R. Holt	Greenwich, R	1887
John H. Perry	Fairfield, R	1889
Allen W. Paige	Huntington, R	1891
Isaac W. Brooks	Torrington, R	1893
Samuel Fessenden	Stamford, R	1895
Joseph L. Barbour	Hartford, R	1897
Frank B. Brandegee	New London, R	1899
John H. Light	Norwalk, R	1901
Michael Kenealy	Stamford, R	1903
Marcus H. Holcomb	Southington, R	1905
John Q. Tilson	New Haven, R	1907
Elmore S. Banks	Fairfield, R	1909
Frederick A. Scott	Plymouth, R	1911
Morris C. Webster	Harwinton, R	1913
Frank E. Healy	Windsor Locks, R	1915,17
James F. Walsh	Greenwich, R	1919
Frederick W. Huxford	Stamford, R	1921
Leonard J. Nickerson	Cornwall, R	1923
Elbert L. Darbie	Killingly, R	1925
John H. Hill	Shelton, R	1927
Samuel A. Eddy	North Canaan, R	1929

[5]Resigned June 16, 1870, having been chosen Judge of Supreme Court of Errors and Alfred A. Burnham of Windham was chosen to fill the vacancy.

Name	Town & Pol.	Term of Service
Howard W. Alcorn	Suffield, R	1931
William Hanna	Bethel, R	1933,35
J. Mortimer Bell	Salisbury, R	1937
Walter Howe	Litchfield, R	1939
Hugh Meade Alcorn, Jr.	Suffield, R	1941
Harold E. Mitchell	West Hartford, R	1943
E. Lea Marsh, Jr.	Old Lyme, R	1945
Frederick H. Holbrook	Madison, R	1947
John R. Thim	Hamden, R	1949
Mansfield D. Sprague	New Canaan, R	1951
Arthur E. B. Tanner	Woodbury, R	1953
W. Sheffield Cowles	Farmington, R	1955
Nelson C. L. Brown, II	Groton, R	1957
William J. O'Brien, Jr.	Portland, D	1959
Anthony E. Wallace	Simsbury, R	1961
J. Tyler Patterson, Jr.	Old Lyme, R	1963,65
Robert J. Testo	Bridgeport, D	1967
William R. Ratchford	Danbury, D	1969,71,72
Francis J. Collins	Brookfield Center, R	1973,74
James J. Kennelly	Hartford, D	1975,76, 77,78
Ernest N. Abate	Stamford, D	1979,80, 81,82
Irving J. Stolberg	New Haven, D	1983,84
R. E. Van Norstrand	Darien, R	1985,86
Irving J. Stolberg	New Haven, D	1987,88
Richard J. Balducci	Newington, D	1989,90,91,92
Thomas D. Ritter	Hartford, D	1993,94,95,96

SECTION II

BIOGRAPHIES AND PHOTOGRAPHS

President of the United States

Connecticut Elective State Officers

United States Senators
From Connecticut

United States Representatives
From Connecticut

Leaders of the
1997-1998 Connecticut General Assembly

Justices of the
Connecticut Supreme Court

Judges of the
Appellate Court

WILLIAM J. CLINTON
THE PRESIDENT

WILLIAM J. CLINTON

The President

William Jefferson "Bill" Clinton, elected on November 3, 1992, was sworn in as the 42nd President of the United States on January 20, 1993. He was reelected on November 5, 1996.

Clinton is a fifth generation Arkansan, born William Jefferson Blythe IV in Hope, Arkansas, on August 19, 1946, two months after his father died in a traffic accident. When he was four years old, his mother married Roger Clinton and the family moved to Hot Springs, where Mr. Clinton grew up and attended public schools.

In 1968, Mr. Clinton received his Bachelor's degree from Georgetown University in Washington, D.C. and then spent two years at Oxford University as a Rhodes Scholar. In 1973 he earned a law degree from Yale University Law School.

He began his political career in 1974 with an unsuccessful campaign for Congress. After serving one term as attorney general of Arkansas, Clinton was elected in 1978 to the first of five terms as the state's governor. He became the nation's longest serving governor and only the second person in Arkansas history to serve as long in that position.

During Clinton's tenure as governor, Arkansas led all surrounding states in job growth for several years and became nationally recognized for improvements in its educational system.

In 1988, Clinton led a major effort by the nation's governors to restructure national welfare laws and to secure Congressional and White House approval of the Family Support Act. The act changed the welfare system to require that welfare recipients work toward independence through education, training and work. It was based on a proposal the National Governors' Association adopted in 1987 during Clinton's term as chairman.

The president is a former chairman of the Democratic Leadership Council 1990-91, the National Governors Association, 1986-87, the Education Commission of the States, 1986-87 and the Lower Mississippi Delta Development Commission 1989-90. He co-chaired the NGA Task Force on Healthcare, 1990-91.

Clinton is married to Hillary Rodham, whom he met in 1973, when they both were attending Yale Law School. They have one daughter named Chelsea.

JOHN G. ROWLAND
GOVERNOR

JOHN G. ROWLAND
Governor

On January 4, 1995, John G. Rowland was sworn in as Connecticut's 86th Governor. At 37, Rowland was the youngest person ever elected to the state's highest office. Rowland is also the youngest governor in the nation.

Since taking office, Governor Rowland has made responsible budgeting and holding the line on state spending top priority. Connecticut's state surpluses have totaled $330 million since 1995, due in great part to spending restraints Governor Rowland put in place. Governor Rowland also secured cuts in the state income tax to give Connecticut workers their first real tax cut in years.

To help the state's economy and create jobs, Governor Rowland has worked to improve the state's overall business climate. To make Connecticut competitive with other states the corporation tax is being phased down by 1/3 and state government is becoming more efficient and user-friendly. The Governor also leads an aggressive public/private marketing effort that has attracted more than 100 new businesses and 8,000 new jobs to Connecticut since 1995.

Under Governor Rowland's leadership, Connecticut enacted some of the toughest welfare reforms in the nation, including a 21-month time limit on benefits and incentives to move recipients into the workforce. As of January 1997, more than 40 percent of welfare recipients were working.

To make Connecticut safer for its citizens, Governor Rowland worked to secure a more workable death penalty, measures to better protect children from sex offenders, and laws forcing criminals to serve at least 85% of their sentences. He also called for a constitutional amendment to protect victim's rights.

To help protect abused and neglected children, Governor Rowland has brought the state's child protection system to a new degree of openness. He has worked to hire more social workers, move more staff into the field to work directly with at-risk children, and make it easier to remove at-risk children from abusive homes.

Governor Rowland has a long history of public service. In 1980, at age 23, he was elected to the Connecticut State Legislature to represent the 73rd Assembly District. He served until 1984, when he was elected to the United States House of Representatives at age 27. He represented the Fifth Congressional District until 1990.

Since taking office, Governor Rowland has been elected Chairman of the New England Governors' Conference. The Wall Street Journal has recognized John Rowland as "one of the nation's top ten emerging government leaders."

Governor Rowland's family has lived in Connecticut for more than 200 years and has a 50-year tradition of public service. Governor Rowland's father and grandfather both served as Comptroller for the City of Waterbury. His grandfather was instrumental in uncovering massive municipal corruption during the 1930's. Four generations of the Rowland family have owned an insurance firm, which Governor Rowland has helped to manage.

Governor Rowland has received many public service awards, including both the Malcolm Baldridge and the TIBCO Advocate of the Year awards. He also became the first Governor to receive the Excellence in State Government award. In addition he also received a Yale University Chubb Fellowship, an honorary doctorate of humane letters from Teikyo Post College, and honorary doctor of laws degrees from both the University of Hartford and University of New Haven.

John Rowland has lived his entire life in the Greater Waterbury area. He is a graduate of Holy Cross High School in Waterbury and Villanova University. Governor Rowland and his wife, Patricia, reside in the Governor's Residence in Hartford. They have five children between them: Kirsten, Ryan, Robert John, Julianne, and Scott.

M. JODI RELL
LIEUTENANT GOVERNOR

M. JODI RELL
Lieutenant Governor

M. Jodi Rell is Connecticut's 105th Lieutenant Governor. She is the first Republican to hold that office in 22 years and the first Republican female Lieutenant Governor in the state's history.

As Lieutenant Governor, Mrs. Rell is a member of the Yale Corporation and the State Finance Advisory Committee. Her responsibilities also include presiding over the state senate as its President.

She is the Chairman of the Prison and Jail Overcrowding Commission and the Connecticut Progress Council. She serves as a member of the Governor's Law Enforcement Council and sits on the Executive Committee of the Greater Hartford Downtown Council. She is Chairman of the State of Connecticut/American Red Cross Disaster Cabinet.

In 1995, Mrs. Rell established the "Lieutenant Governor's Commission on Mandate Reform." As part of the Commission's work, the Lieutenant Governor crisscrossed the state, visiting 101 town halls and meeting with officials from all 169 municipalities to discuss state mandates.

Before being elected Lieutenant Governor, Jodi Rell served as the Deputy Minority Leader of the Connecticut House of Representatives. She was first elected to the House of Representatives in 1984, representing Connecticut's 107th Assembly District, and was re-elected four times.

Mrs. Rell is active in the National Order of Women Legislators (NOWL), which includes former and present women legislators from all 50 states and the U.S. territories. She is a past national president of the group. In 1995 she was honored by NOWL along with Diane Sawyer and Helen Thomas at the National Press Club in Washington D.C. as a recipient of their prestigious Leadership Award.

Lieutenant Governor Rell is a member of the Board of Trustees of the Regional YMCA of Western Connecticut and the Candlewood Lions Club.

Born in Norfolk, Virginia, Mrs. Rell attended Old Dominion University and Western Connecticut State University. The Lieutenant Governor and her husband Lou, live in Brookfield. They have two grown children, Meredith and Michael.

MILES S. RAPOPORT
SECRETARY OF THE STATE

MILES S. RAPOPORT
Secretary of the State

Miles S. Rapoport has served as Connecticut's 71st Secretary of the State since January 4, 1995. Secretary Rapoport believes the Secretary of the State's office should be a strong advocate for democracy, civic involvement and participation, and has established programs, policies and partnerships to fulfill that mission.

Under his leadership, the Secretary of the State's office has issued the State's first Report on the *State of Democracy*, established a Citizen Speakers Bureau and Community Citizen Award to promote civic involvement, and was a lead participant in the committee that brought the first Presidential Debate to Hartford in 1996.

The Secretary of the State's office has developed a multifaceted "Project Democracy" that includes a major initiative to increase voter registration in partnership with state agencies, businesses, community groups, and private organizations. Specific programs are also in place to expand voter education and increase the involvement of young people in democracy, including a new law that permits 17-year-olds to pre-register as voters. The office is also establishing Connecticut's first statewide computerized voter registration list—one of the first states in the country to do so.

Secretary Rapoport is also a leading advocate—in Connecticut and nationally—for reforming the financing of elections, firmly believing we should change the system so that money counts for less and people and ideas for more. He is the chair of the committee on campaign finance reform of the National Association of Secretaries of State (NASS), and also serves as national secretary/treasurer and Eastern Regional vice president of the organization.

Secretary Rapoport also advocates the use of technology to better serve the public. This is reflected in stepped up computerization of the corporate records and accountant certifications recorded by the office and formation of a business advisory committee. There has also been an office-wide emphasis on providing excellent public service, including enhanced staff training and dialogue with customers.

Prior to his election as Secretary of the State, Rapoport served for a decade in the Connecticut House of Representatives, including service as House Chair of the Government Administration and Elections Committee and as an Assistant Majority Leader. He was a legislative advocate for expanded voter registration opportunities, citizen access to state computerized information, and disclosure of campaign finance information. Rapoport also fought for asbestos removal from public schools, better, more universal health care, and the establishment of a reporting system and stiffer penalties for crimes motivated by bigotry and bias.

Prior to his years of public service in the Connecticut legislature, Rapoport was the executive director of the Connecticut Citizen Action Group (CCAG), the state's largest citizen organization, from 1979 to 1984. Under Rapoport's leadership, it succeeded in winning legislation for a superfund on hazardous waste cleanup, regulation of toxic air pollution, and helped reduce numerous proposed utility rate increases.

Rapoport 47, graduated from New York University in 1971 with a BA in political science. Miles and his wife, Sandra Luciano, live in West Hartford. They have two children, Jeff and Ross.

CHRISTOPHER B. BURNHAM
TREASURER

CHRISTOPHER B. BURNHAM
Treasurer

Christopher B. Burnham, is the 81st Treasurer of the State of Connecticut. He is an independently elected Constitutional officer, and sole fiduciary of the State's $14 billion public employee pension fund. Since his inauguration in January of 1995, the Office of the Treasurer has striven toward becoming the finest public investment bank in the Nation.

Treasurer Burnham was elected in 1994, with a clear mandate to reform the management of the pension funds and the Second Injury Fund. In keeping with the fundamental themes of his campaign, Burnham ushered through the legislature the landmark "Anti-Shakedown" Bill, which outlaws campaign contributions to Treasurers or candidates for Treasurer from employees of firms who conduct business with the Office. Burnham was honored as the 1995 "Friend of Democracy" by Common Cause Connecticut for his efforts to purge politics from the investment decisions affecting the retirement security of 144,000 pension beneficiaries. Burnham has also gained national attention as the architect of the largest public pension fund restructuring in recent history.

Mr. Burnham earned his B.A. in Political Science from Washington & Lee University, and his Master's degree in Public Administration from the John F. Kennedy School of Government at Harvard University. Prior to his services as Treasurer, Burnham was elected to three terms in the Connecticut General Assembly, as Representative from the 147th district. He distinguished himself as a fierce opponent of wasteful government spending. As Assistant Minority Leader, he helped lead the fight against the 1991 income tax.

Mr. Burnham is an investment banker, who has held positions with Merrill Lynch & Co., First Boston Corporation, and most recently Vice President of Corporate Finance with Advest, Inc. He is also a Major in the United States Marine Corps Reserve, and was called to active duty in the Persian Gulf during Operation Desert Storm.

Treasurer Burnham resides in Stamford with his wife Courtney, and their son George.

NANCY S. WYMAN
COMPTROLLER

NANCY S. WYMAN
COMPTROLLER

Nancy Wyman became the first woman to hold the office of Connecticut State Comptroller on January 4, 1995. Comptroller Wyman believes that the State Comptroller reports to the people of Connecticut as their chief fiscal guardian. She has implemented policies and programs and sponsored legislation to enhance the office's ability to perform as such. Comptroller Wyman issues a public report each year in which she analyzes the state budget as it relates to the economy and other factors. She also issues a monthly report on state finances.

Under Comptroller Wyman's leadership, the Office of State Comptroller has undergone significant changes in its structure and operations to focus on accountability and public service. She has sponsored legislation that would reform the way the state purchases goods and services and improve scrutiny over the awarding of contracts to vendors. Her office includes significant economic and state revenue forecasting capabilities for the first time.

The State Comptroller oversees the state health plan for 166,000 state employees, retirees, and their dependents. She also led a task force to study ways to improve access to health care for Connecticut's uninsured population. The group's work resulted in proposed legislation aimed at expanding Medicaid eligibility to children and providing tax incentives for businesses to offer health insurance to their employees.

Comptroller Wyman sponsored legislation in 1996 that will open the state health plan to municipalities for their employees. This legislation received overwhelming bipartisan support. The municipalities would benefit from the leverage of the state's huge health insurance group and should be able to reduce their per-employee cost for health care insurance.

The Comptroller has lent her time to several non-profit and charitable organizations since taking office. She serves on the board of the Downtown Hartford YMCA and was a key fundraiser in its 1997 Sustaining Campaign. In 1995, she served as government chair for the Greater Hartford United Way/Combined Health Appeal campaign. She has appeared at numerous MADD functions and served as spokesperson for MADD's 1996 holiday season public-service announcement campaign. And she currently serves as president of the Women's Campaign School at Yale University.

Prior to her election as State Comptroller in 1994, Nancy Wyman served as State Representative (1987-1995) from the 53rd District. She was House Chairperson of the Education Committee and Chairperson of the Appropriations Subcommittee on Elementary and Secondary Education. While a legislator, Ms. Wyman was noted for her work in the area of public education and named "Legislator of the Year" by the Connecticut Education Association. In recognition of her dedication to public service, Ms. Wyman also received awards from the Council of Small Towns, the American School for the Deaf, the Connecticut Library Association, the Connecticut Coalition Against Domestic Violence, the Connecticut Coalition for Children, and the National Abortion Rights Action League (NARAL).

From 1979-1987, Comptroller Wyman served on the Tolland Board of Education and was Vice-Chairperson for four of those years. She has contributed to the local, state and national education debate and is known as an ardent champion of public education.

Comptroller Wyman is a former radiological technologist, with a degree from Long Island College Hospital. She and her husband, Michael, have lived in Tolland since 1973 and have two daughters, Stacey and Meryl.

RICHARD BLUMENTHAL
ATTORNEY GENERAL

RICHARD BLUMENTHAL
Attorney General

Richard Blumenthal is the 23rd Attorney General of the State of Connecticut. Attorney General Blumenthal's priorities are protecting consumers, preserving jobs, enhancing the environment, safeguarding the health and well being of our children, and making the law work for people.

The Attorney General's leadership and innovative use of his office has helped to stop the hostile takeover of a major Connecticut employer, drastically reduced unjustified utility rate increases, ensured that chronic polluters ceased endangering people's health, and protected consumers from the misuse of their charitable donations. Attorney General Blumenthal has personally argued in court on critical issues affecting Connecticut's citizens including defending the State's ban on assault weapons and its welfare reform efforts. He has also saved taxpayers money through aggressive litigation, forced companies deceiving consumers to reimburse those consumers, advocated measures to reduce health insurance fraud, and worked hard to preserve access to quality health care and protect the rights of senior citizens.

Attorney General Blumenthal was elected to office in 1990 and re-elected in 1994. Previously, he was a member of the Connecticut State Senate from 1987 to 1990, and the Connecticut House of Representatives from 1984 to 1987.

Richard Blumenthal also served as United States Attorney for Connecticut for four and one-half years (1977-81). His leadership as the chief federal prosecutor in our State resulted in the successful prosecution of many major cases against drug traffickers, organized crime, white collar criminals, civil rights violators, consumer frauds and environmental polluters.

Attorney General Blumenthal also served as administrative assistant to United States Senator Abraham A. Ribicoff, as aide to Daniel P. Moynihan, when Moynihan was Assistant to the President of the United States, and as a law clerk to Supreme Court Justice Harry A. Blackmun. Attorney General Blumenthal graduated with honors from Harvard College (Phi Beta Kappa; Magna Cum Laude) and Yale Law School, where he was Editor-in-Chief of the *Yale Law Journal*. He also served as a sergeant in the United States Marine Corps Reserves.

Attorney General Blumenthal lives in Greenwich with his wife Cynthia and their four children.

CHRISTOPHER J. DODD
UNITED STATES SENATOR

CHRISTOPHER J. DODD
United States Senator

Christopher John Dodd, Democrat, was born in Willimantic, Connecticut on May 27, 1944.

First elected to the United States Senate in 1980, Mr. Dodd is serving his fourth term as a Senator in the 105th Congress. Senator Dodd is a member of the Committee on Foreign Relations and ranking member of its Subcommittee on Western Hemisphere and Peace Corps Affairs. As a member of the Committee on Banking, Housing and Urban Affairs, he is ranking member of the Subcommittee on Securities. He serves on the Committee on Labor and Human Resources and is ranking member of its Subcommittee on Children and Families. Senator Dodd is also a member of the Committee on the Budget and the Committee on Rules and Administration. In 1983, he founded the Senate Children's Caucus.

Prior to his tenure in the Senate, Mr. Dodd served in the 94th, 95th and 96th Congresses, representing the Second District of Connecticut in the House of Representatives. As a member of the house, he served on the Rules Committee, the Judiciary Committee and the Science and Technology Committee. He was also appointed to the Select Committee on the Outer Continental Shelf and the Select Committee on Assassinations.

Mr. Dodd is the son of the late Senator Thomas J. and Grace Murphy Dodd. After graduating from Providence College in 1966, he entered the Peace Corps, serving two years in the Dominican Republic. He enlisted in the Army in 1969, fulfilled his obligation in reserve status, and was honorably discharged in 1975. He graduated from the University of Louisville School of Law in 1972, was admitted to the Connecticut Bar in 1973, and practiced law in New London until his election to Congress in 1974, his first bid for public office. Senator Dodd is the youngest person ever elected to the U.S. Senate in Connecticut history and the first Connecticut son to follow his father to the upper chamber of Congress.

Senator Dodd lives in East Haddam.

Office addresses: U.S. Senate, Washington, D.C. 20510, phone (202) 224-2823; Putnam Park, 100 Great Meadow Road, Wethersfield, Connecticut 06109, phone (860) 240-3470. In-state toll-free phone: (800) 334-5341. On the Internet: E-Mail Address: sen_dodd@dodd.senate.gov and Home Page Address: http://www.senate.gov/~dodd.

JOE LIEBERMAN
UNITED STATES SENATOR

JOE LIEBERMAN
UNITED STATES SENATOR

Joe Lieberman was born in Stamford, Connecticut on February 24, 1942 and attended public schools there. He received his bachelor's degree from Yale College in 1964 and his law degree from Yale Law School in 1967.

Senator Lieberman was elected to the Connecticut State Senate in 1970, and served there for ten years—the last six as Majority Leader. From 1982 to 1988, Senator Lieberman served as Connecticut's 21st Attorney General.

On November 8, 1988, Joe Lieberman was elected to the United States Senate. He was re-elected to a second term winning by the widest margin of any U.S. Senate race in Connecticut history. He serves on the committees on Armed Services, Environment and Public Works, Governmental Affairs, and Small Business. Senator Lieberman is a Deputy Whip of the Senate. In 1995, he became Chairman of the Democratic Leadership Council.

Creating jobs is a top priority for Senator Lieberman. He supports strong enterprise zones, an R&D tax credit, a lower capital gains tax, personal and business IRAs, and expanded trade. As a member of the powerful Armed Services Committee, he has worked to preserve jobs at Connecticut companies that manufacture products that are critical to our national security.

Senator Lieberman has continued to emphasize environmental protection, authoring portions of the Clean Air Act and has worked to prevent oil companies from drilling in the Arctic National Wildlife Refuge. He wrote laws creating Connecticut's first national park site at Weir Farm, a Long Island Sound office in EPA, and the state's first fish and wildlife refuge along the Connecticut River. He also sponsored a law providing the Farmington River with special Wild and Scenic designation, and authored the Pollution Prosecution Act.

Senator Lieberman co-authored the Congressional Accountability Act, which makes Congress live by the same employment, civil rights and health and safety laws that apply to everyone else in the country. Senator Lieberman also supported legislation to reform the welfare system. He fought for a stronger crime bill to help police crack down on gangs and violent crime. He has been a leader in efforts to increase educational programming for children on television and to focus public attention on the problem of trash television talk shows. He also fought for a "chip" and a television rating system to allow parents to protect their children from sex, violence and profanity on television. Senator Lieberman has been an outspoken opponent of rock and "gangsta rap" groups that use obscene lyrics.

In the field of foreign policy, Senator Lieberman called attention to the threat of terrorism and the proliferation of weapons of mass destruction. In 1995, he and Senate Majority Leader Bob Dole co-sponsored legislation to lift the arms embargo that prevents the Bosnians from defending themselves against Serbian aggression.

A major portion of Senator Lieberman's agenda is focused on constituent service. He cuts government "red tape" for thousands of Connecticut residents..

Senator Lieberman is the author of four books: *The Power Broker* (1966), a biography of the late Democratic Party chairman, John M. Bailey; *The Scorpion and the Trantula* (1970), a study of early efforts to control nuclear proliferation; *The Legacy* (1981), a history of Connecticut politics from 1930-1980; and *Child Support in America* (1986), a guidebook on methods to increase the collection of child support from delinquent fathers.

Senator Lieberman lives in New Haven with his wife Hadassah. They have four children, Matthew, Rebecca, Ethan and Hana.

Office addresses: 706 Hart Senate Office Building, Washington, D.C. 20510, phone, (202) 224-4041; Hartford office: 1 State Street, Suite 1420, Hartford, Connecticut 06103, phone (860) 549-8463, or toll-free, (800) 225-5605. E-Mail Address: senator_lieberman@lieberman.senate.gov.

BARBARA B. KENNELLY
U.S. Representative, First District, Connecticut

BARBARA B. KENNELLY

U.S. REPRESENTATIVE, FIRST DISTRICT, CONNECTICUT

Congresswoman Barbara B. Kennelly has represented the First District of Connecticut since 1982, and was most recently re-elected in November, 1996, when she received more than 74 percent of the vote. Congresswoman Kennelly serves on the Ways and Means Committee where she is ranking member of the Subcommittee on Social Security. In addition, she was elected by her Democratic colleagues to their fourth-ranking leadership position, Vice Chair of the Democratic Caucus. She is the first woman to hold this position. Congresswoman Kennelly was also the first woman to serve as a Chief Deputy Majority Whip, and the first to serve on the House Permanent Select Committee on Intelligence.

Among the Congresswoman's accomplishments in the last session of Congress were passage of her plan to reduce the vesting period for multi-employer pension plans, which made one million additional workers eligible for pensions; her plan to allow the terminally ill to collect their life insurance benefits early and tax-free; and her plan to permit tax deductions for individuals and businesses who purchase long-term care insurance. Congresswoman Kennelly is a long-time advocate for children, working particularly to improve the collection of child support payments across state lines. She has fought for child protection programs, foster care, and health care for children, and she has championed the Earned Income Tax Credit, which increases take-home pay for low-income families.

A life-long resident of Hartford, Congresswoman Kennelly received a B.A. in Economics from Trinity College, Washington, D.C. She earned a certificate from the Harvard Business School on completion of the Harvard-Radcliffe Program in Business Administration and a Master's Degree in Government from Trinity College, Hartford. Congresswoman Kennelly holds honorary doctorates from Mount Holyoke College; the University of Hartford; Sacred Heart University; Teikyo Post University; Saint Mary's College, and Simmons College.

Prior to her election to Congress, Congresswoman Kennelly was Secretary of the State of Connecticut and a member of the Hartford Court of Common Council. Her late husband, James, was Speaker of the Connecticut State House from 1975 through 1978. She has three daughters and a son.

Washington address: 201 Cannon House Office Building, Washington, D.C. 20515, phone (202) 225-2265; Hartford office: Eleventh Floor, One Corporate Center, Hartford, Connecticut 06103, phone (860) 278-8888.

SAM GEJDENSON
U.S. Representative, Second District, Connecticut

SAM GEJDENSON

U.S Representative, Second District, Connecticut

Sam Gejdenson (pronounced GA'-DEN-SON), a Democrat, has served the people of Eastern Connecticut in the U.S. House of Representatives since 1981. He has fought to help diversify and strengthen the economic base of defense dependent areas, to expand export markets for U.S. industries making it easier for small and medium sized companies to market their products overseas, to protect the environment, and to enhance retirement and pension security for working men and women.

In 1993, House Speaker Thomas S. Foley named Gejdenson Chairman of a Defense Conversion Committee to coordinate policies aimed at helping communities like Southeastern Connecticut. This appointment capped several years of work in the Congress on economic diversification issues, including the 1990 passage of legislation Gejdenson wrote to establish the nation's first $200 million job creation and retraining program for areas impacted by defense cuts.

To broaden the presence of Connecticut's exporters in international markets, Gejdenson served as Chairman of the House Subcommittee on Economic Policy, Trade and the Environment. Through his chairmanship, Gejdenson secured passage of legislation, "The Jobs Through Exports Act," to help small and medium sized companies start exporting, and create new jobs.

Gejdenson, who grew up on his family's dairy farm in rural Bozrah, Connecticut is committed to preserving the quality of our environment. A senior member of the House Natural Resources Committee, Gejdenson has worked to create a National Heritage Corridor in northeastern Connecticut; protect the Long Island Sound through an active role on the Long Island Sound Congressional Caucus; and ensure safety for the workers and the people who live near nuclear power plants.

Early in the 103rd Congress Gejdenson re-introduced election reform legislation and once again put himself at the center of a national debate over cleaning-up the federal election process. Gejdenson's legislation, which was first introduced in the 102nd Congress, was hailed by Common Cause and other groups as "the most comprehensive campaign finance reform bill in two decades." Although the bill was approved by both the House and Senate, it was vetoed by former President Bush.

Gejdenson also serves as co-chair of the House Democratic Caucus Task Force on Retirement Security. In the 104th Congress, Gejdenson was a lead co-sponsor of sweeping legislation—the Retirement Savings and Security Act—to expand pension coverage to millions of working Americans, create 401(k) plans for small businesses, and strengthen the laws which protect workers' retirement funds from corporate raids.

Gejdenson was born in 1948 in an American displaced persons camp in Eschwege, Germany following World War II. His parents are Holocaust survivors who settled in Bozrah after the war.

Gejdenson attended local schools in Bozrah and Norwich, Connecticut. He graduated from Mitchell College in New London, Connecticut in 1968 with an A.S. and in 1970, graduated with a B.A. from the University of Connecticut, in Storrs.

In 1974, Gejdenson became a full-time legislator in the Connecticut House of Representatives. He served two terms in the state house, and, after working in the administration of former Connecticut Governor Ella T. Grasso, launched his first bid for U.S. Congress in 1980. He is the father of two children, Mia and Ari.

Office addresses: 1401 Longworth House Office Building, Washington, D.C. 20515, phone (202) 225-2076; 2 Courthouse Square, 5th Floor, Norwich, Connecticut 06360, phone (860) 886-0139; 94 Court Street, Middletown, Connecticut 06457, phone (860) 346-1123. E-Mail Address: Bozrah.@Hr.House.Gov. Internet Homepage: http://www.house.gov/gejdenson/welcome.htm.

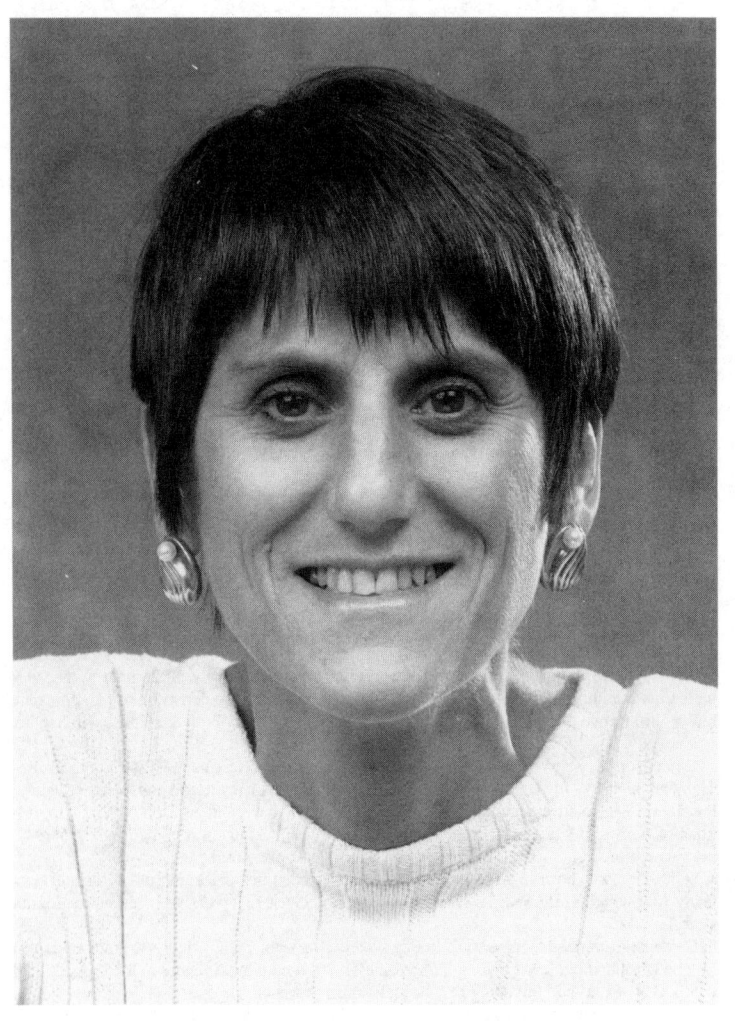

ROSA DeLAURO
U.S. Representative, Third District, Connecticut

ROSA DeLAURO

U.S. Representative, Third District, Connecticut

Congresswoman Rosa DeLauro has worked a lifetime for the people of Connecticut. She was first elected to Congress from Connecticut's Third District on November 6, 1990 and was re-elected in 1992, 1994 and 1996. At the beginning of the 105th Congress, Rosa was named to the Appropriations Committee and sits on the Labor/HHs and Agriculture Subcommittees. Rosa also serves in the Democratic Leadership of the House as a Chief Deputy Whip.

Rosa was born and raised in New Haven's Wooster Square. Her grandmother owned and operated a pastry shop there. Her father, Ted, was an Alderman known for his hard work that earned him the nickname "Mayor of Wooster Square." Her mother, Luisa, is today the longest-serving member of the New Haven Board of Aldermen.

Since coming to Congress, Rosa has made economic improvement a top priority. She authored a proposal to offer tax relief for approximately 130 million middle-income taxpayers, helped write a transportation bill that is bringing 100,000 jobs to Connecticut over six years. She sponsored legislation to help Connecticut's defense-dependent businesses, workers and communities make the transition to a post-Cold War economy.

Rosa has championed job training programs to make Connecticut Workers more competitive and has introduced her own legislation to create 250,000 jobs nationwide through infrastructure development.

Rosa has also focused her attention on efforts to reduce crime and make our communities safer. She formed the Anti-Crime Youth Council with more than 140 high school students, in order to give young people a voice in the national debate on crime and violence. In addition, Rosa helped pass some of the most sweeping anti-crime legislation ever written, helping lead the fight for passage of the Brady Bill and the Assault Weapons ban putting 100,000 new police officers on the streets, and mandating tough sentences for repeat, violent offenders.

A strong supporter of health care reform, Rosa pushed for a plan that would guarantee comprehensive private health insurance to every American. She also introduced legislation to crack down on health care billing fraud, overcharging and other abuses. Rosa was instrumental in increasing funding for breast and cervical cancer research and screenings. She has also introduced a bill to guarantee longer hospital stays for women undergoing mastectomies

Prior to her election to the U.S. House of Representatives, Rosa DeLauro served as Executive Director of EMILY's List, a national organization committed to increasing the number of women in elected office. She served as Executive director of Countdown '87, the national campaign that successfully stopped U.S. military aid to the Nicaraguan Contras. From 1981-1987, Rosa served as Chief of staff to U.S. Senator Christopher Dodd.

A graduate of Marymount College, where she received her B.A. with honors, Rosa received her M.A. in International Politics from Columbia University and studied at the London School of Economics.

Rosa is married to Stanley Greenberg, President of Greenberg Research, Inc., a public issues research and polling firm. Their children—Anna, Kathryn and Jonathan Greenberg—are all grown and pursuing careers and post-graduate education.

Office addresses: 436 Cannon House Office Building, Washington, D.C. 20515, phone (202) 225-3661; 59 Elm Street, New Haven, Connecticut 06510, phone (203) 562-3718.

CHRISTOPHER SHAYS
U.S. Representative, Fourth District, Connecticut

CHRISTOPHER SHAYS

U.S. REPRESENTATIVE, FOURTH DISTRICT, CONNECTICUT

Congressman Christopher Shays was elected to represent Connecticut's Fourth District in a special election in 1987, and to a sixth term in 1996.

According to Politics In America, published by Congressional Quarterly: "Republicans and Democrats have often been in a state of near-war since Shays joined the House in 1987, but he has successfully cut his own path, one that has him siding with Democrats on some high-profile issues and leading the GOP charge on others."

He is a senior member of the House Budget Committee and the Government Reform and Oversight Committee.

Christopher is known for his efforts to get our country's financial house in order and balance the budget; save our trust funds, particularly Medicare, for future generations and transform our "caretaking" social, corporate and agricultural welfare state into a "caring" opportunity society.

On the Budget Committee, Christopher chairs the Working Group on Health Care charged with helping reform Medicare and Medicaid. He has been repeatedly honored by the National Taxpayers Union and Citizens Against Government Waste for his work to balance the budget and strengthen our economy, and was listed as the most "fiscally responsible" House member by the bipartisan Concord Coalition.

On the Government Reform and Oversight committee, he chairs the Subcommittee on Human Resources and Intergovernmental Relations, which has responsibility for investigating waste, fraud and abuse in the Departments of Health and Human Services, Education, Housing and Urban Development, Labor and Veterans Affairs.

Noting that "if a law is right for the private sector, it is right for Congress," Christopher gained national prominence when he co-authored the Congressional Accountability Act, requiring Congress to live by the laws it sets for the rest of the country. In January 1995, the Congressional Accountability Act was the first element of the Republican Contract with America taken up on the opening day of the 104th Congress and was the first bill signed into law in 1995 by President Clinton.

Christopher gained further national prominence by taking a leadership role in helping pass legislation in November 1995 banning gifts to members of Congress and requiring a higher level of disclosure of the activities of lobbyists in Washington. He is now working on a bipartisan basis to enact comprehensive campaign finance reform.

One of only a few Republicans representing an urban district, Chris is a strong voice for cities. In 1992, he and Congressman Kewisi Mfume unveiled their "Urban Marshall Plan to Rebuild our Cities" to bring businesses back to urban areas, create jobs and expand their tax bases. He also helped spearhead the fight to save the comprehensive crime control bill of 1994 by negotiating a bipartisan compromise that reduced the overall cost of the bill and added tough new provisions.

Christopher was born in Stamford in October 1945 to Bud and Peggy Shays of Darien. He graduated from Darien High School and Principia College, and holds an MBA and MPA from New York University. Following college, he married his high school sweetheart, Betsi, and they worked in the Peace Corps as teachers in Fiji. They live in Stamford with their daughter Jeramy.

Office addresses: 1502 Longworth House Office Building, Washington, D.C. 20515, phone (202) 225-5541; district offices: 10 Middle Street, Bridgeport 06604, phone (203) 579-5870; Government Center, 888 Washington Boulevard, Stamford 06901, phone, (203) 357-8277. E-Mail Address: CSHAYS@HR.HOUSE.GOV.

JAMES H. MALONEY

U.S. Representative, Fifth District, Connecticut

JAMES H. MALONEY

U.S. REPRESENTATIVE, FIFTH DISTRICT, CONNECTICUT

James H. Maloney is currently serving his first term representing the people of Connecticut's Fifth Congressional District, made up of the northern parts of New Haven and Fairfield Counties, including the Naugatuck Valley and the cities of Waterbury, Danbury, and Meriden.

Maloney ran for Congress to make a difference in the lives of Connecticut's families. As a former State Senator, he established a strong record as a moderate "can-do" legislator who struck a balance between social and economic issues. In Congress, Maloney intends to strengthen educational opportunities for our nation's youth, create jobs and economic growth, protect seniors, and preserve our environment. Maloney is also a firm believer that to effectively represent the people, one must be actively involved in the community and personally familiar with its concerns. Accordingly, his main priority since winning the election has been establishing a first-rate constituent out-reach and service program in his District and Washington offices.

As a founder of the Housatonic Valley Economic Development Partnership, Maloney understands the importance of bringing leaders from all walks of the community together to stimulate economic growth and enhance economic opportunities for Connecticut's families. He will work from his position on the House Banking and Financial Services Committee to bring new economic opportunities to the district, provide small businesses with the tools necessary to get up and running, facilitate the growth of the financial services sector of Connecticut's economy, address the concerns of larger employers in the area, and expand housing opportunities throughout the district.

He will work to secure continued opportunities for Connecticut's defense contractors and their employees. He is aware that for more than 200 years Connecticut's defense industry has been both a major source of employment for our state and a critical component of America's national security that ensures our United States forces are the best prepared and equipped in the world. Maloney also successfully sought a seat on the House National Security Committee.

Elected to the Connecticut State Senate in 1986, Maloney represented Bethel, Danbury, and New Fairfield for eight years. During his tenure, Maloney was most well-known for stepping up to the plate and passing the first significant reduction in state taxes in nearly a decade. As Chairman of the Finance Committee, he engineered a $260 million tax cut, including reductions in consumer taxes, property taxes, business energy taxes, and corporate taxes. In addition, Maloney was instrumental in securing $30 million in state funding for the construction of the Waterbury Mall, which will create more than 4,000 jobs for our state, and in implementing other innovative capital projects. He also co-authored legislation that successfully improved state government efficiency and financial planning.

Maloney's dedication to improving the lives of Connecticut families extends to other areas as well. While serving as Chair of the Labor Committee, he was an advocate for employee-fair reform of the state's work compensation system and for stronger family-leave and worker safety legislation. Dedicated to preserving our precious environment, he worked to pass measures that protect Connecticut's fresh-water lakes, encourage recycling efforts, and fighing "Greenhouse" pollution.

The oldest of ten children, Maloney was born on September 17, 1948 and is a graduate of Harvard University and Boston University School of Law. He currently lives in Danbury with his wife, Mary, and their three daughters, Adele, Anna and Ellen.

Office addresses: 1213 Longworth Office Building, Washington, D.C. 20515, phone (202) 225-3822, FAX (202) 225-5746; John S. Monagan Federal Building, 135 Grand Street, Waterbury, Connecticut 06702-1911. Tel., (203) 573-1418, FAX (203) 573-9329.

NANCY L. JOHNSON
U.S. Representative, Sixth District, Connecticut

NANCY L. JOHNSON

U.S. Representative, Sixth District, Connecticut

Nancy Johnson represents Connecticut's Sixth Congressional District, which stretches from the urban corridor alongside the Connecticut River north of Hartford to the scenic Litchfield County towns north and west of industrial Waterbury and Danbury. Johnson, who has represented the district since 1982, is working to create jobs, promote economic growth, improve health care, balance the budget and reform education during the 105th Congress.

In 1988, Johnson became the first Republican woman ever named to the House Ways and Means Committee, which is responsible for the nation's tax code, trade policy and issues such as Medicare, unemployment compensation, Social Security and welfare. Johnson also chairs the Subcommittee on Oversight, which oversees the impact of legislative policies once they become law and the effectiveness of federal bureaucracies, such as the Internal Revenue Service. As Chairman, Johnson successfully led the development of the Taxpayer Bill of Rights II, legislation that includes more than 30 new protections for taxpayers and was signed into law in 1996.

Johnson also serves on several congressional caucuses, which focus on specific legislative issues. She is the co-founder and co-chair of the Congressional Bearings Caucus, a bipartisan group of legislators that works to strengthen the nation's industrial base and the U.S. bearing industry. In addition, Johnson devotes time to the Housing Opportunity Caucus, Education Caucus and Rural Health Care Coalition, and serves as the Co-Chair of the Congressional Caucus for Women's Issues and of the New England Council.

Through her work on the Ways and Means Committee, Rep. Johnson has become a nationally recognized leader in health care reform. Ensuring the solvency of Medicare, creating universal access to health care and controlling costs are health care issues on which she has specifically focused and can address as a member of the Subcommittee on Health. Her legislation to expand the community health care delivery system was the only health care bill signed into law during the 102nd Congress (1991-92). In 1995, Congress expanded and made permanent a program introduced by Johnson which allows older Americans the choice to purchase low-cost supplemental health care insurance, and approved another Johnson bill expanding community health centers' ability to offer affordable, quality care to millions more people.

Johnson was very active in the welfare reform debate in the 104th Congress, and served on the House-Senate conference committee that developed the final bill signed into law in 1996. During the conference, she was successful in her efforts to assure medical coverage and day care support for families making the transition from welfare to work. Johnson authored the child support enforcement section of the law which includes new, tougher, interstate enforcement mechanisms, a more effective national parent locator system, and provisions that facilitate paternity establishment.

The Congresswoman's political career began when she ran for Connecticut State Senate in 1976, becoming the first Republican elected to the New Britain seat in 30 years. She held the seat until her election to the House of Representatives. Prior to seeking elective office, Johnson was active in community affairs in New Britain and was a visiting lecturer on political science at Central Connecticut State University.

Johnson, born in Chicago and a graduate of Radcliffe College, is married with three grown daughters.

Office Addresses: 343 Cannon House Office Building, Washington, D.C. 20515, phone (202) 225-4476; 480 Myrtle Street, Suite 200, New Britain, Connecticut 06053, phone (860) 223-8412.

KEVIN B. SULLIVAN
PRESIDENT PRO TEMPORE OF THE STATE SENATE

KEVIN B. SULLIVAN
President Pro Tempore of the State Senate

First elected to the State Senate in 1986, Kevin Sullivan represents West Hartford, Bloomfield, Burlington and Farmington. In 1997, he was chosen to lead the State Senate as President Pro Tempore.

Senator Sullivan served for ten years as Chairman of the General Assembly's Education Committee and is nationallly recognized for his work on school improvement. He is also known for leadership on issues of spending control, economic development, children and the elderly. In 1993, he was selected to participate in the University of Virginia's Program for Emerging Political Leaders.

Long active in community service, Senator Sullivan served on the West Hartford Town Council and as Mayor. He represents Connecticut on the Education Commission of the States and is a member of the Rotary Club, League of Women Voters, Drugs Don't Work Board of Directors, Connecticut-Israel Exchange Commission and Wadsworth Atheneum Board of Electors. He also founded the State Capitol Vietnam Veteran's Memorial.

Senator Sullivan's honors include recognition by the Anti-Defamation League, United Seniors in Action, Greater Hartford Association for Retarded Citizens, Connecticut Association of Boards of Education, Connecticut Conference of Independent Colleges, Coalition for Children, Urban League, Advocates for the Arts, Connecticut Junior Leagues, Connecticut Education Association, American School for the Deaf, Veterans of Foreign Wars and Greater Hartford Jaycees.

Raised in West Hartford, Kevin Sullivan attended local public schools and was the first in his family to have the opportunity to go to college. He graduated from Trinity College in 1971, where he recieved the Samuel Fishzohn Award for Civil Rights Activity, and the University of Connecticut School of Law in 1982. He is a Vice President at Trinity College in Hartford and a business attorney.

Kevin resides in West Hartford with his wife, Carolyn Thornberry.

GEORGE C. JEPSEN

MAJORITY LEADER OF THE STATE SENATE

GEORGE C. JEPSEN
Majority Leader of the State Senate

George Jepsen of Stamford represents the 27th Senatorial District serving the towns of Stamford and Darien.

He is the Senate Majority Leader in his fouth term as a State Senator. Previously, he served as Chairman of the Planning and Development Committee (1991-92), as the Chairman of the Judiciary Committee (1993-94) and as Ranking Member of the Finance, Revenue and Bonding Committee (1995-96). He also served as Minority Whip (1995-96).

Prior to joining the Senate, Jepsen served as an Assistant Majority Leader in the House of Representatives, representing the 148th Assembly District for two terms. During that time, he served as vice-chair of the Insurance and Real Estate Committee and as a member of the Finance, Revenue and Bonding Committee and of the Family and the Workplace Committee.

As a legislator, Jepsen has been a successful advocate of significant legislation on a variety of issues. He championed and co-sponsored Connecticut's 1990 historic pro-choice legislation that affirmed a woman's right to choose. In addition, he has been a leader in expanding Connecticut's Living Will law in 1991and enacting the Assault Weapons Ban in 1993. He was also a powerful voice for passage of several laws confronting domestic violence, that have made Connecticut a leader in this field. Senator Jepsen is also known for his strong support of balanced budgets and tax policies, such as reform of local property tax.

Recognizing his leadership and commitment, numerous advocacy groups have presented Senator Jepsen with awards and honors, including M.A.D.D. (Mothers Against Drunk Driving), for his successful 1995 effort in passing tougher drunk driving legislation, and CCAG (Connecticut Citizens Action Group) for his work against gun violence. Senator Jepsen has also received awards from SACIA (Southwestern Area Commerce and Industry Association), and the National Federation of Independent Businesses for his legislative efforts on behalf of the business community. In addition, the NOW (National Organization of Women) and the NARL (National Abortion and Reproductive Rights League) have honored Jepsen for his efforts on behalf of women's' issues and women's right to choose.

Senator Jepson is an attorney with the law firm of Shipman and Goodwin. He was previously with the law firm of Abate and Fox and also served as general counsel to the Carpenters' Union Local 210. Prior to that, he was a teaching fellow at the Government Department of Harvard University under professors Richard Neustadt and Archibald Cox, teaching the courses "The American Presidency" and "The Supreme Court and Constitutional Development." He has also served as a visiting lecturer of political science for the University of Connecticut in Stamford.

Jepsen graduated Harvard Law School, J.D. Cum Laude in 1982 when he also received a Master of Public Policy degree from the Kennedy School of Government. He graduated from Dartmouth College in 1976 with Summa Cum Laude and Phi Beta Kappa honors.

Jepson was born November 23, 1954. His interests include history, economics, international relations, and current events. As an injured marathoner, his regular exercise now includes bycycling. He enjoys foreign languages, speaking French, Chinese, and Spanish with varying degrees of fluency, and foreign travel, having traveled extensively in Europe, South and Central America, and the Near and Far East. His interests also include cooking.

Senator Jepsen and his wife Diana and their sons Christian and William live at 171 Courtland Avenue in Stamford.

M. ADELA EADS
MINORITY LEADER OF THE STATE SENATE

M. ADELA EADS

MINORITY LEADER OF THE STATE SENATE

State Senator Dell Eads has been serving the Thirtieth Senatorial District since 1981. She represents fifteen towns in Connecticut's Northwest Corner, an area larger than any other in the General Assembly. Before being elected to the Senate, she served two terms as a member of the House of Representatives.

During Senator Ead's tenure in the Senate, her colleagues have elected her to various leadership positions, including Deputy Republican Leader Pro Tempore, Minority Leader and Senate President Pro Tempore. Currently serving as the Senate Republican Leader, Senator Eads has a special responsibility to co-ordinate legislative efforts among members of her caucus with others, including Governor John Rowland.

Senator Eads was appointed Co-Chair of the Select Committee on Children and also serves as Ranking member of the Legislative Management Committee. She is a member of the Executive and Legislative Nominations, Internship and Regulations Review Committees.

Eads prides herself on constituent service and is extremely interested in children's issues. Among recent achievements, she cites her work on implementing measures to facilitate the termination of parental rights in chronic abuse and neglect cases, on establishing Connecticut's Office of the Child Advocate, and on instituting the State's unprecedented Welfare Reform Package. As a leader in the Republican Party, she is a strong supporter of legislation to limit the size of government and to further reduce state taxes.

Dell Eads was born in Brooklyn, New York to parents who were equally fluent in Spanish and English. She attended Sweet Briar College in Virginia and the Katherine Gibbs School in New York City. She has lived in Kent with her husband G. Vernon Eads since 1951 and is a partner in their drop forge equipment business. Mr. and Mrs. Eads have two sons and five grandchildren.

THOMAS D. RITTER
SPEAKER OF THE HOUSE OF REPRESENTATIVES

THOMAS D. RITTER
Speaker of the House of Representatives

Speaker of the House Thomas D. Ritter (D-Hartford) led the General Assembly to one of its most successful legislative sessions in recent memory. Among the many legislative accomplishments of the 1996 session, Speaker Ritter is most proud of his leadership in the fight to protect Connecticut residents' health, including requiring health plans to provide a minimum of inpatient care for mothers and newborns, restricting minors' access to tobacco, non-discrimination in insurance policies against cancer survivors and the creation of a breast and cervical cancer screening program for uninsured women. Other legislative accomplishments under his leadership include an initiative saving municipal taxes by opening the state employee health insurance pool to municipal employees, structural reforms of business taxes to encourage cluster-based economic development and innovative legislation to authorize the creation of charter schools in Connecticut.

Speaker Ritter is currently serving his third two-year term as leader of the House of Representatives and his ninth term representing the citizens of Hartford. He has been recognized by his peers nationally who recently named him President of the National Speakers Association and elected him to the Board of Directors of the State Legislative Leaders Foundation.

Prior to his election as Speaker, Ritter served for six years as the House Chair of the General Assembly's Banks Committee, during which time he oversaw the passage of interstate banking and key legislation helping first-time homebuyers and consumers.

As Banks Chair, Ritter also headed the Task Force on Discrimination in Mortgage Lending, which targeted new mortgage money to eligible participants in urban areas. He also presided over the creation of a panel to review rejected mortgage loans to ensure that there was no bias in loan decisions.

For the eight years prior to his being elected Speaker, Ritter was appointed by his city colleagues to serve as spokesperson for the Hartford delegation in the House.

Ritter belongs to a host of civic and non-profit organizations and has received numerous awards for his work in the General Assembly and in the Hartford community.

Ritter is an attorney and he graduated from Noah Webster School, Loomis School, Amherst College and University of Connecticut Law School. He and his wife, Christine, have two children: Jessica and Matthew.

MOIRA K. LYONS
MAJORITY LEADER OF THE HOUSE OF REPRESENTATIVES

MOIRA K. LYONS

Majority Leader of the House of Representatives

State Representative Moira K. Lyons, of Stamford, was first elected to the House of Representatives in 1981. Subsequent to the 1994 state election, Representative Lyons was chosen to serve as the Majority Leader of the Connecticut House of Representatives. She is the first woman to hold this position.

During her sixteen years in the General Assembly, Representative Lyons has served her constituents with distinction. For six years she co-chaired the Legislature's Transportation Committee. In that capacity, Representative Lyons championed the need for expanded and improved mass transit, the preservation of the Transportation Fund, and the need to restructure programs and services in the Department of Motor Vehicles.

Representative Lyons has been at the forefront of seeking legislation to responsibly balance the need to control health care costs while safeguarding the delivery of quality care.

From 1992-94 Representative Lyons served as Deputy Speaker of the House of Representatives. She is respected for her thoroughness and belief that fairness be an integral part of the legislative process.

In recognition of her leadership skills and dedication to improving the quality of life in Connecticut, Representative Lyons was selected in 1994 as one of thirty-one nationwide recipients of the Henry Toll Fellowship Program. The purpose of this award is to promote excellence in state government for emerging leaders.

Representative Lyons has received acknowledgement for her work in many areas, among them: the AARP Distingquished Legislator Award; the Distinguished Public Service Award from the Business Council of Southwestern Connecticut, the Kings Mark Resource Conservation and Development Area, Inc., Award for Environmentally Sound Programs, and the Connecticut State Medical Society Legislative Award of Excellence.

Though the position of House Majority Leader focuses attention on state issues, Representative Lyons continues to retain strong ties to her local community. In the past she has served on the Stamford Board of Representatives. Currently she is a member of the Board of Directors of the Connecticut Training and Employment Agency; Action Against Chemical Dependency; and the Workplace, Inc.

Representative Lyons received a B.A. degree in English and Sociology from the Georgian Court College in New Jersey.

ROBERT M. WARD
MINORITY LEADER OF THE HOUSE OF REPRESENTATIVES

ROBERT M. WARD

Minority Leader of the House of Representatives

Robert M. Ward of Northford serves as the Minority Leader in the Connecticut House of Representatives. Since 1985 he has represented the people of the 86th District, which currently includes North Branford and parts of East Haven and Guilford.

During his tenure in the house, Representative Ward has served as Deputy Minority Leader and Assistant Minority Leader. He also has been the ranking Member of the Education Committee and has served on the Judiciary and Regulation Review committees as well as the Law Revision Commission.

Representative Ward has distinguished himself in the General Assembly on issues concerning education, particularly the issue of school choice. He was a member of the Governor's Task Force on Quality and Integrated Education.

He was a sponsor of the UConn 2000 initiative to improve facilities at the state's flagship university, a measure to encourage development of the biotech industry through tax incentives, and laws to improve K-12 education for Connecticut school children.

Representative Ward has played a leadership role in changing the state's highly controversial and often-criticized home-release program for prison inmates.

A well-respected lawmaker, he was rated by his house colleagues to be the most effective legislator in a recent survey conducted by *Connecticut Magazine*.

In addition to his legislative service, Representative Ward has served on the North Branford Republican Town Committee since 1982. He is a member of the PTO of North Branford and was a Youth Basketball Coach.

He is a former member and treasurer of the Northford Volunteer Fire Department, Company No. 2, a former member and past president of the North Branford Jaycees, a former member of the Totoket Historical Society and a past member of the North Branford Education Goals Committee and the North Branford Sesquicentennial Committee.

Born November 8, 1952, Representative Ward attended the University of Kentucky from 1970-71 and earned a Bachelor of Arts Degree Cum Laude from the University of Connecticut in 1974. He received a Juris Doctor Degree with honors from the University of Cincinnati in 1978.

Representative Ward was admitted to the Connecticut Bar in October 1978 and the U.S. District Court in November 1978. He is a sole practitioner in the general practice of law maintaining an office in the Town of Branford.

Representative Ward is a former town attorney in East Haven and former assistant town attorney and WPCA attorney in North Branford.

Representative Ward and his wife, Anita Siena Ward, have four children: Michael, Rebecca, Nicole and Sarah.

THE SUPREME COURT

Front (left to right): Justice David M. Borden, Chief Justice Robert J. Callahan, Justice Robert I. Berdon; Rear (left to right): Justice Flemming L. Norcott, Jr., Justice Richard N. Palmer, Justice Francis M. McDonald, Jr., Justice Joette Katz.

CONNECTICUT SUPREME COURT

Chief Justice Robert J. Callahan

Born June 3, 1930, Norwalk, Connecticut. Education: Norwalk High School, 1948; B.S., Boston College, 1952; LL.B., Fordham University, 1955. Admitted to Connecticut Bar, 1955. Fordham University School of Law Dean's Medal of Recognition, 1986; Norwalk High Alumni Wall of Honor, 1995. Member, Norwalk Common Council, 1955-56, 1969-70; U.S. Army, 1956-58; Prosecuting Attorney, Norwalk City Court, 1959-61; Assistant Prosecutor, Circuit Court, 1965-68; Member, Norwalk Parks and Recreation Commission, 1963-69, Chairman, 1966-67; Judge, Circuit Court, 1970-74; Judge, Court of Common Pleas, 1974-76; Judge, Superior Court, 1976-85; Guggenheim Fellowship in Criminal Law, Yale University, 1984-85; Senior Appellate Judges Seminar, Institute of Judicial Administration, New York University, 1985; Member, Board of Pardons, 1985, State Library Board, 1991; Associate Justice, Connecticut Supreme Court, June 22, 1985-September 1, 1996; Chief Justice September 1, 1996.

Associate Justice David M. Borden

Born August 4, 1937, Hartford, Connecticut. Education: Weaver High School, 1955; B.A., Amherst College, magna cum laude, Phi Beta Kappa, 1959; LL.B., Harvard Law School, cum laude, 1962; Admitted to the Connecticut Bar, 1962; Executive Director, Commission to Revise the Criminal Statutes of Connecticut, 1963-71; Chief Draftsman, Connecticut Penal Code, 1963-69; Chief Counsel, Judiciary Committee, 1975-76; Judge, Court of Common Pleas, 1977-78; Judge, Superior Court, 1978-83; President, Connecticut Judges Association, 1981-83; Judge, Appellate Court, 1983-90; Connecticut Law Revision Commission, 1984-88; Administrative Judge for the Appellate System, 1989-1993; Associate Justice, Connecticut Supreme Court, May 10, 1990; chairperson, Rules Committee of the Superior Court, 1992-present; Member, American Law Institute, 1991-present; Connecticut Law Review Award for excellence in legal scholarship and service to the legal community, 1994; Connecticut Moot Court Board Award, 1990; Adjunct Faculty, University of Connecticut School of Law, 1968-70, 1989-92, 1994-present; Honorary Member, Phi Delta Phi Legal Fraternity, 1994-present.

Associate Justice Robert I. Berdon

Born December 24, 1929, New Haven, Connecticut. Education: Hillhouse High School, 1947; B.S., University of Connecticut, 1951; LL.B., University of Connecticut School of Law, 1957; LL.M., University of Virginia School of Law, 1988. Admitted to the Connecticut Bar, 1957. Member: U.S. District Court for Connecticut, 1958; U.S. Supreme Court, 1961. Member: New Haven County Bar Association, Connecticut Bar Association, American Bar Association, American Judicature Society. Awards and Recognitions: Connecticut Housing Finance Authority, 1973; Connecticut State Development Commission for participation and work in the State's Industrial Revenue Bond Program, 1973; Award for the Judiciary, Connecticut Trial Lawyers Association, 1976; Distinguished Alumni Award, University of Connecticut, 1977; Board of Editors, Connecticut Bar Journal, 1982; The Outstanding State Trial Judge in the United States, Association of Trial Lawyers of America, 1982; American Board of Trial Advocates, 1986; Public Service Award, University of Connecticut School of Law Alumni Association, 1989; Judiciary Award, Connecticut Bar Association, 1991. Treasurer, State of Connecticut, 1971-73; Judge, Superior Court, State of Connecticut, 1973-91; Adjunct Professor of Law, University of Bridgeport School of Law, 1986-91; Associate Fellow, Saybrook College, Yale University, 1986-present; Lecturer in Law, University of Connecticut School of Law, 1993; Connecticut Board of Pardons, 1991-92; Associate Justice, Connecticut Supreme Court, September 30, 1991.

ASSOCIATE JUSTICE FLEMMING L. NORCOTT, JR.

Born October 11, 1943, New Haven, Connecticut. Education: The Taft School, 1961; B.A., Columbia College, 1965; J.D., Columbia University School of Law, 1968; admitted to the Connecticut Bar, 1968; LL.D. (Hon.), University of New Haven, 1993. Peace Corps Volunteer (Lecturer in the Faculty of Law, University of East Africa, Nairobi, Kenya); Bedford-Stuyvesant Restoration Corporation Legal Staff; Assistant Attorney General, United States Virgin Islands; Co-founder and Executive Director of the Center for Advocacy, Research and Planning, Inc. (New Haven); Hearing Examiner, Connecticut Commission on Human Rights and Opportunities. Lecturer, Yale Law School and Yale College; Lecturer, University of New Haven, Criminal Justice Program; Board of Governors, University of New Haven; Eastern Collegiate Football Officials Association, New Haven Football Officials Association; Associate Fellow, Calhoun College, Yale University; Member, Omega Psi Phi Fraternity. Board of Trustees, Yale-New Haven Hospital; Board of Directors, Long Wharf Theatre; Judge, Superior Court, 1979-87; Judge, Appellate Court, 1987-92; Associate Justice, Connecticut Supreme Court, July 14, 1992.

ASSOCIATE JUSTICE JOETTE KATZ

Born, February 3, 1953, Brooklyn, New York. Education: Berkeley Institute, 1970; B.A., Brandeis University, 1974; J.D., University of Connecticut School of Law, 1977. Admitted to the Connecticut Bar, 1977. Member: District Court of Connecticut, 2nd Circuit; U.S. Supreme Court; Private Practice, 1977-78; Assistant Public Defender, Appellate Unit, Office of Chief Public Defender, 1978-1981; Assistant Public Defender, 1981-1983; Instructor, University of Connecticut School of Law, 1981-1984; Chief of Legal Services, Public Defender Services, 1983-1989. Judge, Superior Court, 1989-1992; Associate Justice, Supreme Court, October 22, 1992.

ASSOCIATE JUSTICE RICHARD N. PALMER

Born May 27, 1950, Hartford, Connecticut. Education: Wethersfield High School, 1968; B.A., Trinity College, Phi Beta Kappa, 1972; J.D., University of Connecticut School of Law, with high honors, 1977. Admitted to Connecticut Bar, 1977. Member: U.S. District Court for Connecticut, 1978; District of Columbia, 1980; U.S. Court of Appeals for the Second Circuit, 1981. Law Clerk to U.S. District (now Second Circuit Court of Appeals) Judge Jon O. Newman, 1977-78; Associate, Shipman and Goodwin, 1978-1980; Assistant United States Attorney for Connecticut, 1980-83, 1987-90. Partner, Chatigny and Palmer, 1984-86; United States Attorney for Connecticut, 1991; Chief State's Attorney for Connecticut, 1991-93; Associate Justice, Supreme Court, March 17, 1993.

ASSOCIATE JUSTICE FRANCIS M. MCDONALD, JR.

Born January 22, 1931, Waterbury, Connecticut. Education: AB., Holy Cross College, (Worcester, MA), 1953; LL.B., Yale University Law School, 1956. Admitted to Connecticut Bar, 1956; Special Agent, FBI, 1956-57; Assistant U.S. Attorney, District of Connecticut, 1958-60; Assistant Prosecuting Attorney, Circuit Court, 1961-65; Deputy Chief Prosecuting Attorney, Connecticut Circuit Courts, 1965-68; States Attorney at Waterbury, 1968-84; Superior Court Judge, 1984-96; Associate Justice, Connecticut Supreme Court, 1996.

Senior Justice Ellen A. Peters

Born March 21, 1930, Berlin, Germany. Education: Hunter College High School, 1947; B.A., Swarthmore College, 1951; LL.B., Yale Law School, 1954; M.A. (Hon.), Yale University, 1964; LL.D. (Hon.), Swarthmore College, 1983; LL.D. (Hon.), University of Hartford, 1983; LL.D. (Hon.), Georgetown University, 1984; LL.D. (Hon.), Yale University, 1985; LL.D. (Hon.), Connecticut College, 1985; LL.D. (Hon.), New York Law School, 1985; LL.D. (Hon.), Colgate University, 1986; HL.D. St. Joseph College, 1986; LL.D. (Hon.), Trinity College, 1987; LL.D. (Hon.) Bates College, 1987; LL.D. (Hon.), Wesleyan University, 1987; LL.D. (Hon.), DePaul University, 1988; HL.D., Albertus Magnus College, 1990; LL.D., University of Connecticut, 1992; LL.D., University of Rochester, 1994. Admitted to Connecticut Bar, 1957; U.S. District Court for Connecticut, 1965. Recipient, Judiciary Award of Connecticut Trial Lawyer's Association, 1982; Ella T. Grasso Medal, 1982. Citation of Merit, Yale Law School, 1983. Myrtle Wreath Award, Conn. Region of Hadassah, 1986. Pioneer Women Award, Hartford College for Women, 1988. Henry J. Naruk Judiciary Award, Connecticut Bar Association, 1992. Distinguished Service Award, University of Connecticut Law School Alumni Association, 1993. Raymond E. Baldwin Public Service Award, 1995. Connecticut Law Tribune Distinguished Service Award, April 10, 1996; National Center for State Courts 1996 Distinguished Service Award, June 3, 1996; Connecticut Bar Association Special Award, June 3, 1996; Hartford College for Women, Laura A. Johnson Woman of the Year, October 17, 1996. Member, Connecticut Bar Association, American Bar Association, American Judicature Society, American Academy of Arts & Sciences, American Philosophical Society, Conference of Chief Justices, 1984, president, 1994-95; National Center for State Courts Bd. of Directors, 1992, chairperson, 1994-95; American Law Institute, Member of Council, 1984-; Commissioner, Permanent Commission on the Status of Women, 1973-74; Member, Connecticut Law Revision Commission, 1978-84; Member, Connecticut Board of Pardons, 1978-81; Fellow, Yale Corporation, 1986-92. Member, Board of Directors, Hartford Foundation for Public Giving, January 1, 1997. Law Clerk to U.S. Circuit Judge Charles E. Clark, 1954-55; Associate in Law, University of California at Berkeley, 1955-56; Professor, Yale Law School, 1956-78; Professor (Adjunct) of Law, Yale Law School, 1978-84; Associate Justice, Supreme Court, May 10, 1978-Nov. 21, 1984; Chief Justice, Nov. 21, 1984.

THE APPELLATE COURT

Front (left to right): Judge William J. Lavery, Judge Edward Y. O'Connell, Chief Judge Antoinette L. Dupont, Judge Paul M. Foti, Judge Sidney S. Landau; Rear (left to right): Senior Judge Albert W. Cretella, Jr., Judge E. Eugene Spear, Judge Maxwell Heiman, Judge Barry R. Schaller, Judge Francis X. Hennessy, Senior Judge Frederick A. Freedman.

CONNECTICUT APPELLATE COURT

JUDGE ANTOINETTE L. DUPONT
CHIEF JUDGE

Born January 10, 1929, New York, NY. Education: Williams Memorial Institute, 1946; B.A., Brown University, 1950; J.D., Harvard Law School, 1954; Special Counsel, City of New London, 1960-61; Member: Board of Education, New London, 1966-68; Board of Editors, Connecticut Bar Journal, 1969-70; State Bar Examining Committee, 1980-87; Judicial Review Council, 1981-88; President, Connecticut Judges Association, 1983-84; American Law Institute, 1986-present; Fellow, American Bar Foundation, 1986-present; Board of Directors, Day Publishing Co., 1986-present; Board of Trustees, Day Publishing Co., 1989-present; Treasurer, National Conference of Chief Judges of Appellate Court, 1987-88; Executive Committee of National Conference of Chief Judges of Appellate Courts, 1986-90; Co-chairperson, Task Force on Gender, Justice and the Courts, 1987-92; National Task Force on Gender Bias, 1987-92; ABA Appellate Task Force on Reduction of Delay, 1987-91; Judge, Court of Common Pleas, 1977-78; Judge, Superior Court, 1978-83; Chief Administrative Judge, Civil Division, 1983; Annual Judiciary Award, Connecticut Trial Lawyers' Association, 1983; Annual Award, Connecticut Bar Association, Family Law Section, 1988; Annual Award, Hartford Association Women Attorneys, 1990; Annual Commendation Award, Connecticut Bar Association, Women and the Law Section, 1992; Henry J. Naruk Judiciary Award, Connecticut Bar Association, 1994; Judge, Appellate Court, Aug. 15, 1983; Chief Judge, Appellate Court, Nov. 30, 1984.

JUDGE EDWARD Y. O'CONNELL

Born March 12, 1930, Stafford Springs, Connecticut. Education: Stafford Public Schools; Cheshire Academy; Atlantic Air Academy; B.A., University of Connecticut, 1951; J.D., University of Connecticut School of Law, with honors, 1954; National Judicial College, Reno, Nevada, 1979. Military service: U.S. Army, 1947-48; U.S. Air Force Reserve, 1948-77, Lt. Col. Admitted to the Connecticut Bar, 1954, U.S. Supreme Court, U.S. Court of Appeals-2d Circuit, U.S. District Court for Connecticut. Member: American Bar Association, Connecticut Bar Association, Hartford County Bar Association, Tolland County Bar Association. Private law practice, 1954-77; Attorney for the Town of Stafford, 1961-78; President and Chairman of Board of Directors of Johnson Memorial Hospital, 1975-78; President, Stafford Public Library Association, 1970-72; Director, Asnuntuck Community College Foundation, 1975-78. Assistant Prosecuting Attorney, Municipal Court, 1954-55; Judge, Municipal Court, 1955-60; Judge, Probate Court, 1960-77; Judge, Court of Common Pleas, 1978; Judge, Superior Court, 1978-87; Judge, Appellate Court, October 1, 1987.

JUDGE PAUL M. FOTI

Born January 25, 1935, New Haven, Connecticut. Education: Notre Dame High School, 1952; B.S., Fordham University, 1956; J.D., University of Connecticut School of Law, 1959; admitted to Connecticut Bar, 1959; U.S. Army Reserve, 1959-65; Prosecuting Attorney, Circuit Court, Court of Common Pleas, 1965-78; New Haven Pretrial Services Council, 1967-73; Guggenheim Fellowship in Criminal Law, Yale Law School, 1973-74; Advisory Committee, Statewide Organized Crime Investigatory Task Force, 1973-77; Southern Connecticut Criminal Justice Supervisory Board, 1975-77; National Judicial College, Reno, Nevada, 1979; Judicial Bench Book Committee, 1982-87; Connecticut Judges' Institute, 1986-87; Judge, Court of Common Pleas, 1978; Judge, Superior Court, 1978-87; Judge, Appellate Court, November 2, 1987; Evidence Code Drafting Committee, 1994-95.

JUDGE WILLIAM J. LAVERY

Born March 26, 1938, Bridgeport, Connecticut. Education: Fairfield Prep, 1955; A.B., Fairfield

University, 1959; LL.B., Fordham Law School, 1964. Military service: U.S. Army, 1960-61. Admitted to the Connecticut Bar, 1964. Member: Bridgeport Board of Aldermen, 1963-67; Council on Environmental Quality of the State of Connecticut, 1971-74; Commission on Comprehensive Health Planning for the State, 1976-79. State Representative, 1967-71; Chairman, Legislative Public Health and Safety Committee, 1969-71; attorney for Housing Authority, City of Bridgeport, 1969-72; Counsel to the Majority Party in the House of Representatives, 1971-73; Vice-chairman, Commission on Hospitals and Health Care, 1976-81; Former President, Bridgeport Mental Health Association; Newtown Scholarship Committee; Vice-chairman, Newtown Charter Commission, 1974-75; Town and Borough Attorney of Newtown, 1976-81; Vice President, Connecticut Judges Association, 1991-92; President, Connecticut Judges Association 1992-93; Trustee, C. H. Booth Library, Newtown; Director, Family Life Center, Newtown. Judge, Superior Court, 1981-89; Judge, Appellate Court, October 4, 1989.

JUDGE SIDNEY S. LANDAU

Born April 19, 1935, Bronx, New York. Education: Great Neck High School, 1952; B.A., Alfred University, 1956; LL.B., New York University School of Law, 1959. Admitted to the Connecticut Bar, 1960; Admitted to the New York Bar, 1960; Assistant Prosecuting Attorney, State of Connecticut, 1968-71; Attorney for Sewer Commission, City of Stamford, 1971-76; Town Chairman, Democratic Party, City of Stamford, 1971-76; Adjunct Professor of Law, Quinnipiac College School of Law, 1980-present; Breakthru Foundation Director, Youth at Risk, Bridgeport, 1984-86; Quinnipiac College School of Law, Advisory Board; National Judicial College, Reno, Nevada, 1977; New York University Institute of Judicial Administration, 1993-90; Judge, Court of Common Pleas, 1976-78; Judge, Superior Court, 1978-90, Judge, Appellate Court, May 10, 1990.

JUDGE MAXWELL HEIMAN

Born April 24, 1932, Hartford, Connecticut. Education: Farmington H.S., 1950; B.A., University of Connecticut, 1954; J.D., Boston College Law School, 1957; Legislation Director, Annual Survey of Massachusetts Law, 1956-57; Admitted to the Connecticut Bar, 1957; U.S. District Court, Connecticut, 1961; U.S. Court of Appeals for the Second Circuit, 1963; U.S. Supreme Court, 1963; U.S. Tax Court, 1974; Private law practice, Hartford and in Bristol, 1957-87; Newington Board of Education 1970-75; former member, Board of Directors, Jewish Family Services, Hartford Legal Aid Society, 1974-75; Chairman, UMPA Commission; Member, Commission to study the Courts; Commission to Study the Insanity Defense; Member, Judicial Performance Evaluation Committee; State Trial Referee; Board of Directors, Alternative Dispute Resolution Project, Inc.; Professional Advisory Board, Parents Without Partners; Board of Directors, Jewish Family Service; President, Hartford County Bar Association, 1974-75, Connecticut Bar Association, 1981-82; Member, Judiciary Committee of the Connecticut Bar Association, 1972-80, Chair, 1984-86; State Delegate to American Bar Association House of Delegates, 1984-87; Chair, Steering Committee of the Nominating Committee, 1986-87; Member, Board of Governors, American Bar Association, 1987-90; ABA Committee on Selection, Tenure & Compensation of Judges, 1990-93; Member, Judges Advisory Committee on the Standing Committee on Ethics and Professional Responsibility; Fellow, American College of Trial Lawyers; Life Fellow, American Bar Foundation; Member, Research Advisory Committee, 1992-present, Connecticut Judges' Association, Vice President, 1992-93; President, 1993-94; Alternate Member, Judicial Review Council, 1995; Member, Connecticut Bar Examining Committee, 1966; Trustee, The American Muscular Degeneration Foundation, Inc., 1995; Judge, Superior Court, 1987-90; Judge, Appellate Court, December 21, 1990.

JUDGE BARRY R. SCHALLER

Born, November 23, 1938, Hartford, Connecticut. Education: Manchester High School, 1956; B.A., Yale University, 1960; J.D., Yale Law School, 1963. Admitted to the Connecticut Bar, 1963. Member: U.S. District Court for Connecticut; Court of Appeals, 2nd Circuit, U.S. Supreme Court.

Member, Connecticut Bar Association, New Haven County Bar Association, Hartford County Bar Association, American Judicature Society, American Judges Association; Charter Life Fellow, Connecticut Bar Foundation; Private law practice, 1963-74; Co-Counsel, House Minority Leader, 1969. Member, Board of Pardons, 1971-74; Chair, 1973-74; Connecticut Planning Committee on Criminal Administration, Executive Committee, 1972-74; Guggenheim Fellow, Yale Law School, 1975-76, 1984, 1985-86; Visting Lecturer, Yale College; Adjunct Clinical Faculty, Yale Law School; Executive Committee, Yale Law School, 1990-92; Associate Fellow, Branford College, Yale University; Executive Committee, Connecticut Center for Judicial Education, 1989-92; Chair, Superior Court Bench Book Committee, 1985-92; Judicial Leader, National Judicial College; Faculty, American Academy of Judicial Education; Faculty, Connecticut Judges Institute; Director, Connecticut Judges Association, 1990-92. Judge, Circuit Court, 1974; Judge, Court of Common Pleas, 1975; Judge, Superior Court, 1978; Judge, Appellate Court, October 23, 1992.

JUDGE E. EUGENE SPEAR

Born April 18, 1938, Cincinnati, Ohio. Education: Central High School, 1956; B.A., University of Connecticut, 1960; J.D., University of Connecticut Law School, 1963. Admitted to the Connecticut Bar, 1963; Private law practice, 1963-73; Public Defender, 1973-82; Administrative Judge, Fairfield J.D., 1989-91; Chief Administrative Judge, Civil Division, 1991-93; Member, Superior Court Rules Committee, 1985-89, 1991-93; Superior Court Executive Committee, 1985-89; Executive Committee, Connecticut Judges Association, 1988; Criminal Justice Commission, 1985-90; Board of Directors, Hall Neighborhood House, 1965-present, President, 1975-76; Regional Youth Substance Abuse Council, 1990-93; Settlement Education Committee, 1991-92; Board of Trustees, Park City Hospital, 1967-68; Board of Directors, Y.M.C.A., 1990-92; Bridgeport Fire Commission, 1965-67; Bridgeport Board of Education, 1967-71; Recipient, Bridgeport, Connecticut and New England Outstanding Young Man Awards by the Jaycees, 1967; Judicial Award, Connecticut Trial Lawyers Association, 1990; Judge, Superior Court, 1982-93; Judge, Appellate Court, November 5, 1993.

JUDGE FRANCIS X. HENNESSY

Born September 11, 1930, New York City. Education: Cathedral College High School, Fordham College, B.S. Social Sciences, 1957; J.D., University of Connecticut School of Law, 1961; Military Service: 1951-53, U.S. Army, Korea, Purple Heart, Combat Infantryman's Badge; Admitted to the Connecticut Bar, 1961; Private law practice, 1961-76; Commissioner of Special Revenue, 1972-76; Adjunct Faculty Member, St. Joseph College, 1989-95; Chair, Committee on Judicial Evaluations1990-94; Chair, Executive Committee of the Connecticut Center for Judicial Education, 1988-94; Co-Chair, Task Force on Gender, Justice and the Courts, 1988-91; Co-Chair, Connecticut Task Force on Minority Fairness, 1992-95; Member, Executive Committee of the Superior Court, 1988-present; Member, Juvenile Justice Advisory Committee, 1985-95; Member, Sheriff's Advisory Board, 1986-94; Board of Directors, Association of Family and Conciliation Courts, 1984-86; Chair, Connecticut Commission on Child Support Guidelines, 1988-90; Governor's Policy Advisory Council for the Annie E. Casey Foundation Child Welfare Reform Initiative; Member, State Library Board, 1986-present; Distinguished Service Award, Family Law Section Connecticut Bar Association, 1986; Annual Commendation Award, Connecticut Bar Association, Women and Law Section, 1992; Chief Justice Warren Burger Award; National Congress of Men; Judge, Juvenile Court, 1976-78; Judge, Superior Court, 1978-94; Chief Administrative Judge of the Family Division, 1979-86; Deputy Chief Court Administrator, 1986-94; Appellate Court, 1994.

SENIOR JUDGE FREDERICK A. FREEDMAN

Born April 3, 1929, Bridgeport, Connecticut. Education: Bassick High School, 1947; B.A., University of Connecticut, 1951; LL.B., Yale Law School, 1954; admitted to the Connecticut Bar, 1954; Military Service: U.S. Air Force, JAG, 1954-57; Private law practice, 1957-81; Member,

Board of Finance, Monroe, 1960-63; Town Attorney, Monroe, 1961-65; Member, Conservation Commission, Weston, 1972-74; Connecticut Transportation Authority, 1974-75; Commission on Compensation for Elected State Officials and Judges, 1975-81; Vice Chairman 1978-81; Board of Directors, Association of Family and Conciliation Courts, 1984-86; Connecticut Task Force on Gender, Justice and the Courts; Connecticut Bar Association Committee on Liaison with State Courts 1986-92; Chair, Connecticut Commission on Child Support Guidelines 1988-90; Governor's Policy Advisory Council for the Annie E. Casey Foundation Child Welfare Reform Initiative; Fellow, American Bar Association. Judge, Superior Court, 1981-92; Chief Administrative Judge, Family Division, 1986-92; Member, Superior Court Rules Committee 1991-92; Judiciary Award, Connecticut Bar Association, 1990; Judge, Appellate Court, January 10, 1992; Senior Judge, Appellate Court, Sept. 1, 1994; Administrative Judge for the Appellate System, February 1, 1993-August 1, 1994.

SECTION III

STATE GOVERNMENT—LEGISLATIVE

Joint Committee on Legislative Management

Auditors of Public Accounts

Legislative Commissioners' Office

Office of Senate and House Clerks

Finance Advisory Committee

Members and Officers of the
State Senate, 1997-1998

Members and Officers of the
House of Representatives, 1997-1998

Alphabetical Roll of the
Senate and House of Representatives, 1997-1998

Legislative Committees, 1997

Sessions of the
General Assembly Since 1884

Political Division of the Connecticut
General Assembly Since 1887

JOINT COMMITTEE ON LEGISLATIVE MANAGEMENT

Sec. 2-71a, Gen. Stat. Salary, Exec. Dir., $83,733-106,764. Address: Room 5100, Legislative Office Bldg., Hartford 06106. Tel., (860) 240-0100.

Senate Members: Chm., Pres. Pro Tempore, Kevin B. Sullivan, West Hartford, Majority Leader, George C. Jepsen, Stamford. Joseph J. Crisco, Jr., Woodbridge; Eileen M. Daily, Westbrook; Thomas P. Gaffey, Meriden; Alvin W. Penn, Bridgeport; Melodie Peters, Quaker Hill. Minority Leader, M. Adela Eads, Kent. James T. Fleming, Simsbury; Judith G. Freedman, Westport; George L. Gunther, Stratford;.

House Members: Chm., Speaker, Thomas D. Ritter, Hartford; Majority Leader, Moira K. Lyons, Stamford. Reginald G. Beamon, Waterbury; Melody A. Currey, East Hartford; William R. Dyson, New Haven; Mary G. Fritz, Yalesville; Robert D. Godfrey, Danbury; Joan V. Hartley, Waterbury; Wade A. Hyslop, Jr., New London; David B. Pudlin, New Britain; Andrea L. Stillman, Waterford; Richard D. Tulisano, Rocky Hill. Minority Leader, Robert M. Ward, Northford. Richard O. Belden, Shelton; Lawrence F. Cafero, Jr., Norwalk; Raymond V. Collins, West Haven; Ruth C. Fahrbach, Windsor; Brian J. Flaherty, Watertown; F. Philip Prelli, Winsted.

Exec. Dir., George H. Meier, Hartford; *Personnel,* James P. Tracy, Wethersfield; *Finance,* Doris McAusland, Windsor Locks; *Data Processing,* Edward Kingston, Hamden.

AUDITORS OF PUBLIC ACCOUNTS

Sec. 2-89, Gen. Stat. Appointed by the General Assembly, for four years, and until a successor is appointed and has qualified. Salary, $86,620-$110,445. Address: Rooms 114, 116, State Capitol, Hartford 06106. Tel., (860) 566-2119, 5572.

Kevin P. Johnston, Pomfret, July 1, 1997; Robert G. Jaekle, Stratford, July 1, 1999.

LEGISLATIVE COMMISSIONERS' OFFICE

Sec. 2-54, Gen. Stat. Legislative Comrs. appointed by the General Assembly, for four years, and until a successor is appointed and has qualified, Salary, Comrs., $30,539-$37,687; Dir., Legislative Legal Services, $78,738-102,551. Address: Room 5500, Legislative Office Bldg., Hartford 06106. Tel., (860) 240-8410; FAX, (860) 240-8414; E-Mail,lco@lco.state.ct.us.; Internet, http://www.cslnet.ctstateu.edu/clg/lco.htm.

Legislative Comrs., Max S. Case, Milford, June 30, 1997. Robert G. Gilligan, Wethersfield, June 30, 1999.

Dir., Legislative Legal Services, Marcia B. Goodman, Bridgeport.

OFFICE OF LEGISLATIVE RESEARCH

Sec. 2-71c, Gen. Stat. Salary, Dir., $78,738-$102,551. Address: Room 5300, Legislative Office Bldg., Hartford 06106. Tel., (860) 240-8400; FAX, (860) 240-8881.

Dir., L. Allan Green, Hartford.

OFFICE OF FISCAL ANALYSIS

Sec. 2-71c, Gen. Stat. Salary, Dir., $78,738-$102,551. Address: Legislative Office Bldg., Room 5200, Hartford 06106. Tel., (860) 240-0200; FAX, (860) 240-0052.

Acting Dir., Bob Harris, Hamden; *Section Chiefs: Revenues and Bonding,* Dan Schnobrich, Broad Brook; *Expenditure Analysis,* L. Spencer Cain, Enfield; Geary Maher, Berlin.

LEGISLATIVE PROGRAM REVIEW AND INVESTIGATIONS COMMITTEE

Sec. 2-53e, Gen. Stat. Salary, Dir., $78,738-$102,551. Address: State Capitol, Hartford 06106. Tel., (860) 240-0300.

Senate Members: Chm., Fred H. Lovegrove, Jr., Fairfield; Eric D. Coleman, Bloomfield; Eileen M. Daily, Westbrook; George C. Jepsen, Stamford; William H. Nickerson, Greenwich; Win Smith, Jr., Milford.

House Members: Chm., Michael J. Jarjura, Waterbury; Kevin M. DelGobbo, Naugatuck; Brian E. Mattiello, Torrington; Ellen Scalettar, Woodbridge; Peter F. Villano, Hamden; Julia B. Wasserman, Sandy Hook.

Dir., Michael L. Nauer, Glastonbury.

CONNECTICUT LAW REVISION COMMISSION

Secs. 2-86, Gen. Stat. Salary, Exec. Dir., $69,353-$90,226. Address: State Capitol, Rm. 509A, Hartford 06106. Tel., (860) 240-0220.

Appointed by the Governor, William R. Breetz, Jr., Hartford; Louis I. Gladstone, Fairfield, June 30, 1997. Jon P. FitzGerald, Bristol, June 30, 1999. Elliot N. Solomon, Bolton, Colin C. Tait, Norfolk, June 30, 2000.

Appointed by the Pres. Pro Tempore of the Senate, Mark Nielsen, Danbury, June 30, 2000. Robert W. Grant, Wethersfield, June 30, 1998. Designee of the Pres. Pro Tempore of the Senate, Michael W. Lyons, Norwalk. Designee of the Senate Minority Leader, James P. Sandler, Hartford.

Designee of the Speaker of the House, Edmund Schmidt, Darien. Appointed by the Speaker of the House, *Chm.,* I. Milton Widem, Hartford, June 30, 1998. H. Maria Cone, Hartford, June 30, 2000. Designee of the House Minority Leader, Mary Anne O'Neill, Manchester.

Judiciary Committee Co-Chm., Michael P. Lawlor, East Haven, Donald E. Williams, Jr., Thompson, *Ranking Member,* Robert Farr, West Hartford, *Designee of Senate Ranking Member,* Arthur J. O'Neill, Southbury;.

Exec. Dir., David D. Biklen, Hartford.

OFFICE OF SENATE CLERKS

Sec. 2-10, Gen. Stat. Address: Room 305, State Capitol, Hartford 06106. Tel., (860) 240-0500.

Senate Clerk, Thomas P. Sheridan, Glastonbury; *Asst. Senate Clerk,* Marilyn F. Cohen, West Hartford; *Permanent Asst. Senate Clerk,* Vita C. Hardy, Hartford; *Senate Journal Clerk,* Lois F. Latraverse, Dayville; *Senate Calendar Clerk,* Donna G. Moore, Columbia; *Senate Bill Clerk,* Frank A. Forzano, Vernon; *Office Asst.,* Alice A. Joseph, West Simsbury.

OFFICE OF HOUSE CLERKS

Sec. 2-10, Gen. Stat. Address: Room 109, State Capitol, Hartford 06106. Tel., (860) 240-0400.

House Clerk, Garey E. Coleman, Hartford; *Asst. House Clerk,* Cynthia K. Swienton, Simsbury; *Permanent Asst. House Clerk,* Ann M. Clark, Bloomfield; *House Journal Clerk,* Lynn England, Rocky Hill; *House Bill Clerk,* John N. Barry, Southington; *House Calendar Clerk,* Anita DeLorenzo, Bloomfield; *Office Asst.,* Pamela Young, Bristol.

PERMANENT COMMISSION ON THE STATUS OF WOMEN

Sec. 46a-1, Gen. Stat. Salary, Exec. Dir., $63,283. Compensation of members, necessary expenses. Address: 18-20 Trinity St., Hartford 06106. Tel., (860) 240-8300; FAX, (860) 240-8314.

Appointed by the Governor, *Chm.,* Sarah E. McGirr, Groton, June 30, 1997; Ruth L. Pulda, Hartford, June 30, 1998; George Schatzki, West Hartford, June 30, 1999; Cindy R. Slane, Easton, June 30, 2000; Karen L. Giblin, Ridgefield, June 30, 2001.

Appointed by the Pres. Pro Tempore of the Senate, Patricia Russo, Stamford, June 30, 1997; Rosaida M. Rosario, West Hartford, June 30, 1998; Barbara DeBaptiste, Waterbury, June 30, 2000; Jann-Marie Halvorsen, Middlebury, June 30, 2001.

Appointed by the Speaker of the House, Geraldine A. Roberts, Wethersfield, June 30, 1997; Carmen I. Sierra, Hartford, June 30, 1998; Ann Park, Hartford, June 30, 2000; Patricia Hendel, New London, June 30, 2001.

Exec. Dir., Leslie J. Brett, Ph.D., West Hartford.

COMMISSION ON CHILDREN

Sec. 46a-126, Gen. Stat. Compensation of members, necessary expenses. Address, 18-20 Trinity St., Hartford 06106. Tel., (860) 240-0290.

Ex officio, Stephen A. Harriman, Comr. of Public Health; Richard Blumenthal, Attorney General; Michael W. Kozlowski, Secretary of the Office of Policy and Management; John J. Armstrong, Comr. of Correction; Aaron Ment, Chief Court Administrator; Peter H. O'Meara, Comr. of Mental Retardation; Linda D'Amario Rossi, Comr. of Children and Families; two vacancies.

Appointed by the Governor, Judith A. Busch, Southbury; Joan Hubbard, Hamden; Mrs. Tamar H. MacFadyen, South Windham; John R. Raye, M.D., Granby.

Appointed by the Pres. Pro Tempore of the Senate, Ruth Rose, Branford; Lawrence B. Rifkin, Prospect. Appointed by the Senate Minority Leader, Maryanne Campbell,

Gaylordville; Edward Epstein, Kent. Appointed by the Speaker of the House, Shirley West, Hartford; Laura Lee Simon, Westport. Appointed by the House Minority Leader, Elizabeth A. Bozzuto, Waterbury; David Salce, Berlin.

Appointed jointly by the Senate and House Majority Leaders, Toni N. Harp, New Haven; Robert T. Keeley, Jr., Bridgeport; Cameron C. Staples, New Haven; Donald E. Williams, Jr., Thompson.

STATE COMMISSION ON CAPITOL PRESERVATION AND RESTORATION

Sec. 4b-60, Gen. Stat. Compensation of members, none. Address: Room 5100, Legislative Office Bldg., Hartford 06106. Tel., (860) 240-0100.

Ex officio, Theodore R. Anson, Comr. of Public Works.

Appointed by the Governor, Sharon S. Farrelly, Wethersfield; John Ruffalo III, East Haven.

Appointed by the Pres. Pro Tempore of the Senate, *Chm.,* Rev. Joseph A. Devine, Cheshire; M. Adela Eads, Kent. Appointed by the Senate Minority Leader, vacancy. Appointed by the Speaker of the House, Jack Dollard, Hartford; Milton L. Howard, Hartford. Appointed by the House Minority Leader, Paul D. Abercrombie, North Haven.

Appointed by the Chm., Conn. Historical Comm., vacancy; appointments of the Joint Committee on Legislative Management, Wade A. Hyslop, New London; vacancy.

COMMISSION ON COMPENSATION OF ELECTED STATE OFFICIALS AND JUDGES

Sec. 2-9a(a), Gen. Stat. Commission to make recommendations to the General Assembly on or before February 15 of odd numbered years. Address: Room 5100, Legislative Office Bldg., Hartford 06106. Tel., (860) 240-0100.

Appointed by the Governor, Joseph J. Fauliso, Hartford; Denis F. Mullane, West Hartford; Oskar G. Rogg, New Milford.

Appointed by the Pres. Pro Tempore of the Senate, Danforth M. Smith, Milford; Kenneth E. Taylor, New Milford. Appointed by the Senate Minority Leader, *Chm.,* Bruce D. Rubenstein, Hartford; Margaret Sandberg, West Hartford. Appointed by the Speaker of the House, Richard H. Goldstein, West Hartford; Vincent J. Loffredo, Avon. Appointed by the House Minority Leader, Robert J. Berta, Easton; K. Michael Snyder, Newtown.

Admin., Mary Janicki.

COMMISSION ON UNIFORM LEGISLATION

Sec. 2-80, Gen. Stat. Members appointed by the Governor, for a term coterminous with term of the Governor, Compensation, none. Address: State Capitol, Room 509A., Hartford 06106. Tel., (860) 240-0220.

Chm., David D. Biklen, Hartford, William R. Breetz, Hartford; John H. Langbein, Ph.D., Woodbridge; Roger P. Morgan, Stonington; Neal Ossen, Hartford; Joseph Geremia, Jr., Prospect; Roger Whitman, West Hartford.

Admin., George H. Meier.

FINANCE ADVISORY COMMITTEE

Sec. 4-93, Gen. Stat. Address: Secy., Office of Policy and Management, 80 Washington St., Hartford 06106.

Ex officio, Chm., John G. Rowland, Governor; M. Jodi Rell, Lieutenant Governor; Christopher B. Burnham, Treasurer; Nancy S. Wyman, Comptroller.

Appointed by the Pres. Pro Tempore of the Senate, Senators Joseph J. Crisco, Jr., Woodbridge; Robert L. Genuario, Norwalk; Alternates: Senators Judith G. Freedman, Westport; Brian McDermott, Wallingford.

Appointed by the Speaker of the House, Annette Carter, Hartford; William R. Dyson, New Haven; Peter A. Metz, Madison. Alternates: Terry Backer, Stratford; Terry Concannon, Haddam; Peter A. Metz, Madison; Robert M. Ward, Northford.

Clerk, Michael W. Kozlowski, Granby, Secy., Office of Policy and Management; *Asst. Clerk,* Pam Law, Exec. Budget Officer, Budget and Financial Mgmt.

LATINO AND PUERTO RICAN AFFAIRS COMMISSION

Sec. 2-120, Gen. Stat. Compensation of members, none. Address: 18-20 Trinity St., 2nd Floor, Hartford 06106. Tel., (860) 240-8330.

Appointed by the Governor, Maritza Tiru, Waterbury; Salvador Vazquez, Waterbury; Wallie D. Feliciano, Meriden.

Appointed by the Pres. Pro Tempore of the Senate, Rolando T. Martinez, South Glastonbury; Doris Rosado, Meriden. Appointed by the Senate Majority Leader, Alma L. Maya, Bridgeport. Appointed by the Senate Minority Leader, Felipe Reinoso, Bridgeport; Raul A. Rodriguez, Hartford. Appointed by the Speaker of the House, Manuel Diaz, New Haven; Yasha Escalera, Manchester. Appointed by the House Majority Leader, *Chm.,* Americo L. Santiago, Bridgeport. Appointed by the House Minority Leader, Efrain Rosado, New Britain; Ramon A. Serbia, Stamford.

Exec. Dir., Fernando Betancourt.

MEMBERS AND OFFICERS OF THE SENATE OF THE STATE OF CONNECTICUT
JANUARY SESSION, 1997

Note: Legislative statistics concerning past members of the Connecticut General Assembly are on file in the State Library.

President, Lieutenant Governor, M. Jodi Rell; *President Pro Tempore*, Kevin B. Sullivan; *Majority Leader*, George C. Jepsen; *Deputy President Pro Tempore*, Alvin W. Penn; *Deputy Majority Leaders*, Thomas P. Gaffey, Melodie Peters; *Asst. Presidents Pro Tempore*, Biago Ciotto, Eileen M. Daily; *Chief Asst. Majority Leader*, Thomas A. Colapietro; *Asst. Majority Leaders*, Thomas A. Bozek, Eric D. Coleman, Toni N. Harp; *Minority Whip*, Brian McDermott; *Minority Leader*, M. Adela Eads; *Minority Leader Pro Tempore*, James T. Fleming; *Deputy Minority Leaders*, Louis C. DeLuca, George L. Gunther, Thomas F. Upson; *Asst. Leaders*, Judith G. Freedman, Robert L. Genuario, William H. Nickerson, Angelina Scarpetti, Win Smith, Stephen R. Somma; *Minority Whip*, William A. Aniskovich. *Clerk of the Senate*, Thomas P. Sheridan; *Asst. Senate Clerk*, Marilyn F. Cohen; *Permanent Asst. Clerk*, Vita C. Hardy; *Chaplains*, Rabbi Hans Bodenheimer, Msgr. Joseph A. Devine, Dr. Barbara Headley, The Rev. James J. Nock.

Sen. Dist.	Name	Pol.	Birthplace	Occupation	Length of Service
1	JOHN W. FONFARA 23 Fenwick St., Hartford 06114	D	Hartford	marketing consultant	House, 1987, 89, 91, 93, 95
2	ERIC D. COLEMAN 77 Wintonbury Ave., Bloomfield 06002	D	New Haven	attorney	House, 1983, 85, 87, 89, 91, 93. Senate, 1995
3	GARY D. LeBEAU Legislative Office Building, Rm. 2200, Hartford 06106-1591	D	East Hampton, MA	teacher	House, 1991, 93. Senate, 1995.
4	MARY ANN HANDLEY 133 Prospect St., Manchester 06040	D	Manchester	retired professor	
5	KEVIN B. SULLIVAN 32 Walkley Rd., West Hartford 06119	D	Hartford	college administrator	Senate, 1987, 89, 91, 93, 95
6	THOMAS A. BOZEK 32 Ten Acre Rd., New Britain 06052	D	Manchester, NH	analyst	Senate, 1995
7	JOHN A. KISSEL 16 Frew Ter., Enfield 06082	R	Worcester, MA	attorney	Senate, 1993, 95
8	JAMES T. FLEMING Legislative Office Bldg., Rm. 3400, Hartford 06106-1591	R	Teaneck, NJ	dir., community relations	House, 1981, 83, 85, 87, 89. Senate, 1991, 93, 95
9	BIAGIO S. CIOTTO 68 Harris Hill Rd., Wethersfield 06109	D	Hartford	retired	Senate, 1995

MEMBERS AND OFFICERS OF THE SENATE—Continued

Sen. Dist.	Name	Pol.	Birthplace	Occupation	Length of Service
10	TONI NATHANIEL HARP P.O. Box 9434, New Haven 06534	D	San Francisco, CA	homeless project dir.	Senate, 1993, 95
11	MARTIN M. LOONEY 132 Fort Hale Rd., New Haven 06512	D	New Haven	attorney	House, 1981, 83, 85, 87, 89, 91. Senate, 1993, 95
12	WILLIAM A. ANISKOVICH 15 Grove Ave., Branford 06405	R	New Haven	attorney	House, 1991, 93, 95
13	THOMAS P. GAFFEY 50 Pearl St., Meriden 06450	D	Meriden	communications director	Senate, 1995
14	WINTHROP S. SMITH, JR. Legislative Office Bldg., Rm. 2400, Hartford 06106-1591	R	Milford	attorney	Senate, 1993, 95
15	THOMAS F. UPSON 827 Oronoke Rd., 10-1, Waterbury 06708	R	Waterbury	attorney	Senate, 1985, 87, 89, 91, 93, 95
16	STEPHEN R. SOMMA 70 Ellsworth Ave., Waterbury 06704	R	Waterbury	director of development	Senate, 1989, 91, 93, 95
17	JOSEPH J. CRISCO, JR. 1205 Racebrook Rd., Woodbridge 06525	D	New Haven	vice president public affairs	Senate, 1991, 93, 95
18	CATHERINE W. COOK 8 West Mystic Ave., Mystic 06355-2329	R	New London	administrator	Senate, 1993, 95
19	EDITH G. PRAGUE 145 Rte. 87, Columbia 06237	D	Methuen, MA	retired	House, 1983, 85, 87, 89, 91, 93. Senate, 1995
20	MELODIE M. PETERS 10 Tototket Rd., Quaker Hill 06375	D	Springfield, MA	nurse/labor coordinator	Senate, 1993, 95
21	GEORGE L. GUNTHER 890 Judson Place, Stratford 06497	R	Bridgeport	natureopathic physician (ret)	Senate, 1967, 69, 71, 73, 75, 77, 79, 81, 83, 85, 87, 89, 91, 93, 95
22	ANGELINA SCARPETTI 319 Whitney Ave., Trumbull 06611	R	Italy	restaurant consultant	Senate, 1985; 89, 91, 93, 95
23	ALVIN W. PENN 313 Waterview Ave., Bridgeport 06608	D	Cleveland, OH	dir., affirmative action	Senate, 1991, 93, 95
24	MARK NIELSEN 258 Main St., Danbury 06811	R	Hartford	attorney	House, 1993. Senate, 1995

MEMBERS AND OFFICERS OF THE SENATE—Continued

Sen. Dist.	Name	Pol.	Birthplace	Occupation	Length of Service
25	ROBERT L. GENUARIO 2 Singing Woods Rd., Norwalk 06850	R	Norwalk	attorney	Senate, 1991, 93, 95
26	JUDITH G. FREEDMAN 17 Crawford Rd., Westport 06880	R	Bridgeport	teacher	Senate, 1987, 89, 91, 93, 95
27	GEORGE C. JEPSEN Legislative Office Bldg., Rm. 3300, Hartford 06106-1591	D	Hattiesburg, MS	attorney	House, 1987, 89. Senate, 1991, 93, 95
28	FRED H. LOVEGROVE, JR. 431 Catamount Rd., Fairfield 06430	R	Redding	realtor	Senate, 1983, 85, 87, 89, 91, 93, 95
29	DONALD E. WILLIAMS, JR. P.O. Box 201, Thompson 06277	D	Cincinnati, OH	attorney	Senate Spec. Elec. 1993; 95
30	M. ADELA EADS 160 Macedonia Rd., Kent 06757	R	Brooklyn, NY	legislator	House, 1977, 79. Senate, 1981, 83, 85, 87, 89, 91, 93, 95
31	THOMAS A. COLAPIETRO Legislative Office Bldg., Rm. 3505, Hartford 06106-1591	D	Bristol	retired	Senate, 1993, 95
32	LOUIS C. DeLUCA P.O. Box 32, Woodbury 06798	R	Everett, MA	businessman	Senate, 1991, 93, 95
33	EILEEN M. DAILY 103 Cold Spring Dr., Westbrook 06498	D	Boston, MA	legislator	Senate, 1993, 95
34	BRIAN M. McDERMOTT Capitol Office Bldg., Rm. 110, Hartford 06106	D	New Haven	businessperson	Senate, 1995
35	TONY GUGLIELMO 100 Stafford St., Stafford Springs 06076	R	Stamford	insurance agency owner	Senate, 1993, 95
36	WILLIAM H. NICKERSON 35 Quail Rd., Greenwich 06831	R	Glen Cove, NY	real estate	House, 1987, 89. Senate, 1991, 93, 95

Democrats, 19; Republicans, 17; Total, 36.

MEMBERS AND OFFICERS OF THE HOUSE OF REPRESENTATIVES OF THE STATE OF CONNECTICUT
JANUARY SESSION, 1997

Speaker, Thomas D. Ritter; *Majority Leader*, Moira K. Lyons; *Speaker Pro Tempore*, David B. Pudlin; *Deputy Speakers*, Joan V. Hartley, Wade A. Hyslop, Jr.; *Deputy Majority Leaders*, Melody A. Currey, Mary G. Fritz, Robert D. Godfrey, Andrea L. Stillman; *Majority Whips*, Alex Knopp, Ernest E. Newton II, Richard D. Tulisano; *Asst. Majority Leaders*, Reginald G. Beamon, Annette W. Carter, Thomas F. Conway, Nancy A. DeMarinas, Patricia A. Dillon, Louis P. Esposito, Jr., Edna Garcia, Frederick A. Gelsi, Marie L. Kirkley-Bey, John J. Lescoe, John D. Mordasky, Gary Orefice, Joseph Serra, John W. Thompson, Vincent J. Tonucci, Christel H. Truglia; *Minority Leader*, Robert M. Ward; *Deputy Minority Leaders*, Lawrence F. Cafero, Jr., Brian J. Flaherty; *Deputy Minority Leader at Large*, Richard O. Belden; *Minority Whips*, Raymond V. Collins, Ruth C. Fahrbach, John E. Piscopo; *Asst. Minority Leaders*, Ann P. Dandrow, Christopher DePino, Angelo M. Fusco, Robert A. Maddox, Jr., Claudia Powers, F. Philip Prelli, Pamela Sawyer, Lenny T. Winkler. *Clerk of the House*, Garey E. Coleman; *Asst. Clerk*, Cynthia K. Swienton; *Permanent Asst. Clerk*, Ann M. Clark; *Chaplain*, Rev. Michael S. Galasso.

Assembly Dist.	Name	Pol.	Birthplace	Occupation	Length of Service
1	KENNETH P. GREEN 223 Granby St., Hartford 06112	D	Hartford	social worker	1995
2	THOMAS D. RITTER Legislative Office Bldg., Rm. 4100, Hartford 06106-1591	D	New Haven	attorney	1981, 83, 85, 87, 89, 91, 93, 95
3	MINNIE GONZALEZ 68 Heath St., Hartford 06106	D	Adjuntas, PR	legislator	
4	EVELYN C. MANTILLA* 19 Vernon St., Hartford 06106	D	Caguas, PR	independent consultant	
5	MARIE L. KIRKLEY-BEY 39 Ashley St., Hartford 06105-1402	D	New Britain	supv., patient accounts	1993, 95
6	ART J. FELTMAN Legislative Office Bldg., Rm. 2104, Hartford 06106-1591	D	Hartford	lawyer	
7	ANNETTE W. CARTER Legislative Office Bldg., Rm. 4034, Hartford 06106-1591	D	Troy, AL	legislator	Spec. Elec. 1988; 89, 91, 93, 95
8	PATRICK J. FLAHERTY P.O. Box 570, Coventry 06238	D	Hartford	bank economist	1993, 95

MEMBERS AND OFFICERS OF THE HOUSE OF REPRESENTATIVES—Continued

Assembly Dist.	Name	Pol.	Birthplace	Occupation	Length of Service
9	RICHARD D. VELTRI Legislative Office Bldg., Rm. 4078, Hartford 06106-1591	R	Huntington, NY	consultant	1995
10	MELODY A. CURREY 14 Martin Cir., East Hartford 06118-1119	D	Margaretsville, NY	legislator	1993, 95
11	MICHAEL A. CHRIST 117 Michael Ave., East Hatford 06108	D	Hartford	commercial advertising rep.	1995
12	JAMES R. McCAVANAGH Legislative Office Bldg., Rm. 2400, Hartford, 06106-1591	D	Manchester	real estate broker	1983, 85, 87, 89, 91, 93, 95
13	JOHN W. THOMPSON 118 Autumn St., Manchester 06040	D	Staten Island, NY	consultant	1987, 89, 91, 93, 95
14	NANCY E. KERENSKY 35 Berle Rd., South Windsor 06074	D	Denver, CO	speech language pathologist	1995
15	MARY U. EBERLE 205 Duncaster Rd., Bloomfield 06002	D	St. Louis, MO	legislator	1993, 95
16	THOMAS J. HERLIHY 8 Woodcliff Dr., Simsbury 06070	R	Queens, NY	business owner	
17	JESSIE G. STRATTON 33 Bahre Corner Rd., Canton 06019	D	Swarthmore, PA	legislator	1989, 91, 93, 95
18	ANDREW M. FLEISCHMANN Legislative Office Bldg., Rm. 4020, Hartford 06106-1591	D	Hartford	writer	1995
19	ROBERT FARR 90 Whiting La., West Hartford 06107	R	Hartford	attorney	1981, 83, 85, 87, 89, 91, 93, 95
20	JOHN L. RITTER 179 Wood Pond Rd., West Hartford 06107	D	New Haven	attorney/businessman	
21	DEMETRIOS S. GIANNAROS 56 Basswood Rd., Farmington 06032	D	Greece	professor of economics	1995

MEMBERS AND OFFICERS OF THE HOUSE OF REPRESENTATIVES—Continued

Assembly Dist.	Name	Pol.	Birthplace	Occupation	Length of Service
22	ELIZABETH A. BOUKUS Legislative Office Bldg., Rm. 4014, Hartford 06106-1591	D	New Britain	legislator	1995
23	THERESA B. GERRATANA 674 Lincoln St., New Britain 06052	D	New Britain	legislator	1993, 95
24	DAVID B. PUDLIN Legislative Office Bldg., Rm. 4100, Hartford 06106-1591	D	New Britain	adult educator	1989, 91, 93, 95
25	JOHN C. GERAGOSIAN 33 Recano Rd., New Britain 06053	D	New Britain	realtor	1995
26	ANTHONY J. TERCYAK 150 Belridge Rd., New Britain 06053	R	New Britain	legislator	Spec. Elec. 1994; 95
27	DOMINIC MAZZOCCOLI 29 Cinnamon Rd., Newington 06111	R	Hartford	insurance underwriter	1993, 95
28	PAUL R. DOYLE 38 Thornbush Rd., Wethersfield 06109	D	Hartford	attorney	1995
29	RICHARD D. TULISANO 11 Sunny Crest Dr., Rocky Hill 06067	D	Hartford	attorney	1975, 77, 79, 81, 83, 85, 87, 89, 91, 93, 95
30	ANN P. DANDROW 272 Hart St., Southington 06489	R	Cambridge, MA	legislator	1987, 89, 91, 93, 95
31	SONYA F. GOOGINS 74 Forest La., Glastonbury 06033	R	New Haven	legislator	1995
32	JAMES A. O'ROURKE III 7 Forest Rd., Cromwell 06416	D	Boston, MA	legislator	1991, 93, 95
33	JOSEPH C. SERRA P.O. Box 233, Middletown 06457	D	Middletown	secy./treas. public works	1993, 95
34	TERRY CONCANNON 76 Timms Hill Rd., Haddam 06438	D	Ireland	tax consultant	1993, 95
35	ROBERT LANDINO 219 Old Salt Works Rd., Westbrook 06498	D	New Haven	engineer	Spec. Elec. 1995

MEMBERS AND OFFICERS OF THE HOUSE OF REPRESENTATIVES—Continued

Assembly Dist.	Name	Pol.	Birthplace	Occupation	Length of Service
36	CLAIRE SAUER 47 Mitchell Hill, Lyme 06371	D	Valley Stream, NY	legislator	1995
37	GARY J. OREFICE 47 Columbus Ave., Niantic 06357	D	Hartford	insurance underwriter	1993, 95
38	ANDREA L. STILLMAN 5 Coolidge Court, Waterford 06385	D	New York, NY	businesswoman/legislator	1993, 95
39	WADE A. HYSLOP, JR. 32 Beldon St., New London 06320	D	New London	minister	1991, 93, 95
40	NANCY A. DeMARINIS 898 Shennecossett Rd., Groton 06340	D	Glen Ridge, NJ	retired guidance counselor	1993, 95
41	LENNY T. WINKLER 151 Pamela Ave., Groton 06340	R	New London	nurse/legislator	Spec. Elec. 1988, 89, 91, 93, 95
42	MARY K. McGRATTAN 13 Lynn Dr., Ledyard 06339	D	New York, NY	registered nurse	1993, 95
43	ROBERT R. SIMMONS P.O. Box 268, Stonington 06378	R	New York, NY	teacher/soldier	Spec. Elec. 1991; 93, 95
44	MICHAEL A. CARON 158 Pond Hill Rd., Moosup 06354	R	Putnam	sales	1991, 93, 95
45	STEVEN MIKUTEL 152 Bethel Rd., Norwich 06360	D	Norwich	legislator	1993, 95
46	PETER A. NYSTROM 108 Geer Ave., Norwich 06360	R	Norwich	legislator/supervisor	1983; 87, 89, 91, 93, 95
47	JACK MALONE 20 Harland Rd., Norwich 06360	D	Willimantic	dir. of development	1995
48	LINDA A. ORANGE 52 Standish Rd., Colchester 06415	D	Hartford	legislator	1987, 89, 91, 93, 95
49	JOHN J. LESCOE 33 Hewitt St., Willimantic 06226	D	Windham	teacher/business person	1987, 89, 91, 93, 95
50	JEFFERSON B. DAVIS 154 Wade Rd., Pomfret Ctr. 06259	D	Hartford	legislator	1991, 93, 95

MEMBERS AND OFFICERS OF THE HOUSE OF REPRESENTATIVES—Continued

Assembly Dist.	Name	Pol.	Birthplace	Occupation	Length of Service
51	SHAWN T. JOHNSTON 222 Ravenelle Rd., No. Grosvenordale 06255	D	Putnam	electrical consumption analyst	1995
52	JOHN D. MORDASKY 168 Hydeville Rd., Stafford Springs 06076	D	Stafford	dairy farmer	1979; 83, 85, 87, 89, 91, 93, 95
53	MICHAEL J. CARDIN 157 Dockerel Rd., Tolland 06084	D	Rockville	legislator	1995
54	DENISE W. MERRILL 148 Coventry Rd., Mansfield Ctr. 06250	D	San Mateo, CA	attorney/legislator	Spec. Elec. 1994; 95,
55	PAMELA Z. SAWYER 95 South Rd., Bolton 06043	R	Pawtucket, RI	legislator	1993, 95
56	THOMASINA CLEMONS 655-7 Talcottville Rd., Vernon 06060	D	Charleston, WV	retired university admin.	1995
57	EDWARD C. GRAZIANI Legislative Office Bldg., Rm. 1000, Hartford 06106-1591	D	New York, NY	attorney	1991, 93, 95
58	FREDERICK A. GELSI 63 Roosevelt Blvd., Enfield 06082	D	Vineland, NJ	retired	1979; 83, 85, 87, 89, 91, 93, 95
59	STEPHEN M. JARMOC 33 Abbe Rd., Enfield 06082	D	Enfield	farmer	1993, 95
60	CARL J. SCHIESSL 93 Raymond Rd., Windsor Locks 06096	D	Hartford	attorney	1987, 89, 91, 93, 95
61	RUTH C. FAHRBACH P.O. Box 279, Windsor 06095	R	New York, NY	legislator	1981, 83, 85, 87, 89, 91, 93, 95
62	RICHARD F. FERRARI 9 Carriage La., East Granby 06026	R	Hartford	legislator	1991, 93, 95
63	F. PHILIP PRELLI 105 Indian Meadow Dr., Winsted 06098	R	Winsted	insurance agent	1991, 93, 95
64	ANDREW W. RORABACK P.O. Box 357, Goshen 06756	R	Torrington	lawyer	1995

MEMBERS AND OFFICERS OF THE HOUSE OF REPRESENTATIVES—Continued

Assembly Dist.	Name	Pol.	Birthplace	Occupation	Length of Service
65	BRIAN E. MATTIELLO 26 Albany Ave., Torrington 06790	R	Torrington	legislator	1993, 95
66	ROBERT A. MADDOX, JR. 104 Deerwood Dr., Bethlehem 06751	R	Torrington	marketing & sales associate	1987, 89, 91, 93, 95
67	JEANNE W. GARVEY 53 Walker Brook Rd. North, New Milford 06776-2233	R	Bridgeport	realtor	1993, 95
68	BRIAN J. FLAHERTY 21 Neill Dr., Watertown 06795-1706	R	Waterbury	editor	1989, 91, 93, 95
69	ARTHUR J. O'NEILL 1468 Bucks Hill Rd., Southbury 06488	R	Waterbury	lawyer	Spec. Elec. 1988; 89, 91, 93, 95
70	KEVIN M. DELGOBBO 83 Meadow St., Naugatuck 06770	R	Oradell, NJ	international trade consultant	
71	ANTHONY J. D'AMELIO 64 Wellington Ave., Waterbury 06708	R	Waterbury	restaurant owner/realtor	Spec. Elec. 1996
72	REGINALD G. BEAMON Legislative Office Bldg., Rm. 4114, Hartford 06106-1591	D	Waterbury	legislator	1987, 89, 91, 93, 95
73	JOAN V. HARTLEY Legislative Office Bldg., Rm. 4100, Hartford 06106-1591	D	Waterbury	legislator	1985, 87, 89, 91, 93, 95
74	MICHAEL J. JARJURA 6 Gayridge Rd., Unit 306-2, Waterbury 06705	D	Waterbury	atty./business exec.	1993, 95
75	THOMAS F. CONWAY 1136 Hamilton Ave., Waterbury 06706	D	Waterbury	boiler-fireman/funeral director	1987, 89, 91, 93, 95
76	JOHN E. PISCOPO 50 Judson St., Thomaston 06787	R	Waterbury	legislator	1989, 91, 93, 95
77	ROGER B. MICHELE 485 Farmington Ave., Bristol 06010	D	Bristol	real estate broker/ barber	1995

MEMBERS AND OFFICERS OF THE HOUSE OF REPRESENTATIVES—Continued

Assembly Dist.	Name	Pol.	Birthplace	Occupation	Length of Service
78	WILLIAM A. HAMZY 4 Prospect St. Ext., Terryville 06786	R	Torrington	attorney	1995
79	KONSTANTINOS M. DIAMANTIS P.O. Box 197, 201 West St., Bristol 06010	D	Bristol	attorney	1993, 95
80	DENNIS H. CLEARY P.O. Box 6008, Wolcott 06716	R	Waterbury	nursing home admin./r.n.	1993, 95
81	ANGELO M. FUSCO 661 Main St., Plantsville 06479	R	Southington	facilities mechanic	1985, 87, 89, 91, 93, 95
82	EMIL ALTOBELLO, JR. Legislative Office Bldg., Rm. 2803, Hartford 06106-1591	D	Meriden	legislator	1995
83	JAMES W. ABRAMS 91 Midland Dr., Meriden 06450	D	Orange, NJ	attorney	1995
84	CHRISTOPHER G. DONOVAN 188 Atkins St., Meriden 06450	D	Darby, PA	labor rep.	1993, 95
85	MARY M. MUSHINSKY 188 South Cherry St., Wallingford 06492	D	New Haven	legislator	1981, 83, 85, 87, 89, 91, 93, 95
86	ROBERT M. WARD Legislative Office Bldg., Rm. 4200, Hartford 06106-1591	R	Wilmington, DE	attorney	1985, 87, 89, 91, 93, 95
87	STEVE FONTANA 180 Fitch St., North Haven 06473-3705	D	Ann Arbor, MI	lawyer	1995
88	NANCY BEALS 255 Ridgewood Ave., Hamden 06517	D	El Paso, TX	legislator/community volunteer	1993, 95
89	VICKIE O. NARDELLO 8 Laurel La., Prospect 06712	D	Italy	public health dental hygenist	1995
90	MARY G. FRITZ 43 Grove St., Yalesville 06492	D	Cambridge, MA	legislator	1983; 87, 89, 91, 93, 95
91	PETER F. VILLANO 132 Armory St., Hamden 06517	D	New Haven	legislator	1993, 95

MEMBERS AND OFFICERS OF THE HOUSE OF REPRESENTATIVES—Continued

Assembly Dist.	Name	Pol.	Birthplace	Occupation	Length of Service
92	PATRICIA A. DILLON 68 West Rock Ave., New Haven 06515	D	Queens, NY	legislator	1985, 87, 89, 91, 93, 95
93	HOWARD C. SCIPIO 30 Bellevue Rd., New Haven 06511	D	Bridgeport	mortgage broker	1993, 95
94	WILLIAM R. DYSON P.O. Box 2064, New Haven 06521	D	Waycross, GA	teacher/legislator	1977, 79, 81, 83, 85, 87, 89, 91, 93, 95
95	JOHN S. MARTINEZ 7 Arch St., New Haven 06519	D	New York, NY	consultant	1995
96	CAMERON C. STAPLES Legislative Office Bldg., Rm. 3100, Hartford 06106-1591	D	Salem, MA	attorney	1993, 95
97	CHRIS DePINO 1354 Dean St., New Haven 06512	R	New Haven	train conductor	Spec. Elec. 1992; 93, 95
98	PATRICIA M. WIDLITZ 160 Deer La., Guilford 06437	D	Middletown	legislator	1995
99	MICHAEL P. LAWLOR 3 Atwater St., East Haven 06512	D	New Haven	attorney	1987, 89, 91, 93, 95
100	SUSAN BYSIEWICZ P.O. Box 2461, Middletown 06457	D	New Haven	lawyer	1993, 95
101	PETER A. METZ 99 Bishop La., Madison 06443	R	Yonkers, NY	attorney	1993, 95
102	PETER J. PANARONI, JR. 25 Frank St., Branford 06405	D	New Haven	construction/truck driver	
103	CRAIG HENRICI 1135 Main St., Hamden 06514	D	New Haven	lawyer	
104	VINCENT J. TONUCCI 26 Fairview Ter., Derby 06418	D	Derby	real estate broker/ appraiser/investor	1987, 89, 91, 93, 95
105	LEONARD C. GREENE*** 146 Cedar La., Beacon Falls 06403	R	Derby	marketing	

MEMBERS AND OFFICERS OF THE HOUSE OF REPRESENTATIVES—Continued

Assembly Dist.	Name	Pol.	Birthplace	Occupation	Length of Service
106	JULIA B. WASSERMAN 113 Walnut Tree Hill Rd., P.O. Box 848, Sandy Hook 06482	R	West Germany	director of health	1991, 93, 95
107	B. SCOTT SANTA-MARIA P.O. Box 524, Brookfield 06804	R	Danbury	police officer	1995
108	NORMA GYLE 6 Milltown Rd., New Fairfield 06812	R	East Orange, NJ	registered nurse/counselor	1985, 87, 89, 91, 93, 95
109	LEWIS J. WALLACE, JR. 110 Hayestown Rd., Danbury 06811	D	West Germany	public utility manager	
110	ROBERT D. GODFREY 13 Stillman Ave., Danbury 06810-8007	D	Danbury	attorney	1989, 91, 93, 95
111	CHRISTOPHER R. SCALZO P.O. Box 875, Ridgefield 06877	R	Peekskill, NY	legislator	1995
112	WILLIAM J. VARESE 21 Benedict Rd., Monroe 06468	R	Bridgeport	attorney	1991, 93, 95
113	RICHARD O. BELDEN 14 Keron Dr., Shelton 06484	R	Derby	ombudsman	1975, 77, 79, 81, 83, 85, 87, 89, 91, 93, 95
114	ELLEN SCALETTAR Legislative Office Bldg., Rm. 4027, Hartford 06106-0591	D	New York, NY	attorney	1993, 95
115	STEPHEN D. DARGAN Legislative Office Bldg., Rm. 3603, Hartford 06106-1591	D	New Haven	sales	1991, 93, 95
116	LOUIS P. ESPOSITO, JR. 56 Lakeview Ave., West Haven 06516	D	New Haven	garage owner	1993, 95
117	RAYMOND V. COLLINS 6 Morris St., West Haven 06516	R	New Haven	administrative asst.	1985; 1989, 91, 93, 95
118	JAMES A. AMANN 515 Popes Island Rd., Milford 06460	D	Bridgeport	corporate pres.	1991, 93, 95

MEMBERS AND OFFICERS OF THE HOUSE OF REPRESENTATIVES—Continued

Assembly Dist.	Name	Pol.	Birthplace	Occupation	Length of Service
119	RICHARD F. ROY 43 Howe St., Milford 06460	D	Cornwall, NY	free lance writer	1993, 95
120	JOHN A. HARKINS 1035 Whippoorwill La., Stratford 06497	R	Perth Amboy, NJ	real estate appraiser	
121	TERRANCE E. BACKER 125 Jefferson St., Stratford 06497	D	Stamford	long island soundkeeper	1993, 95
122	LAWRENCE G. MILLER 60 Peace Acre La., Stratford 06497	R	Bridgeport	president	1991, 93, 95
123	ELAINE HAMMERS 59 Coventry La., Trumbull 06611	R	New York, NY	human resources	
124	ERNEST E. NEWTON II 190 Read St., Bridgeport 06607	D	Fort Bel Voir, VA	legislator	1989, 91, 93, 95
125	ROBERT T. KEELEY, JR. 816 North Ave., Bridgeport 06606	D	Bridgeport	teacher	1983, 85, 87, 89; 93, 95
126	CHRISTOPHER L. CARUSO 208-B Beechmont Ave., Bridgeport 06606	D	Bridgeport	legislator	1991, 93, 95
127	JACQUELINE M. COCCO 93 Heppenstall Dr., Bridgeport 06604	D	Bridgeport	legislator	1987, 89, 91, 93, 95
128	EDNA I. GARCIA P.O. Box 5887, Bridgeport 06610	D	Humacao, PR	teacher	1991, 93, 95
129	LEE A. SAMOWITZ 851 Clinton Ave., Bridgeport 06604	D	Bridgeport	attorney	1983; 87, 89, 91, 93, 95
130	HECTOR A. DIAZ P.O. Box 2533, Bridgeport 06608	D	Manhattan, NY	caseworker	Spec. Elec. 1995
131	RONALD S. SAN ANGELO 151 Andrew Ave., Apt. 24, Naugatuck 06770	R	Waterbury	sales rep.	1993, 95
132	CARL J. DICKMAN 34 Miro St., Fairfield 06432	R	Rockport, MA	retired	1995
133	PAUL M. TYMNIAK P.O. Box 1051, Fairfield 06430	R	Bridgeport	attorney	1995

MEMBERS AND OFFICERS OF THE HOUSE OF REPRESENTATIVES—Continued

Assembly Dist.	Name	Pol.	Birthplace	Occupation	Length of Service
134	JOHN E. STONE, JR. 195 Carroll Rd., Fairfield 06430	R	Boston, MA	financial services	1995
135	JOHN E. STRIPP 4 Scatacook Trail, Weston 06883	R	New York, NY	corporate financial consultant	1993, 95
136	C. KENNETH BERNHARD 146 Kings Hwy. No., Westport 06880	R	White Plains, NY	attorney	
137	ALEX KNOPP 35 Fifth St., Norwalk 06855-2402	D	Manchester	attorney	1987, 89, 91, 93, 95
138	DAVID J. CAPPIELLO Legislative Office Bldg., Rm. 4200, Hartford, 06106-1591	R	Danbury	legislator	1995
139	KEVIN RYAN 21 Terrace Dr., Oakdale 06370	D	Fitchburg, MA	clinician/adjunct professor	1993, 1995
140	JOSEPH D. CLEMMONS, SR.** 19 Adamson Ave., Norwalk 06854	D		reverend	
141	JOHN J. RYAN 311 Noroton Ave., Darien 06820	R	New Haven	attorney	1995
142	LAWRENCE F. CAFERO, JR. 6 Weed Ave., Norwalk 06850	R	Bridgeport	attorney	1993, 95
143	ANTONIETTA BOUCHER 5 Wicks End La., Wilton 06897	R	Italy	small business owner	
144	JOHN WAYNE FOX 13 Aple Tree Dr., Stamford 06906	D	Stamford	attorney	1981, 83, 85, 87, 89, 91, 93, 95
145	CHRISTEL H. TRUGLIA 7 Gypsy Moth Landing, Stamford 06902	D	Germany	legislator	1989, 91, 93, 95
146	MOIRA K. LYONS Legislative Office Bldg., Rm. 4100, Hartford 06106-1591	D	Trenton, NJ	legislator	1981, 83, 85, 87, 89, 91, 93, 95
147	MICHAEL C. FEDELE 64 Huckleberry Hollow, Stamford 06903	R	Italy	chm./ceo	1993, 95

MEMBERS AND OFFICERS OF THE HOUSE OF REPRESENTATIVES—Continued

Assembly Dist.	Name	Pol.	Birthplace	Occupation	Length of Service
148	ANNE B. McDONALD 53 Courtland Hill St., Stamford 06906-2306	D	Syracuse, NY	legislator	91, 93, 95
149	JANET K. LOCKTON Legislative Office Bldg., Rm. 2105, Hartford 06106-1591	R	New Jersey	legislator	1991, 93, 95
150	MARILYN A. HESS 61 Byram Shore Rd., Greenwich 06830	R	Chicago, IL	legislator	1993, 95
151	CLAUDIA M. POWERS 15 Hendrie Ave., Riverside 06878	R	Key West, FL	retired teacher	1993, 95

Democrats, 96; Republicans, 55
Total, 151.

*Elected February 25, 1997 to fill the vacancy caused by the resignation of Edwin E. Garcia.
**Elected February 25, 1997 to fill the vacancy caused by the resignation of Donnie R. Sellers, Sr.
***Elected March 4, 1997 to fill the vacancy caused by the resignation of John W. Betkoski III.

Pursuant to Section 2-8 of the Connecticut General Statutes, each member of the general assembly, with the exception of officers, receives a base salary of $16,750 for each year of a term. Each member also receives a transportation allowance in the amount of $3,500 in th House of Representatives and $4,500 in the Senate. Officers of the general assembly are compensated as follows: Speaker of the House and President Pro Tempore of the Senate, $23,160; Majority and Minority Leaders of the House and Senate, $22,050; Deputy Speakers of the House and Deputy Majority and Minority Leaders of the House and Senate, $20,620; Assistant Majority and Minority Leaders and Committee Chairmen, $19,300; and, Ranking Members of each Joint Standing Committee, $18,2000. Each officer also receives a $3,500 allwwance for expenses.

LEGISLATIVE REPORTERS—*Associated Press*, Evan Berland, (860) 524-7857, 7858; *Connecticut Post*, Ken Dixon, (860) 549-4670; *Hartford Advocate*, Mike Kuczkowski, (860) 548-9300; *Commercial Record*, Harlan J. Levy, Vincent Valvo, (860) 644-3489; *Conn. Radio Network*, Steve Kotchko, Mark Sims, (860) 527-1901; *Hartford Courant*, Mathew Daly, (860) 241-6617, Christopher Keating, (860) 241-6656; Jon Lender, (860) 241-6524; *Journal-Inquirer*, Gary Kleeblatt, Don Michak, (860) 547-1066; *Meriden Record-Journal*, Peter Urban, (860) 241-9069, (203) 235-1661; *New Haven Register*, Gregory B. Hladky, (860) 524-0719, (860) 240-1798, 1797; *New London Day*, Jennifer Peter, (860) 278-5869; *New York-Times*, Jonathan Rabinovitz, (860) 247-2991; *Norwalk Hour*, Steve Burkholder, (860) 560-6969; *Norwich Bulletin*, Susan Haigh, (860) 549-0192; *Waterbury Republican-American*, Maura Kelly, (860) 727-0460; *News 12 TV*, Jim Murphy, (203) 849-1321; *WFSB TV Channel 3*, Jeffrey Cole, (860) 244-1765; *WTNH TV Channel 8*, Mark Davis, (860) 249-2340, (860) 296-8881; *WVIT TV Channel 30*, Tom Monahan, (860) 246-5506; *WTIC-TV Channel 61*, John Harrington, (860) 727-0082; *WTIC 1080 AM*, Walt Dibble, Judy DiScipio, (860) 522-1080, Ext. 260.

ALPHABETICAL ROLE OF THE SENATE
JANUARY SESSION, 1997

Dist.	Senators	Pol.	Telephone Res.	Bus.
12	ANISKOVICH, WILLIAM A.	R	(203) 483-9280	(860) 240-0596
6	BOZEK, THOMAS A.	D	(860) 223-3880	(860) 240-0411
9	CIOTTO, BIAGIO S.	D	(860) 563-7353	(860) 240-0595
31	COLAPIETRO, THOMAS A.	D	(860) 582-6527	(860) 240-0475
2	COLEMAN, ERIC D.	D	(860) 243-8118	(860) 240-0550
18	COOK, CATHERINE W.	R	....	(860) 536-4418
17	CRISCO, JOSEPH J., JR.	D	(203) 389-8788	(860) 240-0032
33	DAILY, EILEEN M.	D	(860) 399-7342	(860) 240-0447
32	DeLUCA, LOUIS C.	R	(203) 263-4785	(860) 240-0145
30	EADS, M. ADELA	R	(860) 927-3553	(860) 240-8800
8	FLEMING, JAMES T.	R	(860) 651-8192	(860) 240-8800
1	FONFARA, JOHN W.	D	(860) 296-3334	(860) 240-0414
26	FREEDMAN, JUDITH G.	R	....	(860) 240-8800
13	GAFFEY, THOMAS P.	D	(203) 634-3068	(860) 549-6390
25	GENUARIO, ROBERT L.	R	(203) 847-7230	(203) 849-9292
35	GUGLIELMO, TONY	R	(860) 684-4878	(860) 684-4164
21	GUNTHER, GEORGE L.	R	(203) 378-8572	(860) 240-8841
4	HANDLEY, MARY ANN	D	(860) 649-8367	(860) 240-0498
10	HARP, TONI N.	D	(203) 865-2232	(203) 784-0204
27	JEPSEN, GEORGE C.	D	(203) 327-3793	(860) 240-8620
7	KISSEL, JOHN A.	R	(860) 745-0668	(860) 240-0474
3	LeBEAU, GARY D.	D	(860) 598-5818	(860) 240-0488
11	LOONEY, MARTIN M.	D	(203) 468-8829	(203) 777-4716
28	LOVEGROVE, FRED H., JR.	R	(203) 255-0123	(800) 842-1421
34	McDERMOTT, BRIAN M.	D	(203) 294-9198	(860) 240-0099
36	NICKERSON, WILLIAM H.	R	(203) 661-0597	(860) 240-8800
24	NIELSEN, MARK	R	(203) 748-6753	(203) 796-0151
23	PENN, ALVIN W.	D	(203) 335-0299	(860) 240-0589
20	PETERS, MELODIE M.	D	(860) 443-8857	(860) 240-0431
19	PRAGUE, EDITH G.	D	(860) 228-9280	(860) 240-0543
22	SCARPETTI, ANGELINA	R	....	(800) 842-1421
14	SMITH, WINTHROP S., JR.	R	(203) 878-1486	(203) 783-1200
16	SOMMA, STEPHEN R.	R	....	(860) 240-0430
5	SULLIVAN, KEVIN B.	D	(860) 232-4994	(860) 240-8600
15	UPSON, THOMAS F.	R	(203) 753-1193	(203) 755-3007
29	WILLIAMS, DONALD E., JR.	D	....	(860) 928-0481

ALPHABETICAL ROLL OF THE HOUSE
JANUARY SESSION, 1997

Dist.	Representatives	Pol.	Telephone Res.	Bus.
83	ABRAMS, JAMES W.	D	(203) 237-9646	(203) 949-9422
82	ALTOBELLO, EMIL, JR.	D	(203) 634-1692	(860) 240-8585
118	AMANN, JAMES A.	D	(203) 783-1910	(203) 766-4686
121	BACKER, TERRANCE E.	D	(203) 378-8399	(203) 854-5330
88	BEALS, NANCY	D	(203) 248-3243	(860) 240-8585
72	BEAMON, REGINALD G.	D	....	(860) 240-8500
113	BELDEN, RICHARD O.	R	(203) 924-1757	(203) 386-6630
136	BERNHARD, G. KENNETH	R	(203) 227-1274	(203) 334-9421
143	BOUCHER, ANTONIETTA	R	(203) 762-3232	(800) 842-1423
22	BOUKUS, ELIZABETH A.	D	(860) 747-3366	(860) 240-8741
100	BYSIEWICZ, SUSAN	D	(860) 346-0695	(860) 240-0480
142	CAFERO, LAWRENCE F., JR.	R	(203) 854-6769	(203) 853-2700
138	CAPPIELLO, DAVID J.	R	(203) 778-0138	(800) 842-1423
53	CARDIN, MICHAEL J.	D	(860) 875-6598	(860) 240-8488
44	CARON, MICHAEL A.	R	(860) 564-6858	(860) 240-8700
7	CARTER, ANNETTE W.	D	(860) 240-0815	(860) 240-8585
126	CARUSO, CHRISTOPHER L.	D	(203) 374-1655	(860) 240-8374
11	CHRIST, MICHAEL A.	D	(860) 289-3527	(860) 240-8585
80	CLEARY, DENNIS H.	R	(203) 879-6535	(203) 879-8066
56	CLEMONS, THOMASINA	D	(860) 871-2443	(860) 240-8487
140	CLEMMONS, JOSEPH D., SR.	D	(203) 838-6232	(860) 240-8585
127	COCCO, JACQUELINE M.	D	(203) 372-2621	(860) 240-0590
117	COLLINS, RAYMOND V.	R	(203) 933-2428	(860) 240-8797
34	CONCANNON, TERRY	D	(860) 345-4141	(860) 240-8585
75	CONWAY, THOMAS F.	D	(203) 755-1903	(203) 753-6181
10	CURREY, MELODY A.	D	(860) 568-5584	(860) 240-8500
71	D'AMELIO, ANTHONY J.	R	(203) 574-3434	(203) 757-2629
30	DANDROW, ANN P.	R	(860) 621-5660	(860) 240-8700
115	DARGAN, STEPHEN D.	D	(203) 937-1985	(860) 240-0573
50	DAVIS, JEFFERSON B.	D	(860) 974-2917	(860) 240-0550
70	DeLGOBBO, KEVIN M.	R	(203) 720-7503	(203) 757-8777
40	DeMARINIS, NANCY A.	D	(860) 445-8098	(860) 240-8354
97	DePINO, CHRIS	R	(203) 467-9306	(860) 547-0589
79	DIAMANTIS, KONSTANTINOS	D	(860) 582-2993	(860) 585-9500
130	DIAZ, HECTOR A.	D	(203) 366-5659	(203) 576-8474
132	DICKMAN, CARL J.	R	(203) 336-2442	(800) 842-1423
92	DILLON, PATRICIA A.	D	(203) 387-6159	(860) 240-8548
84	DONOVAN, CHRISTOPHER G.	D	(203) 630-3863	(860) 240-0540
28	DOYLE, PAUL R.	D	(860) 257-7952	(860) 240-8585
94	DYSON, WILLIAM R.	D	(203) 777-3460	(203) 946-6937
15	EBERLE, MARY U.	D	(860) 242-6711	(860) 240-0430
116	ESPOSITO, LOUIS P., JR.	D	(203) 397-8588	(860) 240-8586
61	FAHRBACH, RUTH C.	R	(860) 688-0822	(860) 240-8700
19	FARR, ROBERT	R	(860) 236-0175	(860) 233-6336
6	FELTMAN, ART J.	D	....	(860) 240-8585
147	FEDELE, MICHAEL C.	R	(203) 329-2909	(203) 359-8040
62	FERRARI, RICHARD F.	R	(860) 653-2691	(860) 240-8381
68	FLAHERTY, BRIAN J.	R	(860) 274-3673	(860) 240-8700
8	FLAHERTY, PATRICK J.	D	(860) 742-0899	(860) 240-8543
18	FLEISCHMANN, ANDREW M.	D	(860) 523-7424	(860) 240-8585
87	FONTANA, STEVE	D	(203) 234-2240	(860) 240-8768

ALPHABETICAL ROLL OF THE HOUSE—Continued

Dist.	Representatives	Pol.	Telephone Res.	Bus.
144	FOX, JOHN WAYNE	D	(203) 359-4125	(203) 324-6777
90	FRITZ, MARY G.	D	(203) 269-1169	(860) 240-8552
81	FUSCO, ANGELO M.	R	(860) 628-0027	(203) 250-4435
128	GARCIA, EDNA I.	D	(203) 335-5469	(860) 240-8538
67	GARVEY, JEANNE W.	R	(860) 355-0173	(800) 842-1423
58	GELSI, FREDERICK A.	D	(860) 745-7376	(860) 240-8662
25	GERAGOSIAN, JOHN C.	D	(860) 224-1701	(860) 827-3482
23	GERRATANA, THERESA B.	D	(860) 225-5092	(860) 240-0561
21	GIANNAROS, DEMETRIOS S.	D	(860) 674-9543	(860) 240-8357
110	GODFREY, ROBERT D.	D	(203) 778-5127	(860) 240-8500
3	GONZALEZ, MINNIE	D	(860) 236-9654	(860) 240-8500
31	GOOGINS, SONYA F.	R	(860) 633-4237	(860) 240-8750
57	GRAZIANI, EDWARD C.	D	....	(860) 240-0452
1	GREEN, KENNETH P.	D	(860) 242-0277	(860) 289-8131
105	GREENE, LEONARD C.	R	(203) 729-9806	(860) 240-8700
108	GYLE, NORMA	R	(203) 746-4189	(203) 746-6561
123	HAMMERS, ELAINE	R	(203) 452-7048	(860) 240-8765
78	HAMZY, WILLIAM A.	R	(860) 589-7675	(860) 582-5300
120	HARKINS, JOHN A.	R	(203) 377-1019	(203) 378-8085
73	HARTLEY, JOAN V.	D	(203) 757-6267	(860) 240-8500
103	HENRICI, CRAIG	D	(203) 281-3881	(203) 265-2035
16	HERLIHY, THOMAS J.	R	(860) 658-2509	(860) 651-0271
150	HESS, MARILYN A.	R	(203) 531-0003	(860) 240-8722
39	HYSLOP, WADE A., JR.	D	(860) 443-1431	(860) 443-5897
74	JARJURA, MICHAEL J.	D	(203) 757-9191	(203) 757-9191
59	JARMOC, STEPHEN M.	D	(860) 749-0431	(860) 749-7970
51	JOHNSTON, SHAWN T.	D	(860) 923-9656	(860) 240-8588
125	KEELEY, ROBERT T., JR.	D	(203) 384-9888	(860) 240-0490
14	KERENSKY, NANCY E.	D	(860) 648-2866	(860) 240-8585
5	KIRKLEY-BEY, MARIE L.	D	(860) 728-1733	(860) 240-8500
137	KNOPP, ALEX	D	(203) 838-2476	(860) 240-8763
35	LANDINO, ROBERT A.	D	(860) 399-4802	(203) 248-2960
99	LAWLOR, MICHAEL P.	D	(203) 469-9725	(203) 240-0530
49	LESCOE, JOHN J.	D	(860) 423-4793	(860) 240-8585
149	LOCKTON, JANET K.	R	....	(860) 240-8700
146	LYONS, MOIRA K.	D	....	(860) 240-8500
66	MADDOX, ROBERT A., JR.	R	(203) 266-5958	(860) 240-8700
47	MALONE, JACK	D	(860) 889-9994	(860) 240-8585
4	MANTILLA, EVELYN C.	D	(860) 246-0383	(860) 240-8500
95	MARTINEZ, JOHN S.	D	(203) 624-9321	(860) 240-8593
65	MATTIELLO, BRIAN E.	R	(860) 489-8732	(860) 240-8700
27	MAZZOCCOLI, DOMINIC	R	(860) 666-8626	(860) 954-2741
12	McCAVANAGH, JAMES R.	D	(860) 649-5702	(860) 649-3800
148	McDONALD, ANNE B.	D	(203) 357-7310	(860) 240-0560
42	McGRATTAN, MARY K.	D	(860) 464-1204	(860) 464-7079
54	MERRILL, DENISE W.	D	(860) 423-7155	(860) 240-8545
101	METZ, PETER A.	R	(203) 245-2219	(203) 245-2060
77	MICHELE, ROGER B.	D	(860) 582-6838	(860) 582-6838
45	MIKUTEL, STEVEN	D	(860) 376-4615	(860) 240-8583
122	MILLER, LAWRENCE G.	R	(203) 377-1523	(203) 377-0028

ALPHABETICAL ROLL OF THE HOUSE—Continued

Dist.	Representatives	Pol.	Telephone Res.	Bus.
52	MORDASKY, JOHN D.	D	(860) 684-7267	(860) 684-7267
85	MUSHINSKY, MARY M.	D	(203) 269-8378	(860) 240-8585
89	NARDELLO, VICKIE O.	D	(203) 758-4219	(860) 240-8661
124	NEWTON, ERNEST E. II	D	(203) 334-4884	(860) 240-8361
46	NYSTROM, PETER A.	R	(860) 887-4646	(860) 240-0442
69	O'NEILL, ARTHUR J.	R	(203) 264-3951	(203) 264-3112
48	ORANGE, LINDA A.	D	(860) 537-3936	(860) 240-0453
37	OREFICE, GARY J.	D	(860) 739-9583	(860) 240-8500
32	O'ROURKE, JAMES A. III	D	(860) 635-2992	(860) 240-8574
102	PANARONI, PETER J., JR.	D	(203) 481-8342	(860) 240-8561
76	PISCOPO, JOHN E.	R	(860) 283-2155	(860) 240-8700
151	POWERS, CLAUDIA M.	R	(203) 637-1438	(800) 842-1423
63	PRELLI, F. PHILIP	R	(860) 379-1017	(860) 379-7726
24	PUDLIN, DAVID B.	D	(860) 225-2078	(860) 240-8568
20	RITTER, JOHN L.	D	(860) 561-2360	(860) 293-3333
2	RITTER, THOMAS D.	D	....	(860) 240-8500
64	RORABACK, ANDREW W.	R	(860) 491-8617	(860) 489-6880
119	ROY, RICHARD F.	D	(203) 878-8030	(203) 878-8030
141	RYAN, JOHN J.	R	(203) 655-7106	(203) 853-2100
139	RYAN, KEVIN	D	(860) 848-0790	(860) 240-8589
129	SAMOWITZ, LEE A.	D	(203) 367-3483	(203) 335-4540
131	SAN ANGELO, RONALD S.	R	(203) 729-0536	(800) 842-1423
107	SANTA-MARIA, B. SCOTT	R	(203) 775-5702	(203) 744-7900
36	SAUER, CLAIRE	D	(860) 434-2936	(860) 240-8585
55	SAWYER, PAMELA Z.	R	....	(860) 240-8700
114	SCALETTAR, ELLEN	D	(203) 387-2388	(203) 387-2388
111	SCALZO, CHRISTOPHER R.	R	(203) 431-4712	(800) 842-1423
60	SCHIESSL, CARL J.	D	(860) 292-3017	(860) 240-0460
93	SCIPIO, HOWARD C.	D	(203) 562-9233	(860) 842-8267
33	SERRA, JOSEPH C.	D	(860) 347-0119	(860) 240-8362
43	SIMMONS, ROBERT R.	R	(203) 535-2083	(203) 535-8378
96	STAPLES, CAMERON C.	D	(203) 773-9123	(860) 240-0420
38	STILLMAN, ANDREA L.	D	(860) 443-8568	(860) 240-8500
134	STONE, JOHN E., JR.	R	(203) 255-4261	(860) 240-8700
17	STRATTON, JESSIE G.	D	(860) 693-9274	(860) 240-0440
135	STRIPP, JOHN E.	R	(203) 227-8917	(860) 240-8700
26	TERCYAK, ANTHONY J.	R	....	(860) 240-8714
13	THOMPSON, JOHN W.	D	(860) 643-8991	(860) 649-9766
104	TONUCCI, VINCENT J.	D	(203) 734-5206	(203) 736-2111
145	TRUGLIA, CHRISTEL H.	D	(203) 357-7786	(860) 240-8375
29	TULISANO, RICHARD D.	D	(860) 529-5412	(860) 563-9306
133	TYMNIAK, PAUL M.	R	(203) 259-9604	(800) 842-1423
112	VARESE, WILLIAM J.	R	(203) 261-8598	(203) 268-2337
9	VELTRI, RICHARD D.	R	(860) 568-5127	(860) 240-8787
91	VILLANO, PETER F.	D	(203) 562-5251	(800) 842-8267
109	WALLACE, LEWIS J., JR.	D	(203) 730-8441	(203) 797-4539
86	WARD, ROBERT M	R	(203) 484-0339	(203) 481-8226
106	WASSERMAN, JULIA B.	R	(203) 426-9178	(860) 240-8700
98	WIDLITZ, PATRICIA M.	D	(203) 453-9924	(860) 240-0556
41	WINKLER, LENNY T.	R	(860) 446-0097	(860) 240-8700

1997 LEGISLATIVE COMMITTEE ASSIGNMENTS

SELECT COMMITTEE ON AGING

SENATORS PRAGUE, *Chm.,* 19th Dist.; SULLIVAN, *Vice Chm.,* 5th.

SENATOR KISSEL, *Ranking Member,* 7th.

REPRESENTATIVES VILLANO, *Chm.,* 91st Dist.; BOUKUS, *Vice Chm.,* 22nd; BYSIEWICZ, 100th; KERENSKY, 14th; NEWTON, 124th; SCIPIO, 93rd.

REPRESENTATIVES HAMZY, *Ranking Member,* 78th; DELGOBBO, 70th; DEPINO, 97th; HARKINS, 120th.

APPROPRIATIONS

SENATORS CRISCO, *Chm.,* 17th Dist.; HARP, *Vice Chm.,* 10th; BOZEK, 6th; MCDERMOTT, 34th; WILLIAMS, 29th.

SENATORS GENUARIO, *Ranking Member,* 25th Dist.; ANISKOVICH, 12th; COOK, 18th; FREEDMAN, 26th.

REPRESENTATIVES DYSON, *Chm.,* 94th Dist.; BACKER, *Vice Chm.,* 121st; CONCANNON, *Vice Chm.,* 34th; BOUKUS, 22nd; CARDIN, 53rd; CARTER, 7th; CLEMONS, 56th; CURREY, 10th; DIAMANTIS, 79th; DIAZ, 130th; DILLON, 92nd; DONOVAN, 84th; FLEISCHMANN, 18th; FONTANA, 87th; GERAGOSIAN, 25th; JARMOC, 59th; JOHNSTON, 51st; LAWLOR, 99th; MERRILL, 54th; MICHELE, 77th; O'ROURKE, 32nd; ROY, 119th; RYAN, 139th; SCALETTAR, 114th; STILLMAN, 38th; THOMPSON, 13th; TRUGLIA, 145th; TULISANO, 29th.

REPRESENTATIVES METZ, *Ranking Member,* 101st Dist.; CLEARY, 80th; D'AMELIO, 71st; FAHRBACH, 61st; FARR, 19th; FLAHERTY, 68th; GOOGINS, 31st; HERLIHY, 16th; SAN ANGELO, 131st; SIMMONS, 43rd; STONE, 134th; STRIPP, 135th; TYMNIAK, 133rd; VELTRI, 9th; WASSERMAN, 106th.

BANKS

SENATORS FONFARA, *Chm.,* 1st Dist.; COLEMAN, *Vice Chm.,* 2nd.

SENATOR SMITH, *Ranking Member,* 14th Dist.

REPRESENTATIVES MCCAVANAGH *Chm.,* 12th Dist.; MALONE, *Vice Chm.,* 47th; DEMARINIS, 40th; DOYLE, 28th; HENRICI, 103rd; KIRKLEY-BEY, 5th; MICHELE, 77th; NEWTON, 124th; RITTER, 20th; SERRA, 33rd.

REPRESENTATIVES STRIPP, *Ranking Member,* 135th Dist.; BELDEN, 113th; HESS, 150th; PRELLI, 63rd; VARESE, 112th.

SELECT COMMITTEE ON CHILDREN

SENATORS WILLIAMS, *Vice Chm.,* 29th Dist.; SULLIVAN, 5th.

SENATOR EADS, *Chm.,* 30th Dist.

REPRESENTATIVES MUSHINSKY, *Chm.,* 85th Dist.; KERENSKY, *Vice Chm.,* 14th; GONZALEZ, 3rd; HARTLEY, 73rd; THOMPSON, 13th; TRUGLIA, 145th.

REPRESENTATIVES TYMNIAK, *Ranking Member,* 133rd Dist.; BERNHARD, 136th; DANDROW, 30th; TERCYAK, 26th.

COMMERCE

SENATORS McDERMOTT, *Chm.,* 34th Dist.; CIOTTO, *Vice Chm.,* 9th; HARP, 10th.

SENATORS COOK, *Ranking Member,* 18th Dist.; GUGLIELMO, 35th.

REPRESENTATIVES SAMOWITZ, *Chm.,* 129th Dist.; CARUSO, *Vice Chm.,* 126th; AMANN, 118th; BOUKUS, 22nd; CARTER, 7th; CHRIST, 11th; FONTANA, 87th; GIANNAROS, 21st; GREENE, 105th; JARJURA, 74th; JOHNSTON, 51st; MERRILL, 54th; MIKUTEL, 45th; ORANGE, 48th; OREFICE, 37th.

REPRESENTATIVES HESS, *Ranking Member,* 150th Dist.; GOOGINS, 31st; MILLER, 122nd; PRELLI, 63rd; RYAN, 141st; SIMMONS, 43rd; STONE, 134th; STRIPP, 135th.

EDUCATION

SENATORS GAFFEY, *Chm.,* 13th Dist.; HANDLEY, *Vice Chm.,* 4th.

SENATORS FREEDMAN, *Ranking Member,* 26th Dist.; KISSEL, 7th.

REPRESENTATIVES STAPLES, *Chm.,* 96th Dist.; MERRILL, *Vice Chm.,* 54th; BEALS, 88th; CARDIN, 53rd; CURREY, 10th; DIAMANTIS, 79th; DYSON, 94th; EBERLE, 15th; FELTMAN, 6th; FRITZ, 90th; GARCIA, 128th; GIANNAROS, 21st; GREEN, 1st; KERENSKY, 14th; RYAN, 139th; WALLACE, 109th; WIDLITZ, 98th.

REPRESENTATIVES MATTIELLO, *Ranking Member,* 65th Dist.; BOUCHER, 143rd; CAFERO, 142nd; HAMMERS, 123rd; HERLIHY, 16th; POWERS, 151st; SAWYER, 55th; SCALZO, 111th; TYMNIAK, 133rd; VELTRI, 9th.

ENERGY AND TECHNOLOGY

SENATORS PETERS, *Chm.,* 20th Dist.; FONFARA, *Vice Chm.,* 1st; McDERMOTT, 34th.

SENATORS SOMMA, *Ranking Member,* 16th Dist.; NIELSEN, 24th.

REPRESENTATIVES EBERLE, *Chm.,* 15th Dist.; NARDELLO, *Vice Chm.,* 89th; ALTOBELLO, 82nd; FLAHERTY, 8th; OREFICE, 37th; RITTER, 20th; SCIPIO, 93rd; TONUCCI, 104th.

REPRESENTATIVES FERRARI, *Ranking Member,* 62nd Dist.; LOCKTON, 149th; MILLER, 122nd; TERCYAK, 26th; VELTRI, 9th.

ENVIRONMENT

SENATORS DAILY, *Chm.,* 33rd Dist.; HANDLEY, *Vice Chm.,* 4th.

SENATOR FLEMING, *Ranking Member,* 8th Dist.

REPRESENTATIVES STRATTON, *Chm.,* 17th Dist.; McGRATTAN, *Vice Chm.,* 42nd; ABRAMS, 83rd; BACKER, 121st; CARUSO, 126th; DAVIS, 50th; JARMOC, 59th; MIKUTEL, 45th; MORDASKY, 52nd; MUSHINSKY, 85th; ROY, 119th; WALLACE, 109th; WIDLITZ, 98th.

REPRESENTATIVES NYSTROM, *Ranking Member,* 46th Dist.; COLLINS, 117th; FERRARI, 62nd; MADDOX, 66th; PISCOPO, 76th; PRELLI, 63rd; RORABACK, 64th.

EXECUTIVE AND LEGISLATIVE NOMINATIONS

SENATORS JEPSEN, *Chm.,* 27th Dist.; SULLIVAN, *Vice Chm.,* 5th; HARP, 10th; PETERS, 20th.

SENATORS DeLUCA, *Ranking Member,* 32nd Dist.; EADS, 30th.

REPRESENTATIVES GRAZIANI, *Chm.,* 57th Dist.; DARGAN, 115th; GODFREY, 110th; HARTLEY, 73rd; HYSLOP, 39th; McCAVANAGH, 12th; PUDLIN, 24th; RITTER, 20th.

REPRESENTATIVES VARESE, *Ranking Member,* 112th Dist.; GARVEY, 67th; GYLE, 108th; NYSTROM, 46th; PISCOPO, 76th.

FINANCE, REVENUE AND BONDING

SENATORS LOONEY, *Chm.,* 11th Dist.; DAILY, *Vice Chm.,* 33rd; PENN, *Bonding Chm.,* 23rd; FONFARA, *Bonding Vice Chm.,* 1st; GAFFEY, 13th.

SENATORS NICKERSON, *Ranking Member,* 36th Dist.; DeLUCA, 32nd; SMITH, 14th.

REPRESENTATIVES SCHIESSL, *Chm.,* 60th Dist.; GIANNAROS, *Vice Chm.,* 21st; LANDINO, *Vice Chm.,* 35th; MARTINEZ, *Vice Chm.,* 95th; GELSI, *Bonding Chm.,* 58th; LESCOE, *Bonding Vice Chm.,* 49th; ALTOBELLO, 82nd; BEALS, 88th; BEAMON, 72nd; CHRIST, 11th; COCCO, 127th; FELTMAN, 6th; FLAHERTY, 8th; GERRATANA, 23rd; KEELEY, 125th; KNOPP, 137th; McDONALD, 148th; MORDASKY, 52nd; MUSHINSKY, 85th; NEWTON, 124th; SAMOWITZ, 129th; SAUER, 36th; SCIPIO, 93rd; STAPLES, 96th.

REPRESENTATIVES BELDEN, *Ranking Member,* 113th Dist.; CARON, 44th; DANDROW, 30th; DeLGOBBO, 70th; FUSCO, 81st; GYLE, 108th; HESS, 150th; MADDOX, 66th; O'NEILL, 69th; PISCOPO, 76th; SANTA-MARIA, 107th; SCALZO, 111th; WINKLER, 41st.

GENERAL LAW

SENATORS COLAPIETRO, *Chm.,* 31st Dist.; LeBEAU, *Vice Chm.,* 3rd; CIOTTO, 9th.

SENATORS KISSEL, *Ranking Member,* 7th Dist.; UPSON, 15th.

REPRESENTATIVES FOX, *Chm.,* 144th Dist.; CHRIST, *Vice Chm.,* 11th; BOUKUS, 22nd; ESPOSITO, 116th; GREENE, 105th; KIRKLEY-BEY, 5th; SCIPIO, 93rd; TONUCCI, 104th.

REPRESENTATIVES RORABACK, *Ranking Member,* 64th Dist.; CAPPIELLO, 138th; CARON, 44th; METZ, 101st.

GOVERNMENT ADMINISTRATION AND ELECTIONS

SENATORS LeBEAU, *Chm.,* 3rd Dist.; PENN, *Vice Chm.,* 23rd; CRISCO, 17th.

SENATORS LOVEGROVE, *Ranking Member,* 28th Dist.; NIELSEN, 24th.

REPRESENTATIVES BYSIEWICZ, *Chm.,* 100th Dist.; BEALS, *Vice Chm.,* 88th; FLEISCHMANN, 18th; GERRATANA, 23rd; KNOPP, 137th; LANDINO, 35th; MANTILLA, 4th; SAUER, 36th; STRATTON, 17th; WALLACE, 109th.

REPRESENTATIVES SAN ANGELO, *Ranking Member,* 131st Dist.; DICKMAN, 132nd; HAMMERS, 123rd; MAZZOCCOLI, 27th; POWERS, 151st.

SELECT COMMITTEE ON HOUSING

SENATORS HANDLEY, *Chm.,* 4th Dist; JEPSEN, *Vice Chm.,* 27th.

SENATOR LOVEGROVE, *Ranking Member,* 28th Dist.

REPRESENTATIVES FLAHERTY, *Chm.,* 8th Dist.; DIAZ, *Vice Chm.,* 130th; CLEMMONS, 104th; GONZALEZ, 3rd; LESCOE, 49th; O'ROURKE, 32nd.

REPRESENTATIVES SCALZO, *Ranking Member,* 111th Dist.; BOUCHER, 143rd; HERLIHY, 16th.

HUMAN SERVICES

SENATORS HANDLEY, *Chm.,* 4th Dist.; DAILY, 33rd.

SENATOR NEILSEN, *Ranking Member,* 24th Dist.

REPRESENTATIVES KEELEY, *Chm.,* 125th Dist.; ABRAMS, *Vice Chm.,* 83rd; CARDIN, 53rd; CLEMONS, 56th; DIAZ, 130th; HYSLOP, 39th; KIRKLEY-BEY, 5th; THOMPSON, 13th; TRUGLIA, 145th; VILLANO, 91st.

REPRESENTATIVES GARVEY, *Ranking Member,* 67th Dist.; DICKMAN, 132nd; MATTIELLO, 65th; POWERS, 151st; SAWYER, 55th.

INSURANCE AND REAL ESTATE

SENATORS BOZEK, *Chm.,* 6th Dist.; WILLIAMS, *Vice Chm.,* 29th.

SENATOR DeLUCA, *Ranking Member,* 32nd Dist.

REPRESENTATIVES AMANN, *Chm.,* 118th Dist.; ALTOBELLO, *Vice Chm.,* 82nd; CONWAY, 75th; DARGAN, 115th; EBERLE, 15th; FONTANA, 87th; GERAGOSIAN, 25th; HENRICI, 103rd; NARDELLO, 89th; OREFICE, 37th.

REPRESENTATIVES FEDELE, *Ranking Member,* 147th Dist.; CAPPIELLO, 138th; D'AMELIO, 71st; HARKINS, 120th; RYAN, 141st.

INTERNSHIP

SENATORS COLAPIETRO, *Chm.,* 31st Dist.; CRISCO, *Vice Chm.,* 17th; CIOTTO, 9th.

SENATORS SCARPETTI, *Ranking Member,* 22nd Dist.; DeLUCA, 32nd; EADS, 30th;

REPRESENTATIVES SCIPIO, *Chm.,* 93rd Dist.; JARMOC, 59th; TONUCCI, 104th.

REPRESENTATIVES CAPPIELLO, *Ranking Member,* 138th Dist.; CAFERO, 142nd; MADDOX, 66th.

JUDICIARY

SENATORS WILLIAMS, *Chm.,* 29th Dist.; COLEMAN, *Vice Chm.,* 2nd; FONFARA, 1st; LOONEY, 11th.

SENATORS UPSON, *Ranking Member,* 15th Dist.; KISSEL, 7th; SOMMA, 16th.

REPRESENTATIVES LAWLOR, *Chm.,* 99th Dist.; SCALETTAR, *Vice Chm.,* 114th; ABRAMS, 83rd; AMANN, 118th; BYSIEWICZ, 100th; DeMARINIS, 40th; DOYLE, 28th; FELTMAN, 6th; FOX, 144th; FRITZ, 90th; GARCIA, 128th; GODFREY, 110th; GRAZIANI, 57th; GREEN, 1st; HENRICI, 103rd; JARJURA, 74th; MARTINEZ, 95th; McCAVANAGH, 12th; MICHELE, 77th; SAUER, 36th; SCHIESSL, 60th; STAPLES, 96th.

REPRESENTATIVES FARR, *Ranking Member,* 19th Dist.; BERNHARD, 136th; CAFERO, 142nd; CAPPIELLO, 138th; DANDROW, 30th; HAMZY, 78th; MAZZOCCOLI, 27th; NYSTROM, 46th; O'NEILL, 69th; RORABACK, 64th; VARESE, 112th; WINKLER, 41st.

LABOR AND PUBLIC EMPLOYEES

SENATORS PRAGUE, *Chm.,* 19th Dist.; COLAPIETRO, *Vice Chm.,* 31st.

SENATOR GUGLIELMO, *Ranking Member,* 35th Dist.

REPRESENTATIVES DONOVAN, *Chm.,* 84th Dist.; GERAGOSIAN, *Vice Chm.,* 25th; BACKER, 121st; CONWAY, 75th; DeMARINIS, 40th; ESPOSITO, 116th; TULISANO, 29th.

REPRESENTATIVES SANTA-MARIA, *Ranking Member,* 107th Dist.; BOUCHER, 143rd; HAMMERS, 123rd; LOCKTON, 149th.

LEGISLATIVE MANAGEMENT

SENATORS SULLIVAN, *Chm.,* 5th Dist.; JEPSEN, *Vice Chm.,* 27th; CRISCO, 17th; DAILY, 33rd; GAFFEY, 13th; LOONEY, 11th; PENN, 23rd; PETERS, 20th.

SENATORS EADS, *Ranking Member,* 30th Dist.; FLEMING, 8th; FREEDMAN, 26th; GUNTHER, 21st.

REPRESENTATIVES RITTER, *Chm.,* 2nd Dist.; BEAMON, 72nd; CURREY, 10th; DYSON, 94th; FRITZ, 90th; GODFREY, 110th; HARTLEY, 73rd; HYSLOP, 39th; LYONS, 146th; PUDLIN, 24th, STILLMAN, 38th; TULISANO, 29th.

REPRESENTATIVES WARD, *Ranking Member,* 86th. Dist.; BELDEN, 113th; CAFERO, 142nd; COLLINS, 117th; FAHRBACH, 61st; FLAHERTY, 68th; PRELLI, 63rd.

PLANNING AND DEVELOPMENT

SENATORS COLEMAN, *Chm.,* 2nd Dist; GAFFEY, *Vice Chm.,* 13th.

SENATOR GENUARIO, *Ranking Member,* 25th Dist.

REPRESENTATIVES DAVIS, *Chm.,* 50th Dist.; WIDLITZ, *Vice Chm.,* 98th; CARUSO, 126th; CLEMONS, 56th; CLEMMONS, 140th; GREENE, 105th; JOHNSTON, 51st; LANDINO, 35th; PANARONI, 102nd; SAMOWITZ, 129th; SERRA, 33rd.

REPRESENTATIVES LOCKTON, *Ranking Member,* 149th Dist.; BERNHARD, 136th; GOOGINS, 31st; MILLER, 122nd; RYAN, 141st.

PROGRAM REVIEW AND INVESTIGATIONS

SENATORS DAILY, *Ranking Member,* 33rd Dist.; COLEMAN, 2nd; JEPSEN, 27th; LOONEY, 11th.

SENATORS LOVEGROVE, *Chm.,* 28th Dist.; NICKERSON, 36th, SMITH, 14th.

REPRESENTATIVES JARJURA, *Chm.,*74th Dist.; SCALETTAR, 114th; VILLANO, 91st.

REPRESENTATIVES WASSERMAN, *Ranking Member*, 106th Dist.; DELGOBBO, 70th; MATTIELLO, 65th.

PUBLIC HEALTH

SENATORS HARP, *Chm.,* 10th Dist.; PETERS, *Vice Chm.,* 20th; PRAGUE, 19th.

SENATORS GUNTHER, *Ranking Member,* 21st Dist.; COOK, 18th.

REPRESENTATIVES McDONALD, *Chm.,* 148th Dist.; GERRATANA, *Vice Chm.,* 23rd; CONCANNON, 34th; DONOVAN, 84th; FLEISCHMANN, 18th; MALONE, 47th; MARTINEZ, 95th; McGRATTAN; 42nd; MANTILLA, 4th; NARDELLO, 89th; ORANGE, 46th; PUDLIN, 24th; RYAN, 139th.

REPRESENTATIVES GYLE, *Ranking Member,* 108th Dist.; CLEARY, 80th, DICKMAN, 132nd; FAHRBACH, 61st; STONE, 134th; WINKLER, 41st.

PUBLIC SAFETY

SENATORS PENN, *Chm.,* 23rd Dist.; LeBEAU, *Vice Chm.,* 3rd.

SENATOR SCARPETTI, *Ranking Member,* 22nd Dist.

REPRESENTATIVES DARGAN, *Chm.,* 115th Dist.; MIKUTEL, *Vice Chm,* 45th; CARTER, 7th; CLEMMONS, 104th; CONWAY, 75th; ESPOSITO, 116th; GONZALEZ, 3rd; McGRATTAN, 42nd; MANTILLA, 4th; ORANGE, 48th; O'ROURKE, 32nd; PANARONI, 102nd.

REPRESENTATIVES CARON, *Ranking Member,* 44th Dist.; COLLINS, 117th; DEPINO, 97th; FERRARI, 62nd; FUSCO, 81st; SAN ANGELO, 131st; SANTAMARIA, 107th; TERCYAK, 26th.

REGULATIONS REVIEW

SENATORS BOZEK, *Chm.,* 6th Dist.; LOONEY, *Vice Chm.,* 11th; LeBEAU, 3rd.

SENATORS GUNTHER, *Ranking Member,* 21st Dist.; EADS, 30th; FLEMING, 8th.

REPRESENTATIVES KNOPP, *Ranking Member,* 137th; MORDASKY, 52nd; STRATTON, 17th; TULISANO, 29th.

REPRESENTATIVES O'NEILL, *Chm.,* 69th Dist.; CLEARY, 80th Dist.; COLLINS, 117th; FLAHERTY, 68th.

TRANSPORTATION

SENATORS CIOTTO, *Chm.,* 9th Dist.; McDERMOTT, *Vice Chm.,* 34th; BOZEK, 6th; COLAPIETRO, 31st.

SENATORS ANISKOVICH, *Ranking Member,* 12th Dist.; NICKERSON, 36th; SCARPETTI, 22nd.

REPRESENTATIVES COCCO, *Chm.,* 127th Dist.; ROY, *Vice Chm.,* 119th; DOYLE, 28th; GELSI, 58th; GREEN, 1st; LESCOE, 49th; MALONE, 47th; O'ROURKE, 32nd; PANARONI, 102nd; SERRA, 33rd; STILLMAN, 38th.

REPRESENTATIVES SIMMONS, *Ranking Member,* 43rd Dist.; DePINO, 97th; FEDELE, 147th; GARVEY, 67th; HAMZY, 78th; HARKINS, 120th; SAWYER, 55th.

LENGTH OF LEGISLATIVE SESSIONS

From 1887 through 1970, the General Assembly met in biennial sessions pursuant to Amendment XXVII to the Constitution of 1818, adopted October 1884.

Year	Convened	Adjourned
1887	Wednesday, January 5th	Thursday, May 19th
1889	Wednesday, January 9th	Saturday, June 22nd
1891	Wednesday, January 7th	Dead-locked Session
1893	Wednesday, January 4th	Friday, June 30th
1895	Wednesday, January 9th	Tuesday, July 9th
1897	Wednesday, January 6th	Saturday, June 12th
1899	Wednesday, January 4th	Tuesday, June 20th
1901	Wednesday, January 9th	Monday, June 17th
1903	Wednesday, January 7th	Thursday, June 18th
1905	Wednesday, January 4th	Wednesday, July 19th
1907	Wednesday, January 9th	Thursday, August 1st
1909	Wednesday, January 6th	Tuesday, August 24th
1911	Wednesday, January 4th	Tuesday, September 26th
1913	Wednesday, January 8th	Wednesday, June 4th
1915	Wednesday, January 6th	Tuesday, May 18th
1916	Tuesday, September 12th*	Tuesday, September 12th
1917	Wednesday, January 3rd	Thursday, May 17th
1918	Tuesday, March 19th*	Wednesday, March 20th
1919	Wednesday, January 8th	Thursday, May 8th
1920	Tuesday, September 14th*	Tuesday, September 14th
1920	Tuesday, September 21st*	Tuesday, September 21st
1921	Wednesday, January 5th	Wednesday, June 8th
1923	Wednesday, January 3rd	Wednesday, June 6th
1925	Wednesday, January 7th	Wednesday, June 3rd
1927	Wednesday, January 5th	Friday, May 6th
1929	Wednesday, January 9th	Wednesday, May 8th
1929	Tuesday, August 6th*	Tuesday, August 6th
1931	Wednesday, January 7th	Wednesday, May 27th
1933	Wednesday, January 4th	Wednesday, June 7th
1935	Wednesday, January 9th	Wednesday, June 5th
1936	Thursday, November 5th*	Wednesday, December 9th
1937	Wednesday, January 6th	Wednesday, June 9th
1939	Wednesday, January 4th	Wednesday, June 7th
1941	Wednesday, January 8th	Wednesday, June 4th
1942	Monday, October 19th*	Monday, October 19th
1943	Wednesday, January 6th	Wednesday, May 19th
1944	Monday, January 24th*	Friday, January 28th
1944	Monday, June 19th*	Tuesday, June 20th
1945	Wednesday, January 3rd	Wednesday, June 6th
1946	Tuesday, May 7th*	Friday, May 17th

LENGTH OF LEGISLATIVE SESSIONS

Year	Convened	Adjourned
1947	Wednesday, January 8th	Tuesday, June 3rd
1948	Tuesday, February 17th*	Thursday, February 26th
1948	Monday, August 23rd*	Wednesday, August 25th
1949	Wednesday, January 5th	Wednesday, June 8th
1949	Tuesday, June 14th*	Thursday, June 30th[1]
1949	Wednesday, October 5th*	Thursday, October 6th
1949	Wednesday, November 9th*	Thursday, December 1st
1950	Thursday, March 9th*	Friday, May 26th[2]
1950	Tuesday, September 5th*	Friday, September 15th
1951	Wednesday, January 3rd	Wednesday, June 6th
1951	Wednesday, June 13th*	Wednesday, June 13th
1953	Wednesday, January 7th	Friday, May 29th
1955	Wednesday, January 5th	Wednesday, June 8th
1955	Wednesday, June 22nd*	Friday, June 24th
1955	Wednesday, November 9th*	Thursday, December 15th
1957	Wednesday, January 9th	Wednesday, June 5th
1957	Tuesday, September 17th*	Tuesday, October 1st
1958	Tuesday, March 4th*	Friday, April 18th[3]
1959	Wednesday, January 7th	Wednesday, June 3rd
1961	Wednesday, January 4th	Wednesday, June 7th
1963	Wednesday, January 9th	Wednesday, June 5th
1963	Wednesday, June 26th*	Wednesday, June 26th
1964	Tuesday, April 21st*	Thursday, April 23rd
1964	Monday, August 3rd*	Thursday, September 10th
1964	Tuesday, November 10th*	Friday, January 29th, 1965
1965	Tuesday, February 2nd[6]defined.	Wednesday, June 9th
1965	Monday, December 13th*	Monday, December 13th
1967	Wednesday, January 4th	Wednesday, June 7th
1969	Wednesday, January 8th	Wednesday, June 4th
1969	Monday, June 23rd*	Thursday, June 26th
1970	Tuesday, October 6th*	Tuesday, October 6th

LENGTH OF LEGISLATIVE SESSIONS

Beginning in 1971, the General Assembly has met in annual sessions pursuant to Article III of the Amendments to the Constitution of 1965, adopted November 25, 1970. The houses (Senate and House of Representatives) of the General Assembly convene on the same date, but may adjourn on different dates. The dates listed below for the adjournment of the General Assembly indicate the date of adjournment of the house that was last in session.

Year	Convened	Adjourned
1971	Wednesday, January 6th	Wednesday, June 9th
1971	Friday, June 11th*	Thursday, August 12th
1972	Wednesday, February 9th	Wednesday, May 3rd
1972	Tuesday, May 16th*	Tuesday, May 23rd
1972	Monday, June 12th*	Thursday, June 16th
1972	Tuesday, September 19th*	Wednesday, January 3rd, 1973
1973	Wednesday, January 3rd	Friday, June 1st
1974	Wednesday, February 6th	Wednesday, May 8th
1975	Wednesday, January 8th	Wednesday, June 4th
1975	Monday, July 21st*	Friday, August 8th
1975	Monday, December 1st*	Thursday, December 4th
1976	Wednesday, February 4th	Wednesday, May 5th
1977	Wednesday, January 5th	Wednesday, June 8th
1978	Wednesday, February 8th	Wednesday, May 3rd
1979	Wednesday, January 3rd	Wednesday, June 6th
1979	Monday, July 30th*	Monday, July 30th
1979	Monday, July 30th*	Monday August 13th
1979	Wednesday, October 31st*	Tuesday, November 20th
1980	Wednesday, February 6th	Wednesday, May 7th
1981	Wednesday, January 7th	Wednesday, June 3rd
1981	Friday, July 31st*	Friday, July 31st
1981	Thursday, November 19th*	Monday, January 25, 1982
1982	Wednesday, February 3rd	Wednesday, May 5th
1982	Monday, June 28th*	Wednesday, June 30th
1983	Wednesday, January 5th	Wednesday, June 8th
1983	Friday, June 10th*	Wednesday, June 29th
1983	Monday, July 25th*	Monday, July 25th
1983	Tuesday, October 11th*	Thursday, October 13th
1983	Friday, December 9th*	Friday, December 9th
1984	Wednesday, February 8th	Wednesday, May 9th
1984	Monday, June 25th*	Monday, June 25th
1985	Wednesday, January 9th	Wednesday, June 5th
1985	Wednesday, July 24th**	Thursday, July 25th
1986	Wednesday, February 5th	Wednesday, May 7th
1986	Wednesday, May 21st*	Friday, June 6th
1986	Wednesday, June 11th*	Friday, June 13th
1986	Monday, June 23rd*	Monday June 23rd

Year	Convened	Adjourned
1986	Monday, June 23rd*	Tuesday, July 1st
1987	Wednesday, January 7th	Wednesday, June 3rd
1987	Wednesday, July 22nd*	Wednesday, July 22nd
1988	Wednesday, February 3rd	Wednesday, May 4th
1988	Monday, June 20th*	Monday, June 20th
1989	Wednesday, January 4th	Wednesday, June 7th
1989	Monday, July 17th*	Monday, July 17th
1990	Wednesday, February 7th	Wednesday, May 9th
1990	Monday, June 25th*	Monday, June 25th
1991	Wednesday, January 9th	Wednesday, June 5th
1991	Wednesday, June 5th*	Thursday, September 19th
1991	Wednesday, June 12th*	Wednesday, June 12th
1991	Wednesday, June 26th*	Thursday, June 27th
1991	Monday, June 29th*	Monday, July 6th
1991	Wednesday, September 11th*	Monday, September 16th
1991	Monday, November 18th*	Wednesday, December 18th
1992	Wednesday, February 5th	Wednesday, May 6th
1992	Tuesday, May 12th*	Monday, June 1st
1992	Monday, June 22nd*	Monday, July 6th
1993	Wednesday, January 6th	Wednesday, June 9th
1993	Thursday, June 10th*	Thrusday, June 17th
1993	Wednesday, September 22nd*	Monday, September 27th
1993	Wednesday, October 20th*	Wednesday, October 20th
1994	Wednesday, February 9th	Wednesday, May 4th
1994	Friday, May 6th*	Wednesday, May 25
1994	Wednesday, May 25*	Wednesday, May 25
1994	Wednesday, July 6th*	Wednesday, July 13th
1994	Wednesday, July 13th*	Wednesday, July 13th
1994	Wednesday, October 12th*	Monday, November 28th
1994	Monday, November 28th*	Monday, November 28th
1995	Wednesday, January 4th	Wednesday, June 7th
1995	Wednesday, October 25th*	Monday, November 20th[4]
1996	Wednesday, February 7th	Wednesday, May 8th

[1] The Senate adjourned without date June 30th. The Governor, under the provisions of Article 4, Sec. 9 of the Connecticut Constitution, issued a Proclamation ending the Special Session as of June 30. The House of Representatives, however, met on July 6th and then recessed subject to the call of the Speaker of the House.

[2] The House of Representatives adjourned sine die May 25. The Senate adjourned May 26.

[3] The Senate and House of Representatives recessed on March 20 and reconvened on April 8.

[4] The Senate adjourned Nov. 17. The House of Representatives adjourned Nov. 20.

*Special Session.

**Two Special Sessions on same day.

†Special "Regular" Session (1963 holdover General Assembly).

NOTE: As of the 1971 session, the General Assembly convenes on Wednesday following the first Monday of January in the odd-numbered years and adjourns not later than the first Wednesday after the first Monday in June; and convenes on Wednesday following the first Monday of February in the even-numbered years and adjourns not later than the first Wednesday after the first Monday in May.

POLITICAL DIVISION OF THE CONNECTICUT GENERAL ASSEMBLY SINCE 1887

STATE SENATE

Year	Republicans	Democrats	Other Parties
1887	14	10	
1889	17	7	
1891	7	17	
1893	12	12	
1895	23	1	
1897	24	0	
1899	20	4	
1901	22	2	
1903	18	6	
1905	29	6	
1907	27	8	
1909	31	4	
1911	21	14	
1913	14	21	
1915	30	5	
1917	25	10	
1919	24	11	
1921	34	1	
1923	27	8	
1925	33	2	
1927	34	1	
1929	22	13	
1931	20	15	
1933	17	18	
1935	15	17	Soc. 3
1937	9	26	
1939	16	17	Soc. 2
1941	13	22	
1943	22	14	
1945	15	21	
1947	27	9	
1949	13	23	
1951	17	19	
1953	22	14	
1955	16	20	
1957	31	5	
1959	7	29	
1961	12	24	
1963	13	23	
1965*	13	23	
1967	11	25	
1969	12	24	
1971, 72	17	19	
1973, 74	23	13	
1975, 76	7	29	

Year	Republicans	Democrats	Other Parties
1977, 78	14	22	
1979, 80	10	26	
1981, 82	13	23	
1983, 84	13	23	
1985, 86	24	12	
1987, 88	11	25	
1989, 90	13	23	
1991, 92	16	20	
1993, 94	17	19	
1995, 96	19	17	
1997	17	19	

*1963 holdover General Assembly.

POLITICAL DIVISION OF THE CONNECTICUT GENERAL ASSEMBLY SINCE 1887

HOUSE OF REPRESENTATIVES

Year	Republicans	Democrats	Other Parties
1887	137	109	Ind. 2; Vacancy 1
1889	152	96	Ind. 1
1891	133	116	Ind. 1; Vacancy 1
1893	137	113	Proh. 1
1895	204	46	Peoples 1
1897	218	29	Nat. Dem. 5
1899	180	69	Gold Dem. 3
1901	201	52	Ind. 1; Gold Dem. 1
1903	187	68	
1905	219	36	
1907	189	66	
1909	208	47	
1911	159	99	
1913	130	120	Progressive 6; Pro. Rep. 2
1915	196	60	Progressive 1; Ind. 1
1917	194	64	
1919	189	69	
1921	248	13	Ind. 1
1923	210	52	
1925	239	23	
1927	237	25	
1929	220	42	
1931	182	85	
1933	195	72	
1935	180	85	Soc. 2
1937	167	100	
1939	202	63	Soc. 2
1941	185	87	
1943	202	70	
1945	196	76	
1947	227	45	
1949	180	92	
1951	190	87	
1953	221	58	
1955	184	92	Ind. 3
1957	249	30	
1959	138	141	
1961	176	118	
1963	183	111	
1965*	183	111	
1967	60	117	
1969	67	110	
1971, 72	78	99	
1973, 74	93	58	
1975, 76	33	118	

Year	Republicans	Democrats	Other Parties
1977	58	93	
1978	60	91	
1979, 80	48	103	
1981, 82	69	82	
1983, 84	64	87	
1985, 86	85	66	
1987	59	92	
1988	60	91	
1989, 90	63	88	
1991	62	88	Vacancy 1
1992, 93	64	87	
1994	65	86	
1995, 96	60	91	
1997	55	96	

*1963 holdover General Assembly.

OFFICIALS AND THEIR DUTIES

THE SENATE

President of the Senate

The Lieutenant Governor is the President of the Senate by virtue of her office. It is her duty to preside over the Senate, to recognize members wishing to address the Senate, to put all questions to vote, to decide questions of order and to refer bills to committees. In the event of a tie vote, the Lieutenant Governor may cast a vote to break the tie.

President Pro Tempore

The President Pro Tempore is elected by the Senate from its own members. It is his duty to preside over the Senate in the absence of the President and to appoint the Senate members of all committees, except in those instances when committee appointments are made by resolution.

Majority and Minority Leader

The Senate Majority Leader and the Senate Minority Leader are elected by their respective caucuses and serve as their parties' leading spokespersons in floor debate.

Clerk and Assistant Clerk

The Clerk of the Senate is elected by the members. The Clerk appoints an Assistant Clerk who aids him in carrying out his duties. It is the duty of the Clerk to read all bills, resolutions and other documents presented to the Senate, to keep a record of the day's business, to enter upon a Calendar the bills and resolutions received from the House or from committees; to prepare the Journal, to keep a record available to members of the action to date on all resolutions and bills, to see that copy for printing is prepared and that the daily Journal, Bulletin, Calendar and personal mail are distributed to the members and to sign bills upon engrossment.

Messengers and Doorkeepers

The majority and minority leadership of the Senate appoint doorkeepers, messengers, and a sergeant-at-arms. They serve under the direction of the Clerk and are responsible for addressing the needs of the Senate with respect to messenger service and the distribution of documents.

THE HOUSE OF REPRESENTATIVES

Speaker

The Speaker is elected by the House of Representatives from its own members. It is his duty to preside over the House during its sessions, to appoint the House members of all committees not appointed by resolution, to recognize all persons wishing to address the House, to put all questions to vote, to decide questions of order and to refer bills to committees.

Deputy Speakers

Deputy Speakers are appointed by the Speaker of the House and assume the duties of the Speaker in his absence.

Majority and Minority leader

The House Majority Leader and House Minority Leader are elected by their respective caucuses and serve as their parties' leading spokespersons in floor debate.

Clerk and Assistant Clerk

The Clerk of the House is elected by the members and an Assistant Clerk is appointed by resolution. It is the duty of the Clerk to keep adequate records of the proceedings of the House, to read all bills, resolutions and other instruments presented for action, to keep theJournal and a daily Calendar including accurate records of all transactions between the House and Senate, to keep a record available to members of the action to date on all resolutions and bills, to supervise the distribution of the Journal, Bulletin, and Calendar, and to sign bills upon engrossment.

Messengers and Doorkeepers

The majority and minority leadership of the House appoint doorkeepers, messengers and a sergeant-at-arms. They serve under the direction of the Clerk and are responsible for handling the needs of the House with respect to messenger service and the distribution of documents.

COMMITTEES

There are eight classes of committees in the General Assembly: Standing Committees, Statutory Committees, Select Standing Committees, Joint Special Committees, Senate Special Committees, House Special Cornmittees, Conference Committees and Special Interim Committees.

Standing Committees

Standing committees are those to which bills and resolutions are referred. The names of these committees are designated in the rules. If joint rules are adopted, these committees are Joint Committees. If joint rules are not adopted, as was the case in the 1951 and 1955 sessions, each house appoints its separate committees. Senate members on such committees are appointed by the President Pro Tempore and House members by the Speaker. Under the rules, minority party members of the committees are nominated by the minority party leader of each house.

The joint rules prohibit a standing committee from meeting when either house of the General Assembly is meeting in floor session. Committee appointments are usually made on the opening day of a two-year term. The first person named to a committee by the appointing authority (the President Pro Tempore in the Senate and the Speaker in the House) becomes the chair. The rules usually require that the chair or co-chairs of each committee schedule an organizational meeting within three days after appointment of the members. In all meetings of a joint committee, and at all public hearings, the Senate and House chairs mutually agree as to who shall preside. All questions of order and other proceedings and questions relating to evidence are determined by a majority vote. All matters reported on are first reported to the house in which they originate.

Statutory Committees

There are permanent joint committees that exist by statute and are charged with specific tasks and responsibilities. There are four such committees: The Joint Committee on Legislative Management (Sections 2-71a through 2-71s, C.G.S.); The Program Review and Investigations Committee (Sections 2-53d through 2-53j, C.G.S.); The Regulation Review Committee (Section 4-170, C.G.S.); and the Committee for Legislative Internships (Sections 2-81 through 2-83, C.G.S.).

Select Standing Committees

During the 1997-98 term, there are select joint standing committees on Housing and Children. Any bills favorably reported by these select committees have to be referred to the appropriate joint standing committee.

Joint Special Committees

These committees are appointed to perform a special task and are discharged when that task is completed. The number of members is usually determined by the resolution calling for their appointment. Generally, it is the practice that Senate members are appointed by the President Pro Tempore and House members are appointed by the Speaker. Typical committees in this group are the committees to inform the Governor that the House and Senate are in joint session, and special investigating committees to function during the session.

Senate Special Committees

These committees are generally of a temporary nature and arise either from the Senate rules or from specific resolution. Unless otherwise designated, the members are appointed by the President Pro Tempore. Committees in this group may include the committee on Senate appointments and the committee on canvass of vote for State senators.

House Special Committees

These committees are also of a temporary nature and arise either from the House rules or from specific resolution. Unless otherwise designated, the members are appointed by the Speaker. Committees in this group may include the committee on canvass of vote for State representatives and the committee on seating arrangements.

Committee of Conference

When the Senate and House pass differing versions of the same bill, a committee of conference may be appointed to reconcile the differences and propose compromises which may make the matter acceptable to both houses. Any member may request that a committee of conference be appointed and the rules usually provide that such committee shall consist of three or more, and an equal number, from each house, appointed by the President Pro Tempore of the Senate and the Speaker of the House, respectively. At least one of the appointments from each house must be from the non-prevailing side of the vote in that house and at least one of the appointments, from each chamber must be from that chamber's minority party membership.

Special Interim Committees

The General Assembly sometimes finds it desirable to establish special joint study committees to examine a particular topic during the interim period between regular sessions. All standing committees continue in operation during interim periods.

ENACTMENT OF BILLS

Prior to the opening of the odd-year session and for a limited time thereafter (as specified in the joint rules), members and members-elect of the General Assembly may file proposed bills and resolutions in the house in which they serve. In even-year sessions, individual legislators may introduce only those proposed bills and resolutions that are of a fiscal nature. Standing committees may introduce bills on any topic in any regular session of the General Assembly.

Proposed bills are not written in full statutory language. Rather, they state briefly (usually in a single paragraph), the substance of the proposed legislation in informal, nonstatutory language. Bills written in formal statutory language may be introduced only by a committee. Proposed bills may be jointly sponsored by Senators and Representatives, and any member may co-sponsor a proposed bill originating in either house by requesting the Clerk to add his name to the list of sponsors.

The member presents the proposed bill to the Clerk of the House or Senate who assigns it a number. First reading of a proposed bill or resolution is by title and reference to a committee or by acceptance by the house of a printed list, distributed to the members, of the bills and resolutions with their numbers, sponsors, and titles, and the committees to which they have been referred. It is then recorded in the Journal by number and title, with a brief statement of purpose, and is sent to the other house for concurrent reference.

The committee separates the proposed bills referred to it into subject categories and, after providing legislators with time to express their views on these proposed bills, prepares fully drafted bills on those subjects on which it feels bills should be drafted. These are "committee" bills drafted in formal statutory language. A committee may also choose to draft a bill on a wholly new subject. Such bills are called "raised" bills. Committee bills and raised bills are also sent to both houses for a first reading, and then referred to their original committee for consideration.

Public Hearing

The staff of the committee to which the bill is assigned sends notice of the date and place of a public hearing to the member who introduced any proposed bill upon which the committee bill that is being heard is based. Upon request, such notices are also provided to other interested persons. Hearing notices are also published in the Bulletin.

Committee Action

After the public hearing, the committee meets to decide upon its action on the bill. Notice of such meeting is published in the Bulletin and all meetings are open to the public. The committee has several options: (1) A "favorable" report which indicates that a majority of the committee favors the bill and recommends its passage; (2) a "favorable substitute," that is a bill amended by the committee before it is favorably reported; (3) a vote to reject, or to "box," the bill; (4) an "unfavorable" report, which indicates that a majority of the committee opposes the bill and recommends its rejection. A committee may also vote a "change of reference" or a "favorable change of reference" to another committee. As the General Assembly seldom accepts or rejects a bill contrary to a committee's recommendation, it is important for any member interested in its passage or rejection to secure substantial backing and to present convincing arguments on the matter to the committee. The rules permit the members of a committee from each house to act separately in reporting bills to their respective houses. Such a provision may be necessary when the House is controlled by one party and the Senate by another.

The Bill in the House and Senate

Upon a favorable vote, the bill must be first reviewed by the Legislative Commissioners' Office and approved by a Legislative Commissioner before being sent to the house in which it was introduced. The Legislative Commissioners then deliver the bill to the Clerk of the House or Senate, as the case may be, who, under the order of business, "Reports of Committees," presents the report to the particular house. Without discussion, the bill is read the second time (by title only) and laid on the table. Each favorably reported bill is printed and receives a file number distinct from the original bill number. No further action on the bill can be taken until the second day succeeding the day on which it is placed in the files which are provided for the purpose on the desk of each member. Bills are placed on the Calendar by title, file number, and bill number in the order in which they are received from committee. Bills that are ready for action (that is, which have been in the files of the members for two days) are marked with an "XX" on the Calendar. They are taken up in the order in which they appear on the Calendar. The third and final reading of the bill is ordinarily by title only, but any member may request that it be read in full. Following the reading of the bill, a member of the committee which reported it explains the committee's reasons for so doing, and a general debate on the bill is in order. There may be a consent calendar on which bills, designated by the majority and minority leaders of the house in which they are pending, may be placed and passed on motion without debate. Any member may move for removal of a bill from the consent calendar and, when so removed, the bill is considered on the regular calendar.

Amendments must be in typewritten form and may be offered by members at any time prior to final passage. They are prepared in the Legislative Comissioners' Office at the request of a member. If a bill is amended on third reading other than to correct clerical errors or mistakes as to forms or dates, the amendment must be approved by a Legislative Commissioner and the bill, as amended, must be reprinted and returned in its new form to the members' files before it can be passed.

Passage and Engrossment

After a bill has passed on the third reading, it is held for one day for a motion to reconsider, which can only be made by a member on the prevailing side of the vote. If not reconsidered, the bill is transmitted to the other house. If the other house amends the bill, it comes back to the first house for concurrence in the amendments. If the amendments are not concurred in, a conference committee may be appointed to resolve the differences. When passed by both houses, the bill is delivered to the Legislative Commissioners' Office for engrossing and supervision of printing in its final form. It is then signed by a Legislative Commissioner, the Clerk of the Senate and the Clerk of the House, and transmitted by the Clerks to the Secretary of the State who presents it to the Governor for his approval or veto.

Action by the Governor

If the Governor receives the bill while the legislature is in session, he has five calendar days, exclusive of Sundays and holidays, in which to sign it or return it to the house in which it originated with a statement of his objections. In the latter case, the bill may be reconsidered and, if passed by at least two-thirds of the members of each house of the General Assembly, it becomes law. If the Governor does not sign or veto the bill within five calendar days after the same has been presented to him, Sundays and holidays excepted, it automatically becomes law unless the General Assembly has adjourned the regular or special session. If the regular or special session has adjourned, the bill becomes law unless the Governor, within fifteen calendar days after it has been presented to him, transmits it to the Secretary of the State with his objections. In such case, the bill does not become law unless it is reconsidered and repassed by the General Assembly by at least two-thirds of the members of each house of the General Assembly at the time of its reconvening for its constitutionally mandated session to reconsider such vetoes.

Veto Session

If the Governor vetoes any bill or bills after the General Assembly has adjourned, the Secretary of the State must reconvene the General Assembly on the second Monday after the last day on which the Governor is either authorized to transmit or has transmitted every bill to the Secretary with his objections (Section 15 of Article IV of the State Constitution), provided if such Monday falls on a legal holiday the General Assembly is reconvened on the next following day. The reconvened session is for the sole purpose of reconsidering and, if the General Assembly so desires, repassing such bills. The General Assembly must adjourn sine die not later than three days following its reconvening.

SECTION IV

STATE GOVERNMENT
EXECUTIVE AND ADMINISTRATIVE

Elective State Officers
and Personnel

State Departments and Related Agencies
Boards and Commissions

ELECTIVE STATE OFFICERS AND PERSONNEL OF OFFICES

GOVERNOR

Address: Room 200, State Capitol, Hartford 06106. Tel., (860) 566-4840.

Governor, John G. Rowland; *Chief of Staff,* David W. O'Leary; *Deputy Chief of Staff,* Brendan M. Fox; *Legal Counsel,* Mary Ann Hanley; *Legislative Dir.,* George E. Krivda; *Dir. of Communications,* Dean C. Pagani; *Deputy Dir. of Communications,* Nuala A. Forde; *Secy. to Governor,* Kathleen C. Mengacci; *Scheduler for Governor,* Christine D. Corey; *Dir. of Constituent Services,* Michael J. Martone; *Dir. of Urban Affairs,* Dennis J. King.

GOVERNOR'S BRIDGEPORT OFFICE. Rosa J. Correa, Dir., 10 Middle St., 1st Floor, Bridgeport 06604. Tel., (203) 336-8700; FAX, (203) 339-4440.

GOVERNOR'S EASTERN CONNECTICUT OFFICE. Michael F. Doyle, Dir., 171 Salem Tpke., P.O. Box 1007, Norwich 06360. Tel., (860) 886-0555; FAX, (860) 823-3111.

CONNECTICUT'S WASHINGTON OFFICE. Ruth B. Ravitz, Dir., 444 North Capitol St., N.W., Suite 317, Washington, D.C. 20001. Tel., (202) 347-4535; FAX, 347-7151. F*ederal Affairs Asst.,* Maria L. Gamble; *DEP Congressional Liason,* Rachel Towbin.

GOVERNOR'S MILITARY STAFF. *Adjutant General/Chief of Staff,* Maj. Gen. David W. Gay, Manchester; *Asst. Adjutant General (Air)/Deputy Chief of Staff,* Brig. Gen. George A. Demers, Suffield; *Asst. Adjutant General (Army),* Brig. Gen. Frank Avallone, Branford; *Chief of Staff (Air),* Brig. Gen. Kenneth W. Mahon, Windsor; *Senior Pilot,* Col. Albert A. Rubino, Windsor Locks; *Surgeon General,* Col. Joseph P. Wierzbinski, Madison; *Marine Corp Reserve Aide-de-Camp,* Col. Christopher B. Burnham, Stamford; *U.S. Air Force Reserve Aide-de-Camp,* Col. Eugene F. Sullivan, Windsor; *U.S. Marine Corp Reserve Aide-de-Camp,* Col. Carl R. Venditto, Southington; *U.S. Army Reserve Aide-de-Camp,* Col. Lawrence J. Ebner; Wethersfield; *Aides-de-Camp,* Maj. Charles E. Alfano, Somers; Maj. Francis G. Brennan, Waterbury; Col. William A. Cugno, Southington; Col. Aldor J. Dubois, Glastonbury; Col. Mary Ann Epps, Hartford; Maj. J. Timothy Krusko, Watertown; Lt. Comdr. John F. O'Neill, West Hartford; Col. Roy R. Pinette, Avon; Capt. Louis R. Rell, Brookfield; SFC James R. Wagner, Rocky Hill; Maj. Steven K. Wilson, Kensington; Col. Ireneusz J. Zembrzuski, Berlin; *Ex officio members:* Maj. Robert A. Burnham, Enfield, Commandant, First Company, Governor's Foot Guard; Maj. Richard E. Erff, Westbrook, Commandant, Second Company, Governor's Foot Guard; Maj. Richard J. Belliveau, Wallingford, Commandant, First Company, Governor's Horse Guard; Maj. Peter E. Moritz, Ridgefield, Commandant, Second Company, Governor's Horse Guard.

GOVERNOR'S CABINET. *Administrative Services,* Comr. Barbara A. Waters; *Agriculture,* Comr. Shirley Ferris; *Banking,* Comr. John P. Burke; *Children and Families,* Comr. Linda D'Amario Rossi; *Consumer Protection,* Comr. Mark A. Shiffrin; *Correction,* Comr. John J. Armstrong; *Economic and Community Development,* Comr. Peter N. Ellef, *Conn. Development Authority,* Pres./Chm. Arthur H. Diedrick; *Education,* Comr. Theodore S. Sergi; *Environmental Protection,* Comr. Sidney J. Holbrook; *Higher Education,* Comr. Andrew G. De Rocco, Ph.D.; *Insurance,* Comr., George M. Reider, Jr.; *Labor* Comr. James P. Butler; *Mental Health and Addiction*

Services, Comr. Albert J. Solnit, M.D.; *Mental Retardation,* Comr. Peter H. O'Meara; *Motor Vehicles,* Comr. Jose O. Salinas; *Policy and Management,* Secy. Michael W. Kozlowski; *Public Health,* Comr. Stephen A. Harriman; *Public Safety,* Comr. Kenneth H. Kirschner; *Public Works,* Comr. Theodore R. Anson; *Revenue Services,* Comr. Gene Gavin; *Social Services,* Comr. Joyce A. Thomas; *Transportation,* Acting Comr. James F. Sullivan; *Veterans Affairs,* Comr. Eugene A. Migliaro, Jr.

LIEUTENANT GOVERNOR

Address: Room 304, State Capitol, Hartford 06106. Tel., (860) 524-7384.

Lieutenant Governor, M. Jodi Rell; *Chief of Staff,* M. Lisa Moody; *Exec. Secy.,* Marion T. Stearns.

SECRETARY OF THE STATE

Address, Capitol Office: Room 104, State Capitol, 210 Capitol Ave., Hartford 06106. Tel. (860) 509-6200.

Secretary of the State, Miles S. Rapoport; *Dir. of Programs and Communication,* Bernard L. Kavaler; *Capitol Office Dir.,* Bettye Jo Pakulis; *Planning and Program Coordinator,* Brenda Samuels Woods; *Exec. Asst.,* Rebecca M. Doty; *Admin. Asst.,* Jane Axelby.

Address: 30 Trinity St., P.O. Box 150470, Hartford 06115-0470.

Deputy Secretary of the State, Howard G. Rifkin, (860) 509-6212; *Asst. Secretary of the State,* Thomas Corrigan, (860) 509-6215; *Asst. Secretary of the State,* Americo Santiago, (860) 509-6217; *Managing Atty., Commercial Recording,* Maria M. Greenslade, (860) 509-6006; *Election Services Mgr.,* Thomas H. Ferguson, (860) 509-6100; *Management and Support Services Mgr.,* Jane Ellis, (860) 509-6152; *Records and Legislative Services Mgr.,* Peter J. Bartucca, (860) 509-6135; *Human Resources Mgr.,* Jocelyn Dowdy, (860) 509-6152; *Community Involvement Dir.,* Donna Parsons, (860) 509-6216; *Exec. Asst.,* Gerry Simpson, (860) 509-6113; *Exec. Secys.,* Vicki Albert, Mary Vasquez.

STATE BOARD OF ACCOUNTANCY

Appointed by the Governor for a term coterminous with term of the Governor or until a successor is chosen, Sec. 20-280, Gen. Stat. Address: 30 Trinity St., Hartford 06106. Tel., (860) 509-6179.

Chm., Bernard Blum, CPA, Bloomfield; Donald S. Brodeur, Sr., CPA, Old Lyme; Aaron Lutin, PA, West Hartford; Sherryll Margiotta, Wethersfield; James E. Quinn, Middle Haddam; Sandra M. Schork, Stamford; George G. Veily, CPA, Avon.

Exec. Dir., David L. Guay.

TREASURER

Address: 55 Elm St., Hartford 06106. Tel., (860) 702-3000. Internet Address: www.state.ct.us/ott/.

Treasurer, Christopher B. Burnham; *Deputy Treasurer,* Paul J. Silvester; *Asst. Treasurer/Chief of Staff,* J. Vincent Chase; *Deputy Chief of Staff,* Karen L. Jannetty; *Exec. Secy. to Treas.,* Sharon Brainard; *Asst. Treas, Policy,* Taegan D. Goddard; *Legislative Program Mgr.,* Steven C. Casey; *Communications Dir.,* Patrick J. O'Neil.

SECOND INJURY FUND. *Asst. Treas.,* G. Kevin Saba.

CASH MANAGEMENT DIVISION. *Asst. Treas.,* Larry Wilson; *Cash Reporting/ Accounting & Reconciliation,* vacancy; *Bank Control,* Joseph Higgins; *Cash Control and Forecasting,* Ann McLaughlin; *Short Term Investments,* Harold Johnson.

DEBT MANAGEMENT DIVISION. *Asst. Treas.,* David Warren; *Debt Mgmt. Specialist,* Catherine Boone; *Clean Water Fund Financial Admin.,*Sharon Dixon-Peay.

PENSION FUNDS MANAGEMENT DIVISION. *Alternative Investments,* Everett Miller III; *Acting Chief Investment Officer,* Gary L. Carter.

FINANCIAL REPORTING AND CONTROLS DIVISION. *Comptroller of the Treasury,* Ernest McNeill; *Mgr.,* Lisa R. Carver; *Bus. Mgr.,* Ivars Maidelis; *Personnel Officer,* Theodore Janiszewski; *Unclaimed Property Admin.,* Robert Romanelli; *Info.Technology Admin.,* Leon Rippell.

INVESTMENT ADVISORY COUNCIL. Sec. 3-13b, Gen. Stat. Address: State Treasurer, 55 Elm St., Hartford 06106. Tel., (860) 702-3155.

Ex officio, Secy., Christopher B. Burnham, State Treasurer; Michael W. Kozlowski, Secy., Office of Policy and Management.

Public Members: Chm., Steven W. Hart, Darien; Sherry Brown, Hartford; John W. Heilshorn, Litchfield; Robert Killian, Jr., Hartford; Wilson Wilde, West Hartford.

State Teachers Union Representatives: Clare H. Barnett, Waterbury; John J. Quirke, Southbury; Rosalyn Schoonmaker. *State Employees Union Representatives:* Sidney Lipshires, West Hartford; Joel W. Schweidel, West Hartford.

COMPTROLLER

Address: Room 309, 55 Elm St., Hartford 06106. Tel., (860) 702-3301. Internet Address: www.state.ct.us/otc/.

Comptroller, Nancy Wyman; *Deputy Comptroller,* Mark E. Ojakian; *Exec. Secys.,* Peggy Gray, Joelyn Wheeler; *Exec. Assts.,* Martha Carlson, Robert E. King, Carmen I. Sierra, Michael Sullivan; *Accounts Payable Div. Dir.,* A. Douglas Vallee; *Budget and Financial Analysis Div. Dir.,* John Clark; *Computer Services Div. Dir.,* Carl Kask; *Payroll Services Div. Dir.,* Gary J. Reardon; *Policy Evaluation and Review Div. Dir.,* Jeanne C. Berube; *Retirement and Employee Benefits Div. Dir.,* Steven Weinberger; *Support Services Div. Dir.,* Bernard McLoughlin.

STATE EMPLOYEES' RETIREMENT COMMISSION. Sec. 5-155a, Gen. Stat. Address: 55 Elm St., Hartford 06106.

Chm., Peter R. Blum, Hartford; Dominic Badolato, New Britain; Robert D. Baus, New Jersey; Carmen Boudier, Bloomfield; Charles Casella, East Hartford; Robert D. Coffey, Amston; Thomas P. Culley, Avon; David O. Elliot, Collinsville; Edward Marth, Rhode Island; Steve Perruccio, Middletown; Claude Poulin, Washington, D.C.; Joseph G. Wankerl, Southington; Richard D. Wilber, Canterbury; Linda J. Yelmini, Glastonbury; vacancy.

Ex officio, Secy., Nancy S. Wyman, Tolland.

MEDICAL EXAMINING BOARD FOR STATE EMPLOYEE DISABILITY RETIREMENT.

Appointed by the Governor to serve at his pleasure, Sec. 5-169(c), Gen. Stat.

Edward A. Blanchette, M.D., Glastonbury; Robert L. Chesanow, M.D., Cheshire; Anne H. Flitcraft, M.D., New Haven; Karen E. Grimmell, M.D., Hamden; Michael J. Hodgson, M.D., Collinsville; Jacqueline H. Taback, M.D., Newtown; Eileen Storey, M.D., Winsted.

THE OFFICE OF THE CLAIMS COMMISSIONER

Sec. 4-142a, Gen. Stat. Appointed by the Governor, with the advice and consent of the General Assembly, to serve for a term of four years from the first day in July. The Commissioner shall receive such compensation as is fixed under the provisions of Sec. 4-40. Address: 239 Washington St., Hartford 06106. Tel., (860) 566-2024.

Claims Comr., James R. Smith, Middlebury.

ATTORNEY GENERAL

Address: 55 Elm St., Hartford 06106. Tel., (860) 566-3579. Internet Address: www.cslnet.ctstateu.edu/attygenl.

Attorney General, Richard Blumenthal; *Deputy Attorney General,* Aaron S. Bayer; *Associate Attorneys General,* William B. Gundling, Jane S. Scholl, Robert W. Werner; *Dir. of Policy/Communications,* William P. Halldin; *Press Secy.,* Cheryl Y. Fialkoff; *Constituent Services Coordinator,* Kevin T. Mullane; *Special Counsel/Legislation,* Richard F. Kehoe; *Special Counsel/Whistleblower,* Phyllis Hyman; *Special Counsel,* Alvin R. Wilson, Jr.; *Chief Admin. Officer,* Virginia M. Jones; *Exec. Secy.,* Joanne Borysevicz; *Bus. Mgr.,* Kevin Costello; *Law Librarian,* Ann Hayman; *System Mgr.,* Evelyn Godbout; *Citizen Advocacy Team,* Jeffrey A. Meyers, George F. Pekarski; *Personnel Officer,* Richard Campbell.

DEPARTMENT 1—*Antitrust/Consumer Protection:* 110 Sherman St., Hartford, (860) 566-5374. *Dept. Head,* Steven M. Rutstein; Lorrie Lewis-Adeyemi, Valerie J. Bryan, Rachel O. Davis, Garry H. Desjardins, Arnold B. Feigin, Neil G. Fishman, Megan J. O'Neill, Stephen R. Park, Roger F. Reynolds, Phillip Rosario, William M. Rubenstein.

DEPARTMENT 2—*Child Protection:* 110 Sherman St., Hartford, (860) 566-3696. *Dept. Head,* Susan T. Pearlman; Paul J. Bakulski, Michael J. Besso, Renee L. Bevacqua, Beth A. Crawford, Ann Marie DeGraffenreidt, Nina F. Elgo, Hensley M. Flash, Donald R. Green, James Kelly, Michael F. McKenna, Stephen Ment, Kathryn A. Mobley, Maryanne Z. Mulholland, Patricia E. Naktenis, Michael R. O'Connor, Bette L. Paul-Zak, Linda P. Prestley, Anita T. Satti, Carolyn A. Signorelli, Sonia S. Stoloff, Jose A. Suarez, Denise L. Vecchio, Arthur E. Webster, Michael Wertheimer, William J. Wholean, Lawrence G. Widem, Benjamin Zivyon.

DEPARTMENT 3—*Environment:* 55 Elm St., Hartford, (860) 566-2090. *Dept. Head,* Joseph Rubin; Janet Brooks, Brian Comerford, Patricia A. Horgan, Mark P.

Kindall, Mary K. Lenehan, John M. Looney, Kimberly P. Massicotte, Eliot D. Prescott, Robert B. Teitelman, Krista E. Trousdale, Richard F. Webb, David H. Wrinn.

DEPARTMENT 4—*Finance/Public Utilities:* 110 Sherman St., Hartford, (860) 566-4899. *Dept. Head,* John G. Haines; Jonathon L. Ensign, Richard K. Greenberg, Robert L. Klein, Christopher L. Levesque, Shelagh P. McClure, William J. Prensky, Paul M. Scimonelli. One Central Park Plaza, New Britain, (860) 872-1553, Ext. 2114: Robert S. Golden, Mark F. Kohler, Phillip Rosario,Tatiana Sypko.

DEPARTMENT 5—*Child Support:* 55 Elm St., Hartford, (860) 566-4998; 1115 Main St., Bridgeport, (203) 579-6877. *Dept. Head,* Donald M. Longley; Gail M. Barto, Ronald Blanchette, Leo Budnick, Jr., Joseph B. Davis, Wilbur W. Dinegar, Seymour P. Dunn, Andrea Gaines, Kenneth A. Graham, Amy L. Guido, Rochelle Homelson, Thomas H. Hrusa, Stephen J. McGovern, Helene Opocensky, Patricia Pac, Frank J. Rogers, Gail C. Rosenfeld, Robert T. Statchen, Lucia Z. Szarzanowicz, George E. Szydlowski.

DEPARTMENT 6—*Labor Relations:* 55 Elm St., Hartford, (860) 566-3110. *Dept. Head,* Charles A. Overend; Laurie Adler, Thomas R. Clifford, Thadd A. Gnocchi, Beth Z. Margulies, Maria C. Rodriguez, Sharon A. Scully, Richard T. Sponzo, Robert A. Whitehead.

DEPARTMENT 7—*Public Safety/Special Revenue:* 110 Sherman St., Hartford, (860) 566-2832. *Dept. Head,* Margaret Q. Chapple; Henri Alexandre, Richard T. Biggar, Richard T. Couture, Jane B. Emons, Sharon M. Hartley, Loida D. John-Nicholson, Michael J. Lanoue, Ann E. Lynch, Leslie D. McCallum, Madeline A. Melchionne, Stephen J. O'Neill, Terrence M. O'Neill, Stephen R. Sarnoski, Richard M. Sheridan, Steven R. Strom, Robert F. Vacchelli.

DEPARTMENT 8—*Transportation/Public Works/Housing:* 55 Elm St., Hartford, (860) 566-2257. *Dept. Head,* Cornelius F. Tuohy; Michael Arcari, Nancy Arnold, Laurann Asklof, Robert Dagata, George Finlayson, Jr., Priscilla J. Green, Peter R. Huntsman, Robert L. Marconi, Robert T. Morrin, Paul K. Pernerewski, Alan N. Ponanski, Lawrence Russ, Arnold Shimelman, Robert D. Snook, Kenneth N. Tedford, Charles Walsh.

DEPARTMENT 9—*Special Litigation:* 55 Elm St., Hartford, (860) 566-4990. *Dept. Head,* Carolyn K. Querijero; Charles H. Benson, Michael R. Bullers, Susan Q. Cobb, Henry S. Cohn, Gregory T. D'Auria, Thomas J. Davis, Jr., Thomas M. Fiorentino, David E. Ormstedt, Daniel R. Schaefer, Janet A. Spaulding-Ruddell, Paula D. Sullivan, David M. Teed.

DEPARTMENT 10—*Collections/Revenue Enhancement:* 55 Elm St., Hartford, (860) 566-7040. *Dept. Head,* Edward F. Reynolds, Jr.; Judith A. Brown, Judah J. Harris, Denise S. Mondell, Robert A. Nagy, Elizabeth A. O'Dea, Joan E. Pilver, Linda A. Russo, Barbara K. Sperber, Thomas R. Ventre, Gary G. Williams, Glenn A. Woods.

DEPARTMENT 11—*Health/Human Services:* 55 Elm St., Hartford, (860) 566-7334. *Dept. Head,* Richard J. Lynch; Maite Barainca, Hugh Barber, Peter L. Brown, Nyle K. Davey, Karen H. Fritzinger, Patricia A. Gerner, Marianne I. Horn, Jennifer C. Jaff, Patrick B. Kwanashie, Paul J. Lahey, Arnold I. Menchel, Judith A. Merrill,

Edward F. Osswalt, Thomas J. Ring, Henry A. Salton, Christy L. Scott, Felicia R. Suggs, Heather J. Wilson.

DEPARTMENT 12—*Education:* 110 Sherman St., Hartford, (860) 566-7173. *Dept. Head,* Bernard F. McGovern, Jr.; Linsley J. Barbato, Laurie A. Deane, Martha W. Prestley, Ralph E. Urban, James P. Welsh. UCONN Health Center, Farmington, (860) 679-1114: Jane D. Comerford, William N. Kleinman. UCONN, Storrs, (860) 486-4241: Paul M. Shapiro. Conn. State Univ., (860) 493-0115: James J. Grady.

DEPARTMENT 13—*Workers Compensation:* 55 Elm St., Hartford, (860) 566-3495. *Dept. Head,* William J. McCullough; Matthew B. Beizer, Michael J. Belzer, Brewster Blackall, Michael J. Giammatteo, Richard R. Hine, Donna J. Hixon-Smith, Taka Iwashita, Anthony Jannotta, Kenneth H. Kennedy, Jr., Yinxia Long, Sarah J. Posner, Philip M. Schulz, Nancy R. Sussman, Michelle D. Truglia, Ernie R. Walker, Lisa G. Weiss.

CRIMINAL JUSTICE COMMISSION

ARTICLE XXIII of the Amendments to the Connecticut Constitution and Secs. 51-275a, 51-277, and 51-278 Gen. Stat. Said Commission appoints the Chief State's Attorney, Deputy Chief State's Attorney, State's Attorney for a Judicial District and their assistants and deputies. Address: c/o Chm. Francis M. McDonald, 257 Christian Rd., Middlebury 06762.

Appointed by Governor, *Chm.,* Francis M. McDonald, Middlebury; Joyce A. Hopson-King, Burlington; Charles L. Howard, Simsbury; Garrett Moore, Watertown; William J. Sullivan, Waterbury; William L. Wollenberg, Farmington.

Chief State's Attorney, John M. Bailey.

DIVISION OF CRIMINAL JUSTICE

ARTICLE XXIII of the Amendments to the Connecticut Constitution and Sec. 51-276, Gen. Stat. establishes the Division of Criminal Justice as an agency within the executive department, which shall be in charge of the investigation and prosecution of all criminal matters. The division shall have all management rights except appointment of state's attorneys.

Address: 300 Corporate Place, Rocky Hill 06067. Tel., (860) 258-5800. *Chief State's Atty.,* John M. Bailey; *Deputy Chief State's Atty. (Admin., Personnel, and Finance),* Steven M. Sellers; *Deputy Chief State's Atty. (Operations),* Domenick J. Galluzzo.

STATE'S ATTORNEYS
SUPERIOR COURT—JUDICIAL DISTRICTS

Judicial District of Hartford/New Britain: James E. Thomas.
Judicial District of New Haven: Michael Dearington, New Haven.
Judicial District of Waterbury: John A. Connelly, Waterbury.
Judicial District of Fairfield: Donald A. Browne, Bridgeport.
Judicial District of Stamford-Norwalk: Eugene J. Callahan, Stamford.
Judicial District of Litchfield: Frank S. Maco, Litchfield.

Judicial District of Middlesex: John T. Redway, Middletown.
Judicial District of New London: Kevin T. Kane, New London.
Judicial District of Tolland: Patricia A. Swords, Rockville.
Judicial District of Windham: Mark S. Solak, Putnam.
Judicial District of Ansonia/Milford: Mary M. Galvin, Milford.
Judicial District of Danbury: Walter D. Flanagan, Danbury.

SUPERVISORY ASSISTANT STATE'S ATTORNEYS
SUPERIOR COURT—GEOGRAPHICAL AREAS

G.A. # 1: Steven Weiss, Stamford.
G.A. # 2: Joseph Marcello, Bridgeport.
G.A. # 3: Patricia Gilbert, Danbury.
G.A. # 4: Corinne Klatt, Waterbury.
G.A. # 5: Frank McQuade, Derby.
G.A. # 6: James G. Clark, New Haven.
G.A. # 7: Juliett Crawford, Meriden.
G.A. # 8: David Newman, West Haven.
G.A. # 9: Michael Dannehy, Middletown.
G.A. #10: J. Vincent Hauser, New London.
G.A. #11: Mark Stabile, Danielson.
G.A. #12: Cynthia Baer, Manchester.
G.A. #13: John Malone, Enfield.
G.A. #14: Richard Morelli, Hartford.
G.A. #15: Scott Murphy, New Britain.
G.A. #16: John A. O'Reilly, Jr., West Hartford.
G.A. #17: R. Patrick McGinley, Bristol.
G.A. #18: Andrew M. Wittstein, Bantam.
G.A. #19: Nina Rosen, Rockville.
G.A. #20: Robert G. Hall, Jr., Norwalk.
G.A. #21: Thomas M. Griffin, Norwich.
G.A. #22: L. Mark Hurley, Milford.

DEPUTY ASSISTANT STATE'S ATTORNEYS
SUPERIOR COURT—HOUSING SESSIONS

Housing Session at Bridgeport: Judith-Anne Scanlon, Bridgeport.
Housing Session at Hartford: Jessie Bennett, Hartford.
Housing Session at New Britain: Jessie Bennett, New Britain.
Housing Session at New Haven: Judith Rothschild-Rippe, New Haven.
Housing Session at Norwalk: Judith-Anne Scanlon, Norwalk.
Housing Session at Waterbury: Judith Rothschild-Rippe, Waterbury.

JUVENILE PROSECUTORS
SUPERIOR COURT—JUVENILE MATTERS

Administration: Francis J. Carino
Bridgeport: Hillary Bargar

Danbury/Torrington; John H. Kearney
Hartford: Brian Casinghino, Bruce Tonkonow
Middletown: David Cosham
New Haven: Catherine Edwards, Karen S. Hardy-Massaro
Norwalk/Stamford: Joanne Goldberg
Plainville: Joan L. Saglio
Rockville/Willimantic: Joseph J. Kristan, Jr.
Uncasville: William B. Wickwire
Waterbury: Thomas O'Brien

STATE ELECTIONS ENFORCEMENT COMMISSION

Sec. 9-7a, Gen. Stat. Appointed with the consent of the General Assembly. Compensation of members, $50 per day for attendance at commission meetings or hearings, plus reasonable expenses. Address: 410 Asylum St., Room 513, Hartford 06103. Tel., (860) 566-7106; FAX, (860) 566-4402.

Appointed by the Governor, William R. Sokolowski, Ph.D., Wolcott, June 30, 1999.

Appointed by the Pres. Pro Tempore of the Senate, *Vice Chm.,* Albert Rogers, New Haven, June 30, 1997. Appointed by the Senate Minority Leader, *Chm.,* Alice W. Lynch, Westbrook, June 30, 1997. Appointed by the Speaker of the House, Michael H. Handler, Manchester, June 30, 2000. Appointed by the House Minority Leader, Nicholas F. Serignese, Bolton, June 30, 2000.

Exec. Dir./Gen. Counsel, Jeffrey B. Garfield; *Deputy Dir./Asst. Gen. Counsel,* Albert P. Lenge; *Bus. Mgr.,* Kathleen Skomro; *Asst. Bus. Mgr.,* Renee Daignault; *Staff Attys.,* Joan M. Andrews, Ronald M. Gregory; *Investigator,* James F. Mathias; *Auditors,* Ralph V. Hersey, Gregory J. Zepka; *Exec. Secy.,* Joan M. Kalechman; *Clerk,* Lois E. Blackburn.

STATE ETHICS COMMISSION

Chapt. 10, Gen. Stat. Appointed with the consent of the General Assembly. Compensation of members, $50 per day of service, plus necessary expenses. Address: 18-20 Trinity St., Hartford 06106. Tel., (860) 566-4472.

Appointed by the Governor, Maurice T. Fitzmaurice, Wethersfield, Sept. 30, 1997. Kenneth Fellenbaum, Milford, Michael L. O'Connor, Litchfield, Sept. 30, 2000.

Appointed by the Pres. Pro Tempore of the Senate, Jacquelyn Durell, Fairfield, Sept. 30, 1997. Appointed by the Senate Minority Leader, Philip F. DeFronzo, Collinsville, Sept. 30, 1997. Appointed by the Speaker of the House, Evan Dobelle, Hartford, Sept. 30, 1999. Appointed by the House Minority Leader, Stanley H. Burdick, Madison, Sept. 30, 1999.

Exec. Dir./Gen. Counsel, Alan S. Plofsky; *Managing Dir./Comm. Atty.,* Rachel S. Rubin; *Staff Attys.,* Brenda M. Bergeron, Catherine Wassel-Nasto; *Accountant,* Brenda Mathieu; *Clerk,* Cindy Cannata; *Acting Clerks,* Cindy Crelley, France Lee, Sue Read.

FREEDOM OF INFORMATION COMMISSION

Appointed by the Governor, with the advice and consent of either House of the General Assembly, for four years, Sec. 1-21j, Gen. Stat. Compensation of members, $50 per day of service, plus actual and necessary expenses. Address: 18-20 Trinity St., Hartford 06106. Tel., (860) 566-5682; FAX, (860) 566-6474; E-Mail: ERIC.TURNER@PO.STATE.CT.US.

Chm., Frederick E. Hennick, Naugatuck, June 30, 1999. Rosalind Berman, New Haven, June 30, 1997. Andrew J. O'Keefe, Bethlehem, June 30, 1998. Vincent M. Russo, Woodbury, June 30, 1999. Sherman London, Southbury, June 30, 2000.

Exec. Dir./Gen. Counsel, Mitchell W. Pearlman; *Managing Dir./Assoc. Gen.,* Colleen M. Murphy; *Chief Atty.,* Clifton A. Leonhardt; *Dir. of Public Education,* Eric V. Turner; *Comm. Counsel,* Regina M. Hopkins, Barbara E. Housen, Victor R. Perpetua; *Clerk,* Dolores E. Tarnowski; *Bus. Mgr.,* Kathleen L. Skomro; *Asst. Bus. Mgr.,* Renee M. Daignault; *Data Processing Specialist,* Pamela K. Phillips.

STATE DEPARTMENTS AND RELATED AGENCIES, BOARDS AND COMMISSIONS
(As of April 1, 1997)

Office Hours: All state buildings in the Hartford area are open from 8:30 A.M. to 4:30 P.M., Monday through Friday, with the exception of: The State Library and Supreme Court Building, which is open from 8:30 A.M. to 5 P.M., Monday through Friday; 9 A.M. to 1 P.M., Saturday (except holiday weekends). Closed Sundays and holidays.

The Dept. of Motor Vehicles is open from 8:30 A.M. to 4:30 P.M., Tuesday, Wednesday and Friday; 8:30 A.M. to 7:30 P.M., Thursday; 8:30 A.M. to 12:30 P.M., Saturday; closed Monday.

Publications: Each department issues its own serial publications. Requests should be directed to the issuing agency. *Telephone:* For Centrex information and assistance, (860) 566-4200.

DEPARTMENT OF ADMINISTRATIVE SERVICES

COMMISSIONER OF ADMINISTRATIVE SERVICES

Appointed by the Governor, with the advice and consent of either House of the General Assembly, for four years, Secs. 4a-1—4a-2, Gen. Stat. Salary, Comr., $95,000; Deputy Comrs., $83,500. Address: Room 491, State Office Bldg., Hartford 06106. Tel., (860) 566-7528.

Comr., Barbara A. Waters, Southbury, March 1, 1999; *Deputy Comr.,* Alan J. Mazzola, Middletown; *Adm. Mgr.,* Roy B. Dion, Glastonbury; *Process and Quality Improvement Dir.,* Catherine Daly, Cromwell; *Chief Adm. Officer,* Richard M. Cosgrove, Jr., West Hartford; *Communications Specialist,* Donna J. Micklus, Wethersfield; *Dir. of Internal Audit,* Robert Wallace, Coventry; *Dir. of Info. Resources Mgmt.,* Peter R. Hyde, Collinsville; *Policy and Legislative Advisor,* Janis Nome, Canton; *Personnel Admin.,* Steven J. Shapiro, Simsbury; *Dir. of Budget and Fiscal Mgmt.,* James McKenna, Wolcott; *Dir. of Revolving Funds Fiscal Mgmt.,* Elaine Glaski, Berlin; *Dir. of Human Resources Development,* Catherine Bysiewicz-Cluen, Meriden; *Dir. of Internet Services,* William K. Seymour, Glastonbury.

BUREAU OF COLLECTION SERVICES

Sec. 4a-12, Gen. Stat. Address: 363 Russell Rd., Newington 06111. Tel., (860) 666-7503.

Exec. Dir., Wayne R. Seabury, South Glastonbury; *Dir., Info. and Support Services,* Aleksandra Bzdyra, New Haven; *Dir., Revenue Operations,* David H. Swenson, Groton; *Dir., Reimbursement and Recovery Services,* Anil F. Antani, Newington; *Asst. Dir., Operational Measurement and Oversight,* John G. Kearney, Jr., Plymouth.

BUREAU OF TECHNICAL SERVICES

Sec. 4a-2, 51, 75, Gen. Stat. Address: 340 Capitol Ave., Hartford 06106. Tel., (860) 566-7093.

Admin. Mgr., Robert F. Granquist, New Hartford; *Asst. Admin. Mgr., Technical Services,* Mark Bannon, Bloomfield; *Info. Technology Admin.,* Robert A. Mitchell, Thomaston; *Mgr., Business Office Support Systems,* Josephine A. Fox, Storrs; *Dir., Mgr., Computer Support,* Robert Zalucki, Simsbury; *Mgr., Computer Operations,* Michael Mangini, West Hartford; *Mgr., Telecommunications,* William Hastedt, Glastonbury; *Mgr., Technical Support,* Patrick J. Tierney, West Hartford.

BUREAU OF BUSINESS SERVICES

Secs. 4a-2, 51, 4a-75, Gen. Stat. Address: Address: 460 Silver St., Middletown 06457. Tel., (860) 638-3267. Fleet Operations, 190 Huyshope Ave., Hartford 06106. Tel., (860) 566-5940.

Procurement Dir., Edward Jones, Middlefield; *Dir., Fleet Operations,* Stephen Dygus, Kensington.

EMPLOYEES' REVIEW BOARD. Appointed by the Governor, for three years, and until a successor is appointed, Sec. 5-201, Gen. Stat. Compensation of members, $150 per day in lieu of expenses. Address: c/o Chm., DAS Personnel Div., P.O. Box 806, Hartford 06106. Tel., (860) 566-2901.

Chm., Robin E. Miller, Stonington; Paul D. Abercrombie, North Haven; David C. Anderson, West Hartford; Wendella A. Battey, Westbrook; Laurie G. Cain, Simsbury; David A. Dee, Avon; Richard M. McCostis, East Norwalk.

BUREAU OF HUMAN RESOURCES

Sec. 5-199, Gen. Stat. Address: Room 403, State Office Bldg., Hartford 06106. Tel., (860) 566-3081.

Deputy Comr., Alan J. Mazzola, Middletown; *Dir. of Organizational Analysis,* Christina Lawson, Windham; *Adm. Mgr.,* Peter Rozantes, West Granby; *Labor Relations Chief,* Peter Allen, Killingworth; *Workers' Compensation Admin.,* Michael Barletta, Cheshire.

CAREER MOBILITY COMMITTEE. Sec. 4-61t, Gen. Stat. Address: DAS, 165 Capitol Ave., Hartford 06106. Tel., (860) 566-7528.

Ex officio, Chm., Barbara A. Waters, Southbury, Comr. of Adm. Services.

Thelma Ball, Middletown, repr. Dept. of Administrative Services; Barbara Barnwell, Trumbull; Donna Dickson, Portland; Jim French, Plainfield; Oscar Gomez, Springfield, MA; Louida O. Jones, Norwich, repr., Comm. on Human Rights and Opportunities; Joseph J. Kanachovski, Bristol; Laila Maidelis, South Windsor, repr. Office of Policy and Mgmt.; Janis Nome, Canton; Barbara Potopowitz, Niantic, repr. Permanent Comm. on the Status of Women; Brenda Taplin, Middletown; Dale Ursin, East Hampton; Carlos Velez, Bristol; Shirley Williamson, Winsted.

SENIOR EXECUTIVE SERVICE BOARD. Appointed by the Governor for four year terms, Sec. 5-236(d), Gen. Stat. Compensation of members, actual and necessary expenses. Address: DAS Bureau of Human Resources, State Office Bldg., Hartford 06106. Tel., (860) 566-3081.

Joseph A. Belanger, Vernon; Charles Condon, Simsbury; Wayne Dailey, Windham; Patricia Day, West Hartford; James T. Fornabaio, Prospect; J. Robert Tank, Glastonbury.

STANDARDIZATION COMMITTEE. Appointed by the Governor, to serve at his pleasure, Sec. 4a-58, Gen. Stat. Address: Room 491, State Office Bldg., Hartford 06106. Tel., (860) 566-7528.

Chm., Barbara A. Waters, Comr. of Adm. Services; Theodore R. Anson, Comr. of Public Works; Christopher B. Burnham, State Treasurer; James F. Sullivan, Acting Comr. of Transportation; Michael W. Kozlowski, Secy., Office of Policy and Mgmt; Joyce A. Thomas, Comr. of Social Services; Nancy Wyman, State Comptroller.

COMMISSION ON HUMAN RIGHTS AND OPPORTUNITIES

Sec. 46a-52, Gen. Stat. Salary, Dir., $82,500. Compensation of members, none. Address: 21 Grand St., Hartford 06106. Tel., (860) 541-3400. Regional Offices: Capitol Region, 1229 Albany Ave., Hartford 06112. Tel., (860) 566-7710. Eastern Region, 100 Broadway, Norwich 06360. Tel., (860) 886-5703. Southwest Region, 1057 Broad St., Bridgeport 06604. Tel., (203) 579-6246. West Central Region, 50 Linden St., Waterbury 06702. Tel., (203) 596-4237.

Appointed by the Governor, *Chm.,* Ramon Martinez, Jr., Tolland, July 15, 2000. Carmen E. Boudier, Bloomfield; Rev. Christopher L. Rose, West Hartford, July 15, 1998. Hugh L. Carolan, Brookfield; Benjamin F. Rhodes, Jr., Waterbury, July 15, 2000.

Appointed by the Pres. Pro Tempore, Dennis King, Waterbury, July 14, 1999. Appointed by the Senate Minority Leader, Russell C. Williams, Hartford, July 14, 1999. Appointed by the Speaker of the House, Jane L. Glover, New London, July 14, 1999. Appointed by the House Minority Leader, Robert A. Massa, Wethersfield, July 14, 1999.

Exec. Dir., Louis Martin; *Deputy Dir. for Enforcement,* Jewel E. Brown; *Deputy Dir. of Diversity, Education* and *Prevention Programs,* Louida Jones.

HEARING OFFICERS. Appointed by the Governor, to serve at his pleasure, Sec. 46a-57, Gen. Stat., to conduct hearings relative to violations of the Human Rights and Opportunities Law. Compensation, $125 and necessary expenses for each day while conducting hearings.

Ruben E. Acosta, East Hartford; John D. Adams, Enfield; Merle Berke-Schlessel, New Haven; Dennis G. Ciccarillo, New Britain; John F. Daly III, West Hartford; John R. Flores, Newington; Deborah S. Freeman, Hartford; Ronald C. Harris, Windsor; Robert W. Heagney, Simsbury; Donald R. Holtman, East Granby; Carolyn W. Kone, New Haven; Gail S. Kotowski, Guilford; Barbara G. Lifton, Hamden; Thomas C. McNeill, Jr., Avon; Jane B. Monahan, West Hartford; Neil F. Murphy, Jr., Bristol; Margaret D. Northrup, Stamford; Brendan J. O'Rourke, Ridgefield; Helen Z. Pearl, New Britain; Jon L. Schoenhorn, West Hartford; Lea N. Shedd, Hamden; Roxanne E. Sinclair, Waterbury; John F. Stafstrom, Jr., Bridgeport; three vacancies.

STATE INSURANCE PURCHASING BOARD

Appointed by the Governor for a term coterminous with term of the Governor or until a successor is chosen, Sec. 4a-19, Gen. Stat. Compensation of members, necessary expenses. Address: 55 Elm St., Room 118, Hartford 06106. Tel., (860) 566-2148, 6292.

Ex officio, Nancy S. Wyman, State Comptroller.

Chm., Robert J. McLucas, West Hartford; Dorothea E. Brennan, Fairfield; David W. Clark, Simsbury; Cynthia L. DiSano, Ph.D., Branford; Thomas Fitzpatrick, Wethersfield; Robert L. Hill, West Hartford; David M. Landsberg, Durham; Joseph G. Lynch, Portland; William S. Miko, Jr., Monroe; Leslie I. O'Lear, West Hartford; Richard S. Sarnowski, Avon.

MANAGEMENT ADVISORY COUNCIL

Exec. Order 6, dated January 25, 1983. Representatives and alternates elected from managers of each state department defined in Sec. 4-38c of the Gen. Stat. and the Offices of the Attorney General, Comptroller, Secretary of the State, and Treasurer. Agencies assigned to departments for administrative purposes as described in Sec. 4-38f of the Gen. Stat. are considered part of said department for purposes of Council membership.

Chm., David Guay, Secretary of the State; *Vice-Chm.,* Dr. Elise Gaulin-Kremer, Public Health; *Secy.,* Debra Freund, Motor Vehicles; *Past Chm.,* Gary R. Siegel, Mental Health and Addiction Services; *Credentials Chm.,* Hedy Gryszan, Children and Families.

Representatives (R) and Alternates (A) are: *Adm. Services,* C. Thomas Carson (R), David Swenson (A); *Agriculture,* Frank Intino (R); Gabriel F. Moquin (A); *Attorney General,* Ann DeGraffenreidt (R), Priscilla Green (A); *Banking,* Sebastian Scarfe (R), Randolph Connolly (A); *Children and Families,* Hedy Gryszan (R), Al Duran (A); *Comptroller,* Bernard McLoughlin (R), John Clark (A); *Consumer Protection,* Laurence Hannafin (R), Allan M. Nelson (A); *Correction,* Lawrence Mayer (R), Frank Hall (A); *Economic and Community Development,* Ed Dombroskas (R), Meg Yetishefsky (A); *Education,* Robert Babcock (R), Dominic Spera (A); *Environmental Protection,* Joanne Driver (R), vacancy (A); *Higher Education,* vacancy (R), vacancy (A); Patricia Downs (A); *Insurance,* Allen Elstein (R), Jack Gies (A); *Labor,* Carl Buzzelli (R), Jan Schuyler (A); *Connecticut State Library,* Patricia L. Owens (R), David Peck (A); *Mental Health and Addiction Services,* Gary R. Siegel (R), Fred Ferris (A); *Mental Retardation,* John Howard (R), vacancy (A); *Motor Vehicles,* Deborah Freund (R), Nancy McCorkle (A); *Policy and Management,* Kathy Dempsey (R), vacancy (A); *Public Safety,* Paul Fitzgerald (R), Cathleen Simpson (A); *Public Health,* Dr. Elise Gaulin-Kremer (R), Joel Milzoff (A); *Public Utilities Control,* Robert J. Murphy (R), Nicholas Neeley (A); *Public Works,* Joseph Patterson (R), Bruce Cornish (A); *Revenue Services,* Frederick Clark (R); John Kutsukos (A); *Secretary of the State,* David L. Guay (R), Peter J. Bartucca (A); *Social Services,* James Laban (R), Ron DeLuca (A); *Transportation,* David Labossiere (R), Leon Alford (A); *Treasurer,* vacancy (R), Joseph Higgins (A); *Veterans Affairs,* Hugo Adams (R), vacancy (A); *Legislative Management Observer,* James Tracy (R).

STATE PROPERTIES REVIEW BOARD

Sec. 4b-3, Gen. Stat. Compensation of members, $150 per diem up to a maximum of $25,000 annually. Address: Room 123, State Office Bldg., Hartford 06106. Tel., (860) 566-4608; FAX, (860) 566-1314.

Appointed by the Pres. Pro Tempore of the Senate and Speaker of the House, *Vice Chm.,* Jeffrey A. Gebrian, West Hartford, June 30, 1997; Lisa A. Musumeci, Hartford, June 30, 1998; Kenneth M. Fleming, West Hartford, June 30, 1999.

Appointed by the Senate and House Minority Leaders, *Chm.,* Rowland Ballek, Lyme, June 30, 1998; *Secy.,* Pasquale A. Pepe, Ansonia, June 30, 1997; Edwin S. Greenberg, Stamford, June 30, 1999.

Exec. Dir., George D. Edwards.

DEPARTMENT OF AGRICULTURE

COMMISSIONER OF AGRICULTURE

Appointed by the Governor, with the advice and consent of either House of the General Assembly, for four years, Secs. 4-5—4-8, Gen. Stat. Salary, Comr., $75,500. Address: Room 273, State Office Bldg., Hartford 06106. Tel., (860) 566-4667.

Comr., Shirley Ferris, Newtown, March 1, 1999; *Dir., Bureau of Regulation/Inspection,* Dr. Bruce A. Sherman, Brooklyn; *Asst. Dir., Bureau of Regulation/Inspection,* Gabriel F. Moquin, Stafford Springs; *Dir., Bureau of Marketing/Technology,* Robert R. Pellegrino, Enfield; *Fiscal Admin,* Dawn L. Cassada, Newington; *Dir. of Personnel,* Emilie M. Andrews, Branford; *Asst. Dir., Bureau of Marketing/Technology,* Frank A. Intino, South Windsor; *Dir., Bureau of Aquaculture,* John H. Volk, Milford; *Dir., Farmland Preservation,* Joseph J. Dippel, Enfield; *State Veterinarian,* Dr. Jack Meister, Hampton; *Dir., Agriculture Techlnology*, Jane M. Slupecki, MA; *Legislative Liaison,* Melanie J. Attwater; *Exec. Dir., Conn. Marketing Authority*, Robert Badal.

STATE MILK REGULATION BOARD. Appointed by the Governor for a term coterminous with term of the Governor or until a successor is chosen, with the advice and consent of either House of the General Assembly, Sec. 22-131, Gen. Stat. Compensation, $75 per diem.. Address: Dairy Div., Room 273, State Office Bldg., Hartford 06106. Tel., (860) 566-5894.

Ex officio, Chm., Shirley Ferris, Comr. of Agriculture; Stephen A. Harriman, Comr. of Public Health.

Appointed by the Governor, Robert Jacquier, East Canaan; Neil R. Marcus, Redding; Joseph N. Ruwet, Torrington; Frank A. Starvel, Old Greenwich; Mae S. Schmidle, Newtown; Austin I. Tanner, Brooklyn.

GOVERNOR'S COUNCIL FOR AGRICULTURAL DEVELOPMENT. Sec. 22-26e, Gen. State. Compensation, none. Address: c/o Dept. of Agriculture, 165 Capitol Ave., Hartford 06106. Tel., (860) 566-4667.

Ex-officio, Chm., Shirley Ferris, Newtown, Comr. of Agriculture.

Appointed by the Governor, William R. Brophy III, East Granby; Lawrence L. Carville, Vernon; W. A. Cowan, Storrs; Keith A. Frosceno, Hamden; William Hopkins, New Preston; Dorothy R. Jacquier, East Canaan; Robert Kofkoff, Bozrah; Grace C. Nome, West Hartford; John Olsen, Voluntown; Henry M. Rose, South Glastonbury; Michael Smyth, Enfield; Willard C. Stearns, Storrs; Leonard Van Wingerden, Somers; Richard Wyckoff, Granby.

Appointed by the Pres. Pro Tempore of the Senate, Norma O'Leary, Thompson; Lewis A. Tanner, New Preston. Appointed by the Senate Majority Leader, Susan Sankow, Lyme; vacancy. Appointed by the Senate Minority Leader, two vacancies. Appointed by the Speaker of the House, Brian Kelliher, Enfield; Mark Polek, Somers. Appointed by the House Majority Leader, Richard L. Lyons, Stamford; Peter A. Sepe, Sandy Hook. Appointed by the House Minority Leader, Frank J. Papandrea, Cheshire; Stewart Ramsey, Southington.

CONNECTICUT EQUESTRIAN CENTER CORPORATION. Sec. 22-452a, Gen. Stat. Compensation, none. Address: c/o Dept. of Agriculture, 165 Capitol Ave., Hartford 06106. Tel., (860) 566-2683.

Ex-officio, Maj. Richard J. Belliveau, Wallingford; Robert W. Brooks, East Lyme; Kathleen M. McManus, Glastonbury.

Frank A. Intino, South Windsor, Dept. of Agriculture designee; Randall May, Mansfield Ctr., Dept. of Environmental Protection designee; vacancy, Department of Economic and Community Development designee; Patricia E. Lawson-Kelly, Bloomfield, Mayor of Hartford designee; Eric D. Coleman, Bloomfield, Mayor of Bloomfield designee; Stewart W. Beckett, D.V.M., Glastonbury; Mayor of Windsor designee; Appointed by the Friends of Keney Park, Jeffrey A. Stewart, Hartford.

Appointed by the Pres. Pro Tempore of the Senate, Wilson H. Faude, West Hartford. Appointed by the Senate Majority Leader, Joseph D. Pullen, Canton Center. Appointed by the Senate Minority Leader, vacancy. Appointed by the Speaker of the House, John D. Mordasky, Stafford Springs. Appointed by the House Majority Leader, Carol A. Molony, Stratford. Appointed by the House Minority Leader, Richard C. Shaw, South Glastonbury.

CONNECTICUT MARKETING AUTHORITY

Sec. 22-63, Gen. Stat. Salary, Exec. Dir., $70,888. Compensation of members, necessary expenses. Address: Regional Market, 101 Reserve Rd., Hartford 06114. Tel., (860) 527-5047.

Chm., Shirley Ferris, Newtown, Comr. of Agriculture; *Vice Chm.,* Robert R. Pellegrino, Comr. of Economic Development designee.

Appointed by the Governor, John J. Varanelli, Jr., Bethlehem; Maurice E. Yandow, Jr., Wethersfield; vacancy.

Appointed by the Pres. Pro Tempore of the Senate, vacancy. Appointed by the Senate Minority Leader, Frank J. Papandrea, Cheshire. Appointed by the Speaker of the House, Richard Steer, Simsbury; Appointed by the House Minority Leader, George W. Betts, Bristol.

Exec. Dir., Robert A. Badal, Bristol.

DEPARTMENT OF BANKING

BANKING COMMISSIONER

Appointed by the Governor, with the advice and consent of either House of the General Assembly, for four years, Secs. 4-5—4-8, Gen. Stat. Salary, Comr., $87,000; Address: 260 Constitution Plaza, Hartford 06103. Tel., (860) 240-8299; Internet, http://www.state.ct.us/dob/.

Comr., John P. Burke, Middlebury, March 1, 1999; *Dir., Government Relations and Communications,* Robert J. Carragher, South Windsor; *Fiscal Adm. Mgr.,* Michelle Heineman, Wallingford; *Personnel Officer,* Anne Sblendorio, Rocky Hill; *Admin., Depository Institutions,* Joseph A. Pandiscia, Newington; *Bank Div. Dir.* (Bank Examination), Howard F. Pitkin, Jr., Vernon; *Bank Div. Asst. Dirs.* (Bank Examination), Thomas J. Catania, Enfield; Glenn W. Hayes, Wallingford; *Bank Div. Supervising Examiners,* Mary Ellen O'Neill, Cheshire, Sebastian F. Scarfe, Kensington; *Bank Div. Dir.* (Credit Unions), Thomas J. Zaleski, West Hartford; *Bank Div. Dir.* (Consumer Cr.), Robert C. Focht, Glastonbury; *Bank Div. Asst. Dir.* (Consumer Cr.), William Nahas, Jr., Newington; *Bank Div. Dir.* (Securities and Business Investments), Ralph A. Lambiase, Marlborough; *Bank Div. Asst. Dirs.* (Securities and Business Investments), Cynthia Antanaitis, Hartford; Eric J. Wilder, Enfield; *Securities Div. Supervising Examiner,* Sidney A. Igdalsky, West Hartford; *Info. Systems Mgr.,* Michael G. Bannon, New Britain; *Bank Supervising Adm. Atty.,* Gayle S. Fierer, West Hartford; *Communications Specialist,* Gregory E. Futoma, Wallingford; *Communications Officer,* David Tedeschi, Jr., Newington.

DEPARTMENT OF CHILDREN AND FAMILIES

COMMISSIONER OF CHILDREN AND FAMILIES

Appointed by the Governor with the advice and consent of either House of the General Assembly, for four years, Secs. 4-5—4-8, Sec. 17a-5, Gen. Stat. Salary, Comr., $96,305; Deputy Comr., $83,500. Address: 505 Hudson St., Hartford 06106-7107. Tel., (860) 550-6300.

Comr., Linda D'Amario Rossi, Hartford, March 1, 1999; *Deputy Comr./Chief of Staff,* Susan M. Omilian, West Hartford.

CHILD PROTECTION CARELINE, 24-Hour emergency number for reporting abuse or neglect of a child: (800) 842-2288 (TDD: (800) 624-5518). Connecticut Adoption Resource Exchange: (800) 842-6347. Public Affairs and Info. Office: (860) 566-2497.

REGIONAL OFFICES

SOUTHWESTERN REGION—3885 Main St., Bridgeport 06604. Tel., (203) 365-6200.

Reg. Admin., Andrea Routh.

SUB-OFFICE—1616 Washington Blvd., Stamford 06902. Tel., (203) 348-5865.

SUB-OFFICE—25 Van Zant St., Suite 15A, Norwalk 06854.

SOUTH CENTRAL REGION—One Long Wharf Dr., New Haven 06511. Tel., (203) 786-0500.

Acting Reg. Admin., Mary Ellen Tatten.

SUB-OFFICE—Undercliff Rd., Bldg. 2, Meriden 06451. Tel., (203) 238-6185.

SUB-OFFICE—121 Main St.Ext., Middletown 06457. Tel., (860) 638-2100.

EASTERN REGION—2 Courthouse Sq., Norwich 06360. Tel., (860) 886-2641.

Reg. Admin., Thomas Gilman.

SUB-OFFICE—1320 Main St., Willimantic 06226. Tel., (860) 450-2000.

NORTH CENTRAL REGION—250 Hamilton St., Hartford 06105. Tel., (860) 418-8000.

Reg. Admin., Leticia Lacomba.

SUB-OFFICE—364 West Middle Tpke., Manchester 06040. Tel., (860) 533-3600.

SUB-OFFICE—1 Grove St., New Britain 06053. Tel., (860) 832-5200.

NORTH WESTERN REGION—395 West Main St., Waterbury 06702. Tel., (203) 759-7000.

Reg. Admin., Ray Farrington.

SUB-OFFICE—62 Commercial Blvd., Torrington 06790. Tel., (860) 496-5700.

SUB-OFFICE—131 West St., Danbury 06810. Tel., (203) 797-4040.

STATE ADVISORY COUNCIL ON CHILDREN AND FAMILIES. Appointed by the Governor to serve at his pleasure, Sec. 17a-4, Gen. Stat. Compensation of members, necessary expenses. Address: 505 Hudson St., Hartford 06106. Tel., (860) 566-3536.

Ex officio, Linda D'Amario Rossi, Comr. of Children and Families.

Jean A. Adnopoz, Hamden; Albert S. Alissi, D.S.W., Simsbury; Karen Bartis, Hartford; John W. Blanton, Jr., M.D., New Haven; Jane C. Bourns, West Hartford; Donald A. Gaskill, Guilford; Donna Hartigan, Willimantic; Sang Hee Hartigan, Willimantic; Virginia B. Raymond, Storrs; Rick Salwen, M.D., Danbury; Herbert T. Schact, Quaker Hill; Joseph Woolston, M.D., Madison; three vacancies.

ADOPTION SUBSIDY REVIEW BOARD. Sec. 17a-117(c), Gen. Stat. Address: 505 Hudson St., Hartford 06106.

Linda D'Amario Rossi, Comr. of Children and Families; *Dept. of Children and Families;* Janet L. Jackson, West Hartford, *Child Placing Agencing Repr.;* Sandra Killion, Wolcott, *Adoptive Parent Repr.;* vacancy.

HIGH MEADOWS. Facility of Dept. of Children and Families, Sec. 17a-23, Gen. Stat. Value of real property, $8,513,218. Address: 825 Hartford Tpke., Hamden 06517. Tel., (203) 281-8300.

Supt., Gabriel Viada.

LONG LANE SCHOOL. Facility of Dept. of Children and Families, Sec. 17a-3, Gen. Stat. Value of real property, $8,561,322. Address: Long La., Middletown 06457. Tel., (860) 344-2800.

Supt., John Lachapelle.

RIVERVIEW HOSPITAL. Facility of Dept. of Children and Families, Sec. 17a-31, Gen. Stat. Value of real property, $31,191,764. Address: 915 River Rd., Middletown 06457. Tel., (860) 344-2700.

Supt., Carl Sundell.

STATE RECEIVING HOME. Facility of Dept. of Children and Families, Sec. 17a-94, Gen. Stat. Value of real property, $1,664,467. Address: 36 Gardner St., Warehouse Point 06088. Tel., (860) 292-4000.

Supt., James Brown.

WILDERNESS SCHOOL. Facility of Dept. of Children and Families. Value of real property, $1,977,306. Address: P.O. Box 298, East Hartland 06027. Tel., (860) 566-4146.

Dir., Thomas Dyer.

INTERSTATE COMPACT ON JUVENILES. Appointed by the Governor, Secs. 46b-151—46b-151g, Gen. Stat. Address: Interstate Compacts Administration, Undercliff Rd., White Hall Bldg. 2, Meriden 06451. Tel., (203) 238-6405.

Admin., Linda D'Amario Rossi, Comr., Dept. of Children and Families; *Deputy Admin.,* Polly U. Champ.

INTERSTATE COMPACT ON MENTAL HEALTH. Appointed by the Governor, Secs. 17a-615—17a-618, Gen. Stat. For children and youth under the age of 18. Address: Interstate Compacts Administration, Undercliff Rd., White Hall Bldg. 2, Meriden 06451. Tel., (203) 238-6405.

Admin., Linda D'Amario Rossi, Comr., Dept. of Children and Families; *Deputy Admin.,* Polly U. Champ.

INTERSTATE COMPACT ON THE PLACEMENT OF CHILDREN. Appointed by the Governor, Secs. 17a-175—17a-182. Gen. Stat. Address: Interstate Compacts Administration, Undercliff Rd., White Hall Bldg. 2, Meriden 06451. Tel., (203) 238-6405.

Admin., Linda D'Amario Rossi, Comr., Dept. of Children and Families; *Deputy Admin.,* Polly U. Champ.

ADOPTION REVIEW BOARD

Sec. 45a-763, Gen. Stat. Compensation of members, none. Address: 186 Newington Rd., West Hartford 06110. Tel., (860) 566-7897.

Chm., F. Paul Kurmay, Stratford, Probate Court Admin.; Patrick J. Johnson, Jr., West Hartford, Officer of a Child-Placing Agency; Jean Watson, Dept. of Children and Families.

COUNCIL TO ADMINISTER THE CHILDREN'S TRUST FUND

Appointed by the Governor, Sec. 17a-50(b), Gen. Stat. Compensation, none. Address: c/o Children and Families, 505 Hudson St., Hartford 06106. Tel., (860) 550-6473.

Ex officio, Linda D'Amario Rossi, Hartford, Comr., Dept. of Children and Families.

Appointed by the Pres. Pro Tempore of the Senate, Laurie Campbell, Simsbury; vacancy. Appointed by the Senate Minority Leader, Kathleen A. Murphy, Hartford; Richard Sussman, Hartford. Appointed by the Speaker of the House, Matthew J. Broder, Hamden; Frances G. DiFiore, Wethersfield. Appointed by the House Minority Leader, two vacancies.

DEPARTMENT OF CONSUMER PROTECTION

COMMISSIONER OF CONSUMER PROTECTION

Appointed by the Governor, with the advice and consent of either House of the General Assembly, for four years, Secs. 4-5—4-8, Gen. Stat. See Sec. 19-170. Salary, Comr., $75,500. Address: Room 103, State Office Bldg., Hartford 06106. Tel., (860) 566-4999.

Comr., Mark A. Shiffrin, New Haven, March 1, 1999; *Comrs. Office, Chief of Staff,* Raeanne V. Curtis, Hamden; John J. Phelan, Guilford; Anna M. Carbonaro, Plymouth; Thomas P. Cerasulo, Waterbury; Ralph E. Marcarelli, New Haven; George V. Phelan, Norwalk; Diane Chace, New Britain; Marilyn Szemanczky, Rocky Hill.

Attorneys: Neale S. Belgrade, Tolland: Elisa A. Nahas, Newington; Steven J. Schwane, Mansfield Center; Michael D. Spagnoli, Windsor.

Central Licensing Div. Dir., Timothy D. West, New London; *Communications Dir.,* June S. Neal, West Hartford; *Consumer Action Center Coordinator,* Linda D. Becker, Norwich; *Drug Control Div. Dir.,* William P. Ward, Rocky Hill; *Fiscal Admin.,* Susan K. Gray, West Hartford; *Food Div. Dir.,* John F. McGuire, Enfield; *Trades Practices Div. Dir.,* Lois R. Bryant, Glastonbury; *Legislative Liason,* Gordon J. Frassinelli; *Liquor Div. Dir.,* Gerald C. Langlais, Watertown; *Personnel Admin.,* Stephen Caliendo,

Windsor Locks; *Real Estate/Professional Trades Div. Dir.,* Laurence L. Hannafin, Norfolk; *Weights and Measures Div. Dir.,* Allan M. Nelson, Southington.

LIQUOR CONTROL COMMISSION

Commissioner of Consumer Protection serves as Chairman; members appointed by the Governor to serve at his pleasure; Sec. 30-2, Gen. Stat. Salary, members, $42,514. Address: State Office Bldg., Hartford 06106, Tel., (860) 566-4687.

Chm., Mark A. Shiffrin, New Haven; Gary M. Koval, Mansfield Center; Domenic L. Mascolo, Waterbury.

ARCHITECTURAL LICENSING BOARD

Appointed by the Governor for a term coterminous with term of the Governor or until a successor is chosen, Sec. 20-289, Gen. Stat. Address: State Office Bldg., Hartford 06106. Tel., (860) 566-3290.

Norman S. Baier, Jr., New Hartford; Paul H. Bartlett, Fairfield; Laura J. Bordeaux, Hebron; Carole W. Briggs, Hampton; Robert B. Hurd, Rockville.

CONNECTICUT STATE BOARD OF LANDSCAPE ARCHITECTS

Appointed by the Governor for a term coterminous with term of the Governor or until a sucessor is chosen, Sec. 20-368, Gen. Stat. Address: State Office Bldg., Hartford 06106. Tel., (860) 566-3290.

Chm., Vincent C. McDermott, Bethlehem; Dickson F. DeMarche, Bethel; Rudy J. Favretti, Storrs; John Holmes, Vernon; Marianne Pollak, Stamford; Shavaun Towers, Guilford; vacancy.

STATE BOARDS FOR OCCUPATIONAL LICENSING

Appointed by the Governor for a term coterminous with term of the Governor or until a successor is chosen, Sec. 20-331, Gen. Stat. Address: State Office Bldg., Hartford 06106. Tel., (860) 566-3290, 3291.

ELECTRICAL WORK EXAMINING BOARD. Thomas A. Delnicki, South Windsor; Patrick Donahue, Newtown; Ross H. Garber, Hartford; Roger L. Johnson, Jr., Bridgeport; Kenneth B. Leech, Broad Brook; Lewis J. Stanio, Orange; Raymond A. Turri, Torrington; Laurence A. Vallieres, Glastonbury; Frank J. White, Jr., Woodbridge.

ELEVATOR INSTALLATION, REPAIR AND MAINTENANCE WORK EXAMINING BOARD. *Chm.,* John R. DeRosa, Jr., South Windsor; Gerald L. Brown, Jr., Monroe; Paul B. Farnsworth, Northford; Michael D. Griffin, Ellington; Jeffrey J. Hogan; Thomas J. O'Reilly, Brooklyn; vacancy.

FIRE PROTECTION SPRINKLER SYSTEM BOARD. Roger H. Brake, Jr., Trumbull; William A. Fiondella, Guilford; Richard J. Kopchyak, Fairfield; Michael R. Livingstone, Harwinton; John V. Maher, Meriden; Anthony D. Moscato, East Haven; Joseph H. Versteeg, Torrington; Richard Wirth, West Hartford; vacancy.

HEATING, PIPING AND COOLING WORK EXAMINING BOARD. Robert H. Barrieau, West Hartford; Joseph R. Blumberg, Woodbury; Cameron G. Champlin, Jr., Waterford; Michael T. Connor, Waterbury; James M. Eschert, Canton Center; David G. Foster, Westbrook; Joseph Leggo, Newington; Francis J. Limone, East Haven; Leonard F. Murray, Granby

PLUMBING AND PIPING WORK EXAMINING BOARD. Richard T. Chapman, South Glastonbury; Russell W. Fucci, Clinton; Everet L. Gawendo, Norwich; Brian T. Kronenberger, Middletown; Leonard A. Maselli, West Haven; John M. Nettle, Shelton; James Piccoli, Berlin; Peter Romaniello, Waterbury; George C. Sima, Higganum; John R. Sullivan, Winsted; R. Bradley Wolfe, East Granby; R. John Wilcox II, Greenwich.

COMMISSION OF PHARMACY

Appointed by the Governor for a term coterminous with term of the Governor or until a sucessor is chosen, Sec. 20-163, Gen. Stat. Address: State Office Bldg., Hartford 06106. Tel., (860) 566-3290.

Chm., William J. Summa, Jr., R.Ph., Waterbury; Edith G. Goodmaster, New Haven; Robert S. Guynn, R.Ph., Durham; David H. Johnson, Suffield; Domenic A. Sammarco, New Canaan; Frederick C. Vegliante, Killingworth.

STATE BOARD OF EXAMINERS FOR PROFESSIONAL ENGINEERS AND LAND SURVEYORS

Appointed by the Governor for a term coterminous with term of the Governor or until a successor is chosen, Sec. 20-300, Gen. Stat. Address: State Office Bldg., Hartford 06106. Tel., (860) 566-3290.

Chm. Anthony L. D'Andrea, Riverside; Adrienne Camilli, Greenwich; Joseph A. Cermola, New Haven Frank S. Chuang, Wethersfield; John T. DeWolf, Storrs; Andrew G. Farkas, North Haven; William Giel, Milford; Robert Grossenbacher, New Milford; Terry D. McCarthy, Vernon; Curtiss B. Smith, Middlebury; Stanley A. Swimmer, Woodbridge; vacancy.

CONNECTICUT REAL ESTATE COMMISSION

Appointed by the Governor for a term coterminous with term of the Governor or until a successor is chosen, Sec. 20-311a, Gen. Stat. Address: State Office Bldg., Hartford 06106. Tel., (860) 566-5131, 5132.

Chm., John H. Frey, Ridgefield; Janet P. Buckley, West Hartford; Bruce H. Cagenello, Simsbury; Maggie A. Claud, Hartford; Donna M. Hohider, Watertown; Rae D. Tramontano, New Haven; Leonard E. Wells, Mansfield Center; vacancy.

CONNECTICUT REAL ESTATE APPRAISAL COMMISSION

Appointed by the Governor for a term coterminous with term of the Governor or until a successor is chosen, Sec. 20-502, Gen. Stat. Address: State Office Bldg., Hartford 06106. Tel., (860) 566-1546.

Chm., Donato D. Maisano, West Hartford; David F. Ertman, New Haven; Robert J. Kennedy, West Hartford; Gerald V. Rasmussen, Fairfield; Linda M. Sepso, Stratford; A. Howard Spargo, Avon; Nicholas J. Tetreault, Waterbury; vacancy.

STATE BOARD OF TELEVISION AND RADIO SERVICE EXAMINERS

Appointed by the Governor for a term coterminous with term of the Governor or until a successor is chosen, Sec. 20-343, Gen. Stat. Address: Room G-5, State Office Bldg., Hartford 06106. Tel., (860) 566-3290.

Chm., Vincent A. Lanteri, Waterbury; John Bortniak, Stratford; Jack B. Halpert, Bridgeport; Stanley E. Pencikowski, Bristol; vacancy.

STATE TREE PROTECTION EXAMINING BOARD

Appointed by the Governor for a term coterminous with term of the Governor or until a successor is chosen, Sec. 23-61a(b), Gen. Stat. Address: 165 Capitol Ave., Hartford 06106. Tel., (860) 566-3290.

Ex officio, George R. Stephens, North Haven; vacancy.

Chm., Kenneth Bombaci, Essex; Edward Corbett, Coventry; Michael J. Kennedy, Cheshire; Saul Rich, Hamden; vacancy.

BOARD OF PROTECTION AND ADVOCACY FOR PERSONS WITH DISABILITIES

Appointed by the Governor to serve at his pleasure, Sec. 46a-9, Gen. Stat. Address: 60-B Weston St., Hartford 06120-1551. Tel., (860) 297-4300, toll free and TDD (800) 842-7303, TDD (860) 566-2102.

Chm., Stephen Greenspan, Andover; Quincy Abbot, West Hartford; Kathryn Coffin, East Hartford; Durcell Dillon, New Haven; Eileen M. Furey, Ashford; Nora Ellen Groce, Essex; Karen Kangas, West Hartford; Lawrence Kaplan, M.D., Essex; Edward M. Kennedy, Jr., New Haven; Howard Klebanoff, West Hartford; Edward Mambruno, Waterbury; Arthur Pepine, Hamden; Zaida Santiago, Hartford; Suzanne Tucker, Hamden; Phyllis Zlotnick, Newington.

Exec. Dir., James D. McGaughey.

OFFICE OF PROTECTION AND ADVOCACY FOR PERSONS WITH DISABILITIES

Dir. appointed by the Governor to serve at his pleasure, Sec. 46a-10, Gen. Stat. Salary, Exec. Dir., $59,657. Address: 60-B Weston St., Hartford 06120-1551. Tel., (860) 297-4300, toll free and TDD (800) 842-7303, TDD (860) 566-2102.

Exec. Dir., James D. McGaughey, Glastonbury; *Asst. Dir.,* Stanley J. Kosloski, Cromwell.

MOBILE AND MANUFACTURED HOME ADVISORY COUNCIL

Appointed by the Governor for a term coterminous with term of the Governor or until a successor is chosen, Sec. 21-84a, Gen. Stat. Address: c/o Consumer Protection, State Office Bldg., Hartford 06106. Tel., (860) 566-3290.

Appointed by the Governor, Robert Burns, East Hartford; Joseph F. Caccamo, Jr., Bristol; Catherine Conderino, Colchester; Marilyn Denny, West Hartford; Glenna Easton, Danbury; Kristian Jensen, Jr., Southington; Lee Ross, West Hartford; Jeffrey P. Ossen, Mansfield Center.

Appointed by the Pres. Pro Tempore of the Senate, Norman J. DeAngelis, Goshen. Appointed by the Senate Majority Leader, William Fash, Southington. Appointed by the Senate Minority Leader, Marcia Stemm, Plainville. Appointed by the Speaker of the House, Bennett Pudlin, Hamden. Appointed by the House Majority Leader, Myriam Clarkson, Old Lyme. Appointed by the House Minority Leader, Rocco Facinto, East Hartford.

DEPARTMENT OF CORRECTION

COMMISSIONER OF CORRECTION

Appointed by the Governor, with the advice and consent of either House of the General Assembly, for four years, Secs. 4-5—4-8, Gen. Stat. See Sec. 18-80, Gen. Stat. Salary, Comr., $95,000; Deputy Comrs., Operations, $83,500; Programs, $83,500. Address: 24 Wolcott Hill Rd., Wethersfield 06109. Tel., (860) 692-7481.

Comr., John J. Armstrong, March 1, 1999; *Deputy Comr. of Operations,* Peter Matos, Tel. (860) 692-7486; *Deputy Comr. of Programs,* Jack Tokarz, Tel., (860) 692-7493.

COMPLEX 1 FACILITIES

Complex Warden., Daniel K. Benwell, Salary, $83,279. Address: New Haven CC, 245 Whalley Ave., New Haven 06530. Tel., (203) 781-2350.

GARNER CORRECTIONAL INSTITUTION. Warden appointed by the Comr. of Correction, Sec. 18-82, Gen. Stat. Salary, Warden, $72,580. Number of Inmates as of Oct. 1, 1996, 719. Value of real property, $60,693,126. Address: 50 Nunnawauk Rd., Newtown 06470. Tel., (203) 270-2800.

Warden, Remi Acosta, Jr.; *Deputy Wardens,* Carl Capen, Richard Miele.

COMMUNITY CORRECTIONAL CENTERS

BRIDGEPORT CORRECTIONAL CENTER. Warden appointed by the Comr. of Correction, Sec. 18-82, Gen. Stat. Salary, Warden, $74,758. Number of inmates as of Oct. 1, 1996, 827. Value of real property, $28,358,389. Address: 1106 North Ave., Bridgeport 06604. Tel., (203) 579-6131.

Warden, Bruce Grotta; *Deputy Wardens,* Sandra Bundy, Thomas Langner.

NEW HAVEN CORRECTIONAL CENTER. Warden appointed by the Comr. of Correction, Sec. 18-82, Gen. Stat. Salary, Warden, $86,066. Number of inmates as of Oct. 1, 1996, 754. Value of real property, $19,827,040. Address: 245 Whalley Ave., New Haven 06530. Tel., (203) 789-7111.

Warden, Theresa Lantz; *Deputy Wardens,* Dennis Jones, Mary Kilroy.

COMPLEX 2 FACILITIES

Complex Warden, Frank Crose, Salary, $90,701. Address: Cheshire Correctional Institution, 900 Highland Ave., Cheshire 06410. Tel., (203) 250-2744.

JOHN R. MANSON YOUTH INSTITUTION. Warden appointed by the Comr. of Correction, Sec. 18-82, Gen. Stat. Salary, Warden, $76,994. Number of inmates as of Oct. 1, 1996, 643. Value of real property, $37,456,900. Address: 42 Jarvis St., Cheshire 06410. Tel., (203) 271-0818.

Warden, Robert Ronne; *Deputy Warden,* Guy P. Prarie.

CHESHIRE CORRECTIONAL INSTITUTION. Warden appointed by the Comr. of Correction, Sec. 18-82, Gen. Stat. Salary, Warden, $65, 149. Number of inmates as of Oct. 1, 1996, 1,266. Value of real property, $51,118,161. Address: 900 Highland Rd., Cheshire 06410. Tel., (203) 250-2602.

Warden, John Tarascio; *Deputy Wardens,* Patricia M. Calcirari, Richard Floodquist.

WEBSTER CORRECTIONAL INSTITUTION. Warden appointed by the Comr. of Correction, Sec. 18-82, Gen. Stat. Salary, Warden, $55,407. Number of inmates as of Oct. 1, 1996, 430. Value of real property, $11,356,611. Address: 111 Jarvis St., Cheshire 06410. Tel., (203) 250-8689.

Warden, Oreste P. Bona; *Deputy Wardens,* Thomas Lebuis, Judy Madigan.

COMPLEX 3 FACILITIES

Complex Warden, James E. Huckabey, Salary, $78,496. Address: 199 West Main St., Niantic 06357. Tel., (860) 691-6508.

J. B. GATES CONNECTICUT CORRECTIONAL INSTITUTION. Warden appointed by the Comr. of Correction, Sec. 18-82, Gen. Stat. Salary, Warden, $80,827. Number of inmates as of Oct.1, 1996, 617. Value of real property, $12,570,156. Address: 131 North Bride Brook Rd., Niantic 06357. Tel., (860) 691-4713.

Warden, Robert J. Gillis; *Deputy Warden,* Mary Maynard.

YORK/NIANTIC CORRECTIONAL INSTITUTION (MAXIMUM AND MINIMUM SECURITY). Warden appointed by the Comr. of Correction, Sec. 18-82, Gen. Stat. Salary, Warden, $65,149. Number of inmates as of Oct. 1, 1996, 1,112. Value of real property, York, $44,484,110; Niantic, $23,447,871. Address: 201 West Main St., Niantic 06357. Tel., (860) 691-6508.

Warden, Eileen Higgins; *Deputy Wardens,* James Jarvis, James Warren.

COMPLEX 4 FACILITIES

Complex Warden, Brian K. Murphy, Salary, $77,746. Address: Corrigan Correctional Institution, 986 Norwich-New London Tpke., Uncasville 06360. Tel., (860) 848-5860.

BROOKLYN CORRECTIONAL INSTITUTION. Warden appointed by the Comr. of Correction, Sec. 18-82, Gen. Stat. Salary, Warden, $60,000. Number of inmates as of Oct. 1, 1996, 473. Value of real property, $19,554,420. Address: 59 Hartford Rd., Brooklyn 06234. Tel., (860) 566-2480.

Warden, Gurukaur Khalsa; *Deputy Warden,* Marvin T. Blue.

CORRIGAN CORRECTIONAL INSTITUTION. Warden appointed by the Comr. of Correction, Sec. 18-82, Gen. Stat. Salary, Warden, $74,758. Number of inmates as of Oct. 1, 1996, 761. Value of real property, $31,964,907. Address: 986 Norwich-New London Tpke., 06382. Tel., (860) 848-5700.

Warden, Mary Johnson; *Deputy Wardens,* Robert E. Gurn, Kelly Smayda.

NORTHEAST CORRECTIONAL INSTITUTION. Warden appointed by the Comr. of Correction, Sec. 18-82, Gen. Stat. Salary, Warden, $68,681. Number of inmates as of Oct. 1, 1996, 346. Value of real property, $19,944,007. Address: 251 Middle Tpke., Storrs 06268. Tel., (860) 487-4450.

Warden, Evelyn Bush; *Deputy Warden,* Joseph Bonocchi.

RADGOWSKI CORRECTIONAL INSTITUTION. Warden appointed by the Comr. of Correction, Sec. 18-82, Gen. Stat. Salary, Warden, $67,000. Number of inmates as of Oct. 1, 1996, 436. Value of real property, $13,378,765. Address: 982 Norwich-New London Tpke., Uncasville 06382. Tel., (860) 848-5000.

Warden, George K. Wezner; *Deputy Warden,* Rosetta Jones.

COMPLEX 5 FACILITIES

Complex Warden, Hector L. Rodriguez, Salary, $84,886. Address: MacDougall Correctional Institution, 1153 East St. South, Suffield 06080. Tel., (860) 627-2240.

MacDOUGALL CORRECTIONAL INSTITUTION. Warden appointed by the Comr. of Correction, Sec. 18-82, Gen. Stat. Salary, Warden, $65,149. Number of inmates as of Oct. 1, 1996, 959. Value of real property, $55,419,778. Address: 1153 East St. South, Suffield 06080. Tel., (860) 627-3100.

Warden, Mark Strange; *Deputy Wardens,* James Murdoch, Brian O'Connell.

WALKER RECEPTION/SPECIAL MANAGEMENT UNIT. Warden appointed by the Comr. of Correction, Sec. 18-82, Gen. Stat. Salary, Warden, $61,426. Number of inmates as of Oct. 1, 1996, 521. Value of real property, $26,851,049. Address: 1151 East St. South, Suffield 06078. Tel., (860) 292-3400.

Warden, Mary Morgan; *Deputy Warden,* Wayne Choinski.

COMMUNITY CORRECTIONAL CENTER

HARTFORD CORRECTIONAL CENTER. Warden appointed by the Comr. of Correction, Sec. 18-82, Gen. Stat. Salary, Warden, $79,314. Number of inmates as of Oct. 1, 1996, 1,029. Value of real property, $24,381,834. Address: 177 West St., Hartford 06120. Tel., (860) 240-1800.

Warden, Edward T. Arrington.

COMPLEX 6 FACILITIES

Complex Warden, Pamela Richards, Salary, $78,496. Address: Robinson Correctional Institution, 285 Shaker Rd., Enfield 06082. Tel., (860) 763-8400.

ENFIELD CORRECTIONAL INSTITUTION. Warden appointed by the Comr. of Correction, Sec. 18-82, Gen. Stat. Salary, Warden, $72,580. Number of inmates as of Oct. 1, 1996, 726. Value of real property, $12,267,831. Address: 289 Shaker Rd., Enfield 06082. Tel., (860) 763-7310.

Warden, David Marcial; *Deputy Wardens,* Curtiss A. Boyle, Anthony Lorenzano.

CARL ROBINSON CORRECTIONAL INSTITUTION. Warden appointed by the Comr. of Correction, Sec. 18-82, Gen. Stat. Salary, Warden, $65,149. Number of inmates as of Oct 1, 1996, 1075. Value of real property, $28,435,332. Address: 285 Shaker Rd., Enfield 06082. Tel., (860) 763-6200.

Warden, Larry Myers; *Deputy Warden,* John M. Smialowski.

WILLARD CORRECTIONAL INSTITUTION. Warden appointed by the Comr. of Correction, Sec. 18-82, Gen. Stat. Salary, Warden, $54,719. Number of inmates as of Oct. 1, 1996, 434. Value of real property, $11,055,610. Address: 391 Shaker Rd., Enfield 06082. Tel., (860) 763-6174.

Warden, David N. Strange; *Deputy Warden,* Christopher A. Dion.

COMPLEX 7 FACILITIES

Complex Warden, Donald C. DeVeau, Jr., Salary, $76,209. Address: Northern Correctional Institution, 287 Bilton Rd., Somers 06071. Tel., (860) 763-8731.

OSBORN CORRECTIONAL INSTITUTION. Warden appointed by the Comr. of Correction, Sec. 18-82, Gen. Stat. Salary, Warden, $65,149. Number of inmates as of Oct. 1, 1996, 190. Value of real property, $27,472,000. Address: 287 Bilton Rd., Somers 06071. Tel., (860) 763-8600.

Warden, Leslie E. Brooks.

NORTHERN CORRECTIONAL INSTITUTION. Warden appointed by the Comr. of Correction, Sec. 18-82, Gen. Stat. Salary, Warden, $65,149. Number of inmates as of Oct. 1, 1996, 190. Value of real property, $27,472,000. Address: 287 Bilton Rd., Somers 06071. Tel., (860) 763-8600.

Warden, Giovanny Gomez.

CYBULSKI CORRECTIONAL INSTITUTION. Warden appointed by the Comr. of Correction, Sec. 18-82, Gen. Stat. Salary, Warden, $60,847. Number of inmates as of Oct. 1, 1996, 411. Value of real property, $8,753,090. Address: 264 Bilton Rd., Somers 06071. Tel., (860) 763-6501.

Warden, Sandra W. Sawicki; *Deputy Warden,* John K. Crotty.

NEW ENGLAND BOARD OF INTERSTATE CORRECTIONS COMPACT. Sec. 18-104, Gen. Stat. Address: Walker Reception Center, 1151 East St., South, Suffield 06078. Tel., (860) 292-3404.

Admin., John J. Armstrong, Comr. of Correction; *Deputy Admin.,* Jack Tokarz, Deputy Comr. of Programs; *Interstate Compact Supvr.,* Lynn Milling.

INTERSTATE COMPACT FOR PAROLE AND PROBATION SUPERVISION. Sec. 54-133, Gen. Stat. Address: Walker Reception Center, 1151 East St., South, Suffield 06078. Tel., (860) 292-3404.

Admin., John J. Armstrong, Comr. of Correction; *Deputy Admr.,* Jack Tokarz, Deputy Comr. of Programs; *Interstate Compact Supvr.,* Lynn Milling; *Dir. of Offender Classification and Population Mgmt.,* Frederick Levesque.

DEPARTMENT OF ECONOMIC AND COMMUNITY DEVELOPMENT

COMMISSIONER OF ECONOMIC AND COMMUNITY DEVELOPMENT

Appointed by the Governor, with the advice and consent of either House of the General Assembly, for four years, Secs. 4-5—4-8, Gen. Stat. Salary, Comr., $83,500; Deputy Comrs., $75,500. Address: 505 Hudson St., Hartford 06106. Tel., (860) 566-4180.

Comr., Peter N. Ellef, Avon, March 1, 1999; *Deputy Comrs.,* Richard N. Cianci, Southington; vacancy.

CONNECTICUT DEVELOPMENT AUTHORITY

Appointed by the Governor, Sec. 32-11a, Gen. Stat. Compensation of members, necessary expenses. Address: 845 Brook St., Rocky Hill 06067. Tel., (860) 258-7800.

Ex officio, Peter N. Ellef, Comr. of Economic and Community Development; Christopher B. Burnham, State Treasurer; Michael W. Kozlowski, Secy., Office of Policy and Management.

Appointed by the Governor, *Chm./Pres.,* Arthur H. Diedrick, Morris; Edwin R. Chadwick, Goshen; L. Scott Frantz, Riverside; Richmond W. Glover, Avon.

Appointed by the Pres. Pro Tempore of the Senate, Richard T. Mulready, West Hartford. Appointed by the Senate Minority Leader, Anthony J. Nania, North Caanan. Appointed by the Speaker of the House, Thomas Mullaney, Jr., West Hartford. Appointed by the House Minority Leader, Dennis Hrabchak, Northford.

HOUSING ADVISORY COMMITTEE. Appointed by the Governor, and the General Assembly, Sec. 8-385, Gen. Stat. Address: 505 Hudson St., Hartford 06106. Tel., (860) 566-4149.

Mary L. Mauriello, Waterbury, representing the homeless; David A. Pels, Newington, representing an attorney employed by a legal service agency; Adele F. Strelchun, Waterbury, representing a community development association, vacancies.

CONNECTICUT HOUSING FINANCE AUTHORITY

Sec. 8-244, Gen. Stat. Address: 999 West St., Rocky Hill 06067-4005. Tel., (860) 721-9501.

Ex officio, John P. Burke, Banking Comr; Christopher B. Burnham, State Treasurer; Peter N. Ellef, Comr. of Economic and Community Development; Michael W. Kozlowski, Secy., Office of Policy and Management.

Appointed by the Governor, *Chm.,* Arthur H. Diedrick, Morris; Sandra J. Brown, Stratford; Anthony J. Campanelli, West Hartford; Raymond J. Devlin, Litchfield; Orest T. Dubno, New Haven; Joseph H. Fisher, West Simsbury; Edmund F. Schmidt, Darien.

Appointed by the Pres Pro Tempore of the Senate, Edward J. Fennell, Stratford. Appointed by the Senate Minority Leader, Ronald Smoko, Hamden. Appointed by the Speaker of the House, Walter Pawelkiewicz, Windham. Appointed by the House Minority Leader, Leslie R. Kenny, Glastonbury.

Pres./Exec. Dir., Gary E. King, Killingworth; *Gen. Counsel,* William A. Dickerson, Cromwell; *Vice Pres., Finance and Admin.,* John K. Craford, Old Saybrook; *Vice Pres., Programs and Operations,* Bruce H. Perry, Manchester.

CONNECTICUT TOURISM COUNCIL. Sec. 32-301, Gen. Stat. Address: 865 Brook St., Rocky Hill 06067-3405. Tel., (860) 258-4287.

Ex officio, Chm., Peter N. Ellef, Comr. of Economic and Community Development; William Keish, Comr. of Transportation designee; Mrs. John Rowland, Comr. of Environmental Protection designee.

Appointed by the Governor, Robert Boissevain, North Stonington; Gregg Dancho, Stratford; Patrick McCaughey, New Haven; Lawrence D. McHugh, Middletown.

Appointed by Pres. Pro Tempore of the Senate, Rolf Hammer, New Milford. Appointed by the Senate Majority Leader, H. Scott Phelps, Old Lyme. Appointed by the Senate Minority Leader, Carl A. Carbone, Sr., Hartford. Appointed by the Speaker of the House, Eileen E. Axenroth, Enfield, Rita M. Schmidt, Mystic. Appointed by the House Majority Leader, Eileen J. Sweeney, Manchester. Appointed by the House Minority Leader, Edward Dresel, Southington.

NAUGATUCK VALLEY LOAN FUND ADVISORY COMMITTEE. Appointed by the Governor to serve at his pleasure. Address: Dept. of Economic and Community Development, 865 Brook St., Rocky Hill 06067-3405. Tel., (860) 258-4200.

Chm., Gerald Heffernan, Ansonia; *Members,* William Brennan, Shelton; John S. Driscoll, Bristol; David Einbinder, Ansonia; Robert H. Foster, Oxford; Dan L. Griffith, Huntington; Francis Hennessy, Torrington; Zena Temkin, Torrington.

COMMITTEE FOR THE RESTORATION OF HISTORIC ASSETS IN CONNECTICUT. Sec. 32-6a, Gen. Stat. Address: Dept. of Economic and Community Development, 865 Brook St., Rocky Hill 06067-3405.

Chm., Peter N. Ellef, Comr. of Economic and Community Development; Wilson H. Faude, West Hartford, Chm., Historical Comm.; Ann Y. Smith, Roxbury; Elizabeth V. Varcoe, West Redding.

Edward D. Dombroskas, Staff.

CONNECTICUT INNOVATIONS, INCORPORATED

Sec. 32-35(b), Gen. Stat. Address: 40 Cold Spring Rd., Rocky Hill 06067. Tel., (860) 563-5851; FAX, (860) 563-4877.

Ex officio, Andrew G. De Rocco, Ph.D., Comr. of Higher Education; Peter N. Ellef, Comr. of Economic and Community Development; Bruce Carlson., Secy., Office of Policy and Management designee.

Appointed by the Governor, *Chm.,* Arthur H. Diedrick, Morris; Anthony J. Campanelli, West Hartford; Timothy H. Coppage, West Hartford; Geraldine U. Foster, Essex; Scott Guilmartin, Suffield; George Lewson, Danbury; John W. Olsen, Greenwich; vacancy.

Appointed by the Pres. Pro Tempore of the Senate, Katherine Vick, Kent. Appointed by the Senate Minority Leader, Thomas J. Clark, West Hartford. Appointed by the Speaker of the House, E. Charles McClenachan, Greenwich. Appointed by the House Minority Leader, Alan Greene, Darien.

Exec. Dir., Victor R. Budnick, New Haven.

CONNECTICUT FILM, VIDEO AND MEDIA COMMISSION

Sec. 32-87, Gen. Stat. Compensation, necessary expenses. Address: 865 Brook St., Rocky Hill 06067-4301. Tel., (860) 258-4301.

Ex officio, John W. Betkoski, Beacon Falls; Peter N. Dibble, Deputy Comr. of Economic and Community Development; Anthony Guglielmo, Stafford Springs; Thomas P. Gaffey, Meriden; Marilyn Hess, Greenwich, Ranking Members, Commerce and Exportation Committee. Michael Price, East Haddam, Chp., Commission on the Arts;

Appointed by the Governor, Frank P. Borres, Bridgeport; Susan M. Delia, Granby; Robert H. Gray, Tolland; Ross J. Joel, West Hartford; Hon. Kevin F. Rennie, South Windsor; Lawrence Rifkin, Prospect; vacancy.

Appointed by the Pres. Pro Tempore, *Chm.,* Douglas J. McAward, Brookfield. Appointed by the Senate Majority Leader, James F. Vicevich, Simsbury. Appointed by the Senate Minority Leader, Thomas A. Sheridan, Quaker Hill. Appointed by the Speaker of the House, Martha Ritter, West Hartford. Appointed by the House Majority Leader, Donald D. Sagarino, Jr., New Britain. Appointed by the House Minority Leader, Leslie Jacobs, New Britain.

DEPARTMENT AND BOARD OF EDUCATION

COMMISSIONER OF EDUCATION

Appointed by the Board of Education, for four years, Sec. 10-3a, Gen. Stat. Salary, Comr., $106,000; Deputy Comr., $86,566. Address: Room 305, State Office Bldg., 165 Capitol Ave., Hartford 06106. Tel., (860) 566-5061; FAX, (860) 566-8964; Internet, www.state.ct.us/sde.

Comr., Theodore S. Sergi, West Hartford; *Deputy Comr.,* Benjamin Dixon, Windsor.

STATE BOARD OF EDUCATION. Appointed by the Governor, with the advice and consent of the General Assembly, Sec. 10-1, Gen. Stat. Compensation of board members, necessary expenses. Address: Room 300, State Office Bldg., 165 Capitol Ave., Hartford 06106. Tel., (860) 566-5371; FAX, (860) 566-8964.

Ex officio, Andrew G. De Rocco, Ph.D., Comr. of Higher Education.

Chm., Craig E. Toensing, Falls Village; Feb. 28, 2001; Allan B. Taylor, Hartford; Feb. 28, 1997; Amparo Adib-Samii, Suffield; Janet M. Finneran, Bethany; Edythe J. Gaines, Hartford; Terri L. Masters, Wolcott; Timothy J. McDonald, Waterbury; Feb. 28, 1999; Beverly P. Greenberg, West Hartford; Michael Helfgott, Storrs; Feb. 28, 2001.

Secy., Theodore S. Sergi, Comr. of Education; *Asst. Secy.,* Pamela V. Bergin.

Div. of Educational Programs and Services, Leslie Averna, Acting Assoc. Comr.; *Bureau of Adult Education and Training,* Roberta Pawloski; *Acting Bureau of Applied Curriculum, Technology and Career Info.,* Roberta Pawloski; *Bureau of Early Childhood Education and Social Services,* George Coleman; *Acting Bureau of Special Education and Pupil Services,* Leslie M. Averna; *Div. of Finance and Adm. Services,* John Coroso, Assoc. Comr.; *Bureau of Fiscal Services,* Bruce C. Ellefsen; *Bureau of Grants Processing Services,* Robert A. Brewer; *Bureau of Human Resources,* Richard Wilber; *Office of Info. Systems,* Gregory P. Vassar; *Div. of Teaching and Learning,* Betty J. Sternberg, Assoc. Comr.; *Bureau of Certification and Professional Development,* Abigail Hughes; *Bureau of Curriculum and Instructional Programs,* Mitchell D. Chester; *Bureau of Evaluation and Student Assessment,* Douglas A. Rindone; *Bureau of Research and Teacher Assessment,* Raymond L. Pecheone; *Vocational-Technical School System,* Juan Lopez, Supt.; *Asst. Supt., Instruction and Professional Development,* Joan S. Briggaman; *Asst. Supt., School Operations,* Dominic Spera, Jr.; *Office of Urban and Priority School Dists.,* Elliott Williams, Chief.

VOCATIONAL-TECHNICAL SCHOOL SYSTEM

Supt., Juan S. Lopez; *Asst. Supt., Instruction and Professional Development,* Joan S. Briggaman; *Asst. Supt., School Operations,* Dominic Spera, Jr.

REGIONAL VOCATIONAL—TECHNICAL SCHOOLS—1996-97

Address	School	Director	Secondary & Full-Time Adult Day
141 Prindle Ave., Ansonia 06401	Emmett O'Brien	Eileen Fredericks	441
500 Palisade Ave. Bridgeport 06610	Bullard-Havens	Joseph LaVorgna	933
431 Minor St. Bristol 06010	E. C. Goodwin Satellite	John Tarnuzzer	159
Hayestown Ave. Danbury 06810	Henry Abbott	Mario DiLorenzo	650
Maple St. Danielson 06239	H. H. Ellis	Ernest Gelinas	595
170 Elm St. Enfield 06082	Howell Cheney Satellite	Lewis Randall	58
189 Fort Hill Rd. Groton 06340	Ella T. Grasso Southeastern	Susanna Spera	654
71 Jones Rd. Hamden 06514	Eli Whitney	Cecil Robinson	605
500 Brookfield St Hartford 06106	A. I. Prince	Silas Shannon	716
791 W. Middle Tpke. Manchester 06040	Howell Cheney	Lewis Randall	394
Oregon Rd. Meriden 06451	Horace C. Wilcox	Andrew Jakab	625
60 Daniels St. Middletown 06457	Vinal	Thomas Scharrett	487
600 Orange Ave. Milford 06460	Platt	Gale Tirrell	809
735 Slater Rd. New Britain 06053	E. C. Goodwin	John Tarnuzzer	758
590 New London Tpke. Norwich 06360	Norwich	Charles Salerno	445
P.O. Box 1416 Stamford 06904	J. M. Wright	Daniel Kushman	392
Great Meadow Rd. Stratford 06497	Sikorsky Satellite	Gale Tirrell	42
75 Oliver St. Torrington 06790	Oliver Wolcott	William Perlotto	561
43 Tompkins St. Waterbury 06708	W. F. Kaynor	Georgia Smith-Jennings	721
210 Birch St Willimantic 06226	Windham	Charles Wilt	521
		TOTAL	10,610

Courses include: Air conditioning and refrigeration, automobile body repair, automotive mechanics, aviation mechanics, avionics, baking, barbering, building maintenance, carpentry, computer repair, culinary arts, dental assistant, dental lab technician, digital microprocessor technician, drafting-architectural, bio-environmental technology, drafting-construction design, drafting-machine, electrical, electromechanical, electronics, engine repair-diesel and small engine-internal combustion, environmental systems, fashion technology, graphic communications, hairdressing, cosmetology and barbering, health technology, heating, ventilating and airconditioning (HVAC), home-health aide/CNA, hospitality hotel management, manufacturing technology, masonry, medical assistant, metal trades technology, microcomputer software technology, painting and decorating, plumbing, practical nurse education, signal and communication, surgical technician, and welding.

ADVISORY COUNCIL ON SPECIAL EDUCATION. Sec. 10-76i, Gen. Stat. Address: 25 Industrial Park Rd., Middletown 06457-1543. Tel., (860) 638-4265.

Appointed by the Comr. of Education, June Goodman, Danbury; Ann Seigel, West Hartford. Appointed by the Comr. of Mental Retardation, Margaret Braddon, East Hartford; Bonnie Moran, New Fairfield. Appointed by the Comr. of Children and Families, Gary Blau, Glastonbury; Dolores Woodward, Hartford.

Appointed by the Pres. Pro Tempore of the Senate, Judith G. Freedman, Westport; Joan Gay, West Hartford; Elizabeth R. Harkins, Old Greenwich. Appointed by the Senate Majority Leader, Gary L. Fitzherbert, Washington; vacancy. Appointed by the Senate Minority Leader, John Mattas, Southington; John M. P. Thatcher III, Greenwich; three vacancies. Appointed by the Speaker of the House, Corinne Berglund, Branford; Sherry Earle, Danbury; vacancy. Appointed by the House Majority Leader, Mary U. Eberle, Bloomfield; Geoia Liberty, Stamford; vacancy. Appointed by the House Minority Leader, Judith R. Merida, Middletown; Frank Morisano, Collinsville; Mariann Rossi-Ondusky, Deep River; Claudia Powers, Riverside; Joseph Sak, Kensington.

ARBITRATION PANEL. Appointed by the Governor, with the advice and consent of the General Assembly, for two year terms, Sec. 10-153f, Gen. Stat. Compensation of members, per diem fee. Address: Room 306, State Office Bldg., 165 Capitol Ave., Hartford 06106. Tel., (860) 566-2135; FAX, (860) 566-3585.

Peter R. Blum, West Hartford; Susan Boyan, Tolland; Gerald H. Braffman, Woodbridge; Lynn Alan Brooks, Wethersfield; Laurie Cain, Simsbury; Brian Clemow, West Hartford; Donald Deneen, Windsor; James G. Doyle, Patrick G. Eaglin, Canton; Bristol; Lynn Freedman, West Hartford; John M. Gesmonde, Northford; Martin A. Gould, West Hartford; Donald F. Houston, Fairfield; Robert J. Landsman, Wilton; Loren Lettick, Wallingford; Frank Logue, New Haven; John Malsbenden, Colchester; Robert A. Massa, Wethersfield; Albert J. McGrail, Glastonbury; Susan Meredith, New Haven; Albert G. Murphy, West Hartford; Victor M. Muschell, Torrington; Richard D. O'Connor, Old Lyme; John M. Romanow, New Haven; Thomas J. Staley, Cheshire; vacancy.

STATE COMMISSION ON THE ARTS

Sec. 10-369, Gen. Stat. Salary, Exec. Dir., $50,663. Compensation of members, necessary expenses. Address: 755 Main St., 1 Financial Plaza, Hartford 06103. Tel., (860) 566-4770; FAX, (860) 566-6462.

Appointed by the Governor, *Chm.*, Michael P. Price, Chester; Barbara Davitt, Prospect; James Kelley, Sr., Deep River; Ann Y. Smith, Roxbury; Cynthia H. Twardy, Stamford.

Appointed by the Pres. Pro Tempore of the Senate, June Goodman, Danbury; Vita Muir, Washington; Benjamin Palagonia, Sherman; Robert Schnurr, Sharon; Tim Wolf, West Hartford. Appointed by the Senate Minority Leader, Douglas Evans, Hartford; Paul E. Pozzi, New Haven; vacancy. Appointed by the Speaker of the House, Barbara Anderson, West Hartford; Peter D. Hirschl, Hartford; Vivien White, Stamford; Barbara Schwartz, West Hartford; Mitzi Yates-Waterhouse, Hartford. Appointed by the House Minority Leader, Louise L. DeMars, Bristol; Lynda Smith, Old Saybrook; Ted Yudain, Stamford.

Members, William Bailey, George White, National Council on the Arts; vacancy.

Exec. Dir., John E. Ostrout.

POET LAUREATE. Sec. 3-110f, Gen. Stat. Compensation, none. Address: c/o Commission on the Arts, 755 Main St., 1 Financial Plaza, Hartford 06103.

Poet Laureate, Leo Connellan, Hanover.

CONNECTICUT HISTORICAL COMMISSION

Appointed by the Governor to serve at his pleasure, Sec. 10-321, Gen. Stat. Compensation of members, necessary expenses. Address: 59 South Prospect St., Hartford 06106. Tel., (860) 566-3005.

Katherine W. Bennett, Middletown; Richard Buel, Jr., Ph.D., Essex; Christopher Collier, Ph.D., Orange; Frances B. Devlin, Litchfield; Kevin G. Ferrigno, Manchester; Barbara A. Hudson, Bristol; Richard L. Hughes III, West Hartford; Harold D. Juli, Waterford; Jean R. Kelley, Guilford; Edwin R. Ledogar, Dayville; Marsha Lotstein, West Hartford; Eva M. Potts, Essex.

Dir., John W. Shannahan.

THE CONN. TRUST FOR HISTORIC PRESERVATION. Address: 940 Whitney Ave., Hamden 06517-4002. (A nonprofit organization created pursuant to Special Act No. 75-93, Sec. 3.)

Bd. of Trustees: Chm.., Frederick Biebesheimer, Old Lyme; *Vice Chm.,* Charles C. Kingsley, Branford; *Vice Chm.,* Lee Kuckro, Wethersfield; *Secy.,* Theodore Tucci, Hartford; *Treas.,* William C. G. Swift, Jr., Madison; David H. Barkin, Wallingford; Russell L. Brenneman, Hartford; Bruce W. Chambers, Hamden; William Champagne, Preston; Evan Cowles, Farmington; Robert B. Dannies, New Haven; Gerald Farrell, Jr., Wallingford; Emil Frankel, Weston; Mrs. G. S. B. Gilbert, Greenwich; Frederick D. Hill, Warren; Mary-Michelle U. Hirschoff, Bethany; Alice Houston, Stonington; Jay W. Jackson, Hartford; Martin J. Kenny, Hartford; Joan P. Kerr, New Haven; Susie

Kim, New Haven; Charles Lee, Greenwich; Clifton A. Leonhardt, Farmington; Khalid Lum, Hamden; Joseph McGee, Fairfield; C. Roderick O'Neill, Hartford; Errol Rhoden, Stamford; Craig Schiavone, New Haven; Janet S. Stulting, West Hartford; Deanne H. Winokur, Greenwich; Susan G. Zielenbach, West Hartford.

Exec. Dir., Laura Clarke.

STATE LIBRARY

STATE LIBRARY BOARD. Chief Justice of the Supreme Court or his designee; the Commissioner of Education or his designee; the Chief Court Admin. or his designee, and five members appointed by the Governor, Sec. 11-1, Gen. Stat.

Francis X. Hennessy, Judge of the Appellate Court; Robert Leuba, Deputy Chief Court Admin.; Benjamin Dixon, Ed.D., Dept. of Education.

Appointed by the Governor, Robert R. Gallucci, Waterbury; Mollie Keller, Trumbull; John T. Short, Avon; Edmund B. Sullivan, Ed.D., Suffield; Edwin E. Williams, Stonington.

Appointed by the Pres. Pro Tempore of the Senate, vacancy. Appointed by the Senate Minority Leader, E. Frederick Petersen, Falls Village. Appointed by the Speaker of the House, Ann M. Clark, Bloomfield. Appointed by the House Minority Leader, Mary Etter, South Windsor.

STATE LIBRARY-STATE LIBRARIAN. Appointed by the State Library Board, Sec. 11-1, Gen. Stat. Salary, Librarian, $86,999.91. Address: State Library and Supreme Court Bldg., 231 Capitol Ave., Hartford 06106. Tel., (860) 566-4301.

STATE LIBRARIAN, Richard G. Akeroyd, Jr.; *Admin. Services Div. Dir.,* Richard Kingston; *Personnel/Affirmative Action Program Mgr.,* David A. Peck; *Information Services Div. Dir.,* Lynne Newell; *Cataloging,* Stephen Slovasky; *Collection Mgmt.,* Kristin O. Johnson; *History and Genealogy,* Richard Roberts; *Library for the Blind and Physically Handicapped Head,* Carol Taylor; *Government Information Services,* Julie Schwartz; *Law and Legislative Reference,* Denise Jernigan.

Library Development Div. Dir., Sharon Brettschneider; *Middletown Library Service Center Head,* Mary Engels, 786 South Main St., Middletown 06457, (860) Tel., (860) 344-2972; *Acting Willimantic Library Service Center Head,* Susan Cormier, 1216 Main St., Willimantic 06226. Tel., (860) 456-1717.

State Archivist, Mark Jones; *Public Records Admin.,* Eunice DiBella; *Raymond E. Baldwin Museum of Connecticut History and Heritage, Admin.,* Dean Nelson.

DEPARTMENT OF ENVIRONMENTAL PROTECTION

COMMISSIONER OF ENVIRONMENTAL PROTECTION

Appointed by the Governor, with the advice and consent of either House of the General Assembly, Secs. 4-5—4-8, Gen. Stat. Salary, Comr., $83,500. Address: 79 Elm St., Third Floor, Hartford 06106. Tel., (860) 424-3001.

Comr., Sidney J. Holbrook, Westbrook, March 1, 1999; *Asst. Comrs.*, Susan C. Lajoie, Waterbury; David K. Leff, Collinsville; Arthur J. Rocque, Storrs.

Chief, Bureau of Financial and Support Services, William Evans, Cromwell; *Chief, Bureau of Air Mgmt.,* Carmine DiBattista, Lebanon; *Chief, Bureau of Waste Mgmt.,* Richard Barlow, Canton; *Chief, Bureau of Water Mgmt.,* Robert Smith, Tolland; *Chief, Bureau of Natural Resources,* Edward C. Parker, Rocky Hill; *Chief, Bureau of Outdoor Recreation,* Richard Clifford, Canton.

Eastern Dist.—Address: 209 Hebron Rd., Marlborough 06447. Tel., (860) 295-9523.

Western Dist.—Address: 230 Plymouth Rd., Harwinton 06791. Tel., (860) 485-0226.

Marine Hdqtrs.—Address: 333 Ferry Rd., Old Lyme 06371. Tel., (860) 434-6148.

STATE PARKS, FORESTS, FISH HATCHERIES AND STATE MONUMENTS
CAMPING AREAS

State Parks

Name	District	Town	Acres	No. of Sites	Facilities*
Black Rock	W	Watertown	444	96	f,h,p,s,x
Burr Pond (Taylor Brook Campground)	W	Torrington	438	40	b,f,h,l,p,s,w,x
Devil's Hopyard	E	East Haddam	1,000	20	f,h,l,p
Hammonasset Beach	E	Madison	936	558	f,l,p,s,x
Hopeville Pond	E	Griswold	554	82	b,f,h,p,s,x
Housatonic Meadows	W	Sharon	452	104	f,h,p
Kettletown	W	Southbury	599	72	f,h,p,s
Lake Waramaug	W	Kent	95	88	f,l,p,s,x
Macedonia Brook	W	Kent	2,302	84	f,h,l,o,p
Mashamoquet Brook	E	Pomfret	917	55	f,h,l,o,p,s,w,x
Rocky Neck	E	East Lyme	712	69	f,h,l,p,s,x

State Forests

Name	District	Town	Acres	No. of Sites	Facilities*
American Legion (Austin Hawes Campground)	W	Barkhamsted	789	30	f,h,j,w
Pachaug	E	Voluntown	24,504	40	b,f,h,j,p,s,w

OTHER STATE PARKS

Name	District	Town	Acres	Facilities*
Above All	W	Warren	31	
Beardsley	W	Bridgeport	184	f,p,x
Beaver Brook	E	Windham	401	

Name	District	Town	Acres	Facilities*
Becket Hill	E	Lyme	260	
Bigelow Hollow	E	Union	513	b,f,h,p
Bluff Point	E	Groton	778	f,h
Bolton Notch	E	Bolton	69	
Brainard Homestead	E	East Haddam	25	
Campbell Falls	W	Norfolk	102	f,h,p
Chatfield Hollow	E	Killingworth	356	f,h,l,p,s,w,x
Collis P. Huntington	W	Bethel	883	f,h,w
Conn. Valley Railroad	E	Essexdefined.	300	h,m,o,x,
Dart Island	E	Middletown	2	
Day Pond	E	Colchester	180	f,h,l,p,s
Dennis Hill	W	Norfolk	240	h,p
Dinosaur	W	Rocky Hill	80	h,m,p
Fort Griswold	E	Groton	17	m,o
Gay City	E	Hebron	1,569	f,h,o,p,s,w
George D. Seymour	E	Haddam	222	
George C. Waldo	W	Southbury	150	
Gillette Castle	E	Lyme	185	h,l,m,o,p,x
Haddam Island	E	Haddam	14	
Haddam Meadows	E	Haddam	175	b,f,p,w
Haley Farm	E	Groton	198	h,p
Harkness Memorial	E	Waterford	147	f,o,p
Haystack Mt.	W	Norfolk	284	h,p
Higganum Reservoir	E	Haddam	147	f,h
Hopemead	E	Bozrah	60	
Horseguard	W	Avon	146	
Humaston Brook	W	Litchfield	147	
Hurd Park	E	East Hampton	991	f,h,l,p
Indian Well	W	Shelton	153	b,f,h,l,p,s,x
Ivy Mt.	W	Goshen	50	
John A. Minetto	W	Torrington	715	f,h,j,l,p,s,w
Kent Falls	W	Kent	307	f,h,p
Killingly Pond	E	Killingly	162	
Lamentation Mt.	W	Berlin	47	
Lovers Leap	W	New Milford	40	
Mansfield Hollow (Federal Lease)	E	Mansfield	251	b,f,h,p,w
Mianus River	W	Stamford	335	
Miller's Pond	E	Durham	280	f,h
Minnie Island	E	Salem	1	
Mohawk Mt.	W	Cornwall	273	h,l,p,w
Mt. Bushnell	W	Washington	139	
Mt. Riga	W	Salisbury	315	
Mt. Tom	W	Litchfield	232	f,h,p,s,x

Name	District	Town	Acres	Facilities*
Old Furnace	E	Killingly	134	f,h,p
Osbornedale	W	Derby	417	f,h,l,m,p,w
Penwood	W	Bloomfield	787	h,l,p,w
Platt Hill	W	Winchester	125	p
Pomeroy	E	Lebanon	104	
Putnam Memorial	W	Redding	183	h,l,o,p
Quaddick	E	Thompson	116	b,f,l,p,s,x
Quinebaug Lake	E	Killingly	181	
Quinnipiac River	W	North Haven	342	h,j
Red Cedar Lake	E	Lebanon	340	f,h
Rocky Glen	W	Newtown	45	h
Ross Pond	E	Killingly	242	
Scantic River	E	Enfield	639	b,f,h
Selden Neck	E	Lyme	531	
Seth Low Pierrepont	W	Ridgefield	305	h
Sherwood Island	W	Westport	238	f,l,p,s,x
Silver Sands	W	Milford	297	f
Sleeping Giant	W	Hamden	1,456	f,h,l,p
Southford Falls	W	Oxford	126	f,h,l,p,w
Squantz Pond	W	New Fairfield	172	b,f,h,p,s,w,x
Stillwater	W	Torrington	226	
Stoddard Hill	E	Ledyard	55	b,f,p
Stratton Brook	W	Simsbury	148	f,h,l,p,s,w
Sunnybrook	W	Torrington	444	
Sunset Rock	W	Plainville	15	
Talcott Mt.	W	Bloomfield	574	h,l,o,p
Trimountain	W	Durham	157	
Wadsworth Falls	W	Middlefield	286	f,h,p,s,w
West Rock Ridge	W	Hamden	1,601	f,h,l,o,p,w
Wharton Brook	W	Wallingford	96	f,h,l,p,s,w,x
Whittemore-Larkin Bridle Trail	W	Naugatuck	251	h
Windsor Meadow	W	Windsor	132	
Wooster Mt.	W	Danbury	359	Skeet

(*)
b. boating   l. shelter (picnic)   s. swimming
f. fishing   m. museum   w. winter sports
h. hiking   o. historic   x. concession
j. hunting   p. picnicking

OTHER STATE FORESTS

Name	District	Town	Acres
Algonquin	W	Colebrook	2,979
Cockaponset	E	Haddam	16,443

Name	District	Town	Acres
Enders	W	Granby	1,576
Housatonic	W	Sharon	10,438
James L. Goodwin	E	Hampton	2,003
Massacoe	W	Simsbury	503
Mattatuck	W	Watertown	4,536
Meshomasic	E	Portland	8,142
Mohawk	W	Cornwall	3,640
Mohegan	E	Scotland	395
Nassahegon	W	Burlington	1,227
Natchaug	E	Eastford	13,215
Nathan Hale	E	Coventry	1,272
Naugatuck	W	Beacon Falls	3,500
Nehantic	E	East Lyme	4,011
Nepaug	W	New Hartford	1,200
Nipmuck	E	Union	9,108
Nye-Holman	E	Tolland	779
Paugnut	W	Torrington	1,627
Paugussett	W	Newtown	1,947
Peoples	W	Barkhamsted	2,942
Pootatuck	W	New Fairfield	1,055
Quaddick	E	Thompson	972
Salmon River	E	Colchester	6,517
Shenipsit	E	Stafford	6,126
Topsmead	W	Litchfield	512
Tunxis	W	Hartland	9,215
Wyantenock	W	Cornwall	3,595

FISH HATCHERIES

Name	District	Town	Acres
Burlington	W	Burlington	124
Kensington	W	Berlin	43
Quinebaug	E	Plainfield	1,488

STATE MONUMENTS

Name	District	Town	Type
Continental Army Hospital	W	West Hartford	Site of Hospital
Fort Griswold	E	Griswold	Battlefield
Industrial Monument	W	North Canaan	Iron Furnace
Israel Putnam	E	Brooklyn	Burial Place
John Mason	E	Groton	Burial Place
Miantonomo	E	Norwich	Burial Place
Nathan Hale	E	Coventry	Burial Place
Nathaniel Lyon	E	Eastford	Burial Place
Swamp Fight	W	Fairfield	Battlefield

ACREAGE SUMMARY

	Acres
State Parks	31,729
State Forests	144,768
Total	176,497

CONNECTICUT EMERGENCY RESPONSE COMMISSION. Sec. 22a-601, Gen. Stat. Address: c/o Dept. of Enviornmental Protection, 79 Elm St., 4th Fl., Hartford 06106-5127. Tel., (860) 424-3373.

Ex-officio, Vice Chm., David Leff, Comr., Environmental Protection designee; *Secy.,* Paul J. Connelly, State Fire Marshall designee; James F. Byrnes, P.E., Comr. of Transportation designee; Maria Johnson, Comr. of Public Health designee; George E. Luther, Comr. of Public Safety designee; Stuart Mahler, Secy. of the Office of Policy and Management designee; Jeffrey J. Morrissette, State Fire Admin.; Richard Palo, Comr. of Labor designee; Robert A. Plant, Dir., Office of Emergency Management.

Appointed by the Governor, *Chm.,* Gerard P. Goudreau, Hamden, repr. owners or operators of facilities; Robert J. Araujo, Shelton, public member; George P. Dunn, Middletown, public member; Wyldon K. Fishman, West Hartford, public member; Arthur J. Higgins, Jr., Middletown, chief of volunteer fire dept.; Robert J. Klancko, Woodbridge, repr. owners or operators of facilities; John E. Obier, Jr., North Haven, chief of a municipal fire dept. whose employees are compensated for their services; Thomas J. Wontorek, Farmington, public member; vacancy.

COUNCIL ON ENVIRONMENTAL QUALITY. Sec. 22a-11, Gen. Stat. Address: 79 Elm St., 6th Fl., Hartford 06106. Tel., (860) 424-4000.

Appointed by the Governor, *Chm.,* Ronald J. Thomas, Darien; Daniel J. Alfieri, Amston; Marian Chertow, New Haven; Donal C. O'Brien, Jr., New Canaan; vacancy.

Appointed by the Pres. Pro Tempore of the Senate, Stephen A. Bolton, Andover; Wesley L. Winterbottom, West Hartford. Appointed by the Speaker of the House, Susan Merrow, East Haddam; Richard Sherman, Mansfield Center.

Exec. Dir., Karl J. Wagener, Glastonbury.

CONNECTICUT COUNCIL ON SOIL AND WATER CONSERVATION. Sec. 22a-315(c), Gen. Stat. Address: c/o Dept. of Environmental Protection, 79 Elm St., Hartford 06106. Tel., (860) 424-3060.

Ex officio, Nancy Bull, Cooperative Extension System; Jack Claussen, Storrs Agricultural Experiment Sta.; Vincent Majchier, Exec. Dir., Consolidated Farm Services Agency; Abigail Maynard, Conn. Agricultural Experiment Sta.; Donald Smith, Jr., DEP Bureau of Forestry; Margo Wallace, State Conservationist, USDA-Natural Resources Conservation Service.

Chm., Tom O'Dell, Westport, Middlesex County Soil and Water Conservation Dist.; *Vice Chm.,* Fred Banach, Baltic, Comr. of Environmental Protection designee; *Secy./ Treas.,* Joseph Dippel, Comr. of Agriculture designee; John Breakell, Conn. Assoc. of Conservation Dists.; Deane DiPietro, East Hartford, Hartford County Soil and Water Conservation Dist.; Frank Indorf, New Haven County Soil and Water Conservation Dist.; Norma O'Leary, Windham County Soil and Water Conservation Dists.; Robert

Smith, Rocky Hill Conn. Extension Advisory Council; Art Spielman, New London County Soil and Water Conservation Dist.

Exec. Dir., Allan R. Bennett.

CONNECTICUT UNDERGROUND STORAGE TANK PETROLEUM CLEAN-UP REVIEW BOARD. Sec. 22a-449d(b), Gen. Stat. Address: c/o Dept. of Environemntal Protection, 79 Elm St., 4th Fl., Hartford 06106-5127. Tel., (860) 424-3370.

Ex officio, Vice Chm., Richard J. Barlow, Comr. of Environmental Protection designee; Thomas Bazzolo, Bureau of State Fire Marshall designee; *Secy.,* Marc Papandrea, Comr. of Revenue Services designee; John Radacsi, Secy., Office of Policy and Management designee.

Appointed by the Governor, Henry E. Voegeli, Bethany.

Appointed by the Pres. Pro Tempore of the Senate, Kenneth C. Gostyla, Bloomfield; Appointed by the Senate Majority Leader, Charles Matties, West Hartford; Appointed by the Senate Minority Leader, *Chm.,* John Mitchell, South Windsor; Appointed by the Speaker of the House, Thomas H. Fitzpatrick, Hartford; Bernard Schilberg, South Windsor; Appointed by the House Majority Leader, Paul McCullough, Stamford; Appointed by the House Minority Leader, Albert J. Barr, Stamford.

ATLANTIC STATES MARINE FISHERIES COMMISSION. Sec. 26-297, Gen. Stat. Compensation of members, expenses. Address: Room 011, State Capitol, Hartford 06106. Tel., (860) 240-0100.

Ex officio, Sidney J. Holbrook, Comr. of Environmental Protection, repr. by Ernest E. Beckwith, Jr., Dir., Fisheries Unit; Sen. George L. Gunther, Stratford.

Appointed by the Governor, Lance Stewart, Ph.D., Noank, June 30, 1996.

Admin., George Meier.

INTERSTATE SANITATION COMMISSION. Appointed by the Governor, for four years, and until a successor is appointed and has qualified, Sec. 22a-295, Gen. Stat. Compensation, actual expenses. Address: Howard Golub, Dir., Room 201, 311 West 43rd St., New York, NY 10036; Tel., (212) 582-0380; FAX, (212) 581-5719.

Ex officio, Richard Blumenthal, Attorney General; Stephen A. Harriman, Comr. of Public Health; Sidney J. Holbrook, Comr. of Environmental Protection.

Appointed by the Governor, John Atkin, Norwalk; Jeannette A. Semon, Darien.

MID-ATLANTIC STATES AIR POLLUTION CONTROL COMPACT. Sec. 22a-166, Gen. Stat.

Ex officio, Governor John G. Rowland. Alternate member, Sidney J. Holbrook, Comr. of Environmental Protection.

NEW ENGLAND COMPACT ON RADIOLOGICAL HEALTH PROTECTION. Sec. 22a-160, Gen. Stat.

Admin., Sidney J. Holbrook, Comr. of Environmental Protection, repr. by Kevin McCarthy, Dir., Monitoring and Radiation.

NEW ENGLAND INTERSTATE WATER POLLUTION CONTROL COMMISSION. Appointed by the Governor to serve at his pleasure, Sec. 22a-308, Gen. Stat.

Compensation, actual expenses. Address: Ronald F. Poltak, Exec. Dir., N.E. Interstate Water Pollution Control Comm., 255 Ballardvale St., 2nd Fl., Wilmington, MA 01887.

Ex officio, Stephen A. Harriman, Comr. of Public Health; Robert Smith, Comr. of Environmental Protection designee.

Appointed by the Governor, Teresalee Bertinuson, Broad Brook; Astrid T. Hanzalek, Suffield; Edwin Pearson, Ridgefield.

NORTHEASTERN FOREST FIRE PROTECTION COMMISSION. Appointed by the Governor to serve at his pleasure, Sec. 23-54, Gen. Stat. Compensation, expenses. Address: 79 Elm St., Hartford 06106. Tel., (860) 424-3630.

Robert Chatfield, Prospect; John D. Mordasky, Stafford Springs; Don Smith, Jr., Meriden.

CONNECTICUT RIVER VALLEY FLOOD CONTROL COMMISSION. Appointed by the Governor to serve at his pleasure, with the advice and consent of the Senate, Sec. 25-100, Gen. Stat. Compensation, none. Address: Conn. River Valley Flood Control Comm., P.O. Box 511, Greenfield, MA 01302.

Charles E. Berger, Jr., Torrington; John Carl Thomas, Hanover; Benjamin A. Warner, Barkhamsted.

THAMES RIVER VALLEY FLOOD CONTROL COMMISSION. Appointed by the Governor to serve at his pleasure, with the advice and consent of the Senate, Sec. 25-102, Gen. Stat. Address: Dept. of Environmental Protection, 79 Elm St., Hartford 06106.

Charles E. Berger, Jr., Torrington; John C. Thomas, Hanover (Sprague); Benjamin A. Warner, Barkhamsted.

FIVE MILE RIVER COMMISSION

Appointed by the Governor to serve at his pleasure, Sec. 15-26a, Gen. Stat. Address: P.O. Box 119, Rowayton 06853. Tel., (203) 853-2436.

Chm., Jane Gillespie, Darien; James F. Crane, Darien; Matthew A. Marion, Rowayton; Theodore G. O'Neill, Jr., Norwalk.

CONNECTICUT RIVER GATEWAY COMMISSION

Sec. 25-102d, Gen. Stat. Address: Gateway Comm., P.O. Box 778, Old Saybrook 06475. Tel., (860) 388-3497.

Chm., Irwin Wilcox, Deep River; *Vice Chm.,* Maura K. Finan, Old Saybrook; *Secy.,* Robert Myers, Haddam; *Treas.,* Rudi Besier, Old Lyme; Robert Boulware, East Haddam; Paul de Brigard, Higganum, Midstate RPA; Sandra Huber, Essex, Conn. River Estuary RPA; Kevin Mazer, Lyme; Donald McGannon, Chester; Jay Northrup, Hartford, Repr. Dept. of Environmental Protection; Richard Rieder, Essex.

CONNECTICUT INDIAN AFFAIRS COUNCIL

Appointed by the Governor, Sec. 47-59b, Gen. Stat. Address: 79 Elm Street, Hartford 06106. Tel., (860) 424-3066.

Appointed by the Governor, Michael J. Coady, Manchester; Keith L. Knowlton, Brooklyn; Lee R. Tyrol, Westbrook.

Appointed by the respective tribes, *Mohegan,* Bethany Seidel, Uncasville; *Schaghticoke,* Paulette Crone-Morange, Monroe; *Mashantucket Pequot,* Richard Hayward, Ledyard; *Golden Hill Paugussett,* Chief Aurelius Piper, Trumbull; *Paucatuck Eastern Pequot,* vacancy.

CONNECTICUT RESOURCES RECOVERY AUTHORITY

Appointed by the Governor, with the advice and consent of the General Assembly, Chm. designated by the Governor to serve at his pleasure, Sec. 22a-261(b), Gen. Stat. Address: 179 Allyn St., Hartford 06103. Tel., (860) 549-6390.

Ex officio, James F. Sullivan, Acting Comr. of Transportation; Peter N. Ellef, Comr. of Economic and Community Development; Michael W. Kozlowski, Secy., Office of Policy and Management.

Appointed by the Governor, *Chm.,* Peter N. Ellef, Avon; John C. Chapin, Jr., Farmington; Frank N. Nicastro, Bristol; Edward B. St. John, Middlebury; Theodore T. Tansi, Old Saybrook. Ad Hoc members: Alphonse S. Marotta, Hartford, Peter B. Webster, Essex (Mid-Connecticut Project); Anthony P. Rescigno, North Haven, Louis L. Rubenstein, Wallingford (Wallingford Project); Walter Blanker, Groton; Milton Y. Suzich, Waterford, Thomas R. Rylander, Madison (Southeast Project); Dominick M. DiGangi, Bethany; John Neary, Easton (Bridgeport Project).

Appointed by the Pres. Pro Tempore of the Senate, Kathleen Collins, Hartford; Gary F. Flynn, Farmington; vacancy. Appointed by the Senate Minority Leader, Louis Timolat, Falls Village. Appointed by the Speaker of the House, Bernard Schilberg, South Windsor; Bernard Sullivan, South Windsor. Appointed by the House Minority Leader, Richard O. Belden, Shelton.

BOARD OF GOVERNORS FOR HIGHER EDUCATION

COMMISSIONER OF HIGHER EDUCATION

Appointed by the Board of Governors for Higher Education, Sec. 10a-5(a), Gen. Stat. Salary, Comr., $117,420. Address: Dept. of Higher Education, 61 Woodland St., Hartford 06105-2391. Tel., (860) 566-3910, 3913.

Comr., Andrew G. De Rocco, Ph.D., Hartford, March 1, 1999; *Deputy Comr.,* Valerie F. Lewis, Vernon.

BOARD OF GOVERNORS FOR HIGHER EDUCATION. Sec. 10a-2, Gen. Stat. Address: Dept. of Higher Education, 61 Woodland St., Hartford 06105-2391. Tel., (860) 566-3910, 3913.

Appointed by the Governor, *Chm.,* Logan Clarke, Jr., East Haddam; Jeremiah J. Lowney, Jr., D.D.S., M.S., Lebanon; Lile R. Gibbons, Greenwich; Joan B. Kemler, West Hartford; Dorothy B. Leib, M.D., New London; Maria I. Mojica, Hamden, March 1, 1999; Thomas P. Mondani, Haddam, March 1, 2001.

Appointed by the Pres. Pro Tempore of the Senate, James H. Bates, Lakeville, March 1, 1999. Appointed by the Senate Minority Leader, Alice V. Meyer, Easton, March 1, 1997. Appointed by the Speaker of the House, Albert B. Vertefeuille, South Windham, March 1, 1999. Appointed by the House Minority Leader, William A. Bevacqua, Trumbull, March 1, 1997.

ADVISORY COMMITTEE TO THE BOARD OF GOVERNORS. Sec. 10a-3, Gen. Stat. Address: Dept. of Higher Education, 61 Woodland St., Hartford 06105-2391.

One trustee, administrator, faculty member and student appointed by each of the boards of trustees of the community-technical colleges, Connecticut State University, University of Connecticut and an independent college; one representative of the Board for State Academic Awards; one representative from the accredited private occupational schools of Connecticut.

NEW ENGLAND BOARD OF HIGHER EDUCATION. Sec. 10a-62, Gen. Stat. Address: 45 Temple Pl., Boston, MA 02111. Tel., (617) 357-9620.

Appointed by the Governor, Michael A. Gerber, Bloomfield; Christine Niekrash, D.M.D., Farmington, Oct. 24, 2000.

Appointed by the Pres. Pro Tempore of the Senate, Thomas P. Gaffey, Meriden, Jan. 31, 1999; two vacancies. Appointed by the Speaker of the House, Andrew G. DeRocco, Ph.D., Hartford; Stephen H. Keller, Wethersfield, Jan 31, 99; vacancy.

Pres., John C. Hoy.

EDUCATION COMMISSION OF THE STATES. Secs. 10-374, 375, Gen. Stat. Address: 707 17th St., Suite 2700, Denver, Colorado 80202. Tel., (303) 299-3600; FAX, (303) 296-8332.

Ex officio, John G. Rowland, Governor.

Appointed by the Governor, Francis G. Brennan, Waterbury; Cheryl C. Dickinson, Ed.D., Torrington; Theodore S. Sergi, West Hartford; Patricia G. Sidas, Wilton.

Appointed by the Pres. Pro Tempore of the Senate, Sen. Kevin B. Sullivan, West Hartford. Appointed by the Senate Minority Leader, Judith G. Freedman, Westport. Appointed by the Speaker of the House, Edna Garcia, Bridgeport. Appointed by the House Minority Leader, Paul J. Knierim, Simsbury.

Pres., Frank Newman, Ph.D.

UNIVERSITY OF CONNECTICUT

Salary, Pres., $255,000. Compensation of trustees, traveling expenses. Total enrollment: 22,316, full-time 16,242, part-time 3,750, non-degree students, 2,324. Number of alumni, approximately 123,000. Value of land, buildings and equipment in excess of $480 Million. Address: Storrs 06269. Tel., (860) 486-2000.

BOARD OF TRUSTEES OF THE UNIVERSITY. Sec. 10a-103, 4-9a, Gen. Stat.

Ex officio, Pres., John G. Rowland, Governor; Theodore S. Sergi, Comr. of Education; Shirley Ferris, Comr. of Agriculture.

Appointed by the Governor, *Chm.,* Lewis B. Rome, Bloomfield; James F. Abromaitis, Unionville; Louise Bailey, West Hartford; William R. Berkley, Greenwich; Michael H. Cicchetti, Waterbury; John R. Downey, Redding; Lewis C. Heist, Old Greenwich; Lenworth M. Jacobs, M.D., West Hartford; Claire R. Leonardi, Harwinton; Irving R. Saslow, Hamden; Jennifer C. Smith, West Hartford; Richard Treibick, Greenwich.

Elected by alumni, Louise Berry, Danielson, Aug. 31, 1997. Frank Napolitano, Manchester, Aug. 31, 1999.

Elected by the students, Michael Bellafiore, West Hartford, June 30, 1998. Kingsley Stewart, Storrs, June 30, 1997.

Pres., Phillip E. Austin.

CONNECTICUT MUSEUM OF NATURAL HISTORY. Secs. 10-112a-c, Gen. Stat. Address, c/o The University of Connecticut, 75 North Eagleville Rd., U-23, Storrs 06269-3023. Tel., (860) 486-4460.

Public Info., Carol Davidge.

OFFICE OF ARCHAEOLOGY. Appointed by the Board of Directors of the State Museum of Natural History. Sec. 10a-112, Gen. Stat. Address: U-23, UConn, Storrs 06269-3023. Tel., (860) 486-5248.

State Archaeologist, Nicholas Bellantoni, Ph.D.

STATE HISTORIAN. Appointed by the Trustees of the University of Connecticut, Sec. 11-1, Gen. Stat. Address: Wood Hall, U-103, UConn, Storrs 06269-2103. Tel., (860) 486-3453.

Christopher Collier, Ph.D.

STATE MUSEUM OF ART. Sec. 10a-112g, Gen. Stat. Address: The William Benton Museum of Art, U-140, UConn., Storrs 06269-2140. Tel., (860) 486-4520.

Acting Dir., Thomas Bruhn.

CONNECTICUT SEA GRANT COLLEGE PROGRAM. Address: 1084 Shennecossett Rd., Groton 06340-6097. Tel., (860) 405-9110.

Dir., Edward C. Monahan; *Public Info.,* Margaret Van Patten.

UNIVERSITY OF CONNECTICUT HEALTH CENTER

JOHN DEMPSEY HOSPITAL

Address: 263 Farmington Ave., Farmington 06030. Tel., (860) 679-2000. *Vice Pres./Provost for Health Affairs/Exec. Dir. of the Health Center,* Leslie S. Cutler, D.D.S.; *Hospital Dir.,* Andria Martin.

THAMES RIVER CAMPUS

Address: 401 West Thames St., Norwich 06360. Tel., (860) 823-4600.

CONNECTICUT POISON CENTER

Sec. 10a-132, Gen. Stat. Address: University of Connecticut Health Center, Farmington Ave., Farmington 06030. Tel., (860) 679-3456, (800) 343-2722. 24 hour service.

Admin. Dir., Mary McCormick; *Medical Dir.*, Marc Bayer, M.D.

THE UNIVERSITY OF CONNECTICUT COOPERATIVE EXTENSION SYSTEM

Address: UConn, 1376 Storrs Rd., U-36, Storrs 06269-4036. *Assoc. Dean/Assoc. Dir.*, Nancy H. Bull; *Asst. Dir.*, Roger Adams. *Extension Centers/Field Faculty,* working with individuals, families, and communities to address food and fiber, environmental, family youth and community issues. *Cooperative Extension Centers: Brooklyn Ext. Ctr. Coord..,* Latif Lighari, 139 Wolf Den Rd., 06234-1729; *Haddam Ext. Ctr. Coord..,* Mary Ellen Welch, 1066 Saybrook Rd., Box 70, 06438-0070; *Norwich Ext. Ctr. Coord.,* Norman Bender, 562 New London Tpke., 06360-6599; *Torrington Ext. Ctr. Coord.,* Richard Meinert, 1304 Winsted Rd., 06790-2940; *Vernon Ext. Ctr. Coord.,* Rosemarie Syme, 24 Hyde Ave., 06066-4599; *West Hartford Ext. Ctr. Coord.,* Norm Gauthier, 1800 Asylum Ave., 06117-2600; *Bethel Ext. Ctr. Coord.,* Lynne Grant, 67 Stony Hill Rd., 06801; *North Haven Ext. Ctr. Coord.,* Wanda Little, 305 Skiff St., 06473-4451.

THE UNIVERSITY OF CONNECTICUT COOPERATIVE EXTENSION SYSTEM COUNCILS AND FOUNDATIONS

CONN. 4-H DEVELOPMENT FUND, INC. Address: The University of Connecticut, U-36, 1376 Storrs Rd., Storrs 06269-4036. *Chm.,* Tom Baldwin, Wethersfield.

FAIRFIELD COUNTY AGRICULTURAL EXTENSION COUNCIL, INC. Address: 67 Stony Hill Rd., Bethel 06801-3056. *Pres.,* Bernard Ozielinski, Ridgefield; *Vice Pres.,* Rick Peck, Newton; *Secy.,* Krista Parente, Brookfield; *Treas.,* Kathleen S. Peck, Newtown.

HARTFORD COOPERATIVE EXTENSION COUNCIL, INC. Address: 1800 Asylum Ave., West Hartford 06117-2600. *Pres.,* Mark Sullivan, West Hartford; *Vice Pres.,* Linda Labenski, West Hartford; *Secy.,* Marenda Brown-Stitzer, Kensington; *Treas.,* Roger Bogart, Danbury.

LITCHFIELD COUNTY COOPERATIVE EXTENSION ASSOC., INC. Address: 1304 Winsted Rd., Torrington 06790-2940. *Pres.,* Robert Towne, Jr., Morris; *Vice Pres.,* Ellen Paine, Simsbury; *Secy.,* Judith Hannan, Southbury; *Treas.,* Carll Pallokat, Harwinton.

MIDDLESEX COUNTY EXTENSION COUNCIL, INC. Address: Extension Center, 1066 Saybrook Rd., P.O. Box 70, Haddam 06438. *Pres.,* Roy Hajek, Moodus; *Secy.,* Linda Zanelli, Higganum; *Treas.,* Bill Lowry III, Cromwell.

NEW HAVEN COUNTY COOPERATIVE EXTENSION RESOURCE COUNCIL, INC. Address: 43 Marne St., Hamden 06514-3610. *Pres.,* Kenneth Blazo, Hamden; *Vice Pres.,* vacancy; *Secy.,* vacancy; *Acting Treas.,* Betty Randall, Hamden.

NEW LONDON COUNTY AGRICULTURAL EXTENSION COUNCIL, INC. Address: Extension Center, 562 New London Tpke., Norwich 06360. *Pres.,* Dominic DiPollina, New London; *Vice Pres.*, David DeNoia, Waterford; *Treas.,* Jessie N. Hazen, East Hampton.

TOLLAND COUNTY EXTENSION COUNCIL, INC. Address: 24 Hyde Ave., Vernon 06066. *Pres.,* Richard Sievers, South Windsor; *Vice Pres.,* Ray Axelrod, Willimantic; *Secy.,* Priscilla Couch, Somers; *Treas.,* John Crowley, Stafford Springs.

WINDHAM COUNTY AGRICULTURAL EXTENSION COUNCIL, INC. Address: Cooperative Extension Center, 139 Wolf Den Rd., Brooklyn 06234. *Pres.,* Ross Eddy, Fabyan; *Vice Pres.*, Donal Geer, Hampton; *Secy.,* Joyce Hart, Canterbury; *Treas.,* Preston Roberts, Grosvenordale; *Advisor,* Latif Lighari, Cromwell.

ADVISORY COMMITTEE FOR A CENTER FOR REAL ESTATE AND URBAN ECONOMIC STUDIES AT THE UNIVERSITY OF CONNECTICUT SCHOOL OF BUSINESS ADMINISTRATION

Secs. 10a-124, 4-9a, Gen. Stat. Address: UConn, U-41RE, 368 Fairfield Rd., Storrs 06269-2041. Tel., (860) 486-1268.

Ex officio, Chm., Thomas Gutteridge, Dean of the School of Business Admin., UConn.

Appointed by the Governor, Andrew Brecher, Newington; Joyce G. Epstein, Manchester; William H. Farley, West Simsbury; John H. Frey, Ridgefield; Laurence L. Hannafin, Norfolk; Linda Lara, Niantic.

Appointed by the UConn Board of Trustees, Dr. William A. McEachern, Willington; Dr. Jack E. Stephens, Storrs; Dr. John C. Thompson, Storrs.

Dir., C. F. Sirmans.

BOARD OF TRUSTEES FOR CONNECTICUT STATE UNIVERSITY

Secs. 10a-88, 4-9a, Gen. Stat. Salary, Chancellor, $152,485. Compensation of trustees, necessary expenses. Address: 39 Woodland St., Hartford 06105-2337. Tel., (860) 493-0011.

Chancellor, William J. Cibes, Jr.

Appointed by the Governor, *Chm.,* Lawrence D. McHugh, Middletown; *Vice Chm.,* Karl J. Krapek, Avon; *Secy.,* Emily V. Melendez, Ledyard; Richard J. Balducci, Newington; William Detrick, New Britain; John A. Doyle, Southington; Gregg S. Hannah, Pomfret Center; Lynn M. Hathaway, Stamford; Nancy W. Kaplan, Mystic; L. David Panciera, Rocky Hill; A. Searle Pinney, Brookfield; William Ramirez, Waterbury; Mertie L. Terry, Cromwell; Linda L. Thomsen, New Canaan.

Elected by the students, Christopher M. Borajkiewicz, New Haven, Oct. 31, 1997. Martin Moore, Danbury, Oct. 31, 1998.

CENTRAL CONNECTICUT STATE UNIVERSITY. 1615 Stanley St., New Britain 06050-4010. Tel., (860) 832-3000. Total enrollment 11,646, full-time 6,111, part-time 5,535. Number of alumni, approx., 45,552. *Pres.,* Richard L. Judd, Ph.D.

EASTERN CONNECTICUT STATE UNIVERSITY. 83 Windham St., Willimantic 06226-2295. Tel., (860) 465-5221. Total enrollment 4,527, full-time 2,983, part-time 1,544. Number of alumni, approx., 12,047. *Pres.,* David G. Carter, Sr., Ph.D.

SOUTHERN CONNECTICUT STATE UNIVERSITY. 501 Crescent St., New Haven 06515-1355. Tel., (203) 392-5250. Total enrollment 11,412, full-time 6,163, part-time 5,249. Number of alumni, approx. 46,000. *Pres.,* Michael J. Adanti, M.S.

WESTERN CONNECTICUT STATE UNIVERSITY. 181 White St., Danbury 06810-6885. Tel., (203) 837-8300. Total enrollment 5,397, full-time 2,774, part-time 2,623. Number of alumni, approx. 18,169. *Pres.,* James R. Roach, Ph.D.

BOARD OF TRUSTEES FOR COMMUNITY-TECHNICAL COLLEGES OF CONNECTICUT

Appointed by the Governor, Sec. 10a-71, Gen. Stat. Salary, Chancellor, $138,950; Deputy Chancellor, $109,224. Compensation of trustees, necessary expenses. Address: 61 Woodland St., Hartford 06105. Tel., (860) 566-8760.

Appointed by the Governor, *Chm.,* Lawrence J. Zollo, Waterbury; Bryan N. Anderson, New Haven; Maureen M. Baronian, West Hartford; Louise S. Berry, Danielson; Rev. David Cannon, Preston; Eleanor D. Coltman, Manchester; Thomas F. Dowd, Jr., Bloomfield; Lawrence S. Fox, West Hartford; George Frantzis, Middlebury; William R. Johnson, Glastonbury; Gretchen H. Kingsley, Branford; Jules Lang, East Norwalk; Raymond Rivard, Middlebury; Hector Rodriguez, Bridgeort; Marie M. Spivey, Bloomfield; Nancy Stolfi, Wolcott; six vacancies.

Elected by the students, Frank Reyes, Hartford; Stanley Vitzoski, Waterbury.

Chancellor, Bruce H. Leslie, Ph.D.; *Deputy Chancellor,* Marc S. Herzog, M.S.

COMMUNITY-TECHNICAL COLLEGES

ASNUNTUCK COMMUNITY-TECHNICAL COLLEGE. 170 Elm St., Enfield 06082. Tel., (860) 253-3000. Total enrollment 2,063 full-time 299, part-time 1,764. *Pres.,* Harvey S. Irlen, Ph.D.

CAPITAL COMMUNITY-TECHNICAL COLLEGE. Woodland Campus, 61 Woodland St. Hartford 06105-2354; Flatbush Campus, 401 Flatbush Ave., Hartford 06106. Tel., (860) 520-7800. Total enrollment 2,828, full-time 540, part-time 2,288. *Pres.,* Ira Rubenzahl, Ph.D.

GATEWAY COMMUNITY-TECHNICAL COLLEGE. Long Wharf Campus, 60 Sargent Dr., New Haven 06511-5970; North Haven Campus, 88 Bassett Rd., North Haven 06473. Tel., (203) 789-7071. Total enrollment 4,537 full-time 1,096, part-time 3,441. *Pres.,* Diana VanDer Ploeg, Ph.D.

HOUSATONIC COMMUNITY-TECHNICAL COLLEGE. 510 Barnum Ave., Bridgeport 06608. Tel., (203) 579-6400. Total enrollment 2,653, full-time 472, part-time 2,181. *Pres.,* Janis Wertz, Ph.D.

MANCHESTER COMMUNITY-TECHNICAL COLLEGE. P.O. Box 1046, 60 Bidwell St., Manchester 06040-1046. Tel., (860) 647-6000. Total enrollment 5,523, full-time 1,549, part-time 3,974. *Pres.,* Jonathan M. Daube, Ed.D.

MIDDLESEX COMMUNITY-TECHNICAL COLLEGE. 100 Training Hill Rd., Middletown 06457. Tel., (860) 343-5800. Total enrollment 2,611, full-time 629, part-time 1,982. *Pres.,* Dianne Williams, M.S.

NAUGATUCK VALLEY COMMUNITY-TECHNICAL COLLEGE. 750 Chase Pkwy., Waterbury 06708-3089. Tel., (203) 575-8044. Total enrollment 5,238, full-time 1,536, part-time 3,702. *Pres.,* Richard L. Sanders, Ed.D.

NORTHWESTERN CONNECTICUT COMMUNITY-TECHNICAL COLLEGE. Park Place East, Winsted 06098-1798. Tel., (860) 738-6300. Total enrollment 1,885, full-time 462, part-time 1,423. *Pres.,* R. Eileen Baccus, Ph.D.

NORWALK COMMUNITY-TECHNICAL COLLEGE. 188 Richards Ave., Norwalk 06854. Tel., (203) 857-7000. Total enrollment 5,357, full-time 1,251, part-time 4,106. *Pres.,* William H. Schwab, Ph.D.

QUINEBAUG VALLEY COMMUNITY-TECHNICAL COLLEGE. 742 Upper Maple St., Danielson 06239-1440. Tel., (860) 774-1130. Total enrollment 1,170, full-time 308, part-time 862. *Acting Pres.,* Casey Crabill.

THREE RIVERS COMMUNITY-TECHNICAL COLLEGE. Mohegan Campus, Mahan Dr., Norwich 06360-2479; Thames Valley Campus, 574 New London Tpke., New London 06360. Tel., (860) 886-1931. Total enrollment 3,707, full-time 888, part-time 2,819. *Pres.,* Booker T. DeVaughn, Jr., Ed.D.

TUNXIS COMMUNITY-TECHNICAL COLLEGE. 271 Scott Swamp Rd., Farmington 06032-3187. Tel., (860) 677-7701. Total enrollment 3,468, full-time 901, part-time 2,567. *Pres.,* Catheryn L. Addy, Ph.D.

STATE OF CONNECTICUT HEALTH AND EDUCATIONAL FACILITIES AUTHORITY. Sec. 10a-179, Gen. Stat. Address: Ten Columbus Blvd., 7th Floor, Hartford 06106-1976. Tel., (860) 520-4700.

Ex officio, Christopher B. Burnham, Treasurer; Michael W. Kozlowski, Secy., Office of Policy and Management.

Appointed by the Governor, *Chm.,* Paul J. Silvester, West Hartford; *Vice Chm.,* John A. Barone, Ph.D., Fairfield, James R. Birle, Greenwich; William J. Cibes, Jr., Ph.D., West Hartford; Phyllis C. DeLeo, Ph.D., Wolcott; James G. Pettit, West Hartford; Barbara Rubin, Glastonbury; Herbert B. Price, Stamford; Laurence R. Smith, Jr., Collinsville.

Exec. Dir., Richard D. Gray, Cheshire; *Managing Dir./CFO,* Jeffrey A. Asher, Manchester; *Managing Dir./Gen. Counsel,* David K. Eikenberry, Glastonbury.

BOARD FOR STATE ACADEMIC AWARDS

Appointed by the Governor, Sec. 10a-143, Gen. Stat. The Board administers Charter Oak State College, an institution of higher education awarding college degrees by validation of credit and by examination. Address: 66 Cedar St., Newington 06111-2646. Tel., (860) 666-4595.

Chm., Chandler J. Howard, Farmington; *Secy.,* Joseph R. Halloran, Middlebury; Astrid T. Hanzalek, Suffield; Thomas W. Johnson, Windsor; Doris F. Knight, Orange; Sharon Levinsky, Beacon Falls; Richard A. Lickwar, Old Lyme; Joseph P. McDonough, Farmington; Vincent A. Socci, New Canaan.

Exec. Dir., Merle W. Harris, Ed.D.

CONN. STUDENT LOAN FOUNDATION. Sec. 10a-203, Gen. Stat. Address: 525 Brook St., P.O. Box 1009, Rocky Hill 06067. Tel., (860) 257-4001.

Bd. of Dirs.: Andrew G. De Rocco, Ph.D., Comr. of Higher Education; Logan Clarke, Jr., Chm., Bd. of Governors for Higher Education.

Appointed by the Governor, *Chm.,* T. Brian Condon, Cheshire; *Vice Chm.,* William J. Lucas, Trumbull; *Secy.,* Stephen B. Keogh, Norwalk; *Treas.,* William P. Hawkins, Danbury; Gregory C. Davis, East Hartford; Patrick B. O'Sullivan, Orange; Robert C. Schatz, Newington.

Appointed by the Pres. Pro Tempore of the Senate, Mary Ann Handley, Manchester. Appointed by the Senate Minority Leader, vacancy. Appointed by the Speaker of the House, Denise W. Merrill, Mansfield Ctr. Appointed by the House Minority Leader, Claudia Powers, Riverside.

Pres., Mark W. Valenti.

DEPARTMENT OF INSURANCE

INSURANCE COMMISSIONER

Appointed by the Governor, with the advice and consent of either House of the General Assembly, for four years, Secs. 4-5—4-8, Gen. Stat. Salary, Comr., $87,000; Deputy Comr., $83,872. Address: P.O. Box 816, Hartford 06142-0816. Tel., (860) 297-3800; FAX, (860) 566-7410.

Comr., George M. Reider, Jr., Farmington, March 1, 1999; *Deputy Comr./Dir. of Market Conduct,* William J. Gilligan, Wethersfield; *Acting Dir. of Property and Casualty Div.,* Walter S. Bell, Glastonbury; *Dir., Examination Div.,* Frances J. O'Connor, Avon; *Dir., Life and Health Div.,* Mary Ellen Breault, Newington; *Acting Dir., Licensing and Investigations,* Raymond T. Claytor, Manchester; *Dir., Consumer Affairs Div.,* William J. Mulhall, Waterbury; *Fiscal Adm. Mgr.,* Carolyn A. Carey, Newington; *Counsel,* Jon E. Arsenault, East Hartford.

DEPARTMENT OF LABOR

LABOR COMMISSIONER

Appointed by the Governor, with the advice and Consent of either House of the General Assembly, for four years, Secs. 4-5—4-8, Gen. Stat. Salary, Comr., $83,500; Deputy Comrs., $75,500. Address: 200 Folly Brook Blvd., Wethersfield 06109-1114. Tel., (860) 566-5160; FAX, (860) 566-1520.

Comr., James P. Butler, Fairfield, March 1, 1999; *Secy.,* Diane Y. Morgan, Higganum; *Deputy Comr.,* William R. Bellotti, Middlebury; *Secy.,* Judy C. Garafalo, Middletown; *Deputy Comr., Employment and Training,* John E. Saunders III, Bloomfield; *Secy.,* Donna M. Chamberlain, Manchester; *Deputy Comr.,* Jean E. Zurbrigen, Marlborough; *Secy.,* Veronica Benedetto, Cromwell; *Affirmative Action Admin.,* Haskell O. Kennedy, Jr., Ed.D., Springfield, MA; *Personnel Admin.,* W. Lee Palmer, Glastonbury; *Dir. of Operational Support,* Alice Carrier, West Hartford; *Dir. of Program Policy,* George M. Wentworth, Wethersfield; *Dir. of Marketing,* Rie Poirier, West Hartford; *Dir. of Research,* Roger F. Therrien, Higganum; *Info. Technology Dir.,* Richard Flower, East Hartford; *Chief of Adm. and Fiscal Services,* Robert J. Merola, Plantsville; *Regional Dirs.,* John Bialobrzeski, Meriden; Nancy Calabrese, Waterbury; Ernest Carrasquilla, Windsor; Charles McGlew, Meriden; *Dir. of Staff Development,* Sandi Hastings, Bolton.

DIVISION OF OCCUPATIONAL SAFETY AND HEALTH. *Dir.,* Samuel C. Moore, Hartford; *Asst. Dir.,* Donald A. Heckler, Meriden. Tel., (860) 566-4550, 6916.

CONNECTICUT OCCUPATIONAL SAFETY AND HEALTH REVIEW COMMISSION. Appointed by the Governor to serve at his pleasure, Sec. 31-376. Compensation of members, $125 per diem. Address: Dept. of Labor, 38 Wolcott Hill Rd.., Wethersfield 06109-1114. Tel., (860) 566-4389.

Scott P. Belanger, Wethersfield; Lazarus S. Donabedian, West Hartford; William M. Ducci, New Hartford; Thomas H. Greenleaf, Southington; Michael C. Jainchill, Avon.

WAGE AND WORKPLACE STANDARDS. *Dir.,* Gary K. Pechie, Wethersfield; *Asst. Dir.,* Ronald J. Marquis, Wethersfield. Tel., (860) 566-3450; FAX, (860) 566-6693.

CONNECTICUT STATE BOARD OF LABOR RELATIONS. Appointed by the Governor to serve at his pleasure, with the advice and consent of the General Assembly, Secs. 31-102, 4-9a, Gen. Stat. Compensation of members, $150 per day in lieu of expenses. Address: Dept. of Labor, 38 Wolcott Hill Rd., Wethersfield 06109-1114. Tel., (860) 566-4398; FAX, (860) 566-7035.

Chm., John H. Sauter, West Hartford; C. Raymond Grebey, Stamford; Thomas G. Gutteridge, Ph.D., Tolland.

Agent, John W. Kingston, West Haven; *Gen. Counsel,* Joseph Celentano, Manchester.

CONNECTICUT EMPLOYMENT AND TRAINING COMMISSION

Appointed by the Governor in accordance with Sec. 122(a) (2) of P.L. 97-300, the Federal Job Training Partnership Act and Sec. 31-3i, Gen. Stat. Address: Dept. of Labor, 200 Folly Brook Blvd., Wethersfield 06109-1114. Tel., (860) 566-4388.

Chm., Wallace Barnes, Bristol; Robert E. Burgess, South Norwalk; James P. Butler, Comr. Dept. of Labor; Carmine D'Agostino, Stamford; Andrew G. De Rocco, Ph.D., Comr., Dept. of Higher Education; Peter N. Ellef, Comr. Dept. of Economic and Community Development; Frank Esposito, Norwalk; Michael Ferrucci, North Haven; Murray Gallant, Branford; Rep. Sonya Googins, Glastonbury; Adele Gordon, Stamford; Bennie Jennings, New London; Lauren W. Kaufman, Farmington; Sam D. Koutas, Fairfield; Jane Z. Mahler, Waterbury; Julio Mendoza, Windsor; Lewis A. Miller, Darien; William Moore, Old Saybrook; Shaw Mudge, Stamford; John W. Olsen, Clinton; Raymond R. Oneglia, Litchfield; Richard Pearson, West Hartford; JoAnn Peters, Oxford; Michael P. Peters, Hartford; Laurie Prytko, Manchester; Rosaida Rosario, West Hartford; Louis D. Saloom, Southington; Dr. Theodore S. Sergi, Comr., Dept. of Education; Joyce A. Thomas, Comr., Dept. of Social Services; Anne Wingate, Collinsville.

Deputy Comr., John E. Saunders, Bloomfield.

CONNECTICUT BOARD OF MEDIATION AND ARBITRATION. Appointed by the Governor to serve at his pleasure, Secs. 31-91, 4-9a, Gen. Stat. Compensation of members, $150 at conclusion of proceedings in lieu of expenses. If proceedings extend beyond two days, each member shall receive $50 for each additional day provided the extension has prior approval of the commissioner. Address: Dept. of Labor, 38 Wolcott Hill Road., Wethersfield 06109-1114. Tel., (860) 566-4394; FAX, (860) 566-6914.

Members, Chm., Peter R. Blum, West Hartford; Donald Bardot, West Cornwall; Laurie G. Cain, Simsbury; Michael J. Ferrucci, Jr., North Haven; David A. Ryan, Milford; Raymond D. Shea, West Hartford.

Mediators, Albert V. Burgess, Middlefield; Joseph Egan, Cheshire; James F. Hendricks, West Haven; John A. McCarthy, Sandy Hook; Frank J. Rocco, New Britain; Thomas F. Sweeney, Norwich.

Dir., Catherine J. Serino, Middletown.

JOB CENTERS

Local Office	Address	Telephone
Ansonia	555 Main St., 06401	(203) 736-1060
Bridgeport	500 State St., 06604	(203) 579-6288
Bristol	55 South St., P.O. Box 1629, 06011-1629	(860) 314-2592
Danbury	152 West St. P.O. Box 737, 06813-0737	(203) 797-4151
Danielson	95 Westcott Rd., 06239	(860) 779-5847
Enfield	620 Enfield St., 06082	(860) 741-4284
Hamden	37 Marne St., 06514	(203) 789-7741
Hartford	3580 Main St., 06120	(860) 566-7551

Local Office	Address	Telephone
Manchester	587 East Middle Tpke., 06040	(860) 649-4558
Meriden	290 Pratt St., 06450	(203) 238-6100
Middletown	170B Main St., 06457	(860) 344-3084
New Britain	260 Lafayette St. P.O. Box 1088, 06050	(860) 827-7870
New London	Shaw's Cove 6, 06320	(860) 447-6211
Norwich	6 Cliff St., 06360	(860) 892-2257
Stamford	111 High Ridge Rd., P.O. Box 3831, 06905-0831	(203) 425-2438
Torrington	Torrington Parkade, 486 Winsted Rd. P.O. Box 627, 06790	(860) 626-6227
Waterbury	249 Thomaston Ave., 06702	(203) 596-4150
Willimantic	Tyler Sq., 1320 Main St. 06226	(860) 423-2521

EMPLOYMENT SECURITY BOARD OF REVIEW AND REFEREE SECTION. Chm. appointed by the Governor from civil service list, Sec. 31-237c, Gen. Stat. Salary, $86,913. Chief Referee appointed by Chm., Sec. 31-237i(b). Salary, $70,505. Address: Dept. of Labor, Chm., 38 Wolcott Hill Rd., Wethersfield 06109-1114. Tel., (860) 566-3045; FAX, (860) 566-6932.

BOARD OF REVIEW: *Chm.,* Bennett Pudlin, Hamden; *Counsel,* Lynne M. Knox, Windsor; *Bd. Members,* William F. Jones, Waterbury; Alan M. Kyle, Lyme; *Staff Attys.,* Stephen Lattanzio, Wethersfield; Amy Stillman-Kulig, East Granby; Sheila Wells, Wethersfield.

Chief Referee, W. Burke Reilly, Naugatuck; *Principal Appeals Referees,* Dominick L. Alberino, North Haven; Richard T. Carney, Meriden; Janice Dombrowski, Rocky Hill; Geraldine H. Hawthorne, Hamden; James J. Kendzior, East Hampton; Janice M. San Souci, Wethersfield; *Associate Appeals Referees,* Frederick A. Billings, Fairfield; John Blair, Shelton; James Cesario, North Haven; Denese Chisholm, Hartford; Charles C. Dearborn, Wallingford; Christian M. Dechent, Wolcott; Ralph V. Dorsey, New Haven; Grace M. Grant, Windsor; Karen Hager, Bloomfield; Susan E. Leslie, South Windsor; Sherwin M. Nelson, South Windsor; Janice A. Nordstrom, Cheshire; Charles Russo, Cheshire; Jill Sizensky, West Haven; Lee Terry, Storrs; John P. Vagnini, Seymour; Joan K. Willin, Newington; Matthew A. Wynne, South Windsor.

CONNECTICUT STATE APPRENTICESHIP COUNCIL. Appointed by the Governor to serve at his pleasure, Secs. 31-51b, 4-9a, Gen. Stat. Compensation of members, reimbursed for necessary expenses incurred in the performance of their duties.

Labor Representatives: Leonard F. Dube, Torrington; Giro Esposito, Jr., North Haven; Richard S. Monarca, Middletown; John M. Nettle, Shelton.

Industry Representatives: Robert R. Bosco, Wolcott; John B. Farnham, Glastonbury; Mary Ellen Dombrowski, Wethersfield; vacancy.

Public Representatives: *Chm.,* John E. Saunders III, Bloomfield; Susan Bucknell, West Hartford; Edward J. Rybczyk, Naugatuck; Beatrice Tinty, Haddam.

ADVISORY COUNCIL ON DISPLACED HOMEMAKERS.

Appointed by Comr. of Labor, Sec. 31-3g, Gen. Stat. Address: Dept. of Labor, 200 Folly Brook Blvd., Wethersfield 06109-1114. Tel., (860) 566-2450.

Chm., Betty Kuehnel, East Hartford; Leslie Brett, West Hartford; George S. Brusznicki, New Britain; Robyn Bugbee, Bristol; Carolyn Benvenuti, Waterford; Lillie Crosby, Monroe; Lynn M. Dallas, Meriden; Barbara DeBaptiste, Waterbury; Gwen Gardner, East Hartford; Zena Kovack, West Hartford; Maria-Luz Samper, Storrs; Sally Connolly, Woodbridge; Marjorie Valentin, Lebanon; June Rosen, Avon; Barbara Stracka, Stratford.

WORKERS' COMPENSATION COMMISSION

Appointed by the Governor, for five years, Sec. 31-276, Gen. Stat. Salary, Chm., $100,411, other members, $94,411-$99,411. Address: Chm., Capitol Place, 21 Oak Street, Fourth Floor, Hartford, 06106. Tel., (860) 493-1500; FAX, (860) 247-1361.

Commission Chm., Jesse M. Frankl, West Hartford, March 11, 2002.

Comrs. at Large, Nancy A. Brouillet, March 17, 1998; Robin W. Waller, March 31, 1998; Linda B. Johnson, April 30, 1998; Thomas G. Cotter, May 17, 1998; Michael S. Miles, Amado J. Vargas, Robin L. Wilson, March 29, 1999; James Metro, April 30, 1999; John A. Mastropietro, George A. Waldron, March 31, 2000; Angelo L. dos Santos, Donald H. Doyle, July 10, 2000; Stephen B. Delaney, Roberta S. Tracy, A. Thomas White, Jr., March 11, 2002.

Dist.	Address	Telephone
1	999 Asylum Ave., Hartford 06105	(860) 566-4154
2	90 Sachem St., Norwich 06360	(860) 823-3900
3	700 State St., New Haven 06511	(203) 789-7512
4	350 Fairfield Ave., Bridgeport 06604	(203) 382-5600
5	95 Thomaston Ave., Waterbury 06702	(203) 596-4207
6	1 Lake St., New Britain 06052	(860) 827-7180
7	1515 Summer St., Stamford 06905	(203) 325-3881
8	90 Court St., Middletown 06457	(860) 344-7453

CONNECTICUT GOVERNOR'S COMMITTEE ON EMPLOYMENT OF PEOPLE WITH DISABILITIES

Sec. 31-136-4, Regs. State Agencies. Compensation of members, necessary expenses. Address: Dept. of Labor, 200 Folly Brook Blvd., Wethersfield 06109-1114. Tel., (860) 566-8061.

Honorary Co-Chm., John G. Rowland, Governor; James P. Butler, Comr. of Labor; John E. Saunders, III, Deputy Comr. of Employment and Training; *Chm.,* Sam McKnight, New Haven; Robert Babcock, Hartford; Michael Bean, Ledyard; Marty Burnham, East Hartford; Kay Carver, Bristol; Deborah Ferrigno, West Hartford; Thomas Flanagan III, Norwalk; Tom Foran, West Hartford; Karen Halliday, Middletown; Robert Inman, Wethersfield; Robert Kelsey, Meriden; Tracy Kralik, New Britain; Richard Lawrence, Manchester; Jack LeBlond, Windsor; Ed Mambruno, Hartford;

Shirley Monk, Windsor; Kathy Morrone, Hartford; Kay Rieman, Hartford; Christopher Samulowitz, Waterbury; Mertie Terry, Waterbury; Stephen Thal, Hartford; Diane Uttaro, Hartford; James Zygmont, Plantsville.

Coordinator, Marcia S. Glasper, West Haven

STATE OCCUPATIONAL INFORMATION COORDINATING COMMITTEE

Mandated in 1977 by Federal Public Law 94-482, Education Amendments of 1976; Title II, Vocational Education. Established by Exec. Orders 22, 28, and 12. Additional mandate provided by Federal Public Laws 97-300, Job Training Partnership Act of 1982 and 101-392, Charles D. Perkins Vocational and Applied Technology Education Act. Address: 200 Folly Brook Blvd., Wethersfield 06109. Tel., (860) 566-5368.

Members: Chm., John E. Saunders III, Deputy Comr., Dept. of Labor; Richard G. Akeroyd, Jr., State Librarian; Leslie Averna, Acting Assoc. Comr., Div. of Educational Programs and Services, Dept. of Education; William R. Belloti, Deputy Comr., Dept. of Labor; Jeffrey Blodgett, Dir. of Research and Planning, Dept. of Economic and Community Development; Benjamin Dixon, Deputy Comr., Dept. of Education; John Halliday, Dir., Bureau of Rehabilitation Services; Zena Kovack, Planning Analyst, Dept. of Social Services; Dennis McNeil, Planning Analyst for Policy Development and Planning Div., Office of Policy and Management; Roberta Pawloski, Chief, Bureau of Adult Education and Training, Dept. of Education; Robert Suerken, Supt. of Schools, Dept. of Correction; Dr. Joseph Zikmund II, Assoc. for Research and Policy Support, Dept. of Higher Education.

Exec. Dir., Roger Therrien.

DEPARTMENT OF MENTAL HEALTH AND ADDICTION SERVICES

COMMISSIONER OF MENTAL HEALTH AND ADDICTION SERVICES

Appointed by the Governor, with the advice of the Board of Mental Health and Addiction Services, for four years, Sec. 17a-450, Gen. Stat. Salary, Comr., $92,000; Deputy Comr. for Mental Health, $83,500; Deputy Comr. for Addiction Services, $83,500. Address: 410 Capitol Ave., Hartford 06134. Tel., (860) 418-7000.

Comr., Albert J. Solnit, M.D., New Haven, March 1, 1999; *Deputy Comr. for Mental Health,* Raymond J. Gorman, M.H. S.A., Southington; *Deputy Comr. for Addiction Services,* Thomas A. Kirk, Jr., Ph.D., Ridgefield; *Dir. of Admin. and Operations,* Karen Snyder, South Windham; *Dir. of Mental Health Div.,* Peter Mendelson, Barkhamsted; *Medical Dir.,* vacancy; *Chief, Div. of Safety Services,* Robert Taylor, Oxford; *Chief of Admin. and Fiscal Services,* David Crompton, New Haven; *Dir., Info. Systems Div.,* Charles Hoadley, East Granby; *Dir. of Affirmative Action,* Lamar Eberhardt, Hartford; *Dir. of Community Education,* Karen A. Kangas, Ed.D., West Hartford; *Dir. of Mental Health Community Services,* John Simsarian, Middle Haddam; *Dir. of Forensic Services,* Deborah Scott, A.C.S.W., Guilford; *Dir. of Human Resources,* Jeannette Deschesnes, M.H.S.A., East Hampton; *Dir. of Addiction Treatment and Coordination,*

Robert Savage, West Hartford; *Dir. of Planning, Addiction Services,* Clifford Laube, Southbury; *Dir. of Prevention, Intervention and Training, Addiction Services,* Karen Ohrenberger, Tolland; *Dir. of Psychological Services,* Susan Essock, Ph.D., West Hartford; *Dir. of Public Info. and Media Relations,* Claudette Carveth, Bloomfield; *Dir. of Addictions Program Monitoring,* Jose Ortiz, Bridgeport; *Dir., Quality Assessment and Improvement,* Lynne Garner, Middletown; *Legislative Program Mgrs.,* Doreen DelBianco, Waterbury; Sue Tanner, Glastonbury.

BOARD OF MENTAL HEALTH AND ADDICTION SERVICES. Sec. 17a-456, Gen. Stat. Address: 410 Capitol Ave., Hartford 06134. Tel., (860) 418-7000.

Ex officio, Albert J. Solnit, M.D., Comr. of Mental Health and Addiction Services.

Appointed by the Governor, Chm., Mary W. Brackett, Ph.D., Wilton; *Vice Chm.,* Philippa M. Coughlan, Ph.D., Middletown; *Secy.,* Claire C. Phelan, Woodmont; Mario T. Gaboury, J.D., Ph.D., Bridgeport; J. Kevin Kinsella, Ed.D., Hamden; Joseph F. Legg, Ph.D., East Lyme, Donald G. Miller, Tolland; Sarah B. Palmer, Lebanon; Susan Patrick, West Hartford; Carlos H. Salguero, M.D., New Haven; Kenneth G. Schooff, Coventry; Samuel R. Segal, Litchfield; William H. Sledge, M.D., New Haven.

Chm. and Designee of Regional Mental Health Boards: REGION I - *Pres.,* Claire Fray, Southport; Louis Schulman, Norwalk. REGION II - *Pres.,* Stella Cretella, West Haven; Alan Dann, Woodbridge. REGION III - *Chm.,* Carol Noil-Freda, Gales Ferry; Curt Beck, Ph.D., Storrs. REGION IV - *Chm.,* Mary Hess, Plainville; Ernie Hearion, Hartford. REGION V— Chm., Richard Stanco, Brookfield; Renato Ricciuti, Waterbury.

Exec. Dirs. of Regional Action Councils: Robert Brex, Wauregan; Nelson J. Forman III, Plainville; Robert Francis, Bridgeport; Marlene F. McGann, Wallingford; Theodore Nikolla, New London; Rochelle Ripley, East Hartford; Carl Rush, Stamford; Ruth Ann Sforza, Waterbury; Janet Sharkis, Norwalk; John Sponauer, Shelton; Pat Surprenant, Brookfield; Lori Zehe, Avon; vacancy.

INTERSTATE COMPACT ON MENTAL HEALTH. Sec. 17-259, Gen. Stat. Address: Dept. of Mental Health and Addiction Services, 410 Capitol Ave., Hartford 06134. Tel., (860) 418-7000.

Admin. for Mentally Ill Adults, Albert J. Solnit, M.D.; *Admin. for Mentally Deficient,* Peter O'Meara; *Admin. for Mentally Ill Children and Youth,* Linda D'Amario Rossi.

TREATMENT FACILITIES

CONNECTICUT VALLEY HOSPITAL, MIDDLETOWN. Advisory board members appointed by the Supt., Sec. 17a-470, Gen. Stat. Salary, Supt. $114,370; Number of hospital beds, Gen. Psych., 199; Addiction Services 100; Forensic, 173. Address: Box 351, Middletown 06457. Tel. (860) 344-2666.

Gen. Psychiatric Div. Advisory Bd.: Chm., Jay Bingham, East Hampton; *Vice Chm., 1st* Claire Phelan, Milford; Gay Blair, East Haven; Charlotte Inglehardt-Suraci, North Haven; Ronald Mead, Seymour; Mary Jean Michel, Ansonia; Michael Niman, Meriden; Jerry Ross, New Haven; Leona Ruggiero, Middletown; Marion Sulima, Meriden; Raymond Wing, Middletown; *Special Status,* George Lacoske, Meriden.

Whiting Forensic Div. Advisory Bd.: Chm., Joseph E. Milardo, Middletown; Robert Adnopoz, Hamden; Stephen Fleck, M.D., New Haven; Leslie M. Lothstein, Ph.D., ABPP, West Hartford; Frank J. McCoy, Vernon; Peggy Miller-Hill, ACSW, Monroe; Harold I. Schwartz, M.D., Hartford; Albert J. Solnit, M.D., Comr. of Mental Health and Addiction Services. *Ex officio,* Michael A. Norko, M.D.

Chief Exec. Officer, Garrell S. Mullaney; *Dir. of General Psychiatry Div.,* Judith Normandin; *Acting Dir. of Addiction Services Div.,* Dennis Carroll; *Dir. Whiting Forensic Div.,* vacancy; *Dir. of Human Resources and Patient Central Services,* R. Kearcher; *President of the Medical Staff,* R. Johnson, M.D.; *Dir. of Patient Care Services and Quality Improvement,* Karen Peterkin; Dir. *of Fiscal Services and Plant Operations,* R. Spector; *Dir. of Health Care Services,* J. Zimerman, M.D.

CEDARCREST REGIONAL HOSPITAL. Sec. 17a-470, Gen. Stat. Salary, Supt., $99,551. Number of hospital beds, psychiatric, 90, substance abuse, 90. Address: 525 Russell Rd., Newington 06111. Tel., (860) 666-4613.

Advisory Bd.: Acting Chm., Dennis Keenan, Andover; *Acting Vice Chm.,* Mert Coulombe, New Britain; Mary Ambler, Newington; Evelyn Black, Wethersfield; Warren Bourque, Newington; Rip Holmes, Hartford; Hilda LaRosa, Hartford; Mary Fran Libassi, West Hartford; vacancy.

Supt., Andrew J. Phillips, Ed.D.; *Chief of Professional Services,* Roger Coleman, M.D.; *Mental Health Services Fiscal Dir. I,* Thomas U. Seydewitz; *Dir. Of Hospital Operations and Nursing Services,* Helene Vartelas, M.S.N., R.N., C.S.; *Dir. of Community Services,* Ralph Matteo, A.C.S.W.; *Dir. of Substance Abuse Services,* James Catalanotto; *Dir. of Inpatient Mental Health Services,* Tony Nucifora.

LOCAL MENTAL HEALTH AUTHORITIES

Regional Mental Health Bds. Sec. 17-484, Gen. Stat. REGION I - *Exec. Dir.,* Vicki S. Smith, 83 East Ave., Suite 310, Norwalk 06851. Tel., (203) 857-0565. REGION II - *Exec. Dir.,* Catherine Ferry, Conn. Valley Hospital, P.O. Box 351, Middletown 06457. Tel., (860) 344-2790. REGION III - *Exec. Dir.,* Sheryl Breetz, 26 Dogwood Cir., Newington 06111. Tel., (860) 667-6388. REGION V - *Exec. Dir.,* Leah Lentoche, 20 East Main St., Room 328, Waterbury 06702. Tel., (203) 757-9603.

CONNECTICUT MENTAL HEALTH CENTER, NEW HAVEN. Operated by DMHAS in collaboration with Yale University, Sec. 17a-460, Gen. Stat. Address: 34 Park St., New Haven 06519. Tel., (203) 789-7300. *Dir.,* Selby Jacobs, M.D.

Advisory Bd.: William Farrell, New Haven; Susan Godshall, J.D., New Haven; Willie Greene, New Haven; Claire A. Hendricks, New Haven; Marta E. Moret, M.P.H., New Haven; Beverly A. Nelson, M.S.N., R.N., New Haven; Miriam Niederman, Bethany; Norman G. Roth, New Haven; Ezra E.H. Griffith, M.D., New Haven; vacancy.

CAPITOL REGION MENTAL HEALTH CENTER, HARTFORD. Sec. 17a-450, Gen. Stat. Address: 500 Vine St., Hartford 06112. Tel., (860) 297-0800. *Dir.,* Lillian Tamayo, A.C.S.W.

RIVER VALLEY SERVICES, MIDDLETOWN. Address: P.O. Box 351, Silver St., Middletown 06457. Tel., (860) 344-2040. *Dir.,* Howard Reid.

Advisory Bd.: Chm., Brian Ladr, Middletown; Karen Anderson, Middletown; Jay Bingham, East Hampton; Nancy Brault, Middletown; Terry Carbone, Middletown; Rudi Funke, Jr., Old Lyme; Martha McVerry, Old Saybrook; Richard Murphy, Portland; Kathleen Welch, Deep River; Tom Whitin, Higganum.

SOUTHEASTERN MENTAL HEALTH AUTHORITY, NORWICH. Address: P.O. Box 508, Norwich 06360. Tel., (860) 823-5305. *Dir.,* Douglas R. Davies, Jr.

Advisory Bd.: Chm., Thomas J. Hyland, Mystic; Jacqueline Aronson, Niantic; Margaret S. Ayer, No. Franklin; Lawrence W. Barrett, New London; Constance Bement, Norwich; Jeffrey Bowens, Norwich; Richard E. DesRoches, Norwich; Al Fecteau, Norwich; Lynn Flanagan, Niantic; Jeanne Green, Niantic; Marc Jacques, Norwich; Dolores Jeter, New London; Peggy Morningstar, Norwich; Sarah Palmer, Lebanon; Bruce Thornton, Norwich; Alison Vaughn, Old Lyme; Stanley E. White, Voluntown; William J. Willetts, Jr., East Lyme.

SOUTHWEST CONNECTICUT MENTAL HEALTH SYSTEM, BRIDGEPORT. Address: 211 State St., 4th Floor, Bridgeport 06604. Tel., (203) 696-3368. *Chief Exec. Officer,* David K. Hunter, Ph.D.

WESTERN CONNECTICUT MENTAL HEALTH NETWORK. Address: P.O. Box 5599, Newtown 06470. Tel., (203) 426-4613. *Dir.,* Karen Evertson, MSW, East Hampton.

PSYCHIATRIC SECURITY REVIEW BOARD

Appointed by the Governor with the advice and consent of either House of the General Assembly. Sec. 17a-581, Gen. Stat. Compensation of members, if not a fulltime state employee, $75.00 for each day member is engaged in the performance of official duties, plus expenses. Address: 505 Hudson St., 2nd Floor, Hartford 06106. Tel., (860) 566-1441.

Sylvia Cancela, South Windsor; Robert B. Berger, Enfield, Janet E. Williams, M.D., West Hartford, June 30, 1997. Julia R. Grenier, Collinsville, June 30, 1999. John T. Ryan, Newington, June 30, 2000.

Exec. Dir., Martha E. Lewis, West Hartford.

DEPARTMENT OF MENTAL RETARDATION

COMMISSIONER OF MENTAL RETARDATION

Appointed by the Governor on advice of the Council on Mental Retardation, with the advice and consent of either House of the General Assembly, Secs. 4-5—4-8, Gen. Stat. Salary, Comr., $95,000; Deputy Comr., $83,500. Address: 460 Capitol Ave., Hartford 06106. Tel., (860) 418-6000.

Comr., Peter H. O'Meara, Hartford, March 1, 1999; *Deputy Comr.,* Linda Goldfarb, West Hartford.

COUNCIL ON MENTAL RETARDATION. Appointed in accordance with Sec. 17a-270 Gen. Stat. Compensation of members, necessary expenses. Address: 460 Capitol Ave., Hartford 06106.

Ex officio, Peter H. O'Meara, Comr. of Mental Retardation.

Appointed by the Governor, Richard C. Brown, Enfield; Margery M. Cole, Farmington; J. C. David Hadden, Simsbury; Samuel R. Hyman, Danbury; Margaret O. Lahda, Manchester; James F. Leckman, M.D., Hamden; Albert Lognin, Hartford; Eleanor N. Steere, Groton.

Appointed by the Pres. Pro Tempore of the Senate, Stuart Perlow, Westport. Appointed by the Senate Minority Leader, Sheila S. Mulvey, Cheshire. Appointed by the Speaker of the House, John Andreini, West Hartford. Appointed by the House Minority Leader, Beatrice Krawiecki, South Norwalk.

Appointed by the Southbury Training School Board of Trustee, Lou Richards, Wolcott.

STATE PLANNING COUNCIL ON DEVELOPMENTAL DISABILITIES

Appointed by the Governor for three year terms, Public Law 103-230. Developmental Disabilities Act of 1994. Address: 460 Capitol Ave., Hartford 06106.

Robert L. Board, Cheshire; Suzanne S. Brown, North Stonington; Kiley J. Carlson, Middletown; Pamela DonAroma, Kensington; Sarah W. Dunion, Norwich; John J. Eusko, Jr., East Hartford; Andrew A. Feinstein, Avon; Stephen F. Frazzini, West Hartford; June S. Freeman, Meriden; Marjorie S. Freeman, Trumbull; Stephen Greenspan, Andover; John F. Halliday, Bloomfield; Claude Holcomb, Hartford; Stanley J. Kosloski, Jr., Cromwell; Anthony J. LaCava, Jr., Bethany; Kevin H. Loveland, Farmington; James McGaughey, Glastonbury; Joanne Miller, Greenwich; Philip Myrun, West Hartford; Enid M. Negron, Hartford; Laurie Santerson, Unionville; Jerome J. Spears, Willimantic; Samantha Waddell, West Hartford; James Walker, Norwalk; Louzett Williams, Forestville.

Exec. Dir., Edward T. Preneta.

REGIONAL OFFICES

Dept. of Mental Retardation, Sec. 17a-210, Gen. Stat.

NORTHWEST REGION

Address: 250 Freight St., Waterbury 06702. Tel., (203) 596-4371. *Dir.,* Steven Staugaitis, Ph.D. Salary, Dir., $76,218-$97,766.

Advisory and Planning Council: Joe Colombatto, Mary Conklin, Dorothea LaBelle, Dawn Lambert, Christine Steele.

CHESHIRE OFFICE

Address: 25 Creamery Rd., Cheshire 06410. Tel., (203) 250-3096.

DANBURY OFFICE

Address: 400 Main St., Danbury 06810. Tel., (203) 797-4133.

TORRINGTON OFFICES

Address: 195 Alvord Park Rd., Torrington 06790. Tel., (860) 482-0196.

883 Main St., Torrington 06790. Tel., (860) 496-4116.

NORTH CENTRAL REGION

Address: The Exchange, 270 Farmington Ave., Suite 245, Farmington 06032. Tel., (860) 679-7000. *Dir.,* Kathleen McClellen. Salary, Dir., $76,218-$97,766.

Advisory and Planning Council: Ann Anderson, Marie Gannati, Marie Gibson, Michael Kinney, Lizabeth Mannino, John Quattrocchi, Mark Ritter.

NEWINGTON OFFICE

Address: 71 Mountain Rd., Newington 06111. Tel., (860) 679-7000.

EASTERN REGION

Address: 401 West Thames St., Unit 202, Norwich 06326. Tel., (860) 859-5400. *Dir.,* vacancy. Salary, Dir., $76,218-$97,766.

Advisory and Planning Council: Chm., Eleanor Steer; Betty Berthiaune, Kathleen Bradley, Norma Cassettari, Emmet Cosgrove, Sherrilyn Flannery, Mary Ann Forshaw-O'Keefe, Robert Gorman, Gardner Johnson, Gilbert LaHaie, Jan Lehrman, John J. McGrath, Jr., Ruth Newth, Katharine Porter, Cynthia Strickett, Gerard Sudowski, William Whelan, Katherine Wolf.

JOHN N. DEMPSEY CENTER

Address: 376 Pomfret St., Putnam 06260. Tel., (860) 928-7751.

WILLIMANTIC OFFICE

Address: 90 South Park St., Willimantic 06226. Tel. (860) 456-6327.

MYSTIC EDUCATION CENTER

Address: 240 Oral School Rd., Mystic 06355. Tel., (860) 572-7221.

SOUTHWEST REGION

Address: 115 Virginia Ave., Bridgeport 06610. Tel., (203) 579-6725. *Dir.,* Linda Underwood. Salary, Dir., $76,218-$97,766.

Advisory and Planning Council: Theresa Brown, Peter Carbine, Cheryl Cook, Brenda Dye, John Gibson, Alan Jaffe, Alfred Jennings, Fred Hurley, Marian Lewis, Frank Neulle, Patty Richards, Richard Saunders, Lisa Schwab, Perii Skolnick.

ELLA T. GRASSO CENTER

Address: Armory Rd., Stratford 06497. Tel., (203) 579-6906.

LOWER FAIRFIELD COUNTY CENTER

Address: 142 Silvermine Ave., Norwalk 06850-1607. Tel., (203) 846-9531.

SOUTH CENTRAL REGION

Address: 104 South Turnpike Rd., Wallingford 06492. Tel., (203) 294-5049. *Dir.,* Kathryn duPree. Salary, Dir., $76,218-$97,766.

Advisory and Planning Council: Alene Clancy, Shirley Fritz, Brad B. Gallant, Sylvia Hare, Shirley Heiney, Lorraine Laydon, Pat McGalliard, Jim McGrath, Joseph Parente, Alice Pomper.

MERIDEN CENTER

Address: 35 Undercliff Rd., Meriden 06451. Tel., (203) 238-6300.

SOUTHBURY TRAINING SCHOOL

Address: P.O. Box 872, South Britain Rd., Southbury 06488-0901. Tel., (203) 262-9602. *Dir.,* Charles Hamad, Ph.D. Salary, Dir., $76,218-$97,766.

Bd. of Trustees: Gertrude K. Berman, Southbury; Philip K. Bondy, Woodbridge; Ann Dougherty, Shelton; Richard J. Rawson, Riverside; Louis E. Richards, Waterbury; Irving J. Sloan, Danbury; Joan Taylor, Southbury.

DEPARTMENT OF MOTOR VEHICLES

COMMISSIONER OF MOTOR VEHICLES

Appointed by the Governor, with the advice and consent of either House of the General Assembly, for four years, Secs. 4-5—4-8, Gen. Stat. Salary, Comr., $83,500; Deputy Comrs., $75,500. Address: 60 State St., Wethersfield 06161. Tel., (860) 566-2240.

Comr., Jose O. Salinas, Rocky Hill, March 1, 1999; *Deputy Comrs.,* Joseph D. Shilinga, New Britain; Joseph G. Wankerl, Southington.

LOCAL BRANCH OFFICES

Office	Address	Manager	Tel. No.
Bridgeport	1825 East Main St., 06608	Judith Corbett	(203) 579-6223
Danbury	25 Tamarack Ave., 06811-4884	Carolyn Sinnott	(203) 797-4170
Enfield	4 Pearson Way, 06082	Charlotte Cardona	(860) 623-5124
Hamden	1985 State St., 06517-9998	Jack Melia	(203) 789-7520
New Britain	1185 W. Main St., 06053	Karen Lackey	(860) 827-7743
Norwalk	540 Main Ave. 06851	Pauline Oliver	(203) 840-1993
Norwich	173 Salem Tpke., 06360-0969	Marilyn Quayle	(860) 887-2535
Old Saybrook	7 Custom Dr., 06475	Peggy Nanfito	(860) 399-8353
Waterbury	2210 Thomaston Ave., 06704	Janice Hughes	(203) 596-4481

Office	Address	Manager	Tel. No.
Wethersfield (Main Office)	60 State St., 06161	Susan Houle	(860) 566-2640
Willimantic	1557 West Main St., 06226	Ann Kuczma	(860) 423-1688

PHOTO LICENSE CENTERS

Office	Address	Manager	Tel. No.
Hamden	37 Marne St.	Jack Melia	(203) 789-7520
Middletown	Clocktower Shops	Peggy Nanfito	(860) 399-8353
Milford	Parsons Government Complex	Judith Corbett	(203) 579-6223
New London	New London Mall	Marilyn Quayle	(860) 887-2535
New Milford	Bank & Trust	Carolyn Sinnott	(203) 797-4170
Stamford	Train Station	Pauline Oliver	(203) 840-1993
Torrington	City Hall	Janice Hughes	(203) 596-4481

MOBILE PHOTO UNITS

Visits	Manager	Tel. No.
Avon, Bloomfield, Bristol, Colchester, Derby, Greenwich, Groton, Hamden, Kent, Litchfield, Meriden, Putnam, Salisbury, Southington, Vernon, Waterford, Westport, Wolcott.	Branch Operations	(860) 566-3090

SATELLITE OFFICES

Office	Address	Manager	Tel. No.
Putnam	165 Kennedy Ave.	Ann Kuczma	(860) 423-1688
Stamford	888 Washington Ave.	Pauline Oliver	(203) 840-1993
Winsted	151 Torrington Rd.	Janice Hughes	(203) 596-4481

LICENSING AGENTS

Automobile Assoc. of America (AAA)	Manager	Tel. No.
Avon, Cromwell, Enfield, Manchester, Plainville, Waterford, West Hartford.	Branch Operations	(860) 566-3090

OFFICE OF POLICY AND MANAGEMENT

SECRETARY OF THE OFFICE OF POLICY AND MANAGEMENT

Appointed by the Governor, with the advice and consent of the General Assembly, for four years, Secs. 4-5—4-8, Gen. Stat. Salaries, Secy., $95,000; Deputy Secy., $90,000; Under Secretaries: Budget and Financial Mgmt., $64,000-$87,000; Intergovernmental Policy, $64,000-$87,000; Policy Development and Planning, $64,000-

$87,000; Management and Performance Evaluation, $64,000-$87,000. Address: 450 Capitol Ave., P.O. Box 341441, Hartford 06134-1441. Tel., (860) 418-6200; FAX, (860) 418-6487.

Secy. of the Office of Policy and Management, Michael W. Kozlowski, Granby, March 1, 1999; *Deputy Secy.,* Donald W. Downes, New Britain; *Under Secretaries: Exec. Budget Officer,* Pam Law, Tolland; *Intergovernmental Policy,* Barbara A. Petitjean, Simsbury; *Policy Development and Planning,* Leonard D'Amico, Beacon Falls; *Mgmt. and Performance Evaluation,* Roderic Rahe, Darien.

STATE BOND COMMISSION. Sec. 3-20(c), Gen. Stat. Address: Secy., Office of Policy and Management, 450 Capitol Ave., MS#55SEC, P.O. Box 341441, Hartford 06134-1441.

Chm., John G. Rowland, Governor; *Secy.,* Michael W. Kozlowski, Secy., Office of Policy and Management; Christopher Burnham, State Treasurer; Nancy Wyman, State Comptroller; Richard Blumenthal, Attorney General; Theodore R. Anson, Comr. of Public Works; State Sen. William H. Nickerson and State Rep. Carl J. Schiessl, Co-Chm. of the Joint Legislative Committee on Finance, Revenue and Bonding; State Sen. George Jepsen and State Rep. Richard O. Belden, Ranking Minority Members of the Joint Legislative Committee on Finance, Revenue and Bonding.

EXPRESSWAY BOND COMMITTEE. Sec. 13a-199(b), Gen. Stat. Address: Secy., Office of Policy and Management, 450 Capitol Ave., MS#55SEC, P.O. Box 341441, Hartford 06134-1441.

Ex officio, Chm., John G. Rowland, Governor; *Secy.,* Michael W. Kozlowski, Secy., Office of Policy and Management; Christopher Burnham, State Treasurer; Nancy Wyman, State Comptroller; Richard Blumenthal, Attorney General; Theodore R. Anson, Comr. of Public Works.

MUNICIPAL FINANCE ADVISORY COMMISSION. Appointed by the Governor to serve at his pleasure, Sec. 7-394b, Gen. Stat. Address: 450 Capitol Ave., P.O. Box 341441, Hartford 06134-1441. Tel., (860) 418-6400.

Appointed by the Governor, Paul C. Beaulieu, Cromwell; Katherine H. Campbell, Woodbury; Douglas W. Gillette, West Hartford; Jack E. Miller, Seymour; Edward T. O'Neill, Jr., Cheshire; Barbara A. Petitjean, Simsbury; Marie V. Phelan, Killingworth; Jeffrey H. Smith, Storrs.

CONNECTICUT ENERGY ADVISORY BOARD. Sec. 16a-3, Gen. Stat. Address: 450 Capitol Ave., P.O. Box 341441, Hartford 06134-1441. Tel., (860) 418-6297.

Ex officio, James F. Sullivan, Acting Comr. of Transportation; Mortimer A. Gelston, *Chm.,* Connecticut Siting Council; Sidney J. Holbrook, Comr. of Environmental Protection; Peter N. Ellef, Comr. of Economic and Community Development; Theodore R. Anson, Comr. of Public Works; Reginald J. Smith, Chm., Public Utilities Control Authority.

Appointed by the Governor, Charles S. Isenberg, North Granby; Frank J. Johnson, Forestville; William E. Cratty, Bethel; Lorraine Tinsley, Bristol.

Appointed by the Pres. Pro Tempore of the Senate, Mary J. Healy, Meriden; Glenda C. Reed, Farmington; James P. Sandler, Bloomfield. Appointed by the Speaker of the House, *Chm.*, Michael Casella, New Britain; Barry Ilberman, West Hartford; Paul Popinchalk, West Hartford.

CONNECTICUT ADVISORY COMMISSION ON INTERGOVERNMENTAL RELATIONS

Sec. 2-79a, Gen. Stat. Compensation of members, necessary expenses. Address: 450 Capitol Ave., P.O. Box 341441, Hartford, 06134-1441.

James O'Leary, Goshen, Designee of the Pres. Pro Tempore of the Senate; Jefferson B. Davis, Pomfret, Designee of the Speaker of the House; Stephen J. Hudd, New Haven, Designee of the Senate Minority Leader; *Vice Chm.*, Alice V. Meyer, Easton, Designee of the House Minority Leader; Barbara A. Petitjean, Designee of the Secy. of Policy and Management; Andrea Pereira, Designee of the Comr. of Economic and Community Development; David Leff, Designee of the Comr. of Environmental Protection; Karen Flanagan, Designee of the Comr. of Education.

Appointed by the Governor, John J. Allison, Jr., West Hartford; Paul Audley, Fairfield; Katherine H. Campbell, Woodbury; Timothy Campbell, Canton; Sonya F. Googins, Glastonbury; Bruce Gresczyk, New Hartford; Sandra Klebanoff, West Hartford; Walter Pawelkiewicz, Windham; Michael S. Peters, Hartford; Johanne A. Presser, Suffield.

Appointed by the Pres. Pro Tempore of the Senate, Lewis B. Rome, Bloomfield. Appointed by the Senate Minority Leader, Theodore Brindamour, Manchester. Appointed by the Speaker of the House, Howard Rifkin, Hartford. Appointed by the House Minority Leader, Margaret Wirtenberg, Ph.D., Weston. Appointed by the Connecticut Conference of Municipalities, Joel Cogen, Hamden. Appointed by the Council of Small Towns, George Hill, Mansfield.

Exec. Dir., David W. Russell; *Research Analyst,* Brian E. West.

CONNECTICUT STATE OFFICE OF INFORMATION AND TECHNOLOGY

Sec. 16a-110, Gen. Stat. Address: c/o Office of Policy and Management, 450 Capitol Ave., P. O. Box 341441, Hartford 06134-1441. Tel., (860) 418-6218.

Acting Dir., George E. Fox, Ph.D.

THE CONNECTICUT AGRICULTURAL EXPERIMENT STATION BOARD OF CONTROL

Established 1875. Sec. 22-79, Gen. Stat. Compensation of members, none. Address: Box 1106, New Haven 06504. Tel., (203) 789-7214.

Ex officio, Pres., John G. Rowland, Governor; Shirley Ferris, Comr. of Agriculture; *Dir./Treas.,* John F. Anderson.

Appointed by the Governor, *Secy.,* John Lyman III, Middlefield; Norma O'Leary, Thompson. Appointed by Bd. of Trustees of Wesleyan Univ., *Vice Pres.,* Gregory S.

Horne, Middle Haddam, July 1, 1999. Appointed by Bd. of Trustees of Univ. of Conn., Leon J. Zapadka, Bolton, July 1, 1999. Appointed by Governing Bd. of Sheffield Scientific School, Richard H. Bowerman, Orange, July 1, 1998.

JUVENILE JUSTICE ADVISORY COMMITTEE

Appointed by the Governor to serve at his pleasure. Address: c/o Office of Policy and Management, Policy Development and Planning Div., 450 Capitol Ave., MS#52CPD, Hartford 06134-1441.

Chm., Curtis H. Roggi, Glastonbury, Charles E. Alfano, Somers; Glenda M. Armstrong, Danbury; Robert M. Balboni, Farmington; Richard Barton, Rocky Hill; Henry O. Crawford, Stamford; Eileen M. Daily, Westbrook; Linda D'Amario Rossi, Hartford; Thomas G. Ganley, Newington; Altarik J. Harmon, New London; Ginger Hermann, West Haven; Paul R. Hoey, Wethersfield; Tasha Hunt, Hamden; Tonya L. Lewis, Bridgeport; Evelyn Mendoza, Waterbury; Frank N. Nicastro, Bristol; George R. Oleyer, Oxford; Nicholas Pastore, New Haven; Peggy M. Perillie, Trumbull; Leigh A. Piscitelli, Branford; Alicia Roman, Waterbury; Anthony J. Salius, Harwinton; Norma Schatz, Avon; Theodore S. Sergi, West Hartford; Palmirarelis Torres, Hartford; Robert Troup, New Milford; Terrence L. Weaver-Bey, Bloomfield; Kevin D. J. Witkos, Canton; Kay Wyrick, Waterbury.

COMMISSION ON PRISON AND JAIL OVERCROWDING

Secs. 18-87j, 18-87k, Gen. Stat.

Ex officio, Hon. Aaron Ment, Chief Court Admin.; John J. Armstrong, Comr., Dept. of Correction; Kenneth H. Kirschner, Comr., Dept. of Public Safety; John M. Bailey, Chief State's Atty.; Gerard A. Smyth, Chief Public Defender; Paul E. Brown, Chief Bail Comr.

Appointed by the Governor, *Chm.,* M. Jodi Rell, Brookfield; Robert J. Bosco, Colchester, John E. Meeker, Washington Depot, *Representing Government Officials;* Joseph P. Faughnan, West Haven, *Police Chief;* Robert M. Balboni, Farmington, *Conn. Halfway House, Inc., Offender Services;* Gary J. Merton, *Victim Services;* Walter A. Borden, Bloomfield, Robert Cascella, Newtown, *Public Members.*

CONNECTICUT PARTNERSHIP FOR LONG TERM CARE

Sec. 17b-252, Gen. Stat. Address: Office of Policy and Management, 450 Capitol Ave., MS#52LTC, P.O. Box 341441, Hartford 06134-1441. Tel., (860) 418-6318.

Project Dir., David J. Guttchen, Wethersfield.

DEPARTMENT OF PUBLIC HEALTH

COMMISSIONER OF PUBLIC HEALTH

Appointed by the Governor, with the advice and consent of either House of the General Assembly, for four years, Secs. 4-5—4-8, 19a-2, Gen. Stat. Salary, Comr.,

$95,000. Address: 410 Capitol Ave., P.O. Box 340308, Hartford 06134-0308. Tel., (860) 509-8000; FAX, (860) 509-7286.

Comr., Stephen A. Harriman, Colchester, March 1, 1999. Tel., (860) 509-7101.

Chief of Staff, Elizabeth M. Burns, Wethersfield. Tel., (860) 509-7101.

BUREAU OF REGULATORY SERVICES. Address: 410 Capitol Ave., P.O. Box 340308, Hartford 06134-0308. Tel., (860) 509-7406.

Bureau Chief, Warren Wollschlager.

BUREAU OF COMMUNITY HEALTH. Address: 410 Capitol Ave., P.O. Box 340308, Hartford 06134-0308. Tel., (860) 509-7655.

Bureau Chief, Ardell A. Wilson, D.D.S., M.P.H.

BUREAU OF ADMINISTRATIVE AND SUPPORT SERVICES. Address: 410 Capitol Ave., P.O. Box 340308, Hartford 06134-0308. Tel., (860) 509-7218.

Bureau Chief, Elise Gaulin-Kremer, Ph.D.

OFFICE OF POLICY, PLANNING AND EVALUATION. Address: 410 Capitol Ave., P.O. Box 340308, Hartford 06134-0308. Tel., (860) 509-7120. *Office Dir.,* Marie Roberto, Ph.D.

OFFICE OF SPECIAL SERVICES. Address: 410 Capitol Ave., P.O. Box 340308, Hartford 06134-0308. Tel., (860) 509-7101. *Office Dir.,* Mark F. Brennan.

VARIOUS HEALTH SERVICE BOARDS

CONNECTICUT EXAMINING BOARD FOR BARBERS, HAIRDRESSERS, AND COSMETICIANS. Appointed by the Governor to serve at his pleasure, Sec. 20-235a, Gen. Stat. Address: 410 Capitol Ave., P.O. Box 340308, Hartford 06134-0308. Tel., (860) 509-7648.

Chm., Reno R. Pelletier, Plantsville; Peter Aiello, Hartford; Amy Cobuzzi, Berlin; Alice Hummel, North Haven; Richard C. Nardiello, Woodbury; Susan Rood, Windsor Locks; Patricia Verna, Wallingford; two vacancies.

STATE BOARD OF CHIROPRACTIC EXAMINERS. Appointed by the Governor to serve at his pleasure, Sec. 20-25, Gen. Stat. Address: 410 Capitol Ave., P.O. Box 340308., Hartford 06134-0308. Tel., (860) 509-7648.

Chm., Agostino A. Villani, East Hampton; Linda Boger, Naugatuck; Brendan T. Canty, Ridgefield; James P. Cianciolo, D.C., Guilford; Ronald M. Clukey, D.C., Milford; Robert J. Porzio, D.C., Waterbury; Kenneth Sheptoff, Avon; vacancy.

STATE DENTAL COMMISSION. Appointed by the Governor to serve at his pleasure, Sec. 20-103a, Gen. Stat. Address: 410 Capitol Ave., P.O. Box 340308, Hartford 06134-0308. Tel., (860) 509-7648.

Chm., Roger Ostrander, Jr., D.M.D., Waterbury; William M. Bridgeford, Jr., D.D.S., Middlefield; Jay D. Edwards, D.D.S., Wethersfield; Robert Friedman, D.D.S., Fairfield; David M. Lynch, D.D.S., New Milford; Walter L. Mitchell, Waterbury; David W. Perkins, D.M.D., Southington; Raymond Stabinsky, Norwalk; vacancy.

CONNECTICUT BOARD OF EXAMINERS OF EMBALMERS AND FUNERAL DIRECTORS. Appointed by the Governor to serve at his pleasure, Sec. 20-208, Gen. Stat. Address: 410 Capitol Ave., P.O. Box 340308, Hartford 06134-0308. Tel., (860) 509-7648.

Chm., Celia Pinzi, Orange; Jevera K. Hennessey, Stamford; Donald F. McSweegan, Rocky Hill; Jeffrey R. Thurston, New Britain; Morton L. Weinstein, Farmington.

CONNECTICUT HOMEOPATHIC MEDICAL EXAMINING BOARD. Appointed by the Governor to serve at his pleasure, Sec. 20-8, Gen. Stat. Address: 410 Capitol Ave., P.O. Box 340308, Hartford 06134-0308. Tel., (860) 509-7648.

Acting Chm., Ahmed N. Currim, M.D., Fairfield; Jose M. Mullen, M.D., Colchester; Sarah Najamy, Weston; Diane Servos-Newman, Monroe; William E. Shevin, M.D., Woodstock.

BOARD OF EXAMINERS OF HYPERTRICHOLOGISTS. Appointed by the Governor to serve at his pleasure, Sec. 20-268, Gen. Stat. Address: 410 Capitol Ave., P.O. Box 340308, Hartford 06134-0308. Tel., (860) 509-7648.

Chm., Lawrence M. Jacoby, M.D., West Simsbury; Marsha A. Adams, Hamden; Tova Conners, Orange; Elsie Gasuk, New Britain; Anna Z. Kasprak, New Britain.

CONNECTICUT MEDICAL EXAMINING BOARD. Appointed by the Governor to serve at his pleasure, Sec. 20-8a, Gen. Stat. Address: 410 Capitol Ave., P.O. Box 340308, Hartford 06134-0308. Tel., (860) 509-7648.

Chm., Richard M. Ratzan, M.D., West Hartford; Edward J. Fredericks, M.D., Farmington; Howard L. Goodkind, Litchfield; Carl A. Jaeger, M.D., Greenwich; Velandy Manohar, M.D., Haddam; Bruce M. McDonald, M.D., Southport; Sarah E. McGirr, Groton; Rosalind L. Moldwin, New Britain; Pamela A. Nole, Bethlehem; Dennis G. O'Neill, M.D., Glastonbury; Donna J. Rescorl, Vernon; vacancy.

STATE BOARD OF NATUREOPATHIC EXAMINERS. Appointed by the Governor to serve at his pleasure, Sec. 20-35, Gen. Stat. Address: 410 Capitol Ave., P.O. Box 340308, Hartford 06134-0308. Tel., (860) 509-7648.

Chm., Robert M. Murphy, N.D., Bantam; Merrill R. Eisenberg, Ph.D., Portland; Jonathan S. Raistrick, N.D., Waterbury.

CONNECTICUT STATE BOARD OF EXAMINERS FOR NURSING. Appointed by the Governor to serve at his pleasure, Sec. 20-88, Gen. Stat. Address: 410 Capitol Ave., P.O. Box 340308, Hartford 06134-0308. Tel., (860) 509-7648

Chm., Nancy L. Bafundo, R.N., Newington; Armand S. Amendola, Guilford; Susan Brown, Stamford; Patricia H. Casey, A.P.R.N., Waterbury; Joan H. Dobbins, Southington; Joyce Hunt, Wethersfield; Andrea B. O'Connor, Ed.D., Sherman; Mary E. O'Hurley, R.N., Glastonbury; Mary B. Prybylo, R.N., Plantsville; Linda R. Sacheli, Enfield; Bernard D. Shea, Ph.D., West Hartford; Douglas A. Wade, Berlin.

CONNECTICUT BOARD OF EXAMINERS FOR OPTICIANS. Appointed by the Governor to serve at his pleasure, Sec. 20-139a, Gen. Stat. Address: 410 Capitol Ave., P.O. Box 340308, Hartford 06134-0308. Tel., (860) 509-7648.

Chm., Douglas H. Parker, Meriden; Oliver Clark, Wolcott; Genevieve Kapelewski, Middletown.

CONNECTICUT BOARD OF EXAMINERS FOR OPTOMETRISTS. Appointed by the Governor to serve at his pleasure, Sec. 20-128a, Gen. Stat. Address: 410 Capitol Ave., P.O. Box 340308, Hartford 06134-0308. Tel., (860) 509-7648.

Chm., Edward F. Pinn, O.D., Old Saybrook; Leora A. Berns, O.D., Simsbury; Anthony Manzella, Pawcatuck; Kay A. Molochko, Norwich; John N. Sienko, O.D., Wallingford; Eugene A. Winakor, O.D., Norwich; vacancy.

CONNECTICUT OSTEOPATHIC EXAMINING BOARD. Appointed by the Governor to serve at his pleasure, Sec. 20-15, Gen. Stat. Address: 410 Capitol Ave., P.O. Box 340308, Hartford 06134-0308. Tel., (860) 509-7648.

Chm., Nicholas Palermo, D.O., Manchester; Kenneth Adams, D.O., Wethersfield; Foster Clark, D.O., Litchfield; two vacancies.

CONNECTICUT STATE BOARD OF EXAMINERS FOR PHYSICAL THERAPISTS. Appointed by the Governor to serve at his pleasure, Sec. 20-67, Gen. Stat. Address: 410 Capitol Ave., P.O. Box 340308, Hartford 06134-0308. Tel., (860) 509-7648.

Chm., Christine J. Kasinskas, Cheshire; Joan Grey, West Hartford; Eileen M. Ilberman, West Hartford; Krystyna Piotrowska-Nyerick, M.D., Derby; vacancy.

CONNECTICUT BOARD OF EXAMINERS IN PODIATRY. Appointed by the Governor to serve at his pleasure, Sec. 20-51, Gen. Stat. Address: 410 Capitol Ave., P.O. Box 340308, Hartford 06134-0308. Tel., (860) 509-7648.

Acting Chm., Martin M. Pressman, D.P.M., Orange; Richard Cutler, D.P.M., Farmington; Harold S. Diamond, D.P.M., North Haven; Everett A. Gamble, Enfield; Marc S. Mandell, Norwich.

BOARD OF EXAMINERS OF PSYCHOLOGISTS. Appointed by the Governor to serve at his pleasure, Sec. 20-186, Gen. Stat. Address: 410 Capitol Ave., P.O. Box 340308, Hartford 06134-0308. Tel., (860) 509-7648.

Chm., James J. Monahan, Ph.D., Pomfret Center; Joseph DeVito, Ph.D., Middletown; Gary L. Gendron, Dayville; Leigh Ann Hutchinson, Andover; Elizabeth S. Thayer, Ph.D., Avon.

CONNECTICUT BOARD OF VETERINARY MEDICINE. Appointed by the Governor to serve at his pleasure, Sec. 20-196, Gen. Stat. Address: 410 Capitol Ave., P.O. Box 340308, Hartford 06134. Tel., (860) 509-7648.

Chm., Jordan R. Dann, D.V.M., Ridgefield; Marcia B. Gest, Wilton; Ferris G. Gorra, D.V.M., Marble Dale; Richard E. Lau, D.V.M., Cheshire; Cynthia Walstedt, South Glastonbury.

OFFICE OF HEALTH CARE ACCESS

Appointed by the Governor for a term coterminous with the term of the Governor, or until a successor is chosen, Sec. 19a-612, Gen. Stat. Salary, Comr., $79,693. Address: 410 Capitol Ave., P.O. Box 340308, Hartford 06134-0308. Tel., (860) 418-7001; FAX, (860) 418-7053.

Acting Comr., William Diamond, Windsor.

COMMISSION ON MEDICOLEGAL INVESTIGATIONS

Appointed by the Governor to serve at his pleasure, Sec. 19a-401, Gen. Stat. Compensation of members, actual expenses. Address: 11 Shuttle Rd., Farmington 06032. Tel., (860) 679-3980; FAX, (860) 679-1257.

Ex officio, Stephen A. Harriman, Comr. of Public Health.

Chm., S. Evans Downing, M.D., Guilford; Robert E. Cone, Ph.D., Unionville; Francis R. Coughlin, Jr., M.D., J.D., New Canaan; Steven B. Duke, J.D., New Haven; Todd D. Fernow, Simsbury; Harry S. Gaucher, Jr., J.D., Willimantic; Regina M. Hitchery, Farmington; W. Raymond James, M.D., Essex.

OFFICE OF THE CHIEF MEDICAL EXAMINER

The Chief Medical Examiner appointed by the Commission on Medicolegal Investigations, Sec. 19a-403, Gen. Stat. Salary, Chief Medical Examiner, $159,135. Address: 11 Shuttle Rd., Farmington 06032. Tel., (860) 679-3980; FAX, (860) 679-1257.

Chief Medical Examiner, H. Wayne Carver II, M.D., Avon; *Deputy Chief Medical Examiner,* Edward T. McDonough, M.D., Bethel; *Associate Medical Examiners,* Thomas F. Gilchrist, M.D., Ira Kanfer, M.D., Arkady Katsnelson, M.D., Malka B. Shah, M.D.; *Dir., Toxicology Lab,* Sherwood Lewis, Ph.D.; *Admin.,* Thomas J. Baziak.

ASSISTANT MEDICAL EXAMINERS

Justin Ahamad, M.D., Washington Depot
Celedonio Asuncion, M.D., Hartford
Aileen T. Ong Bacay, M.D., Manchester
David H. Blumin, M.D., Bridgeport
Frank Braza, M.D., Danbury
Edward S. Breakell, M.D., Stamford
David Bregman, M.D., New Haven
Joseph Brenes, M.D., Wolcott
Paul C. Broomhead, M.D., Thomaston
Carlon M. Colker, M.D., Greenwich
Michele Conlon, M.D., Marlborough
Craig Czarsty, M.D., Oakville
Joseph Czarsty, M.D., Oakville
Joseph Daly, M.D., Waterbury
Joel Danisi, M.D., Kent
Charles J. Dayton, M.D., Southington
George Donahue, M.D., Enfield
Richard Dutton, M.D., Winsted
Harry Engle, M.D., Milford
Sa-id Esfahanian, M.D., Norwich
Donald Evans, M.D., Newtown
Leonardo Fernandez, M.D., Guilford
Sebastian J. Gallo, M.D., Middletown
James D. Garrity, M.D., Monroe
Anthony Giangrasso, M.D., Trumbull
James R. Gill, M.D., New Haven
Susan M. Gobel, M.D., Hartford
Richard Goldberg, M.D., Kensington
Richard Gritzmacher, M.D., Old Saybrook
Robert Grossman, M.D., Danbury
G. S. Gudnernatch, M.D., Salisbury
H. Patterson Harris, Jr., M.D., Southport
Carl W. Johnson, M.D., Enfield
Michael E. Keenan, M.D., Coventry
Michael Kelleher, M.D., Bridgeport
Michael Kilgannon, M.D., Willimantic
Leslie S. Kish, M.D., Bristol
Charles Kochan, M.D., Stratford
Gregory Kresel, M.D., Torrington
John Kritz, M.D., Thompson
David J. Krugman, M.D., New Britain
David Kurish, M.D., Sharon
Ralph J. LaGuardia, M.D., Mansfield Ctr.

Stephen Leach, M.D., Willimantic
Lewis I. Levenson, M.D., Enfield
Clarence Lipkoff, M.D., Milford
Anne M. Lorenzo, M.D., Cromwell
Joyce E. Millette, M.D., West Hartford
Henry D. Minot, M.D., Ridgefield
Vittorio Mirabelli, M.D., Bristol
George Molnar, M.D., Westport
Richard Monticciolo, M.D., Rocky Hill
Jon S. Morrow, M.D., Ph.D., New Haven
Dennis G. O'Neill, M.D., Manchester
Devbala Patel, M.D., Manchester
Edward Pendagast, Jr., M.D., Easton
Marjorie Petro, M.D., Willimantic
Boris Pukay, M.D., Mystic
Theodore Safford, Jr., M.D., Ridgefield
Harold Scanchez, M.D., New Britain
Francis R. Scifo, M.D., Stratford
Charles Scribner, M.D., Canton
Bernard Sheehan, M.D., Old Saybrook
Bernard Sherlip, M.D., Bridgeport
Warren Silliman, M.D., Windsor
John Sinard, M.D., New Haven
Neena Singh, M.D., Vernon
Jacob Slepian, M.D., Ansonia
Melvin Spielberg, M.D., Warehouse Point
Ismail Tarkhan, M.D., Milford
Leroy N. Testerman, M.D., Manchester
Dean F. Uphoff, M.D., Hartford
Benjamin Weisman, M.D., Bridgeport
Paul Wong, M.D. Putnam
Arthur Woolfson, M.D., Unionville
Jared B. Zelman, M.D., Sharon
Ronald A. Zlotoff, M.D., Waterbury

DEPARTMENT OF PUBLIC SAFETY

COMMISSIONER OF PUBLIC SAFETY

Appointed by the Governor, for four years, Secs. 4-5—4-8, Sec. 29-1b, Gen. Stat. Salary, Comr., $95,000. Administration offices, 1111 Country Club Rd., Middletown 06457-9294. Tel., (860) 685-8000.

Comr. of Public Safety, Kenneth H. Kirschner, Southington, March 1, 1999; *Deputy Comr., Div. of Fire, Emergency and Building Services,* George Luther; *Affirmative Action,* Phyllis Harden; *Labor Relations,* Sgt. Robert Tolomeo; *Government Affairs,* Lt. Paul Fitzgerald; *Conn. Forensic Science Laboratory,* Dr. Henry Lee.

DIVISION OF STATE POLICE

Dir. of Personnel, Ronald Savitski; *Info. and Telecommunications,* James Zelle; *Fiscal Services,* George Killeen; *Health/Safety Services,* Linda Gervais; *Facilities Mgmt.,* Louis LaPorto.

Units: *Office of Field Operations,* Lt. Col. William McGuire; *Office of Admin. Services,* Lt. Col. Matthew Tyszka; *Professional Standards,* Lt. Thomas Snyder; *Bureau of Criminal Investigations,* Maj. Richard Covello; *Statewide Narcotics Task Force,* Lt. Frank Griffin; *Statewide Organized Crime Investigative Task Force,* Lt.Charles McIntyre; *Statewide Cooperative Crime Control Task Force,* Lt. Edward Kasche; *Casino Unit,* Lt. Bradley Beecher; *Training Academy,* Lt. Ralph Carpenter; *Public Info.,* Sgt. Dale Hourigan; *Research and Planning,* Capt. Danny Stebbins.

STATE POLICE BARRACKS

CENTRAL DISTRICT—Capt. Mark Leahy
 294 Colony St., Meriden 06450-2098
 Tel., (203) 238-6191
 Major Crime Unit . . . . Lt. John Mannion

Troop "F"—Westbrook 06498 . . . . Lt. Clifford M'Sadoques
 Connecticut Tpke., West, I-95, P.O. Drawer F
 Tel., (860) 566-4527

Troop "H"—Hartford 06106 . . . . Lt. Michael Woodson
 100 Washington St. (Rear)
 Tel., (860) 566-5990

Troop "I"—Bethany 06525 . . . . Lt. Edward Brunt
 631 Amity Rd.
 Tel., (203) 789-7720

Troop "W"—Windsor Locks 06096 . . . . Lt. Roy Beavers
 Bradley International Airport
 Tel., (860) 566-7833

EASTERN DISTRICT—Capt. Richard Wheeler.
 Uncas-on-Thames Hospital, 401 West Thames St.
 P.O. Box 711, Norwich 06360-7156
 Tel., (860) 566-8037
 Major Crime Unit . . . . Sgt. Thomas Davoren

Troop "C"—Tolland 06084 . . . . Lt. Louis Lacaprucia
 1320 Tolland Stage Rd.
 Tel., (800) 318-7633

Troop "D"—Danielson 06239 . . . . Lt. Eugene Sullivan
 Westcott Rd.
 Tel., (860) 566-4666

Troop "E"—Montville 06382 . . . . Lt. George Constantine
 I-395 East, P.O. Box 306, Uncasville
 Tel., (860) 566-4468

Troop "K"—Colchester 06415 . . . . Lt. Philip Cameron
 Hartford Rd.
 Tel., (860) 566-4015

WESTERN DISTRICT—Capt. Manfred Bridean
 452-B Bantam Rd., Rte. 202, Litchfield 06759
 Tel., (860) 567-3137
 Major Crime Unit . . . . Lt. Timothy Barry

Troop "A"—Southbury 06488 . . . . Lt. James Sazzano
 Lakeside Rd.
 Tel., (860) 566-7492

Troop "B"—Canaan 06018   Lt. David Werner
Route 7, North Canaan
Tel., (860) 566-7350

Troop "G"—Bridgeport 06604   Lt. Peter Warren
149 Prospect St., Bridgeport 06604
Tel., (860) 566-7834

Troop "L"—Litchfield 06759   Lt. Benjamin Pagoni
452-B Bantam Rd., Rte. 202
Tel., (860) 566-7490

NEW ENGLAND STATE POLICE ADMINISTRATORS' COMPACT. Sec. 29-162, Gen. Stat. Address: 1111 Country Club Rd., P.O. Box 2794, Middletown 06457-9294. Tel., (860) 685-8000.

Member, Kenneth H. Kirschner.

POLICE OFFICER STANDARDS AND TRAINING COUNCIL. Appointed by the Governor to serve at his pleasure, Sec. 7-294b, Gen. Stat. Compensation of members, actual expenses involved in the performance of duties. Address: 285 Preston Ave., Meriden 06450. Tel., (203) 238-6505.

Ex officio, Kenneth H. Kirschner, Comr. of Public Safety, Southington; Merrill S. Parks, Jr., F.B.I., Special Agent-in-Charge, New Haven.

Chiefs of Police: Chm., Wilfred J. Blanchette, Jr., Baltic; John P. Ambrogio, Hamden; Joseph F. Croughwell, Jr., Hartford; Kenneth R. Cruz, Guilford; Thomas E. Flaherty, Milford; Edmund H. Mosca, Old Saybrook; Thomas J. Sweeney, Bridgeport; James M. Thomas, Glastonbury; *Mayors:* Robert J. Chatfield, Prospect; Philip A. Giordano, Waterbury; *Faculty at UConn,* Catherine M. Havens, West Granby; *Public Members:* Carol S. Bryan, Branford; Kurt P. Cavanaugh, Glastonbury; Thomas A. Johnson, Guilford; Thomas P. O'Dea, Jr., Hartford; Craig Z. Zendzian, Southington.

Exec. Dir., T. William Knapp, Wethersfield.

STATEWIDE NARCOTICS TASK FORCE POLICY BOARD. Sec. 29-179, Gen. Stat. Address: 1111 Country Club Rd., P.O. Box 2794, Middletown 06457-9294. Tel., (203) 238-6616.

Ex-officio: Kenneth H. Kirschner, Comr. of Public Safety; John M. Bailey, Chief State's Attorney; Michael Priore, Resident Agent-in-Charge, U.S. Drug Enforcement Admin.; Chief Kenneth Cruz, Guilford Police Dept./Pres. Conn. Chiefs of Police Assoc.

Chiefs of Police: Chm., Thomas M. Falvey, Groton Town; *Vice Chm.,* Robert E. Mossman, Stratford; Joseph F. Croughwell, Jr., Hartford; Michael E. Metzler, Seymour; William Perry, Southington.

STATEWIDE COOPERATIVE CRIME CONTROL TASK FORCE POLICY BOARD. Sec. 29-179i, Gen. Stat. Address: 1111 Country Club Rd., P.O. Box 2794, Middletown 06457-9294. Tel. (203) 238-6616.

Ex-officio: *Chm.,* Kenneth H. Kirschner, Comr. of Public Safety; Judge Aaron Ment, Chief Court Admin.; John M. Bailey, Chief State's Attorney; John J. Armstrong, Comr. of Correction; T. William Knapp, Exec. Dir., Municipal Police Training Council; Lt. Joe Davis, CO, Statewide Cooperative Crime Control Task Force.

DIVISION OF FIRE, EMERGENCY AND BUILDING SERVICES

Units: Legal Counsel, Janet Ainsworth; *Public Info.,* Florence Sinow.

OFFICE OF THE STATE FIRE MARSHAL, Sec. 29-250, Gen. Stat. Address: 1111 Country Club Rd., P.O. Box 2794, Middletown 06457-9294. Tel., (860) 685-8380.

Deputy State Fire Marshal, Douglas B. Peabody.

Units: Bureau of Boilers, James W. Corcoran; *Bureau of Elevators,* Louis Orsini; *Bureau of Engineering,* Paul Connelly; *Bureau of Investigation and Enforcement,* Sgt. Joseph Versteeg; *Bureau of Licensing and Permits,* Philip E. Bourgeois; *Bureau of Education and Data Mgmt.,* Wayne Maheu.

OFFICE OF STATEWIDE EMERGENCY TELECOMMUNICATIONS, Sec. 28-24, Gen. Stat. Address: 1111 Country Club Rd., P.O. Box 2794, Middletown 06457-9294. Tel., (860) 685-8080.

Supvr., George Pohorilak.

CRANE OPERATORS EXAMINING BOARD

Appointed by the Governor to serve at his pleasure, Sec. 29-222, Gen. Stat. Address: c/o Bureau of License and Permits, 1111 Country Club Rd., P.O. Box 2794, Middletown 06457-9294. Tel., (860) 685-8470.

Chm., Edward B. St. John, Middlebury, repr. Public; Richard DeJulio, Newtown, repr. Operators; William W. Glowacki, Niantic, repr. Owners; Francis McMahon, Vernon, repr. Public; Joseph W. Sudol, North Haven, repr. Dept. of Public Safety.

OFFICE OF STATE BUILDING INSPECTOR. Secs. 29-251-29-282, Gen. Stat. Address: 1111 Country Club Rd., P.O. Box 2794, Middletown 06457-9294. Tel., (860) 685-8310.

State Building Inspector, Ramon A. Serbia, Stamford.

Units: Codes and Standards, Licenses/Training, Technical Services; Daniel Tierney, Supvr. Public Bldg. Safety Official.

STATE CODES AND STANDARDS COMMITTEE

Appointed by the Comr. of Public Safety, Sec. 29-251, Gen. Stat. Address: 1111 Country Club Rd., P.O. Box 2794, Middletown 06457-9294. Tel., (860) 685-8310.

Chm., Michael D. Macri, Stamford, repr. Building Officials; *Vice Chm.,* Marjorie F. Shansky, New Haven, repr. Public; *Secy.,* Philip A. Burton, Simsbury, repr. Engineers; Leo Belval, Manchester, repr. Building Officials; James E. Doherty, Cheshire, repr. Fire Marshals; Laurence M. Ford, Redding, repr. Public; Louis J. Free, Bridgeport, repr. Architects; Donald A. Harwood, Wallingford, repr. Public; Daniel J. Herzig, Sr.,

P.E., Bloomfield, repr. Engineers; Wayne D. Holmes, Hartford, repr. Engineers; Thomas A. Hunter, Westport, repr. Public; Roger Langlois, Torrington, repr. Health; Christopher R. Laux, Woodbridge, repr. Architects; Debbie Sampson, West Haven, repr. Advocacy; Lawrence Tryon, Suffield, repr. Building Contractors; John R. Vendetta, Hartford, repr. Fire Marshals; vacancy, repr. Labor;

STATEWIDE EMERGENCY 911 COMMISSION

Appointed by the Governor for three years, Sec. 28-29a, Gen. Stat. Address: 1111 Country Club Rd., P.O. Box 2794, Middletown 06457-9294. Tel., (860) 685-8080.

Frank B. Connolly, Northford, June 30, 1999, repr. Conn. Conference of Municipalities; David Dagon, East Hartford, June 30, 1996, Municipal Fire Chief; George L. Davis, Woodstock Valley, June 30, 1999, repr. Technical Support Services Unit, Div. of State Police; Ernest N. Herrick, Storrs, June 30, 1999, Volunteer Firefighter; Chief Milton J. King, North Windham, June 30, 1999, Municipal Police Chief; Craig A. Miner, Litchfield, June 30, 1996, repr. Council of Small Towns; Jeffrey J. Morrissette, Wethersfield, June 30, 1996, State Fire Admin.; Robert A. Plant, Coventry, June 30, 1996, repr. Office of Emergency Management; Gordon K. Shand, West Hartford, June 30, 1999, repr. Office of Emergency Medical Services.

OFFICE OF EMERGENCY MANAGEMENT. Sec. 28-2(a), Gen. Stat. Salary, Dir., $65,841. Address: 360 Broad St., Hartford 06105. Tel., (860) 566-3180.

Dir., Robert A. Plant.

Area Coordinators: Area 1, Bridgeport, Gary Summa; *Area 2,* Middletown, Pedro Melendez; *Area 3,* Rocky Hill, Paul Pascarelli; *Area 4,* Colchester, Anthony Scalora; *Area 5,* Litchfield, Johnny Cooper.

INTERSTATE CIVIL DEFENSE AND DISASTER COMPACT. Sec. 28-23, Gen. Stat. Address: 360 Broad St., Hartford 06105. Tel., (860) 566-3180.

Admin., Robert A. Plant, Emergency Mgmt. Dir.

BOARD OF FIREARMS PERMIT EXAMINERS

Appointed by the Governor for a term coterminous with term of the Governor or until a successor is chosen, Sec. 29-32b, Gen. Stat. Compensation of members, reasonable subsistence and travel allowances. Address: Secy., 251 Maxim Rd., Hartford 06114-1607.

Chm., G. Eric Doerschler, Wethersfield; *Secy.,* Arthur C. Carr, Canton; George M. Carolan, North Granby; Dennis P. DeCarli, East Haddam; William P. Longo, Litchfield; James J. McMahon, Sr., Southington; Thomas J. Rotunda, Jr., Chief of Police, Ridgefield.

MILITARY DEPARTMENT

Adjutant General appointed by the Governor, for four years, and until a successor is appointed and has qualified, Sec. 27-19, Gen. Stat. Address: National Guard Armory, 360 Broad St., Hartford 06105. Tel., (860) 524-4953; FAX, (860) 524-4898. For information concerning the Governor's Foot Guard, Governor's Horse Guard, the National Guard and Naval Militia, contact the Military Dept., Tel., (860) 524-4967.

The Adjutant General, MG David W. Gay; *Asst. Adjutants General* BG Frank A. Avallone, BG George A. Demers; *Property and Procurement Officer,* David I. Thomas; *U.S.P. and F.O. for Conn.,* Col. I. J. Zembrzuski; *State Judge Advocate,* Lt. Col. Michael Tuohy; *State Comd. Sgt. Major,* CSM Stephen Primett.

STATE ARMORIES

Ansonia—5 State St. 06401
Branford—87 Montowese St. 06405
Bristol—61 Center St. 06010
Enfield—Route 5 & 1635 Mullen Rd. 06082
Hartford—360 Broad St. 06105
Hartford (Hartford Brainard Airport) 251 Maxim Rd. 06114
Manchester—330 Main St. 06040
Meriden—241 E. Main St. 06450
Naugatuck—619 Rubber Ave. 06770
New Britain—855 Stanley St. 06051
New Haven—290 Goffe St. 06511
New London—249 Bayonet St. 06320
Niantic—Camp Rowland, 38 Smith St. 06357
Norwalk—290 New Canaan Ave. 06850
Norwich—Industrial Park, 38 Stott Ave. 06360
Putnam—25 Keech St. 06260
Rockville—120 West Rd. 06066
Southington—590 Woodruff St. 06489
Stratford—63 Armory Rd. 06497
Waterbury—64 Field St. 06702
Westbrook—37 Brookside Ave. 06498
Windsor Locks—Camp Hartell, Rte. 75, 06096

AIR NATIONAL GUARD

Bradley Air National Guard Base, Nicholson Rd., East Granby 06026

Orange Air National Guard Station, U.S. Rte. 1, 206 Boston Post Rd., Orange 06477

AVIATION FACILITIES

Groton—Connecticut Aviation Classification Repair Activity Depot (AVCRAD), 139 Tower Ave., Groton/New London Airport, Groton 06340

Hartford—Maxim Rd., Brainard Airport, 06114

Windsor Locks—Rte. 75, Ella Grasso Hwy., Bradley International Airport, 06096

FIELD TRAINING SITES

Windsor Locks, Camp Hartell, Rte. 75, 06096—Niantic, Camp Rowland, 38 Smith St., 06357—East Lyme, Stone's Ranch, Military Reservation, U.S. Rte. 1, 462 Boston Post Rd., 06333

GOVERNOR'S GUARD FACILITIES

Avon—First Company, Governor's Horse Guard, 232 West Avon Rd., R.F.D. 2, 06001

Newtown—Second Company, Governor's Horse Guard, Fairfield Hills Hospital, Wildlife Dr., P.O. Box 5525, 06470

Hartford—First Company, Governor's Foot Guard, 159 High St., P.O. Box 1771, 06101

New Haven—Second Company, Governor's Foot Guard, 290 Goffe St., P.O. Box 9670, 06536

OTHER FACILITIES

Rifle Range, 591 No. High St., East Haven 06512

State Military Depot—Bldg. 154, Bradley Field, Rte. 75, Windsor Locks 06096

DEPARTMENT OF PUBLIC UTILITY CONTROL

PUBLIC UTILITIES CONTROL AUTHORITY

Appointed by the Governor, with the advice and consent of the General Assembly, Sec. 16-2, Gen. Stat. Salary, Chm., $97,112. Address: 10 Franklin Sq., New Britain 06051. Tel., (860) 827-1553; FAX, (860) 827-2613.

Chm., Reginald J. Smith, New Hartford, June 30, 1997. Thomas Benedict, Newington, June 30, 1997; Glenn Arthur, Gales Ferry; Jack Goldberg, Waterbury; Janet Polinsky, New London, June 30, 1999.

Exec. Dir., Paul Corey, Waterbury.

DEPARTMENT OF PUBLIC UTILITY CONTROL. *Dir. of Advocacy and Regulatory Operations,* Nicholas E. Neeley, New Haven; *Dir. of Utility Regulation and Research,* Renee Poirier, Wethersfield; *Dir. of Adjudication,* Peter J. Jenkelunas, Farmington; *Asst. Atty. Gen.,* Robert S. Golden, Jr., West Hartford.

CONNECTICUT SITING COUNCIL. Sec. 16-50j, Gen. Stat. Compensation of Council members, $150 per day of service and necessary traveling expenses. Address: 10 Franklin Sq., New Britain 06051. Tel., (860) 827-2935; FAX, (860) 827-2950.

Energy and Telecommunications Facilities, Ex officio, Sidney J. Holbrook, Comr. of Environmental Protection; Reginald J. Smith, Chm., Public Utilities Control Authority.

Hazardous Waste, Low Level Radioactive and Ash Residue Disposal Facilities. Ex officio, Stephen A. Harriman, Comr. of Public Health; Kenneth H. Kirschner, Comr. of Public Safety.

Appointed by the Governor, for terms coterminous with term of the Governor, *Chm.,* Mortimer A. Gelston, East Haddam; Gloria Dibble Pond, Woodbury; William H. Smith, Ivoryton; Colin C. Tait, Norfolk; Edward S. Wilensky, Wolcott.

Appointed by the Pres. Pro Tempore of the Senate, William J. Huber, Westport. Appointed by the Speaker of the House, Albert Gary, Hartford.

Four Ad Hoc Members for Hazardous Waste Facilities and Low Level Radioactive Waste Facilities appointed by the chief elected official of the municipality they represent for hazardous waste and low level radioactive waste facilities.

OFFICE OF CONSUMER COUNSEL. Appointed by the Governor, with the advice and consent of either House of the General Assembly, for five years, Sec. 16-2a, Gen. Stat. Salary, $67,755-86,913. Address: 10 Franklin Sq., New Britain 06051. Tel., (860) 827-2900.

Consumer Counsel, Guy R. Mazza, Ridgefield; *Asst. to the Consumer Counsel,* Eugene M. Koss, Tolland.

DEPARTMENT OF PUBLIC WORKS

Sec. 4-125, Gen. Stat. Salary, Comr., $83,500; Deputy Comr., $75,500. Address: Room 425, State Office Bldg., Hartford 06106. Tel., (860) 566-3360.

Comr., Theodore R. Anson, Bridgewater, March 1, 1999; *Deputy Comr.,* P. J. Delahunty, Jr., Southington; *Bureau Head, Admin.,* Dennis F. Kerrigan, Wethersfield; *Bureau Head, Facilities Design and Construction,* Richard F. Piotrowski, Plainville.

Chief Financial Officer, Joseph P. Patterson, Wethersfield.

FACILITIES MANAGEMENT. *Admin.,* Gary A. Gallucci, Westchester.

CLIENT PLANS AND PROGRAMS. *Acting Admin.,* Richard J. Tedder, Unionville.

LEASING AND PROPERTY TRANSFER. *Dir.,* Anthony M. Ciarlone, New Haven.

DEPARTMENT OF REVENUE SERVICES

OFFICE OF THE COMMISSIONER

Appointed by the Governor, with the advice and consent of either House of the General Assembly, for four years, Secs. 4-5—4-8, Gen. Stat. Salary, Comr., $83,500. Address: 25 Sigourney St., Hartford 06106. Tel., (860) 297-5650.

Comr., Gene Gavin, Westport, March 1, 1999; *Exec. Secy.,* Patricia A. Hicks, West Hartford. *Chief of Staff,* Joseph W. Mooney, Branford; *Exec. Secy.,* Gail J. Hanna, Trumbull; *Asst. Comr.,* Barbara J. Chisholm, Southbridge, MA.

Appellate Div. Dir., Scot R. Anderson, Wethersfield; *Admin. Asst.,* Darlena R. Pehr, Vernon; *Tax Unit Mgr.,* Ellen M. Pliskowski, Farmington; *Tax Appellate Specialists,* Albert J. Babbitt, Broad Brook, Lynn D. Bisighini, Bloomfield, John B. King, Storrs; *Tax Appellate Officers,* Janice W. DellaCamera, North Haven, Richard C. Heitz, Southington; Donna L. Kapij, Rocky Hill, Ann M. Keating, West Hartford; Stephen T. Kuraska, Ellington, Michael J. O'Sullivan, Jr., Wallingford, Hans Romaine, Norwalk; Robert E. West, East Hartford.

ADMINISTRATION DIVISION. *Chief of Fiscal Adm. Services,* Kevin G. Forsa, Southington; *Admin. Asst.,* Vivian M. Positano, Bristol; *Personnel Admin.,* Bruce F. Chamberlain, Hebron.

AUDIT DIVISION. *Dir.,* Hans G. Spalter, Southington; *Admin. Asst.,* Mary Ellen Dyjak; *Div. Chiefs,* Michael J. Hayes, Southington; Paul P. Roulier, South Windsor; Robert H. Slattery, Madison; Joseph A. Thomas, Waterbury; *Unit Mgrs.,* Rosemary A. Cleary, West Hartford; Patrick J. Crowley, West Hartford; Timothy L. Gove, Durham; Paul Greenfield, Coventry; Edward E. Hall, Lebanon; George Hary, New Britain; Bruce A. Innes, Watertown; Edward C. Kozlenko, Berlin; John H. Kutsukos, South Glastonbury; David J. Lepri, Wolcott; John C. Libby, South Windsor; William D. McKellar, Thomaston; Raymond A. Perkins, Manchester; James M. Schweppe, Storrs; Harry J. Yost, Seymour.

REGIONAL OFFICES

Location	Address	Telephone
Bridgeport	10 Middle St., 06601	(203) 579-6252
New Haven	2105 State St., 06517	(203) 789-8003
Norwich	2 Cliff St., 06360	(860) 889-2660
Waterbury	24 Wooster Ave., 06708	(203) 596-4311

COLLECTION AND ENFORCEMENT DIVISION. *Dir.,* Hans G. Spalter, Southington; *Asst. Div. Chiefs,* Ronald Dirienzo, East Granby; Robert Wilcox, Marlborough; Keith Wilson, Storrs; *Supvrs.,* Pamela Calachan, Norwich; Wayne Chykirda, East Berlin; William Clato-Day, Windsor; Hibeh Dilzer, New Britain; Pamela Doolan, Newington; Elaine Kowaleski, Middletown; Timothy Martin, West Hartford; Philip Kozlak, Torrington; John McLoughlin, Hamden; Calvin Mellor, Norwich; Frances Misseri, Manchester; Laura Niski, Oxford; Denis Ratte, Prospect; James Seaman, Plantsville; Leo Soucy, Windsor; *Tax Hearing Officers,* John Hussey, West Hartford; Doris Reckert, Plainville; Lisa Rustek, Southington, Linda Sheary, West Hartford.

INFORMATION SERVICES DIVISION. *Dir.,* Frances V. Moffett, Poquonock; *Agency Data Processing Mgr.,* Gary M. Cyr, Plainville; *Office Automation System Specialist,* Mary Jane Talley, Bolton.

INHERITANCE TAX DIVISION. *Managing Atty.,* John M. Dunham, West Hartford; *Inheritance Tax Attys.,* Robert L. Eddy, Simsbury; Stuart H. Gollinger, Rocky Hill; Maurice J. Sturm, Bloomfield; *Tax Inheritance Supvr.,* David A. Burke, Andover.

LEGAL AND TECHNICAL SERVICES. *General Counsel/1st Asst. Comr.,* Richard D. Nicholson, South Windsor; *Managing Atty.,* Frederick P. Clark, West Hartford; *Adm. Asst.,* Armida Crowley; *Tax Attys.,* Louis P. Bucari, Waterbury; Donna F. Haghighat, West Hartford; Felicia S. Hoeniger, Bridgewater; Kelly J. Kennedy, West Hartford; Stacey A. King-Pavano, New Haven; Diana L. Leyden, Glastonbury; Jean E. Morrison, Cromwell; Jane C. Steinmetz, Wethersfield; Peter A. Teeuwissen, Farmington.

OPERATIONS DIVISION. *Dir.,* Donald B. Pecor, Glastonbury; *Adm. Asst.,* I. Shirley Zeppa, Manchester; *Asst. Dirs.,* Henry M. Kerr, Vernon; Edward H. Mehmel,

Southington; Robert J. Rinaldi, Simsbury; *Supvrs.,* Kathleen M. Davis, West Hartford; Gary Dowling, Glastonbury; Susanna Esposito, Orange; Richard Hyatt, Westbrook; Brenda Lauzier, Winsted; Brian McGovern, West Hartford; Beverly Rice, Coventry; Penny Ross, Bristol; Angela Starkowski, Wethersfield.

TAXPAYER SERVICE DIVISION. *Dir.,* Elaine M. Leon, Preston; *Unit Mgr.,* Sandra G. Wilcox, Marlborough.

DIVISION OF SPECIAL REVENUE

Exec. Dir. appointed by the Governor, Sec. 12-557c, Gen. Stat. Salary, $75,000. Address: 555 Russell Rd., Newington 06111. Tel., (860) 594-0501.

Acting Exec. Dir., George F. Wandrak, Southington; *Deputy Exec. Dir.,* vacancy; *Unit Chief, Admin.,* William J. McMahon, Bridgeport; *Acting Unit Chief, Integrity and Assurance,* James Vance, Coventry; *Unit Chief, Planning and Research,* Pamela A. Raposa, East Hartford; *Acting Unit Chief, Security,* John Cotter, South Windsor.

GAMING POLICY BOARD. Appointed by the Governor, with the advice and consent of both Houses of the General Assembly, Sec. 12-557d, Gen. Stat. Compensation of members, $50 per day of service, plus necessary expenses. Address: 555 Russell Rd., Newington 06111. Tel., (860) 566-2756.

Ex officio, George F. Wandrak, Acting Exec. Dir., Div. of Special Revenue.

Chm., Nelson C. L. Brown, Glastonbury; Gilbert Lebovitz, Rocky Hill; Daniel Marchitello, Cheshire; Henrietta M. Mead, Norfolk; vacancy.

DEPARTMENT OF SOCIAL SERVICES

Appointed by the Governor, with the advice and consent of either House of the General Assembly, for four years, Secs. 4-5—4-8, Gen. Stat. Salary, Comr., $95,000; Deputy Comrs., $83,500, $84,182. Address: 25 Sigourney St., Hartford 06106. Tel., (860) 424-5008.

Comr., Joyce A. Thomas, Milford, March 1, 1999; *Deputy Comrs.,* Sarah G. Miller, Windsor; Michael P. Starkowski, Rocky Hill.

REGIONAL OFFICES

Region	Regional Admin.	Address	Phone
Eastern	Ron DeLuca	279 Main St., Norwich 06360	(860) 823-5050
North Central	Pat Wilson-Coker	3580 Main St., Hartford 06120	(860) 566-5730
Northwest	Robert Lucash	249 Thomaston Ave., Waterbury 06702	(203) 597-4000

	Regional Admin.	Address	Phone
South Central	JoAnn Diglio	194 Bassett St., New Haven 06511	(203) 789-7992
Southwest	Frances Freer-Tripp	925 Housatonic Ave., Bridgeport 06606	(203) 579-6837

REGIONAL OFFICES

	Field Mgr.Contact	Address	Phone
Eastern	Kathryn Talbot	31 Commerce St., Killingly 06737	(860) 779-9730
	Kathryn Talbot	670-676 Main St., Willimantic 06226	(860) 450-7657
North Central	Sandee Sorel-LeDuc	50-100 North Main St., Bristol 06010	(860) 583-1671
	Beverly Miller Joaquim Soares	330 Broad St., Manchester 06040	(860) 647-5901
	Charles Callegari	270 Lafayette St., New Britain 06053	(860) 827-7149
Northwest	Al Matheson	405 Main St., Danbury 06810	(203) 797-4039
	Marc Paletsky	62 Commercial Blvd., Torrington 06790	(860) 626-6600
South Central	Jim Laban	55 West Main St., Meriden 06451	(203) 238-6221
	Amelia Reilly Lucio Hidalgo	117 Main St. Ext., Middletown 06457	(860) 344-2101
Southwest	Elizabeth Turner	7 Concord St., Norwalk 06854	(203) 866-0704
	Evelyn Balamaci	1642 Bedford St., Stamford 06905	(203) 357-8144

COMMISSION ON AGING

Sec. 17b-420(a). Salary, Exec. Dir., $73,544. Address: 25 Sigourney St., Hartford 06106. Tel, (860) 424-5360.

Appointed by the Governor, Ethel M. Austin, Hartford; Bernice Corbo, Waterbury; Mary Ann Norelli, Bethlehem; Walter L. Schlenker, Westport; Agnes W. Timpson, Hamden.

Appointed by the Pres. Pro Tempore of the Senate, Joan Quinn, Wethersfield; by the Senate Majority Leader, Kathi M. Bissell, Milford; by the Senate Minority Leader, *Chm.,* Nancy Gyurko, Torrington; by the Speaker of the House, Thomas P. Connors, Milford; by the House Majority Leader, Carmen Romano, North Haven; House Minority Leader, Mary Wilcox, Berlin.

Exec. Dir., A. Cynthia Matthews.

AREA AGENCIES ON AGING

Area	Address	Phone	Health Insurance Info.
Eastern	401 West Thames St., Norwich 06360	(860) 887-3561	(800) 994-9422
North Central	2 Hartford Sq. West, Hartford 06106	(860) 724-6443	(800) 994-9422
South Central	201 Noble St., West Haven 06516	(203) 933-5431	(800) 994-9422
Southwestern	955 Main St., Bridgeport 06604	(203) 333-9288	(800) 994-9422
Western	249 Thomaston Ave., Waterbury 06702	(203) 757-5449	(800) 994-9422

STATE OMBUDSMAN *State Ombudsman,* Barbara Frank, Hartford. Tel., (860) 424-5200.

ELDERLY SERVICES DIVISION

REGIONAL OMBUDSMEN

Southwest Region: 1 Lafayette Cir., Bridgeport 06604. Tel. (203) 579-6919. Alba Ferrari, Julie Lillibridge.

South Central Region: 414 Chapel St., New Haven 06511. Tel. (203) 789-7508. Betty Ann Avery, Jeanette Thomas.

Eastern Region: 100 Broadway, Rm. 108, Norwich 06360. Tel., (860) 886-7425. Cathie Brady, Andrea Costick.

North Central Region: 56 Arbor St., Hartford 06106. Teresa Cusano, Tel., (860) 566-5343. Vicki DeMartino, Shirley Homar, Michael Michalski.

Northwest Region: 249 Thomaston Ave., Waterbury 06702. Tel., (203) 596-4473. Sheila Hayden.

BUREAU OF REHABILITATION SERVICES

Location	Dir.	Phone
Bridgeport	Paul Diana	(203) 579-6300
Hartford	Thomas Calo	(860) 566-4100
New Haven	Robert Igo	(203) 789-7867
Norwich	Joseph Kane	(860) 887-3546
Waterbury	Lorene Castle	(203) 578-4550

STATE COMMISSION ON THE DEAF AND HEARNG IMPAIRED

Sec. 46a-28, Gen. Stat. Salary, Exec. Dir., $57,000. Address: 1245 Farmington Ave., West Hartford 06107-2668. Interpreting, Voice and TDD, Tel., 566-7414; General Info., (860) 561-0196; after hour emergencies, (860) 242-7698.

Ex-officio, Chm., Winfield McChord, Supt., American School for the Deaf; John Purdy, Dept. of Education; Albert Pimentel, Pres., Conn. Council of Organizations Serving the Deaf.

Tara Parikh, M.D., Dept. of Health Services; Carolyn Isakson, Dept. of Education; Dr. Donald Rightmer, Dept. of Mental Health and Addiction Services; Luz Aillon, Dept. of Children and Families; Irene Mason, Dept. of Social Services, Marcia Smith Glasper, Dept. of Labor.

Appointed by the Governor, *Chm.,* Luisa J. Gasco-Soboleski, Southington; Karen A. Avena, Middletown; Judith Dandrow, Southington; Raymond DeRosa, Wallingford; Thomas A. Meehan, New Hartford; Katherine H. Robinson, West Hartford; Lucille S. Rose, Plainville; Mary M. Silvestri, Danbury; Gloria W. White, Norwich; vacancy.

Exec. Dir., Valerie R. Marino.

BOARD OF EDUCATION AND SERVICES FOR THE BLIND

Appointed by the Governor to serve at his pleasure, Sec. 10-293, Gen. Stat. Salary, Exec. Dir., $65,000. Compensation of board members, none. Address, Exec. Dir., 170 Ridge Rd., Wethersfield 06109. Tel., (860) 566-5800; FAX, (860) 278-6920.

Ex-officio, Joyce A. Thomas, Comr. of Social Services.

Appointed by the Governor, *Chm.,* Richard G. Fairbanks, Ph.D., Old Greenwich; Eileen Akers, Norwich; Mary R. Brunoli, Hartford; Salvatore D'Amico, Wethersfield; Kenneth Olson, New Britain; Shirley Phelon, East Hartford.

Exec Dir., Kenneth R. Tripp.

CHILD DAY CARE COUNCIL

Appointed by the Governor, to serve at his pleasure, Sec. 19a-78, Gen. Stat. Compensation of members, necessary expenses. Address, c/o Department of Social Services, 25 Sigourney St., Hartford 06106. Tel., (860) 424-5006.

Ex-officio members, Stephen A. Harriman, Comr. of Public Health; Joyce A. Thomas, Comr. of Social Services; Linda D'Amario-Rossi, Comr. of Children and Families; Peter N. Ellef, Comr. of Economic and Community Development; Theodore Sergi, Comr. of Education.

Appointed by the Governor, Joyce Abate, Norwalk, repr. child day care center provider; Nora Barker-Joseph, New Haven, repr. family day care provider; Audette Bisaillon, Stamford, repr. family day care provider; Carol Brezezon, Seymour, repr. family day care provider; Judith E. Carroll, Middle Haddam, repr. advocacy group concerned with young children; Rita I. Decker, Hartford, repr. parent with a child enrolled in a child day care service; Deborah A. Flis, Rocky Hill, repr. Permanent

Comm. on the Status of Women; Ida B. Gilbert, Hartford, repr. community action programs; Susan Holland, Simsbury, repr. parent with a child enrolled in a child day care service; Lisa M. McGuire, South Windsor, repr. Conn. Business and Industry Assoc.; Darlene C. Ragozzine, Woodbridge, repr. higher education with program in early childhood education; Merle E. Stoner, Glastonbury, repr. community council; Barbara M. Tacchi, Bristol, repr. child day care center provider; Robert Windom, M.D., New Haven, repr. American Academy of Peidatrics; Elaine Zimmerman, North Haven, repr. Comm. on Children; three vacancies.

DEPARTMENT OF TRANSPORTATION

COMMISSIONER OF TRANSPORTATION

Appointed by the Governor, with the advice and consent of either House of the General Assembly, for four years, Secs. 4-5—4-8, Gen. Stat. Salary, Comr., $95,000. Address: 2800 Berlin Tpke., Newington 06131-7546. Tel., (860) 594-3000.

Acting Comr., James F. Sullivan, Wolcott, March 1, 1999; *Secy. to Comr.,* Madeleine P. Makiaris, Niantic; *Deputy Comr.,* Harry P. Harris; *Secy. to Deputy Comr.,* Lorraine T. Fiducia, Rocky Hill; *Legislative Program Mgr.,* W. David Gilbert, Marlborough; *Dir. of Communications,* Susan Reynolds, Wethersfield; *Public Hearings Specialist,* John J. Wallace, South Windsor; *Transp. Counsel,* Cornelius Tuohy, Naugatuck; *Dir. of Mgmt. Services,* Norman Dupuis, Cromwell; *Equal Employment Opportunity Assurance Admin.,* Margo S. Kilbon, Simsbury.

BUREAU OF FINANCE AND ADMINISTRATION

Address: 2800 Berlin Turnpike, Newington 06131-7546. Tel., (860) 594-2201.

Bureau Chief, Charles E. Canane, Jr., Vernon; *Transp. Business Admin./Info. Systems,* Thomas J. Perrone, Wethersfield; *Admin./Operation and Support,* Joseph A. Pirolo, Coventry; *Info. Systems Dir.,* Robert A. DiScipio, Glastonbury; *Dir. of Budget Service,* Kenneth J. Donahue, Rocky Hill; *Dir. of Contract Admin.,* Valerie C. Joyner, Windsor; *Dir. of Property and Facilities Services,* Arthur F. Keating, Stratford; *Dir. of Purchasing and Material Mgmt.,* Edward G. Saller, Hebron; *Personnel Admin.,* Frederick J. Sanders, Rocky Hill; *Dir. of External Audits,* William P. Scholl, Milford; *Dir. of Accounting Services,* Charles Jeski, Newington; *Dir. of Capital Services,* Anne P. Choquette, Rocky Hill.

BUREAU OF AVIATION AND PORTS

Address: 2800 Berlin Tpke., Newington 06131-7546. Tel. (860) 594-2529.

Bureau Chief, Robert F. Juliano, Granby; *Dir. of Engineering,* Edwin J. Fijol, P.E., Longmeadow, MA; *Fiscal Admin.,* Barbara Wells, West Willington; *Dir. of Marketing and Development,* Andre J. Libert, Fairfield; *Aviation Admin.,* Kenneth J. Robert, East Hartford; *Maritime Programs Mgr.,* D. Douglas Brown, Norwich.

STATE AIRPORTS—Bradley International Airport, Windsor Locks, *Acting Asst. Airport Admin.,* William F. Palmer; Groton-New London Airport, Groton, *Mgr.,vacancy;* Hartford-Brainard Airport, Hartford, *Mgr.,* Barry R. Pallanck; Danielson Airport, Killingly, *Contract Mgr.,* Gary Boroughf; Waterbury-Oxford Airport, Oxford, *Mgr.,* Peter J. Zguzenski; Windham Airport, Windham, *Contract Mgr.,* Norvald Oygard.

BUREAU OF ENGINEERING AND HIGHWAY OPERATIONS

Address: 2800 Berlin Tpke., Newington 06131-7546. Tel. (860) 594-2700.

Bureau Chief, James F. Sullivan, Wolcott; *Transp. Chief Engr.,* James F. Byrnes, Jr., P.E., Colchester; *Dir. of Fiscal/Special Projects,* Richard J. Haley, Rocky Hill.

Engineering Admin., Earle R. Munroe, P.E., Wethersfield; *Mgr. of State Design,* Bradley J. Smith, P.E., Bolton; *Mgr. of Consultant Design,* Stephen M. Barton, P.E., Glastonbury; *Mgr. of Design Services,* Joseph J. Obara, P.E., Somers; *Mgr. of Bridge Safety and Evaluation,* James P. Loersch, P.E., Bolton; *Transp. Utilities Engr.,* Kenneth F. Rapoza, Rocky Hill; *Mgr. of Research and Materials Testing,* Charles E. Dougan, PH.D., P.E., Enfield; *Asst. Mgr. for Materials Testing,* Keith R. Lane, P.E., Haddam; *Asst. Mgr. for Research,* James M. Sime, P.E., East Hartford; *Mgr. of Traffic Engineering,* Walter H. Coughlin, P.E., Rocky Hill; *Asst. Mgr. of Traffic Engineering,* John A. Vivari, Old Saybrook; *Construction Admin.,* Arthur W. Gruhn, P.E., Guilford; *Mgr. of Construction Operation*s, L. Brian Castler, Cheshire; *Mgr. of Survey Operations,* John Puglisi, Wethersfield; *Maintenance Admin.,* Louis R. Malerba, Durham; *Transp. Maintenance Dir.,* Michael D. Turano, Canterbury; *Dir. of Highway Operations,* William W. Stoeckert, Torrington; *Transp. Maintenance Mgr.(Planning),* Joseph A. Misbach, Wallingford; *Mgr. of Bridge Maintenance,* Franco R. Liberatore, Rocky Hill; *Transp. Maintenance Mgr. (Operations),* Vincent A. Guntner; Oakdale; *Principal Engineer,* John D. Micali, Newington; *Rights of Way Admin.,* James E. Lewis, South Windsor; *Div. Chief (Titles),* Lawrence Orvis, Wethersfield; *Div. Chief (Appraisal),* Gene E. Gisselbrecht, Torrington; *Div. Chief (Property Mgmt.),* David L. Labossiere, Windsor; *Div. Chief (Adm.),* Richard C. Allen, Tolland; *Div. Chief (Acquisition-Relocation),* John P. Randazzo, New Britain; *Governor's Highway Safety Repr.,* Susan C. Maloney, Cromwell.

DISTRICT NO. 1—ROCKY HILL—1107 Cromwell Ave., 06067. Tel., (860) 258-4601. *Dist. Engr.,* Leon M. Alford, P.E., Windsor; *Asst. Dist. Engr.,* Dennis J. Purcell, Middletown; *Transp. Maintenance Dir.,* Victor LaBarre, Taftville; *Dist. Maintenance Supervising Planner,* David Cahill, Southington; *Transp. Maintenance Mgrs.,* Richard Annino, Middletown, Stephen Cochrane, Seymour, Charles Woodworth, Willington; *Dist. Special Services Section Mgr.,* Vincent J. Urban, Jr., Vernon.

DISTRICT NO. 2—NORWICH—171 Salem Tpke., 06360. Tel., (860) 823-3204. *Dist. Engr.,* Michael E. Lavallee, P.E., Plainfield; *Asst. Dist. Engr.,* Charles Panteleakos, Dayville; *Transp. Maintenance Dir.,* Wayne McAllister, Chester; *Dist. Maintenance Supervising Planner,* Marcella C. Maiorano, Salem; *Transp. Maintenance Mgrs.,* Richard Annino, Middletown, Joseph Durante, West Haven; Richard D. LaLiberte, Sprague; *Dist. Special Services Section Mgr.,* Gary Fitch, Canterbury.

DISTRICT NO. 3—NEW HAVEN—140 Pond Lily Ave., 06525. Tel., (203) 389-3100. *Dist. Engr.,* Joseph DeMarco, P.E., Glastonbury; *Asst. Dist. Engr.,* Paul H. Breen, Hamden; *Transp. Maintenance Dir.,* Norman S. Hannibal, Washington; *Dist. Supvervising Planner,* Raymond Daly, Cheshire; *Transp. Maintenance Mgrs.,* Joseph J. Czarnecki, Naugatuck, William Papp, Stratford; Ralph L. Smith, Huntington; *Dist. Special Services Section Mgr.,* Michael Magda, Branford.

DISTRICT NO. 4—THOMASTON—359 South Main St., Thomaston 06787. Tel., (860) 585-2800. *Dist. Engr.,* Wayne Blair, P.E., Niantic; *Asst. Dist. Engr.,* Peter L. Curcio, P.E., West Hartford; *Transp. Maintenance Dir.,* Richard Poole, Lebanon; *Dist. Maintenance Supervising Planner,* Gene W. Parsons, New Milford; *Transp. Maintenance Mgrs.,* Robert P. Mongillo, Southington, William Papp, Stratford; Raymond C. Smith, Beacon Falls; *Special Services Section Mgr.,* C. Richard Hagstrom, Bridgewater.

BUREAU OF POLICY AND PLANNING

Address: 2800 Berlin Tpke., Newington 06131-7546. Tel. (860) 594-2003.

Bureau Chief, Richard A. Martinez, Berlin; *Transp. Policy and Planning Admin.,* William H. Messner, Southington; *Transp. Dir. of Inventory and Forecasting,* Stuart D. Leland, South Windsor; *Transp. Dir. of Intermodal Policy,* Maribeth Demma, Kensington; *Transp. Dir. of Environmental Planning,* Edgar T. Hurle, Middletown.

BUREAU OF PUBLIC TRANSPORTATION

Address: 2800 Berlin Tpke., Newington 06131-7546. Tel., (860) 594-2800.

Bureau Chief/Deputy Transp. Comr., Harry P. Harris, Fairfield; *Rails Admin.,* Lawrence J. Forbes, Clinton; *Transit Admin.,* Michael Sanders, Chester; *Mgr., Motor Transport,* Robert Cumpstone, Wethersfield; *Chief, Fiscal/Adm. Services,* Thomas G. Anderson, Wethersfield.

CONNECTICUT PUBLIC TRANSPORTATION COMMISSION. Sec. 13b-11a, Gen. Stat. Compensation of members, necessary expenses. Address: 2800 Berlin Tpke., Newington 06131-7546. Tel., (860) 594-2852.

Ex officio, Sidney J. Holbrook, Comr. of Environmental Protection; Michael W. Kozlowski, Secy., Office of Policy and Management; James F. Sullivan, Acting Comr. of Transportation; Sen. William A. Aniskovich, Rep. Jacqueline M. Cocco, Co-Chm., General Assembly Transportation Committee.

Appointed by the Governor, *Chm.,* Paul A. Ehrhardt, Simsbury; Timothy J. Grandfield, Madison; Morton Katz, Avon; Joseph B. Kittredge, New Haven; Yvonne Loteczka, Newington; Alice R. A. Pinsince, Ivoryton; Frank C. Schroll, Glastonbury; Russell G. St. John, Granby; two vacancies.

Appointed by the General Assembly Leadership, W. Dudley Birmingham, Wethersfield; Richard C. Carpenter, East Norwalk; Thomas Hubbard, Litchfield; Borden P. Steeves, West Haven; Elinor F. Wilber, Fairfield; three vacancies.

RIGHTS OF WAY SCREENING COMMITTEE—Appointed by the Governor, Ralph J. Biondi, Waterbury; Kathryn S. Ekstrom, Cromwell; Paige J. Everin, West Hartford; Donald G. Leavitt, Newington; Edward D. Schwartz, Meriden; James F. Shugrue, Wethersfield.

STATE HARBOR COMMISSIONERS FOR NEW HAVEN HARBOR. Appointed by the Governor for a term coterminous with term of the Governor, with the advice and consent of the Senate, Special Laws, Vol. VII, 1872, pp 287, 748; Sec. 13b-51, Gen. Stat. Compensation, none.

Vice Pres., Arthur N. Ferrucci, New Haven; *Clerk,* Nicholas N. Colonese, 758 Main St., West Haven; Frank M. Grazioso, New Haven; John P. Wynne, Jr., New Haven, vacancy.

HARBOR MASTERS

Appointed by the Governor, for the duration of appointment, and until a successor is appointed and qualified, Sec. 15-1, Gen. Stat.

Harbor	*Master*
Branford	Ronald Reis
Bridgeport	Joseph C. Savino, Jr.
Chester	F. Thomas Crowley, Jr.
Clinton	Jeffrey P. Colvin
Darien	Robert P. Price
Deep River	Thomas J. Griffin
East Hartford	John J. Barry, Jr.
East Haven	Matthew Belmonte
Essex	Paul F. Riggio
Glastonbury	Thomas N. DePasquale
Greenwich	Joseph A. Siciliano
Groton	Aubrey J. Hamilton
Groton Long Point	John B. Sebastian
Guilford	William J. Moher, Jr.
Hartford	Joseph Musumeci
Lord's Point (Stonington)	Robert W. Tabor
Lyme	Gary H. Reynolds
Madison	Ernest W. Small
Masons Island/Ram's Island/Enders Island	Rufus Allyn
Middletown	Charles W. Snow, Jr.
Milford	Mead W. Batchelor
Mystic River	James A. Friedlander
New Haven	Edward T. Flanagan
New London	Richard M. Brown
Niantic	Joseph L. Selden, Jr.
Noank	James Giblin
Norwalk	Michael Griffin
Norwich	Peter R. Przekop
Old Lyme	Richard G. Sagan

Harbor	Master
Old Saybrook	Grant W. Westerson
Pawcatuck River (Stonington)	Mark W. Tebbets
Southport	Patrick L. Carroll
Stamford	Kevin J. Malloy
Stonington	Andrew C. Heublein
Stratford	John J. Flynn
Waterford	John W. Lane
Westbrook	Leonard J. Mierzejewski
Westport	John J. Giunta, Jr.
Wethersfield Cove	David G. Santoro

DEPUTY HARBOR MASTERS

Harbor	Deputy Master
Branford	vacancy
Bridgeport	Clinton J. Stites
Chester	Lance S. Parker, Jr.
Darien	Eugene E. McGarry
Essex	Raymond A. Rubenbauer
Guilford	vacancy
Milford	Richard N. Neilson
Mystic River	Herbert A. Holmstedt
Niantic	vacancy
Norwalk	Clyde J. Mount
Old Lyme	Glen S. Abrahamsson
Stamford	Mark Johnson,
Stamford	Joseph L. Santagata
Stonington	Nancy H. Gibson
Stratford	E. Scott Corner
Westbrook	David K. Russell
Westport	John J. Giunta, Jr.

STATE BOUNDARY MARKS. Agent appointed by the Governor, Sec. 3-8, Gen. Stat. Address: 2800 Berlin Tpke., Newington 06131-7546. Tel., (860) 594-3000.

Authorized Agent, James F. Sullivan, Acting Comr. of Transportation.

STATE TRAFFIC COMMISSION. Sec. 14-298, Gen. Stat. Compensation of members, none as State Traffic Commission. Address: Richard J. Howard, Exec. Dir., 2800 Berlin Tpke., Newington 06131-7546. Tel., (860) 594-3025.

James F. Sullivan, Acting Comr. of Transportation; Jose O. Salinas, Comr. of Motor Vehicles; Kenneth H. Kirschner, Comr. of Public Safety.

BRADLEY INTERNATIONAL AIRPORT COMMISSION

Sec. 15-101r, Gen. Stat. Compensation of members, fifty dollars for each meeting and necessary expenses. Address: Bradley International Airport, Admin. Offices, Terminal B, Windsor Locks 06096. Tel., (860) 292-2001; FAX, (860) 627-3594.

Appointed by Governor, *Chm.,* Charles P. Watras, Suffield, July 1, 1999; Carl E. Meyer, Jr., Darien; Vincent A. Rocco, West Hartford, July 1, 1997. George P. Howard, Deep River.

Appointed by the Pres. Pro Tempore of the Senate, Mary Ellen Flynn, Hartford; Michael T. Long, Simsbury, July 1, 2001. Appointed by the Senate Majority Leader, Timothy Brignole, East Granby, July 1, 2000. Appointed by the Senate Minority Leader, Felix DeFronzo, Collinsville, July 1, 1997. Appointed by the Speaker of the House, Paul D. Estefan, Danbury; Phil Schonberger, Bloomfield, July 1, 1997. Appointed by the House Majority Leader, Randall Graff, Windsor, July 1, 1999. Appointed by the House Minority Leader, Mrs. Astrid T. Hanzalek, Suffield, July 1, 1997. Appointed by the Chief Elected Officials of their respective towns, Everett Dowe, Windsor; David K. Kilbon, First Selectman, East Granby; Warren Packard, Suffield; Victor Puia, First Selectman, Windsor Locks, July 1, 1999; vacancy.

DEPARTMENT OF VETERANS' AFFAIRS

Appointed by the Governor with the advice and consent of either House of the General Assembly, for four years, Secs. 4-5—4-8, 27-102l, Gen. Stat. Salary, Comr., $75,500. Deputy Comr., $64,500. Address: Dept. of Veterans Affairs, 287 West St., Rocky Hill 06067. Tel., (860) 721-5891.

Comr., Eugene A. Migliaro, Jr., Wolcott, March 1, 1999; *Deputy Comr.,* S. Derek Phelps, Waterford; *Veterans Affairs Dir. of Planning,* John L. Levitow, Rocky Hill; *Agency Personnel Admin. 2,* Eileen Cantin, Cromwell; *Fiscal/Admin. Mgr. 2,* Burton W. Deane, Jr., Rocky Hill; *Affirmative Action Admin I,* Noreen Sinclair, Waterbury; *Dir. of Safety and Security,* Hugo Adams, Rocky Hill.

Bd. of Trustees, David D. Boland, Brooklyn; John G. Chiarella, Sr., Waterbury; Richard W. Lewis, Waterbury; Dr. Michael Mittelmann, West Hartford; William J. Pomfret, Middletown; John N. Roberto, Norwalk; Linda S. Schwartz, Pawcatuck; Judith A. Torpey, Wethersfield; Stanley F. Zebzda, Wethersfield.

OFFICE OF ADVOCACY AND ASSISTANCE

Address: Dept. of Veterans' Affairs, Office of Advocacy and Assistance, 287 West St., Rocky Hill 06067. Tel., (860) 721-5892.

Deputy Comr., S. Derek Phelps, Waterford; *Service Officers: 1st Dist.,* George E. Doyle, Jr., South Windsor; William V. Loder, Elmwood; *2nd Dist.,* Walter Lachack, Jr., North Franklin; Donna Meskony, Willimantic; *3rd Dist.,* James Gaines, Bloomfield; Michael Szumigala, Waterbury; *4th Dist.,* William J. Gambino, Stamford; *5th*

Dist., Peter DiMaria, Watertown; Robert Genovese, Waterbury; *6th Dist.,* Ronald J. Eisen, Simsbury.

Office of Advocacy and Assistance-Supvr., Maurice L. Collin, Manchester.

VETERANS HOME AND HOSPITAL

Address: Dept. of Veterans Affairs, Veterans Home and Hospital, 287 West St., Rocky Hill 06067. Tel., (860) 721-5891.

Rated capacity, 753. Home, 500. Hospital, 253. Total enrollment, July 1, 1996, 561. Value of real property, July 1, 1996, $39,506,890.

Hospital Admin., Sharon R. Wood, Rocky Hill; *Dir. of Residential and Rehab. Services,* James J. McKinnon III, Rocky Hill.

UNAFFILIATED STATE AGENCIES, BOARDS AND COMMISSIONS

ADVISORY COMMISSION ON AMERICAN AND FRANCOPHONE CULTURAL AFFAIRS

Appointed by the Governor to serve at his pleasure, Exec. Order #23. Address: Chm., 250 Shadduck Rd., Middlebury, 06762. Tel., (203) 758-2042.

Chm., Yolande Bosman, Middlebury; Jini J. Dyer, Watertown; Arlette Lippincott, Glastonbury; Evelyn Sirois, Windsor; Joanne E. Yurso, Windsor.

STATE CHEMISTS

Appointed by the Governor, for two years, Sec. 4-22, Gen. Stat. Compensation of members, none. Address: 88 Charlton Hill, Hamden 06518.

Lester Hankin, Ph.D., Hamden.

OFFICE OF STATE FIRE ADMINISTRATION

Sec. 7-323o, Gen. Stat. *State Fire Admin.,* Jeffrey J. Morrissette. Address: Perimeter Rd. P.O. Box 3383, Windsor Locks, 06096. Tel., (860) 627-6363, ext. 230; FAX, (860) 654-1889; E-Mail, jeff.morrissette@po.state.ct.us.

COMMISSION ON FIRE PREVENTION AND CONTROL

Appointed by the Governor, Sec. 7-323k, Gen. Stat. Address: Perimeter Rd., P.O. Box 3383, Windsor Locks, 06096. Tel., (860) 627-6363; FAX, (860) 654-1889; E-Mail, CFDC@po.state.ct.us.

Ex officio voting members, Kenneth H. Kirschner, Comr. Public Safety; Bruce H. Leslie, Ph.D., Chancellor, Community-Technical Colleges.

Appointed by the Governor, *Chm.,* Peter S. Carozza, Jr., Waterbury, Aug. 31, 1999; *Vice Chm.,* John R. Vendetta, Hartford, Aug. 31, 1998; *Secy.,* Chief Edward F. Haber,

Ret., Berlin, Aug. 31, 1999; Robert J. Chatfield, Prospect; Daniel Milewski, Stratford; Chief Peter F. Mullen, Ret., Branford; Aug. 31, 1998. Jon W. Andresen, Windsor; Chief William S. Johnson, Jr., West Haven; Kevin J. Kowalski, Simsbury; Maurice M. McCarthy, Jr., Waterbury; Chief Richard H. Nicol, Ret., Middlebury; Aug. 31, 1999; vacancy.

CONNECTICUT FIRE ACADEMY

Dir. of Training, Adrian Ouellette, Address: Perimeter Rd., P.O. Box 3383, Windsor Locks 06096-3383. Tel., (860) 627-6363, ext. 236; FAX, (860) 654-1889; E-Mail, andy.ouellette@po.state.ct.us.

GREATER HARTFORD FLOOD COMMISSION

Appointed by the Governor, Special Acts, November Special Session, 1955, No. 72, as amended by Special Act No. 292, 1957. Compensation of members, necessary expenses. Address: 525 Main St., Hartford 06103. Tel., (860) 722-6206.

Chm., Harry R. Holland, Newington; *Secy.,* Aldo P. Provera, Hartford; John S. Pinney, Bloomfield; Benjamin Ramsharran, Hartford; Dale A. Richter, Hartford; Harry B. Schaechter, West Hartford, vacancy.

Exec. Dir., John H. McGrane; *Counsel,* Kenneth B. Kaufman.

CONNECTICUT HAZARDOUS WASTE MANAGEMENT SERVICE

Sec. 22a-134bb, Gen. Stat. Chm. and one director from each Congressional District appointed by the Governor for a term of four years or until a successor is chosen. Compensation of Directors, $100.00 per day of service plus travel expenses. Compensation of Chm. set by the board within available resources. Address: 50 Columbus Blvd., 4th Floor, Hartford 06106-1910. Tel., (860) 244-2007; FAX, (860) 244-2017.

Ex officio, James F. Sullivan, Acting Comr. of Transportation; Michael W. Kozlowski, Secy., Office of Policy and Management; Stephen A. Harriman, Comr. of Public Health; Sidney J. Holbrook, Comr. of Environmental Protection.

Chm., Robert C. Blake, Litchfield; *First Cong. Dist.,* Robert H. Lutts, Hartford; *Second Cong. Dist.,* Wallace C. Pringle, Jr., Ph.D., Haddam; *Third Cong. Dist.,* William C. Summers, New Haven; *Fourth Cong. Dist.,* Samuel C. Stowell, Greenwich; *Fifth Cong. Dist.,* Barbara H. McWhirter, Cheshire; *Sixth Cong. Dist.,* Richard J. Heller, Farmington.

CONNECTICUT HIGHER EDUCATION SUPPLEMENTAL LOAN AUTHORITY

Appointed by the Governor, Sec. 10a-224, Gen. Stat. Address: 29 South Main St., Town Center, Suite 304 N, W. Hartford 06107. Tel., (860) 561-2180.

Ex officio, Andrew G. De Rocco, Ph.D., Comr., Dept. of Higher Education; Michael W. Kozlowski, Secy., Office of Policy and Management; Christopher B. Burnham, State Treasurer.

Appointed by the Governor, *Chm.*, Edwin G. Below, Durham; *Vice Chm.*, Frank R. A. Resnick, West Hartford; Morrison H. Beach, West Hartford; Winifred E. Coleman, West Hartford; Michael E. McKeeman, Middlebury.

STATE HISTORICAL RECORDS ADVISORY BOARD

Appointed by the Governor, 36 CFR pt. 1206.38.

Patricia Bodak-Stark, Lyme; Rev. Robert G. Carroon, Ph.D., West Hartford; Eunice G. DiBella, C.R.M., Rocky Hill; Catherine K. Fields, Litchfield; Leo N. Flanagan, Waterbury; Lawrence B. Goodheart, Ph.D., Hampton; Joan M. Hyde, Westport; Mollie Keller, Ph.D., Trumbull; Sharon B. Laist, Orange; Paul C. Lasewicz, Vernon; Janice Mathews, Hartford; Donna Siemiatkoski, Windsor; Bruce P. Stark, Ph.D., Lyme; Patricia B. Stark, Lyme; Robert W. Storm, West Hartford; Christine Weidman, Ph.D., Hamden; Sandra L. Wheeler, Farmington; Everett C. Wilkie, Jr., Ph.D, Simsbury.

Chm./Historical Records Coordinator: Mark H. Jones, Ph.D., West Hartford. Tel., 566-5650.

Deputy Coordinator, Mollie Keller, Ph.D., Trumbull. Tel., (203) 576-8192.

CITIZENS ADVISORY COUNCIL FOR HOUSING MATTERS

Appointed by the Governor, Sec. 47a-71a, Gen. Stat. Address: 104 Beacon St., Hartford 06105. Tel., (860) 232-7748.

Chm., Raphael L. Podolsky, Hartford; *Vice Chm. for Hartford-New Britain,* Houston P. Lowry, Avon; *Vice Chm. for New Haven-Waterbury,* Sheldon Hosen, New Haven; *Vice Chm. for Bridgeport-Norwalk,* William I. Haslun, Cos Cob; *Vice Chm. for Eastern Connecticut,* Morris Czaczkes, North Franklin; *Secy.,* Linda P. Francois, Bethany; *Treas.,* Barbara Perry, South Windsor; Miguel Ayala, Derby; Nadine Baldetti, Hamden; Peter Blasini, New Haven; Carolyn Comerford, Trumbull; Jane Courville, Norwalk; Elaine DeNigris, New Britain; Linda Drew, Mansfield Center; Glenn Falk, Madison; Sr. Susanne Gebrian, North Grosvenordale; Robin Hammeal-Urban, East Hampton; Ivan A. Hirsch, Fairfield; Robert Kor, West Hartford, Doris Latorre, Bridgeport; Gail MacLean, Norwalk; Lorraine A. Martin, North Haven; John J. McGrath, Windham; Tito S. Molina, Trumbull; Carmen R. Neale, New Hartford; Antonio C. Robaina, Deep River; Peter W. Rotella, Groton Long Point; John Rowland, Middletown; Edward Sanady, West Hartford; Lois Stevenson, Hartford; Richard L. Tenenbaum, Norwalk; James White, Rocky Hill; Joseph Wincze, Jr., Milford; Odessa Young, Bridgeport; Joseph Zibbideo, Avon.

JUDICIAL REVIEW COUNCIL

Sec. 51-51k, Gen. Stat. Address: Exec. Dir., 505 Hudson St., Hartford 06106-0099. Tel., (860) 566-5424; FAX, (860) 566-6617.

Appointed by the Governor, *Chm.,* Hugh F. Keefe, Orange, December 1, 1998; Veronica Airey-Wilson, Hartford; G. Sarsfield Ford, Fairfield; Long Point; Richard Ohanesian, Canton, December 1, 1998; Stanley Cohen, Windsor; Bernard D. Gaffney,

New Britain; William F. Meyer, Newtown, December 1, 1999. William T. Dunn, Jr., Southington; Sandra V. Leheny, Danbury; Robert Schneider, Manchester, Bernard M. Slater, Lyme, December 1, 2000. Alternates, Angelo L. dos Santos, West Hartford; Raymond J. Fontana, Clinton; Maxwell Heiman, Newington; Katherine Y. Hutchinson, Andover; Edward R. Karazin, Jr., Westport; Maynard R. Miller, Jr, West Hartford; Jeffrey R. Partridge, Stratford; Claire Smith, Westbrook, December 1, 1997.

Exec. Dir., Donald B. Caldwell, Bolton.

JUDICIAL SELECTION COMMISSION

Sec. 51-44a, Gen. Stat., Compensation, necessary expenses. Address: State Office Bldg., Room 241, Hartford 06106. Tel., (860) 566-1078; FAX, (860) 566-1678.

Appointed by the Governor, *Chm.,* Rosemary E. Giuliano, Woodbury; William F. Dow III, New Haven; Dale P. Faulkner, New London; Peter M. Nolin, Norwalk; James K. Robertson, Watertown; George D. Royster, Jr.

Appointed by the President Pro Tempore, John Harney, Salisbury. Appointed by the Senate Majority Leader, Ronald E. Brodeur, Sr., Waterbury. Appointed by the Senate Minority Leader, Gayle D. Wilson, Ledyard. Appointed by the Speaker of the House, Hernan LaFontaine, Hartford. Appointed by the House Majority Leader, *Vice Chm.,* Michael J. Buckmir, Stratford. Appointed by the House Minority Leader, Frank J. Morgan, Norwalk.

Exec. Dir., Diane S. Yannetta, West Hartford.

LOW-LEVEL RADIOACTIVE WASTE ADVISORY COMMITTEE

Sec. 22a-163u, Gen. Stat. Compensation none, necessary expenses. Address: c/o Connecticut Hazardous Waste Management Service, 50 Columbus Blvd., 4th Floor, Hartford 06106. Tel., (860) 244-2007; FAX, (860) 244-2017.

Appointed by the Governor, Wolf R. Koste, Glastonbury; Carl C. Noonan, Madison; Edward L. Wilds, Jr., Griswold.

Appointed by the Pres. Pro Tempore of the Senate, Jacqueline Smith, South Windsor; Nancy Way, Ellington. Appointed by the Senate Minority Leader, Raymond E. Jossick, Stratford; vacancy. Appointed by the Speaker of the House, James Okun, Ellington; Rita Provatas, Waterford. Appointed by the House Minority Leader, Carl M. Fink, Simsbury; Arnold Gundersen, Warren.

MARTIN LUTHER KING, JR. COMMISSION

Sec. 10-29b(a), Gen. Stat., Compensation, none. Address: Secretariat, Conn. Commission on Human Rights and Opportunities, 90 Washington St., Hartford 06106. Tel., (860) 566-3350.

Appointed by the Governor, *Chm.,* Dennis J. King, Waterbury; Timothy Crumpton, Hartford; Sarah Diaz, Waterbury; William L. Dixon, New Haven; Michael F. Doyle,

New London; Rev. King T. Hayes, South Windsor; Adele L. Kusnitz, Monroe; Benjamin F. Rhodes, Jr., Waterbury; Sabrina J. Washington, Hartford; two vacancies.

Appointed by the Pres. Pro Tempore of the Senate, two vacancies. Appointed by the Senate Minority Leader, Holly J. Hart, Bloomfield; vacancy. Appointed by the Speaker of the House, Anthony Gray, Hartford; Rev. Alvan Johnson, Bloomfield. Appointed by the House Minority Leader, Beatrice F. Sullivan, Hartford, vacancy.

CONNECTICUT METRO NORTH NEW HAVEN RAIL COMMUTER COUNCIL

Sec. 13b-212b, Gen. Stat., Compensation, none. Address: Box 15125, Park Square Station, Stamford 06904.

Chm., Rodney Chabot, New Canaan; John Anglace, Jr., Shelton; Timothy Batler, Stamford; Eric Bosch, Wilton; James Cameron, Darien; Eugene Colonese, NY; Lawrence Forbes, Newington; Stephanie Harwood, New Canaan; Carl Leaman, Westport; Joseph McGee, Fairfield; Peter S. Meyers, Milford; James Mohs, Milford; Edward Montague, Westport; Benjamin S. Thompson, New Canaan; Joan Ventrilio, Guilford; Edward Zimmerman, New Canaan; two vacancies.

COMMISSIONERS OF THE METROPOLITAN DISTRICT WITHIN THE COUNTY OF HARTFORD

Appointed by the Governor, Legislature and municipalities, P.A. No. 93-380, Sec. 16. Compensation, none. Address: P.O. Box 800, 555 Main St., Hartford 06142-0800. Tel., (860) 278-7850.

Anthony H. Galicchio, Newington, Dec. 31, 1996. Martin B. Courneen, Wethersfield; James A. Crowley; Thomas F. Sarubbi, Wethersfield; Harry B. Schaechter, West Hartford; Joseph A. Visgilio, East Hartford, Dec. 31, 1997. Lawrence F. DelPonte, East Hartford; Bruno W. Mazzulla, Hartford; Randall H. Pease, Jr., West Hartford; Paul M. Ritter, Hartford; Hector M. Rivera, Hartford; Richard M. Torpey, East Hartford; Richard F. Wareing, Hartford; John E. Waters, Windsor; Everett I. Weaver, Newington, Dec. 31, 1998. Michael C. Bellobuono, Wethersfield; Marilyn F. Cohen, West Hartford; Timothy J. Fitzgerald, Windsor; Daniel E. Lilly, Hartford; William J. O'Brien, West Hartford; Steven D. Park, Hartford; Albert F. Reichin, Bloomfield; Dale A. Ryan, Hartford; Pasquale J. Salemi, East Hartford; Raymond Sweezy, Rocky Hill, Dec. 31, 2000. Allen Hoffman, West Hartford, Dec. 31, 2001. Daniel A. Camiliere, Wethersfield; Gertrude M. Cwikla, Hartford; William A. DiBella, Hartford; John M. Grottole, East Hartford; Louis G. LaPorto, Rocky Hill; Trude H. Mero, Hartford; Richard B. Vannie, West Hartford, Dec. 31, 2002; Louis O. Gagliardi, New Britain, (with vote on water matters only).

Dist. Chm., Anthony H. Gallicchio; *Vice Chm.,* Gertrude M. Cwikla; *Dist. Mgr.,* Anthony V. Milano; *Dist. Counsel,* Bourke G. Spellacy; *Dist. Treas.,* vacancy; *Dist. Clerk,* Robert A. Hagan.

BOARD OF PARDONS

Sec. 18-24a, Gen. Stat. Compensation of members, per diem. Address: Secy., Trumbull Park Business Center, 935 White Plains Rd., Suite 203, Trumbull 06611. Tel., (203) 261-0551.

Appointed by the Governor, Chm., Howard G. Iger, M.D., Bloomfield; Vanessa L. Bryant, Hartford; Ronald DeLuca, Norwich; Joseph S. Elder, West Hartford; James R. Smith, Middlebury.

Secy., Burton S. Yaffie, Trumbull.

BOARD OF PAROLE

Appointed by the Governor for a term coterminous with term of the Governor or until a successor is chosen, with the advice and consent of either House of the General Assembly, Sec. 54-124a, Gen. Stat. Compensation of members, Chm., $70,000; other members, $110 for each day spent in performance of duties, plus necessary expenses. Address: 21 Grand St., Hartford 06106. Tel., (860) 692-7400; FAX, (860) 566-2048.

Chm., John E. Meeker, Washington Depot; *Acting Vice Chm.,* Robert J. Moran, Woodbury; Kathleen J. Armentano, Enfield; Priscilla August, Windsor; Cicero B. Booker, Jr., Waterbury; Rubye Daniels, New Haven; Carmen F. Donnarumma, Waterbury; James Gatling, Southington; Daniel M. McCabe, Stamford; Robert L. Minch, Somers; Robert W. Neil, Bolton; Edward H. Simpson, West Simsbury; Gina Solak, Willimantic.

GOVERNOR'S COMMITTEE ON PHYSICAL FITNESS

Appointed by the Governor to serve at his pleasure. Compensation, none. Address: Dr. Keith Overland, 46 Breeds Hill Pl., Wilton 06897. Tel. (203) 834-0307; FAX, (203) 853-2078.

Co-Chm., Dr. Keith Overland, Wilton, Robert E. Stauble, Jr., Glastonbury; *Vice Chm.,* Michael A. Tommasi, Rocky Hill; *Past Chm.,* Linda Wooster, Bethany, North Haven; *Secy.,* Carolyn Vanacore, North Haven; *Treas.,* Brian J. Kennedy, Norwalk; Robert L. Backlund, Glastonbury; Lorraine Baiz, Stamford; Will Berger, Ph.D., Bridgeport; Edward Bonello, Norwalk; Charles Byron, Meriden; David Camaione, Ph.D., Newington; Glenn V. Colarossi, Stamford; Palmer F. Collier III, Brookfield; Frank DeGregorio, East Hartford; Harvey C. Ebel, Ph.D., Stamford; Marc J. Garofalo, Derby; John P. Gawlak, Stamford; William Hamzy, Terryville; Edward J. Hines, Brookfield; Melanie A. Hoben, Middletown; Harvey M. Kramer, M.D., West Redding; Dr. Joseph Kristan, Rockville; Connie Kunkel, Plainville; Gerard J. Lawrence, M.D., South Windham; Roberta Westover, Ed.D., Brookfield.

SOLDIERS', SAILORS' AND MARINES' FUND

Sec. 27-138, Gen. Stat. Salary, Admin., $66,494; Asst., $63,939. Address: 101 South St., West Hartford 06110. Tel., (860) 953-4345; FAX, (860) 953-4317.

Admin., Edward D. Barry; *Asst. Admin.,* Martin J. Campion.

Trustee, Christopher B. Burnham, State Treasurer.

TEACHERS' RETIREMENT BOARD

Secs. 4-9a, 10-183l, Gen. Stat. Salary, Admin., $86,913. Compensation of members, necessary expenses. Address: Admin., Room 202, State Office Bldg., Hartford 06106. Tel., (860) 566-3241.

Ex officio, Theodore S. Sergi, Comr. of Education; Joyce A. Thomas, Comr. of Social Services.

Elected by the Retirement System, *Chm.,* Clare H. Barnett, Waterbury, June 30, 1999; Mary Nicholas, Vernon; Martin Rudnick, North Haven, June 30, 1997; Marion S. Jewell, Stamford;. Rosalyn B. Schoonmaker, Southbury, June 30, 1999.

Appointed by the Governor, public members, Eugene Cimiano, Hartford; Deborah Freedman, Simsbury; Elaine T. Lowengard, West Hartford; Augustine M. Masiello, Woodstock; Charles E. Moller, Jr., Wethersfield.

Admin., John R. Shears.

SECTION V

STATE GOVERNMENT—JUDICIAL

Supreme Court

Appellate Court

Superior Court

Practice of Law—Admission to the Bar

Probate Courts

STATE COURTS

(Justices of the Supreme Court, Judges of the Appellate Court, and Judges of the Superior Court are appointed by the General Assembly, on nomination by the Governor from a list of candidates submitted by the Judicial Selection Commission, for terms of eight years.)

SUPREME COURT
CHIEF JUSTICE

(Salary, $123,576 as of July 1, 1996), Robert J. Callahan, Norwalk; office, Supreme Court Bldg., Hartford, September 1, 1996 through June 21, 2001.

JUSTICES
(As of January 30, 1997)

(Salary, $113,042 as of July 1, 1996), David M. Borden, West Hartford; office, Supreme Court Bldg., Hartford, May 10, 1990-May 7, 1998. Robert I. Berdon, Branford; office, Supreme Court Bldg., Hartford, September 4, 1991-March 3, 2000. Flemming L. Norcott, Jr., New Haven; office, Supreme Court Bldg., Hartford, July 14, 1992-February 16, 2001. Joette Katz, Fairfield; office, Supreme Court Bldg., Hartford, October 22, 1992-February 16, 2001. Richard N. Palmer, Cromwell; office, Supreme Court Bldg., Hartford, March 18, 1993-March 16, 2001. Francis M. McDonald, Jr., Middlebury; office, Supreme Court Bldg., Hartford, September 1, 1996-March 27, 2000.

APPELLATE COURT
(As of January 30, 1997)

CHIEF JUDGE

(Salary, $111,600 as of July 1, 1996), Antoinette L. Dupont, New London; office, Judicial Dist. Courthouse, 95 Washington St., Hartford, Aug. 15, 1983-March 13, 2000.

JUDGES

(Salary, $105,111 as of July 1, 1996), Edward Y. O'Connell, Wethersfield; office, Judicial Dist. Courthouse, 95 Washington St., Hartford, Oct. 1, 1987-March 8, 2004. Paul M. Foti, Branford; office, Judicial Dist. Courthouse, 95 Washington St., Hartford, Nov. 2, 1987-March 8, 2004. William J. Lavery, Newtown; office, Judicial Dist. Courthouse, 95 Washington St., Hartford, October 4, 1989-March 13, 1998. Sidney S. Landau, Stamford; office, Judicial Dist. Courthouse, 95 Washington St., Hartford, May 10, 1990-May 7, 1998. Maxwell Heiman, Newington; office, Judicial Dist. Courthouse, 95 Washington St., Hartford, December 21, 1990-February 5, 1999. Barry R. Schaller, Madison; office, Judicial Dist. Courthouse, 95 Washington St., Hartford, October 23, 1992-February 16, 2001. E. Eugene Spear, Bridgeport; office, Judicial Dist. Courthouse, 95 Washington St., Hartford, January 3, 1994-March 29, 2002; Francis X. Hennessy, West Hartford; office, Judicial Dist. Courthouse, 95 Washington St., Hartford, September 23, 1994-November 27, 2002.

Sr. Associate Judge, Frederick A. Freedman, Weston; office, Judicial Dist. Courthouse, 95 Washington St., Hartford, January 10, 1992-March 3, 2000.

Adm. Judge of the Appellate System, Joette Katz, Justice, Supreme Court, 231 Capitol Ave., Hartford; P.O. Box address, Drawer N, Station A, Hartford 06106.

Chief Clerk of the Supreme Court, Atty. Francis J. Drumm, Jr., Supreme Court Bldg., Hartford; P.O. Box address, Drawer Z, Station A, Hartford 06106.

Reporter of Judicial Decisions, Atty. Emily J. Lebovitz, Supreme Court Bldg., Hartford; P.O. Box address, Drawer N, Station A, Hartford 06106.

Chief Staff Attorney, Atty. Barbara Rodgers, Supreme Court Bldg., Hartford 06106; P.O. Box address, Drawer N, Station A, Hartford 06106.

SUPERIOR COURT
(As of January 30, 1997)

JUDGES
(Salary, $100,411 as of July 1, 1996)

Name	Residence	Term
Harold H. Dean	Darien	1974—February 11, 1999
Howard J. Moraghan	New Milford	1978—June 30, 2002
JoAnne K. Kulawiz	Orange	1978—June 30, 2002
Edward F. Stodolink	Redding	1978—June 30, 2002
G. Sarsfield Ford	Fairfield	1978—June 30, 2002
James M. Higgins	Haddam	1978—June 30, 2002
Aaron Ment	Fairfield	1978—June 30, 2002
Arthur L. Spada	Hartford	1978—June 30, 2002
L. Scott Melville	Bridgeport	1978—June 30, 2002
Mary R. Hennessey	Hartford	1978—June 30, 2002
John P. Maiocco, Jr.	Stratford	1978—June 30, 2002
Samuel S. Freedman (until 7/5/97)	Westport	1978—February 6, 2003
William J. Sullivan	Waterbury	1978—February 6, 2003
William P. Murray	Southington	1979—February 6, 2003
Herbert Barall	East Hartford	1979—February 21, 2003
Ronald J. Fracasse	Cheshire	1979—February 23, 2003
John F. Mulcahy, Jr.	Glastonbury	1979—May 13, 2003
Joseph J. Purtill (until 8/31/97)	Pawcatuck	1979—March 11, 2004
John J. P. Ryan	Greenwich	1980—February 10, 1997
Barbara A. Coppeto	Milford	1981—March 9, 1998
David M. Barry	Manchester	1981—March 9, 1998
Lawrence C. Klaczak	Somers	1981—March 9, 1998
John P. Maloney	West Hartford	1981—March 9, 1998
Leander C. Gray	New Haven	1981—March 9, 1998

Dennis F. Harrigan	Greenwich	1982—March 16, 1998
Wendy W. Susco	Canton	1982—February 8, 1999
Bernard D. Gaffney	New Britain	1982—February 8, 1999
John M. Byrne	Middletown	1982—February 8, 1999
Charles D. Gill	Litchfield	1983—March 13, 2000
Joseph A. Licari, Jr.	North Haven	1983—March 13, 2000
Joseph B. Clark	New Haven	1984—March 13, 2000
Thomas G. West	Danbury	1984—March 13, 2000
John J. Ronan	Milford	1984—April 30, 2000
Thomas P. Miano	Hartford	1984—February 12, 2001
Anne C. Dranginis	Litchfield	1985—May 29, 2001
George N. Thim	Trumbull	1985—May 5, 2001
Socrates H. Mihalakos	Cheshire	1985—March 11, 2002
Joseph P. Flynn	Ansonia	1985—March 11, 2002
Lawrence L. Hauser	East Norwalk	1985—March 11, 2002
Salvatore F. Arena	Portland	1985—March 11, 2002
Richard A. Damiani	North Haven	1985—March 11, 2002
Jonathan J. Kaplan	South Windsor	1985—March 11, 2002
Joseph Q. Koletsky	Waterford	1985—March 11, 2002
Karen Nash Sequino	New Haven	1985—March 11, 2002
Raymond R. Norko	Hartford	1985—March 11, 2002
Thomas J. Corradino	Branford	1986—April 27, 2002
Stuart M. Schimelman	East Lyme	1986—February 10, 2003
Samuel Freed (until 5/8/97)	West Hartford	1986—February 10, 2003
Thomas V. O'Keefe, Jr.	North Branford	1986—February 10, 2003
Robert C. Leuba	Mystic	1986—February 10, 2003
Myron R. Ballen	Fairfield	1986—February 10, 2003
Richard J. Stanley	Centerbrook	1986—February 10, 2003
Robert F. Stengel	Rocky Hill	1986—February 10, 2003
John T. Downey	New Haven	1987—March 8, 2004
Joseph T. Gormley, Jr.	Trumbull	1987—March 8, 2004
Michael Hartmere	Milford	1987—March 8, 2004
Christina G. Dunnell	Newington	1987—March 8, 2004
Joseph L. Steinberg	Hartford	1987—March 8, 2004
Leonard M. Cocco	Trumbull	1987—March 8, 2004
Beverly J. Hodgson	New Haven	1987—March 8, 2004
Edward J. Leavitt	West Haven	1987—March 8, 2004
Edward J. Mullarkey	Rocky Hill	1987—March 8, 2004
John J. Langenbach	West Hartford	1988—March 8, 2004
Russell F. Potter, Jr.	Windham	1988—March 8, 2004
Thelma A. Santos	West Hartford	1988—March 8, 2004
Sidney Axelrod	Madison	1988—March 8, 2004
William F. Hickey, Jr.	Stamford	1988—March 8, 2004
Bruce W. Thompson	Branford	1988—March 8, 2004
Marshall K. Berger, Jr.	Canton	1988—February 7, 1997
Andre M. Kocay	West Hartford	1997—January 27, 2005

Elaine Gordon	Madison	1997—January 27, 2005
A. William Mottolese	Stamford	1997—January 27, 2005
Robert F. McWeeny	Hartford	1997—January 27, 2005
Clarance J. Jones	Madison	1989—April 18, 1997
Terence A. Sullivan	Willington	1989—April 18, 1997
Jon C. Blue	Hamden	1989—April 18, 1997
Christine S. Vertefeuille	Cheshire	1989—March 6, 1998
Philip R. Dunn	West Hartford	1989—March 6, 1998
Roland D. Fasano	North Haven	1990—March 6, 1998
Patrick J. Clifford	Madison	1990—March 6, 1998
Joseph H. Sylvester	Stratford	1990—March 6, 1998
Samuel J. Sferrazza	Somers	1990—March 6, 1998
Samuel H. Teller	Bolton	1990—May 7, 1998
Joseph W. Doherty	Naugatuck	1990—May 7, 1998
Richard A. Walsh	West Hartford	1990—May 7, 1998
Howard Scheinblum	West Hartford	1990—May 7, 1998
Romeo G. Petroni	New Haven	1990—May 7, 1998
Joseph H. Pellegrino	Hamden	1990—May 7, 1998
Sandra Vilardi Leheny	Danbury	1990—May 7, 1998
Julia L. Aurigemma	Cromwell	1990—May 8, 1998
Robert L. Holzberg	Middletown	1990—May 8, 1998
Edward R. Karazin, Jr.	Westport	1990—June 24, 1998
Thomas F. Parker	West Hartford	1990—February 5, 1999
Robert A. Martin	New London	1990—February 5, 1999
John W. Moran	Milford	1990—February 5, 1999
E. Curtissa R. Cofield	Glastonbury	1991—June 6, 1999
Michael R. Sheldon	Canton	1991—June 6, 1999
William B. Rush	Fairfield	1991—June 6, 1999
Jonathan E. Silbert	Guilford	1991—June 6, 1999
Carmen Elisa Espinosa	Southington	1992—March 10, 2000
David L. Fineberg	Avon	1992—March 3, 2000
Bruce L. Levin	Orange	1992—March 3, 2000
Linda K. Lager	Woodbridge	1992—March 3, 2000
Eddie Rodriguez, Jr.	Easton	1992—March 3, 2000
L. Paul Sullivan	West Hartford	1992—February 16, 2001
Richard M. Rittenband	South Windsor	1992—February 16, 2001
Patty Jenkins Pittman	Hamden	1992—February 16, 2001
Kevin E. Booth	Niantic	1992—February 16, 2001
Nicola E. Rubinow	West Hartford	1992—February 16, 2001
Douglas C. Mintz	Norwalk	1993—January 26, 2001
Kevin P. McMahon	Niantic	1993—February 2, 2001
Susan B. Handy	Pawcatuck	1993—February 2, 2001
Robert J. Devlin, Jr.	Guilford	1993—February 2, 2001
Douglas S. Lavine	West Hartford	1993—February 2, 2001
Peter E. Wiese	Avon	1993—May 17, 2001
Francis J. Foley III	Hanover	1993—May 18, 2001
Jon M. Alander	Hamden	1993—March 29, 2002

Christine E. Keller	Hartford	1993—March 29, 2002
Frank H. D'Andrea, Jr.	Stamford	1993—March 29, 2002
Alexandra D. DiPentima	Hartford	1993—March 29, 2002
David W. Skolnick	Woodbridge	1993—March 29, 2002
Kevin Tierney	Greenwich	1994—March 29, 2002
H. Maria Cone	Hartford	1994—April 29, 2002
Richard W. Dyer	Manchester	1994—November 27, 2002
Thomas L. Nadeau	Wilton	1994—November 27, 2002
Thomas A. Bishop	North Stonington	1994—November 27, 2002
Richard J. Tobin	Stamford	1994—November 27, 2002
John F. Kavanewsky, Jr.	East Norwalk	1994—November 27, 2002
George Levine	Hartford	1994—November 27, 2002
Lynda B. Munro	Clinton	1994—November 27, 2002
John C. Driscoll	Norwich	1994—November 27, 2002
Maureen D. Dennis	Southport	1994—November 27, 2002
Richard F. Comerford, Jr.	Stamford	1994—November 27, 2002
Joseph M. Shortall	Bloomfield	1994—November 27, 2002
Jack L. Grogins	Redding	1994—November 27, 2002
James T. Graham	Bloomfield	1994—November 27, 2002
Barry K. Stevens	Stratford	1994—November 27, 2002
Jorge A. Simon	Glastonbury	1996—March 8, 2004
Burton A. Kaplan	Orange	1996—March 8, 2004
Robert E. Beach, Jr.	Glastonbury	1996—March 8, 2004
Richard E. Arnold	Orange	1996—March 8, 2004
Patrick L. Carroll III	Shelton	1996—March 8, 2004
Frank A. Iannotti	North Haven	1996—March 8, 2004
C. Ian Mclachlan	Farmington	1996—March 8, 2004
A. Susan Peck	West Hartford	1996—March 8, 2004
Elliott N. Solomon	Bolton	1996—March 8, 2004
Bradford J. Ward	West Hartford	1996—March 8, 2004
William Holden	Bridgeport	1996—May 9, 2004
Barbara M. Quinn	Chester	1997—February 27, 2005
Patricia L. Harleston	Hartford	1997—February 27, 2005
Carmen L. Lopez	Bridgeport	1997—February 27, 2005
William L. Wollenberg	Farmington	1997—February 27, 2005
Frank M. D'Addabbo	New Britain	1997—February 27, 2005
Peter T. Zarella	West Hartford	1997—February 27, 2005
Robert T. Resha	Danbury	1997—February 27, 2005
John Turner	Hamden	1997—February 27, 2005
Gary J. White	Stamford	1997—February 27, 2005
Dale W. Radcliffe	Trumbull	1997—February 27, 2005

Senior Judges
(As of March 28, 1996)
(Sec. 51-165, Gen. Stat.)

Name	Residence	Term
Richard T. O'Connell	Old Saybrook	1984—February 12, 2001
Martin L. McKeever	Orange	1978—June 30, 2002
William M. Shaughnessy, Jr.	West Hartford	1980—March 11, 2004
Jerrold H. Barnett	Bethany	1983—March 13, 2000
Martin L. Nigro	Greenwich	1977—June 30, 2002
William J. McGrath	Fairfield	1978—June 30, 2002
Stanley Novack	Stamford	1978—June 30, 2002
Morton I. Riefberg	Danbury	1985—March 11, 2002
William B. Lewis	Riverside	1983—February 8, 1999
Edgar W. Bassick III	Fairfield	1986—March 11, 2002
Seymour L. Hendel	New London	1978—June 30, 2002
Allen W. Smith	Glastonbury	1979—March 11, 2004

State Referees, Supreme Court, Appellate Court and Superior Court—(Sec. 52-434, Gen. Stat.) Herbert S. MacDonald, North Haven; *Alva P. Loiselle, Willimantic; Anthony E. Grillo, Hamden; *Joseph F. Dannehy, Willimantic; *Arthur H. Healey, New Haven; *David M. Shea, Hartford; *Robert D. Glass, Waterbury; *Angelo G. Santaniello, New London; *William C. Bieluch, West Hartford; *George D. Stoughton, West Hartford; *Daniel F. Spallone, Deep River; *John J. Daly, Hartford; *Albert W. Cretella, Jr., North Haven; Philip R. Pastore, New Haven; *Max H. Reicher, New Britain; Eli L. Cramer, Norwich; *Simon S. Cohen, West Hartford; Paul J. Driscoll, Norwich; *Michael J. Sicilian, Fairfield; *George A. Saden, Bridgeport; *Jay E. Rubinow, Manchester; *Douglass B. Wright, West Hartford; *John M. Alexander, Windsor; *Harold M. Missal, Bristol; *Milton H. Belinkie, Bridgeport; Maurice J. Sponzo, West Hartford; *Harold M. Mulvey, Hamden; *Margaret C. Driscoll, Bridgeport; *John D. Brennan, East Hartford; *John Ottaviano, Jr., Cheshire; *Julius J. Kremski, New Britain; *Francis J. O'Brien, Meriden; *John N. Reynolds, Hamden; William Beale Ramsey, New Haven; *John C. Flanagan, Hamden; *Robert J. Hale, Glastonbury; *Robert Satter, Avon; *Philip E. Mancini, Jr., Westville; *Francis R. Quinn, Norwich; *Frank S. Meadow, Woodbridge; *Donald T. Dorsey, Meriden; *Donald W. Celotto, Woodbridge; *Frances Allen, Avon; *Hugh C. Curran, Milford; *Anthony V. DeMayo, East Haven; *Paul M. Vasington, Norwich,*James F. Bingham, Stamford; Edward R. Doyle, Wethersfield; *Samuel S. Goldstein, West Hartford; *Harry N. Jackaway, West Hartford; *Walter R. Budney, Ivoryton; *William L. Hadden, Jr., Hamden; *George W. Ripley II, Shelton ; *Joseph H. Goldberg, Avon; *Howard F. Zoarski, Branford; *Norris L. O'Neill, West Hartford *Robert P. Burns, Branford; Walter M. Pickett, Jr, New Preston; *Frederica S. Brenneman, Glastonbury; *Jerry Wagner, Bloomfield; Hadley W. Austin, Madison; D. Michael Hurley, Niantic; Arnold W. Aaronson, Avon; Sabino P. Tamborra, Norwich; Harry Hammer, Rockville; Thomas H. Corrigan, Wethersfield; Michael P. Conway, Baltic; Morton I. Riefberg, Danbury (from 3/31/97); Samuel Freed, West Hartford (from 5/8/97); Samuel S. Freedman, Westport (from 7/5/97); Joseph J. Purtill, Pawcatuck (from 8/13/97).

State Referees, Juvenile Court—John F. McLinden, Waterbury; Thomas D. Gill, West Hartford.

Chief Family Support Magistrate—Katherine Y. Hutchinson, Andover.

Family Support Magistrates—Harris T. Lifshitz, Rocky Hill; Edmund H. Miller, Stamford; Ronald M. Sullivan, Bridgewater; Elliot A. Ginsberg, West Hartford; Deborah A. Kochiss-Frankel, Stratford; Sandra S. Sosnoff, New Haven; Wilson J. Trombley, Wolcott; Paul Matasavage, Waterbury.

Family Support Magistrate Referees—Norman A. Buzaid, Danbury; Alan E. Steele, Middletown;

---

*Judge Trial Referees by appointment from Chief Justice for one year from July 1, 1996.
Chief Family Support Magistrate designated by the Chief Court Administrator.

OFFICE OF CHIEF COURT ADMINISTRATOR

CHIEF COURT ADMINISTRATOR

(Appointed by, and serves at the pleasure of, the Chief Justice; Salary, $118,068 as of July 1, 1996.) *Chief Court Administrator,* Hon. Aaron Ment; *Deputy Chief Court Administrator,* (Salary, $102,877 as of July 1, 1996.) Hon. Robert C. Leuba. Address: Supreme Court Bldg., 231 Capitol Ave. (Drawer N, Station A) Hartford 06106. Tel., (860) 566-4461.

ADMINISTRATIVE SERVICES
75 Elm St. (Drawer N, Station A), Hartford 06106
(Unless otherwise noted)

Exec. Dir. of Adm. Services, James O. Cavanaugh (Address: 231 Capitol Ave.)

Commission on Official Legal Publications—Sec. 51-216a, Gen. Stat.

Chm., Ex officio, Robert J. Callahan, Chief Justice of the Supreme Court; Aaron Ment, Judge, Chief Court Administrator.

Appointed by the Chief Justice, David M. Shea, Judge Referee; George D. Stoughton, Judge Referee; James O. Cavanaugh, Exec. Dir., Admin. Serv., Joseph D. D'Alesio, Exec. Dir. of Operations, Superior Court/Exec. Secy.; Emily J. Lebovitz, Reporter of Judicial Decisions.

Publications Dir., Richard J. Hemenway, 111 Phoenix Ave., Enfield 06082; *Forms Mgr.,* Michael Piela..

Dir. of Facilities, Joseph P. McMahon; *Mgr. of Facilities,* Gerald F. Rucci; *Mgr. of Security,* Robert W. Kilpatrick; *Dir. of Financial Services,* Joseph F. Camilleri; *Mgr. of Financial Services,* Thomas N. Sitaro; *Mgr. of Budget,* Dean P. Skevas; *Dir. of Human Resource Mgmt.,* Robert D. Coffey; *Personnel Mgr. (Automated Systems and Employee Benefits),* Eileen R. Rausch; *Personnel Mgr. (Recruitment, Employee Services and Compensation),* Eileen L. Finn; *Mgr. of Labor Relations,* William F. Risley;

Dir. of Internal Auditing, Danny C. Taylor; *Dir. of Mgmt. and Policy Analysis,* Bruce Borre; *Dir. of Materials Mgmt.,* Cortez White; *Mgr. of Purchasing,* Veda Shimkowitz.

Judicial Info. Systems (Data Processing) Unit, (340 Capitol Ave., Hartford 06106): *Dir. of Judicial Info. Systems (Data Processing),* Stephanie B. Kwasnicki; *Mgr. of Systems Development,* Elizabeth Bickley; *Mgr. of Office Technology,* Anne Marie Martin; *Mgr. of Technical Support,* Darryl Hamblett.

AFFIRMATIVE ACTION/EMPLOYMENT DISCRIMINATION

Address: 75 Elm St., Hartford 06106. Tel., (860) 722-5872. *Affirmative Action and Employment Discrimination Program Coordinator,* Moira Butler.

EXTERNAL AFFAIRS
231 Capitol Ave. (Drawer N, Station A), Hartford 06106. Tel., (860) 566-8210.

Dir. of External Affairs, Melissa A. Farley; *Mgr. of Communications,* Karen A. Berris; *Staff Atty.,* Deborah J. Fuller.

SUPERIOR COURT OPERATIONS
75 Elm St., Hartford 06106-1692
(Unless otherwise noted)

Exec. Dir. of Operations, Superior Court/Exec. Secy., Joseph D. D'Alesio; *Legal Counsel,* Mary B. O'Connor; *Dir. of Admin.,* Frank L. Cassello; *Deputy Dir., Program and Staff Development,* Salvatore A. D'Amico; *Mgr. of Admin. Services/Superior Court,* Ronald J. Macchio; *Chief Court Interpreter,* William Alvarado; *Examiner of Seized Property,* Charles A. Esau.

Court Operations, Dir. of Court Operations, James R. Maher; *Deputy Dir., Automated Systems,* Frank M. Goetz; *Chief Clerk, Housing Matters,* Suzanne Colasanto (121 Elm St., New Haven 06510); *Mgr., Dispute Resolution Program (Housing Specialist),* Cynthia Teixeira (121 Elm St., New Haven 06510).

Centralized Court Services, Dir. of Centralized Court Services, Sherry Antonacci; (Infractions mailing address: P. O. Box 5044, Hartford 06102-5044; All other mail: P.O. Box 1140, Hartford 06143-1140. Tel., (860) 529-0510. *Clerk,* Sherry Antonacci; *Mgr.,* Pamela Frank-Brown.

Superior Court Records Ctr., 111 Phoenix Ave., Enfield 06082. Tel., (860) 741-3714; *Mgr.,* Patrick McGuire.

Jury Admin., 225 Spring St., Wethersfield 06109. Tel., (860) 566-7497; *Jury Admin.,* Richard Gayer.

JUDGE SUPPORT SERVICES

Address: 100 Washington St., 3rd Floor, Hartford 06106. Tel., (860) 566-5914.

Dir. of Judge Support Services, Faith P. Arkin; *Deputy Dir. of Continuing Education,* Anthony B. Fisser, (100 Washington St., 2nd Floor, Hartford 06106); *Staff Develop-*

ment Officer, Evelyn F. Eisenhardt; *Deputy Dir. of Law Libraries,* Maureen D. Well; *Deputy Dir. of Legal Research,* Alberta Slattery, (121 Elm St., New Haven 06510); *Admin., Judicial Performance Evaluation,* Margery M. Wilber.

CONNECTICUT JUDICIAL BRANCH—LAW LIBRARY SYSTEM
(Sec. 11-19a, Gen. Stat.)

BRIDGEPORT—Willie Jackson
    Law Library at Bridgeport
    Courthouse, 1061 Main St.
    Bridgeport 06604
    Tel., (203) 579-6237

DANBURY—Nita Hirshon
    Law Library at Danbury
    Courthouse, 146 White St.
    Danbury 06810
    Tel., (203) 797-2731

HARTFORD—Carole Martin
    Law Library at Hartford
    Courthouse, 95 Washington St.
    Hartford 06106
    Tel., (860) 548-2866

LITCHFIELD—Peter Jenkins
    Law Library at Litchfield
    Courthouse, 15 West St.
    Litchfield 06759
    Tel., (860) 567-0598

MIDDLETOWN—Lawrence Cheeseman, Jr.
    Law Library at Middletown
    Courthouse, 1 Court St.
    Middletown 06457-3374
    Tel., (860) 343-6560

NEW HAVEN—Martha J. Sullivan
    Law Library at New Haven
    Courthouse, 235 Church St.
    New Haven 06510
    Tel., (203) 789-7889

NEW LONDON—Jane Burke
    Law Library at New London
    Courthouse, 70 Huntington St.
    New London, CT 06320
    Tel., (860) 442-7561

NORWICH—Barbara Bradley
    Law Library at Norwich
    Courthouse, 1 Courthouse Sq.
    Norwich 06360
    Tel., (860) 887-2398

PUTNAM—Donna Izbicki
    Law Library at Putnam
    Courthouse, 155 Church St.
    Putnam 06260
    Tel., (860) 928-3716

ROCKVILLE—Roseann Canny
    Law Library at Rockville
    Courthouse, 69 Brooklyn St.
    Rockville 06066
    Tel., (860) 872-3824

STAMFORD—Jonathan Stock
    Law Library at Stamford
    Courthouse, 123 Hoyt St.
    Stamford 06905
    Tel., (203) 359-1114

WATERBURY—Mary Fuller
    Law Library at Waterbury
    Courthouse, 300 Grand St.
    Waterbury 06702
    Tel., (203) 596-4044

WILLIMANTIC—vacancy
    Law Library at Willimantic
    Courthouse, 108 Valley St.
    Willimantic 06226
    Tel., (860) 423-8491

ADMINISTRATIVE—Maureen D. Well
    Dir. of Law Libraries
    100 Washington St., 3rd Floor
    Hartford 06106
    Tel., (860) 566-7850

LEGAL SERVICES

100 Washington St. (P.O. Box 150474), Hartford 06115-0474. Tel., (860) 566-3835. (Unless otherwise indicated)

Dir. of Legal Services, Carl E. Testo; *Atty./Legal Services,* Martin R. Libbin; *Counsel/Legal Services,* Joseph J. Del Ciampo; *State Bar Counsel,* Daniel B. Horwitch, (287 Main St., East Hartford 06118-1885); *Admin. Dir., State Bar Examining Committee,* R. David Stamm (287 Main St., 2nd Floor, Suite 1, East Hartford 06118-1885).

ADULT PROBATION

Secs. 54-103—54-107, Gen. Stat. Address: 2275 Silas Deane Hwy., Rocky Hill 06067. Tel., (860) 563-1332.

Dir., Robert J. Bosco; *Deputy Dir. for Admin.,* Terry M. Borjeson; *Deputy Dir. for Operations,* Michael Santese.

DISTRICT MANAGERS

1st Dist., Meredith Moses; 2nd Dist.; Anthony Alves; 3rd Dist., Catherine Jaundrill.

ALTERNATIVE SANCTIONS

1155 Silas Deane Hwy., Wethersfield 06109. Tel., (860) 257-1904. *Dir.,* William H. Carbone; *Deputy Dir., Operations,* John F. Brooks; *Deputy Dir., Program and Staff Development,* James Greene.

BAIL COMMISSION

Address: 2275 Silas Deane Hwy., Rocky Hill 06067. Tel., (860) 529-6193. *Chief Bail Comr.,* Paul F. Brown; *Asst. Chief Bail Comr. of Operations,* Jo-Ann L. White; *Deputy Chief Bail Comr., of Administration,* Louis J. Palumbo; *Supervised Release Mgr.,* vacancy.

FAMILY DIVISION

Address: 225 Spring St., 4th Floor, Wethersfield 06109. Tel., (860) 529-9655. *Dir.,* Anthony J. Salius; *Deputy Dir., Juvenile Matters,* Frank M. Driscoll; *Deputy Dir., Adm. Services,* Richard D. Byam; *Deputy Dir., Family Matters,* Robert I. Tompkins.

DIVISION OF JUVENILE DETENTION SERVICES

Address: 1155 Silas Deane Hwy., Wethersfield 06109. Tel., (860) 529-7659. *Dir.,* Thomas F. White; *Deputy Dir.,* Robert F. Cunningham; *Mgr.,* Dennis E. Kane.

SUPPORT ENFORCEMENT

287 Main St., East Hartford 06118-1885. Tel., (860) 569-6233. *Dir.,* John T. Keegan; *Deputy Dir. of Admin.,* George Dombroski.

OFFICE OF VICTIM SERVICES

Address: 1155 Silas Deane Hwy., Wethersfield 06109. Tel., (860) 529-3089. *Dir.,* Carol R. Watkins; *Victim Compensation Supvr.,* Irene Mikol; *Victim Services Supvrs.,* Karen Corney, Charles Lexius.

Edwin Pearson, Richard W. Shettle, Sarah F. Summons, Susan Wolfson.

Dir., Carol R. Watkins.

SENTENCE REVIEW DIVISION

(Appointed by the Chief Justice, Sec. 51-194, Gen. Stat.) *Chm.,* Hon. Joseph J. Purtill, Pawcatuck; Hon. Lawrence C. Klaczak; Hon. Raymond R. Norko; *Alternates,* Hon. Thomas P. Miano, Hon. Richard J. Stanley. *Exec. Secy.,* Paul M. Palten, Esq., 100 Washington St., Hartford 06106.

SUPERIOR COURT OFFICERS

JUDICIAL DISTRICTS

JUDICIAL DISTRICT OF ANSONIA-MILFORD.—(Towns of Ansonia, Beacon Falls, Derby, Milford, Orange, Oxford, Seymour, Shelton, West Haven.) Address: 14 West River St. (P.O. Box 210), Milford 06460. Tel., (203) 877-4293. *Trial Court Admin.,* Nancy L. Kierstead, Tel., (203) 878-4910; *Chief Clerk,* Nellie Jo Dubin; *State's Atty.,* Mary M. Galvin, Tel., (203) 874-3361; *Public Defender,* David F. Egan, Tel., (203) 874-8857; *Lead Family Relations Counselor,* Allen B. Rubin, Tel., (203) 877-0001; *Support Enforcement,* 172 Golden Hill St., Bridgeport 06604. Tel., (203) 579-6590; *Official Reporter,* Alice Masterson, Tel., (203) 874-8523; *Adult Probation.,* Joseph Callahan, 44-64 River St., Milford 06460. Tel., (203) 877-1253.

JUDICIAL DISTRICT OF DANBURY.—(Towns of Bethel, Brookfield, Danbury, New Fairfield, Newtown, Redding, Ridgefield, Sherman.) Address: 146 White St., Danbury 06810. Tel., (203) 797-4400. *Trial Court Admin./Chief Clerk,* Therese A. Servas, Tel., (203) 797-4400; *Deputy Chief Clerk,* Robin J. Smith, Tel., (203) 797-4400; *State's Atty.,* Walter D. Flanagan, Tel., (203) 797-4073; *Public Defender,* Robert F. Field, 146 White St., Danbury 06810. Tel., (203) 797-4405; *Family Services Supvr.,* Paul J. Bevins, Tel., (203) 797-4029; *Support Enforcement,* Walter Biesadecki, 71 Main St., Danbury 06810. Tel., (203) 731-2940; *Official Reporter,* Ronald DeSimone, Tel., (203) 797-4175; *Adult Probation,* Frank Travisano, 319 Main St., Danbury 06810. Tel., (203) 797-4414.

JUDICIAL DISTRICT OF FAIRFIELD.—(Towns of Bridgeport, Easton, Fairfield, Monroe, Stratford, Trumbull.) Address: 1061 Main St. (P.O. Box 110), Bridgeport 06601. Tel., (203) 579-6527. *Trial Court Admin.,* Bernard J. Luckart, Tel., (203) 382-8400; *Chief Clerk,* Donald J. Mastrony, Tel., (203) 579-6527; *Deputy Chief Clerks,* David Bristo, vacancy, Tel., (203) 597-6527; *State's Atty.,* Donald A. Browne, Tel., (203) 579-6506; *Public Defender,* Preston Tisdale, Tel., (203) 579-6501; *Family Services Supvr.,* Janet Esposito-Daigle, Tel., (203) 579-6513; *Support Enforcement Services Supvr.,* Eileen Rodman, 172 Golden Hill St., P.O. Box 821, Bridgeport 06604.

Tel., (203) 579-6590; *Official Reporter,* Shirley Sambrook; *Adult Probation,* Thomas Coughlin, 1127 Main St., Bridgeport 06604. Tel., (203) 579-6241.

JUDICIAL DISTRICT OF HARTFORD-NEW BRITAIN.—(Towns of Avon, Berlin, Bloomfield, Bristol, Burlington, Canton, East Granby, East Hartford, East Windsor, Enfield, Farmington, Glastonbury, Granby, Hartford, Manchester, Marlborough, New Britain, Newington, Plainville, Plymouth, Rocky Hill, Simsbury, Southington, South Windsor, Suffield, West Hartford, Wethersfield, Windsor, Windsor Locks.) Addresses at Hartford: Civil, 95 Washington St. (Drawer D, Station A), Hartford 06106. Tel., (860) 548-2700; Criminal, 101 Lafayette St. (Drawer D, Station A), Hartford 06106. Tel., (860) 566-1630. *Trial Court Admin.,* David M. Jackson, Tel., (860) 548-2780; *Chief Clerk,* Michael J. DiDonato; *State's Atty.,* James E. Thomas, Tel., (860) 566-3190; *Public Defender,* M. Fred DeCaprio, 101 Lafayette St., Hartford 06106. Tel., (860) 566-4284; *Family Services Supvr.,* Robert Colucci, 18 Trinity St., Hartford 06106. Tel., (860) 566-3140; *Support Enforcement Services Supvr.,* Diane Harvey, 4th Floor, 999 Asylum Ave., Hartford 06105. Tel., (860) 566-8723; *Official Reporter,* Harold J. Moan; *Adult Probation Supvr.,* E. Flynn O'Keefe, 643 Maple Ave., Hartford 06114. Tel., (860) 566-8350.

ADDRESS AT NEW BRITAIN: 177 Columbus Blvd., New Britain 06051. Tel., (860) 827-7133. *Chief Clerk,* Margaret Moser; *Family Services Supvr.,* Charlotte J. Stamos, 74 Vine St., New Britain 06052. Tel., (860) 827-7130; *Adult Probation,* Steven Chatlas; *Support Enforcement,* Richard Palladino, 74 Vine St., New Britain 06052. Tel., (860) 827-7100.

JUDICIAL DISTRICT OF LITCHFIELD.—(Towns of Barkhamsted, Bethlehem, Bridgewater, Canaan, Colebrook, Cornwall, Goshen, Hartland, Harwinton, Kent, Litchfield, Morris, New Hartford, New Milford, Norfolk, North Canaan, Roxbury, Salisbury, Sharon, Thomaston, Torrington, Warren, Washington, Winchester.) Address: Courthouse, 15 West St. (P.O. Box 247), Litchfield 06759. Tel., (860) 567-0885. *Trial Court Admin.,* Scott A. Hartley, Tel., (860) 567-5438, (203) 596-4027; *Chief Clerk,* Brian J. Murphy; *State's Atty.,* Frank S. Maco, Tel., (860) 567-0871; *Public Defender,* Christopher M. Cosgrove, 63 West St., P.O. Box 944, Litchfield 06759-0944. Tel., (860) 567-3101; *Family Services Supvr.,* Stephen R. Grant, Litchfield Commons, Rte. 202, P.O. Box 307, Litchfield 06759. Tel., (860) 567-9463; *Official Reporter,* Charles H. Dukes; *Support Enforcement,* Karen Archambault, 11 Scovill St., Waterbury 06702.

JUDICIAL DISTRICT AT MERIDEN.—Address: 54 West Main St., Meriden 06451. Tel., (203) 238-6666. *Chief Clerk,* Joseph M. Dudra; *Housing Specialist,* Elizabeth Casey, Tel., (203) 238-6667; *Lead Family Relations Counselor,* Kathryn Ceruti, Tel., (203) 238-6140; *Support Enforcement Services,* 414 Chapel St., New Haven 06511. Tel., (203) 789-7485.

JUDICIAL DISTRICT OF MIDDLESEX.—(Towns of Chester, Clinton, Cromwell, Deep River, Durham, East Haddam, East Hampton, Essex, Haddam, Killingworth, Middlefield, Middletown, Old Saybrook, Portland, Westbrook.) Address: 1 Court St., Middletown 06457. Tel., (860) 343-6400. *Trial Court Admin./Chief Clerk,* Michael Kokoszka; *Deputy Chief Clerk,* Jonathan Field; *State's Atty.,* John T. Redway, Tel.,

(860) 343-6425; *Public Defender,* Richard F. Kelly, Tel., (860) 343-6480; *Family Services Supvr.,* Joanne R. Ventre, Tel., (860) 343-6460; *Support Enforcement,* Joseph Silva, 484 Main St., Middletown 06457. Tel., (860) 344-3095; *Official Reporter,* Gerald Rankin, Tel., (860) 343-6515; *Adult Probation,* Dennis A. Fennessey, 484 Main St., Middletown 06457. Tel., (860) 344-2998.

JUDICIAL DISTRICT OF NEW HAVEN.—(Towns of Bethany, Branford, Cheshire, East Haven, Guilford, Hamden, Madison, Meriden, New Haven, North Branford, North Haven, Wallingford, Woodbridge.) Address: 235 Church St., New Haven 06510. Tel., (203) 789-7908. *Trial Court Admin.,* Nicholas J. Cimmino, Tel., (203) 789-7949; *Chief Clerk,* William Sadek; *Deputy Chief Clerk,* George Fasanella; *State's Atty.,* Michael Dearington, Tel., (203) 789-7894; *Public Defender,* Thomas J. Ullman, Tel., (203) 789-7891; *Family Services Supvr.,* George Manning, Tel., (203) 789-7903; *Support Enforcement Supvr.,* Jodye Decrescenzo, 414 Chapel St., New Haven 06511. Tel., (203) 789-7485; *Official Reporter,* Sabrina G. Santoro; *Adult Probation,* Richard Pavasaris, 867 State St., New Haven 06511. Tel., (203) 789-7876.

JUDICIAL DISTRICT OF NEW LONDON.—(Towns of Bozrah, Colchester, East Lyme, Franklin, Griswold, Groton, Lebanon, Ledyard, Lisbon, Lyme, Montville, New London, North Stonington, Norwich, Old Lyme, Preston, Salem, Sprague, Stonington, Voluntown, Waterford.) Address: Courthouse, 70 Huntington St., New London 06320. Tel., (860) 443-5363. *Trial Court Admin.,* William J. Novi, Tel., (860) 437-0544; *Chief Clerk,* Jeffrey W. Feldman; *Deputy Chief Clerk,* David S. Gage; *State's Atty.,* Kevin Kane, Tel., (860) 443-2835; *Public Defender,* Bruce A. Sturman, Tel., (860) 443-0490; *Family Services Supvr.,* David Henriques, Tel., (860) 443-2826; *Support Enforcement Supvr.,* Thomas Daniels, 99 Main St., Norwich 06360. Tel., (860) 886-2694; *Adult Probation,* Norman Shove, 302 State St., New London 06320. Tel., ((860) 442-9426.

Address at Norwich: 1 Courthouse Sq., Norwich 06360. Tel., (860) 887-3515. *Chief Clerk,* Jorene M. Couture.

JUDICIAL DISTRICT OF STAMFORD-NORWALK.—(Towns of Darien, Greenwich, New Canaan, Norwalk, Stamford, Weston, Westport, Wilton.) Address: 123 Hoyt St. (P.O. Box 3245, Ridgeway Station), Stamford 06905. Tel., (203) 965-5307. *Trial Court Admin.,* Lorraine A. Murphy, Tel., (203) 965-5268; *Chief Clerk,* John C. Morrow; *Deputy Chief Clerk,* Pasquale V. Spinelli; *State's Atty.,* Eugene J. Callahan, Tel., (203) 965-5215; *Public Defender,* Joseph J. Bruckmann, 115 Hoyt St., Stamford 06905. Tel., (203) 965-5245; *Family Services Supvr.,* Roger Grenier, Tel., (203) 965-5282; *Support Enforcement Supvr.,* John J. Maxwell, 115 Hoyt St., Stamford 06905. Tel., (203) 965-5228; *Official Reporter,* Susan Wandzilak; *Adult Probation,* Dennis White, 115 Hoyt St., Stamford 06905. Tel., (203) 324-9518.

JUDICIAL DISTRICT OF TOLLAND.—(Towns of Andover, Bolton, Columbia, Coventry, Ellington, Hebron, Mansfield, Somers, Stafford, Tolland, Union, Vernon, Willington.) Address: 69 Brooklyn St., Rockville 06066. Tel., (860) 875-6294. *Trial Court Admin.,* Howard E. Emond, Jr., Tel., (860) 875-0672; *Chief Clerk, (Civil),* Kathleen F. Chase, Tel., (860) 875-6294; *Chief Clerk (Criminal),* Roy Smith, Jr., Tel., (860) 870-3200; *State's Atty.,* Patricia A. Swords, Tel., (860) 870-3270; *Public Defender,* Phillip N. Armentano, 1 Court St., Rockville 06066. Tel., (860) 870-3280; *Family*

Services Supvr., Peter H. Myers, 1 Court St., Rockville 06066. Tel., (860) 872-4088; *Support Enforcement,* Amy Olem, 30 Lafayette Sq., Rockville 06066. Tel., (860) 870-4010; *Official Reporter,* Marijean McKeon; *Housing Specialist,* Kathleen Solazzo.

JUDICIAL DISTRICT OF WATERBURY.—(Towns of Middlebury, Naugatuck, Prospect, Southbury, Waterbury, Watertown, Wolcott, Woodbury.) Address: 300 Grand St., Waterbury 06702. Tel., (203) 596-4023. *Trial Court Admin.,* Scott A. Hartley, Tel., (203) 596-4027, 4057; *Chief Clerk,* Philip H. Groth; *Deputy Chief Clerk,* Richard L. Haas, Jr.; *State's Atty.,* John A. Connelly, Tel., (203) 596-4210; *Public Defender,* Alan D. McWhirter, Tel., (203) 596-4040; *Family Services Supvr.,* William F. Rosa, Tel., (203) 596-4018; *Official Reporter,* Richard M. Walsh; *Adult Probation,* Peter Trombley, 11 Scovill St., Waterbury 06702. Tel., (203) 596-4195; *Support Enforcement Supvr.,* Karen Archambault, 11 Scovill St., Waterbury 06702. Tel., (203) 596-4188.

JUDICIAL DISTRICT OF WINDHAM.—(Towns of Ashford, Brooklyn, Canterbury, Chaplin, Eastford, Hampton, Killingly, Plainfield, Pomfret, Putnam, Scotland, Sterling, Thompson, Windham, Woodstock.) Address: 155 Church St. P.O. Box 191, Putnam 06260. Tel., (860) 928-7749. *Trial Court Admin.,* Howard E. Emond, Jr., Tel., (860) 928-7749; *Chief Clerk,* Francis A. Orszulak; *State's Atty.,* Mark S. Solak, Tel., (860) 928-5695; *Public Defender,* Ramon J. Canning, 108 Valley St., Willimantic 06226. Tel., (860) 928-7679; *Family Services Supvr.,* Joseph J. Nash, 50 Canal St., Putnam 06260. Tel., (860) 928-0478; *Support Enforcement,* Donald Fiore, 50 Canal St., P.O. Box 191, Putnam 06260. Tel., (860) 963-2580; *Official Reporter,* Kathleen O'Callaghan.

GEOGRAPHICAL AREAS (GA's)

G.A. #1.—(Towns of Darien, Greenwich, Stamford.) Address: 115 Hoyt St., Stamford 06905. Tel., (203) 965-5208. *Clerk,* Rita Connolly; *Supvervisory Asst. State's Atty.,* Steven Weiss, Tel., (203) 965-5255; *Bail Comr.,* Anna D. Stamatin; *Adult Probation,* Dennis White, Tel., (203) 324-9518; *Supervisory Asst. Public Defender,* Nancy Kekac, Tel., (203) 965-5245.

G.A. #2.—(Towns of Bridgeport, Easton, Fairfield, Monroe, Stratford, Trumbull.) Address: 172 Golden Hill St., Bridgeport 06604. Tel., (203) 579-6568. *Clerk,* Victoria Toenshoff; *Supervisory Asst. State's Atty.,* Joseph Marcello, Tel., (203) 579-6555; *Bail Comr. Supvr.,* Marilyn W. Holden; *Adult Probation,* Thomas Coughlin; *Supervisory Asst. Public Defender,* Andrew S. Liskov, Tel., (203) 579-6551.

G.A. #3.—(Towns of Bethel, Brookfield, Danbury, New Fairfield, Newtown, Redding, Ridgefield, Sherman.) Address: 146 White St., Danbury 06810. Tel., ((203) 797-4400. *Clerk,* Louis A. Pace, Jr.; *Supervisory Asst. State's Atty.,* Patricia M. Gilbert, Tel., (203) 797-4073; *Bail Comr.,* John A. Feulner; *Family Relations Supvr.,* Paul J. Bevins, P.O. Box 912, Danbury 06810. Tel., (203) 797-4410; *Adult Probation,* Frank Travisano; *Public Defender,* Robert F. Field, Tel., (203) 797-4405.

G.A. #4.—(Towns of Middlebury, Naugatuck, Prospect, Southbury, Waterbury, Watertown, Wolcott, Woodbury.) Address: 7 Kendrick Ave., Waterbury 06702. Tel., (203) 596-4050. *Clerk,* Betty A. Little; *Supervisory Asst. State's Atty.,* Corinne L. Klatt,

Tel., (203) 596-4066; *Bail Comr. Supvr.,* Gary A. Roberge; *Adult Probation,* Peter Trombley; *Supervisory Asst. Public Defender,* Gregory Barnes, Tel., (203) 596-4063.

G.A. #5.—(Towns of Ansonia, Beacon Falls, Derby, Orange, Oxford, Seymour, Shelton.) Address: 106 Elizabeth St., Derby 06418. Tel., (203) 735-7438. *Clerk,* Jo-Ann Miller; *Housing Specialist,* Elizabeth Casey, Tel., (203) 735-9625; *Supervisory Asst. State's Atty.,* Frank McQuade, Tel., (203) 735-7480; *Supvr. Bail Comr.,* Michael J. Hoban; *Lead Family Relations Counselor,* Ray Sadler, Tel., (203) 735-9595; *Supervisory Asst. Public Defender,* Susan Brown, Tel., (203) 735-8616.

G.A. #6.—(Towns of Bethany, New Haven, Woodbridge.) Address: 121 Elm St., New Haven 06510. Tel., (203) 789-7461. *Clerk,* Louis P. Fagnani, Jr.; *Supervisory Asst. State's Atty.,* James Clark, Tel., (203) 789-7455; *Bail Comr. Supvr.,* Janet A. Carnevale; *Adult Probation,* Richard Pavasaris; *Supervisory Asst. Public Defender,* Joan A. Leonard, Tel., (203) 789-7458.

G.A. #7.—(Towns of Cheshire, Hamden, Meriden, North Haven, Wallingford.) Address: 54 West Main St., Meriden 06451. Tel., (203) 238-6130. *Clerk,* Gerri Duggan; *Supervisory Asst. State's Atty.,* Juliett Crawford, Tel., (203) 238-6125; *Bail Comr.,* Betsy K. Bryan; *Supervisory Asst. Public Defender,* Richard V. Ackerson, Tel., (203) 238-6135.

G.A. #8.—(Towns of Branford, East Haven, Guilford, Madison, North Branford.) See listing for G.A. #6 above. *Supervisory Asst. State's Atty.,* David Newman, Tel., (203) 789-7855; *Bail Comm. Supvr.,* Janet A. Carnevale; *Supervisory Asst. Public Defender,* David G. Kaplan, Tel., (203) 789-7857.

G.A. #9.—(Towns of Chester, Clinton, Cromwell, Deep River, Durham, East Haddam, East Hampton, Essex, Haddam, Killingworth, Middlefield, Middletown, Old Saybrook, Portland, Westbrook.) Address: 1 Court St., Middletown 06457-3377. Tel., (860) 343-6445. *Clerk,* Patricia M. Byrne; *Supervisory Asst. State's Atty.,* Michael Dannehy, Tel., (860) 343-6300; *Bail Comr.,* Robert J. Christiano; *Adult Probation,* Dennis Fennessey; *Public Defender,* Richard F. Kelly, Tel., (860) 343-6480.

G.A. #10.—(Towns of East Lyme, Groton, Ledyard, Lyme, New London, North Stonington, Old Lyme, Stonington, Waterford.) Address: 112 Broad St., New London 06320. Tel., (860) 443-8343. *Clerk,* Linda Connors; *Housing Specialist,* Tais Ericson, Tel., (860) 443-8346; *Supervisory Asst. State's Atty.,* J. Vincent Hauser, Tel., (860) 443-8444; *Bail Comr. Supvr.,* Michael P. Amanti; *Adult Probation,* Norman Shove; *Supervisory Asst. Public Defender,* Thomas J. Haley, Tel., (860) 443-5356.

G.A. #11.—(Towns of Ashford, Brooklyn, Canterbury, Chaplin, Eastford, Hampton, Killingly, Plainfield, Pomfret, Putnam, Scotland, Sterling, Thompson, Windham, Woodstock.) Address: 172 Main St., Danielson 06239. Tel., (860) 774-8516. *Clerk,* Christopher M. Burke; *Housing Specialist,* Kathleen Solazzo, Tel., (860) 774-8516; *Supervisory Asst. State's Atty.,* Mark Stabile, Tel., (860) 774-7237; *Bail Comr.,* Michael Sullivan; *Family Relations Supvr.,* Joseph J. Nash, 50 Canal St., Putnam 06260. Tel., (860) 928-0478; *Adult Probation,* vacancy, 183 Main St., Danielson 06239. Tel., (860) 774-5735; *Public Defender,* Ramon J. Canning, 108 Valley St., Willimantic 06226. Tel., (860) 423-6038.

G.A. #12.—(Towns of East Hartford, Glastonbury, Manchester, Marlborough, South Windsor.) Address: 410 Center St., Manchester 06040. Tel., (860) 647-1091. *Clerk,* vacancy; *Supervisory Asst. State's Atty.,* Cynthia Baer, Tel., (860) 649-4779; *Bail Comr.,* Brenda Joy; *Lead Family Relations Counselor,* Deborah Derrick. Tel., (860) 643-2481; *Adult Probation,* Brett Capshaw, 341 Broad St., Manchester 06040. Tel., (860) 649-1650; *Supervisory Asst. Public Defender,* Michael H. Handler, Tel., (860) 649-6484.

G.A. #13.—(Towns of East Granby, East Windsor, Enfield, Granby, Simsbury, Suffield, Windsor, Windsor Locks.) Address: 111 Phoenix Ave., Enfield 06082. Tel., (860) 741-3727. *Clerk,* Maria L. Reed-Cook; *Supervisory Asst State's Atty.,* John Malone, Tel., (860) 741-3743; *Bail Comr.,* Terrence Antrum; *Lead Family Relations Counselor,* MaryAnn Reid-Gill, Tel., (860) 741-3697; *Supervisory Asst. Public Defender,* Sandra Davis, Tel., (860) 741-3741.

G.A. #14.—(City of Hartford.) Address: 101 Lafayette St., Hartford 06106. Tel., (860) 566-1630. Small Claims, Tel., (860) 566-1680. *Clerk,* Michele D. Catapano; *Supervisory Asst. State's Atty.,* Richard Morelli, Tel., (860) 566-5996; *Supvr. Bail Comr.,* Lois J. Elsesser; *Adult Probation,* E. Flynn O'Keefe; *Supervisory Asst. Public Defender,* John F. Barry, Tel., (860) 566-5090.

G.A. #15.—(Towns of Berlin, New Britain, Newington, Rocky Hill, Wethersfield.) Address: 125 Columbus Blvd., New Britain 06051. Tel., (860) 827-7106. *Clerk,* Joanne L. Matos; *Supervisory Asst. State's Atty.,* Scott Murphy, Tel., (860) 827-7108; *Supvr. Bail Comr.,* James Carollo; *Adult Probation,* Steven Chatlas; *Supervisory Asst Public Defender,* Lorenzo Smith, Jr., Tel., (860) 827-7110.

G.A. #16.—(Towns of Avon, Bloomfield, Canton, Farmington, West Hartford.) Address: 105 Raymond Rd., West Hartford 06107. Tel., (860) 236-4551. *Clerk,* Catherine Nicolay; *Supervisory Asst. State's Atty.,* John O'Reilly, Tel., (860) 236-3533; *Bail Comr.,* Charles Cyr; *Supervisory Asst. Public Defender,* Martin Epstein, Tel., (860) 232-9684.

G.A. #17.—(Towns of Bristol, Burlington, Plainville, Plymouth, Southington.) Address: 131 No. Main St., Bristol 06010. Tel., (860) 582-8111. *Clerk,* vacancy; *Supervisory Asst. State's Atty.,* R. Patrick McGinley, Tel., (860) 584-8564; *Bail Comr.,* Wilfred L. Beloin; *Lead Family Relations Counselor,* David R. Williams, Tel., (860) 583-1835; *Adult Probation,* Gordon Mason, 225 North Main St., Bristol 06010. Tel., (860) 584-0073; *Supervisory Asst. Public Defender,* John S. Papa, Jr., Tel., (860) 589-5976.

G.A. #18.—(Towns of Bethlehem, Barkhamsted, Bridgewater, Canaan, Colebrook, Cornwall, Goshen, Hartland, Harwinton, Kent, Litchfield, Morris, New Hartford, New Milford, North Canaan, Norfolk, Roxbury, Salisbury, Sharon, Thomaston, Torrington, Warren, Washington, Winchester.) Address: 80 Doyle Rd, P.O. Box 667, Bantam 06750. Tel., (860) 567-3942; *Clerk,* Eric R. Groody; *Supervisory Asst. State's Atty.,* Andrew M. Wittstein, Tel., (860) 567-3944; *Bail Comr.,* Roberta M. Bento; *Housing Specialist,* Elizabeth Casey; *Family Relations Supvr.,* Stephen R. Grant, Litchfield Commons, Rte. 202, Litchfield 06759. Tel., (860) 567-3948; *Supervisory Asst. Public Defender,* Carol Goldberg. Tel., (860) 567-3946.

G.A. #19.—(Towns of Andover, Bolton, Columbia, Coventry, Ellington, Hebron, Mansfield, Somers, Stafford, Tolland, Union, Vernon, Willington.) Address: 20 Park St., P.O. Box 980, Rockville 06066. Tel., (860) 870-3200. *Clerk,* Roy Smith, Jr.; *Supervisory Asst. State's Atty.,* Nina N. Rosen, Tel., (860) 870-3277; *Bail Comr.,* Joann Vaughan; *Public Defender,* Phillip N. Armentano, Tel., (860) 870-3280.

G.A. #20.—(Towns of New Canaan, Norwalk, Weston, Westport, Wilton.) Address: 17 Belden Ave., Norwalk 06850. Tel., (203) 846-3237. *Clerk,* Efrain Vargas; *Supervisory Asst. State's Atty.,* Robert G. Hall, Jr., Tel., (203) 847-4527; *Bail Comr.,* Gabriella Galasso; *Lead Family Relations Counselor,* Jill K. Lesser, Tel., (203) 847-5826; *Adult Probation,* James McGinnis, 606 West Ave., Norwalk 06850. Tel., (203) 866-5025; *Supervisory Asst. Public Defender,* James P. Ginocchio, Tel., (203) 846-9519.

G.A. #21.—(Towns of Bozrah, Colchester, Franklin, Griswold, Lebanon, Lisbon, Montville, Norwich, Preston, Salem, Sprague, Voluntown.) Address: 1 Courthouse Sq., Norwich 06360. Tel., (860) 889-7338. *Clerk,* Julia S. Schaeffer; *Housing Specialist,* Tais Ericson, Tel., (860) 889-7338; *Supervisory Asst. State's Atty.,* Thomas M. Griffin, Tel., (860) 889-5284; *Bail Comr.,* Lois Dupointe; *Adult Probation,* Edward Dalenta, 100 Broadway, Norwich 06360. Tel., (860) 889-8351; *Supervisory Asst. Public Defender,* Edward O'Regan, Tel., (860) 889-3838.

G.A. #22.—(Towns of Milford, West Haven.) Address: 14 West River St., Milford 06460. Tel., (203) 874-1116. *Clerk,* Eileen L. Whelan; *Supervisory Asst. State's Atty.,* L. Mark Hurley, Tel., (203) 874-3017; *Bail Comr.,* Ralph O'Connor; *Lead Family Relations Counselor,* Allen B. Rubin, Tel., (203) 877-0001; *Adult Probation,* Joseph Callahan, 44-46 River St., Milford 06460. Tel., (203) 877-1253; *Public Defender,* David F. Egan, Tel., (203) 874-8857.

HOUSING SESSIONS

HOUSING SESSION AT BRIDGEPORT: 172 Golden Hill St., Bridgeport 06604. Tel., (203) 579-6936; *Clerk,* Jeffrey Hammer; *Housing Specialists,* Maureen Desjardin, John Savino; *Asst. State's Atty.,* Judith-Anne Scanlon.

HOUSING SESSION AT HARTFORD: 18 Trinity St., Hartford 06106. Tel., (860) 566-8550; *Clerk,* Victor Feigenbaum; *Housing Specialists,* Roberta Palmer, Richard Tynan; *Asst. State's Atty.,* Margaret Flynn. Tel., (860) 566-1387.

HOUSING SESSION AT NEW BRITAIN: 177 Columbus Blvd., New Britain 06051. Tel., (860) 827-7111; *Clerk,* Michael J. Flynn; *Housing Specialists,* Roberta Palmer, Richard Tynan; *Asst. State's Atty.,* Margaret Flynn.

HOUSING SESSION AT NEW HAVEN: 121 Elm St., New Haven 06510. Tel., (203) 789-7937; *Chief Clerk,* Suzanne Colasanto; *Mgr. of Dispute Resolution Programs,* Cynthia Teixeira; *Housing Specialists,* Marie A. Langan, Heriberto Villafane; *Asst. State's Atty.,* Judith H. Rothschild-Rippe. Tel., (203) 789-7056.

HOUSING SESSION AT NORWALK: 17 Belden Ave., Norwalk 06850. Tel., (203) 846-4332; *Clerk,* Marie E. Mangines; *Housing Specialists,* Maureen Desjardin, John Savino, *Asst. State's Atty.,* Judith-Anne Scanlon.

HOUSING SESSION AT WATERBURY: 300 Grand St., Waterbury 06702. Tel., (203) 596-4061; *Clerk,* Dana M. Guiliano; *Housing Specialists,* Marie A. Langan, Heriberto Villafane; *Asst. State's Atty.,* Judith H. Rothschild-Rippe. Tel., (203) 596-4061.

JUVENILE MATTERS

BRIDGEPORT OFFICE: 784 Fairfield Ave., 06604. *Supvr.,* Eugene Kuruc, 299 Washington Ave., Bridgeport 06604. Tel., (203) 579-6588; *Lead Juvenile Probation Officers,* William B. Carlos, Georgia Shaffner, Tel., (203) 579-6588; *Clerk,* Margaret Gosselin, (203) 579-6544; *Detention Supvr.,* Peter Dobson, 790 Fairfield Ave., Bridgeport 06604. Tel., (203) 579-6548.

DANBURY OFFICE: 71 Main St., 06810. *Supvr.,* John R. Roorbach, Tel., (203) 797-4407; *Clerk,* Antoinette Beal.

HARTFORD OFFICE: 920 Broad St., 06106. *Supvr.,* Bruce Dana, Tel., (860) 566-8296; *Lead Juvenile Probation Officers,* Michele Hall, Tel., (860) 566-8292, Awilda Nunez, Tel., (860) 566-8290; *Clerk,* Elizabeth Flynn, Tel., (860) 566-8270; *Detention Supvr.,* Leo Arnone, Tel., (860) 566-8280.

MIDDLETOWN OFFICE: 230 Main St. Ext., 06457. Tel., (860) 344-2986. *Supvr.,* Robert Hindle; *Clerk,* Twanetta Merrill.

NEW HAVEN OFFICE: 239 Whalley Ave., 06511. *Supvr.,* Richard Aldridge, Tel., (203) 786-0305; *Clerk,* Cynthia L. Cunningham, Tel., (203) 786-0337; *Detention Supvr.,* David Konefal, Tel., (203) 786-0343; *Lead Juvenile Probation Officer,* Michael Zucarelli, Tel., (203) 786-0306; Maria Knight, Tel., (203) 786-0313.

NORWALK OFFICE: 11 Commerce St. 06850, Tel., (203) 866-9275. *Lead Juvenile Probation Officer,* James Baldwin; *Clerk,* vacancy.

PLAINVILLE OFFICE: 31 Cooke St., 06062. Tel., (860) 747-5701. *Supvr.,* John Reddick; *Clerk,* Dianne G. Polletta.

ROCKVILLE OFFICE: 25 School St., 06066 Tel., (860) 872-7143. *Supvr.,* Albert L. Chase; *Clerk,* June Russell.

STAMFORD OFFICE: 91 Prospect St., 06901. Tel., (860) 348-7355. *Supvr.,* Joseph H. Paquin, Jr.; *Clerk,* Yolanda Smith.

TORRINGTON OFFICE: 139 New Litchfield St., 06790. Tel., (860) 489-0201. *Lead Juvenile Probation Officer,* James Kearney *Clerk,* Nicholene Marciano.

UNCASVILLE (MONTVILLE) OFFICE: 869 Norwich-New London Tpke., P.O. Box 462, 06382. Tel., (860) 848-9213. *Supvr.,* Julia O'Leary; *Clerk,* Suzanne A. Polomski.

WATERBURY OFFICE: 83 Prospect St., 06723. Tel., (203) 596-4202. *Supvr.,* Timothy Leece; *Clerk,* Jo-Ann Pickles.

WILLIMANTIC OFFICE: 316 Pleasant St., 06226. Tel., (860) 423-7743. *Lead Juvenile Probation Officer,* Louise Hyyppa; *Clerk,* Carmen Echevarria.

JUVENILE DETENTION CENTERS

Bridgeport: 790 Fairfield Ave., 06604. *Supvr.,* Peter Dobson, Tel., (203) 579-6548.

Enfield: 287 Shaker Rd., 06082. *Supvr.,* D. James Barton, Tel., (860) 763-7076, (Temporary Office)

Hartford: 920 Broad St., 06106. *Supvr.,* Leo Arnone, Tel., (860) 566-8280.

New Haven: 239 Whalley Ave., 06511. *Supvr.,* David Konefal, Tel., (203) 786-0343.

DIVISION OF PUBLIC DEFENDER SERVICES
(Sec. 51-289, 51-290, Gen. Stat.)
PUBLIC DEFENDER SERVICES COMMISSION

Commission members, *Chm.,* Carl D. Eisenmann; Hon. E. Curtissa Cofield; The Rev. Msgr. William A. Genuario; Richard P. Gilardi; Hon. John F. Kavanewsky; Linda Kelly; Diane E. Randall.

OFFICE OF CHIEF PUBLIC DEFENDER

Chief Public Defender, Gerard A. Smyth; *Deputy Chief Public Defender,* Susan O. Storey; *Chief of Trial Services,* Patrick J. Culligan. Address: One Hartford Sq. West, Suite 201, Hartford 06106. Tel., (860) 566-5328.

Chief of Legal Services, G. Douglas Nash. (Address: 121 Elm St., New Haven 06510. Tel., (203) 789-7477.)

PUBLIC DEFENDERS

SUPERIOR COURT-JUDICIAL DISTRICTS

Judicial District of Hartford/New Britain: M. Fred DeCaprio.
Judicial District of New Haven: Thomas A. Ullman.
Judicial District of Waterbury: Alan D. McWhirter.
Judicial District of Fairfield: Preston C. Tisdale.
Judicial District of Stamford: Joseph J. Bruckman.
Judicial District of Litchfield: Christopher M. Cosgrove.
Judicial District of Middlesex: Richard F. Kelly.
Judicial District of New London: Bruce A. Sturman.
Judicial District of Tolland: Phillip N. Armentano.
Judicial District of Windham: Ramon J. Canning.
Judicial District of Ansonia/Milford: David F. Egan:
Judicial District of Danbury: Robert F. Field.

SUPERVISORY ASSISTANT PUBLIC DEFENDERS

JUVENILE MATTERS

Bridgeport Juvenile Matters: George R. Oleyer.
New Haven Juvenile Matters: Raymond P. Kosinski.
Hartford Juvenile Matters: Christine Rapillo.

PRACTICE OF LAW

ADMISSION TO THE BAR. The Admission of attorneys to practice before the Courts of this state is regulated by rules adopted by the Judges of the Superior Court. These rules, together with the regulations made by the committees set forth below, and information for candidates appear in the Rule Book which may be obtained from the Adm. Dir. of the Committee. Prospective applicants are advised to contact the committee during the summer between the second and third year of law school for information on admission rules then in effect.

STATE BAR EXAMINING COMMITTEE

Address: 287 Main St., 2nd Fl., Suite 1, East Hartford 06118-1885. Tel., (860) 568-3450. *Admin. Dir.,* R. David Stamm.

Chm., Raymond W. Beckwith, Trumbull; *Vice Chm.,* Barbara M. Quinn, Niantic; *Secy.,* Irving H. Perlmutter, New Haven; *Treas.,* John W. Barnett, New Haven.

Richard F. Banbury, Hartford; John D. Boland, Putnam; Deborah L. Bradley, West Hartford; Hon. Anne C. Dranginis, Litchfield; Patricia C. Farrell, Middletown; Hon. Joseph P. Flynn, Waterbury; Hon. Maxwell Heiman, Hartford; Arthur A. Hiller, Bridgeport; Shirley V. Hoogstra, New Haven; Amy Beth Levy, Waterbury; Adam Mantzaris, Wallingford; Robert W. Marrion, New London; Gail E. McTaggart, Waterbury; Hon. Aaron Ment, Hartford; Joseph A. Moniz, Hartford; David A. Moraghan, Torrington; Denise M. Phelan, Hartford; Michael J. Whelton, East Hartford; Allen L. Williams III, Stamford; Mary K. Zackrison, Bridgeport.

The Bar Examining Committee prepares a comprehensive bar examination administered in February and July. The Committee also investigates the character and fitness of applicants for admission to the bar.

Standing Committees on Recommendations for Admission

Hartford County.—Vincent L. Diana, Manchester, *Chm.;* Richard R. Brown, Hartford; Gary Friedel, New Britain; Monica L. Harper, Hartford.

New Haven County.—Ruth Beardsley, New Haven, *Chm.;* Jack H. Evans, New Haven; ; W. Fielding Secor, Waterbury; John R. Donovan, Meriden; Steven J. Errante, New Haven.

New London County.—Leo J. McNamara, New London, *Chm.;* Frederick C. Berberick, Jr., Norwich; Thomas B. Wilson, New London.

Fairfield County.—Cindy L. Robinson, Bridgeport, *Chm.;* Donald A. Browne, Bridgeport; Auden Grogins, Fairfield; Carolyn R. Linsey, Trumbull; John Merchant, Bridgeport; W. Patrick Ryan, Stamford.

Windham County.—Noah H. Starkey, Willimantic, *Chm.;* Gina M. Pickett, Putnam; Rachel S. Poulos, Danielson.

Litchfield County.—Frank H. Finch, Jr., Winsted, *Chm.;* Jill B. Brakeman, Torrington; Louise F. Brown, Sharon.

Middlesex County.—Myron Poliner, Middletown, *Chm.;* William Howard, Middletown.

Tolland County.—Abbot B. Schwebel, Rockville, *Chm.;* Joseph P. Capossela, Vernon; Susan Boyan, Tolland.

The Standing Committees on Recommendations for Admission for each county are appointed by the Judges of the Superior Court in such county. All applications for admission on motion and applications for admission by examination which have been identified by the Bar Examining Committee as presenting possible character and fitness problems are referred to the Standing Committee for the county of the applicant's residence.

STATEWIDE GRIEVANCE COMMITTEE. Sec. 51-90, Gen. State. Office: 287 Main St., East Hartford 06118-1885. Tel., (860) 568-5717.

Appointed by the Judges of the Superior Court, Alfred R. Belinkie, Bridgeport; Thomas Cloutier, Old Saybrook; David A. Cury, West Hartford; Salvatore C. DePiano, Bridgeport; Carmen Donnarumma, Waterbury; Anne R. Hoyt, Moosup; Lewis A. Hurwitz, Milford; Carol E. Johnson; Robert J. Kor, West Hartford; Margaret P. Mason, New Haven; Marcus R. McCraven, Hamden; Thomas J. McKiernan, Darien; Mary Ellen Smith, Niantic; Kerry A. Tarpey, Rockville; M. Katherine Webster-O'Keefe, New Milford.

Bar Counsel, Daniel B. Horwitch.

PROBATE COURTS

See Constitution of Connecticut, Art. V, Sec. 4; Chapt. 774, Gen. Stat. Judges of Probate are elected quadrennially on the Tuesday after the first Monday in November in years having an even number, and for the term of four years from the Wednesday after the first Monday of January next succeeding their election. There are 132 Probate Districts in the State of Connecticut. Names in *italics* denote the Judges of Probate.

PROBATE COURT ADMINISTRATOR. Appointed by the Chief Justice of the Supreme Court, Sec. 45a-74, Gen. Stat. Salary, $100,411. Hon. F. Paul Kurmay, Stratford. Office address: 186 Newington Rd., West Hartford 06110. Tel., (860) 566-7897. *Chief Counsel,* Linda A. Dow; *Asst. to Admin.,* Thomas E. Gaffey.

CONNECTICUT PROBATE ASSEMBLY. Sec. 45a-90, Gen. Stat. Office: 186 Newington Rd., West Hartford 06110-2320. Tel., (860) 566-7897. *Chief Judge and Pres.,* Hon. Earl F. Capuano, Westport; *1st Vice Pres.,* Hon. Robert K. Killian, Jr., Hartford; *2nd Vice Pres.,* Hon. Linda M. Salafia, Norwich; *Rec. Secy.,* Hon. Sheila M.

Hennessey, Newington; *Exec. Secy.,* Hon. Norman E. Rogers, Jr., New Hartford; *Treas.,* Hon. Paul E. Cravinho, Stonington.

COUNCIL ON PROBATE JUDICIAL CONDUCT. Sec. 45a-62, Gen. Stat. Compensation of members, not to exceed $100 per diem and necessary expenses. Address: 186 Newington Rd., West Hartford 06110. Tel., (860) 566-7897.

Chm., Hon. Arthur H. Healey, Trial Referee, New Haven; Hon. Philip D. Main, Probate Judge, Granby; Thomas J. Gallagan, Brookfield; Cameron F. Hopper, Greenwich; Janet M. Wildman, Washington, Sept. 30, 1999.

Exec. Dir., Richard F. Banbury, One State St., Hartford 06103. Tel., (860) 549-1000.

Hartford County

AVON. Constituted May session, 1844, from Farmington. *D. Stephen Gaffney.* Location: Town Hall, 60 West Main St., 06001. Hours: 9 A.M.-12 Noon, Mon. through Fri. Tel., (860) 409-4348; FAX, (860) 677-8428.

BERLIN (Berlin, New Britain). Constituted June 2, 1824, from Farmington, Hartford and Middletown. *Walter A. Clebowicz.* Location: Court House, 177 Columbus Blvd., P.O. Box 400, New Britain 06050-0400. Hours: 9 A.M.-4 P.M., Mon. through Fri. Tel., (860) 826-2696; FAX, (860) 826-2695.

BLOOMFIELD. Constituted January 9, 1991, from West Hartford. *Steven M. Zelman.* Clerk, Juliet Lavissiere. Location: Bloomfield Town Hall, 800 Bloomfield Ave., 06002. Hours: 9 A.M.-1 P.M., 2-4:30 P.M., Mon. through Fri., and by appointment. Tel., (860) 769-3548; FAX, (860) 769-3598.

BRISTOL. Constituted June 4, 1830, from Farmington. *Andre D. Dorval.* Location: City Hall, 06010. Hours: 9 A.M.-5 P.M., Mon. through Fri. Tel., (860) 584-7650; FAX (860) 584-3818.

BURLINGTON. Constituted June 3, 1834, from Farmington. *Charles W. Bauer.* Clerk, Patricia DeSanto. Location: Town Hall, Rte. 4, 200 Spielman Hwy., 06013. Hours: 9 A.M.-1 P.M., Fri., and by appointment. Tel., (860) 673-2108.

CANTON. Constituted June 7, 1841, from Simsbury. *Raymond B. Green.* Clerk, Marygale Bouldin. Location: Canton Town Hall, 4 Market St., (P.O. Box 175, Collinsville 06022). Hours: 8:30 A.M.-1:30 P.M., Tues. through Thurs.; Fridays by appointment. Tel., (860) 693-7851.

EAST GRANBY. Constituted July 4, 1865, from Granby. *Paul A. Ridgeway.* Location: Town Hall, 9 Center St., Probate Office, Rm. 13, P.O. Box 542, 06026. Hours: 9 A.M.-12 Noon, Tues. through Thurs., and by appointment. Tel., (860) 653-3434.

EAST HARTFORD. Constituted May, 1887, from Hartford. *Ann K. Fulco.* Clerk, Patricia Robillard. Location: Town Hall, 740 Main St., 06108. Hours: 9 A.M.-4:30 P.M., Mon. through Fri. Tel., (860) 291-7278.

EAST WINDSOR (East Windsor, South Windsor). Constituted May session, 1782, from Hartford and Stafford. *William E. Grace.* Clerk, Lauren E. DeLoreto. Location:

Town Hall, 1540 Sullivan Ave., South Windsor 06074. Hours: 8 A.M.-1 30 P.M., Mon. through Thurs.; 8 A.M.-4:30 P.M., Fri.; other hours by appointment. Tel., (860) 644-2511, Ext. 271; FAX, (860) 644-3781.

ENFIELD. Constituted May 26, 1831, from East Windsor. *Susan L. Warner.* Location: 820 Enfield St., 06082. *Clerks,* Linda Chrzanowski, Rita M. Kemp. Hours: 9 A.M.-4:30 P.M., Mon. through Fri; 9 A.M.-7 P.M., 1st Mon. of each month. Tel., (860) 253-6305; FAX, (860) 253-6357.

FARMINGTON. Constituted January, 1769, from Hartford. *J. David Morrissey.* Clerk, Arlene Burns. Location: Town Hall, 1 Monteith Dr., 06032-1053. Hours: 9 A.M.-4 P.M., Mon. through Fri. Tel., (860) 673-8250; FAX, (860) 673-8262.

GLASTONBURY. Constituted January 8, 1975, from Hartford. *Donald L. Hamer.* Clerk, Allene M. Scaglia. Location: 2155 Main St., 06033-6523. Hours: 9:30 A.M.-4:30 P.M., Mon. through Fri., and by appointment. Tel., (860) 652-7629, 7631.

GRANBY. Constituted May session, 1807, from Simsbury and Hartford. *Philip D. Main.* Clerk, Susan B. Christian. Location: Town Hall, 15 No. Granby Rd., 06035. Hours: 9 A.M.-12 Noon, Tues., Wed., Fri. Tel., (860) 653-8944.

HARTFORD. Constituted May session, 1666, as a County Court. *Robert K. Killian, Jr.* Clerk, June C. Fialkoff. Location: 10 Prospect St., 06103. Hours: 9 A.M.-4 P.M., Mon. through Fri.; 4-6:30 P.M., Mon., by appointment only. Tel., (860) 522-1813.

HARTLAND. Constituted June 3, 1836, from Granby. *Beatrice Y. Isabelle.* P.O. Box 100, West Hartland 06091. Location: Town Hall Annex Bldg., 22 South Rd., East Hartland. Hours: 10 A.M.-1 P.M., Mon., Fri., and by appointment. Tel., (860) 653-9710, (860) 379-8625.

MANCHESTER. Constituted June 22, 1850, from East Hartford. *John W. Cooney.* Clerk, Sandra Haun. Location: Hall of Records, 66 Center St., 06040. Hours: 8:30 A.M.-12 Noon, 1-4:30 P.M., Mon. through Fri.; 6-8 P.M. Thurs. for informal question/answer sessions. Tel., (860) 647-3227; FAX, (860) 647-3236.

MARLBOROUGH. Constituted June 11, 1846, from Colchester. *William J. Heslin III.* Location: Town Hall, P.O. Box 29, 26 No. Main St., 06447. Hours: 9 A.M.-12 Noon, Mon.; 6-8 P.M., Tues.; 12 Noon-4 P.M., Thurs. or by appointment. Tel., Bus., (860) 295-6200.

NEWINGTON (Newington, Rocky Hill, Wethersfield). Constituted January 8, 1975, from Hartford. *Sheila M. Hennessey.* Clerk, Rose Anne Adamowich. Location: Center Place, 66 Cedar St., Rear, 06111. Hours: 9 A.M.-4 P.M., Mon. through Fri. Tel., (860) 665-1285; FAX, (860) 665-1331.

PLAINVILLE. Constituted May, 1909, from Farmington. *Heidi Famiglietti,* Location: Plainville Municipal Center, 1 Central Sq., 06062. Hours: 9 A.M.-3 P.M., Mon. through Thurs.; 9 A.M.-1 P.M., Fri. Tel., (860) 793-0221, Ext. 250; Res., (860) 747-5985.

SIMSBURY. Constituted May session, 1769, from Hartford. *Glenn E. Knierim.* Clerk, Lydia B. Chidsey. Location: Belden Town Office Bldg., 933 Hopmeadow St.,

P.O. Box 495, 06070. Hours: 9 A.M.-1 P.M., 2-4:30 P.M., Mon. through Fri.; other hours and evenings, by appointment. Tel., (860) 658-3277.

SOUTHINGTON. Constituted May 24, 1825, from Farmington. *Carl J. Sokolowski.* Clerk, Jean P. Parzych. Location: Town Office Bldg., Main St., P.O. Box 165, 06489. Hours: 8:30 A.M.-12 Noon, 1-4:30 P.M., Mon. through Fri; Sat. and evenings, by appointment. Tel., (860) 276-6253.

SUFFIELD. Constituted May session, 1821, from Hartford and Granby. *Beverly T. Patterson.* Clerk, Judith A. Remington. Location: Town Hall Bldg., 06078. Hours: 8 A.M.-12 Noon, Mon., Fri.; 8 A.M.-3 P.M., Tues, Wed., Thurs; afternoons, evenings and weekends by appointment. Tel., (860) 668-3835, 6748; FAX, (860) 668-3898.

WEST HARTFORD. Constituted January 5, 1983, from Hartford. *John A. Berman.* Asst. Clerks, Lori A. P. Errico, Janice D. Reynolds. Location: Town Hall, Rm. 318, 50 So. Main St., 06107. Hours: 8:30 A.M.-4:40 P.M., Mon. through Fri. Tel., (860) 523-3174; FAX, (860) 236-8352.

WINDSOR. Constituted July 4, 1855, from Hartford. *Brian T. Griffin.* Clerk, Katie Chiodo. Location: Town Hall, 275 Broad St., 06095. Hours: 8:30 A.M.-4:30 P.M., Mon. through Thurs.; 8:30 A.M.-12 Noon, Fri. Tel., (860) 285-1976.

WINDSOR LOCKS. Constituted January 4, 1961, from Hartford. *William C. Leary.* Clerk, Laurie A. Roberts. Location: Town Hall, Church St., 06096. Hours: 9 A.M.-2 P.M., Mon. through Thurs. Tel., (860) 627-1450.

New Haven County

BETHANY. Constituted July 4, 1854, from New Haven. *Guy D. Yale.* Location: Town Hall, 40 Peck Rd., 06524. Hours: 9-11:30 A.M., Tues., Thurs., and by appointment. Tel., (203) 393-3744.

BRANFORD. Constituted June 21, 1850, from Guilford. *John E. Donegan.* Clerk, Leslie S. George. Location: Town Hall, 1019 Main St., P.O. Box 638, 06405. Hours: 9 A.M.-12 Noon, 1-4:30 P.M., Mon. through Fri. Tel., (203) 488-0318.

CHESHIRE (Cheshire, Prospect). Constituted May 27, 1829, from Wallingford. *Raymond F. Voelker.* Clerk, Audrey B. Disbrow. Location: Town Hall, 06410. Hours: 8:30 A.M.-12:30 P.M., 1:30-4 P.M., Mon. through Fri. Tel., (203) 271-6608.

DERBY (Derby, Ansonia, Seymour). Constituted July 4, 1858, from New Haven. *Clifford D. Hoyle.* Location: City Hall, Ansonia 06401. Hours: 9 A.M.-4:30 P.M., Mon. through Fri.; Sat., by appointment only. Tel., (203) 734-1277; FAX, (203) 734-0922 .

EAST HAVEN. Constituted January 5, 1955, from New Haven. *Thomas J. Giaimo.* Location: Town Hall, 06512. Hours: 9:30 A.M.-1 P.M., 2-3:30 P.M., Mon.; 9:30 A.M.-1 P.M., Tues., Wed.; 9:30 A.M.-1 P.M., 2-4:30 P.M., Thurs. Tel., (203) 468-3895.

GUILFORD. Constituted October session, 1719, from New Haven and New London. *Joel E. Helander.* Location: Town Hall, 31 Park St., 06437. Hours: 9 A.M.-12 Noon, 1-4 P.M., Mon., Tues., Thurs., Fri.; 9 A.M.-12 Noon, Wed. Tel., (203) 453-8006.

HAMDEN. Constituted January 8, 1945, from New Haven. *Salvatore L. Diglio.* Clerk, Christine L. Panzo. Location: Hamden Memorial Town Hall, 2372 Whitney Ave., 06518. Hours: 8:30 A.M.-4:30 P.M., Mon. through Fri. Tel., (203) 287-2570; FAX, (203) 287-2571.

MADISON. Constituted May 22, 1834, from Guilford. *George G. McManus, Jr.* Clerk, Carol B. Lougee. Location: Town Campus, 8 Campus Dr., P.O. Box 205, 06443. Hours: 9 A.M.-3 P.M., Mon. through Fri. Tel., (203) 245-5661.

MERIDEN. Constituted June 3, 1836, from Wallingford. *John F. Papandrea.* Clerk, Janet Firulli. Location: Rm. 113, City Hall, 06450. Hours: 8:30 A.M.-7 P.M., Mon.; 8:30 A.M.-4:30 P.M., Tues. through Fri. Tel., (203) 630-4150; FAX, (203) 630-4043.

MILFORD. Constituted May 30, 1832, from New Haven. *Bernard F. Joy.* Location: Parsons Municipal Complex, 06460. Hours: 9 A.M.-5 P.M., Mon. through Fri. Tel., (203) 783-3205.

NAUGATUCK (Naugatuck, Beacon Falls). Constituted July 4, 1863, from Waterbury. *Robert M. Siuzdak.* Location: Town Hall, 06770. Hours: 9 A.M.-4 P.M., Mon. through Fri. Tel., (203) 729-4571, Ext. 220.

NEW HAVEN (New Haven). Constituted May session, 1666, as a County Court. *John A. Keyes.* Location: 200 Orange St., 4th floor, P.O. Box 905, 06504. Hours: 9 A.M.-4 P.M., Mon. through Fri. Tel., (203) 946-4880.

NORTH BRANFORD. Constituted April 14, 1937, from Guilford and Wallingford. *Frank J. Forgione.* Clerk, Diane B. Whalen. Location: Town Hall, Foxon Rd., 06471. Mailing Address: P.O. Box 214, 06471. Hours, 9 A.M.- 12 Noon, Mon. through Fri. Tel., (203) 481-0829.

NORTH HAVEN. Constituted January 5, 1955, from New Haven. *Eileen B. Donahue.* Clerk, Valerie A. Dondi; Asst. Clerk, Lucy D. Puglia. Location: Town Hall, 18 Church St., P.O. Box 175, 06473-0175. Hours: 8:30 A.M.-4:30 P.M., Mon. through Thurs. Tel., (203) 239-5321, Ext. 775.

ORANGE. Constituted January 8, 1975 from New Haven. *Robert W. Carangelo.* Location: High Plains Community Center, 525 Orange Center Rd., 06477. Hours: 9 A.M.-12 Noon, Mon. through Fri. Tel., (203) 891-2160; FAX, (203) 891-2161.

OXFORD. Constituted June 4, 1846, from New Haven. *John W. Fertig, Jr.* Clerk, Eugenia Purcella. Location: Town Hall, 06478. Hours: 7-9 P.M., Mon.; 1-5 P.M., Tues., Wed.; 9 A.M.-5 P.M., 7-9 P.M., Thurs., and by appointment. Tel., Bus., (203) 888-2543; Res., (203) 888-0363.

SOUTHBURY. Constituted January 4, 1967, from Woodbury. *Mary Kay Flaherty.* Clerk, Cynthia Wadman. Location: Town Hall Annex, 421 Main St. South, P.O. Box 674, 06488. Hours: 9 A.M.-4:30 P.M., Mon. through Fri., and by appointment. Tel., (203) 262-0641; FAX, (203) 264-9310.

WALLINGFORD. Constituted May session, 1776, from New Haven and Guilford. *Philip A. Wright, Jr.* Clerk, Margaret J. Coogan. Location: Town Hall, 45 South Main St., Rm. 114, 06492. Hours: 9 A.M.-5 P.M., Mon. through Fri. Tel., (203) 294-2100.

WATERBURY (Waterbury, Middlebury, Wolcott). Constituted May session, 1779, from Woodbury. *James J. Lawlor.* Location: City Hall Annex, Chase Bldg., 236 Grand St., 06702. Hours: 9 A.M.-4:45 P.M., Mon. through Fri.; 9 A.M.-6 P.M., Thurs and 9 A.M.-12 Noon, Sat., Memorial Day through Labor Day. Tel., (203) 755-1127.

WEST HAVEN. Constituted January 4, 1943, from New Haven. *E. Michael Heffernan.* Location: City Hall, 06516. Hours: 9 A.M.-4 P.M., Mon. through Fri. Tel., (203) 937-3552, 3553, 3554.

WOODBRIDGE. Constituted January 7, 1987, from New Haven. *Robert H. Horowitz.* Clerk, Jo-Marie Tamburrino. Location: 11 Meetinghouse La., 06525. Hours: 3-7 P.M., Mon.; 9 A.M.-1 P.M., Wed. Tel., (203) 389-3410.

New London County

BOZRAH. Constituted June 3, 1843, from Norwich. *Stanley A. Mokrzewski.* Clerk, Jessie Friedrich. Location: 486 Fitchville Rd., P.O. Box 35, Gilman 06336. Hours: By appointment. Tel., (860) 886-1997; FAX, (860) 887-7571.

COLCHESTER. Constituted May 29, 1832, from East Haddam; contains the records of East Haddam from October session, 1741 to May 29, 1832. *Kevin Kennedy.* Location: 127 Norwich Ave., 06415. Hours: 12:30-4:30 P.M., Mon., Tues., Thurs., Fri.; 9 A.M.-1 P.M., Wed., and by appointment. Tel., (860) 537-7290; FAX, (860) 537-0547.

EAST LYME. Constituted June 2, 1843, from New London. *Leo J. McNamara.* Location: East Lyme Town Hall, P.O. Box 519, 108 Pennsylvania Ave., Niantic 06357. Hours: 8:30 A.M.-12:30 P.M., Mon. through Fri.; afternoon hours by appointment. Tel., (860) 739-6931; FAX, (860) 739-6930.

GRISWOLD. Constituted January 3, 1979, from Norwich. *George L. Kennedy.* Location: Town Hall, School St., Jewett City 06351. Hours: 1 P.M.-3 P.M., Mon., Tues.; 9-11 A.M., Wed., 5-7 P.M., Thurs., and by appointment. Tel., (860) 376-0216.

GROTON. Constituted May 25, 1839, from Stonington. *Frederick W. Palm, Jr.* Clerk, Helen M. Falvey. Location: Town Hall, 45 Fort Hill Rd., 06340. Hours: 9 A.M.-12:30 P.M., 1:30-4:30 P.M., Mon. through Fri., and by appointment. Tel., (860) 441-6655; FAX, (860) 441-6657.

LEBANON. Constituted June 2, 1826, from Windham. *Geraldine E. McCaw.* Location: Town Hall, 06249. Hours: 10 A.M.-12 Noon, Tues., Fri.; 4-6 P.M., Thurs. Tel., (860) 642-7429; by appointment, (860) 642-7092.

LEDYARD. Constituted June 6, 1837, from Stonington. The records of Ledyard from May, 1666 to October, 1766, are in New London; from October, 1766 to June 6, 1837, are in Stonington. *Gertrude B. Smith.* Clerk, Jane E. Perry. Location: Town Hall, 06339-0038. Hours: 9:30 A.M.-12:30 P.M., Mon. through Fri., by appointment. Tel., (860) 464-8740, Ext. 219.

LYME. Constituted July 5, 1869, from Old Lyme. Probate records concerning Lyme, from May 1, 1666 to June 4, 1830, are in New London; from June 4, 1830 to July 4, 1869, are in Old Lyme; from July 4, 1869 to date, are in Lyme. *William T.*

Koch, Jr. Location: Town Hall, Route 156, Lyme, P.O. Old Lyme 06371. Hours: 9 A.M.-12 Noon, Mon., Fri., and by appointment. Tel., (860) 434-7733.

MONTVILLE. Constituted June 27, 1851, from New London. *Linda J. Mott.* Location: Town Hall, Uncasville 06382. Hours: 9 A.M.-1 P.M., Mon., Tues., Thurs., Fri.; 9 A.M.-5 P.M., Wed. Office Tel., (860) 848-9847.

NEW LONDON (New London, Waterford). Constituted May session, 1666, as a County Court. *Mathew H. Greene.* Location: Municipal Bldg., 06320; Mailing address: P.O. Box 148, 06320. Hours: 9 A.M.-4 P.M., Mon. through Fri. Tel., (860) 443-7121; FAX, (860) 437-8155.

NORTH STONINGTON. Constituted June 4, 1835, from Stonington. *Teresa A. Pensis.* Location: 391 Norwich-Westerly Rd., P.O. Box 204, 06359-0204. Hours: 9 A.M.-12 Noon, Mon., Wed.; 1-4 P.M., Tues., Thurs., Fri., and by appointment. Tel. and FAX, (860) 535-8441.

NORWICH (Norwich, Franklin, Lisbon, Preston, Sprague, Voluntown). Constituted October, 1748, from New London; contains the records of Griswold to January 3, 1979. *Linda M. Salafia.* Clerk, Eileen M. Petrowski. Location: City Hall, 100 Broadway, 06360. Hours: 9 A.M.-4:30 P.M., Mon. through Fri. Tel., (860) 887-2160; FAX, (860) 887-2401.

OLD LYME. Name of district changed from Lyme to Old Lyme, July 24, 1868. Probate records concerning Old Lyme, from May 1, 1666 to June 4, 1830, are in New London; from June 4, 1830 to date, are in Old Lyme. *Sylvia L. Peterson.* Clerk, Josephine McCulloch. Location: Memorial Town Hall, 52 Lyme St., 06371. Hours: 9 A.M.-12 Noon., 1-4 P.M., Mon. through Fri. Tel., (860) 434-1406; FAX, (860) 434-9283.

SALEM. Constituted July 9, 1841, from Colchester and New London. *William C. Kollman, II* (Hartford Rd., Salem 06415). Location: Town Office Bldg., Rte. 85. Hours: 9 A.M.-5 P.M., Mon. through Fri.; evening and weekend hours by appointment. Tel., (860) 859-3873.

STONINGTON. Constituted October session, 1766, from New London. *Paul E. Cravinho.* Location: Town Hall Bldg., 152 Elm St., P.O. Box 312, 06378. Hours: 9 A.M.-12 Noon, 1-4 P.M., Mon. through Fri. Tel., (860) 535-5090; FAX, (860) 535-0520.

Fairfield County

BETHEL. Constituted July 4, 1859, from Danbury. *Daniel W. O'Grady.* Clerk, Marlene H. Ruiz. Location: Bethel Municipal Ctr., 1 School St., P.O. Box 144, 06801. Hours: 9 A.M.-1 P.M., Mon. through Fri.; other hours, by appointment. Tel., (203) 794-8508.

BRIDGEPORT. Constituted June 4, 1840, from Stratford; contains the records of Stratford from May session, 1782 to June 4, 1840, and the records of Easton, which include the records of Weston, Easton being a district of its own from July 22, 1875, until March 4, 1878. *Jonas J. Meyer III.* Clerk, Geraldine C. Nargi. Location: McLevy

Hall, 202 State St., 06604. Hours: 9 A.M.-4 P.M., Mon. through Fri. Tel., (203) 333-4165.

BROOKFIELD. Constituted June 19, 1850, from Newtown. *Jeffrey W. Reinen.* Clerk, Lorrie A. Clark. Location: Town Hall, P.O. Box 5192, 06804-5192. Hours: 1:30-4:30 P.M., Mon. through Fri., and by appointment. Tel., (203) 775-3700; FAX, (203) 740-9008.

DANBURY. Constituted May session, 1744, from Fairfield. *Dianne E. Yamin.* Clerk, Marjorie L. Cerveniski. Location: City Hall, 155 Deer Hill Ave., 06810. Hours: 8:30 A.M.-4:30 P.M., Mon. through Fri. Tel., (203) 797-4521.

DARIEN. Constituted May 18, 1921, from Stamford. *William H. Atkinson.* Clerk, Jean M. Fitzmaurice. Location: Town Hall, 2 Renshaw Rd., 06820. Hours: 9 A.M.-12:30 P.M., 1:30-4:30 P.M., Mon. through Fri.; 9 A.M.-12:30 P.M., Fri., July through Labor Day. Tel., (203) 656-7342.

FAIRFIELD. Constituted May session, 1666, as a County Court. *Daniel F. Caruso.* Clerk, Dolores Terek. Location: Independence Hall, 725 Old Post Rd., 06430. Hours: 9 A.M.-5 P.M., Mon. through Fri.; 9 A.M.-4:30 P.M., July and August. Tel., (203) 256-3041.

GREENWICH. Constituted July 4, 1853, from Stamford. *David R. Tobin.* Clerk, Barbara Carbino. Location: Town Hall, 101 Field Point Rd., 06830. Hours: 8:30 A.M.-4:30 P.M., Mon. through Fri.; 8:30 A.M.-12 Noon, Fri., July, August, and first Fri. in September. Tel., (203) 622-7879.

NEW CANAAN. Constituted June 22, 1937, from Norwalk. *Richard E. Burke.* Clerk, Joan D. Nowak. Location: Town Hall. Mailing address: Box 326, 06840. Hours: 8:30 A.M.-1 P.M., 2-4:30 P.M., Mon. through Fri.; 8:30 A.M.-12 Noon, Fri., July, Aug., and first week of Sept. Tel., (203) 972-7500; FAX, (203) 966-5555.

NEW FAIRFIELD. Constituted January 8, 1975, from Danbury. *Peter R. Larkin.* Clerk, Nancy Larkin. Location: Town Hall, 4 Brush Hill Rd., 06812. Hours: 9 A.M.-12 Noon, Wed., Thurs. Tel., (203) 746-8160, 1605.

NEWTOWN. Constituted May session, 1820, from Danbury. *Margot S. Hall.* Clerk, Margaret L. Gross. Location: Edmond Town Hall, 45 Main St., 06470. Hours: 8:30 A.M.-12 Noon, 1-4:30 P.M., Mon. through Fri. Tel., (203) 270-4280; FAX, (203) 270-4205.

NORWALK (Norwalk, Wilton). Constituted May session, 1802, from Fairfield and Stamford. *John E. Vallerie, Jr.* Clerk, Mary Jane Johnston. Location: 125 East Ave., P.O. Box 2009, 06852-2009. Hours: 9 A.M.-4:30 P.M., Mon. through Fri. Tel., (203) 854-7737.

REDDING. Constituted May 24, 1839, from Danbury. *Richard L. Emerson.* Clerk, Carol N. Conklin. Location: Town Hall, Rte. 107, P.O. Box 1125, 06875. Hours: 9 A.M.-1 P.M., Mon. through Fri., and by appointment. Tel., (203) 938-2326; FAX, (203) 938-8816.

RIDGEFIELD. Constituted June 10, 1841, from Danbury. *Joseph A. Egan, Jr.* Clerk, Ann T. Buccitti. Location: Town Hall, 400 Main St., 06877. Hours: 9 A.M.-5 P.M.,

Mon. through Fri.; closed Wed. afternoons, July and Aug. Tel., (203) 431-2776, Ext. 25.

SHELTON. Constituted May, 1889, from Bridgeport and Derby. Name changed from Huntington to Shelton, August 29, 1919. *Fred J. Anthony.* Clerk, Norine Nedavaska. Location: 40 White St., 06484. Hours: 9 A.M.-12 Noon, 1-4:30 P.M., Mon. through Fri. Tel., (203) 924-8462; FAX, (203) 924-8943.

SHERMAN. Constituted June 4, 1846, from New Milford. *Barbara J. Ackerman.* Location: Town Hall, 06784. Hours: 9 A.M.-12 Noon, Tues., and by appointment. Tel., (860) 355-1821. If no answer, call (860) 354-9930.

STAMFORD. Constituted May session, 1728, from Fairfield. *Gerald M. Fox, Jr.* Clerk, Nina Turnbull. Location: Government Center, P.O. Box 10152, 888 Washington Blvd., 06904-2152. Hours: 9 A.M.-4 P.M., Mon. through Fri. Tel., (203) 323-2149; FAX, (203) 964-1830.

STRATFORD. Constituted May session, 1782, from Fairfield. The records of Stratford previous to June 4, 1840, are in Bridgeport. *F. Paul Kurmay.* Location: Town Hall, 2725 Main St., 06497. Hours: 9:30 A.M.-4:30 P.M., Mon. through Fri. Tel., (203) 385-4023; FAX, (203) 375-6253.

TRUMBULL (Trumbull, Easton, Monroe). Constituted January 7, 1959, from Bridgeport. *John P. Chiota.* Clerk, Mary L. Dupnik. Location: Town Hall, 5866 Main St., 06611-5416. Hours: 9 A.M.-4:30 P.M., Mon. through Fri. Tel., (203) 452-5068, 5062, 5063.

WESTPORT (Westport, Weston). Constituted May session, 1835, at the time of the incorporation of the town of Westport. The territory was taken from Fairfield, Norwalk and Weston. *Earl F. Capuano.* Clerk, Shirley A. DeLuca. Location: Town Hall, 110 Myrtle Ave., 06880. Hours: 9 A.M.-4:30 P.M., Mon. through Fri. Tel., (203) 341-1100.

Windham County

ASHFORD. Constituted June 4, 1830, from Pomfret. *Dennis R. Poitras.* Location: Tremko House, 20 Pompey Hollow Rd., Box 61, 06278. Hours: 1-3:30 P.M., Thurs., and by appointment. Tel., (860) 429-4986.

BROOKLYN. Constituted June 4, 1833, from Pomfret and Plainfield. *James K. Kelley.* Clerk, Khamleuang V. Kelley. Location: Town Hall, 06234. Hours: 11:30 A.M.-4:30 P.M., Tues.; other hours and evenings by appointment. Tel., (860) 774-5973, 2778, 2497.

CANTERBURY. Constituted May 27, 1835, from Plainfield. *Juliette S. Stadnicki.* Location: Town Office Bldg., P.O. Box 26, 06331. Hours: 9:30 A.M.-4:30 P.M., Wed., and by appointment. Tel., (860) 546-9605, 6159.

EASTFORD (Eastford, Chaplin). Constituted June 21, 1849, from Ashford. *Reid R. Samuelson.* Location: Town Office Bldg., Westford Rd., 06242. Hours: 10 A.M.-12 Noon, Wed., and by appointment. Tel.,(860) 974-1885, 3240.

HAMPTON. Constituted June 2, 1836, from Windham. *Jeannine L. Lamont.* Location: Town Office Bldg., 06247. Hours: 9 A.M.-12 Noon, Thurs., and by appointment. Tel., (860) 455-0201, Office Tel., (860) 455-9132.

KILLINGLY. Constituted June 4, 1830, from Pomfret and Plainfield. *Bertram J. Anderson.* Clerk, Dorothy A. Shurilla. Location: Town Hall, 172 Main St., Danielson 06239. Hours: 1-4:30 P.M., Mon. through Fri. Tel., (860) 779-5319.

PLAINFIELD. Constituted May session, 1747, from Windham. *Kathleen Sendley Barry.* Location: Town Hall, 8 Community Ave., 06374. Hours: 12:30-4:30 P.M., Mon., Thurs.; 8:30 A.M.-12:30 P.M., Tues., Wed., Fri., and by appointment. Tel., (860) 564-0019.

POMFRET. Constituted May session, 1752, from Windham and Plainfield. The records of Pomfret were burned January 5, 1754. *Cecile D. Stoddard.* Location: 5 Haven Rd., 06259. Hours: 10 A.M.-4 P.M., Tues. through Thurs.; Sat. and evenings, by appointment. Tel., (860) 974-0186; FAX, (860) 974-3950.

PUTNAM. Constituted July 5, 1856, from Thompson. *Nicholas R. Scola..* Location: Town Hall, 126 Church St., 06260. Hours: 9 A.M.-12 Noon, Mon. through Fri. Tel., (860) 963-6868.

STERLING. Constituted June 17, 1852, from Plainfield. *Signe L. Nowosadko* (P.O. Box 157, Oneco 06373). Location: 1114 Plainfield Pike, Rte. 14-A, Oneco, 06373. Hours: 8:30 A.M.-12 Noon, Mon., Wed., and by appointment. Tel., Courthouse, (860) 564-8488; Bus., (860) 885-2960.

THOMPSON. Constituted May 25, 1832, from Pomfret. *Aileen A. Witkowski* (Box 74, North Grosvenor Dale 06255). Location: Town Bldg., North Grosvenor Dale 06255. Hours: 9 A.M.-12 Noon, Mon. through Fri.; Sat. and evenings, by appointment. Tel., (860) 923-2203.

WINDHAM (Windham, Scotland). Constituted October session, 1719, from Hartford and New London. *Patrick M. Prue.* Location: Town Hall Bldg., P.O. Box 34, Willimantic 06226. Hours: 9 A.M.-1 P.M., Mon. through Thurs.; 9 A.M.-12 Noon, Fri. Tel., (860) 465-3049; FAX, (860) 465-3012.

WOODSTOCK. Constituted May 30, 1831, from Pomfret. *Nancy M. Gale.* Location: Town Hall, 06281. Hours: 3-6 P.M., Wed.; 1:30-4:30 P.M., Thurs.; all other times by appointment. Tel., (860) 928-2223; FAX, (860) 963-7557.

Litchfield County

BARKHAMSTED. Constituted June 5, 1834, from New Hartford; contains the records of New Hartford, from May 27, 1825 to June 5, 1834. *Curtis K. Case* (P.O. Box 185, Pleasant Valley 06063-0185). Location: Town Office Bldg., 67 Ripley Hill Rd., Pleasant Valley. Hours: 10 A.M.-1 P.M., Mon. through Wed.; all other times by appointment. Tel., (860) 379-8665.

CANAAN (Canaan, North Canaan). Constituted June 6, 1846, from Sharon. *Diana J. Matheson.* Location: Town Hall, North Canaan, P.O. Box 905, Canaan 06018. Hours: 9 A.M.-1 P.M., Mon. through Fri., and by appointment. Tel., (860) 824-7114.

CORNWALL. Constituted June 15, 1847, from Litchfield. *Margaret D. Cooley.* Location: Town Office, Pine St., 06753. Hours: 9 A.M.-12 Noon, Tues., Thurs., and by appointment. Tel., (860) 672-2677.

HARWINTON. Constituted May 27, 1835, from Litchfield. *John W. Pickard.* Location: Town Offices, 100 Bentley Dr., 06791. Hours: 9 A.M.-1 P.M., Wed., and by appointment. Tel., (860) 485-1403.

KENT. Constituted May 26, 1831, from New Milford. *Barbara L. Miller.* Location: Town Hall, 06757. Hours: 9 A.M.-12 Noon, Tues., Thurs., and by appointment. Tel., (860) 927-3729.

LITCHFIELD (Litchfield, Morris, Warren). Constituted October session, 1742, from Hartford, Woodbury and New Haven. *Arleen G. Keegan.* Location: Town Office Bldg., 06759. Hours: 9 A.M.-1 P.M, Mon. through Fri., and by appointment. Tel., (860) 567-8065; FAX, (860) 567-2538.

NEW HARTFORD. Constituted May 27, 1825, from Simsbury. The records of New Hartford previous to June 5, 1834, are in Barkhamsted. *Norman E. Rogers, Jr.* Location: Town Hall, P.O. Box 308, 06057. Hours: 9 A.M.-12 Noon, Tues., Thurs., or by appointment. Tel., (860) 379-3254.

NEW MILFORD (New Milford, Bridgewater). Constituted May session, 1787, from Woodbury, Sharon and Danbury. *Suzanne L. Powers.* Clerk, Ellen E. Moore. Location: Town Hall, 10 Main St., 06776. Hours: 9 A.M.-12 Noon, 1-5 P.M., Mon. through Fri.; 9 A.M.-12 Noon, Fri., July through Labor Day. Tel., (860) 355-6029; FAX, (860) 355-6002.

NORFOLK. Constituted May session, 1779, from Simsbury and Litchfield. *Linda F. Riiska.* Clerk, Anne R. Moses. Location: 19 Maple Ave., 06058. Hours: 9 A.M.-12 Noon, Tues., Thurs., and by appointment. Tel., (860) 542-5134; FAX, (860) 542-5876.

PLYMOUTH. Constituted May 31, 1833, from Waterbury. *Sonja J. deSousa.* Location: Town Hall, 80 Main St., Terryville 06786. Hours: 9 A.M.-1 P.M., Mon. through Fri., and by appointment. Tel., (860) 585-4014.

ROXBURY. Constituted June 6, 1842, from Woodbury. *Jeannette M. Puglio.* Location: Town Hall, 29 North St., 06783. Hours: 9 A.M.-12 Noon, 1 P.M.-3 P.M., Tues., Thurs. Tel., (860) 354-1184; FAX, (860) 354-0560.

SALISBURY. Constituted June 16, 1847, from Sharon. *Richard T. Fitzgerald.* Clerk, Patricia Laitala; Asst. Clerk, Maureen Erickson. Location: Town Hall, 06068. Hours: 9 A.M.-12 Noon, Mon. through Fri., and by appointment. Tel., (860) 435-5183.

SHARON. Constituted October session, 1775, from Litchfield. *Suzanne J. Xanthos.* Location: Town Hall, Main St., 06069. Hours: 3-5 P.M., Mon., Tues., Wed., Fri. Tel., (860) 364-5514; FAX, (860) 364-5789.

THOMASTON. Inc. July, 1875, from Plymouth. *Susan H. Kaniewski.* Location: Town Hall Bldg., 158 Main St., 06787. Hours: 9 A.M.-12 Noon, Mon. through Fri., and by appointment. Tel., (860) 283-4874.

TORRINGTON (Torrington, Goshen). Constituted June 16, 1847, from Litchfield. *Joseph J. Gallicchio.* Clerk, Eda Sullivan. Location: Municipal Bldg., 140 Main St., 06790. Hours: 9 A.M.-12 Noon, 1:30-5 P.M., Mon. through Fri. Tel., (860) 489-2215.

WASHINGTON. Constituted May 22, 1832, from Litchfield and Woodbury. *Victoria M. Cherniske.* P.O. Box 295, Washington Depot. Clerk, Kathleen M. Gollow. Location: Bryan Memorial Town Hall, Washington Depot 06794. Hours: 9 A.M.-12 Noon, 1-3 P.M., Mon., Wed., Fri., and by appointment. Tel., (860) 868-7974.

WATERTOWN. Constituted June 3, 1834, from Waterbury. *Carey R. Geghan.* Clerk, Gail D. Cesarello. Location: Town Hall, 06795. Hours: 9 A.M.-12 Noon, 1-3 P.M., Mon. through Fri.; Tel., Bus., (860) 945-5237; Res., (860) 945-0781.

WINCHESTER (Winchester, Colebrook). Constituted May 31, 1838, from Norfolk. *Alan M. Barber.* Location: Town Hall, 338 Main St., Winsted 06098. Hours: 9 A.M.-12 Noon, 1-4 P.M., Mon. through Fri. Tel., (860) 379-5576.

WOODBURY (Woodbury, Bethlehem). Constituted October session, 1719, from Hartford, Fairfield and New Haven. *Mary D. Donaldson.* Asst. Clerk, Robyn F. Moran. Location: P.O. Box 84, 281 Main St. South, Shove Bldg. 06798. Hours: 9 A.M.-12 Noon, 1-4 P.M., Tues., Thurs., and by appointment. Tel., (203) 263-2417; FAX, (203) 263-2748.

Middlesex County

CLINTON. Constituted July 5, 1862, from Killingworth. *William L. Dunn.* Clerk, Margaret A. Schroeder. Location: Eliot House, P.O. Box 130, 06413. Hours: 9 A.M.-12 Noon, 1-4 P.M., Mon. through Fri. Tel., (860) 669-6447.

DEEP RIVER. Constituted January 5, 1949, from Saybrook. *Patricia L. Damon.* Clerk, Valerie N. Shickel. Location: Town Hall, 174 Main St., P.O. Box 391, 06417. Hours: 9 A.M.-12 Noon, 1-4 P.M., Tues., Fri., and by appointment. Tel., (860) 526-6026; FAX (860) 526-6094.

EAST HADDAM. Constituted October session, 1741, from Hartford. The records of East Haddam previous to May 29, 1832, are in Colchester. *Paul D. Buhl.* Clerk, Marge B. Calltharp. Location: East Haddam Town Office (River House), 06423. Hours: 10 A.M.-2 P.M., Mon. through Fri., and by appointment. Tel., (860) 873-5028, 2000; FAX, (860) 873-5025.

EAST HAMPTON. Constituted June 1, 1824, from Middletown and East Haddam. The records of Chatham previous to January 6, 1915, are in Portland. *Anne C. McKinney.* Clerk, Elizabeth E. Welch. Location: 20 East High St., Town Hall Annex, 06424. Hours: 9 A.M.-2 P.M., Mon. through Thurs., and by appointment. Tel., (860) 267-9262.

ESSEX. Constituted as Old Saybrook, July 4, 1853, from Saybrook and included what are now the three towns of Essex, Old Saybrook and Westbrook. Name changed to Essex in 1859. Contains Old Saybrook probate records from July 4, 1853 to July 4, 1859. *Deborah M. Pearl.* Clerk, Valerie N. Shickel. Location: Town Hall, 24 West Ave., 06426. Hours: 9 A.M.-1 P.M., Mon. through Fri.; afternoons by appointment. Tel., (860) 767-4347.

HADDAM (Higganum, Haddam Neck). Constituted June 3, 1830, from Middletown and Chatham. *Sharon G. Kapitulik.* Clerk, Charles F. Riordan. Location: Town Office Bldg., 30 Field Park Dr., 06438. Hours: 10 A.M.-2 P.M., Tues. through Thurs., and by appointment. Tel., (860) 345-8531; FAX (860) 345-3730.

KILLINGWORTH. Constituted June 3, 1834, from Saybrook (now Chester). *Judith P. Lentz.* Location: Town Hall Office Bldg., 323 Rte. 81, 06419. Hours: 9 A.M.-12 Noon, Mon., Wed., Fri., and by appointment. Tel., Bus., (860) 663-2304; Res., (860) 663-1361.

MIDDLETOWN (Middletown, Cromwell, Durham, Middlefield). Constituted May session, 1752, from Hartford, Guilford and East Haddam. *Joseph D. Marino.* Location: 94 Court St., 06457. Hours: 8:30 A.M.-4:30 P.M., Mon. through Fri. Tel., (860) 347-7424; FAX, (860) 346-1520.

OLD SAYBROOK. Constituted July 4, 1859, from Essex. Old Saybrook probate records between 1666-1719, are in New London and New Haven; records between 1719-1780, are in Guilford; records between 1780-1853, are in Chester; records between 1853-1859, are in Essex; records from 1859 to the present, are in Old Saybrook. *Roger W. Goodnow.* Clerk, Kathleen M. Delaney. Location: Town Hall, 302 Main St., 06475. Hours: 9 A.M.-1 P.M., Mon. through Fri., and by appointment. Tel., (860) 395-3128; FAX, (860) 395-3125.

PORTLAND. Constituted April 22, 1913, from Chatham. Contains the records of the District of Chatham previous to January 6, 1915. *Richard J. Guliani.* Location: Town Hall, 265 Main St., 06480. Hours: 9 A.M.-12 Noon, Mon. through Fri., and by appointment. Tel., (860) 342-6739; FAX (860) 342-0001.

*SAYBROOK. Constituted May session, 1780, from Guilford. *Helen B. Bennet* (P.O. Box 628, Chester 06412). Location: 65 Main St., Chester. Hours: 9:30 A.M.-12:30 P.M., Tues., Thurs., and by appointment. Tel., (860) 526-0007.

WESTBROOK. Constituted July 4, 1854, from Old Saybrook. *Constance J. Vogell.* Clerk, Josephine McCulloch. Location: Town Hall, 06498. Hours: 2-5:30 P.M., Mon. through Fri., and by appointment. Tel., (860) 399-5661; FAX (860) 399-9568.

*The District of Saybrook serves only the Town of Chester.

Tolland County

ANDOVER (Andover, Bolton, Columbia). Constituted June 27, 1851, from Hebron; contains the records of Hebron from May session, 1789 to June 27, 1851. *Elaine N. Camposeo.* Location: 222 Bolton Ctr. Rd., Bolton 06043. Hours: 9 A.M.-4 P.M., Mon., Wed.; 9 A.M.-3 P.M., Fri.; Tues. evenings and Thurs., by appointment only. Tel., (860) 649-8066.

COVENTRY. Constituted June 19, 1849, from Hebron. *David C. Rappe.* Location: 1712 Main St., Town Office Bldg., 06238. Hours: 9 A.M.-12 Noon, Wed., Thurs.; 7:30-9 P.M., Tues. Tel., (860) 742-4070.

ELLINGTON (Ellington, Vernon). Constituted May 31, 1826, from East Windsor and Stafford. *Thomas F. Rady III.* Clerk, Susan E. Nash. Location: 14 Park Place, P.O.

Box 268, Rockville 06066. Hours: 9 A.M.-4 P.M., Mon. through Fri.; other hours by appointment. Tel., (860) 872-0519.

HEBRON. Constituted May session, 1789. The records of Hebron previous to June 27, 1851, are in Andover Probate District. *Kevin C. Connors.* Location: Town Office Bldg., 15 Gilead St., 06248. Hours: 8 A.M.-4 P.M., Tues; 3-7 P.M., Thurs.; 9 A.M.-12 Noon, Fri., and by appointment; July and August by appointment only. Tel., (860) 228-9406; FAX (860) 228-4859.

MANSFIELD. Constituted May 30, 1831, from Windham. *George E. Hill.* Location: Probate Court, Audrey P. Beck Bldg., 4 So. Eagleville Rd., Storrs 06268. Hours: 2-5 P.M., Tues., Wed., Thurs., and by appointment. Tel., Bus., (860) 429-3313; Res., (860) 429-5177.

SOMERS. Constituted June 3, 1834, from Ellington. *Francis W. Devlin, Jr.* Location: Town Hall, 600 Main St., 06071. Hours: 9 A.M.-1 P.M., Tues., Thurs., and by appointment. Hearings and conferences by appointment. Tel., (860) 763-8212.

STAFFORD (Stafford, Union). Constituted May session, 1759, from Hartford and Pomfret. *Thomas J. Fiore.* Clerk, Carol Parizek. Location: Warren Memorial Town Hall, Stafford Springs 06076. Hours: 9 A.M.-12 Noon, 1-4:30 P.M., Mon.; 9 A.M.-12 Noon, Tues. through Fri. Tel., (860) 684-3423.

TOLLAND (Tolland, Willington). Constituted June 4, 1830, from Stafford. *George A. Baker.* Clerk, Diane D. DuBaldo. Location: Town Hall, 21 Tolland Green. Hours: 12:30-4:30 P.M., Mon.; 9 A.M.-12 Noon, Wed., Fri.; 5:30-8:30 P.M., Thurs., and by appointment. Willington: 6-8 P.M., Mon. Tel., (860) 871-3640; FAX, (860) 871-3663. Emergency Tel., (860) 429-0799.

SECTION VI

COUNTIES

County Sheriffs

Composition of Counties

THERE ARE NO COUNTY SEATS IN CONNECTICUT

County government was abolished effective October 1, 1960; counties continue only as geographical subdivisions.

COUNTY SHERIFFS ADVISORY BOARD/COUNTY SHERIFFS AGENCY. Address: 84 Wadsworth St., Hartford 06106. *Chm.,* Gerard Egan; *Adm. Dir.,* Patricia C. Lempicki.

CONNECTICUT STATE SHERIFFS ASSOCIATION. Address: One Court St., Middletown 06457-8312. *Pres.,* Joseph E. Bibisi, Middletown; *Vice Pres.,* Walter J. Kupchunos, Jr., Hartford; *Secy.,* James P. L. Kenney, Windham; *Treas.,* Michael Piccoli, Storrs; *Exec. Dir.,* William L. Mehlhorn, Fairfield.

Exec. Committee: Gerry Egan, New London County; Jay Kenney, Windham County.

COUNTY SHERIFFS

Sheriffs are elected for the term of four years, Art. IV, Sec. 25, Conn. Const.

HARTFORD COUNTY (Constituted, 1666)

Sheriff, Walter J. Kupchunos, Jr., June 1, 1999. Salary, $37,000. Office: 101 Lafayette St., Hartford 06106; P.O. Box 260847, Hartford, 06126. Tel., (860) 566-4930. **Chief Deputy,** vacancy.

Deputy Sheriffs—Berlin, Donald Lee Ward, 43 Oak Ridge Dr., 06037 **Bloomfield,** Allen DeLorenzo, 112 Cottage Grove Rd., 06002; Bennett Millstein, 112 Cottage Grove Rd., 06002. **Bristol,** Arthur B. Cyr, P.O. Box 302, 06011; John T. Fiorillo, P.O. Box 1557, 06010; Bruce M. Suchinski, P.O. Box 393, 06010. **East Hartford,** Henry P. Guerrette, 126 Wickham Dr., 06118; John R. Johnston, P.O. Box 281175, 06128; Anthony J. Roberto, 1780 Main St., 06108; Bruce W. Schatz, P.O. Box 280534, 06108. **East Windsor,** Marshall E. Lamenzo, P.O. Box 363, 06028. **Enfield,** Theodore J. Plamondon, Jr., 109 South Rd., 06082. **Farmington,** Mary Ann Douglas, 9 Field Stone Run, 06032; Edward F. Sitnik, 38 Hotchkiss Rd., 06032. **Glastonbury,** Charles Fisher, P.O. Box 180, 06033; Barbara Hill, 21 Woodpond Rd., 06033; James F. Noonan, P.O. Box 372., 06033 **Hartford,** Joseph L. Antinerella, P.O. Box 340-667, 06134; Walter J. Fonfara, P.O. Box 340-753, 06134; Joseph Homelson, 234 Pearl St., 06103; Roberta L. Jones, 111 Chatham St., 06112; Joseph A. LaCava, 30 Henry St., 06114; Roland E. Mailloux, 39 Russ St., 06106; Herman Milton, 70 Burlington St., 06112; Aaron B. Mounds, 3 Cambridge St., 06120; Joseph Musumeci, 39 Russ St., 06106; William U. Myers, 1229 Albany Ave., 06112; Michael P. Pane, P.O. Box 340-667, 06134; William R. Smith, 678 Garden St., 06112; Robert J. Tasillo, 30 Woodland St., 06105; Wilmer J. Woolford, P.O. Box 320477, 06134. **Manchester,** Richard L. LaPointe, 55 Wadsworth St., 06040; Lisa H. Stevenson, 46 Kennedy Rd., 06040. **New Britain,** Charles S. Conochalla, 85 Vance St., 06052; John A. Lepito, P.O. Box 305, 06050; Paul A. Ruel, Jr., P.O. Box 1675, 06052; Joseph J. Vitelli, 78 Dwight St., 06051; Alex J. Zaniewski, P.O. Box 545, 06050. **Newington,** Timothy J. Bennett, P.O. Box 310837, 06131; Edward J. Carey, 42 Churchill Dr., 06111; John R. Griffin, P.O. Box 11287, 06111; Paul S. Uccello, 32 Tunxis Rd., 06111. **Plainville,** John W. Tarca, P.O. Box

494, 06062. **Rocky Hill,** Frederick DiNardi, 169 Valley Crest Dr., 06067; Louis M. LaPorto, 2 Evans Rd., 06067. **Simsbury,** Edward Cosgrove, 6 Eagle La., 06070. **Southington,** David F. Hubbs, 127 Shwekey La., 06489. **South Windsor,** Abraham Glassman, P.O. Box 533, 06074. **West Hartford,** Douglas A. Conant, P.O. Box 370022, 06137; Charles P. Ferrato, P.O. Box 10043, 06110; Michael F. Gentile, 1373 Farmington Ave., 06107; Edward W. Jurgelas, P.O. Box 330444, 06133; Scott M. Kraimer, P.O. Box 271621, 06107; Thomas J. O'Neill, Jr., 116 White Ave., 06119; Peter J. Perone, P.O. Box 330531, 06133; John F. Tracey, Jr., 10 North Main St., 06107. **Wethersfield,** Albenie Gagnon, 49 Orchard Brook Dr., 06109; Francis T. Ragonese, 275 Pine La., 06109. **Windsor,** Erwyn B. Glanz, P.O. Box 612, 06095; Albert C. Graham, 50 Grande Ave., 06095; Daniel L. Lynch, P.O. Box 99, 06095. **Windsor Locks,** Grant S. Carragher, 22 Oak Ridge Dr., 06096.

NEW HAVEN COUNTY (Constituted, 1666)

Sheriff, Frank J. Kinney III, 42 Bradley Ave., Branford 06405, June 1, 1999. Mailing address, P.O. Box 200, New Haven 06510. Salary, $37,000. Office: State Court House, 235 Church St., New Haven 06510. Tel., (203) 789-7883. **Chief Deputy,** Domenic Jannetty, 60 Center St., Waterbury 06702.

Deputy Sheriffs—Ansonia, Carl Badamo, 30 Holbrook St; Richard Krueger, 4 Remer St. **Branford,** Joseph Nardini, 57 Piscitello Dr. **Derby,** John F. Getlein, P.O. Box 396. **East Haven,** Benjamin Mazzucco, 76 Paul St. **Hamden,** Robert Aceto, P.O. Box 5392; Willard Allen, 59 Katherine Dr.; H. Mark DeAngelis, P.O. Box 5471; Aniello Longobardi, 55 Renshaw Rd.; Anthony Mentone, 541 Hill St.; Dennis Panagrossi, P.O. Box 6441; Thomas J. Russo, 61 Park Ave. **Meriden,** Jules Awdziewicz, 84 Higby Dr.; Michael Cassidy, 152 Reynolds Dr.; Joseph Marinan, 9 Sylvan Valley Rd.; Joseph J. Salafia, 304 Dexter Ave.; Sanford Sheftel, 14 Dove Dr. **Milford,** George J. Amato, Jr., 10 Orchard Rd.; Donald Creller, 65 Trumbull Ave.; Robert Hardiman, 468 Burnt Plains Rd.; Kevin Norman, 58 Naugatuck Ave.; William Stuart, P.O. Box 551. **Naugatuck,** Joseph Butler, 25 Fairchild St. **New Haven,** Arthur T. Barbieri, 199 Crown St.; Lonnie W. Barnes, 311 Bassett St.; Gerald Cappiello, 289 Willow St.; Edward DiLieto, 135 Townsend Ter.; William Illingworth, 746 Quinnipiac Ave.; Robert Miller, 45 Court St.; Alphonse Paolillo, 151 Huntington Rd.; Fred Wilson, 308 Huntington St. **North Branford,** Frank Baldo, P.O. Box 212; T. Jerry Juliano, P.O. Box 155. **Northford,** Andrew Esposito, P.O. Box 162. **North Haven,** Peter Criscuolo, 15 Fawn Ridge Rd.; Arthur Concilio, 48 Postman Hwy. **Orange,** Ronald Mangano, 272 Hyland Ter. **Oxford,** Peter E. Karpovich, Jr., 51 Chestnut Tree Hill Ext. **Seymour,** Arthur Davies, 124 Middle Benham Rd. **Wallingford,** Howard Marshall, Jr., 6 Briarwood La.; Timothy Wall, P.O. Box 297. **Waterbury,** Thomas Denihan, P.O. Box 3356; Thomas Gahan, 196 Harwood Rd.; Brian Hobart, 206 Columbia Blvd.; Robert Mulcahy, P.O. Box 3244; John Murray, P.O. Box 2614; Dominic Rosa, P.O. Box 3356; Joseph Sullivan, Jr., P.O. Box 3356. **West Haven,** Timothy Borer, 17 Alexander Dr.; John Burgarella, P.O. Box 229; Norris Horton, 20 Dix St.; James Morrissey, P.O.

Box 551; William J. Nolan, 26 Sharon Ave; Charles Vingiano, 15 Sycaway St. **Wolcott,** Vincent Messina, P.O. Box 6292. **Woodbridge,** Anthony DeVito, 17 Burma Rd.

NEW LONDON COUNTY (Constituted, 1666)

Sheriff, Gerry Egan, 140 West Thames St., Norwich 06360, June 1, 1999. Salary, $37,000. Office: State Court House, P.O. Box 671, 70 Huntington St., New London 06320. Tel., (860) 443-5400. **Chief Deputy,** Thomas A. Connors, 364 Glenwood Ave., New London 06320. Tel., (860) 447-0218; FAX, (860) 437-3297.

Deputy Sheriffs—Bozrah, John Sullivan, 468 Fitchville Rd., 06334. **East Lyme,** Joseph L. Corbett, 20 McElaney Dr., Niantic; Margaret LaBranche, P.O. Box 639. **Groton,** Richard J. Andriola, P.O. Box 982; **Montville,** Neil Feinberg, 849 Chesterfield Rd., Oakdale; Harry Lakowsky, 59 Woodland Rd., Uncasville. **New London,** Joseph C. Heap, II, 34 School St.; Joseph LoGioco, P.O. Box 1224; Josh Martin, 254 Lower Blvd.; George Morgan, 21 Gorton St.; Boleslas Murach, Jr., 302 Bayonet St. **Norwich,** Thomas J. Burke, P.O. Box 966; John B. McGuire, P.O. Box 1153; Robert Spayne, 23 Harland Rd. **Stonington,** Lester Duncklee, 50 West Vine St., Pawcatuck 06379. **Waterford,** Maurice Blinderman, 198 Shore Rd.; Thomas F. McKittrick, 4 Cherry St.; Leonard Weinberg, P.O. Box 442; James Sullivan, 1180 Hartford Tpke.

FAIRFIELD COUNTY (Constituted, 1666)

Sheriff, Edwin S. Mak, 364 Ellsworth St., P.O. Box 3321, Bridgeport, June 1, 1999. Salary, $37,000. Office: 1061 Main St., Bridgeport 06604. Tel., (203) 579-6239. **Chief Deputy,** William L. Mehlhorn, P.O. Box 622, Trumbull 06611. Tel., (203) 579-6230. Office: 1061 Main St., Bridgeport 06604.

Deputy Sheriffs—Bethel, Edward W. Plate, 53 Rockwell Rd. **Bridgeport,** Terry L. Brown, 80 Cartright St., #8L; Gerald V. Cappiello, Jr., P.O. Box 613; Thomas Fraher, 338 McKinley Ave.; Sara Laden, P.O. Box 3634; Paul M. Post, 62 Chatham Ter.; Willie J. Smith, 101-A Karen Ct.; Charles Valentino, 76 Waverly Pl. **Danbury,** Roger F. Delsin, 97 Kohanza; Steven Pichiarallo, P.O. Box 736, Bethel; Gary Renz, 8 Eustis Ave.; J. Stephen Woods, P.O. Box 371. **Fairfield,** Ronald Z. Kadar, P.O. Box 183; Joan A. Swanson, P.O. Box 1524. **Greenwich,** Jack Bart, 98 Byram Shore Rd.; Siegrun Pottgen, P.O. Box 84, Glenville Sta.; Joseph P. Purcell, P.O. Box 11033. **Monroe,** Albert W. Caliendo, 10 Nutmeg Cir.; John J. Cotter, 15 Old Zoar Rd.; Richard A. Orr, 40 Woodlawn Rd.; Robert Zwierlein, 500 Monroe Tpke., Suite 181. **Newtown,** Frank DeLucia, P.O. Box 811. **Norwalk,** Lawrence F. Cafero, 60 Rampart Rd.; Alan Freedman, P.O. Box 628; E. K. Makowski, P.O. Box 245, Belden Sta.; Richard A. Moccia, 106 East Rocks Rd.; William D. Wiest, P.O. Box 2107, Belden Sta. **Ridgefield,** James E. Sullivan, P.O. Box 136. **Shelton,** Richard J. Chaffee, Sr., P.O. Box 811; Patricia A. Randall, 58 Brownson Dr. **Stamford,** Mark Pesiri, P.O. Box 373; Paul Verille, 1856 Summer St.; Anthony D. Verrico, 12 Tyler Dr.; Frank J. Zezima,

56 Stephen St. **Stratford,** Thomas W. Allen, P.O. Box 1230; Thomas English, P.O. Box 442; Edward J. Fennell, P.O. Box 648. **Trumbull,** George F. Hammel, 115 Canoe Brook Rd.; Donald W. Mattice, 53 Twitch Grass Rd. **Westport,** Fausto Carusone, P.O. Box 3008.

WINDHAM COUNTY (Constituted, 1726)

Sheriff, James P. L. Kenney, P.O. Box 311, Thompson 06277, June 1, 1999. Salary, $35,000. Office: Superior Court Bldg., 155 Church St., P.O. Box 191, Putnam 06260. Tel., (860) 928-5181. **Chief Deputy,** Frank A. Zak, Jr., Box 406, Central Village 06332.

Deputy Sheriffs—Ashford, Caroline Makray, 91 Waterfall Rd. **Plainfield,** Nicholas Yonta, 153 Prospect St., Moosup. **Putnam,** Arthur P. Johnston, 6 Park Rd. **Willimantic,** Louise Clifford, P.O. Box 341; David Page, P.O. Box 532; Thomas W. White, P.O. Box 913.

LITCHFIELD COUNTY (Constituted, 1751)

Sheriff, Richard L. Zaharek, Salary, $35,000. Office: Litchfield County Court House, P.O. Box 735, Litchfield 06759. Tel., (860) 567-0844; FAX, (860) 567-3135. **Chief Deputy,** Kevin P. McGrady, Office: Litchfield County Court House, P.O. Box 735, Litchfield 06759. Tel., (860) 567-0844; FAX, (860) 567-3135.

Deputy Sheriffs—Bethlehem, Jeremy W. Buswell, P.O. Box 670. **Canaan,** Elissa P. Wernan, Box 321. **Goshen,** James D. Hiltz, P.O. Box 288. **Harwinton,** David J. Carey, 31 Pineridge Rd.; Armand O. Gauthier, P.O. Box 22; Paul J. Krenitsky, P.O. Box 71; Thomas T. T. Telman, 126 Woodchuck La. **New Milford,** David E. Pare, P.O. Box 336; Michelle P. Wittstein, P.O. Box 1870. **Thomaston,** Julianne Ingham, P.O. Box 175. **Torrington,** Richard Perry, 20 Linden St. **Watertown,** John J. Hayes, 629 Guernseytown Rd. **Winsted,** James J. Barber, R.F.D. 4; Michael S. Nicosia, P.O. Box 125. **Woodbury,** Roger P. Rose, Jr., P.O. Box 550.

MIDDLESEX COUNTY (Constituted, 1785)

Sheriff, Joseph E. Bibisi, June 1, 1999. Salary, $35,000. Office: State Court House, One Court St., Middletown 06457. Tel., (860) 343-6550; FAX, (860) 343-6557. **Chief Deputy,** Sebastian J. Milardo, State Court House, One Court St., P.O. Box 1601, Middletown 06457. Tel., (860) 343-6550.

Deputy Sheriffs—Cromwell, Louis Corneroli, P.O. Box 132; Theodore W. Herrmann, 1 Kim Ileen Court. **Middletown,** Louis Aresco, P.O. Box 208; David Bish, P.O. Box 2452; Raymond Klick, P.O. Box 54; Philip C. Schiro, P.O. Box 156; Relford M. Ward, Sr., P.O. Box 325; Stuart E. Woods, P.O. Box 1893; William E. Wrang, Jr.,

P.O. Box 1015. **Old Saybrook,** Joseph Passanesi, P.O. Box 676. **Portland,** Robert Supple, Box 723. **Westbrook,** Michael Casserino, P.O. Box 533.

TOLLAND COUNTY (Constituted, 1785)

Sheriff, Mike Piccoli, 507 North Eagleville Rd., Storrs 06268, June 1, 1999. Salary, $35,000. Office: State Court House, 20 Park St., P.O. Box 316, Rockville 06066. Tel., (860) 870-3260. **Chief Deputy,** Sharon Uhlman, 23 Hillcrest Dr., Stafford Springs 06076. State Courthouse, 20 Park St., Rockville 06066.

Deputy Sheriffs—Bolton, J. Frederick Audette, 8 Meadow Rd. **Columbia,** Gregory Woodruff, P.O. Box 285. **Coventry,** Kathleen Ullmar, 143 Forest Rd. **Ellington,** Alfred Francis, 82 Main St. **Hebron,** Aaron Reid, 422 Church St., Amston. **Mansfield,** Michael Schor, P.O. Box 677; Timothy A. Quinn, 101 Depot Rd., P.O. Box 22, Mansfield Depot. **Somers,** Michael Pio, 50 Dillenback Rd. **Stafford Springs,** Sharon Uhlman, 23 Hillcrest Dr. **Tolland,** Joseph A. Nedwied, 32 Walbridge Hill Rd.; Richard Stawiarski, 567 Old Post Rd. **Vernon,** John Drost, III, P.O. Box 31; Tim Poloski, 38 Risley Rd.

COMPOSITION OF COUNTIES IN THE STATE OF CONNECTICUT

FAIRFIELD COUNTY
Bethel
Bridgeport
Brookfield
Danbury
Darien
Easton
Fairfield
Greenwich
Monroe
New Canaan
New Fairfield
Newtown
Norwalk
Redding
Ridgefield
Shelton
Sherman
Stamford
Stratford
Trumbull
Weston
Westport
Wilton

HARTFORD COUNTY
Avon
Berlin
Bloomfield
Bristol
Burlington
Canton
East Granby
East Hartford
East Windsor
Enfield
Farmington
Glastonbury
Granby
Hartford
Hartland
Manchester
Marlborough
New Britain
Newington
Plainville
Rocky Hill
Simsbury
Southington
South Windsor
Suffield
West Hartford
Wethersfield
Windsor
Windsor Locks

LITCHFIELD COUNTY
Barkhamsted
Bethlehem
Bridgewater
Canaan
Colebrook
Cornwall
Goshen
Harwinton
Kent
Litchfield
Morris
New Hartford
New Milford
Norfolk
North Canaan
Plymouth
Roxbury
Salisbury
Sharon
Thomaston
Torrington
Warren
Washington
Watertown
Winchester
Woodbury

MIDDLESEX COUNTY
Chester
Clinton
Cromwell
Deep River
Durham
East Haddam
East Hampton
Essex
Haddam
Killingworth
Middlefield
Middletown
Old Saybrook
Portland
Westbrook

NEW HAVEN COUNTY
Ansonia
Beacon Falls
Bethany
Branford
Cheshire
Derby
East Haven
Guilford
Hamden
Madison
Meriden
Middlebury
Milford
Naugatuck
New Haven
North Branford
North Haven
Orange
Oxford
Prospect
Seymour
Southbury
Wallingford
Waterbury
West Haven
Wolcott
Woodbridge

NEW LONDON COUNTY
Bozrah
Colchester
East Lyme
Franklin
Griswold
Groton
Lebanon
Ledyard
Lisbon
Lyme
Montville
New London
North Stonington
Norwich
Old Lyme
Preston
Salem
Sprague
Stonington
Voluntown
Waterford

TOLLAND COUNTY
Andover
Bolton
Columbia
Coventry
Ellington
Hebron
Mansfield
Somers
Stafford
Tolland
Union
Vernon
Willington

WINDHAM COUNTY
Ashford
Brooklyn
Canterbury
Chaplin
Eastford
Hampton
Killingly
Plainfield
Pomfret
Putnam
Scotland
Sterling
Thompson
Windham
Woodstock

SECTION VII

LOCAL GOVERNMENT

Dates of Town, City and Borough Elections

Cities and Boroughs in Connecticut
with Dates of Incorporation

Grand Lists, Tax Rates and Due Dates

Towns, Cities and Boroughs—
Officers and Statistics

Regional Planning Agencies

Regional Councils of Governments

Regional and Municipal Transit Districts

Population of Connecticut by Counties

Population of Towns, 1800-1990

Post Offices in Connecticut
(Towns, Villages and Districts with
Post office of Same Name)

Distances to all Towns in Connecticut
from Hartford

Connecticut Towns in the Order
of their Establishment

TOWN ELECTIONS

Biennially, odd years, first Monday in May

Andover	Bethany	Naugatuck	Woodbridge
Avon	Bolton	Sherman	
Barkhamsted	Farmington	Union	

Biennially, odd years, Tuesday after the first Monday in November

Ansonia	East Windsor	New Britain	Southbury
Ashford	Ellington	New Canaan	Southington
Beacon Falls	Enfield	New Fairfield	South Windsor
Berlin	Essex	New Hartford	Sprague
Bethel	Fairfield	New Haven	Stafford
Bethlehem	Franklin	Newington	Stamford
Bloomfield	Glastonbury	New London	Sterling
Bozrah	Goshen	New Milford	Stonington
Branford	Granby	Newtown	Stratford
Bridgeport	Greenwich	Norfolk	Suffield
Bridgewater	Griswold	North Branford	Thomaston
Bristol	Groton	North Canaan	Thompson
Brookfield	Guilford	North Haven	Tolland
Brooklyn	Haddam	North Stonington	Torrington
Burlington	Hamden	Norwalk	Trumbull
Canaan	Hampton	Norwich	Vernon
Canterbury	Hartford	Old Lyme	Voluntown
Canton	Hartland	Old Saybrook	Wallingford
Chaplin	Harwinton	Orange	Warren
Cheshire	Hebron	Oxford	Washington
Chester	Kent	Plainfield	Waterbury
Clinton	Killingly	Plainville	Waterford
Colchester	Killingworth	Plymouth	Watertown
Colebrook	Lebanon	Pomfret	Westbrook
Columbia	Ledyard	Portland	West Hartford
Cornwall	Lisbon	Preston	West Haven
Coventry	Litchfield	Prospect	Weston
Cromwell	Lyme	Putnam	Westport
Danbury	Madison	Redding	Wethersfield
Darien	Manchester	Ridgefield	Willington
Deep River	Mansfield	Rocky Hill	Wilton
Derby	Marlborough	Roxbury	Winchester (Winsted)
Durham	Meriden	Salem	Windham
Eastford	Middlebury	Salisbury	Windsor
East Granby	Middlefield	Scotland	Windsor Locks
East Haddam	Middletown	Seymour	Wolcott
East Hampton	Milford	Sharon	Woodbury
East Hartford	Monroe	Shelton	Woodstock
East Haven	Montville	Simsbury	
East Lyme	Morris	Somers	
Easton			

CITY ELECTIONS
*Town and city consolidated or co-extensive.

Biennially, odd years, first Monday in May

Groton

Biennially, odd years, Tuesday after the first Monday in November

	*Meriden	*Norwalk	*West Haven
*Ansonia	*Middletown	*Norwich	
*Bridgeport	*Milford	*Shelton	
*Bristol	*New Britain	*Stamford	
*Danbury	*New Haven	*Torrington	
*Derby	*New London	*Waterbury	
*Hartford			

BOROUGH ELECTIONS
*Town and borough consolidated.

Biennially, odd years, first Monday in May

Bantam (Litchfield)
Danielson (Killingly)
Fenwick (Old Saybrook)
Jewett City (Griswold)
Litchfield

*Naugatuck
Newtown
Stonington
Woodmont (Milford)

(Where the name of the borough is other than the town in which it is located, the town location is given in parentheses.)

CITIES IN CONNECTICUT WITH DATE OF INCORPORATION

City	County	Date Incorporated
New Haven	New Haven	January session, 1784
New London	New London	" 1784
Hartford	Hartford	May session, 1784
Middletown	Middlesex	" 1784
Norwich	New London	" 1784
Bridgeport	Fairfield	" 1836
Waterbury	New Haven	" 1853
Meriden	"	" 1867
New Britain	Hartford	" 1870
Danbury	Fairfield	January session, 1889
Ansonia	New Haven	" 1893
Derby	"	" 1893
Norwalk	Fairfield	" 1893
Stamford	"	" 1893
Bristol	Hartford	" 1911
Shelton	Fairfield	" 1915
Winsted (Winchester)	Litchfield	named January session, 1917
Torrington	"	" 1923
Milford	New Haven	" 1959
West Haven	New Haven	Home Rule Act, June 1961
Groton	New London	" " " May 4, 1964

BOROUGHS IN CONNECTICUT WITH DATE OF INCORPORATION

Borough	County	Date Incorporated
Stonington	New London	May session, 1801
Newtown	Fairfield	" 1824
Danielson (Killingly)	Windham	" 1854
Litchfield	Litchfield	January session, 1879
Naugatuck	New Haven	" 1893
Jewett City (Griswold)	New London	" 1895
Fenwick (Old Saybrook)	Middlesex	" 1899
Woodmont (Milford)	New Haven	" 1903
Bantam (Litchfield)	Litchfield	" 1915

MUNICIPAL GRAND LISTS AND TAX RATES

Source: Office of Policy and Management

(All property is assessed at a uniform rate of 70% of value, Sec. 12-62a, Gen. Stat.)

Town	Net Grand List 1994	Tax Rate 1996-97 Mills	Tax Due Date Real Property 1996-97	Indebtedness 1995	Date of Last Revaluation
Andover	$ 120,903,554	30.4	July-Oct., Jan.-Apr.	$ 1,818,168	1992
Ansonia	262,485,440	28.9	July-Jan.	8,427,600	1995
Ashford	109,006,560	26	July-Jan.	3,760,440	1995
Avon	1,423,295,910	20.85	July-Jan.	17,465,810	1987
Barkhamsted	224,999,065	20.5	July-Jan.	2,957,074	1989
Beacon Falls	204,047,763	25	July-Jan.	2,460,599	1992
Berlin	949,014,222	34.4	July	17,520,000	1986
Bethany	297,602,875	24.15	July-Jan.	6,775,490	1989
Bethel	1,146,046,977	19.41	July-Oct., Jan.-Apr.	21,709,710	1988
Bethlehem	229,170,801	19.24	July-Jan.	1,213,603	1989
Bloomfield	959,008,243	28.33	July	12,020,100	1990
Bolton	266,535,490	24.76	August	9,455,000	1989
Bozrah	111,302,237	21	July-Jan.	6,260,000	1992
Branford	1,884,115,885	22.19	July-Jan.	24,236,308	1991
Bridgeport	2,327,796,454	67.5	July-Jan.	155,665,747	1983
Bridgewater	173,924,497	19.45	July-Jan.	1,691,209	1989
Bristol	2,590,922,433	26.5	July-Jan.	41,857,000	1987
Brookfield	1,004,414,715	23.8	Aug.-Jan.	18,296,645	1993
Brooklyn	264,403,209	20	July-Oct., Jan.-Apr.	15,082,694	1990
Burlington	519,736,144	19	July-Jan.	11,199,458	1988
Canaan	71,196,853	29	July-Jan.	95,003	1987
Canterbury	184,605,344	20.77	Aug.-Jan.	7,064,577	1990
Canton	608,990,108	21.35	July-Jan.	12,007,194	1988

MUNICIPAL GRAND LISTS AND TAX RATES—Continued

Town	Net Grand List 1994	Tax Rate 1996-97 Mills	Tax Due Date Real Property 1996-97	Indebtedness 1995	Date of Last Revaluation
Chaplin	$ 117,737,760	18.7	July-Jan.	$ 4,541,195	1988
Cheshire	1,557,488,278	26.1	July-Jan.	70,107,464	1988
Chester	280,534,215	19.35	July-Jan.	4,532,353	1989
Clinton	691,692,851	27.89	July-Jan.	12,198,778	1990
Colchester	545,966,005	25.02	July-Jan.	37,097,100	1991
Colebrook	113,036,066	22.33	July-Jan.	1,333,085	1990
Columbia	249,762,260	20.5	July-Jan.	10,695,000	1992
Cornwall	167,809,974	17.75	July-Jan.	2,692,636	1992
Coventry	458,836,960	23.2	July-Jan.	8,069,078	1991
Cromwell	729,704,120	22.95	July-Jan.	6,280,000	1988
Danbury	4,444,257,600	19.13	July-Oct., Jan.-Apr.	56,580,047	1987
Darien	2,800,800,253	15.32	July-Jan.	11,993,231	1988
Deep River	235,690,511	22.4	July-Jan.	3,522,636	1992
Derby	436,620,750	29	July-Jan.	17,502,788	1991
Durham	333,700,885	26.05	July-Jan.	6,417,277	1990
Eastford	52,618,862	32.29	July-Jan.	1,037,962	1986
East Granby	355,352,040	21.9	July-Jan.	8,140,000	1989
East Haddam	384,509,990	25.17	July-Jan.	13,505,000	1994
East Hampton	567,205,657	22.91	July-Jan.	26,261,627	1990
East Hartford	1,538,307,940	42.81	July-Jan.	13,702,949	1993
East Haven	934,722,998	37.12	July-Jan.	44,500,000	1991
East Lyme	813,769,064	27	July-Jan.	29,155,608	1991
Easton	666,321,847	23.4	July-Jan.	14,159,392	1994
East Windsor	386,228,155	24.5	July-Jan.	4,724,500	1995
Ellington	527,014,877	25	July-Jan.	8,266,915	1990

MUNICIPAL GRAND LISTS AND TAX RATES—Continued

Town	Net Grand List 1994	Tax Rate 1996-97 Mills	Tax Due Date Real Property 1996-97	Indebtedness 1995	Date of Last Revaluation
Enfield	$1,668,542,443	28.95	July-Jan.	$16,559,431	1993
Essex	611,090,375	13.2	July-Jan.	4,586,352	1989
Fairfield	4,141,357,445	24.8	July-Oct., Jan.-Apr.	32,845,000	1993
Farmington	1,679,687,466	21.6	July-Jan.	32,009,472	1994
Franklin	126,178,965	20.95	July-Jan.	4,080,354	1989
Glastonbury	1,504,115,422	29.6	July-Jan.	10,336,000	1995
Goshen	200,240,465	23.6	July-Jan.	2,266,687	1986
Granby	561,227,510	26.02	July-Jan.	13,349,184	1987
Greenwich	9,412,789,240	15.62	July-Jan.	32,116,512	1993
Griswold	319,612,974	22.25	July-Jan.	24,878,250	1992
Groton	1,700,798,131	22.3	July-Jan.	31,290,000	1992
Guilford	1,018,309,555	28.5	July-Jan.	37,335,000	1995
Haddam	994,509,549	21.5	July-Jan.	3,690,064	1991
Hamden	2,331,309,427	34.14	July-Jan.	33,069,251	1991
Hampton	75,101,699	24.55	July-Jan.	3,872,073	1988
Hartford	5,960,680,293	32.4	July-Oct., Jan.-Apr.	109,289,479	1989
Hartland	112,550,648	20.75	July-Jan.	1,985,000	1992
Harwinton	370,555,170	19.2	July-Jan.	8,717,386	1988
Hebron	335,979,428	29.04	July-Jan.	12,354,924	1993
Kent	267,510,930	17.69	July-Jan.	1,082,791	1989
Killingly	528,533,684	20	July-Oct., Jan.-Apr.	22,078,022	1994
Killingworth	290,325,428	26	July-Jan.	2,910,115	1992
Lebanon	332,697,862	17.5	July-Jan.	11,548,640	1989
Ledyard	548,652,999	28.9	July-Jan.	4,474,780	1992
Lisbon	140,027,374	16.5	July-Jan.	3,455,460	1991

MUNICIPAL GRAND LISTS AND TAX RATES—Continued

Town	Net Grand List 1994	Tax Rate 1996-97 Mills	Tax Due Date Real Property 1996-97	Indebtedness 1995	Date of Last Revaluation
Litchfield	$678,495,073	19.14	July-Jan.	$6,220,609	1988
Lyme	273,627,230	11.75	July	532,905	1989
Madison	1,393,573,349	22.2	July-Jan.	6,141,066	1990
Manchester	2,562,044,560	24.26	July-Jan.	18,273,770	1990
Mansfield	471,327,510	25.56	July-Jan.	10,164,082	1990
Marlborough	258,870,321	28.8	July-Jan.	4,354,761	1993
Meriden	1,711,561,010	35.8	July-Oct., Jan.-Apr.	67,043,643	1992
Middlebury	435,854,472	27.95	July-Jan.	9,785,013	1992
Middlefield	213,652,470	26.85	July-Jan.	3,761,036	1992
Middletown	2,154,819,203	23.1	July-Jan.	57,506,000	1987
Milford	2,560,288,486	30.81	July-Jan.	53,749,354	1991
Monroe	1,220,541,840	22.43	July-Jan.	8,604,027	1988
Montville	654,038,196	26.1	July-Jan.	28,310,810	1991
Morris	165,247,515	23.13	July-Jan.	605,754	1991
Naugatuck	540,976,860	55.6	July-Jan.	34,393,000	1980
New Britain	1,460,543,209	49.83	July-Jan.	108,477,000	1985
New Canaan	2,838,341,430	15.64	July-Jan.	15,687,471	1988
New Fairfield	834,703,945	23.1	July-Jan.	20,765,773	1991
New Hartford	408,651,475	19.45	July-Jan.	3,249,403	1989
New Haven	2,164,487,416	61.14	July-Jan.	158,422,189	1991
Newington	1,548,413,175	25.25	July-Jan.	9,653,412	1991
New London	914,357,060	27.3	July-Jan.	26,090,000	1988
New Milford	1,375,115,755	26.25	July-Jan.	21,627,671	1992
Newtown	1,069,052,600	25	July-Jan.	24,327,819	1995
Norfolk	166,935,509	21.32	July-Jan.	1,813,687	1988

MUNICIPAL GRAND LISTS AND TAX RATES—Continued

Town	Net Grand List 1994	Tax Rate 1996-97 Mills	Tax Due Date Real Property 1996-97	Indebtedness 1995	Date of Last Revaluation
North Branford	$ 601,095,523	26.21	July-Jan.	$ 15,776,824	1992
North Canaan	177,207,150	22	July-Jan.	4,392,904	1987
North Haven	1,801,447,275	23.38	July-Jan.	34,813,950	1991
North Stonington	280,874,141	24	July-Jan.	10,442,333	1990
Norwalk	3,315,460,761	46.48	July-Jan.	78,684,942	1983
Norwich	1,399,566,205	24.34	July-Jan.	32,503,284	1988
Old Lyme	762,415,211	17.8	July-Jan.	5,166,550	1990
Old Saybrook	1,137,918,579	14.66	July-Jan.	17,458,073	1989
Orange	1,140,920,069	24.12	July-Jan.	19,724,887	1990
Oxford	430,203,913	29.04	July-Jan.	14,505,250	1990
Plainfield	475,803,800	20.5	July-Jan.	27,104,227	1987
Plainville	817,348,230	26.6	July-Jan.	21,543,600	1991
Plymouth	413,882,030	31.8	July-Jan.	22,204,599	1993
Pomfret	162,318,105	19.34	July-Jan.	5,896,048	1991
Portland	420,686,747	28.76	July-Jan.	9,700,219	1992
Preston	190,161,670	19.5	Aug.-Jan.	1,626,235	1987
Prospect	343,516,882	22.8	Sept.-Jan.	4,757,763	1990
Putnam	349,444,870	14.25	Aug.-Jan.	11,134,333	1988
Redding	917,883,017	19	July-Jan.	5,573,462	1987
Ridgefield	2,189,299,573	21.38	July-Oct., Jan-Apr.	22,998,008	1986
Rocky Hill	1,173,704,750	22	July-Jan.	6,963,577	1989
Roxbury	249,496,753	17.9	July-Jan.	3,471,461	1986
Salem	170,701,080	26.25	July-Jan.	6,753,800	1991
Salisbury	475,480,820	14.1	July-Oct., Jan-Apr.	4,868,270	1990
Scotland	65,876,119	22.25	July-Jan.	2,103,646	1989

MUNICIPAL GRAND LISTS AND TAX RATES—Continued

Town	Net Grand List 1994	Tax Rate 1996-97 Mills	Tax Due Date Real Property 1996-97	Indebtedness 1995	Date of Last Revaluation
Seymour	$ 402,440,245	40.54	July-Jan.	$ 17,864,519	1993
Sharon	294,554,168	16	July-Oct, Jan.-Apr.	3,886,013	1989
Shelton	2,083,271,140	21.62	July-Jan.	20,965,646	1993
Sherman	333,625,793	13.70	July-Jan.	2,534,120	1989
Simsbury	1,308,564,478	29.2	July-Jan.	9,292,031	1994
Somers	395,324,896	21.41	July-Jan.	22,291,550	1994
Southbury	1,551,846,403	17.5	July-Jan.	5,234,220	1987
Southington	1,921,104,844	25.8	July-Jan.	27,721,778	1993
South Windsor	962,539,739	33.71	July-Jan.	24,990,214	1994
Sprague	122,952,885	19.5	July-Jan.	1,310,000	1990
Stafford	466,439,048	24.8	July-Jan.	24,183,918	1990
Stamford	7,525,164,948	29.1	July-Jan.	160,373,553	1993
Sterling	114,046,246	19.5	July-Jan.	1,995,000	1987
Stonington	1,083,369,054	22.6	July-Jan.	23,340,439	1994
Stratford	2,272,818,010	32.49	July-Jan.	79,090,298	1991
Suffield	715,106,970	23.5	July-Jan.	23,576,362	1989
Thomaston	352,127,236	25.05	July-Jan.	5,707,860	1989
Thompson	332,707,081	17.56	July-Jan.	5,992,907	1990
Tolland	527,637,597	26.5	July-Jan.	5,512,703	1991
Torrington	1,605,423,651	26.13	July-Jan.	51,552,396	1988
Trumbull	2,426,934,696	24.1	July-Oct, Jan.-Apr.	37,382,920	1990
Union	47,762,810	16.14	July-Jan.	221,551	1989
Vernon	1,101,726,940	28.9	July-Jan.	20,657,280	1991
Voluntown	86,736,642	22.3	July-Jan.	3,403,967	1991
Wallingford	2,133,122,711	24.8	July-Jan.	13,657,000	1991

MUNICIPAL GRAND LISTS AND TAX RATES—Continued

Town	Net Grand List 1994	Tax Rate 1996-97 Mills	Tax Due Date Real Property 1996-97	Indebtedness 1995	Date of Last Revaluation
Warren	$ 107,290,768	20.75	July	$ 318,809	1986
Washington	466,636,988	16.5	July-Jan.	4,526,474	1989
Waterbury	1,500,975,583	74.64	July-Jan.	49,021,766	1980
Waterford	3,474,840,050	14.46	July-Jan.	5,005,000	1986
Watertown	1,144,434,546	20.21	July-Jan.	15,743,085	1989
Westbrook	462,869,352	21	July-Jan.	20,783,607	1991
West Hartford	3,745,405,315	29.61	July-Jan.	37,399,000	1989
West Haven	1,699,100,798	35.21	July-Jan.	62,953,530	1991
Weston	1,176,859,181	21.52	July-Jan.	10,402,620	1989
Westport	3,001,194,386	23.4	July-Oct, Jan.-Apr.	24,345,000	1985
Wethersfield	1,751,743,725	22.41	July-Jan.	13,191,523	1989
Willington	282,076,920	19.1	July-Jan.	3,225,481	1988
Wilton	1,888,042,840	21.69	July-Jan.	25,495,890	1994
Winchester	410,804,906	27.56	July-Jan.	6,292,622	1994
Windham	508,816,618	23.33	July-Jan.	8,054,013	1993
Windsor	1,956,222,110	20.5	July	30,965,000	1989
Windsor Locks	951,627,723	15.73	July-Jan.	1,140,000	1989
Wolcott	613,297,552	26.25	July-Jan.	16,147,513	1991
Woodbridge	699,540,005	27.61	July-Jan.	11,437,722	1991
Woodbury	648,930,715	18.35	July-Jan.	3,083,800	1988
Woodstock	293,611,896	24.70	Aug.-Jan.	12,085,014	1991

TOWNS, CITIES AND BOROUGHS

The following listings of municipal officers, justices of the peace, and town, city and borough statistics were compiled from annual reports submitted to the Secretary of the State by municipal clerks through January 1, 1997, and the accuracy of the information in this section is dependent on those reports. The area of the towns (total area of land and inland water) is taken from "Area Measurement Reports, Areas of Connecticut, 1990" by the U.S. Dept. of Commerce, Bureau of the Census. The populations of towns are taken from the estimated populations as of July 1, 1995, by the Conn. State Dept. of Public Health.

ANDOVER. Tolland County.—(Form of government, selectmen, town meeting, board of finance.)—Inc., May 18, 1848; taken from Hebron and Coventry. Area, 15.7 sq. miles. Population, est., 2,815. Voting district, 1. Principal industries, agriculture, small wood and machine shops. Transp.—Passenger: Served by the buses of Bonanza Bus Lines, Inc. from Hartford, and Willimantic. Post office, Andover, covered by two rural free deliveries.

TOWN OFFICERS. Clerk and Reg. of Vital Statistics, Marjorie R. Anderson; Hours, 8:30 A.M.-12 Noon, 1-4 P.M., Mon. through Thurs.; 5-7 P.M., Mon.; 8:30 A.M.-12:30 P.M., Fri.; Address, Town Office Bldg., 17 School Rd., P.O. Box 328, 06232-0328; Tel., (860) 742-0188.—**Asst. Clerk and Asst. Reg. of Vital Statistics,** Charlotte Atherley.—**Selectmen,** 1st, Edward F. Turn, Sr. (R) Tel., (860) 742-7305, Steven O. Fish (R), David H. Rhinelander (D).—**Treas.,** Morgan B. Steele.—**Bd. of Finance,** Susan P. B. Losee, Chm., Ylo Anson, Rene Chouinard, Gerald Hardisty, Mary M. Keenan, Kenneth A. Lester, John F. Phelps, John M. Zabkar III; Alternates, John V. Furan, Leroy R. Krewson.—**Tax Collector,** Carol A. Houghton; Asst., Jean Cochrane.—**Bd. of Assessment Appeals,** Jan M. Neumeth, Chm., Andrew F. Gasper, Jr., Diane Santese.—**Assessor,** Joan LeBlond.—**Registrars of Voters,** Beverly W. Bennett (D), Louise F. Parkington (R).—**Supt. of Schools,** F. William Davis.—**Bd. of Education,** Joan V. Foran, Chm., Elisabeth Houle, Diane M. Rea, Donald Rey, 1999; George C. Elliott, Theodore Sakelarakis, Voncille Wright, 2001; Jay K. Linddy, Donald P. Rea, 2003.—**Planning and Zoning Comm.,** Robert F. Burbank, Chm., Suzanne J. Dower, Susan C. England, Leigh A. Hutchinson, Erich Siismets; Alternates, David Buffum, Anne Rhinelander, Robert Russell.—**Zoning Bd. of Appeals,** Richard L. Higgins, Chm., Wayne Besaw, Marianne Jensen, William P. Kralovich, Joan C. Madore, Mary C. McNamara, Kevin B. Sheehan; Alternates, Richard Busch, Kathleen D. Cadrin, Evelyn H. Saygert.—**Inland Wetlands Comm.,** Steven Reade, Chm., Suzanne J. Dower, John England, Gerald Hardisty, James McCann; Alternates, Donald Denley, vacancy.—**Agents for the Elderly,** Valerie Jacobs, Adele McBride.—**Dir. of Health,** Rozanne Venti, M.D.—**Library Directors,** Samuel Davis, Jr., Linda H. Fish, Jean S. Gasper, Daniel O'Neil, Alfred H. Pepin, Jr., Julia A. Victoria.—**Recreation Comm.,** Jay Linddy, Chm., Joan Foran, William Dakin, William Foley, Thomas Moynihan, Jeffrey Rea.—**Building Inspector,** Robert Moreland.—**Chief of Police,** Edward F. Turn.—**Chief of Fire Dept.,** Curtis W. Dowling; Deputy, Shawn Covell.—**Fire Marshal,** Wallace Barton.—**Bd. of Fire Comrs.,** William Breadheft, Chm., Wallace E. Barton, William D. Covell, William D. Hegener, Jay K. Linddy, Henry G. Parkington.—**Civil Preparedness Dir.,** Edward F. Turn.—**Town Atty.,** Stanley Falkenstein.—**Justices of the Peace,** Marjorie R. Anderson, Wayne F. Besaw, Sr., Deborah C. Fuger,

Katharine Koonze, Kenneth A. Lester, Jay K. Linddy, Cynthia McGilton, Charlotte L. Neal, Henry G. Parkington, Erich Siismets, Elizabeth A. Spear, Margaret Wilt.

ANSONIA. New Haven County.—(Form of government, mayor, board of aldermen.)—Town and city consolidated, Inc., April, 1889; taken from Derby. Area, 6.2 sq. miles. Population, est., 17,825. Voting districts, 7. Birthplace of Gen. David Humphreys. Principal industries, manufacture of copper and brass, plastics, latex foam, electronics, automatic screw machine products, novelties. Transp.—Passenger: Served by Metro North Commuter Railroad Co. and buses of Conn. Transit from New Haven; and Valley Transit District buses cover Ansonia, Derby, Seymour, Shelton. Freight: Served by Boston & Maine Railroad and numerous motor common carriers. Post office, Ansonia.

CITY AND TOWN OFFICERS. City Clerk, Town Clerk and Reg. of Vital Statistics, Florence K. Hoinski; Hours, 8:30 A.M.-4:30 P.M., Mon. through Fri.; Address, City Hall, 253 Main St., 06401; Tel., (203) 736-5980.—**Asst. City and Town Clerk, Asst. Reg. of Vital Statistics,** Madeline H. Bottone.—**Mayor,** Nancy Valentine (R); **Dir. of Adm. Affairs,** William C. Nimons.—**Bd. of Aldermen,** 1st Ward, Peter J. Danielczuk, Pres., Cathy L. Prestiano; 2nd Ward, John Bellis, Jane B. Della Volpe; 3rd Ward, David P. Lysak, Kathleen B. Samela; 4th Ward, Carol A. Gabianelli, Edward C. Norman; 5th Ward, Louis R. Macero, Charles Marrone, Paul E. Schumacher III; 6th Ward, James A. Dempsey, Richard J. Miller, Jr.; 7th Ward, David S. Cassetti, Judith A. Nicolari.—**Treas.,** Ronald V. Greski.—**Comptroller,** vacancy.—**Bd. of Apportionment and Taxation,** Roy Tidmarsh, Chm., Timothy S. Ahearn, Nicholas Amico, Sr., Gale M. Banks, Kevin M. Blake, Joseph Confinante, Jr., Robert W. Hultgren, Michael A. Kalweit, Edward Lane, Donald W. Mark, Stephen J. Strumello, vacancy.—**Finance Asst./Purchasing Agent,** vacancy.—**Tax Collector,** Roy Vacca.—**Bd. of Assessment Appeals,** Louis R. Macero, Chm., Patricia Fers, Susan A. Nargi, Ellen Troy.—**Assessor,** Margaret M. Dzwonchyk.—**Registrars of Voters,** John Erlingheuser (D), Callie Vartelas (R).—**Supt. of Schools,** Ruth F. Connors.—**Bd. of Education,** William Evans, James A. Fainer, Christine J. Shortell, 1997; Beverly L. Tidmarsh, Chm., Julius I. Douglas, Bartholomew R. Flaherty III, Richard Thayer, 1999.—**School Building Comm.,** James A. Fainer, Chm., Timothy Ahearn, Gale M. Banks, Julius Douglas, William Ives, Elaine Kalweit, Edward Lane, Charles Marrone, William Nimons, Edward Norman, Paul E. Schumacher III, Beverly L. Tidmarsh.—**Personnel Dir./Affirmative Action Officer,** Claude L. Perry, Sr.—**Retirement Bd.,** Donald Mark, Chm., Joseph Confinante, Jr., Carol Gabianelli, Ronald V. Greski, Florence K. Hoinski, David Lysak, Albertha Smoot.—**Planning and Zoning Comm.,** Richard T. Sturges, Chm., Bert Berardelli, James T. Della Volpe, David Ford, John Hunt, Nunzio Parente, William A. Schuchmann, Sr., Earl Williams; Alternate, Paul Mudry.—**Zoning Bd. of Appeals,** Gary Merlone, Chm., Frank J. Baxter, Karl Dombroski, Laura Gagnon, Russell Garcia, Jeremiah F. Kennedy; Alternates, Gary Cassetti, John Maricondi, Susan G. Vacca.—**Zoning Enforcement Officer,** Peter Crabtree.—**Fair Housing Officer,** Claude L. Perry, Sr.—**Development Comm.,** Stephen I. Blume, Chm., Michael J. Adanti, George Boath, Dean Ford, Ralphine Ford, Linda Gentile, Blanche Johnson, Richard Sturges, James J. Tyma; Claude L. Perry, Sr., Admin.—**Housing Auth.,** Vincent W. Malerba, Jr., Chm., Juanita Coleman, John A. Della Volpe, John D. Lawlor, Kevin McDuffie; A. Pat Ambrogio, Exec. Dir.—**Bd. of Ethics,** Joyce Clark, Chm., Bruce Goldson, Gail Kryvanis, Joseph Palmucci, Anthony Ruggiero, Jr.—**Conservation Comm.,** William Urban, Chm., Randolph Carroll, Robert Ives, John Killeen, Jr., Richard Lauer, Frank V. Pergola, Edward Sokolnicki, Jr.—**Inland Wetlands Comm.,** William Urban, Chm., David Ford, Robert Ives, John Izzo, Jr., Richard Lauer, William Malerba, Earle Williams.—**Historic Dist. Comm.,** Helen Ptak, Chm., Mary Connors, John Gentile, Mary Hennessey, Phyllis Judd, George Pritchard, Cecilia Rafalowski.—**Municipal Historians,** Marie C. Balco, Margaret J. Gibbs.—**Historical Comm.,** Michael Impellitteri, Jr., Chm., Randolph Carroll, Thomas P. Clifford III, Margaret Gibbs, William McDonnell, Jr., George W. Pritchard, Carol L. Starkey.—**Comm. for Elderly Services,** Donald Poehailos, Chm., Maureen A. Baron, Francis J. Burleigh, Henry Jemioto, Theresa Kurkowski, Josephine Pietrosante, Ann Marie Pitney, Diane Stroman, Sophie Wilder.—**Bd. of Welfare,** Florence Camilleri, Chm., Arlene Applebaum, George Burnett, Maureen C. Levine; Ann Marie Caporale, Dir.—**Dir. of Health,** Leon J. O'Connor, M.P.H.—**Health District,** John R. Calderwood, Chm., Thomas P. Clifford III, Joanne Evans.—**Library Directors,** Susan I. Hawley, Chm., Lisa Bellaria, Marcia Dobrowski, Lynda Frattalone, Stanley Kapinos, John J. Lonergan, Jr., Violet A. O'Donnell, Carol Sardinha, Margaret Sullivan.—**Recreation Comm.,** Anthony Cieplak, Chm., Dennis Banks, Jeffrey W. Burkitt, Karl King, Leonard Kirpas, Thomas Pepe, Alfonso Smith.—**Bd. of Public Works,** Jeffrey W. Burkitt, James DeGennaro, Jr., Leonard Marazzi, Albertha Smoot.—**Building and Refuse, Flood Control/Streets and Bridges,** Joseph Maffeo, Acting Supt.—**City Engineer,** Donald W. Smith, Jr.—**Water Pollution Control Auth.,** Richard Krueger, Chm., Conrad Gagnon, Robert Ives, Spero Jordanides, Howard Madigosky, Charles Marrone, Albertha Smoot.—**Municipal Parking Auth.,** Alex Bakunowich, Jr., Pres., Stephen C. Bodak, John Lotto, Edward Sabatini.—**Building Inspector,** Nicholas Behun.—**Plumbing Inspector,** Anthony Sattaneo.—**Electrical Inspector,** Robert J. Dunn.—**Building Bd. of Appeals,** Carmen Pitney, Sr., Chm., David Blackwell, Nicholas T. Macero, Jr., Norman Smith, Jr.—**Chief of Police,** James J. McGrath.—**Bd. of Police Comrs./Traffic Auth.,** Eugene K. Baron, Pres., Samuel Baranowsky, Brian Phipps.—**City Sheriffs,** Della Hubbard, Louis R. Macero, Marion Norman, John Rafalowski, Robert A. Wargo.—**Chief of Fire Dept.,** James Fleming, Jr.; Assts., Judd Blaze, Robert Caruso, Michael Stahl, John Thomson, Jr.—**Fire Marshal,** Norman Smith, Jr.; Deputies, John Granatie, Jr., Joseph Kingston, Jr., Carl Smith, Jr.—**Bd. of Fire Comrs.,** Edward C. Norman, Chm., Paul E. Schumacher III.—**Rescue and Medical Services Comm.,** James A. Dempsey, Chm., Kenneth Blake, Frank Halpin, David P. Lysak; Robert W. Reichelt, Dir.—**Labor Counsel,** Saranne Murray.—**Corporation/ Claims Counsel,** Richard S. Bruchal.—**Civil Preparedness Dir.,** Robert Reichelt.—**Justices of the Peace,** Jack L. Abbels, Gloria Badamo, Jeffrey W. Burkitt, Randall F. Carroll, Michael Dalton, Sr., Carol M. Duhaime, Patricia J. Fers, Robert F. Fogarty, John W. Gatison, Jr., Brad Harris, Hazel Hummel, Elaine C. Kalweit, Michael A. Kalweit, Patricia A. Pirritino, Cecilia Rafalowski, Sandra L. Soltesz, Rita St. Jacques, Edward J. Sokolnicki, Jr., Nancy Valentine.

ASHFORD. Windham County.—(Form of government, selectmen, town meeting, board of finance.)—Inc., Oct., 1714. Area, 39.5 sq. miles. Population, est., 3,969. Voting district, 1. Principal industry, agriculture. Transp.—Freight: Served by numerous motor common carriers. Post office, Ashford.

TOWN OFFICERS. Clerk and Reg. of Vital Statistics, Barbara B. Metsack; Hours, 8:30 A.M.-3 P.M., Mon., Tues., Wed., Fri.; 7-9 P.M., Wed.; Address, Knowlton Memorial Town Hall, Rte. 44, 25 Pompey Hollow Rd.; Tel., Storrs, (860) 429-7044.— **Asst. Clerks and Asst. Regs. of Vital Statistics,** Cheryl A. Bowen, Beverly G. Ference.—**Selectmen,** 1st, John M. Zulick (D) Tel., (860) 429-2750, Jennie Atkins (D), William A. Falletti (R).—**Treas.,** Anne M. Supina.—**Bd. of Finance,** William R. Becker, Chm., Jean N. McCarthy, Gerald P. Nagy, Donald Protheroe, Merrill P. Simpson, Michael J. Zambo; Alternates, Thomas R. Lackman, Steven K. Reviczky, Brian J. Rossman.—**Tax Collector,** Mary Ann J. Simpson.—**Bd. of Assessment Appeals,** Gordon M. Cole, Ellen M. Nemecek, James Reviczky.—**Assessor,** Emily M. Kasacek.—**Registrars of Voters,** Alvah H. Phillips (D), John S. Cowen (R).—**Supt. of Schools,** Richard H. Butler.—**Bd. of Education,** Stephen B. Galinat, Sr., Chm., Rhonda M. Kincaid, Charles H. McCaughtry, 1997; Newton R. Emerson II, Linda G. Gagne, Carl H. Pfalzgraf, Donna Jean Tuller, 1999.—**Planning and Zoning Comm.,** Sidney E. Organ, Jr., Chm., Alexander Hastillo, Gary H. Lawrence, Hank Levaur, Gerald P. Nagy, George J. Quirk, Brian J. Rossman, Malcolm K. White; Alternates, John W. Bartok, Jr., Brian E. Specyalski, Stanley A. Whitehouse.—**Zoning Bd. of Appeals,** Charles L. Atkins, Chm., William C. Barr, Charles E. Johnson, Paul G. Pekarovic, Emery E. Zambo; Alternates, William J. Alape, William A. Kerensky, Mark Naylor.—**Zoning Enforcement Officer,** Rudolph E. McKray.—**Conservation and Inland Wetlands Comm.,** Richard E. Dziadus, Chm., John S. Barclay, Thomas R. Lackman, Gary R. Lipstreu, V. Peter Piecyk III, David Rechel, Richard Zulick; Alternates, Evangeline Abbot, Beata T. Metsack.—**Comm. on Aging,** P. Jules Girardet, Chm., Teresa Costello, Marie McGuire, Catherine R. Muska, Anita Pyne, Mary Tremko; Carrie Chebro, Agent for the Elderly.—**Dir. of Health,** Bruce D. Lundgren.— **Sanitarian,** Northeast District Dept. of Health.—**Library Directors,** Evelyn T. Pfalzgraf, Chm., Cynthia Curry, Sue E. Harkness, Shirley A. Johnson, Gerald P. Nagy, Donna L. Viel.—**Municipal Historian,** Barbara B. Metsack.—**Recreation Comm.,** Thomas Proctor, Chm., Jeffrey J. Bond, Elizabeth A. Delhaie, Cornelius J. Harper, Judith S. Knowles, Craig Krest, Bette Stern.—**Housing Auth.,** Carrie Chebro, James F. Dineen, Sr., Dorothy Lackman, Kevin R. Pratt, Jr., Theodore P. Simmons.—**Building Inspector,** Terry Bellman.—**Building Code Bd. of Appeals,** John Ference, Jr., Leslie C. Hobby, John P. Reviczky.—**Tree Warden,** Hank Levaur.—**Chief of Police,** John M. Zulick.—**Constables,** Charles B. Reviczky, Robert Viel.—**Chief of Fire Dept.,** Richard E. Whitehouse; Deputy, Bruce Fletcher.—**Fire Marshal,** Richard E. Whitehouse.—**Civil Preparedness Dir.,** Robert T. Burr.—**Town Atty.,** Dennis J. O'Brien (55 Church St., Willimantic).—**Justices of the Peace,** Helen M. Barr, William R. Becker, Joan E. Bowley, Lucia M. Britton, Robert T. Burr, Carolyn W. Chebro, John S. Cowen, Geraldine T. Dunphy, Linda G. Falletti, William A. Falletti, Stephen B. Galinat, Teresa M. Galipeau, David M. Gardner, Anthony J. Horn, Anne J. Keenan,

William A. Kerensky, Henry Levaur, Patricia A. Lockey, Joanne L. Lovell, Jean N. McCarthy, Kevin T. A. McCarthy, Charles H. McCaughtry, Michael A. McGuire, Paul M. Metsack, Ellen M. Nemecek, William F. Paradis, Paul G. Pekarovic, Joseph F. Peters, Carl H. Pfalzgraf, Evelyn T. Pfalzgraf, Michael Pfalzgraf, David J. Rechel, James Reviczky, Joan A. Riviczky, John P. Reviczky, Steven K. Reviczky, Mark A. Sullivan, Harold Upton, Kay M. Warren, Gail A. Zaicek, Malorzata L. Zan-Phillips.

AVON. Hartford County.—(Form of government, town manager, town council, board of finance.)—Inc., May, 1830; taken from Farmington. Area, 23.5 sq. miles. Population, est., 14,143. Voting district, 1. Principal industries, insurance, printing, manufacture of time devices, jet engine testing equipment, concrete products and poultry processing, reflective tapes, fiber optics. Transp.—Passenger: Served by buses of the Arrow Line, Inc. from Hartford, Winsted and Torrington, and Conn. Transit. Freight: Served by numerous motor common carriers. Post office, Avon. Rural free delivery.

TOWN OFFICERS. Clerk and Reg. of Vital Statistics, Caroline B. LaMonica; Hours, 8:30 A.M.-4:30 P.M., Mon. through Fri.; 8 A.M.-4:45 P.M., Mon. through Thurs.; 8 A.M.-12:30 P.M., Fri., July, Aug.; Address, 60 West Main St., 06001; Tel., Farmington, (860) 409-4310; FAX, (860) 677-8428.—**Asst. Clerk and Asst. Reg. of Vital Statistics,** Elinor S. Burns.—**Town Manager,** Philip K. Schenck, Jr.; Asst., Karen L. Levine.—**Town Council,** Richard W. Hines, Chm., Diane S. Hornaday, S. Edward Jeter, William J. Shea II, Joseph C. Woodford.—**Treas.,** Edward J. Doyle.—**Bd. of Finance,** Arthur L. Herrmann, Chm., John F. Carlson, Thomas A. Gugliotti, Thomas F. Harrison, William R. Hooper II, Peter R. Sorensen, R. Lewis Zacchera.—**Tax Collector,** Mary C. Bowman.—**Bd. of Assessment Appeals,** Russell C. Peckham, Chm., Richard S. Connel, William B. Cooper, James R. McCarthy, Donald A. Stern.—**Assessor,** Harry derAsadourian.—**Registrars of Voters,** Marilyn B. Dumas (D), Ann J. Tilson (R).—**Supt. of Schools,** Philip A. Streifer.—**Bd. of Education,** Thomas S. Becker, Paula P. Erickson, Paul E. Potanka, David T. Shopis, 1997; Pamela P. Friedman, Chm., Thomas C. McNeill, Jr., Vincent E. Roche, Martin Toyen, David S. Wolansky, 1999.—**Planning and Zoning Comm.,** Robert N. Meyers, Chm., Carol K. Griffin, Patrick J. Shea, Duane E. Starr, Sylvia K. Stieber, Douglas C. Thompson, Barnard Tilson; Alternates, Henry R. Frey, Jr., Linda H. Keith, Elaine G. Primeau.—**Town Planner,** Steven M. Kushner.—**Zoning Bd. of Appeals,** John E. Drew, Chm., David B. Beizer, Jonathan C. Belden, Harry Garfinkel, Linda B. Meyers; Alternates, John F. Brooks, George M. Catrambone, Stephen Philbrick.—**Inland Wetlands Comm.,** H. Scott Smith, Chm., Rebecca Blankenbicker, Walter J. Ives, Joseph W. Lester, Jr., Joanne Reilly, Rosalie R. Renfrew, Dale H. Tasker.—**Natural Resources Comm.,** Mary C. Harrop, Chm., Dean S. Applefield, Michael R. Beauchamp, Charles L. D. Chin, Dana L. Downing, Scott F. Lewis, Janice S. Titus.—**Committee on Aging,** Miriam D. McWilliams, Chm., Gloria L. Farrell, Alice W. Herrmann; Alan E. Rosenberg, Agent/Dir. of Social Services.—**Medical Advisor,** Ralph Rosenberg, M.D.—**Library Directors,** Anne R. Paine, Pres., Ami Belsky, T. Dean Daniels, H. Edward DeRoehn, Joan Gugliotti, Rose Ann McLaury, Michael Monts, Paul Potanka, Aric Schichor, Keith Sherman, vacancy.—**Parks and Recreation Advisory Committee,**

Leslie J. Chaput, Henry R. Frey, Jr., Stanley J. Phillips, Jr.; Glenn M. Marston, Dir.—**Town Engineer,** Thomas A. Daukas.—**Tree Warden,** Rudolph W. Fromm.—**Building Inspector/Fire Marshall,** Donald Washburn.—**Building Code Bd. of Appeals,** William D. Barnett, William L. Brown, James H. Eacott III, Paul E. Potanka, Louis N. Usich, Jr.—**Water Pollution Control Auth.,** Milton P. Anstey, Chm., George W. England, Robert M. Loebell, Stephen J. McGuff, James E. Speich.—**Dir. of Health/Sanitarian,** Farmington Valley Health Dist.—**Chief of Police,** James A. Martino, Jr.—**Constables,** Nicholas Cecere, Rene Ruez.—**Chief of Fire Dept.,** James W. DiPace; Deputy, Clarence Evans.—**Civil Preparedness Dir.,** Philip K. Schenck, Jr.—**Town Atty.,** Robert C. Hunt, Jr.—**Justices of the Peace,** Jonathan B. Alter, Marilyn B. Dumas, Ilene D. Kaplan, Morton N. Katz, William Kes, Rosalie S. Lester, Heidi A. Lewis, Robert M. Loebell, Richard B. McCall, James R. McCarthy, William G. Oechslin, Rosalie R. Renfrew, Kove J. Schwartz, Fern L. Sprung, Richard A. Stahl, Sylvia K. Stieber, Ann J. Tilson, Penelope R. Woodford.

BANTAM.* BOROUGH OFFICERS. P.O. 569, c/o Clerk, 35 Circle Dr., Bantam 06750. Tel., (860) 567-0396.—**Warden,** Richard J. Sheldon.—**Burgesses,** Stuart Clem, Peter Dauten, Joseph A. Kowalec, Jr., Victoria J. Meaney, Scott Parsons, Geary Roberts.—**Clerk,** Cynthia McPhee.—**Tax Collector,** Michelle Wetmore.—**Assessor,** Beth Snihatsch.—**Treas.,** Pauline Keith.—**Planning and Zoning,** Kent Gilyard, Chm.—**Zoning Bd. of Appeals,** Joanne Creedon, Chm., Tom Gillman, William Smith, Nancy Waldvogel, vacancy; Alternates, Pat Stanton, two vacancies.—**Building Inspector,** James H. Graham.—**Chief of Fire Dept.,** Scott Parsons; Asst., John Campbell.—**Fire Marshal,** Fletcher Cooper; Asst., David Cooper.—**Borough Atty.,** Peter Litwin.

---

*See Town of Litchfield.

BARKHAMSTED. Litchfield County.—(Form of government, selectmen, town meeting, board of finance.)—Inc., Oct., 1779. Area, 38.8 sq. miles. Population, est., 3,494. Voting district, 1. Principal industries, agriculture and the manufacture of chairs, dies, gauges, craft materials and special machinery. Transp.—Freight: Served by numerous motor common carriers. Post offices, Pleasant Valley and Riverton. Rural free delivery from Winsted, New Hartford, Collinsville and North Canton.

TOWN OFFICERS. Clerk and Reg. of Vital Statistics, Maria V. Mullady; Hours, 9 A.M.-4 P.M., Mon. through Thurs.; 9 A.M.-1 P.M., Fri.; Address, Town Hall, Rte. 318, Box 185, Pleasant Valley 06063; Tel., Winsted, (860) 379-8665; FAX, (860) 379-9284; Internet: http://159.247.0.202/MUNIC/BARKHAMSTED/barkhamsted.htm; E-Mail: duster@esslink.com.—**Asst. Clerk and Asst. Reg. of Vital Statistics,** Nancy N. Winn.—**Selectmen,** 1st, Michael D. Fox (D), Carmella M. Lattizori (D), Richard T. Winn (R).—**Treas.,** Brian E. Noe.—**Bd. of Finance,** Andrew R. Bray, Chm., Maurice D. Grasso, Carol A. Grenier, Alvin R. Krassner, Lewis H. Patchett, Anthony R. Prete; Alternates, David R. Moulton, Debra H. Parrott.—**Tax Collector,** Teresa T. Collins.—**Bd. of Assessment Appeals,** Michael S. Day, Chm., George M. Murphy,

Linda S. Murphy.—**Assessors,** Mary E. Ringuette, Chm., Francis J. Lattizori, Daniel K. Mullady.—**Registrars of Voters,** Helen M. Ahles (D), Susan L. Day (R).—**Supt. of Schools,** Judith B. Condon.—**Bd. of Education,** Lynda M. Masselle, Chm., Anita M. Deschenes-Desmond, Stephen M. Raftery, Reed M. Vincent, 1997; Kevin D. Case, Joan S. Egbertson, Scott T. Jeffrey, 1999.—**Planning and Zoning Comm.,** Christina Lavieri, Chm., Storm M. Connors, James H. Hart, David R. Moulton, Maureen E. Wehner; Alternates, David W. Boratko, Gregory M. Cantwell, John R. Greaser.—**Zoning Bd. of Appeals,** Stuart E. Reed, Chm., Dennis J. Halnon, Jeffrey Kayser, Eugene Longo, Jr., Patricia E. Pasqualucci; Alternates, Richard A. Bitzer, Martha N. Patchett, Bryan J. Woods.—**Zoning Enforcement Officer,** Karl Nilsen.—**Conservation Comm.,** Robert Judd, Chm., Edward A. Boratko, Irving Hart, Frederica Irish, Julia Pattison, Heather Robotham, vacancy; Alternates, two vacancies.—**Inland Wetlands Comm.,** Robert Ringuette, Chm., Gene Brunell, Barbara Dileo, Roger Hurlbut, Jon J. Starn, George Terwilliger, vacancy; Alternates, two vacancies.—**Municipal Historian,** Douglas E. Roberts.—**Agent for the Elderly,** Robert Judd.—**Dir. of Health,** Richard H. Matheny, Jr., M.P.H.—**Recreation Comm.,** Vivian Irwin, Chm., Pamela Brunell, Doreen Daneault, Marilyn Holcomb, three vacancies.—**Supt. of Highways,** Joseph Marek.—**Building Bd. of Appeals,** George Hazlehurst, Chm., Donald Antonucci, Paul Beauchene, John Greaser, Robert Lamson.—**Building Inspector,** Mark Melanson.—**Tree Warden,** Theodore Church.—**Chief of Police,** Michael D. Fox.—**Constables,** Brian L. Baldwin, Robert J. Baldwin, Gerald J. Bergman, Donald J. Breininger, Matthew Butwill, Michael J. Carl, Thomas F. Chappell, Thomas H. Goodwin, Jr., Mark R. Granquist, Paul H. Johnson, David G. Krom, Lennart S. Nicholson.—**Chief of Fire Dept.** (Barkhamsted East), William LeGeyt, Jr.; (Pleasant Valley), John Andryzeck; (Riverton), Michael VanNess.—**Fire Marshal,** Michael VanNess; Deputies, David Tripp, Richard Winn.—**Civil Preparedness Dir.,** Carl Nebelsky.—**Town Atty.,** Stephen Allaire.—**Justices of the Peace,** Helen M. Ahles, Franklin T. Batson, Clinton F. Billups, Edward A. Boratko, Bonnie W. Boyle, William A. Boyle, Pamela T. Brunell, Teresa T. Collins, Michael S. Day, Carol A. Grenier, Frank A. Herrick, James A. Hughes, Alvin R. Krassner, Cara S. Lattizori, Carmella M. Lattizori, Eugene Longo, Jr., Joan L. Markure, Frank R. McCormick, Willard C. Minton, David R. Moulton, George M. Murphy, Brian E. Noe, Thomas F. O'Brien, Martha N. Patchett, Raymond P. Pech, Betty R. Reed, Mary E. Ringuette, Samuel J. Rulli, Sr., Christopher M. Smith, Joyce K. Sperow, Donald S. Stein, Ann Sugdinis, Betty Ann A. Sweeney, Mark A. Telford, Carol A. Wallace, Maureen E. Wehner.

BEACON FALLS. New Haven County.—(Form of government, selectmen, town meeting, board of finance.)—Inc., June, 1871, taken from Bethany, Oxford, Seymour and Naugatuck. Area, 9.9 sq. miles. Population, est., 5,351. Voting district, 1. Principal industries, agriculture, warehouse storage and manufacture of plastic molding, and small hardware. Public Transp.: Metro North Commuter Railroad. Transp.—Freight: Served by Boston & Maine Corporation and numerous motor common carriers. Post office, Beacon Falls.

TOWN OFFICERS. Clerk and Reg. of Vital Statistics, Paula D. Balanda; Hours, 9 A.M.-12:30 P.M., 1-4:30 P.M., Mon. through Fri.; 7:30-9 P.M., Tues., Thurs.; Address, 10 Maple Ave., 06403; Tel., Naugatuck, (203) 729-8254.—**Asst. Clerk and Asst. Reg. of Vital Statistics,** Linda H. Beckwith.—**Selectmen,** 1st, Susan A. Cable (D) Tel., (203) 729-4340, Richard L. Rydzik (R), David R. Scott (U).—**Treas.,** Stanley J. Pokora.—**Bd. of Finance,** Thomas J. Trzaski, Chm., Robert F. Doiron, Peter V. Galla, Mary Anne Holloway, James P. Mooney, James W. Woodward, Jr.—**Tax Collector,** John C. Flach.—**Bd. of Assessment Appeals,** William S. Gillen, Chm., Walter J. Plankey, Thomas A. Pratt.—**Assessors,** Stanley H. Kersten, Chm., Anton W. Sirch, Robin S. Trzaski.—**Registrars of Voters,** Katherine G. Grace (D), Helen K. Mis (R).—**Supt. of Schools,** Helene Skrzyniarz.—**Planning and Zoning Comm.,** Gerard F. Smith, Chm., James T. Canning, Frank G. Crossley, Frank D'Angelo, Manuel R. Gandarillas, Mary E. Harvey, Arthur S. Koeller, Evelyn E. Sirowich, vacancy.—**Zoning Bd. of Appeals,** Christopher G. Betkoski, Chm., Richard P. Hebert, Jr., Edward S. Korzon, Vivian L. Molleur, Terry T. Stryjewski; Alternates, Helen A. Jurzynski, Nancy A. King, David W. Moran.—**Zoning Enforcement Officer,** A. Joseph Tarascio.—**Economic Development Comm.,** Anthony San Angelo, Chm., Roy Bachinsky, Edward S. Korzon, Joseph W. Norton, Raymond A. Shea, David F. Shugdinis, James W. Woodward, Jr.—**Inland Wetlands Comm.,** Donald J. Molleur, Chm., Mary E. Harvey, Stephen J. Knapik, Richard J. Minnick, Walter J. Opuszynski, Jr., Edward J. Smith, Jr., Dominick S. Sorrentino.—**Historical Comm.,** John D. Packer, Chm., Clementina M. Cardow, William Cardow, Edith M. Minnick, Dorothy B. Thurston.— **Municipal Historian,** Michael Krenesky.—**Comm. on Aging,** Gloria McGeever, Chm., Helene Colburn, Leonard Kvedas, Charlotte A. Magnuson, Dorothy Rotko; Katherine G. Grace, Social Services Clerk.—**Dir. of Health,** Leon J. O'Connor, M.P.H. (P.O., Shelton).—**Library Directors,** Susan M. Slater, Chm., Lisa A. Betkoski, Sheree J. Butcaris, Susan R. Levine, Wanda Mulinski, Lisa R. Willadsen.—**Parks and Recreation Comm.,** Arthur Daigle, Jr., Chm., Robert M. Bradley, Donna Cole, Daniel A. French, Sharon L. Haversat, Donald J. Molleur, Dominick S. Sorrentino, Bill Weed, Jr.—**Dir. of Public Works,** Frank DelVecchio.—**Town Engineer,** Robert Peck.— **Building Inspector,** John Peterson.—**Water Pollution Control Auth.,** Joseph Fitzpatrick, Chm., Raymond J. Belisle, Robert P. Bovienzo, Glenn A. Broadbent, Lars E. Edgren, David Rupsis.—**Waste Water Treatment Dir.,** Brian Fitzpatrick.—**Civil Preparedness, Dir.,** Jeremy C. Rodorigo.—**Chief of Police,** Susan A. Cable.—**Peace Officers,** Brian D. Blakeman, Edward V. Doll, Jr., Charles A. Dudac, Gregory J. Gallo, Joseph H. Kuntz, Leonard Rubbo, William T. Serrano.—**Chief of Fire Dept.,** William Lee.—**Fire Marshal,** Sean Lennon; Asst., Kenneth Ventresca.—**Town Atty.,** Laura M. Mooney (P.O., Naugatuck).—**Municipal Agent,** Dolores S. Gandarillas.—**Justices of the Peace,** William J. Abromaitis, Jr., Allan A. Banyacsky, John W. Betkoski III, Robert P. Bovienzo, Susan A. Cable, Peter A. Christensen, John M. Criscuolo, Leonard F. D'Amico, Frank P. D'Angelo, Mabel A. DelVecchio, Robert F. Doiron, Kenneth E. Egan, Jill A. Falbo, Katherine G. Grace, Leonard C. Greene, Robin M. Greene, Mildred M. Jurzynski, Gary M. Kamarowsky, Mary Ellen Kingsley, Michael Krenesky, William F. Mariano, Jr., Edmund A. Mis, Helen K. Mis, Joan M. Morris, Stanley J. Pokora, Raymond A. Shea, Brior Stack-Sweeney, Margaret F. Trzaski, Robin S. Trzaski, Chester J. Uszakiewicz.

BERLIN. Hartford County.—(Form of government, town manager, town council.)—Inc., May, 1785; taken from Farmington, Wethersfield and Middletown. Area, 27.0 sq. miles. Population, est., 16,792. Voting districts, 7. Principal industries, over 125 small to medium size manufacturers call Berlin home, producing everything from precision machine tools to paper cups; the corporate headquarters of Northeast Utilities is located here. Transp.—Passenger: Served by Amtrak, New Britain Transp. Co., and by Greyhound. Freight: Served by Conrail and numerous motor common carriers. Post offices, Berlin, East Berlin and Kensington.

TOWN OFFICERS. Clerk and Reg. of Vital Statistics, Joanne G. Ward; Hours, 8:30 A.M.-4:30 P.M., Mon. through Wed.; 8:30 A.M.-7 P.M., Thurs.; 8:30 A.M.-1 P.M., Fri.; Address, P.O. Box 1, Kensington 06037; Tel., (860) 828-7035; all other town offices, 240 Kensington Rd., Kensington 06037; Tel., New Britain, (860) 828-7000.—**Asst. Town Clerks,** Marsha Busnarda, Cheryl DeFurio, Roberta Lugli.—**Asst. Regs. of Vital Statistics,** Marsha Busnarda, Cheryl DeFurio, Roberta Lugli.—**Treas.,** Nancy J. Lockwood.—**Collector of Revenue,** Denise M. McNair.—**Bd. of Assessment Appeals,** William Diskin, Sally Murdoch, Raymond A. Ruta.—**Registrars of Voters,** John F. Miller (D), Elizabeth A. Tedeschi (R).—**Town Manager,** Bonnie L. Therrien.—**Town Council,** Ida M. Ragazzi, Mayor & Chm., Mary J. Agostini, Paul C. Argazzi, Frederick J. Jortner, John P. McIntosh, Eileen M. Meskill, Arthur B. Powers,, Bruce A. Trevethan, Thomas J. Veronesi.—**Supt. of Schools,** Richard J. Paskiewicz.—**Bd. of Education,** Pamela A. DonAroma, Kevin Porter, Gary McPhee, 1996; Darryl E. Johnson, Gale B. Kiade, vacancy, 1997; Robert A. Argazzi, Teresa M. Dorsey, Richard Zaccardo, 1998.—**Design Review Committee,** Joseph Strattner, Chm., Keith Bostrom, Marilyn Brierley, John Gemmell, Robert Johnson, Ingeborg Lukens; Anthony Dalfino, Agent.—**Planning and Zoning Comm.,** Bruce Moore, Chm., Joan Carey, Diane Jorsey, Kathryn Kearns, Kenneth Jovin, Robert Weiss, Timothy Zigmont; Alternates, Edward Egazarian, Martin Harwin, Robert Holmes.—**Public Building Comm.,** James Ouellette, Chm., Charles Bertagna, Arthur France, Robert Poglitsch, Peter Shackford, Jerome Skolnick, Earl H. Wicklund.—**Zoning Bd. of Appeals,** John J. Aguzzi, Jr., Audrey A. Bertagna, Robert Clark, Robert Facey, Jr., Edward W. Sampt; Alternates, Thomas A. Gerdis, Donald R. Guite, William Traverse, Jr.—**Economic Development Comm.,** Edward Egazarian, Donald P. Geschimsky, Dennis Phaneuf, Laurence J. Siembab, Ronald Stack, Thomas Stregowski, Scott D. Veley; Charles Karno, Dir.—**Housing Auth.,** Frank Stavola, Chm., Helen G. Bolles, Eugene T. Lubas, Gustav Pletz, Elizabeth Thureson.—**Conservation Comm.,** Richard Schmidt, Chm., Christina Berger, Michael Delorenzo, Catherine Jortner, Michele Spacek, William Welch; Alternates, Richard A. Glidden, Rachel A. Symonaitis.—**Inland Wetlands Comm.,** Robert Estabrook, Jr., Raymond Jarema, James McCarthy, Constance B. Marshall, Ralph Simeone, Charles Warner; Alternates, Michael Balinskas, Sherry R. Lang, Joseph Monzillo.—**Board of Ethics,** James L. McNair, Mark Russak, vacancy; Alternates, Vincent F. Biscoglio, Jr., Charles C. Davis.—**Historic Dist. Comm.,** Patricia Cheko, Raphael Collazo, Jr., Brian J. Hull, Karoll Wiater; Alternates, Norma Harss, Daniel Race, Lucy Traverse.—**Municipal Historian,** Ann W. Borthwick.—**Comm. for the Aging,** Lorraine Clark, Chm., Elizabeth Baldyga, Marilyn Meigs, Leo J. Melowicz, Hugh Penney, Mary Wilcox; Ellen Burbridge, Dir.—**Dir. of**

Social Services, Antoinette Pajor.—**Youth Services Advisory Bd.,** Lida Huggins, Chm., Sheila Cartelli, Nicholas Caveliere, Jon Demko, Gail Dwyer, Christopher J. Godfrey, Thomas Hodolitz, Monica Kaczor; Douglas Truitt, Coordinator.—**Dir. of Health,** Mary Ann Cherniak.—**Public Health Nursing Service,** David Cornwall, Pres., Mary Armetta, Barbara Brigandi, Larry Broisman, M.D., Roberta Chant, Pamela Lamore, John Matulis, Sherry Papandrea, John Roman, Stanley Sangeloty, Roberta Satalina, Carolyn Wysocki.—**Comr. for the Disabled,** Susan Buckley.—**Berlin-Peck Library Bd.,** David Borthwick, Chm., Michael J. Allen, Beatrice Desper, Donna Moore, Joseph Pandolfo, Sharon Powell, Rosalie Punkunas, Allison Turkowski, Carol Welz.—**Parks and Recreation Comm.,** William Baccaro, Chm., David W. Bush, Edward Giana, Philip Maule, Victor Salce, Sebastian Senia, Leonard Zielinski; Stephen Kelly, Dir.—**Dir. of Public Works/Town Engineer,** Morgan Seelye; Deputy, Joseph Paskiewicz.—**Supt. of Highways,** Brian Griswold.—**Town Planner,** Brian J. Miller.—**Building Inspector,** Nicholas Chirico.—**Building Code Bd. of Appeals,** Peter Fletcher, Patrick Kinney, Richard Yale, two vacancies.—**Water Control Comm.,** Pierre Bennerup, Chm., Bruce LaRoche, Penelope Pease, Frederick Sorbo III, Irving Warner; Alternates, Frank Horbal, Dolores Nye, Arvid Ritchie.—**Sanitarian,** Joseph Paskiewicz.—**Chief of Police,** Gerald Charamut.—**Police Comm.,** Thomas F. Heavren, Jr., Chm., Angelo Barcella, Robert E. Clark, Anthony Legnani, Richard A. Olson.—**Constables,** Michael Anderson, Frances Brautigam, Paul Eshoo, Joseph J. Farone, William Gelmini, Norman Johnson, Michael Nelson.—**Chief of Fire Dept.,** James Simons (Berlin), David Jorsey (East Berlin), Mark Lewandowski (Kensington), Ronald Lindgren (South Kensington).—**Fire Marshal,** Steven Waznia; Deputy, Edward J. Haber.—**Consumer Protection Advisor,** Robert A. Johnson.—**Bd. of Fire Comrs.,** Ronald Lindgren, Chm., Glen Fongemie, Clifford Gorneault, Chester Haber, Vincent Lewandowski, Norman Martinelli, Robert Zotter.—**Emergency Management Dir.,** Matthew Odishoo; Assts., Patrick Buckley, Brian Heavren.—**Corporation Counsel,** Stephen J. Anderson.—**Justices of the Peace,** John J. Aguzzi, Jr., Emil T. Albert, Michael Anderson, Elizabeth S. Baldyga, Angelo J. Barcella, Bernard H. Basiliere, Jr., Frances R. Brautigam, Arnold W. Carlson, Judith K. Church, Robert E. Clark, Ralph Cobuzzi, Loren E. Dickenson, Frank Dobeck, Jr., Barbara P. Edelson, Robert E. Facey, Jr., David E. Felth, John J. Gerdis, Thomas F. Heavren, Jr., Karen M. Horwedel, Norman K. Johnson, Lillian R. Klotz, Richard J. Kuziak, Anthony E. Legnani, Ronald Lindgren, Norman J. Martinelli, Marilyn N. Meigs, Robert F. Nieman, Robert J. Peters, Norma H. Ross, Peter A. Rosso, Victor M. Salce, Albert T. Scapellati, Joseph F. Scheyd, Albert Squillacote, Virginia W. Stelmack, Lois P. Szczepanik, Eugene. T. Sullivan, Jr., Theresa A. Tonina, Charles W. Warner, Robert A. Weiss, Mary S. Wilcox, Diane L. Wolf.

BETHANY. New Haven County.—(Form of government, selectmen, town meeting, board of finance.)—Inc., May, 1832; taken from Woodbridge. Area, 21.4 sq. miles. Population, est., 4,845. Voting district, 1. Principal light industry, agriculture; mostly a suburban residential town. Freight: Served by numerous motor common carriers. Mail is taken from Amity Station, New Haven, and delivered by rural free delivery. Bethany Community post office is operable with post office boxes and for normal purchasing and posting requirements. Express offices, Naugatuck and New Haven. Voted package store liquor permits, grocery store and restaurant beer permits, 1971. Also voted restaurant wine and beer permit on May 4, 1981.

TOWN OFFICERS. Clerk and Reg. of Vital Statistics, Joan C. Simpson; Hours, 9:30 A.M.-4:30 P.M., Mon. through Fri.; Address, Town Hall, 40 Peck Rd., 06524-3322; Tel., New Haven, (203) 393-0820; FAX, (203) 393-0821.—**Asst. Clerks and Asst. Regs. of Vital Statistics,** Nancy A. McCarthy, Hertha B. Russell.—**Selectmen,** 1st, John E. Ford III (R) Tel., (203) 393-2100, Craig A. Stahl (R), Michael P. Stearne (D).—**Treas.,** Nancy C. Grom.—**Bd. of Finance,** Russell D. von Beren, Jr., Chm., Frank A. Altieri, Benny DiCenzo, Marcel J. Lamy, Rose Tressel, Richard G. Van Horn.—**Tax Collector,** Leon Grabowski.—**Bd. of Assessment Appeals,** Joseph A. Geremia, Jr., Chm., Gary J. Ross, vacancy.—**Assessor,** Francis J. Barta; Clerk, Jean Rushworth.—**Registrars of Voters,** Marion Ash (D); Deputy, Derrylynn Gorski, (D); Linda Thiel (R); Deputy, Gail Q. Civitello, (R).—**Supt. of Schools,** Corinne S. Berglund.—**Bd. of Education,** Douglas A. Pfenninger, Chm., David Gewirtz, John E. Scanlon, Jr., 1997; David Berg, Janet Brinton, Joseph A. Geremia, Jr., 1999; Nancy F. Connito, Sandra A. McSherry, William E. Sim, 2001.—**Planning and Zoning Comm.,** Newton H. Borgerson, Jr., Chm., Bernard O. Bachenheimer, Sharon J. Huxley, Melissa Martincich-Spear, David I. Tressel; Alternates, Bonnie L. Amendola, Edward F. Czepiga, Jr., John B. Gardner.—**Zoning Bd. of Appeals,** Janice Jasiorkowski, Chm., Joseph R. Cenotti, Jerome M. Eisenstadt, Phyllis C. Epstein, Janet M. Finneran; Alternates, Walter G. Briggs, Louis B. Cohen, Raymond G. Martino.—**Zoning Enforcement Officer,** Peter Giovacchino; Asst., Robert H. Brinton.—**Economic Development Comm.,** John W. Caldwell, Chm., William F. Gorski, Joel M. Nesson, vacancy; Alternates, two vacancies.—**Conservation Comm.,** Audrey Eisenstadt, Mary Ann Lincoln, Kenneth W. Martin, Stephen W. Press, Susan Welch.—**Inland Wetlands Comm.,** Brian P. Blake, Malcolm Evans, Eric L. Stone, Co-Chm., Charles Famularo, Andrew Liveten; Alternates, Sandra Breslin, Robert H. Brinton, Jr.—**Municipal Historian,** Robert H. Brinton.—**Dir. of Human Resources,** Jeanne Del Vecchio.—**Dir. of Health,** Ronald Zlotoff, M.D.—**Parks and Recreation Comm.,** Ellen Meyers, John A. Paugus, June Riley, Marcia Royster-Clark.—**Bethany Animal Control Reps.,** Gary Ross, Craig A. Stahl.—**Regional Canine Officers,** Robert Roy, Sr., Fred Sills.—**Building Official,** Peter Giovacchino; Asst., John Miklos.—**Road Foreman,** Herbert G. Howard.—**Recycling and Solid Waste Committee,** Benny DiCenzo, Chm., Herbert Howard, Mary Ann Lincoln, Todd Ryker, Jeanne Sharon.—**Sanitarian,** Lester Warner.—**Tree Warden,** Raymond W. Pantalone, Jr.—**Chief of Police,** John E. Ford III.—**Constables,** Walter Briggs, Douglas Bushman, Herbert G. Howard, Cliff Rosson.—**Chief of Fire Dept.,** George H. Quinn, Jr.—**Fire Marshal/Civil Preparedness Dir.,** Herbert G. Howard.—**Jury Committee,** Marian N. Ash, Gail Q. Civitello, Marguerite Cody.—**Town Counsel,** John K. Knott (P.O., Cheshire).—**Justices of the Peace,** Lisa J. Anderson, Robert H. Brinton, Jr., William E. Gilbert, Nancy C. Grom, Clark D. Hurlburt, Steven A. Ledewitz, Paul K. Manger, June G. Riley, Doras P. Sarkady, Reva B. Schwartz, Pamela F. Stearne.

BETHEL. Fairfield County.—(Form of government, selectmen, town meeting, board of finance.)—Inc., May, 1855; taken from Danbury. Area, 16.9 sq. miles. Population, est., 17,921. Voting districts, 4. Principal industries, electronics, chemicals, and wire. Transp.—Passenger: Served by Metro North Commuter Railroad Co. and buses of the Candlewood Valley Bus Co. Freight: Served by Conrail and numerous motor common carriers. Post office, Bethel.

TOWN OFFICERS. Clerk and Reg. of Vital Statistics, Judith A. Novachek; Hours, 9 A.M.-5 P.M., Mon. through Fri., 9 A.M-7 P.M., Thurs.; Address, Town Hall, 1 School St., 06801-0003; Tel., Danbury, (203) 794-8505; FAX, (203) 794-8588.— **Asst. Clerks and Asst. Regs. of Vital Statistics,** Carole A. Ritch, Sheila C. Zelensky.—**Selectmen,** 1st, Charles A. Steck III (R) Tel., (203) 794-8501; FAX, (203) 794-8552, J. Philip Gallagher (D), John L. Thiele (R).—**Treas.,** Robert L. DiMatteo.—**Bd. of Finance,** Iri Luts, Chm., James A. Bryan, Donald Buonomo, Richard P. Kerivan, Richard E. Merritt, Matthew Paulsen, Martin W. Ryan.—**Tax Collector,** Regina Whitlock.—**Bd. of Assessment Appeals,** Mildred Thiele, Chm., John J. Mullaney, Jr., Paul B. Tripi.—**Assessor,** Kristina Maddocks.—**Registrars of Voters,** Mary O'Leary (D), Mary Legnard (R).—**Supt. of Schools,** Robert Gilchrest.—**Bd. of Education,** Fred DeNigris, Ann Marie P. Heering, Deborah Rizzo, Chris Trodahl, 1997; Francis S. Infurchia, Chm., Jeremiah M. D'Amura, Thomas D. Kearns, Robert Mancusi, Randy Rodgers, 1999.—**Planning and Zoning Comm.,** Denis Riordan, Chm., William G. Doling, Kitty Grant, Alice Hutchinson, Michael J. Mannion, J. Richard Shannon, Emily A. Yager; Alternates, Charles Down, Kevin J. Gallagher, Frederick R. Jones, Jr.— **Zoning Bd. of Appeals,** Treadwell Lewis, Chm., John R. Cleary, Frank A. Kovacs, Brendan P. McCollam, John R. Streaman; Alternates, Spruille Braden, Jr., Hugo Greco, Robert F. Pitt, Jr.—**Economic Development Comm.,** Charles M. McCollam, Jr., Chm., Jeremiah D'Amuria, Robert Haig, John Holbrook, William Luts, Frank Rotella, Joseph Vannucci.—**Insurance/Pension Comm.,** Charles Grant, Chm., Brian E. Andreoli, Steven Baklas, Michael Becher, Edward J. Tomasko.—**Purchasing Agent,** David Norvig.—**Housing Auth.,** William Cratty, Chm., Marilyn Caravetta, Dorothy Clarke, Elsie Del Monte, Francis Novachek; Jane Hall, Exec. Dir.—**Inland Wetlands Comm.,** Joyce Dixon, Chm., Donald Dempsey, Joan Gereg-Bradley, Heide Lock, Julie T. Sorcek; Alternates, Alfred Dennis, Salvatore A. Maniscalco.—**Committee on the Aging,** Joseph W. Tarrant, Jr., Chm., Muriel Connolly, Mary Morgan, Dorothy Owens, Kathryn Yannantuono.—**Acting Dir. of Social Services,** Eileen Clark.—**Dir. of Health,** Laura Vasile.—**Library Directors,** Constance Booth, Chm., Robert Antanaitis, F. Carl Berry, Gerald DeLeo, William Freeman, Eileen Goodrich, Julia A. Gallagher, Carol Lawlor, Tracy Parsons, Michael B. Quigley, Margaret Reynolds.—**Municipal Historian,** Patrick Wild.—**Parks and Recreation Comm.,** Dave Olson, Chm., Robert Heering, Elsie Kapteina, Patrick Morton, Charles Smith, Sue Westerberg, Harold Zuvich; Timothy Burke, Dir.—**Youth Comm.,** Richard Kerivan, William Oberacker, Patricia Rees, Monica Walters, Stacey Zimmerman.—**Public Utilities Comm.,** Donald Cheh, vacancy.—**Supt. of Highways,** Edward Flynn.—**Dir. of Public Works/ Town Engineer,** Hemraj Khona—**Supvr. of Public Works,** Clarence Rees.—**Tree Warden,** Rolf Brandt.—**Comptroller,** Barry Curina.—**Building Inspector,** Raymond Rubley.—**Building Code Bd. of Appeals,** Joseph Loya, Randall Noe.—**Permanent**

Building Committee, Richard Straiton, Chm., Donald Cote, Thomas Dixon, Geraldine Mills, David Norvig, Richard Schlemmer, Jeremiah Spillane; Alternates, John Rondano, Roger J. Walsh.—**Chief of Police,** John P. Basile.—**Police Comm.,** Susanne Bitterman, Robert J. Legnard, Tom Mason, Ronald White.—**Chief of Fire Dept.,** Edwin J. Read.—**Fire Marshal,** Peter Valenti.—**Civil Preparedness Dir.,** Clarence Rees.—**Town Atty.,** Daniel W. O'Grady.—**Justices of the Peace,** Steven Baklas, Floyd Banzhaf, Jane E. Bickford, Susanne Bitterman, Frederick F. Carpenter, Jr., Michael F. Clarke, Rose Ann Clarke, John R. Cleary, George J. Davis, Elsie Del Monte, Alfred J. Dennis, E. Joyce Dixon, Jean M. Dube-Brown, William I. Duff, Patricia M. Duff-Mancusi, Jeanne B. Feingold, J. Philip Gallagher, Stephen C. Gallagher, Nicholas J. Gazetos, Rose Gorman, Jane E. Hall, Anne Marie P. Heering, Clifford J. Hurgin, Alice M. Hutchinson, Frederick J. Jones, Jr., Donna R. Kiah, Richard H. Kolwicz, Anthony Landi, Carol J. Lawlor, Martin J. Lawlor, Jr., James R. Legnard, Robert J. Legnard, Carl Lemb, Treadwell M. Lewis, Scott T. Lindstrom, Sharen L. Lindstrom, Robert Mancusi, Geraldine L. Mannion, Katherine M. Mannion, Brendan P. McCollam, Charles M. McCollam, Jr., Mary G. McCollam, Carol McDowell, Richard E. Merritt, Edward J. Mills, Geraldine F. Mills, Lawrence J. Mills, Patrick C. Morton, John J. Mullaney, Jr., Jeffrey E. Muthersbaugh, Daniel W. O'Grady, George L. O'Keefe, Mary R. O'Leary, Thomas O'Leary, Jr., Forrest C. Palmer, John K. Parsons, Jr., Arthur L. Paulsen, Matthew A. Paulsen, Susan R. Paulsen, Robert F. Pitt, Jr., Patricia M. Rees, Margaret M. Reynolds, Wendy S. Reynolds, Martin W. Ryan, Thomas P. Ryan, Jane E. Shannon, William P. Shannon, E. O'Malley Smith, Roland D. Smith, Jerry F. Spillane, Claudia J. Stephan, Richard Straiton, John C. Streaman, John R. Streaman, John W. Szewczuk, Joseph Tarrant, Jr., Allen L. Tate, Paul B. Tripi, Christopher M. Trodahl, Jean Uzwiak, Peter J. Valenti, Dawn E. Whaley, Patrick T. Wild.

BETHLEHEM. Litchfield County.—(Form of government, selectmen, town meeting, board of finance.)—Inc., May, 1787; taken from Woodbury, and known as "North Purchase." Area, 19.7 sq. miles. Population, est., 3,324. Voting district, 1. Principal industries, agriculture and dairy products. Transp.—Freight: Served by numerous motor common carriers. Post office, Bethlehem. Rural delivery covers entire town. Express office, Waterbury or Woodbury.

TOWN OFFICERS. Clerk and Reg. of Vital Statistics, Lucy N. Palangio; Hours, 9 A.M.-12 Noon, Tues. through Sat.; Location, 36 Main St., South; Mailing Address, P.O. Box 160, 06751; Tel., Woodbury, (203) 266-7510.—**Asst. Clerk and Asst. Reg. of Vital Statistics,** Kathleen Gallo.—**Selectmen,** 1st, Robert F. Gallo (R) P.O. Box 160, Tel., (203) 266-7677, James V. Kacerguis (D), Eileen M. Mendyka (R).—**Treas.,** Michael J. Devine.—**Bd. of Finance,** Richard K. Russell, Jr., Chm., Leonard J. Assard, Leo S. Bulvanoski, Carl E. Meister, Harry J. Traver, Patricia J. Whelan.—**Tax Collector,** Edith M. Rupe.—**Bd. of Assessment Appeals,** Margaret Langlois, Chm., Edward A. Roden, Helen H. Woodard.—**Assessors,** Charles C. Parmelee, Chm., Carolyn B. Nadeau, Joseph D. O'Rourke.—**Registrars of Voters,** Majorie C. Bennett (D), Ellen R. Samoska (R).—**Supt. of Schools,** Joseph Sabatella.—**Planning Comm.,** Evelyn S. Paluskas, Chm., Matthew C. Cowles, Thomas M. Donegan, Jeffrey Hamel,

David P. Thompson; Alternates, Donna M. Dickinson, Paul J. Manning, Millicent M. Roden.—**Inland Wetlands Comm.,** Paul E. Reid, Chm., Ruth Avitabile, Margaret Langlois, Vincent G. Mirabilio, Richard D. Schempp, Robert L. Ueberbacher, Rand S. Wheeler; Alternates, Chris Butterfield, Peter J. Charest, William G. Sambrook.— **Historic Dist. Comm.,** Doris B. Nicholls, Chm., Walter Hunt, Richard Iller, Beverly B. Mosch, John P. Wildman; Alternates, Gary Grenfell, Robert Piazza, Douglas Sherman.—**Municipal Historian,** Evelyn S. Paluskas.—**Dir. of Social Services,** Robert F. Gallo.—**Library Directors,** Nancy Feola, Janet L. McDermott, Carolyn B. Nadeau, Pamela A. Nole, Jeanne A. Sargent, Walter M. Seiderer.—**Recreation Committee,** Robert DeJoseph, Mark DePietro, Judith A. Diemond, Kenneth M. Leclerc, Barbara A. Merriam, Carolyn B. Nadeau, Collette Poletta, Martin J. Rajcok, Melissa Russell, Donald Swendsen, Robert Waldron.—**Road Foreman,** James Kacerguis.—**Town Engineer,** Edward J. Sweeney.—**Building Code Bd. of Appeals,** Donald L. Banks, Anthony Bosko, Paul Molzon, James C. Selby, Douglas B. Sherman.—**Building Inspector,** Paul E. Woike.—**Lake Auth.,** James Brody, Lawrence J. Feola, Leland W. Krake III, Jean M. Loren, Frederick J. Mendyka, Peter T. Miller, Robert G. Stephen, Steven J. Sweeney, Jr.—**Chief of Police,** Robert F. Gallo.—**Constables,** Harold G. Austin, Joseph Orsini, Stephen Sorriero, Jr., John Twining, William Vienneau, Anthony L. Viola.—**Chief of Fire Dept.,** Thomas C. O'Neil.—**Fire Marshal,** John Rudzavice.— **Town Atty.,** David Losee.—**Justices of the Peace,** Victor J. Allan, Lance G. Beckley, Marjorie C. Bennett, Kenneth J. Curran, MaryAnn T. Eggert, Thomas B. Farrell, Valerie M. Hunt, Eileen O. Mendyka, Stephen J. Paluskas, David M. Rosa, Arnold E. Smith, John P. Wildman, John A. Zarrella.

BLOOMFIELD. Hartford County.—(Form of government, town manager, town council, town meeting.)—Inc., May, 1835; taken from Windsor. Area, 26.2 sq. miles. Population, est., 18,546. Voting districts, 6. Principal industries, insurance, aerospace products, specialized tools, electronics, gold and diamond products, diversified industries and agriculture. Transp.—Passenger: Served by buses of Conn. Transit from Hartford. Freight: Served by Boston & Maine Corporation and numerous motor common carriers. Post office, Bloomfield. Rural free delivery. Voted limited liquor permit, 1970, and additional liquor permits, 1981.

TOWN OFFICERS. Clerk and Reg. of Vital Statistics, Marguerite Phillips; Hours, 9 A.M.-5 P.M., Mon. through Fri.; Address, Town Hall, 800 Bloomfield Ave., P.O. Box 337, 06002; Tel., Hartford, (860) 769-3500.—**Deputy Clerk and Deputy Reg. of Vital Statistics,** Rita A. Rousseau.—**Asst. Clerk and Asst. Reg. of Vital Statistics,** Frances E. Wiggins.—**Town Manager,** Louie Chapman, Jr.—**Town Council,** Faith McMahon, Mayor (D); Richard A. Days, Alfred I. Dyce, Anne P. Fetzner, Joseph P. Merritt, Larry Pleasant, Carl Reisner, Sydney T. Schulman, Deputy Mayor, Michael S. Wagner.—**Selectmen,** Quree P. Carter, Allan DeLorenzo, Hyman Sloate, Donald N. Thatcher, vacancy.—**Dir. of Finance,** William T. Bailey.—**Treas.,** Althea Jenkins.—**Tax Collector,** Jean G. Kitchens.—**Bd. of Assessment Appeals,** Anita E. Delorenzo, Edwin E. Gittleman, Anthony J. Kapsis.—**Assessor,** Peter R. Marsele.— **Registrars of Voters,** Sandra J. Wilson (D), Angelita K. Tolly (R).—**Supt. of Schools,** Paul Copes.—**Bd. of Education,** Martin Bush, Wayne Hypolite, Robert W. Ike, Barbara G. Thornton, 1997; Robert H. Berman, Silas Shannon, Jr., Shirley W. Thompson, 1999.—**Town Plan and Zoning Comm.,** Jonathan C. Colman, Chm., Barry J. Berson, Daisy Chavez, Fannie R. Gabriel, Nicholas H. Panke, Shirley Y. Williams; Alternates, Philip Small, Daphne Thomas, Patricia H. Yorgensen.—**Dir. of Planning,** Thomas B. Hooper.—**Zoning Bd. of Appeals,** Jacqueline J. Isaacson, Chm., Woodrow Dixon, William Z. Goldstein, Joel J. Neuwirth, Joeannah H. Stinson; Alternates, Valeria Caldwell-Gaines, Robert Horn, Charles D. Strouse.—**Conservation, Energy and Environment Comm.,** Benjamin C. Berliner, Lee Comar, Alden Giddings, Alison Hunt, Mohammad S. Keshwarz, Nicholas Panke, William Peterson, Vikki Reski, Donald N. Thatcher, Paul Wilusz.—**Inland Wetlands and Water Courses Comm.,** Philip N. Small, Chm., Benjamin C. Berliner, Alan Budkofsky, Jonathan C. Colman, Donald Evans, Alden Giddings, Laurianetta Huguley, John Lobon, Nicholas Panke.—**Comm. on Aging,** Lucille Morisse, Chm., Barbara F. Bagnall, Philip Cohn, Patricia H. Fitt, Fannie R. Gabriel, Virginia Hallisey, John Lertora, Albert Martin, Grace Oettle, Paul Pelletier, Rose Schaefer, Ann Shapiro, Bette Tuttle.—**Agent for the Elderly,** Yvette Huyghue-Pannell.—**Human Relations Comm.,** Barbara Barber, Thomas McNeil, eleven vacancies.—**Dir. of Social Services,** Edythe Latney.—**Dir. of Health,** Steven J. Huleatt.—**Library Directors,** Nancy S. Kamins, Chm., Gloria T. Dowdell, Doris L. Jordan, I. Beatrice Llewellyn, Jean P. Martin, Betty L. Storrs.—**Parks and Recreation Committee,** Louis Blumenfeld, Michael Chambers, Norman Fenichel, Robert Green, Carlyle Hinds, Errol F. Hosein, Chester Jelks, Carolyn R. Jones, Sylvestus Martin, Else Spitzer, Helena Spoor, Daphne Thomas, David Patrick Triumph, A. Weaver, Jr., Aaron West, Paul Wilusz; Harold Barenz, Dir.—**Building Official,** William R. Boyens.—**Chief of Police,** Richard C. Mulhall; Capt., vacancy.—**Chiefs of Fire Dept.,** Daniel Canfield, Chief; William Riley, Asst.; Deputies, Roger Michalman, Roger Nelson (Center). Edmund A. Lescoe, Jr., Chief; vacancy; Deputy, Theodore Hansen, (Blue Hills).—**Fire Marshals,** Carl G. Booker, Sr., Roger Nelson; Deputy, John Birse (Center).—**Fire Comrs.,** John W. Leavitt, Jr., Chm., Raymond McMahon, Benjamin Snyder, Sr. (Center); Jimmy Davis, Chm., Alfred Allison, Barbara Bagnall (Blue Hills).—**Town Atty.,** Marc N. Needelman.—**Justices of the Peace,** David A. Baram, Sandra D. Belliveau, Eva M. Bennett, Cynthia S. Bercowetz, Edward J. Brooks, Seena Brown, Barbara S. Canfield, Susan A. Carlson, Edward R. Clark, Everett A. Clark, Lawrence J. Cohen, Naomi K. Cohen, William H. Coleman, Martha R. Collins, Annquenette S. Cotton, Margaret N. Cunnane, Jimmy Davis, Doris B. Davitt, Richard A. Days, Anita E. DeLorenzo, Ann DeMonte, Samuel DuBosar, Norman S. Fenichel, Anne P. Fetzner, Charles A. Forrest, Marjorie Fortner, Renee Fritz, Harvey L. Frydman, Howard S. Frydman, Ruth W. Fuller, Fannie R. Gabriel, Alden R. Giddings, Susan Giddings, Terrence P. Gilbert, Edwin A. Gittleman, William Z. Goldstein, Mellanee Harris, Angela R. Hauptman, Robert Horn, Robert W. Ike, Jeff Jacobs, Franklin D. Johnson, Thelma N. Johnson, Doris L. Jordan, John W. Leavitt, Alan Lebow, William E. Mahoney III, Mary C. Major, Faith McMahon, Joseph P. Merritt, Elizabeth A. Merrow, Brenda C. Milner, Na'eem Muhammad, Grace M. Nome, Theodore S. Norman, Nicholas H. Panke, Jeff Powell, Albert F. Reichin, Linda C. Reichin, Barbara L. Reisner, Carl Reisner, Burton B. Rosenfield, Sharon D. Sandler, Bernice C. Schaefer, Martin V. Serignese, Margaret V. Shaw, Hyman Sloate, Reginald S. Smith, Gershon J. Sosin, Joeannah H. Stinson, Charles D. Strouse, Marilyn S. Sumberg, Michael

C. Swan, Gerald I. Swilling, Joseph M. Tapper, Jane F. Thaller, Donald N. Thatcher, Daphne Thomas, Shirley W. Thompson, Angelita K. Tolly, David H. Tolly, Blanche L. Ward, Raymond H. Watkins, Jr., Robert L. Watkins, Yvonne L. Weaver-Bey, William Weissenburger, Jr., Alice J. Williams, Shirley Y. Williams, Gordon Willoughby, Jr., Linda M. Woike, Ronald H. Wolpoe, Evelyn Wurdig, Laura Yopp.

BOLTON. Tolland County.—(Form of government, selectmen, town meeting, board of finance.)—Inc., Oct., 1720. Area, 14.7 sq. miles. Population, est., 4,792. Voting districts, 2. Principal industry, agriculture, manufacture of printed circuits, commercial cleaning solvents, candy manufacturing, small machine shop. Transp.—Passenger: Served by buses of Arrow Line, Inc. from Hartford and Willimantic and by Conn. Transit. Freight: Served by numerous motor common carriers. Post office, Bolton.

TOWN OFFICERS. Clerk and Reg. of Vital Statistics, Susan M. DePold; Hours, 9 A.M.-4 P.M., Mon., Wed., Thurs.; 9 A.M.-5 P.M., 6-8 P.M., Tues; 9 A.M.-3 P.M., Fri.; Address, 222 Bolton Center Rd., 06043; Tel., Manchester, (860) 649-8066.—**Asst. Clerk and Asst. Reg. of Vital Statistics,** Nancy V. Soma.—**Selectmen,** 1st, Carl A. Preuss (R) Tel., (860) 643-7230, Stasi Morianos (D), Robert R. Morra (R), Robert W. Neil (R), Richard A. Pelletier (D); Joyce M. Stille, Admin. Officer.—**Treas.,** Catherine H. Peterson.—**Bd. of Finance,** James G. Roscoe, Chm., Susan B. Bosworth, Michael W. Eremita, Michael S. Hassett, Robert D. Lessard, Wiliam R. Pike, Cecily I. England.—**Tax Collector,** Lori Converse.—**Bd. of Assessment Appeals,** Virginia M. Wickersham, Chm., Arthur E. Mensing, Leslie K. Shea.—**Assessor,** Charles P. Danna, Jr.—**Registrars of Voters,** Monita Hebert (D), Priscilla M. Dooley (R).—**Supt. of Schools,** Dr. Mark Cohan.—**Bd. of Education,** James H. Marshall, Chm., William F. Blafkin, Dennis E. Esliger, 1997; Karen L. Bergin, Paul V. Edelen, Susan S. Hein, Ceila A. Robbins, 1999.—**Planning and Zoning Comm.,** Loren H. Otter, Chm., Kenneth L. Caya, Douglas T. Cheney, Carol S. Hewey, Eric M. Luntta, Don L. Palmer, Jr., Alan C. Wiedie; Alternates, Renato Cocconi, Marilyn Moonan, Jeffrey A. Scala, vacancy.—**Zoning Enforcement Officer,** Lincoln B. White.—**Zoning Bd. of Appeals,** John H. Roberts, Chm., John F. Audette, Joel E. Hoffman, Henry M. Kelsey, Jonathan M. Treat; Alternates, David G. Lynn, William R. Pike, Robert D. Rouleau.—**Conservation Comm.,** Rodney E. Parlee, Chm., Michael Kempf, Dorothy Reiss, Helen J. Wolfgram, vacancy; Alternate, Hope Grunske.—**Inland Wetlands Comm.,** Gwen E. Marrion, Chm., Louis N. Cloutier, Jr., David T. Pistritto, R. Barry Schempf, Wayne K. Shorey; Lincoln B. White, Agent; Alternate, James B. Bousfield.—**Economic Development Comm.,** Marian Z. Kelsey, Chm., Stephen G. Devereaux, Cecily I. England, Joshua Hawks-Ladds, Robert B. Hewey, Richard M. Jennings, Kathleen M. Johnson.—**Senior Citizens Committee,** Daniel J. Buckson, Chm., Theresa D. Cusano, Jane Maneggia, Patricia H. Morianos; Dorothy A. Whitehead, Agent for the Elderly.—**Senior Services,** Cheryl Schardt.—**Welfare Dir.,** Cheryl Schardt.—**Bd. of Health,** Ruth C. Mensing, Chm., Jane Devereaux, Dolores A. Mulcahy, Laura C. Toomey, three vacancies; C. Wendell Wickersham, M.D., Dir.; Serge Poulin, M.D., Asst. Dir.—**Municipal Historian,** George L. Larned.—**Library Trus-**

tees, Jennifer J. Geisler, Chm., Thomas A. Boyd, Jr., Elise M. Fiorentino, Anja Hoffman, Thomas A. Hoops, Karen S. Miller, Paul Stillman; Elizabeth Thornton, Dir.—**Recreation Comm.,** Raymond J. Boyd, Jr., Gwen D. Campbell, Betty Caruso, John P. Chiaputti, Bruce S. Davies, James Dayton, Dennis S. Esliger, Randall J. Potterton, Robert E. Yaps.—**Open Burning Officials,** Elna C. Dimock, Joyce Stille.—**Public Works Foreman,** Donato Rattazzi, Jr.—**Building Inspector/Sanitarian,** Lincoln B. White.—**Town Engineer/Planner,** Robert Grillo.—**Building Code Bd. of Appeals,** James R. Bousfield, Lawrence A. Converse III, Joseph P. Lorenzini, Thomas A. Manning, Alan C. Wiedie.—**Public Building Comm.,** Arthur E. Mensing, Chm., James R. Bousfield, Douglas T. Cheney, Leslie K. Shea, Jonathan F. Spooner; Alternates, Stephen G. Miller, William R. Pike.—**Chief of Police,** Carl A. Preuss.—**Constables,** William Edwards, Jr., Anthony Fasanelli, Rocco Fierravanti, Robert A. Highter, James J. Prior III, Paul M. Smith, Steven T. Schiavi, Alan R. Stosuy, Walter C. Waddell, two vacancies.—**Chief of Fire Dept.,** N. James Preuss.—**Fire Marshal,** Peter H. Massolini; Deputy, Michael W. Eremita.—**Bd. of Fire Comrs.,** Henry M. Kelsey, Chm., Ronald G. Dube, John P. Morianos, Wendy J. Scott, Raymond P. Soma.—**Civil Preparedness Dir.,** Corey Violette.—**Town Atty.,** Richard L. Barger.—**Justices of the Peace,** Karen L. Bergin, Douglas T. Cheney, Rachel L. Evans, Mark Johnson, Marian Z. Kelsey, Donna M. Kinney, Patricia H. Morianos, Robert R. Morra, Don L. Palmer, Jr., Richard A. Pelletier, Robert W. Peterson, Pamela Z. Sawyer, Leslie K. Shea, Norma P. Tedford, Robert C. Vaughn, Helen J. Wolfgram.

BOZRAH. New London County.—(Form of government, selectmen, town meeting, board of finance.)—Inc., May, 1786; taken from Norwich. Area, 20.2 sq. miles. Population, est., 2,309. Voting district, 1. Principal industries, agriculture, cement mixing, manufacturing of plastics, sporting equipment, insulation, small tools, padding goods, Air Separation plant. Transp.—Freight: Served by numerous motor common carriers. Post offices, Bozrah and Gilman.

TOWN OFFICERS. Clerk and Reg. of Vital Statistics, Donna J. Long; Hours, 9 A.M.-4 P.M., Tues., Wed., Thurs.; 9 A.M.-12 Noon, Sat., and by appointment; Address, Town Hall, 1 River Rd., 06334; Tel., Norwich, (860) 889-2689.—**Selectmen,** 1st, Raymond C. Barber (D) P.O. 158, Bozrah; Tel., (860) 889-2680, 2689, Linda A. Adelman (D), Keith Robbins (R).—**Treas.,** Evelyn M. Casavant.—**Bd. of Finance,** William E. Ballinger III, Charles Connell, Ray Dows, Dennis E. Main, Michael J. O'Connor, Dale B. Speerli.—**Tax Collector,** Donna J. Long.—**Bd. of Assessment Appeals,** Douglas R. Barber, Henry A. Granger, Barbara A. Speerli.—**Assessors,** John E. Graham, Chm., William M. Fishbone, Marguerite B. Smith.—**Registrars of Voters,** Marilynn Sullivan (D), Adele Fishbone (R).—**Supt. of Schools,** David Easterly.—**Bd. of Education,** Robert A. Kofkoff, Donald E. LaPre, Jane K. Seder, Thomas Weber, 1997; Charles Frey, Chm., Amy McAdoo-Mattingly, Sheilagh Morgan, 1999.—**Planning and Zoning Comm.,** Seymour Adelman, Chm., Ralph G. Fargo, John S. Gural, Stephen Seder, Doris Wilyer; Alternates, M. Earl Lathrop, Terrence K. Smith, Nancy Taylor.—**Zoning Bd. of Appeals,** Arnold S. Kaplan, Chm., Ernest V. Jensen, Robert A. Kofkoff, Maria Lindo-Diskin, Thomas Ververis; Alternates, Scott S. Barber, Henry A. Granger, vacancy.—**Conservation and Inland Wetlands Comm.,** William Fishbone, Arthur Goulart, Jr., Gary LaLima, Howard McGarvey, Jonathan Records, John Sullivan, Donna Tardiff.—**Municipal Historian,** John Orr, Jr.—**Agent for the Elderly,** Jane Seder.—**Dir. of Health,** Michael G. Betten, M.D. (P.O. 158, Bozrah).—**Parks and Recreation Comm.,** Charles L. Long, Chm.; Joseph F. Angelico, Mark Easter, Nancy R. Morgan, Henry Rianhard, John P. Sullivan, Marilynn Sullivan.—**Building Inspector,** David Atkinson.—**Sanitarian,** Steven L. Brunetti.—**Tree Warden/Open Burning Official,** Raymond C. Barber.—**Lake Auth.,** Henry Granger, Jr., Donald LaPre, John Wilyer.—**Chief of Police/Civil Preparedness Dir.,** Raymond C. Barber.—**Constables,** Jonathan C. Gilman, Ralph G. Fargo, Henry A. Granger, Antone Goulart III, John E. Graham, Fred K. Potter, Stephen F. Seder.—**Chief of Fire Dept.,** Thomas Main; Deputy, Michael Smith.—**Town Atty.,** Kevin Conway (P.O., Mystic).—**Justices of the Peace,** Douglas R. Barber, Katherine N. Booth, Maria L. Chiangi, Timothy T. Coleman, William M. Fishbone, Jonathan C. Gilman, Timothy Gilman, Claire R. Granger, Stanley A. Mokrzewski, Bradley W. Ruth, Warren A. Strong, John M. Wilyer.

BRANFORD. New Haven County.—(Form of government, representative town meeting, selectmen, board of finance.)—Named, 1653. Area, 28.0 sq. miles. Population, est., 28,043. Voting districts, 5. Principal industries, wire, electronics and ignition parts. Transp.—Passenger: Served by buses of Conn. Transit from New Haven and Clinton. Freight: Served by Conrail and numerous motor common carriers. Post offices, Branford, Short Beach and Stony Creek.

TOWN OFFICERS. Clerk and Reg. of Vital Statistics, Georgette A. Laske; Hours, 9 A.M.-4:30 P.M., Mon. through Fri.; 4:30-6:30 P.M., first and third Thurs. of the month; Address, Town Hall, 1019 Main St., P.O. Box 150, 06405; Tel., (203) 488-6305.—**Asst. Clerks and Asst. Regs. of Vital Statistics,** Nancy N. Brierley, Marian C. Tansey, Jessica Weller, Melinda C. Yester.—**Representative Town Meeting,** Adrienne M. Ahern, Nancy M. Barbieri, Mark D. Barnes, Peter A. Berdon, Beth D. Bryan, Jonathan D. Clark, Kim A. Conlin, Robert B. Denhardt, Jr., Janet M. Dermer, Ann C. Devlin, Robert J. Dingus, William R. Donaruma, Brian C. Festa, Dennis T. Flanigan, Dominic Giordano, Richard T. Goodwin, Richard K. Greenalch, Jr., Stephen P. Hanchuruck, Michael B. Kinney, Frank P. Malinconico, Judith Myjak, Jodi L. Paviglionite, Albert Petrosino, Joseph Pinski, Tim Raynor, Paul V. Riccio, Jr., Kurt M. Schwanfelder, John A. Smith, Victor J. Tohak, Jr., Frank B. Twohill, Jr.—**Selectmen,** 1st, Dominic A. Buonocore (R) Tel., (203) 488-8394, FAX, (203) 481-5561, Warren F. Collins (D/T), Jo-anne W. McGuigan (R).—**Treas.,** Edward J. Maloney, Jr.; Asst., Doran M. Podoloff.—**Bd. of Finance,** Donald Jackson, Chm., Robert T. Bouley, Michael F. Giordano, Joseph W. Mooney, Charles F. Shelton, Jr., Lorraine K. Young; Richard A. Belden, Dir.—**Tax Collector,** Janet A. Kaminsky.—**Bd. of Assessment Appeals,** Connie Cestari, Joseph D. Chandler, Alfred T. Harrington.—**Assessors,** James Janz, Chm., Michael Cerrito, Mark A. Del Rocco.—**Registrars of Voters,** Lucille M. Pascarella (D), Marion E. Burkard (R).—**Supt. of Schools,** Dr. Bruce E. Storm.—**Bd. of Education,** Maria Diamantis, Edward Struzinsky, 1997; Frank J. Kinney III, James J. Mendillo, Randina A. Prete, 1999; Anthony Uzzo, Chm., Marilyn J. Brown, Robert S. Dargan III, Arthur H. Lombard, 2001.—**Planning and Zoning**

Comm., Ellsworth McGuigan, Chm., Joan Berdick, Philip Fischer, Michael Laudano, Joseph Vaiuso; Alternates, R. Charles Andres, Stephen Duhamel, Stephen Laden.—**Zoning Bd. of Appeals,** David Jacobs, Chm., Joshua Brown, Raymond Ferguson, Lawrence Fisher, Robert Harrington, Walter Kreske; Alternates, Steven Errante, Scott Schrimp, vacancy.—**Zoning Enforcement Officer,** Justine K. Gillen.—**Economic Development Comm.,** Frank Zemina, Chm., Cornelius Crowley, Jr., Robert Dow, Kenneth Graham, Edward Johnson, Jr., Rhoda Loeb, Roberta McColl, John Moss, William T. O'Brien, Jr.—**Housing Auth.,** Edan Calabrese, Chm., John Caruso, Douglas Denes, Anna Herr, Richard Ryan.—**Conservation/Environmental Comm.,** Chester Bloomquist, Chm., Robert Davis, Arthur Howe, Elmer Kropp, Christine Macchia, William Reed, Lisa Santacroce, Eleanor Saulys, Pamela Schreiber, Harriet Seligson, vacancy.—**Inland Wetlands Comm.,** Daniel Shapiro, Chm., Florence Bennett, Joan Berdick, Peter H. Borgemeister, James Perito, Truman Sherk, Robert Valley; Alternates, Helen W. Mulvey, two vacancies.—**Flood and Erosion Control Bd.,** Peter Banca, Chm., Charles Bohn, Richard Coyle, John Lipkvich, Herbert Ross.—**Water Comm.,** Barbara Brennan, Acting Chm., Salvatore Consiglio, Robert Criscuolo, Frank Palumbo, Louis Vitelli.—**Branford Solid Waste Management Comm.,** Anthony Giardiello, Chm., Richard Bauerfeld, Vladimir Cherni, Stuart Fitts, Carlene Kulisch, Mary Jo Riddle, Alain St. Thomas; Margaret Hall, Solid Waste Mgr.—**Comm. on Services for Elderly,** Diane Anderson, Phyllis Batrow, Nancy Borgmeister, Jacqueline Cohen, Ann Freeman, Ann Laird, Luba P. Mebert, Alex Murphy, Blossom Rose; Matthew Brady, Dir.; Dagmar B. Ridgway, Asst. Dir.—**Welfare Supvr.,** Veronica Wright.—**Dir. of Health,** Dennis Johnson, R.S., M.P.H.—**Bd. of Public Health,** Anna Schilder, Chm., Frank Dumark, Arlene Granata, George Guertin, Robert Jacobs, Dennis Nastri, Jessica Parlato, Lois Shine.—**Library Directors,** Willoughby Wallace Library: Chester Cooke, Chm., Josephine Buchanan, Kendall Lewis, Diane McGuire, Ellen D. Page, Margaret Thoms, Bill Tower; Susan Donovan, Library Dir. Blackstone Memorial: Joan Berdick, Pres., Robert Conroy, John Moughty, Craig Newton, Jr., David Reif, Susan Spear; Marlene Palmquist, Library Dir.—**Municipal Historian,** Jane P. Bouley.—**Recreation Bd.,** Scott Temple, Chm., William Aniskovich, Sr., Vincent Cassella, Carol Meglio, William T. O'Brien, Jr.—**Dir. of Parks and Recreation,** Alex Palluzzi.—**Dir. of Public Works,** Edward Masotta.—**Town Engineer,** Stephen Dudley.—**Purchasing Agent,** Nancy Porto.—**Building Inspector,** Perry Smart.—**Sewer Auth.,** Doran Podoloff, Chm., Peter Brainard, Eric Larson, Jr., Richard Matz, vacancy.—**Shell Fish Comm.,** Regis Vetrano, Chm., Michael Infantino, Jr., Edwin Kelsey III.—**Tree Warden,** vacancy.—**Supt. of Sanitation,** Peter Stallings.—**Chief of Police,** William Holohan; Deputy, Robert Gill.—**Police Comm.,** Neil Velleca, Chm., Carol Bryan, Jon Grossman, John Mooney, Ernest Peterson, James Ryan.—**Constables,** Donald M. Austin, Sr., Edward A. Cooke, Daniel P. Kinney, George D. Lepre, Joyce N. Tipping, Harold E. Wilkinson III, Robert Zettergren.—**Chief of Fire Dept./ Fire Marshal,** Peter Buonome; Asst. Chief, Robert Massey, Sr.; Deputies, Peter P. DaRos, Edwin Kelsey, Robert Massey, Jr.—**Bd. of Fire Comrs.,** Anthony DaRos, Chm., Madeline Clem, Ernest Collins, Mark Gilyard, Kenneth Kaminsky, Charles Marsh.—**Civil Preparedness Chief,** Peter Mullen.—**Town Atty.,** Alphonse Ippolito.—**Justices of the Peace,** Lucy A. Bello, Eileen Cavanaugh, Doris Freund, Nancy G. Gaylord, Robert D. Gott, Arthur J. Howe, Kristin L. Johnson, Rhoda Loeb, Ann B.

Lynch, Rose V. Rabovsky, Edward L. Reynolds, Bonnie Samson, Jessica Weller, Catherine K. Xeller.

BRIDGEPORT. Fairfield County.—(Form of government, mayor, city council.)—Town inc., May, 1821; taken from Stratford and Fairfield; city inc., May, 1836; town and city consolidated, 1836. Area, 19.4 sq. miles. Population, est., 136,817. Voting districts, city elections, 23; state elections, 32. Principal industries, manufacture of electric apparatus and appliances, steam specialties and industrial instruments, machine tools and accessories, plastic, wiring devices, aluminum and zinc castings. Transp.—Passenger: Served by Amtrak and Metro-North Commuter R. R. Co., steam boat from Port Jefferson, LI and buses of Arrow Lines, Vermont Transit, Human Services Transportation Consortium (HSTC), Metro Pool, Inc., Conn. Limousine, Conn. American (Charter), Greyhound and Trailways; locally by Bonanza Bus Lines, Inc., People Mover of the Bpt. Transit District and Chieppo Bus Co. (Charter). Freight: Served by Conrail, ferryboat from Port Jefferson, LI and numerous motor common carriers. Also located here is a Municipal Airport. Post office, Bridgeport.

CITY AND TOWN OFFICERS. Town Clerk, Hector Diaz; Hours, 9 A.M.-4:30 P.M., Mon. through Fri. Address, City Hall, Rm. 124, 45 Lyon Ter., 06604; Tel., (203) 576-7207.—**Asst. Town Clerks,** Alba L. Rodriguez, Ann Marie Thibodeau.—**Reg. of Vital Statistics,** vacancy; Address, 202 State St., Rm. 105, 06604; Tel., (203) 576-7445.—**Asst. Reg. of Vital Statistics,** Patricia McCoy.—**City Clerk,** Fleeta C. Hudson; Hours, 9 A.M.-4:30 P.M., Mon., Wed., Fri., 9 A.M.-1 P.M., Tues.; Address, City Hall, Rm. 204, 45 Lyon Ter., 06604; Tel., (203) 576-7081.—**Asst. City Clerk,** Candace A. Palmer-Pelton.—**Mayor,** Joseph P. Ganim (D).—**City Council Pres.,** Lisa Parziale.—**Council Members,** 130th Dist., Patrick C. Crossin, Auden C. Grogins; 131st Dist., Joel Gonzalez, Alberto Negron; 132nd Dist., Lisa Parziale, Robert S. Walsh; 133rd Dist., John M. Brannelly, Jr., Audrey F. Martinsky; 134th Dist., Josephine M. Covino, John M. Fabrizi; 135th Dist., Sybil O. Allen, Alan Stein; 136th Dist., William A. Finch, James P. McGinnis; 137th Dist., Alberto J. Ayala, Lydia Martinez; 138th Dist., J. Edward Green, Michael J. Marella, Jr.; 139th Dist., Shirley Bean, James Holloway.—**Chief Adm. Officer,** Dennis C. Murphy.—**Chief Financial Officer,** Jerome Baron.—**Treas.,** Sharon Lemdon.—**Chief of Staff,** Patrick Coyne.—**Dir. of Labor Relations,** Marie D. Dukes.—**Comptroller,** vacancy.—**Tax Collector,** Robert G. Tetreaut.—**Assessor,** Pamela K. Davis.—**Registrars of Voters,** Lucille E. Bruno (D), Frances L. Bociek (R).—**Supt. of Schools,** James A. Connelly.—**Bd. of Education,** Michael C. Bisciglia, James W. Horne, Jr., Nancy Hornyak, Max Medina, Jr., Joan K. Nobriga, 1997; Lydia Falcon, Inacia Geter, Susie R. Laffitte, Michael A. Lanese, 1999.—**Personnel Dir.,** John Colligan.—**Civil Service Comm.,** John M. Fabrizi, Pres., Ralph Ford, Leanor Guedes, Joseph Ianniello, Carmen Marcano.—**City Planner,** Michael P. Nidoh.—**Planning and Zoning Comm.,** Joann Collins, Barbara Freddino, John Ehnot, Dorothy Guman, Gene Memoli, Lucille Sullivan, Marie Tedesco, Clarence Williams, vacancy; Alternates, Mary T. DeStefano, Eldridge Dorsey, Sheila Lungi.—**Zoning Enforcement Officers,** Dennis Buckley, William Shaw.—**Zoning Bd. of Appeals,** Richard Bepko, Chm., Anthony J. Lancia, Sr., Cruzmilda Maldonado-Stodolski, Ernest Seabrook, vacancy; Alternates, Linda Grace, Stanley Kisiel, vacancy.—**Economic, Industrial and Development Comm.,** John F. O'Connell, Chm., Roy O'Neil, Pres., Philip H. Burdett, Ph.D., James Carbone, David E. Carson, Robert Conklin, David D'Addario, Bruce Dillingham, Peter Donovan, E. Terry Durant, Venoal Fountain, Richard S. Freeman, Richard Grossi, Don Heyward, Richard Hoyt, Ralph Kelly, Sam D. Koutas, Philip J. Kuchma, Michael Leone, Ralph LoStocco, Anthony Macleod, Joseph Maloney, Jack McGregor, John Phelan, E. Cortright Phillips, John C. Stawarky, Jr., Robert G. Tetreault, Paul S. Timpanelli, James F. Tomchik; Mayor Joseph P. Ganim, Philip Trager, Counsel.—**Redevelopment and Housing Site Development Agency,** Kevin Agee, John Kleps, Samuel Liskov, Joan Magnusen, Dennis O'Malley.—**Housing Auth.,** Leona Belcher, Jeri Boyd, Carlos M. Garcia, Wayne Hashack, Roberto Rodriguez; Clarence Craig, Exec. Dir.—**Historic Dist. Comm.,** Anne Brignolo-Hourcle, Guy Horvath, Charles Jones, Duane Wetmore; Alternates, Stuart Sachs, two vacancies.—**Municipal Historian,** Charles W. Brilvitch.—**Senior Citizens Comm.,** Tillie Bograd, Helen Carroll, Joseph Celantano, Frances Cidorwich, Marjorie Hamilton, Michael Lanese, Julia Vargara, Frank Welcome.—**Welfare Dir.,** Iris Molina.—**Dir. of Public Health,** Roslyn Hamilton.—**Library Bd. of Directors,** John Arcudi, Pres., John J. Driscoll, Harry L. Green, William Holden, Helen Liskov, James E. O'Donnell, John G. Phelan, Roberto Rodriguez, Sheryl J. Rosander; Nancy Johmann, City Librarian.—**Comm. for People with Disabilities,** Edith Ahronson, Lorene Castle, James Catalanetto, Porter Cleveland, Douglas Dupee, David Goldstein, Evelyn Kennedy, Cynthia Knapp, Iris Ramos, Jimmy Smith, Helen Thomas, Joseph Vincenzi.—**Park Comm.,** Cruz Rosa, Pres., Joe D'Amicol, Melissa Dancy, Ernest Garcia, Timothy Holleran, Earl King, James Lesko, William Stewart.—**Dir. of Public Facilities,** John Marsilio.—**City Engineer,** Barry Skinner.—**Purchasing Agent,** William Czerwinski, Jr.—**Sealer of Weights and Measures,** Anthony Innacell.—**Municipal Building Official,** Peter J. Paajanen; Building Insp., Thomas Duda.—**Acting Dir. of Environmental Health/Sanitarian,** vacancy.—**Admr. of Human Resources Development,** Vernon Thompson.—**Chief of Police,** Thomas J. Sweeney.—**Police Comm.,** Rachel Berarducci, Kevin Boyle, Carolyn Jackson, Raymond Larracuente, Al Losada, Robert Morton.—**Sheriffs,** Antonio D. Diaz, Lee V. Grisby, Michael L. Moretti, Domingo L. Robles, Dennis Scinto, Cecil Young.—**Acting Chief of Fire Dept.,** David Schiller.—**Fire Marshals,** Joseph Micalizzi, Angelo Noccioli.—**Bd. of Fire Comrs.,** J. Edward Caldwell, Pres., George Arias, Charles Feroleto, Jonas Meyer, Kenneth Moales, Wendell Randolph, Stuart Rosenberg.—**Civil Preparedness Dir.,** Scott Appleby.—**City Atty.,** Mark J. Anastasi; Deputy, John D. Guman.—**Justices of the Peace,** Michelina Accettullo, Rose Adao, Vidal Agosto, Pauline H. Alexay, William A. Allen, Alberto J. Ayala, Manuel Ayala, Paul T. Barnum, Therese M. Basso, Lucille Bish, Raymond E. Blank, Warren Blunt, Rudolph Bociek, Tillie Bograd, Joseph J. Borges, Jr., Joyce L. Boston, Julian Braxton, Wendy J. Bridgeforth, Lucille E. Bruno, Thomas V. Caco, Sara F. Carson, Christopher L. Caruso, Fedela Cidorowich, George H. Comer, Augustine S. Corica, Rosa J. Correa, Hector Diaz, Gelsmina Disora, Robert Dortenzio, Willie A. Dyer, Nancy E. Eads, Anne Ehnot, Walter J. Faherty, Melva Falberg, Joanne G. Feher, Luz Flores, Michael D. Freddino, Jr., Joseph P. Ganim, Paul J. Ganim, Thomas G. Ganim, Anna L. Garcia, Joseph J. Garmella, Bill Gouveia, Linda A. Grace, Edward J. Green, Joseph S. Hatrick, Sr., Peter J. Holecz, James Holloway, Michael J. Horvath, Joseph W. Ianniello, Jr., Frank C. Iossa, Linda P. Kentosh, Joan

Killelea-Nobriga, Michael A. Lanese, Clifford S. LaRose, Richard H. Lee, Bobby D. Lindsay, Samuel Liskov, Joan K. Magnuson, Michael J. Marella, Jr., Lydia Martinez, Willie Matos, Ethel L. Matthews, Alma L. Maya, John F. McCarthy, Jr., Joseph Mendro, Joseph W. Messineo, Anthony J. Minutolo, Joseph Minutolo, Karen A. Morton, Ernest L. Nichols, Eugene R. O'Neill, Diane H. Osborne, Marie A. Pastor, Lillian J. Phillip, Richard P. Porto, Amy Powell, Edward Radzvilla, Nina Ramos, Jose A. Rivera, Jr., Daniel S. Roach, Bonita M. Robinson, Domingo L. Robles, Xiomara Rodriguez, Linda A. Sanzo, Dennis C. Schilli, Rafael Segarra, Annette Segarra-Negron, George J. Sigona, Philip L. Smith, Willie J. Smith, John A. Soares, Linda Spearman, Audrey J. Stabler, Robert F. Thornton, Irene Valentino, Enrique Vasquez.

BRIDGEWATER. Litchfield County.—(Form of government, selectmen, town meeting, board of finance.)—Inc., May, 1856; taken from New Milford. Area, 17.3 sq. miles. Population, est., 1,724. Voting district, 1. Principal industry, agriculture. Transp.—Freight: Served by numerous motor common carriers. Post office, Bridgewater. Voted No Liquor Permit, 1935.

TOWN OFFICERS. Clerk and Reg. of Vital Statistics, Cheryl L. Pinkos; Hours, 8 A.M.-12 Noon, Mon., Wed., Fri.; 8 A.M.-5 P.M., Tues.; Address, Town Hall, Main St., 06752; Tel., office, New Milford, (860) 354-5102.—**Asst. Clerks and Asst. Regs. of Vital Statistics,** Karen Eddy, Ann C. Harvey, Mary C. Semenetz.—**Selectmen,** 1st, William T. Stuart (D) Tel., (860) 354-5250, Neil A. Cable (D), Charles R. Hagstrom (R).—**Treas.,** Amy D. Allingham.—**Bd. of Finance,** Richard L. Falwell, Chm., George D. Allingham, Joseph C. Hogan, Pierre P. Lachance, Donald Shail, Molly Stratton.—**Tax Collector,** Wendy E. Jones.—**Bd. of Assessment Appeals,** Virginia M. Herron, James R. Mulvey, Harold Rannestad.—**Assessors,** Ann C. Harvey, Chm., Elizabeth M. Nelson, Maureen Warner.—**Registrars of Voters,** Helen L. Worden (D), Mary H. Roberts (R).—**Supt. of Schools,** Robert Nicoletti.—**Planning and Zoning Comm.,** Thomas E. Gilmore, Chm., Robert A. Hacker, Felicia S. Hoeniger, Laszlo L. Pinter, vacancy; Alternates, Peter Blicher, Jr., Timothy J. Egan, Leo P. Null.—**Zoning Bd. of Appeals,** Lois S. Carreira, Chm., Mary J. Allen, Edward R. Bennett, James B. Coffey, Frances J. Lachance; Alternates, Arthur Foote, Margaret Khare, Arthur J. Murphy.—**Conservation and Inland Wetlands Comm.,** Curtis Read, Chm., William Douma, Sharon Y. Gawe, Alex McNaughton, Victor Nelson, Strother Purdy, Robert Stuart; Alternates, Michael Chelminski, vacancy.—**Municipal Historian,** Dorothy A. Gustafson.—**Agent for the Elderly,** David Ledbetter.—**Dir. of Health,** Josef J. Burton, M.D.—**Recreation Comm.,** Michael Cioppa, Chm., Mary J. Allen, David Harvey, Lillian Murphy, Richard Ryerson, Daniel Storrs, Julianne Stuart.—**Supt. of Highways,** William T. Stuart.—**Tree Warden,** Bernard T. Wright, Jr.—**Building Inspector,** Thomas O'Loskey.—**Building Code Bd. of Appeals,** John P. Roma.—**Resident State Trooper,** TFC Daniel J. Semosky.—**Chief of Police,** William T. Stuart.—**Constables,** Glenn Knapp, Michael Lasagna, two vacancies.—**Chief of Fire Dept.,** James R. Sullivan.—**Acting Fire Marshal,** Wayne Gravius; Deputy, Charles Smith.—**Civil Preparedness Dir.,** Rolland D. Harvey.—**Town Atty.,** Fred Baker (P.O., Danbury).—**Justices of the Peace,** Robert S. Brown, Neil A. Cable, Hila C. Colman, Joseph S. Giordano, Robert T. Gumpper, Shirley G. Gumpper, Jennifer A. Hacker, Robert A.

Hacker, Charles R. Hagstrom, Elizabeth M. Nelson, Mary H. Roberts, William T. Stuart, Margaret J. Sullivan, Marie R. Synnestvedt, Maureen Warner, Marie R. White.

BRISTOL. Hartford County.—(Form of government, mayor, city council.)—Town inc., May, 1785; taken from Farmington. Town and city co-extensive, 1911. Area, 26.8 sq. miles. Population, est., 59,658. Voting districts, 10. Principal industries, springs, timing devices, brass products, screw machine products, cutting and creasing rules, synchronous electric motors, variable transformers, automatic voltage regulators, electric connectors; brass, bronze and copper sheet, rod and wire; brass and aluminum forgings, wire forms, paper punches, various metal products to specifications, machine tools, metal stamping, counting devices; automobile parts, jewelry, etc. Transp.—Passenger: Served locally by New Britain Transportation Co. Buses with commuter routes by Conn. Transit and Bonanza Bus Lines, Inc. from Hartford and Waterbury and from New York City via Danbury, by Greyhound. Freight: Served by Boston & Maine Corporation and numerous motor common carriers. Post office, Bristol, with classified station at Forestville. Three rural delivery routes.

CITY AND TOWN OFFICERS. City Clerk, Town Clerk and Reg. of Vital Statistics, Florence McAuliffe; Hours, 8:30 A.M.-5 P.M., Mon. through Fri.; Address, City Hall, 111 North Main St., 06010; Tel., (860) 584-7656.—**Asst. City and Town Clerk,** Dolores C. Nocera.—**Asst. Regs. of Vital Statistics,** Mary Lou Lakovitch, Dolores C. Nocera, Grace B. Stranieri.—**Mayor,** Frank N. Nicastro, Sr. (D).—**City Council: Council Members,** Frank N. Nicastro, Sr., Mayor, Chm., ex officio, Richard D. Colbert, Jr., Gerard Couture, J. Harwood Norton, Jr., Thomas J. Ragaini, Arthur J. Ward, Joseph P. Wilson.—**Treas.,** Patti D. Ewen.—**Comptroller,** Theodore N. Hamilton.—**Bd. of Finance,** John A. Letizia, Jr., Chm., Audrey H. Dubay, Roald M. Erling, Gail M. Hartmann, Richard J. Miecznikowski, Frank N. Nicastro, Sr., Mayor, ex officio, Allan F. Plourde, Jeanne E. Radcliff, Frederick J. Walker.—**Tax Collector,** Esmonde J. Phelan, Jr.—**Bd. of Assessment Appeals,** Gail Fuller, Peter A. Giola, Gary M. Schaffrick.—**Bd. of Ethics,** Donna Fortier, Chm., Morris Euley, H. Phillips Jesup, Charles E. McCormick, Carol L. Zesk; Alternates, Jane Anastasio, Cheryl E. Hricko, vacancy.—**Assessor,** Richard J. Lasky.—**Registrars of Voters,** Marie Jo O'Meara (D), Eleanore K. Klapatch (R).—**Supt. of Schools,** Edward J. Maher.—**Bd. of Education,** Beverly R. Bobroske, Barbara Y. Doyle, Julie M. Luczkow, Janet L. Moylan, Patricia B. Petosa, Kathleen Roberge, Richard P. Saporito, Reinhard L. Walker, Cheryl Yetke, 1999.—**Personnel Dir.,** James Byer.—**Personnel Appeals Bd.,** Donald J. Aiudi, Thomas L. Kenyon, Phillip LaFlamme, Dominick A. Lucenti, vacancy.—**Retirement Bd.,** Louise H. Rohner, Chm., John Boi, Gail M. Hartmann, Gregory M. Miller, Frank N. Nicastro, Sr., Mayor, City Treas., Comptroller, ex officio, David J. Preleski, Arthur Ward.—**Planning Comm.,** Michael J. Girouard, Chm., John Mastrobattista, Kenneth G. Scott, John J. Soares, William J. Veits; Alternates, Domenic A. Busto, Brian D. Ewings, Marie C. Keeton.—**Zoning Comm.,** Frank J. Johnson, Chm., John A. Lodovico, Jr., Kenneth E. Nairne, Edward J. Paul, Carl E. Staggers; Alternates, Louis Galgano, Leilani D. O'Connor, Robert W. Pachesa.—**Zoning Bd. of Appeals,** Bertrand F. Bouvier, Chm., Gilles H. Angers, Michael D. Goulet, Richard A. Newcity, Jerald A. Rafaniello; Alternates, Theresa Pac, Jeffrey P. Twombly, Mark J. Young.—

Housing Auth., Peter G. Imperator, Chm., Delores J. Capers, Joan M. Courchaine, Nayda T. Roper, Mark E. Schulz; Laurel Robinson, Exec. Dir.—**Transportation Comm.,** Edmund S. Luczkow, Chm., Michael A. Barrette, Barbara Hackney, Thomas J. Ragaini, Rita M. Shone, Alan Weiner, vacancy.—**Wetlands and Watercourses Comm.,** Lee W. Levesque, Jr., Chm., Norman R. Beaudoin, Greg A. Klimek, Jeffrey G. Merrow, Norman Taillon, Ellen A. Zoppo; Alternates, Robert M. Chaisson, William J. Englert, vacancy.—**Comm. on Aging,** Barbara B. Morrocco, Chm., Keith D. Graham, Jr., Willard E. Kellert, Francis P. Labriola, Bernard E. O'Keefe, David L. Page, Walter E. Siel; John K. Pringle, Jr., Exec. Dir.—**Comm. on the Handicapped,** Catherine D. Cassin, Chm., Gary S. Allen, Barbara Badore, Christopher Caccamo, David A. Hartley, David J. Kelly, Laurie J. Metzger.—**Welfare Supt.,** Katherine M. Plourde.—**Bd. of Public Welfare,** Pamela M. Messier, Chm., Lance W. Chase, Wilfredo Hernandez, Frank N. Nicastro, Sr., Mayor, ex officio, Paul E. Nicoletti, Kathi J. Sorey.—**Bristol-Burlington Health District, Dir.,** Patricia Checko.—**Bd. of Health (Bristol-Burlington Health District),** Thomas P. O'Brien, Chm., Merton F. Baehr, William J. Brownstein, M.D., Ronald B. Herriott, Daniel J. Scopetta.—**Library Directors,** E. Bartlett Barnes, Georgine D. Cawley, Carol A. Denehy, Mildred T. Donaghy, Donna Papazian, P. Everett Weed.—**Municipal Historian,** Dorothy A. Manchester.—**Bd. of Parks Comrs.,** Frank N. Nicastro, Sr., Mayor, Chm., ex officio, James R. Cleveland, James R. Dumont, John J. Fortunato, Philip E. Leary, Francis W. Mullins, Coral P. Richardson; Dennis N. Malone, Supt.—**Youth Comm.,** Mayra I. Berrios, Ronald G. Burns, Gerard J. Couture, Patricia M. Kalat, Lori Kuntz, Linda Lowery, Michael Negron, Carole C. Rosano, Peter J. Sassu, Jr., David M. White; Eileen McNulty, Coordinator.—**Bd. of Public Works,** Frank N. Nicastro, Sr., Mayor, Chm., ex officio, Edward L. Corbeil, Gerard Couture, J. Harwood Norton, Jr., Donald V. Padlo, David R. Waggoner, Arthur J. Ward.—**Dir. of Public Works,** Ronald H. Smith.—**City Engineer,** Paul Strawderman.—**Sealer of Weights and Measures,** Angelo Lapadula.—**Asst. of Streets and Sanitation,** Claud Bourret.—**Purchasing Agent,** Clifford B. Carlson.—**Dir. of Veterans/Handicapped Services,** Alphonse Santucci.—**Building Official,** Vincent J. D'Andrea.—**Building Code Bd. of Appeals,** David Butts, Chm., Philip C. Ferraro, Augustine F. Lepore, Jr., George Moskowicz, Robert W. Wentland; Sub., Harry A. Herold, Jr.—**Bd. of Water Comrs.,** Joel B. Wulff, Chm., Robert A. Badal, Wayne F. Bolduc, Angelo Lapadula, Anthony R. Lodovico; Leonard Valentino, Supt.—**Supt. Water Pollution,** Joseph Mercieri.—**Claims Inspector,** Stephen Rybczyk.—**City Sanitarian,** Phyllis Amodio.—**Chief of Police,** William R. Kohnke.—**Bd. of Police Comrs.,** Frank N. Nicastro, Sr., Mayor, Chm., ex officio, Robert Chmieleski, Richard D. Colbert, Jr., Rae Fredrickson, William L. Greger, Edward C. Krawiecki, Sr., Ercole J. Labadia.—**Constables,** Mark J. Anderson, Karen Dolce, Norman A. Fortier, Jr., Patrick J. O'Meara, Trina J. Theriault, Algier G. Weeks.—**Chief of Fire Dept.,** Anthony D. Basile; Deputies, Henry Gaski, Robert Greisner, Armand Lemieux, Jon Pose.—**Fire Marshal,** Denis J. Pieri.—**Bd. of Fire Comrs.,** Frank N. Nicastro, Sr., Mayor, Chm., ex officio, James T. Beaucar, Gerard J. Couture, Stephen P. Damiano, Donald G. Goranson, Jr., Frank V. O'Meara, Robert J. Tenerowicz.—**Civil Preparedness Dir.,** Richard B. Ladisky.—**Corporation Counsel,** Richard E. Lacey; Assts., Ann T. Baldwin, Wyland D. Clift, Dean B. Kilbourne.— **Justices of the Peace,** Thomas M. Abbott, Donald J. Aiudi, Susan L. Alden, Mark J.

Anderson, Gilles H. Angers, Lorraine B. Arburr, Bruce R. Avritch, Robert A. Badal, Carlyle F. Barnes, Alan J. Beals, Sr., Douglas A. Beals, Douglas A. Beals, Jr., James T. Beaucar, Lori N. Beaucar, Mayra I. Berrios, Whit Betts, Beverly R. Bobroske, Gerhardt L. Bobroske, John J. Boi, Kimberly A. Bonola, Margaret L. Bonola, Bertrand F. Bouvier, Maureen G. Brightman, Daniel W. Britt, Domenic A. Busto, Janet E. Carlson, Donald Cassin, Robert M. Chaisson, Richard G. Chapman, Lance W. Chase, Robert W. Chase, J. Roger Chasse, Roger E. Chiasson II, Sondra S. Clement, Wyland D. Clift, Richard D. Colbert, Jr., James J. Collin, Thomas W. Conlin, Ann Copjec, Paul D. Corcoran, Phillip R. Courchaine, Gerard J. Couture, John L. Cyr, Roman J. Czuchta, Jerome Davis, Judith deBear, Ann P. Degnan, Judy L. Dellaera, Kathy A. DeLuco, Kosta Diamantis, Nicholas J. DiBattista, Chester F. Dobrowolski, Maria Dorval, Barbara Y. Doyle, Michele A. Dubois, Stephen J. Duffy, Faye L. Duquette, Mary T. Dutcher, Donna L. Eriksen, Christopher T. Evans, Patti D. Ewen, Robert E. Ewen, Anthony S. Fabrizio, Suzanne Fabrizio, Carlo M. Faienza, Cindy Faienza, Helen G. Fenn, Maxine R. Fippinger, Joan C. Fitzgerald, Jon P. FitzGerald, Kathryn A. Forader, Donna L. Fortier, Norman A. Fortier, Jr., Barbara H. Franklin, Constance M. Frateroli, Gail Fuller, Louis Galgano, Frank J. Garfi, Jr., Rosemarie K. Garfi, Mary Ann A. Giola, Peter A. Giola, Michael J. Girouard, Nora B. Gleim, Carol Gosler, Gertrude Greenleaf, Diana Gregoire, Bruce A. Guillemette, Albert R. Haddad, Patricia M. Hardy, Gail' M. Hartmann, Voncile J. Hartmann, Jesse H. Haskell, James E. Herens, Anne C. Houlihan, Cheryl E. Hricko, Sylvia M. Imperator, Richard J. Jackson, Sr., Thomas W. Janek, James C. Johnson, Beryl P. Josephson, Carl H. Josephson, Gerald E. Kaczenski, Andrea Kapchensky, Thomas L. Kenyon, Dean B. Kilbourne, Kimberly A. Kilbourne, Eric L. King, Ellie Klapatch, Myron H. Klosowski, Thaddeus J. Klosowski, Edward C. Krawiecki, Edward C. Krawiecki, Jr., Angelo D. Lapadula, Fanny Lapadula, Thomas L. Lavigne, Rowena S. Lavoie, Michael D. Leahy, John J. Leone, Jr., Denise A. Lepage, Lee W. Levesque, Jr., Edward P. Lorenson, Marianne Lydem, Nicole R. Massicotte, Jahn A. Mastrianni, Jr., Robert R. McFadden, Phyllis V. McMahon, Eileen M. McNulty, Edward T. McPhee, Jr., Tyrone J. Mellon, Anita J. Michele, Rodney D. Michele, Roger B. Michele, Kevin T. Mihaly, Gregory M. Miller, James H. Minella, Craig M. Minor, Art Mocabee, Edward J. Monahan, Sean M. Moore, Joseph J. Mudry, Jr., Francis W. Mullins, Frank N. Nicastro, Sr., J. Harwood Norton, Jr., Peter J. Nye, Leilani D. O'Connor, Frank V. O'Meara, Marie Jo O'Meara, Patrick J. O'Meara, Robert J. O'Meara, Mary L. M. O'Neil, Noelle M. Owens, Robert W. Pachesa, Jr., Terry A. Parker, Linda J. Paul, Daniel R. Pelletier, Judy A. Perry, Patricia B. Petosa, Janet L. Pose, Anthony J. Potocki, Richard F. Prindle, Max Rabin, Thomas J. Ragaini, Paula J. Ray, Michael R. Read, Virginia P. Read, Beverly A. Redman, Chester B. Reed, Jr., Bryan Ricci, Jeffrey Rimcoski, Michael B. Rimcoski, Jeffrey A. Rindfleisch, Terry Roach, Robert G. Robles, Anne P. Ruquist, Richard P. Saporito, Sebastian F. Saraceno, Debra R. Saucier, Cathy A. Savino, Gary M. Schaffrick, Joan V. Seguljic, Rita M. Shone, Gary A. Simpson, Kathleen Smith-Cashman, Jean R. Sonstrom, Phyllis E. Spooner, Jane M Steadman, William T. Stortz, John A. Stupak, Jr., Brian S. Suchinski, Trina J.. Theriault, John F. Torrence, Jr., Daniel O. Tully, Phyllis R. Van Gorder, David R. Waggoner, Art Ward, Algier G. Weeks, Lynn Wentland, Marie S. Werner, Michael L. Werner, Charles W. Whelan, David M. White, James E. White, Mark K. Winter, Diane L. Winters, Michael J. Winters, Otto J. Winters, Jr., William M. Wolfe, Jr., Gardner E. Wright, Jr., Joel B. Wulff, Mark J. Young, Bart J. Zelechowski, Christopher Ziogas, Ellen A. Zoppo, Michael C. Zoppo.

BROOKFIELD. Fairfield County.—(Form of government, selectmen, town meeting, board of finance.)—Inc., May, 1788; taken from Danbury, New Milford and Newtown. Area, 20.4 sq. miles. Population, est., 14,691. Voting districts, 2. Principal industries, lithography, manufacturing of connectors and R. F. components, custom built metal products to blueprints and specifications, machine and tool making shops and assembly of electronic equipment. Transp.—Passenger: Served by buses of the Housatonic Area Regional Transit. Freight: Served by Conrail and numerous motor common carriers. Post offices, Brookfield.

TOWN OFFICERS. Clerk and Reg. of Vital Statistics, Ruth B. Burr; Hours, 8:30 A.M.-4:30 P.M., Mon. through Fri. (call for summer hours); Address, Brookfield Municipal Center, Pocono Rd., P.O. Box 5106, 06804-5106; Tel., Danbury, (203) 775-7313.—**Asst. Clerks and Asst. Regs. of Vital Statistics,** Sheelah F. Adams, Ann S. Elges.—**Selectmen,** 1st, Bonnie P. Smith (R) P.O. Box 5106, Tel., (203) 775-7300, John Osborne (D), Allan D. Sniffin (R).—**Treas.,** David A. Scribner.—**Bd. of Finance,** William R. Davidson, Chm., Charles S. Galda, Judith A. Heise, Howard Lasser, Joseph R. Loughlin, Fred G. Standt.—**Tax Collector,** Georgia B. Lawrence.—**Bd. of Assessment Appeals,** Thomas J. Gallagan, Chm., Sandra J. Schroder, John H. Will, Jr.—**Bd. of Ethics,** Barton C. Conant, Mark Lyon, Janet M. Robinson.—**Assessor,** Joseph Kusiak.—**Registrars of Voters,** Adelaide M. Marek (D), Deanne L. Sniffin (R).—**Supt. of Schools,** David C. Bristol.—**Bd. of Education,** Arthur O. Kerley, Chm., George E. Hope, Jr., Catherine C. Lasser, 1997; Steven R. DeVaux, William N. Tinsley, Barbara Y. Wolff, vacancy, 1999.—**Planning Comm.,** Richard A. Miller, Chm., Bruce F. Hunton, James K. Knight, Stephen J. O'Reilly, Jon A. VanHise; Alternates, Aeloa Delaney, Fred Weisman, vacancy.—**Zoning Comm.,** James P. Gleason, Joan A. Gould, Stanley C. Parker, Ralph E. Ragette, William E. Schappert; Alternates, James P. Gleason, Katherine M. Hurley, vacancy.—**Zoning Bd. of Appeals,** Josephine G. Spinella, Chm., Paul E. Gibson, Charles E. Keller, Douglas J. Lewis, Anthony J. Porrazzo; Alternates, Gerald Barra, Lawrence J. Mix, vacancy.—**Land Use Enforcement Officer,** Paul Johnson.—**Economic Development Comm.,** Kenneth V. Keller, Chm., Stephen J. Breckley, John T. Carroll, Martin J. Foncello, Jr., Alfred J. Garzi.—**Housing Auth.,** Douglas W. Fisher, Chm., Janet Drohan, Emily Kane, Ethel Pliska, Ann M. Wendt, Karen N. Wuhrer.—**Conservation Comm.,** Fred C. Ball, Chm., Paul W. Davis, Alice W. Dew, Dorothy Evans, Aart W. Hoogenboom; Alternates, Joseph P. Barsky, Stephanie Landis, Christine Schappert.—**Inland Wetlands Comm.,** Stanley J. Kurpiewski, Chm., Angela J. Abercrombie, James A. Blake, George A. Chaber, John A. Smoligia; Alternates, Joseph P. Barsky, vacancy.—**Historic Dist. Comm.,** Jacqueline A. Salame, Chm., Rosemary Fawcett, Harold Proudfoot, Elaine Rajcula, vacancy; Alternates, Peter J. Bertolami, Robert R. Brown, Elizabeth deLambert.—**Municipal Historian,** Marilyn S. Whittlesey.—**Youth Comm.,** Kathleen VanDuzee, Chm., Wendy Andrews, Joan Gillroy, Wendy Seiffer, vacancy.—**Comm. on Aging,** Theresa Eberhard, Chm., Joan DeMores, Bertha Schladitz, Ann R. Sheinhouse; Alternates, Barbara Lewis, two vacancies.—**Dir. of Social Services,** Barbara Roche.—**Dir.**

of Health, Robert A. Mascia, M.D.—**Library Bd. of Trustees,** Marie M. Lombardi, Chm., Margaret C. Drapeau, Lynn Harrison, Sherry Reuter, Serena Stanley; Alternates, Martin J. Ford, W. Clark Harrington, Seymour Wofsey.—**Parks and Recreation Comm.,** Linda A. Mitten, Chm., Brian G. Berardi, Robert S. Blick, Gerard W. Friedrich, Doris Tyransky; Dennis R. DiPinto, Dir.; Alternates, David M. Kettunen, Barbara Murphy, Edward J. Smith.—**Dir. of Public Works,** Ronald Klimas.—**Tree Warden,** Walter Loesch.—**Building Inspector,** William M. Andricovich.—**Municipal Bd. of Appeals,** Donald G. Westenhofer, Chm., Eugene Golaszewski, John L. Martino, two vacancies.—**Controller,** Raymond Bolek.—**Water Pollution Control Auth.,** William B. Tappan, Jr., Chm., Allan R. Chichester, Josephine G. Spinella, George R. Sutter, Guy R. Sutter; Alternates, John Osborne, Thomas Perrotta, Louise Trojanowski-Marconi.—**Lake Authorities,** Candlewood: Theresa Gereg, Steven I. Zoltan, vacancy; Lillinonah: Joseph J. Antosh, Robert J. DiTullio, Ann Schiessl.—**Sanitarian,** Michael P. McCarthy.—**Chief of Police,** John W. Anderson.—**Police Comm.,** Peter B. Sanderson, Chm., Harry A. Gerowe, Sr., John L. Martino, Russell R. Reynaga, Joseph T. Siklos; Alternates, David C. Keefe, Robert L. Marconi, Louis R. Rell.—**Chiefs of Fire Dept.,** Wayne A. Gravius (Brookfield); Gary W. Gramling (Candlewood).—**Fire Marshal,** Wayne A. Gravius.—**Civil Preparedness Dir.,** Wayne A. Gravius.—**Town Atty.,** William J. McNamara, Jr.—**Justices of the Peace,** Angela J. Abercrombie, Richard Amorossi, Joseph E. Baker, Henry S. Barsky, James A. Blake, Lucille A. Blessey, Arlene Bucci, Fred W. Busch, Marjorie B. Carmody, John T. Carroll, Glenn E. Christy, Mariann Cioffi, James R. Conant, Joseph A. Consalvo, James J. Davies, Aeloa Delaney, Joan A. DeMoraes, Elizabeth M. Esandrio, James F. Fiddner, Douglas W. Fisher, Martin J. Foncello, Jr., William J. Fuchs, Sr., Charles S. Galda, Jr., Thomas J. Gallagan, James P. Gleason, Eugene L. Golaszewski, Joan A. Gould, David S. Grossman, Yolanda R. Hague, Judith A. Heise, Kathleen C. Hill, George E. Hope, Jr., Joseph Ingardia, Jeffrey R. Kass, Richard D. Kast, Stanley W. Kaswer, Adrienne G. Keller, Charles E. Keller, Kenneth V. Keller, Catherine C. Lasser, Howard Lasser, Michele L. Lee, Edgar A. Locke, Joseph R. Loughlin, Mary M. Loughlin, Carolyn F. Lyon, Mark S. Lyon, Winifred M. Manton, Adelaide M. Marek, M. Robert Markowitz, Joseph Martone, Richard A. Miller, Patrick J. Morgan, Stephen J. O'Reilly, John Osborne, Joan G. Park, Roger P. Prinz, Jeffrey W. Reinen, Louis R. Rell, M. Jodi Rell, Paula J. Schneider, Sandra J. Schroder, Agnes E. Schullery, David A. Scribner, Greg Seabury, Ann R. Sheinhouse, Georgia Siklos, Allan D. Sniffin, Peter J. Socci, Josephine G. Spinellla, James C. Sutherland, George R. Sutter, Janet H. Terrill, Louise Trojanowski-Marconi, Jack T. Tyransky, Maureen G. Van Hise, Steven J. Villodas, Loretta M. Wachter, Peter L. Walrath, Anneliese G. Westenhofer, Leo C. Wilderman, Constance M. Will, John H. Will, Jr., Theresa A. York, Shirley J. Zaccara, Edith B. Zoltan.

BROOKLYN. Windham County.—(Form of government, selectmen, town meeting, board of finance.)—Inc., May, 1786; taken from Pomfret and Canterbury. Area, 29.1 sq. miles. Population, est., 6,642. Voting districts, 1. Principal industries, agriculture and manufacture of electrical goods. Transp.—Passenger: Served by buses of Bonanza Bus Lines, Inc. and Northeastern Conn. Transit Dist. Freight: Served by numerous motor common carriers. Post office, Brooklyn.

TOWN OFFICERS. Clerk and Reg. of Vital Statistics, Leona Mainville; Hours, 9 A.M.-4:30 P.M., Mon. through Wed., 9 A.M.-6 P.M., Thurs., 9 A.M.-1 P.M., Fri.; Address, Town Hall, P.O. Box 356, 06234; Tel., Danielson, (860) 774-9543.—**Asst. Clerks and Asst. Regs. of Vital Statistics,** Marilyn L. Benson, Eileen M. Theroux.—**Selectmen,** 1st, Donald S. Francis (D) Tel., (860) 779-3411, Maurice F. Bowen (D), Tamsen H. Harris (R).—**Treas.,** Leona A. Mainville.—**Bd. of Finance,** Chris D. Berris, Chm., Mark Brouillard, Deborah Cornman, Roger Engle, Lyn A. LaCharite, Steven H. Townsend.—**Tax Collector,** Susan Gibeault.—**Bd. of Assessment Appeals,** Robert L. Dragon, John K. Harris, Jr., Diane K. Wimmer.—**Bd. of Ethics,** Howard B. Denslow, Lucinda H. Hogarty, Robert J. Kelleher, Sonia L. Klemm, Michael J. Niejadlik.—**Assessor,** Melissa L. Baer; Asst., Marilyn L. Benson.—**Registrars of Voters,** Eleanor L. Warren (D); Cassandra L. Leach (R).—**Supt. of Schools,** Louise S. Berry.—**Bd. of Education,** Thomas A. Dziki, Caroll E. Marston, Blair G. Mondor, Chris C. Silva, Kenneth J. Swartz, David M. Teed, 1997.—**Planning and Zoning Comm.,** Bruce Parsons, Chm., Wayne Dube, Thomas Hogarty, Hans Koehl, Barbara Lambert, Steven Sondak, Austin I. Tanner, John Wilcox, Ronald Wood, Andrew Young; Alternates, Edward Homonoff, Eugene Kozlow, James Monstream.—**Town Planner,** vacancy.—**Zoning Bd. of Appeals,** Dan G. Ross, Chm., Donald LoRusso, Albert Luciano, Joseph Mathieu, Gary Sposato; Alternates, John Filchak, two vacancies.—**Zoning Enforcement Officer,** Chester Dobrowski.—**Economic Development Comm.,** Robert Brandriff, Thomas Dziki, Jeffrey Jones, Mae Lyons, Bruce Randall, Carol Ross, Paul Sorel.—**Conservation Comm.,** Alice Choquette, William E. Carver, Bruce Fitzback, Mae Lyons, Joyce Meader, William Morales, Andrew Rzeznikiewicz; Alternates, David Loos, Joel I. Rosenberg, vacancy.—**Inland Wetlands Comm.,** Henry Moses, Chm., Richard Booth, Ray Ducharme, Nathan Ives, Wayne Logee, Joanne Smith, vacancy; Alternates, Theodore W. Niejadlik, Andrew Rzeznikiewicz, Donna Weisenberger.—**Housing Auth.,** Aida Bissonnette, Chm., Ronald A. Glaude, David Heilemann, James K. Kelley, Jean Westerfield.—**Brooklyn Resource Recovery Auth.,** Thomas Doherty, Cynthia Parsons, Clifford Pohudniak; Alternate, vacancy.—**Agent for the Elderly,** Tamsen H. Harris.—**Library Dir.,** Katherine Stellitano, Pres.—**Parks and Recreation Comm.,** Mike Barry, Pamela Child, Stephen Danna, Nancy Dziki, Roger Engle, Charles Morrison, Chris C. Silva, Marjolaine Townsend, James A. Warren, Sr.—**Building Inspector,** John Berard.—**Building Code Bd. of Appeals,** William J. Kuchy, Jr., William Pakulis, James E. Rose.—**Water Pollution Control Auth.,** John K. Harris, Jr., Chm., Frank Juhasz, Jean P. Trudeau, John A. Weber.—**Tree Warden,** Frank Rich.—**Chief of Police,** Donald S. Francis.—**Constables,** Nancy H. Booth, John DonFrancisco, Robert L. Dragon, Gerald Mainville, Jr., John J. Zurowski.—**Chiefs of Fire Dept.,** Shawn Drszulak (E. Brooklyn), Jeffrey B. Otto (West Wauregan and Mortlake).—**Fire Marshal,** Paul D. Kisby.—**Bd. of Fire Comrs.,** Chris Berris, Hartley Field, Norman Nault, Dan Ross, William R. Skene.—**Civil Preparedness Dir.,** Paul D. Kisby.—**Town Attys.,** Jackson, Harris, Burlingame & Huber.—**Justices of the Peace,** Lois A. Baker, Maurice F. Bowen, Deborah Cornman, Robert L. Dragon, Marie C. Dusseault, John K. Harris, Robert J. Kelleher, Sonia L. Klemm, J. Gloria Lee, Hugh M. MacKenzie, Sr., Viola H. Robillard, James W. Stuyniski, David M. Teed.

BURLINGTON. Hartford County.—(Form of government, selectmen, town meeting, board of finance.)—Inc., May, 1806; taken from Bristol. Area, 30.4 sq. miles. Population, est., 7,656. Voting districts, 1. Transp.—Freight: Served by numerous motor common carriers. Post office, Burlington.

TOWN OFFICERS. Clerk and Reg. of Vital Statistics, Barbara A. Soden; Hours, 8:30 A.M.-4 P.M., Mon. through Fri.; Address, 200 Spielman Hwy., 06013; Tel., Farmington, (860) 673-2108.—**Asst. Clerk and Asst. Reg. of Vital Statistics,** Gloria M. DeForge.—**Selectmen,** 1st, Theodore C. Scheidel, Jr. (D) Tel., (860) 673-6789, Mary Ann Schwarzmann (R), George A. Zurles (D).—**Treas.,** Salvatore V. Vitrano.—**Bd. of Finance,** Arthur W. Johanson, Jr., Chm., John C. Bombara, Frederick J. Chard, Jr., Michael A. Chowaniec, Roger L. Powell, Michael S. Sage.—**Tax Collector,** Linnea B. Lomnicky.—**Bd. of Assessment Appeals,** Raymond A. Goshdigian, Chm., Sharon D. Powers, Thomas J. Turick.—**Assessor,** Gail P. Sartori.—**Registrars of Voters,** Joan H. Tharau (D), Lena R. Spielman (R).—**Supt. of Schools,** Robert W. Goldman.—**Planning and Zoning Comm.,** Robert J. Coates, Chm., James Chard, Edward J. Lockwood, Richard A. Miller, John N. Norton, Gaeton Poulin, Lucien V. Rucci; Alternates, James H. Fenner, Samuel Romanzi, Michael Vollono.—**Zoning Bd. of Appeals,** Gregory M. Szydlo, Chm., David Kuziak, Philip C. Smith, Howard R. Sussdorf, Gerard P. van Noordennen; Alternates, Mitchell Kogut, Maureen M. Lovejoy, Peter Perkins.—**Economic Development Comm.,** Michael B. Best, Chm., Ronald H. Lesieur, F. Patrick O'Sullivan, Stephen J. Savino, Abraham Shapiro, William J. Starr; Alternates, Carol A. Emond, vacancy.—**Inland Wetlands Comm.,** David B. Sherman, Chm., John Bombara, John Bubick, Aniello L. DePascale, James Desmarais, Richard C. Fetzer, Frances X. Lynch, Jonathan R. Schwartz, Gregory F. Ugalde.—**Municipal Agent for the Elderly,** Virginia L. Mills.—**Comm. on Senior Citizens Services,** Joann B. McBrien, Chm., William E. Furniss, Christine A. Griswold, Walter J. Krawiec, Virginia L. Mills, Mary Anne Schwarzmann, Loretta Szymanski.—**Dir. of Health,** Patricia Checko (P.O., Bristol).—**Library Directors,** P. Michael Ragaisis, Chm., Beryl M. Chard, Jenny Mantel, Sanford M. Mazeau, Patricia L. Miller, James Mills, Marie F. Purcell, Carol O. Troiani, vacancy.—**Recreation Comm.,** Robert D. Sheriffs, Chm., Gerald Falvey, Kathleen Freese, Ann Ibbotson, Thomas Nestico, Paul Stawarz, three vacancies; Joanne McBrien, Dir.—**Tree Warden,** Albert Wilusz.—**Building Official,** Charles Kirchofer Tel., (860) 673-1000.—**Building Code Bd. of Appeals,** Alan R. Chandler, Frederick J. Chard, Jr., William M. Coyle, Edward F. Lepore, vacancy.—**Sewer Comm.,** Paul Bystrak, Chm., Joseph W. Backes III, Barbara Cole, John Jozwik, Charles J. Lanfair, Jr., William Parente.—**Water System,** David G. Liberty.—**Chief of Police,** Theodore C. Scheidel, Jr.—**Constables,** Richard Bond, Peter Fernald, Kenneth R. Soden.—**Chief of Fire Dept.,** Richard J. Higley.—**Fire Marshal,** Joseph J. Fioretti; Deputy, Timothy J. Tharau.—**Civil Preparedness Dir.,** vacancy.—**Town Atty.,** Charles W. Bauer.—**Justices of the Peace,** Joseph W. Backes III, Alvina E. Furniss, Clara N. Hamernick, Thomas L. Kobylarz, Edward J. Muzynski, Jr., Audrey N. Norton, Dewey E. O'Dell, Sandra M. O'Dell, Grace M. Platt, Birchard Taylor, Kathleen Taylor, Joanne L. West.

CANAAN. Litchfield County.—(Form of government, selectmen, town meeting, board of finance.)—Inc., Oct., 1739. Area, 33.3 sq. miles. Population, est., 1,272. Voting district, 1. Principal industries, agriculture and manufacture of lime and limestone, and pre-engineered homes. Freight: Served by numerous motor common carriers. Post office, Falls Village. Rural free delivery, daily.

TOWN OFFICERS. Clerk and Reg. of Vital Statistics, Mary M. Palmer; Hours, 9 A.M.-3 P.M., Mon. through Fri. Address, Town Hall, P.O. Box 47, 107 Main St., Falls Village 06031; Tel., (860) 824-0707.—**Asst. Clerks and Asst. Regs. of Vital Statistics,** Susan J. Kelsey, Patrice D. McGrath, Karen A. Surdam.—**Selectmen,** 1st, Peter G. Lawson (R) P.O., Falls Village, Tel., (860) 824-0707, Patricia A. Mechare (D), Louis G. Timolat (R).—**Treas.,** Linda S. Paviol.—**Bd. of Finance,** Thomas Coolidge, John P. Holland, S. William Jenks, Charles J. Lemmen, James March, James P. McGuire, Ann Z. Miller.—**Tax Collector,** Linda S. Paviol.—**Bd. of Assessment Appeals,** Warren Buck, Hazel K. McGuire, Frank N. Ruotolo.—**Assessors,** Norma Grusauskas, Susan J. Kelsey, Joan C. Manasse.—**Registrars of Voters,** Jane Anne S. Worthington (D), Mary C. Petersen (R).—**Supt. of Schools,** Marvin Maskovsky.— **Bd. of Education,** R. Allen Cockerline, Chm., Gail Sinclair, Carol M. Staats, 1997; Margaret Ruotolo, Melissa J. Steines, 1999.—**Planning and Zoning Comm.,** William L. Fox, Chm., L.A.S. McCabe, Joan Manasse, Robert Reid, John P. Steines, Jr., Richard H. Stone; Alternate, Mike DeMazza.—**Zoning Bd. of Appeals,** Richard L. Kubarek, Chm., David S. Jacobs, Charles J. Lemmen, Louise M. March, Ellery W. Sinclair; Alternates, Melinda B. Belten, William L. Dickinson, John P. Holland.—**Zoning Officer,** Raymond C. Pomaski.—**Conservation and Inland Wetlands Comm.,** Susan J. Kelsey, Chm., Mark Burdick, Geraldine Nebor, Ellery W. Sinclair, Louis G. Timolat.—**Agent for the Elderly,** Patricia D. McGrath.—**Dir. of Health,** Dennis J. Kobylarz.—**Library Directors,** Ellery W. Sinclair, Pres., Kay C. Blass, Elizabeth Germon, Barbara Kelsey, Charles Lemmen, Barbara Lindsay, David Lindsay, Pat Mechare, Erica Palmer, Victor Valla.—**Municipal Historian,** Marion Stock.—**Recreation Comm.,** James March, Chm., John Holland, Richard L. Kubarek, John Raffanello, Betsy Rosenbloom.—**Tree Warden,** Peter G. Lawson.—**Building Inspector,** Bill Conrad.—**Building Code Bd. of Appeals,** Eugene F. Wright, Chm.—**River Comm.,** Charles Lewis.—**Water Comm.,** William S. Blass, Chm., Gregory Carlson, Faye H. Lawson, Edward McGuire, Fred Petersen.—**Sanitarian,** Louis G. Timolat.—**Energy Coordinator,** Patrice D. McGrath.—**Constables,** Charles Adams, John P. Holland, Susan J. Kelsey, James A. March, James P. McGuire, Ellery W. Sinclair, Louis G. Timolat.—**Chief of Fire Dept.,** Curt A. Mechare.—**Fire Marshal,** Stanley MacMillan, Jr.—**Bd. of Fire Comrs.,** Thomas P. Gaisford, Chm., Curt A. Mechare, Edward G. McGuire, E. Fred Petersen, Jean Vallette.—**Civil Preparedness Dir.,** Noel F. Ambery.—**Town Atty.,** Judith Dixon.—**Justices of the Peace,** James J. Belter, Gregory Carlson, H. Stephen Casey, Susan J. Kelsey, Peter G. Lawson, Charles Lemmen, Louise M. March, Carole K. McGuire, Hazel K. McGuire, James P. McGuire, Patricia Mechare, Mary M. Palmer, E. Frederick Petersen, Margaret R. Ruotolo, Allan M. Schwaikert, Louis G. Timolat, Harry Wilhelm, Jane Anne S. Worthington.

CANTERBURY. Windham County.—(Form of government, selectmen, town meeting, board of finance.)—Inc., Oct., 1703; taken from Plainfield. Area, 40.2 sq. miles. Population, est., 4,658. Voting district, 1. Principal industries, agriculture and dairy products. Transp.—Freight: Served by Providence & Worcester Railroad co. and numerous motor common carriers. Post office, Canterbury. Rural free delivery from Canterbury. Voted Grocery Store Beer Permit, 1971; Restaurant Beer and Wine Permit, 1987; Restaurant All Alcohol Permit, 1990.

TOWN OFFICERS. Clerk and Reg. of Vital Statistics, Marilyn E. Burris; Hours, 9:30 A.M.-4:30 P.M., Mon. through Wed.; 9:30 A.M.-7 P.M., Thurs.; 9:30 A.M.-2 P.M., Fri.; Mailing Address, P.O. Box 27, 06331; Tel., (860) 546-9377.—**Asst. Clerk and Asst. Reg. of Vital Statistics,** Beth L. Heon.—**Selectmen,** 1st, Neil A. Dupont, Sr. (R) Tel., (860) 546-9693, Paul R. Goyette (R), Raymond A. Guillet (D).—**Treas.,** Donna M. Sharp.—**Bd. of Finance,** Edith B. Kinsey, Chm., Lloyd L. Anderson, Lewis J. Gray, Steven K. Pelletier, Kenneth H. Rawn, John Waskiewicz, Sr.—**Tax Collector,** Marilyn E. Burris.—**Bd. of Assessment Appeals,** Eric M. Arnio, Joseph A. Delli-Carpini, George R. Weeks.—**Assessor,** Judy E. Moffitt.—**Registrars of Voters,** Loreen F. Hegan (D), Mary L. Bergeron (R).—**Supt. of Schools,** Robert Gutzman.—**Bd. of Education,** Joseph S. Rodowicz, Richard Veilleux, Robert E. Stearns, 1997; Patricia D. Arnio, Paul R. Cady, Lorna L. Champagne, Douglas N. Czaja, 1999.—**Planning and Zoning Comm.,** Francis X. Brey, Anthony Denning, Robert J. Droesch, Aili H. Galasyn, Daniel P. Harazim, David J. Norell, Stanley Rodowicz, Jr., Mark O. Weeks, Leslie M. Wrigley, Jr.; Alternates, Michael R. Hogan, Kenneth M. Quimby, Charles H. Savarese.—**Zoning Bd. of Appeals,** Donald D. Bryant, John H. Kivela, Thomas F. Lord, William J. Pechka, Sr., vacancy; Alternates, Christopher J. Ferris, Patricia E. Sullivan, George R. Weeks.—**Zoning Enforcement Officer,** Jared Wibberley.—**Economic Development Comm.,** Paul H. Bergeron, Anthony Denning, David G. Ginnetti, Edward R. Grab, Daniel P. Harazim, Luther E. Thurlow, Mark O. Weeks, Christian C. Wellinghausen.—**Inland Wetlands Comm.,** David McKinley, Chm., Blanche J. Boyle, Jeffrey S. Davis, David J. Hart, Norman T. Miller, Francis L. Strmiska, Jr., John A. Tetreault; Jared Wibberley, Enforcement Officer; Alternates, William J. Chalfant, James Strmiska, John J. Sullivan.—**Municipal Agent for the Elderly,** Patricia Rice.—**Welfare Admin.,** Piper L. Clerkin.—**Recreation Comm.,** Lewis J. Gray, Chm., Richard O. Fish, Carl E. Nelson, Sally E. Peavey, John A. Sullivan, Donna J. Way.—**Municipal Building Comm.,** Carl Boecherer III, Paul R. Goyette, Daniel P. Harazim, Michael R. Hogan, Carl E. Nelson, Joseph Stajduhar, R. Glen Veit.—**Building Inspector,** Robert Kerr.—**Chief of Police,** vacancy.—**Constables,** Robert C. Kinne, Shirley A. Guillet, John S. Nelson, Jr., David J. Norell, Alan W. Patridge, Sr., Kalervo J. Ruuskanen.—**Chief of Fire Dept.,** David Veit.—**Fire Marshal,** Paul Yellen.—**Civil Preparedness Dir.,** Luther Thurlow.—**Town Atty.,** John D. Boland.—**Justices of the Peace,** Kathleen L. Brey, Robert J. Droesch, Aili H. Galasyn, Shirley A. Guillet, David J. Norell, Roy W. Rautio, Edith B. Roberts, Juliette S. Stadnicki, Charles A. Thurlow, Linwood Tracy.

CANTON. Hartford County.—(Form of government, selectmen, town meeting, board of finance.)—Inc., May, 1806; taken from Simsbury. Area, 25.0 sq. miles. Population, est., 8,453.

Voting district, 1. Principal industries, manufacture of chemicals, wrought iron, brass, electro magnetic clutches and brakes, moment of inertia measuring instruments, art galleries, antique shops. Transp.—Passenger: Served by buses of Conn. Transit Auth. from Hartford. Freight: Served by numerous motor common carriers. Post offices, Collinsville, Canton, Canton Center and North Canton.

TOWN OFFICERS. Clerk and Reg. of Vital Statistics, Shirley C. Krompegal; Hours, 8:30 A.M.-4:30 P.M., Mon. through Fri. (for information on summer hours, call Town Clerks office); Address, 4 Market St., P.O. Box 168, Collinsville 06022; Tel., (860) 693-7870.—**Asst. Clerks and Asst. Regs. of Vital Statistics,** Beryl Cole, Joan Roncaioli.—**Selectmen,** 1st, Kathleen C. Corkum (D) P.O., Collinsville, Tel., (860) 693-7847, Noel G. Baker (R), Louis M. Daniels (R), Mary B. Tomolonius (D), Mark A. Wroblewski (R).—**Treas.,** Diane Napier.—**Chief Adm. Officer,** Frederick E. Turkington.—**Bd. of Finance,** Richard A. Stratton, Chm., Charles Klem, Mark E. Lowell, Richard Ohanesian, George Thimot, William H. Tribou III.—**Tax Collector,** Marilyn S. Drs.—**Bd. of Assessment Appeals,** Paul F. Volovski, Chm., Robert L. Porter, Mark Quattro.—**Registrars of Voters,** James M. Keane (D), Carl S. Svensen, Jr. (R).—**Supt. of Schools,** David Quattropani.—**Bd. of Education,** Robert E. Bessel, Susan R. Bush, Susan J. Norland, 1997; Catherine T. DeSimas, Chm., Daniel B. LeGeyt, Giorgio Pinton, 1999; Robert J. Bridgman, Jill Cromwell, Carryl J. L. Sinish, 2001.—**Zoning Comm.,** Christopher Winsor, Chm., Howard Bahre III, Douglas Bok, Peter Clarke, Katherine Hooker, Jay Weintraub, two vacancies; Alternates, Timothy Nardi, Mark Petty, vacancy.—**Planning Comm.,** Adolph Yekel, Chm., Rosemary Aldridge, James Carpenter, Dana Schreiber, Alan Weiner; Alternates, Esther L. Davidson, Mark Higby, James Miner.—**Town Planner,** Eric Barz.—**Zoning Bd. of Appeals,** Paul F. Volovski, Chm., Anthony DeVito, Jay Eustace, Katherine Jenkins, Robert Sigman; Alternates, Robert Brainard, Peter Stein, vacancy.—**Economic Development Comm.,** Mark Quattro, Chm., Marcy Campbell, Susan Grawford, Mark Lange, Rowena Okie, Mary Tomolonius.—**Housing Auth.,** Bruce Hoben, Chm., Nancy R. Bowden, David Fisher, Jr., Ethel Kuehn.—**Conservation Comm.,** Sarah Leff, Chm., Jean Darlington, Scott Kania, Karen McIntyre, Gary St. Peter, Roger Thrall, Cassandra Vorisek.—**Inland Wetlands Comm.,** David J. Markowitz, Chm., Richard Dalphin, Barbara Green, Philip Ostapko, Philip Royer; Alternates, Russell W. Askloff, Paul Czaplicki, Timothy Wheeler.—**Canton Center Historic Dist. Comm.,** Edward Pepin, Chm., Timothy LeGeyt, Margaret Perry, Charles Wall, vacancy; Alternates, Betty Stanley, Barbara Sulaviki, vacancy.—**Collinsville Historic Dist. Comm.,** David Leff, Chm., Roger Clarke, Eric Jackson, Dawn Wolff.—**Comm. on Aging,** Rose Stepnick, Chm., Carol Barlow, Katherine Hartnett, Mildred Merrill, Thomas Stribula, Sandra Trionfini; Alternates, Mary K. D'Atri, Mary E. Fletcher.—**Agent for the Elderly,** Carol Barlow.—**Dir. of Social Services,** Kathleen Corkum.—**Dir. of Health,** Richard H. Matheny.—**Pension Comm.,** Richard Anderson, Chm., Mark Homan, Ramon Smith, Wilbur Thomas, John A. T. Wilson.—**Library Directors,** Joanna Eickenhorst, Chm., Caroline Aho, Pamela Alverez, Diana Boorjian, Denise Duffee, Patricia Owen; three vacancies.—**Parks and Recreation Comm.,** Susan Crawford, Mark Homan, Pamela Keagan, S. Scott McAlindin, Lynn Seiden-Preminger, Michael Spescia, J. Patrick Stumbras.—**Dir. of Public Works,** Richard Negro.—

Town Engineer, R. Kenneth Wassel.—**Purchasing Agent,** Dorothy Shackleford.—**Building Inspector,** Francis Jasmin.—**Building Code Bd. of Appeals,** Christopher Winsor, Chm., L. Lawton Miner, Russell Richardson, Jr., Charles Whitney, vacancy.—**Water Pollution Control Auth.,** Robert Sutmiller, Chm., Edward Herbert, Robert Leach, William Mattes, Larry D. Minichiello.—**Sanitarian,** David Knauf.—**Chief of Police,** Lowell Humphrey.—**Constables,** Thomas Dowd, John H. Penfield, Margaret H. Perry, William H. Tribou III, Mark A. Wroblewski, Hershel Zamechek, Richard A. Zommer, vacancy.—**Chief of Fire Dept.,** Richard Hutchings; Donald Capen, Harold Freytag, Matthew Hartnett, Station Chiefs.—**Fire Marshal,** Michael Yacovino.—**Civil Preparedness Dir.,** Joseph Ulcikas.—**Town Attys.,** Levy and Droney.—**Justices of the Peace,** Noel G. Baker, Diana Boorjian, Margaret P. Colavecchio, Kathleen C. Corkum, Louis M. Daniels, Mary E. Fletcher, Samuel S. Humphrey, Rita Kozlak, Diane Krzanowski, Shirley C. Krompegal, Timothy P. Legeyt, Michael Lockaby, Donald L. MacKie, Mary Tomolonius, Carol G. York.

CHAPLIN. Windham County.—(Form of government, selectmen, town meeting, board of finance.)—Inc., 1822; taken from Windham, Mansfield and Hampton. Area, 19.6 sq. miles. Population, est., 2,183. Voting district, 1. Principal industry, agriculture. Post office, Chaplin. Rural free delivery for part of the town from Chaplin, North Windham and Mansfield Center post offices.

TOWN OFFICERS. Clerk and Reg. of Vital Statistics, Jane S. Hampton-Smith; Hours, 9 A.M.-3 P.M., Mon., Thurs., Fri.; 9 A.M.-1 P.M, 7-9 P.M., Tues.; Address, Town Hall, Rte. 198, P.O. Box 286, 06235; Tel., Willimantic, (860) 455-9455.—**Asst. Clerks and Asst. Regs. of Vital Statistics,** Janice Fitts, Linda T. Nielsen, Judith M. Spencer.—**Selectmen,** 1st, William E. Philbrick (R) Tel., (860) 455-0073, Eugene Boomer, Jr. (R), Raymond J. Helmer (D).—**Treas.,** Janice R. Fitts.—**Bd. of Finance,** David Morris, Chm., Donald Donofrio, Steven Gilbert, Robin Graves-Hoagland, Irene Schein, Richard Theriaque.—**Tax Collector,** Linda T. Nielsen.—**Bd. of Assessment Appeals,** Donald E. Fitzgerald, Ken Powchak, Keith Purdy.—**Assessor,** Herbert F. Braasch.—**Registrars of Voters,** Geraldine Helmer (D), Doris B. Silliman (R).—**Supt. of Schools,** Rodger Wutzl.—**Bd. of Education,** Bruce Kinzer, Marsha S. Purdy, Lisa A. Rose, Kamala P. Willey, 1997; Thomas A. Hoagland, Chm., Susan M. Peifer, Rickey T. Serwanski, 1999.—**Planning and Zoning Comm.,** Eugene Boomer, Jr., Chm., Gustav A. Birkmanis, Paul J. Carbone, David P. Garceau, Dale Kopek, Robert Northrop, Paul E. Peifer; Alternates, Randy J. Godaire, Gerald E. Robinson, Sr., Irene Schein.—**Zoning Bd. of Appeals,** Victor N. Boomer, Chm., Steven Chuk, Marvin Cox, Timothy Shashok, Steven J. Smith; Alternates, Edward Birkmanis, Richard H. Cahill, John Meyer.—**Zoning Enforcement Officer,** Raymond Murphy.—**Building Inspector,** Terry Bellman.—**Inland Wetlands Comm.,** Scott R. Matthies, Chm., Edward H. Bullard, John D. Fitts, Stephen Lanzit II, Steven Laume, Juan Sanchez, Jr., Randall J. Weiss; Alternates, William Ireland III, Lesley Sweeney, vacancy.—**Historic Dist. Comm.,** Marvin Cox, Chm., John D. Fitts, Carl Lindquist, Paul Peifer, Johanne Philbrick; Alternates, Charles Avila, Scott Matthies .—**Welfare Dir./Agent for the Elderly,** Gertrude I. Linkkila.—**Dir. of Health,** Peter Jones, M.D. (P.O., Willimantic).—**Library Directors,** Johanne Philbrick, Chm., Diane Cox, Nancy A. Goodrich,

Jane S. Hampton-Smith, Sally A. Ireland, Ellen V. Kinzer, Charlene Meyer, Marsha Purdy, Teresa Ridgeway, Anne Sicilian.—**Recreation Comm.**, Richard Theriaque, Chm., Chris Blair, Douglas Cates, Randy Godaire, Steven Guay, Brian Kelleher, Julie LaCasse, Anthony J. Pinto, Linda Sargent, Joyce St. Lawrence.—**Building Code Bd. of Appeals,** Paul Carbone, four vacancies.—**Road Foreman,** Anthony E. Burelle.—**Tree Warden,** Ronald Bertothy.—**Sanitarian,** John Valente.—**Chief of Police,** Wm. E. Philbrick.—**Chief of Fire Dept.,** Steve Guay; Deputy, Jim McDonough.—**Fire Marshal,** Robert Dubos.—**Burning Official,** Christopher Knight.—**Civil Preparedness Dir.,** Grove A. Baker.—**Town Atty.,** John Boland (P.O., Putnam).—**Justices of the Peace,** Victor N. Boomer, Patricia D. R. Boyd, Phyllis E. Garrison, Joan Gerdsen, Roger D. Golden, Bert D. Gunn, George H. Hamlin, Henry E. Hansen, Julie A. LaCasse, Stephen R. Lanzit II, Gertrude I. Linkkila, Dmitry L. Petrik, Kenneth Powchak, Gerald E. Robinson, Sr., Geraldine A. Siggins, Frederick A. Surridge, Lloyd D. Whitman, Sr.

CHESHIRE. New Haven County.—(Form of government, town manager, town council.)—Inc., May, 1780; taken from Wallingford. Area, 33.4 sq. miles. Population, est., 26,691. Voting districts, 4. Principal industries, agriculture and manufacture of brass goods and heavy machinery. Transp.—Passenger: Served by buses of Conn. Transit from New Haven and Waterbury. Freight: Served by Boston & Maine Corporation and numerous motor common carriers. Post office, Cheshire.

TOWN OFFICERS. Clerk and Reg. of Vital Statistics, Carolyn Z. Soltis; Hours, 8:30 A.M.-4 P.M., Mon. through Fri.; Address, Town Hall, 84 South Main St., 06410; Tel., (203) 271-6601.—**Asst. Clerks and Asst. Regs. of Vital Statistics,** Laura Brennan, Arnett T. Talbot, Elizabeth A. Walesky.—**Town Manager,** Edward T. O'Neill, Jr.—**Town Council,** Sandra R. Mouris (R), Chm. and Mayor; Alfred C. Adinolfi, David J. Borowy, Kathleen S. Held, Michael O'Brien, David E. Orsini, Thomas Stretton, Judy C. Villa, vacancy.—**Finance Dir.,** Michael A. Milone.—**Tax Collector,** Donald E. Holley.—**Bd. of Assessment Appeals,** Edward R. Ulozas, Chm., John L. Campbell, Martin L. Lambert.—**Assessor,** Mario J. Panagrosso, Jr.—**Registrars of Voters,** Sheila S. Kelly (D), Kathleen E. Nankin (R).—**Supt. of Schools,** Ralph Wallace.—**Bd. of Education,** Dennis C. Deninger, John A. Gremelsbacker, Richard E. Lau, 1997; Tod Dixon, Chm., Raymond F. Angelo, Jr., Dennis P. Clark, Carolyn H. Engelhardt, 1999.—**Planning and Zoning Comm.,** Joseph J. Traester, Chm., Barbara E. Barlok, Toby S. Brimberg, Richard Bruno, Daniel C. Esty, Kathleen E. Gannon, Kenneth G. Irish, Ranald P. Jones, Robert J. Reihl; Alternates, David A. Pelletier, Keith E. Robertson, Kathryn H. Smith.—**Town Planner,** Richard A. Pfurr; Asst., Lisa Murphy.—**Zoning Bd. of Appeals,** Robert J. Knowles, Chm., Harold W. Mosher, William P. O'Hara, Jr., Robert J. Sepp, Louis P. Todisco; Alternates, Roy Andersen, Jack Bush, Robert G. Capo.—**Zoning Enforcement Officer,** Lisa J. Murphy.—**Economic Development Comm.,** Richard A. Dice, Chm., Robert Babcock, Beatrice D. Fiorino, Arthur Hostage, John Hyslop, Lee McParland, David Schrumm, .—**Environmental Planner,** James Sipperly.—**Housing Auth.,** Harvey B. Boutwell, Chm., Albert C. Graziosa, Ruth Johnson, Brian J. Miller, John Souther, Richard A. Ziegler.—**Inland**

Wetlands Comm., Jack M. Pasquale, Chm., Robert G. Berner, Robert DeJongh, Charles W. Dimmick, Talivaldis Maidelis, Tiffany Masterson, Kristen Wolfe.—**Energy Comm.,** Roger F. Waszmer, Chm., Jack Altobello, Jack Bush, Ken Cianci, James R. Humphrey, David Wilder, Carol Wilson.—**Safety Comm.,** Walter Kulow, Chm., James M. Clark, Martha Ryzak.—**Town and Police Retirement Bd.,** Alan J. Craig, Chm., Carmen Civitello, Thomas Denne, Andrew Falvey, Edward Saad.—**Committee on Aging,** Diane Link, Chm., William Dunn, Mark J. Fernandez, Ebenezer Foster, David Hunter, Jay Kaplan, Rodney Lane, M. John Lyons, Edward Scott; Doreen Pulisciano, Agent.—**Dir. of Human Services,** Robert W. Bohannon.—**Dir. of Health,** Thomas J. Wegrzyn.—**Library Bd.,** Emmett Shutts, Chm., Joy Hostage, Daryl Marty, Becky Merrill, Nelle Mokrzynski, George Pawlush.—**Municipal Historian,** Arthur Hostage.—**Parks and Recreation Comm.,** James Nankin, Chm., Don Baillie, Matthew Bowman, Patrick Duffy, Lori Rusnack, Susan Saundry, Douglas Van Wie.—**Youth Services Committee,** William S. Ricker, Chm., Michael Balfe, William Freitag, Susan Harris, Elaine R. Lau, Christopher Pasquale, Herb J. Rosenfield.—**Dir. of Public Works,** Thomas F. Crowe, Jr.—**Tree Warden/Town Engineer,** Thomas F. Crowe, Jr.—**Building Inspector,** Leonard Cunningham.—**Building Code Bd. of Appeals,** John Bates, Steven Durkee, Patrick Euley, James Sakonchick.—**Water Pollution Control Auth.,** Kenneth E. Neumann, Chm., Steve Eberle, Timothy Pelton, Arthur Repak, Kenneth C. Stevens, Jr., David Veleber.—**Supt. of Sanitation,** James Theriault.—**Sanitarian,** Lorraine DeNicola.—**Chief of Police,** George R. Merriam; Deputy, Joseph Ferry.—**Constables,** John L. Campbell, Carmen M. Civitello, M. John Lyons, Joseph W. Raines.—**Public Building Comm.,** Philip Sapper, Chm., James H. Biggart, Lewis Cohen, C. Anthony Edge, Thomas H. Hughes, Jr., James McKenney, Frank W. Miner, John S. Purtill, Richard Sawyer.—**Chief of Fire Dept.,** Jack Casner.—**Fire Marshal,** James E. Doherty; Deputies, John Bates, Jeff Boland.—**Civil Preparedness Dir.,** George R. Merriam, Acting.—**Town Atty.,** John K. Knott, Jr.—**Justices of the Peace,** Sylvia V. S. Abbate, Alfred C. Adinolfi, John D. Altobello III, Raymond F. Angelo, Jr., Robert H. Averack, Josephine D. Banach, John W. Birkenberger, David J. Borowy, Janice M. Borowy, Harvey B. Boutwell, George E. Bowman, Paul A. Bowman, Pennie S. Branden, Jack Bush, Robert G. Capo, Dorothy M. Cassidy, Sandra A. Chase, Martin E. Cobern, Richard W. Conrad, Carol A. Dempsey, Wanda L. Dewey, Louis M. DiMauro, Charleen F. Dimmick, Theresa A. Dinicola, Ernest A. DiPietro, Jr., Tod Dixon, Kerrie Dunne, Lucy V. Earley, Stephen H. Eberle, Ellen M. Elsner, Daniel C. Esty, Stephen M. Ezer, Stephen F. Gabriel, Ronald A. Gagliardi, Kathleen E. Gannon, Elizabeth Giardino, John A. Gremeslbacker, Kathleen S. Held, Richard A. Held, Linda D. Hershman, Arthur Hostage, Joy W. Hostage, John J. Jakabauski, Kathleen A. Kaplan, Maryann M. Keane, Sheila S. Kelly, Robert J. Knowles, Michael J. Laden, Martin R. Lambert, Charles W. Liedke, Sr., Talivaldis Maidelis, David Mercugliano, Brian J. Miller, Frank W. Miner, Harold W. Mosher, Sandra R. Mouris, James A. Nankin, Sheila W. Pastor, George G. Pawlush III, John E. Reihl, James J. Rodgers, Hilary Rutberg, Henry Schissler, Linda Schissler, Raymond S. Shocki, Jr., Kathryn H. Smith, Laraine M. Smith, Thomas C. Smith, Thomas J. Staley, Raymond C. Stewart, Jr., Louis P. Todisco, Mickey M. Ulizio, Edward R. Ulozas, David S. Veleber, Judy C. Villa, Carol A. Wilson, Ann V. Zeiger.

CHESTER. Middlesex County.—(Form of government, selectmen, town meeting, board of finance.)—Inc., May, 1836; taken from Saybrook, now Deep River. Area, 16.8 sq. miles. Population, est., 3,621. Voting district, 1. Principal industries, windows, mailing equipment, emergency lighting equipment and metal goods manufacturing. Transp.—Passenger and Freight: Chester Airport and numerous motor common carriers. Post office, Chester.

TOWN OFFICERS. Clerk and Reg. of Vital Statistics, Debra G. Calamari; Hours, 9 A.M.-12 Noon, 1-4 P.M., Mon., Wed., Thurs.; 9 A.M.-12 Noon, 1-7 P.M., Tues.; 9 A.M.-12 Noon, Fri.; Address, Town Office Bldg., 65 Main St., P.O. Box 328, 06412; Tel., Deep River, (860) 526-0006.—**Asst. Clerks and Asst. Regs. of Vital Statistics,** Deborah A. Alldredge, Margaret C. Meehan.—**Selectmen,** 1st, Martin L. Heft (D) Tel., (860) 526-0013, Joseph F. Bergonzi (D), John S. Conant (R).—**Treas.,** Elizabeth A. Netsch.—**Bd. of Finance,** John R. Ivimey, Jr., Chm., Suzanne H. Carlson, Jennifer M. Janecek, Thomas E. Marsh, Edmund J. Meehan, Thomas S. Moore; Alternates, Wayne T. McAllister, Carl G. Nilsson, Elizabeth A. Perreault.—**Tax Collector,** Joyce A. Aley.—**Bd. of Assessment Appeals,** Bruce H. Watrous, Chm., Dudley W. Clark, Jr., Daniel M. Watts.—**Assessors,** William J. Hamel, Chm., Geoffrey L. Jacobson, Cynthia N. Stevens.—**Registrars of Voters,** Sandy Hesser (D), George Cusack (R).—**Supt. of Schools,** John H. Proctor.—**Bd. of Education,** Pamela M. Christman, Chm., Amy S. Conderino, Susan C. Hainsworth. Linda J. Hicks, Rebecca H. Johnson, Anna S. Sweeney, 1997; Marian L. Bairstow, Denise L. Learned, Robert J. Narducci, 1999.—**Planning and Zoning Comm.,** Michael W. Joplin, Chm., Janet C. Good, Christian F. Hamilton, Robert J. Miceli, William K. Paynter, Christopher J. Pearson, Priscilla R. Robinson, Natalie J. Williams, vacancy; Alternates, John M. Brodzinski, John J. DeLaura, Jr, Errol F. Horner.—**Zoning Bd. of Appeals,** Frank D. Lavezzoli, Chm., Deborah A. Alldredge, Jil N. Kaplan, Eugene T. Smith, Andrew J. Vomastek; Alternates, Mario S. Gioco, Kim V. Mendonsa, Elizabeth A. Sader.—**Zoning Enforcement Officer,** Larry Gilliam.—**Municipal Economic Development Comm.,** Thomas S. Moore, Chm., Margaret S. Bernier, William J. Kotchen, Lorraine Lieberman, Harry Meissner, Carl G. Nilsson, Charles Park, Joel P. Severance, Bruce H. Watrous, Leo V. Zavatone.—**Conservation Comm.,** John B. Ball, Chm., Albert G. Bisacky, William H. Burr, Richard Holloway, Thomas M. Kablik, George T. Trevisani, Jr., vacancy; Alternates, George H. Foulds, Nancy B. Kluck, Patricia A. Pendergast.—**Agent for the Elderly,** Ellen Redmount.—**Dir. of Social Services,** Lynn Legan.—**Dir. of Health,** Russell Munson, M.D.—**Retirement Bd.,** Scott K. Baker, Chm., David L. Burr, Donald A. Croteau, Jennifer M. Janecek, Whitelaw Wilson.— **Library Bd.,** Margaret C. Meehan, Chm., Edward C. Hull, Jill F. Jones, Katherine M. Marsh, Jane W. Paynter, Jeanne M. Ross.—**Municipal Historian,** Robert J. Miceli.— **Parks and Recreation Comm.,** J. Brian Buckley, Chm., William S. Drain, Darlene F. Decker, Susan C. Hainsworth, Beth Mularski, James L. Ready, Scott W. Smith; Elizabeth A. Netsch, Dir.—**Building Inspector,** Ronald Rose.—**Water Pollution Control Auth.,** William Reddy, Chm., Joseph F. Bergonzi, John S. Conant, Martin L. Heft, James K. Pease.—**Tree Warden,** Martin L. Heft.—**Resident State Trooper,** Thomas Heinssen.—**Constables,** Todd Belcourt, Richard J. Ciecierski, Steven Fuelner, Russell Gingras II, Edward Naples, Kenneth J. Reid, Charles Vincelette, six vacancies.—**Police Comrs.,** Joseph F. Bergonzi, Charlene O. Janecek, Helen E. Raffuse, Jeffrey H. Ridgway, Peter J. Zanardi.—**Chief of Fire Dept.,** Edward F. Perkins III; Asst., Charles Greeney, Jr.—**Fire Marshal,** Bernard F. Negrelli; Deputy, John L. Simcheski.—**Bd. of Fire Comrs.,** Joel P. Severance, Chm., Francis D. Lavezzoli, Bernard Negrelli, Edward F. Perkins III, Richard M. Schreiber.—**Emergency Mgmt. Dir.,** Elizabeth Perreault; Deputy, Raymond Narducci.—**Town Atty.,** John Bennet (Essex).—**Justices of the Peace,** Phyllis A. Bevington, Dawn C. Burr, John S. Conant, Joseph Friend, John C. Giddings, Emily S. Miller, Elizabeth A. Perreault, Harvey E. Redak, Anna S. Sweeney, Jerry A. Walden, Mary Wheeler, Whitelaw Wilson.

CLINTON. Middlesex County.—(Form of government, selectmen, town meeting, board of finance.)—Inc., May, 1838; taken from Killingworth. Area, 19.0 sq. miles. Population, est., 13,137. Voting districts, 2. Principal industries, agriculture, fishing, and the manufacture of face creams, toilet preparations, facial tissues, plastics, wire and small boat building. Transp.—Passenger: Served by buses of Conn. Transit and Shoreline Service from New Haven and Shore Line Rail. Freight: Served by Conrail and numerous motor common carriers. Post office, Clinton.

TOWN OFFICERS. Clerk and Reg. of Vital Statistics, Karen L. Marsden; Hours, 9 A.M.-4 P.M., Mon. through Fri.; Address, 54 East Main St., 06413; Tel., (860) 669-9101.—**Asst. Clerk and Asst. Reg. of Vital Statistics,** Pollyanne I. Brown.—**Selectmen,** 1st, James M. McCusker, Jr. (D) Tel., (860) 669-9333, James R. Cave (R), Paul D. Jakubson (D), Lewis J. Perry, Jr. (D), Dan D. Shaw (R).—**Treas.,** William E. Lofgren; Asst., Anna Rubino.—**Bd. of Finance,** Stuart W. Fox, Chm., Jeffrey A. Cissell, Barbara H. Webb, G. Curtis Whelan, Sandra M. Woodbridge, Richard A. Zimmerman; Rosemary Fallknor, Dir.; Alternates, SueAnn Cunningham, William B. Robbins.—**Tax Collector,** Dolly G. Mezzetti.—**Bd. of Assessment Appeals,** Gary P. Bergeron, Chm., James E. Burris, James M. Conklin.—**Assessor,** Christine Barta.—**Registrars of Voters,** Diane L. Shepard (D), Donna Chrostowski (R).—**Supt. of Schools,** David B. Erwin.—**Bd. of Education,** John W. Corvo, Jr., Deborah T. Grass, Glynis P. Houde, Robert M. Smalley, 1997; James Aiello, Jr., William L. Calvert, Susan M. Skidmore, 1999.—**Bd. of Ethics,** Miguel A. Escalera, Margery C. Scully, Russell D. Woodbridge.—**Communications Committee,** Peter Finch, Charles Hynes, James M. McCusker, Jr., Peter Seale, Melanie Yanus.—**Planning and Zoning Comm.,** Kim Barrows, Chm., Anne B. Caldwell, Gale W. Miller, Michael J. Mozzochi III, Kimberly Ann Neri, Raymond J. Rigat, Gary F. Sheldon, Nancy Taubman, Marye T. Wagner; Alternates, Jane A. Cerri, two vacancies.—**Zoning Bd. of Appeals,** Mark W. Richards, Chm., Noreen T. Braza, George Doerrer, Joel A. Douglas, Lauren Santos; Alternates, Martin K. Lane, Kenton P. Moore, Jeff M. VanTienan.—**Zoning Enforcement Officer,** Barbara Swan.—**Economic Development Comm.,** Daniel A. Vece, Jr., Chm., James E. Burris, III, David C. Grimm, Peter Moore, Carl A. Neri, two vacancies.—**Housing Auth.,** John Neri, Chm., Gordon E. Folsom, Sr., Edward J. O'Brien, Janet Schrensky, vacancy.—**Inland Wetlands Comm.,** Carol G. Carlough, Kenton P. Moore, Co-Chm., Beth E. Davies, Lynn Holland, Michael J. Nejdl, Kevin J. Zawoy, vacancy; Alternates, Kathryn F. Bozzi, Sueanne Cunningham, Judith M. McGuinness.—**Historic Dist. Comm.,** Carl L. Bixby, Jr., Chm., Sally V. Bergeron, Siobhan C. Doherty-Rogers, Florence M. Heck, Nancy Taubman; Alternates, Gregory Bartels, G. Clive Cowper, Josephine J. Elliot.—**Municipal Historian,** Ernest C. Burnham, Jr.—**Agent for the Elderly/Veterans Affairs,** Miguel A. Escalera.—**Dir. of Social Services,** Charles Lennerton.—**Dir. of Health,** Arnold C. Winokur.—**Youth and Family Services Bureau,** Nancy D. Hayes, Cheryl J. Hill, David M. Konefal, Pamela L. Perry, John P. Quinn, Lois A. Ruggiero, Doreen Sambuco, Susan B. Schreck, Gary F. Sheldon, Catherine Wall.—**Park and Recreation Comm.,** Harold A. Swaun, Chm., Michael J. Brochu, Dennis M. Donovan, Barbara A. Lye, Mark Scagliarini, Joseph E. Schettino, Jr., Michael L. Sutyla; Robert Potter, Dir.—**Public Works Comm.,** Gerald J. Cotter, Chm., William A. Comeau, James L. Forchielli, Joseph F. Novajosky, David Sousa; Edward Vailette, Dir.; Alternates, George C. Heck, Peter A. Neff.—**Building Official,** Louis E. Siegle.—**Water Pollution Control Auth.,** Robert J. Grabarek, Chm., Thomas A. McKernan, Robert F. Nielson, Karen L. Rigat, Gary J. Russo, Selwyn L. Taubman, William Walter.—**Harbor Management Comm.,** Steven D. Hayes, Chm., Bradley J. Fallon, Lorraine B. Joel, Ronald D. Nash, Gregory H. Nazarian, John D. Sullivan, William W. Webster.—**Shell Fish Comm.,** Thomas A. Brennan, Chm., David Kaplan, Henry T. Stebbins.—**Chief of Police,** Joseph P. Faughnan.—**Police Comm.,** Carl F. Swan, Chm., James A. Beardsley, Robert E. DiBona, Lorraine B. Joel, Angelo V. Lupone.—**Constables,** William Hoffman, Paul F. King, William B. Robbins, Peter E. Rogers.—**Chief of Fire Dept.,** Hugh D. Allen.—**Fire Marshal,** Hugh D. Allen.—**Civil Preparedness Dir.,** Peter B. Finch.—**Town Atty.,** John S. Bennet.—**Justices of the Peace,** James A. Beardsley, Noreen T. Braza, Patricia K. Butler, Patricia Cook, James B. Diamond, Richard L. Hershatter, Condile Kunkel, Stephanie Lemay, Lewis J. Perry, Jr., Joseph Schettino, Jr., Michael Teodosio, Louise D. Welch, Virginia D. Zawoy.

COLCHESTER. New London County.—(Form of government, selectmen, town meeting, board of finance.)—Inc., 1698; named, Oct., 1699. Area, 49.8 sq. miles. Population, est., 11,906. Voting district, 1. Principal industries, agriculture and manufacture of leather novelties, plastics and ladies' coats, machine shop, metal fabrication. Transp.—Passenger: Served by buses of Connecticut Transit Auth. from Hartford and New London; Barstow Bus Transp. from Norwich. Freight: Served by numerous motor common carriers. Post office, Colchester. Five rural free deliveries from Colchester and one from East Hampton.

TOWN OFFICERS. Clerk and Reg. of Vital Statistics, Patricia A. LaGrega; Hours, 8:30 A.M.-4:30 P.M., Mon. through Fri.; 8:30 A.M.-7 P.M., Thurs.; Address, Town Hall, 127 Norwich Ave., 06415; Tel., (860) 537-7215.—**Asst. Clerks and Asst. Regs. of Vital Statistics,** Nancy Bray, Joyce Kelley.—**Selectmen,** 1st, Jenny Contois (D) Tel., (860) 537-7220, William Wagner (R), Goldie Liverant (D), Keith Marvin (R), James Sinclair (D).—**Treas.,** Donald Stanavage.—**Bd. of Finance,** Bruce Hayn, Chm., Dean Conrad, Ronald Goldstein, Gregory Kehaya, Robert Kell, Jon Sandberg.— **Tax Collector,** Sharon Dailey.—**Bd. of Assessment Appeals,** Robin Havelin, John Sawchuk, Arthur Standish.—**Registrars of Voters,** Dorothy Mrowka (D), Barbara Gibbons (R).—**Supt. of Schools,** Michael Riley.—**Bd. of Education,** William Hettrick, Chm., Maureen Connolly, Jay Einhorn, Donna Maltempo, 1997; Mark A. Balaban, John Mazzarella, Jean M. Stawicki, 1999.—**Planning and Zoning Comm.,** Robert Weeks, Chm., Derek Amidon, Michael Ciccone, Jeffrey Ferro, Kenneth Fragnoli, Paul Maxwell, Robert O'Hagan, John Poniatowski, Ronald S. Vasques, two vacancies.—**Zoning Bd. of Appeals,** Dorothy Mrowka, Chm., Donald Emond, Linda Sablitz, Fay Sherman, Arthur Shilosky; Alternates, Kenneth Judd, Darryl J. Lowden, Al Zaremskas.—**Housing Auth.,** Eleanor Feldman, Cheryl Good, Doris L. Krause, Janet LaBella, Roselyn Plotkin; Dorothy Shiff, Exec. Dir.—**Fair Rent Comm.,** Laura Flom, Neil Gervasi, Steven Petty, Dorothy Shiff, Richard Squires, Odessa Turner.—**Conservation and Inland Wetlands Comm.,** Gary Avery, Susan Bruening, Morris Epstein, Nicholas Norton, Mark Saternis; Alternates, Kurt Prochorena, two vacancies.—**Historic Dist. Comm.,** H. Jean Smith, Chm., Alma Alpert, Theresa Congdon, Kip Morrissett, Irving Plotkin; Alternates, Janice Adams, Nancy J. Anderson, Andrew George.—**Arts Comm.,** Bette Avery, Naomi B. Kearns, Debbie Nericco, Martha Rhodes, Cheryl Ringo.—**Comm. on Aging,** Catherine Conderino, Chm., Fanny Bray, Joan DeVore, Amy Ferling, Margaret Loomis, Ann Smyk, Muriel Zehntner, Robert W. Zehntner.—**Youth Comm.,** Fred Briger, Elizabeth D'Atri, Shirley Holt, Carla Johnson, Lorraine Marvin, Lynn Noyes, Carla Schwartz.—**Welfare Dir.,** Lyn Mara.—**Dir. of Health,** Lynn Poniatowski, R.N.M.S.—**Library Directors,** Lynn Norton, Chm., Aldene Bauchman, Virginia Campbell, Celia Conrad, Jenny Contois, A. Victor Horvitz, Audrey Saly, Robert Warren, Erica Wimber.—**Parks and Recreation Comm.,** Norman Kaplan, Chm., David Anderson, Cathy Costello, Paul Knutsen, David McElroy, Anita Miazga, David O'Brien, Diane Zettervall; Alternate, Ronald Yuchniuk.—**Dir. of Public Works,** Mark Decker.—**Zoning Inforcement Officer,** Alicia Lathrop.—**Building Inspector,** Timothy York.—**Sewer and Water,** Scott Bayden, Anthony Cerino, Gregory Cordova, Rick LeMay, Nancy Riella, William Stepule, Carey Stollman, Robert Tarlov, Robert Washburn.—**Sewer Auth.,** Bd. of Selectmen.—**Police Comm.,** Robert Bromley, James Kennedy, Linda Orange, Steve Petty, George White.—**Chief of Fire Dept.,** Jess McMinn.—**Fire Marshal,** Reed Gustafson.—**Civil Preparedness Dir.,** Reed Gustafson.—**Town Attys.,** Shipman and Goodwin.—**Justices of the Peace,** Pamela A. Adams, David K. Anderson, Mark Balaban, Patricia A. Barton, Francis E. Blume, James W. Ciaglo, Jr., John D. Cohen, Theresa I. Congdon, Celia B. Conrad, Jenny Contois, Andrew J. Cournoyer, David E. Cournoyer, Jason D. Cournoyer, Amy Beth Coyle, Rosemary Coyle, Stephen A. Coyle, Diane M. Donle, Sam Downey, Jay R. Einhorn, Louis A. Eguren, Kenneth E. Fargnoli, Eileen S. Fazekas, John F. Fedus, James A. Felciano, Richard Finkelstein, Rosalinde Finkelstein, Maureen Gammo, Richard W. Gibbons, Irving S. Goldberg, Bruce I. Goldstein, H. Renee Goldstein, Raymond A. Hastings, Valerie C. Hopkins-McGriff, Arthur V. Horvitz, Sheila S. Horvitz, Joseph J. Joaquin, Kenneth C. Judd, Stephen J. Jurovaty, Gregory E. Kehaya, Robert Kell, Virginia M. Kriedel, Diane M. LaGrega, Merja Lehtinen, Sandra L. Lewis, Andrew S. Liverant, Goldie Liverant, John D. Long, Edward L. Mack, Thomas M. Maikshilo, Cathy C. Marvin, Everett W. Marvin, Keith R. Marvin, Loren W. Marvin, John Mazzarella, Jess J. McMinn, Jakob Mincengendler, Dorothy A. Mrowka, Lucien C. Mrowka, Selma S. Nirenstein, John J. Nolan, Ana K. Norton, Andrew M. Norton, Linda A. Orange, Albert A. Ouellette, Jr., Bernard G. Park, Elyse R. Park, Ronald E. Pepin, Adam Piekarz, Helen Piekarz, Margaret A. Popek, Michael Popek, Michael A. Popek, Nancy W. Riella, Burton C. Ryan, Linda R. Sablitz, Audrey

V. Sally, Walter L. Sanchi, John W. Sawchuk, Walter Sawchuk, Jr., William Sawchuk, Steven A. Schuster, Mary Jane Scott, James S. Sinclair, Donald A. Stanavage, Susan G. Standish, Gloria A. Sypher, Frank D. Tamburrino, Sr., Francis H. Tarnowski, William F. Wagner, Nancy Wasniewski.

COLEBROOK. Litchfield County.—(Form of government, selectmen, town meeting, board of finance.)—Inc., Oct., 1779. Area, 32.9 sq. miles. Population, est., 1,347. Voting district, 1. Principal industry, agriculture. Freight: Served by numerous motor common carriers. Post office, Colebrook; rural delivery from Riverton and Winsted.

TOWN OFFICERS. Clerk and Reg. of Vital Statistics, N. Joyce Nelson; Hours, 10 A.M.-4:30 P.M., Mon., Fri.; 1-4:30 P.M., Tues., Wed., Thurs.; Address, Town Hall, 558 Colebrook Rd., P.O. Box 5, 06021; Tel., Winsted, (860) 379-3359; FAX (860) 379-7215.—**Asst. Clerk and Asst. Reg. of Vital Statistics,** Lorraine C. Washington.—**Selectmen,** 1st, George M. Wilber (D) Tel., (860) 379-3359, Isidore P. Jasmin III (D), Ralph W. Hazen, Jr. (R).—**Treas.,** Richard E. Blankenship.—**Bd. of Finance,** Sylvia J. Virgilio, Chm., Judith A. Bottomley, Diane E. Johnstone, Barbara G. Spiegel, Janet B. Stason, Thomas A. Travaglin.—**Tax Collector,** N. Joyce Nelson.—**Bd. of Assessment Appeals,** Mark A. Lett, Chm., Nadia M. Corvo, Jerome F. Rathbun.—**Assessors,** Joan M. Durant, William E. Nelson, Helga I. Poreda.—**Registrars of Voters,** Richard H. Hemingson (D), Eleanor E. Russo (R).—**Supt. of Schools,** David Wittmer.—**Bd. of Education,** Thomas L. Hodgkin, Chm., Joyce C. Hemingson, Douglas M. Kenneson, 1997; Joseph J. Alciati, Donald Barr, Sarah W. Estock, Stephen W. Kravitz, 1999.—**Planning and Zoning Comm.,** Evelyn W. Crane, Chm., Howard G. Estock, Michael F. Jasmin, Anthony W. Komarnsky, Theodore V. Wilber; Alternates, Gordon S. Coleman, Bruce A. Desmond, vacancy.—**Zoning Bd. of Appeals,** Richard F. White, Chm., Sandra J. Brennan, Thomas E. Lawton, Charles S. Whitney, Fred P. Williams; Alternates, Edward J. Banas, Siegfried W. Poreda, Frank R. Trager.—**Inland Wetlands Comm.,** Norman F. Thompson III, Chm., Thomas E. Adams, Vernon H. Dunbar, Diana A. Holcomb, Raymond L. Swanton; Alternates, Leroy E. Millard, Jr., Keith Sleeper, vacancy.—**Historic Dist. Comm.,** Nancy P. Blum, Chm., Joyce C. Hemingson, John Hooker, Frank W. Jones, Jr., Olga H. Lossin; Alternates, Evelyn W. Crane, Marcella C. Miller, Harriet L. Smith.—**Dir. of Health,** Farmington Valley Health Dist.—**Recreation Bd.,** Raymond A. Winn, Chm., Peter P. Case, James P. Davidson III, Theresa J. Kenneson, Julie King.—**Building Inspector,** Charles J. McCarthy.—**Tree Warden,** George M. Wilber.—**Chief of Police,** George M. Wilber.—**Constables,** H. Spencer Coleman, Christopher L. Johnstone, John H. Lossin, Gerald J. Peters.—**Chief of Fire Dept.,** John T. Boutin.—**Fire Marshal,** Joseph Beadle.—**Civil Preparedness Dir.,** Alan R. White.—**Town Atty.,** David A. Moraghan (P.O., Torrington).—**Justices of the Peace,** Holly M. Bodycoat, Barbara B. Case, Sally A. Coleman, Samuel W. Franklin III, Carol J. Googins, Robert E. Jasmin, Sr., Diane E. Johnstone, Peter J. Kennedy, Patricia M. Marshall, John C. Miller, Marcella C. Miller, William E. Nelson, Jr., John P. Parisi, Janet H. Rathbun, James E. Rogers, Barbara G. Spiegel, Sidney S. VanLeer, Lorraine C. Washington, Penelope F. White, Gloria M. Wilber.

COLUMBIA.

Tolland County.—(Form of government, selectmen, town meeting.)—Inc., May, 1804; taken from Lebanon. Area, 22.0 sq. miles. Population, est., 4,845. Voting district, 1. Principal industry, manufacturing. Summer resort. Transp.—Passenger: Served by Bonanza Bus Lines, Inc. Freight: Served by numerous motor common carriers. Post office, Columbia. Rural free delivery of mail from Columbia post office.

TOWN OFFICERS. Clerk and Reg. of Vital Statistics, Robin M. Kenefick; Hours, 9 A.M.-3 P.M., Mon. through Fri.; 6-8 P.M., Mon.; Address, Yeomans Hall, 323 Rte. 87, 06237; Tel., (860) 228-3284.—**Asst. Clerks and Asst. Regs. of Vital Statistics,** Elaine P. Trask; Sub. Reg., Paul J. Cichon.—**Selectmen,** 1st, Adella G. Urban (D) Tel., (860) 228-0110, Robert C. Baldwin, Jr. (R), Louis J. Scotti (D).—**Treas.,** Linda C. Spector; Asst., Nancy R. Smith.—**Financial Planning and Allocation Comm.,** Mark A. Allen, Kevin C. Donohue, Marshall A. Martin, William P. O'Brien, Stephen G. Ruff, Catherine U. Treuting, Lynne Urban.—**Financial Planner,** Paula L. Stahl.—**Tax Collector,** Carol Price; Asst., Erminia D. Lowman.—**Bd. of Assessment Appeals,** Peter A. Nichols, Helmut Traichel, Herbert W. Winkler.—**Assessor,** Eunice G. McDermott; Asst., Deborah E. German.—**Registrars of Voters,** Astrid S. Belanger (D), Evelyn F. Cafrella (R).—**Supt. of Schools,** Dean T. Toepfer.—**Bd. of Education,** Marjorie Golden-Mossberg, Marjorie M. Inzinga, Felicia N. O'Brien, 1997; Sandra S. Figoten, Cathy N. Klein, Wendy T. Peters, Jonathan S. Zorn, 1999.—**Town Planner/Zoning Enforcement Officer,** Martha A. Fraenkel.—**Planning and Zoning Comm.,** Edwin J. Johnston, Jr., Chm., Walter Deptula, Russell P. Inzinga, Edward F. Mathieu, Jr., Anthony A. Morascini, Peter A. Nichols, William C. Peck; Alternates, Gloria J. Boque, Nancy A. Hammarstrom, Richard B. Lavigueur.—**Zoning Bd. of Appeals,** Joseph J. Narkawicz, Chm., Michael J. Berube, Ann B. Blanchard, Matthew J. Fredette, Gregory L. Woodruff; Alternates, Robert J. Boque, John F. Haggerty, Joseph P. Szegda.—**Conservation Comm.,** Charles L. Phillips III, Chm., Diane Duva, Joan M. Hill, Irene M. Laskow, James E. Parker, Carole J. Williamson, two vacancies.—**Inland Wetlands Comm.,** Clarke L. Robinson, Chm., Thomas Archambault, Donald P. Cianci, Claude A. Garritt, Jr., John F. Haggerty, Charles W. Sanborn, Ronald J. Wikholm; John Valente, Agent; Alternates, two vacancies.—**Solid Waste Comm.,** Elisabeth P. Andrews, Henry Golan, Peter Naumec, Mary Ratti, vacancy.—**Municipal Historian,** Anita F. Ramm.—**Comm. on Aging,** Myron Berkowitz, Sally C. Broderick, Betty S. Eigner, Sophie Golan, Warren P. Jurovaty, Phyllis G. Starkel, Irving L. Tannenbaum.—**Municipal Agent for the Elderly,** Patricia M. Moon.—**Social Services Admr.,** Patricia M. Moon.—**Senior Services Coordinator,** Katherine Eves.—**Dir. of Health,** Ralph Laguardia, M.D.—**Recreation Council,** Gary Reynolds, Pres., Jerry A. James, Jean Murphy, Jeanne Nuhfer.—**Building Inspector,** Robert S. Moreland.—**Sanitarian,** John Valente.—**Building Code Bd. of Appeals,** Helmut Traichel, four vacancies.—**Road Foreman,** Henry J. Ausburger.—**Public Works Dir.,** Peter Naumec.—**Public Safety Comm.,** Peter J. Moeckel, Chm., Carey M. Bilyeu, Santo Franzo, Michael J. Lester, David R. Shaffer.—**Chief of Police,** Adella G. Urban.—**Conservation Constables,** Peter J. Moeckel, Robert Zahansky.—**Open Burning Officials,** Peter J. Moeckel Peter J. Starkel.—**Chief of Fire Dept.,** Jerry A. James; Deputy, Michael J. Lester.—**Fire Marshal,** Leslie A. Kittle, Jr.; Deputy, Michael J. Lester.—**Civil Preparedness Dir.,** Frances Sullivan.—**Town Atty.,** Stanley Falkenstein (P.O., Manchester).—**Justices of the Peace,** Joan F. Baldwin, Henry M. Beck, Kevin C. Donohue, Russell P. Inzinga, Gary A. Littlefield, Hugh M. MacKenzie, Frances A. Malek, William P. O'Brien, Carl H. Schwartz, Elaine P. Trask, Mark A. Vining.

CORNWALL. Litchfield County.—(Form of government, selectmen, town meeting, board of finance.)—Inc., May, 1740. Area, 46.3 sq. miles. Population, est., 1,498. Voting district, 1. Rural residential community. Served by numerous motor common carriers. Post offices, Cornwall, Cornwall Bridge, West Cornwall and rural free delivery from Falls Village, Litchfield, West Cornwall and Cornwall Bridge.

TOWN OFFICERS. Clerk and Reg. of Vital Statistics, Cheryl C. Evans; Hours, 9 A.M.-4 P.M., Mon. through Thurs.; Address, Town Office, 26 Pine St., P.O. Box 97, 06753; Tel., (860) 672-2709.—**Asst. Clerks and Asst. Regs. of Vital Statistics,** Barbara C. Dakin, Vera L. Dinneen.—**Selectmen,** 1st, Gordon M. Ridgway (D) Tel., (860) 672-4959, William E. Brecher (D), J. W. Preston (R).—**Treas.,** D. Stevenson Hedden.—**Bd. of Finance,** Ralph C. Gold, Chm., Kenneth C. Baird, Hendon Chubb, Peter M. Hammond, William Hurlburt, Willis Ocain; Alternates, Denten E. Butler, Jr., Celia Senzer.—**Tax Collector,** Helen Migliacci.—**Bd. of Assessment Appeals,** John E. LaPorta, Jean Pond, Phyllis H. Wojan.—**Assessor,** Barbara S. Johnson.—**Registrars of Voters,** Jayne Ridgway (D), Lisa K. Cruse (R).—**Supt. of Schools,** Marvin Maskovsky.—**Bd. of Education,** Katherine E. Gannett, Chm., Philip W. Hart, Anne Zinsser, 1997; Philip S. Bishop, Robin Freydberg, James Terrall, 1999.—**Planning and Zoning Comm.,** William Lyon, Chm., John A. Frost, Kenneth E. Keskinen, Lynn Scoville, Doc Simont, James Whiteside; Alternates, Vera L. Dinneen, Anne Kosciusko, Jr., Isabelle C. Osborne.—**Zoning Bd. of Appeals,** Huntington Williams, Chm., Anne Chamberlain, Ella L. Clark, Klaus W. Edler, John L. Miller, Phyllis Nauts; Alternates, Donald Bardot, Phyllis Wojan, Joanne Wojtusiak.—**Zoning Enforcement Officer,** John E. Calhoun.—**Conservation Comm.,** George F. Brown, Chm., Chris Hopkins, Timothy Locke, Michael B. Redmond, Michael Root, Lori B. Welles.—**Inland Wetlands Agency,** D. Stevenson Hedden, Chm., Jean Bouteiller, William Hurlburt, Charles C. Osborne, Doc Simont; Alternates, Arthur F. Lorch, James Prentice.—**Committee for the Aging,** Liane Dunn, Jill E. Gibbons, Paula V. Holmes, Lucy R. Kling.—**Agent for the Elderly,** Jill E. Gibbons.—**Parks and Recreation Comm.,** Martha Bruehl, Chm., Deirdre A. Fischer, Joe Gwazdauskas, Hugh I. Hunt, Brian Kavanagh, Caren Nelson, Mark Pastre, Craig I. Simons; Alternates, Diane L. Cole, Sharon L. Sawicki.—**Municipal Historian,** Michael G. Gannett.—**Building Inspector,** William Jenks.—**Fire Marshal,** Stanley MacMillen, Jr.—**Tree Warden,** George F. Brown.—**Chief of Police,** Gordon M. Ridgway.—**Chief of Fire Dept.,** David Williamson.—**Civil Preparedness Dir.,** Richard Lynn.—**Town Atty.,** Perley H. Grimes (P.O., Litchfield).—**Justices of the Peace,** Donald Bardot, William W. Beecher, Carla S. Bigelow, Philip S. Bishop, Denton E. Butler, Jr., Gordon S. Cady, Hendon Chubb, Patricia T. Collins, Richard B. Dakin, Klaus W. Edler, Jane Giddens-Jones, Montgomery Hare, Donald Hedden, Kenneth E. Keskinen, Barbara Klaw, Elizabeth H. Lansing, John F.

Leich, Phyllis Nauts, Marie Prentice, Ann M. Schillinger, Julia M. Scott, Stephen Senzer, Pauline Sobotka.

COVENTRY. Tolland County.—(Form of government, town manager, town council, town meeting.)—Inc., May, 1712. Area, 38.4 sq. miles. Population, est., 10,905. Voting districts, 3. Principal industries, agriculture, varying, the manufacture of sutures, and varied small industries. Principally residential. Transp.—Freight: Served by numerous motor common carriers. Post office, Coventry; seven rural delivery routes.

TOWN OFFICERS. Clerk and Reg. of Vital Statistics, Ruth E. Benoit; Hours, 8:30 A.M.-4:30 P.M., Mon. through Wed.; 8:30 A.M.-6:30 P.M., Thurs.; 8:30 A.M.-1:30 P.M., Fri.; Address, Town Office Bldg., 1712 Main St., P.O. Box 189, 06238; Tel., (860) 742-7966.—**Asst. Clerks and Asst. Regs. of Vital Statistics,** Susan J. Cyr, Cheryl A. McIntire.—**Town Manager,** John A. Elsesser.—**Town Council,** Joan A. Lewis, Chm., Mark S. Allaben, Michael Donohue, Matthew D. O'Brien, Denise M. Savageau, Claire C. Twerdy, M. Deborah Walsh.—**Treas.,** Ruth E. Benoit.—**Tax Collector,** Shirley D. Martin.—**Bd. of Assessment Appeals,** Rose M. Fowler, Chm., Lester T. Hill, John C. Howard, Jr., Kathleen A. Joy, Anthony J. Mancuso.—**Assessor,** Lindell Braasch.—**Registrars of Voters,** 1st Dist., Marjorie L. Roach, 2nd Dist., Barbara K. Johnson, Dist. 2A, Mary Ann Hall (D); 1st Dist., Janice K. Hall, 2nd Dist., Sandra D. Ashley Dist. 2A, Inge Pope (R).—**Supt. of Schools,** Michael J. Malinowski.—**Bd. of Education,** Linda A. Scussel, Chm., Peter DePaola, Michael P. Enders, Jonathan B. Kreisberg, Karen L. Post, Kathleen Ryan, Pamela S. Sewel, 1997.—**Personnel Appeals Bd.,** Roberta Falana, Lawrence J. Golden, Robert J. Haas, Peter L. Halvorson, G. Richard Messier, Patricia A. White, vacancy.—**Pension and Retirement Comm.,** Sandra D. Ashley, Marilyn S. Chase, Laurence Diamond, Katherine Muraski, William J. Zenko; Richard Dziadus, Agent.—**Planning and Zoning Comm.,** Darby L. Pollansky, Chm., Michael P. Enders, Richard Hines, David A. Ruth, Joann L. Terry; Alternates, George W. Dolleris, two vacancies.—**Town Planner,** Eric M. Trott.—**Zoning Bd. of Appeals,** Matthew G. Anderson, Chm., Bruce A. Bergeron, Donald L. Ferry, William G. Hoffman, Pamela B. Parkinson; Alternates, Jean M. Cardinal, Lionel G. Jean, Christopher Sarli.—**Zoning Enforcement Officer,** Stephen T. Wallace.—**Inland Wetlands Comm.,** William Saganich, Jr., Chm., Brian D. Coss, Lori J. Mathieu, Darby L. Pollansky, Beau Thurnaver; Alternates, Steven Klimkoski, vacancy.—**Economic Development Comm.,** Sondra A. Stave, Chm., Michael F. Farina, Richard E. Giggey, Raymond P. Giglio, James N. Ladd, Jr., Mark Lavitt, John A. Ohlund III, Richard C. Pelletier, Donald A. Scussel.—**Housing Auth.,** Albert E. Bradley, Chm., Charlotte C. Kennedy, James N. Ladd, Jr., Constance Lathrop, Mary Walsh.—**Housing Code Bd. of Appeals,** Debra Freund-Bother, Clifford Johnson, Joseph Malon, David Mortlock, John Motycka, Curtis Reynolds.—**Conservation Comm.,** Eric D. Thomas, Chm., Pauline Arendt, Arthur W. Hall, Leroy A. Lowe, Jr., William Saganich, two vacancies.—**Municipal Historian,** Arnold E. Carlson.—**Arts Comm.,** Herman W. Dahl, Chm., Constance Ballou, Allison Bayer, Christine A. Coss, Joelen Gates, Elizabeth R. Murphy; Alternates, Tanzzy Cooley-Castonguay, Michael F. Farina, Jr., Diane Fitzgerald.—**Human Rights Comm.,** Albert E. Bradley, Chm.,

Debra Freund-Bothur, David Meldrum, Patricia White, vacancy; Dorothy M. Grady, Officer.—**Human Services Admr.,** Dorothy M. Grady.—**Youth Advisory Bd.,** Carol M. Bonnano, Barbara Caldwell, Terrie D. Carpenter, Cathy I. Cemetina, Paul Manzone, Kate Norris, Gladys M. Rychling, Walter Solinski, Susan B. Weikel; Donna H. Newton, Coordinator.—**Medical Advisor,** Robert P. Bowen, M.D.—**Dir. of Health,** Robert M. Bowen.—**Parks and Recreation Comm.,** Orlo B. Smith, Chm., Terrie O. Carpenter, Richard J. Cromie, Robert C. Ferguson, Kenneth J. Jones, Marsha L. Kolodziej, Warren K. Little; Mark Paquette, Recreation Dir.—**Supt. of Public Works,** Walter Veselka.—**Town Engineer,** Weston & Sampson.—**Building Inspector,** Robert J. Bach.—**Building Code Bd. of Appeals,** David A. Eddy, Chm., Michael F. Cleary, John N. Motycka, Richard C. Pelletier, James T. Rowley, Jr.—**Insurance Advisory Comm.,** Donald J. Edwards, Chm., Laurence Diamond, Clifford Johnson, Irene J. Kwiatowski, Terrance S. McCarthy.—**Water Pollution Control Auth.,** Denise E. Alexander, Katherine Fowler, John P. Ianni, Donald A. Scussel, Matthew J. Twerdy.—**Tree Warden,** Charles Conkling.—**Chief of Police,** Frank V. Trzaskos.—**Constables,** two vacancies.—**Chiefs of Fire Dept.,** Michael LaChappelle (Coventry), Charles Greenbacker (North Coventry).—**Fire Marshal,** Noel E. Waite.—**Burning Official,** Lester T. Hill, Noel E. Waite.—**Civil Preparedness Dir.,** Kenneth A. Hicks.—**Town Atty.,** Michael A. Zizka.—**Justices of the Peace,** Constance B. Anderson, John M. Barrett, Bruce A. Bergeron, Albert E. Bradley, Marilyn J. Chase, Michael F. Cleary, H. F. Falana, Jr., John J. Gally, Dorothy M. Grady, Roland C. Green, Brian R. G. Heath, John C. Howard, Jr., Musa M. Jatkowski, Paul F. Jatkowski, Lionel G. Jean, Pamela G. Papanos, Sondra A. Stave.

CROMWELL. Middlesex County.—(Form of government, selectmen, town meeting, board of finance.)—Inc., May, 1851; taken from Middletown. Area, 12.9 sq. miles. Population, est., 12,709. Voting district, 1. Principal industries, horticulture, aircraft components and manufacture of tools. Transp.—Passenger: Served by buses of Conn. Transit from Middletown and Hartford. Freight: Served by numerous motor common carriers. Post office, Cromwell.

TOWN OFFICERS. Clerk and Reg. of Vital Statistics, Bernard Neville; Hours, 8:30 A.M.-4 P.M., Mon. through Fri.; Address, 41 West St., 06416; Tel., (860) 632-3440.—**Asst. Clerks and Asst. Regs. of Vital Statistics,** Darlene DiProto, Lori Grillo.—**Selectmen,** 1st, Ryk Nelson (D) Tel., (860) 632-3410, David I. Murphy (D), Deputy; Anthony V. Amenta, Jr. (R), Kathryn S. Ekstrom (R), John M. Flanders (D), Richard Newton (R), Anthony Varricchio, Sr. (D).—**Treas.,** Bernard Neville.—**Bd. of Finance,** Raymond B. Thiesen, Chm., Paul C. Beaulieu, Richard J. Becker, Donna Caswell, Arthur Director, Michael H. Gengler; Alternates, Jill Ferraiolo, Robert Jahn, Edwin Maley, Jr.—**Tax Collector,** D. Jane Johnson.—**Bd. of Assessment Appeals,** Robert Milardo, Chm., H. Blake Anderson, Margaret M. Reidy.—**Assessor,** Robert C. Kemp.—**Registrars of Voters,** Elizabeth H. Haines (D), Angela A. Incerti (R).—**Supt. of Schools,** James Gere.—**Bd. of Education,** Oma Kelley, Chm., Shirley J. Banic, Mary E. DeMaio, Minnie M. Libera, Glen Macko, 1997; James N. Gibson, Latif Lighari, Martha L. Rennie, vacancy, 1999.—**Planning and Zoning Comm.,** Arthur G. Johnson, Jr., Chm., Brian Armet, Bonnie Anderson, Susan B. Anderson, Joe

D'Eugenio, Stanley E. Jasiecki, Michael Nadeau, Brian Turner, David P. Visconti; Alternates, Anthony Scierka, Maurice Villano.—**Zoning Bd. of Appeals,** Gregory I. Godston, Chm., Joseph R. Morin, Madeline O'Brien, Michael L. Shonta, Diana M. Varese; Alternates, Carolyn St. Paul, Susan Ye, vacancy.—**Zoning Enforcement Officer,** Frederic Curtin.—**Economic Development Comm.,** Ernest Lacore, Chm., Kathy Ekstrom, Richard Haines, Robert Jahn, Karen Rohr.—**Inland Wetlands Comm.,** Madelyn O'Brien, Chm., Kenneth Cichon, Thomas McDermott, Wynn Muller, Corey Smith, vacancy; Alternates, Anita Bengston, Ronald Eddy.—**Elderly Comm.,** Paul Harrington, Chm., George Byrne, Florence Dombrowski, David Gellman, Camille Mollo, Ester Slossberg, Jane Sullivan.—**Dir. of Social Services/Human Services,** Al Kaplan.—**Youth Services Coordinator,** Ann France.—**Elderly Services Coordinator,** Theresa Frazier.—**Committee for the Handicapped,** Elizabeth Gaulton, Chm., Ann Camp, Karen Cosker, Luella Landis, Nancy Liddell, Camille Mollo, Mary Lou Murphy, Ronald Safranski.—**Dir. of Health,** Alan Rutner, M.D.—**Library Comm.,** William Dickerson, Chm., Alessandrina Beaulieu, Margaret M. Colella, Barbara J. Grotheer, Bernard Neville, Martha Rennie, Mithu Saderanghani.—**Municipal Historian,** vacancy.—**Parks and Recreation Comm.,** Richard Nobile, Chm., Nancy Amenta, David Beauchemin, Thomas Franklin, Phil Gregory, Diane Hasz, Patricia Madej, Margaret Mullen, Mertie Terry.—**Dir. of Public Works,** Michael Marino.—**Building Inspector,** David Jolley.—**Water Polution Control Auth.,** William Lowry, Chm., Brian Armet, Victor F. Cassella, Sr., Mary Konopka, Sandra Muller.—**Capital Expenditures Comm.,** Glen Johnson, Acting Chm., Amber Caverly, Steve Lowrance, Brian Robertson, Mark Rose.—**Sanitarian,** Tom Armentano.—**Chief of Police,** Anthony Salvatore.—**Police Comm.,** Bd. of Selectmen.—**Chief of Fire Dept.,** William Lee; Russ Johnson, Deputy; Asst., David J. Colligan.—**Fire Marshal,** Todd Gagnon; Supt., S. William Jarzavek.—**Bd. of Fire Comrs.,** Louis F. Spada, Jr., Chm., Edward C. Clapp, Kenneth Going, John Hamlin, Howard Nielson, Ronald Platt, George Schmaltl, Donald H. Swanson, Anthony Villaggio.—**Civil Preparedness Dir.,** Fred Curtin.—**Town Attys.,** Mark K. Branse, Pepe & Hazard.—**Justices of the Peace,** John M. Flanders, Elizabeth H. Haines, Diane Hasz, Mary Konopka, William D. Lowry III, Arthur J. Mollo, Jr., Sandra K. Muller, Madelyn E. O'Brien, Jean O. Partridge, Eugene P. Rohr, Paul C. Slaters, Douglas A. Sienna, Timothy B. Walsh.

DANBURY. Fairfield County.—(Form of government, mayor, common council.)—Settled, 1687; named, Oct., 1967, Inc., town, May, 1702; city, 1889. Town and city consolidated, Jan. 1, 1965. Area, 44.3 sq. miles. Population, est., 67,370. Voting districts, 7. Principal industries: pharmaceuticals, electronic components, chemicals, medical instruments and equipment, metal fabrication and special machinery, precision bearings, high tech optical instruments and equipment, printing and publishing, ultrasonic equipment, high tech research and development, and several corporate headquarter locations. Transp.—Passenger: Served by Metro North Railroad Co. from New York City and Norwalk, Bonanza Bus Co., Housatonic Area Regional Transit (HART). Freight: Served by Conrail and numerous motor common carriers. Post office, Danbury.

CITY AND TOWN OFFICERS. Town Clerk and Reg. of Vital Statistics, Michael R. Seri; Hours, 8:30 A.M.-4:30 P.M., Mon. through Fri.; Address, City Hall,

155 Deer Hill Ave., 06810; Tel., (203) 797-4531.—**Asst. Clerks,** Louise I. Oliva, Joan W. Schmiedel, Catherine R. White.—**Asst. Reg. of Vital Statistics,** Lori A. Kaback.—**City Clerk,** Elizabeth A. Crudginton; Hours and address, same as Town Clerk; Tel., (203) 797-4515.—**Asst. City Clerk,** Jimmetta L. Samaha.—**Mayor,** Gene F. Eriquez (D).—**Common Council,** 1st Dist., Warren M. Levy, Harry W. Scalzo; 2nd Dist., Helena Abrantes, Paul E. McAllister, Jr.; 3rd Dist., Thomas J. Arconti, Eileen S. Coladarci; 4th Dist., Ernest M. Boynton, John J. Esposito; 5th Dist., Emile G. Buzaid, Jr., Thomas J. Valeri; 6th Dist., Valdemiro D. Machado, Connie E. Shuler; 7th Dist., Louis T. Charles, Jr., Robert P. Gomez; At Large Members, Pauline Basso, Janet A. Butera, Marcia T. Fox, Matthew P. Gallagher, Albert S. Mead, Jr., Vincent P. Nolan, Jr., Christopher C. Setaro.—**Treas.,** Thomas R. Green.—**Comptroller/Dir. of Finance,** Dominic A. Setaro, Jr.—**Risk Mgr.,** Thomas Fabiano.—**Tax Collector,** Catherine Skurat.—**Bd. of Assessment Appeals,** William Hajj, John Scozzafava, Marion Smith, vacancy.—**Assessor,** Robert F. Coyne; Asst., Irene Simonelli.—**Registrars of Voters,** George F. Schmiedel (D), Jean A. Natale (R).—**Acting Supt. of Schools,** Herbert Pandiscio.—**Bd. of Education,** Michael A. Christian, Gladys B. Cooper, Larry Dorris, Michael S. Fazio, Ellen Morelock, George O'Loughlin, Louis A. Rotello, 1997; Abner Burgos-Rodriquez, Brian E. Cotter, Carlo J. Marano, Nancy Marcus, 1999.—**Personnel Dir.,** Emanuel Merullo; Asst., Julio Lopez.—**Civil Service Comm.,** Rafael Pina, Chm., Frank Caracanci, Eleanor Lewis; Julio Lopez, Acting Chief Examiner.—**Zoning Comm.,** Theodore Haddad, Jr., Chm., John N. Ashkar, Alfred E. Cipriani, Anthony G. DiCaprio, Antonio M. Fernandes, Michael J. Gallagher, Cristal Loubriel, Anthony P. Mazza, vacancy; Alternates, Robert D. Lynch, Jack D. Mackay, vacancy.—**Planning Comm.,** Joseph Justino, Chm., John Deeb, Debbie Gogliettino, Frank Malone, Steve Zaleta; Alternates, Mark Boughton, Alice Hyman.—**City Planner,** Dennis Elpern.—**Zoning Bd. of Appeals,** Richard S. Jowdy, Chm., Phyllis Garavel, Michael Sibbit, Peggy H. Stewart, Beverly White; Alternates, Dom Chieffalo, Joseph DaSilva, Jr., vacancy.—**Redevelopment Agency,** John J. Sullivan, Chm., John J. Addessi, Joseph Canale, Jr., Art Colley, Jack Green, Robert Peat, Arthur Roberts, Barbara Susnitzky, vacancy.—**Housing Auth.,** Samuel Deibler, Chm., Willie Brown, Bernard Fitzpatrick, Robert Kovacs, Gladys McFarland, vacancy.—**Fair Rent Comm.,** Steven Gillotti, Chm., Reuben L. Bush, Sylvia Esposito, Felix Merante, Robert Petterson, Margaret Williams, Lydia Yaglenski, two vacancies; Alternates, two vacancies.—**Conservation Comm.,** Barbara Monsky, Chm., Michael Halas, Loraine Herger, James O'Connell, Mary Reynolds, Dennis W. Stubelt.—**Environmental Impact Comm.,** Mike Zotos, Chm., David Athans, John Gogliettino, Bruce Lees, Lawrence Rinaldo, Matthew Rose, Mark Verna; Alternates, three vacancies.—**Comm. on Aging,** Sigrid Benyei, Chm., John Durzik, Olita Grigors, John Grimes, Elisabeth McKee, Thomas Quinn, Seth Sanford, Kathryn Santuro, Walter Wayman; Alternates, Millie Siegel, Roland Soronson, vacancy.—**Comm. on Persons with Disabilities,** Grace Scire, Chm., Dr. Larry Cohen, Cathie DiBuono, Jane Davis, John Gentile, Janet Ross, Thomas Sjovall, Gudrun Sterling, vacancy; Alternates, three vacancies.—**Equal Rights and Opportunities,** Julio Lopez, Affirmative Action Officer.—**Welfare Dir.,** Deborah MacKenzie.—**Dir. of Health,** William Campbell.—**Library Bd. of Directors,** John W. Hoffer, Chm., Joan Damia, Tom Frizzell, William Goodman, Betty Jane Hull, Edward Moore, William Sullivan, Harold Wibling, vacancy.—**Cultural Comm.,**

Benjamin DaSilva, Jr., Chm., Mary Burke, Harvey Center, John Cherry, Evelyn Durgy, Robert Feinson, Ada Humphreville, Helen Masterson, Chris Rotello, Mel Schwartz, vacancy.—**Parks and Recreation Comm.,** Robert Gentry, Chm., Richard W. Cyr, Creighton Lee, George Rivard, Carol Smith, Mario Tiani, Ed Walsh, Norman Winnerman, vacancy.—**Parks and Recreation Dept.,** Robert G. Ryerson, Dir.—**Public Works Dirs.,** William Buckley, Jack Schweitzer.—**Building Inspector,** Leo Null.—**Building Code Bd. of Appeals,** John Plecity, Chm., Frank Figueredo, Roger LeBlanc, John A. Schweitzer, vacancy.—**Sanitarian,** Peter Dunn.—**Tree Warden,** Richard Smith.—**Purchasing Agent,** Warren Platz.—**Parking Auth.,** Jerry Lefebvre, Chm., Frank Cappiello, Peter Damia, Tom Devine, Felice Plain.—**Candlewood Lake Auth.,** Sally Conroy, James Panzica, Robert Smart.—**City Engineer,** Jack Schweitzer.—**Chief of Police,** Nelson Macedo; Deputy, Leo Gantert.—**Constables,** Donald T. Crudginton, Paul D. Estefan, Harold Garofolo, Francis J. Kieras, Glenn C. Wicklund.—**Chief of Fire Dept.,** Carmen J. Oliver; Deputy, Peter Siecienski.—**Fire Marshal,** Alan Schacht.—**Civil Preparedness Dir.,** Paul Estefan.—**Asst. Corporation Counsel,** Daniel Casagrande.—**Justices of the Peace,** John Ashkar, Pauline Basso, Allyson J. Bernard, Al Cipriani, Helen Collischonn, Elizabeth Crudginton, Lillian Cyr, Marianne E. Dahill, Charles DeFranco, Christina M. Dudas, Gene F. Eriquez, John Esposito, Sandra Falzone, Harold Garofalo, Robert Godfrey, Richard L. Goldstein, Alfred P. Hazard, Warren Joli, Sr., Irene King, Frank Klecha, Eleanor Lewis, Julio A. Lopez, Robert Ogden, Kenneth J. O'Neill, Michael Ortega, Jr., Mary Ann Rickert, Joseph Scozzafava, Stanford Smith, Sr., Virginia Swenson, Lynn Waller, Steven Zaleta, Nicholas Zotos.

DANIELSON. BOROUGH OFFICERS. (See Town of Killingly for assessor, building inspector, bd. of education, director of health, highways, housing, sewerage treatment plant, bd. of assessment appeals, registrar of vital statistics, registrars of voters.) c/o Clerk, Box 726, 06239; Tel., Danielson, (860) 774-4159.—**Pres.,** Elaine Lippke.—**Clerk/Treas.,** Bernice C. Gendreau.—**Council,** Susanne Allard, Eugene Audet, Philip A. Hoyt, Lynn Laberge, Elizabeth Martin, Edmond M. Raheb.—**Tax Collector,** Denise A. King.—**Chief of Fire Dept.,** Richard Levola.—**Borough Atty.,** Stephen J. Burlingame.

DARIEN. Fairfield County.—(Form of government, representative town meeting, selectmen, board of finance.)—Inc., May, 1820; taken from Stamford. Area, 23.4 sq. miles. Population, est., 19,171. Voting districts, 5. Residential community; no industries. Clubs: Wee Burn Country Club, Woodway Country Club, Country Club of Darien, Tokeneke Beach Club, Noroton Yacht Club, Darien Boat Club, Ox Ridge Hunt Club, Nutmeg Curling Club, Middlesex Swimming Club, Old Kings Highway Tennis Club. Transp.—Passenger: Served by Metro North Commuter Railroad Co. and buses of Conn. Transit from Stamford and Norwalk. Freight: Served by Metro North and numerous motor common carriers. Post offices, Darien, Noroton and Noroton Heights.

TOWN OFFICERS. Clerk and Reg. of Vital Statistics, Marilyn M. Van Sciver; Hours, 8:30 A.M.-4:30 P.M., Mon. through Fri.; Address, 2 Renshaw Rd., 06820; Tel., (203) 656-7307.—**Asst. Clerks and Asst. Regs. of Vital Statistics,** Ann Marie

Kvinge, Judith A. Symeon.—**Selectmen,** 1st, Henry M. Sanders (R) Tel., (203) 656-7338, Jane F. Branigan (R), Joseph D. Miceli (R), Enid J. Oresman (D), Charlotte T. Suhler (D).—**Moderator Representative Town Meeting,** Richard C. Casey.—**Town Admin.,** Norman A. Lucas.—**Treas.,** William T. McIntire II.—**Bd. of Ethics,** Joseph H. Burchenal, Anne D. Carnahan, Ursula W. Forman, Lynn N. Hamlen, Clara C. Sartori.—**Bd. of Finance,** Theodore B. Covert, Chm., Douglas C. Curtis, Jr., John R. Hamilton, Peter F. Hovell, Edward B. Kostin, Robert O. White, Saralyn L. Woods.—**Tax Collector,** Carolyn D. Miller.—**Bd. of Assessment Appeals,** Bruce S. Kough, Chm., John C. Bell IV, Judith P. Tibbetts.—**Tax Assessor,** Joseph A. Cullen.—**Registrars of Voters,** Thomas R. Dunn (D), Donald P. Smith (R).—**Supt. of Schools,** Eileen Gress.—**Bd. of Education,** Elizabeth A. Fenton, Chm., John A. Fixary, Laurie E. Williamson, 1997; Evonne G. Klein, Janis J. Rehlaender, Van M. Roberts, 1998; Adele M. Conniff, Sallie Raleigh, Joseph R. Warren, 1999.—**Planning and Zoning Comm.,** William K. Flanagan, Jr., Chm., Frederick B. Conze, Mark R. Costello, Patrick J. Damanti, Kevin D. Gray, Jon C. McEwan; Raymond D. Nurme, Dir.; David J. Keating, Asst. Dir.—**Zoning Enforcement Officer,** David J. Keating.—**Zoning Bd. of Appeals,** Margaret Y. Walker, Chm., M. Ramsey Bell, Frederick Kolbe, Georgia A. von Schmidt, John J. Walker; Alternates, Michael P. Castine, Michael Jones, James Von Klemperer.—**Beautification Comm.,** Daniel Benton, Chm., Robin Barnum-Sokolow, Susan Bhirud, Joanne Costello, Elizabeth duPont, Susan Faulkner, Christopher McGoldrick, Wendy Megroz, Stephen Nightingale, Margaret S. Papp, Patricia Parlette, Edward V. R. Spurgeon, Pauline S. Tuck.—**Housing Auth.,** Alfred J. Senese, Chm., Kaye Barker, Francine E. Buchanan, Bonnie F. Dora, Ralph Lim; A. Vincent Falcioni, Exec. Dir.—**Environmental Protection Comm.,** Herman Heideklang, Chm., Basil Andriuk, Jon C. McEwan, Susan Purnell, Vicki Secrest, Charles Stamm, Ronald Thomas.—**Municipal Historians,** Marian Castell, Louise McLean.—**Comm. on Aging,** Alexander T. Liu, Chm., Patricia Carpenter, Suzanne Flynn, Mary G. Giarratana, Ronald M. Heinbaugh, May Lechak, Rosemary Mace, Laura Manning, Fred R. Sammis, Sonja Smith, Linda Verbeck.—**Youth Comm.,** Langdon Clarke, Chm., Karen Briganti, Susan Blanker, Gwynne Campbell, Keeley Kriskey, Rick Oakford; Alicia Sillars, Dir.—**Dir. of Social Services,** Judith Morrison.—**Dir. of Health,** Margaret M. McLaughlin, M.D.; Asst., Bernard Rosenberg, Ph.D.—**Parks and Recreation Comm.,** Barbara Thorne, Chm., Dulcy Brainard, Sal Giarratana, Francis Gilmartin, Richard Groppa, Donald Hamson, E. Carey Holcomb, Francis Jones, Meryl Sheetz; Susan M. Swiatek, Admr.—**Supt. of Public Works,** Robert Steeger.—**Building Inspector,** Charles A. Saverine.—**Sewer Comm.,** William Doughman, Chm., John Fisher, Arthur E. VanSciver, Peter VanWinkle; Robert A. Riith, Supt., Sewer Services.—**Sanitarian,** Bernard Rosenberg.—**Tree Warden,** Marshall A. Cotta.—**Chief of Police,** Hugh McManus.—**Police Comm.,** Douglas Campbell, Chm., J. Paul Johnson, Peter L. Truebner.—**Constables,** David W. Morgan, Phillips G. Terhune, Jr., Russell P. Tiano.—**Chiefs of Fire Dept.,** John Winking (Darien), Robert J. Buch (Noroton), Marc McEwan (Noroton Heights).—**Fire Marshal,** Robert J. Buch; Deputy, vacancy.—**Bd. of Fire Comrs.,** Michael P. Vitti, Chm., Daniel J. Brown, Robert J. Buch, Ronald J. Falcioni, Douglas Lockhart, Marc McEwan, Martin O'Reilly, Steven J. Palmer, John Winking.—**Civil Preparedness Dir.,** John Jordan.—**Town Atty.,** John D. Hertz.—**Justices of the Peace,** Edward M. Axelrod, Benjamin A.

Bruno, Eugene F. Coyle, A. Vincent Falcioni, Lynn N. Hamlen, Cathy A. Hauck, Debra W. Hertz, Anthony T. Improta, Anthony J. Leone, Phoebe C. MacKenzie, Ann S. Mandel, Enid J. Oresman, Joseph Pankowski, Jr., Marian T. Persico, William L. Rylander, Anne W. Shaw, Charlotte T. Suhler, Russell P. Tiano, Arlene F. Tulacro, Georgia A. von Schmidt, George V. Zengo.

DEEP RIVER. Middlesex County.—(Form of government, selectmen, town meeting, board of finance.)—Settled, 1635 as Saybrook; united with Connecticut, Dec., 1644; name changed to Deep River, July 1, 1947. Area, 14.2 sq. miles. Population, est., 4,408. Voting district, 1. Principal industries, agriculture and manufacture of plax and plastic goods, electric soldering irons, business forms. Transp.—Freight: Served by numerous motor common carriers. Post office, Deep River. Outlying section of town served by rural free delivery.

TOWN OFFICERS. Clerk and Reg. of Vital Statistics, Jeanne G. Nickse; Hours, 9 A.M.-12 Noon, 1-4 P.M., Mon. through Fri.; Address, Town Hall, 174 Main St., 06417; Tel., (860) 526-6024.—**Asst. Clerks and Asst. Regs. of Vital Statistics,** Donna Nelson, Jean M. Ressler.—**Selectmen,** 1st, Richard H. Smith (D) Tel., (860) 526-6020, Richard R. Daniels, Jr. (D), Richard C. Marvin (R).—**Treas.,** Thomas W. Lindner.—**Bd. of Finance,** Paula R. Strobel, Chm., Gregory Alexander, Joseph D. Griffith, Frederick J. Hellmers, Janice Kollmer, Rita Samuels.—**Tax Collector,** Arthur R. Thompson.—**Bd. of Assessment Appeals,** William Frank, Chm., Thomas Griffin, Roberta A. Ziobron.—**Assessor,** Robin L. O'Loughlin.—**Registrars of Voters,** Cathy Malcarne (D), Frances T. Strukus (R).—**Supt. of Schools,** John H. Proctor.—**Bd. of Education,** Antonio Robaina, Chm., Linda Hall, Kathleen Lalikos, Nathan Schatz, 1997; Karen Conniff, Susan E. Germini-Humble, Lori J. Guerette, Cathie Jefferson, Pamela V. Potter, 1999.—**Planning and Zoning Comm.,** Peter Nucci, Jr., Chm., Karen Conniff, Thomas Griffin, Jonathan Kastner, Antonio Robaino, Henry Stocek, Robin Weinberger; Alternates, John T. Attridge, Christine Elliott, Frederick J. Hellmers.—**Zoning Bd. of Appeals,** Donald Grohs, Chm., Jerome Ackerman, William Cotter, Margot G. Marvin, Charles Rayner; Alternates, Edward Judd, Thomas McGrath, Richard M. Nelson.—**Zoning Enforcement Officer,** Cathie Jefferson.—**Economic Development Comm.,** Stan Kirla, Ted MacKenzie, Robert R. Stalsburg.—**Conservation and Inland Wetlands Comm.,** John Kennedy, Chm., Peter Crosby, Eric Roise, Nancy Shea, Janet Stone, John Underhill, vacancy; Alternates, Joseph Miezejeski, Brenda Sampson.—**Agent for the Elderly,** Nellie Johnson.—**Welfare Dir.,** Eunice Howard.—**Dir. of Health,** Roy D. Eichengreen, M.D. (P.O., Chester).—**Bd. of Public Health,** Richard R. Daniels, Jr., Pres., Audrey Ely, Catherine Lambert, Michelle Peckham, Richard Ross, Audrey Taber, Deborah Wolfe, Flo Zaremba, vacancy.—**Library Directors,** Lorraine Ballsieper, Patricia Hellmers, Jean Kelley, Sandra L. Louthain, Arlene Macmillan, Edward K. Morrissey, Michaele M. Ward, Cindy Warm, vacancy.—**Parks and Recreation Comm.,** Roy Jefferson, Chm., Gail Adams, Douglas Carlson, Richard Conniff, Teresa Dee, Sue Graham, Tim Haut, Cathy Jefferson, Ann Joy, Janet Klinck, Daniel Kollmer, Barbara Malcarne, Cathy Malcarne, Donna Nelson, David Pollock, Jennifer Scott, Kerry Wittel, Charles Wolfe, Debra Ziobron.—**Town Engineer,** Thomas Metcalf.—**Building Inspector/Sanitarian,** Richard Leighton.—**Water Pollution Control Auth.,** Robert Stalsburg, Chm., Julia Bushnell, Ted MacKenzie, James Mayne, Rita Samuels; Alternates, Edward Godfrey III, vacancy.—**Resident Trooper,** Ben Liberatore.—**Constables,** Peter H. Lewis, Robert Seibert, Richard Smith, Cleon Springer, Raymond Sypher.—**Chief of Fire Dept.,** Robert Raymond; Deputy, James Budney.—**Fire Marshal,** Keith Nolin; Deputy, Charles Greeney, Jr.—**Bd. of Fire Comrs.,** Peter L. Woodcock, Chm., Roger Bineau, Richard W. Bogart.—**Civil Preparedness Dir.,** Keith Nelson; Deputy, Jerry Clark.—**Justices of the Peace,** Sarah Adams, Barbara Barlow, Elizabeth A. Becker, Roger Bineau, Daniel J. Connors, Richard R. Daniels, Jr., Edward E. Dennis, Patricia J. Jones, John Larson, Thomas W. Lindner, Joseph Miezejeski, Patricia Morrissey, Valerie L. Nucci, Kevin M. O'Brien, Darlene A. Pollock, Thomas E. Reed, Jean M. Ressler, Donald R. Sampson, Rita Samuels, John L. Simcheski, Lindsay Smith, Robert R. Stalsburg, Henry Stocek, Chris Strukus, Kenneth A. Wood, Jr., Mary D. Zawacki.

DERBY. New Haven County.—(Form of government, mayor, board of aldermen.)—Named, May, 1675. Town inc., May 13, 1775. City inc., June 7, 1893. Town and city consolidated, June 7, 1893. Area, 5.4 sq. miles. Population, est., 11,774. Voting districts, 3. Principal industries, telecommunications, photography, printing, and manufacture of castings, forgings, heavy machinery (metal) heat treating, rubber goods, nail clippers and manicure implements. Transp.—Passenger: Served by Metro North Commuter Railroad Co. and buses of Conn. Transit from Bridgeport and New Haven; Valley Transp. Co. from Bridgeport and Waterbury, and by Valley Transit District. Freight: Served by Conrail and numerous motor common carriers. Post office, Derby.

CITY AND TOWN OFFICERS. Town Clerk and Reg. of Vital Statistics, Barbara R. Moore; Hours, 9 A.M.-5 P.M., Mon. through Fri.; Address, City Hall, 35 Fifth St., 06418; Tel., (203) 736-1462.—**Asst. Town Clerk and Asst. Reg. of Vital Statistics,** Vera Novelli.—**City Clerk,** Joan Williamson; Hours and address, same as Town Clerk; Tel., (203) 736-1456.—**Asst. City Clerk,** Barbara Toni.—**Mayor,** Alan Schlesinger (R).—**Aldermen,** 1st Ward, Dina L. Weissman, Pres., Ann D. Massa, Elmer Voytek, 2nd Ward, Paul A. Kluk, Bruce Sill, Peter Tascione; 3rd Ward, Bonnie B. Chevarella, Laura Ann Wabno, Erwin Williams.—**Bd. of Ethics,** David Ahearn, Chm., Leo DiSorbo, John Kowarik, John Moran; Alternates, Richard Cerritelli, Pasquale DeRosa, Lucille Rubino.—**Finance Committee,** Carmine Durante, Ronald M. Sill.—**Treas.,** Keith A. McLiverty.—**Bd. of Apportionment and Taxation,** Henry J. Domurad, Jr., Chm., Robert A. Cerritelli, Edwin Cuevas, Barbara Dybas, Donald Goldberg, Sharon Hughes, Jenniegrace A. Izzo, Angelo Mongillo, Beverly Moran, Cornelia Tarnoski.—**Tax Collector,** Fay M. Foy.—**Bd. of Assessment Appeals,** Henry J. Domurad, Jr., Dina L. Weissman.—**Assessment Officer,** Paul Dinice.—**Registrars of Voters,** Leila Beltrone (D), Hazel J. Knapp (R).—**Supt. of Schools,** Nathan Chesler.—**Bd. of Education,** Donna S. DiGianvittorio, Richard M. Froehle, Mary S. Kluk, Cheryl Pereiras, Christine J. Robinson, 1998; James V. Gildea, Chm., Mark T. Domurad, Tracy A. Gildea, Colleen P. Mancini, 2000.—**Pension Bd.,** Joseph Babjak, Joseph Bassi, Donald Goldberg, Joyce Kaye, Keith McLiverty, Ronald Sill, Peter Tascione, Barbara Toni.—**Parking Auth.,** Joseph E. Moore, Walter Nizgorski, Anthony Staffieri, Nicholas Teodosio, Bernard Williamson.—**Planning Comm.,** Nicholas Valentino,

Chm., Stephen Dripchak, Charles Lippi, Carmine Menillo, Michael Piscioneri.—**Zoning Comm.,** Leonard Waleski, Chm., Vincent Guardiano, Sharon Hughes, Themis Klarides, Thomas Lionetti, Ken Moffat, Gerald Moscariello.—**Zoning Bd. of Appeals,** William Eustace, Chm., Madeline Miani, Earl T. Robinson, Ann Searles, Carol Senfield; Alternates, Leo Disorbo, John Izzo.—**Zoning Enforcement Officer,** David Dodes.—**Economic Development Comm.,** John Rak, Chm., Joseph Daddio, Paul Dinice, Jr., Joseph E. Moore, James Rogers, Walter Skowronski, Jay Witek.—**Housing Auth.,** Henry Lionetti, Chm., Francis Barretto, Richard Chudoba, Carolyn Duhaime, Peter Montini.—**Conservation Comm.,** Thomas Voytek, Chm., James Anton, Fred Columbo, Jr., Roberta Getlein, Karen Kemmesies, Thelma Stepan, Leonard Waleski.—**Inland Wetlands Comm.,** Fred Columbo, Jr., Chm., Carl Carloni, Karen Kemmesies, Edgar Lansing, Phillip Marcucio, William Vertrees, Jr., Thomas Voytek.—**Elderly Comm.,** Angelina Vitali, Chm., Virginia Costigan, Clarence Douglass, Mary Jeanetti, Mary Pitney, Patricia Rondini, Anne Scaife, Alice Stobierski, Josephine Taylor.—**Dir. of Health,** Leon J. O'Connor, M.P.H.—**Welfare Dir.,** Fay M. Foy.—**Library Directors,** Charles M. Stankye, Jr., Pres., Christopher Carson, Marie Cecarelli, Lillian Comboni, Frances Fallon, Marie Kopjanski, Elizabeth Micci, two vacancies.—**Municipal Historian,** Charles Rotteck, Jr.—**Parks and Recreation Comm.,** James L. Mascolo, Jr., Linda Stonaha, Mario Tessitore, John Walsh.—**Parks Dir.,** William Clynch.—**Recreation Dir.,** Dennis O'Connell.—**Dir. of Public Works,** Gary Parker.—**City Engineers,** Milone & MacBroom, Inc.—**Sealer of Weights and Measures,** Flavio Orazietti.—**Building Inspector,** David Kopjanski.—**Sewer Auth.,** Bd. of Aldermen.—**Lake Housatonic Auth.,** Brian Anderson, Chm., Edmund Everetts, Hazel Knapp.—**Chief of Police,** Andrew Cota.—**Police Comm.,** John De Barbieri, Chm., Thomas McGowan, Stanley Muzyk.—**City Sheriffs,** Pasquale T. Martone, Walter Nizgorski.—**Chief of Fire Dept.,** Kelly Curtis.—**Fire Marshal,** vacancy.—**Fire Comr.,** James Butler.—**Civil Preparedness Dir.,** Vincent Vizzo.—**Corporation Counsel,** Winnick, Vine, Welsh, Donnelly & Teodosio.—**Justices of the Peace,** Marc J. Garofalo, Ernestine Gaudio, James V. Gildea, Richard A. Grande, JennyGrace A. Izzo, Harry Kinney, Hazel J. Knapp, John W. Kowarik, Keith A. McLiverty, Madeline Miani, Lorraine C. Moore, Stanley F. Muzyk, Jr., Asher Nickelsberg, Flavio Orazietti, Eleanor C. Pivirotto, Kathleen Riordan, Alan Schlesinger, Vincent J. Tonucci, Laura Ann Wabno, John S. Witek.

DURHAM. Middlesex County.—(Form of government, selectmen, town meeting, board of finance.)—Named, May, 1704. Inc., Oct., 1708. Area, 23.8 sq. miles. Population, est., 6,223. Voting district, 1. Principal industries, manufacture of metal boxes and cabinets, electrical supplies and tools. Transp.—Freight: Served by numerous motor common carriers. Post office, Durham.

TOWN OFFICERS. Clerk and Reg. of Vital Statistics, Laura L. Francis; Hours, 9 A.M.-4:30 P.M., Mon. through Fri.; 10 A.M.-12 Noon, Sat., except for holiday weekends; Address, Town Hall, 30 Town House Rd., P.O. Box 428, 06422; Tel., Middletown, (860) 349-3452.—**Asst. Clerk and Asst. Reg. of Vital Statistics,** vacancy.—**Selectmen,** 1st, Henry A. Robinson (D) Tel., (860) 349-3625, Gene L. Brown (R), Brian C. Curtis (D).—**Treas.,** Francis E. Korn.—**Bd. of Finance,** George M.

Eames IV, Chm., Loraine A. Coe, Kenneth Gregory, Paul M. Keurajian, Gladys B. Lavine, Rosemarie Naples.—**Tax Collector,** Joanne B. Salva.—**Bd. of Assessment Appeals,** Kristan M. Higgins, Joyce M. Tubby, Margaret Q. Yeomans.—**Assessor,** Henry S. Philip, A.S.A., CCMA.—**Registrars of Voters,** Natalie A. H. Church (D), Althea M. Parmelee (R).—**Supt. of Schools,** William D. Breck, Ph.D.—**Planning and Zoning Comm.,** Lewis G. Hinman, Jr., Chm., Brian Ameche, George M. Eames III, Patricia A. Eick, Richard G. Eriksen, Robert E. Francis, Janice L. Melnick, Dian O'Neal, R. B. Schoonmaker, Jr.; Alternates, Warren C. Hadley, Eugene Riotte, Michael R. Trusty.—**Town Planner,** Geoffrey Colegrove.—**Zoning Bd. of Appeals,** Mark P. Gregg, Chm., M. Clark Kearney, Vincent Marino, Patricia A. Page, Elwin L. Stannard; Alternates, Katherine Forline, James M. Kowolenko, Jr., Malcolm B. Pearce, Jr.—**Economic Development Comm.,** Fred O. Raley, Chm., Joan Hughes, Paul Keurajian, James Kowolenko, Patricia Paganetti, Richard Spooner.—**Conservation Comm.,** Brian Ameche, Chm., Raymond Bahr, John S. Donadio, Warren Herzig, Frederick A. Huntley, Frank LaBella, William LaFlamme, Robert Melvin, Christine Wilmanns.—**Personnel Policy Bd.,** Roger L. Quinley, Chm., Joan Hughes, Bruce Sievers, John Stengel, Gerry Turner.—**Inland Wetlands Comm.,** George R. Zeeb, Chm., Steven B. Comen, Robert Czarnecki, John Hastings, Warren Herzig, Alois J. Petrzel, Leo V. Willett, Jr.; Alternates, Scott Douglas, Richard Eriksen, Joel LaBella.—**Historic Dist. Comm.,** James McLaughlen, Chm., Lynne Riotte, Patricia Wallace, George R. Zeeb; Alternates, Marilyn Ackerman, Sharon McCormick, vacancy.—**Agent for the Elderly,** Margery Stahl.—**Human Services Admr.,** Janet S. Muraca.—**Dir. of Health,** Leo V. Willett, Jr., M.D.—**Library Directors,** Jane R. Eriksen, Chm., Lynn Johnson, David Lavine, Cathy R. Moore, Anne J. Mueller, Elizabeth Richards, Michael Spier, R. David Turley, Dorothy Willett; Valerie Harrod, Librarian.—**Municipal Historian,** Francis E. Korn.—**Recreation Comm.,** Wendy Manemeit, Chm.—**Highway Foreman,** Kurt Bober.—**Building Code Bd. of Appeals,** Ronald Westford, Chm., Rolf A. Florin, Roger Kleeman, Ronald G. Markham, Gaetano Puglisi.—**Building Inspector,** Anthony Satagaj.—**Animal Control Officer,** Bruce A. Rau.—**Tree Wardens,** Lewis G. Hinman, Robert White.—**Town Engineer,** Ralph Zimbouski.—**Sanitarian,** William Milardo, Jr.—**Chief of Police,** Henry A. Robinson.—**Chief of Fire Dept.,** Steven Levy.—**Fire Marshal,** Robert J. Morpurgo.—**Open Burning Official,** George Planeta, Jr.—**Civil Preparedness Dir.,** Paul Roberts.—**Town Atty.,** Vincent J. McManus, Jr. (P.O., Wallingford).—**Justices of the Peace,** Kathleen Bert, Judy Caturano, Cory Cullen, George M. Eames, III, Barbara Eckert, Richard Eriksen, Ethel Heyl, Patricia C. John, David Lavine, Ronald J. Markham, Jane S. Mauro, James W. McLaughlin, Diane Moore, Nicholas Nyhart, Michael Pierce, Robert Poliner, Boyd Timanus, Scott Wright.

EASTFORD. Windham County.—(Form of government, selectmen, town meeting.)—Inc., May, 1847; taken from Ashford. Area, 29.2 sq. miles. Population, est., 1,367. Voting district, 1. Principal industries, metal fabricating, and horticulture. Transp.—Freight: Served by numerous motor common carriers. Post office, Eastford; also rural delivery from Chaplin, Pomfret Center. Voted No Liquor Permit, 1978.

TOWN OFFICERS. Clerk and Reg. of Vital Statistics, Mary P. Shamback; Hours, 10 A.M.-12 Noon, 1-4 P.M., Tues., Wed.; 9 A.M.-12 Noon, 2nd and last Sat. of each month; Address, Town Office Bldg., 16 Westford Rd., P.O. Box 273, 06242; Tel., Putnam, (860) 974-1885.—**Selectmen,** 1st, Russell H. Mayhew, Jr. (R) Tel., (860) 974-0133, Mary A. Duncan (D), Robert L. Reiss (R).—**Treas.,** Thomas O. Latham.—**Tax Collector,** Marilyn J. Adams.—**Bd. of Assessment Appeals,** Bette Danielson, Thomas French, C. Robert Small.—**Assessor,** Carol Crawford, CCMA.—**Registrars of Voters,** Dagmar Noll (D), Cynthia Anderson (R).—**Supt. of Schools,** Stephen B. Hosmer.—**Bd. of Education,** Eva C. Beermann, Linda Torgeson, Chm., Christopher J. Whitehouse, Richard L. Woodward, Steven Zinn, 1997; Herman E. Barlow, Jr., Meryl S. Kronisch, 1999.—**Planning Comm.,** Thomas R. Goodwin, Guy Grube, Kristina Schultz, Marian Slye, Steven Sokoloski, vacancy; Alternates, John Buell, Effie Vinal.—**Conservation Comm.,** Deborah Lee, Chm., Michael Adam-Kearns, Patricia Green, Clifford Noll, Jr., John Revill.—**Inland Wetlands Comm.,** Deborah Lee, Chm., Michael Adam-Kearns, Dean Bunnell, Thomas Dejohn, Thomas Goodwin, Patricia Green, John Revill.—**Agent for the Elderly,** vacancy.—**Dir. of Social Services,** Patricia Jones.—**Library Directors,** Maureen Morley, Chm., Deborah L. Adams, Suzanne Anderson, Patricia Bak, Terry L. Cote, Joyce T. Small, Cynthia Woodward, two vacancies.—**Municipal Historian,** Edward J. Jezierski.—**Recreation Comm.,** Cynthia F. Anderson, Audrey Carabeau, Edith Hulburt, Susan Shead, Debra Thompson.—**Building Inspector,** Alvin Kilburn.—**Tree Warden,** Norman Green.—**Chief of Police,** Russell H. Mayhew, Jr.—**Constables,** Kenneth B. Anderson, Joseph P. Meier, Robert Newton, William Parker.—**Chief of Fire Dept.,** Kevin Barlow; Deputy, John Paquin.—**Fire Marshal,** Richard Whitehouse.—**Civil Preparedness Dir.,** Edward F. Staveski.—**Town Atty.,** Nicholas Kepple (New London).—**Justices of the Peace,** Patricia K. Anderson, Stephen W. Bowen, Oscar B. Brockmeyer, Dean E. Bunnell, Bette L. Danielson, Mary A. Duncan, Sharon L. Griswold, Joseph Kozey, Jr., Nancy L. Mayhew, Robert B. McKay, Joyce E. Merlo, Paul E. Nissen, Robert L. Reiss, Reid R. Samuelson, Jeffrey O. Sandness, A. Stephen Sokoloski, Linda A. Torgeson.

EAST GRANBY. Hartford County.—(Form of government, selectmen, town meeting, board of finance.)—Inc., June, 1858; taken from Granby and Windsor Locks. Area, 17.6 sq. miles. Population, est., 4,374. Voting districts, 2. Principal industries, manufacturing and quarrying. Transp.—Freight: Served by numerous motor common carriers. Post office, East Granby.

TOWN OFFICERS. Clerk and Reg. of Vital Statistics, Elisabeth W. Birmingham; Hours, 9 A.M.-Noon, 1-4 P.M., Mon. through Thurs.; 9 A.M.-1 P.M., Fri.; Address, Town Hall, 9 Center St., P.O. Box T C, 06026, all other offices, P.O. Box 1858; Tel., Simsbury, (860) 653-6528.—**Asst. Clerk and Asst. Reg. of Vital Statistics,** Laura B. LaFond.—**Selectmen,** 1st, David K. Kilbon (D) Tel., (860) 653-2576, David R. Barnes (R), Mary Ellen Brown (D).—**Treas.,** J. Rodman Birmingham.—**Bd. of Finance,** Timothy J. Mulligan, Chm., Gordon F. Granger, Jr., Suzanne B. Lazar, Joseph L.Tardif, William W. Westervelt, William R. Zenga; Alternates, Charles F. Hunderlach, Jr., William A. Ullman.—**Tax Collector,** Karen M. Short.—**Bd. of Assessment Appeals,** Joann Cornelius, Chm., Chester M. DeGray, Jr., Robert G. Yeaton.—

Assessors, Mary Ellen Brown, Chm., Harold C. Holly, Jr., Edward F. Phillips.—**Registrars of Voters,** Sandra A. Poirer (D), Thelma A. Wilmot (R).—**Supt. of Schools,** Brenda L. Needham.—**Bd. of Education,** William A. Ullman, 1997; Edith J. S. Doherty, William F. O'Brien, Jr., Caryl T. Ryan, 1998; Linda K. Lawton, Steven C. Sullivan, 2000; James J. Feeney, Chm., Christine A. Durkin, Patrick J. Majewski, 2002.—**Planning and Zoning Comm.,** Fredrick T. O'Brien, Chm., Lee P. Echert, Franklyn H. Kilby, R. Daniel Methot, Frances A. Perkins, Richard F. Rumohr; Alternates, June T. Cameron, Virginia N. Howard, Mary Ann Kaiton.—**Zoning Bd. of Appeals,** David M. Lawton, Chm., John H. Colbeck, Jr., Henry G. Ernst, Robert C. Lindberg, Patricia G. Louison; Alternates, Margaret G. Bedortha, John P. Corcoran, Jeanne M. Dube.—**Zoning Enforcement Officer,** Albert F. Biddleman.—**Jury Committee,** Nancy M. Biddleman, Sandra A. Poirier, Thelma A. Wilmot.—**Economic Development Comm.,** Arnold E. Cohen, Chm., David R. Barnes, Thomas W. Henry, Thomas F. Howard, Sally B. Picard, Robert D. Shangraw, Michael J. Sullivan; William W. Pratt, Officer.—**Conservation Comm.,** Clifford E. Amirualt, Chm., Margaret G. Bedortha, Nancy L. Collins, George E. Cornelius, Jr., Brian F. Florin, Richard A. Livingston, John M. McIsaac, Jr.; Alternates, Joyce Kennedy-Raymes, John J. Manfreda.—**Municipal Historian,** Marguerite F. Guinan.—**Comm. on Aging,** Loraine D. Fleming, Chm., Beatrice B. Adams, Lucille T. Begley, Donald T. Burger, Ann F. Fahr, Dorothy F. Higgins, Amy Hunderlach, Grace K. Keating, Frank S. Marino.—**Health Officer,** Richard H. Matheny, Jr. (P.O., Avon).—**Animal Control Officer,** Linda L. Rossetti.—**Open Burning Official,** C. Edward Chatey.—**Comm. on Youth Services,** Gerald M. Brady, Chm., Joy Guiliano, Charles Hines, Lyn C. Hyman, David J. McNally; Wendy O'Donnell, Deborah S. Ribaudo, Lawrence Terra; Cynthia M. Garrey, Dir.; Student Members, four vacancies.—**Parks and Recreation Comm.,** Luanne M. Echert, Chm., Jay M. Aronson, Patricia Ann Beliveau, Jillann K. DeGray, Karen W. Hines, Kurt K. Larsen, Jon E. Scherer, Matthew T. Short, Elizabeth B. Waterman; Nancy A. Lawton, Dir.—**Building Inspector,** Richard A. Nelson.—**Town Engineer,** Charles V. Francis, Jr.—**Water Pollution Control Auth.,** Charles V. Francis, Jr., Chm., June T. Cameron, Richard L. Evans, Daniel J. Lizdas, Robert G. Yeaton.—**Tree Warden,** vacancy.—**Sanitarian,** Richard H. Matheny, Jr.—**Chief of Police,** David K. Kilbon.—**Constables,** Mark J. Dysart, Thomas J. Jacius, Jr., Gerald J. Peters, Jr., Andrew R. Rossetti, Daniel J. Thibault.—**Chief of Fire Dept.,** C. Edward Chatey; Deputy, Donald D. Zessin.—**Fire Marshal,** Kenneth F. Beliveau; Deputies, Chester M. DeGray, Jr., William S. Graham.—**Civil Preparedness Dir.,** vacancy; Deputy, Mark J. Dysart.—**Town Atty.,** Donald R. Holtman.—**Justices of the Peace,** David R. Barnes, Edward V. Barth, Mary Ellen Brown, Laura B. Brunelle, Charles W. Chatey, Shirley A. Cooper, Joann Cornelius, Henry G. Ernst, Ann F. Fahr, Richard F. Ferrari, Mary H. Hausmann, Thomas F. Howard, Charles F. Hunderlach, Jr., David K. Kilbon, Karen A. Mosher, Carolyn B. Phillips, Joy R. Turner, Frederick A. Webster, William R. Zenga.

EAST HADDAM. Middlesex County.—(Form of government, selectmen, town meeting, board of finance.)—Inc., May, 1734; taken from Haddam. Area, 56.6 sq. miles. Population, est., 7,375. Voting district, 1. Principal industries, manufacture of nylon and cotton twine, custom injection plastic molders, fish nets, printing, custom built bicycles, plumbing and heating products, boat manufacturing, lamp shades, kite manufacturing and assembly, concrete products; numerous summer resorts and the Goodspeed Opera House are located here. Transp.—Passenger: Served by buses of Greyhound. Freight: Served by numerous motor common carriers. Post offices, East Haddam, Moodus and Hadlyme.

TOWN OFFICERS. Clerk and Reg. of Vital Statistics, Mildred E. Quinn; Hours, 9 A.M.-12 Noon, 1-4 P.M., Mon., Wed., Thurs., 9 A.M.-12 Noon, 1-7 P.M., Tues., 9 A.M.-12 Noon, Fri.; Address, Town Office Bldg., P.O. Box K, Goodspeed Plaza, 06423; Tel., Moodus, (860) 873-5027.—**Asst. Clerks and Asst. Regs. of Vital Statistics,** Edith W. Bogue, Ruth Gobelle.—**Selectmen,** 1st, Susan D. Merrow (D) Tel., (860) 873-5020; FAX (860) 873-5025, Jack Drumm (D), John E. Galliot (R).—**Treas.,** John J. Gowac.—**Bd. of Finance,** Andrew J. Tarpill, Chm., Peter Dean, Ellen W. Kamm, Peter S. Ligas, David F. Meade II, R. Steven Parady.—**Tax Collector,** Janet C. Tucker.—**Bd. of Assessment Appeals,** Michael E. Gross, Rudolph Hoffmann, Joanne S. Roczniak.—**Assessor,** Ellen Lakowsky; Asst., Edith W. Bogue.—**Registrars of Voters,** Joyce Simon (D), Mary Dean (R).—**Supt. of Schools,** Daniel J. Thompson.—**Bd. of Education,** John F. Fielding, Chm., Barbara Free, Nicholas Iacovelli, Jack Wyman, 1997; Joene M. Hendry, Arthur J. Vachon, 1999; Robert W. Ballek, Pamela B. Gourlie, Walter J. Wassil, 2001.—**Planning and Zoning Comm.,** Dan J. D'Amelio, Chm., Erik W. Dill, Bruce M. Dutch, George Fellner, George B. Giesey, Emmett Lyman III, Lloyd Neudecker; Alternates, Susan D. Sienko, Mark Trotochaud, vacancy.—**Zoning Bd. of Appeals,** Stuart Wood, Chm., Norman Gobelle, Christopher Hankins, Lenoir Roberge, Daniel Tierney; Alternates, Joseph G. Daigle, Andrea Pascal, vacancy.—**Economic Development Comm.,** Ed Thereault, Chm., Kristin DiErrico, Walter Golec, James Johnson, Lloyd Neudecker, Pamela D. Rubenbauer, Andrea Skwarek.—**Fair Housing Officer,** Lillian B. Molle.—**Conservation Comm.,** Michael Sewell, Chm., Ruth Bennett, Gregory McHone, John Modica, John Morris, Richard Urban, vacancy.—**Inland Wetlands Comm.,** Randolph W. Dill, Chm., Mary Augustiny, Valerie Bodner, Nancy McHone, Kathy Reynolds; Alternates, Irving Davis, vacancy.—**Water Pollution Control Auth.,** Norman Gobelle, Chm., Richard Fiala, Richard J. Hoffmann, Andrew Lord, Louis R. Piscatelli, John Russell; Alternate, Bruce Dutch.—**Historic Dist. Comm.,** William Brady, Chm., Ron Brennan, David Nelson, Anita Sherman; Alternates, John Russell, Karl Stofko, two vacancies.—**Municipal Historian,** Karl Stofko.—**Committee for the Aging,** Mary Dean, Robert Garthwaite, Joanne Ligas, Victor Ottavi, Mildred Radway, Marie Speck, Carl Viggiani; Joanne Roczniak, Agent; Alternates, Eleanor Hopkin, Nancy Stockburger.—**Dir. of Health,** Baker Salsbury.—**Library Directors,** Walter J. Bielot, Chm., Christine P. Antaya, Judith Lee Bos, Kathleen Des Rosiers, Arthur Donnellan, Jr., Lucille Gardner, Walter J. Golec, Melba Helmboldt, Evelyn M. Maynard, Josephine McMullen, Kristine M. Paul, Bertha Pear, Elsie T. Snell, Mary A. Tomasi, Helen Tylec, Patrice M. Veselak, Brian W. Whitehill.—**Recreation Comm.,** JoAnn Parady, Chm., Ann Forbotnick, Kevin Maynard, Roy Parker, Walter Parkus, Jr., Steven Quinn, Martin Ryczek, Michael Weaver, Walter Ziobron, Jr.; Amanda Roczniak, Dir., Trish Landa, Asst.—**Tree Warden,** Richard Hoffman.—**Open Burning Official,** Daniel Barry.—**Building Inspector,** Wayne Greene.—**Dog Warden,** Priscilla La Fountain; Asst., Larry La Fountain.—**Street Light and Safety Committee,** Walter Bielot, Chm., Stanley Kurek, George Ryczek, two vacancies.—**Jury Committee,** Beatrice Balvin, Kate Boylston, Robert Calltharp.—**Building Code Bd. of Appeals,** Daniel Maus, Jr., Chm., James Curtin, George Fellner, Rudolph Hoffmann, Julius Schwab; Alternates, Hans Lohse, Daniel Necle.—**Chief of Police,** Susan D. Merrow.—**Constables,** George Corbeil, Lawrence Golet, Thomas M. Griffith, Jr., Norman R. Gustafson, Craig Mansfield, David Papallo, Reginald B. Patchell, Benjamin Quinones, Robert M. Weronik.—**Chief of Fire Dept.,** John J. Blaschik, Jr.; Asst. Chief, Jerry Boynton.—**Fire Marshal,** John Shanaghan; Deputies, John J. Blaschik, Jr., Norman D. Jamieson.—**Bd. of Fire Comrs.,** Peter Dean, Chm., Matthew Cashman, Edward Smith III.—**Emergency Management,** Matthew Cashman, Stuart Coleman, Jr., Don Jones, Kevin MacNeil, Henry Schmittberger, Joseph Szczech, Jr.; Burton Clark, Dir.—**Town Atty.,** John Bennet.—**Justices of the Peace,** Joanne B. Bernard, Harriet G. Cummings, Edwin P. DesRosiers, Randolph W. Dill, Thomas J. Dudchik, Bruce M. Dutch, Lynn C. Eimutis, Elizabeth J. Gross, Jacquelyn M. Hall, Everett L. Herden, Robert L. Johnson, Mary Ellen Klinck, Adele Miller, Bradley P. Parker, Leonard Swan.

EAST HAMPTON. Middlesex County.—(Form of government, town council, town manager, board of finance, town meeting.)—Inc., as Chatham, Oct., 1767; taken from Middletown. Area, 36.8 sq. miles. Population, est., 11,021. Voting districts, 1. Principal industries, manufacture of bells, paper boxes, witch hazel, tools and dies, forestry. Freight: Served by numerous motor common carriers. Post offices, Cobalt, East Hampton and Middle Haddam.

TOWN OFFICERS. Clerk and Reg. of Vital Statistics, Pauline L. Markham; Hours, 8 A.M.-4 P.M., Mon., Wed., Thurs.; 8 A.M.-7:30 P.M., Tues.; 8 A.M.-12:30 P.M., Fri.; Address, Town Hall, 20 East High St., 06424; Tel., (860) 267-2519.—**Asst. Clerk,** Jean Siena.—**Asst. Regs. of Vital Statistics,** Jean Siena, William B. Spencer.—**Town Council,** Donald Markham, Chm. (D) Tel., (860) 267-4468, Donald Coolican (R), William F. Farrell, Jr. (D), Jane French (D), Robert Heidle (R), Wayne Rand (R), James Standish (D).—**Town Manager,** Alan H. Bergren.—**Finance Dir.,** Carol G. Souppa.—**Bd. of Finance,** Thomas Pastorello, Chm., Raymond Cramer, Steven Greco, Steve Maynard, Francis T. McAuliffe, Beverly Warga, vacancy.—**Tax Collector,** Marie Durkin.—**Bd. of Assessment Appeals,** Patrick A. Fales, Chm., Claudia J. Magrath, Karen L. Olson.—**Assessor,** Donna Brodowski.—**Registrars of Voters,** Debra Markham (D), Jane Christopher (R).—**Supt. of Schools,** John DeGennaro.—**Bd. of Education,** Gail Hamm, Chm., Lynda Blau, Thomas A. Donnelly, Winnie A. Edmonds, Raymond P. Krupa, David Lee, Gregory Pugatch, Peter Strickland, K. Richard Trojanoski, Jr., 1999.—**Planning and Zoning Comm.,** Jacqueline Fantasia, Chm., Peter Aarestad, Douglas Bonoff, Frederick Hansen, Christine Palazzo, Mark Philhower, James Sennett; Alternates, Judson Landon, William MacDonald, Francis Shugrue, Jr.—**Zoning Bd. of Appeals,** Charles Nichols, Chm., James Brown, Nancy Flannery, Willie Fuqua, Suzanne E. Redfield, Nancy Zimmer; Alternates, Charles Dutch, Dianne Gorrick, Brendan Flannery.—**Zoning Enforcement Officers,** James Carey.—**Citizens Advisory Committee,** vacancies.—**Housing Code Bd. of Appeals,** Richard Betts, Willie Fuqua, John Hansen, William Krauth, Dennis Lavigne.—**Economic Develop-**

ment Comm., Robert States, Chm., Arlene Bielefield, John Durkin, Martha Hitchcock, George Looby, vacancy; Alternate, Kathleen Nowakowski.—**Housing Auth.,** Wilbur Bornman, Chm., Olga Booth, Paul Doran, Patricia DuFour, Bonnie Geysen.—**Inland Wetlands Comm.,** Jeffry Foran, Chm., David Boule, John Calvocoressi, Robert Dillard, Rowland Rux, Raymond Zatorski; Alternates, Alison Walck, two vacancies.—**Jury Committee,** James Costello, Alice Fancher, John Reilly.—**Historic Dist. Comm.,** Gerald Peterson, Chm., Ned Costello, Robert DeWar, Catherine Hogan, Alford Olson; Alternates, Tim Murray, Jane Phillips, Paul Rapo.—**Municipal Historian,** James Hansen, Jr.—**Librarian,** Ann Davis.—**Agent for the Elderly/Senior Citizens Coord.,** Martha Frappier.—**Welfare Dir.,** Alan H. Bergren; Social Worker, Hollis Block.—**Dir. of Health,** Thad King.—**Town Cemetery Bd.,** George White, Chm., James Costello, Arthur Jacobson, Elise Roenigk.—**Parks and Recreation Comm.,** James Wild, Chm., James Ahearn, Linda Billiel, Debra McKinney, Richard Norkun, Paul Provost, Maria Rand, Jeffrey Robinson, Joseph Shomberg; David Putnam, Dir.—**Dir. of Youth Services,** Wendy Regan.—**Dir. of Public Works,** Robert Drewry.—**Highway Foreman,** Philip Wall.—**Public Utilities Admin.,** Bradford Kargl.—**Tree Warden,** Davis Strong.—**Animal Control Officer,** Paul Carlson.—**Town Engineer,** Cummings & Lafayette.—**Building Code Bd. of Appeals,** Fred Hecht, Chm., Joseph Becker, Ralph Gross, John Nilsen, John Youngs.—**Water Pollution Control Auth.,** George White, Chm., David A. Hitchcock, , Edward Jackowitz, David Kelsey, Richard Labas, Dag Lindland, Frederick Pereau.—**Sanitarian,** Thad King.—**Chief of Police,** Eugene B. Rame.—**Constables,** Benjamin Burdick, Jr., Dennis Erickson, Fred Everett, Lary Selavka.—**Chief of Fire Dept./Fire Marshal,** Philip Visintainer.—**Bd. of Fire Comrs.,** Richard Brown, Chm., Charles Gotta, Dean Michelson, Alfred Royce, Jr., David Simko.—**Civil Preparedness Dir.,** Michael Scranton.—**Town Atty.,** Richard W. Tomc.—**Justices of the Peace,** Susan Brown, John L. Calvocoressi, Nancy Cramer, William Devine, Maria Durkin, Robert A. Dutch, William D. Grady, Gail K. Hamm, Phyllis Hansen, Jessie Hazen, William Helveston, Lynn B. Horne, Carol Lane, William MacDonald, Dean P. Markham, Ann R. McLaughlin, Maria F. Rand, Suzanne Redfield, Richard F. Wall.

EAST HARTFORD. Hartford County.—(Form of government, strong mayor, town council.)—Inc., Oct., 1783; taken from Hartford. Area, 18.8 sq. miles. Population, est., 48,125. Voting districts, 10. Principal industries, the manufacture of precision parts and aircraft engines, steel fabrication, banking and insurance, paper manufacturing, appliances, television and radio, stamp and die plates, small tools, machinery, metal working, bulk oil storage and distribution, bottling plants, storage warehouses, retail sales, and automobile dealerships. Transp.—Passenger: Served by buses of Conn. Transit from Hartford, Manchester, Rockville, South Windsor and Glastonbury; The Eastern Bus Lines, Inc. from Enfield; Post Road Stages, Inc. from Stafford Springs; and The Arrow Line, Inc. from East Hartford. Freight: Served by Conrail and numerous motor common carriers. Post office, East Hartford (branch of Hartford post office).

TOWN OFFICERS. Clerk and Reg. of Vital Statistics, Anne R. Fornabi; Hours, 8:30 A.M.-4:30 P.M., Mon. through Fri.; Address, Town Hall, 740 Main St., 06108; Tel., Hartford, (860) 291-7100; FAX (860) 289-0831.—**Asst. Clerk,** Donna L. Lavado.—**Asst. Reg. of Vital Statistics,** Patricia Tozzoli.—**Mayor,** Robert M. DeCrescenzo (D).—**Town Council,** Richard P. Gentile, Chm., Stephen Bates, Donald M. Currey, Allan T. Driscoll, Marylee A. Hickey, Richard F. Kehoe, Susan G. Kniep, Joanne S. LeBeau, James S. Parker.—**Selectmen,** Craig J. Popielarczyk, Chm., Steven R. Hudak, J. Roger Pelletier.—**Treas.,** Henry J. Genga.—**Bd. of Ethics,** John Rovaldi, Chm., Esther B. Clarke, Julia C. Tischofer; Alternates, Isolde Bates, George Duggan, Lois Gero.—**Dir. of Finance,** Barbara J. Avard.—**Tax Collector,** Barbara Bertrand.—**Bd. of Assessment Appeals,** Robert DePietro, Chm., James H. Korp, James Lusby.—**Assessor,** Richard S. Buchanan, Deputy, Delman Wolf.—**Personnel Dir.,** Thomas Dawkins.—**Personnel Appeals Bd.,** Shaun Jones, Chm., Elizabeth Kuehnel, vacancy; Alternates, Rudy Buck, Mary Weech, vacancy.—**Registrars of Voters,** Margaret A. Byrnes (D), Mary J. Mourey (R).—**Supt. of Schools,** George B. Drumm.—**Bd. of Education,** Hilde J. Mayranen, Chm., Joseph P. Balesano, Robert J. Damaschi, Joseph P. Haley III, Kathleen Randall, 1997; Lee Griffin, Michael J. Hartigan, Jill Upton, Prescille F. Yamamoto, 1999.—**Planning and Zoning Comm.,** Anthony F. Kayser, Chm., Elaine Carey, Dennis Conroy, Robert DePietro, John M. Grottole, L. P. Morton Hickey, Jr., Janet Lynch; Alternates, Kathleen Duran, Lois Gero, vacancy.—**Town Planner,** Michael J. Dayton.—**Zoning Bd. of Appeals,** Robert Burns, Chm., Joseph P. Balesano, Mary Finnegan, Austin Harlow, William Horan; Alternates, Robert S. Fortier, Michael Morelli, J. Lucien Plante.—**Economic Development Comm.,** Maurice Belanger, Chm., Lawrence DelPonte, Patricia Gately, James Korp, Joanne S. Lebeau, James S. Parker, Jacques Pelletier, Thomas Rup, Craig Stevenson.—**Redevelopment Agency,** Maurice Belanger, Chm., Gayle S. Fisher, Dominic Fulco III, William D. Miller, Firmo Noiva.—**Housing Auth.,** Arthur O'Brien, Chm., Leo J. Bond, Wanda Z. Franek, Constance O'Brien, Raymond A. St. Peter; John B. Roughan, Exec. Dir.—**Public Bldg. Comm.,** Russell Richards, Chm., Martin Burnham, Lamar Burt, Donald M. Currey, Robert Damaschi, Daniel DePietro, David Holmes, Hilde Mayranen, Robert Musheno.—**Inland Wetlands/Environment Comm.,** Gordon R. Macfarlane, Chm., Mary Dowden, Dawn Holmes, Michael Malinguaggio, Rosemarie O'Dea, Richard Pire, Judith Shanahan; Alternates, Albert Anderson, Cyril M. Mizla, Victor Serrambana, Jr.—**Historic Dist. Comm.,** Doris Suessman, Chm., David Holmes, Steven T. Hudak, Robert Pasek, Raymond E. Tubbs; Alternates, Mary Dowden, Florence Schroeter, Mark Weinberg.—**Comm. on Services for the Elderly,** Frances Rival, Chm., Dorothy Glover, Priscilla Lancaster, John Rival, Mary Robinson, Ralph Serignese, Evelyn Uhrig.—**Comm. on Services to the Handicapped,** Martin A. Burnham, Chm., Jeanette Lareau, Kathleen McNamara, Steve Solimene.—**Retirement Bd.,** Henry J. Genga, Chm., Stephen Bates, Robert Fournier, Estelle McCarthy, Paul Williams.—**Human Rights Comm.,** Janet Lynch, Chm., Paul Di Santo, Lucille Farmer, Lee Griffin, Elizabeth Harlow, Thomas Reardon, Terry Reno, Donna Salemi, Ulises Toledano.—**Dir. of Social Services,** John Choquette.—**Dir. of Health,** Charles I. Motes, Jr., M.P.H., R.S.—**Emergency Medical Services Comm.,** Henry Genga, Chm., Stephen D. Bates, Lori Cerone, David Dagon, Robert A. Derr, Marylee Hickey, Ken Loock, Charles I. Motes, James Shay.—**Municipal Historian,** Doris D. Sherrow.—**Dir. of Libraries,** Patrick Jones.—**Library Comm.,** Cynthia Reik, Chm., Marsha Balet, Patricia Begley, Shirley Bornhiem, Mayme Casady, Betty Ghagan, Patrick Jones, Andrew W. Nelson, Betty Squires, Alice Wilson.— **Dir. of Youth Services,**

Gary Shea.—**Beautification Comm.,** Patricia Sirois, Chm., Helen Boardman, Dennis Conroy, Marylee Hickey, Delores Kehoe, Elizabeth Kilgariff, Sharon Miller, Mary Mourey, Antonio Russo.—**Fine Arts Comm.,** Judith Okeson, Chm., Lorraine Arcari, Regina Barall, Terrye Blackstone, Lillian Goodberg, Karen Howe, Hilde Mayranen, Glynnis McKenzie, Jeannette Mullen, Maureen Rodgers, Dan L. Russell, Florence Schroeter, Prescille Yamamoto, two vacancies.—**Dir. of Parks and Recreation,** Deborah Mockus.—**Dir. of Public Works,** Roger J. Mullins; Asst., Richard Toce.—**Purchasing Agent,** John R. Martin.—**Town Engineer,** Michael Mancini.—**Dir. of Licences and Inspections/Zoning Enforcement Officer,** Donald J. Vigneau.—**Development Dir.,** James F. Dunn.—**Sealer of Weights and Measures,** vacancy.—**Building Code Bd. of Appeals,** Charles Brewer, Chm., Robert Damaschi, Herb Evans, James Kate, two vacancies.—**Sanitarians,** Robert Keating, Raymond T. Quinn.—**Chief of Police,** James W. Shay.—**Constables,** Robert G. Adams, Richard L. Begley, Joseph R. Carlson, Austin S. Harlow, Soulivanh Khamvongsay, James W. Shelmerdine, Jr., Albert J. Thomas, Jr.—**Chief of Fire Dept.,** David Dagon.—**Fire Marshal,** David Roth.—**Emergency Management Coord.,** Kenneth Loock.—**Corporation Counsel,** Janis Small.—**Justices of the Peace,** Fred Balet, C. Edwin Carlson, Esther B. Clarke, Dennis Conroy, William B. Dailey, Jr., Rose M. DeMonte, Henrietta Dill, Rocco A. Faccinto, Richard R. Flower III, Anne R. Fornabi, Ida Funk, Lois Gero, Anthony Gochee, Ana Gould, Marylee A. Hickey, James Korp, Patricia Labbe, Anita L. Malcolm, Cyril M. Mizla, Mary J. Mourey, Richard L. Mourey, Mary A. Paquette, James S. Parker, Elizabeth K. Pauski, Roland A. Pepin, Robert P. Perrault, J. Lucien Plante, Berta C. Scott, Ralph A. Serignese, Raymond St. Peter, James A. Trail, Richard D. Veltri.

EAST HAVEN. New Haven County.—(Form of government, mayor, town council, board of finance.)—Inc., May, 1785; taken from New Haven. Area, 13.4 sq. miles. Population, est., 26,651. Voting districts, 5, with 2 subdistricts. Principal industry, wholesale distribution and warehousing, electronic components and equipment, architectural castings, high-tech welding equipment; research and development, printing, insurance and investments. Served by buses of Conn. Transit from New Haven and Branford. Freight: Served by Conrail and numerous motor common carriers. Post office, East Haven.

TOWN OFFICERS. Clerk and Reg. of Vital Statistics, Elizabeth C. Leary; Hours, 9 A.M.-5 P.M., Mon. through Fri.; Address, 250 Main St., 06512; Tel., New Haven, (203) 468-3201.—**Asst. Clerk,** Rosemarie Calamita.—**Asst. Regs. of Vital Statistics,** Rosemarie Calamita, Victoria Pollio, Lorene Russell.—**Mayor,** Henry J. Luzzi (D).—**Town Council,** 1st Dist., Vincent A. Camera, James M. Dougherty, Fred J. Parlato; 2nd Dist., Francis J. Gravino, Chm., Mariam D. Amendola, Michael J. Michaud; 3rd Dist., Paul L. Burns, Patricia Travaglino, Carl J. Ruggiero; 4th Dist., Edward R. Foley, Sam J. Giglio, Richard Lucibello, Jr.; 5th Dist., Leon G. Archambault, Jessie Caruso, Carol D. Massaro.—**Selectmen,** Joseph F. Buonome (D), Jean Donarumo (R), Charles G. Parrett (D).—**Bd. of Ethics,** Norman DeMartino, Charles Schlegel, Matthew Shanley.—**Treas.,** Patricia A. Mellion.—**Bd. of Finance,** Mayor Henry J. Luzzi, Chm., ex officio, Steven J. Carleton, Richard DePalma, Mario Giaimo,

Paul R. Karbowski, Mark J. Petonito, Anthony Serio; vacancy, Dir.; Ralph Mauro, Deputy.—**Civil Service Comm.,** Patricia Mellion, Chm., Carolyn DeChello, Paul Esposito.—**Tax Collector,** Louise Fodero.—**Bd. of Assessment Appeals,** Jerald Volpe, Chm., Arthur Inglese, Steven Loban.—**Assessor,** Michael J. Milici.—**Registrars of Voters,** Janet A. Cianelli (D), Donna Norman (R).—**Supt. of Schools,** Dr. Denise Hexom.—**Bd. of Education,** Sidney Isenberg, Chm., Linda A. Abbott, Clara DiMartino, Joann T. Esposito, Salvatore Follo III, Patricia Mellion, Steven J. O'Donnell, Marilyn M. Vitale, Ronald J. Vestuti, 1997.—**Planning and Zoning Comm.,** Gene Ruocco, Chm., Meyer Biller, Robert Celentano, Charles Coyle, Ronald Mazzucco; Alternates, Leo Ahern, Steven Carleton, Matthew Limoncelli.—**Zoning Enforcement Officer,** George Mingione.—**Town Planner,** Anthony Panico.—**Zoning Bd. of Appeals,** Peter Cianelli, Madelyn Cianelli, Co-Chm., Andrew Grillo, Joseph Levatino, Rose S. Staplins; Alternates, Donald Hemstock, Jr., Michael Liso, vacancy.—**Economic Development Comm.,** Donald DeChello, Chm., Richard Augur, John Prato, James Vincent, Ralph Vitale.—**Urban Renewal/Housing Agency,** Peter DeSantis, Albert Fucci, Anthony Geraci, Anthony Moscato, William Parker.—**Housing Auth.,** John Barber, Chm., Stephen Cuddy, Herman Hackbarth, Arthur Pagliuca, Rose Tryanow.—**Airport Comm.,** Joseph Porto, Michael Romei.—**Inland Wetlands Comm.,** Ronald Andrade, Chm., Biagio Fronte, Fred Rossomando, Guy Rozier, Christine Sanford; Alternates, Laura Cifarelli, vacancy.—**Flood and Erosion Control Bd.,** Bernard Shields, Chm., Robert Affie, Edward Donroe, Jr., Catherine McGarry, Dominic Passarelli; Alternates, Paul DeNegre, David Okraska.—**Agent for the Elderly,** Regiano Marini.—**Counseling and Community Service.,** Donald Franco, Chm., Barbara Connally, Janet McCaul, Kenneth Sitnick, vacancy.—**Welfare Dir.,** Magdalen Sparaco.—**Dir. of Health,** Dennis Johnson.—**Library Bd.,** Eileen DeMayo, Chm., Linda Amarante, Myrtle Bruce, Sandra Carbone, Patricia Criscuolo, Sylvia DePalma, Michaleyn Vegliante, Lynn Velleca, Kathleen Yuse; William Basel, Dir.—**Recreation and Athletic Complex Comm.,** Steven Narracci, Chm., Anthony Criscuolo, Joseph DePalma, Henry Martone, Patrick Paulsen.—**Public Services Dir./Town Engineer,** Anthony Ferraro.—**Building Official,** Asher Nickelsberg.—**Water Pollution Control Auth.,** Robert Limoncelli, Chm., James Kennedy, Neil Longobardi, John Luzzi, Raymond Pompano.—**Chief of Police,** James Criscuolo.—**Police Comm.,** Robert Nastri, Chm., Andrew Esposito, Alphonse Lauro, Paul McCormick, Sandra Wright.—**Constables,** Barbara Coppola, Nancy Evans, Charlene A. Giagrande, Andrew Gianelli, Wayne Whitehead, William D. Wolcott, Jr.—**Chief of Fire Dept./Civil Preparedness Dir.,** Wayne Sanford.—**Fire Marshal,** Anthony Moscato.—**Bd. of Fire Comrs.,** Fred DePalma, Chm., Fred Marotti, Vincent Palmer, John Porto, Wendy Shields.—**Town Atty.,** Michael Albis; Assts., Alfred J. Cronk, Hugh Keefe.—**Justices of the Peace,** Linda A. Abbott, Alberta Bagnoli, Merelyn R. Criscuolo, Arthur L. DeSorbo, Clara L. DiMartino, Jean M. Donarumo, James A. Fletcher, Ronald D. Gambardella, Richard F. Iaguessa, Sidney W. Isenberg, Carmel Limoncelli, Raymond A. Marsico, Jr., Doris Martin, Geraldine M. Narracci, Van Nastri, Maryann K. Pacelli, Lynn D. Pizzorusso, Maryann Sgrignari, Anthony J. Teodosio, Marilyn M. Vitale.

EAST LYME. New London County.—(Form of government, selectmen, town meeting, board of finance.)—Inc., May, 1839; taken from Lyme and Waterford. Area, 42.0 sq. miles. Population, est., 16,031. Voting districts, 3. Principal industries, boat marinas, sport fishing, tourism. Transp.—Passenger: Served by SEAT and Amtrak. Post offices, East Lyme and Niantic.

TOWN OFFICERS. Clerk and Reg. of Vital Statistics, Esther B. Williams; Hours, 8:30 A.M.-4:30 P.M., Mon. through Fri.; Address, Town Hall, 108 Pennsylvania Ave., P.O. Box 519, Niantic 06357; Tel., Niantic, (860) 739-6931, Ext. 334; FAX, (860) 739-6930.—**Asst. Clerks and Asst. Regs. of Vital Statistics,** Lesley Blais, Mary A. Duke.—**Selectmen,** 1st, David L. Cini (D) P.O. Box 519, Niantic, Tel., (860) 739-6931, Rose Ann Hardy (D), Edwin J. Jutila (D), Jeffrey McNamara (R), Gary Lakowsky (D), F. Kent Sistare, Jr. (R).—**Treas.,** William J. Ebersole, Jr. (P.O., Niantic).—**Bd. of Finance,** David W. Jacobs, Chm., Robert G. Jones, Jean E. Petersen, Joseph F. Segal, Barbara H. Sokolov, Allan R. Taylor.—**Tax Collector,** Ruth E. Ames.—**Bd. of Assessment Appeals,** Jill K. Carini, William Dwyer, Jr., James Lagrotteria, Gregory P. Massad, Margaret A. Prokop.—**Assessor,** Catherine G. DaBoll.—**Registrars of Voters,** Donna C. Jutila (D), Catherine Devine (R).—**Supt. of Schools,** Jack Reynolds.—**Bd. of Education,** Mary Broderick, Chm., Ilaina Clement, T. Kevin Murphy, Robert C. Wilson, 1997; Ted Jablkowski, John E. Johnson, Bryan B. Mahon, Susan F. Reardon, Laura A. Rotchford, Glenn Shapiro, 1999.—**Planning Comm.,** Alice E. Johnson, Chm., Walter P. Cullen, Harold L. Kaplan, Mario P. Locarno, Stephen J. Rebelowski, Richard M. Waterman; Alternates, Ann J. Hamilton, Joseph J. Kwasniewski, Glenn A. Landers.—**Town Planner,** L. Jean Davies.—**Zoning Comm.,** Wayne L. Fraser, Chm., Athena D. Cone, William Dwyer, Sr., Paul Formica, Christopher Mullaney, Norman B. Peck III; Alternates, Donn Jourdan, Shawn M. McLaughlin, Kent G. Presley.—**Zoning Enforcement Officer,** William Mulholland.—**Zoning Bd. of Appeals,** Francis H. Hunt, Chm., Peter P. Mariani, Jr., Edwin T. McDonough, Jr., William Mountzoures, George Petetin; Alternates, Linda M. Goff, Arthur Saunders III, vacancy.—**Economic Development Comm.,** Christopher Barrett, Chm., John J. Devine, Robert S. Foster, Richard Gada, Catherine Irwin, John Jensen, William H. Kowenhoven.—**Conservation Comm.,** Thomas Ramotowski, Chm., Edmund W. Hafner, Russell J. Hausman, David L. Larson, Joseph B. Moore, Roy Smith, vacancy; Alternates, James Harris, Ron Nichols, vacancy.—**Comm. on Aging,** Mary Broga, Chm., Donald Barry, Russell H. Beckwith, Beverly DeFord, Ann J. Hamilton, Ilene Harris, Jane H. Powers; Cathy Wilson, Citizen Admin.—**Welfare Dir.,** Susan Saunders.—**Dir. of Health,** David D. Thompson, Jr. (P.O. Niantic)—**Town Historian,** Olive Tubbs Chendali; Deputy, Wilbur Beckwith.—**Parks and Recreation Comm.,** Robert D. Tobin, Chm., Edward H. Dzwilewski, Charles Fenick, Frederick R. Hollendonner, Melville A. Manwaring, J. Robert Pfanner, William J. Willetts, Jr.; Samuel M. Peretz, Dir.—**Dir. of Public Works,** Frederick G. Thumm.—**Town Engineer,** Philip Bergeron.—**Supt. of Highways,** Charles Holyfield.—**Building Inspector,** J. Claude Jean.—**Building Code Bd. of Appeals,** Richard C. Caulkins, John Cutillo III, three vacancies.—**Supt. of Sewers,** Gary Fritz.—**Water and Sewer Comm.,** David L. Cini, Chm., Bruce R. Brailey, Mary N. Cahill, Joseph C. Care, Stephen DiGiovanna, Fred Kral, Joseph J. Mingo, Edward T. Ramotowski, Michael S. Tinkel.—**Senior Sanitarian,** George C. Calkins.—**Sanitarian,** vacancy.—**Tree Warden,** Wesley Jezierski.—**Chief of Police,** David L. Cini.—**Constables,** Bruce W. Babcock, Delmar Carter, Jean Cavanaugh, Joseph Dunn, Edward Geneski, Joseph Jones, Eric Kwasniewski, James Levandoski, Donald Marr, Michael Masucci, Linda J. Nott, Paul Renshaw, Joseph San Juan, Terry Saffioti, Thomas Smith, James Weekley, Robert C. Wilson.—**Chiefs of Fire Dept.,** Ronald Pringle (Niantic), William Rix (Flanders).—**Fire Marshal,** Richard E. Morris.—**Emergency Mgmt. Dir./Public Safety Dir.,** Robert P. Heal; Deputy, Pearl F. Rathbun.—**Town Atty.,** Robert W. Marrion (P.O., New London).—**Justices of the Peace,** Judith E. Allen, Paul F. Anger, Robert S. Aniello, Beverly M. Barnard, Chris M. Barrett, James R. Benn, Barbara L. Birmingham, Paul L. Bobinski, Brenda Brewster, Barbara M. Brown, Sarah B. Budds, Robert J. Bulmer, David L. Cini, Holly Cini, Matthew W. Cini, Sally W. Cini, Donald P. Cone, Catherine W. Devine, Christopher W. Devine, John J. Devine, William P. Donovan, Constance Dwyer, William Dwyer, Jr., William Dwyer, Sr., Edward H. Dzwilewski, William J. Ebersole, Jr., Richard Fabricant, Abraham I. Fisher, Sandra Fisher, Patricia C. Foley, Paul M. Formica, Wayne Fraser, Dorothy B. Gerick, Ann J. Hamilton, Rose Ann Hardy, John T. Hoye, June M. Hoye, Francis H. Hunt, Janis R. Hutchinson, Ted Jablkowski, Stephen L. Jackson, Robert J. Janovic, Alice E. Johnson, Dale H. Johnson, Robert G. Jones, Edwin J. Jutila, Susan K. Karnes, Kathleen K. Kushman, Joseph Kwasniewski, Mario P. Locarno, Lisa Massad, Cherylann T. McCarthy, Barbara McCredie, Paul J. McDonough, Madeline V. Miller, Lewis J. Mostowy, Regina B. Mostowy, Donna L. Orefice, Gary J. Orefice, Dorothy R. Perkins, Tennyson G. Perkins, Barbara Potopowitz, Jane H. Powers, Mark H. Powers, Maura M. Powers, William P. Powers, John G. Prokop, Jr., Margaret A. Prokop, Joanne S. Reeves, Robert Rue, Louis D. Salerno, Arthur C. Saunders III, Mabel N. Schimelman, Dawn Seery, Kevin Seery, F. Kent Sistare, Jr., Mary Grace Smith, Paul B. Solyn, Joseph Steele, Lorraine A. Steele, Allan R. Taylor, David D. Thompson, Jr., Leonard W. Tourville, Edward S. Tregger, Robert S. Tuneski, Arthur S. Tuttle, Mary Jane Wharton, William J. Willetts, Jr., Esther B. Williams, Diane D. Zukowski.

EASTON. Fairfield County.—(Form of government, selectmen, town meeting, board of finance.)—Inc., May, 1845; taken from Weston. Area, 28.6 sq. miles. Population, est., 6,489. Voting district, 1. Residential community. Transp.—Freight: Served by numerous motor common carriers. Post office, Easton (branch of Bridgeport post office).

TOWN OFFICERS. Clerk and Reg. of Vital Statistics, Elizabeth A. Pander; Hours, 8:30 A.M.-4:30 P.M., Mon. through Fri.; Address, Town Hall, 225 Center Rd., 06612; Tel., Bridgeport, (203) 268-6291.—**Asst. Clerk and Asst. Reg. of Vital Statistics,** Janice J. Greiser.—**Selectmen,** 1st, Anthony J. Colonnese (R) Tel., (203) 268-6291, Dolores M. Schwartz (D), Stephen L. Zakos (R).—**Treas.,** Leon E. Induni.—**Comptroller,** Joy Haller.—**Bd. of Finance,** Andrew R. Kachele, Chm., Robert Lessler, Thomas H. Partridge, Phillip Petron, Velma Worth; Robert F. Moffitt, Clerk; Alternates, Roberta Cable, C. Lee Hanson, vacancy.—**Bd. of Ethics,** Philip Baroff, Barbara Broderick, Arlene Millbauer, Sandra Ostreligh, Robert Petrucelli.—**Tax Collector,** Patrice Hildenbrand.—**Bd. of Assessment Appeals,** Hugh J. Barry, Chm., Walter Finick, Victor R. Goldmerstein.—**Assessor,** Teresa Raineri; Deputy, Rachael Schwartz.—**Registrars of Voters,** Jean B. Bromer (D), Eunice K. Hanson (R).—**Supt. of Schools,** Kenneth R. Freeston.—**Bd. of Education,** Phyllis C. Machledt, Chm.,

Steve Hedges, 1997; Elliot H. Kraut, Karin H. Swanson, 1999; Ruth Powell, Joseph W. Schwartz, 2001.—**Pension and Employees Benefit Comm.,** James F. Kenney, Manuel A. Bernardo, James J. Broderick, Anthony J. Colonnese, Alan Goldbecker, Thomas McCafferty, G. Webster Miller, Laurie Richardson.—**Planning and Zoning Comm.,** Robert H. Albrecht, Chm., Philip G. Luckhardt, Robert E. Maquat, James J. Mellen, John J. Neary; Alternates, Thomas Savard, Sherman Turner, Emmett Wallace.—**Zoning Enforcement/Soil Erosion Control Officer,** Mario Garofalo.—**Zoning Bd. of Appeals,** Donald J. Jordan, Chm., J. Brian Fatse, Raymond W. Ganim, Victor George, Mitchell H. Greenberg; Alternates, Patricia Berlin, John Harris, Thomas Herrmann.—**Open Burning Official,** Peter G. Neary.—**Conservation Comm.,** Phillip A. Doremus, Chm., Gail W. Bromer, Stephen Edwards, Robert B. Factor, William S. Florczak, Eleanor Sylvestro, Dori M. Wollen; Alternates, Sharon Cregeen, Robert Falkenhagen, Bruce LePage; Mario Garofalo, Enforcement Officer.—**Dir. of Social Services,** Josephine Stenqvist.—**Comm. for the Aging,** John Bromer, Ann Fiyalka, Dorothy Pavlick; Patricia R. Finick, Municipal Agent; Alternates, Marvin B. Gelfand, Sal Santella, Ann Zowine.—**Dir. of Health,** Edward Pendagast, M.D.—**Emergency Medical Services Comm.,** Charles B. Watson, M.D., Chm., Jonathan Maisel, Martin A. Ohradan, Richard Schwartz, Steven Soberman, M.D.—**Bd. of Library Directors,** Patricia Pond, Chm., Leopold G. Bourret, Sarah Factor, Karen Lee Gunther-Chung, Les Kozerwitz, Anne Lindquist.—**Park and Recreation Comm.,** John Cunningham, Chm., Thomas Cable, Cheryl Everett, Michael Fleischer, Robert Menegay, Kathleen A. Roach, Kathleen Smith; Karen McGuire, Dir.—**Dir. of Public Works/Town Engineer,** Edward L. Nagy, P.E.—**Tree Warden,** Richard McLaughlin.—**Building Inspector,** Emil W. Martin.—**Building Bd. of Appeals,** John Marsilio, Harry Ruzicka, three vacancies.—**Insurance Comm.,** James F. Tomchik, Chm., Anthony J. Colonnese, Jay Hereford, Peter Pisaretz, Joseph W. Schwartz.—**Road Comm.,** Larry Edwards, P.E./L.S., Chm., Anthony Grosso, vacancy.—**Chief of Police,** John Solomon.—**Police Comm.,** Philip J. D'Eramo, Chm., Charles R. Feld, William Freeman, Robert J. Nicola, George E. Scrivani.—**Constables,** George A. Beno, John M. Gordon, Paul R. Greiser, Sr., Richard F. Greiser, Charles Laskay, Jr., Clinton H. Salko, vacancy.—**Chief of Fire Dept.,** David H. Buchanan.—**Fire Marshal,** Peter G. Neary; Deputies, Lucey E. Crossman, Schuyler D. Sherwood.—**Bd. of Fire Comrs.,** Robert J. Connell, Chm., Ralph T. Altieri, Kevin Collins, Charles N. Laskay, Jr., Edward Pendagast.—**Civil Preparedness Dir.,** David H. Buchanan; Asst., Anthony Casubolo.—**Town Atty.,** Ronald D. Williams.—**Justices of the Peace,** Frank S. Beckerer, George A. Beno, John J. Bromer, Anthony J. Colonnese, Philip J. D'Eramo, Catherine M. diCecco, Phillip A. Doremus, Ronald J. Dougiello, Charles R. Feld, Mary Ann C. Freeman, Maria E. Gaines, George W. Ganim, Joann M. Gelfand, Victor S. George, Janice J. Greiser, Richard F. Greiser, Alfred W. Hamann, Eunice K. Hanson, Robert F. Hennessey, Clarence E. Jennings, Donald J. Jordan, Andrew R. Kachele, Monte Klein, Edward J. Kovac, Robert H. Lessler, Phyllis C. Machledt, Albert A. Mansi, James J. Mellen, John J. Neary, Peter G. Neary, Robert J. Nicola, Elizabeth A. Pander, Ann C. Partridge, James P. Schwartz, Joseph L. Silhavy, Irving Silverman, Barbara Shields, Nicholas V. Soares, Jr., Gerald F. Solisiak, Patricia Soltisiak, Elaine H. Spicer, Alfred M. Treidel, Maria S. Watson, Ronald D. Williams, Andrew H. Wolff, Velma V. Worth, Pauline Yatrakis, Stephen L. Zakos.

EAST WINDSOR.

Hartford County.—(Form of government, selectmen, town meeting, board of finance.)—Inc., May, 1768; taken from Windsor. Area, 26.8 sq. miles. Population, est., 9,700. Voting districts, 2. Principal industries, agriculture, support system facilities, and manufacture of small tools, paper boxes, electronics, aluminum by-products, farm implements and fertilizers. Freight: Served by numerous motor common carriers. Post offices, Broad Brook and East Windsor.

TOWN OFFICERS. Clerk and Reg. of Vital Statistics, Claire S. Badstubner; Hours, 8:30 A.M.-4:30 P.M., Mon. through Wed.; 8:30 A.M.-7:30 P.M., Thurs.; 8:30 A.M.-12:30 P.M., Fri.; Address, Town Hall, 11 Rye St., P.O. Box 213, Broad Brook 06016; Tel., Windsor Locks, (860) 623-9467.—**Asst. Clerk and Asst. Reg. of Vital Statistics,** Karen W. Gaudreau.—**Selectmen,** 1st, John E. Rajala (D) P.O. Box 366, Broad Brook, Tel., (860) 623-8122, Kenneth C. Crouch (R), Frances M. Kinsellar (D), Linda L. Roberts (R), Denise E. Sabotka (D).—**Treas.,** Reginald E. Bancroft, Jr.—**Ethics Comm.,** Donald Arcari, Natalie Bancroft, Robert H. Cathcart, Sr., Andrew J. Tripp, vacancy.—**Bd. of Finance,** Charlotte Foley, Chm., Barbara J. Bertrand, Kurt W. Johansen, Daniel A. Mickey, Peter Nevers, vacancy.—**Tax Collector,** Janet L. Regina.—**Bd. of Assessment Appeals,** Marilyn F. Butenkoff, James M. Lenegan, Elaine A. Stevens.—**Assessors,** John M. Bassinger, Chm., Ronald J. Drolett, Herbert R. Tschummi.—**Registrars of Voters,** Marilyn S. Rajala (D), Linda C. Sinsigallo (R).—**Supt. of Schools,** Philip I. Morton.—**Bd. of Education,** William S. Kolodziej, Chm., Joan C. Eckel, Louise D. Lyke, Christopher Mickey, vacancy, 1997; JoAnne Holigan, Ruth W. Howell, Judith E. Paquin, Mary M. Tarbell, vacancy, 1999.—**Planning and Zoning Comm.,** Edward Filipone, Frank Gowdy, Barry S. Howell, Susan Kiss, Sonia Morell; Alternates, Brian C. Chisholm, Gary G. Guiliano, David U. Lockwood.—**Town Planner,** Jose Giner.—**Zoning Enforcement Officer,** William Carrington.—**Zoning Bd. of Appeals,** Thomas V. Arcari, Robert H. Caldon, Earl F. Larson, Clifford L. Nelson, Wade W. Signor; Alternates, William G. Raber, Jr., Dennis Soucy, vacancy.—**Economic Development Comm.,** Richard L. Covill, Timothy Ellison, Robert A. Grant, Herbert Holden, James Karat, Francis A. Salva, Jr., James H. Spencer.—**Housing Auth.,** Karen Boutin, John P. Grace, Barbara R. LaMay, Beverly Percoski, Anthony J. Razzano.—**Conservation and Inland Wetlands Comm.,** Richard Gwozdz, John E. Malin, John Maslak, Emil A. Mulnite, Robert J. Raber, Michael Sawka, Leo Szymanski; Alternates, Alan Brewer, two vacancies.—**Elderly Comm.,** Earl O. Hemingway, Patricia D. Kirchhof, Gay F. Richard, H. Stuart Woodard, Bonnie K. Yosky; Nicholas Annelli, Municipal Agent.—**Social Services Coordinator,** Elizabeth Burns.—**Dir. of Health,** William Blitz (P.O., Enfield).—**Parks and Recreation Comm.,** Sandra B. Foster, Chm., Suzie Boice, Robert Healy, Robert R. Russell, Blaine G. Simpkins.—**Highway Foreman,** David Fisck.—**Building Inspector,** Michael T. Agnew.—**Water Pollution Control Auth.,** Paul Catino, Thomas F. Davis, Patricia Pond, John Sauerhoefer, Frank J. Smith.—**Chief of Police,** Thomas J. Laufer.—**Police Comm.,** D. James Barton, Jr., Marie E. DeSousa, Steven D. Knibloe, Melvin S. Meacham, Linda C. Sinsigallo.—**Constables,** Michael T. Balf, Frank L. Kirchhof, Jr., Richard P. Pippin, Jr., Joseph F. Roberts, Blaine G. Simpkins, Leo Szymanski, George H. Ulitsch.—**Chiefs of Fire Dept.,** William A. Loos, Jr. (Broad Brook), Thomas J.

Clynch III (Warehouse Point).—**Fire Marshal,** Blaine G. Simpkins (East Windsor), Thomas J. Clynch III (Warehouse Point); Acting Deputy, Donald Arcari (East Windsor).—**Pension and Retirement Comm.,** D. James Barton, Jr., Charlotte Foley, William S. Kolodziej, Louise Lyke, Daniel Mickey, Peter Nevers, Denise Sabotka, Donald S. Wagner.—**Civil Preparedness Dir.,** Mary Buckley.—**Town Attys.,** Goodman, Rosenthal & McKenna.—**Justices of the Peace,** Janice M. Albetski, Claire S. Badstubner, Calvin A. Bancroft, Reginald E. Bancroft, D. James Barton, Jr., Walter E. Bass, Jr., Barbara J. Bertrand, Paul E. Bertrand, George G. Butenkoff, Marilyn F. Butenkoff, Robert J. Cormier, Ronald J. Drolett, Teresa M. Drolett, Harold T. Flaherty, Joan C. Galinski, Lillian Gudzunas, Walter Gudzunas, Frances M. Keenan, Frances M. Kinsellar, Steven D. Knibloe, Louise D. Lyke, Robert K. Lyke, Jr., Caroline G. Madore, Maria Martineau, Barbara Mazurek, Faye C. Meacham, Melvin S. Meacham, Harald M. Mikkelsen, Clifford L. Nelson, Peter J. Nevers, Raymond Noble, Judith E. Paquin, Beverly W. Percoski, Kathleen B. Pippin, Pauline T. Putriment, John E. Rajala, Marilyn S. Rajala, Alfred Regina, Joseph F. Roberts, Linda L. Roberts, Denise E. Sabotka, Betty Ann Sheridan, Jane S. Simpkins, Linda C. Sinsigallo, Charles J. Szymanski, Lorraine A. Vines, Robert M. Watts, Carl H. Weymouth, Jr., Gloria Weymouth, Carol S. Yeomans.

ELLINGTON. Tolland County.—(Form of government, selectmen, town meeting, board of finance.)—Inc., May, 1786; taken from East Windsor. Area, 34.6 sq. miles. Population, est., 11,817. Voting districts, 2. Principal industry, agriculture. Transp.—Passenger: Served by buses of Post Road Stages, Inc. from Stafford Springs and Rockville. Freight: Served by numerous motor common carriers. The town is served by rural delivery from the Ellington post office.

TOWN OFFICERS. Clerk and Reg. of Vital Statistics, Cynthia J. Lacaprucia; Hours, 9 A.M.-7 P.M. Mon.; 9 A.M.-4:30 P.M., Tues. through Fri.; Address, 55 Main St., P.O. Box 187, 06029; Tel., Rockville, (860) 875-3190.—**Asst. Clerk,** Nancy A. Lemek.—**Asst. Regs. of Vital Statistics,** Nancy A. Lemek, Diane H. McKeegan.—**Selectmen,** 1st, Michael P. Stupinski (R) Tel., (860) 875-0787, Peter J. Charter (R), Theodore C. Graziani (D), Douglas D. Hill (R), Robert S. Wallace (R), Nancy O. Way (R), Rachel L. Wheeler-Rossow (D).—**Bd. of Finance,** Michael P. Scudieri, Chm., Robert J. Clements, Dennis W. Frawley, Mark D. Leighton, Robert K. Pagani, Barry C. Pinto; Nicholas J. DiCorleto, Jr., Finance Officer.—**Tax Collector,** Pamela Lombardo.—**Bd. of Assessment Appeals,** Leonard Johnson, Chm., Thomas J. Stack, Francis Yost.—**Assessor,** Frances Keenan.—**Registrars of Voters,** Cheryle Halleran (D), Margaret R. Dawson (R).—**Supt. of Schools,** Dr. Richard E. Packman.—**Bd. of Education,** Gary J. Blanchette, William F. Harford, Donald M. Weekes, 1997; Maurice W. Blanchette, Chm., Kenneth J. Brennan, Wendy J. Ciparelli, Cynthia P. Costanzo, Richard E. Currey, Susan J. Luginbuhl, John N. O'Shaughnessy, 1999.—**Planning and Zoning Comm.,** Francis J. Prichard, Jr., Chm., Clifford L. Aucter, Francis C. Shea, Lori L. Spielman, Stanley L. Tetrault, Emery L. Zahner; Alternates, Ann Harford, William Hogan, Marlene Weinert.—**Town Planner,** Joseph Baker.—**Zoning Bd. of Appeals,** Betty Jane Bergstrom, Kenneth M. Braga, Dean Kloter, Robert E. McMullen, Michael E. Riley, Margo Wheeler; Alternates, Alfred Francis, Beverly Fries, vacancy.—**Economic Development Comm.,** Edwina Thirsher, Chm., Brian Griffin, Joyce Joy, Patricia Schuiten, Douglas Townsend.—**Housing Auth.,** Stephen Schindler, Chm., Margaret Bean, Evelyn M. Cassel, Gloria Cohen, Frank Graziani; Alex Ross, Exec. Dir.—**Conservation and Inland Wetlands Comm.,** Kenneth Braga, Chm., Art Barber, Stephen Olander, Vincent J. Purnhagen, Lori Spielman, Margo Wheeler.—**Social Services Coordinator,** Doris Crayton.—**Health Dir.,** William H. Blitz, M.P.H.R.S. (P.O., Enfield).—**Human Services Comm.,** Deborah Bellizzi, Yale Cantor, Helen Filloramo, Sandra-Anne Orsini, Sharon Schall, Susan Stack, Bonnie Tessman, Marlene Weinert.—**Library Directors,** Mary K. Clements, Robert Eddy, Ruth L. Helme, Marjorie R. Helme-Brother, Beverly B. Lewis, Nancy L. Lombard.—**Municipal Historian,** vacancy.—**Parks and Recreation Comm.,** Thomas Boscarino, Chm., Neal Breen, Kathy Korchari, Jess Kupec, Allan Martindale, Audrey Monti, Darlene Sutton, James Vozzolo, Peter Weiti; Robert Tedford, Dir.—**Dir. of Public Works/Tree Warden,** Peter H. Michaud.—**Town Engineer,** James Thompson.—**Building Inspector,** Thomas J. Connelly.—**Building Code Bd. of Appeals,** Howard Reckert, Chm., James W. Alexander, Robert McKinney, Peter Williams, Ronald Zemanek.—**Water Pollution Control Auth.,** Michael Weinert, Chm., Edward Duell, George Shaw.—**Chief of Police,** Michael P. Stupinski.—**Constables,** Michael Bard, Joseph Belliveau, Arthur Carlson, Michael Caron, Michael DuBois, Douglas Fornal, Robert Hoffman, Maureen Lowe, Michael Nieliwocki, three vacancies.—**Chiefs of Fire Dept.,** John Turner (Center), Allen D. Harvell (Crystal Lake).—**Fire Marshals,** Robert Dabica (Crystal Lake), Allan Lawrence (Ellington).—**Civil Preparedness Dir.,** Allan Lawrence.—**Town Atty.,** Atherton B. Ryan.—**Justices of the Peace,** Clifford L. Aucter, Maurice W. Blanchette, Kenneth M. Braga, Peter J. Charter, Robert J. Clements, Robert M. Dawson III, Ann Harford, William F. Harford, Leonard A. Johnson, Robert A. Ludwig, Sr., Beatrice McConville, John T. Millane, Robert K. Pagani, Barry C. Pinto, Francis J. Prichard, Jr., Bernard G. Stein, Iris T. Stein, John A. Strom, Robert S. Wallace, Nancy O. Way, Donald M. Weekes.

ENFIELD. Hartford County.—(Form of government, town manager, town council.)—Named and inc., by Massachusetts, 1683; annexed to Conn., May, 1749. Area, 34.2 sq. miles. Population, est., 45,451. Voting districts, 9. Principal industries, insurance, manufacture of toys, water filtration systems, specialized machinery, aluminum and magnesium castings, wooden reels for wire and cables, silk screening, games, greeting cards, tools and gauges, envelopes, laser beam welding, warehouse distribution of toys, clothing and pharmaceuticals, manufacture of electronic assemblies, processing of food and dairy products, ice cream, vegetable and tobacco farming. Located on Rte. I-91, 18 miles north of Hartford and 8 miles south of Springfield, MA. Transp.—Passenger: Public transportation by Conn. Transit Bus lines, and by Pioneer Valley Transit Auth. Freight: Served by Conrail, Boston & Maine Corporation and numerous motor common carriers. Post office, Enfield; carrier and RFD.

TOWN OFFICERS. Clerk and Reg. of Vital Statistics, Suzanne F. Olechnicki; Hours, 9 A.M.-5 P.M., Mon. through Fri.; Address, 820 Enfield St., 06082; Tel., (860) 253-6440; FAX (860) 253-6310; Internet: http://www.state.ct.us.—**Deputy Clerk and Asst. Reg. of Vital Statistics,** Jean E. Blaser.—**Asst. Clerk and Asst. Reg. of Vital**

Statistics, Joyce P. Mascena.—**Town Manager,** Scott A. Shanley; Asst., Daniel T. Vindigni.—**Town Council,** Dist. 1, William R. Vayda; Dist. 2, Adam Pierz; Dist. 3, Scott R. Kaupin; Dist. 4, Michael S. Ludwick; Councilmen at Large, Giovanni Carollo, Frank P. Dodd, Sr., William Edgar, Jr., Alice Egan, Deputy Mayor Peter J. Falk, Sean M. McGuire, Mayor Mary Lou Strom.—**Ethics Comm.,** Clayton M. Grey, Carol A. Hall, John F. McCafferty, Richard J. Michaels, vacancy; Alternates, Leonara J. DeBella, vacancy.—**Treas.,** Gregory Simmons.—**Dir. of Finance,** David E. Minnich.—**Tax Collector,** Suzanne R. Longo.—**Bd. of Assessment Appeals,** August Jasminski, Rudolph S. Kuraska, Gretchen E. Pfeifer-Hall.—**Assessor,** Joyce M. Jacius.—**Registrars of Voters,** Mary Lou Flynn (D), Vaughan O. Vanderscoff (R).—**Supt. of Schools,** John Gallacher.—**Bd. of Education,** Ann S. Maloney, Chm., Charles A. Fuller, Jr., Nelson E. Gamage, Michael L. Hanlon, Roger W. Jones, Nicholas D. Sinsigalli, Jr., William V. Thomson, Jr., Scott M. Vining, Jr., W. Franklin Wood, 1997.—**Planning and Zoning Comm.,** Charles A. Duren, Chm., Edgar H. Butcher, Arnold H. Christensen, Francis P. Costanzo, Anthony M. DiPace, Nicles Lefakis, Jack Mancuso; Alternates, Elizabeth A. Ballard, Leonard J. Theriault, John H. Waller.—**Town Planner,** Robert A. Burke.—**Dir. of Economic Development,** Raymond L. Warren.—**Economic Development Comm.,** Celeste Bergman-Moore, Gregory Caravella, Ralph J. Cerrato, John Gual, Claire P. Hunt, Harvey Irlen, David Navarro, E. Patrick Storey, Jr., vacancy.—**Zoning Bd. of Appeals,** Francis J. Gonynor, John L. Ledoux, Jr., Gerald M. Legault, Lisa M. Raymond, Richard A. Zaczynski; Alternates, Patrick J. Crowley, Edward H. Furey, S. Harry Madler.—**Zoning Enforcement Officer,** Wayne T. Bickley.—**Development/Redevelopment Agency,** Gerald K. Fitzsimons, Stephen L. Niemitz, E. Patrick Storey, Jr., Thomas A. Terrall, Jr., Rosario T. Vella, vacancy.—**Housing Auth.,** William J. Ballard, June E. Bouffard, Tadeus Buczkowski, Gerald Crowley, Richard L. Gonyea, Robert Rookey; Mary Ellen Kuraska, Exec. Dir.—**Housing Code Appeals Bd.,** Samuel Albano, Dorothy C. Allen, Paul E. Censki, Karen H. Chadderton, Richard M. Szewczak; Alternates, Constance P. Harmon, Lawrence P. Tracey, Jr.—**Fair Rent Comm.,** Louis A. DeCaro, Adam Gwozdz, Donna L. Koseian, Samuel McGill, Jr., Kenneth H. Murray, Clinton G. Williams, vacancy.—**Conservation Comm.,** Mary E. Goodhouse, Robert J. Grunert, Jr., Joanne D. Kneiss, Roger L. Olsen, Gretchen E. Pfeifer-Hall, George P. Rigatti, Michael A. Schnitzler, vacancy; Alternates, Robert A. Egan, Edward T. Mokrycki, Russell L. Scull.—**Historic Dist. Comm.,** Arthur Cote, Francis J. Gonynor, Joanne Lynch, Richard M. Tatoian, Samuel C. Worthen; Alternates, F. Russell Meyer, Nancy Smyth, Lillian Troiano.—**Comm. on Aging,** Rodney E. Almeida, Joan W. Cass, Pauline L. Christian-Strom, Esther R. Hannum, Mary Jablonski, Omer S. Muchmore, Jr., M. Louise B. Stevens, Eileen C. Stroiney, vacancy.—**Human Relations Comm.,** Christopher S. Burzynski, Louis A. DeCaro, Diane L. Duggan, Cynthia Mangini, Mary McGuire, Loretta M. Nelson, Michael P. Reissig.—**Social Services Dir.,** Dorothy C. Allen.—**Dir. of Health,** William H. Blitz.—**Chief Sanitarian,** Michael Caronna.—**Library Bd. of Trustees,** Ann Duren, Diane M. Laroche, Francis J. Martin.—**Supt. of Parks and Recreation,** William E. Davis.—**Purchasing Agent,** Michael Alexopoulos, Jr.; Asst., Cathy Cherpak.—**Dir. of Public Works,** John J. Kazmarski.—**Cultural Arts Comm.,** Robert J. Albom, Eileen Axenroth, Patricia Folmsbee, Jacqueline S. Horner, Priscilla D. McManus, Marie-Louise Starski, vacancy.—**Town Engineer,** Jeffrey Bord.—**Supt. of**

Highways, Albert A. Kneiss, Jr.—**Building Official,** Stuart F. VanWagner.—**Building Code Bd. of Appeals,** Kenneth J. Bergeron, Louis A. DeCaro, Gary C. Herrick, Joseph F. Petronella, Gary L. Sullivan.—**Water Pollution Control Auth.,** Town Council.—**Supt. of Sanitation,** Marvin E. Serra.—**Chief of Police,** Ronald G. Marcotte, Sr.—**Constables,** Charles J. Abronze, Arthur Cote, Joan N. Garini, Ronald J. Gregory, Sr., Roger L. Olsen, Theodore J. Plamondon, Jr., vacancy.—**Fire Depts.,** Enfield: Edward N. Richards, Chief; John P. Vacon, Fire Marshal. Hazardville: John J. Flanagan, Chief/Fire Marshal. North Thompsonville: Earl Provencher, Chief/Fire Marshal. Shaker Pines: Raymond Aiken, Chief; David Senatore, Fire Marshal. Thompsonville: George J. Belanger, Chief; Paul E. Censki, Fire Marshal.—**Civil Preparedness Dir.,** Harold Spillane.—**Town Atty.,** Christopher W. Bromson.—**Justices of the Peace,** Charles J. Abronze, Claudette P. Alaimo, Esther Alaimo, Cindy B. Andersen, Elizabeth A. Ballard, Paul D. Batchelder, Tom Baziak, Neil T. Begley, Mary Ann Beiler, Jo Ann Bellantuono, Fred M. Bergamini, Mary T. Bergamini, Bridgette Birchall, Deborah J. Bonanno, Sandra G. Butcher, Andrea E. Campbell, Ronald L. Campbell, Lindsey M. Carlson, Teresa C. Carlson, Giovanni Carollo, John A. Castle, Cynthia E. Chapin-Howell, David G. Cheney, Jill M. Conklin, George Contois, Robert L. Corbin, Patrick J. Crowley, Eleanor B. D'Amato, James P. D'Amato, Louis A. DeCaro, Edward J. Dolinsky, Diane L. Duggan, Ann Duren, Charles A. Duren, Alice Egan, Robert A. Egan, Carri L. Ewing, Janice K. Ewing, Peter J. Falk, John G. Fenner, Sr., Salvatore J. Fiore, Gerald K. Fitzsimons, Liane A. Flynn, Mary Lou Flynn, Edward H. Foley, David J. Fredrick, Linda E. Fredrick, James Frost, Richard G. Furey, Joan N. Garini, Flora Gates, Nicholas J. Giaccone III, Nelson S. Giddings, Kevin J. Gordon, Kenneth P. Gorzkowski, Jeffrey A. Gowdy, Ronald J. Gregory, Sr., Gladys M. Grip, Gloria K. Guillemette, Russell T. Hack, Sr., Stephen J. Haley, Edward J. Harris, Mary Ann Harris, Russell F. Hayward, Kenneth L. Heitman, Jacquelyn V. Hethcoat, Mary Ann Howell, Karen Howland-Falk, Eleanor M. Jarmoc, Robert W. Jones, Scott R. Kaupin, Mary Ellen Killeen, Charles S. Koseian, John C. Koseian, Shakea D. Koseian, Stephan H. Koseian, Joseph P. Kowalski, Jr., Ferdinand P. Kula, Jr., Richard D. Laffargue, Beverly J. Lanouette, John H. Ledoux, Jr., Nicles Lefakis, Deborah A. Legault, Gerald M. Legault, Kymberly B. Lessard, Michele R. Lizee, Donald R. Lord, Jr., Michael S. Ludwick, Gilbert J. MacKenna IV, Westy T. MacNeil, Lila A. Mailman, Cynthia Mangini, James Massaro, John W. Maznicki, William P. McGuire, Priscilla D. McManus, Erika L. Melnick, Edward T. Mokrycki, John Mokrycki, Jr., Dianne C. Nabors, Paul A. Nabors, Randa S. Nesman, Stephen L. Niemitz, Michael Q. Nosal, Tophie K. Nowak, Gayle Obregon, Patricia Olsen, Roger L. Olsen, Josephine A. Ouellette, Richard G. Ouellette, Karen I. Owens, Lucinda Peck, Margaret Perry, Linda M. Pilch, Edward J. Poremba, Jr., Kelly M. Poudrette, Yvonne D. Prestwich, Lynn Provencher, Mary Jane Pych, James M. Ranta, Lisa M. Raymond, Joan C. Reuter, Roger Russell, Michael W. Ryan, Monica C. Ryan, Charles E. Salamone, John C. Salamone, Ellen P. Sawn, Frederick Schmalz, Martha J. Schmalz, Irma G. Schober, Lynn A. Scull, Russell L. Scull, Nicholas D. Sinsigalli, Jr., Jeanne Smith, Raymond F. Stanio, Sylvia Stanio, Edward G. Stentaford, Jr., E. Patrick Storey, Jr., Eileen C. Stroiney, Mary Lou Strom, Anthony H. Sullivan, Gary L. Sullivan, Linda Sullivan, Daniel S. Swenson, John T. Tait, Peter S. Targonski, Lawrence L. Telmosse, Leonard J. Theriault, Sharon L. Theriault, Michael A. Tippo, Robert W. Tkacz, Vaughan O. Vanderscoff, Rosario T. Vella, Jeanne Watton, Karen A. Weseliza, Blair A. White, James A. White, Clinton G. Williams, Joanne M. Williams, W. Franklin Wood, Cynthia M. Yakoubian, Thomas P. Yakoubian, John R. Young, John H. Zdebski, William G. Zimmerman.

ESSEX. Middlesex County.—(Form of government, selectmen, town meeting, board of finance.)—Inc., Sept. 13, 1852, as Old Saybrook; taken from Saybrook. Name changed, July 8, 1854 to Essex. Area, 11.8 sq. miles. Population, est., 5,855. Voting districts, 3. Principal industries, boat building and repair, turbine blades, machine parts, novelties, naval lighting equipment and bent wire products. Transp.—Freight: Served by numerous motor common carriers. Post offices, Essex, Centerbrook and Ivoryton.

TOWN OFFICERS. Clerk and Reg. of Vital Statistics, Betty J. Gaudenzi; Hours, 9 A.M.-4 P.M., Mon. through Fri.; Address, Town Hall, 29 West Ave., P.O. Box 98, 06426; Tel., (860) 767-4344; E-Mail, EssexCT@AOL.com; Internet, http://www.state.ct.us/MUNIC/ESSEX/essex.htm.—**Asst. Clerk and Asst. Reg. of Vital Statistics,** Elisa C. Young.—**Selectmen,** 1st, Peter B. Webster (R) Tel., (860) 767-4348, Alvin G. Wolfgram (D), William F. Werwaiss (D).—**Treas.,** Betty J. Gaudenzi.—**Bd. of Finance,** Richard F. Gamble, Chm., Ward L. Johnson, Kenneth W. Kells, Chester W. Kitchings, Jr., Paula McManus, Peter J. Philpot.—**Tax Collector,** Nancy L. Stadalnik.—**Bd. of Assessment Appeals,** Lois Ely, Frank J. Flores, Jr., Kathleen M. Rubenbauer.—**Assessor,** Judith Rivers.—**Registrars of Voters,** 1st, 2nd & 3rd Dists., Dolores Budney (D); Elizabeth G. Schellens (R).—**Supt. of Schools,** John Proctor.—**Bd. of Education,** W. Campbell Hudson, Chm., Terry Stewart, 1997; Laura A. Berry, Vincent Pacielo, 1999; James C. Childress, Richard R. Rodelli, 2001.—**Planning Comm.,** Laura Champion, Linda Herman, August Pampel, Russell Smith, William Swartzbaugh; Alternates, Edward Cook, Geraldine Lombard, Richard Mela.—**Zoning Comm.,** Gregory H. Ellis, Chm., Peter Hance, Joel Marzi, Thomas Melvin, Sally Wiseman; Alternates, Thompson Crosby, Donna Hyde, vacancy.—**Zoning Bd. of Appeals,** Stuart Ingersoll, Chm., Betty Bevan, Burton Churchill, Thomas McManus, Norman Needleman; Alternates, John Ducan, Michael Perkins, John Senn.—**Zoning Enforcement Officer,** Larry Gilliam.—**Housing Auth.,** Selene Sweck, Chm., Sally Cochran, William Foster, Ruth Schumacher, Anthony J. Shea.—**Conservation Comm.,** John Leach, Chm., Eric P. Bierre, Robert Dunn, Jean Hanor, Robert Russo, Kathleen Tucker, vacancy.—**Inland Wetlands Comm.,** Laura Champion, Charles Corson, Daniel Lapman, John Leach, Jean Leuchtenburg, Alice Powers, vacancy; Alternates, William Doane, Ted Sullivan, vacancy.—**Harbor Management Comm.,** Jeffrey Going, Chm., Edward Birch, Carl Lombard, Walter Schieferdecker, Michael Viscuso; Alternates, Paul Dubey, Walter Wiegert.—**Agent for the Elderly,** Dyan Lombardi.—**Welfare Dir.,** Virginia Zeleznicky.—**Dir. of Health,** Christopher W. Goff, M.D.—**Town Historian,** Donald Malcarne.—**Parks and Recreation Comm.,** Cecelia Brown, Chm., Jon Alverez, Jacqueline Doane, Robert Hammer, Strickland Hyde III, John Johns, Donald Mesite; Alternates, Elizabeth Easley, Virginijus Jonynas, Barbara Pirruccio.—**Supt. of Highways,** David Caroline.—**Building Inspector,** Richard Leighton.—**Sanitarian,** Carol L. Speer.—**Tree Warden,** August F. Pampel, Jr.—

Town Engineer, Doane Engineering.—**Building Code Bd. of Appeals,** Robert Harper, Chm., Rudolph Besier, Edward Binder, Frederick A. Radcliffe, C. Talcott Scoville.—**Sanitary Waste,** Alvin Wolfgram, Chm., Elizabeth Pierson, Robert Potts, Kenneth Wexler, William Rutan; Alternates, Alice Pinsince, vacancy.—**Chief of Police,** Peter B. Webster.—**Constables,** Patrick Bowers, Nicholas Incerti, Richard Leighton, Kenneth R. Savage, Robert J. Schmid, Joseph Sparaco.—**Chief of Fire Dept.,** Paul Fazzino.—**Fire Marshal,** Richard Leighton.—**Civil Preparedness Dir.,** William Buckridge.—**Town Atty.,** David M. Royston.—**Justices of the Peace,** Betty J. Bevan, Virginia C. Cook, Charles N. Doane III, Paul Dubey, Linda K. Dwyer, David W. Galligan, Alda M. Gaudenzi, Fay F. Gerritt, Sean Gilligan, Bruce Glowac, JoAnn Greenwood, Lino Grillo, Jean R. Hanor, Richard Hertz, Ward Johnson, Carl S. Kaufmann, Jack Lazare, Roger B. LeCompte, Geraldine A. Lombard, Richard Manning, William C. Mitchel, Douglas W. Paul, Ingjerd Philpot, Peter Philpot, Alice R. Pinsince, Peter E. Pool, Richard Rieder, Heidi M. Samuelson, Linda Savitsky, Elizabeth Schellens, Dorothy M. Shugrue, Frank P. Simkowski, Peter J. Trantino, William P. Veillette, Michael Viscuso, Peter Webster, Gary J. Weymer.

FAIRFIELD. Fairfield County.—(Form of government, representative town meeting, selectmen, board of finance.)—Settled, 1639; named 1645; included in Connecticut Colony, May, 1685. Area, 31.3 sq. miles. Population, est., 53,057. Voting districts, 10. Principal industries, the manufacture of bearings, gears, wire screens, and coated fabrics, refining precious metals, steel company, location of General Electric International Corporate Hdqrs., Fairfield Univ. and Sacred Heart Univ. Transp.—Passenger: Served by Metro North Commuter Railroad Co. and buses of the Bridgeport Transit Auth. Freight and Express: Served by numerous motor common carriers. U.S. Route 1, Merritt Parkway and Conn. Turnpike pass through town, east and west. Post offices, Fairfield, Southport and rural free delivery.

TOWN OFFICERS. Clerk and Reg. of Vital Statistics, Marguerite H. Toth; Hours, 8:30 A.M.-5 P.M., Mon. through Fri.; 8:30 A.M.-4:30 P.M., 3rd Mon. in June through Labor Day; Address, Town Hall, 611 Old Post Rd., 06430; Tel., (203) 256-3090, all other offices, (203) 256-3000.—**Asst. Clerks and Asst. Regs. of Vital Statistics,** Ann E. Hradsky, Ann Roche.—**Moderator, Representative Town Meeting,** Bryan LeClerc.—**Selectmen,** 1st, Paul A. Audley (R) Tel., (203) 256-3030, Kenneth A. Flatto (D), Jill Kelly (R).—**Treas.,** Stephen Galpin.—**Bd. of Ethics,** W. Bradley Morehouse, Chm., Dorothea Brennan, Noel Newman, Julia Thiele, vacancy.—**Fiscal Officer,** John P. Leahy.—**Bd. of Finance,** Paul H. Hiller, Jr., Chm., Susan P. Barrett, Robert J. Bitar, William J. Fitzpatrick III, Mary K. Frost, H. Penny Hug, Samuel J. Lazinger, John P. McCarthy, Andrew P. Toal.—**Tax Collector,** Stanley Gorzelany.—**Bd. of Assessment Appeals,** Edward Crowley, Scott Gerard, Frederick Miller, John Steeneck III, Harold Sutphen.—**Assessor,** Thomas F. Browne, Jr.—**Registrars of Voters,** Patricia S. Como (D), Joan K. O'Rourke (R).—**Supt. of Schools,** Carol Harrington.—**Bd. of Education,** Joan B. Maguire, Chm., Joan Madeo, 1997; Deborah M. Dowd, Richard O'Shea, Richard Z. Popilowski, Barbara Rifkin, 1999; Clifton Freedman, Jeffrey L. Matthews, Kathleen O'Brien, 2001.—**Personnel Dir.,** Donald Agard.—**Planning and Zoning Comm.,** Charles R. Eick, Jr., Barbara Findlay, Kevin

Gumpper, Myron J. Hinckley, Stephen W. Lang, Stephen Maggiola, Lois Smith; Alternates, Daniel Forbes, Michael Tetreau, Felicia Watson.—**Town Planner,** Joseph E. Devonshuk, Jr.—**Zoning Bd. of Appeals,** Robert Brennan, Kathleen Howard, Frank A. Johnson, John Milici, Richard G. Osborne; Alternates, Francis Halas, Kathleen Maxham, Dianne E. Young.—**Zoning Enforcement Officer,** vacancy.—**Economic Development Comm.,** James Callahan, Donna E. Milne, Peter A. Penczer, Lawrence J. Roberts, Harvey Sussman, Paul Vimini, vacancy.—**Housing Auth.,** Carolyn H. Durgy, Chm., Anne R. Jackson, Henry Morris, Alice Sabanosh, Richard I. Steiber.—**Conservation and Inland Wetlands Comm.,** Michael Giaquinto, Chm., Michael Bologna, Joseph Carcusa, Jr., Catherine Doyle, Robert Erskine, Robert J. Filotei, Charles S. Jankovski.—**Flood and Erosion Control Bd.,** Russell B. Jennings, Chm., Albert F. Grauer, Harry Sheketaff, Timothy Wallace, Eileen Wilcox.—**Conservation Dir.,** Thomas Steinke.—**Historic Dist. Comm.,** Robert E. Hatch, Chm., Jeanne Anderson, David S. Parker, Melanie Smith, Catherine Tymniak; Alternates, Joan Homa, Judith Proctor, vacancy.—**Human Services,** Laurence Sarezky, Chm., Ann Atkinson, Mark Edinberg, Patricia Hart, Carol Landsman, Jennifer Moorin, Ellen Wolf, vacancy.—**Dir. of Social Services,** Marcia Salko.—**Bd. of Health,** William Evans, Carol Jakab, William Kueffner, M.D., Bruce M. McDonald, Rita Waterman; Arthur Leffert, Dir.—**Library Trustees,** Barbara Bressler, Claire Fray, Gretchen Goether, Kenneth Hanson, George Longstreth, Peter Mott.—**Park Comm.,** Gail R. Usher, Chm., Kenneth Dalling, Donald Knuth, Brian Silvestro, vacancy.—**Bd. of Recreation,** William M. Johnson, Jr., Chm., Gretchen Hauser, Donald Knuth, Elizabeth Oderwald, Andrew J. Skroly.—**Dir. of Public Works,** Richard White.—**Purchasing Agent,** Michael Pettee.—**Town Engineer,** Ron Caton.—**Building Inspector,** Larry Gress.—**Building Bd. of Appeals,** Steven Canaiy, Stanley C. Forstrom, Sutiri Giavara, John R. Leverty.—**Water Pollution Control Auth.,** Stephen Demetri, Chm., Arthur R. Hersh, Daniel Jennings, Jill Kelly, vacancy.—**Tree Warden,** Kenneth Placko.—**Chief of Police,** Ronald Sullivan.—**Police Comm.,** William J. Wenzel, Chm., Harold Adams, Edward Gleason, George Lacovera, Myrtle G. Miller.—**Constables,** Nicholas A. Fabian, Jr., Ronald Kadar, Anthony Mazzeo, Francis D. Rowe, Eugene Short, Ruth A. Smey, Michael Terek.—**Chief of Fire Dept.,** Daniel Gardiner.—**Fire Marshal,** Harry Ackley.—**Bd. of Fire Comrs.,** Joan Rasmussen, Chm., Patrick Carroll, Michael Dowling, Victor L. Durgy, Jr., Charles Ross.—**Town Atty.,** Thomas Walsh, Jr.; Asst., James Rice.—**Justices of the Peace,** Alba Allard, Thomas Angelo, Paul A. Audley, Vincent J. Biondi, John B. Blank, Stephanie Cavallaro, Richard S. Cellar, Patricia A. Coffey, Edward V. Crowley, Jr., Susan DeLeon, Susan B. Felner, John C. Ford, Meg Francis, Barbara T. Garrison, Michael Girardi, Stephen Grathwohl, Sheila W. Greenspan, Leo F. Gregg, Joanne M. Instone, Kevin P. Kiley, Edward S. Kosciolek, Chester S. Kubel, Joan Kulick, Bryan L. LeClerc, Howard Z. Lehrman, Stanton H. Lesser, Robert Loftus, Keith A. Lorch, Anthony Mazzeo, Joseph F. McKeon, Jr., Estelle M. McMaster, Frederick E. Miller, Jr., Deborah J. Myles, Rose Marie Olexovitch, Robert K. O'Rourke, Barbara Papretz, Americo Perlini, Ellery E. Plotkin, Eve F. Schare, Jeffrey C. Seymour, Eugene Short, Ruth A. Smey, Michael A. Terek, Rosalie Vento-Kaufman, Jeffrey Weiner.

FARMINGTON. Hartford County.—(Form of government, town manager, town council, town meeting.)—Inc. and named, Dec., 1645. The Town of Farmington, Borough of Unionville and Borough of Farmington were consolidated in 1947. Area, 28.8 sq. miles. Population, est., 21,197. Voting districts, 2. Principal industries, textile specialties, manufacture of ball bearing spindles, steel balls, springs, steel hatches, fans, heating tapes, sakrete products, flow and level switches, lighting fixtures, poultry equipment, leather products, wooden boxes and excelsior, compressor blades and vanes, metal stampings, rubber and plastic parts. Transp.—Passenger: Served by buses of Conn. Transit from Hartford. Freight: Served by Boston & Maine Corporation and numerous motor common carriers. Post offices, Farmington and Unionville.

TOWN OFFICERS. Clerk and Reg. of Vital Statistics, Edgar A. King; Hours, 8:30 A.M.-4:30 P.M., Mon. through Fri.; Address, Town Hall, 1 Monteith Dr., 06032-1053; Tel., (860) 673-8200.—**Asst. Clerks and Asst. Regs. of Vital Statistics,** Frances L. Bassett, Alice W. Colburn, Joan B. Creel.—**Town Manager,** Thomas J. Wontorek.—**Town Council, At Large,** Arline B. Whitaker, Chm.; 1st Dist., Bruce Chudwick, Elizabeth R. Gray, William J. Raymond; 2nd Dist., Robert DiPietro, Nicholas S. Scara, Michael J. Schloss.—**Treas.,** Daniel Costello; Deputy, Julie Albert.—**Tax Collector,** Teresa Colton.—**Bd. of Assessment Appeals,** James M. Fusco, Richard C. Mathews, Elliott Mini, Kyle Ondrush, Ruth Robbins, Jeremiah Wadsworth.—**Assessor,** Linda I. Arnold.—**Registrars of Voters,** Lorraine P. Neff (D), Betty D. Coykendall (R).—**Supt. of Schools,** Robert Villanova.—**Bd. of Education,** Jean B. Baron, Kenneth Koos, Paula B. Ray, Timothy Reagan, Tory Stempf, 1997; Nancy A. Nickerson, Chm., Judith A. DeVincke, Mary G. Reed, Alan D. Sibarium, 1999.—**Planning, Zoning and Inland Wetlands Comm.,** James H. Pogson, Chm., Donald L. Banta, Barbara A. Brenneman, Christian R. Hoheb, Charlie Martin, Deborah B. Quigley; Alternates, Jeffrey Apuzzo, Ronald Harrison, John W. Vibert.—**Town Planner,** Jeffrey Ollendorf.—**Zoning Bd. of Appeals,** George V. Lawler, Chm., Eric Knapp, Patricia L. LeBouthillier, Sharon G. Mazzochi, John H. Miller, Jr., Laurence S. Witkin; Alternates, Paul J. Hawkins, Mary Ellen Lyons, William A. Wadsworth.—**Housing Auth.,** Howard H. Coe, Chm., David H. Andrews, John DeMeo, M. Jane Inrig, Justin J. Pagano, vacancy.—**Conservation Comm.,** John T. Hickey, Chm., W. Bruce Ashworth, Anne E. DiPietro, Daniel Dornfeld, Jody Gordon, Eileen Marks, Paul Orth, Jeremiah Wadsworth, Marian M. Webb.—**Historic Dist. Comm.,** Lucius Whitaker, Chm., Terry Feder, Charles Leach, Tim McLaughlin, Marian M. Webb; Alternates, Ann Bissell, Mark Fey, Alison Howe.—**Municipal Historian,** Jean Johnson.—**Services for the Elderly,** Nancy Walker, Chm.—**Human Relations Committee,** Ruth Grobe, Richard M. Harty, Lydia Klatsky, Zalman Nakhimovsky.—**Dir. of Human Resources,** Alan Hutchinson.—**Dir. of Parks and Recreation,** Bruce L. Till.—**Supt. of Streets,** Lee Mahannah.—**Town Engineer,** James Grappone.—**Building Inspector,** Mark St. Pierre.—**Building Code Bd. of Appeals,** Lawrence R. Dorman, Donald Hammerberg, Jr., Elliot H. Mini, J. David Morrissey, Henry Schadler.—**Water Pollution Control Auth.,** G. William Saxton, Chm., James Foote, John P. Matava, Joseph O'Flaherty, Richard M. Stockwell.—**Treatment Plant Supvr.,** William Kaminski.—**Chief of Police,** LeRoy Bangham.—**Constables,** Robert J. Costello, Richard M. Harty, Richard Rogers.—**Chiefs of Fire Dept.,** John Nelson (East

Farms), Donald Antigiovanni (Farmington), Barry Knight (Tunxis).—**Fire Marshal,** Vincent DiPietro.—**Town Atty.,** Day, Berry & Howard (P.O., Hartford).—**Justices of the Peace,** Donald L. Banta, Nancy E. Chellgren, James M. Fusco, Paul A. Hoha, Christian R. Hoheb, Bernice G. Kaplin, John P. Karwoski, Lydia Klatsky, Christopher L. Montes, Mary G. Reed, Roberta Skripol, Robert M. Smith.

FENWICK.* BOROUGH OFFICERS. Office Address: 580 Maple Ave., P.O. Box 126, Old Saybrook 06475.—**Warden,** Lafayette Keeney.—**Clerk,** J. Waide Howley.—**Treas.,** Charles Chadwick.—**Tax Collector,** E. Lewis Bartlett, IV.—**Burgesses,** Millicent Benner, Peter B. Brainard, Charles Chadwick, C. Douglas Collins, Mark McCann, Louise D. Riggio.

---

*See Town of Old Saybrook.

FRANKLIN. New London County.—(Form of government, selectmen, town meeting.)—Inc., May, 1786; taken from Norwich. Area, 19.6 sq. miles. Population, est., 1,757. Voting district, 1. Principal industries, agriculture, dairying and poultry products, egg processing plant, grain feed mills, truck terminals. Home of a multi-million dollar mushroom growing facility. Home of The Savings Institute Branch. Transp.—Freight: Served by Central Vermont Railway and numerous motor common carriers. Post office, North Franklin. Rural free delivery.

TOWN OFFICERS. Clerk and Reg. of Vital Statistics, Debra S. Beisiegel; Hours, 9 A.M.-4 P.M., Mon.through Thurs.; 6-8 P.M., Tues.; Address, 7 Meeting House Hill Rd., Town Hall, North Franklin 06254; Tel., Lebanon, (860) 642-7352.—**Asst. Clerk and Asst. Reg. of Vital Statistics,** Barbara J. Curran.—**Selectmen,** 1st, James R. Handfield (R) Tel., (860) 642-6055, Linda A. Bartlett (D), Thomas M. Curran (R).—**Treas.,** Elizabeth J. Churchill.—**Bd. of Finance,** A. Bruce Dougherty, Chm., Russell C. Beisiegel, Louise Fisher, William B. Hayden, David Levanto, Brian Southworth.—**Tax Collector,** Grace B. Sterry.—**Bd. of Assessment Appeals,** Margaret S. Ayer, Charles W. Grant, Jr., vacancy.—**Assessor,** John Chaponis.—**Registrars of Voters,** James F. Ward, Jr. (D), Thomas Manning (R).—**Supt. of Schools,** Richard Olsen, Ph.D.—**Bd. of Education,** Ronald V. DeCarolis,Gary W. Ladyga, Debra A. Luberto, James F. Ward, 1997; Richard A. Handfield, Gail Piotrkowski, vacancy, 1999.—**Planning and Zoning Comm.,** Richard A. Handfield, Chm., Anne Angelastro, Louise Fisher, Gary Fontaine, Robert Laudette; Alternates, Leonard Angelastro, Leo A. Bienvenue, Gary Ladyga.—**Zoning Bd. of Appeals,** Robert Constant, Chm., John J. Carboni, A. Bruce Dougherty, Alden A. Miner, William J. Postler; Alternates, James W. Auwood, Robert G. Jello, James W. Kingsley.—**Economic Development Comm.,** David Walter, Chm., Boris S. Avdevich, Christopher C. Darrow, Jessie Laudette, Thomas Manning.—**Inland Wetlands and Watercourses Comm.,** Herman Weingart, Chm., John A. Avila, Jack Bienvenue, Leo Bienvenue, Charles W. Grant, Jr.; Alternates, Bruce Korenkiewicz, Donald Smith, vacancy; Charles Grant, Jr., Enforcement Officer.—**Municipal Agent on Aging,** Kathy Hamilton.—**Dir. of Health,** David L. Schoon, M.D. (P.O., Norwich).—**Recreation Comm.,** Mark Heinonen, Chm., Nancy Constant, John R. Crowe, William Farrell, Wallace Gagnon, Lee Johnson, Gary Kropp,

Alden Miner, James Miner, Tim O'Hearn, Thomas E. Rec, Jr., Don Richmond, Brian Southworth, Peter Yednorowicz.—**Tree Warden,** Milton F. Beckwith.—**Building Inspector,** Curtis Garry.—**Sanitation Engineer/Zoning Enforcement Officer,** Ronald Chalecki.—**Chief of Police,** James R. Handfield.—**Constables,** Michael Coady, David Henneforth, Joseph Kapzukiewicz, Donald P. Konow, Henry M. Konow, Sr., William Postler.—**Chief of Fire Dept.,** John H. Marcotte III.—**Fire Marshal/Civil Preparedness Dir.,** William Eyberse.—**Town Atty.,** Frederick C. Berberick, Jr. (P.O., Norwich).—**Justices of the Peace,** Anne Angelastro, Boris S. Avdevich, Anne B. Ayer, Margaret S. Ayer, Stori L. Beckwith, Debra S. Beisiegel, Grace B. Curran, A. Bruce Dougherty, John B. Harty, Richard B. Hiscox, Stephen M. Jennes, Barbara Konow-Ward, John L. Laterra, Grace W. Linden, Vincent R. Majchier, Thomas A. Manning, John C. McGuire, Barbara Z. Philipp, Craig M. Plante, Gina M. Plante, Todd C. Postler, William J. Postler, Thomas J. Shakun, Eunice P. Spicer, Grace B. Sterry, Thomas H. Warbin, James F. Ward, Jr., Herman R. Weingart, Jr., Richard H. Weingart, Juliana C. Woodworth.

GLASTONBURY. Hartford County.—(Form of government, town manager, town council, board of finance.)—Inc., May, 1693; taken from Wethersfield. Area, 52.3 sq. miles. Population, est., 28,238. Voting districts, 8. Principal industries, agriculture, business machines, insurance, poultry research and breeding, and manufacture of machine tools. Transp.—Passenger: Served by buses of Conn. Transit from Hartford. Freight: Served by numerous motor common carriers. Post offices, Glastonbury, South Glastonbury and East Glastonbury. Three rural free deliveries.

TOWN OFFICERS. Clerk and Reg. of Vital Statistics, Edward J. Friedeberg; Hours, 8 A.M.-4:30 P.M., Mon. through Fri.; Address, 2155 Main St., 06033; Tel., (860) 652-7616.—**Asst. Clerks and Asst. Regs. of Vital Statistics,** Brenda J. Dione, Suzanne S. Espenshade.—**Town Manager,** Richard J. Johnson.—**Town Council,** Joe Broder, Kurt P. Cavanaugh, Marti Curtis, Thomas F. Flanagan, Stephen N. Giamalis, H. David Megaw, Paul M. Nye, George M. Purtill, Judith A. Stearns.—**Treas./Dir. of Admin. Services,** G. Ted Ellis.—**Bd. of Finance,** Diane L. Northrop, Chm., Constantine Constantine, Edward B. Dingledy, Walter F. Hemlock, Edward F. McCabe, James R. McIntosh.—**Tax Collector,** Madeline G. Rettberg.—**Bd. of Assessment Appeals,** Robert D. Bowden, Dennis C. Cavanaugh, William Holmes, David Motycka, Shaun O'Rourke.—**Assessor,** Leon J. Jendrzejczyk.—**Registrars of Voters,** Joan D. Kemble (D), Carolyn S. Larsen (R).—**Supt. of Schools,** Jacqueline Jacoby.—**Bd. of Education,** Michelle Fontaine, Catherine B. Geraci, Lewis A. Parker, 1997; Suzanne Galvin, Chm., Richard C. Brown, Paul Collins, Paul F. Haas, Jr., Helen Stern, 1999.—**Town Plan and Zonning Comm.,** Michael F. Lepore, Chm., Mark K. Branse, H. Buhl Kent, Scott Lessne, Patricia V. Low, Barbara Nebb; Alternates, Patricia Bussa, Jane Sleath, Robert E. Thorne.—**Town Planner/Dir. of Community Development,** Kenith Leslie.—**Environmental Planner,** Thomas Mocko.—**Zoning Bd. of Appeals,** Robert Gamer, Chm., Michael H. Clinton, John C. Linderman, Sandra R. O'Leary, Dorothy S. Peltzer; Alternates, Jeanie Babineau, Carl E. Hein, Matthew Klos.—**Economic Development Comm.,** Robert Mulcahy, Chm., Walter Erley, John Farley, David M.

Hallowes, Richard Katz, James M. Lynch, B. Kent Sleath.—**Housing Auth.,** James F. Noonan, Chm., Craig Fontaine, Richard H. Inman, Zelda Lessne, Frances W. Young; Ivan M. Pour, Exec. Dir.—**Conservation and Inland Wetlands Comm.,** Peter M. Stern, Chm., James Bingham, Judith Harper, William Patrick, Charles J. Reed, Edward A. Richardson, Gerhard D. Schade.—**Historic Dist. Comm.,** Mary Lou Barrett, Chm., E. Marston Moffatt, Galen Sheperd, Thomas Theurkauf, Louise Walker; Alternates, Charles L. Miller, Marcia Olsson, Dennis Pepe.—**Library Directors,** Gloria Avitabile, Chm., Jane Brown, H. Kennedy Hudner, Blakeslee Lloyd, Martha A. Poole, Della Schultz.—**Municipal Historian,** Marjorie McNulty.—**Fine Arts Comm.,** Carol Ahlschlager, David Blanchard, Bonnie Ferris, Cynthia Fitton, Ann Larson, Cynthia Lattanzio, Steven Molaver, Jack Morris, Doris S. O'Rourke, Philomena Pappa, Natalie Rice, Candace Satin, Mary Jane Sullivan, Charlene Vehlies, Fran Waldman.—**Community Beautification Committee,** Elizabeth Lynch, Chm., Toni Easterson, David Flattery, Lewis Middleton, Donald B. Reid, Robert G. Shipman, Della Winans.— **Comm. on Aging,** Frank B. Dibble, Elizabeth Giamalis, Warren Kreiner, William McGaw, Jr., Audrey Quinlan, Ernest F. Reale, Monica Shea.—**Human Relations Comm.,** Lisbeth Becker, John C. Glezen, Sandra Hassan, Kim McClain, Maureen Shannon.—**Social Services Dir.,** Jo-Ann Dorn.—**Dir. of Health,** David Boone.—**Recreation Comm.,** Betsy Katz, Chm., Fred Clark, Jr., J. Bayliss Earle, Lynn Hazard, Lew Lassow, Jollie Steffens.—**Dir. of Parks, Recreation and Facilities,** Raymond Purtell.—**Youth and Family Resources Comm.,** Steven Jacoby, Chm., Tricia Dougherty, Shana Ellovich, Richard King, Karen Klingensmith, Luci Leone, Thomas J. McKee, Susan Motycka, Cathy Vacchelli.—**Purchasing Agent,** John A. Makiaris.— **Town Engineer/Mgr. of Physical Services,** vacancy.—**Engineering Supt.,** Chester Hamlin.—**Supt. of Highways,** Scott Zenke.—**Building Official,** Edward P. Pietrycha.—**Building Code Bd. of Appeals,** Charles W. Brown, Calvin J. Carini, David B. Cox, James W. Dutton, Graham Tyrol.—**Housing Code of Appeals Committee,** Kristine Brown, Nelson C. L. Brown, Patricia Moriarty.—**Public Building Comm.,** David B. Cox, Chm., Edward J. Kamis, Jr., W. Michael Low, Robert Martino, Scott Tyrol.— **Water Pollution Control Auth.,** Bradley E. Northrop, Chm., Louis M. Accornero, Carmine Biello, Nils G. Carlson, John Gavin, William Habicht, Robert Jordan.— **Safety Committee,** Whitney Smith, Chm., Brian Comerford, Carole Hilton, Janet T. Jefford, Helen Litwin, Kevin A. Randolph, Gloria Zwirn.—**Supt. of Sanitation,** Michael Bisi.—**Sanitarian,** David Boone.—**Chief of Police,** James M. Thomas.—**Chief of Fire Dept.,** Stephen Haines.—**Fire Marshal,** Christopher N. Siwy.—**Bd. of Fire Comrs.,** Gilbert D. Spencer, Chm., Peter Deich, Norman Fierravanti, Arnold H. Higgins, Chandra Stino, Brian E. Tyrol.—**Civil Preparedness Dir.,** Robert F. DiBella.— **Town Attys.,** Halloran & Sage.—**Justices of the Peace,** Mario L. Accornero, George P. Adamson, William L. Baldwin, Lynn Baronas, Margaret Y. Berg, Barbara A. Bernacki, Richard R. Brown, Dennis C. Cavanaugh, Nanette T. Char-Lifshitz, Robert Cramer, Esther M. Derench, Robert F. DiBella, Patricia A. Dougherty, Mary Foley, Lloyd Frauenglass, Carlene Harris, Florence Z. Henderson, Arnold H. Higgins, Harvey A. Katz, Henry A. Kinne, Mary R. Lamphire, Elliot G. Macht, Marilyn V. Messenger, Donna Plank, Lucretia Seidel, Susan J. Spector, James M. Spencer, Richard H. Turcott, Sr., W. Gilbert Wolf, Marlene Zola.

GOSHEN. Litchfield County.—(Form of government, selectmen, town meeting, board of finance.)—Inc., Oct., 1739. Area, 45.2 sq. miles. Population, est., 2,478. Voting district, 1. Dairy community, attractive lakes. Nearly 1,400 acres of Mohawk State Forest are situated in Goshen. The Appalachian Trail passes through this heavily wooded wildlife sanctuary. Transp.—Freight: Served by numerous motor common carriers. Post office, Goshen; rural delivery from Norfolk, Litchfield and Falls Village.

TOWN OFFICERS. Clerk and Reg. of Vital Statistics, Barbara L. Allen; Hours, 9 A.M.-12 Noon, 1-4 P.M., Mon. through Fri.; Address, Town Office Bldg., 42 North St., P.O. Box 54, 06756; Tel., Torrington, (860) 491-3647; FAX, (860) 491-9162.— **Asst. Clerk and Asst. Reg. of Vital Statistics,** Patricia M. Rudnyai.—**Selectmen,** 1st, James P. O'Leary (R) P.O. Box 187, Tel., (860) 491-2308, Thomas J. Christian, (R), Henrietta C. Horvay (D).—**Treas.,** James A. Bernard.—**Bd. of Finance,** Alfred E. Wright, Chm., Marilyn M. Brennan, Russell A. Day, Johanna B. Kimball, Charlene B. O'Neil, vacancy; Alternates, Edwin R. Chadwick, David K. Reising.—**Tax Collector,** Arthur W. Wistrom.—**Bd. of Assessment Appeals,** William H. Bligh, Jr., Chm., James D. Hiltz, David K. Reising.—**Co-Assessors,** Patricia Braislin, Lauren Elliott.—**Bd. of Assessors,** John M. Kelley, Chm., Walter L. Arbo, Joan M. Lang, James D. Upton, John M. Wadhams.—**Registrars of Voters,** Cynthia A. Barrett (D), Walter M. Horvay (R).—**Supt. of Schools,** Timothy M. Breslin.—**Planning and Zoning Comm.,** John T. Breakell, Chm., Jean O. Breakell, Mark C. Fraher, Robert P. Valentine, Christopher J. Wright; Alternates, Walter C. Burcroff, Nathaniel T. Hall, vacancy.—**Zoning Bd. of Appeals,** Stephen W. Dunn, Chm., John M. Buslewicz, Robert W. Darr, Richard C. Hippner, Gail J. Lavoie; Alternates, Vincent A. Mainella, two vacancies.—**Zoning and Inland Wetlands Enforcement Officer,** Martin J. Connor.—**Conservation Comm.,** John W. Ross, Chm., Norman DeAngelis, Russell B. Hurley, Barnett D. Laschever, Anders A. Nygren, three vacancies.—**Inland Wetlands Comm.,** Martin G. Bothroyd, Chm., Jane Bakker, Frederick D. Griswold, Robert H. Hedus, Linda Quasnitschka, Anthony J. Savarese, Thomas R. Stansfield.—**Agent for the Elderly,** Marilyn M. Brennan.—**Library Directors,** Rosemary E. Bonaguide, Rebecca J. Burcroff, Ginette P. Clement, Judith F. Hippner, Joan K. Kelley, vacancy.— **Municipal Historian,** Margaret K. Wood.—**Health Officer,** Stephen W. Mordenti.— **Recreation Comm.,** Arthur Machen, Chm., Francis S. Goodhouse, Richard W. Hadden, Helen P. Loomis, Gregory S. Mitchell, Robert H. Perez.—**Building Inspector,** Paul E. Woike.—**Building Bd. of Appeals,** Theodore A. Panasci, George H. Schuster, Christopher J. Wright, two vacancies.—**Water Pollution Control Auth.,** David T. Bonaguide, Chm., Russell B. Hurley, Wayne E. Robinson, John J. Rudnyai, vacancy.—**Animal Control Officer,** Donald W. Gustafson.—**Tree Warden,** Joseph L. Sarri.—**Chief of Police,** James P. O'Leary.—**Constables,** Joanne Buslewicz, Martin J. Connor, Francis S. Goodhouse, Robert B. Hall, Jerry M. Harmon, Mark E. Murphy, David K. Reising.—**Chief of Fire Dept.,** Peter A. Grusauskas.—**Fire Marshal,** Scott M. Fraher.—**Bd. of Fire Comrs.,** William J. Hageman, Chm., Roland W. Clinton II, Wayne E. Robinson.—**Jury Committee,** Anders A. Nygren, Katherine F. Vaill, Patricia D. Wright.—**Civil Preparedness Dir.,** R. Christopher Mitchell.—**Town Attys.,** Roraback & Roraback.—**Justices of the Peace,** Suzette L. Barker, Diana Y. Bernard,

Edwin R. Chadwick, Margaret C. Dranginis, Bernice B. Firestone, Maureen M. Goodhouse, Peter A. Grusauskas, Holly H. Herold, Darlene A. Krukar, Ronald F. Nodine, A. Michele Rotatori, Peter Rotatori, Jr., Alfred H. Wright, Jr.

GRANBY. Hartford County.—(Form of government, selectmen, town manager, board of finance.)—Inc., Oct., 1786; taken from Simsbury. Area, 40.8 sq. miles. Population, est., 9,441. Voting districts, 2. Rural residential community with a variety of community retail, service and office commercial developments designed to meet the needs of the residential community. Transp.—Passenger: Served by buses of the Connecticut Transit from Hartford and Granby. Freight: Served by numerous motor common carriers. Post offices, Granby, North Granby and West Granby.

TOWN OFFICERS. Clerk and Reg. of Vital Statistics, Carol J. Smith; Hours, 9 A.M.-4 P.M., Mon. through Fri.; Address, Town Hall, 15 North Granby Rd., 06035; Tel., Simsbury, (860) 653-8949.—**Asst. Clerks and Asst. Regs. of Vital Statistics,** Yolanda G. Stillwell, Betsy McWilliams.—**Town Manager,** William F. Smith, Jr.—**Selectmen,** 1st, William J. Simanski (R), Ronald F. Desrosiers (D), John B. Flint (R), Sally S. King (D), James W. Oates (R).—**Treas.,** David W. Russell.—**Bd. of Finance,** Michael B. Guarco, Jr., Chm., Ronald J. Begansky, Paul M. Giblon, Douglas W. Porter, Gail B. Promboin, Robert A. Verrengia.—**Tax Collector,** Lauren C. Stuck.—**Bd. of Assessment Appeals,** Lowell C. Johnson, Chm., James R. Sansone, Wyman B. Ward.—**Assessor,** Patricia J. Juda.—**Registrars of Voters,** Katharine L. Riley (D), Doris S. Ellis (R).—**Town Moderator,** Donald P. Wilmot.—**Supt. of Schools,** Gwen Van Dorp.—**Bd. of Education,** Joseph A. Bischof, Ann Crimins, William Eisenman, Howard Gaynor, 1997; Terri-Ann Hahn, James C. Heminway, Jr., Daniel J. Wolfe, Jr., 1999.—**Planning and Zoning Comm.,** Paula Johnson, Chm., Daniel P. Brown, Jr., Margaret A. Chapple, Charles Kraiza, Eric Lukingbeal, John M. Morgan, Frederick O. Wilhelm.—**Zoning Bd. of Appeals,** William M. A. Wilson, Chm., Walter J. Burke, J. Holden Camp, Jr., Wayne E. Chapple, James J. Ryan; Alternates, Judy A. Goff, James F. Olsen, Arthur E. Phillips.—**Development Comm.,** Robert Daglio, Chm., Al Guarco, Herbert H. Hulbert, Esther K. Jones, Bruce Murtha.—**Conservation Comm.,** Richard J. Van Nostrand, Chm., Roy Champagne, Natica G. Jones, Charles J. Katan, Nicole Morganthaler, Jane Reardon, John R. Schumann.—**Inland Wetlands Comm.,** Charles J. Katan, Chm., Barry Avery, Sally S. King, Neil W. Kraner, Richard H. Martindale, David W. Tolli, Richard Van Nostrand.—**Comm. on Aging,** Bernice Perret, Chm., George L. Bronsord, John S. Budek, Therese Dell, Margaret S. Francolini, Anna L. Lyons, Marie Zidel; Paula Johnson, Municipal Agent.—**Library Bd.,** Carol Y. Bressor, Chm., Shawn E. Ball, Elaine B. Jones, John E. Jones, Dianne H. Koprowski, Nancy L. Olsen, Norton L. Shapiro, Laura F. Waldron, Deborah J. Woodsome; Joan Fox, Dir.—**Municipal Historian,** Carol Reid.—**Municipal Historian,** Carol Laun.—**Park and Recreation Bd.,** Bengt Wennberg, Chm., Thomas W. Grant, Judy Guarco, Gregory LaRocque, Kathryn C. Lawson, Harold Smith, Russell G. St. John.—**Recreation Dir.,** Kay Woodford.—**Dir. of Public Works,** William Lyons.—**Town Engineer,** Edward Sweeney.—**Building Inspector,** Henry M. Miga.—**Sanitarian,** Richard Matheny.—**Dir. of Community Development,** Francis G. Armentano.—**Chief of Police,** Jeremiah P. Marron, Sr.—**Constables,** Edward E. Bucken, Roger A. Grover.—**Chief of Fire Dept.,** Allen Christensen.—**Fire Marshal,** John H. Oates.—**Civil Preparedness Dir.,** Joanne Foster.—**Town Atty.,** Donald R. Holtman.—**Justices of the Peace,** Florence M. Bischoff, Loren J. Bressor, Ronald F. Desrosiers, Doris S. Ellis, Fred B. Feins, Judy A. Goff, Evelyn E. Hall, William Haslun, Lowell C. Johnson, Elaine B. Jones, Joseph Mattavi, Nancy L. Olson, Christopher S. Riley, James R. Sansone, Judith A. Shapiro, William J. Simanski, William F. Smith, Jr., William H. Stewart, Russell G. St. John.

GREENWICH.

Fairfield County.—(Form of government, representative town meeting, selectmen, board of finance.)—Settled, 1640, submitted to Connecticut, Oct. 6, 1656. Area, 76.7 sq. miles. Population, est., 57,732. Voting districts, 12. Transp.—Passenger: Served by Metro North Commuter Railroad Co. and buses of Conn. Transit between Old Greenwich and Stamford; from Stamford and Port Chester, NY, and buses of Greyhound and Trailways. Freight: Served by Conrail and numerous motor common carriers. Post offices, Greenwich, Cos Cob, Glenville, Old Greenwich and Riverside.

TOWN OFFICERS. Clerk and Reg. of Vital Statistics, Carmella C. Budkins; Hours, 8 A.M.-4 P.M., Mon. through Fri.; Address, Town Hall, 101 Field Point Rd., P.O. Box 2540, 06836; Tel., (203) 622-7897, 7898.—**Asst. Clerk,** Dorothea Meilinggaard.—**Asst. Reg. of Vital Statistics,** Barbara Lowden.—**Moderator, Representative Town Meeting,** Thomas J. Byrne.—**Selectmen,** 1st, Tom R. Ragland III (R) Tel., (203) 622-7710, 7711, Lolly H. Prince (R), David Singer (D).—**Treas.,** Catherine Brown.—**Bd. of Ethics,** Victor R. Coudert, Jr., Chm., William Genuario, Miles F. McDonald, David G. Ormsby, Mary B. Sullivan.—**Comptroller,** Robert Morgan.—**Tax Collector,** James L. Branca.—**Bd. of Assessment Appeals,** Louis C. Caravella, Clifford C. Frost, Rowland D. Harris, Mary B. McNamee, George Rich.—**Bd. of Estimate and Taxation,** Richard F. Kriskey, Chm., Jara N. Burnett, Peter J. Crumbine, Lawrence M. Crutcher, Henry J. Fisher II, Robert Gilhuly, Kathryn K. Guimard, Edward T. Krumeich, Jr., Frank E. Mazza, Alice P. Melly, Stephanie Raia.—**Assessor,** vacancy.—**Registrars of Voters,** Sharon Vecchiolla (D), Veronica B. Musca (R).—**Supt. of Schools,** John Whritner.—**Bd. of Education,** James W. Cuminale, Chm., Phyllis A. Matthews, Anne P. Simpson, John L. Vecchiolla, 1997; Lile R. Gibbons, Elizabeth R. Harkins, Margaret J. Kavounas, Genny Krob, 1999.—**Planning and Zoning Comm.,** Peter K. Joyce, Chm., Truman Eustis III, Mrs. Swan Grant, Lora S. Siefert, vacancy.—**Town Planner,** Diane Fox.—**Zoning Bd. of Appeals,** Barbara Hopkins, Acting Chm., William Frattarola, Harry LeBein, Edward Manuel, Paul McDonald, Clifford O'Hara, William Rader, David Shields.—**Housing Auth.,** Sue McClenachan, Chm., Louis Cozolino, William Haslun II, Carolyn Lewis, Alma Rutgers.—**Conservation Comm.,** Phil Bartels, Chm., Nancy Dickinson, Lisette Henrey, Marjorie Mountain, William Rutherford, Renee Seblatnigg, Mary Young; Alternates, Thomas R. Baptist, Eric V. Brower, Stephanie Sanchez.—**Wetland Agency,** Michael A. Aurelia, Dir.—**Inland Wetlands and Water Courses Agency,** Raymond J. Heimbuch, Chm., Eugene Blanche, Suzanne B. Graham, David J. O'Brien, Sarah Sawyer, Emerson Stone, Ferdinand S. Veith; Alternates, Peter Benedict, David J. Menegon, Matthew J.

Popp.—**Historic Dist. Comm.,** David Donald, Chm., Peter A. Alexander, Fred Mascioli, Richard G. McClung; Alternates, Jo Conboy, Richard Cosse, Frank Nicholson.—**Municipal Historian,** William E. Finch.—**Flood and Erosion Control Bd.,** Raymond Haney, Anthony McCleod, Edward J. Schmeltz.—**Comm. on Aging,** Wilmot Harris, Chm., Florence Damon, Lindsey Dodge, Sylvia Gordon, Betty Hauptman, Barbara Posey, Bernadette Settlemeyer, Sydney A. Wood-Cahusac.—**Bd. of Social Services,** Regina Benvenuto, Duncan Burke, Nancy Burke, Elizabeth Deming, Ann Isaacson, Donna Nickitas; Carol A. Femia, Comr.—**Dir. of Health,** James Lieberman, M.D.—**Bd. of Public Health,** David Hopper, Chm., Edith Beck, M.D., Vin Cam, Vincent R. DeFina, James Rosenblum, Elaine Suchman.—**Library Directors,** Greenwich: Elizabeth Maniero; Perrot Memorial: Michael Hagen.—**Bd. of Parks and Recreation,** Lisbeth Beck, Rocco Benvenuto, Andrew Burke, David J. D'Andrea, John J. Kavanagh, Gary Oztemel, Stephen Rupp, C. Thomas Richardson, Toni Wyman.—**Dir. of Public Works,** Marcos Madrid; Asst., Robert Kalm.—**Town Engineer,** Garo Garabedian.—**Supt. of Highways,** Joseph Roberto.—**Tree Warden,** Laurence A. Cooper.—**Purchasing Agent,** Joan Sullivan.—**Sealer of Weights and Measures,** Anthony F. Belmont.—**Building Inspector,** William Marr.—**Building Code Bd. of Appeals,** Edward Ahneman, Thomas Cholnoky, Michael Franco, Peter Ogden, Harry E. Peden, Jr.—**Supt. of Sanitation, Sewer Div.,** Stephen J. Demetri.—**Nuisance Abatement Officer,** vacancy.—**Chief of Police,** Kenneth Moughty.—**Constables,** James E. Clifford, William Fassuliotis, Lawrence A. Infante, Siegrun K. Pottgen, Dominick R. Romeo, Jr., Marcelle W. Sherwood, Joseph D. Zeranski.—**Chief of Fire Dept.,** Noel Padden.—**Town Atty.,** John Meerbergen.—**Justices of the Peace,** Sigmund A. Beck, Sandra K. Bendfeldt, Rocco Benvenuto, James Boskello, Louis C. Caravella, Michael Chiappetta, James Clifford, Stuart F. Coan, Sheldon Coleman, Jr., Forbes Delaney, Peter G. DiLeo, William Ferenc, Karen Fox, William Frattarola, Betty Hauptman, Anthony Hayden, Cynthia P. Hliva, Lawrence A. Infante, Ann S. Isaacson, Edward Krumeich, Jr., Lawrence Larson, Roger Lourie, Mary Ann Mullen, Helen Neilsen, Stephanie Raia, Dominick Romeo, Mary Romeo, Marcelle W. Sherwood, Fred Sibley, Anne Simpson, Emil Smeriglio, Michael W. Stein, Cynthia von-Keyserling.

GRISWOLD. New London County.—(Form of government, selectmen, board of finance, town meeting.)—Inc., Oct., 1815; taken from Preston. Area, 37.1 sq. miles. Population, est., 10,110. Voting districts, 2. Principal industries, warehousing, agriculture and poultry farming, machine products, wire and cable. Transp.—Passenger: Served by buses of SEAT. Freight: Served by Conrail and numerous motor common carriers. Post office, Jewett City.

TOWN OFFICERS. Clerk and Reg. of Vital Statistics, Ellen W. Dupont; Hours, 8:30 A.M.-4 P.M., Mon., Tues., Thurs., Fri.; 8:30-12 Noon, Wed.; Address, Town Hall, 32 School St., P.O. Box 369, Jewett City 06351-2398; Tel., Jewett City, (860) 376-7063; FAX (860) 376-7070.—**Asst. Clerk and Asst. Reg. of Vital Statistics,** Valerie Pudvah.—**Selectmen,** 1st, Paul J. Brycki (D), Tel., (860) 376-7061, Steve Mikutel (D), William D. Stetson (R).—**Treas.,** Donald F. Ouillette.—**Bd. of Finance,** Joseph Przylucki, Jr., Chm., Keith Burzycki, Chris C. Clark, Christopher Hoddy, Richard J. Malek, Jeffrey F. Petersen, John Wolkowski.—**Tax Collector,** Richard Grabowski.—**Assessor,** Cynthia Kata.—**Bd. of Assessment Appeals,** John Curran, Maria Edmond, Carlton Miller.—**Registrars of Voters,** 1st Dist., Lucille Gibeault, 2nd Dist., Mary Ingvas (D); 1st Dist., Mary Koziol, 2nd Dist., Carol Seaman (R).—**Supt. of Schools,** Edward Malvey.—**Bd. of Education,** Aleta DeRoy, Marie C. Quinn, Claudia L. Zatorski, 1997; Raymond M. Blanchard, Jacquie P. Burzycki, Alfred E. Covino, Richard Grabowski, 1999.—**Planning and Zoning Comm.,** Philip Anthony, Jr., Daniel Deguire, Charles E. Gagne, Jr., Gail J. Rooke-Norman, F. Clyde Seaman; Alternates, Nicholas Holowaty, Sr., Ernest Norman, Richard J. Yonta.—**Town Planner,** Mario Tristany.—**Zoning Bd. of Appeals,** Ronald C. Anthony, Alfred F. Covino, Dorothy Faulise, Theodore A. Faulise, Ronald Jodoin; Alternates, Charles J. Joseph, Jr., Blanche Sedgwick, William Sharkey, Jr.—**Housing Auth.,** Maria Edmond, Chm., Raymond Blanchard, Terry Blanchard, Paul DesChamps, Mary Miller, Frances Watson.—**Conservation and Inland Wetlands Comm.,** Aleta DeRoy, Chm., Gary Czeczotka, Daniel Deguire III, Rae Grasso, Aristede Johnson, Courtland Kinnie, Byron Waterman; Alternates, Richard Mackin, Mark Roy.—**Municipal Historian,** Mary R. Deveau.—**Comm. on Aging,** Donna Szalls, Agent.—**Dir. of Social Services,** Ruth A. Wolinski.—**Dir. of Health,** A. G. Gosselin, M.D.—**Public Health Nursing Bd.,** Norman Gileau, Chm., Paul J. Brycki, Annabelle Curran, Betty Curran, Barbara Duda, Maria Edmond, Irene Gifford, A. G. Gosselin, M.D., Margaret Kuzyk, Phyllis McCullough, Donald F. Ouillette, Hermine Purvis, Ann Stearns, Katherine Sweet, Elizabeth Wojtkun, Ruth Wolinski, James Wright.—**Recreation Comm.,** Richard Sikorski, Chm., Louis Beam, Alan Geer, Francis LaPointe, Stephen McDougal; David Drobiak, Dir.—**Dir. of Public Works,** Paul J. Brycki.—**Tree Warden,** Philip Yurechko.—**Building Inspector,** Peter Zvingilas.—**Sanitarian,** Albert Gosselin, Jr.—**Sewer Auth.,** John J. Curran, Jr., Chm., Aleta DeRoy, Bruce Smith.—**Chief of Griswold Volunteer Fire Dept.,** Richard Harrelle.—**Fire Marshal,** Steve Merchant, Jr.—**Civil Preparedness Dir.,** Steve Merchant, Jr.—**Town Atty.,** Peter Gianacoplos.—**Justices of the Peace,** Elaine Berlute, Cathlene Briody, Kenneth Briody, Catherine Brycki, Alfred F. Covino, William Czmyr, William Demicco, Aleta Deroy, Maria Edmond, Patricia Drobiak, Mary Beth Duda, Ellen Dupont, F. Thurston Fields, Lawrence J. Fowler, Jr., Norman Gileau, Mary Holowaty, Charles Joseph, Jr., George Kennedy, Mary Koziol, Steve McDougal, Carlton E. Miller, Stuart Norman, Jr., Sylvia Nyszczy, Carol A. Ouillette, Joseph Przylucki, Jr., Marie Quinn, Benjamin Podurgiel, Carol Seaman, Blanche Sedgwick, Laverne Stetson, William D. Stetson, Normand Sylvestre, Shirley M. Walsh, Ruth A. Wolinski.

GROTON. New London County.—(Form of government, town manager, town council, representative town meeting.)—Inc., May 10, 1705; taken from New London. Area, 45.2 sq. miles. Population, est., 44,029. Voting districts, 9. Principal industries, construction of submarines, precision castings, shipbuilding, and manufacture of pharmaceuticals, piers and bridge work, bricks and blocks. Transp.—Passenger: Served by Amtrak and by buses of Southeast Area Transit (SEAT) from New London and Norwich and Barstow Transp. from Dayville. Freight: Served by Providence & Worcester Co. and numerous motor common carriers. Airplane service to all major cities. Post offices, Groton, West Mystic, Noank, Groton Long Point, City of Groton, Old Mystic, Mystic, Submarine Base.

TOWN OFFICERS. Clerk and Reg. of Vital Statistics, Barbara Tarbox; Hours, 8:30 A.M.-4:30 P.M., Mon. through Fri., 9 A.M.-4:30 P.M., Thurs.; Address, Town Hall, 45 Fort Hill Rd., 06340; Tel., (860) 441-6600.—**Deputy Town Clerk,** Janet L. Downs.—**Asst. Town Clerks,** Robin I. Cedio, Antoinette Pancaro.—**Asst. Regs. of Vital Statistics,** Robin I. Cedio, Janet L. Downs, Antoinette Pancaro.—**Town Manager,** Ronald P. LeBlanc.—**Town Council,** Dolores E. Hauber, Mayor; Rose Marie Althuis, Lori N. Bartinik, Jane S. Dauphinais, Catherine Kolnaski, Rick Norris, Frank O'Beirne, Jr., Harry Watson, Chaz Zezulka.—**Moderator, Representative Town Meeting,** George Edwards.—**Treas.,** Cindy R. Landry.—**Dir. of Finance,** Sal Pandolfo.—**Town Tax Collector,** Nancy L. Dytko.—**Bd. of Assessment Appeals,** Richard D. Haviland, Chm., Robert S. Gillies, Paul C. van Dyke.—**City and Town Assessor,** Anne Dougherty; Asst., Loreta Zdanys.—**Registrars of Voters,** Leonora V. Lewis (D), Victoria M. Rossman (R).—**Supt. of Schools,** Dr. George Reilly.—**Bd. of Education,** Joann Jones, Meredith E. Russell, Frederick J. Spellman, Beverly H. Washington, 1997; Ellen C. Brown, G. Michael Hewitt, Larry Hurley, Elizabeth R. Montgomery, Robert L. Zuliani.—**Planning Comm.,** James R. Sherrard, Chm., Peter Roper, John Spinner, Hank Steinford, Jean Wood; Alternates, Richard Bradley, Elizabeth P. Padgett, vacancy.—**Zoning Comm.,** Steven Hudecek, Chm., Robert O'Neill, Kenneth Reid, John F. Scott, David Winkler, Jr.; Alternates, Barbara Caron, George Marcus, vacancy.—**Zoning Bd. of Appeals,** Edward Stebbins, Chm., Richard Fitzgerald, Floyd Kravits, Tom Manning, James L Young; Alternates, Scott Russotto, two vacancies.—**Economic Development Comm.,** Lian Obrey, Chm., L. Paul Benda, Jim Csisar, Frank DelCampo, Thomas J. Haling, Ernest P. Romano, Peter W. Rotella, Joseph Waszkelewicz, vacancy.—**Housing Auth./ Redevelopment Agency,** Peter S. Gianacoplos, Chm., Margaret Burbank, Ruth Ficken, Ludwig Pulaski, vacancy.— **Housing Code Bd. of Appeals,** William Fontaine, Anne Jenssen, Sally Sawyer, William Story, vacancy; Alternates, Patricia Anderson, John Sullivan.—**Fair Rent Comm.,** Virginia Cowell, June DeCarlo, Margaret Howard, Michael T. Marcy, vacancy; Alternates, Doreen Damble, Wes Sprinkel.—**Harbor Management,** Paul Bates, Chm., Francis L. Crowley, David Ferrell, Ann S. Rankin, Kenneth Steere; Alternates, Richard Dixon, Marshall Parsons.—**Retirement Bd.,** Ronald P. LeBlanc, Chm., William Ames, Maier Freedman, Philip Greene, William Jervis, Marten Schoonman.—**Personnel Appeals Bd.,** Nancy C. LaCapra, Robert H. Moore, three vacancies.—**Conservation Comm.,** Brae Rafferty, Chm., Thomas E. Bogue, Cathi deLisle, Lois F. Geary, Gail Munn, vacancy.—**Inland Wetlands Agency,** David Scott, Chm., Barbara Block, Girard Keeler, Eunice Sutphen, Barbara Williams; Alternates, Edward Eckelmeyer, R. Quincy Robe.—**Permanent School Building Committee,** John Webster, Chm., Marjorie Buckley, Wayne Chiapperini, James Jewett, Robert Morrison.— **Historic Dist. Comm.,** Richard Seager, Chm., David C. Beckwith, Ruth Keyes, Nancy A. Mitchell, Theodore C. Rice; Alternates, C. William Coldwell, John P. Walsh, Eva Wright.—**Municipal Historian,** Carol W. Kimball.—**Agent for the Children,** Sandra Easton.—**Agent for the Elderly,** Lee deLisle.—**Dir. of Social Services,** Marjorie D. Fondulas.—**Dir. of Ledge Light Health Dist.,** Mary Jane Engle.—**Library Bd.,** Paul

K. Dufault, Acting Chm., Paul Bowles, Barbara Haviland, Kay Janney, Joyce M. Kaiser, Rosemary Palmer, Eleanor Steere, Harriet G. Weaver, vacancy; Alan Benkert, Dir.—**Parks and Recreation Comm.,** Colleen Sullivan, Chm., Calvin McCoy, Robert E. Perozzotti, Pat Russack, two vacancies; Lee deLisle, Dir.—**Dir. of Public Works,** Gary J. Schneider.—**Purchasing Agent,** John Piacenza.—**Tree Warden,** Marten Schoonman.—**Building Inspector,** Mark W. Tebbets.—**Building Code Bd. of Appeals,** William F. Hermann, Jr., Chm., Charles E. Feeney, Russell E. Sergeant, Robert S. Smith, Lou Venditti.—**Water Pollution Control Auth.,** Cameron Cutler, Chm., Thomas S. Davies, Harley Moore, David G. Williams, vacancy.—**Shellfish Comm.,** Ronald Chappell, Chm., Stephen Jones, Joseph D. McNeil, Roger Sherman, Richard Wood; Alternates, Elmer Edwards, Edward Martin, David Wilson.—**Chief of Police,** David Vanasse.—**Fire Depts.,** Center Groton: James Wilson, Chief; Richard Branche, Marshal. Groton Long Point: Doug Perina, Chief. Mystic: Frank C. Hilbert, Chief; Richard Perkins, Sr., Fire Marshal. Noank: Richard Latham, Chief. Old Mystic: Ken Richards, Chief/Marshal. Poquonnock Bridge: Edward B. Amatrudo, Chief; Christian Killam, Fire Marshal. West Pleasant Valley: Donald Rollins, Fire Marshal.—**Civil Preparedness Dir.,** Carl R. Sawyer.—**Town Atty.,** James F. Brennan, Jr.—**Justices of the Peace,** Margaret R. Burbank, Tony DeMarinis, Richard Dixon, Shirley Dunbar-Rose, Lawrence E. Gemma, Betty Gibson-Pierce, Leonard R. Grimes, Aubrey Hamilton, Lillian L. Hansen, Dolores R. Harrell, Graham G. Herwerth, Jr., Charlene Hill, Mark Hogan, Lawrence E. Hurley, Nancy Kaplan, Frances Kapolowicz, Lian Obrey, Ethel M. Orkney, Dolores Ortiz-Rigg, Philip Plouffe, Dennis Popp, Theresa Qualich, Sally M. Sawyer, Donald Schoolcraft, Rose Sheetz, John R. Small, Alma R. Venditti, Chaz Zezulka III.

CITY OFFICERS. For recording of all legal instruments see Town of Groton above. (Form of government, mayor, council.) Inc. as a borough, Jan., 1903; inc. as a city, May 4, 1964. Voting districts, 3.—**City Clerk,** Barbara L. Frucht; Hours, 8 A.M.-4:30 P.M., Mon. through Fri.; Address, 295 Meridian St., 06340; Tel., (860) 446-4103; FAX (860) 445-4058.—**Mayor,** Bette J. Giesing (R).—**Councilors,** Daniel C. Kelley, Deputy Mayor; Mark H. Ciliano, Elizabeth S. Duarte, Lori T. Hesch, Andrew M. Parrella, William C. Spicer.—**Treas.,** Barbara L. Frucht.—**Dir. of Finance,** Anthony Timpano.—**Retirement Bd.,** Bette J. Giesing, Mayor, Chm., Jay Buckley, Alexander Chisholm, Mark Ciliano, Lawrence Gerrish, Ellis Hartman, Julius Panucci, Jeffrey Sherman, Frank Winkler.—**City Planner,** Michael Murphy.—**Planning and Zoning Comm.,** Debra Jenkins, Chm., Henry Buermeyer, Howard S. Dodd, Jr., Wallace Frankopoulos, Kenneth Jones, James L. Streeter, vacancy; Alternates, Marion Orkney, two vacancies.—**Zoning Bd. of Appeals,** Dwaine Rugh, Chm., Alfred Collins, Harry Gore, Charles Kosloskey, Keith Ruhe; Alternates, Andrea Buermeyer, Eleanor Gergen, Waldron Higgins.—**Rental Housing Code Bd. of Appeals,** Michael Coleman, Dolores Ortiz-Rigg, Alan Palmer, William Rabitaille, vacancy; Alternates, Raymond Holmes, vacancy.—**Eastern Point Historic District Comm.,** Robert Geary, Chm., Michael R. Boucher, Mildred Carlson, Robert Hauptmann, Mary L. Johnson; Alternates, Althea King, Robert LaFrance, vacancy.—**Conservation and Inland Wetlands Comm.,** Longene J. Chmura, Chm., Mannie J. Cooper, Julie Maisch, Lorraine Santangelo, Charles Wright; Alternates, David Paskausky, vacancy.—**Utility Comm.,**

Bette J. Giesing, Chm., Jay S. Buckley, Biaggio Donatelli, Julio Leandri, Dwight Norris.—**Bozrah Utility Comm.,** Bette J. Giesing, Chm., Raymond C. Barber, Jay S. Buckley, Biaggio Donatelli, Robert Kokoff, Ralph W. Lathrop, Julio Leandri, Dwight Norris, Joyce Okonuk.—**Beach and Park Committee,** Alfred Restivo, Chm., Omar Allvord, Richard Aspinwall, Arthur Callahan, Ann G. Crooks, Thomas Hill, Barbara Teehan.—**Parks and Recreation Dir.,** William Sanford.—**Purchasing Agent,** Robert Champagne.—**Harbor Management Comm.,** Horace Newbury, Chm., Thomas Clay, Sr., Syma A. Ebbin, Lawrence Jacobsen, Richard J. Stark; Alternates, Charles Pierce, Robert S. Smith, vacancy.—**Supt. of Highways,** Robert H. Morse.—**Public Works Building Comm.,** Albert Chapman, Chm., Alexander Chisholm, Jack Friedstein, Eleanor Gergen, William Spicer.—**Zoning and Building Official,** David L. Atkinson.—**Ledge Light Health Dist. Dir.,** Mary Jane Engle.—**Building Code Bd. of Appeals,** Peter L. Racich, Sr., Andrew Walz, two vacancies; Alternates, Guy Scribner, two vacancies.—**Chief of Police,** Wilfred Blanchette, Jr.; Deputy, James Schmitt.—**Chief of Fire Dept./Fire Marshal,** Donald Rollins; Deputy Chief, John Cunningham.—**Civil Preparedness Dir.,** Philip Tuthill.—**City Atty.,** Peter Gianacoplos.

GUILFORD. New Haven County.—(Form of government, selectmen, town meeting, board of finance.)—Settled, 1639; named, July 6, 1643. Area, 49.7 sq. miles. Population, est., 20,315. Voting districts, 4. Principal industries, agriculture and manufacturing. Transp.—Passenger: Served by buses of Conn. Transit from New Haven, and by Greyhound and Trailways. Freight: Served by Conrail and numerous motor common carriers. Post office, Guilford. Eleven rural free delivery routes.

TOWN OFFICERS. Clerk and Reg. of Vital Statistics, Janice G. Teft; Hours, 8:30 A.M.-4:30 P.M., Mon. through Fri.; Address, Town Hall, 31 Park St., 06437; Tel., (203) 453-8001.—**Asst. Clerks and Asst. Regs. of Vital Statistics,** Anna J. Dwyer, Jean B. McGrady.—**Selectmen,** 1st, Edward J. Lynch (D) Tel., (203) 453-8015, Samuel D. Bartlett (R), Barbara W. Puffer (R).—**Treas.,** Edward Creighton.—**Finance Officer,** Andy Potochney.—**Bd. of Finance,** Matthew T. Hoey, Chm., Peter F. Culver, Kenneth Gamerman, Frank Grundman, Robert J. Hartmann, Sr., Joseph S. Mazza, Marianne Sullivan.—**Tax Collector,** Barbara A. Kohls.—**Bd. of Assessment Appeals,** Joseph M. Montesano, Jr., Frederick J. Trotta, vacancy.—**Assessor,** Larry C. Hall.—**Registrars of Voters,** Anne C. Weir (D), Elizabeth C. Bartlett (R).—**Supt. of Schools,** Thomas R. Giblin.—**Bd. of Education,** Richard Beatty, Keith Bishop, William L. Dwyer, Kaaren A. Janssen, Sandra M. Whelan, 1997; J. Michael Brown, Chm., Stephen G. Rieben, Randy Ruotolo, Gordon Strothers, 1999.—**Planning and Zoning Comm.,** Frederick I. Kingsbury, Chm., Elizabeth C. Bartlett, Dennis Dostert, David W. Fisher, Robert Guadagno, Timothy Pacileo, Beryl Weinstein; Alternates, Ralph S. Brown, Salvatore Catardi, Joseph M. Montesano, Jr.—**Town Planner,** George Kral.—**Zoning Bd. of Appeals,** Robert J. Carroll, Chm., C. Eugene Bishop, Ann Endyke, Eugene Sivek, Alex Sommers; Alternates, William G. Coale, Jr., Louis Federici, Elliot J. Wilcox.—**Zoning Enforcement Officer,** M. William McAvoy, Jr.—**Historic Dist. Comm.,** Ann C. Street, Chm., Thomas Lodge, Alison L. Page, Joan Shrewsbury, Erica Udoff; Alternates, Ellen C. McFarland, Sara Nelson, Priscilla W.

Norton.—**Municipal Preservation Bd.,** Elizabeth Mills Brown, Jane P. Greene, Jane S. Hanson, Frederick N. Vogt, vacancy.—**Economic Development Comm.,** Charles Havrda, Chm., Stephen S. Brown, John Delay, Robert Deutsch, Jeffrey Mobley, George Page, Jr., Sandra Rux; Alternates, Stephanie Erb, Sara Ann Ferland, Robert O'Such, Glen Weston-Murphy.—**Housing Auth.,** John Crawford, Chm., Beatrice Duryea, James Goodridge, Rosemary Iannotti, Jeanne H. Thomsen.—**Conservation Comm.,** Jerome Silbert, Chm., Greg Bugbee, Raymond L. Dudley, Robert Eber, Toini Jaffe, Robert Kloepfer, Michael Pochan; Alternates, Bill Johnson, William A. Lichtenfels, Bill Yule.—**Inland Wetlands Comm.,** Robert Light, Chm., E. Robert Eber, Charles L. Johnson, Edward Kreidel, Timothy Pacileo, David Skelton, Earl Swan; Alternates, David Egan, Gwen Gunn, Anthony Picagli.—**Harbor Management Comm.,** Edwin H. Fisher, Jr., James Kleinkauf, Rick Maltby, David North, Jerry Theise.—**Flood and Erosion Control Bd.,** Edward J. Lynch, Chm., Samuel Bartlett, James Portley, Barbara Puffer, John Volpe.—**Shellfish Comm.,** Daniel R. Biemesderfer, Chm., Gary Frohlich, David North, Sarah Richards, John Schroeder; Alternates, Todd Davenport, Ronald Moalli, Michael Nicholson.—**Welfare Dir.,** Tammy C. DeFrancesco.—**Agent for the Elderly,** Angela Ross.—**Human Services Council,** Dreux Beirne, Gregory Buckley, Natalie Feingold, Michael Hayes, Janice Markham, Susan Moore, Marilyn Peterson, Barbara Puffer, Mary Ann H. Quinn.—**Dir. of Health,** John M. Brogden, M.D.—**Library Directors,** Tassy Walden, Pres., Trudy Barnes, Charles Conti, Jr., William J. Cox III, Audrey Eisenlohr, Virginia Foster, Betsy Gribble, Gordon Halstead, Mark Kravitz, Joseph Marshal, Laura Page, Thomas Pugh, vacancy.—**Municipal Historian,** Joel E. Helander.—**Recreation and Park Comm.,** Craig Helmrich, Chm., Kurt Burkle, Rose Dostert, Charles Ehlert, Barry Erb, Barbara Hemming, Arthur Larson, Jr., Ralph Schipani, Jr.; Rick Maynard, Recr. Dir.—**Dir. of Youth Services,** Michael Regan.—**Dir. of Public Works,** John Volpe.—**Acting Tree Warden,** John Volpe.—**Building Inspector,** George Gdovin.—**Building Code Bd. of Appeals,** Kent C. Bloomer, E. Carleton Granbery, Jr., Byron W. McCandless, Harry Shepard, Frederick N. Vogt; Alternate, Gary M. Tierney.—**Water Pollution Control Auth.,** Anne Weir, Chm., Nancy Deutsch, Henry J. Graver, Jr., SueEllen Heinrich, Everett L. MacLeman, Calvin Page.—**Marina Comm.,** Gerald Clapp, Chm., William J. Moher, Jr., Tim Reiss, Jerry Theise, Veronica Wallace.—**Chief of Police,** Kenneth R. Cruz; Deputy, Thomas Terribile.—**Police Comm.,** Frederick Trotta, Chm., Arthur J. Benson, Allen Jacobs, Edwin Lombard, Joseph Montesano.—**Chief of Fire Dept.,** Charles E. Herrschaft, Jr., Asst. Chief, David Moffat.—**Fire Marshal,** Charles E. Herrschaft, Jr.—**Bd. of Fire Comrs.,** Paul Hemming, Frank V. Larkins, Jr., George F. Sullivan, Jr.—**Civil Preparedness Dir.,** Charles Herrschaft, Jr.—**Town Attys.,** Tyler, Cooper & Alcorn.—**Justices of the Peace,** Hugh A. Baird, Rose A. Dostert, Nancy R. Duffy, William L. Dwyer, Marguerite A. Edwards, Diane Freeman, Paul B. Hemming, William A. Lichtenfels, Eleanor H. McKernan, Leslie Naylor-Corey, Gloria A. Nemczuk, Richard W. Steeves, Veronica Wallace.

HADDAM. Middlesex County.—(Form of government, selectmen, town meeting, board of finance.)—Inc., Oct. 8, 1668. Area, 46.4 sq. miles. Population, est., 7,226. Voting districts, 4. Principal industries, atomic energy plant, lumber yards, marinas, and manufacture of metal-working machinery, printed circuits, wire products, plastics, molding, extruding and offset printing. Transp.—Freight: Served by numerous motor common carriers. Post offices: Haddam, Haddam Neck and Higganum.

TOWN OFFICERS. Clerk and Reg. of Vital Statistics, Ann P. Huffstetler; Hours, 9 A.M.-4 P.M., Mon. through Wed.; 9 A.M.-7 P.M., Thurs.; 9 A.M.-12 Noon, Fri.; Address, Town Office Bldg., 30 Field Park Dr., P.O. Box 87, 06438; Tel., Middletown, (860) 345-8531.—**Asst. Clerk and Asst. Reg. of Vital Statistics,** Susan Bailey.— **Selectmen,** 1st, Marjorie W. DeBold (D) Tel., (860) 345-8531, Harvey T. Clew (D), Walter A. Czaja, Jr. (R).—**Treas.,** Richard J. Hickish.—**Bd. of Finance,** JoAnn R. Woickelman, Chm., Keith R. Ainsworth, Paul L. Bohner, Donald G. Galletti, Jr., Clare M. Hoover, Jacob Levine; Alternates, Wayne M. Rutty, Lucille Silvestrini, Joel Wolak.—**Tax Collector,** Dorothy M. Morrell.—**Bd. of Assessment Appeals,** Kenneth T. Hampton, Frances J. Oktavec, Marie A. Salemi.—**Assessor,** Robert Coates.—**Registrars of Voters,** 1st Dist., Shelley L. Bensenhaver, 2nd Dist., Gary G. Butler, 3rd Dist., Mabel V. Andrews, 4th Dist., Helen V. Bernhardt (D); 1st Dist., Helen P. Ehlers, 2nd Dist., Paul A. Hoover, 3rd Dist., Ann E. Pender, 4th Dist., Edward Vynalek (R).— **Supt. of Schools,** Charles Sweetman.—**Planning and Zoning Comm.,** Mark A. Dubois, Chm., Steven W. Hitchcock, Virginia L. Marshall, Joseph O'Sullivan, Peter J. Petrini, Donald A. Smith, Charles F. Steinhilper, Jr.; Alternates, Robert M. Baranoff, Stasia T. DeMichele, Paul A. Hoover.—**Town Planner,** vacancy.—**Zoning Bd. of Appeals,** David P. Kapitulik, Chm., Thomas G. Berchulski, Terrence J. Danaher, Deborah A. Prior, Marie A. Salemi; Alternates, Daphne J. Messick, Loreen R. Lundgren, James F. Sibley.—**Zoning Enforcement Officer,** Roger Alsbaugh.—**Conservation and Inland Wetlands Comm.,** Leslie Starr, Chm., Daniel Iwanicki, Philip Leavenworth, Robert Myers, Dennis Unites, two vacancies; Alternates, Raul deBrigard, Robert W. Scully, Jr.—**Committee for the Aging,** John Rogerson, Chm., Mable Andrews, Mary Arrigoni, June Fuller, Clara Galanto, Joan Higgins, Ruth Oktavec, Philip Porter, Cora Rich, Adele Vynalek.—**Dir. of Health,** John Korab, M.D. (P.O., Higganum).— **Library Directors,** Edward Munster, Chm., Mary Aduskevich, Peter Aduskevich, Clare Hoover, Catherine C. Lassen, Diana Link, Bruce Ricker, Bruce Root, Malcolm Stearns, Jr., Paul Sturges, Alberta Tuohy, Karen Wildeman.—**Municipal Historian,** Libby Kaye.—**Parks and Recreation Comm.,** John Coggins, Chm., Robert Duval, Michael Jordan, Arleen Stannard.—**Tree Warden,** Philip Goff.—**Town Engineer/ Sanatarian,** Robert Tommell.—**Building Code Bd. of Appeals,** Ellsworth Beckwith, Chm., John Bacon, Thomas Dondero, Roger Ohlson, vacancy.—**Chief of Police,** Marjorie W. DeBold.—**Constable,** vacancy.—**Building Official/Fire Inspector,** Robert Rothstein.—**Chiefs of Fire Dept.,** Co. No. 1, John Dowling; Co. No. 2, Michael Stevens.—**Fire Marshal,** Scott Brookes.—**Civil Preparedness Dir.,** Howard McAuliffe.—**Town Attys.,** Howard & McMillan.—**Justices of the Peace,** Peter D. Aduskevich, Eric J. Andrews, Bonye Baroni, Shelly B. Bensenhaver, Raymond W. Bogdan, Barbara E. Casey, Jeannetta U. Coley, William J. Conners, Samuel D. Crum, Jr., Richard C. DeBold, Emilie R. deBrigard, Raul deBrigard, Robert R. Delvecchio, Helen P. Ehlers, Marilyn L. Fowler, Donald G. Gilletti, Jr., William M. Huffstetler, Theodore S. Kulak, Ginny M. LaBella, Christopher C. Lassen, Mark P. Lundgren, Janet Lynch, Thomas H. Lynch II, Jack Michael, Jacqueline Michael, Elizabeth H.

Mosca, Judith H. Munster, Francis X. Murphy, Frances J. Oktavec, Lloyd A. Pearson, Elizabeth J. Reynolds, Marie A. Salemi, Jonathan W. Sibley, Eleanor C. Tomaszewski, Felicia M. Wisneski, Raymond E. Wisneski.

HAMDEN.
New Haven County.—(Form of government, mayor, legislative council.)— Inc., May, 1786; taken from New Haven. Area, 33.3 sq. miles. Population, est., 51,093. Voting districts, 9. Principal industries: retail trade, computer products, manufacturers of wire and cable, concrete, pump mixer products, fabricated metals, construction and business services. Transp.— Passenger: Served by buses of Conn. Transit from New Haven. Freight: Served by Conrail and numerous motor common carriers. Post offices, Hamden, Mount Carmel and Whitneyville, branches of New Haven post office.

TOWN OFFICERS. Clerk and Reg. of Vital Statistics, Vera A. Morrison, Hours, 9 A.M.-4 P.M., Mon. through Fri.; Address, Memorial Town Hall, 2372 Whitney Ave., 06518; Tel., (203) 287-2510; FAX (203) 287-2518.—**Asst. Clerks and Asst. Regs. of Vital Statistics,** Cynthia Esposito, Linda M. Melillo, Gilda A. Robinson.—**Mayor,** Lillian D. Clayman (D).—**Legislative Council: Councilmen at Large,** Craig Henrici, Pres., Peter Garofalo, Benjamin A. Gorman, Eric L. Kuselias, Robert Miller, Mattie Mims; 1st Dist., Anne Ramsey; 2nd Dist., Frank Cesare; 3rd Dist., Henry Candido; 4th Dist., Stephen J. Mayer; 5th Dist., Margaret DeVane; 6th Dist., Nicholas Troiano; 7th Dist., Pasquale Corso; 8th Dist., Carol Longo; 9th Dist., Marie Scharf.—**Dir. of Finance,** Thomas Pesce.—**Bd. of Ethics,** John L. Connolly, Chm., Jerome Jason, Stuart Pearl, Owen Sanderson, Rita Sullivan; Alternates, Vernell Reid, vacancy.—**Tax Collector,** Barbara Tito.—**Bd. of Assessment Appeals,** Bernard Nitkin, Chm., Charles Hermann, Ronald Meneo.—**Chief Assessor,** James Clynes; Deputy, Helen Totz.— **Registrars of Voters,** John Flanagan (D), Louise Pilon (R).—**Supt. of Schools,** Alida Begina.—**Bd. of Education,** Michaela Degnan, Chm., Peter Brown, Alice Fischer, Frances S. Nelson, R. Thomas Rousseau, Nanette Vece, 1997; Edward Beaudette, Lyn Campo, Myron Hul, 1999.—**Personnel Appeals Bd.,** Rabbi Herbert Brockman, Patty Pittman, James O. Walsh, vacancy.—**Civil Service Comm.,** Theodora Howell, Chm., A. J. Raccio, Joan Rudolph.—**Retirement Bd.,** Mayor Lillian D. Clayman, Chm., Robert Anthony, John Ambrogio, James T. Doherty, Frank Erba, Robert Maturo, Thomas Pesce, Patricia Riccitelli, Louise Sault, Thomas Terrace, Michael Veno.— **Planning and Zoning Comm.,** Joseph McDonough, Chm., Diane Abbott, Philip DeCaprio, Peter Fortini, James Garrett, Robert Roscow, Michael Sansone, Geneva White, vacancy; Alternates, Laura Cruickshank, Gerald Nolan, vacancy.—**Town Planner,** Daniel Kops.—**Zoning Bd. of Appeals,** Wayne Chorney, Chm., Gerald Dimenstein, Harold Fitch, Karen Kleinerman, Beatrice LaRoche; Alternates, Matthew Fitch, Robert Gianquinto, vacancy.—**Zoning Enforcement Officer,** Joseph Venditto.— **Community Development Advisory Council,** Phyllis Mulcahy, Chm., Henry L. Blue, John Corso, Jr., Cynthia Dematteis, Harrison H. Mero, Dorna Stover, Duane Wetmore, vacancy.—**Economic Development Comm.,** Gary Kleinerman, Chm., Arthur Giulietti, Howard Leavitt, Dennis Proto, Anthony Sacchetti, Matthew Susman, Mary Jean Sweeney, John L.Wonneberger, vacancy.—**Housing Auth.,** Irwin A. Snyder, Chm., Charles D. Aitro, William Hindinger, Edith Sokoloff, Carolyn Young; Hazelann Cook,

Dir.—**Fair Rent Comm.,** Bennett Pudlin, Chm., Frank DeLuca, Kathleen Murphy, Anthony Simone; Alternate, Les Walhimer.—**Conservation and Inland Wetlands Comm.,** Thomas E. Farver, Chm., Shay Atluru, Joseph Backer, Nancy Bostwick, Virginia Dowd, Thomas Fortuna, Michael Montgomery, James Moore, Mark Scott, Thomas Vocelli; John Raccio, Jr., Insp. Officer; Alternates, Michael Mauro, Robert Smith.—**Agent for the Elderly,** Carol Ireland.—**Mental Health Catchment Area Council,** Mary Dinmore.—**Welfare Supvr.,** Judith Rich.—**Dir. of Health,** Leslie A. Balch.—**Quinnipiack Valley Health Dist.,** Joy Donaldson, Leona Haddad, Doris Morrison-Little, Myra Rochow, Richard Wallace; Alternates, Peter Marone, Jr., Gregory Tignor.—**Comm. on Disabilities,** Beth McArthur, Chm., Josephine Burgh, Margaret Christianson, Katherine Davis, Marcia Nigro, Peter Rumbin, Suzanne Tucker.—**Cable Advisory Council,** George Alexander, William Ellison, Marshall Marcus; Citizens Television, C.F. Prece.—**Arts Comm.,** Thomas Duffy, Chm., Susan Abramson, Shirley Fidler, Patricia Ford, Abraham Gelbart, Joyce Gherlone, Helen Herzig, Kenneth Hilliard, Charles Kortsep, Arnold Lerner, Marvin Michaelsen, Christian Rendiero, Carol Robson, Alphonse Savarese, Sandra Schiff, Evelyn Skelly; Mimsie Coleman, Coordinator.—**Human Services Comm.,** Ellen Andrews, Melissa T. Bowles, Peggy Gallup, Martha Hirsch, Carol Quinn, Gayle Wilder, Steven Wilson.—**Library Bd.,** James McKeon, Chm., Sary M. Aiden, Catherine Berman, Franz Douskey, Lester Hankin.—**Municipal Historian,** Martha Becker.—**Flood and Erosion Control Bd.,** Pauline Sargolini, Chm., Alphonse A. Raiano, Mary Ann Seastrand, John Smoko, Dino Vagnini.—**Parks and Recreation Comm.,** Bernard T. Brennan, Chm., Richard Altieri, Dennis Massaro, Cosino Melillo, Thaddeus Watson.—**Dir. of Parks and Recreation,** Frank Rizzuti.—**Farmington Canal Comm.,** David Schaefer, Chm., Michael D'Agostino, Joseph DiNicola, Michael Flynn, Michael Glynn, Kristin Hawkins, Campbell Stubbs.—**Tree Warden,** Charles DeMatteo.—**Youth Services Bureau Coordinator,** Barbara R. Robinson.—**Dir. of Public Works,** Joseph Velardi.—**Personnel Dir.,** Victor Binkoski.—**Purchasing Agent,** Judi Kozak.—**Building Inspector/Acting Town Engineer,** Joseph Raiola.—**Supt. of Highways and Streets,** Greg DiCrosta.—**Building Bd. of Appeals,** Kristian Larsen, Chm., Thomas Athan, Edward P. Grimshaw, Louis Palmieri, vacancy.—**Water Pollution Control Auth.,** Mayor Lillian Clayman, Chm., Renato Bergami, Joseph Barba, Thomas Dobkowski, James Sette, vacancy.—**Chief of Police,** John Ambrogio.—**Police Comm.,** James Couzens, Robert Lewis, John Morrison, Donald Pritchard, H. Martin Ruff.—**Chief of Fire Dept.,** Tim Sullivan; Asst., Edward Badamo.—**Fire Marshal,** Robert Westervelt; Asst., vacancy.—**Fire Comm.,** Marsha Walsh, Chm., Patricia Afragola, Carl Secola, Sr., Peter Vining, vacancy.—**Civil Preparedness Dir.,** Tim Sullivan.—**Town Atty.,** Burton Rosenberg; Susan Gruen, Michael Kamp, Carl Secola, Assts.; Carla Munroe, Staff Atty.—**Jury Committee,** Joan Bonyai, Patricia D'Ambrose, Stephanie Criscuolo, Janet Fitch, Mona Rhone, Geraldine Tobin.—**Justices of the Peace,** Josephine Baroncini, Joseph C. Bertini, Jr., Harry Brooks III, Ann M. Celone, Francis Cesare, William Cocking, William Cohen, Irma Coleman, Harold F. Fitch, Jr., Thomas Fortuna, Joseph R. Frasier, Martin Friedler, Martina J. Garris, Joseph Gause, Peter Gherlone, Arthur Giulietti, Mary E. Grabowski, Seymour Hatkin, Marie B. Higgins, Eleanor R. Kacy, Geoffrey Kanner, Jacqueline Karn, Elliott Kerzner, Judi Kozak, Deborah Laffin, Carol Longo, Stephen Mayer, Gerald Migliaro, Cosino A. Melillo, Henry Mims, Drew Mogridge,

Evelyn Naples, Bernard Nitkin, Karen E. O'Brien, Colin G. Odell, Myra Rochow, Robert Sadler, Stanley Saslafsky, Fred Sette, Milton Stitzel, Mary A. Velardi, Elizabeth S. Wetmore.

HAMPTON. Windham County.—(Form of government, selectmen, town meeting.)—Inc., Oct., 1786; taken from Windham, Pomfret, Brooklyn, Canterbury and Mansfield. Area, 25.5 sq. miles. Population, est., 1,701. Voting district, 1. Principal industry, agriculture. Transp.—Passenger: Served by buses of Bonanza Bus Lines, Inc. from Hartford and Danielson, and by Greyhound. Freight: Served by numerous motor common carriers. Post office, Hampton; R.F.D. 1 from Hampton; R.F.D. 1 from North Windham.

TOWN OFFICERS. Clerk and Reg. of Vital Statistics, Margaret A. Fox; Hours, 9 A.M.-4 P.M., Tues. and Thurs.; 9 A.M.-12 Noon, Sat. and by appointment; Address, Town Office Bldg., 164 Main St., P.O. Box 143, 06247; Tel., Willimantic, (860) 455-9132; FAX (860) 455-0517.—**Asst. Clerk and Asst. Reg. of Vital Statistics,** Mary Kennan.—**Selectmen,** 1st, Walter A. Stone (R) Tel., (860) 455-9078, Daniel Meade (R), Noel Waite (D).—**Treas.,** Ellen M. Rodriguez.—**Tax Collector,** Loretta P. Stone.—**Bd. of Assessment Appeals,** Joel Bogner, Douglas E. Fox, Paul D. Osypuk.—**Assessors,** Nicole D. Lintereur, Chm., Carol T. Crawford, Joanne Z. Litke.—**Registrars of Voters,** Claire M. Winters (D), Eunice B. Fuller (R).—**Supt. of Schools,** A. Rodger Wutzl.—**Bd. of Education,** Rose Bisson, Kathleen A. Donnelly, Walter A. Stone, Jr., 1997; Katherine Newcombe, Ellen M. Park, Dennis Timberman, 1999; Laurie Berard, Allan R. Cahill, James E. Ianonni, vacancy, 2001.—**Planning and Zoning Comm.,** Robert E. Inman, Chm., Edward N. Adelman, Brian C. Caya, Philip Russell, Guila G. Wagner; Alternates, Robert Burgoyne, William Koennicke, two vacancies.—**Zoning Bd. of Appeals,** Joanne Z. Litke, Chm., L. Bowman Banford, Morris L. Burr, Michael Chapel, William L. Pearl, Felix J. Winters; Alternates, three vacancies.—**Zoning Enforcement Officer,** Martha Fraenkel..—**Inland Wetlands Comm.,** Robert Burgoyne, Chm., Bruce Krupula, Alan Marshall, Muriel Miller, Jeff Weiler; Harold Haraghey, Agent/Flood Ins. Officer.—**Agent for the Elderly/Dir. of Social Services,** Mary Kennan.—**Dir. of Health,** T. Wegrzyn (P.O., Brooklyn).—**Building Inspector,** John Berard.—**Building Code Bd. of Appeals,** Wendell Davis, Chm., Leon O. Berard, Edward J. Halbach.—**Sanitarian,** Northeast District Dept. of Health.—**Supt. of Highways,** Robert Corey.—**Chief of Police,** Walter A. Stone.—**Constables,** Brian Caya, Harold Haraghey, Jr., Laurier J. Henri, Roger W. B. Smalley.—**Chief of Fire Dept.,** Noel Waite; Deputy, David A. DeMontigny.—**Fire Marshal,** Noel Waite.—**Civil Preparedness Dir.,** Carrol Waite.—**Town Atty.,** Noah H. Starkey (P.O., Willimantic).—**Justices of the Peace,** Josiah H. Brown, Hildred M. Chapel, Doris Clapp, Wendell Davis, Thomas A. Gaines, Susan E. Kirsch, Robert J. McDermott, Rhoda M. Micocci, Louise J. Oliver, John Parson, Joyce P. Rodriquez.

HARTFORD. Hartford County.—(Form of government, city manager, court of common council.)—Settled in 1635; inc., 1784; city inc., May, 1784. Town and city consolidated, April, 1896. Area, 18.0 sq. miles. Population, est., 135,750. Voting districts, 27. Principal industries, electrical and telephone equipment, tools, automatic and special machines, automobile parts, precision machines, firearms, plastics, castings, vacuum systems, turbine and marine engines, drop forgings, oil burners, valves, glass machinery, sound equipment; home office of thirty-eight insurance companies and home of the Hartford Whalers. Transp.—Passenger: Served by Amtrak and buses of Conn. Transit locally and from Middletown, Farmington, Bloomfield, Windsor, Rockville, Manchester, Glastonbury, New Britain and Newington; Bonanza Bus Lines, Inc. from Providence, RI, Danielson, Willimantic, Bristol, Waterbury, Danbury and New York City; Greyhound from Hartford to Boston and New York City; Post Road Stages, Inc. from Hartford to Rockville and Stafford Springs; The Arrow Line, Inc. from Albany, NY, Torrington, Winsted, and the University of Conn. at Storrs; Conn. Transit from Manchester and East Hartford; The Airfield Service Co. from Simsbury, Granby and Windsor Locks; The Short Line of Conn., Inc. from New Haven, Meriden and Wallingford; Dattco Inc. from Windsor Locks, Thompsonville and Springfield, MA; Eastern Bus Lines, Inc. from New London and Colchester; New Britain Transp. Co. (Commuter), and Trailways of New England, Inc. from Hartford to Boston and New York City. Freight: Served by Conrail and numerous motor common carriers. Post office, Hartford, Main Office, 141 Weston St.; Station A, 510 Park St.; Central, 80 State St.; Barry Square, 641 Maple Ave.; Blue Hills, 433 Woodland St.; Unity Plaza, 271 Barbour St.; classified branches in East Hartford, West Hartford, Wethersfield, Elmwood, Bishop's Corner (West Hartford), and Newington; eleven contract stations.

CITY AND TOWN OFFICERS. City and Town Clerk, Daniel M. Carey; Hours, 8:30 A.M.-4:30 P.M., Mon. through Fri.; Address, Municipal Bldg., 550 Main St., 06103; Tel., (860) 543-8581.—**Deputy City and Town Clerk,** Delores Lamar.—**Asst. Town Clerks,** Susan DiNardi, Irena Lee, Antonia St. Pierre.—**Regs. of Vital Statistics,** Alexander Marcellino.—**Asst. Regs. of Vital Statistics,** Jacqueline Baker, Minnie Collier, Hathor T. Dell, Jacqueline Woodberry.—**City Manager,** Saundra Kee-Borges; Deputies, Henry Langley, Patricia M. Williams; Linda Bayer, Asst.—**Mayor,** Michael P. Peters (D).—**Court of Common Council,** Deputy Mayor Frances Sanchez, Veronica Airey-Wilson, Luis A. Ayala, Anthony F. DiPentima, Art J. Feltman, Michael T. McGarry, John B. O'Connell, John B. Stewart, Jr., Louis Watkins, Jr.—**Selectmen,** Ellen Jackson, Donald Obedzinski, Jesse J. Smith, Basil S. Thomas, Ludella P. Williams.—**Treas.,** Denise L. Nappier.—**Dir. of Finance,** William J. Hogan.—**Tax Collector,** William L. Donlin.—**Bd. of Assessment Appeals,** William R. Smith, Chm., Allen A. Ackerman, Richard DeNoia.—**Assessor,** Robert Hartzell, Jr.; Asst., Larry Labarbera.—**Registrars of Voters,** Tony Mein , Deputy, Olga Aviles, Asst., Marie Hamilton (D); Joseph DeLorenzo, Deputy, Salvatore A. Bramante, Asst., Alice S. Jenkins (R).—**Supt. of Schools,** Dr. Patricia Daniel.—**Bd. of Education,** Arthur A. Brouillet, Jr., Ted Carroll, Thelma E. Dickerson, Stephanie S. Lightfoot, Elizabeth B. Noel, 1997; Patrice Bazzano-Villalobos, Stephen E. D. Fournier, Ruth E. Hall, Donald V. Romanik, 1999.—**Personnel Bd.,** Francisco DeJesus, Chm., Dolores Bielawiec, Larry Reynolds; Patricia Washington, Dir.—**Pension Comm.,** Thomas M. Malloy, Chm., Scott M. Brady, Hylan T. Hubbard III, Melvin E. Johnson.—**Comm. on the City Plan,** Robert A. LaPorte, Chm., Sandra Bobowski, Femi Bogle-Assegai, Andrew J. Gold, Barnaby W. Horton, Raul A. Rodriquez, Basil S. Thomas; Alternates, Raul Gonzalez, Michael Lupo, Nancy C. Racker; Ralph Knighton, Dir.—**Zoning Bd. of Appeals,** Ronald Bielawiec, David Bobowski, Valerio Giadone, Peter Leonidas, William R. Smith; Alternates, Aida R. Claudio, Helen Nixon, vacancy.—**Zoning Enforcement Officer,** Abraham Ford.—**Redevelopment Agency,** Collin B. Bennett, Chm.,

Cynthia R. Jennings, Rafael Lopez-Hernandez, John Lupo, Jr., Steven D. Park; Madelyn Colon, Exec. Dir.—**Housing Auth.,** Charles W. Groce, Jr., Chm., Michael S. Coyne, Margarita Ortiz, Mollie Shelton, Rosa Velez; John Wardlaw, Exec. Dir.—**Housing and Community Development Dir.,** Ralph Knighton.—**Economic Development Dir.,** Norris V. Bacho—**Fair Rent Comm.,** Kyle Anderson, Henry Brown, Victoria J. Christie, Ella L. Cromwell, Barbara A. Davis, Carol S. Jestin, Lizzie J. McCall, Talia R. Orr, Raul A. Rodriguez.—**Inland Wetlands Agency,** Mayor Michael P. Peters, Chm., Court of Common Council; Daniel M. Carey, Clerk.—**Greater Hartford Flood Comm.,** Mario Navarra, Aldo P. Provera, Margaret Reidy, James E. Reik.—**Cultural Affairs Comm.,** Juan Brito, Susan R. Brown, Jonathan Bruce, Alfred Chambers, Valencia Coleman, Ellis Echevarria, Wilson H. Faude, Alexandra S. Friedman, Allen Jones, William P. Katz, Anthony S. Keller, Clarice S. McLean, Vernon Martin, Gladys N. Hernandez, Elizabeth Pite, Rona L. Reynolds.—**Comm. on Aging,** Marie Alston, Fannie S. Arnum, Juan M. Fuentes, Pearl Haley, James G. Harris, Jr., Roberta L. Jones, Michael Kary, Shirley J. Kemp, Laura M. Kirven, Bessie McGarrah, Olga Mele.—**Coordinator for the Elderly,** Lawrence Zarbo.—**Human Relations Comm.,** Ernestine Brown, Ann Darling, Patricia Lawson, Donna E. MacDonnell, Minerva Molina, Senobia R. Nelson, Iris Ortiz, Nancy C. Parker, Frederick E. Smith, Sue Tenorio, Henry Walker, vacancy.—**Jury Committee,** Ethel M. Austin, Anthony F. DiPentima, Blanche G. Jackson.—**Dir. of Human Services,** Roman Rojano.—**Dir. of Health,** Katherine M. McCormack.—**Public Health Council,** Sandra B. Bobowski, Esther Bush, Evans H. Daniels, M.D., Luis Diez-Morales, M.D., Candida Flores, Linda J. Schofield.—**Library Directors,** Morton A. Elsner, Pres., Rudolph P. Arnold, Paul Basch, John L. Bonee, Lynne O. Burfeind, Stephen B. Goddard, Mary M. Hennessey, William M. Large, Jacquelyn Lilly, Worth Loomis, Mayor Michael P. Peters, Cynthia Reik, Paul Shipman, Jeffrey A. Stewart, Shirley A. Surgeon, Antonina P. Uccello, Robert A. Weinerman.—**Municipal Historian,** Robert Pawlowski.—**Parks and Recreation Advisory Comm.,** Blanche G. Jackson, Chm., Alan Arteche, Gloria M. Cardillo, Victoria J. Christie, Mario DeCapua, Paulette S. Griffin, Ruth E. Hall, Richard Kemp, Linda W. Kinsella, Dorothy J. Payne, Franklin Perry, Cleaven Royster, Maxine K. Stewart, Russell C. Williams.—**Chief of Parks,** Thomas Wallace.—**City Engineer,** John McGrane.—**Supt. of Streets,** vacancy.—**Dir. of Public Works,** Thomas E. Johnson; Asst. Dir., John McGrane.—**Purchasing Agent,** Nancy Haynes.—**Dir. of Licenses and Inspections,** Abraham Ford; Deputy Dir., Joseph Hewes.—**Building Bd. of Appeals,** Lawrence F. Buck, Joseph M. Hallisey, Daniel J. Herzig, Milton L. Howard, Louis Treviso; Alternates, Paul D. Bemis, Brandon Clarke, David Desiderato—**Manager of Waste and Recycling,** Bryan West.—**Chief of Police,** Joseph F. Croughwell.—**Constables,** Ronald Bielawiec, Henry J. Cwikla, Abraham L. Giles, Basilio E. Gonzalez, Ellen N. Nurse, Hector M. Rivera, Tracy K. Sparmer.—**Chief of Fire Dept.,** Robert E. Dobson; Assts., Michael Parker, Billy L. Smith.—**Fire Marshal,** John R. Vendetta.—**Emergency Planning Dir./Fire Chief,** Robert E. Dobson.—**Corporation Counsel,** Kevin G. Dubay.—**Justices of the Peace,** Ada J. Acosta, Maria L. Acosta, Phillippa Y. Adams, Khilesh Adhin, Dawn Amore-Balula, Daniel J. Andrews, Earlean S. Andrews, Druecilla Anglin, Abdul-Shahid Ansari, Imani Ansari, Michael P. Aparo, Janet A. Appellof, Ramon L. Arroyo, Nilsa M. Artau, James W. Austin, Olga I. V. Aviles, Lillian Banks, Paul Banville, Stephen C. Barone, William Barone, Joseph S.

Bascetta, John Bazzano, Maria D. Bell, Adrienne L. Belyeu, Collin Bennett, Lisa C. Bennett, Daniel R. Bielawiec, Dolores W. Bielawiec, Ronald Bielawiec, Rafaela Black, Charles L. Blount, David W. Bobowski, Sandra B. Bobowski, Femi M. Bogle-Assegai, Anna C. Bramante, Salvatore A. Bramante, Frank J. Brown, Henry L. Brown, Barbara C. Browne, Jonathan Bruce, Jorena W. Bruce, Peter F. Brush, Francis J. Buckley, William Camby, Jennie M. Camerato, Gloria M. Cardillo, Daniel M. Carey, William H. Carey II, Bosa E. Carmona, Yolanda Castillo, J. Roman Castro, Alfred A. Chambers, Denese L. Chisholm-Langley, Victoria J. Christie, Eugene Cimiano, Clinton D. Clarke, Eric J. Clarke, Barbara J. Clayton, Glenn M. Coakley, Kathleen D. Collins, Michael C. Collins, Harold G. Comulada, Olga A. Concepcion, Edward V. Conran, Sandra B. Cooper, Luis Cora, Carmen Cordero, Ella L. Cromwell, Gaetano J. Dambrosio, Jr., Rupert Daniels, Robert F. Davis, Margaret C. Davoren, Ann Marie L. DeCapua, Mario A. DeCapua, Francisco DeJesus, Joseph W. DeLorenzo, Mary C. DeLorenzo, Laurie R. DeLuca, John F. DeLucco, Vincenza M. DeLucco, Richard J. Denoia, Thelma E. Dickersohn, Harriet Douglas, Roland Douglas, W. Michael Downes, John J. Dubois, Kathleen J. Duncan, Betty Eldridge, Sheila N. Ellison, Wendy I. Escobales, Leopoldo M. Espejo, Marcela J. Espejo, Kathy Evans, Carl Faggaini, Virginia Falcon, John J. Farley-Blackshire, Art J. Feltman, Louis C. Fennell, Joseph Ferlazzo, Carmen C. Figueroa, Harry L. Figueroa, Christine B. Floyd, Fleetie L. Floyd, Edrick Flynn, Beverly Fonfara, Isabel Fontanez, Charles J. Ford, Janice R. Ford, Marian S. Fothergill, William C. Fothergill, James J. Francoline, Edgard B. French, Juan M. Fuentes, John N. Fusco, John Q. Gale, Gloria F. Garay, Jose Garay, Sr., Victor M. Garay, La Tonya Garner, Sally M. Gaston, Joan H. Gibson, Juanita Giles, Anna M. Gomez, Minnie Gonzalez, Errol G. Goodison, Melmoth A. Grant, Anthony Gray, Kenneth P. Green, Pearline R. Greene, Blanche S. Greenfield, Ruth E. Hall, Susan E. Halperin, Kenneth C. Hamilton, Kenneth W. Hamilton, Marie G. Hamilton, Nichelle M. Hamilton, Paul Hamilton, Flourine B. Harris, Kourtney M. Harris, Pauline Harris, Steven M. Harris, Harry W. Hartie, Felisha W. Henderson, Mary M. Heslin, Eileen D. Hickey, Ernest L. Hodnett, Carol F. Holbrook, Georgiana E. Holloway, Virginia A. Holloway, Myles N. Hubbard, Warren Huertas, Jolean F. Hughes, Syed Hussain, Stacy Iverson, Blanche G. Jackson, Ellen Jackson, Portia Jackson, Gwendolyn M. Jasper, Alice S. Jenkins, Calvin Johnson, Shelley M. Johnson, Riley D. Johnson, Jr., Bradley G. Jones, Roberta L. Jones, Willie J. Joseph, Clarke King, Norman C. King, Kelly G. Kirkley-Bey, Marie L. Kirkley-Bey, Estella V. Knight, Armand A. Korzenik, Ursula G. Korzenik, Delores Lamar, Robert A. Laporte, Edythe S. Latney, Geraldine Lauray, Brenda D. Lawrence, Oddie E. Lawrence, Edward Lazu, Hyacinth D. Ledbetter, Charles E. Lewis, Daniel E. Lilly, Jacquelyn C. Lilly, Wanda B. Litke, Alfred Long, Rafael Lopez, John P. Lupo, Jr., Noemy Maldonado, Joseph R. Marfuggi, Alphonse S. Marotta, Charles Martin, Odell B. Martin, Margarita Martinez, Leo C. Mazotas, Bruno W. Mazzulla, Bertha G. McGarrah, Marguerite F. McGarry, Michael T. McGarry, John A. McKenna, David O. McKinley, Tony Mein, German Melendez, Angel L. Mendez, Ramona Mercado-Espinoza, Sylvia S. Merced, Trude J. Mero, Irene J. Mieszkowicz, Mark S. Mieszkowicz, Patricia A. Miller, Irma R. Milton, James Mitchell, Janis Mitchell, Minerva Molina, Beverly J. Monts, Helen B. Monts, Grady Moorehead, Iris D. Morales, Rosa Morales, Barbara J. Morehead, Richard O. Morehead, Aaron B. Mounds, Clare T. Murphy, Joseph Musumeci, Lisa Musumeci, Anthony J. Napoleon, Senobia R. Nelson, Janice M. Newell, Rigoberto Nieva, Nancy G. Noli, Virginia Nunes, Ellen S. Nurse, Carol J. O'Connell, John B. O'Connell, John B. O'Connell III, Ruth S. Odoms, Talia R. Orr, Isabel Osorio-Vasquez, Charles Oxley, Santo Pantano, Anya O. Park, Steven D. Park, Carol T. Parrish, Muriel C. Paschall, Edgar Perez, Edwin R. Perez, Leora P. Perry, Virginia Pertillar, Michael P. Peters, Wanda T. Piotrowicz, Hipolita Pizarro, Jessica A. Poland, Sebastian M. Polo, Sandra L. Poulin, Elizabeth D. Pratt, Aldo P. Provera, James E. Quint, Jane E. Rainwater, Olive Ramsey, Albert L. Reaves, Dora B. Reddick, Robert B. Redman, Damaris Reyes, Georgette E. Reyes, Thomas D. Ritter, Hector M. Rivera, Richard O. Rivera, Valerie Robertson, Barbara Robinson, Edwin Robles, Americo S. Rodrigues, Alejandro Rodriguez, Candida G. Rodriguez, Carmen M. Rodriguez, Efrain C. Rodriguez, Joaquina V. Rodriguez, Nancy Rodriguez, Raul A. Rodriguez, Jose Rolon, Jose Roman, Donald V. Romanik, Luz Rosado, Mark Rudewicz, Donald J. Rully, Emma B. Russ, Irene D. Ryan, Rosa A. Santos, Maria Serrano, Patricia A. Shepard, Carmen Sierra, George J. Sirois, Agnes D. Smith, Jesse J. Smith, Ricky D. Smith, Carol Smith-Jestin, Andrew J. Sokolik, Clorinda Soldevila, Rocco A. Sorano, Antonia D. St. Pierre, Jeffrey A. Stewart, Troy C. Stewart, Shirley A. Surgeon, Louella H. Tate, Juan Torres, Beverly H. Tucker, Beverly E. Tuttle, Elba I. Valdivieso, Rosaria B. Valente, Virginia P. Valente, Miriam Valentin, Herminio Valle, Jr., Eva Vargas, Radames V. Vasquez, Wanda I. Vasquez, Wilbert Vazquez, Kerry Vega, Kevin Vega, Manuel Velez, Nicole M. Washington, H. John Waterhouse, David A. Waters, Sharon C. Weaver, Christopher C. Webb, Beulah G. Williams, Carl A. Williams, Frankie E. Williams, Jane E. Williams, Lorene B. Williams, Ludella P. Williams, Ronnie J. Williams, Jacqueline M. Wilson, John E. Wilson, Henry A. Wilus, Willia T. Wooden, Ollie G. Worrell, Patricia J. Wrice, Doreen Wright, Nora Wyatt, Jr.

HARTLAND. Hartford County.—(Form of government, selectmen, town meeting, board of finance.)—Inc., May, 1761. Area, 34.6 sq. miles. Population, est., 1,916. Voting district, 1. Principal industries, agriculture and manufacture of wood products. Transp.—Freight: Served by numerous motor common carriers. Mail service twice daily from Granby to East Hartland and from New Hartford to West Hartland. Post offices, East Hartland and West Hartland.

TOWN OFFICERS. Clerk and Reg. of Vital Statistics, Peder T. Pedersen; Hours, 1-4 P.M., Mon., Tues., Wed.; 7-8 P.M., Tues.; Address, Town Office Bldg., 22 South Rd., East Hartland 06027; Tel., Simsbury, (860) 653-3542.—**Asst. Clerks and Asst. Regs. of Vital Statistics,** Dorothy L. Fernsten, Evelyn G. Pedersen, Lynn A. Skaret.—**Selectmen,** 1st, William L. Hodge (D) P.O., East Hartland, Tel., (860) 653-6800, Robert W. Hilbrecht (R), Norman H. Hoidalen (R).—**Treas.,** Robert W. Narvesen.—**Bd. of Finance,** Leon Stoltze, Chm., William A. Blecher, Jeffrey L. Forman, Robert N. Pedersen, Jr., Arthur D. Rhea, Todd R. Shelansky; Alternates, Charlotte A. Anderson, John A. Ferro, vacancy.—**Tax Collector,** Nancy A. Huber.—**Bd. of Assessment Appeals,** Alice H. Kimball, Chm., William W. Bakken, Beatrice Y. Isabelle.—**Assessors,** Philip H. Groth, Gloria Y. Nelson, Gordon C. Wright.—**Registrars of Voters,** Jean R. Salling (D), Thelma K. Olsen (R).—**Supt. of Schools,** Alfred E. Tracy.—**Bd. of Education,** Alana Bordewieck, Daniel A. Bowler, Shirley Green, William P. Ryan,

Peter C. Stred, 1997; Warren K. Haag, Karen L. McNulty, MIchelle D. Viksnes, 1999; Carlene C. Rhea, 2001.—**Planning and Zoning Comm.,** John K. Bannister, David W. Barrett, William H. Emerich, Jr., Warren K. Haag, Stephen F. Hennessey; Alternates, Laurie Adler, Roy D. Fisher, vacancy.—**Zoning Bd. of Appeals,** Russell F. Newton, Chm., Patrick A. Broderick, Christopher P. Eseppi, David L. Faye, Elliott E. Jessen; Alternates, Julia DuFresne, Penelope K. Ziarnik, vacancy.—**Inland Wetlands Comm.,** William W. Bakken, David W. Barrett, Thomas Daukas, William H. Emerick, Jr., David Isabelle, Raymond E. Konikowski, Henry S. Prussing, Brian Watkins.— **Agent for the Elderly,** Carlene Rhea.—**Dir. of Health,** Farmington Valley Health Dist.—**Comm. on Aging,** Gordon C. Wright, Chm., Wayne R. Cromack, Jean A. Delton, Susan Fitch, Janet E. Gentile, Beatrice Y. Isabelle, Ole Lillestolen, Christine M. Martocchio, Mary Ransom, Jean R. Salling.—**Library Directors,** Penelope R. Ziarnik, Chm., Nancy Groth, Carolyn S. Irwin, Pamela L. Kohan, Karen L. McNulty, Anastasia C. Newton, Phyllis Ransom, Jean R. Salling, Ernest W. Smith, Jr.—**Recreation Comm.,** Jeffrey Forman, Chm., Cynthia Dabrowski, Jerry Gunderson, Sheryl L. Kemp, Richard Madara, Robert N. Pedersen, Jr.—**Building Code Bd. of Appeals,** Joseph S. Alicata, Thomas A. Daukas, Paul J. Eseppi, Donald E. Hawley, Norman Hoidalen; Alternate, Robert J. Isabelle.—**Building Inspector,** Henry M. Miga.—**Chief of Police,** William L. Hodge.—**Constables,** Roy D. Fisher, Elliott E. Jessen, Daniel T. Mitchell, Kenet G. Nielsen, Frederick G. Wright, Gordon C. Wright.—**Chiefs of Fire Depts.,** Robert Mueller (East Hartland), Timothy Corcoran (West Hartland).— **Fire Marshal,** Peter P. Sevetz, Jr.—**Civil Preparedness Dir.,** Theodore A. Jansen.— **Town Atty.,** Cohn & Birnbaum, Hartford.—**Justices of the Peace,** Melissa H. Bellerose, James S. Devlin, Philip H. Groth, Robert W. Hilbrecht, Ronald E. Hille, William L. Hodge, Marianne M. Holtham, Carolyn M. Jessen, Thomas J. Prosser, Michael A. Silkey, Ernest W. Smith, Gordon C. Wright.

HARWINTON. Litchfield County.—(Form of government, selectmen, town meeting, board of finance.)—Inc., Oct., 1737. Area, 31.1 sq. miles. Population, est., 5,337. Voting district, 1. Principal industries, agriculture, retail services, construction, landscaping, tools and dies. Transp.—Freight: Served by numerous motor common carriers. Post office, Harwinton.

TOWN OFFICERS. Clerk and Reg. of Vital Statistics, Patricia K. Williamsen; Hours, 8:30 A.M.-4 P.M., Mon. through Fri.; Address, Town Hall, 100 Bentley Dr., 06791; Tel., (860) 485-9613.—**Asst. Clerks and Asst. Regs. of Vital Statistics,** Sharon E. Bandzak, Cherie D. Shanley, Marion B. Thierry.—**Selectmen,** 1st, Marie M. Knudsen (R) Tel., (860) 485-9051; FAX (860) 485-0051, Peter P. Salwocki (D), Peter B. Thierry (D).—**Treas.,** Eleanor G. Woike; Asst., Bradley R. Cagenello.—**Bd. of Finance,** Robert Ferraresso, Chm., James Carros, Salvo N. Falzone, George Nashe, James A. Savanella, Lloyd T. Shanley, Jr.—**Tax Collector,** John H. Thrall; Asst., Jane W. Thrall.—**Bd. of Assessment Appeals,** Alan J. Eckstrand, Vance Taylor, vacancy.—**Assessors,** Barbara J. Bigos, Chm., Mary-Jane Febbroriello, Elizabeth Goodwin.—**Registrars of Voters,** Carol M. Pyrzenski (D), Patricia M. Goodenough (R).— **Supt. of Schools,** Robert W. Goldman.—**Zoning Comm.,** John Byrnes, Chm., Clarence M. Caldwell, Jr., Robert D'Amato, James E. Sawyer, Marilie VanWie; Alternates,

Nina Callahan, George A. Schneider, Edward A. Zielinski.—**Planning Comm.,** Lawrence Connors, Chm., John J. Christian, Jr., Joseph J. Scarpelli, Wiliam J. Tracy, Jr., Earl O. Weingart; Alternates, Edwin G. Booth, Jr., John McNabney, Michael J.Orefice.—**Zoning Bd. of Appeals,** Thomas J. Rotondo, Chm., Michael F. Durstin, Anne T. Gioia, R. Peter Grady, Patrick J. Wall; Alternates, Rosemary P. Carros, John D. Pyrzenski, Nick Terlecky.—**Historic Dist. Comm.,** Francis J. Chiaramonte, Chm., Catherine M. Betts, Helen E. Callahan, Alec Frost, Alphonsus Manzi; Alternates, Kathryn H. Baker, Phyllis Manzi.—**Municipal Historian,** Lloyd T. Shanley, Jr.—**Housing Auth.,** George F. Griben, Chm., Stuart Bronson, Mary Doremus, Cornelius A. Duyser, Jr., Concetta Rajcok.—**Conservation Comm.,** Susan Alender, Chm., Colleen Butcher, Terrence P. Ferrarotti, John D. Goodno, Jeffery Grech, Joan Jordan-Rinaldi, P. Thomas Schoenemann.—**Inland Wetlands Comm.,** Bruce Burnett, Chm., Paul R. Carrier, Jerome A. Deprey, Suzanne Ferrarotti, Anthony A. Gioia, Jr., Bruce Perran, Richard E. Robillard.—**Comm. on Aging,** Diane J. Bock, Chm., Celine M. Griben, Robert Pease, Concetta Rajcok, Lena Silano; Kathryn Berenson, Municipal Agent.—**Dir. of Social Services,** Loda Sheehan.—**Library Bd.,** Elizabeth R. Booth, Cornelius A. Duyser, Jr., Pamela G. French, Carol Gould, Thomas H. Maccalous, Judi Mandl, Glen Richardson, David T. Ryan, Patrick J. Wall.—**Recreation Comm.,** Frank Arigoni, Meredith Brown, Nicholas Caputi, John W. Combs, Wayne Harrigan, MaryAnn Lockhart, Bruce Novatko; Suzanne Stich, Dir.—**Recycling Coord.,** Renee Skarp.—**Highway Supvr.,** Thomas Pollack.—**Land Use Coord.,** James T. Kavanaugh.—**Open Burning Official,** William Rinko, Jr.—**Tree Warden,** Thomas Pollack.—**Town Engineers,** Barnhart, Johnson, Francis and Wild, Inc.—**Building Inspector,** Frank Rybak.—**Water Pollution Control Auth.,** Robert G. Pease, Chm., Alexander J. Carros, Steven G. Criss, Gilbert A. Roberts, J. Matthew Tomasko; Alternates, Andrew J. Kasznay, Jr., Andrew Robbins.—**Emergency Services Committee,** Collette V. Achilli, Patrick Doyle, Scott Kellogg, Thomas Mahoney, Gary A. Pomeroy, Andrew J. Robbins, Robert Santamaria, Lincoln H. Taylor, Jr., Vincent Wheeler.—**Constables,** Richard Bond, Philip J. Bialoglowy II, James Harding, Gary Pomeroy, Francis Zubrowski, vacancy.—**Chiefs of Fire Dept.,** John D.Fredsall (East Side), Lincoln Taylor (West Side).—**Fire Marshal,** Daniel Lowe.—**Civil Preparedness Dir.,** Lincoln Taylor.—**Town Attys.,** Guion, Stevens & Ryback.—**Justices of the Peace,** Richard Achee, Janice J. DeNegre, Louis Fasano, Mary-Jane Febbroriello, Patricia M. Goodenough, R. Peter Grady, Richard D. Kelley, Marie M. Knudsen, Russell Manchester, Lawrence J. Mitnick, Thomas T. T. Telman, Peter B. Thierry, Eleanor G. Woike.

HEBRON. Tolland County.—(Form of government, selectmen, town meeting, board of finance.)—Inc., May 26, 1708. Area, 37.3 sq. miles. Population, est., 7,735. Voting district, 1. Principal industry, agriculture. Transp.—Freight: Served by numerous motor common carriers. Post offices, Hebron and Amston; also rural free delivery from Hebron and Amston.

TOWN OFFICERS. Clerk and Reg. of Vital Statistics, Marian Celio; Hours, 8 A.M.-4 P.M., Mon. through Wed.; 8 A.M.-7 P.M., Thurs.; 8 A.M.-12:30 P.M., Fri.; Address, Town Office Bldg., 15 Gilead St., P.O. Box 156, 06248; Tel., (860) 228-9406.—**Asst. Clerk and Asst. Reg. of Vital Statistics,** Evelyn D. Croston.—**Chief**

Adm. Officer, Robert E. Lee.—**Selectmen,** R. William Garrison, Chm. (R) Tel., (860) 228-9406, James Pasqurell, Jr. (R), Randall G. Peteros (R), W. Fred Schott (D), Elaine M. Zavistoski (U).—**Financial Admin.,** Joanne Gyure.—**Bd. of Finance,** John E. Hibbard, Chm., Katherine L. Higgins, Mark W. Houle, John W. Minnick, Robert McKay, Ann R. Stravalle-Schmidt.—**Tax Collector,** James L. Derby, Jr.—**Bd. of Assessment Appeals,** Thomas A. Covill, Chm., Frederick L. Speno, Jr., Robert A. Tilden.—**Assessor,** Robert Musson; Asst., Eula M. Berglund.—**Registrars of Voters,** John O'Sullivan (D), James L. Derby, Jr. (R).—**Supt. of Schools,** F. William Davis.—**Bd. of Education,** Daniel J. Alfieri, Joseph V. Fiumara, Mary Jaglowski, Mary E. Rudewicz, Willard J. Skehan, 1997; Maria McKeon, Chm., Alan M. Finn, Philip B.Mathews, Judith S. Thompson, 1999.—**Planning and Zoning Comm.,** Karen Strid, Chm., Patricia A. Ayars, George W. Cox III, Bob L. Jones, Steven A. Ross; Alternates, Richard T. Julius, Joseph T. Snyder, vacancy.—**Town Planner,** Michael O'Leary.—**Zoning Bd. of Appeals,** Gerald F. Green, Chm., Vincenzo Basile, Patricia K. Bowler, Gail C. McDonnell, Helen Reardon, Kathleen Shapazian; Alternates, Robert S. Schadtle, Cheryl J. Speno, vacancy.—**Economic Development Committee,** Joan Landon, Chm., John Aissis, Kevin Baldwin, Elizabeth Harrison, Lawrence Preston.—**Housing Auth.,** Martha E. Close, Chm., Carleton Czaikowski, Robert H. Jones, Edith Long, Joseph A. Lusky, two vacancies.—**Conservation and Inland Wetlands Agency,** James Cordier, Chm., John Blake, Thomas Brancato, Christopher G. Bush, Sue-Ellen K. Loeser, James H. McClintock, vacancy.—**Town Historian,** Hebron Historical Society.—**Comm. on the Aging,** Margaret Bonelli, Chm., Laura M. Bennett, Evelyn G. Bendel, Maeril Bennington, Maralyn Porter, Don Raymond, Elizabeth J. Schmeizl, Marjorie Simon, Linda Skoglund, two vacancies; Susan Cromie, Municipal Agent.—**Dir. of Health,** Rozann Venti, M.D. (P.O., Amston).—**Parks and Recreation Comm.,** Victoria Avelis, Chm., Gregory M. Cariglia, Donna M. Chandler, Robert Davis, David P. Jackson, Terence J. McGuire III, Brian D.O'Connell, Robert Raiola, two vacancies.—**Building Inspector,** John Barnecki.—**Public Safety Committee,** Robert E. Croston, Sidney Jones, Virginia Peterson, James Waitkus, three vacancies.—**Municipal Bd. of Appeals,** Barry Miller, four vacancies.—**Water Pollution Control Auth.,** Joan M. Rowley, Chm., Lori Granato, Philip J. LoBianco, Helen Sudal, Charles Wallace, Linda P. Wright, vacancy.—**Sanitarian,** Steven Knauf.—**Constables,** William D'Ambrosio, Anthony Fasanelli, Kenneth Gervais, three vacancies.—**Chief of Fire Dept.,** William Horton; Asst. Chief, David Lynch.—**Fire Marshal,** Raymond Griswold.—**Office of Emergency Management,** J. Peter Carbone.—**Town Atty.,** Donald R. Holtman.—**Justices of the Peace,** Margaret Bonelli, Patricia K. Bowler, Beatrice L. Champagne, James P. Cordier, Evelyn D. Croston, Robert E. Croston, James L. Derby, Jr., Norman J. Dorval, Phyllis M. Garrison, Marjory W. Graham, Katherine L. Higgins, John D. Hooker, John J. Hooker, Gary D. Hummel, Richard A. Keefe, Valerie V. LaVake, Salvatore J. Mastandrea, Robert J. McKay, John W. Minnick, Emily Mitchell, Robert E. Owens, Paul L. Pomprowicz, Brenda J. Quinn, Helen K. Reardon, Joseph J. Reardon III, Joseph J. Reardon, Jr., John F. Richmond, Sandra J. Rini, Steven A. Ross, Joan M. Rowley, Kathleen Shapazian, Ann R. Stravalle-Schmidt, Robert N. Warner, Margaret Yetishefsky.

JEWETT CITY.* BOROUGH OFFICERS. 32 School St., Town Hall, Jewett City 06351; Tel., (860) 376-7082.—**Warden,** Donald H. Ouillette.—**Burgesses,** F. Thurston Fields, Richard Kata, Madeline Locas, Dianne Slopak, Patrick Sullivan.—**Clerk,** John E. Hoddy.—**Treas.,** Cynthia Kata.—**Assessor,** Cynthia Kata.—**Bailiff,** Alan Geer.—**Tax Collector,** Virginia Hoddy.—**Dir. of Health,** Albert G. Gosselin, M.D.—**Civil Preparedness Dir.,** Steven Merchant, Jr.—**Chief of Fire Dept.,** Donald Ouillette.

---

*See Town of Griswold.

KENT. Litchfield County.—(Form of government, selectmen, town meeting, board of finance.)—Inc., Oct., 1739. Area, 49.6 sq. miles. Population, est., 3,104. Voting district, 1. Principal industries, agriculture and the manufacture of transformers and electric cloth cutting machines. Site of Bull's Bridge, one of two remaining covered bridges open to vehicular traffic in Conn. Transp.—Freight: Served by numerous motor common carriers. Post offices, Kent and South Kent.

TOWN OFFICERS. Clerk and Reg. of Vital Statistics, Marcia Scholl; Hours, 9 A.M.-12 Noon, 1-4 P.M., Mon. through Fri.; Address, Town Hall, P.O. Box 678, 41 Kent Green Blvd., 06757-0678; Tel., (860) 927-3433.—**Asst. Clerks and Asst. Regs. of Vital Statistics,** Dorothy Osborne, Marjorie A. Vreeland.—**Selectmen,** 1st, Dolores R. Schiesel (D) Tel., (860) 927-4627, Andrew C. Ocif (R), Mary C. Williams (R).—**Treas.,** Jack C. Kinney, Jr.—**Bd. of Finance,** Joan M. Oros, Chm., Stephen M. Davids, Rufus P. deRham, George W. Jacobsen, Jr., James A. Palmer, Jane Soule.—**Tax Collector,** Deborah J. Devaux.—**Bd. of Assessment Appeals,** Karen J. Casey, Chm., Harriet Bernstein, James J. Marden.—**Assessor,** Patricia Braislin.—**Registrars of Voters,** Marjorie H. Wells (D), Judith Howland (R).—**Supt. of Schools,** Marvin Maskovsky.—**Bd. of Education,** Carolyn R. Echols, Norman F. Vandervoort, 1997; Mary Anne Orioles, Chm., Margaret J. Solomon, 1999; Vincent D. LaFontan, Katherine A. Sawyer, 2001.—**Planning and Zoning Comm.,** C. H. Moore, Jr., Chm., Anne C. Bisenius, Margaret A. Callahan, Betsy D. Eaton, Janet E. Gordon, John A. Johnson, Margaret W. McAvoy, Dwight R. Soule, Marjorie A. Vreeland; Alternates, Catherine Bachrach, Barbara H. Lasch, vacancy.—**Zoning Bd. of Appeals,** Virginia Giles, Sherman Green, Richard T. Kent, Cheryl L. McDowell, Margaret G. Rundall; Alternates, John H. Lindsay, Richard P. Novick, Julie Swaner.—**Zoning Enforcement Officer,** Judith Wick.—**Inland Wetland/Conservation Comm.,** Lynn Werner, Chm., Edward F. de Villafranca, Joan M. Larned, William Newton, Patrick Redmond; Alternates, Bruce Carlson, Eric Houston.—**Historic Dist. Comm.,** Marc E. DeVos, Chm., Roger J. Gonzales, Jr., Emily M. Hopson, Jeffrey P. Morgan, Anne P. Todd; Alternates, Christine Hoene, Darrell Lund.—**Agent for the Elderly,** Bernard Lederman; Gen. Asst. Admin., Susan M. Eads.—**Municipal Historian,** Emily Hopson.—**Parks and Recreation Comm.,** John Quirk, Chm., Scott Eldridge, Alan Gawel, Frances A. McCann, Jay F. Strobino; Alternates, Lori-Jo Carlson, Kevin P. McDougal.—**Building Inspector,** William Jenks.—**Town Engineer,** Edward Fabbri—**Sewer Comm.,** Robert H. Bauer, Chm., Timothy M. Casey, Clifford C. Gustafson, Joseph H. MacRitchie, Jonathan W. Moore, Arthur Seabury.—**Sanitarian,** Torrington Area Health Dist.—**Dog Wardens,** Brenda Sheldon, Lee Sohl.—**Tree Warden,** Bruce B. Bennett.—**Lake**

Waramaug Auth., Christopher Allsop, Kevin Brady, Gary Davis.—**Housatonic River Comm.,** Paul Moroz; Alternate, Valerie Jorrin.—**Chief of Police,** Dolores R. Schiesel.—**Chief of Fire Dept.,** Robert Soule.—**Fire Marshal/Open Burning Official,** Stanley MacMillan.—**Civil Preparedness Dir.,** Robert H. Bauer.—**Town Atty.,** Jeffrey Sienkiewicz.—**Justices of the Peace,** Lori-Jo Carlson, Karen A. Chase, Ruth S. Epstein, William C. Gawel, Martha H. Holcombe, Gail O. Leo, Barbara A. Miller, Randy L. Miller, Paul J. Moroz, Joan M. Oros, John Raabe II.

KILLINGLY. Windham County.—(Form of government, town council, town manager, town meeting.)—Inc., May, 1708. Area, 50.0 sq. miles. Population, est., 16,140. Voting districts, 6. Principal industries, molded rubber products, plastic products, surgical supplies, glass containers, molded circuits, transformer board, poron, electrical insulation, computer bus bars, knives, snack foods. Transp.—Passenger: Served by buses of Bonanza Bus Lines, Inc. from Hartford, Willimantic and Providence, RI, and by Greyhound. Freight: Served by Providence & Worcester Railroad Co. and numerous motor common carriers. Post offices, Attawaugan, Danielson, Dayville, Ballouville, East Killingly, Rogers and South Killingly.

TOWN OFFICERS. Clerk and Reg. of Vital Statistics, Joan A. Cyr; Hours, 8:30 A.M.-12 Noon, 1-4:30 P.M., Mon. through Fri.; Address, 172 Main St., 06239; Tel., Danielson, (860) 779-5308.—**Asst. Clerk and Asst. Reg. of Vital Statistics,** Lisa M. Wood.—**Town Manager,** R. Thomas Homan Tel., (860) 779-5335; Asst., Mark A. Skocypec.—**Town Council,** Dist. 1, Philip A. Hoyt, Peter Menounds; Dist. 2, Donald Bernier, John E. Burke, Jr.; Dist. 3, David A. Griffiths, Peter B. Mann; Dist. 4, John Hallbergh, Kevin Hubert; Dist. 5, Raymond F. Parlato.—**Treas.,** Michelle Weiss.— **Tax Collector,** Patricia Monahan.—**Bd. of Assessment Appeals,** Constance B. Bordonaro, Lorraine J. LaGarde, Kevin Reid.—**Assessor,** Melissa Bonin.—**Registrars of Voters,** Rita LaBelle (D), Emily Harrington (R).—**Supt. of Schools,** David A. Cressy.—**Bd. of Education,** Candace Derosier, Susanne Gaudreau, Peggy D. Muscente, Carol Robbins, 1997; Laurie D. LeClerc, Helen K. Lupien, Janice L. Thurlow, Allen R. Tiebout, Jr., Paul J. Trifone, 1999.—**Planning and Zoning Comm.,** Frederick Moffett, Chm., Bradford Gauthier, Eldon Griffiths, Demeter Lakatzis, Jeffrey Dow; Alternates, John Holland, Gail Pratt, vacancy.—**Planning and Development Dir.,** Larry Dunkin.—**Zoning Bd. of Appeals,** Heidi Eddins, Chm., Patrick Garrity, Mitchell Malek, John Shears, Paul Whitehead, Jr.; Alternates, John Labossiere, Jeff Moore, Anselmo Toni.—**Zoning Officer/Planning Asst.,** George Brown.—**Economic Development Comm.,** Ronald Robinson, Chm., Theodor Altdorf, Fred Duda, John Kettelle, Peter Kissa; Elsie Bisset, Coordinator; Alternates, Patrick Donlon, Rozanne Pappas.—**Housing Auth.,** Charles Beauregard, Chm., Alfonzo DePesco, Al Ducat, George Lakatzis; George White, Tenant Comr.—**Municipal Historian,** Margaret Weaver.— **Environmental Planner,** Linda E. Walden.—**Inland Wetlands Comm.,** Sandy Eggers, Chm., Scott Billington, Brian Boldt, John T. Dalton, William Gazzola, Joan Golrick, Carol Ann Violette-Smith; Alternates, Gerald Perry, vacancy.—**Conservation Comm.,** Mark Rollins, Fred Ruhleman, Ellen Smith, Jim Vance, vacancy; Alternates, two vacancies.—**Agent for the Elderly,** George Kesaris.—**Welfare Dir.,** Cheryl Desjardin.—**Parks and Recreation Comm.,** Mervin Whipple, Chm., Marc Allard, Gene

Blain, Leslie Moore, Scott Tetreault; Richard Calarco, Dir.—**Town Engineer,** Patrick Mclaughlin.—**Dir. of Public Works,** vacancy.—**Purchasing Agent,** Mark A. Skocypec.—**Building Inspector,** Alvin Kilburn.—**Building Bd. of Appeals,** Steven Barry, Raymond Brien, Paul Gazzola, John Ludka, vacancy.—**Sewer Auth.,** J. Ann Hamer, R. Howard Smith, Andrew Whitehead.—**Constables,** Richard D. Allen, Conrad J. Bernier, Brian L. Cole, Craig M. Fisk, Thomas Higgins.—**Town Attys.,** Jackson, Harris & Burlingame.—**Justices of the Peace,** Elaine L. Bernier, John E. Burke, Jr., Stephen Burlingame, Sandy Eggers, Gary L. Gendron, David Griffiths, Elizabeth Halstead, Roger Harrington, John Holland, Margaret Holland, Marie L. LaBelle, Cynthia L. Lavigne, Elaine B. Lippke, Roxanne T. Pappas, Eileen F. Parlato, Linda L. Peters, Terry Sandsbury, Janice L. Thurlow, Alan M. Turner, Mervin Whipple.

KILLINGWORTH. Middlesex County.—(Form of government, selectmen, town meeting, board of finance.)—Named, May, 1667. Area, 35.8 sq. miles. Population, est., 5,257. Voting district, 1. Principal industries, agriculture and steel fabricating. Transp.—Freight: Served by numerous motor common carriers. Post office, Killingworth.

TOWN OFFICERS. Clerk and Reg. of Vital Statistics, Susan S. Adinolfo; Hours, 9 A.M.-12 Noon, 1-4 P.M., Mon. through Fri.; Sat. A.M., by appointment; Address, Town Office Bldg., 323 Route 81, 06419; Tel., (860) 663-1616; FAX, (860) 663-3305.—**Asst. Clerk and Asst. Reg. of Vital Statistics,** Linda M. Dudek.—**Selectmen,** 1st, W. David LeVasseur (R) Tel., (860) 663-1765, Louis C. Annino (D), David L. Denvir (R).—**Treas.,** Michael E. McGuinness.—**Bd. of Finance,** Arthur B. Haesche, Jr., Chm., Alfred F. Dudek, Jr., Leslie A. Riblet, Jeffrey J. Usakewicz, Mark F. Williams, Virginia Wohlstrom.—**Tax Collector,** Ruth Patrick.—**Bd. of Assessment Appeals,** Richard B. Blythe, John D. Mashia, A. Edward Winkler.—**Assessor,** Donna E. Shanoff.—**Registrars of Voters,** Linda A. Gates (D), Pauline J. Lally (R).—**Supt. of Schools,** Charles F. Sweetman.—**Planning and Zoning Comm.,** Charles E. Martens, Jr., Chm., Louis C. Annino, Jr., Richard M. Darin, Suzanne Davenport, Thomas L. Lentz, John R. Speicher; Alternates, I. Joseph Armenia, Larry G. Gilliam, Edward F. Hayash, Jr.—**Zoning Bd. of Appeals,** Bruce E. Dodson, Chm., Rebecca M. Albrecht, Eric W. Auer, William M. Leahy, Edward J. Sipples; Alternates, Cindy Lou Adametz, Pamela M. Ahearn, Nancy Usakewicz.—**Zoning Enforcement Officer,** Cathie Jefferson.—**Conservation Comm.,** Patricia Smulders, Chm., Andrew Annino, Deborah Butler, Virginia A. Lane, Franklyn B. Matthies, Andrea Schull.—**Inland Wetlands Comm.,** Wayne W. Addy, Chm., Roy P. Alexander, Gaylord Rockwell, Derrick R. Schull, Robert T. Tanko, Wendy K. Welter, vacancy.—**Area Agency Dept. on Aging,** Marilyn U. Skipton.—**Municipal Agent to the Aging,** David A. Tuckerman; Asst., Elizabeth B. Tuckerman.—**Dir. of Social Services,** Anne Twarowski.—**Dir. of Health,** Arnold C. Winokur, M.D.—**Public Health Agency,** Joanna L. Boccia, Chm., Carolann F. Annino, Louis C. Annino, Sr., Cynthia B. Croce, Ann LeVasseur, Elaine B. Polson, Kathryn D. Weiss, Catherine Wonneberger, three vacancies.—**Municipal Historian,** Sandra E. Smith.—**Recreation Bd.,** Robert H. Burley, Mark S. Harwood, Stephen A. Hollander, Brian S. Kochan, Erin E. Leahy, Edward J. Sipples, vacancy.—**Town Engineer,** vacancy.—**Building Inspector,** Richard E. Leighton.—**Water Pol-**

lution Control Auth., Peggy Ann Wallace, Chm., Fie Budzinsky, Barbara W. Klein, Chris A. Lundberg, Charles F. Wonnenberger, Jr.—**Sanitarian,** Richard E. Leighton.—**Tree Warden,** Harold L. Pope.—**Chief of Police,** W. David LeVasseur.—**Special Constable,** Walter G. Albrecht.—**Chief of Fire Dept.,** Alfred F. Dudek; Deputy, Brian M. Ahearn.—**Fire Marshal,** Raynor W. Clark.—**Bd. of Fire Comrs.,** Francis A. Dooley, Michael J. Wallace.—**Emergency Mgmt. Dir.,** Alan T. Chapman; Deputies, Donald McDougall, Robert G. Sawyer, Eugene S. Slota.—**Town Atty.,** William Howard.—**Justices of the Peace,** Rebecca M. Albrecht, Michael J. Butler, R. Richard Croce, John D. Henderson, Joyce Hirschhorn, Barbara W. Klein, Jack R. Kneale, W. David LeVasseur, J. Morann, Susan G. Otto, Patricia Smulders, Mark F. Williams.

LEBANON. New London County.—(Form of government, selectmen, town meeting, board of finance.)—Inc., Oct., 1700. Area, 55.2 sq. miles. Population, est., 6,327. Voting districts, 2. Principal industry, agriculture. Transp.—Freight: Served by Central Vermont Railway and numerous motor common carriers. Post office, Lebanon.

TOWN OFFICERS. Clerk and Reg. of Vital Statistics, Joyce A. McGillicuddy; Hours, 9 A.M.-4 P.M., Mon., Tues., Fri.; 9 A.M.-7 P.M., Thurs., Address, Town Hall, 579 Exeter Rd., 06249; Tel., (860) 642-7319.—**Asst. Clerk and Asst. Reg. of Vital Statistics,** Judith A. Smith.—**Selectmen,** 1st, Joyce R. Okonuk (D) Tel., (860) 642-6100, Donald C. Johnson (R), Robert A. Leone (D).—**Treas.,** James Forrest.—**Bd. of Finance,** Ronald E. Bender, Chm., Pierre A. Belisle, Kathy S. Dziadosz, Cornelius V. Shea, Robert M. Slate, Timothy H. Wentworth; Alternates, Russell G. Blakeslee, Richard P. Kane, Charles T. Pogmore.—**Tax Collector,** Joyce A. Hofmann.—**Bd. of Assessment Appeals,** T. Allan Palmer, Chm., Patrick B. Mullarney, Mary E. Webb.—**Assessors,** John E. Bass, Jr., Patricia G. Hedwall, Richard A. Schleicher, vacancy.—**Registrars of Voters,** Mary Beth Yarmac (D), Carol A. Milvae (R).—**Supt. of Schools,** James McKenna.—**Bd. of Education,** Robert M. Gentes, Chm., Judy E. Pflum, Timothy A. Smith, 1997; James E. Blake, Jr., Alvin H. Macke, Betsy E. Petrie, 1999; Peter R. Kline, Margaret T. McCaw, Sandra J. Tremblay, 2001.—**Planning and Zoning Comm.,** Harold Liebman, Chm., Berthier R. Bosse, Robin A. Chesmer, Alan F. Lamb, Raymond J. Manning, Michael D. Procter, Robert G. Williams; Alternates, David M. Geligoff, Barbara A. Griffin, Gregory R. Jones.—**Zoning Bd. of Appeals,** N. Alicia Wayland, Chm., Norman P. Bessette, Mark C. Favrow, Theodore E. Littlefield, Gilbert M. Risley; Alternates, Ellen MacAuley, James W. Megson, Donald Williams.—**Inland Wetlands Comm.,** James E. McCaw, Chm., John Drum, Dean Gustafson, James Hallene, Dennis Hanczar, Robert M. Slate, Robert H. Wentworth.—**Flood and Erosion Control Bd.,** Harold Liebman, Chm., Carlton Hathaway, John Meli, Michael Melville, A. Timothy Smith; Alternates, Joyce Okonuk, two vacancies.—**Economic Development and Industrial Comm.,** Mary Holt, Chm., Robert Korten, John McShea, Edward Schernau.—**Solid Waste Comm.,** Raymond Yarmac, Chm., Leo Bibeau, Robert Leone, Ronald Lyman, Cheryl Wheaton, Robert Wilder, vacancy; Alternates, Richard Patton, Michael Wallace.—**Comm. on Aging,** Geraldine E. McCaw, Chm., Evelyn Buckley, Jane Cady, Susan Cone, Sharon Ledbetter, Theodore E. Littlefield, George Randall, Marion Russo.—**Municipal Agent on Aging,**

Priscilla Donnelly.—**Municipal Agent for Children,** Bonlyn L. Craig.—**Dir. of Health,** Ralph LaGuardia, M.D. (P.O., Willimantic).—**Library Directors,** Susan H. Kane, Chm., Christine R. Bendoraitis, Julie M. Culp, Linda G. Heatherly, Helen F. Krause, Marjorie A. Page, Lynn S. Russo, Joan Russoniello-Goba, Barbara J. Wengloski, vacancy.—**Recreation Comm.,** David Stygar, Chm., Brian F. Edwards, Joseph Halbardier, Margaret Lageman, Sandra Lambert, Christine Nieminen, James Worth.—**Building Inspector,** Peter Zvingilas.—**Building Code Bd. of Appeals,** Jeffrey A. Anderson, Harold A. Krause, Harold A. Wilhelm.—**Tree Warden,** Joan Nichols.—**Constables,** Diane Dolan, Brice F. Padewski, Rusell Pouliot, George S. Smith, Basil P. Spedaliere, Robert Uccello, Thomas A. Winspear, George Winters.—**Chief of Fire Dept.,** Robert L. Cady; Deputies, Robert L. Cady, Jr., Raymond Voght III.—**Chief of Police/Civil Preparedness Dir.,** Joyce R. Okonuk.—**Town Atty.,** Mary Driscoll.—**Justices of the Peace,** Loretta K. Anderson, Mary P. Anderson, Raymond F. Andrews, Rudolph Antonios, Ellen L. Bauwens, Richard R. Bauwens, Pierre A. Belisle, Edward M. Bender, Berthier R. Bosse, Bernyce M. Brennan, Sandra L. Chalifoux, Maris B. Cornell, John A. Cwikla, Ronald L. Davis, Sr., Lucia L. Day, Kenyon D. Gardner, Robert M. Gentes, Philip J. Godeck, Sr., Robert F. Gregory, Walter Jakoboski, Helen F. Krause, Ronald E. Lake, Kenneth H. Lathrop, Bonnie L. LeBlanc, Robert A. Leone, Helen M. Littlefield, E. Marilyn Lowney, Jeremiah Lowney, Joyce A. McGillicuddy, Patricia McKelvey, Rose A. Miller, Raymond S. Milvae, Joyce R. Okonuk, Wayne L. Page, T. Allan Palmer, Nancy A. R. Schweitzer, William T. Wadsworth, Karen A. K. Wax, Robert H. Wentworth.

LEDYARD. New London County.—(Form of government, mayor, town council.)—Inc., June, 1836; taken from Groton. Area, 40.0 sq. miles. Population, est., 14,661. Voting districts, 2. Principal industries, manufacture of chemicals, plastics, concrete and light sheet metal work, indian casino, orchards and nurseries. Rural residential community. Transp.—Freight: Served by Providence & Worcester Co. and numerous motor common carriers. Railway Express Agency and air freight out of Groton/New London Airport, Groton. Post offices, Gales Ferry, rural routes 1, 3, 5, and 8; Ledyard, rural routes 2, 4, 6, and 7; Mystic, R.F.D. 1.

TOWN OFFICERS. Clerk and Reg. of Vital Statistics, Patricia Karns; Hours, 8:30 A.M.-4:30 P.M., Mon. through Fri.; Address, Town Hall, 741 Col. Ledyard Hwy., P.O. Box 38, 06339; Tel., (860) 464-8740, Ext. 229.—**Asst. Clerks and Asst. Regs. of Vital Statistics,** Calvin K. Brouwer, L. Marie Dambach, Dorothy T. Tedeschi.—**Mayor,** Wesley J. Johnson, Sr. (D) Tel., (860) 464-8740, Ext. 222.—**Town Council,** Susan S. Anderson, Cynthia Brewster, Andy Depta, Terry Jones, Richard C. Lightle, Susan Mendenhall, John A. Rodolico, Christopher R. Ruest, Sharon L. Wadecki.—**Treas.,** Nancy Gosslin.—**Tax Collector,** Yvonne Bell.—**Bd. of Assessment Appeals,** Charles Gerke, Robert E. Holman, Stanley Juber.—**Assessor,** Anna M. Reiners.—**Registrars of Voters,** Hazel M. Gorman (D), Lucille DeShong (R).—**Supt. of Schools,** John H. Gillespie.—**Bd. of Education,** Peter W. Champagne, Laurie P. Fratoni, Charles J. Merlo, Jann Nielsen, Thomas C. Reynolds, Robert E. Simpson, Kathleen P. Troyanowski, 1997.—**Planning Comm.,** Elaine M. Bono, Chm., Mary DiGiacomo-Cohen, Robert Grenger, B. Kenneth Koe, J. Mark Venable; Alternates,

Richard Gill, Bill O'Reilly, vacancy.—**Town Planner,** William R. Haase IV.—**Zoning Comm.,** William E. Geer, Chm., Arthur Farago, James T. Mandeville, Louis Rose, Eric Treaster; Alternates, Kenneth Blomstedt, Richard Cerini, Thomas Staigers.—**Zoning Bd. of Appeals,** James L. Mathews, Chm., Fred B. Allyn, Jr., Vincent D. Godino, Allan H. Huhtala, Richard D. Tashea; Alternates, Beatrice Mortensen, John K. Proctor, Stuart N. Uschmann.—**Zoning Enforcement Officer,** Lee Treadway.—**Economic Development Comm.,** Glen N. Arthur, Robert D. Bajorin, Phillip DeRose, Robert Lighton, David Schlecter, Robert Simpson, Richard Smith.—**Housing Auth.,** Anthony Attanasio, Marjorie Brown, George Dieter, Ruth B. Dyer, Arthur Farago.—**Conservation Comm.,** Gordon W. Thomson, Chm., David Foltz, Edmund Lamb II, Daniel P. Panosky, Harry O. Tobiassen, Lisa Wahle, Walter G. Wanamaker III.—**Inland, Wetlands and Watercourses Comm.,** Lynn Marie R. Thompson, William A. Birtcher, Conrad C. Gardner, Robert D. Geer, Adele D. Gorham, Henry Morgan, James R. Roediger, Leland Wilmonen, vacancy.—**Historic Dist. Comm.,** James F. Bowersett, Chm., Janice W. Bell, John Dirlam, William D. Fossum, Sheila Godino; Alternates, Anne G. King, Lance Mayers, Margaret Wilson.—**Permanent Comm. for Senior Citizens,** Vern Brasel, Lillian M. Davis, George Dieter, Ruth P. French, C. J. Garrett, Stuart Murray, Frances Ohler, Helen Scheiber, vacancy.—**Agent for the Elderly,** Edith Dyer.—**Dir. of Social Services,** Eileen King.—**Dir. of Health,** Peter J. Gates, M.D.—**Bd. of Public Health Nursing Service,** Diane Carberry, Chm., Kathy Arbuckle, Vickie A. Barker, Noreen Beaudoin, Nancy Brewer, Thomas Cregeur, Georgia Dunterman, Sandi-Wood Eilenberger, Diane Geer, Annette Guillet, Laurie Gwin, Viola Leonard, Barbara Miller, Jean Nash, Kyle Parkinson, Lorraine Simmons, Deborah Skoglund, Joseph Smey, Laura Wiemann.—**Library Comm.,** William Michaud, Jr., Frank Murray, Patricia Nielsen, Mary Ellen Osborne, Charlotte Sanford, Jean Scialabba, Sandra Seaton, Mary Stuart, Deborah Vessells.—**Municipal Historian,** Janice W. Bell.—**Parks and Recreation Comm.,** John D. Purdy, Chm., Sondra Deeds, Pasquale DeMuria, Melinda Dowsett, Charles R. Esposito, Carol S. Gauthier, Marie Holman, Michelle Leighton, Jane Perry.—**Dir. of Public Works,** Wesley Johnson, Sr.—**Supt. of Highways/Tree Warden,** James Martin.—**Town Engineer,** Steven Masalin.—**Finance Dir.,** Anna Johnson.—**Building Inspector/Sanitarian,** Randy Dalton.—**Building Code Bd. of Appeals,** Wayne Chiapperini, Chm., William L. Ballestrini, Ernest A. Maynard, Jr., Hubert G. Sokolski, Gabriel Stern.—**Water Pollution Control Auth.,** Julien Lupienski, Chm., Greg Bixby, Donald A. Cameron, Lionel S. Harvey, Andrew J. Stackpole, Larry Williamson; Advisory Members, Cynthia Cross, Eugene Jambor, vacancy.—**Chief of Police,** Wesley Johnson, Sr.—**Constables,** Wilfred J. Blanchette III, Joseph B. Burdick, Sr., John M. Craig, Michael T. Finkelstein, Carl F. Fowler, Daniel Gagnon, Craig Getter, John Gorman, James A. Grzesiak, David R. Guiher, Troy C. Johnson, Alfred L. LaMarche, Robert E. Orzechowski, Richard J. Pasqualini, Jr., Scott Petersen, Larry Pudvah, Michael J. Ravenelle, Elizabeth B. Smith.—**Resident Trooper,** William Griffin.—**Chiefs of Fire Dept.,** 1st Dist., George Chapman; Deputy, William Waterhouse; 2nd Dist., Sean McGuckin; Deputy, Michael LaFlamme.—**Fire Marshal,** Randy Blais; Deputy, Donald H. Casavant.—**Dir. of Civil Preparedness,** Robert Heal.—**Town Atty.,** Thomas B. Wilson, Jr.—**Justices of the Peace,** Tony Attanasio, G. Standish Beebe, Robert G. Brown, Thomas A. Dreimiller, Walter G. Eichler, Jr., Lois A. Gardner, Jospeh R. Grills, William R. Haase IV, Paul

O. Holdridge, Jr., Wesley J. Johnson, Sr., Barbara E. Jones, Stanley C. Juber, Peter G. Kallan, B. Kenneth Koe, Jack McGee, Mary K. McGrattan, Jane E. Perry, Ernest V. Plantz, Eleanora M. Quin, Robert R. Smith, Richard D. Tashea, Jerry V. Tobias, Kenneth C. Tucker, Spiros Vitouladitis, Sharon L. Wadecki.

LISBON. New London County.—(Form of government, selectmen, town meeting, board of finance.)—Inc., May, 1786; taken from Norwich. Area, 16.6 sq. miles. Population, est., 3,876. Voting districts, 2. Principal industry, agriculture. Transp.—Freight: Served by Providence & Worcester Railroad Co. and numerous motor common carriers. Post office, Jewett City. Rural free delivery Route 2 and 3 from Jewett City supplies mail facilities for a great part of the town. The northern portion of the town receives its mail from Canterbury, the eastern portion from Jewett City, and the western portion from Versailles and Baltic.

TOWN OFFICERS. Clerk and Reg. of Vital Statistics, Betsy M. Barrett; Hours, 9 A.M.-4 P.M., Mon., Tues., Thurs.; 9 A.M.-4 P.M., 6-8 P.M., Wed.; 9 A.M.-2 P.M., Fri.; 9 A.M.-12 Noon, Sat.; Address, Town Office Bldg., 1 Newent Rd., 06351; Tel., Jewett City, (860) 376-2708.—**Asst. Clerk and Asst. Reg. of Vital Statistics,** Ann E. Leffler.—**Selectmen,** 1st, James M. Wright (R) Tel., (860) 376-3400, Albert G. Gosselin (R), Jeremiah A. Shea (D).—**Treas.,** Nancy R. Gosselin.—**Bd. of Finance,** Audrey Babbitt, Chm., Steven M. Beck, Michelle Joly, Felix Prokop III, Thomas W. Sparkman, Stephen S. Woodruff; Alternates, Stephen Barrett, Donald J. Grant, Daniel W. Teper.—**Tax Collector,** Gail Izbicki.—**Bd. of Assessment Appeals,** Robert D. Adams, Maurice Rocheleau, Joanne A. Wright.—**Assessor,** Susan Rainville.—**Registrars of Voters,** Ivy Mather (D), Mary Grant (R).—**Bd. of Education,** Gilbert Milone, Chm., John G. Acosta, Randall Baah, Paul A. Messier, 1997; Barbara Glenney, Tricia Maynard, Timothy J. Teper, 1999; Arthur J. LaBrie III, vacancy, 2001.—**Planning and Zoning Comm.,** Frans Eyberse, Chm., Robert D. Adams, Lawrence Alice, William Belisle III, William. L. Kuusela, Dennis R. Savage, Frank Sofia, Joseph A. Turano, Raymond R. Yorz; Alternates, Joseph Cormier, Felix Prokop III, Nathan Wise.—**Zoning Bd. of Appeals,** Ronald Babbitt, Chm., Robert Chubka, Regina E. DeMay, Sharon R. Gabiga, vacancy; Alternates, B. Estelle Houle, Laura Gosselin, Thomas Sparkman.—**Conservation and Inland Wetlands Comm.,** Hans Kvist, Chm., Robert Dempsky, Charles Mares, Mark Sullivan, Leonora J. Szruba.—**Agent for the Elderly,** vacancy.—**Comm. on Aging,** Ivy Mather, Chm., Kathy Beck, Edwin Brown, Barbara Burzycki, Joseph Cormier, Laura Gosselin, Mary Grant, Judy Jencks, Colleen Williams.—**Dir. of Health,** Albert G. Gosselin, M.D.—**Municipal Historian,** Richard Herrmann.—**Recreation Committee,** Paula Adams, Randall Baah, Robert Browne, Kim Campbell, Traci Gwiazdowski, Francis Houle, Jr., Gail Izbicki, Daniel Ostrowski, Marguerite Phillips.—**Tree Warden,** vacancy.—**Building Inspector,** Rex Champany.—**Sanitarian,** Albert Gosselin, Jr.—**Acting Chief of Police,** James M. Wright.—**Constables,** Robert P. Chubka, Walter L. Geer, Roger Hamel, John H. Mather, Robert A. Murphy.—**Chief of Fire Dept.,** Richard Hamel.—**Fire Marshal,** John Pellett.—**Civil Preparedness Dir.,** Robert Murphy.—**Town Atty.,** James Kirker.—**Justices of the Peace,** Geraldine M. Brickey, Estelle B. Houle, Burton R.

Jernstrom, Arthur R. Mellor, Terry Nash, Richard R. Pepin, Susan Rainville, Leonora Szruba, Alvina B. Williams, Victoria Yorz.

LITCHFIELD.
Litchfield County.—(Form of government, selectmen, town meeting, board of finance.)—Inc., May, 1719. Area, 56.8 sq. miles. Population, est., 8,584. Voting districts, 4. Principal industry, agriculture. The town is a well known summer resort. Transp.—Passenger: Served by buses of the Kelly Transit Co., Inc. from Torrington and New Milford. Freight: Served by Boston & Maine Corporation and numerous motor common carriers. Post offices, Litchfield and Bantam. Five R.F.D. routes.

TOWN OFFICERS. Clerk and Reg. of Vital Statistics, Evelyn N. Goodwin; Hours, 9 A.M.-4:30 P.M., Mon. through Fri.; Address, Town Office Bldg., 74 West St., P.O. Box 488, 06759; Tel., (860) 567-7561.—**Asst. Clerk and Asst. Reg. of Vital Statistics,** Phyllis N. Bunnell.—**Sub Reg. of Vital Statistics,** Bradford H. Rowe.—**Selectmen,** 1st, Craig A. Miner (R) Tel., (860) 567-7550, Audrey B. Blondin (D), James B. Crampton (R), Edward L. Olcese (D), Jerry R. Zinn (R).—**Treas.,** David T. Wilson.—**Bd. of Finance,** Joseph Hill, Chm., Mark A. Beebe, Helen R. Bunnell, Richard F. Dauphinais, Jeffrey A. French, Albert Harnicar.—**Tax Collector,** Nancy W. Southard.—**Bd. of Assessment Appeals,** Ernest C. Bunnell, Chm., Joseph A. Cushing, Harold J. Fairchild.—**Assessor,** Harold Ducey.—**Registrars of Voters,** 1st Dist., Janet E. Katzin, 2nd Dist., June Anderson, 3rd Dist., Martha Dauphinais, 4th Dist., Joanne L. Bertrand (D); 1st Dist., Carolyn F. Baldwin, 2nd Dist., Barbara A. Padella, 3rd Dist., Carol H. Goslee, 4th Dist., Jean F. Erickson (R).—**Supt. of Schools,** Robert Lindgren.—**Bd. of Education,** Brenda B. Pickert, Chm., Thomas F. Hogan, Celinda W. Lester, 1997; Diane V. Knox, Sharon W. McCoy, Paul D. Sapiro, 1999; James D. Cleminshaw, James L. Katzin, Stephanie Tinfo, 2001.—**Planning and Zoning Comm.,** Anne Talcott, Chm., Carol G. Bramley, William V. Fogarty, Nancy Goldring, Thomas V. Griffin, Eleanordawn R. Hughes, William L. Wilson; Alternates, Laura T. Cleminshaw, Katherine Davis, vacancy.—**Zoning Bd. of Appeals,** Joseph M. McDevitt, Chm., James F. Burke, Jr., Allyn H. Claman, Marybeth Dunning, Robert Frank; Alternates, Andrew Ide, Brian McKernan, Grayce Rogers.—**Land Use/Zoning Enforcement Dir.,** Martin J. Connor.—**Housing Auth.,** Harold Colvocoresses, Chm., Lillian B. Merrill, Frederick Minck, Peter Zajac; Helen Fitch, Exec. Dir.—**Conservation and Inland Wetlands Comm.,** Edward S. Lancaster, Jr., Chm., Barbara Brower, Lynda Hallock, Susan Kennedy, Robert Miller, Frederick Minck, Arthur B. Webster, Jr.—**Milton Historic Dist. Comm.,** Edward Weik, Chm., Webster Janssen, Paul Laird, John Winter; Alternates, Robert V. Fischer.—**Municipal Historian,** Arthur W. Lindh.—**Committee on Aging,** Wilma Hubbard, Chm., Joseph Frascarelli, Doris Lynch, John Ravenscroft, vacancy.—**Social Services Bd.,** Nancy Amrich, John Donohue, Doris Kinder; Jana Engle, Agent.—**Dir. of Health,** James K. Rokos (P.O., Torrington).—**Park and Recreation Comm.,** Roy Conklin, Chm., Roberta Andrulis, Elisa Bauer, Sharon Kiely, Steve McDonald, Virginia Mortora, Leo Normandin, Deborah A. Schaaf; Frank Simone, Michael J. Gallagher, Coordinator.—**Public Works Dir.,** Lawrence M. Clough; Gerald Hollins, Supvr.—**Building Inspector,** John T. Worthington.—**Water Pollution Control Authority,** James Crampton, Chm., Richard

Brennan, William Buckley, James Koser, David R. Wilson; Alternates, Thomas Hubbard, Clifford Schmidt.—**Bantam Lake Auth.,** Thomas Weik, Chm., Ross B. Adkins, Matthew Blondin, C. Dallett Hoopes.—**Tree Warden,** vacancy.—**Chief of Police,** Craig A. Miner.—**Chiefs of Fire Dept.,** Litchfield: Thomas F. Rogers; Bantam: Scott Parsons; East Litchfield: Timothy Valuckas; Northfield: Robert F. Johnson.—**Fire Marshals,** Litchfield: Richard T. Healy; Bantam: Fletcher Cooper; East Litchfield: Richard T. Healy; Northfield: Ethan Walker, Jr.—**Bd. of Fire Comrs.,** John Campbell, Chm., Lance Abbott, Ernest Bunnell, Edward Olcese, John Walker.—**Civil Preparedness Dir./Energy Coordinator,** vacancy.—**Town Atty.,** Stephen Allaire.—**Justices of the Peace,** Carolyn F. Baldwin, Audrey B. Blondin, Sandra G. Carpenter, Karen L. Crimmins, Joseph A. Cushing, Marybeth W. Dunning, Robert L. Fisher, Jr., Eleanordawn R. Hughes, Robert F. Johnson, John G. Maches, James B. Noel, Barbara W. Paradise, Paul M. Rosenberg, Victoria B. Sansing, Marie H. Wallace.

BOROUGH OFFICERS. P.O. Box 913, c/o Clerk, 06759; Tel., (860) 567-8866.—**Warden** Susan A. Levine.—**Burgesses,** Oren K. Boynton Marybeth W. Dunning, Charles Finnegan, Peter Gay, Jane B. Hinkel, Thomas W. Witherspoon.—**Clerk,** Wendy Huff.—**Treas.** Wendy Huff.—**Assessor,** Margaret Noel.—**Borough Tax Collector,** Jeannine M. Cooper.—**Historic Dist. Comm.,** John Hula, Chm., Oren K. Boynton, Jean F. Nelson, James Sansing; Alternates, Dennis Belancik, Gail Galloway, Nan Heminway; Priscilla J. Lamond.

LYME. New London County.—(Form of government, selectmen, town meeting, board of finance.)—Named, May, 1667; set off from Saybrook, now Deep River, in 1665. Area, 34.5 sq. miles. Population, est., 1,969. Voting district, 1. Principal industries, agriculture, boat yards and dairying. Fine harbor. Many summer homes. Transp.—Freight: Served by numerous motor common carriers. Post office, Hadlyme; rural free delivery from Old Lyme post office, Routes 2, 3, and 4.

TOWN OFFICERS. Clerk and Reg. of Vital Statistics, Ruth N. Perry; Hours, 9 A.M.-4 P.M., Mon. through Fri.; Address, Town Hall, 480 Hamburg Rd., 06371; Tel., (860) 434-7733.—**Asst. Clerks and Asst. Regs. of Vital Statistics,** Barbara Gustafson, Linda Winzer.—**Selectmen,** 1st, Ralph F. Eno, Jr. (R) Tel., (860) 434-7733, Chauncey H. Eno (R), Thomas J. Mastrianna (D).—**Treas.,** William L. Hawthorne.—**Bd. of Finance,** Gary H. Reynolds, Chm., Carolyn Bacdayan, Nancy Ballek, Gerald O. Dahlke, Judith Duran, John E. Friday, Jr.; Alternates, Steven E. Mattson, John J. Tiffany II, vacancy.—**Tax Collector,** Julia H. Smith.—**Bd. of Assessment Appeals,** Harry P. Broom, Robert Petitt, Peter J. Stelzner.—**Assessors,** Chm., Diana L. Rord, Fredrick Platt, Geraldine P. Ryba.—**Registrars of Voters,** Nancy L. Roche (D), Richard Gustafson (R).—**Supt. of Schools,** Jefferson Prestridge.—**Planning and Zoning Comm.,** Virginia C. Bladen, William T. Koch, Kevin C. Mazer, Leray L. McFarland, David Tiffany, Kelvin Tyler, Robert Winslow.—**Zoning Bd. of Appeals,** Rufus Barringer, Chm., Steven E. Mattson, Ron Philips, Jeanne C. Rutigilano, S. Spencer Scott; Alternates, Eleanor H. Hilsman, Joseph Rhodes III, Richard Yeomans.—**Zoning Enforcement Officer,** Frank Skwarek.—**Conservation and Inland Wetlands Comm.,**

Donald Gerber, Chm., Susan Cole, Roger Dill, Anthony Irving, Frederick Platt, Robert Schneider, Anthony Thurston, Cynthia Willauer, Thomas Wing.—**Agent for the Elderly,** Eleanor O'Connell.—**Dir. of Social Services,** Linda Winzer.—**Dir. of Health,** David Thompson, M.D.—**Library Directors,** Mary L. Catherwood, Marta F. Cone, Eleanor H. Hilsman, Pauline C. Knoll, Judith Lightfoot, David Payne, Jean Rutigliano, Felix T. Trommer, George Willauerm.—**Municipal Historian,** Hiram Maxim III.—**Recreation Comm.,** Rick Hindman, Chm., Jeff Howe, Jean Latham, Tracey Naumowitz, Charlene Negrelli, William Robinson, Tomas Wing.—**Building Inspector,** Ronald Rose.—**Building Code Bd. of Appeals,** Roger Haser, Chm., Roger F. Mayotte, Francis M. Roche, Francis Ross, Roland Wright.—**Water Pollution Control Auth.,** David Cook, Carter Courtney, Melvin Woody.—**Rogers Lake Auth.,** Fredrik D. Holth, Alan Kyle, Robert F. Roach.—**Sanitarian,** George P. Calkins.—**Constables,** James C. Beers, Frederick Bliven, John M. King.—**Chief of Fire Dept.,** Ronald Rose.—**Fire Marshal,** Philip Bliss.—**Civil Preparedness Dir.,** Edward Tanguay.—**Town Atty.,** J. Averum Sprecher (P.O., East Haddam).—**Justices of the Peace,** Charlotte E. Beers, James W. Calkins, John S. Drahan, Thomas J. Mastrianna, Ronald E. Phillips, Gary H. Reynolds, Julia H. Smith, Jack F. Sulger, Jr., Eleanor B. Sutton, Audrey R. Wayland.

MADISON. New Haven County.—(Form of government, selectmen, town meeting, board of finance.)—Inc., May, 1826, taken from Guilford. Area, 36.8 sq. miles. Population, est., 16,155. Voting districts, 2. Transp.—Passenger: Served by buses of Conn. Transit from New Haven, and by Dattco Bus Line. Freight: Served by Shoreline East and Amtrak. Post office, Madison.

TOWN OFFICERS. Acting Clerk and Reg. of Vital Statistics, Ruth F. Harris; Hours, 8:30 A.M.-4 P.M., Mon. through Fri.; Address, Madison Town Campus, 8 Campus Dr., 06443; Tel., (860) 245-5672.—**Asst. Clerk and Asst. Reg. of Vital Statistics,** Dorothy C. Bean.—**Selectmen,** 1st, Thomas R. Rylander (R) Tel., (860) 245-5602, Debra D. Carney (D), Charles L. Cottrell (R), Jeremiah J. Kleutsch (D), Peter R. Pardo (R).—**Bd. of Finance,** Mary Jo Walker, Chm., John F. Beckert, James R. Deephouse, Bill Kobernusz, Donald F. Snow, Jr., Carol L. Speer.—**Tax Collector,** Alma D. Carroll.—**Bd. of Assessment Appeals,** Craig A. Bernard, Charles T. Felder, Neal M. Glaser, Lee M. Harris, Albert C. Sweet.—**Assessor,** Patricia G. Hedwall.—**Registrars of Voters,** James A. Shanley, Jr. (D), Rosalie Maco (R).—**Supt. of Schools,** H. Kaye Griffin.—**Bd. of Education,** Virginia L. Coniff, Susan P. Greaves, Michael P. Isenberg, Chm., Helen B. Regan, vacancy, 1997; Carl R. Iberger, Peter K. Manko, Ronald J. Piombino, Thomas D. Stewart, 1999.—**Planning and Zoning Comm.,** William Bilcheck, Jr., Chm., Vincent Barese, Richard M. Boutilier, Mitchell H. Cohan, John Dean, Robert P. Keim, Garry Leonard, Terrence W. Macy, Robert Rawson.—**Zoning Bd. of Appeals,** Michael A. Haynes, Henry C. Maguire, Jr., Joel Marcus, Catherine M. Nelli, Jay S. C. Wallace; Alternates, Robert D. Auerbach, John F. O'Brien, Jr., Phillip Zuckerman.—**Zoning Enforcement Officer,** William H. McMinn.—**Economic Development Comm.,** Rob Keating, Chm., Irving L. Drabkin, John Herman, Vickie C. Little, Christine Poutot, Judith Stigle, Stanley Ulsh.—**Inland Wetlands Agency,** John Mathieu, Chm., Tia M. Blevins, William A. Boyd, Glenn W.

Falk, David C. Newton, A. Gordon Peterkin, Robert Sonnichsen; Alternates, Rita C. Ryder, John Stoddard, vacancy.—**Flood and Erosion Control Bd.,** David L. Childs, James Keane, Eugene Langan, Christopher D. Stemen.—**Municipal Historian,** Frances M. Donnelly.—**Agent for the Elderly,** Mary Smith.—**Dir. of Social Services,** Barbara Closter.—**Dir. of Health,** John Bowers; Advisor, Ross Sayers, M.D.—**Beach and Recreation Comm.,** Noreen S. Kokoruda, Chm., O. Preston Lowrey, Jr., Flannigan Smith, Deidre Stimpson, Scott Zimmerman.—**Dir. of Public Works/Town Engineer,** D. Stewart MacMillan, Jr.—**Building Inspector,** Alfred Astorino.—**Building Code Appeals Bd.,** Benson Werthan, Chm., Alfred Halliwell, Jr., John A. Matthews, Michael Riccuiti.—**Water Pollution Control Auth.,** Robert Cerosky, Chm., Bedford Byron, Roberta Gould, David LaFemina.—**Shell Fish Comm.,** Michael Eisele, John J. Gould, Merton W. McAvoy, Jr., Michael Moran, Stephen Pynn.—**Sanitarian,** John Bowers.—**Tree Warden,** Nicholas Williams.—**Chief of Police,** James Cameron.—**Police Comm.,** James Mitchell, Chm., Edward J. Farrell, Jr., Paul R. Grabowski, June D. Hearrell, Dale W. Sweitzer.—**Chiefs of Fire Dept.,** Charles Daricek (Madison), Marshall Bontempo (No. Madison).—**Fire Marshal,** Sheldon Inkster.—**Civil Preparedness Dir.,** Gary H. Reynolds.—**Town Atty.,** Richard J. Beatty.—**Justices of the Peace,** Vincent Barese, John A. Clizbe, Mitchell H. Cohan, Herman E. D'Atri, Geraldine W. Dearington, Marie G. Duke, H. George Greim, Edward R. Guenther, Eugene E. Langan, Timothy M. Loughlin, Peter K. Manko, Barbara B. Mantilia, James D. Rode, Preston E. Smith, William O. Sheridan.

MANCHESTER. Hartford County.—(Form of government, general manager, bd. of directors.)—Inc., May, 1823; taken from East Hartford. Area, 27.7 sq. miles. Population, est., 51,210. Voting districts, 12. Principal industries, engineered fibers, steel metal fabrication, plastics, machine tool companies, printing, warehouse/distribution facilities, electronic equipment, aircraft and missile components. Manchester is also home to one of the largest regional retail concentrations in New England. The Buckland Hill area includes the 1.1 million square foot pavilions at the Buckland Hills mall and an additional 1.7 million square feet of retail property. The town also boasts the Cheney Brothers National Register Historic District which includes historic mills and housing, and the downtown Main Street National Historic Register district. Manchester is located halfway between New York and Boston on Interstates 84, I-291, and I-384. Routes 44 and 6 are all located in Manchester. Transp.—Served by buses of Connecticut Transit, Conrail Freight and various common carriers. Post Offices, Manchester, Station A. and two contract stations.

TOWN OFFICERS. Clerk and Reg. of Vital Statistics, Joseph V. Camposeo; Hours, 8:30 A.M.-5 P.M., Mon. through Fri.; Address, Town Hall, 41 Center St., 06040; Tel., (860) 647-3037; Internet, http:/www.ct.manchester.ct.us.—**Asst. Clerks,** Joan M. Lewis, Emily M. Raymond, Mary Ann Sartor.—**Asst. Regs. of Vital Statistics,** Joan M. Lewis, Emily M. Raymond, Mary Ann Sartor, Eileen Wilson.—**General Manager,** Richard J. Sartor; Deputy, Steven R. Werbner.—**Bd. of Directors,** Stephen T. Cassano (D), Chm., Mayor, Timothy H. Becker, Adelino M. Coelho, Josh Howroyd, Joan E. Humphrey, James E. Morancey, Joseph D. Negri, Clifton E. Thompson, vacancy.—**Selectmen,** Joseph J. Diminico, Bettye J. Kramer, Mary E. Warrington.—**Treas.,** Ronald Osella.—**Budget Officer,** Rob Heustis.—**Dir. of Finance,** Alan J.

Desmarais.—**Ethics Comm.,** John Garside, Chm., A. Paul Berte, Anne Campbell-Maxwell, Joy Dorin, Joyce G. Epstein, Edward Hachadourian, Brad N. Mondschein; Alternates, Robert DeMarchi, Andrew Kravitz, Robert Schneider.—**Collector of Revenue,** Joan M. Troy.—**Bd. of Assessment Appeals,** Edward W. Kloehn, Chm., David Dumaine, Pamela Mondschein.—**Assessor,** Michael Bekech.—**Registrars of Voters,** Herbert J. Stevenson (D), Barbara A. King (R).—**Supt. of Schools,** Eddie L. Davis.—**Bd. of Education,** Susan L. Perkins, Janice M. Horn, 1996; Gloria D. DellaFera, Jonathan L. Mercier, John R. Perlstein, 1997; Evelyn Bush, Susan G. Falcetta, Margaret Hackett, 1998; Craig Lappen, Chm., 1999—**Planning, Zoning and Inland Wetlands Comm.,** William Bayer, Chm., Frank J. Daversa, Wilfred Maxwell, Eugene Sierakowski, David Wichman; Alternates, Peter Molchan, Florence Sheils, vacancy.—**Town Planner,** Mark Pellegrini.—**Zoning Bd. of Appeals,** Edward Coltman, Chm., Peter Crombie, Alphonse Reale, Robert Schneider, James Stevenson; Alternates, Michael Barry, Kathleen R. Maffe, James Skulski.—**Zoning Enforcement Officer,** Thomas R. O'Marra.—**Economic Industrial and Development Comm.,** S. Richard Bottaro, Chm., Bernard Apter, John V. Gannon, Andrea Hewitt, George Lee, Thomas J. Matrick.—**Housing Auth.,** John R. Crowley, Chm., Malcolm F. Barlow, Jo-Ann Cormier, Kevin M. O'Brien, William Rood; Carol C. Shanley, Exec. Dir.—**Conservation Comm.,** Mark Connors, Chm., Frank E. Belknap III, Carolyn Egan, Judy Egan, Peter V. Gavarrino, Bea Hicock, John McMahon, Joan Naab, Douglas Smith.—**Cheney National Historic Dist. Comm.,** Vivian F. Ferguson, Chm., Leslie Belcher, S. Lee Bogli, Jo-Ann Cormier, Frank J. Daversa, Margaret Hackett, Edward Kloehn, Beverly Malone, Nancy Pilver, Barbara Place, Mary Tierney, Alex Urbanetti, Marva Williams; Milton K. Adams, Ex officio.—**Comm. on Aging,** Michael Carrozella, Chm., Vincent Diana, Richard Egan, Joyce G. Epstein, Jill Gelinas, Ellen Jones, Barbara King, Linda J. LaPolla, John J. Smith.—**Human Relations Comm.,** Joseph Sweeney, Chm., Robert Albert, Patricia Cook, Janet Cooney, John Deeb, John Foley, Vivian Garside, Virginia Howell, H. John Malone, Joseph Rafala, Teresa Walker.—**Dir. of Social Services,** Beth Stafford.—**Dir. of Health,** Ronald Kraatz.—**Public Health Advisory Bd.,** Theodore Brindamour, Bridget Donovan, Linda Valerie, Mary Warrington.—**Housing Comm.,** Sylvia Hadge, Chm., Leo Juran, Peter Molchan, Joseph Noti, Joan O'Loughlin, Florence Sheils, Daleyne Siwik, Michael J. Thibodeau.—**Fair Rent Comm.,** Ryan P. Barry, Joseph Diminico, James Halloran, Michael Menard, Warren J. Packer, Joseph H. Tully.—**Town Historian,** Herbert Bengston.—**Library Bd.,** Paul McCary, Chm., Hollis U. Cassano, Patricia Ladd, Geoffrey Naab, Timothy O'Neil, Nancy Pilver; Douglas McDonough, Dir.—**Advisory Park and Recreation Comm.,** Joel E. Janenda, Chm., Dennis Cumberbatch, John DiDonato, Jeffrey Dupont, William D. O'Neill, David Prindiville, Thomas Tierney; D. Scott Sprague, Dir.—**Supt. of Parks,** George Murphy.—**Dir. of Public Works,** Peter P. Lozis, Jr.—**Town Engineer,** Mark J. Witek.—**Dir. of General Services,** Gerald Dupont.—**Supt. of Highways,** Lee F. O'Connor.—**Building Committee,** Francis A. Maffe, Jr., Chm., Doris Bourque, Ted Brindamour, Edward Epstein, David Kahn, John Kinsky, Neil Lawrence, Brian Murphy, Ronald Zavarella.—**Chief Building Inspector,** Leo P. Belval.—**Water and Sewer Admin.,** Robert J. Young.—**Sanitarian,** John Salcius.—**Chief of Police,** Henry R. Minor.—**Constables,** John DiDonato, Richard A. Lyman, Warren J. Packer, Joseph S. Rafala, Lisa H. Stevenson, James S. Taylor, Joseph P. Tomkunas.—**Chiefs of Fire**

Dept., John C. Rivosa (Town), John Mace (Eighth Dist.).—**Civil Preparedness Dir.,** Ronald Kraatz.—**Town Atty.,** Michael M. Darby.—**Justices of the Peace,** Margaret R. Churchill, Edwin J. Ciolkosz, Marjorie A. Dakin, Vivian F. Ferguson, Mary E. Fletcher, Kathleen S. Hartigan, Claudette J. Hinds, Wallace J. Irish, Jr., Carol Kuehl, Michael E. Pohl, Alphonse Reale, Robert G. Schneider, Elsie L. Swensson, Mary Tierney, Lucille B. Vincek.

MANSFIELD. Tolland County.—(Form of government, town manager, town council, town meeting.)—Inc., Oct., 1702; taken from Windham. Area, 45.5 sq. miles. Population, est., 18,134. Voting districts, 3. Principal industries, higher education, service/commerce, agriculture. Location of University of Conn. Transp.—Passenger: Served by buses of Bonanza Bus Lines, Inc. from Hartford and Providence, RI; The Arrow Lines, Inc. from Hartford; WRTD Storrs-Willimantic. Freight: Served by Central Vermont Railroad. Post offices, Mansfield Center, Mansfield Depot and Storrs-Mansfield; rural free delivery from Mansfield Center and Storrs-Mansfield. Voted Limited Liquor Permit, 1969.

TOWN OFFICERS. Clerk and Reg. of Vital Statistics, Joan E. Gerdsen; Hours, 8:30 A.M.-4:30 P.M., Mon. through Fri.; Address, 4 So. Eagleville Rd., 06268; Tel., Storrs, (860) 429-3302.—**Asst. Clerks and Asst. Regs. of Vital Statistics,** Joan Quarto, Sharon Tyler.—**Town Manager,** Martin H. Berliner.—**Town Council,** Fred A. Cazel, Jr., Mayor; Philip P. Barry, Bruce A. Bellm, Joan Buck, Peter J. Newcomer, Edwin E. Passmore, Richard Pellegrine, Howard A. Raphaelson, Michael H. Schor, Deputy Mayor.—**Treas.,** Joan E. Gerdsen.—**Dir. of Finance,** Jeffrey Smith.—**Collector of Revenue,** Pamela Wells.—**Bd. of Assessment Appeals,** Crawford L. Elder, Willard C. Stearns, John F. Sunmark.—**Assessor,** William D. Marsele.—**Registrars of Voters,** Mary Stanton (D), Beverly M. Miela (R).—**Supt. of Schools,** Gordon L. Schimmel.—**Bd. of Education,** Sharry L. Goldman, Susan B. O'Connor, Steve Rogers, 1997; Timothy A. Quinn, Dale L. Truman, Christine Winter, 1999; Donna G. Clauson, Sydney A. L. Plum, William P. Simpson, 2001.—**Planning and Zoning Comm., Inland Wetlands Agency,** Aline L. Booth, Chm., Audrey H. Barberet, Gregory F. Cichowski, Rudy J. Favretti, Katherine K. Holt, Steve J. Lofman, Joseph D. Pandolfo, Alexandra C. Shulte, William E. Thorne; Alternates, Joann Goodwin, Donald M. Nolan, vacancy.—**Town Planner,** Gregory Padick.—**Zoning Enforcement Officer,** Curt Hirsch.—**Zoning Bd. of Appeals,** Julie J. Henry, Shirley R. Katz, Stephen Marks-Hamilton, Carol L. Pellegrine, Julie Wright; Alternates, Daniel W. Deptula, Jr., W. Bradford Goodwin, Michael Piccoli.—**Housing Auth.,** Jane A. Bobbitt, Chm., Beryl W. Griffin, Anne D. Jordan-Crouse, Richard P. Long, Esther M. McCabe.—**Conservation Comm.,** Sherman Clebnick, Robert Dahn, James Koch, Janice Shannon, Frank R. Trainor; Alternates, Dirk Fecho, Quentin Kessel, Kenneth Kline.—**Historic Dist. Comm.,** Isabelle K. Atwood, Gail Bruhn, Kristina Elias, Judith C. Mordkoff, Jody Newmyer; Alternates, Rose Baker, Kenneth Forman, Richard Roberts.—**Comm. on Aging,** William Curtin, Janet Eidel, Gladene Fait, Ruth Galligan, Jean W. Gosselin, Esther McCabe, William Rosen, Mark Ross, William Wilson.—**Municipal Historian,** Roberta K. Smith.—**Social Services Dir./Agent for Elderly,** William Kennedy.—**Dir. of Health,** Kenneth R. Dardick, M.D. (P.O., Storrs).—Library Bd., John D. Allie, Chm., Janet Aitken, Sheila Q. Clark, Martha Frappier, Barbara Katz, Carol M. Moulton, Rita Pollack, Compton Rees, Jr., Joan H. Rogers.—**Parks Advisory Committee,** Anne Strutt, Chm., Patricia A. Bresnahan, Susan C. Craig, Samuel G. Dodd, John Hankins, Elizabeth A. Robinson, Bob Rushton, Donald Wetherell, Betty Wexler.—**Recreation Advisory Committee,** Joseph D. Cerreto, Chm., Richard Brooks, Sheldon L. Dyer, Donald J. Field, Anne L. Rash, Matthew Raynor, Joseph J. Soltys, Elliot Stern, Susan Stuart.–Dir. of Recreation, Curt A. Vincente.—**Animal Control Officer,** Diane Collette.—**Building Code Bd. of Appeals,** Gregory Zlotnick, Chm., Gerald E. Bienvenue, Leland E. Hawkins, Charles Lowe, George Zlotnick.—**Dir. of Public Works,** Lon Hultgren.—**Supt. of Highways,** Tim Webb.—**Building Official,** Carl Panciera.—**Environmental Health Officer,** Charles Bradley.—**Solid Waste Management Committee,** Maria Gogarten-Boekels, Fred Keith, Paul Kobulnicky, Kevin McLaughlin, Stella Ross.—**Chief of Police,** Martin H. Berliner.—**Constables,** Keith A. Norling, Richard L. Sawyer, John O. Stanton.—**Chiefs of Fire Dept.,** Alan Hawkins (Mansfield), Richard Palmer Jr. (Eagleville).—**Fire Marshal/Civil Preparedness Dir.,** John Jackman.—**Town Atty.,** Daniel Lamont (P.O., Willimantic).—**Justices of the Peace,** Stephen M. Bacon, Paul Brody, Fred A. Cazel, Jr., Arppie Charkoudian, Celeste Fackrell, Ada T. Hawkins, David A. Ivry, William N. Kinnard, Jr., Irving Kirsch, Gary Koval, Louise M. Lent, Allan R. Maines, Richard J. Meehan, Joe Pandolfo, Edwin E. Passmore, Carol Pellegrine, Joyce C. Recor, Maria M. Russell, Dot Shaw, Elliott Stern, Thomas E. Weston.

MARLBOROUGH. Hartford County.—(Form of government, selectmen, town meeting, board of finance.)—Inc., Oct., 1803; taken from Colchester, Glastonbury and Hebron. Area, 23.4 sq. miles. Population, est., 5,737. Voting district, 1. Residential community. Transp.—Passenger: Served by buses of Eastern Bus Lines, Inc. from Hartford and New London; Barstow Transp. Co. and by Greyhound. Freight: Served by numerous motor common carriers. Post office, Marlborough.

TOWN OFFICERS. Clerk and Reg. of Vital Statistics, Nancy W. Dickson; Hours, 8 A.M.-4:30 P.M., Mon. through Thurs.; 6-8 P.M., Tues.; 8 A.M.-12 Noon, Fri.; Address, North Main St., P.O. Box 29, 06447; Tel., (860) 295-6206.—**Asst. Clerks and Asst. Regs. of Vital Statistics,** Ethel M. Fowler, Barbara C. Murray, Susan S. Wallen—**Selectmen,** 1st, Howard T. Dean, Jr. (D) Tel., (860) 295-6204, Theodore J. May, Jr. (D), Gregory Secord (R).—**Treas.,** Brian Murphy.—**Bd. of Finance,** Donna S. Beaudoin, Richard Couture, Dennis Hawrylko, Charles E. Hickey, Anthony J. Maiorano, vacancy; Alternates, Franz Harter, Joseph A. LaBella, Richard Shonk.—**Tax Collector,** Barbara C. Murray.—**Bd. of Assessment Appeals,** Richard F. Banbury, David J. Busch, John H. Goodrich, Jr.—**Assessor,** Gertrude Gantick.—**Registrars of Voters,** Barbara Brewer (D), Charlene Garnett (R).—**Supt. of Schools,** F. William Davis.—**Bd. of Education,** Lynn C. Traficanti, Chm., James D. Cherry, Jr., Anne H. Jones, Roger Pocock, 1997; Louise L. Concodello, Jennifer Fortin, Catherine Gaudinski, David C. Harding, Donna M. Mosher, 1999.—**Planning Comm.,** Denis Soucy III, Chm., Herbert Archer, Lillian Harter, John E. Larensen III, vacancy; Alternates, John A. Grybko, Jr., Dorothy Nowsch, Mark Peszko.—**Zoning Comm.,** Judith A. Denberg, Elliot B. Dodge, Jr., Theodore A. Lachapelle, Blair MacLachlan, Robert J. McBrair; Alternates, Joseph D. Farrell, Juanita Harper, David McCartney.—**Zoning Bd. of Appeals,** J. Vincent Burns, Mary G. Hocevar, Thomas J. O'Neill III, Steven Reiner, Karen L. Smith; Alternates, Wendy D. Farley, two vacancies.—**Zoning Enforcement Officer,** Marian G. Staye.—**Economic Development Comm.,** John Murray, Chm., Carl Carlson, Richard Gossoo, Peter Klein, Jr., Rosa Taylor.—**Conservation and Inland Wetlands Comm.,** James Monstream, Chm., Erich Aust, John T. Bray, Donald Hautman, Michael Kleinschmidt.—**Municipal Historian,** Raisa L. Bublick.—**Agent for the Elderly,** vacancy.—**Dir. of Health,** Mark D. Tuttle, M.D.—**Welfare Dir.,** V. J. Schwarzmann.—**Parks and Recreation Comm.,** Robert Gaudinski, Chm., Sandra Dougan, Barbara Lazzari, Joseph Santangelo, Robert Sekoll, William L. Tchakirides; Bette Stern, Dir.—**Road Foreman,** Thomas Giola.—**Engineering Aide/Sanitarian,** James Karrenberg.—**Building Inspector,** Patrick G. Looney.—**Planning Coordinator,** Marian G. Staye.—**Tree Warden,** Gregory Barker.—**Resident State Trooper,** Jeff Megin.—**Constables,** Stephen S. Batchelder, Reginald A. Clarke, William D'Ambrosio, Harold Garnett, Kevin Prior, Julius Ransom, vacancy.—**Chief of Fire Dept.,** William Lord.—**Fire Marshal,** Joseph Asklar.—**Bd. of Fire Comrs.,** Walter Kelly, Robert J. Moore, Sr., Ray Weber.—**Civil Preparedness Dir.,** Douglas Knowlton.—**Town Attys.,** Tyler, Cooper & Alcorn.—**Justices of the Peace,** Nicholas P. Daniolos, Gail Garrity, Dennis J. Hawrylko, Judith K. Hayes, Theodore A. LaChapelle, Richard A. Proch, Douglas H. Secord, Rosa M. Taylor, William L. Tchakirides, Diane Teixeira, Joan O. Woodbury.

MERIDEN. New Haven County.—(Form of government, city manager, city council.)—Town inc., May, 1806; taken from Wallingford. City inc., May, 1867. Town and city consolidated, Jan. 1, 1922. Area, 24.1 sq. miles. Population, est., 58,730. Voting districts, 17. Home of the American Silver Museum, Napier Jewelry, MicroGene System, Targetech Inc, Thompson Candy Factory and Walbro Automotive.. Manufactured products are jewelry, aircraft products, electronics, biotech filters, nuclear instrumentation, electrical signalling and communications equipment, tools, dies, molds and patterns, printing presses, phosphorous brass and bronze in sheets, pewter products, automotive warehouse/distribution centers, auto fuel injection devices, automated buffing and deburring machines, women's apparel, filters, plastics, engine gaskets, corrugated boxes, candy, measurement well drilling devices for offshore oil and gas wells, and submersible pumps. Transp.—Passenger: Served by Amtrak and buses of Conn. Transit, The Short Line of Conn., Inc. from Hartford and New Haven; and by Greyhound. Freight: Served by Conrail and numerous motor carriers. Post offices, Meriden, Station A, and three contract stations.

CITY AND TOWN OFFICERS. City Clerk, Town Clerk and Reg. of Vital Statistics, Irene G. Masse; Hours, 9 A.M.-7 P.M., Mon.; 9 A.M.- 5 P.M., Tues. through Fri.; Address, City Hall, 142 East Main St., Room 124, 06450; Tel., (203) 630-4030; FAX, (203) 630-4059.—**Asst. City and Town Clerk,** Marie P. Corte.—**Asst. Regs. of Vital Statistics,** Christine Boganski, Marie P. Corte, Lillian C. Schultz.—**City Manager,** Roger L. Kemp.—**City Council,** Joseph J. Marinan, Jr., (D), Mayor; Lauren E. Coffey, Deputy Mayor; Matthew C. Dominello, Laura M. Gallo, Joseph R. Galotti, Jr., Keith Gordon, Brian F. Kogut, Patricia D. Lynes, Michael S. Rohde, Hilda Santiago, Walter Shamock, Anthony D. Tomassetti, Stephen T. Zerio.—**Dir. of Finance,** Edward F. Murphy.—**Tax Collector,** Linda Makuch.—**Bd. of Relief,** George Maclaughlin, Chm., John Neumon, Timothy Puglielli.—**Assessor,** Steven Hodgetts.—**Bd. of Ethics,** Margaret Carter, Chm., Linda K. Braddock, Gene D. Correale, John Turley.—**Registrars of Voters,** Elizabeth A. Gassman (D), Lillian T. Soboleski (R).—**Supt. of Schools,** Elizabeth Ruocco.—**Bd. of Education,** Frank J. Kogut, Chm., Noreen A. Aresco, Bruce A. Fontanella, Roy Gooding, Leonard Suzio, 1997; Gerard I. Adelman, Paul R. Crone, Robert E. Kosienski, Jr., William M. Lutz, 1999.—**Municipal Pension Bd.,** John Miniter, Chm., John D. Ivers III, Robert Keene, Arthur Lamothe, David Lohman, Edward F. Murphy, Walter A. Shamock, Jr., Anthony D. Tomassetti.—**Planning Comm.,** Roger DeZinno, Chm., Enrico Buccilli, Arthur R. Geary, Jr., Joseph LaRosa, Jr., John Petrella; Alternates, Laura Bennaro-Uhrig, Christopher Carter, Lois Demayo.—**City Planner,** Dominic Caruso; Asst., Lata Krishnarao.—**Zoning Bd. of Appeals,** Jacqueline T. Zdeb, Chm., James Burt, Britt Hall, Edwin J. Jones, Robert Raguckus; Alternates, Kevin Danby, John E. DeMayo, Herbert Edelstein.—**Housing Auth.,** Lucille Malavenda, Chm., Urseline Boutin, Hector Cardona, Sr., Carl Lohmann, Jennie T. Roccapriore; W. James Rice, Exec. Dir.—**Inland Wetland and Watercourse Comm.,** Jeffrey Fournier, Chm., Roger C. DeZinno, Roger Gibson, Frank E. Indorf, Frank B. Lewandowski, Daniel Reardon, John Turley.—**Land Conservation Comm.,** Roger Gibson, Chm., Jeffrey Fournier, Douglas Hoskins III, Peter Massoth, Janet Pagini, Norman Zimmer; Alternates, Dorothy Danaher, Walter Hylwa.—**Human Rights Advisory Bd.,** Hector Cardona, Sr., Irma Howbrigg, Robert Lorenzo, H. Janice Melvin, John Neron, Jose Rivera, Edward Schwartz, Barbara Wimbish; Deborah Moore, Atty.—**Acting Dir. of Social Services,** Isabel Guzman.—**Acting Dir. of Health,** Beth Vumbaco.—**Chief of Environmental Health,** David Rogers.—**Comm. for People with Disabilities,** Joel Kleinman, Chm., Robert Carabetta, Douglas A. Coombs, Eleanor Denenberg, Debbie French, Thomas Higgins, Geralyn Kogut; Alternate, vacancy.—**Library Bd.,** Joan Edgerly, Chm., Virginia Alwang, Christelle M. Aube, Sharon Jodon, Janis M. Lloyd, Zina Oblon, Marianne P. Papandrea, Catherine Prahler, William Williams.—**Dir. of Parks and Recreation,** Mark Zebora.—**Acting Dir. of Public Works,** Mark Zebora.—**City Engineer,** Dawn Jakiela.—**Supt. of Streets/Sanitation,** Richard Graham.—**Building Official,** Louis A. Corte.—**Purchasing Agent,** Wilma Petro.—**Building Code Bd. of Appeals,** William Kroll, William Orsine, Loretta Parisi.—**Public Utilities Comm.,** Gennaro Martorelli, Chm., Charles Kszwanos, Carolann Nettleton, Robert Nordstrom, Michael Tiezzi.—**Parking Comm.,** Allen Schott, Chm., Joseph Belanger, Elizabeth Kielbasinski.—**Water Dept. Mgr.,** David Lohmann.—**Chief of Police,** Robert E. Kosienski; Deputy, Nelson Cossette.—**Constables,** James Belote, Robert Bennett, Keith Gordon, Lawrence Kibner, William Murdy, Brian Sheftel, vacancy.—**Chief of Fire Dept.,** William Dunn; Deputy, Clinton Ross.—**Fire Marshal,** Ray Alix.—**Civil Preparedness Dirs.,** Thomas Cirillo, John Francis.—**Corporation Counsel,** Lawrence J. Kendzior.—**Justices of the Peace,** Zaiga L. Antonetti, Fleurette Belote, Robert A. Bennett, James A. Burt, Hector M. Cardona, Sr., Charlene D. Caudill, Lynn A. Faria, James R. Fusaro, Velma K. Kimball, Brian T. Mahon, Thomas W. Neill, Carolann Nettleton, Grace S. Peterson, Jose R. Rivera, Frances L. Schwartz, E. Jack Shorr, Lillian T. Soboleski, John P. Turley, Nancy L. Whitfield.

MIDDLEBURY

New Haven County.—(Form of government, selectmen, town meeting, board of finance.)—Inc., Oct., 1807; taken from Waterbury, Woodbury and Southbury. Area, 18.5 sq. miles. Population, est., 6,123. Voting districts, 2. Principal businesses, corporate headquarters and manufacture of clocks, watches. Transp.—Passenger: Served by buses of North East Transp. Co., Inc. Freight: Served by numerous motor common carriers. Post office, Middlebury.

TOWN OFFICERS. Clerk and Reg. of Vital Statistics, Alicia H. Ostar; Hours, 9 A.M.-12 Noon, 1-5 P.M., Mon. through Fri.; Address, Town Hall, 1212 Whittemore Rd., P.O. Box 392, 06762; Tel., (203) 758-2557.—**Asst. Clerk and Asst. Reg. of Vital Statistics,** Edith Salisbury.—**Selectmen,** 1st, Edward B. St. John (R) Tel., (203) 758-2430, Thomas O. Proulx (D), Elaine M. R. Strobel (R).—**Treas.,** Kathleen S. Krevetski.—**Bd. of Finance,** Jonathan B. Dayton, Chm., Michael W. Belden, Karl L. Buckley, Kenneth A. Paddyfote, Francis E. Ruccio, Richard Spierto; Alternates, Francis A. DiGiovanna, William J. Raacke, Joseph F. Sullivan, Jr.—**Tax Collector,** Helen B. Delaney.—**Bd. of Assessment Appeals,** Ronald L. Kulpa, Chm., Brian J. Hanlon, vacancy.—**Assessor,** Edmund A. Corapinski—**Board of Assessors,** Charles A. Monagan, Chm., Ronald J. Bekech, Bernard Evans.—**Registrars of Voters,** Virginia Whiteley (D), Nancy S. Robison (R).—**Supt. of Schools,** Louis J. Esparo, Ph.D.—**Planning and Zoning Comm.,** James H. Emison, Chm., Arthur B. Dayton, Jr., John B. Nocera, Jr., Gerald M. Raimo, William J. Stowell; Alternates, Matthew R. Robison, Francis E. Ruccio, Terry Smith.—**Zoning Bd. of Appeals,** Robert L. Bean, Chm., Raymond A. Caruso, Herbert Faller, Dan Shaban, vacancy; Alternates, Francis M. Fitzgerald, Bernadette C. Graziosa, Ronald L. Kulpa.—**Zoning Enforcement Officer,** Paul L. DeRito.—**Conservation Comm.,** Joseph J. Salvini, Jr., Chm., William R. Bellotti, Bruce A. Ewert, Lorraine L. Levesque, Mulayim Ozkan, Edward J. Ryan III.—**Water Comm.,** John J. Proulx, Jr., Chm., Michael Leonetti, Aldo A. Manzi, Raymond Pietrorazio, Lewis J. Zaza.—**Comm. on Aging,** Judith D. Savarese, Chm., Betty-Jane Blick, Margaret E. Folgmann, Walter R. Meier, Olga Reale, Genevieve C. Siperas, Arlene R. Terrill, August J. Wutzl, vacancy; Jo-Ann Cappelletti, Agent.—**Dir. of Health,** William P. Arnold, Jr., M.D.—**Library Directors,** Lloyd F. George, Chm., Marilyn S. Engelman, Paul F. Hally, Joan M. King, Anne L. Madden, Virginia A. Manzi.—**Municipal Historian,** Bradford E. Smith.—**Dir. of Parks and Recreation,** Carole P. Cipriano.—**Building Inspector,** Paul DeRito.—**Pomperaug Valley Water Auth.,** Francis L. Barton, Jr., Michael A. Leonetti, Aldo A. Manzi.—**Water Pollution Control Auth.,** William J. Cass, Chm., George G. Adams, Francis J. Cipriano, Ralph F. Gilnack Jr., Robert W. Smith.—**Sanitary Inspector,** Eric N. Ianantuoni.—**Chief of Police,** Patrick J. Bona.—**Police Comm.,** David A. Osiecki, Chm., Richard C. Brown, Armand D'Agostino, Maurice Falk, James J. Roach.—**Constables,** William J. Pratt, Gerald M. Raimo.—**Chief of Fire Dept./Civil Preparedness Dir.,** Edmond E. Bailly; Deputy Fire Chief, Paul Perrotti.—**Town Attys.,** Carmody & Torrance, W. Fielding Secor, James R. Smith.—**Justices of the Peace,** Russell E. Aronheim, Gregory Barnes, Ralph J. Barra, Walter Blick, Robert O. Bona, Yolande D. Bosman, Alice P. Brown, Ida P. Byram, Anthony D. Calabrese, Rosalyn Ann Cass, Linda L. Charbonneau, Richarda R. Chovau, Julie M. Clark, Angela C. Corcoran, Armand D'Agostino, Barbara D. DeRiu, Francis A. DiGiovanna, Mary Lou A. Duffy,

Delmar M. Dunn, Richard W. Dwyer, Bernard Evans, Carolyn R. Falk, George Frantzis, Elizabeth V. Fumire, George M. Gomes, Francis J. Grady, Bernadette C. Graziosa, David A. Greene, Gayle M. Griffin, Bertha A. Hadzega, Robert A. Haxhi, James C. Hurlbut, Richard J. Kendzior, Lorraine L. Levesque, Harold S. Lynch, Jr., Virginia A. Manzi, Joseph W. Marciano, David R. Marselinas, Charles A. Monagan, Seena C. Monagan, Judith W. Murphy, Richard H. Nicol, Linda L. Norman, Leo F. Ostar, Kenneth A. Paddyfote, David W. Patterson, William J. Raacke, Phil Robinson, Jr., Matthew R. Robison, Francis E. Ruccio, John Salerno, Maryann Santoni, James R. Smith, Elaine M. R. Strobel, Kristin J. Tiso, Nancy D. Vaughan, Michael Wabuda, Virginia M. Whiteley, Nancy S. Wiatr.

MIDDLEFIELD. Middlesex County.—(Form of government, selectmen, town meeting, board of finance.)—Inc., June, 1866; taken from Middletown. Area, 13.3 sq. miles. Population, est., 4,095. Voting districts, 2. Principal industries, agriculture and manufacture of cement products, gun sights and gun parts, novelties in plastics, thermometers, hardware specialties, such as wire cutters, tools, dies, fixtures, machinery, and work holding devices. Transp.—Passenger: Served by buses of Dattco Inc. Freight: Served by Conrail from New Haven and Middletown and numerous motor common carriers. Post offices, Middlefield and Rockfall. Rural free delivery from Rockfall and Middlefield post offices.

TOWN OFFICERS. Clerk and Reg. of Vital Statistics, Linda R. DeMaio; Hours, 9 A.M.-5 P.M., Mon.; 9 A.M.-4 P.M., Tues. through Thurs.; 9 A.M-3 P.M., Fri.; Address, Town Administration Bldg., 393 Jackson Hill Rd., P.O. Box 179, 06455; Tel., (860) 349-7116; FAX, (860) 349-7115.—**Asst. Clerk and Asst. Reg. of Vital Statistics,** Marilyn Wilson.—**Selectmen,** 1st, Charles R. Augur (D) Tel., (860) 349-7114, Joan F. Lombardo (R), William F. Mackey (D).—**Treas.,** Eleanor H. Burgess.—**Bd. of Finance,** Kieran P. Cahill, Timothy J. Grady, Michael D. Greaves, Ruth H. Tewksbury, Michael V. W. Waller, David G.Webster.—**Tax Collector,** Carol A. Skultety.—**Bd. of Assessment Appeals,** Mark Busey, Lawrence M. DiBernardo, Patricia Dubey.—**Assessor,** Marie Hall.—**Registrars of Voters,** Patricia White (D), Barbara Rowe (R).—**Supt. of Schools,** William D. Breck.—**Planning and Zoning Comm.,** Frank St. John, Chm., Lucy Petrella, Steven Shonta, Nicholas Xenelis, vacancy; Alternates, Gary Freemontle, Robert LaMarche, Edward Tulinski.—**Town Planner,** Geoffrey Colegrove.—**Zoning Bd. of Appeals,** Joan Thrall, Chm., Jean Bertman, Roger Brewer, Robert Carlson, Laura Webster, Matthew Willis; Alternates, David Gold, Paul Pizzo, vacancy.—**Zoning Enforcement Officer,** Mark Lundgren.—**Housing Auth.,** Donald Sperl, Acting Chm., Sophie Pacyna, Peter Sibley, Barnard Thayer, Wilma Turner.—**Conservation Comm.,** Michael Augeri, James Candela, Peter Carras, William Earls, John Girardi, Rosalie Lamphier, Dorothy Waller.—**Inland Wetlands Comm.,** Randolph Bernotas, Jon Brayshaw, Michael Cabelus, Stephen Ernst, James Lyman, Sarah Strickland, Charles Zieminski; Alternates, Barbara-Jean DiMauro, Leopold Kokoszka, Nelson Prue.—**Agent for the Elderly,** Antoinette Astle.—**Dir. of Health,** Mark Ludwig, M.D.—**Library Bd.,** Barbara J. DiMauro, Nadine Ernst, Peter Hewes, Jaye Lamarche, Paulette Magee, Sandra Piantek.—**Parks and Recreation Comm.,** Donald Ginter, Chm., Robert Dlugolenski, Michael Fiddler, Delores Tulinski, vacancy.—**Town Engineer,** Nathan Jacobson Associates.—**Sanitarian,** Alex Cinotti.—**Tree Warden,** John Wyskiel.—**Building Inspector,** Anthony Satagaj.—**Building Code Bd. of Appeals,** John Augeri, Chm., Adelbert Cade.—**Chief of Police,** Charles R. Augur.—**Constables,** Scott Halligan, Michael Polansky.—**Chief of Fire Dept.,** Terry Parmelee.—**Fire Marshal,** Stanley C. Atwell, Jr.—**Civil Preparedness Dir.,** Kenneth Kindschi.—**Town Attys.,** Mark K. Branse, Matthew Willis.—**Justices of the Peace,** Sebastan Areoco, Pauline Bladek, James Blois, William Currlin, Barbara Jean DiMauro, Nancy J. Doane, James Gibbons, Donna M. Golub, Robert E. Grenier, Chester Hulkowicz, Robert LaMarche, Joseph Lombardo, Robert Monthei, Mari-Lynn McPhelimy, Norman J. O'Hara, Georgene Smith, Glenn Tewksbury, Kenneth C. Twombly.

MIDDLETOWN. Middlesex County.—(Form of government, mayor, common council.)—Town inc., Sept. 11, 1651, named, Nov., 1653; city inc., 1784, town and city consolidated, 1923. Area, 42.3 sq. miles. Population, est., 43,620. Voting districts, 10. Principal industries, bricks, switches, paper boxes, marine hardware, auto accessories, tools and dies, metal and wire goods, brass hardware, heat elements, training devices, mica mining, sheet metal, chemicals, jet engines and insurance. Transp.—Passenger: Served by buses of Conn. Transit to Hartford and the Middletown Transit (local); Greyhound from East Hampton, New Haven and Willimantic, and by Trailways. Freight: Served by Conrail and numerous motor common carriers. Post office, Middletown.

CITY AND TOWN OFFICERS. City and Town Clerk, Sandra R. Hutton; Hours, 8:30 A.M.-4:30 P.M., Mon. through Fri.; Address, Municipal Bldg., 245 DeKoven Dr. and Court St., P.O. Box 1300, 06457; Tel., (860) 344-3459, Ext. 459, 460, 461, 462.—**Asst. Town Clerk,** vacancy.—**Reg. of Vital Statistics,** Leon Vinci.—**Asst. Regs. of Vital Statistics,** Lydia D. Guere, Camille Salamone, Sharon Solek.—**Mayor,** Maria M. Holzberg (D), Asst., Mary Palladino.—**City Council,** Gerald E. Daley, Joseph E. Milardo, Jr., Francis T. Patnaude, John L. Robinson, Jesse J. Salafia, Robert P. Santangelo, Steven P. Shapiro, Phrances Szewczyk, Domenique Thornton, Joseph J. Vinci, Jr., Gerard F. Winzer, Sr.—**Bd. of Ethics,** John Barton, Edward J. Eldridge, Mary Klaaren, William Roberts, Joel Young; Alternates, Stephen Anderson, Brian Pollard.—**Treas.,** Christine B. Bourne.—**Dir. of Finance,** James M. Reynolds.—**Finance Committee,** John L. Robinson, Chm., Stephenn T. Gionfriddo, Phrances Szewczyk, Stephen P. Shapiro, Joseph J.Vinci, Jr.—**Tax Collector,** Sebastian J. Garafolo; Asst., Jane B. Aresco.—**Bd. of Assessment Appeals,** Grant C. Livingston, Linda Pagano, Mildred Uliano.—**Tax Assessor,** John Ziomek; Asst., Frank Marchese.—**Insurance and Claims Committee,** Gerald E. Daley, Chm., Joseph E. Milardo, Jr., Jesse J. Salafia.—**Registrars of Voters,** John P. Bozzi, Sr. (D), Marilyn Langille (R).—**Supt. of Schools,** David Larson.—**Bd. of Education,** Fred Chappelle, Edward L. McMillan, Jr., Elizabeth L. Morgan, Barbara M. Weiss, 1997; John F. Shaw, Jr., Chm., Linda L. Brooks, Marie E. Derosier, Thomas C. Hutton, Debra A. Moore, 1999.—**Personnel Dir.,** Lawrence Kinch.—**Personnel Appeals Bd.,** Joyce Conklin, William Howard, Raymond Klick, William Wilson.—**Retirement Bd.,** Richard Simone, Chm., Steven Gomes, Mayor Maria M. Holzberg, Hope Kasper, James Kudrak, James Reynolds, Jesse J. Salafia.—**Planning and Zoning Comm.,** William L. Osborne, Chm., Carl W. Bolz,

Corrine Dorsey, Ronald Klattenberg, W. Lee Osborne, Jeffrey D. Pierce, David Roane, Anthony Vasiliou; Alternates, Carl Chisem, James F. Fortuna, William E. Hohenstein.—**Zoning Bd. of Appeals,** Anabelle Resinsky, Chm., Leslie P. Adams, Jr., Judy Pehota, Sheila Walsh, Steven Weiss; Alternates, Christopher Pappas, Evelyn Russo, James Streeto.—**Economic Development Comm.,** Gerald E. Daley, Chm., Joseph E. Milardo, Jr., Robert Santangelo, Stephen T. Shapiro, Joseph J. Vinci, Jr..—**Parking Auth.,** George R. Aylward, Salvatore C. Fazzino, Joseph Gallo, Gregory Harris, Mayor Maria M. Holzberg, William Huff, James P. Lessor, Jack McCormick.—**Housing Auth.,** Mary Dimon, Francis Marino, Mark Maselli, Salvatore L. Monarca, Evelyn Russo.—**Housing Code Enforcement Officer,** Raymond Santostefano; Chief, Nancy Brault.—**Conservation Comm.,** Alan Siniscalchi, Chm., Jane Brawerman, Katchcn Coley, John Czuba, Marie DeRosier, Daniel Filer, Martin Knight, Earl Roberts, Sheila Stoane, Len Tunderman; Alternates, Jonathan Beatty, James Fortuna, Elena Mandia.— **Inland Wetlands and Watercourses Agency,** William VonMahland, Chm., Susan Aiudi, Jonathan Beatty, William Carpenter, Joseph Carta, Joseph Gallo, Mayor Maria M. Holzberg, Salvatore Nesci, Joseph Seaha, Robert Trigo, Robert Whitney, Barbara Wilson; Alternates, Michael Beal, David Broun, Mary Hotstetler, Michael Loman, Christopher Pappas.—**Citizens Advisory Committee,** Vincent Amato, Carl Chisem, Mary Dimon, Corinne Dorsey, Susan Engelhardt, Lauralane Feitel, Idella Howell, Diane Kelly, Anthony Marino, Donna Mitkoski, Lalani Moore, Fran A. Pappas, John L. Robinson, Stephen Shapiro, Linda Wallace.—**Middletown Preservation Bd.,** Jeffrey D. Bianco, Chm., David Brown, Patricia Evans, James Fortuna, Nancy Goff, Elaine Kapetan, Brian Kronenberger, Ann Tommasi, Elizabeth Warner.—**Senior Affairs Comm.,** William Wasch, Chm., Judith Baldwin, Catherine Beinhorn, Jan Daniels, Melanie Derosier, George Keithan, Edward J. Margnelli, Melanie Masztal, Francis T. Patnaude, Phyllis Pollack, Virginia Rollefson, Joseph J. Vinci, Jr..—**Human Relations Comm.,** Alexander Tucci, Chm., Howard Baran, Velma Crumble, Anthony Guanichaux, Jesse Hunter, Joann Massey, William Oliver, Jr., Annette Ward, John Wood.—**Welfare Dir.,** Annette Ward.—**Dir. of Health,** Leon Vinci, M.P.H.—**Bd. of Health,** Daniel Novak, M.D., Chm., Catherine Beinhorn, Frances Ganguli, Connie Gillies, Anthony Guida, Mayor Maria M. Holzberg, Stephen Shapiro, Gerard F. Winzer, Sr., vacancy.—**Russell Library Trustees,** Chester Bladek, Hortense Kabel, Sybil Paton, Kathy Robinson, Louise Russo, Susan Spaeth.—**Municipal Historian,** Bernard Prue.—**Arts and Cultural Comm.,** Barbara Arafeh, Chm., Patricia Evans, Frances Ganguli, Joyce Kirkpatrick, Claudia Mazzotta, Charlotte McCoid, Joseph E. Milardo, John H. Risley, Jr., Louise Russo, James Salonia, David Santacroce, Dominique Thornton.—**Parks and Recreation Comm.,** Gerard F. Winzer, Sr., Chm., Cliff DeRosier, Ernest Garafoli, Stephen T. Gionfriddo, John Marchese, Nick Salafia, Lenora Woods.—**Dir. of Youth Services,** John L. Larosa, Jr.—**Youth Services Comm.,** August DeFrance, Grady Faulkner, Stephen T. Gionfriddo, John Labbadia, Ed McMillan, Kim Quinones, Linda Ozga, Robert Santangelo, Corrinne Tillotta.—**Dir. of Public Works,** Salvatore C. Fazzino.—**Purchasing Agent,** Deborah Wilcox-Loos.—**Sealer of Weights and Measures,** Philip P. Cacciola.—**Building Inspector,** John Parker, Jr.—**Water Pollution Control Auth.,** Dennis J. Purcell, Chm., Robert E. Bohro, Jr., John Cihocki, Joe Gallo, John Giuliano, Francis Patnaude, Joseph J. Vinci, Jr..—**Harbor Improvement Agency,** Edward Dzialo, Jr., Chm., Dennis Bradley, Thomas A.

Chace, Joseph Guida, Jane Hall, Helen Hammond, Claude LaCombe, Edgar Pratt, Domenique Thornton.—**Sewage Plant Supt.,** Guy Vecchitto.—**Sanitary Disposal Dist. Comm.,** Michael Misenti, Chm., Mary Augustine, David Santacroce, Sebastian J. Santacroce, John Uccello.—**Sanitarians,** Henry Solek, Chief, Vincent Mazzotta, James Monopoli.—**Water and Sewer Auth.,** Guy Russo.—**Chief of Police,** George R. Aylward; Deputy Chief, Ronald E. Lee.—**Police Comm.,** Robert P. Santangelo, Chm., Francis T. Patnaude, Jesse J. Salafia.—**Chief of Fire Dept.,** John Cyrulik.—**Fire Chiefs,** Sebastian DiMauro (South); John Cyrulik (Middletown); Art Higgins (Westfield).—**Fire Comm.,** Gerard Winzer, Chm., Joseph E. Milardo, Jr., Domenique S. Thornton.—**Civil Defense Dir.,** Karl Hervey.—**Corporation Counsel,** Daniel Ryan.—**City Atty.,** Trina Solecki-Aucaigne.—**Justices of the Peace,** Leslie P. Adams, Michael E. Amara, Mary Augustine, Joseph E. Bibisi, Arline Blau, Edward J. Bogdan, John P. Bozzi, Sr., Lawrence Cacciola, Marie Carlson, Joseph S. Colonghi, William Corvo, Edward J. Dzialo, Jr., Raymond J. Dzialo, Sandra L. Faraci, James F. Fortuna, Joseph Gallo, Sebastian J. Garafalo, Corinne Gill, Paul Gionfriddo, Stephen T. Gionfriddo, Jeanne Goldner, Maria M. Holzberg, William R. Hohenstein, Jr., Sandra R. Hutton, Marie Kalita, Mary L. LaBella, Anthony R. Lancia, Sr., Helen G. Landry, Marilyn M. Langille, Ann Marie B. Lawson, Victor Liburdi, Sebastian Marino, Ralph Matteo, Willard McRae, Steven H. Meyer, Joseph E. Milardo, Jr., Salvatore Nesci, Marion E. Newberg, Emanuel Pattavina, Christopher Peterson, Anton Petras, Martin J. Reardon, Sr., Phyllis H. Redford, Annabel L. Resnisky, David Roane, John Robinson, Evelyn V. Russo, Helen Ryan, Rose Sbalcio, Anthony Sbona, Joseph C. Serra, Thomas J. Serra, Stephen P. Shapiro, John F. Shaw, Jr., George M. Souto, Richard Thompson, Domenique Thornton, Mildred M. Uliano, Anthony J. Vasiliou, Barbara Weiss.

MILFORD. New Haven County.—(Form of government, mayor, board of aldermen.)—Settled in 1639, under New Haven; named, Nov. 24, 1640; united with Connecticut Colony, 1664. Inc. as a city, June 15, 1959. Town and city consolidated, 1959. Area, 24.7 sq. miles. Population, est., 48,762. Voting districts, 5. Principal industries, retail furniture center, sailmaking, hydraulic lifts, ball point pens, razors, razor blades, lighters, corrugated paper, fabricated metals, instruments, and specialty tools, high tech components, wholesale ice cream making, regional insurance service center, computer center and major distribution, warehousing and common carrier center corporate fast food service international headquarters, major recreational and boating center with municipal marina and boat launching ramps, and Jai Alai Fronton. Transp.—Passenger: Served by Metro North Commuter Railroad Co. and buses of Conn. Transit between Milford and New Haven and Milford Transit for local and service to Stratford. Major corporate headquarters center and limousine service to Hartford, New York, and Newark airports. Post offices, Milford Center, Devon, Pepe's Farm Rd.

CITY AND TOWN OFFICERS. City Clerk, Town Clerk and Reg. of Vital Statistics, Alan H. Jepson; Hours, 8:30 A.M.-5 P.M., Mon. through Fri.; Address, Parsons Complex, 70 West River St., 06460-3364; Tel., (203) 783-3210.—**Asst. Clerks and Asst. Regs. of Vital Statistics,** Sandra Lardiere, Joan Pilvelait.—**Mayor,** Frederick L. Lisman (R).—**Bd. of Aldermen,** Terry J. Munk, Chm., Joseph B. Barnes

III, Thomas Beirne III, Allen E. Cegan, Lawrence F. Ciacci, James R. Coffey, Michele G. Collins, Albert J. DeLuca, Anthony Detoro, Jr., Wayne A. Donaldson, Lloyd Fleming, Barbara L. Genovese, Bernard J. Lickteig, Nancy E. Marino, Albert L. Munroe.—**Treas.,** Anne Loin.—**Bd. of Finance,** Stephen J. Skudlarek, Jr., Chm., Joseph M. Agro, Jr., Samuel Bergami, Jr., Stephen Fogler, Jr., Angelo Leo; Antoinette Anderson, Dir.—**Tax Collector,** Linda L. Harra; Deputy, Judy J. Gabryszewski.—**Bd. of Assessment Appeals,** Michael J. Petrucelli, Chm., Joseph E. Godin, George H. Ward.—**Assessor,** William Gaffney; Assts., Thomas A. Biros, Paul Slattery.—**Registrars of Voters,** M. Lee Tamas (D), Rose I. Scarpa (R).—**Supt. of Schools,** Mary Jo Kramer.—**Bd. of Education,** Jan P. Fugal, Chm., Gerald O. Cavallo, Jeffrey G. Cochrane, Karen A. Craig, Carol C. Faruolo, Margaret H. Filakosky, Pat Giel, Scott Marlow, Raymond J. Watt, Ronald Winfield, 1997.—**Pension and Retirement Bd.,** Joseph Sartor, Chm., Christopher Cody, Richard Elwell, Michael Jagoe, John H. Kane, Katherine Patrick, Alexander Pazsak, Joseph N. Pouliot, Roy Povinelli, Peter Provo, Michael Ryan, William Schempp, James B. Stirling, Joan M. Sullivan, William Vernon.—**Personnel Dir.,** John Boland.—**Civil Service Comm.,** Stephen Studer, Chm., Ruth Dowin, Karen Fitzmaurice, Virginia B. Griffin, David Hill.—**Planning and Zoning Bd.,** Russell Mette, Chm., Richard J. Carey, Jr., Patricia A. Champney, Richard A. Hoffman, Sr., Kevin Liddy, Malcolm J. Palm, Vincent J. Sarullo, Jr., William J. Sayles, Gregory Smith, John A. Wicko.—**City Planner,** Wade Pierce.—**Zoning Bd. of Appeals,** Errol Van Hise, Chm., Dennis Anderson, Thomas Flanders, John L. Marvell, Kevin L. Norman; Alternates, Peter Carroll, Fred Katen, Michael Mercurio.—**Zoning Enforcement Officer,** Richard Vaczek.—**Inland Wetlands Agency,** John Rigely, Chm., Joseph Alves, Richard Austin, Colleen Beirne, Walter Farley, John Ludtke, Katherine Lutz, Kevin Norman, vacancy; Alternates, Mark J. Krom, William J. Sahlman.—**Economic and Industrial Development Comm.,** Robert Kapusta, Chm., Lisa Arenberg, Kenneth Brannin, John Gaynor, Jr., Wendy Weir; Robert Gregory, Exec. Dir.—**Housing Auth.,** Keith Rubenstein, Chm., Jack Diamond, Gladys H. Katen, George Ronkowitz, Jeanne Voss; Arthur E. Miller, Exec. Dir.—**Conservation Comm.,** Letitia C. Malone, Chm., Jeffrey L. DiDonato, Raymond J. Edwards, Eileen G. Farakos, Aileen D. O'Connell, Allen Robles, Henry D. Rotman, John Vanacore, John Westerman, Valerie White, Sheila Woodlock.—**Flood and Erosion Control Bd.,** Gary B. Montano, Chm., Joseph S. DellaMonica, Edward J. Filanowski, Fred Katen, William Phillips.—**Historic Dist. Comm.,** Robert L. Berchem, Chm., Raymond Cable, Timothy Clark, Sandra Elgee, Susan Whitaker; Alternates, Julia Geib, Peter Smith.—**Council on Aging,** Kenneth Stephens, Chm., Anne Alves, Jack D. Benard, Nancy Case, Lillian Holmes, Mary E. Jepson, Robert Kappel, John E. Rigely, Sr., Audrey Thomas-Kimble.—**Human Resources Development Agency,** Robert J. Hamilton, Chm., Albert L. Barnes, Ross DeLeonardo, Stuart Fletcher, George Marshal, Kathleen Nelson, Phyllis Roman, Ralph Vanacore, Wilma Walsh; Joel R. Baldwin, Dir.—**Social Services Dir.,** Wilma Walsh.—**Dir. of Health,** George Kraus, M.D.—**Chief Environmental Officer,** Richard Werner.—**Bd. of Health,** Gregory P. Lynch, Chm., Wiley Bowling, Howard Fink, Ernest Judson, Jr., Mark D. Rego, Joseph Reingold, Constance Young.—**Library Bd.,** Sandra C. Smith, Chm., Marion Ahrens, Ellen Austin, Thomas P. Connors, Linda Creedon, Susan M. Gaydos, Karen O'Neill, Paula Patterson, Richard Smith, vacancy; Salvatore Stingo, Librarian.—**Fine Arts Council,** William Meddick, Exec. Dir.—

Parks, Beaches and Recreation Comm., George Avery, Chm., Stuart Champney, Gail Dixon, Deborah Studer, Daniel W. Worroll, Jr.—**Dir. of Recreation,** Edward Austin.—**Dir. of Public Works,** Bruce Kolwicz.—**City Engineer,** John Casey.—**Purchasing Agent,** Lawrence Tomasco.—**Building Inspector,** Edward Liskiewicz.—**Building Code Bd. of Appeals,** Ray S. Oliver, Chm., Carmen Collucci, Louis J. D'Amato, Richard Jagoe, Steven G. Langley.—**Sewer Comm.,** Lawrence Kaplan, Chm., John Knapp, Lewis Scarpa, Peter Vita, Edward Zukowski.—**Harbor Management Comm.,** James R. Beard, Chm., Mark M. Anstey, Frank K. Bayers, Harry A. Hyatt, Gary B. Montano, Albert L. Munroe, Jr., David Yerxa; Alternates, Joseph Gilbert, vacancy; Richard Hasking, Dir.—**Sanitation Foreman,** Edward O'Donnell.—**Tree Warden,** Tyler Lewis.—**Chief of Police,** Thomas Flaherty; Inspector, William Schultz.—**Police Comm.,** Robert D'Amore, Chm., Charles Bristol, Melvin Eisenhandler, L. Kenneth Fellenbaum, Sheila Fleming, John H. O'Connell, Thomas Zawislinski.—**Constables,** Linda M. Gustafson, Martin B. Hardiman, Robert H. Miller, Ronald Peruzzi, Vincent F. Rositani, Sr, Robert Serrano, Sr., Frank J.Zielinski, Jr.—**Chief of Fire Dept.,** Louis LaVecchia; Fire Marshal/Asst. Chief, Thomas Phelan.—**Bd. of Fire Comrs.,** John Healy, Chm., Edmund Colangelo, Carmen Corvino, John Griffin, Edward J. Obert, Jr., Thomas Riso, Jr., Phillip Ucci.—**Civil Preparedness Dir.,** Louis LaVecchia.—**City Atty.,** Marilyn Lipton.—**Justices of the Peace,** Thomas G. Arsenault, Wiley E. Bowling, Jr., Mary F. Caruso, Linda M. Casey, Allan E. Cegan, Patricia A. Chaco, Patricia A. Champney, Leslie C. Delaney, Albert J. DeLuca, Don DiNapoli, Ruth M. Dowin, Una A. Glennon, Elizabeth M. Griffin, Linda M. Gustafson, Richard A. Hoffman, Sr., Frederick E. Katen, Daniel L. McAllen III, Hazel A. Raigue, James L. Richetelli, Jr., Deborah F. Smith, Marilyn Wardell, Suzanne E. Wasylink, Karen Zaneski-Nettleton, Frank J. Zielinski, Jr.

MONROE. Fairfield County.—(Form of government, selectman, town council, town meeting.)—Inc., May, 1823; taken from Huntington (now Shelton.) Area, 26.3 sq. miles. Population, est., 17,760. Voting districts, 4. Principally residential, varied small industries. Transp.—Freight: Served by Conrail and numerous motor common carriers. Post offices, Monroe and Stevenson. Sixteen rural delivery routes supply the inhabitants with mail daily.

TOWN OFFICERS. Clerk and Reg. of Vital Statistics, Thelma Kay Inderdohnen; Hours, 9 A.M.-5 P.M., Mon. through Fri., or by appointment; Address, Town Hall, 7 Fan Hill Rd., 06468; Tel., (203) 452-5417; FAX (203) 261-6197; Home page address, http://www.state.ct.us/MUNIC/MONROE/monroe.htm.—**Asst. Clerks and Asst. Regs. of Vital Statistics,** Dianne M. Blatchley, Madeline D. Hanlon.—**Selectman,** Karen L. Burnaska (D) Tel., (203) 452-5421.—**Town Council,** Judith J. Stripay, Chm., James G. Ferris, David D. Halliwell, John W. Hansen, Dorothy A. Martin, Robert B. Mitchell, Joseph A. C. Ruel, Jody S. Short, Joseph A. Tuozzoli, Jr.—**Treas.,** Shaun P. Shanley.—**Bd. of Ethics,** Karen Perachio, Acting Chm., Eleanor Bartosik, Alice Deak, Timothy R. Knutson, vacancy; Alternates, Gerald Gaynor, Claudia Tuozzoli, vacancy.—**Bd. of Finance,** David A. Ward, Chm., James E. Bresnahan, John P. Fracassini, Michael J. Lipnicki, Carl E. Tomchik, Stephen J. Vavrek.—**Tax Collector,** Deborah B. Pothier.—**Bd. of Assessment Appeals,** Rudolph C. Beers III, Chm., Richard

A. Orr, Alex Sowchuk.—**Assessor,** Francis W. Kascak.—**Registrars of Voters,** Vivian N. Capoccitti (D), Nancy M. vonGlahn (R).—**Supt. of Schools,** Norman T. Michaud, Ed.D.—**Bd. of Education,** J. Thomas Benek, Chm., Janice W. Martin, Judith M. Miko, Raymond E. Svana, Thomas W. Taylor, 1997; Marsha A. Motter, David S. Rutkin, Margaret J. Villani, Jack Witt, 1999.—**Planning and Zoning Comm.,** Andrew S. Abate, Chm., Robert J. Martin, P. John Millo, Ellen L. Oros, vacancy; Alternates, Leon A. Barnaby, Jr., Alan R. Haven, Edward M. Stuart.—**Planning Admin.,** Daniel A. Tuba.—**Zoning Bd. of Appeals,** Enid Lipeles, Chm., John L. Gaffield, William M. Michaels, Joseph Pardee, James Wendt; Alternates, Stephen J. Chisarik, Raymond W. Knapp, Jr., Donald Nickdow.—**Zoning Enforcement Officer,** Timothy Ryan.—**Economic Development Comm.,** George Massar, Chm., Edward F. Barrett, Edward Deak, Anthony Fischetti, Steven Schapiro, Keith Weindling, vacancy; Charles Spanbauer, Coord.—**Housing Auth.,** James Davison, Chm., Walter Hedden, Nadine Richardson, Alton Spahn, Anastasia O. Zeiner.—**Conservation and Water Resources/Inland Wetlands Comm.,** Nicholas C. Esposito Chm., John Bath, Ignatius Bertone, Jane Gardner, Deborah L. Orwig, John Perachio, Philip White.—**Historic Dist. Comm.,** Barbara Harlacker, Chm., Sylvia Abate, Elizabeth A. Edgerton, Charles Moore, Joan L. Renaud; Alternates, Diana Frascatore, Joanne Quaranta, Gary Scrofani.—**Municipal Historian,** Edward N. Coffey.—**Youth Comm.,** Paula Caparaso, Vida Casubolo, Rudolph D'Ambrosio, Debralee Greenwood, Julie Hass, Noel Walls, vacancy.—**Comm. for the Aging,** Dolores Augustyn, Chm., Barbara Alberts, Julia deLeon, Raymond J. Quinlan, Sr., Rosemary Wishneski, James Wojeck, vacancy.—**Agent for the Elderly,** Joan Tomlinson.—**Welfare Dir.,** Irena Kandybowicz.—**Dir. of Health,** Claude Light, M.D.—**Bd. of Health,** Robert Cargill, Chm., Richard Amato, Claude Light, M.D., Paul A. Moyse, Michael Ringler.—**Emergency Medical Services Comm.,** Michael Perretta, Chm., Kurt Breither, William Miko, Robert Weeks, Sharron Wessel.—**Library Directors,** William Ehlers, Chm., Mildred Fiegel, John Iannarone, Carol Parmelee, Susan Thomas, vacancy; Lynn Rosato, Librarian.—**Jury Committee,** Ursula Gaffield, Chm., Kathryn Antrim, Marie Bresnahan.—**Lake Zoar Auth.,** Robert Hare, Howard Saad, William Soracin.—**Parks and Recreation Comm.,** Jody S. Short, Chm., Frank Bent, Gregory Gagner, Angelo Lisi, Jr., Agostino Modaffari, Jerome Rookasin, David Struss, Gary A. Tincu, vacancy; Ronald Wallisa, Recr. Dir.—**Town Engineer,** Sherwood Lovejoy.—**Highway Foreman,** James Robertson.—**Building Inspector,** James Sandor.—**Building Bd. of Appeals,** David Bjorklund, Chm., Salvatore Morabito, Louis Raab, Richard Smagala, Richard Steiner.—**Sanitarian,** Thomas Monks.—**Tree Warden,** David Solek.—**Chief of Police,** Robert J. Wesche.—**Police Comm.,** Andrew F. Csire, Frank A. Pinto, Linda S. Suhr, Ronald Villani, Robert L. Zwierlein.—**Constables,** Susan A. Koneff, Richard A. Orr.—**Emergency Management Dir.,** Gerald Swartwood.—**Chiefs of Fire Dept.,** William Davin (Monroe), Robert Wickson (Stepney), Frank Schrodl (Stevenson).—**Fire Marshal,** Anthony E. Carpenter.—**Town Atty.,** David O. Chittick.—**Justices of the Peace,** Lewis D. Andrews, Kathryn J. Antrim, Eleanor Bartosik, Karen L. Burnaska, Edward A. Callo, Andrew F. Csire, Pamela A. Galian, Robert B. Gangnath, David D. Halliwell, Malvin L. Karwoski, Angelo Lisi, Jr., Jane McCarthy, Raymond F. McPadden, Sr., Judith M. Miko, P. John Millo, Jerome L. Rookasin, Joseph A. C. Ruel, Beverly A. Stebbins,

Judith J. Stripay, Margaret A. Tranzillo, Joseph A. Tuozzoli, Jr., Margaret J. Villani, Barbara Anne Yaworowski, Gary E. Zenobia.

MONTVILLE. New London County.—(Form of government, mayor, town council, limited town meeting.)—Inc., Oct. 12, 1786; taken from New London. Area, 44.1 sq. miles. Population, est., 16,572. Voting districts, 5. Principal industries, the manufacture of paper board, paper boxes, computer boards, electricity, tachometers, and aluminum doors and windows. Transp.— Passenger: Served by buses of SEAT. Freight: Served by Central Vermont Railway and numerous motor carriers. Post offices, Montville, Uncasville and Oakdale.

TOWN OFFICERS. Clerk and Reg. of Vital Statistics, Margaret E. Skinner; Hours, 9 A.M.-5 P.M., Mon. thru Fri.; Address, Town Hall, 310 Norwich-New London Rd., Uncasville 06382; Tel., Norwich, (860) 848-1349.—**Asst. Clerk and Asst. Reg. of Vital Statistics,** Lorraine F. Coyer.—**Mayor,** Patrick J. Dougherty (D), Tel., (860) 848-3030.—**Town Council,** Max L. Kopko, Chm., Howard R. Beetham, Jr., Robert J. Collins, Leo M. Chupaska, Marie Feinberg, Irving H. Holmes, James A. Knighton.— **Treas.,** Lisa DiMarco.—**Tax Collector,** Joan Zujus.—**Finance Dir.,** Michael S. Hillsberg.—**Bd. of Assessment Appeals,** Adele C. Giulian, Ellen H. Lakowsky, Joseph J. Socha III.—**Assessor,** Darryl DelGrosso.—**Registrars of Voters,** Lorraine Elliott (D), Judith A. MacNeilly (R).—**Supt. of Schools,** Jacob Ludes III.—**Bd. of Education,** Sandra Berardy, Chm., Linda N. Goodman, Norma Leonard, Todd Pomazon, Joseph C. Sheffey, Jr., 1997; Donald E. Dykes, William T. Herrmann, Susannah E. Holmes, Nancy A. Thomas, 1999.—**Town Planner,** Marcia Vlaun.—**Planning and Zoning Comm.,** Gregory Majewski, Chm., Stanley Bellamy, Arthur Charland, Mary Clark-Wilson, Bart Ferrante, Jr., William Tinnel, Russell A. Wallen, two vacancies; Alternates, James T. Cunningham, two vacancies.—**Zoning Bd. of Appeals,** Robert P. Ziegler, Chm., Joseph DeVito III, Keith M. Foster, Joseph W. Jaskiewicz, Robert Shanahan, Jr.; Alternates, Donald Dykes, Ronald K. McDaniel, Jr., vacancy.—**Zoning Enforcement Officer,** Thomas Sanders.—**Economic Development,** Richard Bennett, Chm., JOseph DeVito, Marjorie Gatheral, Judy Larose, Judith A. MacNeilly, Alan Marcus, Jeffrey W. Muttart, Bernard E. Szreders, Katherine West.—**Housing Auth.,** Alice Howarth, Mary Thomas, Georgia A. Tracey, Homer F. Waters, Donald Woodmansee.—**Conservation Comm.,** John Straub, Chm., four vacancies; Alternates, two vacancies.—**Inland Wetlands Comm.,** Douglas K. Brush, Chm., Jeffrey E .Brewer, Jill B. Johnson, Richard A. Larsen, Charles H. McAdams, Horace O'Donnell, Howard V. Riske, Jr., Philip R. Sullivan, Lois D. Taylor.—**Flood and Erosion Control Bd.,** Town Council.—**Municipal Historian,** Helen Aldrich.—**Comm. on Aging,** Albert F. Post, Sr., Chm., Carol J. Lathrop, Barbara A. MacFayden, John T. Munton, Mildred Peck, Willie J. Wells, vacancy.—**Social Services Dir.,** Carol Dawley.—**Youth Advisory Bd.,** Dennis R. Monahan, Jr., Chm., Sandra Berardy, Kelby Chappelle, Donna Ganong, Donna Geary, Scott Geary, Sheila H. Harris, Constance Herrmann, Anthony J. Pescatello. Jr., Charles E. Spicer.—**Youth Services Dir.,** Christine Van Dusen.— **Dir. of Health,** Arthur Cohen (Uncas Health Dist.).—**Parks and Recreation Comm.,** Nancy A. T. Cook, Chm., Joseph S. Berardy, Nancy Delacruz, Stanley J. Gwudz, Kenneth B. Herman, Joseph W. Jaskiewicz, Joseph N. Lavoie, James Loftis, James F.

Orlando; James Butler, Recr. Dir.—**Water and Water Pollution Control Auth.,** Wilfred Bellefleur, Chm., John F. Geary, Bruce Martell, two vacancies.—**Dir. of Public Works,** vacancy.—**Building Code Bd. of Appeals,** John Biederka, Arthur Eisdore, Jr., Bart Ferrante, Jr., William Pieniadz, vacancy.—**Building Inspector,** Russell Stauffer.—**Sewer Admin.,** William Noyes.—**Gardner Lake Auth.,** Joseph Hull, Albert Lyman, vacancy.—**Recycling Admin.,** Fannie Esidore.—**Public Safety Committee,** Fred Avery, Sr., Chm., Paul J. Benyeda, Neil Feinberg, Alexander Hay, Julius Jurkiewicz, Anthony Pescatello, Jr., Thomas West.—**Chief of Police,** Patrick J. Dougherty.—**Constables,** Carl Bourne, Leonard Bunnell, Scott Davis, Grigg Jacobson, Richard Lenda, Jon Lowke, Mark Manley, Dennis Mathers, Dennis R. Monahan, Jr., Carlton Pipping, William Rodenberg, Robin Salvatore, Mahhew Tringe, David Vidal, Russell Wehner.—**Chiefs of Fire Depts.,** Richard McGuigan (Chesterfield), Robert Daegatano (Mohegan), Scott Hurne (Montville), Gary Murphy (Oakdale).—**Fire Marshal/Civil Preparedness Dir.,** Raymond Occhialini.—**Town Atty.,** James J. Devine.—**Justices of the Peace,** Betty J. Allard, Herbert H. Bachelder, Jr., Henri L. Baxter, Raymond F. Bedard, Howard R. Beetham, Jr., Patricia A. Beetham, Merrielee Beetham-Turley, Sandra Berardy, Kenneth G. Brevard, Teri E. Bruce, Frank N. Chalk, Mary E. Clark-Wilson, Robert J. Collins, Patricia A. Danielson, Shelley J. Dennis, Patrick J. Dougherty, Josephine M. Dreessen, Alfred J. Drozdal, Ernest J. Duhaime, Patrick J. Dunion, Donald E. Dykes, Lorraine A. Elliott, Richard H. Fawcett, Marjorie Fisher, Keith M. Foster, Marchita N. Foster, Patrick M. Foster, Marjorie A. Gatheral, Michael J. Grelle, Sr., Harry B. Heller, Ellen L. Hillman, Joseph W. Jaskiewicz, Edward G. Javor, Jill B. Johnson, Victoria Kapilotis, Jerome L. Keel, Kevin J. Klinefelter, James A. Knighton, Max L. Kopko, Eric J. Land, Judith Ann MacNeilly, Ann M. Mattson, Ines Mazzei, Charles H. McPherson, Matthew S. McShane, Ronald Moore, Marie V. Morosky, Shirley I. Morphis, Marjorie P. Murphy, Loretta E. Phillips, John M. Pisczek, Rosemary S. Platt, Kenneth L. Przybysz, Alfred A. Raab, James S. Radgowski, Robert T. Reed, George A. Rice, James F. Rondeau, Kevin Ryan, Elizabeth Schafer, Wayne D. Scott, Jeffrey C. Seeley, Elisabeth P. Sheehan, Joseph J. Socha III, Bernard E. Szreders, Joanne R. Tew, Richard L. Wilson, Eleanor S. Winsor, Theodore Wisniewski, Jr., Alexander Zawacki.

MORRIS. Litchfield County.—(Form of government, selectmen, town meeting, board of finance.)—Inc., June, 1859; taken from Litchfield. Area, 18.7 sq. miles. Population, est., 2,160. Voting district, 1. Principal industry, agriculture and light industry. Bantam Lake, the largest natural lake in the state and a popular summer resort lies mostly within the town. Transp.—Freight: Served by numerous motor common carriers. Post offices, Morris and Lakeside.

TOWN OFFICERS. Clerk and Reg. of Vital Statistics, Ann E. Carr; Hours, 9 A.M.-12 Noon, 1-4 P.M., Mon. through Fri.; Address, 3 East St., P.O. Box 66, 06763; Tel., (860) 567-7433.—**Asst. Clerks and Asst. Regs. of Vital Statistics,** Marilyn Birkett, Laura Halloran.—**Selectmen,** 1st, Philip D. Birkett (R) Tel., (860) 567-9335, Linda B. Tiffany (R), Richard A. Hull, Sr. (ACP).—**Treas.,** Donald B. Lawson.—**Bd. of Finance,** John Dezzuti, James K. Finch II, Sallyann M. Gladych, Patricia G. Goslee, Bill King, Sandra A. Vicari.—**Tax Collector,** Carol J. Whittlesey.—**Bd. of Assess-**

ment **Appeals,** Norval R. Lunan, Chm., David Fenn, Gregory P. Margaitis.—**Assessor,** Barbara Bigos.—**Registrars of Voters,** Laura L. Halloran (D), Suzanne M. Shrady (R).—**Supt. of Schools,** Dr. Timothy M. Breslin.—**Pension Fund Trustees,** Cathy Kohout, Betty Pattison, Eugenia Pedane.—**Planning and Zoning Comm.,** Barbara E. Bongiolatti, Chm., Marilyn W. Birkett, Thomas F. Dougherty, Richard J. Grinvalsky, Joseph F. Margaitis, Michael Maselli, Robert J. McNamara, John Sniffen, Edward T. Sutton, Jr.; Alternates, Gregory P. Margaitis, Stephen S. Paletsky, Daniel K. Thomas.—**Zoning Bd. of Appeals,** Mark Conlon, Nancy S. Fenn, David L. Snyder, Paul J. Tiffany, Clifford M. Wheeler; Alternates, Robert T. Cahill, Jr., Joseph C. Ferraro, Frederick J. McCarthy.—**Zoning Enforcement Officer,** Walter Burcroff.—**Housing Auth.,** Evelyn Rowley, Chm., Margaret Andrulis, Linda Conlon, Peter Dahlin, Mark Paletsky; Dale Kroop, Dir.—**Conservation and Inland Wetlands Comm.,** Eugene A. Mastroianni, Chm., Jamie Delorenzo, Michael Doyle, John Gladych, Jeffrey Greenwood.—**Agent for the Aging,** Marilyn Aligata.—**Senior Center Comm.,** Catherine Hull, Chm., Evelyn Doyle, Kay Healy, Hugh Stiles, Helen Styers, Rosemary Vogini.—**Recreation Dir.,** Diane Lauretano.—**Dir. of Health,** James Rokos, M.P.H. (P.O., Torrington).—**Bd. of Public Health,** JoAnn Battistoni, Tom Dougherty, Patricia Goslee, Carol Keysor, Sandra Vicari, two vacancies.—**Library Directors,** Sarah P. Irwin, Chm., Donna Crepeau, William King, Carol A. Smith, Virginia Towne, Dolores H. Whelan.—**Municipal Historian,** Walter France.—**Beach and Recreation Comm.,** J. Reginald Harrison, Chm., William Downes, Charles E. Liner, Norval Lunan, William A. Nelson, vacancy.—**Building Official,** Paul E. Woike; Asst., Joel Skilton.—**Building Code Bd. of Appeals,** five vacancies.—**Sewer Auth.,** Michael Doyle, Chm., Joann Battistoni, Steven Kohout, Eugene Mastroianni, Mary Nield; Alternates, Scott Personatti, Richard Roberts.—**Bantam Lake Auth.,** Karrie Morris, Gary Stafford, Thomas Weik.—**Chief of Fire Dept.,** Lewis Clark; Deputy, George Humphrey, Jr.—**Fire Marshal,** Joel Skilton.—**Sandy Beach Comm.,** Linnea Bauer, David Fenn, Corinne Houle, Amy VanHorne, Pamela Wray.—**Town Attys.,** Roraback & Roraback.—**Justices of the Peace,** Philip D. Birkett, Lenore T. Blake, Arnold R. Bohanan, Sr., Barbara E. Bongiolatti, Jacqueline R. Costantino, Thomas F. Dougherty, James K. Finch II, Henry J. Grenier, Jr., Bonnie L. Grinvalsky, Laura L. Halloran, Richard A. Hull, Sr., Sarah P. Irwin, Michael T. Keilty, Michelle M. Margaitis, Eugene A. Mastroianni, Frederick C. Neri, Marguerite J. Neri, Jeffrey Nield, David L. Paletsky, Marc A. Paletsky, Carol S. Perham, Robert J. Pivirotto, Evelyn F. Rowley, Albert J. Ruigrok, Michael Schwartz, Richard P. Skilton, John C. Sniffen, David L. Snyder, Edward T. Sutton, Jr., Sandra A. Vicari, Dolores H. Whelan.

NAUGATUCK. New Haven County.—(Form of government, mayor and burgesses.)—Inc., May, 1844; taken from Waterbury, Bethany and Oxford. Borough and town consolidated, 1895. Area, 16.5 sq. miles. Population, est., 31,050. Voting districts, 8. Principal industries, chemicals, brass novelties, plastics, aerosols, moulded aluminum and iron, glass, brass and copper goods, candy, screws, hospital supplies. Transp.—Passenger: Served by Metro North Commuter Railroad Co. and buses of The Northeast Transportation Bus Line; The Arrow Line, Inc. from New Haven and Winsted; Valley Transp. Co. from Bridgeport. Freight: Served by Conrail and numerous motor common carriers. Post offices, Naugatuck and Union City.

TOWN OFFICERS. Clerk and Reg. of Vital Statistics, Sophie K. Morton; Hours, 8:30 A.M.-4 P.M., Mon. through Fri.; Address, Town Hall, 229 Church St., 06770; Tel., (203) 729-4571, Ext. 265.—**Asst. Clerk and Asst. Reg. of Vital Statistics,** Pamela G. Ruccio.—**Asst. Reg. of Vital Statistics,** Nancy Goudreau.—**Mayor,** Timothy D. Barth (R).—**Controller,** Wayne McAllister.—**Selectmen,** Christian A. Herb, John M. Sheedy, Nancy A. Stiber.—**Treas.,** Judy Anderson.—**Bd. of Finance,** Robert Neth, Chm., John Aresta, Joseph Butler, Harry Cashin III, Cindy Herb, Raymond Lennon, Jr., Michael Reilly, William Rosenblatt, Carlos Santos; Alternates, Mayor Timothy D. Barth, Dorothy Hoff, Raymond R. Kloc.—**Tax Collector,** Henry A. Kogut.—**Assessor,** Norma Henderson.—**Board of Assessment Appeals,** Judy Anderson, Steven Gesseck, Martin F. Sullivan.—**Registrars of Voters,** Ann M. Hildreth (D), Jane H. Pronovost (R).—**Supt. of Schools,** Dr. Alice Tufts.—**Bd. of Education,** Rebecca Zandvliet, Chm., Lorraine C. Dibble, Rocco Vitale, 1997; Brian F. Bedard, Arthur E. Dessureau, Jr., Barbara F. Lewis, 1999; George F. Krodel, Jamie M. Nixon, Alec Wargo, 2001.—**Planning Comm.,** Joseph McEvoy, Chm., Frank Cannizzo, Jeffrey S. Croce, E. Harry Jancis, vacancy; Alternates, Jodi M. Gregg, David Macharelli, Ronald White.—**Town Planner,** Anthony Pesanelli.—**Zoning Comm.,** David Straznitskas, Jack Valinho, Co-Chm., Maryanna Barnes, Stephen Krasney, Stephen Moody; Alternates, Thomas Duffy, Michael Garnett, Daniel Ramos.—**Zoning Bd. of Appeals,** Lynn Tata, Chm., Joseph J. Dinneny, Mary Beth Hanks, Charles L. Marino, Diana C. Parady; Alternates, Anthony Battaglia, Daniel Simoes, vacancy.—**Zoning Enforcement Officer,** Michael Mormile.—**Economic Development Comm.,** Anthony Pesanelli, Chm., Dominic Alegi, Josephus Ballenger, Jr., William Hass, Richard A. Hertel, Richard Hoben, Harry Jancis, Theodore Mariano, Joseph Regan; Alternates, Elaine McLaughlin, James Szarzynski.—**Housing Auth.,** Michael F. Rizzuti, Chm., Beatrice Broadrick, Dorothy Mason, Mary Tamosaitis, Florence Volonino; George R. Ronkowitz, Dir.—**Environmental Control Comm.,** James Ackerman, Chm., Walter Harris, Antonio Moura, Harold J. Simons, Paul Smith, Vincent Sosnowski, Annalee VanAllen; Alternates, Emil A. Coviello, Jr., Ann Simons, Robert VanAllen.—**Inland Wetlands Comm.,** Jose J. Pereira, Chm., Stephen Fainer, Janet Ferguson, Michael Piombo, Louis H. Wilmot; Alternates, Thomas Betkoski, Sharon Haynes.—**Comm. on Services for the Elderly,** Marjorie Carlson, Chm., William Braziel, Beatrice Broadrick, Christine Joyce, Carole Mancini, Manuel Medeiros, Olive Rathburn, Peter Ruggeri, George W. Rusnak, Helen Sokoloski; Ann Austin, Agent.—**Human Resources Development Agency,** Steve Rosenblatt, Chm., Maria DaSilva, William Griffin, Franklin Johnson, Susan Moore, Mary Ann Reilly; Robert Woodfield, Liaison.—**Welfare Supt.,** Barbara Schwartz-Dotts.—**Dir. of Health,** Leon J. O'Connor, M.D.—**Library Directors,** Robert Hill, Chm., Nellie Beatty, Wayne Buckmiller, William Hass, Harry Melkonian.—**Dir. of Youth Services,** Jane Lobdell.—**Park Comm.,** Joseph Healy, Chm., Paul Bendler, Brian Dell, Gordon Rossi, Robert Ruccio; Francis McMullen, Supt.—**Supt. of Streets,** Henry J. Witkoski, Jr.—**Town Engineer,** Ronald Mormile.—**Building Inspector,** Michael Salafia.—**Building Code Bd. of Appeals,** Roland Desrosiers, Earl R. Lindgren, Robert J. Oris, Anthony Smith.—**Purchasing Agent,** Wendy Hozer.—**Water Pollution Control Bd.,** James McGrath, Chm., Joseph Bielanos, Robert Butkevicius, William J. Goggin, Sr., David Weeden; John P. Pruchnicki, Exec. Dir.—**Chief of Police,** Dennis Clisham.—**Police Comm.,** Nelson DeFreitas, Chm. Anita

Carriero, George Errico, Ronald Gallant, Annette Woodfield.—**Chief of Fire Dept.,** Kerry Flaherty.—**Fire Marshal,** Mark Seeger.—**Bd. of Fire Comrs.,** Mayor Timothy D. Barth, John W. Ford, Carl J. Herb, Robert Hildreth, Richard Mortensen, Francis E. Smith.—**Civil Preparedness Dir.,** Larry Santoro.—**Town Atty.,** N. Warren Hess.— **Justices of the Peace,** Charles H. Anderson, Rosanne A. Asselin, Thomas E. Betkoski, Madeleine F. Caine, Marjorie A. Carlson, James F. Curran, Kevin M. DelGobbo, Jose DeMatos, Karen A. Dibble, Ralph DiPalma, Joseph D. Fitzgerald, Florence C. Foley, John W. Ford, Michael J. Garnett, Martin J. Gotlibowski, Neal B. Hanlon, Robert W. Hildreth, E. Harry Jancis, John E. Letts, Sr., Tony G. Locke, Wayne A. McAllister, Diane M. Ostuni, Samuel R. Russo, Cele H. Sargeant, Clarence O. Schiller, Richard C. Wilmot, James J. Woermer, Donald J. Zehnder, Jr.

BOROUGH OFFICERS. Mayor, Timothy D. Barth (R).—**Borough Clerk,** Judith E. Crosswait; Hours, 8:30 A.M.-4 P.M.; Address, 229 Church St., 06770; Tel., (203) 729-4571.—**Asst. Borough Clerk,** Rosanne Asselin.—**Burgesses,** Robert J. Burns, Deputy Mayor; Lois A. Ackerman, Robert J. Burns, Jeffrey S. Croce, William J. Goggin, Sr., Kevin G. Knowles, Robert A. Neth, Joan B. Taf, Joseph J. Wojtczak, Jr.— **Treas.,** Judy E. Anderson.—**Tax Collector,** Henry Kogut.—**Controller,** Wayne McAllister.—**Bailiffs,** Thomas E. Betkoski, Florence C. Foley, Gerald J. Garceau, Karen L. Kimball, Carl J. Miele, Thomas G. Pohorilak, Robert P. Wagner, Richard C. Wilmot.—**Borough Planning Comm.,** Joseph McEvoy, Chm., Frank Cannizzo, Jeffrey S. Croce, E. Harry Jancis; Alternates, Jodi M. Gregg, David Macharell.—**Borough Engineer,** Ronald Mormile.—**Street Supt.,** Hank Witkoski, Jr.—**Borough Atty.,** N. Warren Hess III, Peter Mariano, David Labriola.

NEW BRITAIN. Hartford County.—(Form of government, mayor, common council.)—Town and borough, inc., May, 1850; taken from Berlin. City inc., 1871. Town and City consolidated, April, 1905. Area, 13.4 sq. miles. Population, est., 71,911. Voting districts, 19. Principal industries, manufacture of builders' hardware, engineering firms, banking, hoists, mechanics' tools, etc. Transp.—Passenger: Served locally by buses of Dattco Inc., New Britain Transp. Co., Inc., Bonanza Bus Lines, Inc., Conn. Transit and by Greyhound. Freight: Served by Conrail and numerous motor common carriers. Post office, New Britain.

CITY AND TOWN OFFICERS. City Clerk, Town Clerk and Reg. of Vital Statistics, Peter J. Denuzze; Hours, 8:15 A.M.-3:45 P.M., Mon., Tues., Wed., Fri.; 8:15 A.M.-6:45 P.M. Thurs.; Address, City Hall, 27 West Main St., 06051; Tel., (860) 826-3344.—**Asst. Clerks,** Mary Ann Hausman, Audrey Malkemus, Theresa Szmurlo.—**Asst. Regs. of Vital Statistics,** Mary Dzioba, Marie Haze, Jennifer McMahon, Judith McMahon.—**Mayor,** Lucian J. Pawlak (D).—**Mayor Pro Tempore,** Mark H. Bernacki.—**Common Council:** Aldermen, Mark H. Bernacki, Aime J.Brochu, Paul M. Carver, Jeffrey W. Gacek, Nina F. Jankowski, Barbara G. Kirejczyk, Timothy J. Morrell, Gary J. Pescosolido, William C. Rivera, Lori A. Rocha, Edgardo Saavedra, Barbara U. Scully, James A. Simpson, Robin C. Spencer, Barbara L. Yezierski.—**Treas.,** Robert J. Balocki.—**Bd. of Finance,** Richard M.Pokorski, Chm., Ronald Cuttino, Margie Davis, Leslie Eza, Marilyn Kraczkowsky, Lisa McKinnon,

John Murphy, Alan Parlow, Jr., Raymond Roy, John Valengavich, Daniel Wilcox, James Wyskiewicz; John Jedrzejczyk, Dir.—**Ethics Comm.,** James Sullivan, Chm., Diane DeFronzo, Peggy Riotte, Kenneth Slater.—**Tax Collector,** Fred J. Menditto.—**Bd. of Assessment Appeals,** George Sapieha, Chm., Peter A. Oshana, Adam Pokorski.—**Assessor,** Charles G. Agli, Jr.—**Registrars of Voters,** Edward J. Dzwonkowski (D), Dorothy R. Turnrose (R).—**Supt. of Schools,** Dr. James Rhinesmith.—**Bd. of Education,** Paul S. Amenta, Judith K. Guida, Pres., James E. Sanders, Sr., Juan Verdu, vacancy, 1997; Steven W. Horowitz, Peter J. Kochol, Carole A. Langlais, Peter M. Rosa, Timothy J. Stewart, 1999.—**Personnel Dir.,** John R. Byrne.—**Civil Service Comm.,** Curtis Searle, Chm., Philip T. Hall, Claudia Helfgott, Nancy Judd, Marietta Kerr, Robert F. Weber, Jr.—**City Plan Comm.,** Larry P. Levesque, Chm., Howard Belkin, Esther A. Farr, Peter J.Gostin, Anthony S. Montanile, Thomas Mullins.—**Dir. of Planning,** Sarajane Pickett.—**Zoning Bd. of Appeals,** James Carey, Robert Colossale, Craig D'Angelo, Stephen L. Mangan, Kathleen Olandt, Jack Shea, Catherine Spano; Alternates, three vacancies.—**Community and Neighborhood Development,** Peter Spano, Chm., Anthony Bianca, Jr., Alan Bielanski, Naomi Blank, Michael Carrier, Joseph Kuzia, Edward LaChance, Roger Lagasse, Anthony Norris, Rita Perduta, Elizabeth Ratzlaff, Rubin Rodriguez, Richard Rose.—**Housing Auth.,** Donald DeFronzo, Chm., Kyle Anderson, Elene Demos, David Pollowitz, Bienvenido Sanchez; vacancy, Exec. Dir.—**Housing Bd. of Appeals,** Wilfred Beloin, Chm., Louis Amodio, Sr., Christine Burns, Alphonzo Collins, Robert Nowik, Fred Stockman.—**Conservation Comm.,** Michael Dooman, Chm., Jeffrey Bieber, Edmund Helmecki, Felix H. Kummer, George Markow, Kathryn West.—**Comm. on Aging,** Harriet Geragosian, Chm., Rose Mary Delldonna, Henry Kita, Donna Lee, Leo Maffei, Georgianne Pollowitz, Teresa Sapieha, Rose G. Shilinga.—**Human Rights and Opportunities,** Brenda Simmons, Chm., Howard Dyson, Joan Pina, Daniel M. Salerno, Mary Lou Sanders.—**Welfare Dir.,** Gregory Steltner.—**Bd. of Public Welfare,** Diane Baraglia, Chm., Daniel Blanco, Andra Genovese, Stephen Karp, Peter Mozzer, Sakinah Salahu-Din.—**Dir. of Health,** Hudson Birden.—**Bd. of Public Health,** Dr. Frank Gerratana, Chm., Marcia Bergman, Joyce Bray, Philomena Fedor, Aurora Jakubonski, Wanda Radziewicz, Gary Riley.—**Comm. on Persons with Disabilities,** Tracey Kralik, Chm., Barbara Canzonetti, Maria Gomez, Robin B. Hudson, Michael Kinney, Joanne Niedbala, Diane Radziwon-Moriarity.—**Library Directors,** Joan Kelly-Coyle, Chm., Brenda Bemben, Stanley Blewjas, R. Lois Blomstrann, Paul Carver, Victor C. Darnell, Peter J. Denuzze, Patricia Downs, Seth Feigenbaum, TimothyGrace, Deborah Kennedy, Edward T. Lynch, Paul A. Marier, Kevin McCabe, Mary Meaney, Martha Mosley, Lillian Padula, Claire O. Pietras, Lindsley Wellman.—**Parks and Recreation Comm.,** Sebastian Cannamela, Chm., George Brusznicki, Angelo D'Alfonso, Scott Hamel, William Huber, Patricia C. Kozikowski, Peter Steele, Joe Vitelli; R. Peter Ledger, Dir.—**Building Comm.,** Louis Amodio, Joseph Cisz, Kenneth Jones, Arnold Schwartz, Ned Stachen.—**City Hall Comm.,** Phyllis Hammond, Chm., Eileen Gorczyca, Henry Gajda.—**Bd. of Compensation and Assessment,** Melissa D. Aiudi, Frank Bradley, Joan Calvo, Julie Dyson, James Pollowitz, Thomas Talalaj.—**Cemetery Committee,** William A. Forbes, Chm., Patricia A. Sheridan, D. J. Harry Webb.—**Veterans Comm.,** Maurice Ames, Mario Bonola, Tadeusz Galaszewski, Charles Jase, Raymond Lavoie, Marc Pucinski, John Westergom, Clifford Willis; Louis Gentile,

Dir.—**Bd. of Public Works,** Charles Bugnacki, Michael T. Konik, Mildred Reyes, George Rothstein, Joseph Willis; Joseph Carilli, Dir.—**Acting Purchasing Agent,** John Jedrzejczyk.—**Acting City Engineer,** Clarence Corbin.—**Sanitarian,** Robert Jase.—**Sealer of Weights and Measures,** vacancy.—**Acting Building Inspector,** Norman Wnuk.—**Building Code Bd. of Appeals,** George Bartus, Jose Concepcion, Gordon Harrod, John Stepensky, Stanley Yusciewitz.—**Bd. of Water Comrs.,** Louis O. Gagliardi, Chm., Henry Andrzejczyk, Ronald Hanson, Kim Ki Hoon.—**Chief of Police,** William Sencio.—**Police Comm.,** William J. McNamara, Chm., John Fredericks, Roman Nowak, Manuel Reyes.—**Constables,** Jose E. Angulo, Steven C. Belkin, Charles S. Conochalla, Willard J. Crandall, Dominic M. Paventi, Richard Reyes, Frederick C. Stockman, Alex J. Zaniewski.—**Chief of Fire Dept./Fire Marshal,** Thomas D. Keough, Sr.—**Bd. of Fire Comrs.,** Joseph Veneziano, Chm., Howard Begley, William V. Dworski, Leslie Jacobs.—**Civil Defense Dir.,** Eugene Ostrowski.—**Corporation Counsel,** Robert A. Scalise, Sr.—**Justices of the Peace,** Anne G. Adamowich, Peter Adamowich, James Aglio, Carmen T. Aloisi, Paul J. Amenta, Jr., Paul S. Amenta, Kyle D. Anderson, Florence M. Andrews, Henry S. Andrzejczyk, Jose E. Angulo, Betty Ann M. Atkinson, George Balkun, Howard H. Belkin, Louise P. Belkin, Steven C. Belkin, Wilfred L. Beloin, Shirley G. Black, Michael J. Borselle, Rose B. Bouley, Barbara H. Boutin, Thomas A. Bozek, Alison S. Buckwell, Teresa A. Bujnowski, Joan A. Calvo, Anthony A. Cane, Sebastian Cannamela, Joseph Cap, Fred Caracciolo, Lisa R. Carver, Paul M. Carver, John P. Catenzaro, Anthony G. Cervoni, Jr., Robert D. Clinch, Connie W. Collins, Jose M. Colon, Delizia C. Conochalla, Roseann W. Cornelli, Jenny Correa, Willard J. Crandall, Marilynn Cruz-Aponte, Mary-Dawn R. Danielewski, Nicholas E. DeNigris, Peter J. Denuzze, Lillian W. Dorval, William V. Dworski, Edward J. Dzwonkowski, Olga E. Egipciaco, Theodore Faticoni, Constance W. Fazzina, John L. Fredericks, Louis Gagliardi, Zulma M. Garcia, Helen B. Gaydosh, Joseph M. Gaydosh, Joseph W. Gaydosh, Rose S. Gendron, Albert J. Gentile, Evelyn D. Gentile, Louis A. Gentile, Harriet S. Geragosian, Theresa B. Gerratana, Arthur J. Gibney, Sr., Eugenia H. Gil, Eileen Gorczyca, Peter J. Gostin, William A. Grogan, Edward J. Grudzinski, Ronald Hansen, Joseph H. Harper, Jr., Page S. Hartling, Claudia G. Helfgott, Edmund S. Helmecki, Lawrence J. Hermanowski, Brenda S. Humphrey, Miriam Ithier, Edward J. Januszewski, Elizabeth F. Johnson, Francis A. Joyce, Richard L. Judd, Arlene B. Kawecki, Shirley D. Krawczyk, Deborah A. Krawiec, Halina Z. Krawiec, Gregory J. Kwasowski, John A. Kwasowski, Claude R. Leclerc, Patricia B. Luke, Donald S. Malinowski, Kenneth A. Malinowski, Mary E. Malinowski, Paul J. Manafort, Daniel P. Martinook, Leocadia M. McCue, Lisa H. McKinnon, Susan M. McMullen, John N. McNamara, William J. McNamara, Fred J. Menditto, Joseph J. Menditto, Stanley J. Morgiewicz, Timothy J. Morrell, J. Elizabeth T. Nkonoki-Ward, Anthony J. Norris, Carl R. Olandt, Kathleen W. Olandt, Peter A. Oshana, Larayne Parker, Victoria Parsons, Helen Z. Pearl, Jason E. Pearl, Lisa E. Perry, Emma W. Pierce, Adam Platosz, Ann Platosz, Astrid T. Poglitsch, Wanda F. Radzewicz, Carol V. Rocha, Gregory E. Rogala, Reginald Ronzello, Alexander D. Rosenzweig, Norman J. Roy, Daniel M. Salerno, John D. Salvetti, Jr., Louis G. Salvio, James E. Sanders, Sr., Michael F. Sanders, William A. Sanders, Arnold P. Schwartz, Carol E. Shea, William B. Shea, Jr., Joseph D. Shilinga, Carmen D. Sierra, Lucy M. Smith, Genevieve K. Sobell, Catherine M. Spano, Nathalie B.

Spano, Peter Spano, David C. St Laurent, Ned R. Statchen, Irena Stepanczak, Frederick C. Stockman, Kevin A. Stringer, Bessie L. Surratt, Gregory Thibault, Nancy Lee M. Thomson, Eva Torres-Luciano, Dorothy R. Turnrose, Cassandra C. Tyson, Frances A. Urso, Joseph S. Veneziano, Sandra E. Veneziano, Cara A. Vilas, Josephine G. Wells, Maryjayne B. Wierbicki, Michael J. Wierbicki, Jr., Joe C. Willis, Marilyn G. Wills, James A. Wyskiewicz, Alan F. Zaniewski, Kimberly A. Zaniewski, Frank A. Zenobi.

NEW CANAAN. Fairfield County.—(Form of government, selectmen, town council, board of finance.)—Inc., May, 1801; taken from Norwalk and Stamford. Area, 22.5 sq. miles. Population, est., 18,622. Voting districts, 3. Residential community with a compact business district of specialty shops, and some small office buildings. Transp.—Passenger: Served by Metro North Commuter Rail Co. and Conn. Limousine Service to area airports. Freight: Served by Conrail. Post office, New Canaan.

TOWN OFFICERS. Clerk and Reg. of Vital Statistics, Mary L. Ritter; Hours, 8:30 A.M.-4 P.M., Mon. through Fri.; Address, Town Hall, 77 Main St., 06840; Tel., (203) 972-2323.—**Asst. Clerks and Asst. Regs. of Vital Statistics,** Katherine M. Lutter, Ellen S. Wittenberger.—**Selectmen,** 1st, Louis J. Moreno (R) Tel., (203) 972-2311; FAX, (203) 966-0309, Jack W. Foster (D), Vincent A. Socci (R).—**Town Council,** William R. Bach, Chm., Lewis J. Annunziato, Michael A. Apy, George W. Baker, Jr., John W. Hetherington, Christine M. Hussey, Thomas B. Moorhead, Robert C. Mullane, Laszlo Papp, Laurie A. Saggese, Anne-Marie Sutton, Lawrence A. Tomaselli.—**Treas.,** V. Donald Hersam, Jr.—**Bd. of Finance,** Louis J. Moreno, Chm., Robert M. Conner, Harry Durney, Robert Layton, Richard B. McKeough, Roger C. Smith, C. Daniel Ward, James Wilson; Alternates, Richard P. Bond, G. Ann Byrne, Catherine Devereaux.—**Chief Financial Officer/Comptroller,** Gary G. Conrad.—**Tax Collector,** Louise J. Andronaco.—**Bd. of Assessment Appeals,** V. Henry O'Neill, Karen Z. Sneirson, Julie H. Taylor.—**Assessor,** Gordon M. Donley.—**Registrars of Voters,** George E. Cody (D), Claudia A. Weber (R).—**Supt. of Schools,** Gary G. Richards.— **Bd. of Education,** Ronald M. Cowin, Chm., Susan G. Ceresa, Gene W. Goodman, Sally T. Hines, Doreen M. O'Leary, 1997; Marne A. Dubs, Barry J. Kesselman, Sandra S. Richardson, Ditte N. Reifsnyder, 1999.—**Planning and Zoning Comm.,** James H. Bennett, Chm., Lawrence W. DeVito, Walter T. Flaherty, Jr., Jean Grzelecki, Donald Hunziker, Albert J. Kolff, Robert McKay, G. David Scannell, George B. Wendell; Alternates, Robert Coburn, Roger Rothballer, Robert Yaro.—**Town Planner,** Daniel A. Foley.—**Zoning Bd. of Appeals,** Edwin J. Deadrick, Chm., J. Hart Evans, Frank Fredericksen, Stanley E. Jaworowski, Fordyce B. St. John, Jr.; Alternates, Frank Barfuss, Eric Landers, Carroll Yanicelli.—**Housing Auth.,** Richard A. Derbes, Chm., Barbara Ayers, Hans F. Reiss, Henry M. Rowett III.—**Parking Comm.,** Lindy A. Gallagher, Chm., Alan Baker, John Beitler, Robert K. Colville, Richard Franco, Jr.— **Environmental Comm.,** Sven Englund, Chm., James M. Kent, John B. Lee, John J. Morrow, Nancy S. Sessions, Daniel P. Stepanek, Eugene Tonkovich; Alternates, Thomas Conte, George Mandler.—**Historic Dist. Comm.,** Richard Bergmann, Chm., Ann Kallgren, Janet R. Lindstrom, Jens Risom; Alternates, Fielding Bowman, Nina Brown, Wesley Liebtag.—**Personnel Advisory Bd.,** Eugene Kallgren, Chm., Donald

G. Hudson, vacancy.—**Comm. on Aging,** Lois J. Anderson, Chm., David Brown, Mary M. Sherry, Cathleen Vollmer, Penny Young.—**Agent for the Elderly/Dir. of Social Services,** Cheryl A. Pickering.—**Bd. of Social Services,** Barbara Kilner, Chm., Diane Cowin, Leo E. Karl, Jr., Rheba H. Haley, Lynn Lyttle, Manuela Tugman.—**Dir. of Health,** Charlotte R. Brown, M.D.—**Emergency Medical Services Comm.,** Wendy Hilbolt, Chm., Robert N. Clark, Jr., Morey McDaniel.—**Jury Committee,** Howard K. Gray, Chm., Beverly Greenberg, Richard Weber.—**Library Bd. of Trustees,** C. Daniel Ward, Pres., Diane Beck, Jane A. Caulfield, Mik Chwalek, Joan Dam, Robert M. Discipio, Alan R. Donaldson, Robert Drummond, Judy T. Dunn, Jane Fox, Chester B. Hansen, Barbara J. Lapolla, Louis Moreno, Alexandra Potts, Suzanne S. Salomon, Lorna Stengel, John G. Trifero, Jr., Hermoine H. Wade, Christine D. Yordan.—**Parks and Recreation Comm.,** Robert E. Nielsen, Chm., Anne C. Cotton, Mark Dewaele, William F. Hopkins, Halford P. McLane, Alice Parker, Randy Roorbach; Stephen E. Benko, Jr., Recr. Dir.—**Youth Comm.,** Catharine Sturgess, Chm., Dennis Lombard, Mildred Russell, Janet Schmitz, Madaline Winkles, Al Woodhall.—**Dir. of Public Works/Town Engineer,** Frank A. DeNicola.—**Supt. of Highways,** Charles Gallo.—**Chief Building Official,** John J. Picanzi.—**Bd. of Building Appeals,** Murray Albertson, Karl H. Blees, Kenneth L. Waters, William C. Westerhoff, Sr.—**Dir. of Environmental Health/Sanitarian,** A. Briggs Geddis.—**Tree Warden,** William Jordan.—**Chief of Police,** Eric Dam.—**Police Comm.,** James Schlumpf, Chm., Roger Phillips, Dexter Sutton.—**Constables,** William M. Chaffey, Suzanne Conron-Grabarz, Austin O. Furst, Jr., Theodore Jeffrey, Joseph G. Liska, Eileen J. McNamara, vacancy.—**Chief of Fire Dept.,** Stephen E. Benko, Jr.—**Fire Marshal/Civil Preparedness Dir.,** Robert A. Fairty.—**Bd. of Fire Comrs.,** Daniel B. Conron, Chm., Vincent Ferullo, Richard P. Munger.—**Town Atty.,** Edward S. Rimer, Jr.—**Justices of the Peace,** John Antognoli, Alan G. Baker, Patricia K. Brooks, Joan V. Bryk, Henry S. Coleman, Lloyd C. Cook, Sydney L. Greenberg, Arthur B. Guerrero, Hugh Halsell III, George Herhold, Hazel R. Hobbs, Gail Noble, Frances F. Overlock, Ronald Petronella, Mark C. Rearick, Sandra L. Ryan, Robert L. Shafter, Ruth H. Smithers, Jane H. Sweet, Joan Taylor, Bernard Tiani, Mary Ann Walsh, James L. Wilson.

NEW FAIRFIELD. Fairfield County.—(Form of government, selectmen, town meeting, board of finance.)—Inc. May 1740. Area, 25.1 sq. miles. Population, est., 13,143. Voting districts, 2. Principal industries, machined tools and electrical parts; well known summer resort. Transp.—Freight: Served by numerous motor common carriers. Post office, New Fairfield; Brewster, NY, R.F.D. 3.

TOWN OFFICERS. Clerk and Reg. of Vital Statistics, Diana M. Peck; Hours, 8:30 A.M.-5 P.M., Tues. through Fri.; 8:30 A.M.-12 Noon, Sat.; Address, Town Hall, Rte. 39, 4 Brush Hill Road, 06812; Tel., Danbury, (203) 746-8110.—**Asst. Clerk and Asst. Reg. of Vital Statistics,** Gail DeFeo, Beverly Longo, Janice Zackeo.—**Selectmen,** 1st, Cheryl D. Reedy (D) Tel., (203) 746-8101, Art Azzarito (D), Vincent W. Montesano (R).—**Treas.,** Carol L. Kamps, Jr.—**Bd. of Finance,** Dan Reese, Chm., Bill Frederick, Frederick H. Luks, Karen McKernan, Francis Parisette, vacancy; Alternates, John MacDonald, Steve Mendelsohn, Frank J. Mizak, Jr.—**Tax Collector,**

Kerrie L. Greening.—**Bd. of Assessment Appeals,** Patricia D. Hughes, Lawrence C. McGowan. Anthony J. Yorio, Jr.—**Assessor,** Sharon Leahey.—**Registrars of Voters,** Leslie Siegel (D), Mary Ann Carson (R).—**Supt. of Schools,** Rolphe W. Wenner.—**Bd. of Education,** Kim Cesarro, Roy M. Huckabee, Megan Hostler, Richard A. Smith, 1997; John F. Arizzi, Chm., Eugene Arcery, Mike Gismondi, Hugh R. McCarney, Karen P. Milano, 1999.—**Planning Comm.,** John C. Wolf, Chm., Anthony J. DiRocco, Frank J. Fehling, Lawrence C. McGowan, Nancy Mendelsohn; Alternates, Grace W. Perkins, Cynthia Stevens, vacancy.—**Zoning Comm.,** George P. Zerrenner, Chm., William E. Cunningham, Faline S. Fox, Stephen J. Hanrahan, Joseph Letitzia; Alternates, Edward P. Caleca, Philip A. Cammararo, John Moran.—**Zoning Bd. of Appeals,** Donald F. Kamps, Sr., Chm., Steven C. Fiore, Norman Geisinger, James A. Hovanec, Robert Jano; Alternates, John B. Day, George Tremblay, John Wolf.—**Zoning Enforcement Officer,** Mara Porwitzki.—**Conservation and Inland Wetlands Comm.,** Stuart Dickstein, Chm., William Delohery, Joseph Galanti, Karen Anne Huber, William Kivlen, Wayne Van Treuren; Alternates, Joseph G. Galbraith, vacancy.—**Environmental Enforcement Officer,** Robert Cloutier.—**Comm. on Aging,** Greta Cina, Kathleen M. Hull, Beatrice Rebhan, Caryn Reilly, Jeannette Sweeney, Catherine Vetrano, vacancy; Alternates, William J. Gallagher, Therese A. Sciurba, vacancy.—**Dir. of Health,** Timothy Simpkins.—**Library Trustees,** Gail L. Lehman, Chm., William S. Gardner, Patricia J. Gay, Howard J. Hagen, Susan E. Huwer, Frank J. Sweeney.—**Parks and Recreation Comm.,** Terrance P. Hillery, Chm., Charles F. Fenwick, James J. Gorman, Donald Guglielmo, Roman Juskiewicz, Jack Magoon, William O'Keeffe, Robert M. Redenz, Marie A. Tegmier.—**Supt. of Highways,** Thomas Dube.—**Town Engineer,** Walter Fuss.—**Building Inspector,** Ronald Malmberg.—**Building Bd. of Appeals,** William J. Frederick, Frank G. Meier, Dominick Ricci, two vacancies.—**Candlewood Lake Auth.,** Patrick Callahan, Bruce O. Kemble, vacancy.—**Sanitarian,** Timothy Simpkins; Asst., Charlene Taylor.—**Tree Warden,** Larry Hissong.—**Chief of Police,** Cheryl D. Reedy.—**Constables,** Paul Breitzke, William Cario, Kevin Casey, James Dzamko, Anthony S. Farina, Thomas Guman, Joseph Kelly, Michael Manning, Anthony Markert, Joseph Pascento, Robert M. Redenz, Thomas H. Schretzenmayer, three vacancies.—**Chief of Fire Dept./Dir. of Civil Preparedness,** Peter Benzinger.—**Fire Marshal,** Ronald Malmberg.—**Town Atty.,** Michael Lavelle.—**Justices of the Peace,** Eugene N. Arcery, Joanne M. Arizzi, Hillery Bassriel, Mildred Berendsen, Frances J. Blackwell, Edward P. Caleca, Mary Ann Carson, Diane R. Cilento, William E. Cunningham, Peggy Day, Charles E. DeBourbon, Lucille M. DiRocco, William J. DiTullio, Charles F. Fenwick, Jean Fenwick, Joseph A. Galanti, Marilyn O. Galanti, Norman Geisinger, Michael T. Gill, Patricia T. Gill, Sharon G. Giovanniello, Mike Gismondi, John A. Goetz, Annmarie Gorman, Richard T. Grant, Kerrie H. Greening, Bob Gyle, Martha A. Halas, David C. Harrison, Francis R. Hollis, Dale Holly, Roy M. Huckabee, Patricia D. Hughes, Michael A. Iadarola, Margaret A. Imbro, Carol L. Kamps, Donald F. Kamps, Sr., Carol Ann Kissmann, Frank LaBanca, Peter R. Larkin, Raymond C. Lubus, Frederick H. Luks, Mary Jane Magoon, Vincent Mancuso, Nancy Mendelsohn, Steve Mendelsohn, John D. Middleton, Karen P. Milano, Robert T. Miller, Frank J. Mizak, Vincent W. Montesano, Leo D. Montuoro, Thomas Moore, Ward Moss, Lawrence McGowan, Kenneth P. McIlveen, James F. McKernan, Phillip A. Nelson, Earle J. Novak, Jr., Joseph A. Novella,

William O'Keeffe, Diana M. Peck, Grace W. Perkins, Mark S. Prince, Robert M. Redenz, Cheryl D. Reedy, Dan Reese, Caryn M. Reilly, George A. Reitweisner, Robert I. Rosenberg, Philip L. Sanders, John Scott, Brian B. Shea, Leslie Siegel, Seward E. Smith, Cynthia Stevens, Eileen H. Sundstrom, Frank J. Sweeney, Jr., Jeannette H. Sweeney, Douglas E. Thielen, Janice D. Zackeo.

NEW HARTFORD. Litchfield County.—(Form of government, selectmen, town meeting, board of finance.)—Inc., Oct., 1738. Area, 38.1 sq. miles. Population, est., 6,069. Voting districts, 2. Principal industries, furniture making, machine parts, electronic components, blenders, springs, guitars, business forms, plastics. Transp.—Freight: Served by numerous motor common carriers. Post offices, New Hartford and Pine Meadow.

TOWN OFFICERS. Clerk and Reg. of Vital Statistics, Patricia J. Halloran; Hours, 9 A.M.-12 Noon, 12:40-4 P.M., Mon., Tues., Thurs.; 9 A.M.-12 Noon, 1-6 P.M., Wed.; 9 A.M.-12 Noon, Fri.; Address, Town Hall, 530 Main St., 06057; Tel., Winsted, (860) 379-5037; FAX, (860) 379-0940.—**Asst. Clerks and Asst. Regs. of Vital Statistics,** Donna N. LaPlante, Christine Slate.—**Selectmen,** 1st, Bruce H. Gresczyk (R) Tel., (860) 379-3389, Katherine L. Rieger (R), Mary Lou Ringklib (D).—**Treas.,** Linda G. Goff.—**Bd. of Finance,** Neil English, Chm., Joseph H. Bieluch, David J. Bombara, Richard L. Caldwell, David L. Childs, David W. Sessions; Alternates, Gregg B. Kelly, Bernard J. Witte.-**Tax Collector,** Linda M. Sheffield.—**Bd. of Assessment Appeals,** Irving J. Burdick, Jr., Chm., Daniel V. Jerram, Jackie Vincenzo.—**Assessor,** Helga Poreda.—**Bd. of Assessors,** Patricia W. Koch-Lewin, Chm., Helen D. Sellei, Forrest R. Sprague.—**Registrars of Voters,** 1st Dist., Donald O. Garrison, 2nd Dist., Donna P. LaPlante (D); 1st Dist., Barbara D. Elmore, 2nd Dist., Karen Griswold-Nelson (R).—**Supt. of Schools,** Thomas T. James.—**Bd. of Education,** Marshall H. Janes, Marjorie Kacir, Ira Kline, Barbara W. Tota, 1997; Joseph A. Gareis, Chm., Arthur E. Jackman, 1999; George R. Klauber, Maureen Morris, Karen G. Nelson, 2001.—**Planning and Zoning Comm.,** Nicholas V. Labbadia, Chm., Murray O. Gibson, David C. Krimmel, Susan C. Ray, James E. Steadman; Alternates, James Hall, Jonathan D. Hatch, Linda A. Jones.—**Zoning Bd. of Appeals,** John Ferguson, Chm., Jared W. Carroll, John J. Gallagher, Patricia M. Hannon, vacancy; Alternates, William F. Baxter, Polly S. Harris, Terrence Moreschi, Jr.—**Zoning Enforcement Officer,** Karl Nilsen.—**Conservation Comm.,** Allison Murdock, Chm., Charles Carlin, Jean Cronauer, Allan E. Dumont, Harlan Gustafson, S. Patricia Keener, Kathleen Kelleher, John C. McMahon, Ellen Smith, Carleton Taylor.—**Inland Wetlands Comm.,** Alden Ringklib, Chm., Bert Brander, James Hall, S. Patricia Keener, Thomas Legeyt, Albert Linnell, Robert S. Swanke; Paul Volovski, Enforcement Officer; Alternates, Arthur Jackman, Wayne Ryznar.—**Agent for the Elderly,** Doretta Clark.—**Comm. on Aging,** Marcia Anderson, Doretta Clark, Phyllis Dery, Ellen Durstin, Kathleen Gagne, Linda Klauber, George Smith; Alternates, Mary Kent, Lucie Martocchio.—**Welfare Dir.,** Roxanne G. Carroll.—**Retirement Bd.,** William Nolte, Chm., Bruce Gresczyk, Peter O'Brien, Gerald Stevens.—**Housing Authority,** George Jones, Chm., Bertha Beauchemin, Vivian Hickey, Nicholas Labbadia, Anita Milette.—**Recreation Comm.,** Ira Kline, Chm., Dennis Gallo, Daria Hart, Laurie Ann Leach, Nancy

Long, Stephen Nadeau, Todd Sage.—**Historic Dist. Comm.,** Sibyl Pellum, Chm., Barbara Goff, Amy Natale, Theresa Oswell, Frances Stoffer; Alternates, Eugene Falco, Edgar Wilcox, Timothy Yeadon.—**Municipal Historian,** Newman A. Hall.—**Water Pollution Control Auth.,** Anthony Fuschillo, Chm., Bert Brander, Daniel Charest, Arthur Ciccarello, Glenn Fecto, Marlene Geissler, James Smith.—**Town Engineer,** Edward Sweeney.—**Building Inspector,** Paul Volovski.—**Road Foreman,** Victor Vincent.—**Chief of Fire Depts.,** Paul Goodskey (New Hartford); Paul Pobuda (Pine Meadow); John Shaw (South End).—**Fire Marshal,** Michael Ciccarelli.—**Municipal Animal Control Officer,** Stanley Solkowski.—**Civil Preparedness Dir.,** vacancy.— **Town Atty.,** John W. Pickard (P.O., Torrington).—**Justices of the Peace,** Liane H. Adams, Chester Aliano, John A. Austin, Yolanda M. Barrett, William F. Baxter, Bertha V. Beauchemin, Bert Brander, Richard L. Calder III, Kathryn F. Carpenter, John H. Casey, David L. Childs, Pamela A. Churchill, Laura P. Cleinman, John N. Czechowicz, Charlotte S. Dufour, Neil English, Eugene P. Falco, Donald O. Garrison, Patricia M. Hannon, Jonathan D. Hatch, Michael J. Hickey, Robert H. Howson, Linda A. Jones, Gregg B. Kelly, Willard J. King, George R. Klauber, Patricia E. Koch-Lewin, Barbara S. Lautenbach, Arthur E. Lavoie, Diane S. Marr, John C. McMahon, Jr., Frederick S. Mertz, Jr., Joseph J. Monyak, Roberta K. Petit, Earl F. Phillips, James M. Raym, Allison E. Reder, Andrew F. Riess, Mary Lou Ringklib, James A. Schmidt, Helen D. Sellei, Linda M. Sheffield, Sheila M. Smith, Patricia A. Spaziani, Betty Stoutenberg.

NEW HAVEN. New Haven County.—(Form of government, mayor, bd. of aldermen.)—Settled, April, 1638; named, Aug., 1640; Inc., 1784; town and city consolidated, Nov., 1895. Area, 20.3 sq. miles. Population, est., 123,656. Voting districts, 30. Principal industries, manufacture of ammunition, hardware, jewelry, watches, rubber goods, corsets and clothing, machinery, machine tools, wire and wire goods, insulated wire and insulators, paper boxes, automobile radiators, boilers, cigars, razor blades, automobile ignition, replacement equipment, model airplanes, electric and electronic equipment. Transp.—Passenger: Served by Amtrak, Metro North Commuter Railroad Co. and buses of Conn. Transit locally and from Milford, Branford and Wallingford; Cross Country Coach from Bridgeport; The Arrow Line from Waterbury, Torrington and Winsted; Conn. Transit; Empire Bus Lines, Inc. from Danbury, and by Greyhound and Trailways. Freight: Served by Boston & Maine Corporation, Conrail and numerous motor common carriers. Post offices, New Haven, Fair Haven, Westville, Amity, Kilby and Yale Station.

CITY AND TOWN OFFICERS. City Clerk, Stanley Rogers; Hours, 9 A.M.-5 P.M., Mon. through Fri.; Address, Kennedy Mitchell Hall of Records, 200 Orange St., Rm. 204, 06510; Tel., (203) 946-8339.—**Deputy City Clerk,** Sally J. Brown.—**Asst. City Clerk,** Claudia J. Kay.—**Reg. of Vital Statistics,** Michael V. Lynch.—**Deputy Reg. of Vital Statistics,** Carol Longobardi.—**Mayor,** John DeStefano, Jr. (D).—**Aldermen,** 1st Ward, Joshua Civin; 2nd Ward, Olivia C. Martson; 3rd Ward, Anthony Dawson; 4th Ward, Tomas Reyes, Jr.; 5th Ward, Jorge Perez; 6th Ward, Rita R. Krevit; 7th Ward, Esther Armmand; 8th Ward, Luisa DeLauro; 9th Ward, vacancy; 10th Ward, Robert N. Schmalz; 11th Ward, Edward F. Clifford; 12th Ward, Robert W. Bokowski; 13th Ward, Sandy Astarita; 14th Ward, Robin I. Kroogman; 15th Ward, Veronica Nieves; 16th Ward, Raul Avila; 17th Ward, Matt Naclerio; 18th Ward, Anthony Santino; 19th Ward, George D. Gallo; 20th Ward, Ron Smith; 21st Ward, Ronald K. Gattison; 22nd Ward, Maeola Riddick; 23rd Ward, Alvis D. Brooker; 24th Ward, Elizabeth C. McCormack; 25th Ward, Nancy V. Ahern; 26th Ward, David Moakley; 27th Ward, Philip Voigt; 28th Ward, Bruce McClenning; 29th Ward, Carl Goldfield; 30th Ward, Willie J. Moore.—**Bd. of Ethics,** Andrew Gambardella, Jacqueline Harrison, Marsha Perlmutter.—**Controller,** Gregory Brown.—**Tax Collector,** vacancy.—**Bd. of Assessment Appeals,** Robert D'Amato, C. Louise Lytle, two vacancies.—**Assessor,** Larry Hughes.—**Registrars of Voters,** Sharon G. Ferrucci (D), Rae D. Tramontano (R).—**Supt. of Schools,** Reginald Mayo.—**Bd. of Education,** Robert W. McClenahan, Jr., Janette J. Parker, 1997; Arthur J. Bosley, Jr., 1998; John A. Prokop, Jr., Carlos A. Torre, 1999; Patricia McCann-Vissepo, Lester McCorn, 2000.—**Acting Organizational Development Dir.,** Lisa Grasso.—**Civil Service Comm.,** Juliette L. Crawford, Lubbie Harper, Jr., Abigail Padua, Andrea Scott, Anthony M. Solomine.—**Retirement Bd.,** Roy Davidson, Cindy Kissin, Janet Lawrence-Brown.—**City Plan Comm.,** Susan Voight, Chm., Stephen J. Papa, Rodney J. Russell, John Russo.—**Zoning Bd. of Appeals,** Murray Trachten, Chm., Gary Garibaldi, Alphonse Paolillo, Eduardo Perez, Jr., Wesley Thorpe; Alternates, Roxanne Bailey, Martiza P. Gant, Elser H. Richter.—**Zoning Admr.,** Frank Gargiulo.—**Development Comm.,** Josh Venter, Chm., George Clarke, Tony Dawson, Patricia Drax-Pollak, Stephen Garcia, Linda Lorimer, Fred Maretz, Michael Massaro, Matthew Nemerson, Barbara Pearce, Michael Schaffer, James Shure, Teresa Sirico, Charles Turner.—**Redevelopment Agency,** Bishop C. Brewer, Daniel Greer, Harvey Kozim, Rafael Rodriguez, Fred Wilson.—**Housing Auth.,** A. Pasquale Ambrogio, Helen Bosley, Walter Brooks, Jonathan Gillette, Bess Jenkins, Ida Wells.—**Fair Rent Comm.,** Elton McClain, Chm., Connie Fleming, Idalia Garcia, William Kegeles, James Mills, Jr., Charisse C. Townsend, James C. Whitney; Pauline Scipio, Exec. Dir.—**Comm. on Disabilities,** Linda Blair, Agatha Doyle, Co-Chm., Evelyn Belton, Janier Caban-Hernandez, Wilhemenia Christon, Walter Clarke, Sr., David Davis, Patricia Gesualdo, Martha Leo, Deborah McNeill, Sophie Mushin, Abram Phillips, Linda Singer.—**Environmental Advisory Council,** Walter Esdaile, Carla Farrell, Edward E. Gandsman, Karen Gilvarg, Edward Grant, Janet Lindner, Brian McGrath, William P. Quinn, Leonard Smith.—**Historic Dist. Comm.,** Peter Conrad, Fern Drutman, Peter Hall, Richard Hegel, Renata Recknagel; Alternates, Marianne Mazan, Peter S. Conrad, Christopher T. Wuerth.—**Municipal Historian,** Richard Hegel.—**Comm. on Aging,** Louis Aceto, Stanley Barakis, Bessie Boyd, Virginia Davila, Rose D'Agostino, Abraham Fisher, Sylvia Konners, Ann M. LoRusso, Mary McCallum, Ann Merriam, David Miniter, Rose Sorrentino, Mary Sweeten, Sophie N. Turner.—**Welfare Dir.,** Caroline Curry.—**Dir. of Health,** William Quinn, M.P.H.—**Bd. of Health Comrs.,** Ronald Angoff, M.D., James Hadler, M.D., Reid M. Davis, Jack Hughes, M.D., Frank Mongillo III, M.D., Ella L. Thomas.—**Library Directors,** Kathryn F. Bonese, Karl Crawford, MIldred Gray, Peggy McLouth-Pschirrer, Margaret Mitchell, Michael Morand, Ann Walsh, Margaret Watley, vacancy.—**Bd. of Parks Comrs.,** Margaret G. Pastore, Pres., Carmen Aitro, Sandra Astarita, David R. Belowsky, Clifton Bush, Jr., David Santana, Robert Schmalz, Kathleen Wimer.—**Dir. of Parks, Recreation and Trees,** Frank A. Williams, Jr.—**Dir. of Public Works,** Claudette Ford; Deputy, Brian Funk.—**Purchasing Agent,** Elizabeth Sassano.—**City Engineer,** Richard H. Miller.—**Supt. of Streets,** Thomas Simmons.—

Sealer of Weights and Measures, Christine Ciociola.—**Dir., Building Inspector/ Enforcement,** Clarence E. Phillips.—**Supt. of Trees,** Louis Dean.—**Supt. of Refuse Collections,** Frank Ardizzone.—**Dir. of Environmental Health,** Paul Kowalski.— **Chief of Police,** vacancy.—**Police Comm.,** Jonathan Einhorn, Maria Fonseca, Stephen Garcia, Kathy Graves, Jerry Streets.—**Chief of Fire Dept.,** Martin O'Connor.—**Acting Fire Marshal,** Nelson Casillas.—**Bd. of Fire Comrs.,** Stephen M. Kasowitz, Pres., Theodore L. Brooks, William C. Celentano, Jr., Nick Perrelli, Susan Whetstone.— **Civil Defense Dir.,** Chief John E. Smith, Fire Dept.—**Development Admin.,** Walter Esdaile.—**Corporation Counsel,** Patricia Cofrancesco; Deputies, Martin Echter, Michael Koenigsberg.—**Justices of the Peace,** George F. Abel, Sr., Louis A. Aceto, Mark Aceto, Mary D. Aceto, Vivian Acevedo-Rivas, Marie Ackerman, Marexes Adolemaiua-Bey, Bart Adragna, Nancy V. Ahern, Nicholas Aiello, Mary Alford, Charles H. Allen III, Woodrow Allen, Carmen A. Alvarado, Frank Alvarado, Martha Amatruda, Biaggio Amendola, Karen Amores, Mary Jane Anderson, Bryan Anderson, Fannie Anderson, Clorinda Andrea, Gerald Antunes, Josephine Ardito, Frank J. Ardizzone, Michael Argento, Aaron Aronow, Leonard Aronow, Sylvia Arovas, Helen Arsenault, Charles Ashe, Jr., Sandy Astarita, Charles N. Atkinson, Joseph Aveni, Raul Avila, Aida Ayala, Robert Babcock, Thayer Baldwin, Jr., Dominic F. Balletto, Jr., JoAnn Balletto, Jason Balletto, Amos Banks, Rosio Barahona, Leon Barauskas, Kristin Barber, Jean Barker, Ronald A. Barnabei, Jr., Ellie Barrie, Dawn Barros, Bruce J. Barros, Sr., Darlene Battle, William Battle, Addison V. Bechwith, David R. Belowsky, Elizabeth Bennett, Margaret Berg, Diane C. Berg, Arnold Berman, Rosalind Berman, Daniel Blackmon, Linda Blair, Carol Bokowski, Robert Bokowski, Robert Bokowski, Jr., Frank Bombace, Russell Bonaccorso, Jr., Kathryn Bonese, Harriet Bonner, Mabel Bontempo, Arthur Bosley, Helen Bosley, Sharon Bowes, Ann Boyd, Salvatore J. Brancati, Erwin Branch, Byron Breland, Fannie Brooks, Theodore Brooks, Walter S. Brooks, Dora Brown, Lillian Brown, Sally J. Brown, Dorothy Bruckhart, Michael Bruno, Richard Buckholz, Robert E. Buckholz, Robert Burns, Samuel Cabrera, Theresa Camera, Henry C. Campbell, Naomi Campbell, Edward Camposano, Martha Camposano, Barbara Canali, Christopher Canali, Gina Canali, Jose Candelario, Elizabeth Cangiano, Francine Caplan, Robert Caplan, Gerald Cappiello, Jose Caraballo, Eleanor Carbone, Elizabeth Carbone, Mary Ann L. Cardona, William J. Carey, Helen Carocci, Loretta C. Casey, Alphonso Cauley, William Celentano, Jr., Barbara Celotto, Ralph Celotto, Conella Chagares, Ann Chambers, Cantrell Cheeks, Gail Chenault-Camp, Claudine G. Chi, Anthony Ciarlone, Frank Cintron, Harriett Clarke, Leo G. Clarke, Jr., Walbert B. Clarke, Sandra Clendenen, Daphne Clyburn, Pixie Cody, Nick J. Colavolpe, Harriet Collins, Dolores Colon, Rose Lee Comer, John Connelly, Salvatore Consiglio, Jr., Phyllis A. Conte, Elizabeth Coorey, Raye Coppola, Demaria Cordero, Jorge Cordero, Rosieta Cordero, John Corniello, Barbara Coughlin, Lillian Cowan, Linda Cox, Ann Marie Craven, John Cretella, Marcial Cuevas, Ann Curtis, Rose D'Agostino, Vincent D'Agostino, Mary D'Angelo, Arlene Dacis-Rudd, Sandra Dahney-Johnson, James W. Daniel, Elizabeth Darden, Alberta A. Davis, Cameron Davis, Deborah E. Davis, Arlene Davis-Rudd, Anthony B. Dawson, William Decapua, Maria Degaetano, Angelo DeLeo, Alejandria T. DeLeon, Gloria Delgado, Philip DelGuidice, Andrea Delvecchio, Angie Delvecchio, Dianne Delvecchio, Maureen DeMatteo, Rosemarie Dematteo, William Demmons, Michael DePalma, Arlene DePino, Chris

DePino, Frank DePino, John J. DeRosa, John DeStefano, Jr., Katherine DeStefano, Arthur Diadamo, Lorraine Diadamo, Daniel Diaz, Angelo R. Dichello, Norma DiChello, Caroline Dinager, Shirley Dixon, William Dixon, Carol Domorod, Agatha Doyle, Fern Drutman, Linda DuBose, Edmund W. Duenkel II, Mia Duff, Daniel J. Dunn, Daniel J. Dunn, Jr., Margaret Dunn, Roberta Durler, John Dye, William R. Dyson, Christopher Earle, Jonathan J. Einhorn, Kyle D. Einhorn, Vivian M. Elder, James Elefante, Johanna Epperson, John A. Esposito, Philip Evans, John Fabrizio, Thomas Fagan, John Fahey, John Fairchild, Linda Falcigno, Carla Farrell, Victor Fasano, Kathleen T. Faught, Angel G. Fernandez-Chave, Frank Ferriaiolo, Donna Ferrucci, Sharon Ferruccii, Michael Fimiani, Lucille Fiorello, Norman Fleming, Jean Fletcher, Aurea S. Flores, Marcial Flores, Maria Fonseca, Carol Freedman, Jerome Freedman, Damonne Freeman, Robert S. Frew, Anthony Fusco, George Gallo, Andrew A. Gambardella, Derick Gant, Maritza Gant, Igdalia Garcia, Rosalie Garcia, Luis Garcia-Abrines, Salvatore Garibaldi, Jack Garland, Keith Garrett, Shawn Garris, Ronald K. Gattison, Peter Gero, Mae Gibson-Brown, Barbara Glass, Ilan Glenn, Louise E. Glogowski, Theodora Glover, Elizabeth Gomez, Maria Gomez, Nellie Gonzalez, Victoria Gordon, Frederick Gowen, Albert F. Graham, Sharyn Grant, Frank Grasso, Sr., Karl D. Gray, Lorraine Grasso, Lisa Gray, Mildred Gray, Steven Gray, William Gray, Daniel Greene, Gretchen Greenlee, David B. Greensberg, Theresa Grillo, Steven Guttirez, Harold Hack, Florence Hagan, Brian Hagans, Laura Hagfeldt, Peter Hall, Monica Hammie, Walter Hammie, Bertha Hanusiak, Paul Hanusiak, Denise Harris, Jacqueline Harrison, Donald A. Hayden, Catherine Heath, Richard Hegel, Gwen Henderson, Tomas Herazo, Gloria D. Hicks, Mary Hines, Susan Holahan, Thomas R. Holahan, Ora Holmes, Ralph Horning, Morton R. Horwitz, Katherine Hosen, Sheldon Hosen, Willa Houlihan, Jemi Howell, Althen F. Hubbard, Roger W. Hughes, Joseph N. Hull, Ella F. Hunter, Stanley Insler, Louis Iovieno, Jr., Carol Jackson, Andrea Jackson-Brooks, Richard L. Jacobs, John Jacobson, Michael Jefferson, Bessie Jenkins, Brian Jenkins, Joan Jenkins, Tishawn Jenkins, Elizabeth Jeter, Maria M. Jimenez, Otis E. Johnson, Jr., Eunice L. Jones, Nora B. Joseph, Carmella L. Juliano, Barbara Kaczur, Samuel Kearse III, William Kegeles, Anne Kelsey, John F. Kelsey, Barbara O. Kerr, Clifford Keyes, William E. Kilpatrick, Janice M. King, John Klarman, Delores Knight, Ida Knight, Larry Knight, John B. Kozin, Katherine Kras, Walter Kras, Jr., David Kronberg, Charlotte Kroogman, Barbara Kuczar, Gordon C. Lafer, Grace E. Laframboise, Ann Lampo, Gaetano Lampo, Patricia Land, Ralph Landolfi, Josephine Langello, Arlander Langley, Doreen Larson-Oboyski, Jill D. Laudano, Hazel Lee, Helen Leftwich, Leslie Leigh, Rosemarie Lemley, Charles Levene, Sydney Leventhal, Sherman Levine, Leonard Levy, Arthur Lewis, Bonnie Lewis, Odessa D. Lewis, Matthew Lieberman, Loretta Lincoln, Della Lindsey, Harold Lindy, Anthony Little, Loretta Little, George Longyear, Vivian Lopes, Gloria Lopez, Marybelle Lora, Robert Lowell, Jr., Paul Lukasiewicz, Phyllis Lutters, Joseph M. Lynch, Michael V. Lynch, Carrie Lytle, Reggie Lytle, Lisa C. Maccio, Edith Macri, Pat Macri, Catherine Mancini, Heather Mancini, Leslie Marcarelli, Ralph Marcarelli, Pasquale J. Marino, Phyllis L. Marino, Celeste Markle, Charles Marlow, Braulio Martinez, Lucille Masella, Michael J. Massaro, Joseph Mattei, Jr., Joseph Mattei, Sr., Pasquale Mauro, Richard Mazan, Mary McCallum, Bruce Palmer McClean, Joyce McCleese, McClenning, Percy McClure, Elizabeth McCormack, Joseph J. McCormack, Joseph J. McCormack, Jr., Paul McDuffie, Brian

McGrath, Jane McGuirue, Sarah J. McIver, Stephen P. Mednick, Angela Miller, Brenda Miller, Brian Miller, Michael Miller, William Miller, Mary Ellen Mininberg, David Miniter, Myriam Minutillo, David Moakley, Frank Mongillo, George J. Montano, John B. Montano, Andrew Montgomery, Sr., Fabienne Moore, Patricia Moore, Shawnte Moore, Willie J. Moore, David Moulton, Cecelia Muniz, Edgardo Muniz, Soraida Muniz, Grayson Murphy, Sheila R. Murphy, Pearlene Napolean, Marlene Napolitano, Andrew Nastri, Phyllis Nastri, Daniel Newell, Michele Newman, Robert G. Newman, Carol Nista, Beryl S. Normand, Edward Noyes, James O'Connell, Christopher O'Connor, Mary A. O'Connor, Ada Olivo, Lovella O'Morre, David Ortiz, Jr., Maria Pabon, Helen Papa, Stephen Papa, Sr., Janet R. Parker, Janette J. Parker, Ruben Parrilla, Linda Pascale, Lucile Patton, Ana Perez, Dalia Perez, Jorge Perez, William H. Perrotti, John Petraiuolo, Connie Petty, Michaelina Piscitelli, Rita Piscitello, Ann Piscottano, Miguel Pitman, Sandra Pitman, Christina Plass, Frances Plass, Glenn Pollard, Jerry N. Poole, Joyce C. Poole, Lucy Potocsky, Helen C. Powell, Diane Prince, Christopher Proto, Peggy L. Pschirrer, John Querker, John Quiello, P. Christina Quinn, Frank Ragozzino, Benjamin Rand, Jr., Yolanda Rascati, Francine Reid, Dennis Reilly, Norma Reyes, Thomas Reyes, Joelle Rhodes, Gloria Richardson, Linda Richardson, Armond D. Richello, David Riddick, Mae O. Riddick, Ade Rivera, Sally Robertson, Gwendolyn Robinson, Eugene Roddy, Candita Rodriquez, Evelyn Rodriquez, Mark Roffman, Doris Rogers, Kathleen Rogers, Stanley Rogers, Margarita Rolon, Lydia M. Roman, William Rossi, Mark Ryan, Margaret Saars, Dietrich W. Salomon, Muriel Salomon, Santiago Sanchez, Jill Sandes, Stanley Sanders, Joseph Sanford, Joseph Santagata, Anthony M. Santino, Arthur J. Sapienza, Harry K. Sargent, Theresa Scarpellino, Evelyn Schatz, Morris Schatz, Mark J. Schenker, Anna Schildroth, Camille Schimelfanick, Howard C. Scipio, Andrea M. Scott, Hope Segarra, Harold Sessa, Lawrence Shanbrom, Sherry Z. Shanbrom, Michael S. Shea, Jr., Daphne Shepard, Mark Shiffrin, Richard Silverstein, Teresa Sirico, Sesalena D. Smart, Elinor Smith, Shelly Smith, Jesse Snipes, Jr., Teofilo Solivan, Rose Sorrentino, Richard Sperandeo, Edith Spruill, David C. Squeglia, Shirley Stevens, Thomas Strong, Eddie R. Sturdivant, Maxine Sumrell, Catherine Sutton-Dawton, Alice M. Tacinelli, Sally Terry, Eustace D. Theodore, Jeannette Thomas, Fred Thompson, Julia Tomasi, Florence Tomasini, Blanca Torres, Nilda Torres, Charisse Townsend, Henry Townshend, Jr., Marie F. Tramontano, Rae Tramontano, Richard Tramontano, Sr., Lucille Trent, Marlene Tureck, Sophie Turner, A. Jackson Tyson, James Uberti, Elisabeth Van Dyke, Joseph Vanacore, Roger Vann, Israel Vazquez, Mary Vendetto, Gregory M. Ventura, Thomas Verderame III, Ella Vereen, Peter C. Villano, Thomas A. Virgulto, Evo Vitali, Philip Voigt, Susan Voigt, Ronald Waite, John Wakins, Mary N. Wall, Wesley Wallin, James L. Wareck, Ovella Watts, Phebe Wehr, Frankie White, Frankie L. White, Ruby White-Belton, Charles Wiley, Paul Wiley, Willie Williams, Jr., Anthony Willoughby, Diane Wilson, Jonathon P. Wilson, Woodrow Wilson, Virginia Woolums, Joseph Yates, Shah Yusuf, Ed Zabilowski, Kim Zabilowski, Marylou Zabilowski, Tom Zabilowski, Nathan Zeidenberg, Brendon Zunder.

NEWINGTON. Hartford County.—(Form of government, town manager, mayor-town council.)—Inc., July 10, 1871; taken from Wethersfield. Area, 13.2 sq. miles. Population, est.,

28,028. Voting districts, 7. Principal industries, milk processing, and manufacture of airplane parts, dies, gauges, tools and plumbing supplies. Transp.—Passenger: Served by buses of Conn. Transit from Hartford; Dattco Inc. from New Britain; Bonanza Bus Lines, Inc. from Waterbury and Danbury; by Greyhound. Freight: Served by Conrail and numerous motor common carriers. Post office, Newington. Rural free delivery.

TOWN OFFICERS. Clerk and Reg. of Vital Statistics, Roberta N. Jenkins; Hours, 8:30 A.M.-4:30 P.M., Mon. through Fri.; Address, 131 Cedar St., 06111; Tel., (860) 666-8500.—**Asst. Clerks and Asst. Regs. of Vital Statistics,** Sharon R. Dexler, Dianne E. Yusinas.—**Town Manager,** Keith H. Chapman; Asst., vacancy.—**Town Council,** Robert A. Randich (D), Mayor; Myra Cohen, Leon S. Davidoff, Wayne G. Haley, P. Joseph Harpie, John M. Kelly, Joseph L. LaRosa, Thomas B. McBride, Sandra H. Nafis.—**Treas.,** Barbara DeMaio; Deputy Treas., Michael J. Fox.—**Dir. of Finance,** Joan McGovern.—**Tax Collector,** Ruth E. Mangan.—**Bd. of Assessment Appeals,** Louis Califano, Chm., Alfred Binford, Frederick Callahan III.—**Assessor,** Anthony J. Homicki.—**Registrars of Voters,** Marie M. Fox (D), Linda B. Cultrera (R).—**Supt. of Schools,** Ernest L. Perlini.—**Bd. of Education,** Joseph J. Marcellino III, Chm., Robin J. Handleman, Constance L. Harasymiw, Judith C. Igielski, Steven W. Krupa, Donald O. Montanari, Helen W. Nelson, Thomas J. Shields, Stephen R. Woods, 1997.—**Town Plan and Zoning Comm.,** Joseph Klett, Chm., Vincent Camilli, William J. Cariseo, Patricia Genova, Dennis Hebert, Domenic Pane, Bhupen Patel; Alternates, E. Curtis Ambler, Carole Khentigan, John Victorick.—**Town Planner,** Edward Meehan.—**Zoning Bd. of Appeals,** Dennis Doyle, Chm., Thomas J. Boorman, Brian J. Buden, Edmund Tofil, Stephen Woods; Alternates, John Waterman, John Webber, vacancy.—**Zoning Enforcement Officer,** Wayne Bell.—**Development Comm.,** John Carragher, Chm., Paul Cugno, Marie Dowling, Alice Hall, Jonathan A. Harris, Rita A. Hebert, William P. Kelly, George Maciel; Alternates, Thomas S. Mongellow, Linda Spazian, Trudie E. Walker.—**Dir. of Economic Development,** Jack Burke.—**Environmental Quality Comm.,** Michael Fox, Chm., Frank Ancona, Francis E. Brunet, Hyman Braverman, Cheryl A. Holmes, Michael Longo, Jr., Elizabeth A. Ventre, Barbara Wiley, vacancy.—**Housing Auth.,** MacChesney Desmond, Gary Guyette, Francis A. Kelly, Jr., Paul LaRosa, J. William O'Brien; Mary Ann Murphy, Exec. Dir.—**Fair Rent Comm.,** Fred Binford, Karen Gallicchio, Onofrio Mollica, Alfred Pasquini, vacancy; Alternates, Frances Casasanto, Suzanne Reniewicz, vacancy.—**Bd. of Ethics,** Michael Schless, Chm., Angelina A. Emanuele, Wayne V. Estey, Bradford Fenn, Patricia A. Lavery, two vacancies; Alternates, Kathleen Dix, vacancy.—**Conservation and Inland Wetlands Comm.,** Alan Nafis, Chm., John Ferreira, Cathleen Hall, John Igielski, Gary St. Amand, Judith Strong, Alan R. Wengell; Alternates, Vincent Briganti, Donna P. Lin, Deborah Shields.—**Comm. on Aging and the Handicapped,** William A. DeMaio, Chm., Sharon M. Garrard, Cathleen Hall, Maureen H. Klett, Donna Lin, Irene Logan, Rita A. McClean, Diana Robino, Anthony Ruglio; Joyce Lighari, Dir.—**Human Rights Comm.,** April Ann Damato, Chm., Lucy Callahan, Judy Cromack, Orlando Edwards, Susan Erwin, Robin Handleman, Jean Anne McMahon, Nancy Marino, vacancy.—**Dir. of Social Services,** Kenneth Freidenberg.—**Dir. of Health,** Shahnaz Hussain, M.D.—**Library Directors,** Dolores Giantonio, Iris B. Larson, Maureen Lyons, Daniel J. Nahorney, Janet Paklos, Newell Stamm, Jr., vacancy; Maxine Bleiweis, Dir.—**Municipal Historians** Elizabeth S. Baxter, Harry Mandell.—**Parks and Recreation Bd.,** Richard S. Khentigan, Chm., Thomas Bowen, Richard Carbray, Eleanor Fenn, Robert V. Gai, Thomas Lamb, Ronald Procko, Suzanne Reniewicz, Kenneth Tramadeo, Donald Woods, Jr., Kathleen Zolad.—**Supt. of Parks and Recreation,** Robert P. Stanley.—**Recreation Supvr.,** Theodore Fravel.—**Youth Services Coordinator,** Dorothy Revzon.—**Town Engineer,** Peter M. Arburr.—**Supt. of Highways,** Edward Murtha.—**Building Inspector,** Wayne Bell.—**Building Code Bd. of Appeals,** Richard Balducci, Vincent A. Camilli, John P. Carragher, Steven Pizzella, Allan Wengell.—**Public Health Coordinator,** Robert M. Cosgrove.—**Tree Warden,** Nels O. Nelson.—**Chief of Police,** Richard Klett.—**Constables,** John J. Abbate, Thomas G. Ganley.—**Chief of Fire Dept.,** James Trommer; Deputies, Thomas J. Gill, Richard Nadeau, Chris R. Schroeder, Richard Scialabba.—**Bd. of Fire Comrs.,** Timothy F. Kelliher, Jr., Newell A. Stamm, Kent E. Stoddard, Jr.—**Fire Marshal,** Chris R. Schroeder.—**Civil Preparedness Dir.,** Keith Chapman.—**Town Atty.,** Peter J. Boorman.—**Justices of the Peace,** Frank L. Aieta, E. Curtis Ambler, Steven A. Bafundo, Deborah A. Bongiovanni, Frank A. Borowy, David R. Brinkman, Donald N. Brown, Lorraine G. Cariseo, Carolyn A. Carey, Russell H. Correll, James J. Cultrera, Matilda C. DeMaio, Frank V. Eddy, Wayne V. Estey, Karen J. Gallicchio, Patricia M. Genova, Marshall I. Golden, Timothy J. Griffin, Lynette M. Harper, P. Joseph Harpie, Theodore Kowun, Karlyn S. Lempa, Monica W. Lin, Maureen O. Lyons, Harry A. Mandell, Jerilyn K. Nagel, Gilbert J. Peterson, Ronald J. Procko, Suzanne C. Reiniewicz, Nancy S. Schatz, Chris R. Schroeder, Jerome A. Scoler, Thomas J. Shields, Kent E. Stoddard, Jr., Judith A. Strong, Edmond J. Tofil, Everett I. Weaver, Roy C. Zartarian.

NEW LONDON. New London County.—(Form of government, city manager, city council.)—Settled, 1646; named, March 11, 1658. Inc., Jan., 1784. Town and city are co-extensive. Area, 10.8 sq. miles. Population, est., 26,786. Voting districts, 7. Principal industries: steel fabrication, ship building and repair, marine construction, high technology research and engineering, antiques, doors, windows, interior trim, fishing, entertainment and tourism. Transp.—Passenger and freight served by Amtrak and Central Vermont Railroad. Numerous motor common carriers; ferry boat connections with Long Island, Block Island and Fishers Island. International trade through State Pier. Post Office, New London.

CITY AND TOWN OFFICERS. City Clerk, Town Clerk and Reg. of Vital Statistics, Clark van der Lyke; Hours, 8:30 A.M.-4 P.M., Mon. through Fri.; Address, 181 State St., 06320; Tel., (860) 447-5205; FAX, (860) 447-7971.—**City Manager,** Richard M. Brown. Tel. (860) 447-5201; FAX, (860) 447-7971, Keith Harrigan, Asst City Mgr. Personnel; James McDermott, Asst. City Mgr., Public Works.—**City Council,** Jane L. Glover (D), Mayor; Lloyd H. Beachy, Deputy Mayor; Anthony R. Basilica, William M. Cornish, Robert M. Pero, William L. Satti, M. John Strafaci.—**Bd. of Ethics,** John Dauster, Richard L. Humphreville, Hugh F. Lusk, Paul Romano, Scott Sawyer, Eunice Waller, Patricia C. Zalesny.—**Treas.,** Donna Rinehart.—**Bd. of Finance,** Sharon T. Griffis, Pres., Jerome Fischer, Joseph E. Grimmett, William Nahas; Garon Camassar, Dir.—**Tax Collector,** Janice Ballestrini.—**Bd. of Assessment Ap-**

peals, David Massad, Garth Meader, Ruby T. Morris.—**Assessor/Dir. of Real Estate,** vacancy.—**Registrars of Voters,** Dawn Rahilly (D), Barbara Major (R).—**Supt. of Schools,** Rene J. Racette.—**Bd. of Education,** Garrett T. Brennan, Pres., Anthony Bauduccio, Charles A. Brown, Raymond F. Haworth, Arline Krug, Elaine Maynard-Adams, John Satti, 1997.—**Personnel Bd.,** Josephine Esposito, John Etienne, Alvin G. Kinsall, Carl Stoner, Robert C. Weller.—**Pension Committee,** Richard M. Brown, Vaughn Clapp, C. Francis Driscoll, Louis Esposito, Dean Foirer, Peter Gilmore, Donald Gray, Maureen Hammel, Richard Kotecki, Donna Rinehart, Rob Roy.—**Planning and Zoning Comm.,** Lonnie Braxton, Donald Harrington, Joseph C. Heap II, Joseph Logioco, Patricia Romano, Rob Roy, Leah Spitz; Alternates, William Brennan, Gerald Miller, vacancy.—**Zoning Bd. of Appeals,** Salvatore Amanti, Peter T. Burgess, , Ann Keating, Gerald A. Silverman, George Tryopolis.—**Harbor Improvement Agency,** Frances Baldini, John Dauster, Maureen Satti, vacancy.—**Redevelopment Agency,** Frank Delmore, John Duval, Kenneth Foss, Charles E. Matchen, Harold Weiner.—**Housing Auth.,** Minerva Cook, Bruce Patterson, Margaret Reyes, Maria Santiago, Nancy Stanley.—**Bd. of Compensation,** Shirley J. Gillis, Joseph Langello, vacancy.—**Conservation Comm./Inland Wetland Agency,** Carolyn Brotherton, Catherine Cull, Jessie Damon, Marrijo Logan, Paul Raddatz, William Von Winkle, Ronald J. Woffard, Patricia Zalesny.—**Parking Comm.,** Franklin H. Bartol, Alexander K. Bochain, Nancy Cunniff-Cole, Claire P. Hartling, Mario J. Strafaci.—**Historic Dist. Comm.,** Sarah Ryan, Diane K. Smith, David Thompson, Patricia Williams.—**Senior Affairs Comm.,** Frank Griffiths, Mary Kerr, James Lignelli, Joseph Ottaviano, Anibal Salvador, Madeline Tunucci.—**Welfare Dir.,** Michael Rosenkrantz.—**Dir. of Health,** Pamela Kilbrey-Fox.—**Advisory Committee for the Handicapped,** Linda Giesing, Barbara Major, Patricia McCarthy.—**Parks and Recreation Comm.,** Sal Amanti, Salvador Anibal, Nancy Baude, Katherine Nahas, Dawn Rahilly, James Stephenson, Pat Swim, John Williams.—**Citizens Advisory Committee,** Valeda Grills, Phyllis Harris, Charles E. Matchen, Ted Martinez, Pat Modzelewski.—**Equal Employment Opportunity Committee,** Theresa Bohara, Clarence Faulk, Jr., Marie Gravell, Richard Kotecki, Mabel McKissick, Edward T. Samul, Robert Williams.—**Purchasing Agent,** William Hathaway—**Building Board of Appeals,** Garth Meader, vacancy.—**Water and Water Pollution Control Auth.,** Milton Amanti, Keith Christianson, Robert Sommers, Mario Strafaci, Aldo Valentin, Barry J. Weiner, vacancy.—**Chief of Police,** Bruce Rinehart.—**City Sheriffs,** Norman Abell, George Nahas, Kalil Talage.—**Chief of Fire Dept.,** Ronald J. Samul, Sr.—**Fire Marshal,** Calvin Darrow.—**Civil Preparedness Dir.,** Reid Burdick.—**Dir. of Law,** T. Londregan.—**Justices of the Peace,** Shirley Ableman, Catherine Adams, Elizabeth L. Allen, Charles Alloway, Shirley P. Alloway, Anthony J. Basilica, Lorraine J. Basilica, John H. Bray, Bruce Brett, Richard Brown, Reid B. Burdick, Alfred A. Capozza, Gaspare J. Cavasino, Nancy Cole, Mary Coman, Milton L. Cook, Jr., Antonio Cristina, Margaret M. Curtin, Marion E. Doro, Kenneth W. Edwards, Louis J. Esposito, Gloria M. Faulk, Francis J. Ferrigno, Michael J. Fortunato, Daniel J. Gaynor, Raymond J. Gentilella, Shirley J. Gillis, Elizabeth W. Glover, Sandra E. Grady, Marie A. Gravell, Mathew Greene, John A. Grillo, Valeda P. Grills, Donald E. Harrington, Marjorie E. Heap, Richard L. Humphreville, Leo E. Jackson, Howard B. Kaplan, Richard Kotecki, Sr., Norman J. Kozek, Joseph P. Langello, Dorothy B. Leib, J. Levin, Helen Lewis, Emma Lincoln, Demetrios Louziotis,

Evelyn B. Louziotis, Susan P. Mack, Barbara Major, Richard M. Mallove, Seymour I. Manheimer, Patricia McCarthy, Wallace T. McKissick, Gordon T. Miller, Ruby T. Morris, William Nahas, Jeanne Pasqualini, Bob A. Peters, Maureen G. Satti, Michael J. Tranchida, Gretchen van der Lyke, Michael Vendetto, Jr., Walter Watson, Morris Weinstein, Robert C. Weller, Josephine L. Westerberg, Karen Westerberg.

NEW MILFORD. Litchfield County.—(Form of government, mayor, town council, board of finance.)—Inc., Oct., 1712. Area, 63.7 sq. miles. Population, est., 25,132. Voting districts, 6. Principal industries, processing of concentrated foods; manufacture and processing of paper products; electronics and precision instruments production; two hydro-electric plants are located here. New Milford is situated on the eastern shore of Lake Candlewood; Lynn Deming Park is located on the shore of Lake Candlewood. Lake Candlewood and Lake Lillinonah afford recreational facilities. New Milford is the locale of "Naromiyocknowusunkatankshunk Brook." Transp.—Passenger: Bus service by the Housatonic Area Regional Transit District of Danbury, Bonanza Bus Lines and Greyhound. Freight: Served by Conrail and numerous motor common carriers. Post offices, New Milford and Gaylordsville. City and rural delivery.

TOWN OFFICERS. Clerk and Reg. of Vital Statistics, George C. Buckbee; Hours, 9 A.M.-5 P.M., Mon. through Fri.; Address, Town Hall, P.O. Box 360, 06776; all other offices, 10 Main St., 06776; Tel., (860) 355-6020.—**Asst. Clerk and Asst. Reg. of Vital Statistics,** Donna L. Ramsey.—**Mayor,** Arthur J. Peitler (R) Tel., (860) 355-6010.—**Town Council,** Clark J. Chapin, Robert W. Coppola, Patricia A. Greenspan, Peter J. Henderson, Jr., John E. Lillis, Raymond J. O'Brien, Jr., Thomas J. Pilla, Lynn S. Umbarger, Frank E. Wargo.—**Bd. of Finance,** Brian T. Dougherty, Chm., Duane Davin, Jr., Robert A. Mullen, Charles J. Osborne, Jr., William R. Quinnell, Harold L. Taylor; Raymond J. Jankowski, Dir.; Alternates, Brian A. Arnold, William R. Quinnell.—**Tax Collector,** Catherine M. Reynolds.—**Bd. of Assessment Appeals,** Henry A. Brant, Mary King, Virginia H. Smith; Alternate, vacancy.—**Assessor,** Ronald E. Parks.—**Registrars of Voters,** Loretta Brickley (D), Barbara B. Hyatt (R).—**Supt. of Schools,** Raymond E. Avery.—**Bd. of Education,** Robert J. Guendelsberger, Chm., Denise A. Dougherty, Eileen Hickey, Sharon A. Panek, Ann W. B. Rogg, Gary F. Santini, 1997; Lesley M. Bowman, Alexandra K. Johnson, Martin F. Landgrebe, Robert J. McCarthy, Matthew McNally, Diane S. Phillips, 1999.—**Ethics Comm.,** John Byrne, George W. Hermann, Jr., John J. Powers, Patricia Shea, Kenneth E. Taylor.—**Planning Comm.,** Roger J. Szendy, Chm., John T. Knepper, Gerard J. Monaghan, Robert Rush, Damien M. St. James; Alternates, Kristine M. Dahlberg, two vacancies.—**Zoning Comm.,** George P. Doring, Chm., Lawrence M. Greenspan, Ronald C. Lathrope, Donald G. Marsh, Ramona A. Tito; Alternates, Donald F. Babiyan, Charles Raymond, C. Brooks Temple.—**Zoning Bd. of Appeals,** William J. Zehrung II, Chm., Eleanor A. Florio, Jerome E. Hyland, Harry F. O'Brien, James R. Umbarger; Alternates, Walter Bayer, Norman Minto, vacancy.—**Zoning Enforcement Officer,** Loretta Brickiey.—**Inland Wetlands Comm.,** Marsha LaTour, Chm., Elyse Allen, Carlos R. Caridad, Karen Halasi-Kun, Philip G. Lovell, Kathleen Nelson, Robert A. Scalera; James Ferlow, Enforcement Officer; Alternates, Susan E. Simoneali, Danny R. Straub, vacancy.—**Economic Development Comm.,** Howard Spengler, Chm., Agnes M. Knowles, Donald G. Marsh, Martha McMahon, C. James Osborne, Jr., Deborah R. Pritchard, vacancy; Alternates, Naomi Miller, Garland G. Warren.—**Conservation Comm.,** Roger W. Richmond, Chm., Kimberly J. Brown, Adam Halasi-Kun, Robert S. Hutchings, Helen A. Lillis, Lynn Webster.—**Comm. on Aging,** Gretchen O'Shea, Chm., Eleanor B. Baird, Betty Lou Emmons, Alice E. Halpine, Ruth Malins, Christine Pruss, vacancy.—**Welfare Dir.,** Karen Hine.—**Dir. of Social Services,** Patricia Purdy.—**Dir. of Health,** Michael Crespan.—**Library Trustees,** Joanne Lillis, Pres., Joyce Hermonat, Alma Hough, Micki McConaughey, Eileen P. Monaghan, James Reiss, Joseph W. Rush, Barbara W. Street.—**Municipal Historian,** M. Joseph Lillis, Jr.—**Comm. on the Arts,** C. Brooks Temple, Chm., Sarah C. Adams, Charlotte Bostwick, Laura L. Buckbee, Diane D. Dubreuil, Susan Fogarty, Patricia Greenspan, Joanne Lillis, Frank Merkling, Charles Raymond, James Scrimgeour, Deborah A. Swanson.—**Historic Properties Comm.,** William E. Devin, M. Joseph Lillis, Jr., James R. Umbarger.—**Parks and Recreation Comm.,** Peter P. Mullen, Chm., Randy R. Carocci, Victor Consaga, William C. Kamp, Susan C. Lamb, Thomas K. Saunders, Jay A. Solomon; Laurie Albano, Dir.—**Youth Agency,** Gilbert Radday, Chm., Phyllis E. Alesio, John Bachetti, James M. Carmellini, Judith A. Friedman, David I. McCullough, Mary B. Mullen, Lynn Raskin, James Sweeney, Virginia Wall; Mark Mankin, Dir.—**Highway Foreman,** Wayne Rodger.—**Traffic Authority,** Clark J. Chapin, Chm., Richard Hinlicky, Douglas Neelands; Alternate, Alan W. Harris.—**Purchasing Auth.,** Raymond J. Jankowski, Arthur J. Peitler.—**Dir. of Public Works,** William Camosci.—**Building Inspector,** Frank Rybak.—**Building Code Bd. of Appeals,** Harold F. Koehler, Jack Straub, three vacancies.—**Lake Authorities,** Candlewood: Larence J. Liebman, Harold Mayer, Harold Nohe; Lillinonah: Leroy E. Johnson, Jr., two vacancies.—**Sewer Comm.,** William Johnson, Chm., Thomas Altermatt, John M. Friedman, Sr., Gregory McGill, Thomas R. Morey, Patricia Sherry.—**Sanitarian,** Suzanne Eimiche; Asst., Keith Vaughn.—**Tree Warden,** Philip G. Lovell.—**Chief of Police,** James Sweeney.—**Chiefs of Fire Dept.,** Stark Weiner (Northville), Dean Newkirk (Water Witch Hose Co.), John Jejer (Gaylordsville).—**Fire Marshal,** William G. May.—**Civil Preparedness Dir.,** vacancy.—**Town Atty.,** Thomas W. Beecher.—**Justices of the Peace,** John Bachetti, Jr., Loretta Brickley, Barbara B. Buie, Bonnie Butcher-Smith, Carol B. Caldwell, Clark Chapin, Steven J. Defren, John O. Durling, Liba H. Furhman, Joseph Geyer, Maurice A. Goldstein, Robert J. Guendelsberger, Janis Hine, Barbara B. Hyatt, Murray J. Kessler, Esther E. Kibbe, Agnes M. Knowles, Martin Landgrebe, Edwin J. Larson, Arthur L. Lavalette, Jr., M. Joseph Lillis, Jr., Martha C. McMahon, Arthur J. Peitler, Diane S. Phillips, Richard M. Pomerantz, William Quinnell, Joseph Sobel, Kenneth E. Taylor, Mona Tito, Randolph J. Ubben, Virginia V. Wall, Louis C. White.

NEWTOWN. Fairfield County.—(Form of government, selectmen, legislative council, town meeting.)—Inc., Oct., 1711. Area, 59.1 sq. miles. Population, est., 20,971. Voting districts, 4. Principal industries, manufacture of pressure gauges, plastics, paper boxes, wire brushes, biomedical research instruments, corrugated cartons, copper tubing, wire coating, warehouse distribution centers. Transp.—Freight: Served by Conrail and numerous motor common carriers. Post offices, Newtown, Botsford and Hawleyville.

TOWN OFFICERS. Clerk and Reg. of Vital Statistics, Cynthia C. Simon; Hours, 8 A.M.-4:30 P.M., Mon. through Fri.; Address, Edmond Town Hall, 45 Main St., 06470; Tel., (203) 270-4210.—**Asst. Clerks and Asst. Regs. of Vital Statistics,** Blithe M. Dotson, Susan J. Shpunt.—**Asst. Reg. of Vital Statistics,** Jean Salvatore.—**Selectmen,** 1st, Robert A. Cascella (R) Tel., (203) 270-4201, Gary A. Fetzer (D), James M. Mooney, Sr. (R).—**Legislative Council,** A. Winthrop Ballard, Karen H. Blawie, Joe Borst, William A. Brimmer, Jr., John W. Kortze, Joseph J. McGowan, Sr., Melissa M. Pilchard, Pierre Rochman, William F. Rodgers, Jack H. Rosenthal, Lisa B. Schwartz, Donald T. Studley.—**Bd. of Managers,** Sandra R. Motyka, Chm., Edgar W. Beers, David E. Brown, William A. Honan, Jr., Birthe Melville, Marie A. Sturdevant.—**Bd. of Ethics,** Robert E. Daley, Chm., Helen Krueger, David K. Nanavaty, vacancy; Alternates, Maurya Keating, Charles Pilchard.—**Finance Dir.,** Benjamin B. Spragg.—**Tax Collector,** Carol L. Mahoney.—**Bd. of Assessment Appeals,** Charles V. Framularo, Jr., Chm., Eleanor C. Mayer, vacancy.—**Assessor,** Mark DeVestern.—**Registrars of Voters,** Susan S. Fernandes (D), Shirley Lawrenson (R).—**Supt. of Schools,** John R. Reed.—**Bd. of Education,** Amy Dent, Isabelle M. Murray, Herbert C. Rosenthal, 1997; Susan S. Hills, Charles S. Nanavaty, Margaret L. Ulrich-Nims, 1999.—**Pension Committee,** Thomas M. Murtha, Chm., Mark Korotash, Francis A. Krasowski, Jr., David Lydem, Walter Panchniuk, Dunham M. Smith, Edward H. Zeller.—**Planning and Zoning Comm.,** John DeFilippe, Jr., , Chm., John W. Deegan, Thomas C. Paisley, Heidi G. Winslow, vacancy; Alternates, James Boylan, Stephen P. Koch, Daniel C. Rosenthal.—**Zoning Bd. of Appeals,** Charles E. Annett III, Chm., Steven G. Berg, Alan J. Clavette, Richard H. Kessler, Jr., Sally J. O'Neil; Alternates, Timothy J. Cronin, Pat J. Rosato, Earl J. Smith III.—**Zoning Enforcement Officer,** William Nicholson.—**Public Building and Site Comm.,** Frank Krasnickas, Chm., Anthony W. DeCarlo, Paul DesBiens, John Lipusz, Edward F. Muraszkin, Gus Palmieri, Peter Samoskevich; Alternate, Anthony D'Angelo.—**Conservation and Inland Wetlands Comm.,** Donald H. Lawrenson, Chm., Catherine Andrews, Edwin Dudeck, C. Wesley Gillingham, Palma Goodman, Judith Holmes, Lawrence Whippie.—**Environmental Enforcement Officer,** David Thompson.—**Economic Development Comm.,** Evelyn A. Evagash, Robert A. Geckle, James T. Juliano, John F. Klopfenstein, Richard LaBash, Walter S. Motyka, Edward L. Rudisill.—**Dir. of Community Development,** Elizabeth L. Stocker.—**Water Pollution Control Auth.,** Peter L. Alagna, Chm., Timothy LaChapelle, Eleanor C. Mayer, Gary Sheehan, Alan Shepard, Richard B. Zang, Carl J. Zencey.—**Comm. on Aging,** Helen J. Previdi, Chm., Albert R. Brinkman, Katharine E. Dougherty, Merlin Fisk, Jeanne C. Honan, Edna Marks, Dr. Eugene Marks, Leo McIlrath, Jeane Roberts; Karen Hoyt, Municipal Agent; Alternates, Norma H. Gray, Cheryl W. Grenier, Glenna Rees.—**Dir. of Human Services,** Sheila Knox.—**Dir. of Health,** Mark Cooper.—**Library Trustees,** Suzanne Hard, Jeanne C. Honan, Paula M. Hopper, Christopher J. Spiro, Richard L. Sturdevant, Gordon Williams; Janet Woycik, Librarian.—**Lake Authorities,** Zoar: Donald MacKenzie, Peter W. Masella, Robert E. Mitchell; Lillinonah: Ronald Buttner, Michael Daubert, Lillian S. Strickler.—**Hattertown Historic Dist. Comm.,** William Rodgers, Chm., Rosemarie Buckens, Bruce Deegen, Christine Deegan, Brian White; Alternates, Gary A. Bonhiver, William G. Forster.—**Parks and Recreation Comm.,** Lawrence M. Haskel, Chm., Albert D. Borchetta, Jr., William P. Cavanaugh, Roger B. Conner, Sr., Raymond O.

Craven, Patti J. Meyer; Barbara Kasbarian, Recr. Dir.; Ron Moffat, Parks Supt.—**Town Engineer,** Ronald Bolmer.—**Building Inspector,** R. Allen Brinley, Jr.—**Building Bd. of Appeals,** John G. Stiles, Chm., Wendy Beres, Michael F. Porco, Thomas R. Swetts.—**Tree Warden,** John Mead.—**Dir. of Public Works,** Frederick Hurley.—**Chief of Police,** James Lysaght, Jr., Chm., Michael DeJoseph.—**Police Comm.,** Carol Mattegat, Chm., Robert W. Connor, Jr., Gerald J. Frawley, William F. Meyer, James P. Reilly.—**Constables,** George Blantin, Robert W. Connor, Jr., Frank DeLucia, Thomas Goosman, Donald D. MacKenzie, James R. Stiewing, Carl Swanhall, vacancy.—**Fire Marshals,** R. Allen Brinley, Jr., Joseph Cavanaugh, William Halstead, George Lockwood, Henry Stormer.—**Bd. of Fire Comrs.,** Kevin Cragin, Chm., Raul A. Camejo, Lisa Goosman, Frank Johnson, Bill McCarthy, Jeffrey Nezvesky, Kimberly Sharpe.—**Civil Preparedness Dir.,** John Mead.—**Town Atty.,** David Grogins.—**Justices of the Peace,** George E. Blantin, Charles B. Browne III, Gregory J. Bunger, JoAnn M. Connor, Roger B. Connor, Carolyn H. Downing, George R. Gabriel, Lilly Goosman, Cheryl M. Johnson, Edward L. Lucas, Barbara A. O'Connor, Deborah O. Stiewing, Lillian S. Strickler, Kaaren Valenta.

BOROUGH OFFICERS. P.O. c/o Clerk, P.O. Box 164, Newtown 06470; Tel., (203) 426-9497.—**Warden,** Joan G. Crick.—**Clerk,** Darlene Spencer.—**Burgesses,** James O. Gaston, Lee W. Glover, Sr., Gretchen F. Hyde, Betsy Kenyon, Marie F. Walker, James Walker.—**Treas.,** Marie F. Walker.—**Assessors,** Dawn Ford, vacancy.—**Bd. of Assessment Appeals,** John Madzula, Janet Woycik.—**Registrar of Voters,** Linda Connor.—**Tax Collector,** Dawn Ford.—**Zoning Comm.,** Robert W. Connor, Chm., Robert H. Klein, Gregory G. O'Brien, Eugene A. Previdi, Jr., Linda Shepard; Alternates, Edmund P. Breitling, Douglas Nelson, Tami L. Whitlock.—**Zoning Bd. of Appeals,** James W. Crick, Jr., Chm., Walter E. Dzitko, Bea Gellert, John Madzula, Janet Woycik; Alternates, John R. Hilgert, Patrick Hill, Robert Taylor.

NORFOLK. Litchfield County.—(Form of government, selectmen, town meeting, board of finance.)—Inc., Oct., 1758. Area, 46.4 sq. miles. Population, est., 2,108. Voting district, 1. Principal industries, summer resort, agriculture, manufacture of wooden toys and steel balls. Transp.—Passenger: Served by buses of the Arrow Line from Hartford, New Haven, Winsted and North Canaan. Freight: Served by numerous motor common carriers. Post office, Norfolk.

TOWN OFFICERS. Clerk and Reg. of Vital Statistics, Anne R. Moses; Hours, 9 A.M.-12 Noon, 1-4 P.M., Mon. through Fri.; 9 A.M.-12 Noon, Friday, Memorial Day through Labor Day. Address, 19 Maple Ave., P.O. Box 552, 06058; Tel., (860) 542-5679.—**Asst. Clerk and Asst. Reg. of Vital Statistics,** Margaret Cusick.—**Selectmen,** 1st, Arthur S. Rosenblatt (D) Tel., (860) 542-5829, Carl F. Gundlach (R), John A. McGoldrick (D).—**Treas.,** Anne R. Moses.—**Bd. of Finance,** Susan M. Dyer, Chm., Eric B. Anderson, Mark K. Burke, David W. Gourley, Lawrence A. Leifert, J. Michael Sconyers; Alternates, Michael A. Monroe, Colin C. Tait, vacancy.—**Tax Collector,** Eleanor E. LaForge.—**Bd. of Assessment Appeals,** Louis J. Barbagallo, Robert E. Barrett, George V. Phelan.—**Assessors,** Joyce S. Mahoney, Chm., Bonnie M. Gibb, Michael C. Santoro.—**Registrars of Voters,** Kevin M. O'Connor (D), Barbara A.

Tracey (R).—**Supt. of Schools,** Judith Condon.—**Bd. of Education,** Janis B. Graham-Jones, John J. McGinnis, Barbara A. Mulville, 1997; Carolyn B. Conway, Chm., Peter F. Boyle, Schuyler W. Thomson, Robin R. Yuran, 1999.—**Planning and Zoning Comm.,** Robert Mead, Chm., Carolle W. Jenkins, Richard W. Lowe, Patrick McElhorne, Rita K. Tierney, Terrence H. Tirrell, Alexander M. Vagliano; Alternates, Starling W. Childs, Ruthann Olsson, Mary Alice Pilbin.—**Zoning Bd. of Appeals,** Edith Donaldson, Chm., Joanne Munch, Michaela A. Murphy, Louise S. Schimmel, John G. Thew; Alternates, Barbara G. Billings, Ronald T. Zanobi, vacancy.—**Conservation and Inland Wetlands Comm.,** Edward Hinman, Chm., Paul F. Adamson, David Gourley, Michael Halloran, Hartley Mead; Alternates, Christina Hanley, vacancy.—**Historic Dist. Comm.,** Bruce F. Anderson, Robert E. Barrett, George D. Nash, Alan Redford; Alternates, Phyllis M. Diggle, Linda S. Perkins, Reginald W. Whidden.—**Agent for the Elderly,** Paul D. Hosch.—**Dir. of Health,** Torrington Area Health.—**Recreation Comm.,** Marie Lowe, Chm., David Godding, Ann H. Gridley, Aileen Hester, Richard Johnston, Elizabeth Peterson, David Taylor, Beatrice D. Tirrell, vacancy.—**Municipal Historian,** Cay Fields.—**Building Inspector,** Michael LaRosa.—**Sanitarian,** Torrington Area Health.—**Sewer Dist.,** Paul Hosch, Chm., Louis Barbagallo, Ronald T. Zanobi.—**Chief of Fire Dept.,** Steven Osborne.—**Fire Marshal,** Richard Healy.—**Civil Preparedness Dir.,** Sidney W. Toomey.—**Town Atty.,** Levy & Droney (Farmington).—**Justices of the Peace,** Louis J. Barbagallo, Ross K. Burke, Leon A. Deloy, Carl F. Gundlach, Arthur J. Rosenblatt, James J. Stotler, Colin C. Tait, Arnold Tsukroff..

NORTH BRANFORD. New Haven County.—(Form of government, town manager, town council, town budget meeting.)—Inc., May, 1831; taken from Branford. Area, 26.7 sq. miles. Population, est., 13,022. Voting districts, 2. Principal industries, agriculture, trap rock (Tilcon Minerals, Inc. has one of the largest trap rock quarries in the East and ships by rail; has tidewater docks at Pine Orchard), plastic autobody filler, machine products, printing and microfilming, electronic instruments, and solid state control circuitry. Location of New Haven Water Company's largest source of water, man-made Lake Gaillard, and their multi-million dollar water treatment facility. Freight: Served by numerous motor common carriers. Post offices, North Branford and Northford.

TOWN OFFICERS. Clerk and Reg. of Vital Statistics, Lisa A. Valenti; Hours, 8:30 A.M.-4:30 P.M., Mon. through Fri.; Address, Town Hall, 1599 Foxon Rd., P.O. Box 287, 06471; Tel., (203) 481-5369.—**Asst. Clerk and Asst. Reg. of Vital Statistics,** Linda A. Cantore.—**Town Manager,** Frank B. Connolly.—**Town Council,** Joanne S. Wentworth (R), Mayor; Frederick P. Augur, Deputy Mayor; Richard C. Aitro, Alfred Astorino, Jr., Sherman Gomberg, Miriam Miller, Stephen Montesano, Alfred D. Rose, John K. Zephir.—**Treas.,** Anthony P. Esposito, Jr.—**Tax Collector,** Suzanne Kleinkauf.—**Bd. of Assessment Appeals,** Robert Cotton, Carl Negro, vacancy.—**Assessor,** Donna Price.—**Registrars of Voters,** 1st Dist., Laura E. Negro, 2nd Dist., Judith Esposito (D); 1st Dist., Ann Byrne, 2nd Dist., Paulette C. Hart (R).—**Supt. of Schools,** Donald J. McCarthy.—**Bd. of Education,** Ruth Rose, Chm., Genevieve Karbowski-DeMatteo, Vivian Troiano, 1997; Rosemarie Angeloni, Lawrence

J. Casey, Penny Seaman, 1999.—**Planning and Zoning Comm.,** Dennis Hrabchak, Chm., Michael Downey, Joseph Faughnan, Charles Gunn, Frances Lescovich; Richard Schultz, Town Planner; Alternates, Robert Fitch, John Greening, Stephen Scavo.—**Zoning Bd. of Appeals,** Michael Solakian, Chm., Paul Bradley, Michael Downes, Steven Kenning, vacancy; Alternates, Harry Tietjen, two vacancies.—**Economic Development Comm.,** Angela Mazzoli, Chm., Richard Hart, John Mancini, Annaliese Milici, Sara Querfled.—**Housing Auth.,** Mary Ann Augur, Shirley Gagne, William Lovelace, Kathryn Meagher, Jill Vaspasiano.—**Conservation and Inland, Wetlands and Watercourses Agency,** Cookie Aitro, Dino Esposito, Robert Fitch, Stephen Scavo, Christopher Smith, Craig Stoeckle, Carol Zebb; Alternates, Corinne Casanova, vacancy.—**Agent for the Elderly,** Alphonse A. DeRuccio.—**Human Relations Committee,** Denise Greening, Chm., Nancy Davitt, Joseph A. Marino, Fr. Daniel McSheffrey, three vacancies.—**Asst. Welfare Dir.,** Luisa Breen.—**Library Bd.,** Marion Dufourny, Catherine Johnson, Judy Neubig, George Zimmer, vacancy.—**Municipal Historian,** Janet Gregan.—**Park & Recreation Comm.,** Ronald Bergmark, Edward Davitt, Brian Lynch, Ronald Tracz, vacancy; Alphonse A. DeRuccio, Dir.—**Town Engineer,** Kurt Weiss.—**Building Official/Zoning Enforcement Officer,** David Maiden.—**Building Code Bd. of Appeals,** William Neubig, James Petonito, Alfred Petrillo, Scott Small, vacancy.—**Water Pollution Control Auth.,** Joanne S. Wentworth, Chm., Richard C. Aitro, Alfred Astorino, Jr., Frederick P. Augur, Sherman Gomberg, Miriam Miller, Stephen Montesano, Alfred D. Rose, John K. Zephir.—**Dir. of Public Works,** Francis Merola.—**Chief of Police,** Matthew L. Canelli.—**Police Comm.,** Vincent Casanova, Richard Evans, Timothy Ryan, Henry Sondergaard, G. Dan Troiano.—**Constables,** Andrew Esposito III, John Vaspasiano.—**Chief of Fire Dept.,** Ralph N. Thomas.—**Fire Marshal,** Bert Bunnell, Jr.—**Bd. of Fire Comrs.,** Manuel Cabral, Joseph Civitello, Patricia Nagot, Pasquale Sansevero, Angelo F. Tosi, Jr.—**Civil Preparedness Dir.,** Ralph Thomas.—**Town Atty.,** John M. Gesmonde.—**Justices of the Peace,** Robert T. Cotton, Philip J. Dahlmeyer, Jr., William F. Foye, Donald W. Guyer, Richard J. Hart, Marian G. Hawkins, Donald LaBanca, Stanley O. Lyman, Gordon P. McGuire, Carl Negro, John J. Pantalena, John A. Parese, Carlton A. Platt, Jr., Timothy P. Ryan, Carolann K. Slayton, Norma J. Smith, Henry V. Sondergaard, Pasquale Young.

NORTH CANAAN. Litchfield County.—(Form of government, selectmen, town meeting, board of finance.)—Inc., May, 1858; taken from Canaan. Area, 19.5 sq. miles. Population, est., 3,117. Voting district, 1. Principal industries, agriculture, manufacture of medical and surgical instruments, lime and limestone products, magnesium and calcium metals, electrical coils, sand and stone. Transp.—Passenger: Served by buses of The Arrow Line from Albany, NY to Hartford and New Haven, and by Bonanza Bus Lines from Albany to New York City. Freight: Served by Boston & Maine Corporation and numerous motor common carriers. Post offices, Canaan and East Canaan. Rural free delivery from both post offices.

TOWN OFFICERS. Clerk and Reg. of Vital Statistics, Carolyn C. O'Connor; Hours, 9:30 A.M.-12 Noon, 1-4 P.M., Mon. through Fri.; Address, Town Hall, 100 Pease St., P.O. Box 338, Canaan 06018; Tel., (860) 824-3138.—**Asst. Clerks and**

Asst. Regs. of Vital Statistics, Nancy C. Bagnaschi, Jean A. Jacquier, Carroll A. Segalla.—**Selectmen,** 1st, Douglas E. Humes, Jr. (R) P.O. 876, Canaan, Tel., (860) 824-7313, Henry G. Carley, Jr. (R), Nancy L. Gandolfo (D).—**Treas.,** Francis W. McCarthy.—**Bd. of Finance,** Wheaton B. Byers, Chm., Louis E. Allyn II, Shannon L. May-Vernali, Francis D. McGuire, Hatsy Taylor, John F. Warner.—**Tax Collector,** Ross A. Beaujon.—**Bd. of Assessment Appeals,** Edwin K. Gow, David W. Jacquier, Joseph W. Strekas.—**Assessor,** Anthony Barber.—**Registrars of Voters,** Evelyn E. Hedus (D), Clara B. Curtis (R).—**Supt. of Schools,** Marvin Maskovsky.—**Bd. of Education,** William Crepeau, Lisa Richards, Martha A. Scott, Susan E. Warner, 1997; Patricia A. Heinsman, Chm., David A. Beaujon, Gary D. Guerin, Charles E. Moseley, 1999.—**Planning Comm.,** Perry F. Gardner, Acting Chm., Pauline R. Moore, Charles E. Moseley, George W. Schaefer, Robert S. Segalla; Alternates, Warren E. Foley, Edward R. Osborne.—**Housing Auth.,** Beverly A. Becker, Robert G. Palmer, Sally J. Pollard, Norman A. Tatsapaugh, Gertrude Washburn.—**Conservation and Inland Wetlands Comm.,** Suzanne Coe, Chm., Tom Foley, Jr., Frederick Ruggles, N. Bruce Zinke, vacancy.—**Agent for the Elderly,** Nancy E. Laigle.—**Dir. of Health,** Bruce Janelli, M.D. (P.O., Canaan).—**Library Directors,** Oliver F. Eldridge, Edward J. Heinsman, Lynne H. Martin, Bernice E. Olt, Marjorie A. Stevenson, Ruth B. Thompson.—**Municipal Historian,** Fred Hall.—**Recreation Comm.,** Mark W. Hickey, Chm., Patricia J. Boyles, David L. Beaujon, Michael Congloque, Michael Devino, Joanne Gatto, Jill S. Ghi, Debra M. Hester, John H. Matheson.—**Building Inspector,** William Conrad.—**Building Code Bd. of Appeals,** Tony Zavagnin.—**Sanitarian,** Ralph H. Stanton, Jr.—**Chief of Fire Dept.,** Charles P. Perotti; Deputy, Richard J. Weaver.—**Fire Marshal,** Edward J. McGuire.—**Civil Preparedness Dir.,** Edward H. Scott.—**Town Attys.,** Judith Dixon (45 Center St., Winsted), Catherine G. Roraback (P.O. 935, Canaan).—**Justices of the Peace,** Eugene Freund, Anthony G. Gandolfo, Nancy L. Gandolfo, Dori C. Gay, Evelyn E. Hedus, Darinda L. Humes, Richard Koneazny, Lynne H. Martin, Clementine C. McGuire, Margaret B. Schaeffer.

NORTH HAVEN. New Haven County.—(Form of government, selectmen, town meeting, board of finance.)—Inc., Oct., 1786; taken from New Haven. Area, 21.1 sq. miles. Population, est., 21,080. Voting districts, 5. Principal industries, manufacture of aircraft components, paper boxes, miscellaneous non-metallic mineral products, cutlery, tools and general hardware, industrial chemical, miscellaneous wood products, structural clay products, fertilizers, machinery, professional and services equipment, plumbing and heating, manufacture of firearms, commercial printing, sporting goods, electrical and electronic cable and parts, printed circuit boards, aluminum strip mill, steel fabrication, food distribution, die casting, ceramic products, milt and products, scrap reduction. Transp.—Passenger: Served by Amtrak and buses of The Conn. Transit, Inc. from New Haven and Hartford. Freight: Served by Conrail and numerous motor common carriers. Post office, North Haven.

TOWN OFFICERS. Clerk and Reg. of Vital Statistics, Elinor C. Pedalino; Hours, 8:30 A.M.-4:30 P.M., Mon. through Fri.; Address, Town Hall, 18 Church St., 06473; Tel., New Haven, (203) 239-5321, Ext. 765.—**Asst. Clerks and Asst. Regs. of Vital Statistics,** Linda K. Bykowski, Margaret H. Carter.—**Selectmen,** 1st, Anthony P. Rescigno (R) Tel., (203) 239-5321, Ext. 760, Howard L. Luppi (R), Walter J. Nester, Jr. (D).—**Treas.,** Richard J. Guandalini.—**Bd. of Ethics,** Thurl Stalnaker, Chm., Leo Connors, Walter R. Mahon, William F. Mitchell, Pamela Parrella.—**Bd. of Finance,** Albert W. Cretella III, Chm., James B. Curtin, Stanley H. Fontana, Richard F. Gillen, Gary E. Johns, Anthony P. Rescigno, Deborah Ward-O'Brien.—**Dir. of Finance,** Vincent E. Palmeri, Jr.—**Tax Collector,** Elinor C. Pedalino.—**Bd. of Assessment Appeals,** Vincent J. Gangi, Chm., Angelo M. DeCicco, Joan J. Hunt, Jianny Keegan, Claire B. Schulz.—**Assessor,** Robert G. Coates.—**Registrars of Voters,** Phyllis Kaercher (D), Frank J. Riggs (R).—**Supt. of Schools,** Mary Jane Sheehy.—**Bd. of Education,** Anthony R. DeChello, Janice M. Engel, Peter Johnson, 1997; John R. Lambert, Chm., Joseph Ginnetti, James C. Hogan, Jr., 1999; Gerald A. Feinberg, Dolores M. Piscitelli, Eve K. Rocklin, 2001.—**Planning and Zoning Comm.,** Kevin Kopetz, Chm., Dominic M. Palumbo, Jeanne P. Pulleyn, Donald Sbabo, Peter A. Tenedine; Alternates, Vern E. Carlson, William D. O'Hare, Douglas E. Roberts.—**Zoning Bd. of Appeals,** Peter J. Ney III, Chm., James A. Falco, James J. Giulietti, Robert F. Hannon, Nicholas F. Tirozzi; Alternates, Bernard G. Diana, Anthony P. Pileggi, Michael E. Quitko.—**Zoning Enforcement Officer,** Jack Brandt.—**Land Use Admin.,** Robert F. Johnson.—**Economic Development Comm.,** Ralph Durante, Chm., Gennaro Basilio, Susan B. Candido, Angelo DeCicco, Thomas Dunham, William V. Gambardella, Frank Maher, Radha R. Prasad, Daniel Underkofler.—**Housing Auth.,** Richard J. Parrett, Chm., Albert Della Valle, Jr., Louis Guertin, Joseph Marsiglio, John Mulligan.—**Conservation Comm.,** Hugh Davis, Chm., Leela Atluru, Dorie Baker, Lawrence Lazaroff, Ronald Penton, Andrew Sherman, Shelley Wheeler-Carreiro.—**Inland Wetlands Comm.,** Lucille M. Franco, Chm., Edward Bruce, Keane Callahan, Freda Kaplan, Ethel Libson, Michael McGarry, Mark Trojanowski; Alternates, Sandra L. Cummings, Diane C. Jablonski, Cheryl Juniewic.—**Comm. on Aging,** Harriet Cxypoliski, Chm., Frances K. L. Cole, Louis Guertin, David I. Gurniak, Marianne Miranda, Anthony Pacileo, Rodger Salman, Dian Viesselman, Joseph N. Williams; Marjorie Bergin, Agent.—**Dir. of Health,** Leslie A. Balch.—**Community Services Comm.,** Caroline Hansen, Chm., Peter D. Cole, Carol Davis, James Hogan, Jr., Jill Iannone, Frank Kruglik, Eileen Mulqueen, Victor Muzio, Philip Piscitelli.—**Library Bd. of Directors,** John Graef, Jr., Chm., Ann Bacon, David Burke, Jr., Constance Dayton, Joan Hunt, Henry Lozier, Mary Reardon, Paul F. Stuehrenberg, Angelo J. Verdini; Lois Baldini, Dir.—**Parks and Recreation Comm.,** Raymond Gorman, Chm., Richard Connors, William DeMatteo, Jr., John M. Markiewicz, Frank Montagna, Edward J. Morrell, Michael Pomichter.—**Dir. of Public Works,** Richard V. Branigan.—**Supt. of Highways,** Donald White.—**Building Inspector,** John DeMarco.—**Building Bd. of Appeals,** William Buller, Chm., Teresa Hill, Philip Kinsella, Pasquale Rosadini; Alternates, Frank Marino, John Parisella, Daniel Perotto.—**Water Pollution Control Auth.,** Richard Werner, Chm., Lewis Borrelli, Anthony C. Furino, Victor Gomez, William J. Lane, Jr., Bernard Pellegrino, Anthony P. Rescigno.—**Supt. of Scale House/Land Fill,** vacancy.—**Chief of Police,** Kevin Connolly; Deputy, James X. DiCarlo.—**Police Comm.,** Paul D. Abercrombie, Chm., Peggy M. Brennan, Joseph D'Errico, Doris E. Ferner, Edward R. Parisella.—**Constables,** Marguerite H. Carboni, Thomas A. Cxypoliski, Mildred S. Gherlone, Edward Homa, Cheryl A. Juniewic, Frederick J. Kelly.—**Chief of Fire Dept./Fire Marshal,** John E. Obier, Jr.; Deputy, Nicholas Merola; Asst., vacancy.—**Bd. of Fire Comrs.,** Frank Annunziato, Chm., Peter J. Criscuolo, Jr., Edward M. Homa, Frank Porto, Peter E. Ricciardi.—**Civil Preparedness Dir.,** Vincent E. Palmeri, Jr.—**Town Atty.,** Robert K. Ciulla.—**Justices of the Peace,** Kurt D. Anderson, Eileen Borrelli, Catherine A. Brooks, Jeffrey A. Brooks, Frances K. Cole, Harriet Cxypoliski, Victor A. DeBarnardi, Angelo M. DeCicco, Barbara C. Dutra, Freda Kaplan, John M. Markiewicz, William D. O'Hare, Pamela J. Parrella, Lynne M. Rescigno, Carmen Romano, Donald Sbabo, Grace M.Smith.

NORTH STONINGTON. New London County.—(Form of government, selectmen, town meeting, board of finance.)—Inc., May, 1807; taken from Stonington. Area, 55.0 sq. miles. Population, est., 4,826. Voting district, 1. Principal industry, agriculture. Freight: Served by numerous motor common carriers. Post office, North Stonington. Rural deliveries from North Stonington post office and R.F.D. 7 from Ledyard.

TOWN OFFICERS. Clerk and Reg. of Vital Statistics, Patricia P. McGowan; Hours, 9 A.M.-12 Noon, 12:30-4 P.M., Mon. through Fri.; Address, Town Hall, 40 Main St., 06359; Tel., Mystic, (860) 535-2877.—**Asst. Clerk and Asst. Reg. of Vital Statistics,** Joyce G. Main.—**Selectmen,** 1st, Charles E. Elias (R) Tel., (860) 535-0793, Nicholas K. Mullane II (R), Constance N. VanLew (D).—**Treas.,** Connie J. Dean.—**Bd. of Finance,** Bradford P. Borden, Chm., Alicia T. Bauer, Charles R. Marsh, Emil W. Pavlovics, Robert H. Rubio, Lawrence H. Southwick.—**Tax Collector,** Patricia P. McGowan.—**Bd. of Assessment Appeals,** Daniel P. Kitchel, Jeffrey P. Nelson, Susan A. Sweet.—**Assessor,** Joyce M. Elias.—**Registrars of Voters,** Eleanor M. Johnson (D), Barbara C. Perkins (R).—**Supt. of Schools,** Martin C. Gotowala.—**Bd. of Education,** Anita C. Ames, Barbara E. Fontanella, Lawrence M. St Clair, James C. Spavins, 1997; Robert W. Lohmann, Chm., Douglas L. Henderson, John P. Keane, Fred D. Launer, 1999.—**Planning and Zoning Comm.,** Arthur V. Pintauro, Chm., Mary B. Cooper, Anne H. Nalwalk, George P. Panciera, Diana S. Urban; Alternates, Alan J. Pesch, Charles A. Steinhart IV, Allen A. Van Lew.—**Town Engineer,** Patrick Lafayette.—**Zoning Bd. of Appeals,** Arnold S. Herrington, Thomas A. O'Brien, Winifred E. Pattison, Jay W. Ryerson, Allana R. York; Alternates, Raymond A. Geer, Terri B. Mancuso, Helen Quallich.—**Zoning Enforcement Officer,** George C. Brown.—**Economic Development Comm.,** William H. Stoddard, Chm., Warren E. Bishop, Robert H. Boissevain, Richard W. Geiler, Cornelius J. Kluepfel, Marjorie B. Penley.—**Conservation and Inland Wetlands Comm.,** Eugene A. Anderson III, Wayne S. Berardi, James A. Bill, Arthur P. Crofts, Lynne M. Krynicki, Ronald K. Lewis, Palmer N. Miner, Robert J. Miner.—**Dir. of Health,** James F. Brown IV.—**Welfare Dir.,** Janet M. Perkins.—**Recreation Comm.,** William A. Bernard, Chm., Norma J. Holliday, Ronald Modon, Mary T. Sanford, Scott C. Sanford, Kip Taylor, Susan L. White.—**Supt. of Highways,** David Birkbeck.—**Building Inspector,** Timothy E. York.—**Sanitarians,** Theodore A. Faulise, Robert J. Shabunia.—**Chief of Police,** Charles E. Elias.—**Chief of Fire Dept.,** Timothy O. Main II; Deputy, Michael K. Riley.—**Fire Marshal,** George P. Brennan.—**Dir. of Civil Preparedness,** Walter T. Weissmuller.—**Town Attys.,** O'Brien, Shafner, Stuart, Kelly & Morris.—**Justices of the Peace,** Alicia T. Bauer, Rose J. Berg, Joseph J. Bianco, Richard E. Blodgett, Jr., Mary N. Colechia,

Velda M. Hess, Sally A. Humphrey, Cornelius J. Kluepfel, Terri B. Mancuso, Stephen G. Misovich, Nicholas H. Mullane II, Winifred E. Pattison, Barbara C. Perkins, Helen Quallich, Judith A. Rubio, Barbara L. Staunton, Edgar J. Wood, Timothy E. York.

NORWALK. Fairfield County.—(Form of government, mayor, common council.)—Inc., Sept. 11, 1651. Town and city consolidated, Oct., 1913. Area, 36.3 sq. miles. Population, est., 79,358. Voting districts, city elections, 12; state, 14. Principal industries, a wide variety of electronic research and manufacturing companies which produce signaling devices, aircraft radar equipment, optical devices and electronic components; manufacturing of chemicals, machinery and equipment of many kinds, auto accessories, wearing apparel and allied industries, hardware, packaged and frozen foods, lithography and printing. Transp.—Passenger: Served by Metro North Commuter Railroad Co.; buses of Conn. Transit from Stamford, and by Cross Country Coach, Greyhound and Trailways, "Wheels" Local Transit Dist. Freight: Served by Metro North and numerous motor common carriers. Post offices, Norwalk, South Norwalk and Rowayton.

CITY AND TOWN OFFICERS. Town Clerk and Reg. of Vital Statistics, Mary O. Keegan; Hours, 8:30 A.M.-5 P.M., Mon. through Fri.; Address, City Hall, 125 East Ave., P.O. Box 5125, 06856-5125; Tel., (203) 854-7746, 854-7747.—**Asst. Clerks and Asst. Regs. of Vital Statistics,** Ursula Field, Linnea J. Greig.—**City Clerk,** K. C. Senie; Hours, 8:30 A.M.-5 P.M., Monday through Friday; Tel., (203) 854-7701.—**Mayor,** Frank F. Esposito (R).—**Councilmen at Large,** Edward M. Bowers, Andrew T. Conroy, John J. Lombardi, Harold D. McCready, John E. Tobin.—**Common Council,** Dist. A, Richard J. Bonenfant, Richard A. McQuaid; Dist. B, Mathew A. Clark, Sr., Judy Rivas; Dist. C, Guillermo L. Arteaga, Kevin J. Fitzgerald; Dist. D, Ana Maria Aguilar, Charles M. Zinko; Dist. E, Rollo J. Giannini, Peter M. Nolin.—**Selectmen,** Sylvia Meyer, Brian J. Smith, Rocco A. Vita.—**Treas.,** Ralph A. DePanfilis.—**Comptroller,** John F. Smith.—**Dir. of Finance,** Jack E. Miller.—**Bd. of Estimate and Taxation,** David Flewellyn, Chm., Richard Callahan, Mayor Frank Esposito, Jr., Ernest Josem, Cynthia M. Maye, Patricia Richmond, Charles Yost.—**Purchasing Agent,** Mark Turcotte.—**Tax Collector,** Mary K. Ryan.—**Bd. of Assessment Appeals,** Miriam Beyman, Jeanne Soper, Joseph Tavella.—**Tax Assessor,** Kenneth Whitman.—**Registrars of Voters,** Helen A. Carrozelli (D), Ann D. Artell (R).—**Supt. of Schools,** Ralph E. Sloan.—**Bd. of Education,** Richard N. Fuller, Amy K. Jimenez, Jeffrey M. Konspore, Theresa T. Quell, 1996; Thomas J. Cullen, Elizabeth A. Lyons, Roz McCarthy, Rosa Murray, Thomas J. Vetter, 2000.—**Pension Bd.,** James P. Murphy, Chm., Vicki Bove, Diane Campbell, Annaliese Hersom, Rebecca Hoefer, Michael Meany, Jack E. Miller, John Mosby, Donald Nelson, Michael A. Peterson, Charles Pirro III, John Smith, Joseph Tavella.—**Personnel Dir.,** Fredrick Quittell.—**Personnel Committee of the Council,** Harold McCready, Chm., Ana Aguilar, Guillermo Arteaga, Mathew Clark, Charles Zinko.—**Planning Comm.,** Stephen Thomas, Chm., Frank Favano, Virginia Katz, Nicholas Kydes, Walter McLaughlin, Daniel O'Connor, Dennis J. Santella, Eugene Seymour; Michael Greene, Dir.—**Planning Committee of the Council,** John Tobin, Chm., Edward Bowers, Joseph Clemmons, Andrew Conroy, Kevin Fitzgerald, Rollo Giannini, Charles Zinko.—**Zoning Comm.,** Joseph Santo, Chm., Paulette Broder, Lawrence F. Cafero, Sr., Ronnie Coley, Ernest Desrochers,

William LaFontaine, JoAnne Smardin; Alternates, Peter Karadimas, Donald Millar, Nathan Shipp.—**Zoning Bd. of Appeals,** Carmine Cioffi, Ann Greismer, Patrick McBennett, Marjorie Unger, Friedrich Wilms; Alternates, Carl Cooke, Judy H. Cornier, Walter Gogan.—**Zoning Inspector,** James Bradley.—**Redevelopment Agency,** Dominick Montana, Chm., Irving Avrick, Carol Frank, Paul L. Jones, Maritza Marino; Edward Musante, Exec. Dir.—**Sr. Environmental Officer,** Christie Coon.—**Housing Auth.,** Carmen Falcone, Charlotte Josem, Cesar Ramirez, Luis Rivera, B. Tatem; Curtis Law, Exec. Dir.—**Fair Housing Advisory Comm.,** Richard A. Stenhouse, Chm., Mary Corcoran, Carmen Falcone, Lisa H. Ferraro, Anthony Flack, Dominick Montana, Heather Rodin, Bernadine Tatem; vacancy, Fair Housing Officer.—**Fair Rent Comm.,** Richard Booth, Chm., Ismael Cruz-Satt, Patricia Genuario, Taber Hamilton, Mark McElveen, John Mola, two vacancies; Sonja M. Devitt, Dir./Admin.; Alternates, Alfred Ayme, Martin Bernard, Jose Bermudez, Anthony Coppola, Izora Ebron, two vacancies.—**Conservation Comm.,** Lester Bell, Chm., Robert Andre, Beverly Bray, Lynda Kovalik, Anthony Savas, Donald St. John, Wilbur Taylor; Alternates, Arthur Berglund, Jr., Richard Smeriglio, vacancy.—**Historical Comm.,** Valle Fay, Dorothy Girouard, Roger S. Hanford, Ram Hingoran, William Lane, Edna Miller, Kathleen Morrow, Catherine Reischer, Diane Rochelle.—**Municipal Historian,** Ralph C. Bloom.—**Human Relations Comm.,** Lori Torrano, Chm., Barbara Amodio, Ruthie Brown, Sharon Davis, Anthony Flack, Charles Flynn, Joseph Marino, Robert Maslan; Sonja M. Devitt, Dir./Admin.—**Agent for the Elderly,** Laura Epstein.—**Dir. of Health,** Timothy Callahan.—**Bd. of Public Health,** Sharon Donovan, Mary K. Jackson, Kenneth Lalime, Abraham Levine, M.D., Edward J. Tracey, M.D.—**Library Directors,** Josephine Anderson, Chm., Carol Andreoli, Mary T. Brown, Geraldine D'Amato, Anne DiPasquale, James A. Fulton, Grace Vetter, Alonzo Virgil, Johnnie Mae Weldon.—**Dir. of Youth Services,** Linda Wilock.—**Dir. of Public Works,** vacancy.—**Supt. of Highways,** vacancy.—**Sealer of Weights and Measures,** John Schwartz.—**Tree Warden,** Donald Scott.—**Building Inspector,** William Ireland.—**Building Bd. of Appeals,** Dominic Lametta, Chm., Spencer Columbus, Arthur DeSalvo, Sam Resnick, Woody Schempp.—**Shellfish Comm.,** Angelo Rubino, Chm., John Casagrande, John Frank, Sr., Robert Searles.—**Sanitarians,** Erika Bucci, Robert Lichtenberger, Vincent Proto, Kevin Smith.—**Chief of Police,** Harry Rilling; Deputy, vacancy.—**Police Comm.,** George Carroll, Jr., Mayor Frank Esposito, Jr., Charles S. Marshall.—**City Sheriff,** Richard Moccia.—**Constables,** Paul L. Autuore, Fred A. Bondi, S. D. Broder, John A. Campbell, Jr., Carmine C. Cioffi, Alan M. Freedman, Jonathan Major.—**Chief of Fire Dept.,** John E. Yost, Jr.—**Fire Marshal,** James Verda.—**Bd. of Fire Comrs.,** Kenneth Garfunkel, Robert Katz.—**Civil Preparedness Dir.,** John E. Yost.—**Corporation Counsel,** Donald F. Reid.—**Justices of the Peace,** Edmond L. Abel, Ana M. Aguilar, James R. Alvord, James C. Anderson, Carol A. Andreoli, Barbara B. Andrews, Guillermo L. Arteaga, Al Ayme, Alicia Ayme, Karen D. Blackwell, Fred A. Bondi, Richard J. Bonenfant, Edward M. Bowers, Paulette Broder, Mary T. Brown, Otha N. Brown, Jr., John A. Campbell, Jr., Susanna H. Carrillo, Helen A. Carrozelli, Maribel Castillo, Carmine C. Cioffi, Ronnie T. Coley, Andrew T. Conroy, Patrick R. Corridon, Jane E. Courville, Richard A. Cunningham, Robert J. Dagenais, Andrew A. P. D'Alessio, Norma L. Daniel, Charles Donen, Pamela L. Ellis, Louise S. Esposito, Frank T. Favano, Jr., Richard N. Fuller, Rollo J. Giannini, Edward J. Gilmore, Ilene

S. Ginsberg, Viola Green, Colleen Hains, Taber Hamilton III, Ronald E. Kellogg, Stephen B. Keogh, Donna I. King, Jeffrey M. Konspore, Mark M. Kratter, John J. Lombardi, Jacqueline M. Lubell, Angela V. Lyons, Elizabeth A. Lyons, Joseph E. Mann, Joseph J. Mastrianni, Sylvester Maultsby, Scott D. McCoy, Joseph Milici, Michele M. Modugno, Kathleen Morrow, Bettyann Murphy, Harold A. Osgood, Jr., Diana L. Pritkin, Rose Riley-Rodriguez, Ana Rivera, Marina Rivera, John P. Schaberg, Angelina Scombulis, Philip Sherwood, Jr., Philip Siegel, Alan L. Smith, Brian J. Smith, Joseph S. Tamburri, Wilbur S. Taylor, Stephen A. Thomas, Robert J. Tobin, Thelma J. Tourse, John J. Troisi, Jon J. Velez, Susan O. Wallerstein, Patricia Zakhar, Charles M. Zinko, Frank N. Zullo.

NORWICH. New London County.—(Form of government, city council, city manager.)—Settled, 1659; accepted as legal township, May, 1662; city inc., May, 1784; town and city consolidated, Jan. 1, 1952. Area, 29.5 sq. miles. Population, est., 35,356. Voting districts, 10. Principal industries, manufacture of textiles, cartons, plastics, electronics, furniture, plumbing equipment, power tools, wire goods, photo engraving, computer services, marinas. Transp.—Passenger: Served by buses of the Southeast Area Transit, Norwich to Groton and New London. Freight: Served by Central Vermont Railway, Providence & Worcester Co. and numerous motor common carriers. Post offices, Norwich, Yantic and Taftville. Rural free delivery to country districts.

CITY AND TOWN OFFICERS. City Clerk, Town Clerk and Reg. of Vital Statistics, Beverly C. Muldoon; Hours, 8:30 A.M.-4:30 P.M., Mon. through Fri.; Address, City Hall, Room 214, 06360; Tel., (860) 823-3700; FAX (860) 823-3790.—**Asst. City and Town Clerk and Asst. Reg. of Vital Statistics,** DeeAnne Brennan.—**City Manager,** William G. Tallman; Asst., vacancy.—**City Council: Aldermen,** Harry A. Jackson, Pres., Donald Alfiero, Kevin J. Crowley, Mark P. Eaton, Linda D. Kellogg, Edward Martin, John P. Mereen, Raymond L. Ouellet, Mary Ryan-Larkin, Roland R. Trailor, Sr., vacancy.—**Treas.,** William J. Murray.—**Comptroller,** Angelo Sanquedolce.—**Tax Collector,** Theresa Giovanni.—**Bd. of Assessment Appeals,** Charles Gilbert III, Antonio Longo, Philip Shannon.—**Assessor,** Charles Glinski; Asst., Carol Wood.—**Registrars of Voters,** Jane L. Przekop (D), John H. White (R).—**Supt. of Schools,** William Juzwic.—**Bd. of Education,** Anna S. Alfiero, Chm., Mark L. Chenette, Paul F. Chinigo, Ann M. Lafayette, John P. Levangie, Paul D. Maugle, Harry Swatsburg, Bruno Tedeschi, Deborah A. Tennant-Zinewicz, 1997.—**Personnel and Pension Bd.,** Raymond Benoit, Chm., Robert Booth, Daniel LePage, Robert Staley, Elizabeth Yeznach; Richard A. Podurgiel, Personnel Dir.; Alternates, Patricia Adams, Paul Fedeli, John McCann.—**Comm. on the City Plan,** Ralph Page, Chm., Raymond J. Botti, Robert Fargo, Carol A. Napier, Walter Way; Alternates, Mary Driscoll, Pearl Schaen, Margaret Wilson.—**City Planner,** Kathy Warzecha.—**Zoning Bd. of Appeals,** Elizabeth Dougherty, Joseph J. Jacaruso, Eleanor C. Marshall, Arthur Sharron, Dorothy Travers; Alternates, Marc Benjamin, Richard Hamar, Henry Olender, Jr.—**Redevelopment Agency,** Ronald Aliano, Mark Eaton, Anthony Jacobs, Thomas Marien, Dennis Riley, Lottie Scott, Charles Seeman, Thomas Sullivan, Irving Weber.—**Housing Auth.,** Hector Baillargeon, Patricia Bazinet, Alfred Gonsalves, Charlene Jackson, Allison Riley.—**Housing Inspector,** William Sabrowski.—**Inland Wetlands, Watercourses, and Conservation Comm.,** Walter Way, Chm., Paul Burgess, Paul Mathieu, Carl Morello, Barbara Rothstein, Albert Schlager, Gurdon Slosberg; Alternates, Raymond Baribeault, Sherman Chase, Ralph Page.—**Public Utilities Dept. Mgr.,** Richard DesRoches.—**Public Parking Comm.,** Donald Alfiero, Olive Buddington, John Casey, Kevin Crowley, Mark Eaton, Sean Ryan, William G. Tallman.—**Historic Dist. Comm.,** Richard Sharpe, Chm., Cathy Chinigo, Nancy O'Neil, Dale Plummer, Norma Schnip; Alternates, Barbara Bergman, Judith H. Hamblen, Russell Versteeg.—**Municipal Historian,** Dale Plummer.—**Senior Affairs Comm.,** Genevieve Bergendahl, Margaret Aldrich, P. Michael Lahan, Joel J. Ragovin, Jacquelyn Randall.—**Social Services Dir.,** Beverly Goulet.—**Dir. of Health,** Arthur Cohen.—**Recreation Advisory Bd.,** J. Roger Marien, Chm., John Iovino, Carl Morello, Robert Spayne, Angelo Yeitz.—**Supt. of Parks,** vacancy.—**Dir. of Public Works,** Walter Wadja.—**Dir. of Recreation,** Luis DePina.—**Dir. of Youth Services,** Peter Schultheis.—**Supt. of Highways and Streets,** William Daley.—**Purchasing Agent,** William Block.—**City Engineer,** Stephen Garstka.—**Zoning Enforcement Officer,** Ann Brown.—**Building Inspector,** James Troeger.—**Building Code Bd. of Appeals,** Irving Weber, Chm., F. W. Brown, Jr., Joseph E. Caprilozzi, Thomas Fitzpatrick, Robert McKeon.—**Bd. of Public Utilities,** Stanley Israelite, Chm., Frederick C. Barrett, Donald O'Connell, Alan Remondi, Leonard Royce.—**Sanitarian,** Michael Kirby.—**Chief of Police,** Richard J. Abele; Deputy, Louis Fusaro.—**Chief of Fire Dept./Fire Marshal,** James Walsh; Deputy Chief, Ralph Noyes.—**Deputy Fire Marshals,** Raymond Boenig III, Alfred Jonasch, Michael Kirby, Ralph Noyes.—**Civil Preparedness Dir.,** Rita Frechette.—**Corporation Counsel,** Konstant W. Morell.—**Justices of the Peace,** Donald Alfiero, George F. Andrews, Sr., Donna Arico-Bania, Roderick J. Arpin, Calvin F. Baker, Kent S. Baker, Ellen E. Balchunas, Linda D. Becker, Richard C. Benoit, Neil H. Blinderman, Robert L. Booth, Edna M. Brennan, Olive J. Buddington, Steven Caisse, Louis A. Carignan, Sadie Chapman, Harold Cohen, Ernest A. Colburn, Jr., John A. Cotter, James F. Daigle, Jr., Nancy M. Doubleday, Anne T. Doyle, William M. Dugan, James W. Dunion, Thomas J. Dunion, Mark P. Eaton, Stuart Einhorn, Iris D. Fernandez, Beryl I. Fishbone, Carl R. Fleming, Jr., Paul J. Fleming, Elizabeth A. Gentile, Arthur Goldblatt, Ruth C. Goldblatt, Deborah D. Gonet, Linda S. Greenfield, Stuart B. Greenfield, Charles E. Harrington, Pamela V. Hogan, Harry A. Jackson, Linda L. Jackson, Anthony J. Jacobs, Milton L. Jacobson, Diogenes P. John, John P. John, Peter D. John, Louida O. Jones, Mary-Elizabeth Kenyon, George W. Lambert, Jr., Paul J. Lambert, Joy S. Leary, Thomas L. LeClair, John Levanto, Antonio J. Longo III, E. Catherine Marshall, Adelaide D. Masterson, Paul D. Maugle, Joyce F. Maynard, Helen McClafferty, Monica E. McGuire, Janice M. McIntyre, John P. Mereen, Pearl Miller-Schaen, Maria Miranda, Theodore S. Montgomery, Konstant W. Morell, Thomas Morosky, Ralph F. Page, Phyllis S. Porter, Jane L. Przekop, Steven E. Pudlo, Alan Remondi, Gail-Marie Rogers, Josephine M. L. Rogers, Martin M. Rutchik, Sean J. Ryan, Lottie B. Scott, Edward J. Seder, Philip J. Shannon, Arthur J. Sharron, Dorothy A. Sinay, Barbara A. Sipperly, Santa H. Sposato, Thomas F. Sweeney, Stanley P. Taraskiewicz, Dorothy S. Tedeschi, Irving Weber, John H. White, Charles A. Witt, Charles A. Witt, Jr., John H. Wonnacott, Vivian J. Wonnacott, Angelo P. Yeitz, Jr.

OLD LYME.
New London County.—(Form of government, selectmen, town meeting, board of finance.)—Set off from Saybrook, February 13, 1665; Inc., May, 1855, as South Lyme; taken from Lyme; name changed in 1857. Area, 28.8 sq. miles. Population, est., 6,623. Voting district, 1. Residential community and summer resort. Freight: Served by Providence & Worcester Co. and numerous motor common carriers. Post offices, Old Lyme and South Lyme.

TOWN OFFICERS. Clerk and Reg. of Vital Statistics, Irene A. Carnell; Hours, 9 A.M.-12 Noon, 1-4 P.M., Mon. through Fri., 9 A.M.-12 Noon, 1 P.M.-4 P.M.; Address, 52 Lyme St., P.O. Box 338, 06371; Tel., (860) 434-1655.—**Asst. Clerks and Asst. Regs. of Vital Statistics,** Jessie F. Smith, Marian R. Wenck.—**Selectmen,** 1st, Edmund J. O'Brien (D) Tel., (860) 434-1605, James R. Rice (R), Mervin F. Roberts (R).—**Treas.,** Beatrice F. McLean.—**Bd. of Finance,** Timothy C. Griswold, Chm., Frederick E. Acker, Stephen D. Ewers, Michael J. Gaffey, Claire S. Helmboldt, Edward G. Perkins; Alternates, Mark C. Diebolt, Gail F. Roth, David Woolley.—**Tax Collector,** Judith T. Kerr.—**Bd. of Assessment Appeals,** James B. Blair, Jane E. Cable, William F. Groves.—**Assessor,** Walter E. Kent, Jr.—**Registrars of Voters,** Patricia M. McCarthy (D), Roderick M. White (R).—**Supt. of Schools,** Jefferson Prestridge.—**Pension Committee,** Oliver Patrell, Chm., Frederick Acker, Brian Cole, Kathleen Hall, Benjamin Terry.—**Planning Comm.,** Robert Pierson, Chm., Alan Bayreuther, Linda Cotton, Jeffrey W. Flower, Constance Kastelowitz; Alternates, Ralph Griffin, Nancy Strohla, Harold Thompson.—**Zoning Comm.,** Eric V. Fries, Chm., Joan Bozek, George James, Jr., Jane R. Marsh, Thomas Risom; Alternates, Sharon Colvin, Richard Johnston, Clifford Winkel.—**Zoning Bd. of Appeals,** June B. Speirs, Chm., George P. Calkins, Richard A. Moll, Arthur Sibley, vacancy; Alternates, Barbara M. Doyen, Caswell L. Haskell, Jr., Susanne M. Stutts.—**Economic Development Comm.,** three vacancies.—**Conservation Comm.,** David McCulloch, Chm., Thomas J. Degnan, Roger Desnoyers, Lewis G. DiCamillo, Carl A. Kotzan, Mark Lubbers, Kinsley Twining; Alternates, Geraldine Golet, Arnold Sjursen.—**Water Pollution Control Authority,** Thomas Risom, Chm., Corrine Bunce, Jeffrey Flower, Louisa Grogan, George James, Mark Lubbers, Richard Moll, Gary Yuknat; Alternates, Michael Dickey, Joseph O'Connor.—**Flood and Erosion Control Bd.,** H. Perry Garvin III, Chm., Gary D. Smith, Ronald J. Wojcik.—**Shellfish Comm.,** Mervin Roberts, Chm., Kurt Besier, John Seckla.—**Harbor Management Comm.,** John Speirs III, Chm., Glen Abrahamsson, Robert Doyen, Robert Getman, Anthony Licitra, Roderick White; Richard Sagan, Harbor Master; Alternates, John Jolie, Harry Kerop, James Nichols.—**Historic Dist. Comm.,** Jephson O'Connell, Stanley C. Schuler, Co-Chm., Lynn Fairfield-Sonn, Mary L. Lohmann, Barbara S. Traskos; Alternates, David Jones, Kenneth Levin, Nina C. Peck.—**Comm. on Aging,** Francis V. Balboni, Chm., Ruth S. Breitzke, Diane Getman, Robert Halpin, Audrey Hopper, Mary Anne Lombardy, Dorothy Weaver.—**Visiting Nurse,** Linda Camarra.—**Municipal Agent for the Elderly,** Donald Tapper.—**Parks and Recreation Comm.,** Joseph Fulton, Jr., Chm., Mary Ellen Garbarino, Glynnis McAraw, Daria Phelp, Jane Smith-Dell; Timothy Gavin, Dir.—**Building Inspector,** Joseph M. Hart.—**Rogers Lake Auth.,** Norman Carlson, Donald Friday, Mark Lander.—**Tree Warden,** Thomas Degnan.—**Chief of Fire Dept.,** James Jewett.—**Emergency Management Dir.,** David Hoblin.—**Town Atty.,** Marylin C.

Clarke.—**Justices of the Peace,** Patricia A. W. Bennett, Jeanne L. Bliss, Philip J. Bliss, Edith T. Buck, Jane E. Cable, Nancy L. Campbell, Irene A. Carnell, Thomas E. Clements, Jr., Patrick J. Fitzgerald, Verdina Ghirardi, Roger S. Hinze, Lyman B. Hoops, Doris C. Johnson, Robert D. Johnson, Judith T. Kerr, George C. King, Jr., Joseph A. Lacasse, Mark C. Lander, Jerilynn M. Marshall, Barbara Masters, Barbara McBride-Doyen, Patricia M. McCarthy, Agnes Q. O'Connor, Jacqueline M. Opeka, Oliver L. Patrell, Gloria J. Pendleton, Lawrence I. Peterson, Jr., Daria M. Phelps, Mervin F. Roberts, Jennie A. Rubera, Walter O. Seifert, June B. Speirs, Michellee Speirs, Joel S. Suisman, Benjamin C. Thomson, George H. Waugh, Eliisa L. Winkel, Walter O. Zabel.

OLD SAYBROOK.

Middlesex County.—(Form of government, selectmen, town meeting, board of finance.)—Inc., July 8, 1854. Area, 21.6 sq. miles. Population, est., 9,427. Voting districts, 2. Principal industries, electronics, boat building, photographic supplies, printing, tools and dies, and food processing. Transp.—Passenger: Served by Amtrak, and by Greyhound. Freight: Served by Providence & Worcester Co. and numerous motor common carriers. Post office, Old Saybrook.

TOWN OFFICERS. Clerk and Reg. of Vital Statistics, Sarah V. Becker; Hours, 8:30 A.M.-4:30 P.M., Mon. through Fri.; Address, 302 Main St., 06475; Tel., (860) 395-3135.—**Asst. Clerks and Asst. Regs. of Vital Statistics,** Helen G. Fillmore, Sandra Swanson.—**Selectmen,** 1st, Laurence F. Reney (D) Tel., (860) 395-3123, J. Robert Finch (R), William A. Peace (D).—**Treas.,** Gloria C. Fogg.—**Bd. of Finance,** Edward B. Gomeau, Chm., John P. Albertson, Catherine R. Ciardiello, Timothy S. Doyle, Richard B. Dyson, Robert McMahon, Susan G. Townsley.—**Tax Collector,** Olive P. Mulvihill; Asst., Sandra Blasius.—**Bd. of Assessment Appeals,** Ruth M. Fitzgerald, Chm., David W. Chase, Stephen R. Sheehan.—**Assessor,** Lucille B. Kelley.—**Registrars of Voters,** Mildred E. Ploszay (D), Jean B. Winkler (R).—**Supt. of Schools,** Salvatore V. Pascarella, Ed.D.—**Bd. of Education,** Eileen Baker, Karen Brodeur, David G. Brown, Sandra J. Harder, vacancy, 1997; Janet V. Murray, Chm., Albert J. Anderson, Valerie S. Conroy, Milissa A. Rock, 1999.—**Ethics Comm.,** Charles Wiltsie, Jr., Chm., Estelle M. Hepburn, Richard N. Rogers, Harry K. Sedgwick, David A. Tiezzi.—**Planning Comm.,** Judith S. Gallicchio, Robert K. Hallisey, David A. Hoey, Karen J. Marcolini, Velma Thomas; Alternates, Joseph P. Flanagan, Ernest L. Gardner, Jr., Frank R. Jones.—**Zoning Comm.,** Robert Dion, Robert C. Friedmann, Nicholas J. Gorra, Scott K. McBain, Edward F. McSweegan; Alternates, Madeleine B. Fish, Leonard Liggio, Mario Sapia, Jr.—**Zoning Bd. of Appeals,** Allan Fogg, Chm., Eugene M. Chesanek, Christopher Gosselin, Joseph P. Reising, Muriel P. Shemonsky; Alternates, Jean T. Castagno, Patricia L. Ingellis, Rexford H. McCall.—**Zoning Enforcement Officer,** Chester L. Sklodosky.—**Economic Development Comm.,** Robert P. Ganswindt, Chm., David Cole, Valerie Conroy, Ernest L. Gardner, Jr., Paul G. Heroux, George Offerjost, Marilyn C. Reney; Wilma Asch, Exec. Dir.—**Conservation Comm.,** Richard Tietien, Chm., Nathaniel Avery, Jr., Robert B. Boody, Helen Casey, Joan C. Fenger, Gratia F. Lewis, Judith Preston.—**Inland Wetlands Comm.,** Robert P. Ganswindt, Nicholas Gorra, Jr., Judith Preston; At-Large Members, Steven Mazeau,

Charles Monte, Ronald Simms; Alternates, Thomas Burke, Edward Cole, William Steinbuch.—**Agent for the Elderly,** Joan H. Carlson.—**Dir. of Health,** Joseph Fuller, M.D.—**Public Health Nursing Bd.,** Michael R. Galler, Chm., Annemarie Q. Alexa, Gail Antoniac, Andrew Balosie, Jean Hurley, Donna Konarski, Phyllis Wakeham.—**Library Directors,** Michael Galler, Chm., Joan Albertson, Richard B. Dyson, Blanche Gallicchio, Ernest L. Gardner, Jr., Mary Hansen, Suzanne Ladd, Richenda McBain, vacancy.—**Municipal Historian,** Elaine Staplins.—**Parks and Recreation Comm.,** Raymond Dobratz, Chm., James Earles, C. Marston Ladd, Adam P. Laverty, Joyce K. McOmber, Michael Spera, Kevin Wakeham; Vicki Duffy, Dir.—**Supt. of Public Works,** Ronald Baldi.—**Building Inspector/Sanitarian,** Donald Lucas.—**Building Bd. of Appeals,** Robert Harper, Chm., Rudolph Beiser, Edmund Binder, Frederick Radcliffe, C. Talcott Scovill.—**Shell Fish Comm.,** Lawrence P. Bonin, Chm., Jerry E. Cerruti, Howard E. Clark, Jr., Earl Endrich, Sr., Donald G. Gayton.—**Chief of Police,** Edmund Mosca; Deputy, Thomas O'Brien.—**Police Comm.,** Douglas H. Olson, Chm., Paul E. Lutz, Barry S. O'Nell, Ernest Sparaco, Jean B. Winkler.—**Chief of Fire Dept.,** Coleman Bushnell; Deputy, Edward Adanti.—**Fire Marshal,** Coleman Bushnell.—**Emergency Management Dir.,** Ronald Baldi.—**Town Atty.,** Jeremiah F. Donovan.—**Justices of the Peace,** Ivy M. Butler, Joyce L. Cappiello, Susan M. Chase, Dana R. Cosgrove, Susan M. DeBlasiis, Earl Endrich, Allan Fogg, Blanche M. Gallicchio, Ernest L. Gardner, Jr., Frank R. Jones, James J. Leipold, Paul A. Loomis, Barbara J. Maynard, Barry S. O'Nell, Betsy B. Ranelli, Edward J. Root, Marion Sigal, Theodore T. Tansi, William A. Timinskas, John J. Torrenti, Jennifer K. Trantino, Shirley G. VonDassel, Jeremy M. Wilson, Jean B. Winkler.

ORANGE. New Haven County.—(Form of government, selectmen, town meeting, board of finance.)—Inc., May, 1822, taken from Milford and New Haven. Area, 17.4 sq. miles. Population, est., 12,504. Voting districts, 2. Principal industries, printing, woodworking, home building and manufacture of overhead doors, burial vaults, truck bodies, industrial garments, precision equipment, industrial sheet metal, cedar furniture, grafting wax, steel sash, machine screws and communications equipment, candy making, distribution center for automobiles and automotive parts. Transp.—Passenger: Served by buses of Conn. Transit. Freight: Served by Conrail and numerous motor common carriers. Post office, Orange.

TOWN OFFICERS. Clerk and Reg. of Vital Statistics, Jean V. Mitchell; Hours, 8:30 A.M.-4:30 P.M., Mon. through Fri.; Address, Town Hall, 617 Orange Center Rd., 06477; Tel., New Haven, (203) 891-2122.—**Asst. Clerks and Asst. Regs. of Vital Statistics,** Dolores S. Caruso, Ann Trotta.—**Selectmen,** 1st, Robert C. Sousa (D) Tel., (203) 891-2122, Joseph Blake (D), Albert M. Clark III (R), Mitchell R. Goldblatt (D), Laura J. Reid (R), William T. Musco (R).—**Treas.,** Arthur B. Williams III.—**Bd. of Finance,** J. Philip Smith, Chm., Thomas R. Anastasio, Patrick B. O'Sullivan II, Timothy J. Riordan, Richard Slawsky, Brendan E. Williams.—**Bd. of Ethics,** Motier Becque, Deborah Hoffman, Sherman Kramer, William Sherman, Edward Villani.—**Tax Collector,** Julia T. Strawhince; Asst., Deborah L. Estok.—**Bd. of Assessment Appeals,** Anthony DelVisco, Chm., Pamela Galatioto, Jeffrey Sachs; Alternate, Brian Kaligian.—**Assessor,** Mark Branchesi.—**Registrars of Voters,** Carmela N. Apuzzo

(D), Susan S. Blanchette (R).—**Supt. of Schools,** John P. Kowal.—**Bd. of Education,** Sharon Ewen, John Foley, Glenn Pearson, Robert S. Rauch, Christy Anne Somersville, 1997; Richard C. Meisenheimer, Chm., Sue L. Cohen, H. John Hoffman, R. Eugene Torrenti, Carolyn L. Roth, 1999.—**Planning and Zoning Comm.,** Michael J. Paolini, Chm., Roy Cuzzocreo, Mary McMahon, Philip Nizzardo, Jr, Judy Smith-Morgan.— **Zoning Bd. of Appeals,** David Pokras, Chm., Andrew Blanchette, Rudolph Miller, Glenn Pearson, Sue Riordan; Alternates, Charles Barretta, Dave Pite, Suman T. Sabnis.—**Zoning Enforcement Officer,** Paul Dinice.—**Economic Development Comm.,** Gregory J. Mulherin, Chm., Roger W. Boyd, Wilda Hammerman, Frank W. Rogers, Rudy Zimmerman.—**Conservation Comm.,** John G. Dorais, Chm., Robert Archambault, Gerald Butcher, Michael O. Bymachow, Gail Nixon, Paul Ode, Cheryl Serfilippi.—**Inland Wetlands Comm.,** Gerard Butcher, Roy Cuzzocreo, Chm., Walter Bespuda, Aileen DeFeo, Rick Mangione, Frederick O'Brien, Herbert Saunders, Judd W. Smith, William Sperry, Jr.—**Historic Dist. Comm.,** Elizabeth Gesler, Chm., Charles Pelizza, Barbara Scaramozza, Mrs. Lee Schlesinger, Susan T. Wilson; Alternates, Jack Barton, James Ewen, Julia Williams.—**Committee on Aging,** Richard J. Bowllan, Sally Lawson, Alfred Perrone, Philip Pilla, Ann Raccio, two vacancies.—**Human Services Comm.,** Richard Sykes, Chm., Roberta Carlson, Olga Civie, Phoebe Coleman, Eleanor Joyal, Sally Lawson, Rayner Powell, L. Natalie Sandomirsky, Victoria Schneider, Margaret Vernazza, James M. White; Carol D. Nardini, Dir.—**Dir. of Health,** Joseph Zelson, M.D.; Asst., Robert Baltimore, M.D.—**Bd. of Public Health,** Jack Ambrose, Chm., Paul Barash, M.D., Charlotann Dello Russo, Severio Fodero, Kurt Koral, D.D.S., Lynn Gagliola, Rhoda Gorenberg, Marlene Silverstein; Earl Slusky, M.D.; vacancy, Dir., Robert Baltimore, M.D., Asst. Dir.—**Library Directors,** Loretta K. Smith, Chm., Bridget Albert, Hillel Auerbach, Shirley Barton, Wayne Garrick, Leola Gray, Ellen Green, Ursula Hindel, Stephanie Jatlow, Judy Randi, Patricia Rogers, Irene Teller, Virginia Volo; Marilyn Beattie, Librarian.—**Parks and Recreation Comm.,** Ralph Okenquist, Chm., Kim Altschuler, Michael Apuzzo, David Baretta, Alfred Bucknall, John Cifarelli, Janet Lutz, Lee Warncke; Albert T. Baines, Dir.— **Youth Services Coordinator,** Carol Flynn.—**Town Engineer/Dir. of Public Works,** Edwin Lieberman.—**Building Inspector,** Fred A. Trotta.—**Sewer and Building Supt.,** John VanArman; Asst., R. Scott Allen.—**Tree Warden,** Edgar Vaughn, Jr.—**Building Bd. of Appeals,** Giouse Grillo, Elmer Manley, Anthony Marchitto, Kenneth Robinson, Americo Spaziani.—**Water Pollution Control Auth.,** Kevin Gilbert, Chm., Harvey Bletchman, Pacific Giordano, Robert Kleffman, James D. White.—**Sanitarian,** Frederick Schumacher.—**Chief of Police,** Edward Delaney.—**Police Comm.,** Donald Lewis, Chm., Joseph Cuzzocreo, Ernest Leoni, Patricia Pearson, Robert Shanley.— **Constables,** Salvatore A. Apuzzo, Joseph M. Brazier, Edward S. Golembieski, Mark T. Marren, Patricia A. Murdock, Elfo Pol, Lorraine M. Pritchard.—**Chief of Fire Dept.,** Fred Knight.—**Fire Marshal,** Timothy P. Smith.—**Civil Preparedness Dir.,** Donald F. Clark.—**Town Atty.,** John H. Welch, Jr.—**Justices of the Peace,** Carmela N. Apuzzo, Robert E. Bateman, John J. Donohue, William R. Fuhlbruck, Marion A. Hoffman, Arthur F. Jamison, Eleanor B. Joyal, Sherman Kramer, Hymen B. Lender, Marion G. Reid, Fred A. Trotta, Rose Ann Vinglione, Jack L. Weinberg.

OXFORD. New Haven County.—(Form of government, selectmen, town meeting, board of finance.)—Inc., Oct., 1798; taken from Derby and Southbury. Area, 33.4 sq. miles. Population, est., 9,253. Voting district, 1. Principal industry, agriculture and light manufacturing. Transp.— Freight: Served by numerous motor common carriers. Post office, Oxford.

TOWN OFFICERS. Clerk and Reg. of Vital Statistics, Constance E. Koskelowski; Hours, 9 A.M.-5 P.M., Mon. through Thurs.; 7-9 P.M., Mon., Thurs.; Address, 486 Oxford Rd., 06478; Tel., Seymour, (203) 888-2543.—**Asst. Clerks and Asst. Regs. of Vital Statistics,** Margaret A. Spear, Carol A. Zuella.—**Selectmen,** 1st, Kate Cosgrove (D) Tel., (203) 888-2543, Charlie H. Lyons (D), Paul T. Schreiber (R).— **Treas.,** Peter J. Aiksnoras, Jr.—**Bd. of Ethics,** Edward Hardy, Chm., Linda Crowe, Kimberly Drayton, John Joy, William A. Leider, Alphonse Niestemski.—**Bd. of Finance,** Janis F. Williams, Chm., Michael C. Caprio, Robert A. DeBisschop, John J. Fiore, Thomas J. Kelly, Sue Ellen Martino.—**Tax Collector,** Karen M. Guillet.—**Bd. of Assessment Appeals,** Wm. Darrald Atwood, Chm., Lillian B, Frolish, Michael H. Lyon.— **Assessor,** Jeanne F. Shuster.—**Registrars of Voters,** Dorothy M. Bartimole (D), Beulah F. Renker (R).—**Supt. of Schools,** Michael W. Abdalla.—**Bd. of Education,** David M. Babina, Gerald M. Gallant, Linda McIntyre, Chm., David McKane, Kathleen Nelson, 1997; Edward J. Connell, Sheila Kenny, Harold C. Nelson, Barbara Robinson, 1999.—**Planning and Zoning Comm.,** David A Robinson, Sr., Chm., Joseph E. Dempsey, Raymond L. Drapko, Nil J. Guillet, Steven Noga, John G. Tuz, John G. Van Kamerik, Jr.; Alternates, Vincent Vizzo, vacancy.—**Town Planner,** vacancy.—**Zoning Bd. of Appeals,** Calvin E. Fordham, Chm., Paul Aiksnoras, Mark A. Brothers, Scott Mackler, Michael Martino; Alternates, John Barnes, Robert Schlenk.— **Economic Development Comm.,** Delores Morrell, Chm., Frank Coniglio, James Cotter, Marie Hooke, David Marcoux, Charles E. Wright.—**Housing Auth.,** Suzanne Bosek, Chm., Arlene Brooks, Edwina D'Aiuto, Richard Sonnenstuhl, Julia Steinis.— **Conservation and Inland Wetlands Comm.,** David T. Schreiber, Chm., George R. Oleyer, Ken Prowse, Miriam S. Strong.—**Elderly Comm.,** Dorothy Potter, Chm., Nancy Cersonsky, Nellie B. Mosavich, Jane O'Toole, Clark C. Pope; Judith G. Thomas, Agent.—**Dir. of Social Services,** Donna Jurkowski.—**Dir. of Health,** Neal A. Lustig.—**Library Directors,** Susan Decker, James Hanneken, Vincent Martines, Ursala Martino, Suzanne Saggese, vacancy.—**Municipal Historian,** Dorothy A. DeBisschop.—**Park and Recreation Comm.,** Theodore Oczkowski, Chm., Karin O. Burke, Robert Fitzgerald, Colleen Lundgren, Paul McGinnis, Harold Olsen, Enio Pucci, Lorraine Tirella.—**Public Works Dir.,** James T. Dytka.—**Tree Warden,** Glenn Barrett.—**Town Engineer,** Donald W. Smith, Jr.—**Building Official,** Albert DuBois.—**Building Code Bd. of Appeals,** Steven J. Fetyko, Andrew Gazsi, Geraldine M. Hawks, John E. Svehlak, Leonard J. Tomasheski.—**Water Pollution Control Auth.,** William D. Griffin, Chm., John Barnes, Jeffrey Holmes, David A. Robinson, Sr., Albert J. Turcott.—**Lake Authorities,** Zoar: Terry Bogue, Bernard Lintzner, Eugenia Purcella; Housatonic: Steven G. Shingara, Gary D. Spear, vacancy.—**Sanitarians,** Nancy Kontout, Joe Kmetz, Mona LaBissionaire.—**Chief of Police,** Kate Cosgrove.—**Constables,** Arthur M. Antinozzi, Sr., James E. Burr, Jesse R. Burrows, Jr., David M. Conroy, David Ives, Glen M. Thomas, Patrick J. Tisi.—**Chief of Fire Dept./**

510 TOWNS, CITIES AND BOROUGHS

Civil Preparedness Dir., Scott Pelletier.—**Fire Marshal,** Fredrick J. Pommer.—**Town Atty.,** Dominick J. Thomas.—**Justices of the Peace,** James E. Cohen, Harold J. Cosgrove, Kate C. Cosgrove, Linda J. Crowe, Robert A. DeBisschop, John P. DeGennaro, Lila Ferrillo, Lillian B. Frolish, Jeffrey T. Holmes, Joanne P. Jelenik, Thomas J. Kelly, Colleen M. Lieder, Linda P. McIntyre, Linda J. McKane, Alphonse Niestemski, David T. Schreiber, Paul T. Schreiber, George J. Shuster.

PLAINFIELD.
Windham County.—(Form of government, selectmen, town meeting, board of finance.)—Inc., as Quinabaug, May, 1699; named Plainfield, Oct., 1700. Area, 43.0 sq. miles. Population, est., 14,484. Voting districts, 4. Principal industries, cement blocks, chemical products, assembly parts for manufacture of helicopters, automotive rubber strips, rubber laboratory stoppers, plastics and styrene, machine tools and accessories, concrete pipe, rubber molded parts, tools and dies, screen printed materials and electronic components. Transp.—Passenger: Served by buses of Northeast Transit District. Freight: Served by Conrail, Providence & Worcester Railroad Co. and numerous motor common carriers. Post offices, Plainfield, Central Village, Moosup and Wauregan.

TOWN OFFICERS. Clerk and Reg. of Vital Statistics, Helen F. Coombs; Hours, 8:30 A.M.-4:30 P.M., Mon., Tues., Wed., Fri., 8:30 A.M.-6:30 P.M, Thurs.; Address, Town Hall, 8 Community Ave., 06374; Tel., (860) 564-4075.—**Asst. Clerk and Asst. Reg. of Vital Statistics,** Anne Radei.—**Selectmen,** 1st, Paul E. Sweet (D) Tel., (860) 564-4071, Ext. 11), Albert E. Brunsdon (D), Thomas E. Burek (R).—**Financial Officer,** Joseph Gillis.—**Bd. of Finance,** Robert H. Vickers, Chm., Mary E. Attridge-Silvestri, Henry Drobiarz, Lee M. Farland, Susie Thayer, John V. Wakely.—**Tax Collector,** Henry J. Daley.—**Bd. of Assessment Appeals,** Leon J. Couture, Donald M. Gervais, Michael A. Saad.—**Assessor,** Joyce Stangland.—**Registrars of Voters,** Margaret Beausoleil (D), Dawn Burek (R).—**Supt. of Schools,** David Marchesseault.—**Bd. of Education,** Gary P. Beauluc, Helen F. Coombs, Elizabeth B. Kemp, Pasquale Leo, 1997; Robert E. Cloutier, Chm., Monique Allard, Raymond Bogert, 1999; Gary A. Bessette, Virginia Sampietro, 2001.—**Planning and Zoning Comm.,** Dennis P. Jolley, Chm., Joseph R. Breault, Stuart E. Denton, Richard Jacques, Gloria Rizer; Alternates, Gerald C. Carlen, Julie H. Faunce, vacancy.—**Zoning Bd. of Appeals,** Eugene Beausoliel, Ronald L. Fletcher, James Gallow, Carol St. Ament, Frank A. Zak, Jr.; Alternates, Hollis Hooper, Jr., Thomas W. Rizer, Douglas Smith.—**Housing Auth.,** Richard Carroll, Anthony Guglielmi, Lucille Miller, Debra E. Pepin; Lillian Grocki, Exec. Dir.—**Inland Wetlands Comm.,** Mark Andstrom, Chm., Erland Bragg, Ron Desjardins, Francis Gagnon, Jr., Walter McKain, Robert Shaver.—**Municipal Historian,** Carl Plassmann.—**Agent for the Elderly,** David H. Meade.—**Welfare Dir.,** Shirley Martel.—**Recreation Dir.,** Myra Ambrogi.—**Building Inspector,** Robert Kerr.—**Building Code Bd. of Appeals,** Eric Grondahl, Chm., Joseph Bellevance, Alfred Collelo, John C. Stone, Dudley Young.—**Town Engineer,** Reepu D. Singh, P.E.—**Tree Warden,** vacancy.—**Sewer Auth.,** Paul E. Sweet, Chm., Albert E. Brunsdon, Thomas Burek, Michael A. Saad.—**Police Comm.,** Hollis O. Hooper, Chm., Jacqueline Dubois, Mary L. Ravenelle, Edward M. Sylvestre, Harvey Willard.—**Chiefs of Fire Dept.,** Ken Holcomb (Plainfield), Lawrence Despathy (Moosup), Wesley Franz (Central Village), Charles Colli (Wauregan).—**Fire Marshal,** Paul J. Yellen, Deputy, Joseph Bergeron.—**Civil Preparedness Dir.,** Paul J. Yellen.—**Town Atty.,** James Murphy, Jr.—**Justices of the Peace,** Margaret A. Anderson, Leo Andstrom, Eugene C. Beausoleil, Gerard Beausoleil, Leo M. Bernard, Albert E. Brunsdon, Tom Burek, Thomas J. Carlen, Jr., Patricia Carroll, Rosamond Chviek, Robert E. Cloutier, William F. Collelo, Leon Couture, Henry J. Daley, Henry Drobiarz, Jacqueline Dubois, Robert E. Duffney, Shirley Farrell, Stella Faunce, Arlene Fournier, James Gallow, Donald Gervais, Lorraine Gosselin, Rita Holmes, Hollis Hooper, Nadine I. Hoyt, Richard Jacques, Elizabeth Kemp, Ronald E. Knight, Donald J. Lefevre, Paulette Lefevre, Clement Matteau, Diane L. Matteau, William L. Nagel, William E. Nicholson, Allen R. Pierce, Henry J. Plante, Orise J. Poirier, Robert Raymond, John Saad, Carol A. St Ament, James N. Scheibler, James A. Schroth, Herman Sheppard, William G. Smith, Paul E. Sweet, Joseph D. Taverna.

PLAINVILLE. Hartford County.—(Form of government, town manager, town council.)—Inc., July, 1869; taken from Farmington. Area, 9.8 sq. miles. Population, est., 17,213. Voting districts, 5. Principal industries, manufacture of electrical sundries, grinding machines and springs. Transp.—Passenger: Served by buses of New Britain Transp. Co. from Bristol, Bonanza Bus Lines, Inc. from Hartford and Waterbury, and Corbin Coach Lines, Inc. Freight: Served by Boston and Maine and numerous motor common carriers. Post office, Plainville.

TOWN OFFICERS. Clerk and Reg. of Vital Statistics, Peter T. Lennon; Hours, 8:30 A.M.-4:30 P.M., Mon. through Fri.; Address, Municipal Center, 1 Central Sq., 06062; Tel., (860) 793-0221.—**Asst. Clerks and Asst. Regs. of Vital Statistics,** Christine Aldi, Patricia Perry.—**Town Manager,** John Bohenko; Asst., Shirley Osle.—**Town Council,** Helen Bergenty, Chm., Robert P. Cornish, Kevin M. Neary, William A. Petit, Katherine M. Pugliese, James R. Stuart, Robert J. Warnat.—**Treas.,** Daniel P. Ciesielski.—**Dir. of Finance,** Judy L. Doneiko.—**Tax Collector,** Patricia McGarry.—**Bd. of Assessment Appeals,** Anthony Famiglietti, Claire Stuart, Foster White.—**Assessor,** Jane Dickman.—**Registrars of Voters,** Jean Lombardo (D), Mildred D'Antonio (R).—**Supt. of Schools,** James J. Ritchie.—**Bd. of Education,** Richard Clark, Chm., Marliss Kowalczyk, Walter J. Majsak, Ivan Wood, 1997; Carrie L. Burns, John Gasparini, Marilyn Warnat, Thomas Wazorko, Charles O. Zettergen III, 1999.—**Planning and Zoning Comm.,** Fabien Castonguay, Timothy Davenport, William Davison, Conrad Ouellette, Glenn Petit, George Reinwald, Salvatore Santacroce; Alternates, Rene Gauthier, Wayne Gleifert, Frank Pugliese—**Zoning Bd. of Appeals,** Andrew Basile, Peter Dumais, Eustace Mike, Fred Santacrose, Joseph Warner; Alternates, Stephen Cole, Gail Pugliese, Donna Vinelli.—**Economic Development Agency,** Robert Stange, Chm., Joan Deegan, Kenneth Hedman, Kristian Jensen, Jr., Donald St. Pierre.—**Community Development Coordinator,** Richard Corliss.—**Housing Auth.,** Donald G. Wiener, Chm., Robert Berube, Joan St. Pierre, Theresa Smiarowski, William Trepanier.—**Conservation Comm.,** William Dunn, Chm., Robert Anderson, Robin Atwater, Tina Dietzko, Kathleen Kovach, John Marinelli, James E. McQuarrie, Brian Needham, Jason Powell, Michael Sobel, James R. Testa.—**Inland Wetlands Comm.,** Mark DiLoreto, Chm., Shirley Allocca, Robert Curtis, Michael Goulat, Michael Korby, Charles Motes, Richard Negro.—**Senior Citizens Committee,** Helen Marinelli, Chm., Willard Baumgartner, AnnMarie Berarducci, Ann Krupinski, Richard Mitera, Louise Shaw, Joseph Silverio, Sophie Slomski, Marguerite Staskavich.— **Agent for the Elderly,** Shawn Cohen.—**Social Services Dir.,** Beverly Lyons.—**Dir. of Health,** William A. Petit, M.D.—**Youth Services Coordinator,** Roberta Brown.— **Library Directors,** Frank Gagliardi, Chm., Stephen Cole, Patricia Fongemie, Kathryn Lickwar, Barbara Petit, Marilyn Sevigny.—**Town Historian,** Ruth S. Hummel.— **Town Planner,** Mary Hughes.—**Park and Recreation Bd.,** Lawrence Biskupiak, Irene Furman, George Goodall, Denis C. Thompson, Thomas W. Warnat, Tabitha Wazorko.—**Recreation Dir.,** Colin Regan.—**Dir. of Public Works,** Caryl P. Bradt.— **Supt. of Highways,** Frederick Dulac.—**Purchasing Agent,** Shirley Osle.—**Town Engineer,** John Bossi.—**Building Inspector,** Volovski.—**Building Code Bd. of Appeals,** Donald J. Higgins, Leo Labrecque, Ralph Munson, Elmer Saucier, vacancy.— **Supt. of Public Grounds,** Carmen Matteo.—**Supt. of Water Pollution Control,** Joseph Watkins.—**Sanitarian,** Robert F. Finn.—**Chief of Police,** Daniel Coppinger.— **Constables,** Wayne Gleifert, James A. Hanna, Kenneth A. Hedman, Eustace Mike, Philip Sengle, Christopher J. Wazorko, vacancy.—**Chief of Fire Dept.,** Joseph Watkins; Asst., David Laurie.—**Fire Marshal,** William Chamberlin.—**Civil Preparedness Dir.,** Peter T. Lennon.—**Town Atty.,** Robert A. Michalik.—**Justices of the Peace,** Raymond L. Acey, Carol Bartosiewicz, Reade Clemens, Charles A. Cosgrove, Robert N. Curtis, Anthony O. Famiglietti, Domenic J. Forcella, Christine Haddock, Pauline R. Kezer, Aurele Laferriere, Jr., Amy A. Leary, Robert A. Michalik, Eustace Mike, Eugene J. Millerick, Richard R. Mitera, Bruce Morris, Jean C. Nelson, Joan D. Osterag, Peter G. Perakos, Jr., Paul E. Phaneuf, Gail S. Pugliese, Joan R. St. Pierre, John Sartori, Patricia A. Sawczuk, Henry T. Sawicki, Kancace G. Shappy, Robert J. Stange, Deanna Tino, Frank C. Williams, Edgar A. Wynkoop.

PLYMOUTH. Litchfield County.—(Form of government, mayor-town council, limited town meeting.)—Inc., May, 1795; taken from Watertown. Area, 22.3 sq. miles. Population, est., 11,747. Voting districts, 2. Principal industries, agriculture and manufacture of locks, meters, pumps, computers, screw machine products, plastics, electronics, mailable iron castings and hardware. Transp.—Freight: Served by numerous motor common carriers. Post offices, Plymouth, Terryville and Pequabuck. Rural free delivery routes, RFD 1 Plymouth and RFD 2 Terryville.

TOWN OFFICERS. Clerk and Reg. of Vital Statistics, Janet P. Scoville; Hours, 8:30 A.M.-4:30 P.M., Mon. through Fri.; Address, Town Hall, 80 Main St., Terryville 06786-1209; Tel., Bristol, (860) 585-4039; FAX, (860) 585-4015.—**Asst. Clerks and Asst. Regs. of Vital Statistics,** Joan M. Heberle, Doris T. Isbrecht.—**Mayor,** David M. Denis (R) Tel., (860) 585-4002.—**Town Council,** Dist. 8, Michael Ganem (D), Daniel Houlihan (R), David C. Mischke (R); Dist. 31, Roseann Stocker (D), Mark P. Vanoni (D).—**Treas.,** Charles M. Buell.—**Comptroller,** Manuel Gomes.—**Bd. of Finance,** Jeanne E. Hand, Chm., Victoria A. Carey, Kevin Freimuth, Timothy M. Malootian, David V. Merchant, Norma S. Tanguay.—**Tax Collector,** Linda A. Hood.— **Bd. of Assessment Appeals,** Jacqueline S. Stromberg, Chm., Kathleen R. Ciupa, John Dering.—**Assessors,** Albert N. Wollenberg Chm., Richard J. Foote, Jacqueline Landon, Edmund Warkoski.—**Registrars of Voters,** Cheryl J. Gianesini (D), Pamela A. Malley (R).—**Supt. of Schools,** Dr. Thomas Y. McDowell.—**Bd. of Education,** Felix C. Borkowski, Chm., Theodore F. Kosikowski, David J. Sekorski, Barbara P. Spargo, Donna E. Wunsch, 1997; Phillip H. Fowler, Carol R. Kallenbach, Jacqueline T. Landon, Ronald G. Mamrosh, 1999.—**Town Planner,** Leonard Campbell.—**Planning and Zoning Comm.,** Ann Tuleja, Chm., Werner E. Fuerst, Carl W. Kulesa, Steven Panasuk, James R. Tofoe; Alternates, Kevin D. Smith, two vacancies.—**Zoning Bd. of Appeals,** Raymond A. Pelletier, Chm., William S. Hall, Jr., Lisabeth B. Mindera, Daniel J. Murray, Jeffrey Tranchetti; Alternates, Jeffrey Wunsch, two vacancies.—**Zoning Enforcement Officer,** Leonard Campbell.—**Industrial Development Comm.,** John G. Swicklas, Sr., Chm., Charles R. Bombard, Raymond R. Lassy, Jeffrey K. Scott, vacancy.—**Housing Auth.,** Henry F. Klosowski, Chm., Derald L. DeMerchant, Robert W. Johnson, Robert Nelson, Kaye S. Walden; Marilyn Grodecki, Exec. Dir.—**Energy Coordinator,** Warren Dion.—**Conservation and Inland Wetlands Comm.,** Gerard E. Milne, Jr., Chm., Nancy S. Henderson, Louise L. Lake, Thomas W. Zagurski, vacancy; Alternates, Charlene M. White, vacancy.—**Land Use Enforcement Officer,** vacancy.—**Historic Dist. Comm.,** Vincent Klimas.—**Dept. of Aging,** Henry Nypert.—**Dir. of Health,** Antonio Scappaticci, M.D. (Town Hall, 80 Main St., Terryville).—**Human Services Comm.,** Joy Armbruster, Susan Boilard, Janice Burzler, Manmohan B. Harara, Karen Kenney, Janet Spielman, Carol A. Walsh; Denise Bergin, Dir.—**Bd. of Public Health,** Antonio Scappaticci, M.D., Chm., Betty Castle, Margaret Clyma, Nancy Conway, Mayor David M. Denis, Barbara Deschaine, Eveline Finan, George Jabs, Louise Johnson, Anthony Orsini; Judi Blanchet, R.N., ex officio.—**Town Historian,** Matthew O. Malley.—**Library Directors,** Ellen Cifone, Elizabeth L. Norton, Michael D. Drozdick, Rose S. Frazier, Carol L. Houle, Kathryn D. Malley, Cathleen M. Paskus, Dorothy D. Pratt, Mary Jane Wollenberg.—**Parks and Recreation Comm.,** Janet H. Engle, Arthur G. Hamm, Barbara K. Rockwell, Joyce A. Relihan, Janet Speilman, Thomas A. Wollenberg, Karen A. Zagurski; Mary Beth Morelli, Dir.—**Housing Bd. of Appeals,** Donald J. Souza, Chm., Stephan A. Cheney, Edwin R. Ives, Stephen W. Mindera, Jr.; Alternate, Joseph Valaitis.—**Building Inspector,** Joel Skilton.—**Dir. of Public Works/Town Engineer/Tree Warden/ Recycling Coordinator,** Anthony A. Lorenzetti.—**Water Pollution Control Auth.,** Sheila A. Bujnowski, Chm., George F. Andrews, Jr., Philip J. Armbruster, Richard Kallenbach, Ernest J. Pickhardt, Jr.; Terence M. Vigeant, Plant Supvr.; Alternates, two vacancies.—**Sanitarian,** George Jabs.—**Supt. of Highways,** Coe Cleaveland.—**Chief of Police,** David A. Damon.—**Police Comm.,** Ronald N. Wollenberg, Chm., Charles J. DellaCamera, Richard M. Doyle, Sr., Wesley W. Petrin.—**Constables,** Christopher N. Boylan, Tim J. Chapulis, Lawrence Deschaine, Emil H. Golnik, Linda A. Kazmierski, Carl W. Kulesa, John C. Pajeski.—**Chief of Fire Dept.,** Mark Sekorski; Assts., Richard Dwyer, Gary Reed.—**Fire Marshal,** John Schubert; Deputies, Gregory M. Dean, Sr., Stephen Kelsey, Thomas J. O'Hare.—**Bd. of Fire Comrs.,** Stephen J. Fennessy, Sr., Chm., George J. Baraniecki, Wm. A. Hamzy, John Porter III, Stephen Sheak, Vernon C. Wagner, Donna M. Warkoski.—**Civil Preparedness Dir.,** Ronald L. McClain.—**Town Atty.,** Wm. Tracy, Jr.—**Justices of the Peace,** Stephen P. Adamowich, Joan M. Bachand, Arthur F. Blum, Christopher W. Boyland, Victoria A. Carey, George L. Castle, Stephan Cheney, Christine Ciarmella, Michael F. Conway,

James J. Daveluy, Jerry Fedorovich, Stephen J. Fennessy, Sr., Emil H. Golnik, Rajaa A. Hamzy, Rodney G. Houle, Doris T. Isbrecht, Jeannine A. Jandreau, Louise A. Johnson, Catherine G. Kosak, Theodore F. Kosikowski, Jacqueline T. Landon, James A. Landry, Walter R. Lassy, Joseph A. Lewandoski, Roberta B. Marquis, Adeline M. MacDermid, Lizabeth B. Mindera, Michael B. Mindera, Stephen W. Mindera, Jr., Carolyn W. Mueller, Ronald E. Packer, Theodora S. Piotrowski, Edward P. Plaze, Katherine L. Porter, Dorothy B. Pratt, Donald E. Rogers, Eileen A. Ross, James C. Ross, Janet P. Scoville, Barbara P. Sekorski, Hildegarde Siemiatkoski, Roseann Stocker, Florence P. Torok, Lawrence J. Torok, Arden H. Towill, Elizabeth R. Walden, Kaye S. Walden, Donna M. Warkoski, Thomas A. Wollenberg.

POMFRET. Windham County.—(Form of government, selectmen, town meeting, board of finance.)—Named and inc., May, 1713. Area, 40.6 sq. miles. Population, est., 3,355. Voting district, 1. Principal industries, agriculture dairy, forest products, manufacture of cable and cable products, fiberoptics, processing of frozen food dinners. Transp.—Freight: Served by numerous motor common carriers. Post offices, Pomfret, Pomfret Center and Abington.

TOWN OFFICERS. Clerk and Reg. of Vital Statistics, Nora V. Johnson; Hours, 9 A.M.-4 P.M., Mon. through Fri.; Address, 5 Haven Rd., Pomfret Center 06259; Tel., Putnam, (860) 974-0343.—**Asst. Clerk and Asst. Reg. of Vital Statistics,** Cheryl A. Grist.—**Selectmen,** 1st, Stanley S. Sheldon, Jr. (R) Tel., (860) 974-0191, Thomas H. Pahl (D), David I. Patenaude (R).—**Treas.,** Nora V. Johnson.—**Bd. of Finance,** John D. Boland, Chm., Donald F. Burton, Ralph S. Butts, Paul Nelson, Maureen A. Nicholson, Joseph P. Stoddard.—**Tax Collector,** Bonnie J. Duncan.—**Bd. of Assessment Appeals,** James N. Platt, Jr., Chm., Timothy W. McNally, Barry N. Shead.—**Assessors,** Mary G. Page, Kathleen M. Thornton.—**Registrars of Voters,** Norma M. Robbins (D), Elizabeth L. Cartier (R).—**Supt. of Schools,** Stephen Hosmer.—**Bd. of Education,** Henry S. Woodbridge, Jr., Chm., Esther S. Bala, Carolyn A. Hopkins, John R. Rauh, Lois S. Siegmund, 1997; Erik S. Lissfelt, Charles E. Tracy, vacancy, 1999.—**Planning Comm.,** Walter P. Hinchman, Chm., Robert M. Blackmer, Maureen Nicholson, Donald Shaw, Michael W. Wolchesky, vacancy; Alternates, Steven Billington, vacancy.—**Conservation Comm.,** Sandra L. Tosi, Chm., John C. Folsom, Edward Sirrine.—**Inland Wetlands Comm.,** Joseph P. Stoddard, Chm., Donald F. Burton, John E. Casey, Ronald Cusson, Bonnie Duncan, Marshall L. Eaton, Jerome U. Ethier, William B. Hull, Fred R. Sirrine; Alternate, vacancy.—**Economic Development Comm.,** David Flath, Chm., John Bala, Anthony Emilio, Mary Patenaude, Charles Tracy, Ingrid Walker; Alternate, John P. Loos.—**Dir. of Health,** Beth E. Quill (P.O., Brooklyn).—**Library Directors,** Nancy P. Weiss, Chm., Joyce T. Aicher, Susan P. Boland, Georganna D. Dickson, Newell D. Hale, Phyllis A. Lawrence, Carol J. Nelson, Mary E. Patenaude, Anne C. Wolchesky; Marjorie S. Sirrine, Librarian.—**Municipal Historian,** Mary G. Page.—**Recreation Comm.,** Beverly Champany, Chm., Ann Castle, Beth Deschenes, Christine LaCroix, Ann Lengyel, Muriel Mrakovich, Jane L. Navarro, Maureen Nicholson, Dennyse White.—**Tree Warden,** Stanley S. Sheldon, Jr.—**Building Inspector,** Robert H. Fisher III.—**Building Code Bd. of Appeals,** Ronald M. Champany, Raymond Erskine, John N. Paquette.—**Chief of Police,** Stanley S.

Sheldon, Jr.—**Constables,** Patrick D. Gill, Harley J. Hill, Marcel J. Morissette, Robert E. Murray, David P. Platt, Travis F. Sirrine, Fred A. Thornton.—**Chief of Fire Dept.,** Gordon Spink; Deputies, Timothy Morrarty, Ronnie Rondeau.—**Fire Marshal,** Robert H. Fisher, Jr.—**Burning Officer,** Stanley S. Sheldon, Jr.—**Town Atty.,** David M. Hubert.—**Civil Preparedness Dir.,** Harley J. Hill.—**Justices of the Peace,** Edward T. Beauregard, Jr., Katalin Borner, Thomas A. Borner, Elizabeth L. Cartier, John E. Casey, Andrea Cunningham, Georganna D. Dickson, John C. Folsom, Cheryl A. Grist, Robert A. Ikonen, Nora V. Johnson, Sara P. Kivela, Christine M. LaCroix, Stephen R. LaFreniere, Phyllis A. Lawrence, Mary R. Macdonald, Earle R. Maddocks, Jennifer D. Maddocks, Mary G. Page, Thomas H. Pahl, Norma M. Robbins, Milton R. Rollinson, Alton J. Semmelrock, Travis F. Sirrine, Joseph P. Stoddard, Fred A. Thornton, Kathleen M. Thornton.

PORTLAND. Middlesex County.—(Form of government, selectmen, town meeting, finance director.)—Inc., May, 1841; taken from Chatham. Area, 24.9 sq. miles. Population, est., 8,652. Voting district, 1. Principal industries, agriculture, manufacture of automatic packaging machinery and corrugated boxes, precision tools, feldspar quarries and milling, rubber and plastic products, fertilizer, petroleum and bituminous product distributors, 4 boat yards (building, repair and storage). Transp.—Passenger: Served by Greyhound. Freight: Served by Conrail and numerous motor common carriers. Post office, Portland. Village delivery, rural free delivery.

TOWN OFFICERS. Clerk and Reg. of Vital Statistics, Bernadette M. Dillon; Hours, 9 A.M.-4:30 P.M., Mon. through Fri.; Address, Town Hall, 265 Main St., P.O. Box 71, 06480; Tel., Middletown, (860) 342-6743; FAX, (860) 342-0001.—**Asst. Clerks and Asst. Regs. of Vital Statistics,** Mary C. Long, Judith P. McGinley, Rosanne Vecchitto.—**Selectmen,** 1st, Edward L. Kalinowski (P) Tel., (860) 342-6714, Susan Bransfield (D), Richard H. Cote (R), Thomas W. Flood, Jr. (D), James L. Hill (R), Edward J. Leffingwell (R), Barbara R. Phillips (R).—**Finance Dir.,** Donald W. Goodrich.—**Collector of Revenues,** Janet H. Lynch.—**Bd. of Assessment Appeals,** John B. Sterry, Chm., Donald E. Hunt, Richard P. Murphy.—**Assessor,** Paul Labella.—**Registrars of Voters,** Karen J. Soboleski (D), Elaine P. Cote (R).—**Supt. of Schools,** Joseph R. Castagnola.—**Bd. of Education,** Christopher Hetrick, Lynn M. Kennedy, Julia L. Norton, Cynthia R. Varricchio, 1997; Richard F. Conroy, Christopher H. Fox, Jenine A. Olson, 1999.—**Planning and Zoning Comm.,** Rolf O. Bylan, Sara C. Foster, Benjamin P. Lenda, John A. Murray, Theresa D. Supple; Alternates, Joseph C. Balskus, Reed A. Johnson, Charles Woltmann.—**Town Planner,** Raymond Carpentino.—**Zoning Bd. of Appeals,** John V. Flanagan, Chm., Armand F. Arsenault, Karen L. Jacobi, Gary P. Nolan, Raymond G. Tripodina; Alternates, James J. Ruitto, John R. Stewart, Frank E. Tassistro.—**Zoning Enforcement Officer,** Donald Mitchell.—**Economic Development Comm.,** Donald Hunt, Chm., Joseph Amend, Lynn Herlihy, Elizabeth J. Larson, Linda Manchester.—**Housing Auth.,** Donald R. Barrett, Sr., James J. Csere, Wilhelm R. Muller, John Szymaszek, vacancy; Jacqueline Frazee, Dir.—**Housing Code Bd. of Appeals,** Peter A. Lamalfa, Dean E. Phillips, Shirley M. Sullivan, Adolph Tetzlaff, vacancy.—**Housing Code Enforcement Officer,** Donald Mitchell.—**Inland Wetlands Comm.,** Robinson T. Gilbert, Chm., John H. Dillon, Henry E. Fredericks,

Howard R. Goodrich, Joseph R. Organek; Alternates, Guido J. Abramo, Joanne A. Luppi.—**Water and Sewer Comm.,** Thomas J. Bransfield, James E. McCabe, Marilyn McGrath, Charles Montgomery, Jr., Therese D. Supple, Norman D. Ward.—**Dir. of Seniors Program,** Beth Morrisette.—**Dir. of Social Services,** Dean Jacques.—**Dir. of Health,** George M. Rosenfeld, M.D.—**Library Directors,** Judith Bothwell, Chm., Christine B. Arena, Eileen E. Burke, Daniel M. Davis, Christina C. Kelley, George A. Law, Peter J. Marteka.—**Municipal Historian,** Eleanor W. Crowther.—**Parks and Recreation Comm.,** George E. Brede, Chm., Robert J. Agogliati, Lee D. Nordstrom, Avis E. Paddock, Steven B. Wells; Ray E. Foster, Dir.—**Dir. of Youth Services,** William Foreman.—**Dir. of Public Works,** Richard D. Kelsey.—**Building Inspector,** Daniel J. Loos.—**Supt. of Highways,** Donald N. Powers.—**Dir. of Operations,** Robert Darna.—**Animal Control Officer,** Charles Jarzabek.—**Civil Preparedness Coord.,** Robert Ziegler.—**Long Range Capital Planning Comm.,** Donna Benoit, Chm., Wayne J. Carini, James Elder, Brian D. Gouin, William P. Pozzetti.—**Tree Warden,** Harry E. Hetrick; Assts., Arthur Johnson, William H. Long.—**Open Burning Official,** David Powers.—**Town Engineer,** Jeffrey Jacobson.—**Fish, Game and Marine Officer,** Paul Bengston.—**Chief of Police,** Edward L. Kalinowski.—**Constables,** David Bond, Scott Cunningham, Michael Dapkus, Eric Grant, Gary Jarzabek, James Kelly, Ronald J. Milardo, Peter Paranzino.—**Chief of Fire Dept.,** David Powers; Deputy, Robert Petzold.—**Fire Marshal,** Joseph F. Lynch.—**Town Atty.,** Joseph G. Lynch.—**Justices of the Peace,** William Ackerman, Charles D. Anderson, Patricia S. Aresco, Armand F. Arsenault, Donna Benoit, Paul Bonaiuto, Odessa Buttram, Robert E. Cleary, Allen Cohen, Elaine P. Cote, Robert L. Curzan, Bernadette M. Dillon, Joseph A. Dombrowski, Judith A. Elder, Mark J. Finkelstein, Carl E. Fitzgibbons, John E. Flanagan, Arlene R. Flood, Nancy A. Flood, Stanley P. Florkoski, Stanley Florkoski, June B. Forella, Larry S. French, C. Paul Ghent, Marabeth C. Gildersleeve, Gary R. Gomola, Brian Gouin, Lynn R. Herlihy, Robert L. Hodge, Debra Hunt, Donald E. Hunt, Bernie C. Jarzabek, Jr., Charles B. Johnson, Jr., Ivar A. Jozus, Edward L. Kalinowski, Frederick R. Knous, Peter A. LaMalfa, Joseph G. Lynch, Martha L. McCabe, Cyrus C. Miller, William J. Nolan, Keith M. Norton, Paul D. Norton, John W. Otterbein, Edward J. Peters, Jr., Barbara R. Phillips, Arlene W. Piatti, Wesley J. Pierini, Ronald Pinto, Darlene Rice-Kelsey, Ellen Roman, John B. Sterry, Sr., J. Kenneth Stuke, David R. Sundell, Frank Tassistro, Theodore J. Tine.

PRESTON. New London County.—(Form of government, selectmen, town meeting, board of finance.)—Inc., Oct., 1687. Area, 31.8 sq. miles. Population, est., 4,982. Voting district, 1. Principal industries, agriculture and manufacture of brass. Transp.—Freight: Served by numerous motor common carriers. No post office, four rural delivery routes through the town from Norwich and Ledyard.

TOWN OFFICERS. Clerk and Reg. of Vital Statistics, Hattie Wucik; Hours, 9 A.M.-12 Noon, 12:30-4:30 P.M., Tues., Wed., Fri.; 9 A.M.-12 Noon, 12:30-7:30 P.M., Thurs.; Address, Town Hall, 389 Rte. 2, Preston 06365; Tel., (860) 887-9821.—**Asst. Clerks and Asst. Regs. of Vital Statistics,** Nancy Muench, Melinda Roberts.—**Selectmen,** 1st, Robert M. Congdon (R) Tel., (860) 887-5581, Gerald W. Grabarek (D),

Thomas F. Maurer (R).—**Treas.,** Lucille Thoma; Asst., Dorothy Smullen.—**Bd. of Finance,** Morris Fishbone, Chm., William Bartlett, Robert Maurice, Timothy H. Schultz, Randolph F. Stolz, vacancy.—**Tax Collector,** Hattie Wucik.—**Bd. of Assessment Appeals,** Nicholas Kashanski, Wesley Sholes, Parke C. Spicer.—**Assessor,** Mildred Peringer.—**Registrars of Voters,** Barbara Ware (D), Leona Fuller (R).—**Supt. of Schools,** Donald Holder.—**Bd. of Education,** Ann-etta N. Cannon, Chm., Susan J. Beeman, Cynthia L. Lowe, John Moulson, 1997; Nancy Bartlett, Timothy M. Hotchkiss, Ignatz A. Melgey, 1999.—**Planning and Zoning Comm.,** Daniel V. Kulesza, Chm., Roy J. Beauregard, Timothy R. Bowles, Lynwood F. Crary, John H. Kendall, Peter Liebert, John P. Olsson; Alternates, Charles L. Raymond, Leo B. Spicer, vacancy.—**Town Planner,** Richard Serra.—**Zoning Bd. of Appeals,** Allyn L. Brown III, Deborah J. Grabarek, Michael D. House, Terrance W. Pendergast, James Rigney; Alternates, Martha H. Anderson, Richard Dyer, vacancy.—**Zoning Enforcement Officer,** Mildred Peringer.—**Economic Development Comm.,** John Girard, Chm., Roy Beauregard, Joseph Biber, Allyn Brown III, Joseph Bubenicek, Jr., Carol Collette, Arthur Moran, David Paige, John Sasser, John Stuart, Gerard Tardiff, Robert Vescovi.—**Housing Auth.,** Fred McLean, Chm., Janet Harris, Roland Roberts, Ann Spicer, Helen Staubley; Carol Onderdonk, Exec. Dir.—**Conservation/Inland Wetlands Comm.,** Leonard Johnson, Chm., Paul Andruskiewicz, Kent Borner, Constance Capacchione, John Girard, Gerald Grabarek, Norman Marston, John Moulson, Christine Schmidt, Theodore Schulz; David A. Goss, Wetland Agent.—**Senior Affairs Committee,** Antoine Bassette, Joyce Bonnell, Jeannette Girard, Joseph Perrone, Arthur Scoville.—**Agent for the Elderly,** Fran Minor.—**Dir. of Health,** Albert Gosselin, (Norwich).—**Library Director,** Jane Hoddinott, Pres., Janice Bausch, Martha Briggs, Kathleen J. Flaherty, David Hoddinott, JoAnna Holland, Jane Liebert, Raymond Sobanski, Steve Vannais, Ruth Wheeler, Lois Woodmansee.—**Municipal Historian,** Joyce Steffenson.—**Parks and Recreation Comm.,** Leonard Johnson, Chm., David Anderson, Ronald Curtis, James Harnois, Paul Lopresti, Gail Smith, Susan Theve, Harold West, Jr., Brian Witt; Gail Rigney, Secy. Coordinator.—**Building Inspector,** Nelson Webster, Jr.—**Dog Warden,** Tara Toland.—**Tree Warden,** David Martin.—**Acting Sanitarian,** Albert Gosselin, Jr.—**Chief of Police,** Robert M. Congdon.—**Chiefs of Fire Dept.,** Dist. 1, Gerard Frechette; Dist. 2, Russell Holland.—**Fire Marshal,** Gail Burton.—**Civil Preparedness Dir.,** Henry Jorsz.—**Town Atty.,** Frank Manfredi.—**Justices of the Peace,** Alfredo G. Alletto, David Anderson, Gail M. Beauregard, Randy S. Black, David A. Boggis, Alexandria Bosko, Joseph W. Bubenicek, Jr., Robert H. Carden, Nancy Cicchiello, Elizabeth S. Combies, Linda V. Congdon, Lydia A. Crary, Charlene S. Day, John Delesio, Arlene M. Dumais, John P. Fratoni, Leona Fuller, Norman E. Gauthier, Victoria Germani, Ruth E. Going, Deborah J. Grabarek, Gerald W. Grabarek, Claire E. Guiher, Eugene F. Hildreth, James J. Howard, William H. Jacobsen, Gary M. LaCombe, Mark S. Mattern, Thomas F. Maurer, Beverly P. Moulson, David A. Oat, John P. Olsson, Jr., Joseph M. Perrone, Theodore Powell, Susan F. Quinn, William Robinson, Christine F. Schmidt, Heinz Seligman, Denise CB. Sharp, Lucille Slaga, John G. Smiley, Jr., Dorothy A. Smullen, Parke C. Spicer, Lynda C. Stolz, Nancy D. Stuart, Helen W. Staubley, Patricia A. Tunucci, Barbara B. Ware, Shirley L. Woodka, Kenneth L. Zachem, Irene Zuckerbraun.

PROSPECT. New Haven County.—(Form of government, mayor, town council, town meeting.)—Inc., May, 1827; taken from Cheshire and Waterbury. Area, 14.5 sq. miles. Population, est., 8,084. Voting districts, 2. Freight: Served by numerous motor common carriers. Post office, Prospect. Rural delivery of mail Nos. 1, 2, and 3, city Delivery Route Nos. 1203 and 1205, Waterbury.

TOWN OFFICERS. Clerk and Reg. of Vital Statistics, Patricia M. Vaillancourt; Hours, 9 A.M.-4 P.M., Mon. through Fri.; Address, Town Office Bldg., 36 Center St., 06712; Tel., Waterbury, (203) 758-4461.—**Asst. Clerk,** Barbara M. Lombardi.—**Asst. Regs. of Vital Statistics,** Roberta I. Case, Barbara M. Lombardi.—**Mayor,** Robert J. Chatfield (R).—**Town Council,** Douglas B. Merriman, Chm., Gwenn T. Fischer, Dolores A. Franks, Patricia S. Geary, Theresa C. Graveline, Frederick A. Harkins, Joyce K. Jones, Dominic N. Moschella, Shirley M. Sabo.—**Treas.,** James E. Duffy.—**Tax Collector,** Diane M. Lauber.—**Bd. of Assessment Appeals,** Ronald F. Ceccherine, Chm., Cynthia L. Gibbons, Gary V. Hodge.—**Assessor,** Vincent D. Leone.—**Registrars of Voters,** Katherine S. Blinstrubas (D), Kathleen VanderEyk (R).—**Supt. of Schools,** Helene Skrzyniarz, Ph.D.—**Planning and Zoning Comm.,** Marie M. Delage, E. Gil Graveline, Jr., Peter A. Lajoie, Edward J. Miller, George A. Sabo, Jr.; Alternates, Dolores A. Franks, Donald E. Pomeroy, vacancy.—**Zoning Bd. of Appeals,** Dawn E. Krisavage, Chm., Ronald Aliciene, Katherine S. Blinstrubas, Robert Caruso, Carl L. Graveline; Alternates, David L. Curtis, Betty Lou Holley, vacancy.—**Zoning Enforcement Officer,** Clarence O. Schiller.—**Economic Development Comm.,** Jeffrey J. Holley, Peter Hughes, Rosemary K. Marczewski, William J. Nardello, vacancy.—**Conservation Comm.,** George B. Hanover, Michael J. Holley, Jean L. Meehan, Joel H. Meisel, John J. Sullivan.—**Inland Wetlands Comm.,** Arnold A. Koehler, Chm., Brian F. Doody, David C. Holley, John D. Kaufman, Joseph M. Piotrowski; Alternates, Steven A. Iacoviello, William E. Jepson, William F. McCasland III.—**Comm. on Aging,** Frances B. Jackson, Chm., Miriam H. Caouette, Ruby R. DeCosta, Howard L. Hinman, Albert W. Miele, Sr., William H. Nelson, Stephen A. Novicky, Joseph F. Thompson, Ruth Van Wagner; Lucy Smegielski, Agent.—**Welfare Dir.,** Michael S. Rutkowski.—**Dir. of Health,** Thomas J. Wegrzyn, M.P.H. (1247 Higland Ave., Cheshire, 06410).—**Library Bd.,** Susan H. McKernan, Chm., Carmen C. Brown, Kathleen M. Graveline, Mary M. Hinman, Walter Magnavice, Thomas C. Marczewski, Thomas P. Misset, Carole D. Moschella, Georgianna Supra.—**Municipal Historian,** Richard O. Caouette.—**Bd. of Recreation,** William J. Sereduck, Chm., Alexander Bequary, J. Kenneth Clark, Christine Dembishack, Teresa Franz, Philip C. Reed, Kevin Ruane.—**Pension Bd.,** Mayor Robert J. Chatfield, Peter DiLeo, Patricia S. Geary, Douglas B. Merriman, Shirley M. Sabo.—**Asst. Dir. of Public Works,** Eugene J. McCarthy.—**Building Inspector,** William B. Scarpati.—**Building Code Bd. of Appeals,** Raymond T. Caruso, Herwood M. Cochran, Theodore A. Grieder, Eugene C. Lewis, Anthony J. Sasso, Jr.—**Town Engineer,** vacancy.—**Water Pollution Control Auth.,** John L. Schieffer, Jr., Chm., James J. Lehner, Barry W. Mitchell, William J. Nardello, Joy E. Winterhalder.—**Tree Warden,** James D. Wilson.—**Constables,** Kathy Ann Harvey, William E. Jepson, William J. Nardello, Suzanne M. O'Donnell, David Semrow, Joseph L. Welton.—**Chief of Fire Dept.,** Clint F. Brandien; Deputy, Robert J. Chatfield.—**Fire Marshal,** Keith C. Griffin.—**Civil Preparedness Dir.,** Bruce R. Woundy.—**Town Atty.,** John D. Yarbrough, Jr.—**Justices of the Peace,** Carleton J. Benson, Katherine S. Blinstrubas, Pauline B. Boyle, Robert J. Chatfield, Marie M. Delage, Helen M. DeLeon, Donald G. Donahue, Jr., James E. Duffy, Gwen T. Fischer, Patricia S. Geary, Stephanie A. Gomez, Carl L. Graveline, E. Gil Graveline, Jr., Keith C. Griffin, Lynn A. Griffin, Frederick A. Harkins, Gary V. Hodge, Betty Lou Holley, Joyce K. Jones, William E. Jepson, David T. Kluge, Rosemary K. Marczewski, Edward J. Miller, Barry Wms. Mitchell, Dominic N. Moschella, Arline F. Mullins, Mary Nolan, Robert T. O'Brien, Christopher J. Owens, Jr., Lillian R. Pranulis, James F. Quinn, Jr., Jean M. Reilly, George A. Sabo, Jr., Shirley M. Sabo, Dorothy A. Shea, Steven Skrebutenas, Sarah D. Smedes, Patricia M. Vaillancourt, Louis VanderEyk, John M. VanKirk, David Young.

PUTNAM. Windham County.—(Form of government, mayor, selectmen, town meeting, board of finance.)—Town inc., May, 1855; taken from Thompson, Pomfret and Killingly. City inc., Jan., 1895. Town and city consolidated Nov. 8, 1983. The city is a Special Service Dist. Area, 20.4 sq. miles. Population, est., 8,831. Voting districts, 2. Principal industries, agriculture, boilers, phonograph needles, synthetic yarns, buttons, antiques, paper from glass fibers, motor pumps, processing of sail cloth, finishing and dyeing, textile engraving and chrome plating. Freight: Served by Providence & Worcester Railroad Co. and numerous motor common carriers. Post office, Putnam.

TOWN OFFICERS. Clerk and Reg. of Vital Statistics, Sara J. D'Elia; Hours, 8:30 A.M.-12 Noon, 1-4:30 P.M., Mon. through Fri.; Address, Town Hall, 126 Church St., 06260; Tel., (860) 963-6807.—**Asst. Clerk and Asst. Reg. of Vital Statistics,** Norma B. Martell.—**Mayor,** Daniel S. Rovero (D); Deputy Mayor, Dawn H. Hutchings (D).—**Selectmen,** Robert C. Garceau (D), Frederick C. Hedenberg (R), Dawn H. Hutchings (D), Gary A. Kendall (D), Richard C. Place (D), Ower A. Tarr (R).—**Tax Collector,** Patricia Kowal.—**District Auth.,** Maxine F. Mann, Chm., Sharon A. Briere, Barbara Cotnoir, Daniel M. Goyette, Patricia Hedenberg.—**Bd. of Finance,** Anthony Falzarano, Chm., Charles Mahoney, Bruce L. Miller, Allan R. Rawson, Patricia A. Steinbrick; Alternates, Joy C. Child, Sandra J. Ouellette, Mona L. Tremblay.—**Bd. of Assessment Appeals,** Louis F. LaBonte, Linda E. French, vacancy.—**Assessor,** Rande Chmura.—**Registrars of Voters,** Michael D. Duffy (D), Paul A. Bellerose (R).—**Supt. of Schools,** Dr. Virginia J. Grzymkowski.—**Bd. of Education,** Ernest Cotnoir, Chm., Kathleen Noel-Johnson, Joseph Pempek, Karen S. Tidd, 1997; James F. Brezniak, Michael D. Duffy, Roberta A. Hayes, Lillian M. Newth, Peter T. Seraphin, 1999.—**Planning Comm.,** Gerard Cotnoir, Chm., James R. Arnold, Edward Briere, John S. Smith, Sr., John Woodfall; Alternates, Robert Guillot, vacancy.—**Zoning Comm.,** Cynthia Dunne, Chm., Peter E. Benoit, Patricia Hedenberg, Michael Lajeunesse, Walter Popiak; Robert Chenail, Zoning Officer; Alternates, Joseph Vaccariello, vacancy.—**Zoning Bd. of Appeals,** Joseph Nash, Chm., Bruce Bardin, Charles Holbrook, Debra L. Keeler, David J. Vitale; Alternates, James Mahoney, two vacancies.—**Economic Development Comm.,** Paul Grenier, Chm., John Malloy, John Miller, Walter Popiak, Marsha Reed; Alternate, vacancy.—**Conservation and Inland Wetlands Comm.,**

Daniel P. Remian, Chm., Paul A. Bellerose, Eunice R. Bishop, Rene Desaulniers, John Smith, vacancy; Alternates, Amanda Peckham, two vacancies.—**Dir. of Social Services,** Fran Gustavesen.—**Library Directors,** Michael E. Lajeunesse, Chm., Arthur P. Bove, Norma L. Cassettari, Carolyn D. Falzarano, Ruth H. Flagg, Merrilyn J. Garceau, Anne M. Hogan, Raymond B. Leduc, Jane W. St. Onge.—**Municipal Historian,** Robert J. Miller.—**Supt. of Highways,** Gerard Beausoleil.—**Building Inspector,** Robert Fisher.—**Constables,** Richard Bernier, Kenneth Dupre, Arthur Pacheco, tthree vacancies.—**Chief of Police,** Edward Perron.—**Chiefs of Fire Dept.,** John Adams, Norman A. Bernier.—**Fire Marshal,** Normand Perron; Assts., Robert Beaudry, Rickey Hayes.—**Civil Preparedness Dir.,** Ronald P. Saucier.—**Town Atty.,** William H. St. Onge.—**Justices of the Peace,** Wilhelmina E. Beaudreault, William C. Child, Judy H. Clemens, Sara J. D'Elia, David J. Hayes, Frederick C. Hedenberg, Denise G. Lafleur, Paula M. Lajeunesse, Jeannette D. LePire, Lillian M. Newth, Rene W. Richard, Jill M. Scola.

REDDING. Fairfield County.—(Form of government, selectmen, town meeting, board of finance.)—Inc., May, 1767; taken from Fairfield. Area, 32.1 sq. miles. Population, est., 8,152. Voting district, 1. Transp.—Passenger: Served by Metro North Commuter Railroad Co. Freight: Served by Conrail and numerous motor common carriers and railway express from Danbury. Post offices, Redding, West Redding, Georgetown and Redding Ridge.

TOWN OFFICERS. Clerk and Reg. of Vital Statistics, Patricia A. Creigh; Hours, 9 A.M.-4:30 P.M., Mon. through Fri.; Address, Town Office Bldg., 100 Hill Rd., P.O. Box 1028, Rte. 107, 06875-1028; Tel., (203) 938-2377.—**Asst. Clerk and Asst. Reg. of Vital Statistics,** Doneta Dunn.—**Selectmen,** 1st, Henry W. Bielawa (R) Tel., (203) 938-2002, Natalie T. Ketcham (R), Charles P. Mullaney (D).—**Treas.,** Daniel Heller.—**Bd. of Ethics,** Nathaniel Selleck, Chm., Eugene T. Connolly, Jr, Virginia Miller, Beatrice Shilstone, vacancy; Alternates, Henry Merritt, David Stackpole.—**Bd. of Finance,** Alvin Ruml, Chm., James Demaree, Clayton A. Friedberg, Mary Anne Guitar, John Hirschauer, Margaret M. Sullivan.—**Comptroller,** Mary Anne Wiesner.—**Tax Collector,** Patricia J. Moisio.—**Bd. of Assessment Appeals,** Frank J. Kokoska, Chm., Erik A. Lindblom, Edward J. McCarty.—**Assessor,** Daniel J. Kenney.—**Registrars of Voters,** Bess P. Fletcher (D); Marsha K. Berner (R).—**Supt. of Schools,** Kenneth Freeston.—**Bd. of Education,** Hugh Claremont, Tina Miller, Donald Raffety, 1997; William Alvarez, Jr., Kathleen Atkinson, Lynn Eichorn, 1999.—**Planning Comm.,** Diane Taylor, Chm., Doris Almgren, John Downey, Michael Nostin, Jr., Constance Spitzmiller; Alternates, Robert Dean, Fred Hanssen, Robin Linen.—**Zoning Comm.,** Frank J. Taylor, Chm., Thomas R. Baptist, Gerald Casiello, Benjamin L. Gordon, G. Marshall Sanford; Alternates, Andrew Comcowich, Bruce Given, Richard Kasiewicz.—**Zoning Enforcement Officer,** Aimee Pardee.—**Town Consultant,** John Hayes.—**Land Use Coordinator,** Jo-an Brooks.—**Zoning Bd. of Appeals,** John Roche, Acting Chm., Philip D. Bronson, Michael Cardillo, Michael C. Roush, William H. Werfelman, Jr; Alternates, Heloise L. Fahan, Bruce Givens, Robert B. Starrett.—**Conservation Comm.,** David Pattee, Chm., Linda Berger, Victor DeMasi, Carol C. Gilliam, James P. Hanlon, Jeremiah Ross, Fred D. Schroeder.—**Elderly Comm.,** Janet

Metzger, Chm., Catherine Daily, Gertrude Doble, Mary J. Kumke, William Morris, Alice Pardee, Jean Whitham, Tom Wiener, Thomas F.Wylie; Gail Schiron, Agent.—**Dir. of Health,** Matthew A. Miller, M.D. (P.O., West Redding).—**Library Directors,** Lisa Reese, Pres., Warren Bloomfield, Elizabeth Licarie, Lewis Rosen; Helen Stauderman, Dir.—**Parks and Recreation Comm.,** Ann Sunderland, Chm., Harry Adamakos, David Emison, Amy Folkman, Lawrence Kaufman, Patricia Klimaytis, Mary Maday, Patricia A. Werfelman; Roger Moss, Dir.; Kelly Ferris, Asst. Dir.—**Municipal Historian,** Margaret Wixted.—**Town Engineer,** James MacBroom.—**Supt. of Highways,** Roger Harker.—**Building Inspector,** James Hennessey.—**Sanitarian,** Roy C. A. Bradshaw; Consultant, Douglas Hartline.—**Tree Warden,** James McNamara.—**Chief of Police,** Henry W. Bielawa.—**Police Advisory Bd.,** Frederick V. Miller, Chm., Robert Carlson.—**Constables,** Hjalmar W. Anderson, Robert Blum, Robert Carlson, Harvey E. Lehn, Stephen M. Pugner, Henry J. Rasmussen, Jr.—**Chiefs of Fire Dept.,** 1st Dist., James Sugden, Jr.; 2nd Dist., Alfred Landwehr; Georgetown, Michael Heibeck.—**Fire Marshals,** 1st Dist., Jack Hawkins; 2nd Dist., David Sanford; Georgetown, Jack Hawkins.—**Fire Comrs.,** 1st Dist., Per Ola d'Aulaire, Richard Kasiewicz, James McNamara; 2nd Dist., Joseph Hawley, Richard Holmes, Ronald Romano; Georgetown, Albert O. Anderson, Donald E. Heibeck, Lori Withall.—**Civil Preparedness Dir.,** Laurence Ford.—**Town Atty.,** Michael N. LaVelle.—**Justices of the Peace,** John D. Campbell, Andrew Comcowich, Morton Friedman, Dorothee H. Funk, Robert H. Gillette, Michael W. Goodman, Patricia J. Moisio, Alfred D. Pirone, Richard W. Reynolds, Katherine Rook, John F. Rovegno, Alice F. Strouse, Margaret V. Sullivan.

RIDGEFIELD. Fairfield County.—(Form of government, selectmen, town meeting, board of finance.)—Settled, 1708; inc., Oct., 1709; town and borough consolidated, May 11, 1921. Area, 35.0 sq. miles. Population, est., 21,576. Voting districts, 3. Principal industries, pharmaceutical manufacturing, research and development, light manufacturing and building/construction. Transp.—Passenger: Served by Metro North Commuter Railroad Co. Freight: Served by Conrail. Post office, Ridgefield. Four rural routes and one auxiliary route.

TOWN OFFICERS. Clerk and Reg. of Vital Statistics, Barbara Serfilippi; Hours, 8:30 A.M.-4:30 P.M., Mon. through Fri.; Address, 400 Main St., 06877; Tel., (203) 431-2783.—**Asst. Clerks of Vital Statistics,** Marguerite Agresta, Catherine Littleton, Sandra Warner.—**Deputy Regs. of Vital Statistics,** Cynthia Bruno, Ann Tulipani.—**Selectmen,** 1st, Sue W. Manning (R) Tel., (203) 431-2774, Rudolph P. Marconi (D), Abraham N. Morelli (R), Peter V. Yanity (R), Stephen J. Zemo (D).—**Treas.,** Maureen M. Kiernan.—**Finance Dir.,** Jay Wahlberg.—**Bd. of Finance,** Bernard Dzlielinski, Martin F. Heiser, Paul J. Rosa, Jr., John Scarbrough, Timothy J. Sullivan.—**Tax Collector,** Mary H. Foyt.—**Bd. of Assessment Appeals,** Derek S. McClerry, Chm., Joseph M. Dunworth, Victor M. Lampasso.—**Assessor,** Alfred Garzi.—**Registrars of Voters,** Patricia Baker (D), Pauline Moylan (R).—**Supt. of Schools,** Jeffrey Hansen.—**Bd. of Education,** John R. Armato, Marianne Loomis, Joseph F. Sweeney, Hope S. Wise, 1997; Judith Fulkerson, Chm., David C. Bello, Linda M. Bunyan, Frank D'Angelo, Katherine Fischer, 1999.—**Planning and Zoning/Inland Wetlands/Flood and Ero-**

sion Control Bd., Nelson Gelfman, Chm., Michael J. Auturoi, David D. Huntoon, John Katz, Julia B. Masters, James McChesney, Joseph S. Savino, Walter J. Slavin.—**Town Planner,** Oswald Inglese.—**Zoning Bd. of Appeals,** Charles Creamer, Chm., John P. Cooke, Duncan B. Hume, Robert Mannion, E. Leslie Morelli; Alternates, Guy R. Mazza, Marjorie C. McKenna, Robert K. Smith.—**Housing Auth.,** Philip Berquist, Martha Campbell, Kathleen Carney, John E. Dowling, Lynda Hanley, vacancy.—**Zoning Enforcement Officer,** Richard Baldelli.—**Municipal Building Committee,** Susan Chipouras, Chm., John E. Abrassart, Peter Chipouras, Susanne Meaney, Onofrio Piacquadio, Joseph Rabideau, Gloria Stearns, Joseph F. Sweeney, John Thompson, Frank Zarkowsky.—**Conservation Comm.,** William Deane, Paul Jaehnig, Henry Knizeski, Edith Meffley, George Orlan, Philip Quigg, Richard N. Serfilippi, Lillian Willis, Beth Yanity.—**Historic Dist. Comm.,** Kathryn Rosa, Chm., Jill Clapes, John Connors, James Hancock, Richard Venus.—**Town Historian,** Richard E. Venus.—**Comm. on Aging,** Lillian Kehoe, Dorothy Martin, Eileen Means, E. Leslie Morelli, Caroline Multer, Christine Robertson, Veronica Somma; Edna-May Olson, Agent.—**Pension Comm.,** David Campbell, Chm., Christofer Christiansen, Edgar F. Kent, David Kulo, Robert Moriarty, Walter Seiberti, Albert Shagory.—**Dir. of Social Services,** MaryAnn Baldwin.—**Dir. of Health,** Patrick Neligan, M.D.—**Parks and Recreation Comm.,** Howard S. Tuthill, Chm., David Campbell, Frank McPike, Jr., Barbara Polacsek, Jane Rodas, Gary Smith, Wayne Tinker.—**Supt. of Highways,** Frank Serfilippi.—**Town Engineer,** Charles Fisher.—**Building Inspector,** William J. Reynolds.—**Building Code Bd. of Appeals,** John Murren, Chm., David Coffin, Richard DiSalvo, Fred Montanari, Mario Serfilippi.—**Tree Warden,** John Pinchbeck.—**Sanitarian,** Edward Briggs.—**Chief of Police,** Thomas Rotunda.—**Police Comm.,** John W. Carney, Chm., Charles A. Knocke, Carl Lecher, Aldace T. Walker, vacancy.—**Constables,** Richard N. Aarons, William Peatt, Jr., Richard N. Serfilippi, James E. Sullivan, two vacancies.—**Chief of Fire Dept./Civil Preparedness Dir.,** Richard Nagle.—**Fire Marshal,** David Lathrop.—**Town Atty.,** J. Allan Kerr.—**Justices of the Peace,** Marie Adams, Mark D. Allan, Pamela K. Allen, William I. Allen, John R. Armato, Mary Ann E. Baldwin, Patricia A. Baker, Paula S. Bruns, Fred E. Bryant, Herbert V. Camp, Jr., Alice B. Carboni, Martin J. Carr, George R. Catha, Gretchen Celestino, Anthony P. Chianese, John P. Cooke, Glenn H. Cordelli, Dominic D'Addario, Mary H. D'Addario, John A. Delutio, Lucille M. Denovia, James D. Diamond, Lee Dickinson, Eugene S. Dobies, John E. Dowling, Margaret J. Dunnington, Joseph M. Dunworth, Bernard P. Dzielinski, Julie I. Foster, Mary H. Foyt, John H. Frey III, John R. Fulkerson, Jonathon Fulkerson, Judith Fulkerson, Kristen L. Geddis, Karen L. Giblin, Ann M. Gilchrist, Thomas M. Gotimer, Patricia J. Grissmer, Rex E. Gustafson, Michael A. Hagan, John J. Hazel, Joseph H. Heyman, Evelyn S. Hogan, Duncan B. Hume, Joan K. Hume, Ann R. Huntoon, David D. Huntoon, Roberrt R. Jewell, Janet L. Johns, George F. Kain, Nancy Katz, Michael R. Kaufman, W. Jerome Kiernan, Maureen M. Kiernan, L. Timothy Klvana, Victor M. Lampasso, Ruth B. Leibowitz, Jerry V. Leaphart, Christopher K. Leonard, Heather A. Madison, Michael J. Manning, Sue W. Manning, Iris M. McCleery, Barbara R. Manners, Rudolph P. Marconi, Julia B. Masters, Guy R. Mazza, Fred P. Montanari, Salvatore C. Monti, Abraham N. Morelli, Jr., E. Leslie Morelli, Paul J. Morganti, Pauline R. Moylan, Susan M. Mushlin, David E. Nichols, Steven Nissman, Deborah K. Orr, Phyliss Paccadomi, Joan R. Plock, Leo A. Plum, Jr., Kathryn

A. Plum, Todd D. Polley, Catherine M. Quinlan, David L. Raab, Macklin Reid, Patrick J. Reville, Susan S. Reynolds, Thomas F. Reynolds, Michael P. Rizzo, Mark S. Robinson, Paul J. Rosa, Jr., Rodney L. Salvati, John F. Sanders, Joseph S. Savino, Christopher R. Scalzo, Sabina S. Slavin, Bryan E. Smith, Robert K. Smith, Patricia R. Stephens, Joseph P. Stenza, Irene B. Strouse, Jeri L. Taylor, Marjorie Tippett, Sarah E. Tippett, Annie Tulipani, Josette H. Williams, William G. Wyman, Elizabeth Yanity, Peter V. Yanity, Stephen J. Zemo.

ROCKY HILL. Hartford County.—(Form of government, mayor-town council, town manager.)—Inc., May, 1843; taken from Wethersfield. Area, 13.8 sq. miles. Population, est., 16,991. Voting districts, 4. State Veterans Home and Hospital and the new Dinosaur State Park located here. Principal industries, agriculture, castings, bearings, aircraft, and electronics. Transp.—Passenger: Served by buses of Conn. Transit from Hartford and Middletown; Central Conn. Limousine Service to Bradley International Airport; Greyhound and Trailways bus service to New York City and Boston. Freight: Served by numerous motor common carriers. Post office, Rocky Hill.

TOWN OFFICERS. Clerk and Reg. of Vital Statistics, Barbara R. Gilbert; Hours, 8:30 A.M.-4:30 P.M., Mon. through Fri.; Address, Town Hall, 699 Old Main St., P.O. Box 657, 06067; Tel., Hartford, (860) 258-2705.—**Asst. Clerks and Asst. Regs. of Vital Statistics,** Michael Casati, Shirley H. Smith.—**Town Manager,** Philip R. Dunn.—**Town Council,** Donald W. Unwin (R), Mayor and Chm.; Michael J. Gerace, Louis G. LaPorto, Ernest McNeill, Jr., Kenneth Mikulski, Robert E. Mullins, William J. Pacelia, Francis J. Sacerdote, Arthur S. Spada.—**Selectmen,** Donald R. Francis, Rosemary Morganti-Ames, vacancy.—**Treas.,** Karen Rogers.—**Dir. of Finance,** Robert Metcalf.—**Tax Collector,** Patricia M. Milliord.—**Bd. of Assessment Appeals,** Martin K. Hofmann, Marian McDonald, Ronald A. Santos.—**Assessor,** Vivian Bachteler.—**Registrars of Voters,** Angeline Ciarcia (D), Betsy M. Nazzaro (R).—**Supt. of Schools,** J. A. Camille Vautor.—**Bd. of Education,** Michael J. Bocchini, Chm., Laurie J. Boske, Curtis B. Clemens, Sr., Sondra L. Dellaripa, Lori R. Littman, Glenn R. Parent, R. Jeffrey Sands, Frank Szeps, vacancy, 1997.—**Planning and Zoning Comm.,** Stuart Webster, Chm., Cornelius Geldof, Jr., Jesse Harrison, Clifford Hart, Philip Stripinis; Alternates, Barry Goldberg, Cheryl Champagne, William MacDonald.—**Town Planner,** Kimberly Ricci.—**Zoning Bd. of Appeals,** Joseph S. Coelho, Chm., Philip H. Benoit, Salvatore R. Gozzo, Julie A. McManus, Lawrence T. Shiembob; Alternates, John H. Bischoff, Paul L. Maynard, Bruce A. Zawodniak.—**Economic Development Comm.,** Don Warnat, Chm., Ronald Bonola, Marie Johnson, Raj Natarajan, Philip Theroux, Christian Tyrell.—**Redevelopment Agency,** James Ussery, Chm., Donald R. Francis, Stephen Hansen, Jeffrey Horn, Orest Rigoletti, William Seymour, Robert Tangerone.—**Housing Auth.,** Percy Aldridge, Raymond Barrett, Sandra Chandler, Ralph Husband, Cynthia Krawciw.—**Fair Rent Comm.,** Barbara Natarajan, Chm., Richard Lewis, Christian Tyrell, Adrienne Valente, Frank P. Zocco, Jr.; Alternates, Patricia Hughes, John Kriedel, Pamela A. Oliver.—**Open Space and Conservation Comm.,** Frank Szeps, Chm., Francis J. Drumm, Jr., Jeff Horn, Allen Johnson, James Oleksiw, Robert F. Smith, Kevin Walsh; Alternates, Norman A. Topf, two vacancies.—**Insurance Committee,** Roderick A. Wilscam, Chm., Francis A. Begen, Denise Stripinis.—**Public Building Committee,** Daniel Somes, Chm., Edward Ames, Jr., Tim Lewis, Fred Valente.—**Human Relations Committee,** Patricia Beyer, William Donegan, Allen Johnson, Paul Maynard, Rosemary Morganti-Ames, Raj Natarajan, Eleonora Shippy; Alternates, Alexis Carroll, two vacancies.—**Human Services/Welfare Dir.,** Mark A. Williams.—**Dir. of Health,** Paul Hutcheon—**Library Directors,** Douglas Morton, Chm., Claire Clark, Linda Pacelia, Salvatore Pallazzolo, Jr., Dana Whitman, Jr., Shawna Wisnioski, vacancy.—**Parks and Recreation Comm.,** Gail P. Rapoza, Chm., Wendell H. Coogan, James Dennis, Robert Hall, Roberto Solis, Adrienne Valente; Christy Hass, Dir.—**Highway Supt./Dir. of Public Works,** Gerald A. DeRubbo.—**Town Engineer,** James Sollmi.—**Building Inspector,** Peter Langlois.—**Building Code Bd. of Appeals,** John Raffa, Chm., Elton Harvey, Michael McCarthy, Giles Rochefort, Ronald A. Santos.—**Chief of Police,** George Marinelli.—**Constables,** Ronald Bonola, Fred DiNardi, Robert T. Hall, John A. Raffa.—**Chief of Fire Dept.,** Joseph Kohanek.—**Fire Marshal,** Alexander Brilliant, Jr.—**Civil Preparedness Dir.,** Donald W. Unwin.—**Town Atty.,** Curtis Roggi.—**Justices of the Peace,** Patricia Beyer, Edward P. Buckie, James W. Caruso, James S. Ciarcia, John J. Corona, Concetta D'Ambrosio, Robert O. Decker, Michael Desfosses, Donald R. Francis, Michael Gerace, Barry Goldberg, Neil G. Gordes, Robert T. Hall, Miriam Lifshitz-Theroux, Paul L. Maynard, Kenneth E. Mikulski, Betsy M. Nazzaro, Joseph J. Oliva, William Pacelia, Francis J. Sacerdote, Lawrence T. Shiembob, Eleanora Shippy, Richard D. Tulisano, Donald W. Unwin, James E. Ussery, Donald G. Watson, Roderick A. Wilscam, Bruce A. Zawodniak.

ROXBURY. Litchfield County.—(Form of government, selectmen, town meeting, board of finance.)—Inc., Oct., 1796; taken from Woodbury. Area, 26.3 sq. miles. Population, est., 1,927. Voting district, 1. Principal industry, agriculture. Transp.—Freight: Served by numerous motor common carriers. Post office, Roxbury. Voted No Liquor Permit, 1971.

TOWN OFFICERS. Clerk and Reg. of Vital Statistics, Peter A. Hurlbut; Hours, 9 A.M.-12 Noon, 1-4 P.M., Tues., Thurs., 9 A.M.-Noon, Fri.; other times by appointment; Address, 29 North St., 06783; Tel., New Milford, (860) 354-3328.—**Asst. Clerk and Asst. Reg. of Vital Statistics,** Elinor P. Hurlbut.—**Selectmen,** 1st, Edward T. Went (D) Tel., (860) 354-9938, Barbara Henry (R), Elizabeth Hurlbut (D).—**Treas.,** Deborah J. Nelson.—**Bd. of Finance,** Gary R. Adams, Chm., Kenneth R. Allen, Jr., James E. Conway, Charles P. Jackson, Wayne L. Piskura, William T. Trainer.—**Tax Collector,** Brooke J. Wheeler.—**Bd. of Assessment Appeals,** Ray Allen, Kathleen A. Conway, Sharon Maynard.—**Assessors,** Patricia S. Braislin, Lauren Elliott.—**Registrars of Voters,** Judith M. Doran (D), Shirley A. Charpentier (R).—**Supt. of Schools,** Robert Nicoletti.—**Planning Comm.,** Marion J. Skedgell, Chm., Howard M. Bronson, Jr., Robert F. Munson, Jr., Richard Sonder, Dixie Trainer; Alternates, Culver Griffin, David B. Miller, vacancy.—**Zoning Comm.,** Daniel A. Jonker, Chm., Patricia Hermes, James S. Martin, Lorraine Tvrdik, Russell E. Wheeler; Alternates, Hauthaway Mabbett, David A. Poole, vacancy.—**Zoning Bd. of Appeals,** David C. Baron, Norman A. Cover, Douglas R. Erwin, Philo B. Hodge, Mary L. Wright; Alternates, Suzanne G.

Burley, Dudley Diebold, Albert S. Pokrywka.—**Inland Wetlands Comm.,** Lendert T. DeJong, Chm., Richard Crowley, Brian Duda, Robert K. Horrigan, vacancy; Alternates, Ann Marie Casper, Susan Monserud, vacancy.—**Historic Dist. Comm.,** William Ale, Nancy H. Allen, Georgette Miller, Russell E. Poteet, vacancy; Alternates, Phillip N. DeVries, Lindsay E. Law, Thomas B. Zaleta.—**Municipal Historian,** Elmer H. Worthington.—**Agent for the Elderly,** Culver Griffin.—**Dir. of Health,** Josef Burton, M.D.—**Library Directors,** Gloria M. Bevilacque, Barbara W. Cover, Margaret C. Lindheimer, Mary B. Madsen, Robert M. Newman, Jr., Susan G. Purdy, Hugh R. Rawson, Justine A. Smith, Elmer H. Worthington.—**Recreation Comm.,** Jay Kronfeld, Chm., Donna Cloutier, Jane Edwards, Elizabeth R. Garbien, Charles P. Jackson, Charles D. Meade, Nancy N. Meinke, Pamela P. Ruscoe, Charles D. Stauffacher.—**Supt. of Highways,** Edward T. Went.—**Tree Warden,** James F. Lowe.—**Building Inspector/Sanitarian,** Thomas O'Loskey.—**Building Code Bd. of Appeals,** David F. Beglan, Gary Isbell.—**Lake Lillinonah Auth.,** Alfred F. Bevilacque, Leendert T. DeJong, Philip C. Smith.—**Chief of Police,** Edward T. Went.—**Constables,** Thomas Daniels, Michael T. Rice, Philip C. Smith, two vacancies.—**Chief of Fire Dept.,** Gary R. Adams.—**Fire Marshal,** Charles R. Smith; Deputy, Joshua Chabalowski.—**Civil Preparedness Dir.,** Edward T. Went.—**Town Atty.,** Gail E. McTaggart (41 Church St., Waterbury).—**Justices of the Peace,** Ray Allen, Jerry B. Allford, Patricia A. Clark, Shirleyann Charpentier, James H. Diewold, Ernest S. Finch, Joy T. Hodge, Jean G. Murkland, Carol T. Neff, Wayne L. Piskura, Alford H. Rowley, Merlin F. Temple, Jr., Edward T. Went, Elmer H. Worthington.

SALEM. New London County.—(Form of government, selectmen, town meeting, board of finance.)—Inc., May, 1819; taken from Colchester, Lyme and Montville. Area, 29.8 sq. miles. Population, est., 3,554. Voting district, 1. Transp.—Freight: Served by numerous motor common carriers. Post Office, Salem.

TOWN OFFICERS. Clerk and Reg. of Vital Statistics, Cynthia B. Rowin; Hours, 8 A.M.-4 P.M., Mon. through Wed., 8 A.M.-6:30 P.M., Thurs., 8 A.M.-12 Noon, Fri.; Address, Town Office Bldg., 270 Hartford Rd., 06420; Tel., Norwich, (860) 859-3873, Ext. 4.—**Asst. Clerk and Asst. Reg. of Vital Statistics,** Jennifer G. Scace.—**Selectmen,** 1st, Donald W. Bourdeau, Jr. (D) Tel., (860) 859-3504, Peter F. Sielman (D), Frank P. Sroka (R).—**Treas.,** Kimberly A. Siebert.—**Bd. of Finance,** John M. Campion, Charlene Clancy, Horace Lindo, Jr., Chriss R. Miller, Hugh C. Teel, Carol A. Vasquez; Alternates, James Fogarty, Judy Heipel.—**Tax Collector,** Cheryl A. Philopena; Asst., Delaphine E. Hatch.—**Bd. of Assessment Appeals,** Jewell D. James, Valerie Stanavage, Norman B. Wood.—**Assessor,** Debra Sabolesky.—**Registrars of Voters,** Betsy B. Butts (D), Deborah L. Zorn (R).—**Supt. of Schools,** Holden T. Waterman.—**Bd. of Education,** Ruth A. Cole-Chu, Chm., Timothy E. Grilley, Mary Quatroche, Keith Soileau, 1997; Christine M. Gianquinto, Marianne D. Kennedy, 1999; Christopher Constantine, Janet S. Griggs, Anne M. Krodel, 2001.—**Planning and Zoning Comm.,** Michael C. Jensen, Chm., David Burnett, Deborah Cadwell, William C. Miller, Donald B. Mullin, Ann S. Sielman, Lawrence J. Stevens; Alternates, Diana N. Giles, Marilyn L. Haag, Arlene Trust.—**Zoning Bd. of Appeals,** Stephen E.

Buck, Salvatore T. Crisanti, Stephen T. Poole, Rebecca A. Williams, Nancy Winans; Alternates, Denise D. Dube, James D. Fogarty, Chriss R. Miller.—**Zoning Enforcement Officer,** vacancy.—**Inland Wetlands/Conservation Comm.,** Eugene Wilczewski, Chm., Gary H. Alligood, Richard Greene, Douglas Hoefer, Stanley Menitz, James Sipperly, George A. Ziegra; Alternates, Hank Horn, Thomas Howard, vacancy.—**Agent for the Elderly,** vacancy.—**Dir. of Health,** Dr. Michael Feltes.—**Library Directors,** Betsy B. Butts, Chm., Anne W. Bingham, Anne M. Duncan, Janet Nelson-Smith, Denise M. Weinschenker, Joan R. Winters.—**Municipal Historian,** Deanna St. Jean.—**Recreation Comm.,** James Burke, Chm., John Cassidy, Candace Magoon, Jane Marolda, Cheryl Muscarella.—**Purchasing Agent,** Donald W. Bourdeau, Jr.—**Asst. Building Inspector,** Lawrence Stannard.—**Sanitarian,** N. Reed Gustafson.—**Town Planner,** Carl Fontneau.—**Gardner Lake Auth.,** Edward W. Osipowicz, Jr., Chm., Larry Harrington, Helen A. Zaleski.—**Security Police,** H. David Cordell, Michael Westcott.—**Chiefs of Fire Depts.,** James B. Savalle (Gardner Lake); Eugene Maiorano (Salem).—**Fire Marshal,** Donald Bourdeau, Jr.—**Civil Preparedness Dir.,** Donald Bourdeau, Jr.—**Town Atty.,** John W. Butts (P.O., Colchester).—**Justices of the Peace,** Hilmar B. Ahnert, Gary Alligood, Gale Balavender, Raymond S. Beebe, Jr., Janice B. Blonder, Anne C. Bingham, Gary Alligood, Gale Balavender, Donald W. Bourdeau, Jr., Karen H. Buckley, Betsy B. Butts, John W. Butts, Richard Carroll, Mary N. Cikatz, Charlene E. Clancy, Leeland Cole-Chu, Ruth A. Cole-Chu, Joseph S. Dalton, Shirley W. Diamond, Sigmund Diamond, Charles Dye, Mary Jane Edwards, James D. Fogarty, Christine M. Gianquinto, Diana N. Giles, Gregory P. Giles, Delaphine E. Hatch, John Keenan, Erin E. Kennedy, John F. Kennedy III, Mary L. Kollman, Horace Lindo, Marcella C. Maiorano, Mary McGannon-Kollman, Chriss R. Miller, Donita L. Miller, Sharon B. Miller, Michael F. Nortz, Edward W. Osipowicz, Jr., Joseph T. Ploszaj, R. Larry R. Reitz, Francis D. Robinson, Cynthia B. Rowin, Maryanne Sabowski, Alfreda B. Shapere, Ann S. Sielman, Peter F. Sielman, Lauren E. Sipperly, Frank P. Sroka, Lawrence J. Stevens, Hugh C. Teel, Arlene Trust, Carol A. Vasquez, Mary Ann Vesey, Vernon D. Vesey II, Denise Weinschenker, Rebecca A. Williams, Sylvia Winakor, Helen A. Zaleski.

SALISBURY. Litchfield County.—(Form of government, selectmen, town meeting, board of finance.)—Inc., Oct., 1741. Area, 60.1 sq. miles. Population, est., 4,063. Voting district, 1. Rural residential and retirement community. Transp.—Freight: Served by numerous motor common carriers. Post offices, Salisbury, Taconic and Lakeville.

TOWN OFFICERS. Clerk and Reg. of Vital Statistics, Laura H. Johnson; Hours, 9 A.M.-4 P.M., Monday through Friday; Address, Town Hall, 27 Main St., P.O. Box 365, 06068; Tel., Lakeville, (860) 435-5182.—**Asst. Clerks and Asst. Regs. of Vital Statistics,** Patricia P. Gomez, Janet V. Maus, Susan W. Spring; Sub. Regs., Robert G. Palmer, Susan G. Vreeland.—**Selectmen,** 1st, Robert J. Smithwick (R) Tel., (860) 435-5170, Ann M. Cuddy (R), Curtis G. Rand (D).—**Treas.,** Shirley R. Hurley; Asst., Linda Stevens.—**Comptroller,** Joseph Cleaveland.—**Bd. of Finance,** Carl H. Williams, Chm., Zenas Block, Richard T. Fitzgerald, Donald K. Mayland, John A. Rice, Alice B. Yoakum.—**Tax Collector,** Denise M. Rice.—**Bd. of Assessment Appeals,**

Richard J. Cantele, Jr., Michael G. Fitting, J. Dean Hammond.—**Assessor,** Lauren Elliott.—**Registrars of Voters,** Richard O. Walsh (D), Nancy McL. Peck (R).—**Supt. of Schools,** Marvin Maskovsky.—**Bd. of Education,** Mary K. Davidson, Chm., Gordon Johnson, Bill Willis, 1997; Chris T. Brennan, Leo J. Gafney, George D. Kellogg, Jr., W. R. MacKendree, 1999.—**Planning and Zoning Comm.,** Jonathan Higgins, Chm., Val P. Bernardoni, Michael Rogers, J. Leonard Stewart, Susan G. Vreeland; Alternates, Donald E. Hewat, Martin J. Whalen.—**Zoning Bd. of Appeals,** Stephen Victory, Chm., Jeanne C. Bronk, Dale D. Brown, Richard Dee, Robert K. Hydon, vacancy; Alternates, John Bartram, Albert P. Ginouves, Roger C. Rawlings.—**Zoning Enforcement Officer,** Elizabeth M. Hall.—**Conservation and Inland Wetlands Comm.,** Curtis G. Rand, Chm., Stephen T. Belter, David Bowen, Judy Gott, David Heck, Sally Spillane, Audrey M. Whitbeck; Peter K. Oliver, Admin..—**Historic Dist. Comm.,** Lou V. Burgess, Chm., Joseph Brennan, Digby Brown, Candace Cuniberti, Elyse Harney; Alternates, John Eide, David Elwell, Carol Magowan.—**Municipal Historian,** Virginia Moskowitz.—**Comm. on Aging,** Harold Brien, Maureen Brien, Elizabeth Geer, Walter Palmer, Nancy McL. Peck, Kay Stanton, Frank Winters, Mary Winters; Municipal Agent, Patricia Walsh.—**Welfare Dir.,** Barbara Tobias.—**Dir. of Health,** Torrington Area Health District.—**Recreation Comm.,** George DelPrete, Chm., Lou Bucceri, Kim Guy, Mathias Kiefer, David Neilson, Holly Reid; Arthur Wilkinson, Dir.—**Parks and Forest Comm.,** Mathias Kiefer, Chm., Elyse Harney, William F. Morrill.—**Dir. of Public Works/Building Inspector,** Michael G. Fitting.—**Building Code Bd. of Appeals,** George S. Bushnell, William J. Finney, Robert Royce, Christopher Trotta.—**Tree Warden,** George C. Kiefer, Jr.—**Water Pollution Control Auth.,** Robert Royce, Chm., Richard Barton, Nicholas Branchina, Graham Davidson, Neil Scott.—**Committee on Salisbury's Lakes,** Dale Brown, Chm., Michael Beck, Robert Blank, Russel Conklin, Donald K. Maryland, Judy Moore, Donald Preston, Walter C. Shannon, Jr., Jack Silliman, James Worrall.—**Chief of Fire Dept.,** Donald Reid, Jr.—**Fire Marshal,** Michael G. Fitting.—**Civil Preparedness Dir.,** J. Dean Hammond.—**Town Atty.,** Ralph G. Elliot.—**Justices of the Peace,** Rodney G. Aller, David T. Bayersdorfer, Richard G. Bianchi, Laura Brazee, George S. Bushnell, Christopher M. Dakin, George R. Delprete, Thomas P. Drew, William L. Fox, Sandra L. Gomez, Eugene F. Green, J. Dean Hammond, David F. Harris, Charles J. Hayde, Robert K. Hydon, Sue F. Kirber, Jonathan T. Light, Robert F. Longley, Richard T. Meehan, Jr., John C. Mongeau, Michelle P. Nemiroff, Peter K. Oliver, Nancy McL. Peck, Caroline L. Pope, Louis H. Pressman, Fred J. Romeo, Rosina R. Rossire, Robert H. Rout, Robert L. Tapscott.

SCOTLAND. Windham County.—(Form of government, selectmen, town meeting.)—Inc., May, 1857; taken from Windham. Area, 18.7 sq. miles. Population, est., 1,273. Voting district, 1. Principal industry, agriculture. Transp.—Freight: Served by numerous motor common carriers. The northern part of the town is covered by R.F.D. Hampton and R.F.D. Windham comes into the southwestern part of town and R.F.D. from Baltic to the southeastern part. Post office, Scotland.

TOWN OFFICERS. Clerk and Reg. of Vital Statistics, Nancy O'Connor; Hours, 9 A.M.-3 P.M., Mon., Tues., Thurs.; 12 Noon-8 P.M., Wed.; Address, Town Hall, 9

Devotion Rd., P.O. Box 122, 06264; Tel., Willimantic, (860) 423-9634.—**Asst. Clerk and Asst. Reg. of Vital Statistics,** Irene M. Miller.—**Selectmen,** 1st, Elizabeth A. Wilson (D) Tel., (860) 456-7797, Stephanie Abrahams (R), Joseph Savino (D).—**Treas.,** Zane R. Ring.—**Tax Collector,** Nancy O'Connor.—**Bd. of Assessment Appeals,** Charles H. Lasch, Chm., Alphy Bard, Mark Vaughan.—**Assessor,** Claire M. Foltz.—**Registrars of Voters,** Susan Smith (D), Caroline E. Neborsky (R).—**Supt. of Schools,** A. Rodger Wutzl.—**Bd. of Education,** M. Jolene Bowers, Stephen Nelson, Nancy O'Connor, 1997; Douglas T. Stearns, Chm., Linda Patterson, Margaret Perry, Ellen Schreiber, 1999.—**Planning and Zoning, Inland Wetlands Comm.,** Guy Passarello, Chm., Laurence Miller, Milton Moffitt, Jr., George Perry, James Songailo; Alternates, Amos W. Bill II, Frank Bird, Susan Smith.—**Zoning Bd. of Appeals,** David D. Syme, Chm., Bert B. Asselin, Florence Maschka, David E. Miller, Raymond Shafer; Alternates, Charles Alvord, Sr., Frank Pelc, Sr., Zayne Ring.—**Municipal Historian,** Robert B. Leete.—**Agent for the Elderly,** John S. Pizzi.—**Dir. of Health,** Frank Bird, M.D.—**Library Directors,** Charles Brenker III, Warren Haddon, Linda Patterson, Gail Perry, Lori L. Savino, Timothy W. Sullivan, Rebecca Syme, Marjorie Waig, Carol Withington.—**Building Inspector,** George Guay.—**Sanitarian,** John Valante.—**Building Code Bd. of Appeals,** John Spencer.—**Chief of Police,** Elizabeth A. Wilson.—**Constables,** Joseph Gauvin, Walter Neborsky, Frank Pelc, Alan Perry.—**Chief of Fire Dept.,** Daniel Syme; Deputy, D. Andy Syme.—**Fire Marshal,** Noel Waite.—**Civil Preparedness Dir.,** George Guay.—**Town Atty.,** Lloyd Anderson.—**Justices of the Peace,** Charles E. Alvord, Sr., George A. Guay, Robert B. Leete, Guy T. Passarello, George R. Perry, John S. Pizzi, Susan M. Smith.

SEYMOUR. New Haven County.—(Form of government, selectmen, town meeting, board of finance.)—Inc., May, 1850; taken from Derby. Area, 15.0 sq. miles. Population, est., 14,385. Voting districts, 3. Principal industries, agriculture and manufacture of brass and copper mill products of rod, wire and sheet; high quality electric cable for nuclear power plants, industry and railroads; small tools and several specialized machine shops; precast forms; specialized machining and screw machine products; card and paper packaging, communication equipment. Transp.—Passenger: Served by Metro North Commuter Railroad Co. and by buses of Conn. Transit from New Haven to Seymour. Freight: Served by Boston & Maine Corporation and numerous motor common carriers. Post office, Seymour.

TOWN OFFICERS. Clerk and Reg. of Vital Statistics, Esther W. Rozum; Hours, 9 A.M.-5 P.M., Monday through Friday; Address, Town Hall, 1 First St., 06483; Tel., (203) 888-0519.—**Asst. Clerk,** Susan M. Pawluk.—**Asst. Regs. of Vital Statistics,** Anthony V. Chepulis, Franklyn E. Hull, Carl J. Miller III, Susan M. Pawluk.—**Selectmen,** 1st, John O'Toole (D) Tel., (203) 888-2511, Evelyn Dziadik (D), John F. Greco (D), Eugene Severn (D), Clifford P. Strumello, Jr. (R), Walter Trzcinski (R), Louis J. Zaccaro (D).—**Treas.,** Arthur Davies; Asst., Joseph Gido.—**Bd. of Ethics,** Jerrilyn Klubef, Chm., David Dziadik, Linda Giblin, Eugene Kaschel, Walter Trzcinski.—**Bd. of Finance,** Melanie Kalako, Chm., John D. Conroy, Jr., Thomas H. George, Paul S. Hassler, Frank A. Loda, Michael J. Magut, William D. McLean; Alternates, Nancy Savignano, vacancy.—**Tax Collector,** Marie Somma; Asst., Susan R. Haversat.—**Bd. of Assessment Appeals,** Holly C. LaFrance, Anthony F. LoPresti, Paul Pawlak.—**Assessor,** Edward Czernota.—**Registrars of Voters,** Concetta Criscuolo (D), Elly Mihalcik (R).—**Supt. of Schools,** Eugene Coppola.—**Bd. of Education,** David A. Bruner, Chm., Bruce M. Baker, Robert F. Mihalcik, Jr., Susan M. Pawluk, Frederick D. Stanek, 1997; Judith E. Flood, Vincentena Kobasa, Jeanne Loda, Robert Pagliaro, 1999.—**Civil Service Comm.,** John Greco, Chm., Thomas Eighmie, Laura Kulas, Jeanne Loda, Paul Roy, Jonas Sciuckas, Joyce Tarini.—**Planning and Zoning Comm.,** Ronald Skurat, Chm., Jim Baldwin, Arlene Brumer, Clifford Strumello, vacancy; Alternates, Robert Falbo, Joseph Merhill, Marco Rumbin.—**Zoning Bd. of Appeals,** William Sadick, Chm., Thomas Cherry, John Radovich, Joseph Zamoic; Alternates, Theresa Conroy, Norma Moore, Eugene Severn.—**Zoning Enforcement Officer,** Michael Mormeil.—**Economic Development Comm.,** Frank Stuban, Chm., Joseph Cass, Jack Dillon, Frederick Dlugokenski, Wayne Enama, Reno Migani, Paul Roy.—**Housing Auth.,** David J. Keyser, Secy./Exec. Dir., Karen Baker, Marion Fiasconaro, Mary McLaughlin, Patricia Ripperger, Peter Waniga, Brenda White.—**Conservation and Inland Wetlands Comm.,** John L. Hatfield, Chm., David Cox, Michele Damon, Donald Smith, Sr.—**Comm. on Aging,** John DeBarber, Chm., Gene Kaschel, Mary McLaughlin, John Ploski, Jr., Helen Sherwinsky.—**Dir. of Senior Center,** Lucy McConologue.—**Social Services Dir.,** Joanne Micalizzi.—**Welfare Advisory Bd.,** Concetta Criscuolo, Evelyn Dziadik, June Rapuano.—**Dir. of Health,** Leon J. O'Connor, M.P.H.—**Library Directors,** Sharon Brezniak, David Duff, Ann Golebieski, Joyce D. Jarini, Marianne Jelley, Carol A. Kolb, Diane M. Lombardi, Steven Kulas, Carol A. Soisson.—**Head Librarian,** Wayne Gudzinskas.—**Recreation Comm.,** Edward Strumello, Chm., Sue Cassinalli, Janice Moir, John Pappa, Victor Parkosewich.—**Park Comm.,** Dan Dziadik, Chm., Robert Burns, Robert Dorosh, Joan Fowler, Richard Koalchic.—**Tree Warden,** Keith J. Mitchell.—**Dir. of Public Works,** Salvatore Vicari.—**Bd. of Public Works,** Sal Caramo, Chm., John Greco, Russell Kozey, John Magut, William Talamelli.—**Town Engineer,** Alvin MacBrien.—**Purchasing Agent,** Beatrice Falbo.—**Water Pollution Control Auth.,** Louis Zaccaro, Chm., John Bova, Paul Hassler, Nils Osterberg, Ellen Severn.—**Building Inspector,** Peter Giovacchino.—**Sewer Inspector,** Stanley Gryken.—**Lake Housatonic Auth.,** Brian Anderson, Karl Atkins, C. Firmender, Stanley Ptak, Jr.—**Chief of Police,** Michael Metzler.—**Bd. of Police Comrs.,** Salvatore Carano, Chm., Joyce Abramczyk, Francis Conroy, Jr., John Falbo, Gary H. Freeman.—**Fire Marshal,** Michael Driscoll.—**Chief of Fire Dept.,** John M. Cronin, Sr.; Assts., Gene Atkas, Frank Critchett, Patrick Lombardi.—**Bd. of Fire Comrs.,** Joseph Marcinek, Chm., Borden Brooks, Thomas Jensen, James Kazmierski, Charles Pepe.—**Civil Preparedness Dir.,** William Jarvis.—**Town Atty.,** Colleen Fries.—**Justices of the Peace,** Thomas Amico, Thomas Behuniak, David Brummer, Salvatore Carano, Steven Chucta, Jerry Drugonis, Theresa Eaton, John Falbo, John Greco, Robert Kennedy, Roberta King, Robert Koskelowski, Patrick Lombardi, Sharon McGrath, Michael Moher, Michael D. O'Hara, Sr., Lawrence Ouellette, Sr., Frank Sauerman, Linda D. Sochrin, Frederick Stanek, Ann M. Sullo, James Toth, Karl Trybus, Walter Trzcinski.

SHARON. Litchfield County.—(Form of government, selectmen, town meeting, board of finance.)—Inc., Oct., 1739. Area, 59.6 sq. miles. Population, est., 2,980. Voting district, 1. Principal industry, medical. Transp.—Freight and express: Served by motor common carriers. Post office, Sharon; one R.F.D. route from Sharon.

TOWN OFFICERS. Clerk and Reg. of Vital Statistics, Linda A. Wasley, Hours, 9 A.M.-12 Noon, 1-4 P.M., Mon. through Fri.; Address, Town Hall, 63 Main St., P.O. Box 224, 06069-0224; Tel., (860) 364-5224.—**Asst. Clerks and Asst. Regs. of Vital Statistics,** Tina M. Pitcher, Elizabeth H. Casey.—**Selectmen,** 1st, P. Robert Moeller (R) Tel., (860) 364-5789, Thomas H. Bartram (D), John B. Mathews (R).—**Treas.,** Joan B. Loper.—**Bd. of Finance,** Charles D. Brooks, Chm., Deborah K. Anderson, Austin Jackson, Charles S. Mirabile, Barbara Prindle, Harry Rubicam.—**Tax Collector,** Belle E. Becker.—**Bd. of Assessment Appeals,** Robert A. Day, Mary T. Kirby, William R. Riley III.—**Assessors,** Helen W. Humeston, Chm., Deborah E. Reyelt, Christine R. Snyder.—**Registrars of Voters,** Donna Christensen (D), Susan H. McKee (R).—**Supt. of Schools,** Marvin Maskovsky.—**Bd. of Education,** Nancy B. Bird, David Y. Hall, Timothy Parry, Arthur H. Walters, 1997; Thomas F. Casey, Brian F. Kenny, Orlando C. Mo, 1999.—**Planning and Zoning Comm.,** Barclay W. Prindle, Chm., Richard S. Howes, Stanley MacMillan, Jr., William J. Manasse, W. Peter Reyelt, Jr.; Alternates, James DiMartino, Dona M. Ferry, Cynthia Rubicam.—**Zoning Bd. of Appeals,** Nicholas J. Moore, Chm., Robert L. Fisher, John D. Humeston, Thomas Story, Robert G. Wilbur; Alternates, Judith Larsen, Donald Mowry, Jerome Simonson.—**Zoning Enforcement Officer,** Elizabeth Hall.—**Conservation Comm.,** Phyllis Fillow, Chm., Cicily Hajek, Myrtle Hayden, Doris Stroh, William Tingley, two vacancies.—**Inland Wetlands Comm.,** Edward M. Kirby, Chm., Reed Craig, Michael Dudek, Harvey W. Hayden, John D. Humeston, William J. Manasse, Rebecca Thornton; Alternates, Harold Hoyt, vacancy.—**Flood and Erosion Control Bd.,** Stanley MacMillan, Chm.—**Historic Dist. Comm.,** Jeanne Majdalany, Chm., Geoff Haydock, Sally Keating, Muriel Pitcher, Ilse Reese; Alternates, Donald Clarke, Mimi Landis, Carter Smith.—**Bd. of Recreation and Youth,** Terrance Ryan, Chm., Lynn Kearcher, John Mathews, Susan McKenna, Matthew Mette, Deborah Pitcher, Robert Rathbun.—**Agent for the Elderly,** Ella Clark.—**Dir. of Health,** David A. Kurish, M.D.; Asst., G. S. Gudernatch, M.D.—**Bd. of Public Health,** G. S. Gudernatch, M.D., Chm., Mary Kirby, Elizabeth Smith, Claudia Warner.—**Library Directors,** Harry Rubicam, Pres., Pricilla Buckley, Jerome Cramp, James DiMartino, Jo E. Friday, Richard Hayes, Deborah Manasse, Walter Maytham, Matthew Mette, Kathy Metz, Joyce O'Brien, Robert Pierpont, Judy Schwerin, Herbert Susser, Jean VanRosenbergh, Marie B. Wilbur, vacancy.—**Municipal Historian,** Jeanne Majdalany.—**Building Inspector,** Stanley McMillan.—**Water and Sewer Comm.,** Malcolm M. Brown, Chm., Ken Bartram, William Buehrle, Harry Hall, Mary Whitehead; Alternates, Robert Zabelle, vacancy.—**Sanitarian,** Daniel Baroody; Inspector, Jack Riley.—**Tree Warden,** Scott Monroe.—**Chief of Police,** P. Robert Moeller.—**Constables,** Louis Barney, Charles Janssen, David G. Wilbur, two vacancies.—**Chief of Fire Dept.,** Dana Purdy.—**Fire Marshal,** Stanley MacMillan; Deputy, Michael G. Fitting.—**Civil Preparedness Dir.,** Thomas Bartram.—**Town Atty.,** Judith Dixon (P.O., Winsted).—**Justices of the Peace,** Louise Brown, Estelle Gorkofsky, Richard H. Gottlieb, John D. Humeston, Edward M. Kirby, Eugene Lattimer, Judge Manning, Mary J. P. Moore, Charles A. Paton, Tina M.

Pitcher, Barclay W. Prindle, Elizabeth C. Smith, Jane B. Smith, Charles Snyder, Linda A. Wasley, Mary I. Whitehead, Susan Wilbur.

SHELTON. (Formerly Huntington.) Fairfield County.—(Form of government, mayor, board of aldermen.)—Inc., Jan., 1789; taken from Stratford; city inc., 1915; town and city of Shelton, co-extensive. Area, 31.9 sq. miles. Population, est., 35,762. Voting districts, 4. Principal industries, manufacture of abrasive cut off wheels, air pollution control equipment, asphalt, blow mold plastic products, computer systems, cutlery, cutting tools, electronic optical instruments, electronic relays, electroplate parts, eyelet setting tools, gauges, label manufacturing, manicure implements, metal stampers, postage systems, screwdrivers, silicone and rubber molded products, steel molds, swiss army knives, telephone equipment, therapy systems, x-ray equipment, and wooden reels. Transp.—Passenger: Served by buses of the Connecticut Transit to New Haven. Freight: Served by numerous motor common carriers. Post office, Shelton. The outlying districts receive their mail by rural free delivery from Huntington, Pine Rock Park, and Shelton post offices.

CITY AND TOWN OFFICERS. City Clerk, Town Clerk and Reg. of Vital Statistics, Beverly M. Brown; Hours, 8 A.M.-5:30 P.M., Mon. through Fri.; Address, 54 Hill St., P.O. Box 364, 06484; Tel., Huntington, (203) 924-1555.—**Asst. City and Town Clerk,** Jane Barrese.—**Asst. Regs. of Vital Statistics,** Diana Barry, Anna Kovalsky, Margaret Weber.—**Mayor,** Mark A. Lauretti (R).—**Bd. of Aldermen,** 1st Ward, John Finn, David H. Parkins; 2nd Ward, Edward M. Conklin, Eric J. McPherson; 3rd Ward, John F. Anglace, Jr.; Richard J. Chaffee, Sr., 4th Ward, Walter J. Drozeck, John P. Papa.—**Treas.,** Frank C. Pagliaro, Jr.—**Bd. of Ethics,** Anthony Pagoda, Chm., Antonio DeLallo, Lloyd Witmer.—**Dir. of Finance,** Louis Marusic.—**Bd. of Apportionment and Taxation,** Kenneth F. Nappi, Chm., Martin E. Coughlin, Robert J. Dalton, Esteban Hermanowycz, Harry Jordhamo, Edward J. Kisluk .—**Tax Collector,** Deborah Onderko; Asst., Joan Carpenter.—**Bd. of Assessment Appeals,** Phyllis Sochrin, Chm., William Allan, Robert Tonucci.—**Assessor,** Gloria Kovac; Asst., Phyllis Sobczak.—**Registrars of Voters,** John P. Bashar (D), Charles F. Bucher (R).—**Supt. of Schools,** Leon Sylvester.—**Bd. of Education,** James R. Carey, Sr., Joan E. Cameron, William C. Carr, Stephen Chuckta, Sr., Mary Ann Far, Joseph A. Pagliaro, Jr., Helen M. Schilkowski, Richard W. Sutkowski, Thomas Welch, 1997.—**Personnel Dir.,** vacancy.—**Planning and Zoning Comm.,** Joseph A. Pagliaro, Sr., Chm., Timothy J. Burke, Rudolph J. Cassetti, Jr., Allan Cribbins, Jr., Anthony S. Pagoda, Jr., Leon Sylvester; Alternates, William S. Papale, Valerie R. Szondy.—**Planning Admr.,** vacancy.—**Zoning Bd. of Appeals,** Gerald Glover, Chm., John Fitzgerald, Matthew Gallo, Ralph Matto, Edward Toohey; Alternates, Joseph Ballaro, Sr., Peter Kiman, Anthony Smeriglino.—**Zoning Enforcement Officers,** Lawrence Sheridan, Patrick Tisi.—**Economic Development Comm.,** Frederick Musante, Chm., David Brennan, Patrick Lapera, Karen T. McGovern, Michael Petro; vacancy, Exec. Dir.—**Housing Code Enforcement Officer,** vacancy.—**Housing Auth.,** Ralph Matto, Chm., Regina Dinice, Margaret Domorod, Rose Hinman, Shawn Splan; Carole Mihalick, Exec. Dir.—**Conservation Comm.,** Terry Jones, Harriet Wilber, Co-Chm., Teresa Cichucki, Theresa Gallagher, Soren Ibsen, Gillian Leyden, Edward McCreery III, James W. Tate, vacancy.—**Inland Wetlands Comm.,** Alvaro DaSilva, Chm., Joseph Ballaro, Jr., Celeste Beattie, Michael V. Rosso, Norman Santa, Randy Szkola, Gary Zahornasky; Alternates, Richard N. Hayes, Jr., Denis Sheehy.—**Municipal Historian,** Jeannette LaMacchia.—**Municipal Parking Auth.,** Frank Waldhaus, Chm., Ernestine Luise, Jeffrey Merrill, William Papale, Dean Russell.—**Public Employees Appeals Bd.,** Frank Dyer, Chm., Michael Davis, Raymond O'Leary, Norman Santa, vacancy.— **Senior Citizens Comm.,** Robert Weiss, Chm., Linda Hooper, Shirley Keller, Francis Klos, Joseph Lanzi, George Ryan, William Smarz, Regina Zamba.—**Welfare Dir.,** vacancy.—**Valley Health Dist.,** David Beardsley, Mary Casalveri, Grace Monahan, Daniel Taylor.—**Library Directors,** Barbara Glover, Chm., Catherine B. Araujo, Mary R. Bonaccorso, Harriet H. Finn, Shirley Hubbs, Carlyn J. Rehnberg.—**Drug and Alcohol Comm.,** Mary Casalveri, Chm., Patricia Belade, Carol Hellauer, Eileen Litscher, Shirley McEwen, Grace Monahan, vacancy.—**Parks and Recreation Comm.,** John Papa, Chm., Richard Belden, John Browne, Gary Cahill, Joseph DeFilippo, Paul Gabor, Stanley Kudej, Harold LaBonda, Joseph Puopolo, Augustine Riccio, Regina Zamba, Robert Zuraw; Victor Cook, Dir.—**Dir. of Public Works,** Paul DiMauro.—**City Engineer,** Robert F. Kulacz.—**Purchasing Agent,** Thomas Peterson.—**Supt. of Highways,** Edwin J. Hellauer.—**Sealer of Weights and Measures,** Jean Casertano.—**Building Inspector,** Frank Kullberg.—**Building Code Bd. of Appeals,** Wesley Blakeman, Chm., Jules Cayer, L. Harold Jordhamo, Joseph Lanzi, Joseph Salemme.—**Water Pollution Control Auth.,** Matthew Gallo, Chm., Steve Balog, Jr., Frank D'Angelo, G. Michael DeAngelis, Edwin T. Hellauer, William Hurd, Jr., Anthony Luther, Bronislaw Piotrowski.—**Housatonic Lake Auth.,** John Hubyk, Max Jaroszewski, Edward Kisluk.—**Tree Warden,** Dean Cawthra.—**Sanitarian,** Jeffrey Shortell.—**Chief of Police,** Robert White, Jr.—**City Sheriffs,** Richard Olscyk, George Anthony, Patricia Randall.—**Chief of Fire Dept.,** James Lagomarsino; Deputies, Thomas DeMarco, Soren Ibsen.—**Fire Marshal,** James Tortora.—**Bd. of Fire Comrs.,** Charles Sutton, Chm., Kevin Ahern, William Brennan, Bruce Kosowsky, Wayne Travers.—**Civil Preparedness Dir.,** Deane Moss.—**Corporation Counsel,** John Welch; Asst., Ramon Sous.—**Justices of the Peace,** Joseph Ballaro, Allan W. Cameron, Gary J. DeFilippo, Michael DeFilippo, Harriet H. Finn, Susan Finn, Florian F. Folger, Jr., Matthew P. Gallo, Estaban Hermanowicz, John Lauretti, Arch Manzione, Karen McGovern, Dominick C. Mondi, Sandra Nesteriak, Clarence W. Oppel III, Monica Peterson, Jean Polson, Stanley Reichlin, Edward Rockett, Joseph A. Sewack, Edward J. Sheehy, Danielle Smith, Ezio Staffieri, Frank B. Waldhaus, David Zitnay.

SHERMAN. Fairfield County.—(Form of government, selectmen, town meeting.)—Inc., Oct., 1802; taken from New Fairfield. Area, 23.4 sq. miles. Population, est., 3,034. Voting district, 1. Principal industry, agriculture. Transp.—Freight: Served by numerous motor common carriers. Post office, Sherman.

TOWN OFFICERS. Clerk and Reg. of Vital Statistics, Carol L. Havens; Hours, 9 A.M.-12 Noon, 1-4 P.M., Tues. through Fri.; 9 A.M.-12 Noon, Sat.; Address, Mallory Town Hall, 9 Rte. 39, P.O. Box 39, 06784; Tel., (860) 354-5281.—**Asst. Clerk and Asst. Reg. of Vital Statistics,** Ellen M. Grant.—**Selectmen,** 1st, Donna D. Tuck (D), Tel., (860) 355-1139, Michael H. Crawford (R), Anthony V. Hapanowich (R).—

Treas., Ellen M. Grant.—**Tax Collector,** Patricia G. Werme.—**Bd. of Assessment Appeals,** John M. Richards, Chm., Elizabeth S. Beatty, Matthew Lambrech.—**Assessors,** Michelle J. Hansen, Chm., Elizabeth C. Hanson, Richard J. McGoldrick.—**Registrars of Voters,** Joan Oesterling (D), William Tiebout III (R).—**Supt. of Schools,** Michael J. Perrone.—**Bd. of Education,** Joyce F. Kjep, George O. Linkletter, Carol A. Muska, 1997; Pamela R. Bonner, Paul J. Mucci, Carol S. Roberts, Fern L. Wagner, vacancy, 1999.—**Planning and Zoning Comm.,** William R. Jones, Jr., Chm., Margaret Bessel, Tom Joyner, James T. MacGregor, William Tiebout III, John P. Voorhees, Maryann Yanarella; Alternates, Gary Albert, Alex Alexander, Thomas Salat.—**Zoning Bd. of Appeals,** John P. McRoberts, Chm., Helen E. Bray, Kathleen Fazzone, Rosemarie Seligmann, Guido Tino; Alternates, Robert Casazza, Joseph Chiaramonte, Henry Dutton.—**Zoning Enforcement Officer,** Ernest Winkler.—**Conservation Comm.,** James French.—**Inland Wetlands Comm.,** John Bethel, Chm., Donald Coons, Anthony H. Gwyther, Margery Josephson, Wilfried Knaak, Nancy MacGregor, David P. Schneider; Alternates, Laura Baxter, Patricia Endress, Alan Ostrom.—**Historic Dist. Comm.,** Janet Hopkins, Chm., Robert Boone, Alice Schneckenburger, Elizabeth Scholze, Richard Wey.—**Committee on Aging,** Jaye Eike, William Fishwick, Raymond Giddings, Frances Murray, Lloyd R. Thompson.—**Agent for the Elderly,** Linda I. Knaak.—**Dir. of Social Services,** Anthony V. Hapanowich.—**Dir. of Health,** Daniel Baroody.—**Library Directors,** Eileen Rowland, Pres., Judith Brown, Margaret Cook, Jacqueline Crawford, Michelle Hansen, Ann Klueg, Lorraine Kupper, Nancy Mandeville, Lee Martin, Gilbert Singco, Claire Taplin.—**Park and Recreation Comm.,** Frances M. Frattini, Chm., Timothy Beatty, Christine Lent, Henry McDermott, Brian Meenan, Alan Rowburrey.—**Building Inspector,** William Jenks.—**Candlewood Lake Auth.,** William Bray, Hugh Hawkins, Charles Reppenhagen.—**Tree Warden,** James Munch.—**Sanitarian,** Keith Vaughn.—**Chief of Police,** Anthony V. Hapanowich.—**Constables,** Timothy J. Beatty, Gordon Braislin, Joel A. Judd, William F. Knipple, Richard McGoldrick, Benjamin A. Palagonia, Guido Tino.—**Chief of Fire Dept.,** George Barbiero.—**Fire Marshal,** Ernest Winkler.—**Civil Preparedness Dir.,** Anthony V. Hapanowich.—**Justices of the Peace,** Robert D. Bradshaw, Robert A. Casazza, Theodore D. Giddings, Kenneth A. Johnson, Wilfried, Knaak, William F. Knipple, Richard J. McGoldrick, John McRoberts, John D. O'Connor, Benjamin A. Palagonia, Regina Ryan, Guido J. Tino.

SIMSBURY. Hartford County.—(Form of government, first selectman, board of selectmen, town meeting, board of finance.)—Named, May, 1670. Area, 34.3 sq. miles. Population, est., 22,066. Voting districts, 4. Principal industries, agriculture, insurance offices, non-electric blast initation systems, poly propelene fibre manufacturing, and safety and detonating fuse making. Transp.—Passenger: Served by buses of Conn. Transit (Commuter) from Granby and Hartford. Freight: Numerous motor common carriers. Air: Simsbury (private) Airport. Post offices, Simsbury, West Simsbury, Tariffville and Weatogue.

TOWN OFFICERS. Clerk and Reg. of Vital Statistics, Carolyn D. Keily; Hours, 8:30 A.M.-4:30 P.M., Mon. through Fri.; Address, Town Office Bldg., 933 Hopmeadow St., P.O. Box 495, 06070; Tel., (860) 658-3200.—**Asst. Clerks and Asst. Regs.**

of Vital Statistics, MaryAnn C. Lipski, Mary N. Turner.—**First Selectmen,** 1st, Mary A. Glassman (D) Tel., (860) 658-3230; FAX (860) 658-9467, Candace V. Fitzpatrick (R), William F. Garrity (D), Joel Mandell (R), Anita L. Mielert (D), Helen K. Peterson (D).—**Town Moderator,** Donald W. Tuller.—**Treas.,** Kevin G. Kane.—**Bd. of Finance,** Peter K. Askham, James F. Belfiore, Jane L. Carroll, Robert W. Heagney, Paul W. Henault, Michael T. Wade; Kevin G. Kane, Dir.—**Bd. of Ethics,** Joseph E. Grasso, Chm., Richard A. Fortier, Jewel A. Gutman, Glenn E. Knierim, Vincent Kraft, Michael H. Lanza.—**Tax Collector,** Kathleen T. Hayes.—**Bd. of Assessment Appeals,** William G. B. Gardner, Chm., John P. Bruno, Paul F. Pendergast.—**Assessor,** Richard K. Wandy.—**Registrars of Voters,** Lois W. Calvert (D), Sara M. Twitchell (R).—**Supt. of Schools,** Joseph Townsley.—**Bd. of Education,** John O'Neil, Jr., Mary P. Wright, Norman L. Shipley, Jacob Wieselman, 1997; Susanna F. Robillard, Chm., Mary M. Girgenti, Richard A. Hogan, Robert R. Moran, Jr., 1999.—**Zoning Comm.,** Michael J. Bradley, Chm., Austin D. Barney II, Susan M. Case, James W. Gallagher, George T. Neu, Tara D. Willerup; Alternates, Patricia K. Askham, Edward M. Cosgrove, John J. Yorkin.—**Planning Comm.,** Nancy S. Stevens, Chm., Susan Bednarcyk, Deborah Freedman, David Horowitz, Joan W. Howard, Pamela B. Katz; Alternates, Ernest B. Gardow, Duncan R. MacKay, Michael L. Martin.—**Town Planner,** Leonard D. Tolisano.—**Zoning Bd. of Appeals,** Peter A. Stempien, Chm., Valerie E. Beaudreau, James J. Daley, Paul N. Gilmore, Thomas Horan, Bradford Mead; Alternates, Roger M. Eisenstein, Madeleine Gilkey, Robert M. Mule.—**Economic Development Comm.,** Charles D. Houlihan, Jr., Chm., Larry Alan, Peter K. Askham, Jeffrey Blumenthal, Sean M. Fitzpatrick, John J. Molloy, Barbara Petitjean, Maureen Weinberger, Ann Winship.—**Fair Rent Comm.,** Dolores deNagy, Chm., Kathryn Cooper, Michael L. Martin, Angele Mokhiber, Geraldine Muench, Rose Pollock, Norman L. Shipley.—**Public Building Committee,** Richard E. Ostop, Chm., Odvard M. Bergethon, David M. Katz, Mary D. Lyons, Mary Lou Patrina, Alice G. Rowland, Dan Smolnick, C. E. Valentine, vacancy.—**Regional Affairs Sub-Committee,** Anita Mielert, Chm., Suzanne Besser, Paul A. Ehrhardt, Candace Fitzpatrick, Don Jaeckel, Ferguson Jansen, Michael Paine, Helen Peterson, Paul Stein.—**Housing Auth.,** Richard C. Meyer, Chm., Lawrence P. Bock, John Earwaker, Jr., Doris Farmer, Lorry Schwartz; Herbert Salch, Dir.—**Conservation and Inland Wetlands Comm.,** M. Howard Beach, Jr., Chm., Richard A. Miller, Jr., William Nowak, Karl H. Pech, Thomas W. Sharpless, Helene Wade, John E. Yocom; Alternates, Andrew Bucknam, R. Pierce Clayberger.—**Conservation Planning Analyst,** Christie Barton.—**Aging and Disability,** Arline Bidwell, Chm., Priscilla Bergethon, Margaret C. Diachenko, Janet N. Fisk, Dorothy M. Goulart, Elizabeth Horrigan, Gloria K. Knierim, Ann M. Long, Mary P. Mitchell, Nancy M. Roby, Frances M. Sarnecki, Gwendolyn Simpson; Alternates, Esther R. Bartlett, Rose McGurkin-Fuhr, Edward L. LaMontagne, Charlotte Steptoe.—**Health and Welfare Comm.,** Robert A. Dachik, Chm., Allan J. Clark, Anthony L. Drapelick, Marilyn Fierri, Patricia A. LaMontagne, Michael J. Lefebvre, Huguet P. C. Pamcijcr, Marilyn J. Tyszka, vacancy.—**Human Relations Comm.,** Sanjoy K. Goyle, Patricia LaMontagne, vacancy.—**Library Directors,** Gail K. Ryan, Chm., Carol M. Bingham, Kathleen Cockcroft, Ann D. M. Erickson, Barbara C. Gardner, Christopher R. Morkan.—**Historic Dist. Comm.,** James W. Oliver, Chm., William Albert, James Cobbledick, Mark Taub, Elizabeth Woollacott; Alternates, Kennneth Feder, Susanne H.

Lanza, Dianne Mead.—**Culture Parks and Recreation Comm.,** Peter Calnen, Chm., Maureen Celli, Joseph P. Grace, Jr., Linda Johnson, Mary Liljedahl, Charles J. Nicol, Harry Ryan, Jeffrey Siegel, Thomas C. Wassel; Gerard G. Toner, Dir.—**Beautification Committee,** Barbara Howard, Chm., Lois Chase, Linda Domurat, Judith Forbes, Marcia Higgins, Marilyn Yates.—**Dir. of Public Works,** Richard L. Sawitzke.—**Supt. of Highways,** Walter McDonald.—**Town Engineer,** Richard L. Sawitzke.—**Building Official,** Arthur W. Hanke; Assts., Robert J. Campbell, Guy R. Morin.—**Building Code Bd. of Appeals,** Michael A. Girard, Chm., Robert W. Bounds, Emil T. Dahlquist, Thomas Hammick, Paul E. Holland; Alternates, Stephen Garrity, vacancy.—**Water Pollution Control Auth.,** Richard S. Lange, Chm., Richard Buggy, Jr., Phillip A. Burton, Warren B. Coe, Richard S. Order, Terrance Piotrowicz, Martha Schwartz.—**Chief of Police,** Alfred L. Shull.—**Bd. of Police Comm.,** Kathleen Colket, Chm., John E. Carroll, Edward M. Cosgrove, Carl D. Eisenman, Edward H. Simpson.—**Chief of Fire Dept.,** Mark Kerr; Deputy, Kevin J.Kowalski; Assts., James Baldis, James Mead, Thomas Post.—**Fire Marshal,** Kevin J. Kowalski.—**Bd. of Fire Comrs.,** Donald F. Washburn, Chm., Lawrence Gauvain, George Van Wormer.—**Civil Preparedness Dir.,** Reynold L. Hoover.—**Town Attys.,** Cummings & Lockwood.—**Justices of the Peace,** Margaret W. Albert, David C. Balboni, Susan M. Bednarcyk, Arline Bidwell, Peter Calnen, Lois Calvert, Thomas F. Carey, Donna M. Case-Rossato, Albert H. Castricum, Michael J. Daly, Jeanne Delehanty, Dolores G. deNagy, J. Philip Denison, Margaret C. Diachenko, Michael Dropick, Carl D. Eisenman, James Gallagher, Anne Marie Goodrow, Jewel A. Gutman, Kathleen T. Hayes, John K. Jepson, Bertram Kaplan, Robert J. LaMontagne, Jr., Michael Lanza, Gerald L. Lintner, Ann Long, Joel Mandell, Shirley Metzger, John Molloy, James Oliver, Mary Ann Ostop, Barbara A. Petitjean, Suzanne Piotrowicz, Patricia Scanlon, Lorry Schwartz, Scott G. Shanks, Arthur Sokol, Peter A. Stempien, William Tyszka, Michael Wade, Richard D. Wagner, Tara Willerup.

SOMERS. Tolland County.—(Form of government, selectmen, town meeting, board of finance.)—Named, July, 1734; annexed to Connecticut, May, 1749. Area, 28.5 sq. miles. Population, est., 9,996. Voting districts, 2. Principal industries, agriculture and diversified industry. Transp.—Freight: Served by numerous motor common carriers. Post offices, Somers and Somersville. Rural free delivery from Somers post office, four routes.

TOWN OFFICERS. Clerk and Reg. of Vital Statistics, Claire L. Walker; Hours, 8:30 A.M.-4:30 P.M., Mon. through Wed., 8:30 A.M.-7:30 P.M., Thurs., 8:30 A.M.-12:30 P.M., Fri.; Address, Town Hall, 600 Main St., P.O. Box 308, 06071; Tel., (860) 763-8206.—**Asst. Clerk and Asst. Reg. of Vital Statistics,** Ann Marie Logan.—**Selectmen,** Richard H. Jackson III (R), Phillips H. Roland (R), vacancy.—**Treas.,** Edward J. Sullivan.—**Bd. of Finance,** James W. Persano, Chm., John Bowles, Stephen P. Krasinski, Jr., Marilyn W. Pronovost, Timothy J. Vecchiarelli, George F. Warner.—**Tax Collector,** Edward Jekot.—**Bd. of Assessment Appeals,** Gregory J. Pac, Chm., Robert A. Pfeifer, Timothy Vecchiarelli.—**Assessors,** Robert Loubier, Chm., Everett E. Morrill, Joan M. Rivard.—**Registrars of Voters,** Joan M. Rivard (D), Marjory R. Madden (R).—**Supt. of Schools,** Paul Gagliarducci.—**Bd. of Education,** Janice Budington, Chm., Dean P. Hills, Andrew K. Rockett, Julia M. Salerno, Charlotte C. Stopa, 1997; Edward J. Dymek, Jr., Kathryn A. Klein, Janice S. Martin, David Pinney, 1999.—**Planning Comm.,** Richard E. Allan, Chm., Wayne Bickley, Michael Collins, David Palmer, Leonard Viera; Alternates, John Bowles, Elwood A. Clifford, vacancy.—**Zoning Comm.,** Lee Hall, Chm., Patricia A. Jones, Robert E. Landry, Deborah Numrych, Henry Singer; Alternates, three vacancies.—**Zoning Bd. of Appeals,** John Torres, Chm., Ed Mack, Sr., Edna Pellissier, Martin Steinmetz, vacancy; Alternates, Henry Bednarz, Jr., Arnold I. Cowan, Peter L. Klein.—**Zoning Enforcement Officer,** Patrice Carson.—**Conservation and Inland Wetlands Comm.,** Simon Lipton, Chm., Richard E. Allan, Sharon Fales, Joan S. Formeister, Steven P. Kayan, Maurice Rondeau, Donald P. Smith.—**Advisory Committee to the Elderly,** Patricia A. Broer, Alvina C. Burgess, Johanna M. Carr, Ralph Lumb, Harriet K. Osborn, Linda Pease, Dora E. Randall, Arlene Yarnes.—**Agent for the Elderly,** Conrad McIntire, Jr.—**Dir. of Health,** Richard Segool, M.D.—**Housing Auth.,** Raymond Colton, Chm., Donna Allard, Joanne Batchelor, Ernestine Cormier, Bonnie D. Kumiega; Anthony Pellegrino, Exec. Dir.—**Library Directors,** Shirley E. Warner, Chm., Carl Alsing, Kathleen A. Devlin, Darlene A. Lemiech, Patrick Mahon, Marguerite M. McTeague, Dee M. Moak, Laura T. Nesta, Bruce D. Tyler.—**Recreation Comm.,** Peter J. Embriano, Chm., Patricia Bachetti, Thomas A. Chilicki, Gwyn Hight, Peter C. Lewis, Linda R. Nyquist, Peter Stevens; Conrad McIntire, Dir.—**Building Inspector,** Robert Lauzier.—**Building Code Bd. of Appeals,** Alan Seagrave, Chm., Wayne Bickley, Richard W. Larson, Robert Loubier, John Panciera.—**Water Pollution Control Auth.,** James A. Botellio, Chm., Charles Colby, Daniel A. Fraro, Stephen Getman, Charles Gudaitis, Elinor Labutis, Simon Lipton, George W. Vantasel, Jr., vacancy.—**Sanitarian,** Steven Jacobs.—**Chief of Police,** Robert B. Percoski.—**Constables,** David A. Desso, Jr., David C. Desso, Edward Fedorowich, vacancy.—**Chief of Fire Dept.,** Edward F. Pagani, Jr.—**Fire Marshal,** David C. Desso; Asst., Robert Austin.—**Bd. of Fire Comrs.,** Peter Lewis, Chm., Anthony J. Bruno, Robert McCulloch, Jr., Carl Rohrbach, Jr., Gary R. Wysocki.—**Civil Preparedness Dir.,** Eugene E. Allard.—**Town Atty.,** Thomas Fahey.—**Justices of the Peace,** Charles E. Alfano, Harry C. Bergstrom, Ethel S. Botnick, Francis W. Devlin, Jr., Leon Dolby, Donald H. Kennett, Jeffrey M. Lipton, Simon Lipton, Marjory Madden, Marianne H. Myracle, Gregory J. Pac, Edna G. Pellissier, Robert B. Percoski, James W. Persano, Peter B. Smith, Rebecca Smith, Jane M. Tyler, Paul R. Washburn.

SOUTHBURY. New Haven County.—(Form of government, selectmen, town meeting, board of finance.)—Inc., May, 1787; taken from Woodbury. Area, 40.0 sq. miles. Population, est., 15,702. Voting districts, 5. Principal industries, IBM, ice cream and Com-Sat tracking station. Location of Southbury Training School. Transp.—Passenger: Served by buses of Bonanza Bus Lines, Inc. from Danbury, Waterbury, Hartford and New York, and Connecticut Limousine Service to airports. Freight: Served by numerous motor common carriers. Post offices, Southbury and South Britain.

TOWN OFFICERS. Clerk and Reg. of Vital Statistics, Joyce K. Hornbecker; Hours, 8:30 A.M.-4:30 P.M., Monday through Friday; Address, Town Hall, 501 Main

St. South, 06488-2295; Tel., Southbury, (203) 262-0657.—**Asst. Clerks and Asst. Regs. of Vital Statistics,** Geraldine B. DeVoid, Lynn S. Dwyer.—**Selectmen,** 1st, Alfio A. Candido, Jr. (R) Tel., (203) 262-0647, FAX, (203) 264-9762, Donald A. Briggs (R), Mark A. R. Cooper (R), Jeffrey B. Hughes (D), Joan H. King (D), David M. Mathieu (R).—**Treas./Fiscal Officer,** William G. Sarosky.—**Bd. of Finance,** John A. Michaels, Chm., Mark A. Burns, Michael D. Dagostino, Wolcott B. Jones, Arthur J. Mulligan, Richard J. Youdin; Alternates, three vacancies.—**Tax Collector,** Barbara M. Ford.—**Bd. of Assessment Appeals,** Joseph W. Bette, Thomas W. Hill, Stephen M. McCoy.—**Assessor,** Joseph C. Ferraro, Chm.; Asst., Jacqueline P. Demchak.—**Registrars of Voters,** Catherine L. Bedard (D), Sabina F. Andricovich (R).—**Supt. of Schools,** Louis J. Esparo.—**Bd. of Education,** Carol S. Hubert, Stephen P. Moore, Patricia S. Perry, 1997; Steven P. Kammerer, Hendrik E. Mass, Joseph J. Zukoski III, 1999.—**Zoning Comm.,** Donna J. Civitello, Leonard Goldberg, Norman R. Mackie, Edward Wildman, Jr., vacancy; Alternates, Gary J. Giroux, Jeremiah J. O'Brien, Jeri R. Quy.—**Planning Comm.,** Harold W. Davis, Jr., Chm., Tekin Akalin, Donald S. Antilla, James J. Donahue, Gary W. Metcalf, Hugh J. Sullivan; Alternates, Gail DePietro, two vacancies.—**Zoning Bd. of Appeals,** Lemuel G. Johnson, Jr., Chm., J. Peirce Behrendt, Lowell Brody, William Kudon, Jonathan S. Metcalf, Peter W. Peterson; Alternates, Leigh A. Metcalf, Clement L. Segale, Paul E. Sullivan.—**Acting Zoning Enforcement Officer,** Mark D. Cody.—**Economic Development Comm.,** James S. Wilkie, Chm., Gordon M. Cooper, Franklin W. Kennedy, Frank Matula, Richard J. Turner; Alternates, George E. Ritter, James A. Rousmaniere, vacancy.—**Conservation Comm.,** Edward L. Nagy, Chm., Mieke J. Crider, Vincent G. DiCara, Alfred E. Kilgour, Richard D. Matika, Rebecca R. Parsons, John C. Perham.—**Inland Wetlands Comm.,** Paul A. Palmer, Chm., Blair F. Bertaccini, Nelson M. Camp, David W. Liedlich, Scott Martin, William G. Wadman; Deborah Seavey, Enforcement Officer; Alternates, Permelia C. Cognato, William C. Spencer, vacancy.—**Historic Dist. Comm.,** Benjamin Stiles, Chm., Barbara G. Bowen, Laurel A. Casazza, Meta W. Hinze, Beulah H. Tappe; Alternates, Richard S. Cunliffe, R. Carl Kamphausen, Sharon L. Lawler-Guck.—**Municipal Historian,** vacancy.—**Comm. on Services for the Elderly,** Linda P. Salvagne, Chm., Phyllis Burgess, Mary T. Cooper, Carol Damon, Anita Hamilton, Eleanor R. McLellan, Angela S. Rogers; Loryn Ray, Municipal Agent.—**Social Services Dir.,** Sandra Saren.—**Dir. of Health,** Neal A. Lustig.—**Library Directors,** Shirley S. Michaels, Chm., Florence O. Camp, Patricia Clisham, Carol A. Fine, William Lassow, Jeraldine Wenkert-Larson, vacancy; Alternates, Eleanor M. Ackerman, Valerie S. Oliverira, Edwin Suib.—**Parks and Recreation Comm.,** Patrick V. Clark, Chm., Glenn A. Ackerman, Charles C. Guck, Thomas W. Hill, Charles D. Rosa, Robert C. Williams, Gilbert H. Zawadski, Jr.; Patricia Regan, Dir.—**Road Foreman,** George Metcalf.—**Building Inspector,** Mark D. Cody; Asst., vacancy.—**Building Code Bd. of Appeals,** Edward Cox, Arthur E. Olsen, three vacancies.—**Tree Warden,** John F. Hennessey.—**Pomperaug Valley Water Auth.,** Samuel P. Williams III, Chm., two vacancies.—**Water Pollution Control Auth.,** Kevin J. Goyette, Robert Perrella, Jr., Morris Price, two vacancies.—**Lake Authorities,** Zoar: A. Stuart Wilson, Jr., Chm., Peter N. Edmonds, John D. Harold. Lillinonah: James P. Cullinan, Robert C. Gumbardo, Robert H. Moss.—**Sanitarian,** Joseph Kmetz.—**Chief of Police,** Alfio A. Candido, Jr.—**Constables,** Robert F. Bette, Kevin M. Burns, Thomas J. Gugliotti, Jr.,

James E. Houle, Brian C. Hughes, Patrick M. Kenney, Duane S. Manville, Donald L. Nevins III, Michael J. Ohrn, Christopher P. O'Toole, Carl E. Rosa, Cynthia S. Schneider, George J. Slaiby, Francis E. Tierney, Jr., two vacancies.—**Chief of Fire Dept.,** Vincent A. Soares.—**Fire Marshal,** Robert A. Brinley, Jr.—**Civil Preparedness Dir.,** Richard Wildman.—**Town Atty.,** Lawrence Hager.—**Justices of the Peace,** Joseph W. Bette, Lynne M. Campbell, Clarke R. Egeler, Judith A. Eslami, Edmund R. Heebner, Joyce K. Hornbecker, Murray Kass, William Kudon, Norman R. Mackie, John B. McKeone, Eleanor R. McLellan, Sandra G. Moser, Krishnalal I. Nanavaty, Raymond F. Perkins, Albert M. Pichey, Trudy H. Telychka, Silvia F. Tirrell, Louis V. Trifari, William G. Wadman, Granville Weng, William N. Woodward, Jr, Karen R. Zarcone.

SOUTHINGTON. Hartford County.—(Form of government, town manager, town council.)—Inc., Oct., 1779; taken from Farmington. Town and borough consolidated, 1947. Area, 36.6 sq. miles. Population, est., 38,565. Voting districts, 10. Principal industries, agriculture and manufacture of hardware, tinners' and carpenters' tools, plumbing supplies, bolts, aircraft engine parts, grey iron and automobile forgings, brass products, paper boxes, discs, filters, labeling equipment, mixers, pumps, tanks, wood screws, carriage hardware, springs, toys, agitators, bottle fillers, cappers, pallets, hypodermic needles, soap suds, food products. Transp.—Freight: Served by Boston & Maine Corporation and numerous motor common carriers. Post offices, Southington, Plantsville, Milldale and Marion.

TOWN OFFICERS. Clerk and Reg. of Vital Statistics, Leslie G. Cotton; Hours, 8:30 A.M.-4:30 P.M., Mon. through Fri., 8:30 A.M.-7 P.M., Thurs.; Address, Town Office Bldg., 75 Main St., 06489; Tel., (860) 276-6211.—**Asst. Clerks and Asst. Regs. of Vital Statistics,** Mary Dickinson, Kathy Larkin.—**Town Manager,** John Weichsel.—**Town Council,** Andrew J. Meade, Chm., William V. DePaolo, Thomas P. Langdon, Edward M. Malczyk, Leonard Marcheselle, Michael A. Rossi, Sr., Victoria E. Triano, James M. Verderame, James A. Wallace, Jr.—**Treas.,** Richard Lopatosky.—**Bd. of Ethics,** Stephen A. Pomposi, Quito Rossi, Robert Triano, Michael A. Ziebka.—**Bd. of Finance,** Thomas Benevelli, Joseph L. Petrone, Philip Pomposi, Constance C. Proll, Joseph Putala, vacancy; James Bowes, Dir.—**Tax Collector,** Alice Gray.—**Bd. of Assessment Appeals,** Michael Bunko, Thomas E. Gomberg, Theresa Monte.—**Assessor,** Herbert Braasch.—**Registrars of Voters,** Mary Nolan (D), Robert Sherman (R).—**Supt. of Schools,** Louis D. Saloom.—**Bd. of Education,** David J. Derynoski, Richard Montagne, Louis A. Perillo III, Edward S. Pocock III, 1997; Janice McDonald, Chm., Nicholas J. DePaola, Joyce Kogut, Zaya A. Oshana, Elizabeth Platt-Suski, 1999.—**Planning and Zoning Comm.,** Carl P. Verderame, Jr., Chm., Mary Baker, Francis J. Kenefick, Sherri L. Kulas, Dolores Longo, Michael A. Riccio, Frederick Serafino; Alternates, Ann M. Casale, Martin Jansen, David Mastrianni, Robert S. Oshana.—**Town Planner,** Robert Nerney.—**Zoning Bd. of Appeals,** Douglas C. Hageman, Chm., Gail Cianci, Michael Clynes, Richard McDonough, Robert Sherman; Alternates, Doran S. Height, Jr., Joseph LaPorte, Jon Rustek, Robert Y. Salka.—**Zoning Enforcement Officer,** Frank Vinci.—**Economic Development Comm.,** Francis Massucci, Chm., Robert J. Andrews, Anthony D'Angelo, Dominic DiNeno, Russel Hayden, Sr.—**Housing Auth.,** James Shanley, Chm., Jeanne C. Carey, Carol A. Hageman, Joseph Thornton, Jeffrey Wight.—**Conservation Comm.,** Donald Wells, Chm., Madeline Brunelli, Robert Faro, Saverio Longo, Marjorie C. Montague, Eric Monte, M. Stewart Ramsay.—**Comm. on Aging,** Arthur Dellvecchia, Chm., Ann Casale, John D'Angelo, Helene Delahanty, Beverly Perry, Katrina Pocock, Dorothy Riccio, Peter Santago, Sr., Earl M. Temchin.—**Welfare Dir.,** John Weichsel.—**Dir. of Health,** vacancy.—**Library Directors,** Margaret Nevelos, Chm., Allan J. Ballinger, Heidi K. Bittner, Anthony E. D'Angelo, David A. Della Vecchia, Lorenzo W. Langdon, Edward S. Pocock, Susan Reisman, Dorothy M. Testa.—**Parks and Recreation Dept.,** David Kanute, Joseph LaPorte, Joanne Palmieri, Peter P. Sepko, Charles J. Torino; Richard Egidio, Parks Supt.; William Masci, Recr. Supt.—**Tree Warden,** John Calvanese.—**Town Engineer,** Anthony J. Tranquillo.—**Supt. of Sewers,** John DeGioia.—**Supt. of Highways,** John Mayo.—**Building Inspector,** Pascal DellaVecchia.—**Building Bd. of Appeals,** Edward Delahunty, Chm., Philip Foss, Joseph LaPorte, James Putnam, Richard K. White.—**Water Comm.,** Lawrence S. Johnson, Chm., James J. Feltz, David Hubbs, Thomas Janik, Paul Jiantonio, Norman Van Cor.—**Supt. of Water Dept.,** Gilbert Bligh.—**Sanitarian,** John Fazzolari.—**Chief of Police,** William Perry.—**Police Comm.,** William Welch, Chm., Bruce M. Cotton, Henry E. Forgione II, Anthony S. Pizzitola, Francis Verderame.—**Constables,** Jeanne C. Carey, Claudia Castro, Richard Cianci, Michael F. Clynes, George F. Hayes, Joseph Sollack, vacancy.—**Chief of Fire Dept./Fire Marshal,** Richard McDonough; Asst. Chief, Thomas R. Wisner.—**Bd. of Fire Comrs.,** Thomas Kupec, Chm., Felix S. Albrycht, Kevin R. Daly, Leonard Hudak, Edward Maigaire.—**Town Atty.,** David P. Kelley; Asst., John T. Nugent.—**Justices of the Peace,** Harry A. Barron, Jr., John L. Campbell, Michael Carbone, Anthony A. Denorfia, Kenneth W. DiMauro, Douglas J. Gregory, George P. Griffin, Douglas C. Hageman, Doris Hanser, Leonard J. Hudak, Donna-Marie P. Kehoss, Margaret Kennedy, Joseph Klepacki, Dolores L. Longo, Leonard Marcheselle, Theresa D. Monte, Georgette C. Nadeau, John T. Nugent, Constance C. Proll, Tara L. Rich, Rae L Robinson, Robert E. Roy, Robert L. Sherman, Mary Elllen Volscho.

SOUTH WINDSOR. Hartford County.—(Form of government, town manager, town council.)—Inc., May, 1845; taken from East Windsor. Area, 28.7 sq. miles. Population, est., 22,382. Voting districts, 6. Principal industries, fuel cell power plants, automatic numerically controlled drafting machines, digitizers, graphic systems, CAD/CAM systems, photoplotters, artwork generators, electronic and electromechanical controls for aircraft and missle field modular power supplies, computer controlled cloth cutters, automatic grading and marker systems, jet engine/aerospace parts and components, precision machine parts, commercial printing and typesetting, bricks, waste disposal incinerators, fin tube radiation, microflake cigar binders and wrappers, heat transfer decorations, pressure sensitive labels, store fixtures, precious metal recovery, agriculture. Transp.—Passenger: Served by buses of Post Road Stages, Inc. from Hartford and Stafford Springs, and Conn. Transit from Hartford to East Windsor Hill. Freight: Served by Conrail and numerous motor common carriers. Post offices, South Windsor; Bissell Station and East Windsor Hill.

TOWN OFFICERS. Clerk and Reg. of Vital Statistics, Liana T. Kuras; Hours, 8 A.M.-4:30 P.M., Mon., Tues., Wed., Fri.; 8 A.M.-7:30 P.M., Thurs.; Address, Town

Hall, 1540 Sullivan Ave., 06074-2786; Tel., Hartford, (860) 644-2511, ext. 225; FAX (860) 644-3781.—**Asst. Clerks and Asst. Regs. of Vital Statistics,** Gretchen E. Bickford, Theresa G. Samsel.—**Town Manager,** Matthew B. Galligan.—**Town Council,** William E. Aman, (R), Mayor; Ronald P. Morin, Deputy Mayor; Thomas A. Delnicki, Marianne L. Fisher, Kathryn A. Hale, Edward F. Havens, Roy C. J. Normen, Richard Ryan, John J. Woodcock III.—**Selectmen,** Peter T. Anthony, Jr., Josephine C. DeMaio, Ralph A. Giansanti, Sr.—**Treas.,** Matthew S. Streeter.—**Tax Collector/Collector of Revenue,** Joseph Cordani.—**Finance Dir.,** vacancy; Asst., Melanie Crucitti.—**Bd. of Assessment Appeals,** Clarence W. Gay, Chm., Henry Philip, G. Warren Westbrook.—**Assessor,** Edgar Belleville; Asst., Charles Danna.—**Registrars of Voters,** Frances O. Knipple (D), Janis K. Murtha (R).—**Supt. of Schools,** Joseph L. Wood.—**Bd. of Education,** Julie C. Muller, Chm., Raymond J. Cyr, Jr., Kathleen S. Daugherty, John M. Giordano, Nancy J. Merrill, Eugene F. Policelli, William H. Sawyer, Jennifer E. Seamon, Roseann Williams, 1997.—**Planning and Zoning Comm.,** Russell G. Levack, Chm., Frank A. Castro, Louise C. Evans, William T. March, Jr., Walter J. Mealy, Marshall Montana, Maxine S. Parrott; Alternates, Roger Cottle, Sue Larsen, Patricia Porter.—**Dir. of Planning,** Marcia Banach; Asst., Michele Lipe.—**Public Building Comm.,** Howard E. Fitts, Chm., Kenneth Fitzgerald, Alphonse Garcia, Carol S. Kelley, Michael R. Lanza, Charles E. Lyons, Robert Stingle.—**Zoning Bd. of Appeals,** Robert W. Warren, Chm., Marjorie S. Anthony, Joseph J. Carino, Audrey Delnicki, Barbara L. Murray; Alternates, Joel Nadel, Walter Pekala, Daniel Seypura.—**Economic Development Comm.,** Marjorie Anthony, Chm., Joseph Barry, John Buonanducci, Joseph Carino, Joseph Demaio, Joseph Gritzer, M. Terrie Kyc, Marilyn M. Morrison, James Murray, Janis Murtha, Jacqueline J. Smith; Alternates, Deborah Fine, Michael Melocowsky, John Pelkey, Leroy VanderPutten.—**Economic Development Coordinator,** Ralph Hedenberg.—**Housing Auth.,** George Daniels, Jr., Chm., Raymond Donovan, Joan Murphy, Elizabeth Osborne, Faith Weber.—**Elderly Housing Exec. Dir.,** Janet Prior.—**Conservation and Inland Wetlands Comm.,** Elizabeth Warren, Chm., Salvatore Bonanno, Philip Forzley, Carol A. Heffler, Susanne Hannigan, John O'Connell, John Phillips, Susan Smith, Audrey Wasick, vacancy; Alternates, Lynn Abrahamson, Walter Pekala.—**Zoning/Inland Wetlands Enforcement Officer,** Jeffrey Folger.—**Mass Transit/Highway Advisory Comm.,** Stanley Abell, Dorothy Corcoran, Harvey Fine, Susanne Hannigan, Marilyn M. Morrison, Robert L. Murray, Jr., James Neary, Walter Pekala, Bruce Snow.—**Historic Dist. Comm.,** Pamela M. Mahr, Vice Chm., Caroline Alexander, Kathleen Brady, Connie Castro, Charles Nielsen; Alternates, Edwina H. Futtner, Myrtle Odlum, Vernon Petersen.—**Drug and Alcohol Abuse Prevention Comm.,** Harvey Fine, Chm., Paul Burnham, Marjorie Callan, Carol Hart, Elaine K. Holcombe, Walter Pekala.—**Senior Center Dir.,** Margaret Kemp.—**Human Relations Committee,** Elizabeth Asplund, Chm., Monica Barrett, June Cottle, Ellen Falzarano, David Helmin, Debra Mink, Marilyn Pugliese, Nancy Simonds, Robin Trotter.—**Dir. of Health,** Gerald S. Schwartz, M.D.—**Library Bd.,** Gladys Nadel, Chm., Marcia Andrus, Suzanne J. Fitts, Peter Plummer, Kathleen-Mary Sharos, Carole Stroud; Mary Etter, Dir.—**Municipal Historian,** M. Terrie Kyc.—**Park and Recreation Comm.,** Peter D. Anthony, Jr., Patrick Davin, Siamak Dowlatshahi, Joseph Etter, Theodore Hindson, Kevin McCann, Michael Melocowsky, John D. Murphy, Jr., Thomas Sharos, Lavina Wilson, vacancy; Alternates, Alvin Ditman, Leonard Jay.—

Recreation Dir., Ray Favreau; Asst., Michael McCarthy.—**Youth Services Coordinator,** Dennis Sheridan.—**Supt. of Parks/Tree Warden,** Karl Reichle.—**Dir. of Public Works,** Michael Gantick; Asst., C. Fred Shaw.—**Town Engineer,** Jerry Iazzetta.—**Supt. of Highways,** Melvin Stead, Jr.—**Building Inspector,** John Collins.—**Building Code Bd. of Appeals,** Roger Cottle, J. Kirby Holcombe, John Merrill, David Patria, Joseph Vedovato.—**Water Pollution Control Auth.,** Joseph J. Carino, Chm., Robert Dickinson, Anthony Falzarano, Carol Fletterick, Thomas Hindson, James P. Oates, Wayne Tursi.—**Supt. of Pollution Control,** C. Fred Shaw.—**Sanitarian,** Robert Deptula.—**Chief of Police,** Gary K. Tyler.—**Constables,** Peter T. Anthony, Sr., Audrey J. Delnicki, Margaret A. Johnston, Edward W. Kasheta, Jay G. Murtha.—**Chief of Vol. Fire Dept./Fire Marshal,** William R. Lanning.—**Bd. of Fire Comrs.,** William Mitchell, Chm., John Bond, George Cox, Patrick Hankard, Howard Slater.—**Civil Preparedness Dir.,** Robert R. Hornish.—**Town Atty.,** Barry Guliano.—**Justices of the Peace,** Marjorie S. Anthony, Philip P. Apter, Darlene Barrett, Edward Bona, W. Philip Braender, Jr., Marilyn W. Burger, Joseph J. Carino, Frank A. Castro, Helen Conaty, Jean Conaty, Joseph C. DeMaio, Josephine C. DeMaio, Fred S. DeGiacomo, Patrick Edenburn-MacQueen, Carol A. Flagg, Edwina H. Futtner, Thomas F. Griffin, Jay P. Knipple, June V. Lanza, Mark A. Lillis, Muriel A. Mahr, Michelle McCarthy, Marilyn M. Morrison, Barbara C. Murray, Janis K. Murtha, Joel P. Nadel, Maxine Parrott, Anthony J. Pecoraro, Hazel R. Perkins, Elaine M. Pilver, Brenda L. Pines, Julie A. Raymond, Marion R. Roscio, Lincoln H. Streeter, Joan F. Walsh, G. Warren Westbrook, Brian J. Zawodniak, Abraham A. Ziskis.

SPRAGUE. New London County.—(Form of government, selectmen, town meeting, board of finance.)—Inc., May, 1861; acquired from Lisbon and Franklin. Area, 13.8 sq. miles. Population, est., 2,977. Voting district, 1. Principal industries, agriculture and manufacture of paper board and boxes, lithographing, and engraving. Transp.—Freight: Served by numerous motor common carriers. Post offices, Baltic, Hanover and Versailles. The rural free delivery route from Baltic supplies mail facilities for part of Lisbon and Scotland.

TOWN OFFICERS. Clerk and Reg. of Vital Statistics, Claire B. Glaude; Hours, 8:30 A.M.-4 P.M., Mon. through Fri.; 4-6:30 P.M, Thurs.; Address, 1 Main St., P. O. Box 162, Baltic 06330; Tel., Norwich, (860) 822-3001.—**Asst. Clerks and Asst. Regs. of Vital Statistics,** Mary B. Chartier, Marie A. Davis.—**Selectmen,** 1st, Stephen J. Papineau, Sr. (D), P.O. Box 677, Baltic, Tel., (860) 822-3000, Joan M. Charron-Nagle (D), Barry R. Kolar (R).—**Treas.,** Bernice G. Dombkowski.—**Bd. of Finance,** John C. Thomas, Chm., Lisa H. Batten, Carol A. Ham, Diane Hastings, Claude R. Pellegrino, Linda A. Puetz.—**Tax Collector,** Mary L. Thomas.—**Bd. of Assessment Appeals,** Barbara S. Sutcliffe, Chm., Joseph T. Charron, William L. Dombkowski, vacancy.—**Assessor,** Judy Moffitt.—**Bd. of Assessors,** Barry R. Kolar, Daniel T. Nagle, Anthony S. Ozga.—**Registrars of Voters,** Kathleen Z. Boushee (D), Patricia W. Amon (R).—**Supt. of Schools,** Colette B. Trailor, Ph.D.—**Bd. of Education,** Kim M. Begin, Michael W. Bychowsky, Kenneth E. Caisse, 1997; David A. Batten, Deborah A. Deschamps, Warren S. Knight, Anthony S. Ozga, 1999.—**Planning and Zoning Comm.,** John C. Thomas, Chm., Harold J. LaTour, David T. McCaffery, Peter G. Shortoff,

Arthur E. Spielman, Jr., Anna L. Talbot, Richard A. Waterman; Alternates, Brian S. Couture, Charles A. Fortin, Dwight A. Hyde.—**Zoning Bd. of Appeals,** Raymond P. Arpin, Raymond E. Bernier, Sr., James H. Rood, June R. Trainor, vacancy; Alternates, Joseph A. Arpin, vacancy.—**Zoning Enforcement Officer,** Benjamin Hull.—**Economic Development Comm.,** Kim M. Begin, Vincent E. Chrzanowski, John B. Occaso, John C. Thomas.—**Housing Auth.,** Raymond B. Allyn, Chm., Donald G. Allen, Alice Baldwin, Ruth R. Rosiene, Andre Trudelle; Cheryl A. Blanchard, Admin. Asst.—**Conservation and Inland Wetlands Comm.,** Paul Cipriani, Jr., Chm., Jane Cipriani, Leonard Cormier, Edward Semmelrock, Arthur E. Spielman, Jr.; Alternates, Donald Rockwell, Joanne M. Semmelrock.—**Comm. on Aging,** Norman Boulay, Margaret J. Campanelli, Gerard A. Exley, Rosalie Jorczak, Richard King, Dolores A. Knight, JoAnn Lynch, Dorothy Macht.—**Agent for Elderly,** Sophie Generous.—**Dir. of Social Services,** Lena C. Nichols.—**Dir. of Health,** Harold J. Burdo.—**Library Directors,** Glen A. Cheney, Chm., Lorraine Allen, Renee G. Bibeault, Tara Desnoyers, Mae Drescher, Carol Dunn, Yvonne Horelik, Elizabeth Kraemer.—**Municipal Historian,** Dennis R. Delaney.—**Recreation Committee,** Nils Erickson, R. Fugi Fulgueras, Patricia M. Gil, Christine A. Kolar, Elizabeth Kraemer, Cheryl E. Mish, Daniel Nagle, Mary Papineau, Linda A. Puetz, Craig Savageau, Michael Semmelrock, Carol Shefer, Deborah A. St. John, Jan F. Woodworth.—**Dir. of Public Works,** Mark M. Benson.—**Water and Sewer Auth.,** Dudley Geigenmiller, Chm., Edmund F. Conde, David T. McCaffery, Donald Maurice, Walter O. Treat.—**Building Inspector,** Benjamin Hull.—**Sanitarian,** Christopher M. Burdo.—**Supt. of Water and Sewer Dept.,** David H. Rood.—**Tree Warden,** George J. Ozga, Jr.—**Chief of Fire Dept.,** Scott A. Blais; Deputy, Daniel T. Nagle.—**Fire Marshal,** Joseph Grenier; Deputy, Richard A. Hamel.—**Emergency Management Dir.,** Robert Tardif; Deputy, Deneane L. Congdon.—**Town Atty.,** Nicholas Kepple.—**Justices of the Peace,** Dennison L. Allen, Kim M. Begin, Kenneth E. Caisse, Deneane L. Congdon, William E. Deschamps, Bernice G. Dombkowski, Gerard A. Exley, Clifford H. Fortin, Carol A. Ham, Stephen J. Papineau, Sr., June-Clyde Preston.

STAFFORD. Tolland County.—(Form of government, selectmen, town meeting, board of finance.)—Settled, 1719. Area, 58.8 sq. miles. Population, est., 11,890. Voting districts, 3. Principal industries, manufacture of woolen and printed circuits, print goods, paper felting, and filters. Transp.—Freight: Served by Central Vermont Railway and numerous motor common carriers. Post offices, Stafford Springs, Stafford and Staffordville. Other parts of the town are served by rural delivery from Stafford Springs, Somers, and Monson, MA.

TOWN OFFICERS. Clerk and Reg. of Vital Statistics, Pauline Laskow; Hours, 8:30 A.M.-4 P.M., Mon. through Wed.; 8:30 A.M.-6:30 P.M., Thurs.; 8:30 A.M.-12 Noon, Fri.; Address, Warren Memorial Town Hall, P.O. Box 11, Stafford Springs 06076; Tel., Stafford Springs, (860) 684-2532.—**Asst. Clerks and Asst. Regs. of Vital Statistics,** Olive M. Cooley, Carol M. Davis.—**Selectmen,** 1st, John E. Julian (D) Tel., (860) 684-2130, Bruce Dutton (R), Gordon J. Frassinelli, Jr. (D).—**Treas.,** Darlene Dion.—**Bd. of Finance,** Richard Dobson, Chm., Richard Dewey, Elizabeth Heuitson, John Miller, Irene Sfreddo, Sylvan Tetrault.—**Tax Collector,** Cheryl Vail.—**Bd. of**

Assessment Appeals, Theodore W. Rummel, Chm., Sandra Ference, Lida Miller.—**Assessors,** Virginia Guilmette, Chm., Floyd E. Baxter, Maude Emhoff.—**Registrars of Voters,** Joan L. Zelonka (D), Ann E. Haraghey (R).—**Supt. of Schools,** George Apuzzi.—**Bd. of Education,** Jack Kelly, Chm., Lisa Bradway, Juanita Scism, 1997; Georgia Butler, Edward B. Fowler, Michael E. Talamini, Russell E. Vibberts, Jr., 1999.—**Planning and Zoning Comm.,** Francis Benison, Chm., Sandra Collette, John P. Mocko, J. Anthony Morianos, Nancy H. Ravetto.—**Zoning Bd. of Appeals,** Robert Swift, Chm., Harold Finch, Dennis Kaba, Jr., John L. Pisciotta, Jr., Mary Tautic; Alternates, Richard Hartenstein, Richard Martin, Daniel Sarkisian.—**Zoning Enforcement Officer,** Wendell Avery.—**Industrial Development Comm.,** Francis Benison, Bruce Dutton, Michael Fiore, D. Anthony Guglielmo, Peter Locke, John Mordasky, Harry Pragl, Roger Rossi, Theodore R. Satkowski.—**Housing Auth.,** John Richens, Chm., Renato Calchera, Irene Gall, Laura Panciera, Leonard Pollard; John Hurchala, Exec. Dir.—**Conservation Comm.,** Mitchell Muzio, Chm., Arlene Avery, Robert Bourque, Julie Engelke, Nancy Kelly, Gloria Krol, Culver Modisette, Joseph Neafsey, Karen J. Purnell, Michael Richards, Cynthia Rummel.—**Inland Wetlands Comm.,** Barry Locke, Chm., Earl Avery, Louis Bruzzi, Dennis Hodgins, Mitchell Muzio, Ernest Nocerino, Anthony Ostrowski, Cynthia Schaefer, Russell Viberts, John Wilson.—**Social Services Dir.,** Karen Troiano.—**Dir. of Health/Sanitarian,** Bruce Lundgren.—**Arts Comm.,** Kathleen Bachiochi, Chm., Arlene Avery, Dana Bachiochi, David Bartlett, Pamela Buckland, Nancy Dutton, Lida Miller, Florence Polens, Shirley Pufahl, Nancy Tripoli, Jane Waters.—**Municipal Historian,** Duane Beffa-Negrini.—**Recreation Comm.,** David Walsh, Chm., Patricia Bidorini, Catherine Fitzpatrick, Reno Francini, Jr., Louis Harris, H. Blake Hatch, John Howland, John Hurchala, Michael Kaschuluk, Douglas Minich, Carol Parker, Darrell Stark.—**Supt. of Parks,** Peter Williams.—**Dir. of Public Works,** David Hirsch.—**Building Inspector,** Wendell Avery.—**Water Pollution Control Auth.,** David Hirsch, Chm., Earl T. Avery, Albert DePellegrini, Jr., Bruce Dobson, Francis Finch, Herman Perlot, Irwin Polens, Sandra Sullivan.—**Constables,** Keith F. Curnan, H. Blake Hatch, Michael Hurchala, Scott M. Knowlton, Barry Locke, Gary A. Quinn, Joseph W. Satkowski.—**Chiefs of Fire Dept.,** Paul Burns (Staffordville), Joseph Lorenzetti (West Stafford), Edward Grant (Stafford Springs).—**Fire Marshal,** Harold Finch; Deputy, Thomas Finch.—**Civil Preparedness Dir.,** Floyd Baxter.—**Town Atty.,** Thomas Fiore.—**Justices of the Peace,** David W. Baker, Adam Bechta, Zenna D. Brisson, Robert W. Bulter, Sr., Renato Calchera, Keenan P. Clark, Francis Collette, Silvio S. DaDalt, Andrew R. Descheneau, Albert A. DeNunzio, Frederick J. Dion, Elsie B. Enders, Francis T. Finch, Harriet Fiore, Thomas J. Fiore, Edward B. Fowler, Gordon J. Frassinelli, Jr., Patricia Greika, Elizabeth E. Heuitson, Dennis C. Kaba, Jr., Jack Kelly, Scott Knowlton, Marie Leone, Kenneth J. McQuaid, John B. Mitchell, J. Anthony Morianos, Gregory E. Post, Theodore W. Rummel, Dock R. Sellers, Ora P. Sfreddo, Richard G. Speight, Patricia H. Tetrault, Sylvan A. Tetrault, Nicholas G. Volpe, Karen Yencha, Garth A. Yorko, Andrew Zelonka.

STAMFORD. Fairfield County.—(Form of government, strong mayor, board of representatives.)—Settled, 1641, under New Haven jurisdiction; named Town of Stamford in 1642;

submitted to Connecticut, Oct., 1662; in 1893, the City of Stamford, comprising central portion of Town of Stamford, was incorporated. Henceforth, City of Stamford became a composite part of Town of Stamford, resulting in two separate governments—the Town of Stamford and City of Stamford. Town and City of Stamford were consolidated on April 15, 1949 and named City of Stamford. Area, 42.7 sq. miles. Population, est., 110,717. Voting districts, 20. Third largest center of Fortune 500 Corporate Headquarters in the nation. Principal industries, corporate headquarters, reinsurance, investment banking, business and consumer credit, computer software development, magazine publishing, media production and distribution, owner/operators and brokers of bulk cargo ships, research laboratories, management consulting, instruments manufacturing, postage meter manufacturing, plastics. Transp.—Passenger: Served by Amtrak, Metro-North; Conn. Transit local from Darien, Norwalk, and Greenwich; and by Greyhound. Freight: Served by Conrail and numerous common carriers. Post offices, Stamford (four substations), Glenbrook, High Ridge, Ridgeway and Springdale.

CITY AND TOWN OFFICERS. City and Town Clerk, Reg. of Vital Statistics, Lois PontBriant; Hours, 8:30 A.M.-4:30 P.M., Mon. through Fri., except July and Aug., 8 A.M.-4 P.M.; Address, Stamford Government Ctr., 888 Washington Blvd., P.O. Box 891, 06904-0891; Tel., (203) 977-4056; FAX, (203) 977-5222.—**Asst. Clerk,** Ethel K. Feldman.—**Mayor,** Dannel P. Malloy (D), Stamford Government Ctr., 888 Washington Blvd., P.O. Box 10152, 06904-2152; Tel., (203) 977-4150; FAX, (203) 977-5845.—**Bd. of Representatives,** Timothy M. Abbazia, Herman P. Alswanger, John J. Boccuzzi, Lucy F. Corelli, Jeffrey T. Curtis, Sr., Russell Davis, Robert DeLuca, Gloria G. DePina, Carmen Domonkos, Rachel D. Drucker, Paul A. Esposito, Mary L. Fedeli, Alice C. Fortunato, Gerald M. Fox III, Cisco Gaztambide, Joseph A. Gergle, Jr., Philip J. Giordano, George H. Johnson, Ronald Kuzlik, William J. Lasko, John F. Leydon, Jr., Ralph F. Loglisci, William T. MacInnis, David R. Martin, Ellen S. Mellis, Elaine Mitchell, Maria C. Nakian, Peter C. Nanos, Bobby E. Owens, Thomas A. Pia, John L. Ponzini, Richard L. Romaniello, Ronald A. Sabia, Donald B. Sherer, Randall M. Skigen, Annie M. Summerville, Paul J. Ventura, Daniel P. Weiner, Patrick J. White, John R. Zelinsky, Jr.—**Comptroller,** Robert V. Stout.—**Bd. of Ethics,** Lou Pasquino, Chm., David W. Daly, Melvin Grove, Howard Kaplan, Amy LiVolsi; Alternate, Julian Nosenzo.—**Dir. of Admin.,** Thomas S. Hamilton.—**Bd. of Finance,** Ruth H. Powers, Chm., Andrew J. McDonald, Michael G. Mezzapelle, Mary Lou Rinaldi, James M. Rubino, Joseph Tarzia.—**Tax Collector,** Donald LeFevre.—**Bd. of Assessment Appeals,** Joseph Barocas, John J. Hogan, Jr., Philip J. Miolene, Kimberly Norman-Rosedam, Salvan Ross.—**Assessor,** Francis K. Kirwin.—**Registrars of Voters,** Janet Weintraub (D), Barbara McInerney (R).—**Supt. of Schools,** Michael Nast.—**Bd. of Education,** Jill Beaudry, John Mallozzi, James M. Serafino, 1997; Jerry C. Pia, Marc D. Peyser, Dudley N. Williams, Jr., 1998; Eileen M. Iannazzi, Robert E. King, Janet T. Toy, 1999.—**Personnel Comm.,** Marc Teichman, Chm., Frank N. Green, Arnold Kapiloff, Joan Rinaldi, Leroy Terrell; Sim Bernstein, Dir.—**Personnel Appeals Bd.,** Beverly King, Margie Lanier, Margaret Northrop, Rochelle Retleff, Karen Sena.— **Planning Bd.,** Nick Aivalis, John T. Garnjost, Thomas Masone, Gilbert D. Rozier, vacancy; Alternates, Mary Laurie, Harry Orlick, Harry L. Parson.—**Planning and Zoning Dir.,** Robin Stein.—**Zoning Bd.,** Jackie Heftman, Chm., Audrey Cosentini, Hugh F. O'Connell, Phyllis Kapiloff, Irving Slifkin; Alternates, Scott Krowitz, Ronald

Miller, vacancy.—**Zoning Bd. of Appeals,** John A. Sedlak, Chm., Sam Defranco, Claire Friedlander, Raoul Ilaw, Roger Taranto; Alternates, James P. Bartley, Sid Cholmar, Sally Levene.—**Zoning Enforcement Officer,** James Lunney III.—**Redevelopment Comm.,** Neal M. Jewell, Joel Mellis, James Nixon, Stephen Osman, Eric Wormser.—**Economic Development Comm.,** Duane E. Hill, Thomas C. Hunter, Jr., Michael S. Pansini, John T. D. Rich, Joel Selden.—**Housing Auth.,** Sally Silveira, Chm., Tamara Guevara, Robert Harris, Vatella McDowell, Courtney A. Nelthropp; Edward Schwartz, Dir.—**Environmental Protection Bd.,** William Morris, Chm., Louis Levine, Richard Rohr, Paul Weinstein; Gary Klein, Dir.; Alternates, Roberta Barbieri, Joel M. Berns, Gary Stone.—**Comm. on Aging,** Annette Antonelli, Joseph Cottone, Phyllis Doonan, Roxana Kelly, James Kyle, Betty Loughran, Charles Matthews, Michael Meyer, Peter C. Sileo.—**Human Rights Comm.,** Carmine Vaccaro, Chm., Doris Levine, Vincent Martino, Ellen F. Steele, five vacancies.—**Dir. of Public Health, Safety and Welfare,** John Byrne.—**Dir. of Health,** Andrew D. McBride, M.D.—**Health Comm.,** Bert Ballin, D.D.S., Steffi Block, R.N., Bridget Kopek, Angelo Mastrangelo, Jr., M.D., Vincent Mobilio.—**Library Trustees,** Gino Giusti, Chm., Frank D'Andrea, Theodore E. Payne, Frank Rich, Jr., Hinda Rosenthal, James M. Serafino, Richard Taber, Ann Weiss, Anne Works, Peter V. Young.—**Social Services Comm.,** Stephen Chizmadia, Arlene Ettinger, Miguel Garcia, Jack Halpert.—**Parks and Recreation Comm.,** Steven Lesandro, Chm., Nicholas Corbo, Raymond DeLuca, Daniel Lyons, Vincenzo R. Martino.—**Dir. of Operations,** Patricia L. Broom.—**Capital Projects Mgr.,** Thomas Fava.—**Purchasing Agent,** David Vecchia.—**City Engineer,** Norman Liu.—**Sealer of Weights and Measures,** vacancy.—**Building Inspector,** Anthony Strazza.—**Building Bd. of Appeals,** Alfred Giannotti, Louis G. Shanes, Alexander Vanech, two vacancies.—**Water Pollution Control,** Philip Norgren, Chm., Celeste Johnson, Philip Paseltiner, Thomas Romas, Patrick Scarella.—**Solid Waste Supv.,** Louis David.—**Shell Fish Comm.,** Howard Tichauer, Chm., Ruth Fulton, Norman Healy, Kevin Malloy, Adam Valindras.—**Dir., Env. Health,** Peter Dombrowski.—**Chief of Police,** Patrick Tully; Deputies, John Perrotta, Walter Young.—**Police Comm.,** Mark Denham, Chm., Michael Berkoff, Adele Gordon, Winton M. Hill III, David McMahon.—**Constables,** Stacy M. Bogacz, Paul T. Callahan, George E. Christiansen, Jon T. Gallup, Jack Leydon, John J. Liberatore, Ralph J. Serafino, Jr.—**Chief of Fire Dept.,** Ron Graner; Asst., Peter Brown.—**Fire Marshal,** Barry Callahan.—**Bd. of Fire Comrs.,** Richard Lyons, Chm., E. Gaynor Brennan, William Callion, Jr., Marilyn Dussault, J. Ralph Murray.—**Emergency Mgmt. Dir.,** Carl Alton.—**Dir. of Legal Affairs,** Thomas Cassone.—**Justices of the Peace,** Lorna C. Aliperti, Jane R. Austin, Mabel Bannister, Helen E. Baum, Ruby Blackwell, Stephen G. Bowling, Ann S. Brown, Bill Cahill, Richard J. Cichon, Hattie P. Clayburn, Eugene E. Conti, David S. Cunningham, Benjamin Cuttitta, Robert A. Daly, Robert DeLuca, Cheryll A. Duerk, Paul A. Esposito, Victor E. Fazio, Claire Fishman, William H. Flanagan, James Foreman, Jon C. Gallup, Miguel Garcia, Joseph A. Gergle, Jr., Philip J. Giordano, Doris Greenberg, Edwin S. Greenberg, Linda L. Holton, Donald A. Huppert, Lucas Isidro, David C. Jachimczyk, William R. Jarrett, Demetra D. Jones, Mary Laurie, Patzy H. Lavender, Louise P. Levine, Helen J. Liberatore, Ralph L. Lockhart, Donna M. Loglisci, William T. MacInnis, Joseph S. Macklin, Dannel P. Malloy, Vincenzo R. Martino, Barbara A. McInerney, Karen S. Mills, John J. P. Nocerino, Joseph J. Nosal, Bob

E. Owens, Wendy L. Peragine, Ralph A. Pesiri, Thomas A. Pia, Nicolina A. Pierni, Clement L. Raiteri, Jr., Margaret A. Ross, Ronald A. Sabia, Jacqueline Santagata, Jeanne-Lois Santy, Ralph Serafino, Alfonso Sgritta, Sharyn Silberman, Sanchia Spandow, Philip R. Stork, Milton C. Thomas II, Kim Varney, Mariangela Vavala, Paul J. Ventura, Stephen J. Vitka, Alvin M. Wellington, Eleanor H. Yudain, John R. Zelinsky, Jr., Kurt A. Zimbler, John M. Zimmerman.

STERLING. Windham County.—(Form of government, selectmen, town meeting, board of finance.)—Inc., May 4, 1794; taken from Voluntown. Area, 27.3 sq. miles. Population, est., 2,674. Voting district, 1. Principal industries, poultry and dairy farming, manufacturing, stone quarry. Transp.—Freight: Served by numerous motor common carriers. Post offices, Sterling and Oneco.

TOWN OFFICERS. Clerk and Reg. of Vital Statistics, Catherine S. Nurmi; Hours, 8:30 A.M.-3:30 P.M., and by appointment; Address, 1114 Plainfield Pike, Box 157, Oneco 06373; Tel., Moosup, (860) 564-2657.—**Asst. Clerk and Asst. Reg. of Vital Statistics/Treas.,** Carol A. Young.—**Selectmen,** 1st, Robert E. Lewis (R) Tel., (860) 564-2904, Neil H. Cook (R), John F. Firlik (D).—**Bd. of Finance,** J. C. Halbrooks, Chm., Harriet Clowes, Neil Delmonico, Carl Kvist, David Shippee, Gregg O. Wilcox.—**Tax Collector,** Anna M. Franklin.—**Bd. of Assessment Appeals,** Robert P. Jordan, Richard LaHaie, Robert Salisbury.—**Assessor,** Penelope Keith.—**Registrars of Voters,** Christine M. Clancy (D), Loretta Y. Capobianco (R).—**Supt. of Schools,** Frederick Ashton.—**Bd. of Education,** Susan E. McLevy, Debra L. West, 1997; Bernice C. Davis, Darlene Gannon, 1999; Joseph E. Shields, Chm., Gregg O. Wilcox, 2001.—**Planning Comm.,** Patricia Soriero, Chm., Albert Gervasio, Paul Ezzell, Peter Lamb, Ronald Marchesseault; Alternates, Daniel Sefton, Renee Theroux-Keech, vacancy.—**Inland Wetland Comm.,** Robert Mclevy, Chm., Rudy Bawza, Brian Bissonnette, Robert Daigle, Michael Guglielmo, Virginia Shurgot, Norman Talbot, Rodney Young; Alternate, Timothy Hogue.—**Development and Industrial Comm.,** Geoffrey Cooper, Chm., Judith Andrade, Scott Forrest, Kathy Fullerton, Kathy Guglielmo, Kevin Jordan, Michael Molodich, George F. Poland, Eric St. Pierre.—**Welfare Dir.,** Elsie Bisset.—**Library Directors,** Rachel P. Vincent, Chm., Dorothy Capobianco, Marlene Cook, Virginia Navan, Hedwig Russwurm, Holly J. Wood.—**Municipal Historian,** Eileen Sansone.—**Recreation Comm.,** John Brady, Robert Gannon, Chm., Judith Gooslin, Barbara Roberts, John Vitale; Alternate, Nancy Reinwald.—**Building Inspector,** Robert Fisher.—**Water Pollution Control Committee,** Shirl Knox, Chm., Betsy Chamberland, Neil H. Cook, Conrad Langlais, Edmund Morneau.—**Chief of Police/Tree Warden,** Robert E. Lewis.—**Constables,** Bruce N. Etheridge, Albert K. Frink, Walter L. Frink, Wesley A. Love, two vacancies.—**Chiefs of Fire Dept.,** Robert A. Chamberland, Deputy, Charles P. Rabbitt (Sterling); 1st, Peter Capobianco; 2nd, William Livermore; Deputy, Alfred Young (Oneco).—**Fire Marshal,** Thomas Haynes.—**Civil Preparedness Dir.,** Robert A. Chamberland.—**Town Attys.,** Jackson, Harris & Burlingame.—**Justices of the Peace,** Michael J. Bourque, Sr., Mary T. Campbell, Matthew J. Clancy, Jr., Rose M. Deojay, Earl S. Hopkins,

Mark W. Kitchin, Shirl A. Knox, Edmund S. Morneau, Barbara J. Salisbury, Leatrice L. Shippee, Patricia D. Soriero, Rebecca Wood.

STONINGTON. New London County.—(Form of government, selectmen, town meeting, board of finance.)—Settled, 1649; named, 1666. Area, 50.0 sq. miles. Population, est., 16,153. Voting districts, 5. Principal industries, tourism, agriculture, fishing, boat building, oceanographic research and manufacture of machinery, printing presses, plastic products, castings, electrical parts, textiles, screen printing, boat livery, silvercel batteries, harpsicord manufacturing, extrusion machines, photo processing and velvet goods. Transp.—Passenger: Served by Amtrak and buses of Southeast Area Transit (SEAT). Freight: Served by Providence & Worcester Co. and numerous motor common carriers. Post offices, Stonington, Mystic, Old Mystic and Pawcatuck.

TOWN OFFICERS. Clerk and Reg. of Vital Statistics, Ruth Waller; Hours, 8:30 A.M.-4 P.M., Mon. through Fri.; Address, Town Hall, 152 Elm St., P.O. Box 352, 06378; Tel., (860) 535-5060.—**Asst. Clerks and Asst. Regs. of Vital Statistics,** Sally Duplice, Cynthia J. Ladwig.—**Selectmen,** 1st, Donald R. Maranell (D) Tel., (860) 535-5050, William S. Brown (R), William B. McDonough (D).—**Treas.,** Joseph A. Pescatello.—**Bd. of Finance,** Steven E. Donahue, Chm., William Burke, Edith Dunford, Glenn J. Frishman, Frederick Leonard, John P. Walsh.—**Tax Collector,** Susan B. Harrington.—**Bd. of Assessment Appeals,** Michele G. Contino, Chm., Robert E. Ahearn, Stephen M. Palmer.—**Assessor,** Marsha L. Standish.—**Registrars of Voters,** 1st Dist., Teresa S. Grimes, 2nd Dist., Marjorie A. Donahue, 3rd Dist., Gertrude Sullivan, 4th Dist., Patricia Menno-Coveney, 5th Dist., Margaret Woycik (D); 1st Dist., Rita Hoadley, 2nd Dist., Nancy C. Williams, 3rd Dist., Alma Nott, 4th Dist., Virginia K. Deisher, 5th Dist., Barbara L. Read (R).—**Supt. of Schools,** Michael McKee.—**Bd. of Education,** Corinne Kelly, Chm., Gisela Harma, Richard C. Palmer, Sr., Roger Panciera, 1997; Martha Booker, Amanda Lindberg, 1999.—**Planning and Zoning Comm.,** Robert Granato, Chm., Andrew Blanda, Henry P. Bolduc, Jr., Sara Lathrop, James Moody; Alternates, Robert Ahearn, Webster Copp, Kevin T. Riley.—**Town Planner,** Charles Boster.—**Zoning Bd. of Appeals,** John Mershon, Mary Motherway, Jack Steel, James Yacovino, vacancy; Alternates, Karl Kemper, Edward Sullivan, vacancy.—**Housing Auth.,** Paul Cirioni, Chm., Shirley Andrews, Marilyn Graham, Lenore S. Williams.—**Conservation Comm.,** Peter Thacher, Chm., Stuart Cole, Robert Dewire, Howard Eaton, Sheila Lyons, Stanton W. Simm, Jr., John Swenarton.—**Inland Wetlands Comm.,** David Rathbun, Chm., Frank Canfield, John Davis, Marc Mandler, Mark Snyder, Mary Thacher, Myra Wheeler, vacancy; Alternates, Jennifer Scott, vacancy.—**Agent for the Elderly,** Claire Grills.—**Dir. of Social Services,** Carol Umphlett.—**Dir. of Health,** Michael E. Blefeld, M.D. (Sandy Hollow Rd., Mystic).—**Municipal Historian,** Eleanor B. Read.—**Recreation Comm.,** Edward Sheridan, Chm., John Castodio, C. Michael Crowley, Frank Prachniak, Jr., Eugene Spaziani, Joseph Woycik, William Zembruski; James Ballato, Dir.—**Supt. of Highways and Bridges,** Peter L. Balestracci.—**Building Inspector,** Thomas Watkins.—**Building Code Bd. of Appeals,** David Capizzano, Michele G. Contino, Steven D. Grills, Robert Marston, vacancy.—**Water Pollution Control Auth.,** William McDonough, Chm., Charles Beebe, Scott Penley, two vacancies; Harold Storrs, Dir.—**Waterfront Comm.,**

Randy Minor, Chm., Jeffrey Christian, Edward Dennett, Samuel Grimes, Arthur Medeiros, Paul Previty, Sr., Rose Raffo.—**Tree Warden,** Paul Rohacik.—**Sanitarian,** Anthony Bono.—**Chief of Police,** Patrick F. Hedge.—**Police Comm.,** Wayne Greene, Chm., Daniel Booker, David Brown, Lester Duncklee, Dudley Wheeler, Jr.—**Constables,** William B. Cutler, Nancy H. Gibson, Robert C. Johnson, Francis M. Keane, James P. O'Boyle, David J. Santos, Joseph J. Serio, Francis V. Woycik.—**Fire Marshal,** George Brennan.—**Civil Preparedness Dir.,** George Brennan.—**Town Atty.,** Thomas J. Londregan.—**Justices of the Peace,** Paul Altman, Deborah A. Anderson, Peter L. Balestracci, Robert J. Bessette, Dan E. Blackstone, Michael J. Blair, Frank S. Brewer, Linda B. Brown, William S. Brown, Hadlai E. Burdick, Eleanor G. Casey, Mary M. Cleary, Roy L. Cole, Patricia B. Copp, Webster T. Copp, Paul E. Cravinho, William B. Cutler, Virginia K. Deisher, Karen S. Douglass, Robert E. P. Elmer III, Vincent J. Faulise, Barbara M. Fiore, Glenn J. Frishman, Eric Gothberg, Matthew J. Hannon, Dawn V. Jordan, Theodore M. Ladwig, Samuel S. Lamb, Jr., Anthony D. Lombardo, Thomas C. Lyon, James D. MacKenzie, Mary T. McCrea, William B. McDonough, Robin E. Miller, R. Cris Palmer, Antoinette E. Pancaro, Joseph A. Pescatello, Edmund Piver, Frank J. Pucci, Rose V. Raffo, Joseph J. Serio, Cornelius H. Smith, Edward T. Sullivan, Wilmer L. Whitford, Frances H. Wilson, Francis V. Woycik, James P. Yacovino.

BOROUGH OFFICERS. P.O. Box 328, Stonington 06378; Tel., (860) 535-1298.—**Warden,** Eileen C. Jachym.—**Burgesses,** Eleanor G. Casey, William F. Connell, Hervie L. Lamb, Andrew M. Maynard, Christopher S. Rose, Alisa L. Storrow.—**Clerk/Treas.,** Mayada Wadsworth.—**Assessor,** Pamela J. Orkney.—**Tax Collector,** Pamela J. Orkney..—**Planning and Zoning Comm.,** Penny Jones, Chm., Elsa Cole, Anne Eaton, Jane Keener, Sheila Lyons, Bradley Painter, Rosemary Riley; Alternates, David Buck, Peter Thacher.—**Zoning Board of Appeals,** Michael O'Brien, Chm., Leland Abbott, Dean Anderson, Yacomina Nicholas, Maureen Smith; Alternates, Grania H. Ackley, Jane Durborow, Paul Janssens.—**Zoning Enforcement Officer,** Rosalie Maguire.

STRATFORD. Fairfield County.—(Form of government, council-manager.)—Settled, 1639. Area, 19.9 sq. miles. Population, est., 47,230. Voting districts, 10. Principal industries, manufacture of aircraft, air conditioning units, cheese chemicals, electrical parts, hardware, helicopters, machine products, machinery, novelties, plastics, paper products, rubber goods, toys, etc. Home of the "Stratford Shakespeare Theatre". Transp.—Passenger: Served by Metro North Commuter Railroad Co. and by buses of Bridgeport People Mover Co., subsidiary of Greater Bridgeport Transit Dist. Freight: Served by Conrail and numerous motor common carriers. Post Office, Stratford.

TOWN OFFICERS. Clerk and Reg. of Vital Statistics, Patricia P. Ulatowski; Hours, 8 A.M.-4:30 P.M., Mon. through Fri.; Address, Town Hall, Rm. 101, 2725 Main St., 06497-5892; Tel., Bridgeport, (203) 385-4020, 4021, 4022; Fax, (203) 385-4108.—**Asst. Clerks and Asst. Regs. of Vital Statistics,** June Grace, Alice Zawadski.—**Town Manager,** Mark S. Barnhart.—**Town Council: Councilman at Large,** Rudolf J. Weiss.—**Council Clerk,** Laurie Goodsell.—**Councilmen,** 1st Dist., Clement

F. Naples, Chm.; 2nd Dist., Leis Davis, Jr.; 3rd Dist., Richard F. Fredette; 4th Dist., Kent M. Miller; 5th Dist., Raymond S. Voccola; 6th Dist., Anthony J. Schirillo III; 7th Dist., William O. Cabral; 8th Dist., Thomas W. Moore; 9th Dist., David R. Kennedy; 10th Dist., Joseph R. Rainone III.—**Selectmen,** Richard P. Brown, William B. Hansen, vacancy.—**Treas.,** Richard D. Marus.—**Finance Dir.,** Edward B. Gomeau.—**Tax Collector,** Lisa A. P. Biagiarelli.—**Bd. of Assessment Appeals,** William Correia, Chm., Gregory Kelly, Joseph Serino.—**Assessor,** David L. Valente.—**Ethics Comm.,** John Clarke, Carmen Crudo, three vacancies.—**Registrars of Voters,** Richard A. Miron (D), Edward J. Fennell (R).—**Supt. of Schools,** Raymond M. O'Connell.—**Bd. of Education,** Norman A. Aldrich III, Gloria A. Davis, Richard C. Watt, 1997; Deborah A. Rose, Chm., Robert J. Carroll, Michael Koperwhats, Anne T. Wargo, 1999.—**Planning Comm.,** Frederick B. Waugh, Chm., Arthur W. Derbyshire, Kenneth Kellogg, Philip J. Pepin, Robert J. Pitts; Admin., Gary Lorentson; Alternates, Adrien Bonvouloir, Arthur Dritenbas, vacancy.—**Zoning Comm.,** Susan L. Youngquist, Chm., John M. Dempsey, Charles Hess, Helen Patterson, Kathryn Pinkerton; Alternates, Catherine Lawrence, William E. Lindberg, Edward McDonald.—**Zoning Bd. of Appeals,** Robert M. Calzone, Hugh J. Catalano, Theodore Pert, Thomas Torre, Robert C. Watt; Alternates, Charles Burke, Sergio Goncalves, Barry Klein.—**Zoning Enforcement Officer,** John A. Rusatsky.—**Town Planner,** David Killeen.—**Economic Development Comm.,** Howard H. Howes, Chm., Bruce Alessie, Richard Brown, Steve Brown, James Shugrue, Brian Sliva, Arthur Stengel.—**Community Development Agency,** Lewis Davis, Chm., William Cabral, Paul Corvino, William Eaton, Sergio Goncalves, Kent M. Miller, Alvin O'Neal, Florence Rivera, Rudolph Weiss.—**Economic/Community Development Dir.,** Diane C. Toolan.—**Community Services Coordinator,** Patricia Naylor; Asst., Tamara Trojanowski.—**Housing Auth.,** John D. Payton III, Chm., Angela DeClement, Ann DiZenzo, Thomas English, Peter Walkowski; Kevin Nelson, Exec. Dir.—**Fair Housing Officer,** Diane C. Toolan.—**Conservation Comm.,** Robert J. Jontos, Jr., Chm., George P. Fredenburgh, Joseph P. Gresko, Roger Lawson, Gerald F. Sawyer, vacancy; William L. McCann, Environment Conservation Adm.; Alternates, Marcia Stewart, vacancy.—**Comm. on Aging,** Edward Hargus, Chm., Dorothea Anderson, Kathy Brennan, Veronica DiDomenico, Josephine Faggella, Judy Henchar, Helen Hunter, William Kuehn, Milton McDonald, Evelyn Sills, Sophie Wadeka, Josephine Wigglesworth, vacancy.—**Social Serv. Adm.,** Karen Seferi; Asst., Judy Miller.—**Dir. of Health,** Elaine O'Keefe.—**Stratford Library Assoc.,** Marjorie Baird, Edward Fennell, Maxine Goodson, Richard Kleindienst, Sr., Helen Kozma, Doreen Jaekle, William Previs; Edythe M. Landes, Dir.—**Library Operations Review Comm.,** Kent C. Wahlberg, Chm., Dorothy Bradley, Michael Koperwhats, Anthony F. Ross.—**Municipal Historian,** Lewis G. Knapp.—**Supt. of Parks,** Michael Danko.—**Supt. of Recreation,** Patricia L. Patusky.—**Parks and Recreation Committee,** John Harkins, Chm., Michael Buckmir, Gloria Davis, Thomas Fiorella, Richard Fredette, Paul Hoydick, Barry Klein, Edward Matosian, Kent M. Miller, Anthony Ross.—**Human Resources,** Jacques J. Obernesser.—**Dir. of Public Works/Tree Warden,** Michael G. Hudzik.—**Purchasing Agent,** Janet Roberts.—**Town Engineer,** John R. Casey, Jr.—**Building Maintenance Supt.,** Harry Warnstedt.—**Supt. of Highways Div.,** Alan R. Craig.—**Building Official,** John V. Carroll.—**Building Code Bd. of Appeals,** Paul Antinozzi, Chm., John Cowperthwaite,

William DiZenzo, John Jarvis, Robert Mariconda.—**Water Pollution Control Auth.,** Clement F. Naples, Chm., William Cabral, Lewis Davis, Richard Fredette, John Harkins, Kent Miller, Thomas Moore, Joseph Rainone, Anthony Schirillo, Raymond Voccola, Rudolf J. Weiss; Ronald Brenton, Supt.—**Waterfront Harbor Management Comm.,** Robert Sammis, Chm., Manfred Brideau, Gary Caserta, Scott Corner, Robert Gabris, Ross Hatfield, Robert Kekacs, Alan Minter, Richard Perles, Leonard Petrucelli, William Stewart; Alternates, Thomas Allen, Michael Koperwhats.—**Recycling Committee,** William O'Brien, Chm., Pamela Fogarty, Barbara Heimlich, vacancy; Alternates, Kirk Jones, Susan Stevens.—**Supt. of Sanitation,** Gary Catalano.—**Sanitarians,** Edward Knapik, Maureen Hickey.—**Shellfish Comm.,** vacancies.—**Chief of Police,** Robert E. Mossman; Deputy, William B. Knapp III.—**Constables,** Vincent A. Buehler, Jr., Hugh Catalano, J. Anthony Correia, George J. Dirgo, Vincent J. Kostzewski, David J. Martin, Karl Sholanich.—**Chief of Fire Dept.,** Roger L. Macey; Deputy, Ronald C. Nattrass.—**Acting Fire Marshal,** Stephen Pihonak.—**E.M.S. Admr.,** Bruce R. Connery; Asst., Donna N. Best.—**Civil Preparedness Dir.,** Scott Corner.—**Town Atty.,** Richard Buturla; Assts., Richard Gilardi, James Miron, Ellen Morgan Roger Shull.—**Justices of the Peace,** Walter J. Auger, Jonathan Best, Sharon A. Broedlin, Phyllis A. Bronstein, AnnaMarie Buehler, Carol G. Cabral, Kim E. Carroll, Peter F. Carroll, Constantine Chagares, J. Vincent Chase, Tracey S. Chavis, Virginia M. Chittem, Wendy A. Cianfaglione, Paul S. Corvino, Anne DeLottinville, Arthur W. Derbyshire, Sandra Fisher, Lawrence H. Henschel, Daniel J. Jacobs, Irene S. Kostzewski, Patricia A. Kronenberg, Joseph A. Kulikowski, Harold C. Lovell, Jr., Sara F. Martin, Arthur R. Nielsen, James Orlowe, Linda J. Palermo, Frances C. Pascale, Roger A. Pilotti, Brett G. Plucinski, Robert Richard, Linnea A. Scheck, Helen Temple, Margaret H. Voccola, Valerie S. Williams, Donald W. Willis, Karen B. Wiltsie.

SUFFIELD. Hartford County.—(Form of government, selectmen, town meeting, board of finance.)—Inc., May, 1674, by Massachusetts; annexed to Connecticut, May, 1749. Area, 42.9 sq. miles. Population, est., 11,114. Voting district, 1. Principal industries, agriculture, manufacture of ice products, gas, small tools, warehousing. Transp.—Freight: Served by Conrail and numerous motor common carriers. Post offices, Suffield and West Suffield, R.F.D. Nos. 1 and 2 from Suffield office and R.F.D. No. 1 from West Suffield office.

TOWN OFFICERS. Clerk and Reg. of Vital Statistics, Dorothy K. McCarty; Hours, 8:30 A.M.-4:30 P.M., Mon. through Fri.; Summer Hours, 8 A.M.-4:30 P.M., Memorial Day-Labor Day, Mon. through Thurs., 8 A.M.-1 P.M., Friday; Address, Town Hall, 83 Mountain Rd., 06078; Tel., Windsor Locks, (860) 668-3880.—**Asst. Clerks and Asst. Regs. of Vital Statistics,** Jacqueline S. Lathrop, Elaine C. O'Brien.—**Selectmen,** 1st, Roland P. Dowd (U) Tel., (860) 668-3838, Arthur P. Christian (U), Paul A. Kulas (D).—**Treas.,** Edward A. Basile.—**Ethics Comm.,** Robert O. Y. Warren, Chm., Robert J. Clark, Thea Coburn, Richard H. Huleatt, Anne F. Stagg; Alternates, Richard L. Aiken, Jr., Ronald X. Horn.—**Advisory Comm. on Capital Expenditures,** William L. Cannon, Samuel S. Fuller, Edna H. Mann, William J. Steinka, David R. Tagliavini; Alternates, Sarah E. Bourn, Robert J. Frasco.—**Bd. of Finance,** Blair Childs, Jr., Chm., Brian R. Fitzgerald, John R. Henrie, Brian J. Kost,

Warren C. Packard, Stephen E. Smith; Alternates, David S. Berto, Irving J. Friedman, James W. Lennon.—**Tax Collector,** Joan M. McComb.—**Bd. of Assessment Appeals,** Mary Ann Zak, Chm., Chester A. Kuras, Thomas J. O'Malley.—**Assessor,** Susan Altieri.—**Registrars of Voters,** Margaret F. Butler (D), Judith A. Remington (R).—**Supt. of Schools,** Bruce A. Douglas.—**Bd. of Education,** Susan M. Clark, Daniel F. MacKinnon, Elaine C. O'Brien, Thomas R. Sheldon, 1997; Johanne A. Presser, Chm., Eric B. Remington, Phyllis Ryan, Michael J. Smith, Terence T. Stearns, 1999.—**Planning and Zoning Comm.,** Douglas H. Viets, Chm., Brian L. Casinghino, Jeffrey W. Davis, Stephen J. Martin, Robert A. Parks, Jr., Thomas M. Tholany; Alternates, Regina C. Graziani, Sarah S. Peters, Robert H. Skinner.—**Planning Consultant,** William G. Kweder.—**Zoning Bd. of Appeals,** Kenneth Schulte, Chm., Bethany J. Alvord, James Coggins, Brian G. Donnelly, Jay M. Presser; Alternates, Jane P. Fuller, Christine M. Rago, vacancy.—**Economic Development Comm.,** Howard Orr, Jr., Chm., Charles T. Alfano, Jr., Russell T. Cobb, Eugene J. Longo, Paul H. Wabrek; Alexander Carpp, Dir.; Alternates, Susan M. Thorner, Roger F. Tracy.—**Housing Auth.,** Viola Carney, Chm., Sydney F. Fuller, Robert J. Raulukaitis, Sarah S. Skowronski, Anne D. Taylor; Richard Miner, Exec. Dir.—**Conservation Comm.,** Raymond R. Wilcox, Chm., Karl J. Christian, Thomas J. Heffernan, Stephan J. Lefcheck, Glenn A. Neilson, Margot M. Roesberg, Carol S. Rollet; Alternates, two vacancies.—**Historic Dist. Comm.,** Machado Mead, Chm., Gilbert P. Ahrens, Thomas R. Deupree, William S. Moncrief, Gerard H. Riopel; Alternates, Milton M. Edmonds, Jr., Margery C. Warren.—**Dir. of Health,** William H. Blitz, M.P.H., R.S., No. Central District Health Dept. (P.O., Enfield).—**Library Directors,** Claudia G. Hepner, Chm., Ronald P. Borgio, Thomas R. Burton, Muriel P. Coatti, Vincent W. Durnan, Stephen A. Estee, Owen F. Hedden, Samuel E. Johnston III, Jean M. Matejek, Rubina K. Mochon, Edmund B. Sullivan, Robert W. White; Joseph J. Cadieux, Dir.—**Town Historian,** Hawley E. Rising.—**Permanent Building Comm.,** Bobbie C. Kling, Chm., Grace F. Hanrahan, Frederick J. Hanzalek, Bruce L. Kaz, Raymond W. Lozier, Jr., Joseph J. Sangiovanni; Alternates, Milton B. Gardiner, Robert J. Peck.—**Retirement Comm.,** Edward A. Basile, Steven A. Brockett, Roland P. Dowd, Donald M. MacKinnon, Edward G. McAnaney, Warren C. Packard, Robert Williams, vacancy.—**Parks and Recreation Comm.,** John S. Casey, Chm., Robert E. Benson, Jr., Louise H. Cannon, Louis J. Casinghino, Thomas J. DeMaria, Russell E. Mills, Jr., Mary E. Steinka; Wendy Lamontagne, Dir.; Alternates, Steven A. Dunphy, Gail P. Lagasse.—**Tree Warden,** Paul A. Kulas.—**Town Engineer,** Gerald Turbet.—**Building Inspector,** Edward Flanders.—**Building Code of Appeals,** Glenn A. Neilson, Chm., Kerry J. Caldon, Alfred P. Casella, Kevin W. Goff, Stanley C. Szoka.—**Landfill Mgmt. Committee,** Louis G. Boccasile, Chm., Robert J. Borg, Robert R. Roberts, George J. Roebelen, Jr., Deborah L. Smith; Alternates, Donald G. Leis, Jr., Francis K. Tucker.—**Water Pollution Control Auth.,** Hermann Roesberg, Chm., Brendan M. Begley, George E. Philippon, Bruce G. Remington, Amy L. Ruzbasan, William J. Steinka, Maynard Stowe; Bruce C. Williams, Supt., Deborah A. Fabi, Bus. Mgr.—**Sanitarian,** Michael Caronna.—**Chief of Police,** Robert A. Williams.—**Police Comm.,** Matthew J. Conway, Jr., Chm., Philip W. Graham, Michele T. Hall, James W. Lennon, Faith W. Roebelen, Joseph E. Zaczynski.—**Constables,** John S. Casey, Helen K. Corbo, Richard F. Miner, Thomas R. Sheldon, William J. Steinka, Walter E. Szczapa.—**Chief of Fire Dept.,** Thomas L. Bellmore.—

Fire Marshal, George M. Hastings III; Deputies, Steven Brockett, Ronald Carlson, Michael P. Thibedeau.—**Bd. of Fire Comrs.,** Richard F. Miner, Chm., Gerald R. Bland, Frederick E. Hackenyos, Ralph W. Mickelson III, Robert E. Sheridan, Gregory J. Thorner.—**Local Emergency Planning Committee,** Zygmunt F. Dembek, Chm., Thomas L. Bellmore, William Blitz, Arthur J. Boehm, Arthur P. Christian, Roland P. Dowd, Ronald M. Mgrdichian, Stanley Osowiecki, William J. Phelps, Louis Shamback, Stephen Sorrow, Charles Weatherbee, Robert A. Williams.—**Civil Preparedness Comm.,** Thomas L. Bellmore, Roland P. Dowd, Stanley Osowiecki, Richard W. Wilcox, Robert A. Williams; William J. Phelps, Dir.—**Town Attys.,** Justin J. Donnelly, Victoria Spellman.—**Justices of the Peace,** Charles T. Alfano, Jr., Michele M. Basile, Eleanor F. Butler, John S. Casey, Barbara F. Chain, Muriel P. Coatti, Christopher C. Dolnack, Frederick D. George, Regina C. Graziani, Louis N. Hawkins, Gwendolyn S. Houston, Joyce H. Kinsman, Bobbie C. Kling, Sarah A. Kuras, Arthur G. Mandirola, Stephen J. Martin, Joyce K. McIntyre, Beverly T. Patterson, John G. Permatteo, John W. Potter, Suzanne Romano, Robert H. Skinner, William J. Steinka, Joanne M. Sullivan, John W. Wersauckas, Daisy Wilkins-Saunders.

THOMASTON. Litchfield County.—(Form of government, selectmen, town meeting, board of finance.)—Inc., July, 1875; taken from Plymouth. Area, 12.2 sq. miles. Population, est., 7,290. Voting district, 1. Principal industries, injection molding, manufacture of wire, metal pressed sheets and rods, metal shears, electronic equipment and other metal fabrication. Transp.—Freight: Served by Boston & Maine Corporation and numerous motor common carriers. Post office, Thomaston; one R.F.D. route.

TOWN OFFICERS. Clerk and Reg. of Vital Statistics, Catherine DuPont; Hours, 9 A.M.-4:30 P.M., Mon. through Fri.; Address, Town Hall, 158 Main St., 06787; Tel., (860) 283-4141.—**Asst. Clerk and Asst. Reg. of Vital Statistics,** Rosemary L. Martin.—**Selectmen,** Clifford C. Brammer, Jr. (R), Tel., (860) 283-4421, Thomas J. Duffany (D), Roger DuPont (R).—**Treas.,** Paul H. Tracy.—**Bd. of Finance,** Richard M. Chandon, Chm., Michael E. Burr, William Dayton, Kenneth Hopkins, Jr., Richard O'Connell, Joseph F. Wassong, Jr.—**Tax Collector,** Sandra Bruscino.—**Bd. of Assessment Appeals,** Amalia Corey, Cesare J. DelVaglio, Jr., Julianne Ingham.—**Assessors,** Rae Ann Duffy, Chm., Nicholas L. Samela, Alfred Smith.—**Registrars of Voters,** Carol J. Hoebel (D), Barbara Brasche (R).—**Supt. of Schools,** George Counter.—**Bd. of Education,** Lynda Mitchell, Alan Pinard, Catherine Russ, 1997; Michael Kalat, Chm., Steven Dziadik, Karyn L. Pasquella, 1999; Cynthia E. Delvaglio, Delean K. Goldsmith, David Laurentano, 2001.—**Planning and Zoning Comm.,** Paul Biron, Ralph Celone, Douglas Duncan, William Guerrera, Kris Kobryn; Alternates, Shawn Knox, Albion Pelky, Timothy Quinn.—**Zoning Bd. of Appeals,** Joseph F. Wassong, Jr., Chm., Michael S. Bruscino, Jr., Jonathan Foote, Thomas Langlais, James Wilson; Alternates, Cesare J. DelVaglio, Edward Eaton, vacancy.—**Town Planner/ Zoning Enforcement Officer,** Samuel Barto.—**Housing Auth.,** Margaret Conaghan, Alice Langlais, Florence Tillson, John Torrence, Charles Yanavich.—**Conservation Comm.,** Jonathan Foote, Frederick L. Hellerich, Robert A. Mitchell, two vacancies.— **Library Directors,** Peter J. Foley, Jr., Elsa T. Hurlbert, Mary Ann Martin, Karen G.

O'Connell, Kathleen A. Pesce, Barbara Piscopo, Walter G. Robinson, Maryann L. Sandford, Diane Senew, Marilyn Thulin, Kathleen Tobin, Mary Ann K. Torrence.—**Municipal Historian,** Walter Robinson.—**Recreation Comm.,** Terry Costin, Chm., Megan Conaghan, Lester Duffy, Jr., Harry Kryzanowski, William Ryan, Art Williams, Caroline Wilson; Martin Egan, Dir.—**Supt. of Highways,** Gerald Grohoski.—**Building Inspector,** Neil Scala.—**Pollution Control Auth.,** David Baxter, Anthony Cilfone, Charles Fray III, Thomas Mueller, Edward Rohrback, Richard Tingle.—**Tree Warden,** Timothy Chizinski.—**Chief of Police,** Edward Grabherr.—**Constables,** Armand DeFiore, Gary Delaney, Charles R. Fray, Jr., Carol J. Hoebel, Francis A. Wehrle, vacancy.—**Chief of Fire Dept.,** Clifford Brammer.—**Fire Marshal,** Robert Norton, Sr.; Deputy, James O'Neil.—**Bd. of Fire Comrs.,** James Wilson, Chm., Robert Brown, Robert W. Henderson, Robert Ray, Ralph F. Wolf.—**Civil Preparedness Dir.,** Norman Werner.—**Town Atty.,** Michael Rybak.—**Justices of the Peace,** Robert J. Bazin, Diane R. Burr, Armand V. DeFiore, Roger A. DuPont, Beatrice M. Fuller, Carol A. Geddes, Gail A. Lascko, Carol B. Lizotte, Arthur B. Quinn III, John F. Torrence, Nancy F. Wilson.

THOMPSON. Windham County.—(Form of government, selectmen, town meeting, board of finance.)—Inc., May, 1785; taken from Killingly. Area, 48.7 sq. miles. Population, est., 8,780. Voting districts, 4. Principal industries, agriculture, and manufacture of woolen goods, plastics, candy, plumbing goods, synthetics, tool and dye, power equipment, and corrugated boxes. Transp.—Freight: Served by Providence and Worcester Railroad Co. and numerous motor common carriers. Post offices, Thompson, Grosvenor Dale, North Grosvenor Dale and Quinebaug.

TOWN OFFICERS. Clerk and Reg. of Vital Statistics, Rachel C. Haggerty; Hours, 9 A.M.-12 Noon, 1-5 P.M., Mon. through Fri.; 9 A.M.-12 Noon Sat. (except July and August); Address, Town Office Bldg., P.O. Box 899, 815 Riverside Dr., No. Grosvenor Dale 06255; Tel., Putnam, (860) 923-9900.—**Asst. Clerks and Asst. Regs. of Vital Statistics,** Cheryl T. Darling, Paulette J. Hamel.—**Selectmen,** 1st, Norman B. Seney, Jr. (D) Tel., (860) 923-9561, Aaron McGarry (D), James Sali (R).—**Treas.,** Mercedes J. Robbins.—**Bd. of Finance,** Francis J. McGarry, Chm., Donald F. Antonson, Louis P. Faucher, David E. Johnson, Rene J. Morin, Rexford E. Santerre.—**Tax Collector,** Carmen J. Charbonneau.—**Bd. of Assessment Appeals,** Julia J. Rizel, Chm., Cheryl A. Belanger, Dorothy C. Berube.—**Assessor,** Diana M. Couture.—**Registrars of Voters,** James P. Kenney (D), Carl D. Eccleston (R).—**Supt. of Schools,** Edward C. Favolise.—**Bd. of Education,** Jacklyn Bonneau, Susan E. Dumas, Frances E. Roy, 1997; William F. Byrnes, Anastasia E. Kapitulik, James Naum, 1999; Hector L. Morin, Frederick Witkowski, vacancy, 2001.—**Planning and Zoning Comm.,** Charles R. Paquette, Chm., Steven E. Antos, Frederick J. Bates, Randolph C. Blackmer, Jr., Kathryn M. Kuhn, John E. Milas, John J. Rice, Joyce A. Skopek, Stephen W. Small, Francis M. Strong; Alternates, John E. Lamb, David P. Langer, Charles M. Silverston.—**Zoning Bd. of Appeals,** John L. Bell, Sr., Chm., Leona D. Archambault, Robert M. Brodeur, Brian Lynch, Daniel P. Roy, Sr.; Alternates, Raymond P. Faucher, Sr., Joseph G. Garceau, vacancy.—**Zoning Enforcement Officer,** John E. Mahon, Jr.—**Building Inspector,** Ricardo R. Rovero.—**Redevelopment Agency,** David A.

Babbitt, Leta L. Dewey, Kathryn M. Kuhn, James S. Oleksiak, vacancy.—**Housing Auth.,** Lauri Nelson, Chm., Gertrude Leite, Jeannette O'Keefe, Edward J. Prunier, vacancy.—**Conservation and Inland Wetlands Comm.,** Francesca G. Morano, Chm., Robert E. Darling, Bernard H. Davis, Benson R. Gould, Donald R. Hoenig, David E. Johnson, Albert Landry, William K. Pierce, R. Andrew Putnam.—**Conservation Commission Officer,** Carolyn Werge.—**Dir. of Social Services/Agent for the Elderly,** Ada G. Temple.—**Dir. of Health,** Thomas Wegrzyn (P.O. Brooklyn).—**Fair Rent Commission,** Yvette Brissette, Ronald Desrocher, Manfred Isserman, Beverly McDonald, vacancy.—**Small Cities Advisory Bd.,** David A. Babbitt, Chm., Lete Dewey, Shawn Donohoe, Joyce Guilmart, Kathryn M. Kuhn, James S. Oleksiak.—**Library Trustees,** Robert A. LaChance, Chm., Alice M. Bastek, Mary Fatsi, Anna A. Naum, June A. Schoppe, Gladys A. Tucker.—**Municipal Historians,** Donald McGee, Chm., Jeffrey Barske, Linda Mountfort, Jane Vercilli, Susan Vincent.—**Recreation Comm.,** Stanley J. Lesniewski, Chm., Cynthia Antos, Ronald E. Brissette, Jeanne M. Dery, Walter Dudek, Robert Pederson, Michael Santerre, Debra Spinelli, Catherine A. Thomas.—**Building Code Bd. of Appeals,** Edward J. Bibek, Jr., Kenneth R. LeBeau, Roger C. Pelletier, Paul A. Smalarz.—**Water Pollution Control Auth.,** Joseph G. Adiletta, Robert N. Cournoyer, Jr., Charles W. Seney, John A. Zmitrukiewicz, vacancy.—**Chief of Police,** Norman B. Seney.—**Constables,** Joseph G. Garceau, Jean P. Grenier, Peter W. Krawiec, Robert Lary, Jr., Charlotte S. Lenky, Ernest G. Rizel, Claudia Robbins.—**Burning Officer,** Paul H. Grenier.—**Chiefs of Fire Depts.,** Joseph Kudzal (Community Fire Co.), Peter A. Puhlick (W. Thompson), Warren Reynolds (Thompson), Joseph Donovan (Quinebaug), Edward Chrabaszcz (E. Thompson).—**Acting Fire Marshal,** Rick Hayes.—**Civil Preparedness Dir.,** Jean P. Grenier.—**Town Atty.,** William H. St. Onge.—**Justices of the Peace,** Donald A. Brown, Christopher Eichner, Raymond P. Faucher, Sr., Theodore A. Gagne, Linda E. Groh, Michael A. Lajeunesse, Paul F. Lane, Albert J. Marcoux, Jr., Stephen R. Myers, John J. Rice, Frances E. Roy, Luigi C. Salce, Renato T. Schwend, Theodore F. Smith, Catherine A. Thomas, William A. Warner, Douglas J. Williams.

TOLLAND. Tolland County.—(Form of government, town manager, town council.)—Named, May 1715. Inc., May, 1722. Area, 40.3 sq. miles. Population, est., 11,740. Voting district, 1. Principal industry, manufacturing and professional services. Freight: Served by numerous motor carriers. Post office, Tolland.

TOWN OFFICERS. Clerk and Reg. of Vital Statistics, Elaine G. Bugbee; Hours, 9 A.M.-4:30 P.M., Mon. through Thurs.; 5:30-8:30 P.M., Thurs.; 9 A.M.-12:30 P.M., Fri.; Address, Hicks Memorial Municipal Center, 21 Tolland Green, 06084; Tel., Rockville, (860) 871-3630.—**Asst. Clerks and Asst. Regs. of Vital Statistics,** Bernice K. Dixon, Margaret Piazza.—**Acting Town Manager,** David Smith, Tel., (860) 871-3600.—**Town Council,** Joel M. Fain, Chm., (D) Richard J. Field (R), Robert C. Kiehm (D), Carole M. Metcalf-Gordon (D), Charles E. Regan (D), MaryAnn D. Tuttle (D), April C. Teveris (R).—**Treas.,** Elaine G. Bugbee.—**Tax Collector,** Judith E. Lewis.—**Bd. of Assessment Appeals,** Lin Banning, Carl Lesoveck, Mike Penda.—**Assessor,** Walter A. Lawrence.—**Registrars of Voters,** Marion H. Farina (D), Kenneth R. Houck

(R).—**Supt. of Schools,** John Vitale.—**Bd. of Education,** Charles B. Higgins, Chm., Lese C. Amato, Robert F. Benoit, Vicki P. Daniels, Heather R. Gilbert, John C. Lojzim, Joseph R. Mazzarella, Katherine R. Poulos, Gael Stapleton, 1997.—**Planning and Zoning Comm.,** Rebecca Boyden, Chm., Susan K. Errickson, Jennifer M. Nieves, Judith A. Schachner, Richard S. Stawiarski; Alternates, Wayne Johnson, Robert Leonard.—**Town Planner/Zoning Enforcement Officer,** Ronald Blake.—**Zoning Bd. of Appeals,** Robert A. Rubino, Chm., Marilee K. Beebe, Neale Belgrade, Albert J. Boyer, Jr., Elizabeth A. Regan; Alternates, Ramon Martinez, vacancy.—**Economic Development Comm.,** Darrell Chaloult, David Layman, George Mantak, Robert Stewart, William Weigand; Alternates, Robert Leonard, Michael W. Potyra.—**Inland Wetlands Comm.,** Gerald Kerachsky, Chm., Lee Lafountain, Michael Mickiewicz, Naomi Pomper, Arden Tanner; Alternates, Irene Gay, vacancy.—**Housing Auth.,** Conrad Dwire, Chm., Francis L. Bonan, Donald Miller, Debra Simpson, Margaret Zinchuk.—**Dir. of Social Services,** Beverly Bellody.—**Dir. of Health,** Gerald Schwartz.—**Library Bd.,** Barbara Cambria, Kay Cardin, Debra DeVries-Dalton, Kathryn Kusmin, Bettye Jo Pakulis.—**Municipal Historian,** Barbara Palmer.—**Recreation Bd.,** Sharon Bartlett, W. Edwin Errickson, Claire Fazzina, David Geissler, Jim Grassi, Jeffrey A. Maron, Raymond Milvae; Tom Ainsworth, Dir.—**Supt. of Highways,** John Bock.—**Tree Warden,** Theodore Palmer.—**Building Inspector,** Kent Carney.—**Building Code Bd. of Appeals,** Robert Cardin, Stephen Courtney, Stanley Krupowies, Carl Lesoveck, Gilbert Schmeiske.—**Water and Waste Management Comm.,** Robert Fredley, Charles Gardner, Charles Higgins, Kenneth Houck, William Pakulis, Arden Tanner, George Tornatore, two vacancies.—**Sanitarian,** Robert DeVito.—**Constables,** Kendall Keyes, Thomas Martin, three vacancies.—**Chief of Fire Dept./Civil Preparedness Dir.,** Ronald Littell; Deputy, Richard Symonds.—**Fire Marshal,** Richard M. Munichiello.—**Town Atty.,** Dennis O'Brien.—**Justices of the Peace,** Ann Azevedo, Lin M. Banning, Robert W. Bass, Harvey B. Blauvelt, John W. Butler, Michael Cardin, Robert W. Cardin, Stephen E. Courtney, Donato T. DiGenova, Charles A. Gardner, Francis L. Hjarne, Dean Jennings, Kathleen K. Kolpinski, Marilyn R. Kuhnly, James D. Logan, Pamela B. Lord, Carole M. Metcalf-Gordon, Deborah B. Milvae, William K. Pakulis, Peter Palmer, Theodore T. Palmer, Kathleen M. Papillo, Edward L. Sederquest III, Arden Tanner, George S. Tornatore, Nancy S. Wyman.

TORRINGTON. Litchfield County.—(Form of government, mayor, city council.)—Inc. as a town, Oct. 1740; inc. as a city, Oct. 1, 1923. Town and city consolidated, 1923. Area, 40.4 sq. miles. Population, est., 34,031. Voting districts, 6. Principal industries, manufacture of hardware, tools, machinery, kitchen utensils, gaskets, needle bearings, golf shafts, air conditioning equipment. Transp.—Passenger: Served by The Kelley Transit Co., Inc. from New Milford, Danbury and Hartford, and locally by Northwestern Connecticut Transit District, Candy Stripers and rural transit; Freight: Served by Boston & Maine Corporation and numerous motor common carriers. Post office, Torrington.

CITY AND TOWN OFFICERS. City Clerk, Town Clerk and Reg. of Vital Statistics, Joseph L. Quartiero; Hours, 8 A.M.-4:30 P.M., Mon. through Fri.; Address, Municipal Bldg., 140 Main St., 06790; Tel., (860) 489-2236.—**Asst. Town Clerks,**

Marianne Audia, Stella Corey, Maryann Delay, Joan McLaughlin.—**Asst. Regs. of Vital Statistics,** Marianne Audia, Stella Corey, Maryann Delay, Joan McLaughlin.—**Asst. City Clerk,** Joline LeBlanc.—**Mayor,** Mary Jane Gryniuk (D).—**Bd. of Councilmen,** Mary Jane Gryniuk, Chm., Susan F. Cogswell, John J. Dunne, Jr., Virginia K. Kovaleski, Arthur E. Mattiello, Richard J. O'Connor, Thomas P. Scoville.—**Selectmen,** Juliana M. Bray, Jo-An C. Cracco, Edward F. Petrovits.—**Treas./Comptroller,** Richard J. Friday.—**Bd. of Finance,** Mayor Mary Jane Gryniuk, Chm., Gladys Cerruto, Michael Gallicchio, Diane Libby, Peter J. McLaughlin, Carl Michelet, Bertrand J. Theroux.—**Tax Collector,** Joseph Cordani.—**Bd. of Assessment Appeals,** Annette Caputi, Chm., John Fitzgerald, Andrew Lach.—**Assessor,** Joan Oros.—**Insurance Comm.,** Richard J. Friday, Chm., James Fabiaschi, Raymond S. Madeux, Gordon Todd, Albert G. Vasko.—**Registrars of Voters,** James E. Murphy (D), Amelia K. Waldron (R).—**Supt. of Schools,** Dr. John F. Shine.—**Bd. of Education,** James F. McKenna, Chm., Cynthia O. Arnold, Anthony C. Laraia, Douglas K. O'Connell, J. Peter Torrant, 1997; Margaret A. Chadwick, David Mazzaferro, Laurene Pesce, Todd E. Pollutro, Mary Anne Sok, 1999.—**Planning and Zoning Comm./Flood and Erosion Control Bd.,** John T. Hogan, Jr., Chm., Robert Della Donna, David Frascarelli, Doris Murphy, Rita Pacheco; Alternates, Richard Calkins, Janet Iffland, Raymond J. Turri.—**City Planner,** Dana McGuinness.—**Zoning Bd. of Appeals,** Jamie Gregg, Chm., Robert Blenner, James Marinelli, Marie Soliani, Cynthia Vasko; Alternates, Genevieve Gangi, Kathleen Perrotti, Robert Weston.—**Zoning Enforcement Officer,** Thomas Barbero.—**Economic Development Comm.,** Albino Bruno, Gary Giordano, Robert Grier, Cheryl Gruner, Francis A. Hennessy, Grace Koldys, William Mascetti, Robert Panza, Roland Spino.—**Environmental Planner,** Edward Lukacovic.—**Housing Auth.,** Samuel E. Slaiby, Chm., Mario J. D'Angelo, Ken Fuchsman, John F. McCarthy, Catherine Murphy, ; Carmel Ubaldi, Exec. Dir.—**Conservation Comm.,** Raymond Wilcox, Chm., Harry Arsego, Ralph DeAngelo, Robert Hartman-Berrier, John J. Kuzmik, Caroline Minard, vacancy.—**Inland Wetlands Comm.,** Raymond F. Hubert, Chm., Rita Pacheco, William Reardon, Raymond Royals, Paul Sabia, Kathleen Waltos, vacancy.—**Municipal Historian,** Ernest F. Ceder.—**Comm. on Services for the Elderly,** Lena Ostrander, Chm., Chester Bieluch, Rose Galgano, Evelyn Lukes, Virginia Patrick; Anita Post, Albert Signorelli; Alternates, Marty Jakimenko, Raymond Poniatoski, Ann Robustelli.—**Municipal Agent for the Elderly,** Nancy S. Gyurko.—**Dir. of Social Services,** Yvonne Adorno.—**Parks and Recreation Comm.,** Angelo LaMonica, Chm., Jan Dlugokinski, Carol Miasek, Peter Robertson, Thomas Waterfall; Craig Schroeder, Dir.—**Dir. of Public Works/Tree Warden,** Gerald Rollett.—**Supt. of Streets,** Michael A. Bonasera.—**Purchasing Agent,** Charlene Antonelli.—**Sealer of Weights and Measures,** Fletcher Waldron.—**Building Official,** Francis Cardello.—**Building Code Bd. of Appeals,** Daniel F. Farley, Chm., Max Borghesi, Angelo Perugini, Gerald Rollett, Ralph Sabia, Charles White—**City Engineer,** Joseph Cosentino.—**Acting Water Pollution Control Authority Admin.,** Charles Hewitt.—**Personnel Dir.** Thomas Gritt.—**Chief of Police,** Mahlon Sabo; Deputy, Roger Janelle.—**Bd. of Public Safety,** Mary Jane Gryniuk, Chm., Kenneth A. Fuchsman, Philip A. Kozlak, Richard T. McLeod, Robert A. Panza, Richard Purcell, Frank J. Rubino.—**Constables,** Francis A. Gallicchio, Jr., Theodore Miasek, James D. Reginatto, Linda M. Roche, Lori J. Samele, Joseph J. Silano, Robert J. Sorvillo.—**Chief of Fire Dept.,**

Marquam R. Johnson; Deputy, Timothy Schapp.—**Fire Marshal,** Timothy Tharau.—**Civil Defense Dir.,** Arthur Deming, Jr.—**Corporation Counsel,** Albert G. Vasko.—**Justices of the Peace,** Joseph M. Albanese, Jr., Susan Angelini, Gary Arnold, Sidney Axelrod, Floyd D. Baldwin, Addo E. Bonetti, Fred Bruni, Kenneth A. Buckbee, John E. Calkins, Jr., Patsy Capuano, Diana M. Carroll, Susan F. Cogswell, Richard Dalla Valle, James V. DeMaio, Daniel DiGiovanni, Dee Donne, Laurie A. Fillipini, Martha Gallagher, Mary Jane Gryniuk, Christopher C. Healy, Jonathan Hutchinson, Donna L. Isely, Virginia Kovaleski, Anthony Lucia, John D. J. McKeon, Richard T. McLeod, Theodore Miasek, JoAnn O'Connor, Molly S. Oddo, Jeremiah O'Sullivan, Rita Pacheco, Lucille A. Paige, Lloyd Petteway, Eugene T. Redmond, Linda Roche, Fred M. Rose, Fred M. Rose, Jr., Susan Rovezzi-Carroll, Raymond E. Rubino, George B. Ruwet, Leo Senese, Desaree L. Sikora, Marie P. Soliani, Kevin J. Sullivan, Lena L. Tedesco, Edmond N. Tino, Roberta J. Waldron, Robert S. Weston, Edward C. Wilmot, Marion Yonkaitis.

TRUMBULL. Fairfield County.—(Form of government, first selectman, town council, board of finance.)—Inc., Oct., 1797; taken from Stratford. Area, 23.5 sq. miles. Population, est., 31,387. Voting districts, 7. Principal industry, real estate; largely a residential area. Transp.—Passenger: Served by buses of the Greater Bridgeport Transit Dist.; Chestnut Hill Bus Corp. from Bridgeport; The Chieppo Bus Co. from Bridgeport and Danbury; Valley Transp., Inc. from Waterbury and by Greyhound. Freight: Served by numerous motor common carriers. Post office, Trumbull; house deliveries by carriers.

TOWN OFFICERS. Clerk and Reg. of Vital Statistics, Linda M. Lungi; Hours, 9 A.M.-5 P.M., Mon.- Fri.; Address, Town Hall, 5866 Main St., 06611; Tel., (203) 452-5035.—**Asst. Clerks and Asst. Regs. of Vital Statistics,** Susan M. Cole, Gloria S. Murphy.—**First Selectman,** David A. Wilson (D) Tel., (203) 452-5005.—**Town Council,** Dist. 1, Dan E. LaBelle, Chm., Peter Gelderman, Stephen P. Wright; Dist. 2, Angelo D. Cordone, Carol Tenedine, Liz Kedan; Dist. 3, Sandra L. Carey, Neil A. Lieberthal, T. R. Rowe; Dist. 4, Rosemarie Lodice, Jay L. Stollman, vacancy; Dist. 5, Frank Palacino, Leonard J. Roberto, Sr., Risa L. Vine; Dist. 6, Frank E. Altieri, George F. Hammel, Robert L. Minasian; Dist. 7, John T. Cavaliere, Daniel W. Helfrich, Frank D. Verrilli.—**Bd. of Selectmen,** Jane B. Deyoe, Florence L. Pavia, David A. Wilson, Janice L. Winkler.—**Ethics Comm.,** Arthur Friedman, Chm., Michael Dolan, Nancy Phillips, Anthony Pinciaro, Rabbi Jerome Wallin.—**Treas.,** Bruce E. Stern.—**Bd. of Finance,** George B. Baehr, Jr., Chm., Raymond G. Baldwin, Bernard D. Helfrich, Vincent P. Mangiacapra, Fred Radford, Vito Mazza; James Hliva, Dir.; Alternates, Roger Fitzgibbon, Robert Golger, vacancy.—**Tax Collector,** Ross D. Murray.—**Bd. of Assessment Appeals,** Frank Giordanella, Carl Massaro, Jr., Sandra Riley.—**Assessor,** Joseph Simalchik.—**Tax Assessor,** Lee Induni.—**Registrars of Voters,** Robert K. Marconi (D), William S. Holden (R).—**Supt. of Schools,** Edwin T. Merritt.—**Bd. of Education,** Clare Hampford, M. Gloria Maina, Terry Mac Phail, 1997; Arthur Kaiser, Chm., Donna M. Cassidy, William Dunn, 1999.—**Planning and Zoning Comm.,** Anthony Capasso, Chm., Vivian Burr, Kenneth Halaby, Paul Neri, Jack Schlechtweg; Alternates, Anthony Chory, Jeffrey Goldwasser, Daniel Jocis.—**Zoning**

Bd. of Appeals, David Klein, Chm., Frederick K. Bietsch, Frank Kochiss, Michael Muir, Irwin Nabel; Alternates, Russell Friedson, Moufid Makhraz, Frank Rocco.—**Economic Development Comm.,** William Topolski, Chm., John Deeken, Paul Fischer, Gerson Kaufman, Moufrid Makhraz, Raymond Rizio, Gary Ruot, Thomas Tesoro, Norman Winkler, Alphonse Wright.—**Housing Auth.,** Roger Grossbard, Chm., Lori Belmont, Rowena Paumi, Michael Stavish, Ann Stern.—**Conservation Comm.,** David Chardavoyne, Marvin Krumper, Ann Laukkanen-Mones, Lynn O'Donnell-Allen, Thomas O'Neill, Gary Oppedisano, Dwight Smith, Jonathan Spodnick, vacancy.—**Inland Wetlands and Water Course Comm.,** Earl Altieri, Chm., Hugo James, Robert Keogh, Thomas O'Neill, Thomas Schumaker, Jonathan Spodnick, vacancy.—**Flood and Erosion Control Bd.,** Edward M. Curtis, Chm., John Cavaliere, Ronald Farrell, Hugo James, Edward Kulhawik.—**Senior Citizens Comm.,** Rose Pellegrino, Chm., Jean DiBenedetto, Michael DiBenedetto, Frances Hanna, Helen Hayman, Rose Iodice, Teresa Murphy, Joan P. Walsh.—**Dir. of Social Services,** Jean Fereira.—**Emergency Medical Services Comm.,** Vi Watson, Chm., Louise F. Evans, Shelley Ralsten, Joseph Rodriguez, Edwin Rogalewski, D.D.S., Michael Rolleri, Dominick Rutigliano; Charles Evans, Exec. Dir.—**Dir. of Health,** Kenneth J. Maiocco, M.D.—**Bd. of Public Health,** Ann Marie Fekete, Chm., Carole DelVecchio, Joseph Firgelski, M.D., Albert Weinstein, M.D., Benjamin Weisman, M.D.—**Library Directors,** H. Richard Brew, Chm., Daniel Baker, John Cooper, John Hax, Josephine Smith, Jeannine Stauder, Gary Wilson, C. Duncan Yetman, vacancy.—**Municipal Historian,** Trumbull Historical Society.—**Arts Comm.,** Susan Cormier, Renee LeDonne, Margaret Nagourney, Lee Scarpetti, Anne Wright, two vacancies.—**Bd. of Recreation,** Michael Fettig, Chm., Roger McGovern, Mario Rossi, Dennis White, vacancy.—**Parks Comm.,** Robert Ferrigno, Chm., John Behn, Ian Black, Elizabeth Casey, Anthony Chmielewski, Ray Elterich, Thomas Gallo, Arla Wiles.—**Youth Comm.,** Joann Tilghman, Chm., Lisa Andrasko, Brad Day, Helen Kurilec, Enid Rizzo, two vacancies.—**Supt. of Parks,** Vernon Lentz.—**Dir. of Public Works,** Paul A. Kallmeyer; Operations Mgr., Len Provenzano.—**Tree Warden,** Warren Jacques.—**Purchasing Agent,** Stephen Orris.—**Building Official,** Donald Murray.—**Pension Bd.,** J. Robert Lutz, Chm., James Hliva, Thomas Ragonese, Robert Rosenfield, vacancy.—**Building Code Bd. of Appeals,** Joseph Coyne, Edward Malik, August J. Palmieri, Paul Taormina, vacancy.—**Sewer Comm.,** Angelo Memoli, Chm., George Biagioni, Peter Clark, Vincent DiZenzo, Carl S. Koch.—**Chief of Police,** Theodore Ambrosini.—**Police Comm.,** Frank Blanco, Chm., James Butler, Lino Costantini, Nancy DiNardo, Kristine Miklus, Michael Niedermeier.—**Constables,** William Black, Roger Fekete, James Lynch.—**Chiefs of Fire Depts.,** Wayne Schalich (Trumbull Center), John Butz (Nichols), Eugene Miller (Long Hill).—**Bd. of Fire Protection,** Ronald Lewis, Chm., Joseph Adzima, Theodore Ambrosini, George Baehr, Douglas Doyle, Eugene Miller, Ken Montlick, Donald Murray, Wayne Schalich, Wayne Szymyt, David A. Wilson.—**Fire Marshal,** Joseph P. Adzima.—**Civil Preparedness Dir.,** Helen Buswell.—**Town Attys.,** Arthur Hiller, Daniel Schopick, Burton Yaffie.—**Justices of the Peace,** Virginia Bailey, Dana K. Beck, Frank E. Blanco, Joyce M. Campbell, Michael C. Delales, Daniel P. Jocis, Gregory J. Kaufman, Rosemary Malik, Brian E. Murphy, Americo V. Napolitano, Keely M. Papay, Lucille S. Pratt, Donald S. Scinto, Irene Simalchik, Judith M. Szablak.

UNION. Tolland County.—(Form of government, selectmen, town meeting, board of finance.)—Inc., Oct., 1734. Area, 29.8 sq. miles. Population, est., 639. Voting district, 1. Principal industries, agriculture and forestry. Transp.—Passenger: Served by buses of Greyhound and Trailways. Freight: Served by numerous motor common carriers. Rural free delivery from Stafford Springs.

TOWN OFFICERS. Clerk and Reg. of Vital Statistics, Heidi Bradrick; Hours, 9 A.M.-12 Noon, Tues., Thurs.; 9 A.M.-12 Noon, 1-3 P.M., Wed.; Address, Rte. 171, 1024 Buckley Highway, 06076; Tel., Stafford Springs, (860) 684-3770.—**Asst. Clerk and Asst. Reg. of Vital Statistics,** Patricia Brousseau.—**Selectmen,** 1st, Albert L. Goodhall, Jr. (R) Tel., (860) 684-3812, Roy B. Bradrick, Jr. (R), Paul M. Rizner (D).—**Treas.,** Emily Rizner.—**Bd. of Finance,** Richard A. Otto, Chm., Melvin E. Berkey, Jr., Donna H. Corsini, James J. Dabrowski, Peter Tiziani, Launa L. Trinque; Alternates, Curtis M. Berner, Albert L. Goodhall, Gerald C. Leighton III.—**Tax Collector,** Maureen M. Eaton.—**Bd. of Assessment Appeals,** Marguerite Bario, Janet E. Peterson, James J. Smith.—**Assessor,** Joan LeBlond.—**Registrars of Voters,** Carol A. Berner (D), Betty B. Vilandre (R).—**Supt. of Schools,** Richard Butler.—**Bd. of Education,** Carol A. Berner, Emily Rizner, 1997; Brenda A. Burkey, Cheryl L. Gustafson, 1999; Roger Bragdon, Andrea M. Estell, Donna M. S. Jellen, 2001.—**Planning, Zoning, and Inland Wetlands Comm.,** James George, Chm., John S. Geissler, David Heck, David Herr, Michael O'Dette; Alternates, Joseph L. Kratochvil, Robert A. Mihaliak, Diane H. Williams.—**Zoning Bd. of Appeals,** James J. Smith, Chm., Eric Emhoff, Arthur E. Murdock, Janet Peterson, William Scranton, Nathan B. Swift, Jr.; Alternates, Bonnie L. Drabowski, Timothy Goodhall, vacancy.—**Conservation Officer,** Joseph E. Vilandre.—**Comm. on Aging,** Antoinette Gilbronson, Dora Hulse, Margaret Tyler.—**Agent for the Elderly,** Bertha Syphers.—**Dir. of Health/Sanitarian,** Bruce D. Lundgren.—**Library Directors,** Patricia Geissler, Lisa Hackner, Carol Mancini, Steve Szych, Jr., Pamela D. Trinque, Jeannine Upson.—**Municipal Historian,** Jeanine Upson.—**Public Safety Liaison,** Lt. Louis Lacaprucia.—**Tree Warden,** Joseph Prucha.—**Road Foreman,** David D. Eaton.—**Burning Official,** Tom Fitzgerald.—**Building Inspector,** Edward Staveski.—**Solid Waste Management Committee,** David Eaton, Albert L. Goodhall, Sr., Joseph Kratochvil, Robert Mihaliak, Anna M. Pallanck.—**Marine Patrol Officer,** Albert L. Goodhall, Sr.; Assts., James Dabrowski, Paul M. Rizner.—**Constables,** Rudolph Corsini, Michael D'Amico, Albert L. Goodhall, Herbert C. Muller, Joseph Prucha.—**Chief of Fire Dept.,** David D. Eaton; Deputy, William Scranton, Jr.—**Fire Marshal,** Charles Sweetland.—**Civil Preparedness Dir.,** Thomas Fitzgerald; Asst., vacancy.—**Town Atty.,** Michael Devlin.—**Justices of the Peace,** Marguerite Bario, Joan L. Bauer, Carol A. Berner, Bonnie L. Dabrowski, David Eaton, Albert L. Goodhall, Paul M. Rizner, James J. Smith, Kathryn E. Spink, Robert E. Tyler, Jr., Dean Upson.

VERNON. Tolland County.—(Form of government, mayor, town council.)—Town inc., Oct., 1808; taken from Bolton. City of Rockville inc., Jan., 1889. Town of Vernon and City of Rockville consolidated, July 1 1965. Area, 18.1 sq. miles. Population, est., 29,911. Voting districts, 7. Principal industries, anodizing, metal surface treatments, bacteriological media production, communications equipment, fire retardant paints, dyeing and finishing of fabrics, plastics, tools and dies, woodworking. Transp.—Passenger: Served by buses of Conn. Transit from Hartford and Post Road Stages, Inc. from Hartford and Stafford Springs. Freight: Served by numerous motor common carriers. Post offices, Vernon, Rockville and Talcottville.

TOWN OFFICERS. Clerk and Reg. of Vital Statistics, Terri A. Krawczyk; Hours, 9 A.M.-5 P.M., Mon., through Fri.; Address, Memorial Bldg., 14 Park Pl., 06066; Tel., (860) 872-8591.—**Asst. Clerks and Asst. Regs. of Vital Statistics,** Dorothy E. Dove, Lorelei L. Soderlund.—**Asst. Registrar of Vital Statistics,** Alice H. Mellor.—**Town Admin.,** Paul R. Mazzaccaro.—**Mayor,** Tony Muro (D).—**Town Council,** Mayor Tony Muro, Presiding Officer, Jeffrey R. Adamson, Gail P. Faherty, Bill Fox, Marie A. Herbst, Claire L. Janowski, Chester W. Morgan, Mary A. Oliver, Vic Perry, Jr., Paul M. Shimer, Walter W. Simmers, Steven L. Wakefield, Diane R. Wheelock; Terri A. Krawczyk, Council Clerk.—**Treas.,** James M. Luddecke.—**Board of Ethics,** Robert B. Carlson, Chm., Regina T. Daly, Carl M. Dick, MaryJane Oefinger, Timothy Poloski; Alternates, Linda B. Gessay, Nelson H. White, Jr.—**Collector of Revenue,** Peter V. Korbusieski; Asst., Carol S. Nelson.—**Bd. of Assessment Appeals,** Patricia A. Noblet, Chm., Howard G. Abbott, Norman R. Strong.—**Assessor,** John VanOudenhove; Deputy, Jane M. Grigsby.—**Registrars of Voters,** Judith A. Beaudreau (D), Patricia A. Noblet (R).—**Supt. of Schools,** Andrew T. Maneggia.—**Bd. of Education,** Amarjit S. Buttur, Susan N. Hesnan, Peggy A. Jackle, David G. Kemp, Elizabeth Mix, Thomas A. Olsen, 1997; Michelle E. Arn, Chm., Carroll L. Burke, Thomasina C. Russell, 1999.—**Planning and Zoning Comm.,** Christopher A. Crowne, Chm., Juanita L. Bair, Judy H. Fondrk, Joseph M. Tringali, Thomas F. Wagner, Robert F. Warner; Alternates, Carl F. Bard, Alfred L. Pittman, George E. Roraback, Jr.—**Zoning Bd. of Appeals,** Ann F. Bird, Chm., William C. Fredericksen, David F. Haines, Joseph A. Matczak, Roger D. Wiley; Alternates, Michael F. Murray, Mark L. Russell, vacancy.—**Zoning Enforcement Officer,** Gene F. Bolles.—**Conservation Comm.,** Deborah M. Dumin, Chm., William E. Francis, Jr., Gordon P. Gibson, Brian R. Motola, Robert J. Smith; Alternates, Patrick Beron, E. Mason Thrall, Jr.—**Inland Wetlands Regulatory Agency,** William F. Campbell, Chm., Mark W. Davis, Guy D. Minor, Amy B. Paterson, Jacquelyn C. Skillings; Alternates, Jeffrey T. Pescosolido, Ralph E. Zahner.—**Town Planner,** George H. Russell.—**Town Engineer,** DeWilton Timberman III.—**Economic Development Comm.,** John Carter, Chm., Charles W. Ayer, Jr., Charles Hatheway, Nathan B. Karnes, James P. McWalter, Robert K. Mullen, Lucille J. Mulligan, J. John Piela, Brett C. Swihart; Thomas J. Joyce, Jr., Coordinator.—**Housing Auth.,** Mary Lou Menard, Chm., Peter F. Olson, Nancy Osborn, Sally M. Raymond, George W. Russell; Catherine F. Melan, Exec. Dir.—**Energy Conservation Comm.,** Carl Schaefer, Chm., Jimmie Banis, Barry L. Hauser.—**Vernon Arts Comm.,** Edward Adams, Diane Bernier, Joyce A. Deschamps, Linda P. Ferguson, Bridget M. Gilchrist, Margaret A. Hayden, Lisa Marie Letendre, Deborah G. Rodriguez, Phyllis Winkler.—**Municipal Historian,** S. Ardis Abbott.—**Local Historic Properties Comm.,** S. Ardis Abbott, Chm., Rondald Burke, Robert B. Hurd, Myrtle Loftus, Geraldine Strong; Alternates, Steven A. Augustus, James D. Bell, Jean K. Hopkins.—**Agent for the Elderly,** Ella A. Delaney.—**Dir. of Social Services,** Paula Claydon.—**Dir. of Health,** Joseph Kristan, M.D.—**Dir. of Public Works,** David R. Tomko.—**Purchasing Agent,** James M. Luddecke.—**Permanent Municipal Building Com-**

mittee, James J. Beck, Chm., Brendan Flaherty, Jerry F. Kinsman, John P. Leary, Pauline Schaefer, Vincent J. Urban, Mark E. Vesco.—**Building Inspector,** Gene F. Bolles.—**Building Code Bd. of Appeals,** George MacDonald, Chm., Charles H. Blake, John P. Leary.—**Water Pollution Control Auth.,** Carl W. Schaefer, Chm., Howard G. Abbott, John K. Anderson, Jack L. Gorr, Sr., George S. Oprysko.—**Water Pollution Control, Dir.,** David Ignatowicz.—**Pension Bd.,** William J. McManus, Chm., Frank C. Rogers, Anthony P. Zappola.—**Cemetery Comm.,** Wayne E. Ladd, Chm., Scott G. Brown, Virginia D. Hickton, Myrtle D. Loftus, Norman R. Strong.—**Traffic Auth.,** Rudolph Rossmy, Chm., Barbara R. Hofsess, Chester W. Morgan, Jon-Paul Roden, David R. Tomko, Donna Rae Vanderhoff, William G. Viot.—**Chief of Police,** Rudolf M. Rossmy; Capt. Gary L. Mazzone.—**Chief of Fire Dept.,** Robert E. Kelley.—**Fire Marshal,** Donald J. Maguda.—**Town Atty.,** John M. Casey.—**Justices of the Peace,** Jeffrey R. Adamson, Juanita L. Bair, Amarjit S. Buttar, Gloria A. Collins, Susan C. Connell, Robert W. Dotson, Gail P. Faherty, Julie Jacques-Marcotte, Claire L. Janowski, David G. Kemp, Maryann Mierzwa, Dorothy R. Miller, Robert F. North, Nancy Osborn, Nicholas Pawluk, Alfred L. Pittman, Rudolf Rossmy, Pauline A. Schaefer, Gail E. Slicer, Lena J. Thereault, Christy N. Vale, Steven L. Wakefield, Robert F. Warner, Michael A. Winkler.

VOLUNTOWN. New London County.—(Form of government, selectmen, town meeting.)—Inc., May, 1721. Area, 39.8 sq. miles. Population, est., 2,288. Voting district, 1. Principal industry, agriculture, recreation. Transp.—Freight: Served by numerous motor common carriers. Post office, Voluntown. Rural free delivery.

TOWN OFFICERS. Clerk and Reg. of Vital Statistics, Mary Anne Nieminen; Hours, 9 A.M.-2 P.M., Mon. through Thurs.; 6-8 P.M., Tues.; 9 A.M.-12 Noon, Fri.; Sat. by appointment. Tel., (860) 376-4089; Address, Town Hall, Main St., P.O. Box 96, 06384; Tel., Jewett City, (860) 376-4089.—**Asst. Clerk and Asst. Reg. of Vital Statistics,** Cheryl A. Sadowski.—**Selectmen,** 1st, Eric D. Marsh (D) Tel., (860) 376-3927, Paul Whitehead (D), Thomas H. Wilber (R).—**Treas.,** Richard A. Osga.—**Tax Collector,** Frances B. Grenier.—**Bd. of Assessment Appeals,** Gilbert G. Grimm, Chm., John W. Harris, Robert Sirpenski.—**Assessor,** Mildred Peringer.—**Registrars of Voters,** Bridget T. Lee (D), Beth Taylor (R).—**Supt. of Schools,** Anthony Perrelli.—**Bd. of Education,** Wendy K. Gauthier, Jack S. Wesa, 1997; Arthur L. Savona, Chm., Diana M. Ingraham, Arthur F. Ivanick, Donald W. Mann, Nina K. Plumb, 1999.—**Planning and Zoning Comm.,** Kenneth R. Weseman, Chm., Dwayne K. Davis, Charles A. Emmons, Flora Harman, Thomas Smith; Alternates, Lucio A. Almeida, Ruth A. Blanchette, Larry P. Charette.—**Zoning Bd. of Appeals,** David F. Esterquest, Chm., Jeffrey M. Blake, Gregory C. Gardella, James S. Hicks, Jr., Thomas M. Sweet; Alternates, Frank W. Grant, Joan C. Harris, Brett A. Marsh.—**Inland Wetlands Comm.,** Karl Sommers, Chm., Joseph H. Grenier, James S. Hicks, Jr., Thomas E. Kingsbury, David C. Miner; Alternate, David A. Nieminen, Eric J. Williams, Jr.—**Housing Auth.,** Audrey G. Grenier, Debra Grenier, Gertrude Lindell, Joseph Theroux.—**Elderly Comm.,** Frances Grenier, Edgar LaFleshe, Eleanor Morrisette, John Morrisette, John Panko, Mary Panko, Arthur Roode, Vivian Roode.—**Dir. of Health/**

Sanitarian, Town of Griswold.—**Library Directors,** Charles A. Emmons, Georgette F. Grenier, Heather K. Marsh, Gloria J. Matthews, Sandra V. Pellinen, Patricia C. Thevenet.—**Building Inspector,** Daniel P. Kitchel.—**Building Code Bd. of Appeals,** John Rupple.—**Chief of Fire Dept./Fire Marshal,** Joseph H. Grenier.—**Civil Preparedness Dir.,** Robert M. Ruppel.—**Town Atty.,** Nicholas Kepple.—**Justices of the Peace,** Carl D. Anderson, Karen A. Anderson, Beatrice M. Delamater, Walter W. Elomaa, Benjamin K. Gallup, Georgette F. Grenier, Joseph H. Grenier, Edgar D. LaFleshe, Beverly J. Marsh, Eric D. Marsh, Mary Anne Nieminen, Richard A. Osga, Birdsey G. Palmer, Paul Whitehead.

WALLINGFORD. New Haven County.—(Form of government, mayor, town council.)—Named, May, 1670. Town and borough consolidated, Jan. 1, 1958. Area, 39.9 sq. miles. Population, est., 41,276. Voting districts, 14. Principal industries, agriculture and manufacture of silverware, steel, plastic material and hardware. Transp.—Passenger: Served by Amtrak, buses of The Short Line of Conn., Inc.; Conn. Transit from New Haven and Double A Transp. Service locally. Freight: Served by Conrail and numerous motor common carriers. Post offices, Wallingford and Yalesville.

TOWN OFFICERS. Clerk and Reg. of Vital Statistics, Rosemary A. Rascati; Hours, 9 A.M.-5 P.M., Mon. through Fri.; Address, Municipal Bldg., 45 South Main St., P.O. Box 427, 06492; Tel., (203) 294-2145.—**Asst. Clerks and Asst. Regs. of Vital Statistics,** Robin Caruso, Evelyn A. Fernandes.—**Mayor,** William W. Dickinson, Jr. (R).—**Town Council,** Richard Centner, Jr. (R), David J. Doherty (D), Jerry Farrell, Jr. (R), Steven Knight (R), Iris J. Papale (D), Robert F. Parisi (R), Frank A. Renda, Sr. (R), Raymond J. Rys, Sr. (R), Tom Zappala (D).—**Selectmen,** Chester H. Burghoff, Walter Dubar, vacancy.—**Treas.,** Peter Murphy.—**Bd. of Ethics,** Laurie Manke, Chm., G. Randolph Erskine, James L. Kendall, Brendan McCormick; Alternates, Willard Burghoff, Mary Conant, Jack Winkleman.—**Comptroller,** Thomas Myers.—**Tax Collector,** Norman Rosow.—**Bd. of Assessment Appeals,** James Loughlin, Chm., Louis DePonto, Gerald Labriola, Jr.—**Assessor,** Francis J. Barta.—**Registrars of Voters,** C. Mildred Reig (D), Marjorie N. Toth (R).—**Supt. of Schools,** Joseph J. Cirasuolo.—**Bd. of Education,** Carmen Arisco, Joan Barbuto, Patricia Corsetti, Phyllis DeChello, Karen A. Hlavac, Pamela Mangini, Mark A. Moynihan, Valerie A. Nolan, Vincent Testa, 1998.—**Planning and Zoning Comm.,** William Austin, Joseph Chordas, James Fitzsimmons, James Seichter, James Vumbaco; Linda Bush, Town Planner; Alternates, Jay Fishbein, Armand Menard, John Whitney.—**Zoning Bd. of Appeals,** Patricia Carruthers, Barbara Chayer, Steven Hacku, Ellen Mandes, Bonita L. Rubenstein; Alternates, George Lane, A. Jeffrey Somers, vacancy.—**Economic Development Comm.,** Gary Powell, Chm., Bruce Blakey, Joseph Boucher, Ellen Mandes, Richard Nunn, Rosemary Preneta, James Wolfe; Donald Roe, Coordinator.—**Housing Auth.,** Ruth B. Kennedy, Frederick L. Monahan, Jr., Robert Prentice, John Savage, William Ulbrich; Steven Nere, Exec. Dir.—**Conservation Comm.,** William Austin, Chm., John Lathrop, David Mandle, Judith Singer, vacancy.—**Inlands Wetlands Comm.,** James Vitali, Chm., James J. Heilman, Nick Kern, Barbara Lagerstrom, Robert Swick; Alternates, Ellen Deutsch, Vincenzo DiNatale, Matthew Fritz.—**Environ-**

mental Planner, Brent Smith.—**Housing Code Bd. of Appeals,** Nicholas Murano, Chm., H. Lawrence Bourland, Rosario DiNoia, Marc Landow; Carmen Spiteri, Inspector.—**Pension Comm.,** Fred Valenti, Chm., William Farrell, Thomas Myers, Vincent Santacroce, Terence Sullivan.—**Personnel Pensions and Appeals Bd.,** Joseph DaCunto, Richard Doll, Peter Foster, William Lyons, James Rainey, Charles F. Rood.—**Comm. on Aging,** Caryl Ryan, Chm., Ray Cooley, Madeline F. Erskine, William Farrell, Deborah Fitzsimmons, Ronald Granucci, Joan Harlow, Toni Helming, Virginia Isakson, Stewart Kennedy, Marianne Lacy, Videen McGaughey, Eileen McMahon, Ellen Phillips, John J. Sheehy, Jr.—**Welfare Dir.,** Mary Alice Petrucelli-Timek.—**Dir. of Health,** Delbert B. Smith, M.D.—**Bd. of Health,** Andrew Fritz, D.D.S., Chm., William W. Dickinson, Sr., M.D., David Juliano, Elizabeth C. Malko, M.D., J. David McGaughey III, M.D., Robert L. Mullin, M.D., Ellen Phillips.—**Library Bd. of Managers,** Sally Coleman, Charlotte Collins, Lynn DiNallo, Zay Foster, Richard Gaulin, Susan Haakconsen, Frederick Helming, Virginia Isakson, Donald Lunt, Donald Panagrossi, Walter Serbent, John Sienko, Robert Voss, Barbara Webb, Mary Lou Williams; Karen Roesler, Leslie Scherer, Dirs..—**Recreation Comm.,** Patrick Egan, Johanna Fishbein, Charles Johnson, Maynard Parker, Jon Walworth; Tom Dooley, Dir.—**Dir. of Public Works,** Henry McCully; Supt., Edward Niland.—**Purchasing Agent,** Robert N. Pedersen.—**Town Engineer,** vacancy.—**Tree Warden,** Henry McCully.—**PUC,** David Gessert, Chm., George Cooke, Michael Papale; Raymond F. Smith, Dir.—**Sealer of Weights and Measures,** Wilfred Bryand.—**Building Inspector,** Carmen Spiteri.—**Building Bd. of Appeals,** Peter J. Fresina, Chm., George Cotter, Robert DiPasquale, John Prophet, Anthony Roy.—**Electric Div.,** William Cominos.—**Water and Sewer Div.,** Roger Dann.—**Sanitarian,** George P. Yasensky.—**Chief of Police,** Douglas Dortenzio; Deputy, Donald O'Neil.—**Constables,** Robert Allard, William R. Choti, Alvin Gasser, Robert A. Jacques, Michael Mangini, Anthony F. Pragano, Jr., Mary E. Trahan-Kirkland—**Chief of Fire Dept.,** Wayne Lefebvre; Asst., Peter Struble.—**Fire Marshal,** Michael Lamy.—**Civil Preparedness,** Ernest Frattini, Dir.—**Town Atty.,** Janis Small; Corp. Counsel, Adam Mantzaris; Asst., Gerald Farrell.—**Justices of the Peace,** Raymond Arico, Robert Avery, Noma Beaumont, Robert A. DeMarco, Gerald Farrell, Jr., James C. Fitzsimmons, Elaine D. Johnson, Rita Katona, George R. Lane, Eric S. Tangney, Jack Winkleman.

WARREN. Litchfield County.—(Form of government, selectmen, town meeting, board of finance.)—Inc., May, 1786; taken from Kent. Area, 27.6 sq. miles. Population, est., 1,238. Voting district, 1. Principal industry, agriculture. Transp.—Freight: Served by numerous motor common carriers. Postal rural free delivery from New Preston and Cornwall Bridge.

TOWN OFFICERS. Clerk and Reg. of Vital Statistics, Carolyn E. Reynolds; Hours, 10 A.M.-12 Noon, Mon. and Fri.; 10 A.M.-4 P.M., Wed., Thurs.; Address, Town Hall, 7 Sackett Hill Rd., 06754; Tel./FAX, Washington, (860) 868-0090.—**Asst. Clerks and Asst. Regs. of Vital Statistics,** Linda Kennedy, Barbara M. Wasley.—**Selectmen,** 1st, Lewis A. Tanner (R) Tel., (860) 868-9030, Richard K. Abrahams (D), Jack E. Travers (R).—**Treas.,** Samford L. Maier; Deputy, Lori B. Deanne.—**Bd. of Finance,** James P. Richardson, Chm., William L. Hopkins, Paul R. Prindle, William

F. Schnell, David C. Scofield, Michael L. Wiser.—**Tax Collector,** Barbara M. Wasley; Assts., Linda Kennedy, Carolyn E. Reynolds.—**Bd. of Assessment Appeals,** Nancy C. J. Scofield, Chm., Percy R. Allmand, Stephen Jacobs.—**Assessor,** Donald W. Zimbouski.—**Advisory Bd. of Assessors,** Robert B. Reeves, Jr., Chm., Joyce Keith, Bernard E. Tanner.—**Registrars of Voters,** Ruth M. Schnell (D), Josephine W. Vaill (R).—**Supt. of Schools,** Timothy M. Breslin.—**Planning and Zoning Comm.,** Wayne Wilson, Chm., Michael Ajello, Susan Bates, Robert Bolte, Francis A. Breton, Edward Farrell, Philip Gargan, Howard Lethbridge; Alternates, Edward T. Golden, Jr., Allen Moore, Lynn Rosen.—**Zoning Bd. of Appeals,** Ann Martindale, Chm., William F. Hopkins, David C. Scofield, Everett W. Vreeland, Irving Wasley; Alternates, Gary M. Curtiss, James O. Engle, Ronald S. Miller.—**Zoning Enforcement Officer,** Martin Connor.—**Conservation and Inland Wetlands Comm.,** Elwood J. Rahm, Chm., Jeanne Almquist, Frank Beran, Scott Loomis, Paul R. Prindle, Nancy T. Vreeland, Irving J. Wasley; Alternates, Kenneth Conn, Lee Lord, Edward J. Moore.—**Flood and Erosion Control Bd.,** Lewis A. Tanner, Chm., Richard K. Abrahams, Elwood J. Rahm, Jack E. Travers, Wayne Wilson.—**Comm. on Aging,** Suzanne Farrell, Samford Maier, Barbara Wasley.—**Library Bd.,** Suzanne Farrell, Chm., Victoria Chess, Gerald Cowan, Nancy Florio, Arthur Frantz, Connie Miller, Richard Santorelli, Judy Shaw, Martha Winkle, Cathy Yanik.—**Parks and Recreation Comm.,** Michael Wiser, Chm., Ellen Berland, Daniel Dacey, Cathy Keith, Loreen Lethbridge, Kathleen Newton, Mary Stolle, Terry Tanner, Timothy Turrell.—**Building Inspector,** William Jenks.—**Building Code Bd. of Appeals,** William Vogel, Chm.—**Lake Auth.,** Edgar Berner, William Hopkins, Harold Pennington.—**Tree Warden,** Daniel Dacey.—**Chief of Police/Open Burning Control Officer,** Lewis A. Tanner.—**Chief of Fire Co.,** Robert Rumble.—**Fire Marshal,** Stanley MacMillan.—**Civil Preparedness Dir.,** vacancy.—**Town Atty.,** Charles R. Ebersol, Jr.—**Justices of the Peace,** Susan W. Abrams, Kathleen L. Angevine, Robert H. Bolte, Stephen D. Jacobs, Barbara W. Reynolds, Antoinette V. Richardson, Ruth M. Schnell, William F. Schnell, Nancy C. J. Scofield, Constance H. Travers.

WASHINGTON. Litchfield County.—(Form of government, selectmen, town meeting, board of finance.)—Inc., Jan., 1779; taken from Woodbury, Litchfield, Kent and New Milford. Area, 38.7 sq. miles. Population, est., 4,009. Voting district, 1. Transp.—Served by buses of The Kelley Transit Co., Inc., from Torrington, and New Milford. Freight: Served by numerous motor common carriers. Post offices, Washington, Washington Depot and New Preston-Marble Dale.

TOWN OFFICERS. Clerk and Reg. of Vital Statistics, Doris K. Welles, Hours, 9 A.M.-12 Noon, 1-4:45 P.M., Mon., Tues., Thurs., Fri.; 9 A.M.-12 Noon, Wed.; Address, Bryan Memorial Town Hall, P.O. Box 383, Washington Depot 06794; Tel., (860) 868-2786.—**Asst. Clerks and Asst. Regs. of Vital Statistics,** Ruth M. Alex, Briana C. Doran.—**Selectmen,** 1st, Alan J. Chapin (R) Tel., (860) 868-2259, Madeline C. Lyons (D), Beverley E. Miller (R).—**Treas.,** Linda L. McGarr.—**Bd. of Finance,** Michael C. Jackson, Chm., John Boyer, Charles E. Heyman, George D. Ward, Robert G. Weber, Robert G. Whitehead; Alternates, Philip M. Farmer, Valerie Martin, Rexford H. Swain.—**Tax Collector,** Tanya J. Wescott.—**Bd. of Assessment Appeals,** F.

Arthur Potter, Jr., Chm., Ann F. Bruzzi, Katherine A. Connerty.—**Assessor,** Barbara S. Johnson.—**Registrars of Voters,** Constance P. Kaylor (D), Patricia A. Stoeffler (R).—**Supt. of Schools,** Robert Nicoletti.—**Planning Comm.,** Kenneth D. Williams, Chm., Jean P. Averill, George A. Bender, Katherine A. Connerty, Richard G. Dutton; Alternates, Robert C. Buck, Christopher D. Charles, vacancy.—**Zoning Comm.,** Gregory E. Seeley, Chm., Robert K. Borger, Michael Condon, David L. Owen, Susan Werkhoven; Alternates, Frederick Byerly, John M. Larson, Henry R. Martin.—**Zoning Bd. of Appeals,** Nicholas N. Solley, Chm., Reese T. Owens, Bradford S. Sedito, Edmund J. White, vacancy; Alternates, Heman B. Averill, Randolph S. Johnson, Mary J. Roberts.—**Zoning Enforcement Officer,** Janet M. Hill.—**Inland Wetlands/Conservation Comm.,** Alice C. Shusdock, Chm., Elizabeth E. Corrigan, Elaine C. Luckey, Gayle W. Meissner, Stephen G. Solley, Kenneth D. Williams; Janet M. Hill, Insp. Officer; Alternates, William R. McDonald, Debra VanKeuren, vacancy.—**Historic Dist. Comm.,** William H. Smith, Chm., Peter A. Arturi, Peter Talbot, Charles T. Treadway III, vacancy; Janet M. Hill, Insp. Officer; Alternates, Mary R. Harwood, Paul A. Leonard, Alison G. Picton.—**Agent for the Elderly,** Pam Collins.—**Dir. of Health,** Alphonse Altorelli, M.D.—**Dir. of Social Services,** Susan Eads.—**Senior Center Dir.,** Patricia Desmond.—**Parks and Recreation Comm.,** Sheila M. Anson, Chm., Scott B. Barrows, Timothy A. Cook, Joseph B. Fredlund, Joan M. Gauthey, Holly Z. Haas, Raymond W. Reich, James J. White; Denise S. Arturi, Rec. Coord.—**Tree Warden,** R. Dana Gibson.—**Building Inspector,** William Jenks.—**Sanitarian,** Thomas O'Loskey.—**Building Code Bd. of Appeals,** Raymond Kozak, Edward B. Prokop, Jr.—**Lake Auth.,** Julia Casey, Edwin Matthews, Sandy Papsin.—**Resident Trooper,** Gregory J. Kenney.—**Police Officers,** Philip J. Biaglowy, John Colangelo, Ronald Dorazio, James J. Harding, F. Kenneth Fitch, Herbert G. Furhman, Vincent A. Orlando, Joseph Orsini, Caleb Shropshire, John Wyshynski.—**Chief of Fire Dept.,** Thomas R. Osborne.—**Fire Marshal,** Donald S. Etherington.—**Emergency Management Dir.,** Robert Tomlinson; Deputy, Thomas Hearn.—**Town Atty.,** David Miles.—**Justices of the Peace,** Randall J. Breeckner, Ann F. Bruzzi, Christopher B. Combs, Robert Deanne, Jr., Edith C. Johnson, Adam J. Korpalski, William T. McTiernan, John J. Muckstadt, Joshua M. Weiner, Sr.

WATERBURY. New Haven County.—(Form of government, mayor, board of aldermen.)—Town inc., May, 1686; city inc., 1853; town and city consolidated, 1902. Area, 28.9 sq. miles. Population, est., 107,554. Voting districts, 32. Principal industries, manufacture of brass and copper products, clocks, and watches. Transp.—Passenger: Served by Metro North Commuter Railroad Co. and buses of Bonanza Bus Lines, Inc. from Hartford and Danbury; The Conn. Transit from New Haven; North East Transp. Co., Inc. locally. Freight: Served by numerous motor common carriers. Post office, Waterbury.

CITY AND TOWN OFFICERS. Town Clerk, Mary Ellen Ianniruberto; Hours, 8:30 A.M.- 4:50 P.M., Mon. through Fri.; Address, City Hall, 235 Grand St., 06702; Tel., (203) 574-6806.—**Asst. Town Clerk,** Aldona Levanas.—**Reg. of Vital Statistics,** Ulder J. Tillman.—**Asst. Reg. of Vital Statistics,** Eileen Ladden.—**City Clerk,** Vincent T. Graziano; Hours, 8:50 A.M.-4:50 P.M., Mon. through Fri.; Address, 236 Grand

St.; Tel., (203) 574-6741.—**Mayor,** Philip A. Giordano (R), Chm., ex officio of the Bds. of Comrs. of Public Works, City Plan Comm., Inland Wetlands Comm., Public Welfare, Police Comrs., Fire Comrs., Health, Finance, Park Bd., Bd. of Education and Bureau of Assessment.—**Bd. of Aldermen,** Nicholas P. Augelli, Catherine N. Awwad, Paul Bourassa, Sam Caligiuri, Kathy Galullo, Deborah T. Lewis, Lisa E. Mason, Ronald A. Napoli, Nicholas J. Parillo, William J. Pizzuto, William Ramirez, Donald S. Rinaldi, John A. Sarlo, Thomas M. Tremaglio, Linda T. Wihbey.—**Bd. of Voter Admissions,** Joseph W. Diorio, Lana K. Ogrodnik, Zeraida Rosado.—**Treas.,** Michael D. Blumenthal.—**Budget Dir.,** Thomas M. Ariola, Jr.—**Dir. of Audit,** vacancy.—**Operations Admin.,** William Cugno.—**Comptroller,** Pasquale A. Mangini.—**Bd. of Finance,** Philip A. Giordano, Chm., Thomas Ariola, Jr., Nicholas P. Augelli, Michael Blumenthal, Charles R. Giorgio, Pasquale A. Mangini, Donna Marabilio, Ralph A. Minervino, Nicholas J. Parillo, Joseph Yamin.—**Tax Collector,** James R. Walsh.—**Bd. of Assessment Appeals,** Alvera Balanda, Chm., William Perugini, Robert Spataro.—**Assessor,** David Dietsch.—**Registrars of Voters,** Patricia M. Mulhall (D), Susan C. Beatty (R).—**Supt. of Schools,** Roger Damerow, Ph.D.—**Bd. of Education,** Michael A. Andolina, Pres., David Burgos, Lawrence T. Pisapio, Dorothy F. Steward, vacancy, 1997; John F. Alseph, Jr., Paul D. D'Angelo, Deborah Schatzle-Baker, Robert C. Urso, Mary White, 2000.—**Civil Service Comm.,** Paul Bourassa, Paul Conant, Deborah T. Lewis, Jeanette Muccino, Richard Scappini; Edmund Jayaraj, Personnel Dir.—**Retirement Bd.,** Nicholas P. Augelli, David Bozzuto, Genevieve Cavallerano, Pasquale A. Mangini.—**City Plan Comm.,** Richard Handler, Chm., Jeffrey J. Berger, Frank Bonaldi, Leonard Coviello, Domenic Palumbo.—**City Planner,** Keith Rosenfeld.—**Zoning Comm.,** Jack Goldberg, Laurie Singer, Antoinette Spinelli, Thomas Tremaglio, Patrick Zailckas, Jr.—**Zoning Bd. of Appeals,** Kevin Russell Chm., Joseph Caiazzo, Joseph Jaynes, Robert J. Marages, John Palermo; Alternates, Robert Byers, Paul Nogueira, Salvatore Terenzo.—**Zoning Enforcement Officer,** Vincent Viggiano.—**Waterbury Development Agency,** Joseph Healey, Chm., Thomas DiBlasi, John W. Girouard, Carla Murphy, Joseph Murphy, Mildred E. Paris, Alfred J. Perugini, Francis Sullivan, Joseph Tropasso.—**Housing Auth.,** Anthony P. Amabile, Jr., Chm., John Barbino, Valois DeLeon, Jr., William H. Douglas, Jr., Rose Ring, Stephen A. Smith; Silvio Broccoli, Dir.—**Inland Wetlands and Watercourses Comm.,** John DeCesare, Chm., Catherine N. Awwad, Michael DePaulo, Jr., James R. McCarthy.—**Environmental Comm.,** Anthony D'Amelio, Johnson Jones, Bob C. Lubus, Jr., Christine Matlega, Mildred Paris.—**Comm. on Aging,** John Barbino, Anthony Bocci, Sr., Mary K. Gill, Ernie Marino, Louis Orsini, Loretta Robinson, Lisa Shappy, Harold Slater.—**Human Rights Comm.,** Mike CoFrancesco, Deborah T. Lewis, Kathy Galullo, Lillian Maffia, Pat Taylor.—**Bd. of Public Assistance,** Thomas Carusello, Catherine Casey, Jay D'Angelo, Jr., Margarethe Fenske, Raymond Gatling, William Pizzuto, Martin F. Spring, Alan Thibodeau.—**Welfare Dir.,** Carlos Rodriguez.—**Dir. of Health,** Ulder J. Tillman, M.D.—**Bd. of Public Health,** Ulder J. Tillman, M.D., Chm., Fadi Awwad, Sabato D'Ambrosi, Marie Garvin, Mark C. Raad, William Ramirez, Brian St. Onge, William J. Summa, Jr., Giuseppi Tripodi, M.D.—**Library Directors,** Charles G. Baskin, Chm., Anne Bedell, Philip V. Benevento, Jr., Jean Benson, Joanne M. Bergin, Aurora M. Castelano, Genevieve Cavallerano, Mary G. Hutchinson, Consilia Maiorano, Lena M. Napolitano, Lana Ogrodnik, Daniel J. Ryan.—**Council** on Culture, David Bruno, Christen Bulkavitch, Mary Butkevicius, Donna Franks, Maria Giordano, Linda Jacovino, Elizabeth Longo, Meghan Palumbo, Antoinette Spinelli, Barbara Sticco, Linda T. Wihbey.—**Bd. of Park Comrs.,** George Harlamon, Pres., Louis Aucella, George W. Barnhardt, Joseph E. Begnal, Jr., Ernest Marino, Gerardo C. Reyes, Jr., Ben Rhodes, Charles Schaeffer, Jr., Hugh St. Leger, Thomas M. Tremaglio.—**Dir. of Parks and Recreation,** Samuel Leisring.—**Bd. of Public Works,** Mayor Philip A. Giordano, Chm., Catherine N. Awwad, Francis Calabro, Sr., Frank M. Giordano, Frank L. Maffia, Rosario Minnocci, Thomas McDonough, Domenic Piombo.—**Supt. of Streets,** J. Robert Carroll.—**City Engineer,** Ernest Phillips.—**Acting Purchasing Agent,** Michael Ranno.—**Sealer of Weights and Measures,** Harold Traver.—**Building Official,** E. Gil Graveline.—**Supt. of Water,** Kenneth R. Skov.—**Building Code Bd. of Appeals,** Edward Buska, Arthur P. D'Oliveira, Anthony Rubbo, Angelo P. Tedesco; Alternates, John D'Amico, Leon Farr.—**Supt. of Waste Treatment,** Ronald E. Jennings.—**Chief Sanitarian,** Michael Carey.—**Acting Supt. of Police,** John Griffin.—**Police Comm.,** John Blanchfield, Larry Butler, Deborah T. Lewis, Victor Guerrera, Claudio Mancini, Henry McCafferty, Donald M. Rinaldi, Michelle Swanson.—**Constables,** Robert Callahan, Fiore Carusello, Donald M. Cipriano, Nicholas J. Parillo, Thomas Scacco, Joseph A. Synnett, James H. Uriano, Alex J. Velezis.—**City Sheriff,** Richard K. Schnaars.—**Acting Chief of Fire Dept.,** James Trainor.—**Fire Marshal,** Anthony J. Zappone.—**Bd. of Fire Comrs.,** Anthony D'Amelio, Edmond Gerardi, Alphonse Macharelli, Richard M. Marano, Ronald Canarie, Ronald Ferraro, Smith, Rose Spagnoletti, Salvator Vasquez.—**Civil Preparedness Dir.,** Elaine Longino.—**City Atty./Corp. Counsel,** Elena R. Palermo.—**Justices of the Peace,** John F. Alseph, Jr., John R. Barbino, Mitchell M. Berger, Frank J. Bonaldi, David J. Botelle, Thomas Brayton, Henry P. Capozzi, Jr., Antony Casagrande, Genevieve Cavallerano, Dolores Cesare, Michael Cicchetti, F. David Corbett, Leonard Coviello, Gloria Dalton, John D. Dillon, Jr., Timothy J. Fagan, Joseph A. Ficeto, Raymond Gatling, John T. Giannantoni, Brian Goggin, Olga I. Guerrera, Alan H. Hertzmark, Mary Ellen Ianniruberto, Jennie Johnsky, Deborah T. Lewis, Alphonse A. Macharelli, Lillian J. Maffia, Thomas Mallory, Carmen Mallamaci, Richard Marano, Thomas K. McDonough, John J. McGrail, Jr., Robert Mellon, David Moriarty, Timnothy C. Moynahan, Patrick Mulhall, Joseph Murphy, Paul Nogueira, Lana K. Ogrodnik, Nicholas Parillo, Domenic A. Piombo, William Ramirez, Benjamin F. Rhodes, Jr., Nunzio Ricciutti, Thomas V. Riley, Donald J. Rinaldi, Migdalia Rosario, Raymond E. Snyder, Jr., Cecile A. Thomas, Daniel R. Valletta, James R. Walsh, Jean A. Wihbey, F. Patrick Zailckas.

WATERFORD. New London County.—(Form of government, representative town meeting, selectmen, board of finance.)—Inc., Oct., 1801; taken from New London. Area, 44.4 sq. miles. Population, est., 17,312. Voting districts, 4. Suburban Transp.—Freight: Served by Providence & Worcester Co., Central Vermont Railway and numerous motor common carriers. Post offices, Waterford and Quaker Hill.

TOWN OFFICERS. Clerk and Reg. of Vital Statistics, Robert M. Nye; Hours, 8 A.M.-4 P.M., Mon. through Fri.; Address, Town Hall, 15 Rope Ferry Rd., 06385;

Tel., (860) 442-0553.—**Asst. Clerks and Asst. Regs. of Vital Statistics,** Carol Peabody, Catherine M. Reese.—**Representative Town Meeting Moderator,** Donald B. Blevins.—**Selectmen,** 1st, Thomas A. Sheridan (D) Tel., (860) 442-0553, David B. Fairman (D), Leo E. Sullivan (R).—**Treas.,** Elizabeth B. Ritter.—**Bd. of Finance,** George A. Peteros, Chm., Lee J. Adams, Gurdon C. Avery, Jeffrey C. Hall, David T. McDaniel, Robert W. VonAchen; Arthur H. Davis III, Dir.—**Tax Collector,** Germania M. Jensen.—**Bd. of Assessment Appeals,** Julie A. Phelps, Vittorio C. Spera, Robert C. Todd.—**Assessor,** James G. Ramos.—**Registrars of Voters,** Margaret S. Bellucci (D), Jane B. Coville (R).—**Supt. of Schools,** Randall H. Collins.—**Bd. of Education,** William D. Foreman, Joseph A. Parise, David Ruffner, Daniel M. Steward, 1997; Donna L. Martell, Jody M. Nazarchyk, Francis X. Sweeney, George P. Yost, Noel B. Zahler, 1999.—**Planning and Zoning Comm.,** Edwin J. Maguire, Chm., Lawrence J. Levine, Gwen Lombardi, Edward R. Pellegri, Jr., Thomas S. Perkins.—**Planning Dir.,** Thomas V. Wagner.—**Zoning Bd. of Appeals,** James W. Wadlow, Jr., Chm., Pierre Brochu, Donald B. Gallup, Sr., John E. Hagglund, Paul A. Suprin; Alternates, Frederick Behringer, John W. Sheehan, vacancy.—**Zoning Enforcement Officer,** David Martin.—**Economic Development Comm.,** Thomas J. Riley, Chm., Thomas Berube, Kathleen M. Devine, Dennis J. Fallon, Timothy F. Haire, W. Mott Hupfel, Jr., Lynn R. MacMorrow, Theodore Olynciw, Eleanor S. Tabak.—**Housing Code Bd. of Appeals,** John Louziotis, Chm., Matthew N. Condon, three vacancies; Alternates, James Cushing, two vacancies.—**Housing Auth.,** David T. McDaniel, Chm., Larry Bevilacqua, Joan C. Simones.—**Conservation Comm.,** James M. Miner III, Chm., Henry F. Curtis, Markay Malootian, Robert A. Place, Antoni Tabak, Wade M. Thomas; Alternates, Allan L. Elms, Ross Lally.—**Flood and Erosion Control Bd.,** David Benvenuti, Chm., Christopher L. Callahan, Gail L. Hamsher, Gerald E. Holmberg, Lloyd L. Langhammer, Howard B. Russ.—**Personnel Review Bd.,** Robert J. McKeever, Chm., Alan H. Gardiner, Wilma Marsh, George R. Strutt, Rik W. Wells.—**Senior Citizens Comm.,** Joyce Vlaun, Chm., Dorothy V. Avery, Maureen M. Davis, Joyce C. Greineder, Mary Kuhn, Sharon Palmer, Shirley M. Plue, Patricia Ryan, Verna L. Skinner; Susan Turner, Coordinator.—**Agent for the Elderly/Outreach Services Dir.,** Sean P. Kane.—**Welfare Dir.,** Marie Aulenti.—**Dir. of Health,** George Burton, M.D.—**Visiting Nurses of Southeastern CT,** Mary L. Lenzini.—**Library Trustees,** Fred Brucoli, Pres., Bonnie Allison, Clifford Grandjean, Gail Hamsher, John J. Hanrahan, Kay Harbert, Cynthia B. Lawrence, John Merrill, Margaret B. O'Brien, Theodore Olyciw, Rex Pinson, Ephralm Rivard.—**Municipal Historian,** Robert M. Nye.—**Parks and Recreation Comm.,** Fred Brucoli, Chm., Joseph A. Carey, Joseph Filipetti, Ellen Mayo, Barbara Rice, Warren Swanson, Peter M. Thibeau, William Whelan, Jr.; Ronald Bugbee, Dir.; Asst., Paul Eccard.—**Dir. of Public Works,** Edward Steward; Asst., Ronald Cusano.—**Supt. of Highways,** Donald Brigham.—**Tree Warden/Town Engineer,** Edward Steward.—**Building Official,** Frank Hoagland.—**Building Bd. of Appeals,** Donald Macrino, James McGee, Robert Senkow, George W. White, Jr., vacancy.—**Water Pollution Control Auth.,** Peter M. Green, Chm., Harrison Fortier, Sr., Gertrude McKeon, Rita Provatas, Walter L. Varney.—**Waterford/East Lyme Shell Fish Comm.,** Lorenz W. Rinek, Chm., J. Patrick Kelly, Brian T. Sullivan.—**Sanitarian,** Judith A. Wrenn.—**Chief of Police,** Murray Pendleton.—**Police Comm.,** Margaret M. Poulios, Chm., Robert L. Andreoli, Maurice Blinderman, John DiFederico,

Thomas A. Sheridan.—**Chiefs of Fire Dept.,** Thomas Dembek (Goshen); John Mariano (Cohanzie); Eric Munsell (Jordan); Richard T. Kirchhoff (Quaker Hill); Brian Baker (Oswegatchie).—**Fire Marshal,** David Garside; Deputy, Peter Schlink.—**Bd. of Fire Comrs.,** William O. Bartelli, Jr., Chm., Melvin E. Carson, Michael A. Joyce, R. Alan Rheaume.—**Emergency Management Coord.,** Karen Ferrara.—**Town Atty.,** Lois G. Andrews.—**Justices of the Peace,** Gerelyn M. Adcock, Dorothy Avery, Joan H. Bendfeldt, Lawrence J. Bettencourt, Donald B. Blevins, Gertrud G. Blinderman, Marcelle Boisvert, Calvin K. Brouwer, Peter H. Brouwer, Fred Brucoli, Mary M. Burr, Luke P. Cappiello, Mary K. Carlough, Judith A. Coughlin, Jane B. Coville, Loretta A. Cullen, Grace M. Curtis, Luanne E. DeMatto, Leonidas N. Dousis, David B. Fairman, Stuart J. Fishbone, Laura P. Fitch, Brian E. Forshaw, Joseph J. Gangitano, Alan H. Gardiner, Elaine C. Gardner, Catherine D. Geer, Anthony J. Gigliotti, Beth Gigliotti, Sanford Glassman, Edward Gorra, Lee Ann Graham, Paul E. Havener, Jr., Frederick D. Johnston, Ann M. Koletsky, Elizabeth Leonardi, Lawrence J. Levine, Sandra C. Levine, David A. Lewis, Sr., Samuel J. Linder, Judith L. Lupkay, Marie K. Lyall, Mary Anne Madara, Susan A. McCaslin, David T. McDaniel, Gladys H. McFarland, Katie O. McGuire, Martin G. McGuire, Alan D. McNeely, Alan R. Messier, J. Morgan Miner, Jr., James M. Miner III, Mary L. Mingo, Marilyn C. Mitchell, Stephen J. Negri, Ann R. Nye, Robert M. Nye, Raymond R. Olivieri, Sharon M. Palmer, Joseph A. Parise, Carmine J. Parker, Edward R. Pellegri, Jr., Robert R. Pero, George R. Peteros, Earl J. Peters, S. Derek Phelps, Robert Reardon, Sr., Constance C. Reid, David W. Relyea, Elizabeth B. Ritter, Charles E. Rowland, Patricia G. Ryan, Ivan Sadler, Virginia R. Saenger, Gary W. Saunders, Crescentino Secchiaroli, Robert L. Senkow, John W. Sheehan, Thomas A. Sheridan, Patricia M. Smith, Mariea D. Spencer, Vittorio I. Spera, Edward Stein, Andrea L. Stillman, Andonette L. Strazza, George R. Strutt, Leo E. Sullivan, Paul A. Suprin, Robert C. Todd, Sallie E. Unruh, George B. Vachris, Joyce M. Vlaun, Robert W. Von Achen, Lawrence R. Voyer, James W. Wadlow, Jr., Sharon A. Walker, Kristen M. Widham, Jerry A. Winter, Robert P. Zysk.

WATERTOWN. Litchfield County.—(Form of government, town manager, town council, town meeting.)—Inc., May, 1780; taken from Waterbury. Area, 29.6 sq. miles. Population, est., 21,334. Voting districts, 4. Principal industries, manufacture of plastics, rayon, silk, nylon, mattresses, brass goods, metal coloring, wire goods and watches. Transp.—Passenger: Served by buses of North East Transp. Co., Inc. Freight: Served by numerous motor common carriers. Post offices, Watertown and Oakville.

TOWN OFFICERS. Clerk and Reg. of Vital Statistics, Dolores LaRosa; Hours, 9 A.M.-5 P.M., Mon. through Fri.; Address, Town Hall, 37 DeForest St., 06795; Tel., (860) 945-5230.—**Asst. Clerk and Asst. Reg. of Vital Statistics,** Stella C. Orsini.—**Town Manager,** John Salomone; Asst. Town Mgr./Finance Dir., Frank J. Nardelli, Jr.—**Town Council,** Rosalie G. Loughran, Chm., Charles L. Gordon, Jean King, Patricia Kropp, Robert LeBlanc, Scott A. Musselman, Paul H. Rinaldi, Gary Stewart, William Voide.—**Treas.,** Shirley Dorazio.—**Tax Collector,** Mary L. DiSisto.—**Bd. of Assessment Appeals,** John G. Griffith, Chm., Armand Madeux, John Palumbo.—**Assessor,** John Petuch.—**Registrars of Voters,** Walter A. LeMay (D), Armand Madeux (R).—**Supt. of Schools,** Dinoo Dastur.—**Bd. of Education,** Bernard C. Beauchamp, Catherine M. Carney, Michael D. Gambone, Mary Ann Rosa, Denise T. Russ, 1997; Cheryl Carley, Chm., Gary L. Bernier, Joanne H. Pannone, Margaret G. Poulin, 1999.—**Planning and Zoning Comm.,** Judith M. Wick, Chm., Colin Adams, James Blais, Brian DeFoe, Michael Galullo, Stephen McCabe, Billy C. Skyrme.—**Zoning Bd. of Appeals,** Thomas Traver, Chm., Jeffrey Franson, Betsy Muzzicato, Nicholas Reymolds, Enrico Sarandrea; Alternates, Mary Bisson, Allen Chaponis, Roger Phillippe.—**Zoning Enforcement Officer,** vacancy.—**Economic Development Comm.,** Norman Marcoux, Chm., John Bavone, Wilbur Hughes, Gerald C. Langlais, Marion Owen, Nancy Rahuba, John Ritchie, Jack E. Traver, Joseph Wasilauskas.—**Housing Auth.,** Ronald Russo, Chm., Anthony N. Fusco, Andrew Gionta, John McHugh, Olga Pettigrew; Nathan Orfice, Exec. Dir.—**Conservation and Inland Wetlands Comm.,** Wilbur Hughes, Chm., Leo Buonocore, Scott D'Angelis, Michael Garassino, Louis Scozzafava, Peter Tomsheck, Nancy VanDeusen; Alternates, William Breg, Alex Matolosy, vacancy.—**Committee for the Aging,** Helen Williams, Chm., Linda Bernier, Patricia A. Clement, Melanie Flaherty, Martha George, Helen Lukowski, Renee McGee, Karen Sayre, Wanda Witty.—**Public Building Committee,** Francis A. Rinaldi, Jr., Chm., Remo J. Ceniccola, Herbert Darling, Karl Keugler, Alfred Morency, David Pettinicchi, Robert M. Porter, John Orsini, Myroslaw Trojan.—**Agent for the Elderly,** Nancy Wolfe.—**Dir. of Social Services,** Darylle Willenbrock.—**Library Bd. of Trustees,** Deborah Weinberger, Pres., Angela Bozzuto, Roberta Czarsty, Ann Fitzgerald, Charles Frigon, Francis Kaminski, Michael Lamy, Charlotte Morro, Connie Nicholson, Patricia Petro, Susan Ponton.—**Municipal Historian,** Florence Crowell.—**Parks and Recreation Comm.,** John Putetti, Chm., Joe Feero, Gary Lafferty, Norman Marcoux, Teresa Mitchell, Ronald Russo, William Scully; Lisa Carew, Rec. Dir.; Peter Cura, Parks Dir.—**Dir. of Public Works/Tree Warden,** Philip Deleppo.—**Town Engineer,** vacancy.—**Purchasing Agent,** Charles Frigon.—**Building Inspector,** Richard Fusco.—**Water and Sewer Auth.,** Michael J. Vernovai, Sr., Chm., Bruce Austin, Elizabeth Bozzuto, James Carney, Paul Jessell, Conrad Sansoucie, John O. Vitone.—**Chief of Police,** John F. Carroll, Jr.—**Police Comm.,** Ronald Russ, Chm., Sharon A. Demers, Sandra Justin, Robert C. Shuhart, Sherman R. Slavin.—**Constables,** Allen Chaponis, Susan C. Hansen, Barbara Hymel, Mykolas Kumeta, Gary J. Lafferty, Joyce Recchia, vacancy.—**Chief of Fire Dept.,** O'Neill Burrows; Deputy, Larry R. Black.—**Fire Marshal,** O'Neill Burrows.—**Civil Preparedness Dir.,** Robert Marchenko.—**Town Attys.,** Marianne B. Dubuque, Randall S. McHugh.—**Justices of the Peace,** Elaine H. Adams, Lawrence W. Baker, Robert J. Baribault, John Bavone, Bernard C. Beauchamp, John Beeler, Alan R. Blum, John R. Buso, Elizabeth Bozzuto-McHugh, William F. Breg, James E. Brooks, Sr., Sean C. Butterly, Mary B. Canty, Cheryl A. Carley, Lisa M. Cattaneo, Remo J. Ceniccola, Gail D. Cesarello, Mary I. Colangelo, Patricia A. Conti, David C. Dalton, Herbert A. Darling, Audra E. DeFoe, Catherine D. DeLeon, Alexander DellaCamera, Sharon A. Demers, Armand J. Derouin, Gaetano DiMichele, Edmond M. Diorio, Mary I. DiSisto, Kathleen S. Doback, Thomas F. Downey, Ralph J. Fabiano, Tara A. Finley, Fredrick K. Fischer, Susan M. Fitzgerald, J. Andre Fournier, Anthony N. Fusco, Richard Fusco, Charles L. Gordon, Susan C. Hansen, Curtis L. Hickcox, Joseph E. Horzepa, William A. Hosking, Wilbur S. Hughes, Gordon W. James, Sandra M. Justin, Susan L. Kasfeldt, Melita Kelly, August

J. Kiesel, Stephen P. Kiraly, Allan A. Krasnow, J. Timothy Krusko, Robert P. LeBlanc, Rosalie G. Loughran, Helen E. Lukowski, Armand E. Madeux, Carol W. Magee, Barbara Anne Marchand, Joseph D. Masi, Sandra Y. Mattson, Alan D. Mickel, Teresa P. Mitchell, Lynn S. Montambault, Eugene A. Murphy, Jr., John M. O'Brien, Arnold M. Oliver, Jr., John Orsini, Marion A. Owen, Eric J. Palladino, Michelle J. Pannullo, Coreine L. Peluso, Franklin G. Pilicy, Robert M. Porter, Anthony S. Recchia, Joyce M. Recchia, Patricia D. Reilly, Paul H. Rinaldi, Kathleen C. Rizzo, John M. Robb, Sr., Stephen J. Robey, Denise T. Russ, Ronald Russo, Karen C. Schmid, Linda C. Serra, Robert C. Shuhart, Katharine W. Smith, Frederic D. Sorcinelli, Sr., Gary Stewart, Charles Taylor, Edward J. Thompson, Jack E. Traver, Michael J. Vernovai, Sr., Eric W. Voide, Robynne L. Wildman, Jan Wivestad, John N. Zappone.

WESTBROOK. Middlesex County.—(Form of government, selectmen, town meeting, board of finance.)—Inc., May, 1840; taken from Saybrook (Deep River). Area, 21.4 sq. miles. Population, est., 5,404. Voting district, 1. Principal industries, fishing, woodworking, electronics, aircraft and missile parts, emergency lighting, concrete blocks, auto sales, boat rentals and sales, marinas, summer resorts and Westbrook factory stores. Freight: Served by Conrail, Providence & Worcester Co. and numerous motor common carriers. Post office, Westbrook. Rural free delivery.

TOWN OFFICERS. Clerk and Reg. of Vital Statistics, Tanya D. Lane; Hours, 9 A.M.-4 P.M., Mon. through Wed., Fri., 9 A.M.-6:30 P.M., Thurs.; Address, P.O. Box G, 1163 Boston Post Rd., 06498; Tel., (860) 399-3044.—**Asst. Clerks and Asst. Regs. of Vital Statistics,** Dianne C. Annino, Mildred C. Clements.—**Selectmen,** 1st, Franklin D. Lusk (D) Tel., (860) 399-3040, Tony A. Palermo (D), George K. Pytlik (R).—**Treas.,** Sally Greaves; Deputy, Thomas J. Collopy.—**Bd. of Finance,** Dennis J. Hallahan, Chm., William H. Daly, Jr., John W. Doane III, Gerald A. Gartner, Gary F. Gavigan, Melody F. Oryl.—**Tax Collector,** Judith A. Longo.—**Bd. of Assessment Appeals,** Theresa E. Thomas, Chm., Joan M. Carlson, John D. Philbin.—**Assessor,** Patricia Stevenson.—**Registrars of Voters,** Patricia L. Moran (D), Lorraine M. Cenkus (R).—**Supt. of Schools,** Dalton S. Marks, Ph.D.—**Bd. of Education,** Michael M. Dore, Chm., Joanne Lariviere, Frances C. Russell, 1997; Edward P. Braza, Jr., Daniel J. Cyr, Allan C. Johnson, 1999; Richard J. Talpey, John Wargo, Craig S. Wilson, 2001.—**Planning Comm.,** Thomas L. Elliott, Chm., Philip J. Bassett, Thomas M. Maynard, Marilyn M. Ozols, Mary M. Savoie; Alternates, Mary I. Clark, two vacancies.—**Zoning Comm.,** Toni Ann Nolder, Chm., Ernest G. Bodurtha, David G. Diedrick, Kenneth J. Ferrucci, Anthony P. Marino; Alternates, Gilbert E. Nicholls, Harry P. Ruppenicker, Jr., Lawrence E. Savoie.—**Zoning Bd. of Appeals,** John L. Hall III, Chm., Gilbert H. Doel, Stephen A. Doerrer, Richard M. Gallacher, George B. Rehberg; Alternates, Charles A. Lewis, Jr., Beverly C. McNeil, Clifford C. Rimkus.—**Zoning Enforcement Officer,** James R. Taylor.—**Economic Development Comm.,** Jane M. Glaser, Angus McDonald, Jr., Russell J. Mucik, Alec M. Sheard, Jr., Debra A. Williams.—**Conservation Comm.,** Thomas M. ODell, Chm., David G. Diedrick, Philip M. Einsmann, Sr., Robert A. Peterson, Melody J. Sacatos.—**Inland Wetlands/Watercourses Comm.,** John C. Clements, Chm., Paul D'Orio, Raymond E. Fontaine, Richard M. Gallacher, Thomas M. Maynard, Robert A. Peterson, Doris S. Sanstrom; Heidi K.

Wallace, Enforcement Officer; Alternates, John R. Arnold, Kevin Brown.—**Flood and Erosion Control Bd.,** Franklin D. Lusk, Tony A. Palermo, George K. Pytlik.—**Municipal Agent for the Elderly/Dir. of Social Services,** Denise Guite.—**Dir. of Health,** Joseph Fuller, M.D.—**Public Health Nursing Bd.,** Gina Fifield, Chm., Ellen Fredericks, Frank Geissler, Donna Hardy, Georgine Jones, Denise Mason, Ann Mott.—**Library Directors,** Kathleen E. Cietanno, Chm., Knowles Dickey, Louise C. Dibble, Marjorie E. Engel, Teresa S. Gavigan, John S. Hiller, Dorothy E. Holbrook, Shirley S. Lusk, Thomas G. Montefiore, Jr.—**Municipal Historian,** Michael J. Wells.—**Historical Society,** Sally Correll, Pres.—**Bd. of Recreation,** Thomas M. Fredericks, Chm., Richard Annino, Chester Bialicki, Constance Blomquist, Christine Bohannan, Hector Chavez, Lynda M. Fisher, Larry Litevich, Martha B. Meale.—**Tree Warden,** John P. Riggio.—**Building Inspector/Sanitarian,** Paul D'Orio.—**Regional Building Code Bd. of Appeals,** Rudolph Besier, Edmund B. Binder, Robert Harper, Frederick Radcliffe, C. Talcott Scoville.—**Harbor Comm.,** Jonathan Lovejoy, Chm., Philip J. Bassett, Leonard J. Mierzejewski, Alan W. Parker, Rudolph C. Planeta, Jr, Harry P. Ruppenicker; Alternate, Charles C. Bevis.—**Shellfish Comm.,** Robert H. Post, Chm., John J. Lynch III, Leonard J. Mierzejewski, Gary R. Norf, John H. Wilson.—**Constables,** Thomas V. Brady, James Comeau, Mark Comeau, Michael McKenna, Lawrence Merrill, Robert Messercola, Rhea Milardo, Salvatore Milardo, Michael S. Oryl, Jr., Joseph Pucillo, Douglas Senn, Brian Wysocki, vacancy.—**Chief of Fire Dept.,** Patrick M. Murphy; 1st Asst., Carl T. Ponzillo.—**Fire Marshal,** George B. Rehberg.—**Bd. of Fire Comrs.,** Dora R. Green, Chm., Sally H. Correll, Victor S. Mauldin, Jr., Robert T. LaGasse, James B. Tomassetti; Alternate, Jonathan Lovejoy.—**Emergency Management Dir.,** George Pytlik; Deputy, Stephen C. Bettum; Communications Officer, Jose M. Asensio.—**Town Atty.,** Richard J. Beatty.—**Justices of the Peace,** Esther Ann Bettum, Paul M. Brache, Joseph M. Campbell, Nancy S. Carlson, Sally H. Correll, Margery R. Coutermash, William H. Daly, Jr., Evelyn L. Finkel, Nathalie N. Gilmond, Alice W. Lynch, Anthony P. Marino, Angus L. McDonald, Jr., Tony A. Palermo, John D. Philbin, Evelyn C. Smith,

WEST HARTFORD. Hartford County.—(Form of government, town manager, town council.)—Inc., May, 1854; taken from Hartford. Area, 22.4 sq. miles. Population, est., 57,056. Voting districts, 10. Principal industries, manufacture of turbines, automobile parts, coil pipe, ball bearings, electrical supplies, screws, small tools and machinery, precision machinery tools, chucks, dies, chemical products, air conditioning units, and plastics. To a large extent a residential area. Transp.—Passenger: Served by buses of Conn. Transit from Hartford, Farmington, Bloomfield, Newington and Unionville; and Bonanza Bus Lines, Inc. Freight: Served by Conrail and numerous motor common carriers. Post offices, West Hartford, Elmwood and Bishops Corner.

TOWN OFFICERS. Clerk and Reg. of Vital Statistics, Norma W. Cronin; Hours, 8:30 A.M.-4:30 P.M., Mon. through Fri.; Address, Town Hall, 50 South Main St., 06107; Tel., Hartford, (860) 523-3100.—**Asst. Clerk,** Glenda Fournier.—**Asst. Regs. of Vital Statistics,** Marla Famiglietti, Glenda Fournier.—**Town Manager,** Barry M. Feldman.—**Town Council,** Nan Glass (D), Pres. and Mayor; Sandy F. Klebanoff, Deputy Mayor; Robert R. Bouvier, Kevin M. Connors, Liz Gillette, Patrick E. McCabe,

Madeline S. McKernan, John Ritter, Alfred A. Turco—**Town Council Zoning Alternates,** Deborah Buckley, Bernard L. Kavaler, Flo Woodiel; Sub. Alternates, Lance Hultgren, John Tucker.—**Dir. of Finance,** Donna Sims.—**Bd. of Assessment Appeals,** Fred H. Greenwood, Chm., Robert J. Kennedy, Jr., Santa Mendoza.—**Bd. of Assessors,** Joseph Stafford, Chm., P. Michael Margolis, Joseph P. McGuinness, James Tierney, vacancy.—**Dir. of Assessments,** Donna Sims.—**Registrars of Voters,** Eileen S. Horan (D), Selma L. Kaufman (R).—**Supt. of Schools,** David Sklarz.—**Bd. of Education,** Nancy Rion, Chm., Geoffrey G. Fisher, Patricia L. Genser, Wick Sloane, 1997; Joseph DeLucco, Tom Fiorentino, Diane Randall, 1999.—**Town Plan and Zoning/ Inland Wetlands Comm.,** Rochelle Homelson, Chm., John D. Dragat, Thomas J. Ives, Stanley G. Johnson, Jr., Andrew E. Kearns; Alternates, Robert S. Burke, Dennis R. Ferguson, Richard Wirth.—**Town Planner,** Donald Foster.—**Zoning Enforcement Officer,** Eva Espinoza.—**Zoning Bd. of Appeals,** David Hendel, Chm., Karin M. Champagne, Sydney W. Elkin, Scott Franklin, Joseph Gianni; Alternates, Holly Abery-Wetstone, Steven Greenspan, Charles J. Shimkus, Jr.—**Housing Auth.,** Karen E. Bachman, Domenico Gendusco, Lois E. Jainchill, Ilze Krisst, Craig Sylvester; Lynn Koroser, Exec. Dir.—**Conservation and Environment Comm.,** , Richard B. Raport, Chm., Christine Aberg, Harold M. Blinderman, Mary M. Callahan, Gregg W. Gabinelle, Matthew D. Goetz, Alan M. Levere, Mark W. Levy, Kevin F. Morin, Kathleen O'Reilly, Lydia B. Varga.—**Historic Dist. Comm.,** Richard Hughes III, Chm., Barbara Cornelius, Mary M. Donohue, Elizabeth B. Kenna, Anne L. Utz; Alternates, Irene B. Clark, Karl A. Fransson, Christopher M. Roof.—**Senior Citizens Advisory Comm.,** Benjamin T. Taylor, Chm., Peter H. Bigelow, Clifford Q. Christensen, Sylvia K. Feigenbaum, Herbert D. Hoffman, Geraldine B. Hugg, Amy L. Silverman, Archibald Stuart, vacancy.—**Advisory Comm. for Persons with Disabilities,** Steven M. Goldfield, Geraldine P. Heath, Steven J. Heath, Edward J. Howley, Mary Ann Langton, Hollace B. Lorch, Betsy Riley, two vacancies.—**Personnel Bd.,** Jeremy N. Weingast, Chm., William Ankerman, Thomas M. Ganley, Jr., Bernard E. Jacques, Sara R. Shapiro.—**Pension Bd.,** James E. Robinson, Chm., John J. Clay, Anne M. Dowling-Logue, Jacob Hurwitz, Maritsa B. St. Jacques.—**Municipal Historian,** Mims Butterworth.—**Library Bd.,** Janet M. Baillif, Chm., David Harris, Joanne M. Johnson, David G. McMahon, Michael S. Wilder; Denis Lorenz Librarian.—**Human Rights Comm.,** Charles D. Koteen, Chm., Mary Jo Armillotto, Sylvia M. Forster, David K. Jaffe, Abdul-Rahmann R. Muhammad, Dawn S. Rodriguez, Rosemarie Tate, Robert D. Violet.—**Health Planning Bd.,** Joyce E. Schickler, Chm., Miriam S. Cohen, Bernadette Dower-Hirst, Nathan L. Dubin, Gloria A. Maloney, Joseph A. Rossi, Lori E. Sims, vacancy.—**Environmental Sanitarians,** Archie D'Amato, Robert Proctor.—**Parks and Recreation Advisory Bd.,** Steven W. Aronson, Chm., Timothy J. Buckley, Nicole D. Dorman, Eleanor W. Hayes, William F. Healey, Eileen K. Moore, Norman L. Stuart, Barbara F. Wolf.—**Leisure Services Mgr.,** James Capodiece.—**Purchasing Agent,** Arthur Geisel, Jr.—**Town Engineer,** William Farrell.—**Streets and Sanitation Dir.,** Dana Hallenbeck.—**Admin. Services Dir.,** Christopher Johnson.—**Employee Services Dir.,** James Francis.—**Community Services Dir.,** Ronald Van Winkle.—**Human Services Dir.,** Susan Halstead-Fair.—**Chief of Police,** James J. Strillacci; Asst., Robert McCue.—**Constables,** John P. Colangelo, Louis DellaRipa, Robert F. Giovino, Richard Hennessey, Thomas C. McKone, Wilmer L. Newton, Richard E. Parlee, Louis

Salzburg, Leonard A. Teicher.—**Chief of Fire Dept.,** vacancy; Fire Marshal, Richard T. Kane.—**Civil Preparedness Dir.,** Barry M. Feldman.—**Corporation Counsel,** Marjorie S. Wilder.—**Justices of the Peace,** Holly Abery-Wetstone, Ethel L. Adler, Leonard J. Agnew, Victoria F. Albert, Nora B. Anthony, Stephen W. Aronson, George M. Babic, Kenneth C. Barrows, M. Stevens Bartels, Jack Bass, Holly P. Beckett, John F. Begley, Jean P. Berard, Peter H. Bigelow, Mary-Kaye V. Bisaillon, Anthony M. Blassberg, Joanne G. Blume, Sylvia Bornstein, Jay M. Botwick, Rob Bouvier, Phyllis H. Brett, Catherine C. Brewer, Lawrence S. Brick, Pamela S. Brown, Robert W. Burgess, Robert S. Burke, Adele M. Caffrey, Joy E. Campbell, Marie Ann Cantwell, James A. Carabillo, Barbara A. Caraceni, C. Thomas Carson, Edith S. Catler, Karin M. Champagne, Catharine V. Christensen, Dorothy G. Christensen, John E. Claffey, Jr., Martin A. Clayman, Philip A. Cocchiola, Marilyn F. Cohen, Janet S. Cohn, Henry S. Cohn, Gail E. Colangelo, Frederick U. Conard, Jr., Babette F. Connors, Roberta S. Cosby, George R. Crossley, Jack W. Cullin, Steven J. D'Ambrosio, John F. Daly, Frank W. Dantzig, Joseph F. DeLucco, Steven E. Derby, William F. Derby, Loretta H. Devine, Dwight N. Dewey, Angelo N. DiBella, Donald J. Dodd, Francis J. Donahue, Joseph M. Donahue, Margaret Donahue, John D. Dragat, Michael E. Drechsler, Timothy Droney, Nathan L. Dubin, W. James Dyber, Sydney W. Elkin, Arthur Epstein, Eva Espinosa, Robert Farr, Edmund Fedorowicz, Susan P. Fellman, Dennis R. Ferguson, Carmen A. Fiore, Mary L. Flynn, Thomas F. Foley, Jr., Sylvia M. Forster, Brendan M. Fox, Jr., Karl A. Fransson, Marie J. Freuh, Kevin M. Galvin, Thomas M. Ganley, Jr., Patricia Z. Gargano, Domenico Genduso, Alyce Gibbons, Leigh Gold, Samuel Goldberger, Daniel J. Golden, Barbara C. Gordon, Paul G. Grady, James G. Green, Jr., Jacqueline M. Grogan, Harry Grossman, Mary E. Guiney, Bryan F. Gunning, Michael P. Gustafson, Eleanor C. Hamilton, Patricia Anne Hamilton, Eleanor W. Hayes, John I. Haymond, Dorris Heiden, Winston H. Heimer, David S. Hendel, LaVerne I. Hermsen, Dennis G. Hersh, Robert L. Hill, Allen Hoffman, Timothy S. Hollister, Rochelle Homelson, Brien P. Horan, Eileen S. Horan, Dorothy L. Howe, Sheila A. Huddleston, Lance R. Hultgren, Robert Hurvitz, Edward R. Jacovino, David K. Jaffe, Gilbert J. Jones, Scott L. Kaeser, Cynthia A. Kaplan, Selma L. Kaufman, Janina J. Kean, Joan R. Kemler, Joseph E. Kleszczynski, Irving U. Knight, Robert J. Kor, William A. Kovel, Nancy A. Kramer, Ruth P. Kronick, Alice K. Kugelman, Daniel C. Kyker, Jr., Arthur O. LaBranch, Essie S. Labrot, Joseph P. LaPenta, William F. LaPorte, Amelia G. Larkum, Joseph F. Lenihan, Mark W. Levy, Arthur M. Lewis, Bonnie D. Long, Arthur B. Lounder, Jr., Jerome H. Lowengard, Maureen Magnan, Stuart L. Mahler, James Marinan, Moraith Marra-O'Toole, Erik L. Masi, Anne E. McCue, Michael P. McGoldrick, Joseph P. McGuinness, Sheila M. McKay, Lauchlin M. McLean, David G. McMahon, Santa Mendoza, Nancy L. Mercer, Richard F. Messenger, Stanley S. Miller, Paul P. Mitnick, Raymond E. Mortenson, Florence G. Narden, Francis E. Nelson, Julius Newman, Stephanie G. Nielson, Bette P. O'Brien, Elizabeth M. O'Neil, Martin J. O'Toole, Dina M. Odell, Jack S. Opinsky, Louise A. Ouellette, Emma G. Pahuskin, Richard E. Parlee, Betty H. Pavlak, H. Randall Pease, Jr., Lisa C. Petersen, Evan Pitkoff, Geraldine Pizzella, Candice S. Price, David G. Pruyne, John Reeder, Donald P. Reilly, Marilyn S. Rettig, Jerry Rezendes, Carol Ribadeneyra, Penn J. Ritter, Cynthia C. Robertson, Patricia-Beth L. Rome, George W. Rooney, Elliott Rosenberg, Judith Roussis, Marilyn G. Rubin, Barbara S. Sacks,

Bonny N. Salad, Louis M. Salzburg, Edward G. Sanady, Anna T. Sansone, Theresa E. Santomasso, Harry B. Schaechter, Walter B. Schatz, Kenneth M. Scheinblum, William J. Schickler, Gerald Schulman, Ruth G. Scott, Christina M. Sesta, Louise M. Shea, Elizabeth A. Shepardson, Herbert J. Shepardson, Charles J. Shimkus, Jr., Doris J. Shuskus, Arnoldo C. Sierra, Ann F. Simons, Theresa C. Spurr, Joseph S. Stafford, Wendell S. Stephenson, Kaye S. Straw, Carolyn T. Sullivan, Barbara V. Sylvester, Thomas R. Sylvester, William J. Tacy, Rosemarie Tate, Leonard M. Teicher, James S. Tierney, Suzanne B. Todd, Robert S. Tonino, Orwell C. Tousley, Diane L. Tucker, John Tucker, Alfred A. Turco, Barbara B. Ulrich, Sally Van Meter, Richard B. Vannie, Helen R. Vanty, Frank R. Virnelli, Jr., Kimberly A. Wahlberg, John F. Wallace, Jr., Solon L. Weiner, Debora G. Westcott, Irving M. Widem, Richard J. Wirth, S. Steven Wolfson, Florence N. Woodiel, Marcia L. Woolsey, Mona Lisa Wynkoop-Deria, Polly W. Zarella.

WEST HAVEN. New Haven County.—(Form of government, mayor, city council.)—Inc., June 24, 1921; taken from Orange; inc. as a city, June 27, 1961. Area, 11.0 sq. miles. Population, est., 52,477. Voting districts, 10. Principal industries, manufacture of buckles, manufacturing of durable and non-durable goods, textiles, chemicals, pharmaceuticals, artificial stone products. Transp.—Passenger: Served by buses of Conn. Transit from New Haven, Milford and Bridgeport. Freight: Served by Conrail and numerous motor common carriers. Post office, West Haven.

CITY AND TOWN OFFICERS. City Clerk, Town Clerk and Reg. of Vital Statistics, William E. Donegan; Hours, 9 A.M.-5 P.M., Mon. through Fri.; Address, City Hall, 355 Main St., 06516; Tel., West Haven, (203) 937-3534.—**Asst. Clerks,** Deborah Collins, John Pascale.—**Asst. Reg. of Vital Statistics,** Sharon Recchia.—**Mayor,** H. Richard Borer, Jr. (D); Exec. Asst., Douglas Cutler.—**Councilmen at Large,** C. Michael Lennon, John A. Samperi, Wayne Talamelli.—**Councilmen,** 7th Dist., James V. Amendola, Jr., Chm.; 1st Dist., Judith C. Harvey; 2nd Dist., Antonio Buonomo; 3rd Dist., Charles A. Marino; 4th Dist., Albert Towles; 5th Dist., Bernice E. Bowman; 6th Dist., Joseph W. Harvey, Jr.; 8th Dist., Scott J. Smith; 9th Dist., Joseph Cullen, Sr.; 10th Dist., Mary E. Tracy.—**Bd. of Ethics,** Jerome Lacobelle, Sr., Phillip Mancini, Jr., vacancy.—**Treas.,** Michael McGrath.—**Bd. of Finance,** Pasquale Barone, Mayor H. Richard Borer, Jr., Keith Burgess, Genevieve F. Canny, Jessie Terrasi, two vacancies.—**Tax Collector,** Arthur Gilbert.—**Bd. of Assessment Appeals,** Beth V. Denton, David G. Russell, Norman Shove.—**Assessor,** Joan R. Robinson.—**Registrars of Voters,** Emmett J. McDonough (D), JoAnn Callegari (R).—**Supt. of Schools,** George Palerma.—**Bd. of Education,** George Belbusti, Timothy C. Borer, Gerald Calabritto, John E. Erickson, John S. Morgan, Patricia L. Turner, 1997; Jolene Barnes, Chm., Joseph Furman, Treva J. Hackley, Marilyn McDaniel, 1999.—**Personnel Dir.,** Ralph DeLucca, Jr.—**Planning and Zoning Comm.,** James O'Leary, Chm., Raymond Ceccarelli, John Panza, Barbara Simmons, Richard Tracy; Alternates, three vacancies.—**City Planner,** James Hill.—**Zoning Bd. of Appeals,** John Clifford, Richard DeLeo, Sam Girasuolo, Mark Glassman, Pascal Panza; Alternates, Clarence L. Bowman, Dominic Furco, Edmund Wise.—**Zoning Enforcement Officer,** Alfredo

Evangelista.—**Development Comm.,** Peter Maglaris, Chm., Louis A. Buonfiglio, Jr., Clement A. Diana, Joseph Harvey, Sr., Brian F. Smith.—**Redevelopment Agency,** Louis D'Onofrio, Eugene McCarthy, Michael A. Mercuriano, A. Michael Recchia, Theresa Salsone, Sharon Spaziani.—**Housing Auth.,** Willie Homes, Adrienne Hurburt, Joan E. Riccio, Theresa Sansone, Irene Thomas; Michael W. Siwek, Exec. Dir.—**Fair Rent Comm.,** Mary Jane Morrissey, Chm., Elaine Macht, Harold W. Parritt, Eugene Sullivan, David Valente, Richard Watt; Alternates, Galen G. Nally, Francine White.—**Inland Wetlands Comm.,** Edmund Marzano, Chm., John Evangeliste, Kenneth Ferris, Michael T. McCurry; Alternates, Richard Cogswell, Timothy Collins, Christopher Skeens.—**Flood and Erosion Control Bd.,** Thomas Canny, Francis J. Coyle, Jr., Pam Mueller, two vacancies.—**Senior Citizens Comm.,** Lucille A. Cassella, Marqueritte Hambrook, Catherine Howse, Terry Pascarelli, Florence Robinson, Juanita Williams.—**Agent for the Elderly,** vacancy.—**Comr. of Human Resources,** Beth Sabo.—**Dir. of Health,** Eric Triffin.—**Bd. of Health,** Marie Duffy, Maurice Gouin, Ernestine D. Jackson.—**Library Bd. of Directors,** Charles Gunning, Pres., Jennie Annatone, Patricia Bellmore, Francis Blanchette, Barbara Bureau, John Dillman, Eugene Dorsi, Albert E. Forte, Joseph Fortino, Lois King, Thomas Lehman, Stephen Michel, Joseph Pascale; Concetta N. Sacco, Head Librarian.—**Municipal Historian,** Harriet North.—**Parks and Recreation Comm.,** Peter Merola, Chm., Vincent R. Falcone, Carl Guarneri, Ursula Reilly, Donald Wrinn; William Slater, Dir.—**Dir. of Public Works,** Arthur C. Ferris; Asst., Mary V. Annunziata.—**City Engineer,** Abdul Quadir.—**Sealer of Weights and Measures,** Richard Tracy, Sr.—**Building Inspector,** Frank Gladwin; Asst., vacancy.—**Building Code Bd. of Appeals,** Sabino Panza, Chm., George S. Baxter, Harry Catenza, Joseph P. Gorry, Jr., John Markowich.—**Housing Code Appeals Bd.,** Edward Flanders, John Panza, James Roche.—**Water Pollution Control Comm.,** three vacancies.—**Sanitarian,** Raymond A. Puslys, R.S.—**Chief of Police,** Michael Kelly; Deputy, vacancy; Assts., Joseph Innamorato, John Mariano.—**Police Comm.,** Thomas Gallagher, Chm., Paul Bernstein, Alexander Bott, Michael D'Errico, Brendella Coleman-Lokites.—**Constables,** Anthony Bonnanzio, Antonio Buonomo, Louis P. Esposito, Jr., William Nolan, vacancy.—**Chiefs of Fire Dept.,** William S. Johnson, Jr. (First Dist.), James T. Burns (West Shore Dist.), Richard Massaro (Allingtown Dist.).—**Deputy Chiefs/Fire Marshals,** William Mulvey (First Dist.), Robert S. Burns (West Shore Dist.), Richard Sampietro (Allingtown Dist.).—**Bd. of Fire Comrs.,** Stephen D. Dargan, Donald J. Lewis, Bruce Sweeney (First Dist.); John Alexander, David Forsyth, Mark Vere (Allingtown Dist.); Louis D'Onofrio, Richard Fontana, Chm., Frank Hawley, Tina Peckingham (West Shore Dist.).—**Civil Preparedness Dir.,** William M. Welch.—**Corporation Counsel,** Michael Farrell; Assts., Brian G. Enright, Jerome A. Lacobelle, Jr., Henry C. Szadkowsi.—**Justices of the Peace,** John E. Alexander, Martha Bell, Clifford L. Bradley, Gerald Calabritto, JoAnn Callegari, Joyce D. Candido, Nancy Ciarleglio, Linda A. Collins, Joseph Crescenti, Martin DeGrand, John C. Dillman, William Donegan, Marie Duffy, Salvatore S. Eamiello, Kathleen Esposito, Deborah Evangelista, Anthony V. Giordano, Robert J. Guthrie, Joseph Harvey, Jr., Frank E. Hawley, Arthur M. Hubbard, Jr., Beulah Johnson, Douglas Kovacs, Patricia LaValla, Sandra LoRusso, Thomas E. Mansfield, John Morgan, Carol L. Musco, Carl J. Ordazzo, John Pascale, Mary A. Perrone, Francis Skerritt, Borden P. Steeves, Sr., Eugene Sullivan, Mary Tracy.

WESTON. Fairfield County.—(Form of government, selectmen, town meeting, board of finance.)—Inc., Oct., 1787; taken from Fairfield, Inc., 1845, the town was divided and Easton was taken from Weston. Area, 20.7 sq. miles. Population, est., 9,066. Voting district, 2. Residential community; no industries. Transp.—Freight: To South Norwalk. Post office, Weston. Rural free delivery from Weston and Georgetown.

TOWN OFFICERS. Clerk and Reg. of Vital Statistics, Cynthia A. Williams; Hours, 9 A.M.-4:30 P.M., Mon. through Fri.; Address, Town Hall, 56 Norfield Rd., P.O. Box 1007, 06883; Tel., (203) 222-2616.—**Asst. Clerks and Asst. Regs. of Vital Statistics,** Linda Roig, Helen Rosendahl, Sharon C. Shattuck.—**Town Admin.,** Rosemary Cashman; Asst., Carl Tomchik.—**Selectmen,** 1st, George C. Guidera (R) Tel., (203) 222-2656, Harvey D. Attra (R), Harold Shupack (D).—**Treas.,** Robert L. Tranzillo.—**Bd. of Finance,** Emil H. Frankel, Chm., Robert Atkinson, Penny N. Pearlman, Leonard Peterson, Gerald T. Sargent III, Robert I. Siegel, Leslie L. Wolf; Carl Tomchik, Dir.—**Tax Collector,** Charity B. Nichols.—**Bd. of Assessment Appeals,** David M. Brown, Chm., Glenn C. Davis, James T. Shearin.—**Assessor,** Linda Roig.—**Registrars of Voters,** Audrey C. Bartels (D) Eileen S. Buckley (R).—**Supt. of Schools,** David Trigaux.—**Bd. of Education,** Ralph M. Goodmurphy, Lynda J. Hennessey, Linda Pittleman, 1997; John A. Negroni, Chm., Diane L. Forth, Devon J. Pfeifer, Sherrie N. Simerman, 1999.—**Planning and Zoning Comm.,** Jeffrey T. Farr, Chm., David Fridling, Robert J. Osborn, Steven W. Russo, Donald Saltzman, Marguerite Terzian, Michael L. Widland.—**Zoning Bd. of Appeals,** Frederick C. Noyes, Jr., Chm., Carol Falberg, Paul Heifetz, David Simerman, Robert P. Turner; Alternates, Norman L. Herman, W. Macleod Snaith, Richard B. Wolf.—**Zoning Enforcement Officer,** E. Edward Hahne.—**Conservation and Inland Wetlands Comm.,** Stephen R. Patton, Chm., Traute Bushley, J. Thomas Failla, Charles Finkelstein, Wilford A. Lewis, Ellen G. Mason, Paul F. Schultz, Jr.—**Historic Dist. Comm.,** Mary Ann Barr, Chm., Donald C. Bergquist, MacLennan Farrell, Lynn A. Langlois, James T. Shearin; Alternates, Brad Aron, DuBois Morris, Jr.—**Municipal Historian,** Kathleen S. Failla.—**Elderly Comm.,** Richard Miller, Chm., Theresa Castellano, Herbert M. Day, Martha Diamant, Kathleen Messina, Laurie A. Morris, Helen M. Rosendahl; Helen Flores, Agent.— **Dir. of Social Services,** Helen Flores.—**Dir. of Health,** Judith Nelson (P.O., Westport).—**Health Comm.,** Daniel H. Adler, John Conte, Michael Greenberg, Judith Oakes, Barbara Stein.—**Library Committee,** Lynn A. Langlois, Chm., Elllen Aho, Nancy R. Brown, E. Marie Meehan, Johanna Straczek, Helene Weatherill, Helen Welch, David Wiltse.—**Jury Comm.,** Eileen S. Buckley, Jane R. Gray, John Hammerslough.—**Parks and Recreation Comm.,** Catherine A. Iffland, Chm., Prudence Bliss, Nancy Burkholder, Patrick E. Kane, Denise Massengale-Lamb, Val Scansaroli, Robert Uzenoff.—**Building Committee,** Linda Roig, Chm., Audrey C. Bartels, Donald C. Bergquist, David Coprio, Michael Greenberg, Peter Voulgarakis, Richard Wolf.— **Building Bd. of Appeals,** Louis J. Bottone, David Coprio, Thomas Phillips, Peter Voulgarakis.—**Dir. of Public Works,** Joseph Lametta.—**Town Engineer,** John Conte.—**Animal Control Officer,** Mark E. Harper.—**Building Inspector,** E. Edward Hahne.—**Sanitarian,** A. James Smith.—**Tree Warden,** A. James Hoe.—**Chief of Police,** Tony Land.—**Police Comm.,** Phyllis R. McGrath, Chm., Donald Gary, Beth

Gralnick, Blake L. Hampton, Walter Marcus, Peter J. Ottomano, Helen Speck.—**Chief of Fire Dept.,** John Pokorny.—**Fire Marshal,** Frederick J. Moore.—**Civil Preparedness Dir.,** Frederick J. Moore.—**Town Atty.,** Edward S. Rimer, Jr.—**Justices of the Peace,** Cristina M. Arvoy, Jane W. Atkinson, Millicent R. Best, Pamela D. Bochinski, Howard Falberg, Anita M. Field, Alexander R. Formisano, Nancy K. Hammerslough, Paul Heifetz, W. Glenn Major, Alan S. Rasch, Donald L. Saltzman, Joseph O. Spetly, Barbara Stein, Jonathan M. Tendler.

WESTPORT. Fairfield County.—(Form of government, selectmen, representative town meeting, board of finance.)—Inc., May 28, 1835; taken from Fairfield, Norwalk and Weston. Area, 33.3 sq. miles. Population, est., 24,400. Voting districts, 8. Principal industries, retailing and office center for Fairfield County, known for its fine restaurants. Transp.—Passenger: Served by Metro North Commuter Railroad Co. and Minibus. Freight: Served by Conrail and numerous motor common carriers. Post offices, Westport, Saugatuck and Greens Farms. The extreme eastern part of the town is also served by Greens Farms Railroad Station.

TOWN OFFICERS. Clerk and Reg. of Vital Statistics, Joan M. Hyde; Hours, 8:30 A.M.-4:30 P.M., Mon. through Fri.; Address, Town Hall, 110 Myrtle Ave., P.O. Box 549, 06881; Tel., (203) 226-8311.—**Asst. Clerks,** Joyce E. Cotto, Georgette E. Higgs.—**Asst. Regs. of Vital Statistics,** Ruth M. Cavayero, Joyce E. Cotto, Georgette E. Higgs.—**Selectmen,** 1st, Joseph P. Arcudi (R) Tel., (203) 226-8311, Ext. 360, Betty Lou Cummings (R), Nicholas W. Thiemann (D).—**Representative Town Meeting Members, Moderator,** Gordon F. Joseloff. Dist. 1, Catherine S. Herman, Jorgen F. Jensen, William L. Scheffler, Ann E. Sheffer, Joseph J. Valiante, Jr.; Dist. 2, Holton E. Harris, Walter D. Harris, Jeffrey A. Mayer, Mary G. Webber; Dist. 3, Nancy K. Kienzle, William F. Meyer III, Stephen M. Rubin, Harry Traub; Dist. 4, Lewis D. Brey, Janet S. Canning, William Kaufman, Ralph Schwarz, Carol Ann Waxman; Dist. 5, Lawrence O. Aasen, John W. Booth, Ralph Hymans, Janis M. Waserman; Dist. 6, Daniel Boyce, Jamison Daily, Ronald F. Malone, Thomas J. Murphy, William P. Raines; Dist. 7, Stuart Bernard, Paul C. Johnson, Joy M. Miyasaki, Lisa S. Rome; Dist. 8, Irwin Donenfeld, Richard B. Friedman, Gordon F. Joseloff, Linda Merk-Gould, Robert G. Schneider.—**Controller,** Donald J. Miklus; Deputy, John P. Kondub.—**Bd. of Finance,** Edwin K. Dimes, Chm., Penny A. Bray, Diane G. Farrell, Roy E. Fuchs, John A. Laurino, Carl W. Leaman, Joseph D. Warren, Jr.—**Tax Collector,** George Underhill.—**Bd. of Assessment Appeals,** Douglas W. Dunham, J. Drayton Hamm, Garson I. Heller.—**Assessors,** Kenneth Carvell; Deputy, Glenn M. Werfelman; Asst., Dorothy Allen.—**Personnel Dir.,** Carl J. Ingelbrink; Asst., Loretta Hallock.—**Registrars of Voters,** Thelma Ezzes (D), Mabel A. Johnson (R).—**Supt. of Schools,** Paul Kelleher.—**Bd. of Education,** Ira M. Bloom, Chm., Caren C. Gagliano, Steven G. Halstead, Joan A. Irvine, 1997; Cheryl A. Bliss, Eugene E. Cederbaum, Doborah R. Rath, 1999.—**Planning and Zoning Comm.,** Robert D. Graham, Hope Hageman, Eleanor S. Lowenstein, Robert MacLachlan, David R. Marks, Kathryn H. Mimms, Lois S. Porro; Katherine Barnard, Dir.; Carrie Makover, Town Planner; Alternates, Stanley Barnett, William Crowther, vacancy.—**Zoning Bd. of Appeals,** Joanne Leaman, Chm., James C. Ezzes, Barbara R. Herman, John J. McCarthy, John E. Watson

III; Alternates, Robert Allen, Winston Allen, Gregory Altschuh.—**Zoning Enforcement Officer,** Susan Reynolds; Planning Asst., Alicia Mozian; Inspector, Steven Palmer.—**Beautification Committee,** Donald Torrey, Chm., Nancy Carr, Betty Lou Cummings, Claire Ford, Amy Jacques, Patricia Limburg, Helen Muller, Irene Naughton, Tamarra T. Pincavage, Joseph Sexton, Mary Sibley, Joanne Siebrasse, Richard Stein.—**Public Site and Building Comm.,** Alexander Balas, Chm., James Conte, Charles H. Gibbons, Peter Heneage, Edward Kowalcyk, George Petropulos, Richard Pitkin.—**Housing Auth.,** Howard L. Brody, Chm., Ross Burkhardt, Jacqueline Hill, Maurice Reid, John Tursi; Patricia Abbott, Exec. Dir.—**Conservation Comm.,** Stanley Freeman, Chm., Richard Benson, Jo Ann Davidson, Mark Goldstein, Richard Harris, John Horkel, Ann Valiante.—**Environmental Officer,** Frances Pierwola.—**Flood and Erosion Control Bd.,** Walter Schlenker, Chm., James DeStefano, Robert Lasprogato, Charles Martinek, K. Burr McGhee, Robert Seskin, Timothy Walker.—**Historic Dist. Comm.,** Joseph Sledge, Chm., Roy Dickinson, Susan Gunn, Helen Muller, Satenig St. Marie; Alternates, William F. Dohme, Michael Glynn, Diana Heisinger.—**Municipal Historians,** Dorothea Malm, Allen Raymond.—**Comm. for the Elderly,** Paula Leonard, Chm., Dolores Bacharach, Alfred Eiseman, Janis Folsom, Catherine Goldschmidt, Hugh Pickering, Paul Teske; Frances Reynolds, Agent.—**Human Services Comm.,** Irwin Sollinger, Chm., Pamela Driscoll, Venora Ellis, Lauren S. Grosner, Aki Ikeda, Robert Orkand, Kevin Pease; Barbara Butler, Dir.—**Dir. of Health,** Judy Nelson.—**Library Trustees,** Catherine Onyemelukwe, Chm., William Bangser, Jr., Horace Boynton, Dorothy Curran, Joel Davis, Kermit Easton, Jeffrey Jacobs, Barbara Kellerman, Bertram Reisman, Robert Seskin, Joseph Strickland, Faith H. Taylor, Lawrence P. Weisman, Claire Yearwood.—**Parks and Recreation Comm.,** Michael Rea, Chm., Everett Frey, Evan Harding, Donna Hughes, Martha Press; Stuart McCarthy, Exec. Dir.—**Dir. of Public Works,** Stephen Edwards.—**Supt. of Highways,** George Swift.—**Town Engineer,** Daniel Delehanty.—**Building Inspector,** Stephen J. Smith.—**Architectural Review Bd.,** Michael Calise, Chm., George Masumian, Susan Schultz, Joseph Vallone, William Wayman.—**Building Bd. of Appeals,** Anthony J. Izzo, Chm., Winifred S. Allen, Victor Burtsche, Robert McCarthy, John Wanat.—**Sewage Plant Supt.,** vacancy.—**Water Pollution Control Auth.,** Bd. of Selectmen.—**Energy Coordinators,** Albert Kelley, Richard Pitkin.—**Sanitarian,** Eugene J. Tomasky.—**Tree Warden,** Joseph R. Sexton.—**Purchasing Agent,** Richard V. Kilbride.—**Chief of Police,** William J. Chiarenzelli; Deputy, John R. Anastasia.—**Special Police,** Bruce Allen, Richard M. Bayuk, Thomas Candia, Jr., Michael Cantrell, Gary J. Ciuci, William Cribari, Peter D'Amico, Richard J. DeAngelis, Edward G. Frawley, Michael Frawley, Nancy Gale, Gregory Gallo, Stephen N. Geremia, Theodore Gianitti, Richard A. Giunta, Susan Grega, Neil F. Harding, Cynthia Hull, William Hull, Kenneth J. Kelemen, Frederick E. Kellogg, Jr., Karen Kurimsky, David Mortensen, John G. Riordan, Kevin Smith, Todd M. Smith, Raymond A. Tienken.—**Chief of Fire Dept./Fire Marshal,** Richars S. Gough; Deputy, Denis McCarthy.—**Civil Preparedness Dir.,** Donald A. Byington; Deputies, Stephen Edwards, Donald Miklus.—**Town Atty.,** Andrew F. Fink; Asst., Joseph Munro.—**Justices of the Peace,** Martha M. Aasen, Deirdre Abbotts, Ruby C. Allen, Stanley P. Atwood, Myron W. Belaga, Allen S. Bomes, Julia S. Bradley, Paul J. Bray, Howard L. Brody, Peter G. Campbell, Edward J. Capasse, Heidi C. Clark, Carolanne Curry, Judith H. Cuthbert, Theodore Diamond, Edwin K. Dimes,

James J. DiMiceli, Christopher C. Dunham, Douglas W. Dunham, James C. Ezzes, Helen W. Fink, George Francisovich, Carolyn N. Ganz, Joan H. Gillman, Constance Greenfield, Martha S. Hauhuth, Barbara R. Herman, Michael J. Hoherchak, Leonard P. Kaminsky, Peter W. Kardaras, Sylvia Komarow, Sidney B. Kramer, Scott Lerman, Rhona S. Lieberson, Richard A. Lowenstein, Mary W. Madden, Mark Marcus, Emanuel Margolis, John J. McCarthy, Randolph W. Meyer, Seymour J. Mund, Maria S. Nilson, Phyllis R. Nole, Kevin M. O'Grady, Kae Peet, Mark D. Phillips, Barbara L. Plunkett, Lynn D. Quinn, Stephen Rappaport, Estelle M. Reitano, Stephen M. Rubin, Barbara S. Schadt, Robert P. Scholl, Ann E. Sheffer, Edward R. Smolka, Ruth Solway, Scott L. Spitzer, Carl Stitzer, Theodore E. Uly, Agnes Violette-Danzer.

WETHERSFIELD. Hartford County.—(Form of government, town manager, town council.)—Settled, 1634; named, 1637; inc., May, 1822. Area, 13.1 sq. miles. Population, est., 24,004. Voting districts, 10. Principal industries, motel-gas-restaurant motoring trade, marine terminals for gasoline and fuel oils, frozen foods, tools and dies, offices and warehouses food, specialty steel, drug supplies, printing, seedsmen, Connecticut Light & Power Co. Computer Center and Northeast Utilities Service Co. Headquarters; Dept. of Transportation, Labor Dept. and State Motor Vehicles Dept. Transp.—Passenger: Served by buses of Conn. Transit from Hartford and Middletown, and by Greyhound. Freight: Served by B & M and numerous motor common carriers. Site: William H. Putnam Bridge for traffic to Glastonbury and eastern points in Connecticut. Post office, Wethersfield (branch of Hartford post office), with carrier service and also rural free delivery.

TOWN OFFICERS. Clerk and Reg. of Vital Statistics, Dorcas McHugh; Hours, 8 A.M.-4:30 P.M., Mon. through Fri.; Address, Town Hall, 505 Silas Deane Hwy., 06109; Tel., (860) 721-2880.—**Asst. Clerks and Asst. Regs. of Vital Statistics,** Tracy Frankel, Amy L. Morrin, Sandra M. Wieleba.—**Town Manager,** Lee C. Erdmann.—**Town Council,** Wayne J. Sassano, Mayor; Thomas Fitzpatrick, Brendan T. Flynn, Thomas J. Kelly, John J. O'Brien, Jr., Fredrick E. Petrelli, Jr., Gerri Roberts, Richard P. Sparveri, Deputy Mayor, Ronald W. Zdrojeski.—**Selectmen,** Louis E. DelMastro (D), Harry L. Lichtenbaum (D), Beverly M. Noren (D), George A. Ruhe (R), Judith P. Whitehead (R).—**Treas.,** Frances A. Patti; Deputy, Kerry R. Larkin.—**Bd. of Ethics,** Gloria P. McLean, Gail K. Moller, Pamela M. Mooney, Margaret M. Tansey, Joan S. Thorsell; Alternates, Herbert H. Northrop, Stanley F. Zebzda, vacancy.—**Finance Dir.,** Joseph Swetcky, Jr.—**Tax Collector,** Nancy DiGirolamo.—**Bd. of Assessment Appeals,** James M. Sweeney, Chm., Michael F. Egan, Francis R. Sablone.—**Assessor,** John J. Dagata.—**Registrars of Voters,** Carmen A. Pace (D), Mary-Ann E. McFarland (R).—**Supt. of Schools,** Lynne B. Pierson.—**Bd. of Education,** Christine T. Fortunato, Richard M. Gibilsco, Lee N. Johnson, Janet C. Leombruni, Russell A. Morin, John F. Morris, 1997; John F. Cascio, Chm., Penny Stanziale, Patricia M. Strong, 1999.—**Planning and Zoning Comm.,** Robert P. Jurasin, Chm., Ross A. Bouchard, Matthew Cholewa, Joseph L. Hammer, Peter Leombruni, George B. Oickle, Theodore R. Paulding, Richard P. Roberts, Richard H. Sitnick; Alternates, John O'Leary, Darlene A. Oblak, Daniel A. Silver.—**Zoning Bd. of Appeals,** J. Edward Brymer, Jr., Chm., Francis A. Baio, Jr., John Bairos, Louis E. DelMastro, Frank A. Falvo; Alternates, Bruce T. Bockstael, Morris R. Borea, Earle R. Munroe.—**Personnel**

Appeals Bd., Joseph Koneski, Thomas F. Lawton, Jr., Francis T. Ragonese.—**Economic Development and Improvement Comm.,** Fernando G. Rosa, Chm., Greg Bedula, Henry K. Brown, Anthony D. Camilliere, Maria L. DeMarco, Frank Frago, Matthew P. Hallisey, Jon Vining, Christopher White; Alternates, Kenneth J. DeLisa, Craig D. MacGovern.—**Environmental Code Appeals Bd.,** Jeffrey R. Kotkin, Robert F. Murtha, Yolanda S. Preysner; Alternate, Nicolette F. Sposito.—**Insurance Committee,** Stephen M. Mulready, Brian J. Paradee, Jean M. Shea, Debra D. Tietjen.—**Fair Rent Comm.,** Helen C. Bucior, Francis J. Farrelly, John C. Flynn, Patricia R. Poirier, Jeanette E. Soroko, Joan S. Thorsell, vacancy; Alternates, three vacancies.—**Housing Auth.,** Henry Allen, Chm., Donna Jordan, George J. Kelly, Jr., Lisa K. Morgan, vacancy; Jane Rosendahl, Exec. Dir.—**Conservation Comm.,** Joyce J. Bauer, Ingrid Boelhouwer, Richard Crawford, David Gregorio, Robert A. Molloy, Viola H. Morris, Ralph Moyer, Peter O'Keefe, Rebecca M. Zaliznock.—**Inland Wetlands and Water Courses Comm.,** Charles P. Viani, Chm., David D. Ambrose, Lawrence F. Buck, Frederick T. Clark, Joseph M. Hallisey, Frank H. Morris, Michael J. Scenti, James M. Sweeney, vacancy; Alternates, Steven M. Barry, John L. Guilmartin, Penrose Wolf.—**Flood and Encroachment Control Bd.,** George A. Ruhe, Chm., Steven M. Barry, Carolyn A. Ikari, Richard F. Lepore, Paul E. Randazzo; Alternates, John F. Morris, two vacancies.—**Historic Dist. Comm.,** Thomas J. Quarticelli, Chm., Greg Curtin, Deborah S. Susco, Gary D. Vivian, vacancy; Alternates, Alice R. Gold, Clare W. Mead, Vaclav Miglus.—**Senior Citizens Advisory Committee,** Adele J. Antoniou, Kathy Bagley, Marian Conroy, Maryalice B. Czemicki, Marcella Fahey, Sharon Gerrard, Vivian A. Hughes, John A. Rogers, Jane Rosendahl, Donald Schwab, Elizabeth K. Smith, Christine Taylor; Alternates, Dorothy McGurkin, Mary Pezzlo,—**Human Rights and Relations Comm.,** William G. Graeber, Donald P. Guerrini, Gail M. Hensley, Judith S. Hersey, Aurelio Interlandi, John Preysner, Paul E. Randazzo, Pamela M. Rapacz, Barbara J. Ruhe; Alternates, George J. Kelly, Jr., Jeffrey R. Kotkin, vacancy.—**Advisory Committee for People With Disabilities,** Carol C. Keenan, Chm., John F. Cosker, Jr., Illene F. Frank, Joan G. Haines, Paul Hutcheon, John S. Karangekis, Mark L. Leonka, A. Cynthia Matthews, Francis G. Meunier, Jr., Deidre K. Moller, Louise Ryan, Patricia C. Sargent, Lee Sekas, William D. Webb, Stanley Zebzda.—**Agent for the Elderly,** Sharon Gerrard.—**Dir. of Human Services,** John F. Cosker.—**Dir. of Health Dist.** Paul Hutcheon.—**Library Bd.,** Lucille E. Domick, Chm., Patricia P. Erlandson, Victoria F. Meucci, Bradley S. Milvae, David C. Shinn, Yolanda H. Viggiano, Daniel B. Willey, Margaret F. Zacchei, vacancy.—**Municipal Historian,** Dorcas McHugh.—**Committee on Culture and the Arts,** Martha H. Londergan, Chm., Pamela A. Mooney, Sandra C. Mulcahy, Patricia R. Poirier, Sandra Ritter, Ruth A. Schumaker, Carol A. Spaveri, Patricia C. Viani, Patricia M. Warner, five vacancies.—**Advisory Recreation and Parks Bd.,** Raymond F. Schilke II, Chm., Carolyn M. Creed, Richard L. Dobmeier, David Herold, Daniel K. Smith; Thomas A. Ragonese, Dir.; Alternates, Judith P. Whitehead, Charles J. Wood.—**Dir. of Youth Services,** Ken Friedenberg.—**Town Engineer,** James Sheehy.—**Dir. of Public Works,** Lee C. Erdmann; Deputy Dir., James Sheehy.—**Purchasing Agent,** Joseph Swetcky.—**Dir. of Physical Services,** Joseph F. Hart.—**Building Inspector,** Fred P. Valente.—**Bd. of Building Appeals,** Lorenzo Gaudet, Joseph M. Hallisey, Kerry R. Larkin, Robert F. Murtha, vacancy; Alternates, David D. Ambrose, Craig S. Pinney, vacancy.—**Tree Warden,** Joe Hart.—**Chief of Police,** John Karangekis.—**Constables,** Francis A. Baio, Jr., William H. Carey, Jr., George W. Cote, Louis E. DelMastro, Albert G. Kaeser, Jr., Steven A. McFarland, Frank J. Patti.—**Chief of Fire Dept.,** John J. McAuliffe; Asst., Thomas P. Watson; Deputies, William Clark, Theodore H. Schroll, Peter T. Susca.—**Fire Marshal,** Gary S. Santoro.—**Civil Preparedness Dir.,** Lee C. Erdmann.—**Town Atty.,** Charles E. Moller, Jr.; Deputy, John W. Bradley, Jr.—**Justices of the Peace,** Frank A. Baio, Betsy J. Bartlett, F. Diane Boesch, Christine Bradley, Donna L. Campbell, George W. Cote, Edward Czernicki, George A. Dursi, Susan M. Fennelly, Thomas Fitzpatrick, Rita S. Flanigan, Reno Franconi, Saul S. Galinsky, Judith M. Haddad, Susan E. Hoskins, Spencer I. Kanter, Kerry R. Larkin, Harry L. Lichtenbaum, Walter Mayo, Charles A. McFarland, Mary-Ann E. McFarland, Gerhard Merkle, Donna Micklus, John H. Miller, S. Bradley Milvae, Gail K. Moller, Joan M. Pace, Robert T. Pandolfe, Pamela M. Rapacz, Fernando G. Rosa, George A. Ruhe, Genevieve T. Small, Robert W. Smith, Nicolette F. Sposito, Sophie F. Urbanik, Lucille C. Vaughan, Ronald K. Whitehead.

WILLINGTON. Tolland County.—(Form of government, selectmen, town meeting, board of finance.)—Inc., May, 1727. Area, 33.5 sq. miles. Population, est., 6,385. Voting district, 1. Principal industries, agriculture, manufacture of machined parts, electroplating. Transp.—Passenger: Served by buses of the Windham Region Transit District form Storrs to Windham. Freight: Served by Central Vermont Railway and numerous motor common carriers. Post office, Willington. Rural free delivery.

TOWN OFFICERS. Clerk and Reg. of Vital Statistics, Patricia Godbout; Hours, 9 A.M.-2 P.M., Mon. through Fri.; 6-8 P.M., Monday; Address, 40 Old Farms Rd., Willington 06279; Tel., (860) 429-9965.—**Asst. Clerk and Asst. Reg. of Vital Statistics,** Donna J. Hardie.—**Selectmen,** 1st, John Patton (ASP) Tel., (860) 429-5649, John R. Lewis (ASP), Robert W. Perry (R).—**Treas.,** Donna M. Latincsics.—**Bd. of Finance,** Robert Lisewski, Chm., Henry L. Becker, Kathleen K. Blessing, Roger C. Bowen, Lila J. Hisey, Elizabeth S. Robinson; Alternates, Robert A. Hipsky, Jr., Paul A. Williams.—**Tax Collector,** Gay A. St. Louis.—**Bd. of Assessment Appeals,** Carol C. Parizek Chm., Peter S. Andersen, Edward A. Beebe.—**Assessor,** David Gardner.—**Registrars of Voters,** Teddie B. Sleight (D), Judith R. Andersen (R).—**Bd. of Education,** Robert G. Ryder, Chm., Melanie T. Becker, Peter J. Latincsics, 1997; Herbert C. Arico, Edward A. D'Agata, Jerzy J. Debski, Ellen C. Hipsky, 1999.—**Planning and Zoning Comm.,** Ralph Tulis, Chm., Robert A. Begansky, Frederick J. Kaeser, Emil Kalbac, Scott H. Kneeland, Allan D. St. Louis; Alternates, John Blessington, Frank Grimason, Wayne H. Knight.—**Zoning Bd. of Appeals,** Carlton R. Csiki, Chm., Dorothy Brown, Richard Claus, Sr., Paula Enderle, Alfred W. Hyde; Alternates, Sydney R. Goodrich, BonnieLea Stebbins, vacancy.—**Zoning Enforcement Officer,** Susan Jorgensen.—**Conservation Comm.,** Paul Pribula, Chm., Barbara W. Clark, Susan Gagnon, Gary Griffin, Carol M. Jordan, Sarah Smith, Thomas S. Treiber; Alternates, Joseph Gartner, Joseph Phillippi, vacancy.—**Economic Development Comm.,** John Lynch, Chm., Shawn Aldrich, Edward A. Beebe, Robert Deskus, Noreen Passardi; Alternates, Ralph Parizek, vacancy.—**Historic Dist. Comm.,** William Bailey, Chm.,

Mary Beth Caron, Carl Dalbon, Mary Ellen Davis, Thelma King; Alternates, Timothy Blauvert, Lee Dion, Gail Kapinas.—**Municipal Historian,** Isabel B. Weigold.—**Agent for the Elderly,** Georgianna Booth.—**Dir. of Social Services,** Anna Later.—**Dir. of Health,** Gerald Schwartz, M.D. (P.O. Rockville).—**Library Directors,** Teddie B. Sleight, Chm., Mary Bowen, Suzanne Chapman, Ronald Ormiston, Eileen M. Smith, Margaret Winzler.—**Recreation Comm.,** Edward D'Agata, Jr., Chm., Wendy Barbrick, David Chatel, Wendy Knight, Karen Schwanda, Allan St. Louis, Steven Sutcliffe.—**Dir. of Public Works,** Wes Beebe.—**Sanitarian,** Steve Jacobs.—**Building Inspector,** Mary Ann Basile.—**Building Code Bd. of Appeals,** Robert Deskus, Clint Eldredge, Ernest Kucko, Roger W. Perry, Joseph L. Slowinski.—**Chief of Police/Tree Warden,** John Patton.—**Chiefs of Fire Depts.,** Richard Claus, Jr., Richard M. Littell.—**Civil Preparedness Dir.,** George Saba.—**Town Atty.,** Oliver Chapell (P.O. Willimantic).—**Justices of the Peace,** Ruth M. Blessington, Cheryl H. Brown, Calvin C. Cobb, Patricia Godbout, Frances L. Hay, Albert J. Hunyadi, Emily M. Kasacek, Linda C. Makuch, Marianne L. Panciera, Ralph R. Parizek, Robert G. Ryder, Thomas M. Smith.

WILTON. Fairfield County.—(Form of government, selectmen, town meeting, board of finance.)—Inc., May, 1802; taken from Norwalk. Area, 27.4 sq. miles. Population, est., 16,302. Voting districts, 3. Residential community; electronic research development. Transp.—Passenger: Served by Metro North Commuter Railroad Co. Freight: Served by Conrail and numerous motor common carriers. Post offices, Wilton and Georgetown.

TOWN OFFICERS. Clerk and Reg. of Vital Statistics, Joan M. Ventres; Hours, 9 A.M.-5 P.M., Mon. through Fri. (8:30 A.M.-4:30 P.M., Summers); Address, Town Hall, 238 Danbury Rd., 06897; Tel., (203) 834-9205.—**Asst. Clerks and Asst. Regs. of Vital Statistics,** Laraine A. Mott, Teresa W. Servidio.—**Selectmen,** 1st, Robert H. Russell, Jr. (R) Tel., (203) 834-9200, Richard J. Dubow (D), Marilyn C. Gould (R), Gary S. Peak (R), Judith B. Zucker (D).—**Council on Ethics,** Roger R. Valkenburgh, Jr., Chm., Carolyn F. Lenz, Linda Mitchell.—**Treas.,** Katherine L. Chann.—**Comptroller,** Mary J. Anderson.—**Bd. of Finance,** Paul F. Hannah, Jr., Chm., Virginia M. Benin, Paul H. Burnham, John M. Iverson, Curtis R. Welling, Ronald Zibelli.—**Chief Financial Officer,** Joseph A. Dolan.—**Tax Collector,** Richard A. Martin.—**Bd. of Assessment Appeals,** John P. Hickey, Gerald R. Holdridge, Robert W. Wiseman.—**Assessor,** David Lisowski; Deputy, Sharon Carey.—**Registrars of Voters,** Margaret A. Reeves (D), Dita A. McGaughey (R).—**Supt. of Schools,** David F. Clune.—**Bd. of Education,** Charles L. Bruce, Chm., Michael A. Slutsky, Dominick C. Vita, 1997. Carolyn M. Reimers, Howard A. Sherman, Teddy M. Sitter, 1999.—**Planning and Zoning Comm.,** John Ingersoll, Chm., Alice L. Ayers, Calvin C. Braunstein, Thomas C. Gallagher, Henry Gest, Colleen L. Kellman, Doris Knapp, Carol M. Russell, David F. Waters.—**Town Planner,** Wendy Johnston.—**Zoning Bd. of Appeals,** Frank E. Citrin, Roger A. Giler, Edward E. Greene, Robert H. Kelso, John K. Wilson; Alternates, Eric Bosch, Thomas R. Brown, John J. Sweeney.—**Zoning Enforcement Officer,** John Koster.—**Inland Wetlands Comm.,** Eli F. Bleich, Chm., Susan M. Bates, John H. Collier, Robert D. Forster, Nicholas F. Lee, Howard B. Naylor, Jr., Sheila A.

Sommer.—**Conservation Comm.,** Robert A. Sanders, Jr., Chm., Bruce E. Beebe, Nancy N. Faesy, Anthony P. Grassi, Frank Mabley, Steven Mueller.—**Historic Dist. Comm.,** Robert A. Faesy, Jr., Chm., Alice N. Levin, Walter R. T. Smith, Glenn A. Shattuck, Ellen B. Wells.—**Municipal Historian,** Carol M. Russell.—**Comm. on Social Services,** David W. Sherwood, Chm., Inta Adams, Theresa M. Brubeck, George J. Ciaccio, Robert J. Graham, Jorgen Heidemann, Lisa A. Perkins, Kathleen Risley, Linda A. Swayze.—**Agent for the Elderly/Dir. of Social Services,** Suzanne Van Vechten.—**Dir. of Health,** Steven H. Schole.—**Parks and Recreation Comm.,** T. Langdon Allen, J. Casey Healy, Mark A. Ketley, Maria P. Napier, Arthur J. Wall, Jr.—**Environmental Affairs Dir.,** Patricia M. P. Sesto.—**Dir. of Public Works,** Thomas W. Thurkettle.—**Building Inspector,** William T. Connolly.—**Building Code Bd. of Appeals,** Sanford Kellogg, Chm., Anthony Carvutto, Paula B. Reens, Walter R. T. Smith, Donald Winters.—**Water Pollution Control Auth.,** Robert H. Russell, Jr., Chm., David S. Belknap, Robert K. Carson, Frederick C. Herot, Adrian Offinger, Donald Poinier.—**Water Comm.,** Robert H. Russell, Jr., Chm., Edward S. Davis, Frederick C. Herot, Donald Poinier, Albert P. Stauderman, Jr.—**Asst. Sanitarian,** vacancy.—**Tree Warden,** Paul Young.—**Supt. of Highways,** Frank Booth.—**Field Engineer,** William Wiley.—**Chief of Police,** Angelo Toscano.—**Police Comm.,** Jeremiah T. Dorney, Chm., John H. Howard, Richard B. Mitchell.—**Constables,** Robert L. Burns, David A. Flouton, Richard A. Fricke, Christopher Gardner, John D. Manning, Louis M. Miller, vacancy.—**Chief of Fire Dept/Fire Marshall.,** William von Zehle.—**Deputy Fire Chief,** George Peters.—**Deputy Fire Marshall,** David Kohn.—**Fire Inspector,** George Repko.—**Bd. of Fire Comrs.,** James M. Kosakow, William D. Reading, Thomas M. Sinchak.—**Town Atty.,** G. Kenneth Bernhard.—**Justices of the Peace,** Elena Baggio, Bruce Blanchard, Eric Bosch, Lois L. Bruce, Jeffrey A. Cooper, Charles P. Flynn, Edward E. Greene, Louise W. Herot, Erich Lenz, George F. Lenz, George R. Olexo, Thomas M. Sinchak, Roger R. Valkenburgh, Jr., Barbara Wasserman, Judith B. Zucker.

WINCHESTER.* Litchfield County.—(Form of government, town manager, town meeting, selectmen.)—Inc., May, 1771. Area, 33.8 sq. miles. Population, est., 11,338. Voting district, 1. Principal industries, ballbearings, custom cartons, hinges, electrical harnesses and cables, turbine blades, screw machine products, machine tool companies, powdered metal products, pet supplies and business forms. Transp.—Passenger: Served by buses of the Kelly Transit Co., Rural Transit Auth. Freight: Served by numerous motor common carriers. Post offices, Winsted and Winchester Center.

TOWN OFFICERS. Clerk and Reg. of Vital Statistics, William T. Riiska; Hours, 8 A.M.-4 P.M., Mon. through Fri.; Address, Town Hall, 338 Main St., Winsted 06098; Tel., Winsted, (860) 379-2713.—**Asst. Clerk and Asst. Reg. of Vital Statistics,** Sheila S. Sedlack.—**Town Manager,** Paul S. Vayer.—**Selectmen,** 1st, John F. Arcelaschi (R), Virginia Dethy (R), Nancy R. Eisenlohr (D), John R. Forrest (R), Timothy J. Moran (R), Frank Smith (D), Mary Ann Welcome (D).—**Ethics Committee,** Ronald Rosenstein, Chm., Karen Beadle, John Fratini, Anna Harding, Lynn Moran.—**Treas.,** Robert Carfiro.—**Tax Collector,** Ann S. Aust.—**Bd. of Assessment Appeals,** Walter St. Onge, Chm., Peter Walker, Joanne Williams.—**Assessor,** Janice McKie.—**Dir. of**

Finance, Henry L. Centrella.—**Registrars of Voters,** Elizabeth F. Cornelio (D), Dennis F. Moore (R).—**Supt. of Schools,** Raymond W. Powell.—**Bd. of Education,** Kelley S. Babbin, Donna L. Boynton, Marcia A. Hamm, Frank C. Hohmeister, Judith Pavlak, 1997; Dennis F. Moore, Chm., Ray C. Dethy, Joseph C. Fitzgerald, Michael C. Stumo, 1999.—**Planning and Zoning Comm.,** Nancy Eisenlohr, Chm., Anthony Cannavo, Richard Nalette, Patricia Rocco, Steven Sedlack; Alternates, Jane Hutton, Porter G. Griffin III, Henry Tharau.—**Zoning Bd. of Appeals,** Paul Grigg, Chm., Glenn Daniels, Cornelius Hudak, two vacancies; Alternates, David W. Harms, Janie Pavlak, two vacancies.—**Economic Development Comm.,** Rodney A. Bouchard, Chm., Terrence Brennan, Ray C. Dethy, John DiCara, John G. Groppo, Mark Jones, Michael Kane, John Sullivan, Joanne Yorgensen; Joseph J. Stawicki, Dir.; Alternates, Michael Flaherty, John Massicotte, David C. Villa.—**Housing Auth.,** George Mangione, Chm., Harry Briggs, Robert Franz, Robert Shopey, Brian Sullivan; William J. Reilly, Exec. Dir.—**Conservation Comm.,** Gabrielle LaClaire, Chm., Ruth Crane, Pamela Eisenlohr, Francis Gallo, Mary Ann Welcome.—**Inland Wetlands Comm.,** Lynn Moran, Chm., Lawrence Beck, Scott Eisenlohr, David Harms, Philip Hurlbut, Patricia Mills, Stephen Paulinkas, Steven Roberts, Patricia Wass.—**Senior Citizens Comm.,** Carmen F. Bazzano, James Brady, Charles Cooper, Carmen DiGiovanni, Robert Franz, Lee Ann LaClaire, Carl Nordland, Elizabeth C. Sonier; Blanche McCarthy, Agent.—**Senior Center Dir.,** Blanche McCarthy.—**Dir. of Social Services,** Sam Marr.—**Parking Auth.,** Scott Eisenlohr, Mike Monaco, Alan Nero, Del Smith, Rebecca L. Vicks.—**Retirement Adm. Bd.,** Donal Fitzgerald, Chm., Thomas Botticelli, Steve Pray, James Rogers.—**Municipal Historians,** Lee Anne LaClaire, George L. Sherwood.—**Recreation Bd.,** Charles Bunel, Chm., Thomas Bordanaro, James V. DiVita, Debbie Griffin, Charles Marsh, Linda Murphy, Dan Nichols, Louis Petrunti, Wayne Tazzara; vacancy, Dir.; Alternates, Richard Attianese, Joanne Leifert.—**Supt. of Parks/Dir. of Public Works/Tree Warden,** Patrick E. Hague.—**Building Inspector,** John Willnauer.—**BOCA Code Bd. of Appeals,** Roger Griffin, Chm., Richard Dillon, Michael Hamm, Francis Nelligan, Joseph St. Amant.—**Purchasing Agent,** Mark Douglass.—**Water Pollution Control Auth.,** Stephen Vaill, Chm., Roger Griffin, Wayne Keefe, Peter Mellas, Bruce Yorgensen.—**Sanitarian,** Torrington Area Health District.—**Chief of Police,** Anthony J. Paige.—**Constables,** James J. Barber, Michael Nicosia, Robert Shopey, Jr., David C. Villa.—**Chief of Fire Dept./Fire Marshal,** Joseph Beadle.—**Civil Preparedness Dir.,** John J. Phillips.—**Town Atty.,** Kevin Nelligan.—**Justices of the Peace,** Robert G. Blanchette, Sr., Rodney A. Bouchard, Kris A. Cianciolo, Elizabeth F. Cornelio, William J. Darcey, Mary T. Demonstranti, Deirdre H. DiCara, Gemma C. DiMauro, Rosemary Drescher, John L. Fratini, Sarah T. Gauger, Gene A. Gouthier, Deborah G. Jones, Karen P. Jones, Rosemarie Lagueux, Susan R. Mahoney, Patricia A. Martin, Brady Miller, Patricia C. Mills, Timothy J. Moran, Janine M. Pavlak, Frank Prelli, Helene S. Reilly, Jessica M. Shopey, Jerold E. Silverio, Antonio Spera, Walter J. St. Onge, Jr., John R. Sullivan, Gerard H. Trieschmann, Richard P. Wells.

---

*See City of Winsted.

WINDHAM. Windham County.—(Form of government, selectmen, town meeting, board of finance.)—Town inc., May, 1692. City of Willimantic inc., Jan. 1893. Town of Windham and City of Willimantic consolidated July 1, 1983. Area, 27.9 sq. miles. Population, est., 21,846. Voting districts, 5. Principal industries, manufacture of specialty rubber, capacitors, industrial abrasives, radio and electric parts, screw machine products, screws, fasteners, steel, and woven insulation products. Transp.—Passenger: Served by buses of the Bonanza Bus Lines, Inc. from Hartford, Danielson, and Providence, RI; Freight: Served by Central Vermont Railway, Providence and Worcester Railroad Co. and numerous motor common carriers. Post offices, Willimantic, Windham, North Windham and South Windham. Rural free delivery.

TOWN OFFICERS. Clerk and Reg. of Vital Statistics, Ann M. Bushey; Hours, 8:00 A.M.-5 P.M., Mon. through Wed.; 8 A.M.-7:30 P.M., Thurs.; 8 A.M.-12 Noon, Fri.; Address, Town Bldg., 979 Main St., P.O. Box 94, Willimantic 06226; Tel., Willimantic, (860) 465-3013; FAX, (860) 465-3012; Internet: http://159.247.0.202/MUNIC/WINDHAM/Windham.htm. —**Asst. Clerks and Asst. Regs. of Vital Statistics,** Correna Bibeau, Barbara Pittman.—**Selectmen,** 1st, Walter M. Pawelkiewicz (D) Tel., (860) 456-3593, Ext. 208, Daniel M. Haggerty (R), Larry S. Haines (D), Kevin L. Kiss (R), Roger G. Lizee (R), Joseph S. Marsalisi (D), Charlotte S. Patros (D), Mark Shapera (D), Albert B. Vertefeuille (D), Thomas W. White (D), vacancy.—**Treas.,** Ann M. Bushey.—**Controller,** Katherine Maxwell.—**Bd. of Finance,** John E. French, Chm., Andrew J. Carey III, Carlos Flores, Stephen J. LaFlamme, Jo-Anne M. Roberts, Keely A. Santa Lucia, Marjorie R. White.—**Tax Collector,** Linda B. Theriault.—**Bd. of Assessment Appeals,** Samuel M. Bonafine, John E. Nimlo, George H. Patros, C. Lawrence Schiller, Ralph C. Zimmerman.—**Assessor,** Joan E. Paskewich.—**Registrars of Voters,** William J. Sayers, Jr. (D), Maria C. Naumec (R).—**Supt. of Schools,** Patrick Proctor.—**Bd. of Education,** Susan M. Collins, Chm., Dolores Ackley, Mark W. Doyle, Paulette N. Haines, Paula M. Haney, 1997; Manuel A. Diaz, Jr., Leslie A. Johnson-O'Brien, Benjamin S. Vreeland, Lynne P. Weeks, 1999.—**Personnel Dir.,** Robert Tighe.—**Planning Comm.,** David Philips, Chm., Claire Lary, Benjamin Schilberg, Betty Tipton, N. Joseph Underwood; Alternates, Scott Doscher, Russell L. Durfee, vacancy.—**Town Planner,** James E. Finger.—**Zoning Comm.,** Clarence Sylvester, Jr., Chm., Robert Bedard, George Gillette, Genaro Iazzetta, Cynthia Wollner; Alternates, Kenneth Folan, Michael Libertine, vacancy.—**Zoning Bd. of Appeals,** Thomas F. Cronin, Thomas E. DeVivo, Ernest S. Eldridge, Thomas Praaki, Victor L. Rayhall; Alternates, George E. Barton, Melanie S. Keen, Kathryn E. Kiss.—**Zoning Enforcement Officer,** Raymond Murphy.—**Recreation Dir.,** Patricia A. Murphy.—**Social Services Dir.,** Donald Muirhead.—**Librarian,** Theodore Perch.—**Municipal Historian,** Ruth Ridgeway.—**Agent for the Elderly,** Shirley Bombria.—**Dir. of Health and Sanitation,** Steve J. Huleatt.—**Public Works Foreman,** Bradford P. Wojick.—**Housing Auth. Dir.,** Michael J. Westerfield.—**Housing Code Inspector,** Curtis Garry.—**Building Inspector,** Donald Schultz.—**Town Engineer,** Joseph Gardner.—**Sewer Supt.,** Christian Hoffman.—**Water Supt.,** James Reidy.—**Water Pollution Control Auth.,** Henry Roos, Chm., Charles Ferris, Franklin C. Field, Joseph Pernaselli, Gerald Russian.—**Police Chief,** Milton King.—**Constables,** Robert Cahoon, Louis A. Delorme, Jimmy Richards, Larry Rivers, Paul Seretny, two vacancies.—**Fire Chief,**

John Walsh.—**Dir. of Civil Preparedness,** Robert Tighe.—**Town Atty.,** Daniel Lamont.—**Justices of the Peace,** Louis A. Delorme, Mark W. Doyle, Phillip Haddad, Robert J. Haggerty, Larry S. Haines, Nusie M. Halpine, Rebecca H. Kaplan, Ernestine R. Kuter, Melissa M. Kuter, Roger G. Lizee, Joseph A. Mazzola, Richard L. Nassiff, George H. Patros, Lorraine G. Pepin, Matthew A. Piolunek, Thomas Praakli, Nina O. Ricardez, Estelle S. Schiller, Rosa E. Tirado, Lynne P. Weeks.

WINDSOR. Hartford County.—(Form of government, town manager, town council, town meeting.)—Oldest town in Connecticut, settled, Sept. 26, 1633; named, Feb., 1637. Area, 31.1 sq. miles. Population, est., 27,960. Voting districts, 7. Principle industries: power generation, aerospace, insurance, computer aided design and manufacturing software development, medical technology, financial services, manufacturing of computer components, electronics, machine tools, adhesives, measuring devices, automotive parts, air movement equipment, and shade grown tobacco. Transp.—Passenger: Served by Amtrak and buses of Conn. Transit from Hartford. Freight: Served by Conrail and numerous motor common carriers. Post offices, Windsor and Poquonock.

TOWN OFFICERS. Clerk and Reg. of Vital Statistics, Kathleen K. Quin; Hours, 8 A.M.-5 P.M., Mon. through Fri.; Address, Town Hall, 275 Broad St., P.O. Box 472, 06095; Tel., (860) 285-1900.—**Deputy Town Clerks/Deputy Regs. of Vital Statistics,** June T. Cameron, Alice J. Williams.—**Asst. Reg. of Vital Statistics,** Thelma London.—**Town Manager,** Albert G. Ilg.—**Town Council,** Francis J. Brady (D), Mayor; Randall I. Graff, Deputy, William D. Chiodo, Guy B. Jacobs, Michael K. Joy, Robert R. Lydecker, James F. Pacino, L. James Ristas, Donald S. Trinks.—**Selectmen,** 1st, Mary Drost (R), William Donegan (D), Donald J. Higgins (D), Grace Mosdale (D), Arnika M. Mott (R).—**Treas.,** Robert Carroll.—**Bd. of Ethics,** Abraham Morrison, Chm., George T. Griffin, James Mason, George Morganthaler, James Parker.— **Service Unit Leader of Admin. Services,** Donald Cunningham.—**Tax Collector,** Sonia Kessler.—**Bd. of Assessment Appeals,** Domenico B. Albano, George M. Bolduc, John O'Malley.—**Assessor,** Steven Kosofsky.—**Registrars of Voters,** Sandra Suty (D), Karen Andrews (R).—**Acting Supt. of Schools,** Larry Shea.—**Bd. of Education,** Rosemarie A. Miskavitch, Pres., Mark S. Cashman, Timothy Curtis, Audrey M. Garvin, William Herzfeld, Mary A. Isner, Elizabeth B. Kenneson, Violet Nahabedian, Michael C. Stamper, 1997.—**Planning and Zoning Comm.,** Anita Mips, Chm., Michael Bunk, Edward Finnerty, Timothy Fitzgerald, David Kelsey; Alternates, Erwin Booker, Elizabeth Parker, Karl Profe.—**Town Planner,** Mario Zavarella.— **Public Building Comm.,** Joseph Novak, Chm., Robert E. Gustafson, Gary Johnson, George Morganthaler, Robert Pinard.—**Zoning Bd. of Appeals,** Frances Rothenberg, Chm., John Cowan, Max Kuziak, Donald Lopardo, Helene Shay; Alternates, George Bolduc, Joseph Breen, Arthur Machado.—**Economic Development Comm.,** Raymond Donahue, Chm., Robert Geisel, Peter Gross, Agnes Pier, Edward A. Rudolph, William A. Russell, Paul J. Sorbo, Jr., John R. Welch; Harry Freeman, Coord.— **Housing Auth.,** Mary Alexander, Chm., Harold J. DePianta, Ellen Peck, John Pier, Mary Smith.—**Housing Code Board of Appeals,** John Bruno, Chm., Robert Breeding, Andrew Dowe, Frank Jacobs, Jr., Jonathan H. Sasportas.—**Conservation Comm.,**

Mark R. Sussman, Chm., Brian Anderson, Peter Gwyn, Samuel T. Hinckley, Paul Mason, Sarkis Nahabedian, Bruce Whyte, Colette P. Yeich.—**Air and Water Pollution Abatement Comm.,** Domenico B. Albano, Chm., John Ahern, Syed A. Ashraf, Mehran Golbabai, Norman Nadeau, John E. Waters.—**Inland Wetlands and Watercourses Comm.,** Gerald Golden, Chm., Albert J. Boudreau, Ruth Elander, Bernard F. Halligan, Kenneth Herman, Robert Isner, Linda Kollmorgen, Allen Kronick, N. Philip Lord, Jr.; Alternates, Jacqueline Reardon, Barry Walker.—**Historic Dist. Comm.,** Aniela Machernis, Chm., Helen Flynn, Robert Geisel, Marcia Hinkley, Mary Stone; Alternates, Robert Breeding, Diane Kopcinski, William J. Melley.—**Municipal Historian,** Robert T. Silliman.—**Human Relations Committee,** Lucy Goicoechea, Chm., Sonya Dean, John Grant, Max R. Kuziak, Aniela Machernis, Nellie H. Mason, Arnika Mott, Marcia Munoz, Leonard Swade; Alternates, Renata Dixon, Marian Eichner, Steven Erickson, Paul Giampolo.—**Comm. on Aging and Handicapped,** Gale Deming, Chm., Betty Bennett, Viola Borstein, Dorothy Bruno, Maureen A. Donegan, Shirley Hallett, Ruth Jefferis, Joan McVey, Suzanne M. Moriarty, Judith Swade, E; Alternate, Elizabeth Waters.—**Insurance Comm.,** Edward W. Samolyk, Chm., Paul Broxterman, David P. Curley, Edward J. Hill, Margaret Rowe.—**Service Unit Leader of Health and Environment,** Charles J. Petrillo, Jr., Ph.D.—**Service Unit Leader of Family Services,** Thomas Lerario.—**Town Forester,** Dale Gardner.—**Service Unit Leader of Police,** Kevin Searles.—**Constables,** John Drost, Kenneth Herman, Norman Nadeau.—**Fire Chief,** Dale Smith.—**Fire Marshal,** Raymond Walker.—**Civil Preparedness Dir.,** Charles J. Petrillo, Jr.—**Town Attys.,** O'Malley, Deneen, Messina & Oswecki.—**Justices of the Peace,** John J. Ahern, Jr., Domenico B. Albano, Joseph E. Alfieri, Brian J. Anderson, Karen A. Andrews, Robert M. Andrews, Vincenza Aniello, Priscilla A. August, Eric M. Bailey, Sharran S. Bennett, George M. Bolduc, Jr., Ervin Booker, Jr. III, Viola E. Borstein, Michael G. Bunk, Leo C. Canty, Susan M. Canty, Kathleen M. Carroll, Robert F. Carroll, William E. Carter, Stanley L. Cicero, Vivian J. Cicero, Stanley Cohen, Nancy B. Colton, Philip E. Coyne, Rita M. Coyne, Gale H. Deming, Michael A. Donegan, Everett B. Dowe, Jr., John Drost, Marian V. Eichner, Robert L. Ellis, Eric G. Ericson, Margaret R. Ericson, Ruth C. Fahrbach, Edward W. Finnerty, Donald D. Fisher, Dorothy P. Fisher, Helen J. Flynn, Elizabeth H. Freed, Ronald T. Gaylord, David A. Gillette, David L. Guay, Kathleen S. Guay, Laverne S. Gustafson, Robert E. Gustafson, Sandra K. Gustafson, Shirley P. Hallett, Kenneth R. Herman, Joseph P. Hesse, Jr., Ruth P. Jefferis, Marylou W. Karieva, Elizabeth B. Kenneson, Gordon W. Kenneson, Lorraine W. Kirkbride, Thomas J. Laufer, Sr., Thomas J. Laufer, Sr., Vera W. Lavery, Arthur Machado, Aniela Machernis, Marsha L. Mason, Nellie H. Mason, Anita M. Mips, Rosemarie A. Miskavitch, George F. Morganthaler, Arnika M. Mott, Marcia G. Munoz, Laura S. Mycka, Norman G. Nadeau, Theodore R. Nieman, Joseph A. Novak, Jr., Mary Ann Overbaugh, Elizabeth B. Parker, James R. Parker, Robert A. Platt, Sheri Lyn P. Polkey, John E. Purcell, John J. Quigley, Jr., Jacqueline M. Reardon, Mary C. Reardon, Frances R. Rothenberg, Edward W. Samolyk, Alyce S. Schaeffer, Helene H. Shay, Michael D. Spagnoli, Sandra G. Suty, Allan B. Tarbell, Julia H. Tashjian, Glenn C. Thompson, John A. Wall.

WINDSOR LOCKS. Hartford County.—(Form of government, selectmen, town meeting, board of finance.)—Inc., May, 1854; taken from Windsor. Located on west side of Conn.

River, on main route from Hartford to Springfield, MA. Home of Bradley International Airport. Area, 9.4 sq. miles. Population, est., 11,912. Voting districts, 2. Principal industries, food servicing and distribution, manufacture of aerospace products, paper products, electronics and machines. Federal Reserve Clearing House. Transp.—Passenger: Served by Amtrak, transcontinental and transoceanic airlines, buses of Conn. Transit Commuter Express, Dattco Bus, Inc. and Peter Pan Lines service between Springfield, MA, Bradley International and Hartford; limousine service available from Bradley International Airport. Freight: Served by Conrail, all principal airlines and numerous motor common carriers. Post office, Windsor Locks. Carrier service and rural free delivery.

TOWN OFFICERS. Clerk and Reg. of Vital Statistics, William R. Hamel; Hours, 8:30 A.M.-4:30 P.M., Mon. through Fri.; 8 A.M.-1 P.M., Fri., July, Aug., Sept.; Address, Town Office Bldg., 50 Church St., 06096; Tel., (860) 627-1441.—**Asst. Clerks and Asst. Regs. of Vital Statistics,** Jane M. Hall, Elsie C. Nesta, Eileen G. Riner.—**Asst. Reg. of Vital Statistics,** John J. Lee.—**Selectmen,** 1st, Victor J. Puia (D) Tel., (860) 627-1444, John J. Lee (D), Paul Seaha (R).—**Treas.,** David L. Farr; Deputy, Mary Ann Harris.—**Bd. of Finance,** Joseph W. Flynn, Chm., Denise T. Balboni, Dennis J. DeMaine, Barry W. Gray, Malcolm K. Hamilton, Cornelius O'Leary; Alternates, Lois J. Glazier, Mark E. Horan.—**Tax Collector,** Russell C. Gabrielson.—**Bd. of Assessment Appeals,** Michael A. Czarnecki, Beverly G. O'Leary, vacancy.—**Bd. of Assessors,** Catherine M. Jeffery, Chm., Mark E. Cenci, Douglas L. Gilbert.—**Assessor,** Peter R. Marsele.—**Registrars of Voters,** Shirley J. Hespelt (D), Sandra R. Hebert (R).—**Supt. of Schools,** June Hartford-Alley.—**Bd. of Education,** John A. Dowd, Chm., Ann G. Levy, Scott A. Storms, 1997; Sandra M. Kanigowski, Steven N. Wawruck, Jr., 1999.—**Planning and Zoning Comm.,** Ralph W. Leiper, Chm., Marshall H. Brown, Alan M. Gannuscio, James E. Gaylord, Margaret M. Sayers; Mario L. Gatti, ex officio; Alternates, Daniel O. Christian, Peter Michaud, vacancy.—**Zoning Bd. of Appeals,** Joseph C. Becker, Chm., Howard H. Aspinwall, Robert E. Bertrand, Alfred J. Gragnolati, Peter J. Lingua; Alternates, Donna C. Dowd, James P. Gronda, Donna B. LeBlanc.—**Economic and Industrial Development Comm.,** James E. Maitland, Jr., Chm., Daniel O. Christian, Edward A. Ferrari, William C. Hamilton, Patricia K. Julian, Gary M. LaVoye, Nirad Patel, Edward N. Stevensen, Jr., Scott A. Storms.—**Redevelopment Agency,** David G. Parry, Chm., Robert M. Burk, Stephen J. Caliendo, Grant Carragher, Douglas C. Glazier, Chester S. Raynard, three vacancies.—**Housing Code Review Bd.,** Joseph C. Becker, Chm., Mario L. Gatti, Fred R. Miclon, Raymond H. Ouellette, vacancy.—**Housing Auth.,** Edward V. Sabotka, Chm., William C. Hamilton, Bruce F. Holcomb, Loretta H. O'Donnell, Helen P. Olisky, vacancy; L. Jean Glazier, Exec. Dir.—**Conservation Comm.,** Richard J. Frawley, Chm., William A. Howes, Eleanor J. Leonard, Raymond J. Marconi, Thomas K. Unnold; Alternates, Donald B. Lownds, Jr, vacancy.—**Inland Wetlands Comm.,** Paul E. McCarthy, Chm., Howard H. Aspinwall, Marshall H. Brown, Richard J. Frawley, William C. Hamilton, Edward P. Luke, Karen E. Reid, Edward N. Stevenson, Jr., vacancy; Alternates, Gary M. LaVoye, Donna M. Lee.—**Conn. River Assembly,** Richard J. Frawley; Alternate, H. Richard Williams.—**Municipal Resource Recovery Auth.,** John D. McSweegan III, Chm., Carolyn T. Banas, Carol R. Cutler, Joel Levin, Linda S. Mona, Karen E. Reid, Michael G. Wrabel, Jr., vacancy; Alternates, Gary LeClair, vacancy.—**Com-**

mittee on Needs of the Aging, Margaret M. Sayers, Chm., Ruth G. Brunell, Kathleen D. Cienaski, Robert M. Cosgrove, George J. Mumblo, Linda J. Sartori, Delma Taravella, Dolores Walters; vacancy, Municipal Agent; Charlene Kearns, Welfare Coordinator.—**Welfare Dir.,** Victor J. Puia.—**Dir. of Health,** William H. Blitz, M.P.H.R.S. (P.O., Enfield).—**North Central Health Dist. Rep.,** Sandra J. Ferrari, Eileen T. Manning.—**Librarian,** Ronald Hubbs.—**Municipal Historian,** Howard J. White.—**Park Comm.,** Philip F. Famiglietti, Chm., Steven L. Degen, Louis J. Latorra, William J. Marinone, Donald Pisati, vacancy.—**Dir. of Recreation,** David L. Farr.—**Youth Comm.,** Ryan Dowd, Teresa Pappa, Co-Chm., Jennifer Hamilton, Marie Hong, Kethia Ly, Amy Montemerlo, Erin Montemerlo, Andrew Pisati, Jessica Quagliaroli, Jessica Scrivano; Advisors, Paul Angilly, Karen Johnson, Jeffery T. Shovak.—**Dir. of Public Works/Tree Warden,** Michael G. Wrabel, Jr.—**Town Engineer,** Mario L. Gatti.—**Building Inspector,** James Plumridge.—**Housing Code of Appeals Bd.,** Joseph C. Becker, Chm., Melvin E. Hendershot, Shirley O. King, two vacancies; Alternates, Marie L. McGee, vacancy.—**Sewer Comm./Water Pollution Control Auth.,** Victor J. Puia, Pres., Ruth M. Cate, Daniel O. Christian, William R. Hamel, Jeffrey J. Ives, John J. Lee, John D. McSweegan III, Robert C. Oliva; Mario L. Gatti, Michael G. Wrabel, Jr., ex officios.—**Chief of Police,** Capt. William J. Gifford.—**Police Comm.,** Richard Campominosi, Chm., George M. Hall, Edward E. Lanati, Guido J. Montemerlo, Robert F. O'Brien, Patsy F. Ruggiero.—**Constables,** Michael J. Biedrzycki, William J. Fournier, Jr., George M. Hall, Donna M. Lee, Raymond J. Marconi, Thomas L. Marotta, Robert F. O'Brien.—**Chief of Fire Dept.,** William L. Kupernik.—**Fire Marshall,** Michael L. Sinsigalli.—**Bd. of Fire Comrs.,** Russell Gabrielson, Chm., Dennis J. Gragnolati, John J. Lee, Steven R. Mills.—**Civil Preparedness Dir.,** Roger J. Ignazio.—**Town Atty.,** Christopher Stone.—**Justices of the Peace,** Francis J. Aniello, Carolyn T. Banas, Joseph C. Becker, Ruth G. Brunell, Suzanne G. Cannon, Joseph W. Flynn, Saul Goldfarb, Jane V. Hall, William R. Hamel, Edward E. Lanati, Gary M. LaVoye, Paul E. McCarthy, Camille Miller, Margaret M. Sayers, Edward N. Stevensen, Ronald F. Storms, Mary K. Verre.

WINSTED. CITY OFFICERS. (City named, Jan., 1917.)—**Mayor,** John F. Arcelaschi (D).—**Supt. of Police,** Anthony Paige.—**Supt. of Fire Dept.,** Joseph Beadle.—**Supt. of Public Works,** Patrick Hague. (See Town of Winchester for other officials.)

WOLCOTT. New Haven County.—(Form of government, mayor, town council, finance officer.)—Inc., May, 1796; taken from Waterbury and Southington. Area, 21.1 sq. miles. Population, est., 14,293. Voting districts, 3. Principal industries, agriculture and manufacture of tools, novelties, etc. Transp.—Passenger: Served by buses of the Bonanza Bus Lines, Inc. from Waterbury and Hartford. Freight: Served by numerous motor common carriers. Post office, Wolcott.

TOWN OFFICERS. Clerk and Reg. of Vital Statistics, Elaine L. King; Hours, 9 A.M.-4:30 P.M., Mon. through Fri. Address, Town Hall, 10 Kenea Ave., 06716; Tel., (203) 879-8100, Ext. 112.—**Asst. Clerk,** Eleanor M. Maurice.—**Asst. Reg. of Vital Statistics,** Eleanor M. Maurice.—**Mayor,** Steven P. Bosco (R).—**Town Council,** Dist.

1, Thomas G. Dunn, William I. Gauthier, Brian Tynan; Dist. 2, Joan L. Kane, Chm., Roberta E. Leonard, Francis E. Masi; Dist. 3, John J. Cleary, Bonnie Gagnon, Ralph Shove, Jr.—**Treas.,** Roger E. Levesque.—**Bd. of Ethics,** Gerald Masters, Chm., Gerald Baginski, James Johnson, Clarence Pierpont, Ruth-Ann Williams.—**Tax Collector,** Lorraine M. McQueen.—**Bd. of Assessment Appeals,** Harry K. Fitzgerald, Chm., Louis P. Dubois, Jr., John P. Levesque.—**Assessor,** Carolyn F. Byram.—**Registrars of Voters,** Anne R. Forte (D), Esther L. Medford (R).—**Supt. of Schools,** Thomas A. Jokubaitis.—**Bd. of Education,** Patricia B. Najarian, Chm., Gary A. Del Buono, Albert V. Della Volpe, Patricia Deslauriers, Paul DiPietro, Anthony F. Gugliotti, Jr., William F. McKinley, Terri L. Masters, Tracey M. Paquette, 1997.—**Planning and Zoning Comm.,** Henry Fitzgerald, Chm., Mark Bassett, Jay Bonnie, Ronald Perille, Richard Renkun, Stanley Samuolis, Manuel Santos, Theodore Storlazzi.—**Consulting Town Planner,** Central Naugatuck Regional Planning Agency.—**Zoning Bd. of Appeals,** Cynthia M. Hoffman, Chm., Robert P. Castriciano, Keith M. Hill, Brian J. Marino, Esther Medford, Roseanne Monteleone; Alternates, Linda Dominici, John Synnott, vacancy.—**Zoning Enforcement Officer,** Richard P. Longo.—**Industrial and Development Comm.,** Michael Ardry, Chm., Mark Bassett, Bernard Chieffo, Jeff Hubeny, Jean Orsatti, Rito Valletta.—**Housing Auth.,** Jeff Hubeny, Chm., Michael DeNegris, Philip Morytko, Herman Mueller, Marie Smith.—**Conservation Comm.,** Harry Fitzgerald, Charles Hunt, Esther Medford, Lynne Morytko, Raymond Widziewicz.—**Inland Wetlands Comm.,** Michael Walker, Chm., Christopher Borowy, Roger Harbanuk, Richard Homewood, George Leggio, Vernon Russell, Raymond Widziewicz; Alternates, Anne Forte, Sandra McKinley, vacancy.—**Comm. on Aging,** James Baggett, Chm. and Agent, Jeannette C. Baggett, Mayor Steven P. Bosco, Marlene Cossette, Evelyn Duren, Frank Haggard, Helen Lewandoski, Ann Marino, Florence Marino, Michael McCartney, Lorraine McQueen, Anthony Natelle, Udella Tortora, James Watson, Thomas Wegrzyn.—**Welfare Dir.,** James Baggett.—**Dir. of Health/ Sanitarian,** Chesprocott Health Dist. (P.O., Cheshire).—**Library Directors,** Alex Nole, Chm., Constance M. Barker, Lynn Garbacik, Mary Hunt, Emily T. Levesque, Judith Nelson, Sylvia Sheron.—**Municipal Historian,** Patricia Brady.—**Parks and Recreation Comm.,** Harry Najarian, Chm., Larry Albert, Michael Brennan, Paul Garland, Ann Santogatta, Annette Trombley.—**Dir. of Recreation,** Donald Fulmer.—**Purchasing Agent,** Daniel Pagnoni.—**Dir. of Public Works,** Joseph Paulo.—**Building Inspector,** Kenneth J. Smoil.—**Building Code Auth.,** William Gauthier, Chm., Steven Brouillard, James Flynn.—**Water and Sewer Auth.,** Anthony Bell, Chm., David Archambault, Michael Ardry, Christine DeCarlo, Ben Russell.—**Chief of Police,** James Watson.—**Constables,** Michael L. Feola, Paul Gallucci, Peter L. Gelada, Richard A. Homewood, Roger L. Maurice, Jr., Philip M. Morytko.—**Chief of Fire Dept.,** Charles Marcella.—**Civil Preparedness Dir.,** Chester Sergey; Deputy, Philip Culver.—**Fire Marshal,** Philip Culver.—**Town Atty.,** Michael Tansley.—**Justices of the Peace,** Sharon C. Boothroyd, Brian P. Borghesi, Robert P. Castriciano, Marlene C. Cossette, Erminia S. Costa, William I. Gauthier, Arthur A. George, Jr., Ursala A. Guglielmo, Mildred T. Kovic, Emily T. Levesque, Edward L. Lindsly, Rita R. Longo, Brian J. Marino, Eleanor M. Maurice, James M. McQueen, Eugene A. Migliaro, Jr., Alice G. Moss, Patricia A. Najarian, Jean A. Orsatti, William Romaniello, Jr., Lucy R. Rowe, Vernon H. Russell, Michael J. Santogatta, Gary B. Schneider, Stella B. Sirois,

Dolores C. Slater, Norman J. Stanchfield, Theodore E. Storlazzi, William F. Tynan, John C. Vastola, Roland B. Vicedomini, Edward S. Wilensky, Ruthanne T. Williams.

WOODBRIDGE. New Haven County.—(Form of government, selectmen, town meeting, board of finance.)—Inc., Jan., 1784; taken from New Haven and Milford. Area, 19.2 sq. miles. Population, est., 8,091. Voting districts, 2. Principal industry, agriculture; mostly a suburban residential town. Freight: Served by numerous motor common carriers. Post office, R.F.D. Woodbridge. Rural free delivery from New Haven post office. Voted Beer Permit Only, 1935.

TOWN OFFICERS. Clerk and Reg. of Vital Statistics, Stephanie Ciarleglio; Hours, 8:30 A.M.-4 P.M., Mon. through Fri.; Address, Town Hall, 11 Meetinghouse La., 06525; Tel., (203) 389-3422.—**Asst. Clerks and Asst. Regs. of Vital Statistics,** Marcella Naylor, Linda M. Poirier, Anne Walhimer.—**Selectmen,** 1st, Roger M. Harrington (D) Tel., (203) 389-3402, Joseph R. Calistro (R), Rosemary K. DeFilippo (R), Charles C. Goetsch (D), Edward M. Sheehy (D), Genie Schwartz (D).—**Moderator, Town Meeting,** Marshal D. Gibson.—**Treas./Finance Dir.,** Diane Waldron.—**Bd. of Ethics,** Barbara Amatruda, Boyd Johnson, Vincent A. Romei, Rabbi Herbert Weinberg.—**Bd. of Finance,** Matthew Giglietti, Chm., Gregory Egnaczyk, Melanie Gross, Michael Luther, Melvin Stolz, vacancy.—**Tax Collector,** Margaret Pallotto.—**Bd. of Assessment Appeals,** James Gilbert, Chm., William Longa, Barry J. Vine.—**Assessor,** Betsy Nolan.—**Registrars of Voters,** Pamela Blessinger (D), L. Christine Laydon (R).—**Supt. of Schools,** Peter Madonia.—**Bd. of Education,** Freddi Elton, Susan G. Gallo, Jeffrey Kaufman, Denise L. Kelly, Darlene Raggozine, 1997; Elizabeth A. Brett, Bonna M. Greene, James D. Horwitz, Michael P. Shannon, 1999.—**Planning and Zoning Comm.,** Charles B. Swanson, Chm., Jill Countryman, Howard Krantrovitz, Robert McKernan, Genie Schwartz, Benson A. Snaider; Alternates, Robert D'Angelo, Joseph Palmieri, vacancy.—**Town Planner,** Samuel Spielvogel.—**Zoning Bd. of Appeals,** Roger M. Harrison, Chm., Julie T. Block, Stephen Fiore, Marshall D. Gibson, Alan Rice; Alternates, Christopher R. Dickerson, Jodi P. Ellant, Donald Menzies.—**Investment Committee,** Morton Engstrom, Paul R. Greenberg, Melvin Stoltz, Mary Lou Winnick.—**Development and Industrial Comm.,** Stephen Miller, Chm., Robert Bickerton, Frederick Carasone, Romish Mehta, Dominic Proto, Peter Schurman, Jeffrey Tomei.—**Conservation Comm.,** Kathryn Gartland, Chm., John H. Chatfield, Joanne D'Angelo, Charles Goetsch, Charles Griffith, Karen L. Hluchan, Maria K. Kayne.—**Inland Wetlands Comm.,** Robert Blythe, Chm., Samuel Bridgers, John Chatfield, Katherine Hubbard, Alan Lipson; Alternates, Sharon DeKadt, Cathy Shufro.—**Human Services Comm.,** Mimi Setlow, Chm., Lisa Arpaia, Elaine Feldman, Yvonne Klancko, Gloria Kurek, Janice Miller, Lynn Piascyk, Ruth Sachs, Judith Schwartz.—**Dir. of Health,** Susan Addiss.—**Bd. of Health,** Barbara Bradley, Florence A. Ferrell, Michelle Greengarden, Robert L. Lesser, Cheryl Sackler, M.D., Berta Samson.—**Library Directors,** Greydon C. Freeman, Chm., Elias Alexiades, Susan Davidson, Estelle Handler, Beth Heller, Sara Leff, Nancy Ridinger, Darlene Raggozine, Alan Solomon.—**Municipal Historian,** Reverdy Whitlock.—**Recreation Comm.,** Stanley Gedansky, Chm., Harvey Ellis, Robert Goodman, Carolyn Kahn, William Montros, Kenneth Rubin, Mark Sackler; John Adamovich, Dir.—**Sperry Park Comm.,** John

Adamovich, Chm., Nedra Crane, Winchester L. Hubbard, Herbert D. Lewis, Mary Sagarin, Elizabeth Wolff.—**Dir. of Public Works,** vacancy.—**Building Inspector,** Christopher Laux.—**Building Bd. of Appeals,** John Ireland, Chm., Jay Alpert, Edward Cherry, Marvin Schaeffer.—**Sewer Auth.,** John H. Salomon, Chm., Richard Ciarleglio, William Koseki, Dennis Rader, Richard Ridinger.—**Chief of Police/Civil Preparedness Dir.,** Dennis Phipps.—**Police Comm.,** Tina C. Weiner, Chm., Robert Horowitz, Sanford P. Levine, Leonard Lohne, James K. Sabshin.—**Chief of Fire Dept.,** Mark Santoro.—**Fire Marshal,** Kenneth Chamberlin.—**Bd. of Fire Comrs.,** Steven Saslafsky, Chm., Peter Blessinger, Arthur Bogan, Thomas Kelly, Mark Levine.—**Town Counsel,** Alice Miskimin.—**Justices of the Peace,** Caesar Anquillare, Russell Arpaia, Susan C. Baldwin, Elizabeth Brett, Samuel Bridgers, Virginia B. Calistro, Stephanie Ciarleglio, Ann Febbraio, Elaine Feldman, Beth Heller, Peter Hershman, Susan Jacobs, Carrie Kahn, Jeff Kaufman, Gloria Kurek, Susan LaPointe, Arlene Levine, Mark Levine, Sanford Levine, Laura S. Mitler, Joyce Narden, Leonard Plotnick, Darlene Raggozine, Daniel Raucci, Peter Ressler, Alan Rice, Mark Sackler, Ellen Scalettar, Genie Schwartz, Edward M. Sheehy, Ellie Sheehy, William P. Silberberg, Hermine Swimmer, Anna B. Valko, Anne Walhimer, Gerald T. Weiner, Tina C. Weiner, Karen Weinstein, Mary A. Wilson, Mary Lou Winnick.

WOODBURY. Litchfield County.—(Form of government, selectmen, town meeting, board of finance.)—Named, May, 1673. Area, 36.7 sq. miles. Population, est., 8,611. Voting district, 1. Principal industries, machine shops, screw machine shops, welding and woodworking shops. Transp.—Freight: Served by numerous motor common carriers. Post office, Woodbury. Rural free delivery to part of the town.

TOWN OFFICERS. Clerk and Reg. of Vital Statistics, Jane H. Sandulli; Hours, 8:30 A.M.-4:30 P.M., Mon. through Fri. (for information on summer hours, call Town Clerk's Office); Address, 275 Main St., South, Box 369, 06798; Tel., (203) 263-2144.—**Asst. Clerk and Asst. Reg. of Vital Statistics,** Rita Connelly.—**Selectmen,** 1st, Katherine H. Campbell (R) Tel., (203) 263-2141, Mark J. Alvarez (D), Richard W. Crane (R).—**Treas.,** vacancy.—**Bd. of Finance,** Paul D. Hinckley, Chm., Robert B. Cowles, Jane C. DeVries, William T. Drakeley, Timothy J. Johnson, James R. Somers.—**Tax Collector,** Linda G. Lewis.—**Bd. of Assessment Appeals,** Craig M. Leonard, Chm., Dennis R. Galik, Frank Longto.—**Assessor,** Michael G. Moriarty.—**Registrars of Voters,** Abby R. Grondona (D), Ethel E. Follett (R).—**Supt. of Schools,** Joseph Sabatella.—**Planning Comm.,** Andrew Peklo III, Chm., Kenneth G. Green, Eloise E. Smith, Robert W. Travers, vacancy; Alternates, Eugene G. Crawford, Bette Geraci, Sarah Whelan.—**Town Planner/Zoning Enforcement Officer,** Peter Hughes.—**Zoning Comm.,** Vera T. Elsenboss, Ann H. Lilley, Arthur M. Moody III, Theodore Tietz, Jr., vacancy; Alternates, Roberta DePalma, Oswald Rapin, vacancy.—**Zoning Bd. of Appeals,** Peter F. Rutigliano, Chm., Robert W. Bailey, Sandra B. Petkus, Norman C. Taylor, Alexander F. Vitale; Alternates, Donna L. Franceskino, Allan L. Frew, Marion B. Griswold.—**Conservation Comm.,** Frederick R. Leavenworth, Chm., Henry R. DeVries, John Fleming, Allan L. Frew, Virginia Hart, J. Lawrence Pond, Sarah G.Whelan.—**Inland Wetlands Agency,** Wayne Wood, Chm.,

Jeffrey M. Leavenworth, Charles F. Lewis, Daniel Logue, Mary E. Tyrrell; Alternates, Anne Cushman, Earl H. Gillette, Jr., Donald Richards, Jr.—**Historic Dist. Comm.,** Harold J. Perkinson, Chm., Charles Euston, Barbara Gardella, Abby R. Grondona, Peter North; Alternates, Katherine Caroe, Susan Cheatham, Lois Fiftal.—**Municipal Historian,** Frederick T. Strong.—**Comm. for the Elderly,** Grace Carey, Chm., Frank Brennan, Karen Lindahl, Helen Nowak, Virginia Tillson; Alternates, John Calo, Dorothy Russo.—**Municipal Agent,** Mary C. Martin.—**Dir. of Health,** Neal Lustig.—**Library Trustees,** Jane Kendrick, Chm., Sarah Hood, Bernard F. McManus, Jr., Carol Sideli, Susan Southworth, Maureen D. Well.—**Park and Recreation Comm.,** Kathleen Johnson, Chm., Katharine Nichols, Catherine Paoli, Michael Riordan, Vincent Tomkalski; Dana Colla, Dir.; Alternates, Sharlene McEvoy, Ann Vitale.—**Dir. of Public Works,** David Monckton.—**Building Inspector,** Joseph Berger.—**Building Code Bd. of Appeals,** Jeffrey Leavenworth, Acting Chm., James Churchill, Henry W. Hart, Arthur R. Nichols, Michael Novak.—**Water Pollution Control Auth.,** Andrew Peklo III, Chm., Janet Bunch, Kenneth G. Green, Eloise E. Smith, Robert W. Travers; Alternates, Eugene G. Crawford, Bette Geraci, Sarah Whelan.—**Sanitarian,** Nancy Kontout.—**Chief of Police,** Katherine H. Campbell.—**Constables,** Edward Anderson, John Colangelo, Terrance Langin, Dana Lent, Bruce Lyle, Howard A. Northrop, Lawrence Rockhill, Thomas Story.—**Chief of Fire Dept.,** David Bengston; Deputy, Richard Rooney.—**Fire Marshal,** Richard Rooney.—**Bd. of Fire Comrs.,** Richard Hayward, Chm., Kenneth Green, Brewster S. Reichenbach, Daryl Scopino, L. Owen Tooker.—**Civil Preparedness Dir.,** Glen Dains.—**Town Attys.,** Carmody & Torrance.—**Justices of the Peace,** Cynthia B. Boudreau, Audre P. Capaldo, Peter M. Clark, Anne C. Cushman, Louis C. DeLuca, Dana J. Fox, Lawrence M. Genden, Diane B. Heavens, Robert J. Horton, Thomas O. McEvoy, Susan Spielberg, Margaret R. Warner, Kathryn C. Yarhouse.

WOODMONT.* BOROUGH OFFICERS. P.O., c/o Clerk, P.O. Box 5033, Woodmont 06460; Tel., (203) 874-7229.—**Warden,** Richard J. Austin.—**Burgesses,** Edward W. Bonessi, Jr., Jerome G. Fiorentino, Christine A. Frasca, Arnold H. Rutkin, Kimberly C. Waisonovitz, Irvin D. Zeidenberg.—**Clerk,** Barbara E. Harrington.—**Treas.,** Claire N. Zeidenberg.—**Tax Collector,** Patricia Cuzino.—**Constable,** James W. Coleman.—**Auditors,** Ellen Austin, Louis W. Berndtson, Jr.

---

*See City of Milford.

WOODSTOCK. Windham County.—(Form of government, selectmen, town meeting, board of finance.)—Settled, 1686; named New Roxbury; name changed, March, 1690, to Woodstock. Annexed to Conn., May, 1749. Area, 61.8 sq. miles. Population, est., 6,303. Voting district, 1. Principal industries, agriculture and manufacture of electrical switches, jet aircraft components, microporous plastics, fancy soaps, toiletries, gourmet foods, and fiberglass components. Transp.—Passenger: Northeastern Connecticut Transit District. Freight and express: Served by numerous motor common carriers. Post offices, Woodstock, East Woodstock, South Woodstock. Voted Limited Liquor Permit, 1974.

TOWN OFFICERS. Clerk and Reg. of Vital Statistics, Mary Ellen L. Heckler; Hours, 8:30 A.M.-4:30 P.M., Mon., Tues. and Thurs.; 8:30 A.M.-6 P.M., Wed.; 8:30 A.M.-3 P.M., Fri.; Address, Town Office Bldg., 415 Rte. 169, P.O. Box 123, 06281; Tel., Putnam, (860) 928-6595.—**Asst. Clerk and Asst. Reg. of Vital Statistics,** Christine G. French.—**Selectmen,** 1st, Edward A. Neumann, Jr. (R) Tel., (860) 928-0208, Roger W. Gale (R), Denis J. Gobin (D).—**Treas.,** Barbara P. Rich.—**Bd. of Finance,** Charles E. Couture, Chm., Michael L. Alberts, J. Stuart Boldry, Margaret H. Rahloff, Shirley E. Rapose, Eric C. Syriac; Alternates, John Ferland, Paul D. Wolf, vacancy.—**Tax Collector,** Gale C. Garceau.—**Bd. of Assessment Appeals,** W. Lewis Hyde, Edward N. Larson, Nancy J. Nystrom.—**Assessor,** Carol E. Walberg; Asst., Dorothy C. Berube.—**Registrars of Voters,** Constance T. Maynard (D), Elizabeth L. Brooks (R).—**Supt. of Schools,** Linda L. Galton.—**Bd. of Education,** William A. T. Cassedy, Margaret B. Higgins, Lawrence S. Paquette, Cheryl A. Pekarovic, vacancy, 1997; Daniel V. Atwood, Jay Livernois, Nancy W. Young, 1999; Romeo A. Blackmar, Charles G. Snow, Jr., 2001.—**Planning and Zoning Comm.,** Edwin C. Higgins III, Chm., D. Mitchell Eaffy, Todd Looby, Paul J. Miller, Carolyn S. Newmann, H. Douglas Porter, Suzanne H. Woodward, H. Dexter Young, vacancy; Alternates, George S. Hudson, Gary Kennett, Margaret R. Wilson.—**Town Planner,** Design Professionals of South Windsor.—**Economic Development Comm.,** Caroline H. Cheney, Patricia B. Douglas, Donald C. Goodwin, Edward N. Larson, Ellis H. Paine.—**Housing Auth.,** Paul R. Stanton, Chm., Lois A. Banister, Vivian Moulin, Carl Sandberg, Antoinette Snow.—**Conservation Comm.,** Mason S. Belden, Dolores Hunt, Joseph Jackson, Kathleen Koller, Edward M. Munroe, Jr., Victoria Scheufler, William Stehlik, G. Leslie Sweetnam, Edwin Von-Derheide.—**Inland Wetlands and Watercourses Agency,** Michael T. Glinsky, Chm., Paul N. Corrente, John E. Mona, Leo A. Morissette, Charles G. Snow, Jr., Seth L. Spalding, vacancy; Alternates, George D. Atwood, Jack A. Mullin, Sr., Mark A. Parker.—**Zoning Bd. of Appeals,** Gurdon Abell, Robert R. Reichel, Sr., Harold Rohloff, Deborah Sherman, Joel Struebing; Alternates, Nelson E. Douglas, Nancy J. Nystrom, William P. Pekarovic.—**Agent for the Elderly,** Constance T. Maynard.—**Dir. of Social Services,** Joy Bachand.—**Acting Dir. of Health,** Northeast District Dept. of Health.—**Recreation Committee,** Elizabeth L. Brooks, Warren Hunt, Elizabeth C. Murphy, Kathleen O'Connor-Cooper, Ann M. Rathbone, Steven C. Schambach, Victoria Scheufler, seven vacancies.—**Building Official,** Terry Bellman.—**Tree Warden,** William Rathbone.—**Chief of Police,** Edward A. Neumann, Jr.—**Constables,** Paul G. Arvidson, Frederick C. Child, Patsy Converse, Donald Genest, Dennis Hebert, Francis Kelly, Joseph Paulus, vacancy.—**Chiefs of Fire Depts.,** Richard Baron, Joseph Surozenski, H. Dexter Young.—**Acting Fire Marshal,** Richard G. Baron.—**Civil Defense Dir.,** H. Dexter Young.—**Town Counsel,** Tyler, Cooper & Alcorn.—**Justices of the Peace,** Arthur E. Bondy, Clarence H. Child, Paul N. Corrente, Theodore E. Demers, Karen L. Dimock, Denis J. Gobin, Robert Gries, Mary P. Larson, Stephen B. Lincoln, Edward A. Neumann, Jr., Joseph W. A. Parker, David C. Philippi, Deborah C. Sherman, Gregory M. Smith, Teodor M. Teja, John Winstanley.

CONN. TOWN CLERKS ASSOC., INC.—*Pres.*, Lois Pontbriant, Stamford, *1st,* Rachel Haggerty, Thompson, *2nd,* Roberta Jenkins, Newington; *Secy.,* Beverly C. Muldoon, City Hall, Norwich 06360; *Treas.,* Anne R. Moses, Norfolk; *Asst. Treas.,*

Carolyn O'Connor, North Canaan; *County Vice Pres., Hartford County,* Dorcas McHugh, Wethersfield; *New Haven County,* Alan Jepson, Milford; *New London County,* Clark vanderLyke, New London; *Fairfield County,* Marguerite Toth, Fairfield; *Windham County,* Catherine Nurmi, Sterling; *Litchfield County,* Patricia Williamsen, Harwinton; *Middlesex County,* Karen Marsden, Clinton; *Tolland County,* Joan Gerdsen, Mansfield.

REGISTRARS OF VOTERS ASSOC. OF CONN.—*Pres.,* Judith A. Beaudreau, Vernon; *Exec. Vice Pres.,* Elizabeth A. Gassman, Meriden; *Vice Pres.,* Mary Lou Flynn, Enfield; *Secy.,* Margaret A. Reeves, Wilton; *Treas.,* Helen K. Mis, Beacon Falls.

CONN. CONFERENCE OF MUNICIPALITIES. Address: 900 Chapel St., 9th Fl., New Haven 06510-2807. Tel., (203) 498-3000; FAX, (203) 562-6314. *Pres.,* Susan Merrow; *Vice Pres. 1st.,* John DeStefano, Jr., *Vice Pres. 2nd.,* Sandra F. Klebanoff; *Secy.,* Rudolf Weiss; *Treas.,* John Weichsel; *Dirs.,* Paul A. Audley, Nan Birdwhistell, John P. Bohenko, H. Richard Borer Jr., Dominic A. Buonocore, Robert M. DeCrescenzo, Gene Eriquez, William A. Falletti, Donald S. Francis, Joseph P. Ganim, Carmella M. Lattizori, Dannel Malloy, Joseph J. Marinan, Jr., Michael P. Peters, Victor Puia, Robert H. Russell, Philip K. Schenck, Jr., Stanley S. Sheldon, Jr., Beatrice C. Stockwell; *Past Pres.,* Stephen T. Cassano, Walter M. Pawelkiewicz; *Exec. Dir./Gen. Counsel,* Joel Cogen; *Assoc. Dir.,* Lynn McNamara.

THE CONNECTICUT COUNCIL OF SMALL TOWNS. Address: 1245 Farmington Ave., Suite 101, West Hartford 06107. Tel., (860) 676-3069; FAX, (860) 676-3200. **Pres.,** Alan H. Bergren, East Hampton; **Vice Pres.,** Nan M. Birdwhistell, Woodbridge; **Secy.,** Alan J. Chapin, Washington; **Treas.,** Adella G. Urban, Columbia; **Exec. Dir.,** Barton D. Russell, West Hartford; **Bd. of Dirs.,** Kay Campbell, Woodbury; Fred Cazel, Mansfield; Frank B. Connolly, North Branford; Jenny Contois, Colchester; Howard T. Dean, Jr., Marlborough; Donald S. Francis, Brooklyn; Bruce Gresczyk, New Hartford; Martin L. Heft, Chester; John E. Julian, Stafford Springs; Edward L. Kalinowski, Portland; Gordon M. Ridgway, Cornwall; Stanley Sheldon, Jr., Pomfret; William Smith, Jr., Granby; George Wilber, Colebrook.

THE CONN. ASSOC. OF ZONING ENFORCEMENT OFFICIALS. Address: 213 Church St., Naugatuck 06770. Tel., (203) 729-4571, Ext. 283. *Pres.,* Michael Mormile, Naugatuck; *Vice Pres.,* Martin J. Connor, Litchfield; *Secy.,* Linda Farmer, Tolland; *Treas.,* Justine Gillen, Branford.

REGIONAL COUNCILS OF GOVERNMENTS
(Revised to January 1, 1997.)

CAPITOL REGION COUNCIL OF GOVERNMENTS. Office: 221 Main St., Hartford 06106; Tel., (860) 522-2217. **Chm.**, Sandra F. Klebanoff, West Hartford; **Vice Chm.**, Steven Cassano, Manchester, Mary A. Glassman, Simsbury; **Secy.**, Beatrice C. Stockwell, Farmington; **Treas.**, Michael Peters, Hartford.

Participating municipalities and representatives: **ANDOVER,** Edward Turn, Sr. **AVON,** Richard W. Hines. **BLOOMFIELD,** Faith McMahon. **BOLTON,** Carl A. Preuss. **CANTON,** Kathleen C. Corkum. **EAST GRANBY,** David K. Kilbon. **EAST HARTFORD,** Robert DeCrescenzo. **EAST WINDSOR,** John Rajala. **ELLINGTON,** Michael P. Stupinski. **ENFIELD,** Mary Lou Strom. **FARMINGTON,** Beatrice C. Stockwell. **GLASTONBURY,** Paul M. Nye. **GRANBY,** William J. Simanski. **HARTFORD,** Michael Peters. **HEBRON,** R. William Garrison. **MANCHESTER,** Steven Cassano. **MARLBOROUGH,** Howard T. Dean, Jr. **NEWINGTON,** Robert A. Randich. **ROCKY HILL,** Phillip Dunn. **SIMSBURY,** Mary A. Glassman. **SOMERS,** John Bowles. **SOUTH WINDSOR,** Richard Ryan. **SUFFIELD,** Roland P. Dowd. **TOLLAND,** Joel Fain. **VERNON,** Tony Muro. **WEST HARTFORD,** Sandra F. Klebanoff. **WETHERSFIELD,** Wayne J. Sassano. **WINDSOR,** Francis J. Brady. **WINDSOR LOCKS,** Victor J. Puia.

COUNCIL OF GOVERNMENTS OF CENTRAL NAUGATUCK VALLEY. Office: 20 East Main St., Suite 303, Waterbury 06702-2399; Tel., (203) 757-0535. **Chm.**, Kate Cosgrove, Oxford; **Vice Chm.**, Rosalie Loughran, Watertown; **Secy.**, Katherine Campbell, Woodbury; **Treas.**, Steven Bosco, Wolcott; **Exec. Dir.**, Peter G. Dorpalen.

Participating municipalities and representatives: **BEACON FALLS,** Susan Cable. **BETHLEHEM,** Robert Gallo. **CHESHIRE,** Sandra Mouris. **MIDDLEBURY,** Edward St. John. **NAUGATUCK,** William Rado. **OXFORD,** Kate Cosgrove. **PROSPECT,** Robert J. Chatfield. **SOUTHBURY,** Alfio Candido. **THOMASTON,** Clifford Brammer. **WATERBURY,** Philip Giordano. **WATERTOWN,** Rosalie Loughran. **WOLCOTT,** Steven Bosco. **WOODBURY,** Katherine Campbell.

NORTHEASTERN CONN. COUNCIL OF GOVERNMENTS. Address: P.O. Box 759, Dayville 06241; Tel., (860) 774-1253. **Chm.**, Donald S. Francis, Brooklyn; **Vice Chm.**, Stanley S. Sheldon, Jr., Pomfret; **Secy.**, Robert E. Lewis, Sterling; **Treas.**, Daniel S. Rovero, Putnam; **Exec. Dir.**, John Filchak.

Participating municipalities and representatives: **BROOKLYN,** Donald S. Francis. **CANTERBURY,** Neil Dupont, Sr. **EASTFORD,** Russell H. Mayhew, Jr. **KILLINGLY,** John E. Burke, Jr. **PLAINFIELD,** Paul E. Sweet. **POMFRET,** Stanley S. Sheldon. **PUTNAM,** Daniel S. Rovero. **STERLING,** Robert E. Lewis. **THOMPSON,** Barney Seney. **WOODSTOCK,** Edward Neuman.

NORTHWESTERN CONN. COUNCIL OF GOVERNMENTS. Address: 17 Sackett Hill Rd., Warren 06754. Tel., (860) 868-7341. **Chm.**, Gordon Ridgway, Cornwall; **Vice Chm.**, Dolores R. Schiesel, Kent; **Secy.**, Alan Chapin, Washington; **Treas.**, Lewis Tanner, Warren; **Exec. Dir.**, Paul A. Boudreau.

Participating municipalities and representatives: **CANAAN,** Peter G. Lawson. **CORNWALL,** Gordon Ridgway. **KENT,** Dolores R. Schiesel. **NORTH CANAAN,** Douglas Humes, Jr. **ROXBURY,** Edward T. Went. **SALISBURY,** Robert Smithwick.

SHARON, Robert Moeller. **WARREN,** Lewis Tanner. **WASHINGTON,** Alan J. Chapin.

SOUTH CENTRAL REGIONAL COUNCIL OF GOVERNMENTS. Office: 127 Washington Ave., 4th Fl. West, North Haven 06473; Tel., (203) 234-7555; FAX, (203) 234-9850; E-Mail, SCRCOG@CONNIX.COM. **Chm.,** Edward J. Lynch, Guilford; **Vice Chm.,** H. Richard Borer, Jr., West Haven; **Secy.,** John DeStefano, Jr., New Haven; **Treas.,** Joanne S. Wentworth, North Branford; **Exec. Secy.,** vacancy; **Exec. Dir.,** James A. Butler.

Participating municipalities and representatives: **BETHANY,** John E. Ford, III. **BRANFORD,** Dominic A. Buonocore. **EAST HAVEN,** Henry J. Luzzi. **GUILFORD,** Edward J. Lynch. **HAMDEN,** Lillian D. Clayman. **MADISON,** Thomas R. Rylander. **MERIDEN,** Joseph J. Marinan, Jr. **MILFORD,** Frederick L. Lisman. **NEW HAVEN,** John DeStefano, Jr. **NORTH BRANFORD,** Joanne S. Wentworth. **NORTH HAVEN,** Anthony P. Rescigno. **ORANGE,** Robert C. Sousa. **WALLINGFORD,** William W. Dickinson, Jr. **WEST HAVEN,** H. Richard Borer, Jr. **WOODBRIDGE,** Nan M. Birdwhistell.

SOUTHEASTERN CONN. COUNCIL OF GOVERNMENTS. Office: 139 Boswell Ave., Norwich 06360; Tel., (860) 889-2324; FAX, (860) 889-1222. **Chm.,** Dolores Hauber, Groton; **Vice Chm.,** James Wright, Lisbon; **Secy.,** Raymond Barber, Bozrah; **Treas.,** Robert Congdon, Preston; **Exec. Dir.,** Richard B. Erickson.

Participating municipalities and representatives: **BOZRAH,** Raymond Barber. **COLCHESTER,** Jenny Contois, Goldie Liverant. **EAST LYME,** David Cini. **FRANKLIN,** James Handfield. **GRISWOLD,** Paul Brycki. **GROTON (town),** Dolores Hauber, Ron LeBlanc. **GROTON (city),** Bette Giesing. **LEDYARD,** Wesley Johnson. **LISBON,** James Wright. **MONTVILLE,** Patrick Dougherty. **NEW LONDON,** Richard Brown, William Satti. **NORTH STONINGTON,** Charles Elias. **NORWICH,** Harry Jackson, William Tallman. **PRESTON,** Robert Congdon. **SALEM,** Donald Bourdeau, Jr., Carl Iontneau. **SPRAGUE,** Joan Charron-Nagle, Stephen Papineau, Sr. **STONINGTON,** Donald Maranell, George Sylvestre. **STONINGTON (borough),** Dorothy Papp, Alisa Storrow. **VOLUNTOWN,** Eric Marsh. **WATERFORD,** David Fairman, Thomas Sheridan.

VALLEY COUNCIL OF GOVERNMENTS. Office: Derby R.R. Station, Derby 06418; Tel., (203) 735-8688; FAX, (203) 735-8680. **Chm.,** Alan R. Schlesinger, Derby; **Vice Chm.,** Nancy Valentine, Ansonia; **Secy.,** Mark A. Lauretti, Shelton; **Treas.,** John O'Toole, Seymour; **Coordinator,** Richard S. Eigen.

Participating municipalities and representatives: **ANSONIA,** Nancy Valentine. **DERBY,** Alan Schlesinger. **SEYMOUR,** John O'Toole. **SHELTON,** Mark A. Lauretti.

REGIONAL EDUCATION COUNCILS

AREA COOPERATIVE EDUCATIONAL SERVICES (ACES). Address: 205 Skiff St., Hamden 06517-1095; Tel., (203) 407-4700. **Chm.,** Winifred Elton, Woodbridge;

Vice Chm., Carolyn H. Engelhardt, Cheshire; **Fiscal Officer,** Patricia Logioco, Orange; **Exec. Dir.,** Peter C. Young.

Participating municipalities and representatives: **ANSONIA,** Christine Shortell. **BETHANY,** vacancy. **BRANFORD,** Marilyn Brown. **CHESHIRE,** Carolyn H. Engelhardt. **DERBY,** vacancy. **EAST HAVEN,** vacancy. **HAMDEN,** Peter Brown. **MERIDEN,** Josephine Femia. **MIDDLETOWN,** Linda Brooks. **MILFORD,** Carol Faruolo. **NAUGATUCK,** Rebecca Zandvliet. **NEW HAVEN,** Arthur Bosley. **NORTH BRANFORD,** Vivian Troiano. **NORTH HAVEN,** Gerald Feinberg. **ORANGE,** Carolyn Roth. **OXFORD,** Sheila Kenny. **SEYMOUR,** Vincentena Kobasa. **SHELTON,** Richard Sutkowski. **WALLINGFORD,** Karen Hlavac. **WATERBURY,** Deborah Schatzle-Baker. **WEST HAVEN,** George Belbusti. **WOLCOTT,** Patricia Deslauriers. **WOODBRIDGE,** Winifred Elton. **REGIONAL DISTRICTS #5,** Patricia Logioco; **#13,** Kate Thibodeau; **#16,** Peter Christensen.

CAPITOL REGION EDUCATION COUNCIL. Office: 111 Charter Oak Ave., Hartford 06106; Tel., (860) 247-2732. **Chm.,** Kevin Porter, Berlin; **Vice Chm.,** Kathy Randall, East Hartford; **Secy./Treas.,** Frank Szeps, Rocky Hill.

Participating municipalities and representatives: **AVON,** David Wolansky. **BERLIN,** Kevin Porter. **BLOOMFIELD,** Shirley Thompson. **BOLTON,** James Marshall. **BRISTOL,** Beverly Brobroske. **CANTON,** Al Hinds. **CROMWELL,** Shirley Banic. **EAST GRANBY,** Patrick Majewski. **EAST HARTFORD,** Kathy Randall. **EAST WINDSOR,** Robert Grant. **ELLINGTON,** Wendy Ciparelli. **ENFIELD,** Roger Jones. **FARMINGTON,** Mary Grace Reed. **GLASTONBURY,** Lew Parker. **GRANBY,** Cal Heminway. **HARTFORD,** Brad Noel. **HARTLAND,** Peter Stred. **MANCHESTER,** Craig Lappen. **NEW BRITAIN,** Peter Kochol. **NEWINGTON,** Helen Nelson. **PLAINVILLE,** Carrie Burns. **PORTLAND,** Cynthia Varricchio. **ROCKY HILL,** Frank Szeps. **SIMSBURY,** Norman Shipley. **SOMERS,** Charlotte Stopa. **SOUTHINGTON,** David Derynoski. **SOUTH WINDSOR,** Julie Muller. **SUFFIELD,** Susan Miller-Clark. **VERNON,** Susan Norlie-Hesnan. **WEST HARTFORD,** Nancy Rion. **WETHERSFIELD,** Patricia Strong. **WINDSOR,** Audrey Garvin. **WINDSOR LOCKS,** Sandra Kanigowski. **REGIONAL DISTRICT #10,** Robert Finder.

COOPERATIVE EDUCATIONAL SERVICES (CES). Address: 25 Oakview Dr., Trumbull 06611; Tel., (203) 365-8800. **Pres.,** Ralph M. Goodmurphy, Weston; **Vice Pres.,** Marsha Motter, Monroe; **Secy.,** Barbara Rifkin, Fairfield; **Exec. Dir.,** Lawrence Miller.

Participating municipalities and representatives: **BRIDGEPORT,** Lydia Falcon, vacancy. **DARIEN,** Elizabeth Fenton. **FAIRFIELD,** Barbara Rifkin. **GREENWICH,** Peggy Kavounas. **MONROE,** Marsha Motter. **NEW CANAAN,** vacancy. **NORWALK,** Elizabeth Lyons, Terry Quell. **RIDGEFIELD,** vacancy. **STAMFORD,** vacancy. **STRATFORD,** Richard Watt. **TRUMBULL,** M. Gloria Maina. **WESTON,** Ralph M. Goodmurphy. **WESTPORT,** Cheryl Bliss. **WILTON,** Carol Reimers.

EASTERN CONN. REGIONAL EDUCATIONAL SERVICE CENTER (EASTCONN). Address: 376 Hartford Tpke., North Windham 06256; Tel. (860) 455-0707; FAX, (860) 455-0691. **Chm.,** Bernice Davis, Sterling; **Vice Chm.,** Herb Arico, Willington; **Secy./Treas.,** Christine Winter, Mansfield; **Exec. Dir.,** David J. Calchera.

Participating municipalities and representatives: **ANDOVER,** Elisabeth Houle. **ASHFORD,** vacancy. **BOZRAH,** Jane Seder. **BROOKLYN,** Thomas Dziki. **CANTERBURY,** Lorna Champagne. **CHAPLIN,** Kamala Wiley. **COLCHESTER,** John Mazzarella. **COLUMBIA,** Cathy Klein, Mary Ellen Lavalette. **COVENTRY,** Linda Scussel. **EASTFORD,** Herman Barlow. **FRANKLIN,** vacancy. **GRISWOLD,** Jacquie Burzycki. **HAMPTON,** James Iannoni. **HEBRON,** Willard Skehan. **KILLINGLY,** Carol Taylor. **LEBANON,** Judy Pflum. **LISBON,** vacancy. **MANSFIELD,** Christine Winter. **MARLBOROUGH,** vacancy. **PLAINFIELD,** Gary Beaulac, Virginia Sampietro. **POMFRET,** Woody Woodbridge. **PUTNAM,** vacancy. **SCOTLAND,** Charles Carroll. **SPRAGUE,** vacancy. **STAFFORD,** Edward Fowler. **STERLING,** Bernice Davis, Darlene Gannon. **THOMPSON,** Hector Morin. **TOLLAND,** Heather Ricker-Gilbert. **UNION,** Andrea Estell. **VOLUNTOWN,** Nina Plumb. **WILLINGTON,** Herb Arico. **WINDHAM,** Paula Haney, Benjamin Vreeland. **WOODSTOCK,** Cheryl Pekarovic. **REGIONAL DISTRICTS #8,** James Pasqurell; **#11,** vacancy; **#19,** Ralph McNeal, Jr.

LONG RANGE EDUCATIONAL ASSISTANCE FOR REGIONAL NEEDS (LEARN). Address: 44 Hatchetts Hill Rd., P.O. Box 805, Old Lyme 06371; Tel., (860) 434-4800; FAX, (860) 434-4820; E-Mail, vseccomb@learn.k12.ct.us. **Chm.,** Gisela Harma, Stonington; **Vice Chm.,** William Calvert, Clinton; **Secy.,** Robert Narducci, Chester; **Fiscal Officer,** Laura Berry, Essex; **Exec. Dir.,** Virginia Seccombe.

Participating municipalities and representatives: **CHESTER,** Robert Narducci. **CLINTON,** William Calvert. **DEEP RIVER,** Karen Conniff, Pamela Potter. **EAST HADDAM,** LEARN. **EAST HAMPTON,** Gail Hamm. **EAST LYME,** Mary Broderick. **ESSEX,** Laura Berry. **GROTON,** Barbara Montgomery. **GUILFORD,** Kaaren Janssen. **LEDYARD,** Laurie Fratoni. **MADISON,** Ginny Connif. **MONTVILLE,** Norma Leonard. **NEW LONDON,** Ray Haworth. **NORTH STONINGTON,** LEARN. **NORWICH,** Mark Chenette. **OLD SAYBROOK,** Albert Anderson, LEARN. **PRESTON,** LEARN. **SALEM,** Marianne Kennedy. **STONINGTON,** Gisela Harma. **WATERFORD,** Donna Martell. **WESTBROOK,** Allan Johnson. **Regional Districts #4,** Chris Allinson; **#17,** Helen Reeve; **#18,** Susan Fogliano.

EDUCATION CONNECTION. Address: P.O. Box 909, 355 Goshen Rd., Litchfield 06759-0909; Tel., (860) 567-0863. **Pres.,** Herbert Rosenthal, Newtown; **Vice Pres.,** DeLean Goldsmith, Thomaston; **Secy.,** Dolores Whelan, Morris; **Treas.,** Charles Isselee, New Preston; **Exec. Dir.,** Jane Tedder, Ed.D.

Participating municipalities and representatives: **BARKHAMSTED,** Kevin Case. **BETHEL,** Rotating. **BROOKFIELD,** Catherine Lasser. **CANAAN,** vacancy. **COLEBROOK,** Joyce Hemingson. **CORNWALL,** vacancy. **DANBURY,** vacancy. **EASTON,** vacancy. **KENT,** vacancy. **LITCHFIELD,** James Katzin. **NEW FAIRFIELD,** Megan Hostler. **NEW HARTFORD,** vacancy. **NEW MILFORD,** vacancy. **NEWTOWN,** Herbert Rosenthal. **NORFOLK,** Peter Boyle. **NORTH CANAAN,** Martha Scott. **PLYMOUTH,** vacancy. **REDDING,** Kathy Atkinson. **SALISBURY,** Mary Davidson. **SHARON,** vacancy. **SHERMAN,** Joyce Kjep. **THOMASTON,** DeLean Goldsmith. **TORRINGTON,** Todd Pollutro. **WATERTOWN,** Joanne Pannone. **WINCHESTER,** vacancy. **REGIONAL DISRICTS #1,** vacancy; **#6,** Dr. Dolores

Whelan; **#7,** Judith Kochey; **#12,** Charles Isselee; **#14,** John Howard; **#15,** Joseph Zukowski.

REGIONAL LIBRARY COUNCILS

CAPITOL REGION LIBRARY COUNCIL. Serves: Avon, Berlin, Bloomfield, Bristol, Burlington, Canton, East Granby, East Hartford, East Windsor, Enfield, Farmington, Glastonbury, Granby, Hartford, Manchester, Marlborough, New Britain, Newington, Plainville, Rocky Hill, Simsbury, Southington, South Windsor, Suffield, West Hartford, Wethersfield, Windsor, Windsor Locks. Office: 599 Matianuck Ave., Windsor 06095; Tel., (860) 298-5319; FAX, (860) 298-5328; E-Mail, office@crlc.org; Internet, http://www.crlc.org. **Exec. Dir.,** Dency Sargent.

EASTERN CONN. LIBRARIES. Serves Regions 3 and 6.

Region 3—Serves: Andover, Ashford, Bolton, Brooklyn, Canterbury, Chaplin, Columbia, Coventry, Eastford, Ellington, Hampton, Hebron, Killingly, Mansfield, Plainfield, Pomfret, Putnam, Scotland, Somers, Stafford, Sterling, Thompson, Tolland, Union, Vernon, Willington, Windham, Woodstock.

Region 6—Serves: Bozrah, Colchester, East Haddam, East Lyme, Franklin, Griswold, Groton, Lebanon, Ledyard, Lisbon, Lyme, Montville, Moodus, New London, North Stonington, Norwich, Old Lyme, Preston, Salem, Sprague, Stonington, Uncasville, Voluntown, Waterford.

Office: 74 West Main St., Norwich 06360; Tel., (860) 885-2760; FAX, (860) 885-2757; E-Mail, pholloway@ecl.org; Homepage, http://www.ecl.org. **Exec. Dir.,** Patricia Holloway; **Asst. Dir.,** Sandra Brooks.

SOUTHERN CONN. LIBRARY COUNCIL. Region 5—Serves: Ansonia, Bethany, Branford, Cheshire, Chester, Clinton, Cromwell, Deep River, Derby, Durham, East Haddam, East Hampton, East Haven, Essex, Guilford, Haddam, Hamden, Ivoryton, Killingworth, Madison, Meriden, Middlefield, Middle Haddam, Middletown, Milford, Moodus, New Haven, North Branford, North Haven, Old Saybrook, Orange, Portland, Seymour, Shelton, Stony Creek, Wallingford, Westbrook, West Haven, Woodbridge. Office: 2405 Whitney Ave., Suite 3, Hamden, 06518-3235; Tel., (203) 288-5757; FAX, (203) 287-0757; E-Mail, OFFICE@SCLC.ORG. **Exec. Dir.,** Michael A. Golrick.

WESTERN CONN. LIBRARY COUNCIL, INC. Serves Regions 1 and 4.

Region 1—Serves: Beacon Falls, Bethlehem, Bridgewater, Burlington, Canaan, Colebrook, Cornwall, Derby, Falls Village, Goshen, Harwinton, Kent, Lakeville, Litchfield, Middlebury, Morris, Naugatuck, New Hartford, New Milford, New Preston, Norfolk, Northfield, Oakville, Oxford, Pleasant Valley, Plymouth, Prospect, Roxbury, Salisbury, Seymour, Sharon, Sherman, Southbury, South Kent, Terryville, Thomaston, Torrington, Warren, Washington, Waterbury, Watertown, West Cornwall, Winsted, Wolcott, Woodbury.

Region 4—Serves: Bethel, Bridgeport, Brookfield, Danbury, Darien, Easton, Fairfield, Greenwich, Monroe, New Canaan, New Fairfield, Newtown, Norwalk, Old

Greenwich, Redding, Ridgefield, Rowayton, Sandy Hook, Shelton, Southport, Stamford, Stratford, Trumbull, Weston, Westport, West Redding,Wilton.

Office: 530 Middlebury Rd., Suite 210-B, P. O. Box 1284, Middlebury 06762-1284; Tel., (203) 577-4010; FAX, (203) 577-4015; E-Mail, abarney@wclc.org. **Exec. Dir.,** Anita R. Barney.

REGIONAL PLANNING AGENCIES

CAPITOL REGION COUNCIL OF GOVERNMENTS. Office: 241 Main St., Hartford 06106; Tel., (860) 522-2217; FAX, (860) 724-1274. **Chm.,** Sandra Klebanoff; **Exec. Dir.,** Richard J. Porth.

CENTRAL CONN. REGIONAL PLANNING AGENCY (Members also serve as the board of the Central Connecticut Paratransit Service). Office: 225 North Main St., Suite 304, Bristol 06010-4993; Tel., (860) 589-7820. **Chm.,** Michael Parks, Bristol; **Vice Chm.,** Theodore Scheidel, Burlington; **Secy.,** Timothy Zigmont, Berlin; **Treas.,** Severino Bovino, Southington; **Exec. Dir.,** Melvin J. Schneidermeyer, Southington.

Participating municipalities and representatives: **BERLIN,** William Diskin, Timothy Zigmont. **BRISTOL,** Timothy W. Furey, Donald V. Padlo, Michael Parks. **BURLINGTON,** Guy Poulin, Theodore Scheidel. **NEW BRITAIN,** Daniel Karp, Susan McMullen, Helen Z. Pearl, Steve P. Schiller. **PLAINVILLE,** Norman Peltzer, Theodore Poulos. **PLYMOUTH,** Verne Fuerst, Edward Plaze. **SOUTHINGTON,** Joseph Adams, Severino Bovino, Robert Salka.

CONN. RIVER ESTUARY REGIONAL PLANNING AGENCY. Address: 455 Boston Post Rd., P.O. Box 778, Old Saybrook 06475; Tel., (860) 388-3497. **Chm.,** Kenneth W. Kells, Essex; **Vice Chm.,** Harriet Naughton, Old Saybrook; **Secy.,** Patricia Smulders, Killingworth; **Treas.,** Mary Savoie, Westbrook; **Dir.,** Linda B. Krause.

Participating municipalities and representatives: **CHESTER,** Donald Croteau, Natalie Williams. **CLINTON,** Daniel Vece, Jr., Marye Wagner. **DEEP RIVER,** Raymond Hayes, Irwin Wilcox. **ESSEX,** Sandra Huber, Kenneth Kells. **KILLINGWORTH,** Holly Darin, Patricia Smulders. **LYME,** Frank Skwarek. **OLD LYME,** Alan Bayreuther, Jane R. Marsh. **OLD SAYBROOK,** Harriet Naughton, Adam Sokolowski. **WESTBROOK,** Doris Sanstrom, Mary Savoie.

GREATER BRIDGEPORT REGIONAL PLANNING AGENCY. Office: 525 Water St., Bridgeport 06604; Tel., (203) 366-5405. **Chm.,** John E. Wrabel, Fairfield; **Vice Chm.,** John Ehnot, Bridgeport; **Secy.,** John J. Neary, Easton; **Treas.,** Charles T. Poarch, Trumbull; **Exec. Dir.,** James T. Wang.

Participating municipalities and representatives: **BRIDGEPORT,** Cowlis Andrews, John Ehnot, William Finch, two vacancies. **EASTON,** John J. Neary, Wallace Williams. **FAIRFIELD,** James Baldwin, John E. Wrabel. **MONROE,** John Danscuk, Robert Sylvester, Jr. **STRATFORD,** vacancy. **TRUMBULL,** Charles T. Poarch, Barbara Smith, Paul Timpanelli.

HOUSATONIC VALLEY COUNCIL OF ELECTED OFFICIALS. Office: Old Town Hall, Rte. 25, Brookfield 06804; Tel., (203) 775-6256; FAX, (203) 740-9167.

Chm., Anthony Hapanowich, Sherman; **Vice Chm.,** Robert Cascella, Newtown; **Exec. Dir.,** Jonathan Chew; **Senior Planner,** J. David Hannon.

Participating municipalities and representatives: **BETHEL,** Charles Steck III. **BRIDGEWATER,** William T. Stuart. **BROOKFIELD,** Bonnie Smith. **DANBURY,** Gene F. Eriquez. **NEW FAIRFIELD,** Cheryl Reedy. **NEW MILFORD,** Arthur Peitler. **NEWTOWN,** Robert Cascella. **REDDING,** Henry Bielawa. **RIDGEFIELD,** Sue Manning. **SHERMAN,** Anthony Hapanowich.

LITCHFIELD HILLS COUNCIL OF ELECTED OFFICIALS. Office: Goshen Town Hall, 42 North St., Goshen 06756. **Chm.,** Craig Miner, Litchfield; **Vice Chm.,** Marie Knudsen, Harwinton; **Secy.,** William Hodge, Hartland; **Treas.,** James O'Leary, Goshen; **Planning Dir.,** Richard M. Lynn, Jr.

Participating municipalities and representatives: **BARKHAMSTED,** Michael Fox. **COLEBROOK,** George M. Wilber. **GOSHEN,** James O'Leary. **HARTLAND,** William L. Hodge. **HARWINTON,** Marie Knudsen. **LITCHFIELD,** Craig Miner. **MORRIS,** Philip D. Birkett. **NEW HARTFORD,** Bruce Gresczyk. **NORFOLK,** Arthur Rosenblatt. **TORRINGTON,** Mary Jane Gryniuk. **WINCHESTER,** John Arcelaschi.

MIDSTATE REGIONAL PLANNING AGENCY. Address: P.O. Box 139, 100 DeKoven Dr., Middletown 06457; Tel., (860) 347-7214. **Chm.,** Richard Newton, Cromwell; **Vice Chm.,** John Calvocoressi, East Hampton; **Secy./Treas.,** Ronald Klattenberg, Middletown; **Exec. Dir.,** Geoffrey L. Colegrove, Durham.

Participating municipalities and representatives: **CROMWELL,** Arthur Johnson, Richard Newton. **DURHAM,** Richard Eriksen, Henry Robinson. **EAST HADDAM,** Lloyd Neudecker. **EAST HAMPTON,** John Calvocoressi, Mark Philhower. **HADDAM,** Raul deBrigard, Stephen Hitchcock. **MIDDLEFIELD,** John Lyman III, Nicholas Xenelis. **MIDDLETOWN,** Ronald Klattenberg, Steven Meyer, David B. Mylchreest. **PORTLAND,** C. Joseph Seiferman, David Sundell.

NORTHEASTERN CONN. COUNCIL OF GOVERNMENTS. See Northeastern Conn. Council of Governments.

NORTHWESTERN CONN. COUNCIL OF GOVERNMENTS. See Northwestern Conn. Council of Governments.

SOUTH CENTRAL REGIONAL COUNCIL OF GOVERNMENTS—REGIONAL PLANNING COMMISSION. Office: 127 Washington Ave., 4th Fl. West, North Haven 06473; Tel., (203) 234-7555. **Chm.,** Robert Roscow, Hamden; **Vice Chm.,** Philip Bolduc, New Haven; **Secy.,** Jeanne Pulleyn, North Haven; **Alternates,** Gary S. Leonard, Madison; Charles B. Swanson, Woodbridge.

Participating municipalities and representatives: **BETHANY,** Sharon Huxley. **BRANFORD,** Michael Laudano. **EAST HAVEN,** Charles Coyle. **GUILFORD,** James Barry, Jr. **HAMDEN,** Robert Roscow. **MADISON,** Mitchell Cohan, Garry S. Leonard. **MERIDEN,** vacancy. **MILFORD,** vacancy. **NEW HAVEN,** Philip Bolduc, Kenneth Miller. **NORTH BRANFORD,** Dennis E. Hrabchak. **NORTH HAVEN,** Jeanne Pulleyn. **ORANGE,** Judy Smith-Morgan. **WALLINGFORD,** James Fitzsimmons. **WEST HAVEN,** James O'Leary. **WOODBRIDGE,** Charles B. Swanson.

SOUTHWESTERN REGIONAL PLANNING AGENCY. Office: 1 Selleck St., East Norwalk 06855-1106; Tel., (203) 866-5543. **Chm.,** William M. Hutchison, Jr., New Canaan; **Vice Chm.,** Daniel Wilder, Weston; **Secy.,** John W. Timbers, Stamford; **Treas.,** Mary S. Ferry, Greenwich. **Exec. Dir.,** Richard C. Carpenter. **Members, Exec. Committee,** Anthony Flack, Norwalk; Louis Gagliano, Westport; Richard Wheeler, Wilton; George Zengo, Darien.

Participating municipalities and representatives: **DARIEN,** Frederick B. Conze, George Zengo. **GREENWICH,** Mary S. Ferry, Diane Fox, Peter Tesei. **NEW CANAAN,** James Bennett, William M. Hutchison, Jr. **NORWALK,** Anthony Flack, Ram Hingorani, Nicholas Kydes, vacancy. **STAMFORD,** Pamela J. Harris, Robert M. Stein, John W. Timbers, vacancy. **WESTON,** Daniel A. Wilder, Margaret Wirtenberg. **WESTPORT,** Louis Gagliano, Douglas Skalka. **WILTON,** John P. Hickey, Richard Wheeler.

VALLEY REGIONAL PLANNING AGENCY. Office: Derby R.R. Station, Derby 06418; Tel., (203) 735-8688; FAX (203) 735-8680; E-Mail, VRPACT@SNET.NET. **Chm.,** John Erlingheuser, Ansonia; **Vice Chm.,** James Baldwin, Seymour; **Secy./ Treas.,** Charles A. Lippi, Derby; **Exec. Dir.,** Richard S. Eigen.

Participating municipalities and representatives: **ANSONIA,** John Erlingheuser, Richard D. Krueger. **DERBY,** Hazel J. Knapp, Charles A. Lippi. **SEYMOUR,** James Baldwin, George Bashura.

WINDHAM REGIONAL PLANNING AGENCY. Office: 968 Main St., Willimantic 06226; Tel., (860) 456-2221, 2222; FAX, (860) 456-1235. **Chm.,** Hallas Ridgeway, Chaplin; **Vice Chm.,** Steve Reviczky, Ashford; **Secy.,** Nancy Hammarstrom, Columbia; **Treas.,** Oliver J. Manning, Lebanon; **Member-at-Large,** Bruce Bellm, Mansfield; **Planning Dir.,** Marguerite Reich.

Participating municipalities and representatives: **ASHFORD,** Kevin McCarthy, Steve Reviczky. **CHAPLIN,** Dale Kopek, Hallas Ridgeway. **COLUMBIA,** Nancy Hammarstrom, William Peck. **COVENTRY,** Art Hall, David Sumner. **HAMPTON,** Julian Pocius, Guila Wagner. **LEBANON,** Timothy Fields, Oliver J. Manning. **MANSFIELD,** Bruce Bellm, Kay Holt. **SCOTLAND,** David Abraham, vacancy. **WILLINGTON,** Joseph W. Voboril, vacancy. **WINDHAM,** Claire Lary, vacancy.

REGIONAL RESOURCES RECOVERY AUTHORITIES

HOUSATONIC RESOURCES RECOVERY AUTHORITY (HRRA). Office: Old Town Hall, Rtes. 25 & 133, Brookfield 06804; Tel., (203) 775-6256; FAX, (203) 740-9167. **Chm.,** William T. Stuart, Bridgewater; **Dir.,** Robert Palmer.

MIDSTATE REGIONAL RESOURCE RECOVERY AUTHORITY (MRRRA). Office: P.O. Box 139, Middletown 06457; Tel., (860) 347-7214.

NORTHEASTERN CONN. REGIONAL RESOURCE RECOVERY AUTHORITY. Office: P.O. Box 198, Brooklyn 06234; Tel., (860) 774-1253. **Chm.,** R. Thomas Homan, Killingly; **Vice Chm.,** Daniel Rovero, Putnam; **Secy./Treas.,** Claire Vincent, Sterling.

Participating municipalities and representatives: **CANTERBURY,** Neil Dupont. **GRISWOLD,** Paul Brycki. **HAMPTON,** Walter Stone. **KILLINGLY,** R. Thomas Homan. **LISBON,** James D. Wright. **PLAINFIELD,** Paul E. Sweet. **POMFRET,** Stanley S. Sheldon. **PUTNAM,** Stanley S. Sheldon, Jr. **SCOTLAND,** Elizabeth Wilson. **STERLING,** Robert E. Lewis. **THOMPSON,** Barney Seney. **VOLUNTOWN,** Claire Vincent. **WOODSTOCK,** Edward Neuman.

SOUTHEASTERN CONN. REGIONAL RESOURCES RECOVERY AUTHORITY (SCRRRA). Office: 132 Military Hwy., Preston 06365; Tel., (860) 887-9643.

Participating municipalities and representatives: **EAST LYME,** Frederick Thumm. **GRISWOLD,** Paul Brycki. **GROTON,** Mick O'Beirne. **LEDYARD,** John Lawrence. **MONTVILLE,** Fannie Esidore. **NEW LONDON,** Ruby T. Morris. **NORTH STONINGTON,** David Birkbeck. **NORWICH,** Roland Trailor. **PRESTON,** Bob Congdon. **SPRAGUE,** Steven Papineau. **STONINGTON,** Jack Baker. **WATERFORD,** Edward Steward.

REGIONAL SCHOOL DISTRICTS
Sec. 10-46, Gen. Stat.
Source: Conn. Assoc. of Boards of Education

Region 1—Canaan, Cornwall, Kent, North Canaan, Salisbury, Sharon. **Bd. Members,** Frances Besmer, Allan Cockerline, Katherine Gannet, Robert Loucks, Paul Mintz, Lisa Richards, Susan Warner; **Supt.,** Marvin Maskovsky.

Region 4—Chester, Deep River, Essex. **Bd. Members,** Chris Allinson, Jacquelyn Calamari, Whitney Garlinghouse, Bruce Glowac, Allen Graham, Timothy Marth, Alice Proctor, Mariann Rossi-Ontusky, Richard Stebbins; **Supt.,** John Proctor.

Region 5—Bethany, Orange, Woodbridge. **Bd. Members,** Marcia Addil, James Cycon, John Donohue, Russell Faroni, Santo Galatioto, Clark Harris, Karen Keranen, Steven Ledewitz, Lynn Lieb, Patricia Logioco, Michael Lohme, W. Richard Lytle, M. J. McCarthy, Kenneth Mull; **Supt.,** Stephen Gordon.

Region 6—Goshen, Morris, Warren. **Bd. Members,** John Angevine, William Downes, Frances Keilty, David MacKenzie, Aimee Mason, Michael O'Neil, Ellen Prindle, Louisa Roraback, Dolores Whelan; **Supt.,** Timothy Breslin.

Region 7—Barkhamsted, Colebrook, New Hartford, Norfolk. **Bd. Members,** David Cusick, Stephen Egbertson, John Funchion, Curt Hoffman, Judith Kochey, Jean Lafave, Kay Sweeney, Jeffrey Wehner; **Supt.,** Robert Fish.

Region 8—Andover, Hebron, Marlborough. **Bd. Members,** Vincenzo Basile, Samuel Davis, Anthony Heslin, David Lenihan, Dennis Moriarity, Deborah Morocco, James Pasqurell, Jr., Richard Soranno, Michael Zebkar, Dieter Zimmer; **Supt.,** R. William Davis.

Region 9—Easton, Redding. **Bd. Members,** Ronald Anderson, Margaret Brown, Emily d'Aulaire, Larry Edwards, Eric Einstein, John Greenan, William Pond, Maria Watson, Andrew Wolff; **Supt.,** Kenneth Freeston.

Region 10—Burlington, Harwinton. **Bd. Members,** Robert Finder, David Fortin, Bruce Hunt, Mitchell Kogut, Paul Omichinski, Rose Ponte, Robert Sheriffs, Leonardi Thomas, Peter Turner; **Supt.,** Robert Goldman.

Region 11—Chaplin, Hampton, Scotland. **Bd. Members,** Lolly Beer, Jack Collins, Joan Fox, John Insalaco, Michael Jacques, Eva Loew, Richard Rivers, Lisa Stearns, Sharon Wakely; **Supt.,** A. Rodger Wutzl.

Region 12—Bridgewater, Roxbury, Washington. **Bd. Members,** Randall Carreira, Chris Combs, Honora Diebold, Reginald Fairbairn, Patrice Fitch, Jay Hubelbank, Charles Isselee, Robert Lowe, Laszlo Pinter, Nunnally Sharise, Peter Tagley, Karen Waupotic, Mary Weber; **Supt.,** Robert Nicoletti.

Region 13—Durham, Middlefield. **Bd. Members,** Robert Booz, William Currlin, Timothy Dumas, Robert Francis, Norman Hicks, Joyce Kellish, David Montgomery, Kate Thibodeau, Ty Zemelsky; **Supt.,** William Breck.

Region 14—Bethlehem, Woodbury. **Bd. Members,** Cynthia Boudreau, Vincent Bove, T. J. Brennan, John Howard, Karen Miller, David Newell, Barbara Perkinson, Joan Smith; **Supt.,** Joseph Sabatella.

Region 15—Middlebury, Southbury. **Bd. Members,** Joseph Drauss, Carolyn Falk, George Frantzis, Carol Hubert, Steven Kammerer, Hendrik Maas, Stephen Moore, Patricia Perry, Anthony Sebastiano, Joseph Zukoski; **Supt.,** Louis Esparo.

Region 16—Beacon Falls, Prospect. **Bd. Members,** Peter Christensen, Priscilla Cretella, Arthur Daigle, Jr., Lawrence Hutvagner, Stanley Pilat, Edward Scarpati, Frank Sundermeyer, Vicky Zaleski; **Supt.,** Helene Skrzyniarz.

Region 17—Haddam, Killingworth. **Bd. Members,** Robert Bilafer, Jeanetta Coley, Michael Dagostino, Robert Daves, Robert Lentz, Helen Reeve, James Sheppard, Patricia Taylor-Wolak, Ed Vynalek; **Supt.,** Charles Sweetman, Jr.

Region 18—Lyme, Old Lyme. **Bd. Members,** Elizabeth Bowman, Teri Estep, Susan Fogliano, Daniel Hagan, Elizabeth Karter, Peter Krause, Angus McDonald, Bill Wenck, Kurt Zemba; **Supt.,** Jefferson Prestridge.

Region 19—Ashford, Mansfield. **Bd. Members,** Paul Brody, Bruce Clouette, Howard Emond, Jr., Ralph McNeal, Jr., Elaine Newcomb, Judy Paesani, William Paradis, Joseph Peters, Scott Posocco, Lee Terry, Francis VanNostrand, Katherine White; **Supt.,** Bruce Silva.

REGIONAL AND MUNICIPAL TRANSIT DISTRICTS

GREATER HARTFORD TRANSIT DISTRICT. Office: One Union Place, Hartford 06103; Tel., (860) 247-5329. **Chm.,** Paul A. Ehrhardt, Simsbury; **Vice Chm.,** William D. Chiodo, Windsor; **Secy.,** James R. Boesch, Wethersfield; **Asst. Secy.,** Elsie L. Swensson, Manchester; **Treas.,** Gilbert H. Bourgoin. **Asst. Treas.,** Morton A. Elsner. **Exec. Dir.,** Arthur L. Handman.

Participating municipalities and representatives: **BLOOMFIELD,** Sydney T. Schulman. **EAST HARTFORD,** Anthony R. Gochee, William Horan. **EAST WINDSOR,**

Gilbert H. Bourgoin. **ENFIELD,** Stephen F. Mitchell, vacancy. **FARMINGTON,** Evan Cowles. **GRANBY,** Russell G. St. John. **HARTFORD,** Morton A. Elsner, Harry W. Hartie, George Payne, Jesse J. Smith. **MANCHESTER,** Whitney W. Jacobs, Elsie L. Swensson. **NEWINGTON,** Daniel Gallicchio, Walter T. McMahon. **ROCKY HILL,** Frank S. Partridge. **SIMSBURY,** Paul A. Erhardt. **SOUTH WINDSOR,** Joseph S. F. Barry. **VERNON,** Michael J. Gessay, vacancy. **WEST HARTFORD,** Louis L. Cohen, William J. Schickler. **WETHERSFIELD,** James R. Boesch, Richard L. Dobmeier. **WINDSOR,** William D. Chiodo, Rita M. Coyne.

GREATER BRIDGEPORT TRANSIT DISTRICT. Office: One Cross St., Bridgeport 06610; Tel., (203) 366-7070. **Chm.,** Walter J. Auger, Stratford; **Vice Chm.,** Mina DiSora, Bridgeport; **Secy.,** Lee Scarpetti, Trumbull; **Treas.,** Joann Dombek, Fairfield; **Gen. Mgr.,** Ronald W. Dodsworth.

Participating municipalities and representatives: **BRIDGEPORT,** Mina DiSora, John Goodwin, Raul Laffitte, Wilfred E. Murphy. **FAIRFIELD,** Joann Dombek, Louis I. Gladstone. **STRATFORD,** Walter J. Auger, Constantine Chagares. **TRUMBULL,** Ralph L. Palmesi, Lee Scarpetti.

GREATER NEW HAVEN TRANSIT DISTRICT. Office: 2319 Whitney Ave., Hamden 06518; Tel., (203) 288-6282. **Chm.,** Lee Davies, Hamden; **Vice Chm.,** Paul Bauer, West Haven; **Secy.,** Sydney Leventhal, New Haven; **Asst. Secy.,** Rhonda H. Shulman, New Haven; **Treas.,** Marjorie Bergin, North Haven; **Asst. Treas.,** Donna Carter.

Participating municipalities and representatives: **BRANFORD,** Matt Brady, vacancy. **EAST HAVEN,** Henry Luzzi, vacancy. **HAMDEN,** Lee Davies, Nancy Hurlburt. **NEW HAVEN,** John DeStefano, Ninzetter Hattie-Hayes, Sydney Leventhal, Frances Plass. **NORTH HAVEN,** Marjorie Bergin. **ORANGE,** William Fuhlbruck. **WEST HAVEN,** Paul Bauer, H. Richard Borer, Jr. **WOODBRIDGE,** Maryellen LaRocca.

HART (Housatonic Area Regional Transit.) Office: 107 Newtown Rd., Danbury 06810; Tel., (203) 744-4070. **Chm.,** Robert Hoburg, New Milford; **Vice Chm.,** Emanuel Merullo, Danbury; **Secy.,** William A. Honan, Jr., Newtown; **Treas.,** Harry Janofsky, Bethel; **Dirs.,** Sylvester Craig, Danbury; Emil Fusek, Redding; Jerry Kehoe, Ridgefield; Leonard Russell, New Fairfield; **Exec. Dir.,** Thomas Williams.

MERIDEN TRANSIT DISTRICT. Address: 22 West Main St., Meriden 06451; Tel., (203) 235-6851; FAX, (203) 630-4274; E-Mail, JOE.ZAJAC@PRODIGY.COM. **Chm.,** Eugene Munzu; **Secy.,** Vincent Mule; **Comrs.,** Debra French, John Nugent, Cynthia Szymaszek; **Admin.,** Joseph Zajac.

MIDDLETOWN TRANSIT DISTRICT. Office: 340 Main St., Middletown 06457. Tel., (860) 346-0212. **Chm.,** William C. Donahue; **Vice Chm.,** vacancy; **Secy./Treas.,** Stephen P. Shapiro; **Bd. Members,** Robert R. Gatehouse, David LeBoeuf, Salvatore Russo; **Transit Admin.,** Thomas A. Cheeseman; **Grants Admin.,** Elizabeth A. Tucker.

MILFORD TRANSIT DISTRICT. Address: 70 West River St., Milford 06460. Tel., (203) 783-3258. **Chm.,** William Mullarkey; **Secy./Treas.,** Alfred Ahrens, Jr.; **Advi-**

sory Bd., John Fleming, Leona Mitchell, John Picelli, Ralph Vanacore; **Exec. Dir.**, Henry Jadach.

NORTHWESTERN CONN. TRANSIT DISTRICT. Address: Municipal Bldg., 140 Main St., Torrington 06790. **Chm.**, Blanche McCarthy, Torrington; **Vice Chm./Treas.**, Evelyn Lukes, Torrington; **Secy.**, Gertrude O'Sullivan, Litchfield; **Exec. Dir.**, Stephen W. Dunn.

Participating municipalities and representatives: **CANAAN,** Stephen Casey. **NORFOLK,** Patrick O'Connor. **NORTH CANAAN,** Anna McGuire. **WINCHESTER,** Arleen Fecto.

NORWALK TRANSIT DISTRICT. Office: 100 Fairfield Ave., Norwalk 06854. Tel., (203) 853-3338. **Comrs.**, Andrew A. Glickson, Jerome L. Klein; **Admin.**, Louis Schulman.

SOUTHEAST AREA TRANSIT (SEAT). Mailing address: P.O. Box 787, Norwich 06360. Tel., (860) 886-2631; FAX, (860) 886-6097; Delivery address, Rte. 12 & 2A, Preston. **Chm.**, Raymond J. Botti; **Gen. Mgr.**, Thomas F. Kirker, Sr.

VALLEY TRANSIT DISTRICT. Office: 41 Main St., Derby 06418; Tel., (203) 735-6824. **Chm.**, William LaRovera, Seymour; **Vice Chm.**, George Blake, Jr., Ansonia; **Secy.**, Marcel Lajeunesse, Derby; **Treas.**, Patricia Minardi, Derby; **Exec. Dir.**, Joseph A. Ferrigno; **Operations Mgr.**, Joy Thompson.

Participating municipalities and representatives: **ANSONIA,** George Blake, Jr., James Starkey. **DERBY,** Marcel Lajeunesse, Patricia Minardi. **SEYMOUR,** William Anglace, William LaRovera. **SHELTON,** Elizabeth Doane, Walter Petz.

WESTPORT TRANSIT DISTRICT. Office: c/o Norwalk Transit District, 100 Fairfield Ave., Norwalk, 06854; Tel., (203) 226-7171, 853-3338. **Dirs.**, Morton Brod, Joseph Sledge; **Admin.**, Louis Schulman.

WINDHAM REGION TRANSIT DISTRICT. Office: 968 Main St., Willimantic 06226; Tel., (860) 456-2223. **Chm.**, Thomas J. McNally, Jr.; **Vice Chm.**, Dennison Nash; **Secy.**, Thomas King; **Treas.**, Joseph Guinan; **Admin.**, Phil Sulentich.

Participating municipalities and representatives: **ASHFORD,** Thomas King. **COLUMBIA,** Robert Broderick. **COVENTRY,** Joseph Guinan. **HAMPTON,** vacancy. **MANSFIELD,** Dennison Nash. **WINDHAM,** Thomas J. McNally, Jr.

REGIONAL WATER AUTHORITIES

SOUTH CENTRAL CONN. REGIONAL WATER AUTHORITY. Office address: 90 Sargent Dr., New Haven 06511; Tel., (203) 624-6671; FAX, (203) 562-0808. **Chm.**, G. Harold Welch, Jr.; **Vice Chm.**, Joseph A. Cermola; **Secy./Treas.**, Claire C. Bennitt; **Asst. Secy.**, Francis A. Merola, **Asst. Treas.**, Eric L. Stone.

SOUTHEASTERN CONN. WATER AUTHORITY. Office address: P.O. Box 415, Gales Ferry 06335; Tel., (860) 464-0232. **Chm.**, Robert W. Smith, Montville; **Vice Chm.**, Andrew J. Ciminera, Sr., Groton; **Treas.**, Paul Burgess, Norwich; **Members**, Michael P. Conway, Sprague; William B. Stanley, Norwich; **Secy./Gen. Mgr.**, Gregory C. Leonard, Groton.

POPULATION OF CONNECTICUT
BY COUNTIES

	1990	**1995 est.**
Fairfield	827,645	830,728
Hartford	851,783	835,589
Litchfield	174,092	179,316
Middlesex	143,196	148,030
New Haven	804,219	794,785
New London	254,957	250,404
Tolland	128,699	131,604
Windham	102,525	104,206
Total for the State	3,287,116	3,274,662

SQUARE MILES OF CONNECTICUT
BY COUNTIES

Fairfield	837.0
Hartford	750.6
Litchfield	944.6
Middlesex	439.1
New Haven	862.1
New London	771.7
Tolland	417.0
Windham	521.5
Total for the State	5,543.6

POPULATION OF TOWNS OF CONNECTICUT FROM 1800–1990

Compiled from the official returns. The census of 1790 was somewhat imperfect. Of New London county it stated: "The return from this county is so blended that the number in each town cannot be ascertained. The aggregate is 33,000." For the Litchfield County towns not returned, Hartland being at that time included, the aggregate population is estimated at 20,342. Greenwich and Stamford were included with Norwalk.

NOTE: The 1756 census figures are available in the 1949 and previous editions of the State Manual; 1774 census in the 1950 through 1960 Manuals; 1782 census in the 1960 through 1970 Manuals; 1790 census in the 1980 and previous editions. Census figures for the periods between the following years may be found in previous editions.

	Town	1800	1850	1900	1950	1990	
1	Andover		500	385	1,034	2,540	1
2	Ansonia			12,681	18,706	18,403	2
3	Ashford	2,445	1,295	757	845	3,765	3
4	Avon		995	1,302	3,171	13,937	4
5	Barkhamsted	1,437	1,524	864	946	3,369	5
6	Beacon Falls			623	2,067	5,083	6
7	Berlin	2,702	1,869	3,448	7,470	16,787	7
8	Bethany		914	517	1,318	4,608	8
9	Bethel			3,327	5,104	17,541	9
10	Bethlehem	1,138	815	576	1,015	3,071	10
11	Bloomfield		1,412	1,513	5,746	19,483	11
12	Bolton	1,452	600	457	1,279	4,575	12
13	Bozrah	934	867	799	1,154	2,297	13
14	Branford	2,156	1,423	5,706	10,944	27,603	14
15	Bridgeport		7,560	70,996	158,709	141,686	15
16	Bridgewater			649	639	1,654	16
17	Bristol	2,723	2,884	9,643	35,961	60,640	17
18	Brookfield	1,010	1,359	1,046	1,688	14,113	18
19	Brooklyn	1,202	1,514	2,358	2,652	6,681	19
20	Burlington		1,161	1,218	1,846	7,026	20
21	Canaan	2,137	2,627	820	708	1,057	21
22	Canterbury	1,812	1,669	876	1,321	4,467	22
23	Canton		1,986	2,678	3,613	8,268	23
24	Chaplin		796	529	712	2,048	24
25	Cheshire	2,288	1,626	1,989	6,295	25,684	25
26	Chester		992	1,328	1,920	3,417	26
27	Clinton		1,344	1,429	2,466	12,767	27
28	Colchester	3,163	2,468	1,991	3,007	10,980	28
29	Colebrook	1,119	1,317	684	592	1,365	29
30	Columbia		876	655	1,327	4,510	30
31	Cornwall	1,614	2,041	1,175	896	1,414	31
32	Coventry	2,021	1,984	1,632	4,043	10,063	32
33	Cromwell			2,031	4,286	12,286	33
34	Danbury	3,180	5,964	19,474	30,337	65,585	34
35	Darien		1,454	3,116	11,767	18,196	35
36	Deep River†	3,363	2,904	1,634	2,570	4,332	36
37	Derby	1,878	3,824	7,930	10,259	12,199	37
38	Durham	1,029	1,026	884	1,804	5,732	38
39	Eastford		1,127	523	598	1,314	39
40	East Granby			684	1,327	4,302	40
41	East Haddam	2,805	2,610	2,485	2,554	6,676	41
42	East Hampton*	3,295	1,525	2,271	4,000	10,428	42
43	East Hartford	3,057	2,497	6,406	29,933	50,452	43
44	East Haven	1,004	1,670	1,167	12,212	26,144	44
45	East Lyme		1,382	1,836	3,870	15,340	45
46	Easton		1,432	960	2,165	6,303	46
47	East Windsor	2,766	2,633	3,158	4,859	10,081	47
48	Ellington	1,209	1,399	1,829	3,099	11,197	48
49	Enfield	1,761	4,460	6,699	15,464	45,532	49
50	Essex		950	2,530	3,491	5,904	50

†Formerly Saybrook.
*Name changed from Chatham May 4, 1915.

POPULATION OF TOWNS OF CONNECTICUT FROM 1800–1990

	Town	1800	1850	1900	1950	1990	
51	Fairfield	3,735	3,614	4,489	30,489	53,418	51
52	Farmington	2,809	2,630	3,331	7,026	20,608	52
53	Franklin	1,210	895	546	727	1,810	53
54	Glastonbury	2,718	3,390	4,260	8,818	27,901	54
55	Goshen	1,493	1,457	835	940	2,329	55
56	Granby	2,735	2,498	1,299	2,693	9,369	56
57	Greenwich	3,047	5,036	12,172	40,835	58,441	57
58	Griswold	....	2,065	3,490	5,728	10,384	58
59	Groton	4,302	3,743	5,962	21,896	45,144	59
60	Guilford	3,597	2,653	2,785	5,092	19,848	60
61	Haddam	2,307	2,279	2,015	2,636	6,769	61
62	Hamden	1,482	2,164	4,662	29,715	52,434	62
63	Hampton	1,379	946	629	672	1,578	63
64	Hartford	5,347	13,555	79,850	177,397	139,739	64
65	Hartland	1,318	848	592	549	1,866	65
66	Harwinton	1,481	1,175	1,213	1,858	5,228	66
67	Hebron	2,256	1,345	1,016	1,320	7,079	67
68	Kent	1,607	1,848	1,220	1,392	2,918	68
69	Killingly	2,279	4,543	6,835	10,015	15,889	69
70	Killingworth	2,047	1,107	651	677	4,814	70
71	Lebanon	3,652	1,901	1,521	1,654	6,041	71
72	Ledyard	....	1,558	1,236	1,749	14,913	72
73	Lisbon	1,158	938	697	1,282	3,790	73
74	Litchfield	4,285	3,953	3,214	4,964	8,365	74
75	Lyme	4,380	2,668	750	857	1,949	75
76	Madison	....	1,837	1,518	3,078	15,485	76
77	Manchester	....	2,546	10,601	34,116	51,618	77
78	Mansfield	2,560	2,517	1,827	10,008	21,103	78
79	Marlborough	....	832	322	901	5,535	79
80	Meriden	....	3,559	28,659	44,088	59,479	80
81	Middlebury	....	763	736	3,318	6,145	81
82	Middlefield	....	....	845	1,983	3,925	82
83	Middletown	5,001	8,441	17,486	29,711	42,762	83
84	Milford	2,417	2,465	3,783	26,870	49,938	84
85	Monroe	....	1,442	1,043	2,892	16,896	85
86	Montville	2,233	1,848	2,395	4,766	16,673	86
87	Morris	....	....	535	799	2,039	87
88	Naugatuck	....	1,720	10,541	17,455	30,625	88
89	New Britain	....	3,029	28,202	73,726	75,491	89
90	New Canaan	....	2,600	2,968	8,001	17,864	90
91	New Fairfield	1,665	927	584	1,236	12,911	91
92	New Hartford	1,753	2,643	3,424	2,395	5,769	92
93	New Haven	5,157	20,345	108,027	164,443	130,474	93
94	Newington	....	....	1,041	9,110	29,208	94
95	New London	5,150	8,991	17,548	30,551	28,540	95
96	New Milford	3,221	4,508	4,804	5,799	23,629	96
97	Newtown	2,903	3,338	3,276	7,448	20,779	97
98	Norfolk	1,649	1,643	1,614	1,572	2,060	98
99	No. Branford	....	998	814	2,017	12,996	99
100	No. Canaan	....	....	1,803	2,647	3,284	100
101	North Haven	1,157	1,325	2,164	9,444	22,247	101
102	No. Stonington	....	1,936	1,240	1,367	4,884	102
103	Norwalk	5,146	4,651	19,932	49,460	78,331	103
104	Norwich	3,476	10,265	24,637	37,633	37,391	104
105	Old Lyme	....	....	1,180	2,141	6,535	105
106	Old Saybrook	....	....	1,431	2,499	9,552	106
107	Orange	....	1,476	6,995	3,032	12,830	107
108	Oxford	1,410	1,564	952	2,037	8,685	108
109	Plainfield	1,619	2,732	4,821	8,071	14,363	109
110	Plainville	....	....	2,189	9,994	17,392	110
111	Plymouth	1,791	2,568	2,828	6,771	11,822	111
112	Pomfret	1,799	1,848	1,831	2,018	3,102	112

POPULATION OF TOWNS OF CONNECTICUT FROM 1800–1990

	Town	1800	1850	1900	1950	1990	
113	Portland		2,836	3,856	5,186	8,418	113
114	Preston	3,440	1,842	2,807	1,775	5,006	114
115	Prospect		666	562	1,896	7,775	115
116	Putnam			7,348	9,304	9,031	116
117	Redding	1,632	1,754	1,426	2,037	7,927	117
118	Ridgefield	2,025	2,237	2,626	4,356	20,919	118
119	Rocky Hill		1,042	1,026	5,108	16,554	119
120	Roxbury	1,121	1,114	1,087	740	1,825	120
121	Salem		764	468	618	3,310	121
122	Salisbury	2,266	3,103	3,489	3,132	4,090	122
123	Scotland			471	513	1,215	123
124	Seymour		1,677	3,541	7,832	14,288	124
125	Sharon	2,340	2,507	1,982	1,889	2,928	125
126	Shelton*	2,792	1,301	5,572	12,694	35,418	126
127	Sherman		984	658	549	2,809	127
128	Simsbury	2,956	2,737	2,094	4,822	22,023	128
129	Somers	1,353	1,508	1,593	2,631	9,108	129
130	Southbury	1,757	1,484	1,238	3,828	15,818	130
131	Southington	1,804	2,135	5,890	13,061	38,518	131
132	So. Windsor		1,638	2,014	4,066	22,090	132
133	Sprague			1,339	2,320	3,008	133
134	Stafford	2,345	2,940	4,297	6,471	11,091	134
135	Stamford	4,352	5,000	18,839	74,293	108,056	135
136	Sterling	908	1,025	1,209	1,298	2,357	136
137	Stonington	5,437	5,431	8,540	11,801	16,919	137
138	Stratford	2,650	2,040	3,657	33,428	49,389	138
139	Suffield	2,686	2,962	3,521	4,895	11,427	139
140	Thomaston			3,300	4,896	6,947	140
141	Thompson	2,341	4,638	6,442	5,585	8,668	141
142	Tolland	1,638	1,406	1,036	1,659	11,001	142
143	Torrington	1,417	1,916	12,453	27,820	33,687	143
144	Trumbull	1,291	1,309	1,587	8,641	32,016	144
145	Union	767	728	428	261	612	145
146	Vernon		2,009	8,483	10,115	29,841	146
147	Voluntown	1,119	1,064	872	825	2,113	147
148	Wallingford	3,214	2,595	9,001	16,976	40,822	148
149	Warren	1,083	830	432	437	1,226	149
150	Washington	1,568	1,802	1,820	2,227	3,905	150
151	Waterbury	3,256	5,137	51,139	104,477	108,961	151
152	Waterford		2,259	2,904	9,100	17,930	152
153	Watertown	1,622	1,533	3,100	10,699	20,456	153
154	Westbrook		1,202	884	1,549	5,414	154
155	W. Hartford**			3,186	44,402	60,110	155
156	West Haven				32,010	54,021	156
157	Weston	2,680	1,056	840	1,988	8,648	157
158	Westport		2,651	4,017	11,667	24,410	158
159	Wethersfield	3,992	2,523	2,637	12,533	25,651	159
160	Willington	1,278	1,388	885	1,462	5,979	160
161	Wilton		2,066	1,598	4,558	15,989	161
162	Winchester	1,371	2,179	7,763	10,535	11,524	162
163	Windham	2,644	4,503	10,137	15,884	22,039	163
164	Windsor	2,773	3,294	3,614	11,833	27,817	164
165	Windsor Locks			3,062	5,221	12,358	165
166	Wolcott	948	603	581	3,553	13,700	166
167	Woodbridge	2,198	912	852	2,822	7,924	167
168	Woodbury	1,944	2,150	1,988	2,564	8,131	168
169	Woodstock	2,463	3,381	2,095	2,271	6,008	169
	Totals	250,902	370,792	908,420	2,007,280	3,287,116	

*Name changed from Huntington, April 15, 1919.
**The 4,411 credited to West Hartford in the census of 1850 apparently referred to all of the town of Hartford outside of the city limits.

POST OFFICES IN CONNECTICUT

(Source: U.S. Post Office Directory)

This list includes towns, villages and districts which have a post office of the same name.
*Multi-zoned ZIP CODE area.
†Passport applications processed.
#Contract Units are stations, branches and community post offices (CPO) operated under contract by persons who are not postal employees.

ALL POST OFFICES IN THIS STATE ARE MONEY ORDER OFFICES

Post Office, Zip Code Town

Post Office, Zip Code	Town
Abington, 06230	Pomfret
Allingtown 06516	Br. New Haven
Amston, 06231	Hebron
Andover, 06232	Andover
Ashford, 06278	Ashford
Ansonia, 06401	Ansonia
Avon, 06001	Avon
Ballouville, 06233	Killingly
Baltic, 06330	Sprague
Bantam, 06750	Litchfield
Barnum, 06605	Sta. Bridgeport
Barry Square, 06114	Sta. Hartford
Beacon Falls, 06403	Beacon Falls
Beardsley, 06606	Sta. Bridgeport
†Belden, 06852	Sta. Norwalk
Berlin, 06037	Berlin
(Br. Kensington)	
#Bethany, 06524	Br. New Haven
Bethel, 06801	Bethel
Bethlehem, 06751	Bethlehem
†Bishops Corner, 06117	West Hartford
(Br. Hartford)	
Bissell, 06074	Sta. South Windsor
Bloomfield, 06002	Bloomfield
Blue Hills, 06112	Sta. Hartford
Bolton, 06043	Bolton
(Br. Manchester 06040)	
Botsford, 06404	Newtown
Bozrah, 06334	Bozrah
Branford, 06405	Branford
Stations:	
Short Beach, 06405	
Stony Creek, 06405	
†Bridgeport, 066*	Bridgeport
Main Office, 06602	
Branch Post Offices:	
Easton, 06612	
†Stratford, 06497	
†Trumbull, 06611	
Stations:	
Barnum, 06605	
Bayview	
Beardsley, 06606	
Noble, 06608	
Bridgewater, 06752	Bridgewater
†Bristol, 06010	Bristol
(Sta. Forestville, 06010)	
Broad Brook, 06016	East Windsor
Brookfield, 06804	Brookfield
Brooklyn, 06234	Brooklyn
Buckland, 06040	Sta. Manchester
#Burlington, 06013	Burlington
(Br. Unionville)	
#Byram, 06830	Sta. Greenwich
Canaan, 06018	North Canaan
#Candlewood Isle, 06812	Sta. Danbury
Canterbury, 06331	Canterbury
Canton, 06019	Canton
Centerbrook, 06409	Essex
Canton Center, 06020	Canton
Centerville-Mt. Carmel, 06518	Hamden
(Br. New Haven)	
Central Village, 06332	Plainfield
Chaplin, 06235	Chaplin
Cheshire, 06410	Cheshire
Chester, 06412	Chester
Clinton, 06413	Clinton
Coast Guard Academy, 06320	Sta. New London
Cobalt, 06414	East Hampton
Colchester, 06415	Colchester
Colebrook, 06021	Colebrook
Collinsville, 06022	Canton
Columbia, 06237	Columbia
Conn. College, 06320	Sta. New London
Cornwall, 06753	Cornwall
Cornwall Bridge, 06754	Cornwall
(#Br. Warren, 06754)	
Cos Cob, 06807	Greenwich
Coventry, 06238	Coventry
Cromwell, 06416	Cromwell
†Danbury, 06810, 06811	Danbury
(Br. New Fairfield, 06812)	
(#Sta. Candlewood Isle, 06812	
Danielson, 06239	Killingly
Darien, 06820)	Darien
Stations:	
Noroton, 06820	
Noroton Heights, 06820	
Dayville, 06241	Killingly
Deep River, 06417	Deep River
Derby, 06418	Derby
Devon, 06460	Sta. Milford
Durham, 06422	Durham
East Berlin, 06023	Berlin
East Canaan, 06024	North Canaan
East End, 06705	Sta. Waterbury
East Glastonbury, 06025	Glastonbury
East Granby, 06026	East Granby
East Haddam, 06423	East Haddam
East Hampton, 06424	East Hampton
†East Hartford, 06108, 06118	East Hartford
East Hartland, 06027	Hartland
East Haven, 06512	East Haven
(Br. New Haven)	
East Killingly, 06243	Killingly
East Lyme, 06333	East Lyme
East Windsor, 06088	East Windsor
East Windsor Hill, 06028	South Windsor
East Woodstock, 06244	Woodstock

(613)

POST OFFICES IN CONNECTICUT

Post Office, Zip Code Town

Eastford, 06242	Eastford
Easton, 06612	Easton
(Br. Bridgeport)	
Ellington, 06029	Ellington
Elmwood, 06110	West Hartford
(Br. Hartford)	
Enfield, 06082	Enfield
Stations:	
Enfield Street, 06082	
Hazardville, 06082	
Essex, 06426	Essex
Fabyan, 06245	Thompson
Fair Haven, 06513	Sta. New Haven
†Fairfield, 06430	Fairfield
(Sta. Samp Mortar, 06430)	
Falls Village, 06031	Canaan
Farmington, 06032	Farmington
Federal Station, 06510	Sta. New Haven
Forestville, 06010	Sta. Bristol
Gales Ferry, 06335	Ledyard
(Sta. Ledyard, 06339)	
Gaylordsville, 06755	New Milford
Georgetown, 06829	Redding
Gilman, 06336	Bozrah
Glasgo, 06337	Griswold
Glastonbury, 06033	Glastonbury
Glenbrook, 06906	Sta. Stamford
†Glenville, 06831	Sta. Greenwich
Goshen, 06756	Goshen
Granby, 06035	Granby
Greens Farms, 06436	Westport
†Greenwich, 06830	Greenwich
Stations:	
†Glenville, 06831	
†West Putnam Ave., 06830	
Grosvenor Dale, 06246	Thompson
Groton, 06340	Groton
Stations:	
Groton City, 06340	
Groton Long Point, 06340	
Noank, 06340	
Submarine Base, 06349	
Groton City, 06340	Sta. Groton
#Groton Long Point, 06340	Sta. Groton
Guilford, 06437	Guilford
Haddam, 06438	Haddam
Hadlyme, 06439	Lyme
†Hamden, 06514	Hamden
(Br. New Haven)	
Hampton, 06247	Hampton
Hanover, 06350	Sprague
†Hartford, 061*	Hartford
Main Office, 06101	
Branch Post Offices:	
Bishops Corner, 06117	
East Hartford, 06108	
Elmwood, 06110	
Newington, 06111	
Old State House 06103	
Silver Lane, 06118	
West Hartford, 06107	
Stations:	
A, 06106	
Barry Square, 06114	
Blue Hills, 06112	
Unity Plaza, 06120	

Post Office, Zip Code Town

Wethersfield, 06109	
Contract Stations:	
#1, 06106	
#22, 06106	
Maple Hill, 06111	
Harwinton, 06791	Harwinton
(Br. Torrington)	
Hawleyville, 06440	Newtown
Hebron, 06248	Hebron
Higganum, 06441	Haddam
Hillside, 06610	Sta. Bridgeport
#Hotchkiss School, 06039	Sta. Lakeville
Huntington, 06484	Sta. Shelton
Ivoryton, 06442	Essex
Jewett City, 06351	Griswold
Kensington, 06037	Berlin
(Br. Berlin, 06037)	
Kent, 06757	Kent
Kilby, 06519	Sta. New Haven
#Killingworth, 06419	Br. Killingworth
(RFD Deep River)	
Lakeside, 06758	Morris
Lakeville, 06039	Salisbury
(#Sta. Hotchkiss School, 06039)	
Lebanon, 06249	Lebanon
Ledyard, 06339	Sta. Gales Ferry
Litchfield, 06759	Litchfield
Madison, 06443	Madison
(#Sta. North Madison, 06443)	
†Manchester, 06040	Manchester
(Br. Bolton, 06040)	
Broad Street, 06040	
Buckland, 06040	
Mansfield Center, 06250	Mansfield
Mansfield Depot, 06251	Mansfield
Marion, 06444	Southington
Marlborough, 06447	Marlborough
(Br. East Hampton)	
Melrose, 06049	East Windsor
†Meriden, 06450	Meriden
(Sta. A, 06450)	
Middle Haddam, 06456	East Hampton
Middlebury, 06762	Middlebury
Middlefield, 06455	Middlefield
Middletown, 06457	Middletown
Station:	
#Wesleyan, 06459	
†Milford, 06460	Milford
Stations:	
Devon, 06460	
Parcel Post, 06460	
Wildermere Beach, 06460	
Woodmont, 06460	
Milldale, 06467	Southington
Monroe, 06468	Monroe
Montville, 06353	Montville
Moodus, 06469	East Haddam
Moosup, 06354	Plainfield
Morris, 06763	Morris
Mystic, 06355	Groton and Stonington
Naugatuck, 06770	Naugatuck
(Sta. Union City, 06770)	
†New Britain, 060*	New Britain
New Canaan, 06840	New Canaan
New Fairfield, 06812	New Fairfield
New Hartford, 06057	New Hartford

POST OFFICES IN CONNECTICUT

Post Office, Zip Code	Town
†New Haven, 065*	New Haven
Main Office, 06511	
Branch Post Offices:	
#Bethany, 06524	
Centerville-Mt. Carmel, 06518	
East Haven, 06512	
†Hamden, 06514	
†West Haven, 06516	
Whitneyville, 06517	
Stations:	
Amity, 06525	
Fair Haven, 06513	
†Federal Station, 06510	
Finance Unit, 06511	
Kilby, 06519	
Westville, 06515	
Yale, 06520	
†New London, 06320	New London
Stations:	
Coast Guard Academy, 06320	
#Conn. College, 06320	
New Milford, 06776	New Milford
†Newington, 06111	Newington
(Br. Hartford)	
New Preston/Marbledale, 06777	
	Sta. Washington Depot
Newtown, 06470	Newtown
Niantic, 06357	East Lyme
Noank, 06340	Sta. Groton
Noble, 06608	Sta. Bridgeport
Norfolk, 06058	Norfolk
Noroton, 06820	Sta. Darien
Noroton Heights, 06820	Sta. Darien
North Branford, 06471	North Branford
North Canton, 06059	Canton
North Franklin, 06254	Franklin
North Granby, 06060	Granby
North Grosvenor Dale, 06255	Thompson
North Haven, 06473	North Haven
North Stonington, 06359	No. Stonington
North Windham, 06256	Windham
#Northfield, 06778	Sta. Litchfield
Northford, 06472	No. Branford
†Norwalk, 068*	Norwalk
Main Office, 06856	
Stations:	
†Belden, 06852	
Rowayton, 06853	
†South Norwalk, 06854	
Norwich, 06360	Norwich
Oakdale, 06370	Montville
Oakville, 06779	Watertown
Old Greenwich, 06870	Greenwich
Old Lyme, 06371	Old Lyme
Old Mystic, 06372	Stonington
Old Saybrook, 06475	Old Saybrook
Old State House 06103	Sta. Hartford
Oneco, 06373	Sterling
Orange, 06477	Orange
Oxford, 06478	Oxford
(#Br. Seymour)	
Parcel Post, 06460	Sta. Milford
Pawcatuck, 06379	Stonington
(#Br. Westerly, RI)	
Pequabuck, 06781	Plymouth
Pine Meadow, 06061	New Hartford
Plainfield, 06374	Plainfield
Plainville, 06062	Plainville
Plantsville, 06479	Southington
Plaza, 06704	Sta. Waterbury
Pleasant Valley, 06063	Barkhamsted
Plymouth, 06782	Plymouth
Pomfret, 06258	Pomfret
Pomfret Center, 06259	Pomfret
Poquonock, 06064	Windsor
Portland, 06480	Portland
#Preston, 06365	Br. Norwich
Prospect, 06712	Prospect
Putnam, 06260	Putnam
Quaker Hill, 06375	Waterford
Quinebaug, 06262	Thompson
Redding, 06875	Redding
Redding Ridge, 06876	Redding
Ridgefield, 06877	Ridgefield
Ridgeway, 06905	Sta. Stamford
Riverside, 06878	Greenwich
Riverton, 06065	Barkhamsted
Rockfall, 06481	Middlefield
Rockville (See Vernon-Rockville)	
Rocky Hill, 06067	Rocky Hill
Rogers, 06263	Killingly
Rowayton, 06853	Sta. Norwalk
Roxbury, 06783	Roxbury
#Salem, 06420	Salem
Salisbury, 06068	Salisbury
Samp Mortar, 06430	Sta. Fairfield
Sandy Hook, 06482	Newtown
Saugatuck, 06880	Sta. Westport
Scotland, 06264	Scotland
Seymour, 06483	Seymour
Sharon, 06069	Sharon
Shelton, 06484	Shelton
(Sta. Huntington, 06484)	
Sherman, 06784	Sherman
Short Beach, 06405	Sta. Branford
Simsbury, 06070	Simsbury
Somers, 06071	Somers
Somersville, 06072	Somers
South Britain, 06487	Southbury
South Glastonbury, 06073	Glastonbury
South Kent, 06785	Kent
South Lyme, 06376	Old Lyme
South Norwalk, 06854	Sta. Norwalk
South Willington, 06265	Willington
South Windham, 06266	Windham
South Windsor, 06074	South Windsor
(Sta. Bissell, 06074)	
South Woodstock, 06267	Woodstock
Southbury, 06488	Southbury
Southington, 06489	Southington
Southport, 06490	Fairfield
Springdale, 06907	Sta. Stamford
Stafford, 06075	Stafford
Stafford Springs, 06076	Stafford
Staffordville, 06077	Stafford
†Stamford, 069*	Stamford
Stations:	
Atlantic Street, 06904	
Glenbrook, 06906	
Ridgeway, 06905	
Springdale, 06907	
Sterling, 06377	Sterling

POST OFFICES IN CONNECTICUT

Post Office, Zip Code Town

Stevenson, 06491	Monroe
Stonington, 06378	Stonington
Stony Creek, 06405	Sta. Branford
Storrs, 06268	Mansfield
†Stratford, 06497	Stratford
Submarine Base, 06349	Sta. Groton
Suffield, 06078	Suffield
Taconic, 06079	Salisbury
Taftville, 06380	Norwich
Talcottville, 06066	Sta. Vernon
Tariffville, 06081	Simsbury
Terryville, 06786	Plymouth
Thomaston, 06787	Thomaston
Thompson, 06277	Thompson
Tolland, 06084	Tolland
Torrington, 06790	Torrington
†Trumbull, 06611	Trumbull
Turnpike, 06066	Sta. Vernon
Uncasville, 06382	Montville
Union City, 06770	Sta. Naugatuck
Unionville, 06085	Farmington
(#Br. Burlington, 06013)	
Unity Plaza, 06120	Sta. Hartford
Vernon-Rockville, 06066	Vernon
Stations:	
Talcottville, 06066	
Turnpike, 06066	
Versailles, 06383	Sprague
Voluntown, 06384	Voluntown
Wallingford, 06492	Wallingford
(Sta. Yalesville, 06492)	
Warren, 06754	Warren
(#Br. Cornwall Bridge)	
Washington Depot, 06794	Washington
Washington Green, 06793	Sta. Washington Depot
†Waterbury, 067*	Waterbury
Branch Post Offices:	
Prospect, 06712	
Wolcott, 06716	
Stations:	
East End, 06705	
Plaza, 06704	
Waterford, 06385	Waterford
Watertown, 06795	Watertown

Post Office, Zip Code Town

Wauregan, 06387	Plainfield
Weatogue, 06089	Simsbury
Wesleyan, 06459	Sta. Middletown
West Cornwall, 06796	Cornwall
West Granby, 06090	Granby
West Hartford, 061*	West Hartford
(Br. Hartford)	
West Hartland, 06091	Hartland
†West Haven, 06516	West Haven
West Mystic, 06388	Groton
†West Putnam Ave., 06830	Sta. Greenwich
West Redding, 06896	Redding
West Simsbury, 06092	Simsbury
West Suffield, 06093	Suffield
West Willington, 06279	Willington
Westbrook, 06498	Westbrook
Weston, 06883	Weston
(Br. Westport)	
Westport, 06880	Westport
(P.O. Boxes only, 06881)	
(Br. Weston, 06883)	
(Sta. Saugatuck, 06880)	
Westville, 06515	Sta. New Haven
Wethersfield, 06109	Wethersfield
(Br. Hartford)	
Whitneyville, 06517	Hamden
(Br. Hamden)	
Wildermere Beach, 06460	Sta. Milford
†Willimantic, 06226	Windham
Wilton, 06897	Wilton
Winchester Center, 06094	Winchester
Windham, 06280	Windham
†Windsor, 06095	
Windsor Locks, 06096	Windsor Locks
Winsted, 06098	Winchester
Wolcott, 06716	Wolcott
Woodbridge 06525	Sta. New Haven
Woodbury, 06798	Woodbury
Woodmont, 06460	Sta. Milford
Woodstock, 06281	Woodstock
Woodstock Valley, 06282	Woodstock
Yale, 06520	Sta. New Haven
Yalesville, 06492	Sta. Wallingford
Yantic, 06389	Norwich

---

†U.S. Passport Agency, located at 1 Landmark Sq., Stamford, 06901.
Note: For towns without post offices of the same name which do not appear in this list, see the following list.

TOWNS, VILLAGES AND DISTRICTS WITH
NO POST OFFICE OF SAME NAME

Towns, boroughs and villages in Connecticut without post offices of the same name as the given municipality are listed below. Where no numeral is appended to such an entity's name, its post office address is the same as the town in which it is located.

Stations, Villages, etc.	Town	Stations, Villages, etc.	Town
Abington 4 Corners[1]	Pomfret	Beach Pond	Voluntown
Addison	Glastonbury	Beach Street	Litchfield
Alders Bridge[2]	Killingworth	Beacon Hill	Wolcott
Aldrich Heights[3]	Plainfield	Bean Hill	Norwich
Aljen Heights	Ledyard	Bear Hill	Chaplin
Allen Hill	Brooklyn	Bear Hill	New Milford
Allentown[4]	Plymouth	Bear Swamp[2]	Killingworth
Allingtown	West Haven	Beaver Brook	Danbury
Almyville[3]	Plainfield	Beaver Meadow	Haddam
Amenia Union	Sharon	Becket Hill[20]	Lyme
Amesville[5]	Salisbury	Becketville	Danbury
Anchor Beach	Milford	Bedlam	Chaplin
Andrews Island[6]	Stonington	Bee Mountain	Oxford
Anguilla[7]	Stonington	Beebe Hill[5]	Canaan
Anguilla Acres[7]	Stonington	Bell Island[21]	Norwalk
Ashford Lake	Ashford	Bell Town	Glastonbury
Ashwillett[8]	No. Stonington	Belltown	Stamford
Aspetuck	Easton	Berkshire[22]	Newtown
Aspetuck District	New Milford	Berkshire Estates	Southbury
Aspetuck Valley[9]	Redding	Berkshires	New Milford
Attawan Beach[10]	East Lyme	Best View[18]	Waterford
Attawaugan[11]	Killingly	Bethany Wood[23]	Bethany
Atwoodville[12]	Mansfield	Between the Rivers	Old Lyme
Augerville	North Haven	Bidwell Town	Glastonbury
Avery Heights	New Milford	Bigelow	Hampton
Ayer's Gap[13]	Franklin	Bigelow[24]	Union
Ayer's Point	Old Saybrook	Bill Hill[20]	Lyme
Babcock Hill[13]	Lebanon	Birch Groves	New Milford
Baileyville[14]	Middlefield	Birch Heights[13]	Franklin
Bakersville	New Hartford	Birch Mountain	Bolton
Bald Hill	Wolcott	Black Hall	Old Lyme
Ball Pond	New Fairfield	Black Hall Pond	Old Lyme
Bangall	Stamford	Black Hill[25]	Plainfield
Banksville	Greenwich	Black Point[10]	East Lyme
Bantam Terrace[15]	Litchfield	Black Rock District[2]	Killingworth
Baptist Hill	Stafford	Blackville[26]	Washington
Barber Hill	South Windsor	Blissville[27]	Lisbon
†Barkhamsted[16]	Barkhamsted	Blueberry[7]	Stonington
Barkhamsted Center[17]	Barkhamsted	Blue Bonnett Knoll	New Milford
Barrack Mountain[5]	Canaan	Blue Hill[28]	Franklin
Barrett Hill	Brooklyn	Blue Hills	Hartford
Barrett Park	Ledyard	Bluff Point	Groton
Bartlett Point[18]	Waterford	Boardman Manor	New Milford
Bashan	East Haddam	Boardman's Bridge	New Milford
Bashan Hill[19]	Bozrah	Bogus Hill	New Fairfield
Bates Woods Park	New London	Bolton Notch	Bolton
Bayview	Milford	Bonny Brook	New Milford
Bayview Heights	Milford	Boom Bridge	No. Stonington
Beach Park	Clinton	Boulder Lake	Clinton

Post Offices—[1]Abington. [2]Killingworth, RFD Deep River. [3]Moosup. [4]Terryville. [5]Falls Village. [6]Mystic. [7]Pawcatuck. [8]Norwich. [9]Redding Ridge. [10]Niantic. [11]Dayville. [12]RFD, Mansfield Center. [13]North Franklin. [14]Rockfall. [15]Bantam. [16]Pleasant Valley. [17]New Hartford. [18]Quaker Hill. [19]Bozrah. [20]Old Lyme. [21]Rowayton. [22]Sandy Hook. [23]Bethany, New Haven 06525. [24]Stafford Springs. [25]Central Village. [26]Washington Depot. [27]Jewett City. [28]Lebanon. †Town.

(617)

Stations, Villages, etc.	Town	Stations, Villages, etc.	Town
Bowers Hill	Oxford	Candlewood Heights	New Milford
Bozrah Street[1]	Bozrah	Candlewood Hill[14]	Haddam
Bradford Hill	Plainfield	Candlewood Hills	New Fairfield
Branchville	Ridgefield	Candlewood Isle	New Fairfield
Brandy Hill	Thompson	Candlewood Knolls	New Fairfield
Branford Hills	Branford	Candlewood Lake	Danbury
Branford Point	Branford	Candlewood Lake East	Brookfield
Breakneck[2]	Union	Candlewood Lake Estates	Sherman
Bridgewater Center	Bridgewater	Candlewood Point	New Milford
Briggs Hill	Sherman	Candlewood Shores	Brookfield
Brighton Beach	Old Lyme	Candlewood Springs	New Milford
Bristol Terrace	Naugatuck	Candlewood Terrace	New Milford
Broad River	Norwalk	Candlewood Trails	New Milford
Brocketts Point	Branford	Cannondale	Wilton
Brockway's Ferry[3]	Lyme	Canterbury Green	Canterbury
Bromica[4]	Kent	Canterbury Plains	Canterbury
Brookfield Junction[5]	Brookfield	Canton Village	Canton
Brooklyn Center	Brooklyn	Caritas Island	Stamford
Brookrun	New Milford	Carmel Hill	Bethlehem
Brookside[6]	Stonington	Carmel Hill	Woodbury
Brooksvale	Cheshire	Carney's Crossing	Danbury
Brush Hill[1]	Bozrah	Case District	Burlington
Brush Hill[7]	Lyme	Castle Hill[6]	Stonington
Brush Island[8]	Darien	Cat Swamp	Woodbury
Brushy Plain	Branford	Cedar Beach	Milford
Buckingham	Glastonbury	Cedar Hill	Hartford
Bucks Corners	Glastonbury	Cedar Knolls	New Milford
Bull's Bridge[4]	Kent	Cedar Lake	Bristol
Bull's Head	Stamford	Cedar Lake	Chester
Bundy Hill	Lisbon	Cedar Lake	Wolcott
Bungay	Seymour	Cedar Land	Southbury
Bunker Hill[9]	Killingworth	Cedar Lane	Oxford
Burlington Center	Burlington	Cedar Ridge	No. Stonington
Burlington Station	Burlington	Cedar Ridge District	Seymour
Burnetts Corner	Groton	Cedar Swamp[9]	Killingworth
Burr Hill[9]	Killingworth	Cedarland	Southbury
Burrville	Torrington	Cemetery Road[15]	Plainfield
Burtville	Derby	Center	Harwinton
Burwells Beach	Milford	Center District[9]	Killingworth
Bush Hill	Brooklyn	Center District	Trumbull
Bush Hill	Lebanon	Center District[2]	Union
Butler's Island	Darien	Center Groton	Groton
Calhoun Street[10]	Washington	Center Hill[16]	Barkhamsted
Calkinstown	Sharon	Centerville	Hamden
Cambridge Estates	Norwich	Chaffeeville[17]	Mansfield
Camelot Estates	New Milford	Chalker Beach	Old Saybrook
Camp Aquila	Sherman	Chalybes	Roxbury
Campbell's Mills	Voluntown	Chapel Hill[18]	Montville
Camptown	Derby	Chaplin Center	Chaplin
Campville	Harwinton	Chapman Beach	Westbrook
Campville[11]	Litchfield	Charter Oak	Oxford
†Canaan[12]	Canaan	Charter Oak Terrace	Hartford
Canaan Mountain[12]	Canaan	Chase Manor	Norwich
Canaan Valley[13]	North Canaan	Cherry Brook[19]	Canton
Canaan Village	North Canaan	Cherry Hill	Branford
Candleset Cove	New Milford	Cherry Hill[20]	Cornwall

Post offices—[1]Bozrah. [2]Stafford Springs. [3]Old Lyme. [4]South Kent. [5]Brookfield Center. [6]Pawcatuck. [7]Hadlyme. [8]Noroton. [9]Killingworth, RFD Deep River. [10]Washington Depot. [11]Northfield. [12]Falls Village. [13]RFD, East Canaan. [14]Higganum. [15]Central Village. [16]New Hartford. [17]Storrs. [18]Oakdale. [19]Canton Center. [20]West Cornwall. †Town.

TOWNS, VILLAGES AND DISTRICTS

Stations, Villages, etc.	Town	Stations, Villages, etc.	Town
Cherry Hill	Norwich	Crescent Beach[16]	East Lyme
Cheshire Heights	Cheshire	Crescent Lake	Enfield
Chesterfield[1]	Montville	Crestwood	New Milford
Chestnut Hill	Columbia	Crocker Hill[17]	Franklin
Chestnut Hill[2]	Killingly	Cross Brook	Roxbury
Chestnut Hill	Lebanon	Crow Hill	Stafford
Chestnut Hill	Litchfield	Crystal Lake	Ellington
Chestnut Hill	Mansfield	Cummings Point	Stamford
Chestnut Hill[3]	Killingworth	Daleville[18]	Willington
Chestnut Hill District[4]	Oxford	Danbury Quarter[19]	Winchester
Chestnut Hill Manor	New Milford	Dart Hill	South Windsor
Chestnut Land	Oxford	Davenport Point	Stamford
Chestnut Tree Hill	Chaplin	Davis District	Stafford
Chewink	Greenwich	Dean Heights	New Milford
Chickahominy	Bristol	Dean Mills	Stonington
Chippens Hill	Burlington	Deer Island[20]	Morris
Chippens Hill	Ledyard	Deer Run Shores	Sherman
Christy Hill Estates[5]	Southbury	Deerfield	Windsor
Churaevka Village	Washington	Derby Neck	Derby
Church Hill[6]	Ellington	Devil's Backbone	Bethlehem
Cider Mill Heights	Branford	Devil's Den	Weston
Clam Island	New Canaan	Devil's Hopyard	East Haddam
Clapboard Hill	No. Stonington	Devonshire Estates[5]	Ledyard
Clark Falls	Hampton	Diamond Hill[21]	Redding
Clarks Corner[7]	Stonington	Diamond Lake	Glastonbury
Clarksville[8]	Seymour	Dibble Hill11	Cornwall
Clifton	Clinton	Doaneville[22]	Griswold
Clinton Beach	North Haven	Dobsonville	Vernon
Clintonville	Sherman	Dodgingtown	Newtown
Coburn	Waterford	Dogwood Knoll[4]	Killingworth
Cohanzie[9]	Stafford	Double Beach	Branford
Colburn Hill	Ledyard	Dowd's Corner	Canton
Colonial Manor	Norwalk	Downerville[8]	Stonington
Comstock Hill	East Hampton	Drakeville	Torrington
Comstock's Bridge	Mansfield	Duck Hole	Clinton
Conantville[3]	Darien	Dudleytown[23]	Cornwall
Contentment Island	Cheshire	Dufree Hill	Waterford
Cook Hill	Lebanon	Eagleville[24]	Mansfield
Cook Hill[10]	Franklin	East Bristol	Bristol
Cooley Hill[11]	Stafford	East Brooklyn[25]	Brooklyn
Cooper Lane	Cheshire	East Chestnut Hill	Litchfield
Copper Valley	Westbrook	East Cornwall[26]	Cornwall
Coral Sands	Lebanon	East Derby	Derby
Coreyville	Old Saybrook	East District[27]	Union
Cornfield Point	Cornwall	East Great Plain	Norwich
Cornwall Center[12]	Cornwall	East Haddam Landing	East Haddam
Cornwall Hollow[13]	Cornwall	East Hill	Canton
Cornwall Plains	New Hartford	East Iron Works	Brookfield
Cotton Hill	Glastonbury	East Kent[28]	Kent
Cotton Hollow[14]	Stamford	East Litchfield	Litchfield
Cove Island	Clinton	East Morris	Morris
Cow Hill	Killingworth	East Neck	Waterford
Cow Pen Hill[4]	Norwalk	East Norwalk	Norwalk
Cranbury	Bethlehem	East Plymouth[29]	Plymouth
Crane Hollow	Plainfield	East Putnam	Putnam
Cranska Village[15]	Ledyard	East River	Madison
Cranwood Homestead	Cornwall	East Stanwich	Greenwich
Cream Hill[12]			

Post offices—[1]Oakdale. [2]RFD, Dayville. [3]Willimantic. [4]Killingworth, RFD Deep River. [5]Gales Ferry. [6]Washington Depot. [7]North Windham. [8]Pawcatuck. [9]Quaker Hill. [10]Lebanon and Columbia. [11]North Franklin. [12]West Cornwall. [13]Falls Village. [14]South Glastonbury. [15]Moosup. [16]Niantic. [17]Lebanon. [18]West Willington. [19]Winsted. [20]Lakeside. [21]West Redding. [22]Jewett City. [23]Cornwall Bridge. [24]Storrs. [25]RFD, Danielson. [26]Litchfield. [27]Woodstock Valley. [28]South Kent. [29]Terryville.

TOWNS, VILLAGES AND DISTRICTS

Stations, Villages, etc.	Town
East Thompson	Thompson
East Village	Monroe
East Willington[1]	Willington
Eastbury	Glastonbury
Eastern Point	Groton
Eastview Acres	Oxford
Edge Lea[2]	Old Lyme
Edgewood	Bristol
Ekonk[3]	Sterling
Ekonk Hill	Voluntown
Elliott[4]	Pomfret
Ellithorpe's Crossing	Stafford
Ellsworth	Sharon
Elm Hill	Newington
Elmville[5]	Killingly
Elmwood	Bethel
Elys Ferry[6]	Lyme
English Neighborhood	Woodstock
Equivalent[7]	Ellington
Esker Point	Groton
Essex Harbor	Essex
Ettadore Park	Milford
Ethel Acres[8]	Lisbon
Exeter	Lebanon
Fairy Lake[9]	Salem
Fall Mountain	Bristol
Fall Mountain Lake Dist.[10]	Plymouth
Far View Beach	Milford
Farmington Village	Farmington
Fenwick	Old Saybrook
Fenwood	Old Saybrook
Ferriss Estates	New Milford
Ferry Point	Old Saybrook
Ferry Road	Old Lyme
Ferry View Heights[11]	Ledyard
Fitchville	Bozrah
Five Mile River[12]	Norwalk
Flag Swamp	Roxbury
Flanders	Kent
Flanders	Woodbury
Flanders Nature Center	Woodbury
Flanders Village	East Lyme
Flat Rock	Plainfield
Flat Rock Hill	Old Lyme
Flat Rocks[13]	Kent
Flax Hill	Norwalk
Floral Park	Old Saybrook
Fog Plain	Waterford
Forest Glen	Old Saybrook
Forge Hollow	Litchfield
Fort Hill	Groton
Fort Hill	New Milford
Fort Trumbull	New London
Fort Trumbull Beach	Milford
Foundry[14]	Redding
Four Mile River	Old Lyme
Foxon	East Haven
Foxtown	East Haddam
Fox Village	Killingworth
†Franklin[15]	Franklin
Franklin Hill[15]	Franklin
Franklin Square	Norwich
Frog Hollow	Ellington
Furnace Hollow	Stafford
Gallows Hill[16]	Redding
Garden City	Seymour
Gardner Lake[17]	Bozrah
Gardner Lake[17]	Salem
Gary District	Putnam
Gayhead	Canterbury
Geer Mountain[13]	Kent
Georgetown[18]	††
Germantown	Danbury
Giants Neck Beach[19]	East Lyme
Giants Neck Heights[19]	East Lyme
Gilbert Corners	Litchfield
Gildersleeve	Portland
Gilead	Waterford
Glass Factory[1]	Willington
Glen[16]	Redding
Glendale Park	Stamford
Glenwood Park	New London
Glenwoods[11]	Ledyard
Glynville	Stafford
Golden Spur[20]	East Lyme
Golds Mill[21]	Cornwall
Good Hill	Kent
Good Hill	Oxford
Good Hill	Roxbury
Good Hill	Woodbury
Goodsell Point	Branford
Goodyear[22]	Killingly
Goshen	Waterford
Goshen Hill	Lebanon
Goshen Road[23]	Plainfield
Governor's Hill	Oxford
Graham Terrace[8]	Lisbon
Grand View Park	Stonington
Granite Bay	Branford
Graniteville	Waterford
Grasmere	Fairfield
Grassy Hill[6]	Lyme
Grassy Hill	Woodbury
Grassy Plain	Bethel
Great Hammock	Old Saybrook
Great Hill[24]	Cornwall
Great Hill	Oxford
Great Hill	Seymour
Great Hill Lake	Portland
Great Neck	Waterford
Great Plain	Danbury
Green Hollow Road[23]	Plainfield
Green Manorville	Enfield
Green Pond	Sherman
Greenacres[25]	North Canaan
Greenfield Hill	Fairfield

Post offices—[1]West Willington. [2]South Lyme. [3]RFD, Moosup. [4]Pomfret Center. [5]RFD, Danielson. [6]Old Lyme. [7]Stafford. [8]Jewett City. [9]Oakdale. [10]Terryville. [11]Gales Ferry. [12]Rowayton. [13]South Kent. [14]Redding Ridge. [15]North Franklin. [16]West Redding. [17]Colchester. [18]Georgetown 06829. [19]Niantic. [20]East Lyme. [21]West Cornwall. [22]Rogers. [23]Moosup. [24]Litchfield. [25]RFD, Canaan. †Town. ††Towns of Redding, Ridgefield, Weston, Wilton.

TOWNS, VILLAGES AND DISTRICTS

Stations, Villages, etc.	Town	Stations, Villages, etc.	Town
Greenhaven Shores[1]	Stonington	Hemlock Heights[15]	Killingworth
Greenmanville[2]	Stonington	Heritage Circle	Southbury
Green's Harbor Beach	New London	Heritage Crest	Southbury
Greenville	Norwich	Heritage Village	Southbury
Greystone	Plymouth	Hidden Lake[16]	Haddam
†Griswold[3]	Griswold	High Island[17]	Branford
Griswold Point	Old Lyme	High Ridge	Stamford
Griswoldville	Wethersfield	Highland	Middletown
Groton Heights	Groton	Highland Park	Manchester
Grove Beach	Clinton	Highlands	Ledyard
Grove Beach	Westbrook	Highwood	Hamden
Grove Beach Manor	Clinton	Hill and Plain	New Milford
Grove Beach Point	Westbrook	Hilliardville	Manchester
Grove Beach Terrace	Westbrook	Hilltop View	New Milford
Guernsey Hill	Litchfield	Hillyview Drive	New Fairfield
Guilds Hollow	Bethlehem	Hinckley Hill[1]	Stonington
Guilford Lakes	Guilford	Hitchcock Lakes	Wolcott
Gulf Beach	Milford	Hogs Back	Oxford
Gungy[4]	Lyme	Holcomb Hill	New Hartford
Gurleyville[5]	Mansfield	Holiday Point	Sherman
Haddam Neck[6]	Haddam	Holly Hill[13]	Montville
Hall	Stafford	Holt District	Plymouth
Hall Meadow[7]	Goshen	Homestead Circle	Old Lyme
Hall Meadow	Torrington	Hop River	Columbia
Hall's Corners	Old Lyme	Hopeville[3]	Griswold
Hallville[8]	Preston	Hopewell[18]	Glastonbury
Hamburg[4]	Lyme	Horse Hill	Westbrook
Hammonasset	Madison	Horse Pond[19]	Salem
Hampton Springs	Hampton	Hotchkiss Grove	Branford
Hanks Hill[5]	Mansfield	Hotchkissville	Woodbury
Harbor View	Clinton	Howard Valley	Hampton
Harbor View	Norwalk	Huckleberry Hill	Brookfield
Hard Hill	Bethlehem	Hull[20]	Redding
Harris[9]	Salem	Hull's Hill	Oxford
Harris Lake[9]	Salem	Hunt	New Milford
Harris Plains	Litchfield	Hunters Mountain	Oxford
Harrisons Landing[10]	Waterford	Hunting Ridge	Stamford
Harrisville	Woodstock	Huntingtown	Newtown
Hart Hollow	Torrington	Huntsville[21]	Canaan
Hartford Turnpike	Vernon	Hurd Park	East Hampton
†Hartland[11]	Hartland	Hyde	Canterbury
Hat Shop Hill	Bridgewater	Hyde Park	Stafford
Hatchetts Point[12]	Old Lyme	Hyde's Corner[22]	Franklin
Hattertown	Newtown	Hydeville	Stafford
Haughton Cove[13]	Montville	Indian Cove	Guilford
Haughton Park[13]	Montville	Indian Hill	Orange
Haviland Heights	New Milford	Indian Hills	Naugatuck
Hawk's Nest Beach	Old Lyme	Indian Neck	Branford
Hay Island[14]	Darien	Indian Ridge	New Milford
Haycock Point	Branford	Indian Springs[15]	Killingworth
Hayden Station	Windsor	Indian Town[23]	No. Stonington
Hayestown	Danbury	Indian Town	Old Saybrook
Haywardville[9]	East Haddam	Inglenook Development	New Fairfield
Hazel Plain	Woodbury	Iron Works	Brookfield
Head of Meadow	Newtown	Island View	Westbrook
Headquarters	Litchfield	Ives Corner	Cheshire

Post offices—[1]Pawcatuck. [2]Mystic. [3]Jewett City. [4]Old Lyme. [5]Storrs. [6]East Hampton. [7]Norfolk. [8]Norwich. [9]Colchester. [10]Quaker Hill. [11]East Hartland. [12]South Lyme. [13]Uncasville. [14]Noroton. [15]Killingworth, RFD Deep River. [16]Higganum. [17]Stony Creek. [18]South Glastonbury. [19]Oakdale. [20]West Redding. [21]Falls Village. [22]North Franklin. [23]RFD 7, Ledyard. †Town.

TOWNS, VILLAGES AND DISTRICTS

Stations, Villages, etc.	Town
Jacks Hill	Oxford
Jackson's Cove	Oxford
Jepson Island[1]	Branford
Job's Hill	Ellington
Job's Pond	Portland
Johnny Cake	Burlington
Johnnycake Hill	Old Lyme
Johnson Hollow[2]	Cornwall
Johnson's Point	Branford
Johnsonville[3]	East Haddam
John Tom Hill	Glastonbury
Jordan Village	Waterford
Joshuatown[4]	Lyme
Joyce Hill	New Fairfield
Judd's Bridge	Roxbury
Jupiter Point	Groton
Kasson Grove	Bethlehem
Keefe Plains[5]	Stafford
Kelsey Point	Westbrook
Kelseytown	Clinton
Kennedy City[6]	Plainfield
Kennedy Heights	Norwich
Kenosia	Danbury
Kent Furnace	Kent
Kent Hollow	Kent
Kent Hollow	New Milford
Kenyonville[7]	Woodstock
Kettletown	Southbury
Kick Hill	Lebanon
Kidd's Island[1]	Branford
Killam's Point	Branford
†Killingly[8]	Killingly
Killingly Center[9]	Killingly
†Killingworth[10]	Killingworth
Kingswood	No. Stonington
Kinney Hollow[5]	Union
Kishwaukee[11]	Plainfield
Kitemaug[12]	Montville
Knollcrest	Norwich
Knollwood	Ellington
Knollwood Beach	Old Saybrook
Lake Beseck	Middlefield
Lake Bonair	Ellington
Lake Chaffee[5]	Ashford
Lake Compounce	Bristol
Lake Garda	Burlington
Lake Harwinton	Harwinton
Lake Hayward[13]	East Haddam
Lake Lillinonah District	Bridgewater
Lake Plymouth District	Plymouth
Lake Stafford	Stafford
Lake's Pond	Waterford
Lakeside	Ledyard
Lakeside	Southbury
Lakeview	Avon
Land O'Pines[14]	Stafford
Lands End	Newtown
Lane District[10]	Killingworth

Stations, Villages, etc.	Town
Lanesville	New Milford
Lamphier's Cove	Branford
Lantern Hill	Ledyard
Laurel Beach	Milford
Laurel Glen	No. Stonington
Laurel Hill	Norwich
Laurel Hill	Sherman
Laurel Park	Norwich
Lavelle Avenue	New Fairfield
Laysville	Old Lyme
Leach Hollow	Sherman
Ledward Island	Stonington
Ledyard Center	Ledyard
Ledyard Village	Ledyard
Leesville[3]	East Haddam
Leffingwell[15]	Bozrah
Leffingwell[12]	Montville
Leonard Bridge[16]	Lebanon
Liberty Hill	Lebanon
Lillibridge Road	Plainfield
Limekiln[17]	Redding
Lime Rock[18]	Salisbury
Lime Rock Station[19]	Canaan
Lisbon Heights	Lisbon
Little Boston[17]	Redding
Little Haddam	East Haddam
Little Pumpkin Island[1]	Branford
Little Standard Beach	Westbrook
Little Valley	Norwich
Little York[17]	Redding
Lochwood	Clinton
Lockwoods Corners	Stamford
Logger Hill	Waterford
Lone Oak	New Milford
Lonetown[17]	Redding
Long Hill	South Windsor
Long Hill District	Trumbull
Long Meadow Hill	Brookfield
Long Mountain	New Milford
Long Neck Point[20]	Darien
Long Pond	Ledyard
Long Ridge	Danbury
Long Ridge	Stamford
Long Society[15]	Preston
Longview[21]	Ellington
Lord Hill[4]	Lyme
Lord's Point	Stonington
Lordship	Stratford
Lost Acres[22]	Granby
Lower City[19]	Canaan
Lower Merryall	New Milford
Lower Pawcatuck[23]	Stonington
Lydallville	Manchester
†Lyme[4]	Lyme
Lyons Plains	Weston
Macedonia	Kent
Magnolia Hill	Bethlehem
Mago Point	Waterford

Post Offices—[1]Stony Creek. [2]West Cornwall. [3]Moodus. [4]Old Lyme. [5]Stafford Springs. [6]Central Village. [7]Woodstock Valley. [8]Danielson. [9]Dayville. [10]Killingworth, RFD Deep River. [11]Moosup. [12]Uncasville. [13]Colchester. [14]Staffordville. [15]Norwich. [16]Lebanon and Columbia. [17]West Redding. [18]RFD, Lakeville. [19]Falls Village. [20]Noroton. [21]Rockville. [22]North Granby. [23]Pawcatuck. †Town.

TOWNS, VILLAGES AND DISTRICTS

Stations, Villages, etc.	Town	Stations, Villages, etc.	Town
Magonk	Waterford	Mohegan[6]	Montville
Mallett District	Bridgewater	Momauguin	East Haven
Manchester Green	Manchester	Money Island[12]	Branford
Manresa Island	Norwalk	Montowese,	North Haven
†Mansfield[1]	Mansfield	Montville Center[13]	Montville
Mansfield City[1]	Mansfield	Montville Manor[13]	Montville
Mansfield 4 Corners[1]	Mansfield	Moodus Estates[14]	East Haddam
Mansfield Hollow[2]	Mansfield	Moodus Lake Shores	East Haddam
Maple Hill	Newington	Mooreville[10]	Winchester
Maple Hollow	New Hartford	Moose Hill	Oxford
Marne Park[3]	Litchfield	Moose Meadow[15]	Willington
Mashapaug[4]	Union	Moosehorn	Roxbury
Mason Hill	Lebanon	Morningside	Milford
Mason's Island[5]	Stonington	Morningside Park	Waterford
Massapeag[6]	Montville	Morris Cove	New Haven
Matson Hill[7]	Glastonbury	Moss Farm	Cheshire
Mauweehoo Hill	Sherman	Mount Woodbury	Woodbury
Meadow Ridge	New Milford	Mountain Lake[11]	Salem
Meadow Wood	No. Stonington	Mountain View Terrace	New Milford
Meadowbrook	New Milford	Mt. Archer[16]	Lyme
Meadowbrook	Oxford	Mt. Carmel	Hamden
Mechanicsville	Granby	Mt. Hope[2]	Mansfield
Mechanicsville	Thompson	Mt. Tobe	Plymouth
Meeting House Hill[8]	Franklin	Mth. of Scantic	South Windsor
Melrose Park	Norwich	Mullen Hill	Waterford
Merryall	New Milford	Mumford Cove	Groton
Merwin's Beach	Milford	Munger Lane	Bethlehem
Merwin's Point	Milford	Music Mountain[17]	Canaan
Merwinsville	New Milford	Music Vale[11]	Salem
Meshomasic	Portland	Myrtle Beach	Milford
Meshomasick Forest	East Hampton	Mystic Island[5]	Stonington
Miami Beach	Old Lyme	Nash Island[18]	Darien
Mianus[9]	Greenwich	Natchaug	Chaplin
Middle Beach	Westbrook	Naubuc	Glastonbury
Middle Gate	Newtown	Naugatuck Gardens	Milford
Middle Quarter	Woodbury	Nayaug[7]	Glastonbury
Middle River	Danbury	Neck Road	Old Lyme
Middlefield Center	Middlefield	Nepaug	New Hartford
Mile Creek	Old Lyme	Nettleton Hollow	Washington
Milford Point	Milford	New City	Stafford
Mill Brook[10]	Colebrook	New Hartford Center	New Hartford
Mill District	Clinton	New Milford Heights	New Milford
Mill Plain	Danbury	New Preston Hills[19]	Washington
Millington	East Haddam	New Preston/Marbledale Sta.[20]	Washington
Millstone	Waterford	New Sweden	Woodstock
Millstone Ridge	New Milford	New Village	Plainfield
Millville	Naugatuck	Newbury Corners	Torrington
Milton	Litchfield	Newent	Lisbon
Mine Hill	New Milford	Newfield	Middletown
Mine Hill	Roxbury	Newfield	Stamford
Minnie Island[11]	Salem	Newfield	Torrington
Minortown	Woodbury	Newhalville	New Haven
Miry Brook	Danbury	Newington Park	Newington
Mitchell's Woods	New London	Newtown Borough	Newtown
Mitchelltown	Sharon	Niantic Village[21]	East Lyme
Mixville	Cheshire	Nichols Village District	Trumbull
Mohawk Tower	Cornwall	Ninevah Falls[22]	Killingworth

Post offices—[1]Storrs. [2]Mansfield Center. [3]Bantam. [4]Southbridge, MA 01550. [5]Mystic. [6]Uncasville. [7]South Glastonbury. [8]North Franklin. [9]Cos Cob. [10]Winsted. [11]Colchester. [12]Stony Creek. [13]Oakdale. [14]Moodus. [15]West Willington. [16]Old Lyme. [17]Falls Village. [18]Noroton. [19]New Preston. [20]Washington Depot. [21]Niantic. [22]Killingworth, RFD Deep River. †Town.

TOWNS, VILLAGES AND DISTRICTS

Stations, Villages, etc.	Town
Nipsic	Glastonbury
Nonnewaug	Woodbury
Nonnewaug Falls	Bethlehem
Nordon Village	Norwich
Norfield	Weston
Noroton Bay[2]	Darien
Noroton Knoll[3]	Darien
Noroton Manor[2]	Darien
North Ashford[4]	Eastford
North Bigelow	Hampton
North Bloomfield	Bloomfield
†North Canaan[5]	North Canaan
North Colebrook	Colebrook
North Cornwall[6]	Cornwall
North End	Sherman
North Goshen	Goshen
North Guilford	Guilford
North Kent	Kent
North Lyme[8]	Lyme
North Madison	Madison
North Mianus[9]	Greenwich
North Newington	Newington
North Park Avenue[10]	Redding
North Plains[8]	East Haddam
North Society	Canterbury
North Somers	Somers
North Stamford	Stamford
North Sterling	Sterling
North Thompsonville	Enfield
North Wilton	Wilton
North Woodbury	Woodbury
North Woodstock[11]	Woodstock
Northeast	Newington
Northville	New Milford
Northwest Corner[12]	No. Stonington
Norwich Falls	Norwich
Norwichtown	Norwich
Oak Grove Beach[13]	East Lyme
Oak Hill Estates	Oxford
Oak Hill Gardens[14]	Stonington
Oakdale Heights[15]	Montville
Oakdale Manor	Southbury
Oakland	Manchester
Oakland Gardens	Farmington
Oakland Heights	Norwich
Oakwood Knoll	Norwich
Obtuse[16]	Brookfield
Occum	Norwich
Ocean Beach Park	New London
Oenoke Ridge	New Canaan
Ogden's Corner	Vernon
Old Black Point[13]	East Lyme
Old Colony Beach	Old Lyme
Old Hamburg[8]	Lyme
Old Harbor Village	Clinton
Old Lyme Estates	Old Lyme
Old Lyme Shores	Old Lyme

Stations, Villages, etc.	Town
Old Mine Hill[1]	Killingworth
Old Mystic	Groton
Old Quarry	Guilford
Old Village	Plainfield
Old Wethersfield	Wethersfield
Olde Mistick Village[17]	Stonington
Orchard Village	Wethersfield
Orcutville	Stafford
Ore Hill[18]	Kent
Ore Hill[19]	Salisbury
Orford Village	Manchester
Oronoque	Stratford
Oswegatchie	Waterford
Otter Cove	Old Saybrook
Overbrook	Stamford
Ox Hill	Norwich
Oxecosset	Stonington
Oxford Airport District	Oxford
Oxoboxo Lake[15]	Montville
Oyster River	Old Saybrook
Pachaug[20]	Griswold
Packerville	Canterbury
Padanaram	Danbury
Paddy Hollows	Bethlehem
Painter Hill	Roxbury
Palestine	Newtown
Palmertown	Montville
Palomino Estates	New Milford
Paradise Green	Stratford
Park Lane	New Milford
Park Lane Acres	New Milford
Parker Hill[1]	Killingworth
Parker Village	Manchester
Parker's Point	Chester
Parkville	Hartford
Parsonage Hill Manor	Ledyard
Patten	Stafford
Pautipaug[21]	Franklin
Pawson Park	Branford
Pea Hill[1]	Killingworth
Pecausett	Portland
Peck Hollow[21]	Franklin
Pemberwick[7]	Greenwich
Pembroke	Danbury
Pendleton Hill	No. Stonington
Pendleton Hill[22]	Voluntown
Penfield Hill	Portland
Pepper Box Road	Waterford
Pequotsepos[17]	Stonington
Pheasant Run[23]	Ledyard
Phoenixville[24]	Eastford
Pickett District	New Milford
Pickett Road	Plainfield
Pickett's Ridge[25]	Redding
Pillsbury Hill[26]	Vernon
Pilot's Point	Westbrook
Pine Grove[27]	Canaan

Post offices—[1]Killingworth, RFD Deep River. [2]Noroton. [3]Noroton Heights. [4]Woodstock Valley. [5]Canaan. [6]West Cornwall. [7]Riverside. [8]Old Lyme. [9]Cos Cob. [10]Easton. [11]East Woodstock. [12]Norwich. [13]Niantic. [14]Pawcatuck. [15]Oakdale. [16]Brookfield Center. [17]Mystic. [18]South Kent. [19]Lakeville. [20]Jewett City. [21]North Franklin. [22]North Stonington. [23]Gales Ferry. [24]Chaplin. [25]West Redding. [26]Rockville. [27]Falls Village. †Town.

Stations, Villages, etc.	Town	Stations, Villages, etc.	Town
Pine Grove[1]	East Lyme	Pumpkin Hill	New Milford
Pine Orchard	Branford	Putnam Heights	Putnam
Pine Orchard District[2]	Killingworth	Putnam Park[20]	Redding
Pine Point[3]	Norwalk	Putney	Stratford
Pine Rock Park	Shelton	Pyquag Village	Wethersfield
Pines Bridge	Beacon Falls	Quaddick	Thompson
Pineville[4]	Killingly	Quaker Farms	Oxford
Pinney Hill	Stafford	Quaker Ridge[21]	Greenwich
Pisgah Mountain	Oxford	Quaker Ridge	Sherman
Plain Hill	Norwich	Quaker Town	Ledyard
Pleasant Valley[5]	Lyme	Quaketaug Hill[22]	Stonington
Pleasant Valley[6]	Mansfield	Quarryville	Bolton
Pleasant Valley	South Windsor	Quassapaug	Woodbury
Pleasant View	New Milford	Quiambaug[23]	Stonington
Pleasant View Heights	Norwich	Quinnipiac	North Haven
Pleasure Beach	Waterford	Quotonset Beach	Westbrook
Pleasure Hill[7]	Franklin	Rainbow	Windsor
Pleasure Valley[8]	Norwich	Raleigh Estates	New Milford
Plum Bank	Old Saybrook	Ram Island	Stonington
Plumtrees	Bethel	Rathbun Hill[10]	Salem
Pocotopaug Lake[9]	East Hampton	Ratlum[24]	Barkhamsted
Podunk	South Windsor	Ratlum[24]	Canton
Pogwank[10]	Salem	Rattle Snake Ledge[10]	Salem
Point Lookout	Milford	Raymond Hill[25]	Montville
Point O'Woods[11]	Old Lyme	Red City	Oxford
Pointina	Westbrook	Red-White District	Woodstock
Pokono Ridge[12]	Brookfield	Rhodesville	Putnam
Pomfret Landing	Pomfret	Ridge[26]	Redding
Pomperaug	Woodbury	Ridge Acres	Darien
Pond Hill Road	Naugatuck	Ridgebury	Danbury
Pond Hill Road[13]	Plainfield	Ridgebury	Ridgefield
Pond Meadow[2]	Killingworth	Ridgewood	Clinton
Pond Meadow	Westbrook	Ridgewood Park	Waterford
Pond Place	Avon	Rippowam Village	Stamford
Pond Point Beach	Milford	Riverbank	Stamford
Ponset[14]	Haddam	Rivercliff[27]	Milford
Ponus Ridge	New Canaan	Riverside	Burlington
Poquetanuck[15]	Preston	Riverside[28]	Norwich
Poquonock Bridge	Groton	Riverside[29]	Newtown
Porter Hill	Bethlehem	Riverside	Oxford
Porter Plains	Thompson	Riverside	Clinton
Potato Island[16]	Branford	Riverside Beach	Waterford
Potter[17]	Willington	Riverside Park	New London
Poverty Hollow	Harwinton	Riversville[30]	Greenwich
Powder Hill	Middlefield	Riverview	Norwich
Pratt Island[18]	Darien	Riverview	Portland
Presidential Estates	Ledyard	Road Church District	Stonington
†Preston[15]	Preston	Roaring Brook[17]	Willington
Preston City[15]	Preston	Roast Meat Hill[2]	Killingworth
Preston Plains[15]	Preston	Robertsville[31]	Colebrook
Promise Land	Seymour	Rock House Hill	Oxford
Prospect District	New Milford	Rock Meadow[17]	Union
Prospect Hill	Brookfield	Rock-Ell[32]	Ellington
Puckshire	Woodbury	Rockland	Madison
Puddletow	New Hartford	Rockland Park[33]	Branford
Puffingham[21]	Cornwall	Rockwell Hill	Stafford

Post offices—[1]Niantic. [2]Killingworth, RFD Deep River. [3]Rowayton. [4]Dayville. [5]Old Lyme. [6]Willimantic. [7]North Franklin. [8]Baltic. [9]Middle Haddam. [10]Colchester. [11]South Lyme. [12]Brookfield Center. [13]Moosup. [14]Higganum. [15]Norwich. [16]Stony Creek. [17]Stafford Springs. [18]Noroton. [19]Cornwall Bridge. [20]West Redding. [21]Old Greenwich. [22]Old Mystic. [23]Mystic. [24]RFD, Collinsville. [25]Uncasville and Oakdale. [26]Redding Ridge. [27]Devon. [28]Taftville. [29]Sandy Hook. [30]Glenville. [31]Winsted and Riverton. [32]Rockville. [33]Short Beach. †Town.

TOWNS, VILLAGES AND DISTRICTS

Stations, Villages, etc.	Town	Stations, Villages, etc.	Town
Rocky Dundee	Stafford	Sharon Valley	Sharon
Rogers Lake	Old Lyme	Shawondassee	Stonington
Rogers Lake West Shores[1]	Lyme	Shelter Knolls	Danbury
Romford[2]	Washington	Sherman Hill	Woodbury
Roosevelt Park[3]	Litchfield	Sherman's Corner	Chaplin
Rose Hill	Portland	Sherwood Forest[16]	Ledyard
Rose Hill	Wolcott	Shingle Hollow[17]	Glastonbury
Ross Hill[4]	Lisbon	Shippan Point	Stamford
Roton Point[5]	Norwalk	Shunoc	No. Stonington
Round Hill[6]	Greenwich	Sill Lane	Old Lyme
Round Hill[4]	Lisbon	Silver Beach	Milford
Roxbury	Stamford	Silver Bluff	Clinton
Roxbury Falls	Roxbury	Silver Lake	Sharon
Roxbury Station	Roxbury	Silvermine	New Canaan
Russeling Ridge	New Milford	Silvermine	Norwalk
Sachem's Head	Guilford	Silvermine	Wilton
Sadd's Mill	Ellington	Skiff Mountain	Kent
Sagamore Cove	Branford	Skokorat	Seymour
Sagamore Terrace	Westbrook	Skyline Acres[18]	Franklin
Salem Four Corners	Salem	Smith Hill[19]	Winchester
Salem Park	Norwich	Smith Ridge	New Canaan
Salem Straits	Darien	Smith's Corner[18]	Franklin
Salmon River[7]	East Haddam	Smith's Neck	Old Lyme
Salmon River Park	East Hampton	Sodom[20]	Franklin
Salt Works	Westbrook	Solomonville[21]	Stonington
Sand Hill	Ellington	Sound View	Old Lyme
Sanfordtown[8]	Redding	South Avon Tax District	Avon
Sasqua Hills	Norwalk	South Bigelow	Hampton
Satan's Kingdom	New Hartford	South Bolton	Bolton
Saunder's Point[9]	East Lyme	South Canaan[22]	Canaan
Sawyer District	Putnam	South Canterbury	Canterbury
Saybrook Ferry	Old Saybrook	South Chaplin	Chaplin
Saybrook Manor	Old Saybrook	South Kent Road	New Milford
Saybrook Manor Beach	Old Saybrook	South Killingly[23]	Killingly
Saybrook Point	Old Saybrook	South Meriden	Meriden
Scantic	East Windsor	South Plains	Litchfield
Schaghticoke	Kent	South Wilton[24]	Wilton
Schwartz Manor	Norwich	Southfield Point	Stamford
Scitico	Enfield	Southford	Southbury
Scofieldtown	Stamford	Southwest District[25]	Killingworth
Scotch Cap[10]	Branford	Southwood Acres	Enfield
Scott Hill[11]	Bozrah	Special Service District	Putnam
Scott Hill[12]	Lebanon	Spicer Hill[11]	Bozrah
Scott's Cove	Darien	Spindle Hill	Wolcott
Scott's Swamp[13]	Farmington	Spithead	Waterford
Scoville Hill	Harwinton	Sport Hill	Easton
Seaport Heights[14]	Stonington	†Sprague[27]	Sprague
Sears Park	East Hampton	Spring Glen	Hamden
Second Hill	New Milford	Spring Hill[27]	Mansfield
Secret Lake	Avon	Spring Hill	Norwalk
Secret Lake	Canton	Spring Lake	Sherman
Sega Acres	New Milford	Spring Wood	Norwalk
Sentinel Hill	Derby	Squantuck	Seymour
Seymour Park[15]	Newington	Squash Hollow	New Milford
Shailerville	Haddam	Stadley Rough	Danbury
Shaker Pines Lake	Enfield	Stafford Hollow	Stafford

Post offices—[1]Old Lyme. [2]Washington Depot. [3]Bantam. [4]Jewett City. [5]Rowayton. [6]Byram. [7]Moodus. [8]West Redding. [9]Niantic. [10]Short Beach. [11]Fitchville. [12]Colchester. [13]Forestville. [14]Mystic. [15]New Britain. [16]Gales Ferry. [17]South Glastonbury. [18]North Franklin. [19]Winsted. [20]Lebanon. [21]Pawcatuck. [22]Falls Village. [23]Danielson. [24]Georgetown. [25]Killingworth, RFD Deep River. [26]Baltic. [27]Storrs. †Town.

TOWNS, VILLAGES AND DISTRICTS

Stations, Villages, etc.	Town	Stations, Villages, etc.	Town
Stafford Village	Stafford	Todd Hill	Bethlehem
Standish Hill	Lebanon	Todd Hollow[13]	Plymouth
Stannard Beach	Westbrook	Todd's Hill	Branford
Stanwich	Greenwich	Tokeneke	Darien
Starr's Plain	Danbury	Tolles Station[14]	Plymouth
State Line	Stafford	Tophet	Roxbury
Stepney	Monroe	Topstone[6]	Redding
Sterling Center	Sterling	Torringford	Torrington
Sterling City[1]	Lyme	Tousey Mountain	Bethlehem
Sterling Hill[2]	Sterling	Towantic	Oxford
Stetson's 4 Corners	Brooklyn	Tower Hill	Chaplin
Stewart Hill	Portland	Tower Hill[4]	Killingworth
Still Hill	Bethlehem	Town Hill	New Hartford
Still River	New Milford	Town Hill	New London
Stillmanville[3]	Stonington	Town Hill[14]	Plymouth
Stillwater	Stamford	Tracy	Wallingford
Stilson Heights	New Milford	Trading Cove[15]	Montiville
Stone House District[4]	Killingworth	Trading Cove	Norwich
Stone Quarry	South Windsor	Transylvania	Woodbury
Stonehenge	Ledyard	Treasure Hill[16]	Kent
Stonehill Acres	Killingworth	Tunnel Hill[7]	Lisbon
Stony Hill	Bethel	Turkey Hill	Haddam
Straitsville	Naugatuck	Turkey Hill	Orange
Strand	Waterford	Turn of River	Stamford
Stratfield	Fairfield	Tuttles Sandy Beach[1]	Lyme
Sucker Brook[5]	Winchester	Tuttles Sandy Beach	Old Lyme
Sumac Island	Branford	Twin Lakes	Salisbury
Summer Island	Branford	Tyler City	Orange
Summit	Cheshire	Tyler Lake[17]	Goshen
Sunny Brook Park	Plainfield	Tylerville	Haddam
Sunny Valley Road	New Milford	Umpawaug[6]	Redding
Sunset Acres	East Haddam	†Union[18]	Union
Sunset Beach	Branford	Union District[4]	Killingworth
Sunset Hill[6]	Redding	Union District[2]	Plainfield
Sylvandale[7]	Lisbon	Union Square	Norwich
Talmadge Hill	New Canaan	Union Village	Manchester
Tankeroosen	Vernon	Union Village	Plainfield
Tantummaheag	Old Lyme	Unionville Village[19]	Farmington
Tashua District	Trumbull	Upper Merryall	New Milford
Tater Hill	East Haddam	Upper Parish	Weston
Tatnic Hill	Brooklyn	Upper Stepney	Monroe
Taugwonk	Stonington	Valley Forge	Weston
Taunton	Newtown	Vargas Corners	Stonington
Tavern Island[8]	Norwalk	Vedder's Point	Branford
Taylor Terrace	New Milford	Vernon Center	Vernon
Taylor Town[9]	Glastonbury	Vidal Park	Stamford
Thames View[10]	Waterford	Village	Voluntown
Thamesville	Norwich	Village Hill[20]	Lebanon
The Highlands[3]	Stonington	Village Hill	Stafford
The Mines[11]	East Hampton	Village Hill[18]	Willington
Thimble Island[12]	Branford	Vinton Mills	South Windsor
Thompsonville	Enfield	Wallack's Point	Stamford
Tigertown	Naugatuck	Wallen's Hill[5]	Winchester
Timber Trails	Sherman	Wallen's Hill[5]	Barkhamsted
Timber Village	Wethersfield	Waller	New Milford
Titicus	Ridgefield	Walnut Beach	Milford
Tobys Rock Mountain	Oxford	Walnut Tree Hill[21]	Newtown

Post offices—[1]Old Lyme. [2]RFD, Moosup. [3]Pawcatuck. [4]Killingworth, RFD Deep River. [5]Winsted. [6]West Redding. [7]Jewett City. [8]Rowayton. [9]South Glastonbury. [10]Quaker Hill. [11]Cobalt. [12]Stony Creek. [13]RFD 1, Plymouth 06782. [14]Terryville. [15]Uncasville. [16]South Kent. [17]Litchfield. [18]Stafford Springs. [19]Unionville. [20]RFD, Willimantic. [21]Sandy Hook. †Town.

TOWNS, VILLAGES AND DISTRICTS

Stations, Villages, etc.	Town	Stations, Villages, etc.	Town
Wamphassuc Point	Stonington	Westminster	Canterbury
Wangunk	Portland	Westover Park	Stamford
Wapping	South Windsor	Westview Acres	Oxford
Waramaug Lake[1]	Washington	Westville	Danbury
Warehouse Point	East Windsor	Westwood Park	Norwich
Warner's Mills	Roxbury	Wheeler Farms	Milford
Warrenville	Ashford	Wheeler Island[14]	Branford
Washburn District[13]	Stafford	Whigville	Burlington
Washington Hill[2]	Barkhamsted	Whippoorwill	Old Lyme
Washington Square	Norwich	Whipstick	Ridgefield
Wassuc[3]	Glastonbury	Whisconier[15]	Brookfield
Waterside	Stamford	Whitcomb Hill[16]	Cornwall
Waterville	Waterbury	White Birch[17]	Salem
Wauwecus Hill	Norwich	White Hills	Shelton
Wawecus Hill[4]	Bozrah	White Hollow	Sharon
Webber	Stafford	White Oak	Southbury
Weekeepeemee	Woodbury	White Sand Beach	Old Lyme
Wellesville	New Milford	Whites Woods	Litchfield
Wells Quarter Village	Wethersfield	Wig Hill	Chester
Wequetequock[5]	Stonington	†Willington[18]	Willington
West Avon	Avon	Wilson	Windsor
West Bantam[6]	Litchfield	Wilson Point	Norwalk
West Beach	Westbrook	Wilsonville[10]	Thompson
West Cheshire	Cheshire	†Winchester[8]	Winchester
West District[7]	Farmington	Windermere Village	Ellington
West Goshen	Goshen	Windsorville[19]	East Windsor
West Hill[8]	Barkhamsted	Winnipauk	Norwalk
West Hill	New Hartford	Winthrop	Deep River
West Iron Works	Brookfield	Witch Meadow[17]	Salem
West Lane	Ridgefield	Wolf Hill	Wolcott
West Morris[9]	Morris	Wolf Meadow[20]	Killingworth
West Mountain	Ridgefield	Wolf Neck[21]	Stonington
West Neck	Waterford	Wolfpits	Bethel
West Norwalk	Norwalk	Wood Creek	Bethlehem
West Park	Stamford	†Woodbridge[22]	Woodbridge
West Pleasant Valley	Groton	Woodlake	Woodbury
West Putnam District	Putnam	Woodridge Estates[23]	Ledyard
West Shore	West Haven	Woodridge Lake	Goshen
West Side	Goshen	Woodside Acres	Ellington
West Side	Woodbury	Woodtick	Wolcott
West Stafford	Stafford	Woodview	New Milford
West Stamford	Stamford	Woodville[24]	Washington
West Thompson[10]	Thompson	Wooster Village	Danbury
West Torrington	Torrington	Works District	Stafford
West Village	Brooklyn	Wormwood Hill[25]	Mansfield
West Wauregan[11]	Brooklyn	Wrightville	Torrington
West Woods	Sharon	Wylie	Voluntown
West Woodstock[12]	Woodstock	Wyndwood	Wethersfield
Westernview	New Milford	Zoar[26]	Newtown
Westfield	Middletown	Zoar Bridge	Oxford
Westford[13]	Ashford		

Post offices—[1]New Preston. [2]North Canton and East Hartland. [3]South Glastonbury. [4]Norwich. [5]Pawcatuck. [6]Bantam. [7]Unionville. [8]Winsted. [9]Lakeside. [10]North Grosvenor Dale. [11]Wauregan or RFD, Brooklyn. [12]Woodstock, South Woodstock, Woodstock Valley. [13]Stafford Springs. [14]Stony Creek. [15]Brookfield Center. [16]Cornwall Bridge. [17]Colchester. [18]West Willington 06279. South Willington 06265. [19]Broad Brook. [20]Killingworth, RFD Deep River. [21]Old Mystic. [22]Woodbridge, Amity Station, New Haven 06525. [23]Gales Ferry. [24]Marble Dale. [25]Mansfield Center. [26]Sandy Hook. †Town.

DISTANCES TO ALL TOWNS IN CONNECTICUT FROM HARTFORD BY MOTOR CAR

(Source: Bureau of Planning and Research of the State Dept. of Transportation. The figures represent the highway mileage as measured between intersections of commercially passable state roads and highways which are close to the geographical center of such towns as possible. No parkways were used in the routings because of their restriction to non-commercial vehicles.)

	Miles		Miles
Andover	20	Franklin	35
Ansonia	43	Glastonbury	11
Ashford	32	Goshen	34
Avon	15	Granby	19
Barkhamsted	25	Greenwich	82
Beacon Falls	37	Griswold	47
Berlin	12	Groton	48
Bethany	34	Guilford	31
Bethel	54	Haddam	23
Bethlehem	37	Hamden	31
Bloomfield	8	Hampton	38
Bolton	14	Hartford	—
Bozrah	34	Hartland	30
Branford	38	Harwinton	27
Bridgeport	54	Hebron	20
Bridgewater	48	Kent	52
Bristol	17	Killingly	46
Brookfield	54	Killingworth	29
Brooklyn	45	Lebanon	29
Burlington	20	Ledyard	46
Canaan	45	Lisbon	42
Canterbury	40	Litchfield	33
Canton	18	Lyme	38
Chaplin	36	Madison	30
Cheshire	25	Manchester	9
Chester	30	Mansfield	26
Clinton	36	Marlborough	16
Colchester	24	Meriden	18
Colebrook	33	Middlebury	37
Columbia	24	Middlefield	20
Cornwall	40	Middletown	16
Coventry	19	Milford	46
Cromwell	11	Monroe	52
Danbury	56	Montville	38
Darien	72	Morris	38
Deep River	33	Naugatuck	35
Derby	45	New Britain	10
Durham	22	New Canaan	73
Eastford	35	New Fairfield	62
East Granby	16	New Hartford	23
East Haddam	28	New Haven	36
East Hampton	22	Newington	7
East Hartford	3	New London	45
East Haven	36	New Milford	50
East Lyme	42	Newtown	48
Easton	61	Norfolk	36
East Windsor	14	North Branford	32
Ellington	17	North Canaan	42
Enfield	21	North Haven	29
Essex	35	North Stonington	51
Fairfield	59	Norwalk	69
Farmington	10	Norwich	37

DISTANCES OF TOWNS FROM HARTFORD

	Miles		Miles
Old Lyme	40	Stratford	50
Old Saybrook	39	Suffield	20
Orange	44	Thomaston	25
Oxford	41	Thompson	50
Plainfield	47	Tolland	20
Plainville	13	Torrington	28
Plymouth	22	Trumbull	57
Pomfret	40	Union	34
Portland	14	Vernon	13
Preston	44	Voluntown	53
Prospect	30	Wallingford	23
Putnam	49	Warren	45
Redding	60	Washington	43
Ridgefield	65	Waterbury	32
Rocky Hill	8	Waterford	42
Roxbury	43	Watertown	28
Salem	32	Westbrook	39
Salisbury	50	West Hartford	5
Scotland	35	West Haven	40
Seymour	41	Weston	66
Sharon	48	Westport	64
Shelton	49	Wethersfield	4
Sherman	58	Willington	25
Simsbury	14	Wilton	69
Somers	23	Winchester	29
Southbury	40	Windham	31
Southington	18	Windsor	9
South Windsor	11	Windsor Locks	13
Sprague	39	Wolcott	24
Stafford	27	Woodbridge	40
Stamford	81	Woodbury	36
Sterling	51	Woodstock	41
Stonington	55		

Distances, Connecticut River, Hartford, to

	Miles		Miles
Wethersfield	4½	Haddam	36½
Glastonbury	6	East Haddam	40
South Glastonbury	10½	East Haddam (Goodspeed's)	41
Rocky Hill	11	Hadlyme	44
Gildersleeve's	16	Deep River	46
Cromwell	18	Hamburg	49
Portland	21	Ely's	51
Middletown	22	Essex	52
Tibbals	27	Lyme	56
Middle Haddam	28	Saybrook Point	58
Higganum	31	Saybrook bar or Sound	60
Rock Landing	33		

CONNECTICUT TOWNS IN THE ORDER OF THEIR ESTABLISHMENT; WITH THE ORIGIN OF THEIR NAMES

Until 1700 almost the only official action of the colonial government (General Court) in regard to town organization, was to authorize the town name, usually chosen by its leading man, from his home in England. In October, 1700, we find implied or quasi incorporation, such as exists to this day in the records. "This assembly doth grant to the inhabitants of the town of Lebanon all such immunities, privileges and powers, as generally other townes within this Colonie have and doe enjoy." The authoritative legal definition of a town in England, contemporary with the earliest Connecticut settlements is given in the first edition of Coke's Commentaries upon Littleton, published 1628: "It can not be a town in law, unless it hath, or in past time hath had, a church, and celebration of Divine services, sacraments and burials." The churches, which moved bodily, with their pastors, from Massachusetts to Connecticut, proceeded to exercise the secular powers which we regard as those of the town, but the English township is known by its ecclesiastical name of parish. Several of our towns were first set off as parishes from great town-tracts; yet the town in Connecticut colony essentially separated church and state in government, in that it never restricted political suffrage to church members. As to dates, the official colonial records are followed, as soon as they begin, 1636.

As Indian was not a written but a spoken language, its spelling is often a matter of astonishing versatility. Because of mutilation of the Indian names by Colonial scribes and by the Colonial pronunciation it is frequently impossible to arrive at any definite conclusion with regard to the original meaning. The variety of dialects, even in the Algonquin tribe, varied greatly, even among those living within thirty or forty miles of one another. This added greatly to the complications of spelling Indian words in English.

To add to the confusion, the white men continually applied Indian names to features of the landscape that were not at all in the Indian mind when they coined the word. Thus a word meaning a hill might be applied by the white men to all the surrounding territory and come eventually to mean a pond. And so the Indian names, or their Indian approximates, have come down to us not in the names of the towns, which the white men were creating in the tradition of their own race, but in features of the countryside streams, mountains, hills and other natural aspects.

THE COLONY

1. Windsor, settled by a company from Plymouth Colony, arriving with the frame and materials of a trading house on their vessel Sept. 26, 1633. This house was set up, 80 to 100 rods below the mouth of the Farmington River, on a tract previously bought of the original Indian proprietors. Before the summer of 1635, the settlers had bought Great Meadow, north of the Farmington, and placed cattle and servants on their lands. They sold out, 1637 and 1638, to Dorchester, Mass., settlers, who had arrived in their vicinity, 1635, and named their settlement Dorchester. It was named in 1637 from Windsor in Berkshire, now a royal residence.

2. Wethersfield, settled as Watertown 1634; named 1637 from Wethersfield in Essex, England. Indian name, "Pyquag."

3. Hartford, Dutch trading house, "House of Hope," 1633; settled as Newtown in 1635; named 1637 from Hertford in Hertfordshire, Indian name, "Suckiag."

4. Deep River, was formerly Saybrook, fort, soon a settlement, 1635; named 1639 from Lord Say & Sele, and Baron Brook; name changed by act of General Assembly, July 1, 1947. Indian name, "Pattaquasset."
5. New Haven, settled April, 1638; named Aug. 1640, from Newhaven on the south coast of Sussex. Indian name, "Quinnipiac."
6. Milford, settled early in 1639; named November, 1640. Indian name, "Wepawaug."
7. Guilford, settled, 1639; named from Guildford parish in Surrey, July, 1643. Indian name, "Menunkatuck."
8. Stratford, settled in 1639; named in 1643 from Stratford-le-Bow, Essex, or more probably, Stratford-on-Avon. Indian name, "Cupheag."
9. Fairfield, settled 1639; name = fair field; or possibly from Fairfield in Kent. Indian name, "Uncoway."
10. Greenwich, settled by the English and named, July 18, 1640, from Greenwich near London; N.Y. to Ct., transferred, 1656. Indian name, "Patuquapaen."
11. Stamford, settled in 1641; named 1642 from Stamford in Lincolnshire. Indian name, "Rippowam."
12. Farmington, settled in 1640; incorporated and named, Dec. 1645. "Tunxis shall be called Farmington" = farming town.
13. New London, settled as "Pequot," 1646, named from London, England, March, 1658. Old Indian name, "Nameaug."
14. Norwalk, settled 1649; incorporated Sept., 1651, "Norwaukee shall bee a townee," Algonkin noyank, point of land, or more probably from the Indian name, "Naramauke."
15. Stonington, settled 1649; named Souther Towne, by Mass., Oct., 1658; Stonington by Conn., 1666. Indian names, "Pawcatuck" and "Mistack."
16. Middletown, incorporated 1651; named 1653, from position between upper river towns and Saybrook. Indian name, "Mattabeset."
17. Norwich, settled 1659; accepted as legal township, May 1662; named from Norwich in Norfolk, England. Indian name, "Mohegan."
18. Lyme, set off from Saybrook, 1665; named from Lyme Regis in Dorsetshire, May, 1667. Formerly East Saybrook.
19. Killingworth, named Kenilworth, May, 1667, from Kenilworth in Warwickshire. Indian name, "Hammonassett."
20. Haddam, settled in 1662; incorporated, and named Oct., 1668, from Much Haddam parish in Hertfordshire.
21. Simsbury, settled and named May, 1670, from Sim (on) Wolcott, leading settler, or from Simondsbury in Dorset.
22. Wallingford, set off from New Haven and named, May, 1670, from Wallingford in Berkshire. Old name, "East River" or "New Haven Village."
23. Woodbury, named May, 1673, from being well wooded. Indian name, "Pomperaug."
24. Suffield, "abbreviation of Southfield," established in Mass., 1674; annexed to Conn., May 1749.
25. Derby, settled 1651; named May, 1675, from Derby, town and county in England. Indian name, "Paugasset" or "Paugasuck."

26. Enfield, grant of township "called Enfield" by Mass., May, 1683, from Enfield in Middlesex; annexed to Conn., May, 1749. Formerly Freshwater.
27. Branford, settled 1639; named 1653, from Brentford in Middlesex; set off from New Haven, 1685. Indian name, "Totoket."
28. Waterbury, settled May, 1674; incorporated and named May, 1686, from abundant waters. Indian name, "Mattatuck."
29. Danbury, settled 1685, named Oct., 1687, from Danbury parish in Essex; incorporated May, 1702. Named by Gov. Treat. First name, "Swampfield." Indian name, "Paquiage" or "Pahquioque."
30. Preston, incorporated 1686, named 1687, probably from the Preston in Suffolk in honor of the Thomas Parke family.
31. Woodstock, settled as New Roxbury, Mass., 1686; named March, 1690, from Woodstock in Oxfordshire; annexed to Conn., May, 1749.
32. Windham, settled 1686; incorporated May, 1692; named from Windham in Sussex, or from Wymondham in Norfolk.
33. Glastonbury, incorporated May, 1693; set off from Wethersfield, June, 1692; named from Glastonbury in Somersetshire.
34. Colchester, settled 1699; named, Oct., 1699, from Colchester borough and port in Essex. Formerly Jeremiah's Farms.
35. Plainfield, settled 1689; name descriptive; authorized Oct., 1700.
36. Lebanon, named 1697 from Lebanon in Syria; Hebrew name = white; incorporated Oct., 1700.
37. Mansfield, settled 1686; set off from Windham and incorporated Oct., 1702; named from Major Moses Mansfield. Originally called Ponde-town. Indian name, "Noubesetuck."
38. Canterbury, settled 1690; set off from Plainfield and incorporated Oct., 1703; named from Canterbury in Kent. Indian name, "Peagscomsueck."
39. Durham, settled 1699; named May, 1704; from Durham, town and county in England. Indian name, "Cockingchaug," or "Coginchaug."
40. Groton, Inc., from New London, May, 1705; named 1705 from English home town of Gov. John Winthrop.
41. Hebron, settled 1704; named 1707 from Heb. Hebron (derivation doubtful); "An association," "a league," and "confederacy," are meanings given this word by various authorities; incorporated May, 1708.
42. Killingly, settled 1700; incorporated May, 1708; and named from Killingly Manor near Pontefract, Yorkshire. Indian name, "Aspinock."
43. Ridgefield, settled 1708; incorporated 1709; named from its ridges. Indian name, "Caudatowa."
44. Ashford, settled 1710, named Oct., 1710, probably from Ashford in Kent, England; incorporated Oct., 1714. Formerly New Scituate.
45. Newtown, named May, 1708 = a new town; incorporated Oct., 1711. Indian name, "Pootatuck" or "Quonapague."
46. Coventry, settled 1709; named from Coventry in Warwickshire, Oct., 1711; incorporated May, 1712.
47. New Milford, settled from Milford, 1707; named Oct., 1703; incorporated Oct., 1712. Indian name, "Weantinock" or "Weantinogue."

48. Pomfret, settled in 1686; named and incorporated May, 1713, from Pontefract in Yorkshire. Indian name, "Mashamoquet."
49. Tolland, named May, 1715; incorporated May, 1722, from Tolland in Somersetshire, whence Henry Wolcott, grandfather of Gov. Roger Wolcott, chief owner.
50. Litchfield, named and incorporated May, 1719, from Lichfield, a town of Staffordshire. Indian name, "Bantam."
51. Stafford, settled in 1719; named from Stafford, town in Staffordshire.
52. Voluntown, settled 1719; named May, 1708 = volun (teers') town; grant to volunteers in the Narragansett war; incorporated, May, 1721.
53. Bolton, settled 1716; named and incorporated Oct., 1720; named from Bolton in Lancashire, or the Duke of Bolton.
54. Willington, named "Wellington," May, 1725, from Wellington in Somersetshire (birthplace of Henry Wolcott, whose grandson Roger was chief purchaser, 1720), which gave title to the Duke of Wellington, but incorporated May, 1727, as "Willington."
55. East Haddam, "Haddam East Society"; incorporated and named May, 1734. Indian name, "Macki-moodus."
56. Somers, set off from Enfield by Mass., and named from Lord Somers, July, 1734; annexed to Conn., May, 1749. Formerly East Enfield.
57. Union, settled 1727, as "Union Lands"; named 1732; incorporated Oct., 1734 (union of East Stafford and State Lands).
58. Harwinton, settled 1731; named May, 1732, from Har(tford), and Win(dsor), from whence its original proprietors; incorporated Oct., 1737.
59. New Hartford, named May, 1733, from Hartford, whence its proprietors, and incorporated Oct., 1738.
60. Canaan, named May, 1738, from the Bible, Canaan = lowland; incorporated Oct., 1739.
61. Goshen, named May, 1738, from Goshen in Egypt; incorporated Oct., 1739.
62. Kent, named May, 1738, from Kent county, England; incorporated Oct., 1739. Indian name, "Scatacook."
63. Sharon, named and incorporated Oct., 1739, with the Hebrew name, sharon, a plain.
64. Cornwall, named May, 1738, from the southwest county of England; incorporated May, 1740.
65. New Fairfield, settled and named May, 1728, from Fairfield; incorporated May, 1740.
66. Torrington, named May, 1732, from Torrington in Devonshire; incorporated Oct., 1740.
67. Salisbury, named May, 1738 (by Rev. Thomas Noyes), from Salisbury, Wiltshire; incorporated Oct., 1741. Indian name, "Weatogue."
68. Norfolk, named May, 1738, from Norfolk county on the east coast of England; incorporated Oct., 1758.
69. Hartland, named 1733 = Hart(ford) land, because owned by Hartford men; incorporated May, 1761.

70. Redding, made a parish and named Reading from Col. John Read, May, 1729; incorporated as Redding from Fairfield, May, 1767.
71. East Hampton, was Chatham, named 1767, from the importance of its shipbuilding in allusion to Chatham, England; incorporated from Middletown, Oct., 1767; name changed by act of General Assembly, May 4, 1915.
72. East Windsor, settled 1680; incorporated from Windsor and named May, 1768. Formerly Windsor.
73. Winchester, tract named from Winchester in Hampshire, May, 1733; incorporated May, 1771. Called the "Green Woods."
74. Washington, incorporated and taken from Kent, Litchfield, New Milford and Woodbury, Jan., 1779; named from George Washington. Formerly parishes of Judea and New Preston.
75. Barkhamsted, named from Berkhamstead in Hertfordshire, May, 1732; incorporated Oct., 1779.
76. Colebrook, named May, 1732, from Colebrooke in Devonshire, settled 1765; incorporated Oct., 1779.
77. Southington, named Oct., 1726, as south society of Farmington; incorporated from Farmington, Oct., 1779.
78. Cheshire, named New Cheshire, May, 1724, from Cheshire, England; incorporated from Wallingford, May, 1780. Earlier called, "West Farms on Mill River."
79. Watertown, incorporated May, 1780, from Waterbury, which suggested its name. Formerly Westbury.
80. East Hartford, incorporated from Hartford, Oct., 1783. Indian name, "Podunk."
81. Woodbridge, incorporated from New Haven and Milford, Jan., 1784 and named from its pastor, B. Woodbridge. Formerly parish of Amity.
82. Berlin, incorporated from Farmington, Middletown and Wethersfield, May, 1785; named from Berlin, Prussia. Formerly Kensington.
83. Bristol, incorporated from Farmington, May, 1785, and named from Bristol, England. Formerly New Cambridge.
84. East Haven, named May, 1707; incorporated from New Haven, May, 1785. Originally Iron Works Village.
85. Thompson (Parish), named 1728, from its chief owner, Sir Robert Thompson; incorporated from Killingly, May, 1785.
86. Bozrah, incorporated from Norwich, May, 1786, and given Heb. name = enclosure. Formerly New Concord.
87. Brooklyn, named 1752, brook line (the Quinebaug); incorporated from Canterbury and Pomfret, May, 1786. Formerly Mortlake.
88. Franklin, incorporated from Norwich, May, 1786, and named from Benjamin Franklin.
89. Ellington, named 1735, from Ellington in Yorks or Hunts; incorporated from E. Windsor, May, 1786. Originally called the "Great Swamp."
90. Hamden, incorporated from New Haven, May, 1786, and named from John Hampden, English patriot.
91. Lisbon, incorporated from Norwich, May, 1786, and named from Lisbon, capital of Portugal. Formerly Newent parish.

92. Warren, incorporated from Kent, May, 1786, and named from Gen. Joseph Warren.
93. Granby, incorporated from Simsbury, Oct., 1786, and named from the Marquis of Granby (Chas. Manners), or from Granby, Mass.
94. Hampton, incorporated from Brooklyn, Canterbury, Mansfield, Pomfret and Windham, Oct., 1786; named from Hampton in Middlesex. Formerly Kennedy or Windham Village.
95. Montville, incorporated from New London, Oct., 1786; name French for mountville.
96. North Haven, named 1739; incorporated from New Haven, Oct., 1786.
97. Bethlehem, named as society, Oct., 1739; Hebrew = house of bread; incorporated from Woodbury, May, 1787.
98. Southbury, named May, 1731; south part of Woodbury; incorporated from Woodbury, May, 1787.
99. Weston, named and incorporated from Fairfield, Oct., 1787; named as the west town, or settlement of Fairfield. Formerly Northfield. Indian name, "Aspetuck."
100. Brookfield, incorporated from Danbury, New Milford and Newtown, May, 1788; named for Thos. Brooks, first pastor. Formerly Newbury.
101. Shelton, named for Edward N. Shelton, leader in Housatonic Dam project; was Huntington, incorporated from Stratford, Jan., 1789, and named from Gov. Samuel Huntington; name changed by act of General Assembly April 15, 1919. Indian name, "Quorum." Formerly parish of Ripton.
102. Sterling, incorporated from Voluntown, May, 1794, and named from Dr. John Sterling, a resident.
103. Plymouth, incorporated from Watertown, May, 1795, and named by H. Cook, from Plymouth, Mass., of which his grandfather was an early settler. Formerly Northbury.
104. Wolcott, incorporated from Southington and Waterbury, May, 1796, and named from Gov. Oliver Wolcott.
105. Roxbury, named May, 1743, as rockier part of Woodbury, whence incorporated Oct., 1796.
106. Trumbull (North Stratford), incorporated from Stratford, Oct., 1797, and named from Gov. Jonathan Trumbull. Formerly parish of Unity.
107. Oxford, parish, named from Oxford, England, 1741; incorporated from Derby and Southbury, Oct., 1798.
108. New Canaan, named 1731; incorporated from Norwalk and Stamford, May, 1801. Formerly Canaan parish.
109. Waterford, incorporated from New London, Oct., 1801; name descriptive.
110. Wilton, named a society, 1726, from Wilton in Wiltshire; incorporated from Norwalk, May, 1802.
111. Sherman, incorporated from New Fairfield, Oct., 1802, and named from Roger Sherman.
112. Marlborough, named 1747, from great Duke of Marlborough, or from Marlborough, Mass.; incorporated from Colchester, Glastonbury and Hebron, Oct., 1803. Previously Eastbury and New Marlborough.

113. Columbia, incorporated from Lebanon, May, 1804, and given the poetic name for the United States.
114. Burlington, incorporated from Bristol, May, 1806; named (as Burlington, Vt.), prob. from 3d Earl of Burlington. Formerly "West Woods" or "West Britain."
115. Canton, incorporated from Simsbury, May, 1806, and the name Canton suggested by the late Ephraim Mills, is derived from a likeness to a Swiss canton. Original name, "Suffrage."
116. *Meriden, named in a deed 1664, from "Meriden Farms," Dorking, Surrey, Eng.; incorporated from Wallingford, May, 1806.
117. Middlebury, incorporated from Southbury, Waterbury and Woodbury, Oct., 1807; named from its position, 1790.
118. North Stonington, named 1724; incorporated from Stonington, May, 1807.
119. Vernon, incorporated from Bolton, Oct., 1808, and named prob. from the home of Washington at Mount Vernon, Va. Formerly North Bolton.
120. Griswold, incorporated from Preston, Oct., 1815; and named from Gov. Roger Griswold.
121. Salem = Hebrew "peace"; named from Salem, Mass., and incorporated as New Salem, from Colchester, Lyme and Montville, May, 1819.
122. Darien, incorporated from Stamford, May, 1820, and named from the Isthmus of Darien. Formerly parish of Middlesex.
123. Bridgeport, name descriptive, 1800; incorporated from Fairfield and Stratford, May, 1821. Indian name, "Pequonock." Formerly Stratfield or Newfield.
124. Chaplin, society, named 1809 from its deacon, Benjamin Chaplin; incorporated from Windham, Mansfield and Hampton, May, 1822.
125. Orange, incorporated from Milford and New Haven, May, 1822, and named from Wm. of Orange (III of England). Formerly North Milford.
126. Manchester, incorporated from East Hartford, May, 1823, and named from Manchester, England, because of manufacturing. Originally Orford parish.
127. Monroe, incorporated from Huntington, May, 1823, and named from Pres. James Monroe. Formerly parish of New Stratford.
128. Madison, incorporated from Guilford, May, 1826, and named from Pres. James Madison. Formerly East Guilford.
129. Prospect, incorporated from Cheshire and Waterbury, May, 1827; named as fine lookout place. Formerly Columbia parish.
130. Avon, incorporated from Farmington, May, 1830, and named from Avon river at Stratford-on-Avon. Formerly Northington.
131. North Branford, named as society, 1768; incorporated from Branford, May, 1831.
132. Bethany, named as parish, 1762; Heb. = house of dates; incorporated from Woodbridge, May, 1832.

---

*See "A Century of Meriden" (Curtis-Gillespie).

133. Bloomfield, incorporated from Windsor, May, 1835; named from a Hartford family. Formerly Wintonbury.
134. Westport, incorporated from Fairfield, Norwalk and Weston, May, 1835; name descriptive. Indian name, "Saugatuck."
135. Chester, parish 1640, named from Chester in Cheshire; incorporated from Saybrook, May, 1836. Indian name, "Pattaquonk."
136. Ledyard, incorporated from Groton, May, 1836; named from Col. Wm. Ledyard, commander at Fort Griswold, Groton, 1781. Formerly North Groton.
137. Clinton, incorporated from Killingworth, May, 1838, and from Gov. Dewitt Clinton of N.Y.
138. East Lyme, named 1816; incorporated from Lyme and Waterford, May, 1839.
139. Westbrook, parish named 1810 as west parish of Saybrook; incorporated from Saybrook, May, 1840. Indian name, "Pochaug."
140. Portland, incorporated from Chatham, May, 1841, and named from Portland, Dorsetshire, famed for quarries. Originally named Conway.
141. Rocky Hill, name given Stepney parish from a hill in it, 1826; incorporated from Wethersfield, May, 1843.
142. Naugatuck, incorporated from Bethany, Oxford and Waterbury, May, 1844; Algonkin name = one tree. Formerly Salem parish or Salem Bridge. Originally South Farms of Waterbury.
143. Easton, incorporated from Weston, May, 1845; named as east part of Weston.
144. South Windsor, incorporated and named from East Windsor, May, 1845. Formerly Windsor Farms.
145. Eastford, named as east parish of Ashford, 1777; incorporated from Ashford, May, 1847.
146. Andover, parish named 1747, perhaps from Andover, Mass.; incorporated from Coventry and Hebron, May, 1848.
147. New Britain, parish named 1754 from (Great) Britain; incorporated from Berlin, May, 1850.
148. Seymour, incorporated from Derby, May, 1850, and named from Gov. Thomas H. Seymour. Indian name, "Naugatuck"; called Rimmon (1670), Chusetown (1735), Humphreysville (1805).
149. Cromwell, incorporated from Middletown, May, 1851, and named from Oliver Cromwell. Formerly Upper Middletown.
150. Essex, parish named 1820; named from Essex, England; incorporated, Sept. 13, 1852, as Old Saybrook; taken from Saybrook; name changed, July 8, 1854 to Essex. Indian name, "Patapoug."
151. Old Saybrook, incorporated from Essex (then Old Saybrook), July 8, 1854, and named at the same time.
152. West Hartford, named 1806; incorporated from Hartford, May, 1854. Formerly West Division.
153. Windsor Locks, named 1833 from canal locks there; incorporated from Windsor, May, 1854. Formerly Enfield Falls.
154. Bethel, named 1759; Hebrew = house of God; incorporated from Danbury, May, 1855.

155. Old Lyme, incorporated as South Lyme, from Lyme, May, 1855; named Old Lyme, 1857.
156. Putnam, incorporated from Pomfret, Thompson and Killingly, May, 1855; named from Israel Putnam. Indian name, "Quinebaug."
157. Bridgewater, named 1803; name descriptive, incorporated from New Milford, May, 1856.
158. Scotland, parish named by first settler, Magoon, a Scot, 1706; set off, 1732; incorporated from Windham, May, 1857.
159. East Granby, named 1822; incorporated from Granby and Windsor Locks, June, 1858.
160. North Canaan, named 1813; incorporated from Canaan (whence its name), May, 1858.
161. Morris, incorporated from Litchfield, June, 1859, and named from James Morris, prominent resident.
162. Sprague, incorporated from Lisbon and Franklin, May, 1861, and named from W. Sprague, village founder.
163. Middlefield, named 1744, from rural part of Middletown; incorporated from Middletown, June, 1866.
164. Plainville, named 1831 = earlier name "Great Plain"; incorporated from Farmington, July, 1869.
165. Beacon Falls, name descriptive, 1856; incorporated from Bethany, Oxford, Naugatuck and Seymour, June, 1871.
166. Newington, parish named 1721, from Newington in Kent or Stoke-N. Middlesex (London), incorporated from Wethersfield, July, 1871.
167. Thomaston, incorporated from Plymouth, July, 1875; named 1866 from Seth Thomas, clock mfr. there.
168. Ansonia, incorporated from Derby, April, 1889; named from Anson G. Phelps, founder of mfg. village, 1843.
169. West Haven, incorporated from Orange, June, 1921; named when made the west parish of New Haven, about 1720.

SECTION VIII

POLITICAL

State Central Committees

Town Chairpersons and Vice Chairpersons

Election Statistics

DEMOCRATIC STATE CENTRAL COMMITTEE OF CONNECTICUT

380 Franklin Ave., Hartford 06114
Tel., (860) 296-1775
(As of January 1, 1997)

Chm., Edward L. Marcus, 100 Stony Creek Rd., Branford 06405
Vice Chm., Patricia Paniccia, 25 Easton Rd., Monroe 06463
Secy., Dominic Palumbo, 1298 Hartford Tpke., Unit 2E, North Haven 06473
Treas., Maureen Satti, 517 Alewife Pkwy., New London 06320

District

1. Carmen Sierra, 200 Goodrich St., Hartford 06114
   Bruno Mazzulla, 700 Maple Ave., Hartford 06114

2. Ella L. Cromwell, 192 Vine St., Hartford 06112
   Abe Giles, 188 Cleveland Ave., Hartford 06120

3. Marjorie Anthony, 97 Pleasant Valley Rd., South Windsor 06074
   Bud Salemi, 17 Pheasant La., East Hartford 06108

4. Patricia Morianos, 42 South Rd., Bolton 06043
   John J. Sullivan, P.O. Box 1437, Manchester 06040

5. Barbara C. Gordon, 129 Ardmore Rd., West Hartford 06119
   Joseph Lenihan, 73 Bonny View Dr., West Hartford 06107

6. Claudia Helfgott, 12 Brady Ave., New Britain 06052
   John C. King, 469 Lincoln St., New Britain 06052

7. Carl Dudek, 20 Tyler Rd., Enfield 06082
   Julia Tashjian, 31 Basswood Rd., Windsor 06095

8. Elaine Primeau, 12 Towpath La., Avon 06001
   William Rocks, 2 Coppergate Rd., East Granby 06026

9. Mary Viggiano, 20 Garfield Rd., Rocky Hill 06067
   John Carragher, 36 Forest Dr., Newington 06111

10. Andrea Jackson-Brooks, 102 Dewitt, New Haven 06519
    William Gray, 22 Tilton St., New Haven 06511

11. Arthur T. Barbieri, 5 Horsley Ave., New Haven 06512
    Phyllis Marino, 92 Grafton St., New Haven 06513

12. Patricia M. Widlitz, 160 Deer La., Guilford 06437
    Frank J. Kinney III, 42 Bradley Ave., Branford 06405

13. Catherine K. Beinhorn, 374 Pine St., Middletown 06457
    Patsy Papandrea, 48 Holiday Hill Rd., Meriden 06450

14. Robert Hardiman, 468 Burnt Plains Rd., Milford 06460
    Dorothy Hardiman, 468 Burnt Plains Rd., Milford 06460

15. Madeleine Freeman Caine, 282 North Main St., Naugatuck 06770
    Martin Morrissey, Sr., 480 Farmington Ave., Waterbury 06710

16. Thomas Kenny, 87 Bateswood Rd., Waterbury 06706
    Dolores L. Longo, 111 Southington Ave., Southington 06489

17. Judi Kozak, 180 Cannon St., Hamden 06514
    Jerry Weiner, 15 Bishop Dr., Woodbridge 06525

18 Dorothy F. Doucette, 136 Bethel Rd., Norwich 06360
   Thomas Moukawsher, 328 Mitchell St., Groton 06340
19 Deborah Stiggle, 522 New London Tpke., Norwich 06360
   Joseph Socha, 3 Ventura Drive, Oakdale 06370
20 Marcia S. Bell, 20 Keeney La., New London 06320
   Anthony Attanasio, 11 Reuven Dr., Ledyard 06339
21 Richard Buturla, 265 Post Oak Rd., Stratford 06497
   Virginia Chittem, 90 Glenn Dr., Stratford 06497
22 Josephine DiNardo, 61 Suzanne Cir., Trumbull 06611
   John Fabrizi, 120 Doreen Dr., Bridgeport 06604
23 Sybil A. Allen, 785 Chopsey Hill Rd., Bridgeport 06606
   Brian C. Williams, 27 Myrtle Ave., Bridgeport 06604
24 Charles M. McCollam, 8 Mansfield St., Bethel 06801
   Jimmetta Samaha, 208 Southern Blvd., Danbury 06810
25 Donna King, 71 Aiken St., Unit Q-16, Norwalk 06854
   Frank N. Zullo, 24 Sawmill Rd., Norwalk 06851
26 Stuart Smith, 26 Cricket La., Wilton 06897
   Diane Farrell, 125 Weston Rd., Westport 06880
27 John Scanlon, 33 Putter Dr., Stamford 06907
   Sanchia Spandow, 91 Strawberry Hill Ave., #429, Stamford 06902
28 Beatrice D. Steeneck, 260 Shetland Rd., Fairfield 06430
   John Wrabel, 77 Orchard Hill Dr., Fairfield 06430
29 Dawn M. Niles, Lot 14, Evelyn Dr., North Windham 06256
   Daniel S. Rovero, 53 Prospect St., Putnam 06260
30 Roberta S. Willis, P.O. Box 1733, Lakeville 06039
   Owen J. Quinn, 15 College Ave., Torrington 06790
31 Brian Suchinski, 130 Oak Hill Dr., Bristol 06010
   Rosemary Morante, 28 Welch St., Plainville 06062
32 Michael J. Vernovai, Sr., 71 Dalton St., Oakville 06779
   Marjorie C. Bennett, 12 Main St. North, Bethlehem 06751
33 Anthony Marino, 472 Seaside Ave., Westbrook 06498
   Dorothy Mrowka, 399 Lebanon Ave., Colchester 06415
34 Dominic Palumbo, 1298 Hartford Tpke., Unit 2E, North Haven 06473
   Laraine M. Smith, 37 Wallingford Rd., Cheshire 06410
35 Devra Baum, 31 Reed St., Vernon 06066
   Bill Pakulis, 146 Virginia La., Tolland 06084
36 Pete Peck, 15 Skyridge Rd., Greenwich 06831
   Mary McNamee, 190 Milbank Ave., Greenwich 06830

Members of the National Committee

Ellen Camhi, 50 Arnold Dr., Stamford 06905
John Olsen, 23 High St., Clinton 06413
Anthony V. Avallone, 75 Broad St., Milford 06460

REPUBLICAN STATE CENTRAL COMMITTEE OF CONNECTICUT

97 Elm St., Rear, Hartford 06106
Tel., (860) 547-0589
(As of January 1, 1997)

Chm., Chris DePino, 20 Iris St., New Haven 06512
Vice Chm., Patricia A. Longo, 444 Thayer Pond Rd., Wilton 06897
Secy., Judy Ganswindt, 14 Pennywise La., Old Saybrook 06475
Treas., Stephen Bafundo, 93 Littlebrook Rd., Newington 06111

District

1 John O'Connell III, 819 New Britian Ave., Hartford 06106
  John J. Logan, 318 Hartford Ave., Wethersfield 06109

2 Fannie Gabriel, 43 Prospect St., Bloomfield 06002
  Kevin Deneen, 37 Welch Ave., Windsor 06095

3 Fred Balet, 190 Woodmont Dr., East Hartford 06118
  Edwina Futtner, 203 Sandstone Dr., South Windsor 06074

4 B. Kent Sleath, 60 Williams Glen Way, Glastonbury 06033
  John Garside, 77 Strickland St., Manchester 06040

5 Richard Vannie, 34 Lexington Rd., West Hartford 06119
  vacancy

6 Lisa Carver, 286 Garry Dr., New Britain 06052
  Frank Dobeck, 30 Woodland La., Kensington 06037

7 Esther Hannum, 16 Copper Dr., Enfield 06082
  Michael Nesta, 122 Hampten Rd., Somers 06071

8 Marge Diachenko, 28 Lincoln La., Weatogue 06089
  Lilliam Ludlam, 566 Town Hill Rd., New Hartford 06057

9 Steven Bafundo, 93 Little Brook Rd., Newington 06111
  Mark Dean, 34 Pebble Rd., Wethersfield 06109

10 George Gallo, 500 Prospect St., #4-F, New Haven 06511-2166
   Thomas E. Mansfield, 39 Front St., West Haven 06516

11 Ralph Marcarelli, 37 Wooster Pl., New Haven 06511
   Paul Karbowski, 171 Angela Rd., East Haven 06512

12 Art L. DeSorbo, 494 Silver Sands Rd., East Haven 06512
   Beth Bryan, 283 Harbor St., Branford 06405

13 Anthony Vasiliou, 3 Yellow Wood St., Middletown 06457
   Martin Lilienthal, 150 Tulip Dr., Meriden 06450

14 Doris Knight, 414 Old Tavern Rd., Orange 06477
   Gerald Cavallo, 80 Ocean Ave., Milford 06460

15 Tim Longino, 46 Melissa La., Prospect 06712
   Mark Brennan, 6 Rockhurst Dr., Waterbury 06708

16 Richard Cianci, 540 Berlin St., Southington 06489
   Dennis King, 27 Transit St, Waterbury 06704

17 Patricia Fers, 28 West Brookside Ave., Ansonia 06401
   Barbara DiNicola, 10 Dante Pl., Hamden 06514

18 Donald E. Schoolcraft, 350 Ring Dr., Groton 06340
   Steven Wade, 15 Collins Rd., Stonington 06378
19 Edward J. Sedar, 69 Sherwood La., Norwich 06360
   Herman R. Weingart, 446 Lebanon Rd., North Franklin 06254
20 Emma Lincoln, 16 Glenwood Pl., New London 06320
   John Torrenti, 9 Mallard Pt., Old Saybrook 06475
21 Gary DeFilippo, 43 Perch Rd., Shelton 06484
   Richard Gilardi, 1050 Beaver Dam Rd., Stratford 06497
22 Linda A. Grace, 793 Broad Bridge Rd., Bridgeport 06610
   Ann Moore, 19 Coventry La., Trumbull 06611
23 Ralph Segarra, 257 Jane St., Bridgeport 06608
   Michael Garrett, 49 Weber Ave., Bridgeport 06610
24 Robert Yamin, 8 Johnson Dr., Danbury 06810
   Jeff Muthersbaugh, 54 Milwaukee Ave., Bethel 06801
25 Enirco DiPasquale, P.O. Box 669, Norwalk 06852
   John J. Ryan, P.O. Box 1085, Norwalk 06856
26 Jon Frey, P.O. Box 207, 1 Copps Hill Rd., Ridgefield 06877
   Vincent Socci, 88 Forest St., New Canaan 06840
27 Charles Klein, Jr., 60 Vanech Dr., Stamford 06905-3629
   Phillips G. Terhune, Jr., 8 Echo Dr., Darien 06820
28 Paul Tymniak, 225 White Hill La., Fairfield 06430
   Robert Hall, 5 Nettleton Ave., Newtown 06470
29 C. Lawrence Schiller, 33 Bolivia St., Willimantic 06226
   John E. Burke, P.O. Box 145, 3 Lawton La., Dayville 06241
30 Anna-Elysapeth McGuire, 49 Allyndale Rd., North Canaan 06018
   John Morris, 3533 Hall Meadow Rd-Goshen, Norfolk 06058
31 Ellie Klapatch, 44 Arbor Ct., Bristol 06010
   William Petit, P.O. Box 310, 132 Redstone Hill, Plainville 06062
32 Gregg Seabury, 3 Fieldstone Rd., Brookfield 06804
   Andy Munson, P.O. Box 295, Roxbury 06783
33 June Forella, 5 Highland Ave., Portland 06480
   Elizabeth Wagner, 172 Stollman Rd., Colchester 06415
34 Edward R. Ulozas, 52 Williamsburg Dr., Cheshire 06410
   Frank Porto, 145 Buell St., North Haven 06473
35 Frank Falana, 3980 South St., Coventry 06238
   Barry Shead, 4 Fairview Cir., Pomfret 06259
36 Ann Issacson, 45 Willow Rd., Riverside 06878
   Ralph F. Loglisci, 39 Mercedes La., Stamford 06905

Members of the National Committee

John Miller, 1137 Silas Deane Hwy., Wethersfield 06109
Jo McKenzie, P.O. Box 1419, Madison 06443

DEMOCRATIC TOWN CHAIRPERSONS AND VICE CHAIRPERSONS

TOWN	TOWN CHAIRPERSONS	ADDRESS	VICE CHAIRPERSONS	ADDRESS
Andover	Jay Linddy	125 Lake Rd. 06232	Kenneth Lester	188 Lake Rd. 06232
Ansonia	Richard D. Krueger	4 Remer St. 06401	Pauline A. Sampieri	54 Finney St. 06401
Ashford	Garrett Tuller	212 Southworth Dr. 06278	Jean N. McCarthy	436 Bebbington Rd. 06278
Avon	Paul Fox	24 Oak Bluff 06001	Sylvia Stieber	P.O. Box 416, 06001
Barkhamsted	Bette Jane Murphy	Box 176, Pleasant Valley 06063	Andrew W. Bray	65 Ratlum Mountain Rd., Collinsville 06022
Beacon Falls	Tom Trzaski	34 Fairfield Pl. 06403	Pamela Belisle	341 Burton Rd. 06403
Berlin	Charles Warner	121 Timberwood Rd., Kensington 06037	John Aguzi	19 Cole La., Kensington 06037
Bethany	Alexandra Breslin	91 Sperry Rd. 06524	Wesley Spear	220 Bethmour Rd. 06254
Bethel	Martin Lawlor, Jr.	40 Shelley Rd. 06801	Susanne Bitterman	27 Katria Cir. 06801
Bethlehem	Philip W. Thompson	131 Auncient Oak Rd. 06751	Marjorie C. Bennett	12 Main St. North 06751
Bloomfield	Bennett Millstein	46 Cliffmount Dr. 06002	Althea Jenkin	38 Hillfarm Rd. 06002
Bolton	Marian Kelsey	15 Shady La. 06043	Robert D. Lessard	15 Converse Rd. 06043
Bozrah	Robert A. Kofkoff	Box 187, 06334	Maria Chiangi	13 Goulard Dr. 06334
Branford	Edward C. Johnson, Jr.	132 Sunset Hill Dr. 06405	Carol Bryan	283 Harbor St. 06405
	Joan P. Grossman	11 Prospect Hill Rd. 06405	vacancy	
	Anthony Daros	27 Watrous Ave. 06405		
Bridgeport	Mario Testa	920 Madison Ave. 06606	Joan Nobriga	148 Coachlight Sq. 06608
Bridgewater	Ann L. Falwell	250 Old Turnpike Rd. 06752	Felicia Hoeniger	Clatter Valley Rd. 06752
Bristol	Mayra Berrios	125 Shawn Dr., Apt. G-10, 06010	Louis Galgano	64 Long La. 06010
Brookfield	Robert Marconi	125 Whisconier Rd. 06804	John Osborne	2 Bristol Path 06804
Brooklyn	Steven Townsend	169 Barrett Hill Rd. 06234	Rheo Brouillard	48 Fairway Dr., Danielson 06239
Burlington	Warren Baird	64 Barnes Hill Rd. 06013	Gregory F. Uglade	55 Arch St. 06013
Canaan	Carole K. McGuire	P.O. Box 156, Falls Village 06031	John Maloney	42 Deer Rd., Falls Village 06031
Canterbury	Kenneth Rawn	186 Hanover Rd. 06331	Kathleen L. Brey	22 Baldwin Brook Rd. 06331
Canton	William H. Tribou	66 Trailsend Dr. 06019	William Kurtz	11 Sugar Camp Rd. 06022
Chaplin	Marvin Cox	31 Chaplin St. 06235	Irene Schein	95 Miller Rd. 06235
Cheshire	Michael J. Laden	772 Mountain Rd. 06410	Kathleen Kaplan	40 Judson Ct. 06410
Chester	Nancy Mattson	3 Butter Jones Rd. 06412	Kurt Ziemann	P.O. Box 262, 06412
Clinton	Ethelene DiBona	107 Old Post Rd. 06413	Siobhan Doherty-Rogers	15 Thrush Cross Rd. 06413
Colchester	Robert Weeks	181 Taylor Rd. 06415	Dorothy Mrowka	399 Lebanon Ave. 06415
Colebrook	Jerry Peters	P.O. Box 33, 06021	Janet Stason	3 Pinney St., Winsted 06098
Columbia	Kevin Donohue	18 Latham Rd. 06237	Peter J. Moeckel	7 Rte. 87, 06237
Cornwall	Stephen Senzer	37 Cogswell Rd., West Cornwall 06796	Barbara Klaw	280 Cream Hill Rd., West Cornwall 06796
Coventry	Majorie Roach	348 Lewis Hill Rd. 06238	Peter R. Henry	31 John Paul La. 06238
Cromwell	Joseph R. Morin	8 West Street Ter. 06416	Danny Brandt	9 Hawthorne Ct. 06416
Danbury	Joseph Walkovich	208 Southern Blvd. 06810	Eleanor T. Lewis	25 Center St. 06810

DEMOCRATIC TOWN CHAIRPERSONS AND VICE CHAIRPERSONS

TOWN	TOWN CHAIRPERSONS	ADDRESS	VICE CHAIRPERSONS	ADDRESS
Darien	Anne Shaw	5 Hollister La. 06820	Kathy Hammell	36 Phillips La. 06820
Deep River	James Spallone	10 Westbrook Rd. 06417	Valerie Nucci	38 Essex St. 06417
Derby	Mike Kelleher	39 Belleview Dr. 06418	Madeline Miami	12 Selma Ave. 06418
Durham	Gladys Lavine	140 Dead Hill Rd. 06422	Patricia Ann Page	454 Main St. 06422
Eastford	Mary A. Duncan	211 Eastford Rd., Apt. 198, 06242	Cliff Noll	45 French Rd. 06242
East Granby	Thomas Howard	59 Old County Rd. 06026	Michael Sullivan	72 Wynding Hills 06026
East Haddam	Joanne Rozniak	1 Oak Rd. 06423	Bradley Parker	318 Town St. 06423
East Hampton	Philip A. Wheeler	P.O. Box 132, Middle Haddam, 06456	Alan Hurst	1 Spice Hill Rd., Middle Hadam 06456
East Hartford	Pasquale J. Salemi	17 Pheasant La. 06108	Doris T. Curley	72 Anita Dr. 06118
East Haven	Andrew Verderame	81 Bennett Rd. 06512	Alfred Cronk	136 Gene St. 06512
East Lyme	William P. Powers	21 Haigh Ave., Niantic 06357	Yolanda Barracco	16 Elm St. 06512
Easton	Emmett Wallace	25 Knapp St. 06612	Richard B. Fabricant	16 Chapman Dr. 06333
East Windsor	Frances M. Keenan	13 Reservoir Ave. 06016	Alison Bonds	3 Austin Drive Ext. 06612
Ellington	Ronald Blanchette	74 Kibbe Rd. 06029	vacancy	
Enfield	Jack Mancuso	17 Keller Ave. 06082	Mark D. Leighton	40 Blueberry Cir. 06029
Essex	Alvin G. Wolfgram	P.O. Box 863, 06426-0863	Karl Dudek	20 Toyler Rd. 06082
Fairfield	Eileen Wilcox	68 Romanock Pl. 06430	vacancy	
Farmington	Deborah Quigley	486 Main St. 06032	Jonathan Kantrowitz	877 Burr St. 06430
			Justin J. Pagano	10 Girard Ave. 06032
			John Karwoski	17 Red Coat La. 06032
Franklin	Barbara Konow-Ward	45 Baltic Rd., Franklin 06254	John Laterra	19 Pautipaug Hill Rd. 06254
Glastonbury	Nicholas Paindiris	119 Butler Dr. 06033	Alice Maggi	282 Stanley Dr. 06033
Goshen	Marilyn M. Brennan	342 West Hyerdale Dr. 06756	John D. Garvey	239 Beach St. 06756
Granby	Harold Smith	P.O. Box 853, 06035	Margaret Chapple	10 Burleigh Dr. 06035
Greenwich	Sigmund A. Beck	15 Skyridge Rd. 06831	Gwenn Bylinsky	32 Chapel La. 06878
			Harry LeBien	64 Burning Tree Rd. 06831
Griswold	Richard J. Duda	4 Scott Dr., Jewett City 06351	Cynthia Kata	37 Russell St., Jewett City 06351
Groton (Town)	Lian Obrey	53 Monument St. 06340	John McGee	33 Essex St., West Mystic 06340
Groton (City)	Gary Johnson	165 Tyler Ave. 06340	Andrew Parrella	790 Eastern Point Rd. 06340
Guilford	Robert Deutsch	63 Grist Mill Cir. 06437	Tamzon Green	64 Leetes Island Rd. 06437
Haddam	Christopher Lassen	P.O. Box 69, Higganum 06441	Terry Concannon	76 Timms Hill Rd. 06438
Hamden	Arthur J. Giuletti	20 Elliot Dr. 06514	John Morrison	1692 Whitney Ave. 06517
Hampton	Marilyn Higgins	38 Hammond Hill Rd. 06247	Robert McDermott	208 West Old Route 6, 06247
Hartford	Robert Jackson	24 Canterbury St. 06112	Aida Morales	235 Roger St. 06106
Hartland	William Hodge, Acting	22 South Rd., E. Hartland 06027	vacancy	
Harwinton	Mary Jane Febbroriello	47 South Rd. 06791	vacancy	

DEMOCRATIC TOWN CHAIRPERSONS AND VICE CHAIRPERSONS

TOWN	TOWN CHAIRPERSONS	ADDRESS	VICE CHAIRPERSONS	ADDRESS
Hebron	John R. Quinn	10 Mohegan La., Amston 06231	Patricia Bowler	101 Slocomb Rd., Amston 06231
Kent	Edward Epstein	27 Lane St. 06757	vacancy	
Killingly	Raymond F. Parlato	107 Broad St., Danielson 06239	Roxanne Pappas	889 Upper Maple St., Box 503, Danielson 06239
Killingworth	Rick Albrecht	86 Cow Hill Rd. 06419	Mark Williams	274 Roast Meat Hill Rd. 06419
Lebanon	Mark Favrow	5 Hillcrest Heights 06249	Harold Liebman	1593 Exeter Rd. 06249
Ledyard	Frank Gionfriddo	466 Col. Ledyard Hwy. 06339	Colette Crown	49 Harvard Ter. 06335
Lisbon	Leonora Szruba	195 Kimball Rd. 06351	Daniel W. Teper	50 Dogwood Dr. 06351
Litchfield	Michael Dunn	18 McBride Rd. 06759	Linda Bongiolatti,	25 Goodhouse Rd. 06759
Lyme	vacancy		LeRoy McFarland	24-2 Burr Rd. 06371
Madison	Melanie Clark	71 Beekman Pl. 06443	Todd Foust	391 Durham Rd. 06443
Manchester	Theodore R. Cummings	87 Lawton Rd. 06040	Betty Kramer	41 Campfield Rd. 06040
Mansfield	Richard Sherman	43 Pinewoods La. 06250	Betty Gardner	98 Foster Dr. 06226
Marlborough	Philip L. Dimond	110 Jerry Daniels Rd. 06447	Diane M. Teixeira	56 East Hampton Rd. 06447
Meriden	Frank J. Cirillo	85 Briarwood Dr. 06450	Francis L. Schwartz	111 Milton Dr. 06450
Middlebury	Kathleen Krevetski	P.O. Box 355, 06762	Jim Roach	182 Curtis Rd. 06762
Middlefield	Sebastian J. Aresco	11 Elvira Dr., Rockfall 06481	vacancy	
Middletown	Anthony Petruccelli	526 Westfield St. 06457	Sara Vecchitto	1411 Forest Glen #14, 06457
Milford	Kevin McGrath	24 Miles St. 06460	Beverly W. Melzer	166 Herbert St. 06460
Monroe	Gary Zenobia	91 Swendsen Dr. 06468	Vivian N. Capoccitti	88 Swendsen Dr. 06468
Montville	Ronald H. Moore	35 Evergreen La., Oakdale 06370	Joseph DeVito	1494 Old Colchester Rd., Oakdale 06370
Morris	Frederick Neri	79 Slab Meadow Rd. 06763	Stephen Paletsky	Rte. 109, 06763
Naugatuck	William J. Goggin, Jr.	401 Union City Rd. 06770	Joseph R. McEvoy	52 Ruela Dr. 06770
New Britain	John H. McNamara	56 Brighton St. 06053	Caludia Helfgott	12 Brady Ave. 06052
New Canaan	Johnny M. Potts	3 Colonial Court, 06840	Kathleen Vollmer	322 Hoyt Farm Rd. 06840
New Fairfield	Michael Gill	25 West Ridge Rd. 06812	William O'Keefe	19 Donna Dr. 06812
New Hartford	Polly S. Harris	335 Cottin Hill Rd. 06057	John McMahon, Jr.	2 Cedar La. 06057
New Haven	Dominic F. Balleto	366 Townsend Ave. 06512	Linda G. Cox	64 Bristol St. 06511
Newington	Frank L. Aieta	595 Church St. 06111	Suzanne Reniewicz	82 Stuart St. 06111
New London	Anthony R. Basilica	54 Gardner Ave. 06320	Marcia S. Bell	20 Keeney La. 06320
New Milford	Murray Kessler	16 Revere Rd. 06776	Virginia V. Wall	141 Pumpkin Hill Rd. 06776
Newtown	Earl J. Smith	5 Serenity La., Sandy Hook 06482	Daniel Rosenthal	70 Main St. 06470
Norfolk	H. James Stedronsky	P.O. Box 9, Winsted 06098	Mary O'D. Welz	41 Maple Ave. 06058
North Branford	Lawrence Casey	38 Wilford Rd. 06471	vacancy	
North Canaan	Tom Gailes	138 South Canaan Rd. 06018	Nancy L. Gandolfo	316 West Main St. 06018
North Haven	Arthur M. Concilio	48 Postman Hwy. 06473	Peggy Brennan	100 Fitch St. 06473

DEMOCRATIC TOWN CHAIRPERSONS AND VICE CHAIRPERSONS

TOWN	TOWN CHAIRPERSONS	ADDRESS	VICE CHAIRPERSONS	ADDRESS
North Stonington	Jennifer Johnson	P.O. Box 67, 06359	James A. Cunha	646 Lantern Hill Rd. 06359
Norwalk	Donna King	81 Aiken St., Unit Q-16, 06851	Rose Riley-Rodriguez	148 South Main St. 06854
Norwich	Thomas L. Leclair	One American Way 06360	Nancy DePietro	157 Broad St. 06360
Old Lyme	Francis P. McTigue	P.O. Box 402, Lyme 06371	Gloria J. Pendleton	35 Mile Creek Rd., Apt. 2A 06371
Old Saybrook	Robert S. Dion	63 Maple Ave. 06475	C. Marston Ladd	5 Cricket Ct. 06475
Orange	Joseph A. Lembo, Jr.	518 Summit Dr. 06477	Marlene Silverstein	860 Shaghark Dr. 06477
Oxford	Katherine P. Johnson	68 Dorman Rd. 06478	Kathleen Murphy	10 High Ridge Ter. 06478
Plainfield	William A. Holmes	14 Fernwood St. 06374	Gloria Rizer	98 Community Ave. 06374
Plainville	Dan Ciesielski	33 Overlook Dr. 06062	Val Dumais	43 Reliance Rd. 06062
Plymouth	Patrick Perugino	82 Allen St., Terryville 06786	Jerry Fedorovich	38 Harwinton Ave., Terryville 06786
Pomfret	Thomas Pahl	147 Tyrone Rd. 06259	Norma Robbins	189 Deerfield Rd. 06259
Portland	Joseph S. Coatsworth	65 Old Carriage Rd. 06480	Bernadette M. Dillon	22 Waverly Ave. 06480
Preston	Eugene Hildreth	2 Ortega Dr. 06365	Christine Schmidt	3 Lawrence Ct. 06365
Prospect	Steven Skrebutenas	3 Orchard Dr. 06712	Katherine Blinstrubas	24 Maple Dr. 06712
Putnam	Gerry Cotnoir	39 Van Den Noort St. 06260	Paula Lajeunesse	113 Mechanics St. 06260
Redding	Tina Miller	81 Seventy Acre Rd., West Redding 06896	Michael Roush	55 Old Stagecoach Rd., West Redding 06896
Ridgefield	John W. Kukulka	90 Saint Johns Rd. 06877	Barbara R. Maners	109 Round Lake Rd. 06877
Rocky Hill	Glenn R. Parent	31 Berkshire Rd. 06067	Rosemary M. Ames	32 Footehill Rd. 06067
Roxbury	Jacqueline G. Dooley	77 Goldmine Rd. 06783	Wayne Piskura	65 Mollory Rd. 06783
Salem	Leeland J. Cole-Chu	300 Hartford Rd. 06420	James Fogarty	373 Old New London Rd. 06420
Salisbury	Albert Ginouves	22 Meadow St., Lakeville 06039	Sara Zarbock	P.O. Box 180, Lakeville 06039
Scotland	Amy Lake	211 Huntington Rd. 06264	Susan Smith	356 Hanover Rd., Baltic 06330
Seymour	John S. Pizzi	1 South West Rd. 06483	Steve Kulas	38 George St. 06483
Sharon	John Greco	9 Rolling Hills 06069	Jerne Cramp	160 White Hollow Rd. 06069
Shelton	Thomas H. Bartram	66 Geissler Dr. 06484	Harriet Finn	29 East Village Rd. 06484
Sherman	David McGovern	5 Peace Pipe La. 06784	Richard McGoldrick	107 Church Rd. 06784
Simsbury	Christina McDermott	P.O. Box 22, 06070	Tara Willerup	26 Barry Lane 06070
Somers	Adam Sharaf	33 Manse Hill Rd. 06071	Maurice Rondeau	95 Durkee Rd. 06071
Southbury	David B. Palmer	1826 Bucks Hill Rd. 06488	William Liedlich	2 Pomperaug Office Park 06489
Southington	Donna Civitello	111 Southington Ave. 06489	vacancy	
South Windsor	Dolores L. Longo	185 Valley View Dr. 06074	Joel Nadel	135 Windsor Dr. 06074
Sprague	Jacqueline Smith	25 Scotland Rd., Baltic 06330	Mary L. Thomas	17 Salt Rock Rd., P.O. Box 185, Hanover 06350
Stephen J. Papineau, Sr.				
Stafford	Edward M. Muska	2 Penny La., Stafford Springs 06076	Theodore R. Satkowski	167 Upper Rd., Box 218, Staffordville 06077
Stamford	Ellen P. Camhi	50 Arnold Dr. 06905	Vincenzo R. Martino	25 Charles Mary La. 06905
Sterling	John Molodich	Rte 49, Box 633, Moosup 06354	Hedwig Russwurm	RFD Box 105, Oneco 06373

DEMOCRATIC TOWN CHAIRPERSONS AND VICE CHAIRPERSONS

TOWN	TOWN CHAIRPERSONS	ADDRESS	VICE CHAIRPERSONS	ADDRESS
Stonington	Joseph Pescatello	14 Avery St., Pawcatuck 06379	Frank Pucci	35 Hinckley St., Mystic 06355
Stratford	Richard A. Miron	117 Ferry Ct. 06497	Eileen S. Wilson	395 Pilgrim La. 06497
Suffield	Eleanor F. Butler	1174 Blossom St. 06078	Stephen Martin	56 Rasley Rd., West Suffield 06093
Thomaston	Marie Galbraith	290 Walnut Hill Rd. 06787	Beatrice C. Fuller	375 Walnut Hill Rd., P.O. Box 188, 06787
Thompson	Catherine A. Thomas	655 Riverside Dr., Grosvenordale 06246	Christopher Eichner	27 Elliot Hill Rd., North Grosvenordale 06255
Tolland	Bettye Jo Patulis	146 Virginia La. 06084	Charles Higgins	16 Louis La. 06084
Torrington	Jack Dillon	124 Whippoorwill La. 06790	Carolann Kennedy	10 Westledge Dr. 06790
Trumbull	Nancy J. DiNardo	61 Suzanne Cir. 06611	Paul A. Neri	25 Birch St. 06611
Union	James J. Smith	106 Old Brown Rd. 06076	Bonnie Dabrowski	44-40 Crawford Center Dr., Stafford Springs 06076
Vernon	Gloria Collins	164 Box Mountain Dr. 06066	Timothy Polowski	38 Rigley Rd. 06066
			Pauline Schaefer	1 Fox Hill Dr. 06066
Voluntown	Carl D. Anderson	880 Pendleton Rd. 06384	Cindy McGaw	RFD 1, Box 342A 06384
Wallingford	William Fischer	31 Sunrise Cir. 06492	Nicholas Kern	326 Main St. 06492
			Deborah Testa	30 Pipep Dr. 06492
Warren	Richard K. Abrahams	111 Town Hill Rd. 06754	William F. Schnell	16 Strawberry La., New Preston 06777
Washington	Dorothy Hill	51 Nichols Hill Rd. 06794	Adelaide Roberts	9 Shinar Mountain Rd. 06794
Waterbury	Thomas Carusello	162 Geddes Ter. 06705	Antony A. Casagrande	16 Brentwood Ave. 06705
Waterford	Sharon Palmer	9 Laurel Glen Rd., Quaker Hill 06375	Earl Peters	10 Totoket Rd., Quaker Hill 06375
Watertown	Wilbur S. Hughes	370 French St. 06795	Denise Russ	135 Porter St. 06795
Westbrook	Anthony P. Marino	472 Seaside Ave. 06498	Marilyn Ozols	104 Salt Island Rd. 06498
West Hartford	Marilyn F. Cohen	46 Stoneham Dr. 06117	Larry Price	124 Beverly Rd. 06117
West Haven	Wayne Talamelli	28 Fairlea Rd. 06516	Deborah L. Evangelista	23 Leete St. 06516
Weston	James Shearin	1 Old Mill Rd. 06883	Harvey Bellin	70 Birch Hill Rd. 06883
Westport	Martha M. Aasen	31 Ellery La. 06880	Howard Brody	79 Clinton Ave. 06880
Wethersfield	Shirley W. Steinmetz	375 Brimfield Rd. 06109	Robert W. Smith	76 Farmstead Rd. 06109
Willington	Wayne Knight	351 River Rd. 06279	Arthur Forst	7 Penney Hill Rd. 06279
Wilton	Stuart Smith	26 Cricket La. 06897	Margaret Reeves	55 Hemmelskamp Rd. 06897
Winchester	Brian W. Sullivan	362 Tiffany Rd., Winsted 06098	Arnold Travagin	27 Front St., Winsted 06098
Windham	Dennis J. O'Brien	34 Bellevue St., Willimantic 06226	Paulette N. Haines	29 Laurel La. 06280
Windsor	David Guay	413 West Wolcott Ave. 06095	Anita Mips	14 Dudley Town Rd. 06095
Windsor Locks	George Hall	18 Midland Rd. 06096	Edward A. Ferrari	19 Helena La. 06096
Wolcott	Jean M. Orsatti	34 Woodcrest Ave. 06716	Ann R. Forte	6 Deepwood Dr. 06716
Woodbridge	Gerald T. Weiner	15 Bishop Dr. 06525	Nancy Scully	68 Orchard Rd. 06525
Woodbury	Dennis Galik	151 Flanders Rd. 06798	Reed Bertolette	43 Tomlinson Rd. 06798
			Paul Hinckley	135 Cat Rd., P.O. Box 414, 06798
Woodstock	Denis J. Gobin	313 East Quasset Rd. 06281	Shirley Rapose	9 Meehan Rd. 06281

REPUBLICAN TOWN CHAIRPERSONS AND VICE CHAIRPERSONS

TOWN	TOWN CHAIRPERSONS	ADDRESS	VICE CHAIRPERSONS	ADDRESS
Andover	Ylo Anson	138 Boston Hill Rd. 06232	Leigh Ann Hutchinson	38 Bunker Hill Rd. 06232
Ansonia	George Boath, Jr.	10 Dempsey Ct. 06401	vacancy	
Ashford	William Falletti	165 Mansfield Rd. 06278	Merrill Simpson	137 Mansfield Rd. 06278
Avon	Vincent E. Roche	146 Deepwood Dr. 06001	Penelope R. Woodford	687 West Avon Rd. 06001
Barkhamsted	David R. Moulton	5 Deer Run Rd., North Canton, 06059	John Lavieri	P.O. Box 202, Pleasant Valley 06063
			Maria Mullady	22 Robin Dr., Collinsville 06002
			James Hart	100 Park Rd., Pleasant Valley 06063
Beacon Falls	Leonard C. Greene	146 Cedar La. 06403	Christopher B. Sura	2 Ellen Dr. 06403
Berlin	Joseph Bajorski	80 Butternut La. Kensington 06037	Audrey Bertagna	195 Stockings Brook Rd., Kensington 06037
Bethany	Russell D. von Beren	134 Wooding Hill Rd. 06524	Jean T. Raddatz	22 Bethridge Rd. 06524
Bethel	Robert H. Paugh	123 Putnam Park Rd. 06801	John Cleary	112 South St. 06801
Bethlehem	Ingrid Buswell	89 Woodcreek Rd. 06751	Pamela Nole	P.O. Box 6, West Rd. 06751
Bloomfield	Howard Frydman	P.O. Box 932, 06002	vacancy	
Bolton	Mark Johnson	11 Lynwood Dr. 06043	Susan Bosworth	239 Hebron Rd. 06043
Bozrah	Keith Robbins	46 Rosemarie La. 06334	Stephen Sedar	111 Bishop Rd. 06334
Branford	Al Ippolito	16 Indian Woods Rd. 06405	Carol Bryan	283 Harbor St. 06405
Bridgeport	Joan Magnuson	67 Sampson St. 06606	vacancy	
Bridgewater	Randall Carreira	50 Old Town Hwy. 06752	Victor Persbacker	1 Bridgewater Common 06752
Bristol	Carlo Faienza	186 Mountain View Ave. 06010	Art Mocabee	70 Wolcott Rd. 06010
Brookfield	William Fuchs	6 Cannon Rd. 06804	Sandra Schroder	148 Longmeadow Hill Rd. 06804
Brooklyn	Keith Knowlton	30 Canterbury Rd. 06234	Robert Kelleher	122 Day St., Danielson 06239
Burlington	Michael Chowaniec	143 Johnnycake Mtn. Rd. 06013	Lucien Rucci	104 Barnes Hill Rd. 06013
Canaan	Fred Peterson	15 Prospect St. Falls Village 06031	vacancy	
Canterbury	John T. Bennett	48 Barstow Rd. 06331	Luther Thurlow	181 Colburn 06331
Canton	Ronald L. Grenier	85 West Mountain Rd., Collinsville 06020	Vince D'Addeo	9 Highland Dr. 06019
Chaplin	Eugene Boomer, Jr.	137 Bedlam Rd., N. Windham 06256	E. Hill Bullard	42 Shuba La., Mansfield Ctr. 06250
Cheshire	Harold W. Mosher	272 Country Club Rd. 06410	Robert Sepp	805 Broad Swamp Rd. 06410
Chester	Thomas E. Marsh	12 Winthrop Rd. 06412	vacancy	
Clinton	Maryanne Cardone	11 Kings Grant 06413	Joseph Schettino, Jr.	One Hurd Bridge Rd. 06413
Colchester	Raymond A. Hastings	75 Kennedy Dr. 06415	Nicholas Norton	94 Winchester Rd. 06415
Colebrook	John Miller	113 Sandy Brook Rd., Winsted 06098	Penelope White	P.O. Box 26, 06021
Columbia	Bryant Andrews	99 Rte. 87, 06237	Bill Jenkins	17 Thompson Hill Rd. 06237
Cornwall	Don Bardot	Town St., West Cornwall 06796	Lisa Cruse	Cream Hill Rd., West Cornwall 06796
Coventry	Albert Harper	4001 South St. 06238	vacancy	
Cromwell	Paul Beaulieu	468 Main St. 06416	Phyllis Eagle	7 Pondview Dr. 06416
Danbury	Michael A. McLachlan	P.O. Box 4665, 06813	Vincent Nolan, Jr.	12 Hillanda 06811

REPUBLICAN TOWN CHAIRPERSONS AND VICE CHAIRPERSONS

TOWN	TOWN CHAIRPERSONS	ADDRESS	VICE CHAIRPERSONS	ADDRESS
Darien	William D. Glover	24 Brush Island Rd. 06820	Linda Santarella	341 West Ave. 06820
Deep River	Edward Godfrey	187 Essex St. 06417	Karen Armour	35 Fairview Ave. 06820
Derby	Richard Frowhle	19 Iamotti La. 06418	Francis Strukus	62 Bushy Hill Rd. 06417
Durham	Scott Douglass	107 Black Walnut Dr. 06422	Leo Disorbo	7 Benanto Dr. 06418
Eastford	Dean Bunnell	Box 1, 06242	Gene Brown	277 Maple Ave. 06422
East Granby	Gordon F. Granger, Jr.	85 Copper Hill Rd. 06026	Robert L. Reiss	100 Chaplin Rd. 06242
East Haddam	Emmett J. Lyman	136 Town St. 06423	Carolyn B. Phillips	4 Cedar Ridge Rd. 06026
East Hampton	Maria F. Rand	12 Olde Flatbrook Rd. 06424	Randy Dill	Beebe Rd. 06423
East Hartford	Wanda Z. Franek	645 Goodwin St. 06108	Tom Pastorello	15 Barton Hill Rd. 06424
East Haven	Lawrence C. Sgrignari	118 Angela Dr. 06512	James Korp	744 Brewer St. 06118
East Lyme	Paul Formica	20-A Bush Hill Dr., Niantic 06357	Frank Cappelloni	140 Thompson St. Unit 06513
Easton	Maria Gaines	1164 Sport Hill Rd. 06612	Harold Kaplan	8 Hathway 06333
East Windsor	Al Regina	12 Petticoat La., Broad Brook 06016	Alfred Treidel	22 Soundview Dr. 06612
Ellington	Robert K. Pagani	7 Crystal Rd. 06029	Scott Nai	241 South Water St. 06088
Enfield	Lisa Raymond	409 Ashmead Commons 06082	Clifford Aucter	427 Somers Rd. 06029
Essex	James J. Hill	83 North Main St. 06426	Tom Terrall	14 Orbit Dr. 06082
Fairfield	John P. McCarthy	10 Twin Brooks La. 06430	vacancy	
Farmington	Dennis Person	35 Crescent Ave. 06032	Michael Fox	45 Lakeside Dr. 06430
Franklin	Bruce Dougherty	24 Hyde Park Rd., No. Franklin 06254	Kay Olsen	51 Crocus La. 06032
Glastonbury	Robert E. Brown	49 Tall Timbers Dr. 06033	Russell Beisieger	715 Lebanon Rd., North Franklin 06254
Goshen	Susannah E. Curi	175 Pie Hill Rd. 06756	Carl Hein	310 Farmcliff Dr. 06033
Granby	John Adams	3 Westview Dr. 06035	Edwin Chadwick	39 Tamara 06756
Greenwich	Daniel Donahue	22 Normandy La., Riverside 06878	Diane Neumann	60 Haven Dr. 06035
Griswold	Kenneth Briody	119 North Main St., Jewett City 06351	William Lewis	58 East Elm St. 06830
	Stewart Norman	10 School St. 06351	David Schultz	110 No. Eagleville Rd., Storrs 06268
Groton (Town)	Eleanor Steere	144 East Shore Ave., Groton Long Pt. 06340	Glenn Shiffer	39 Church St. Noank 06340
Groton (City)	Thomas Hill	258 Shore Ave. 06340	Debra Jenkins	41 Burgess Pl. 06340
Guilford	James F. O'Keefe	50 Nut Plains Rd. West 06437	George Goss	Duck Hole Rd. 06437
Haddam	Robert Stimolo	P.O. Box 10, 06438	Keith Ainsworth	365 Saybrook Rd., Higganum 06441
Hamden	Joshua A. Winnick	215 Santa Fe Ave. 06517	Austin Cesare	24 Beacon St. 06514
Hampton	Gordon Hansen	282 Main St. 06247	Bill Pearl	42 Cedar Swamp Rd. 06247
Hartford	John B. O'Connell, Jr.	819 New Britain Ave. 06106	Robert Lutts	95 Huntington St. 06105
Hartland	Carolyn Irwin	140 Hartland Blvd., East Hartland 06027	Steven Ryder	98 Hartland Blvd., East Hartland 06027
Harwinton	Rosemary Carros	131 South Rd. 06791	Paul Krenitsky	Clearview Ave. 06791
Hebron	Brian Haskell	322 Skinner La. 06248	vacancy	

REPUBLICAN TOWN CHAIRPERSONS AND VICE CHAIRPERSONS

TOWN	TOWN CHAIRPERSONS	ADDRESS	VICE CHAIRPERSONS	ADDRESS
Kent	Frank P. Orioles	81 No. Main St. 06757	James A. Palmer	132 So. Kent Rd. 06785
Killingly	Gary Gendron	P.O. Box 640, Dayville 06241	vacancy	
Killingworth	Jack R. Kneale	592 Rte 81, 06419	Charles Morgan	53 Green Hill Rd. 06415
Lebanon	Robert Wentworth	177 West Town St. 06249	Jonica Blakeslee	453 Kick Hill Rd. 06249
Ledyard	Christopher Ruest	15 Mathewson Mill Rd. 06339	Raymond Vogel	6 St. Peters Ct. 06339
Lisbon	Thomas Sparkman	20 Ethyl Acres 06351	William Kuusela	350 River Rd. 06351
Litchfield	Susan W. P. Lowenthal	P.O. Box 427, 06759	David Parenti	34 Old Newton Rd. 06759
Lyme	Rowland Ballek	90 Mt. Archer Rd. 06371	Ruth Perry	P.O. Box 783, Old Lyme 06371
Madison	Michael Haynes	1490 Durham Rd. 06443	Jonathan Heflin	25 Derenthal Dr. 06443
Manchester	Clifton Thompson	26 Pondview Dr. 06040	John Deeb	20 Wetherell St. 06040
Mansfield	Leonard E. Wells	P.O. Box 275, Mansfield Center 06250	Gary Koval	26 Charter Oak Sq. Mansfield Ctr. 06250
Marlborough	Frank G. Usseglio II	32 Flood Rd. 06447	Robert Gaudinski	89 Chapman Rd. 06447
Meriden	Richard Antonetti	15 Sachem Cir. 06450	Lois DeMayo	648 Main St., So. Meriden 06451
Middlebury	James R. Smith	11 Strathmore Rd. 06762	Julie Clark	133 Steinman Ave. 06762
Middlefield	Jon Brayshaw	4 Long Hill Rd. 06455	Robert Lamarche	51 Sunrise Ridge 06481
Middletown	Evelyn V. Russo	108 High St. 06457	Corinne Gill	52 Basswood Dr. 06457
Milford	Stephen W. Studer	80 Christine Ter. 06460	Phillip F. Ucci	78 Tumblebrook Dr. 06460
Monroe	Victor Catalano	35 Canterbury La. 06468	Jody Short	31 Stable Ridge Rd. 06468
Montville	Eric Land	516 Raymond Hill Rd., Uncasville 06382	Shelley Dennis	120 Pottys La., Uncasville 06382
Morris	Edward Sutton	P.O. Box 326, 56 Platt Farm Rd. 06763	Paul Tiffany	243 Looking Glass Hill 06763
Naugatuck	Judy Anderson	701 BeaconValley Rd. #21, 06770	Jeffrey Burmeister	1 Glenwood Ave. 06770
New Britain	Joe Willis, Sr.	142 City Ave. 06051	Leslie Jacobs	44 West End Ave. 06052
New Canaan	Dennis J. Taylor	80 Sunset Hill Rd. 06840	John Kelly	132 Turtleback 06840
New Fairfield	Roy Huckabee	4 Drummers La. 06812	Margaret Day	24 Peasant Dr. 06812
New Hartford	Lourena G. Helt	55 Birdsview Ave. 06057	David J. Bombara	24 Country La. 06057
New Haven	Sandy Astarita	140 Summit St. 06513	Jeanette Thomas	205 Ivy St. 06513
Newington	Bob Schatz	239 Maple Hill Ave. 06111	vacancy	
New London	Alvin G. Kinsall	22 Penny La. 06320	Bernard Donihee	33 Lee Ave. 06320
New Milford	Joe Sobel	132 Second Hill Rd. 06776	vacancy	
Newtown	Russ Melita	16 Budd Dr. 06470	Mae Schmidle	Echo Valley Rd. 06470
Norfolk	Carl Gundlach	223 Old Goshen Rd. 06058	Barbara Tracey	Long Meadow Dr. 06058
North Branford	Vincent Casanova	10 Bittersweet Dr. 06471	John Vaspasiano	295 Clintonville Rd. 06472
North Canaan	Douglas Humes	80 Old Turnpike Rd., Canaan 06018	Francis D. McGuire	Allyndale Rd., Canaan 06018
North Haven	Mildred S. Gherlone	100 Blakeslee Ave. 06473	Albert Cretella III	477 Middletown Ave. 06473
North Stonington	Sandra M. Steinhart	56 Hangman Hill Rd. 06359	Marjorie Penley	33 Fowler Rd. 06359
Norwalk	Richard Moccia	17 Ambler Dr. 06851	Carmine Cioffi	130 Fillow St. 06854

REPUBLICAN TOWN CHAIRPERSONS AND VICE CHAIRPERSONS

TOWN	TOWN CHAIRPERSONS	ADDRESS	VICE CHAIRPERSONS	ADDRESS
Norwich	Gerard Kortfelt	30 Elmwood Ave. 06360	James Daigle	9 Shady La. 06360
Old Lyme	Kurt Zemba	28 Champlain Dr. 06371	Richard Johnston	30 Neck Rd. 06371
Old Saybrook	Robert Antoniac	12 Ridgewood Dr. 06475	vacancy	
Orange	William Musco	366 Lambert Rd. 06477	Richard Mason	526 Gospel La. 06477
Oxford	Jay N. Silberkleit	26 Rolling Hills Dr. 06478	Lila Ferrillo	93 O'Neill Rd. 06478
Plainfield	William L. Nagel	32 Highland St. Ext., Moosup 06354	Guy LaPointe	231 Black Hill Rd. 06374
Plainville	David Underwood	4 Littleman Ct. 06062	Robert Berube	17 Eastwood Rd. 06062
Plymouth	Mark Malley	174 Keegan Rd. 06782	John Dering	70 Minor Rd., Terryville 06786
Pomfret	John Bala	80 Covell Rd. Pomfret Ctr. 06259	Mary Patenaude	P.O. Box 127, 06258
Portland	Donna Benoit	P.O. Box 53, 9 Russell Ave. 06480	James Elden	183 Cox Rd. 06480
Preston	Carl Zarkos	119 Old Jewett City Rd. 06365	Parke Spicer	11 Rte. 117, 06365
Prospect	James Duffy	107 Clark Hill Rd. 06712	Robert Hiscox	224 Matthew St. 06712
Putnam	Fred Hedenberg	84 South Main St. 06260	vacancy	
Redding	James D. Cotton	41 Pine Mountain Rd. 06896	William Brown	64 Lonetown 06896
Ridgefield	Susan S. Reynolds	112 Old West Mtn. Rd. 06877	Christopher Leonard	25 Mallory Hill Rd. 06877
Rocky Hill	James S. Ciarcia	234 Whitewood Dr. 06067	vacancy	
Roxbury	Jay Kronfeld	47 South St. 06783	Hugh Teel	19 Blueberry La. 06783
Salem	Diana N. Giles	40 Morgan Rd. 06420	Charles Meade	260 Norwich Rd. 06420
Salisbury	Jeanne Bronk	P.O. Box 501, 06068	John Bartram	120 Undermountain Rd. 06068
Scotland	Stephanie N. Abraham	P.O. Box 346, 06264	Robert B. Leete	39 Station Rd., 06264
Seymour	Robert Kennedy	35 Greenwood Cir. 06483	Pat Lombardi	143 Derby Ave. 06483
Sharon	Rosellen Schnurr	30 Cornwall Bridge Rd. 06069	vacancy	
Shelton	Frank Pagliaro	Vaccaro Heights 06484	Donald Ramia	195 Birdseye Rd. 06484
Sherman	Robert D. Bradshaw	4 Deer Run Trail 06784	Elizabeth Rowburrey	5 Gelston Rd. 06784
Simsbury	Thomas Young	16 Hampden Cir. 06070	Robert Heagney	8 Fawnbrook La. 06070
Somers	Alfred O. Brouillet	20 Gracie Dr. 06071	Hal Vita	247 Hall Hill Rd. 06071
Southbury	Penny Cognato	164 Turrill Brook Dr. 06488	vacancy	
Southington	Ann Dandrow	272 Hart St. 06489	Edward Pocock III	37 Lacey Rd. 06489
South Windsor	Mark Lillis	667 Griffin Rd. 06074	James Trinks	94 Candlewood Dr. 06074
Sprague	Dennison L. Allen	P.O. Box 304, Versailles 06383	Kenneth Caisse	P.O. Box 771, Baltic 06330
Stafford	Dock R. Sellers	36 A Michele Ave., Stafford Springs 06076	J. Anthony Morianos	89 Michelec Rd., Stafford Springs 06076
Stamford	Donna M. Loglisci	39 Mercedes La. 06905	John Liberatore	31 Puritan La. 06906
Sterling	Shirl A. Knox	P.O. Box 297, 131 Main St., 06377-0297	Robert P. Jordan	337 Saw Mill Hill Rd. 06377
Stonington	Robin Miller	698 Pequot Trail 06378	William Brown	340 River Rd., Pawcatuck 06379
Stratford	Benjamin Proto	1877 Broadbridge Ave. 06497	Linnea A. Scheck	72 Howard St. 06497
Suffield	Robert Skinner	1411 No. Grand St., West Suffield 06093	John Murphy	71 East Street North 06078

REPUBLICAN TOWN CHAIRPERSONS AND VICE CHAIRPERSONS

TOWN	TOWN CHAIRPERSONS	ADDRESS	VICE CHAIRPERSONS	ADDRESS
Thomaston	Charles Yanavich	292 Branch Road 06787-0175	Stephen Sordi	P.O. Box 373, 06787
Thompson	James Naum	29 Red Bridge Rd., North Grosvenordale 06255	John Bell	222 Pompeo Rd., No. Grosvenordale 06255
Tolland	Roger Knight	48 Cora Rd. 06084	Jennifer Nieves	400 Old Post Rd. 06084
Torrington	Ann M. Giammattasio	285 Patterson St. 06790	J. Thomas Ferrarotti	119 Kinney St., 1B 06790
Trumbull	William Holden	6 Woodfield Dr. 06611	Wesley A. Radcliffe	32 Sunrise Ave. 06611
Union	Albert Goodhall	69 Cemetery Rd. 06076	Nathan Swift	Buckley Hwy. 06076
Vernon	John Anderson	20 Hemlock Dr. 06066	Nancy Osborn	6 Knollwood Dr. 06066
Voluntown	Thomas Wilber	69 Forge Hill Rd.06348-1305	Donna Brown	41 Congdon Rd. 06384
Wallingford	Robert H. Bolte	608 North Elm St. 06492	Barbara Thompson	136 Colonial Hill 06492
Warren	Andrew Bravo	37 Hardscrabble Rd. 06754	vacancy	
Washington	Ann F. Bruzzi	87 Baldwin Hill Rd., Washington Depot 06794	Thomas Daniels	22 Old Litchfield Rd. 06793
Waterbury	Michael Stolfi	114 Split Rock Dr. 06705	Susan Beatty	28 Valentine St. 06708
Waterford	Luanne E. Dematto	14 Pamela Way 06385	John Parise	41 Devonshire Dr. 06385
Watertown	Paul Jessell	39 Radnor La. 06779	Stephen Kiraly	311 Linkfield Rd. 06795
Westbrook	Harry P. Ruppenicker, Jr.	12 Hammock Dock Rd. 06498	Paula Ferrara	51 Trout Brook Rd. 06498
West Hartford	Herbert Shepardson	41 Westmont 06117	Edward Connors	24 Rumfor St. 06107
			Sally Van Meter	158 Steele Rd. 06119
West Haven	John Isdale	101 Lakeview Ave. 06516	Paul Rapanault	30 North St. 06516
Weston	Thomas A. Aquila	13 Riverfield Dr. 06883	Eileen S. Buckley	248 Lyons Plain Rd. 06883
Westport	Robert Burns	6 Northfield Dr. 06880	vacancy	
Wethersfield	Richard P. Roberts	60 Highview Ave. 06109	Paul Courchaine	481 Main St. 06109
Willington	John Blessington	29 Mason Rd. 06279	Linda Makuch	10 Depot Rd., Unit 1002, 06279
Wilton	Bruce Blanchard	64 Oak Ledge La. 06897	Harold E. Clark	30 Hollow Tree Pl. 06897
Winchester	William W. McCabe	240 Colebrook Rd., Winsted 06098	Debbie Angell	151 Elm St., Winsted 06018
Windham	Sam Shifrin	78 Bricktop Rd. 06280	Roy Quimby	27 Stanley Rd. 06280
Windsor	Paul J. Panos	48 Brookview Rd. 06095	Joseph Mancarella	105 Preston St. 06095
Windsor Locks	Ruth G. Brunell	124 Southwest Ave., S-38, 06096	Michael Czarnecki	246 Main St. 06096
Wolcott	Anthony Bell	32 Joseph Ave. 06716	Patricia Watarian	43 Rocco Dr. 06716
Woodbridge	Donald N. Celotto, Jr.	3 Knollwood Rd. 06525	Lynn Piasyck	80 Woodfield Rd. 06525
Woodbury	Vincent M. Russo	38 Hesseley Meadow Rd. 06798	James Somers	536 Upper Grassy Hill Rd. 06798
Woodstock	Romeo A. Blackmar	13 Northgate Rd., P.O. Box 115, South Woodstock 06267	Erica Bates	275 Senexet Rd. 06281

State Map of Congressional Districts

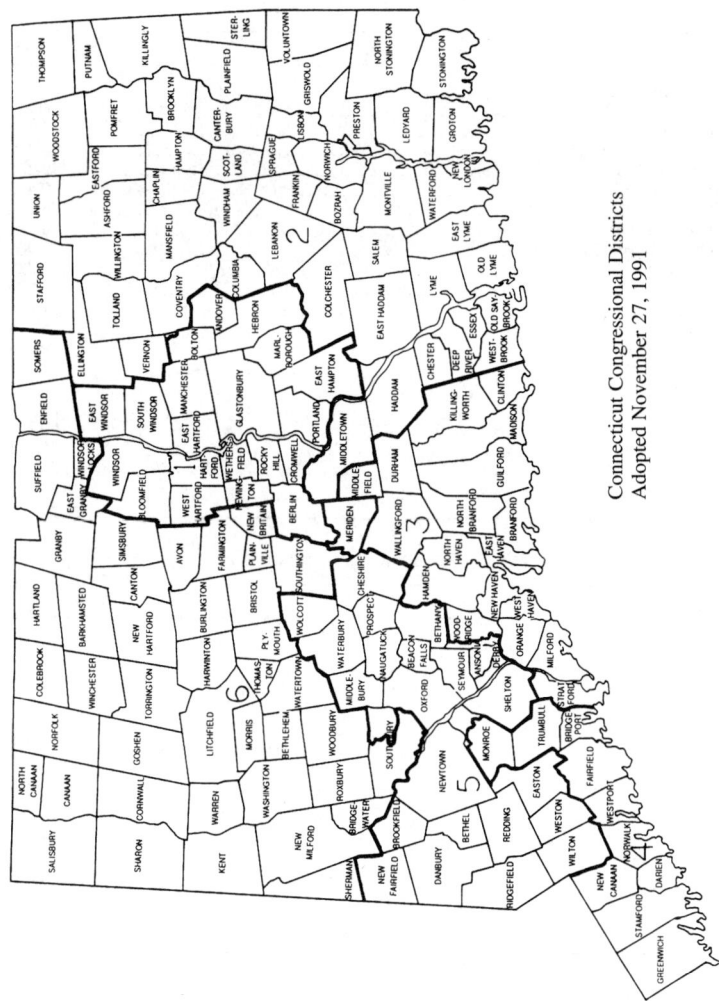

Connecticut Congressional Districts
Adopted November 27, 1991

CONNECTICUT CONGRESSIONAL DISTRICTS
(Adopted November 27, 1991)

CONGRESSIONAL DISTRICT 1

Towns	Population
Andover	2,540
Berlin	16,787
Bloomfield	19,483
Bolton (P)	4,250
Cromwell	12,286
East Hampton	10,428
East Hartford	50,452
East Windsor	10,081
Glastonbury	27,901
Hartford	139,739
Hebron	7,079
Manchester	51,618
Marlborough	5,535
Newington	29,208
Portland	8,418
Rocky Hill	16,554
South Windsor	22,090
West Hartford	60,110
Wethersfield	25,651
Windsor	27,817
Total	548,027

CONGRESSIONAL DISTRICT 2

Towns	Population
Ashford	3,765
Bolton (P)	325
Bozrah	2,297
Brooklyn	6,681
Canterbury	4,467
Chaplin	2,048
Chester	3,417
Colchester	10,980
Columbia	4,510
Coventry	10,063
Deep River	4,332
Eastford	1,314
East Haddam	6,676
East Lyme	15,340
Carried Forward	76,215

CONNECTICUT CONGRESSIONAL DISTRICTS

CONGRESSIONAL DISTRICT 2

Towns	Population
Brought Forward	76,215
Ellington	11,197
Essex	5,904
Franklin	1,810
Griswold	10,384
Groton	45,144
Haddam	6,769
Hampton	1,578
Killingly	15,889
Lebanon	6,041
Ledyard	14,913
Lisbon	3,790
Lyme	1,949
Mansfield	21,103
Middletown	42,762
Montville	16,673
New London	28,540
North Stonington	4,884
Norwich	37,391
Old Lyme	6,535
Old Saybrook	9,552
Plainfield	14,363
Pomfret	3,102
Preston	5,006
Putnam	9,031
Salem	3,310
Scotland	1,215
Sprague	3,008
Stafford	11,091
Sterling	2,357
Stonington	16,919
Thompson	8,668
Tolland	11,001
Union	612
Vernon	29,841
Voluntown	2,113
Waterford	17,930
Westbrook	5,414
Willington	5,979
Windham	22,039
Woodstock	6,008
Total	548,030

CONNECTICUT CONGRESSIONAL DISTRICTS

CONGRESSIONAL DISTRICT 3

Towns	Population
Branford	27,603
Clinton	12,767
Durham	5,732
East Haven	26,144
Guilford	19,848
Hamden	52,434
Killingworth	4,814
Madison	15,485
Middlefield	3,925
Milford	49,938
New Haven	130,474
North Branford	12,996
North Haven	22,247
Orange	12,830
Stratford	49,389
Wallingford	40,822
West Haven	54,021
Woodbridge (P)	6,296
Total	547,765

CONGRESSIONAL DISTRICT 4

Towns	Population
Bridgeport	141,686
Darien	18,196
Fairfield	53,418
Greenwich	58,441
Monroe (P)	15,347
New Canaan	17,864
Norwalk	78,331
Stamford	108,056
Trumbull	32,016
Westport	24,410
Total	547,765

CONNECTICUT CONGRESSIONAL DISTRICTS

CONGRESSIONAL DISTRICT 5

Towns	Population
Ansonia	18,403
Beacon Falls	5,083
Bethany	4,608
Bethel	17,541
Brookfield	14,113
Cheshire	25,684
Danbury	65,585
Derby	12,199
Easton	6,303
Meriden	59,479
Middlebury	6,145
Monroe (P)	1,549
Naugatuck	30,625
New Fairfield	12,911
Newtown	20,779
Oxford	8,685
Prospect	7,775
Redding	7,927
Ridgefield	20,919
Seymour	14,288
Shelton	35,418
Southbury (P)	2,819
Waterbury	108,961
Weston	8,648
Wilton	15,989
Wolcott	13,700
Woodbridge (P)	1,628
Total	547,764

CONGRESSIONAL DISTRICT 6

Towns	Population
Avon	13,937
Barkhamsted	3,369
Bethlehem	3,071
Bridgewater	1,654
Bristol	60,640
Burlington	7,026
Canaan	1,057
Canton	8,268
Colebrook	1,365
Cornwall	1,414
East Granby	4,302
Enfield	45,532
Carried Forward	151,635

CONNECTICUT CONGRESSIONAL DISTRICTS

CONGRESSIONAL DISTRICT 6

Towns	Population
Brought Forward	151,635
Farmington	20,608
Goshen	2,329
Granby	9,369
Hartland	1,866
Harwinton	5,228
Kent	2,918
Litchfield	8,365
Morris	2,039
New Britain	75,491
New Hartford	5,769
New Milford	23,629
Norfolk	2,060
North Canaan	3,284
Plainville	17,392
Plymouth	11,822
Roxbury	1,825
Salisbury	4,090
Sharon	2,928
Sherman	2,809
Simsbury	22,023
Somers	9,108
Southbury (P)	12,999
Southington	38,518
Suffield	11,427
Thomaston	6,947
Torrington	33,687
Warren	1,226
Washington	3,905
Watertown	20,456
Winchester	11,524
Windsor Locks	12,358
Woodbury	8,131
Total	547,765

POPULATION OF CONGRESSIONAL DISTRICTS
1990 U.S. Census

First District	548,027	Fourth District	547,765
Second District	548,030	Fifth District	547,764
Third District	547,765	Sixth District	547,765

Total State Population 3,287,116

State Map of Senatorial Districts

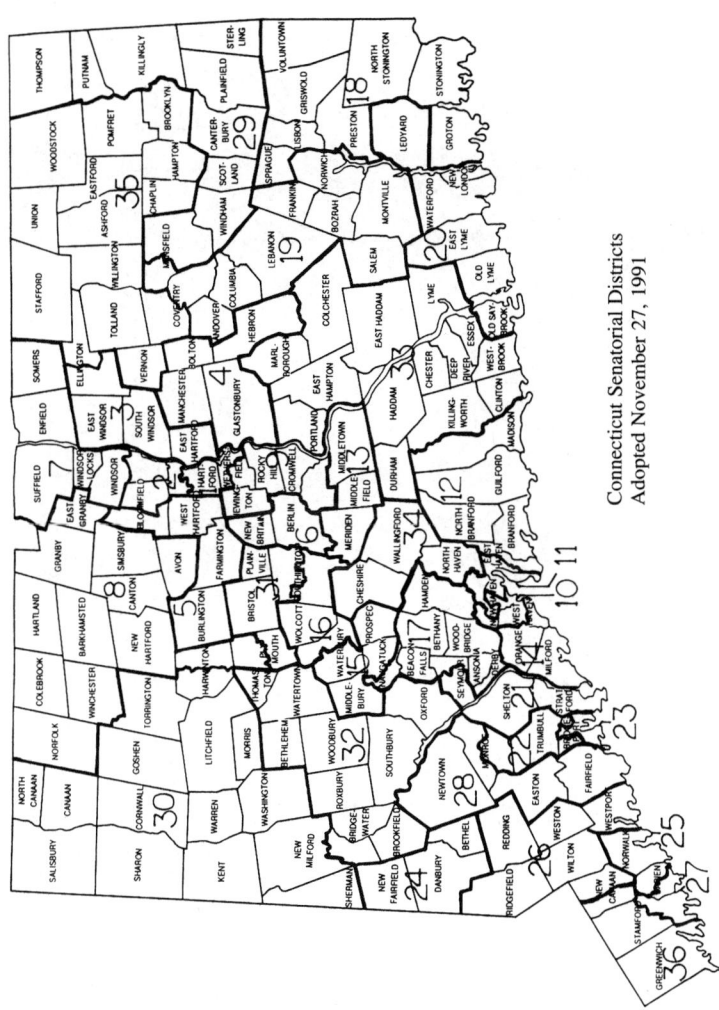

Connecticut Senatorial Districts
Adopted November 27, 1991

SENATORIAL DISTRICTS
(Adopted November 27, 1991)

Senatorial District No.	Towns	Town Population	District Population
1	Hartford (P)	79,185	
	Wethersfield (P)	10,250	89,435
2	Bloomfield (P)	14,277	
	Hartford (P)	60,554	
	Windsor (P)	14,353	89,184
3	East Hartford	50,452	
	East Windsor	10,081	
	Ellington (P)	8,960	
	South Windsor	22,090	91,583
4	Bolton	4,575	
	Glastonbury	27,901	
	Hebron	7,079	
	Manchester	51,618	91,173
5	Bloomfield (P)	5,206	
	Burlington	7,026	
	Farmington	20,608	
	West Hartford	60,110	92,950
6	Berlin	16,787	
	New Britain	75,491	92,278
7	Enfield	45,532	
	Somers	9,108	
	Suffield	11,427	
	Windsor (P)	13,464	
	Windsor Locks	12,358	91,889
8	Avon	13,937	
	Barkhamsted	3,369	
	Canton	8,268	
	Colebrook	1,365	
	East Granby	4,302	
	Granby	9,369	
	Hartland	1,866	
	Harwinton (P)	1,711	
	New Hartford	5,769	
	Norfolk	2,060	
	Plymouth (P)	7,248	
	Simsbury	22,023	
	Winchester	11,524	92,811

SENATORIAL DISTRICTS
(Adopted November 27, 1991)

Senatorial District No.	Towns	Town Population	District Population
9	Cromwell	12,286	
	Middletown (P)	16,065	
	Newington	29,208	
	Rocky Hill	16,554	
	Wethersfield (P)	15,401	89,514
10	New Haven (P)	65,457	
	West Haven (P)	26,237	91,694
11	East Haven (P)	8,657	
	Hamden (P)	18,448	
	New Haven (P)	65,017	92,122
12	Branford	27,603	
	East Haven (P)	17,487	
	Guilford	19,848	
	Madison	15,485	
	North Branford	12,996	93,419
13	Meriden	59,479	
	Middlefield	3,925	
	Middletown (P)	26,697	90,101
14	Milford	49,938	
	Orange	12,830	
	West Haven (P)	27,784	90,552
15	Middlebury	6,145	
	Naugatuck (P)	23,614	
	Prospect	7,775	
	Waterbury (P)	56,242	93,776
16	Southington (P)	27,262	
	Waterbury (P)	52,719	
	Wolcott	13,700	93,681
17	Ansonia	18,403	
	Beacon Falls	5,083	
	Bethany	4,608	
	Derby	12,199	
	Hamden (P)	33,986	
	Naugatuck (P)	7,011	
	Seymour (P)	4,572	
	Woodbridge	7,924	93,786
18	Griswold	10,384	
	Groton	45,144	
	Lisbon	3,790	
	North Stonington	4,884	
	Preston	5,006	
	Sprague	3,008	
	Stonington	16,919	
	Voluntown	2,113	91,248

SENATORIAL DISTRICTS
(Adopted November 27, 1991)

Senatorial District No.	Towns	Town Population	District Population
19	Andover	2,540	
	Bozrah	2,297	
	Columbia	4,510	
	Coventry (P)	5,538	
	Franklin	1,810	
	Lebanon	6,041	
	Mansfield (P)	9,420	
	Montville	16,673	
	Norwich	37,391	
	Salem	3,310	89,530
20	East Lyme	15,340	
	Ledyard	14,913	
	New London	28,540	
	Old Lyme	6,535	
	Old Saybrook	9,552	
	Waterford	17,930	92,810
21	Seymour (P)	9,716	
	Shelton	35,418	
	Stratford	49,389	94,523
22	Bridgeport (P)	49,127	
	Monroe (P)	8,648	
	Trumbull	32,016	89,791
23	Bridgeport (P)	92,559	92,559
24	Bethel	17,541	
	Danbury	65,585	
	New Fairfield	12,911	96,037
25	Darien (P)	11,227	
	Norwalk	78,331	89,558
26	New Canaan (P)	11,016	
	Redding	7,927	
	Ridgefield	20,919	
	Weston	8,648	
	Westport	24,410	
	Wilton	15,989	88,909
27	Darien (P)	6,969	
	Stamford (P)	84,196	91,165
28	Easton	6,303	
	Fairfield	53,418	
	Monroe (P)	8,248	
	Newtown	20,779	88,748

SENATORIAL DISTRICTS
(Adopted November 27, 1991)

Senatorial District No.	Towns	Town Population	District Population
29	Canterbury	4,467	
	Killingly	15,889	
	Mansfield (P)	11,683	
	Plainfield	14,363	
	Putnam	9,031	
	Scotland	1,215	
	Sterling	2,357	
	Thompson	8,668	
	Windham	22,039	89,712
30	Canaan	1,057	
	Cornwall	1,414	
	Goshen	2,329	
	Harwinton (P)	3,517	
	Kent	2,918	
	Litchfield	8,365	
	Morris	2,039	
	New Milford (P)	15,348	
	North Canaan	3,284	
	Salisbury	4,090	
	Sharon	2,928	
	Sherman	2,809	
	Torrington	33,687	
	Warren	1,226	
	Washington	3,905	88,916
31	Bristol	60,640	
	Plainville	17,392	
	Plymouth (P)	4,574	
	Southington (P)	11,256	93,862
32	Bethlehem	3,071	
	Bridgewater	1,654	
	Brookfield	14,113	
	New Milford (P)	8,283	
	Oxford	8,685	
	Roxbury	1,825	
	Southbury	15,818	
	Thomaston	6,947	
	Watertown	20,456	
	Woodbury	8,131	88,983

SENATORIAL DISTRICTS
(Adopted November 27, 1991)

Senatorial District No.	Towns	Town Population	District Population
33	Chester	3,417	
	Clinton	12,767	
	Colchester	10,980	
	Deep River	4,332	
	Durham	5,732	
	East Haddam	6,676	
	East Hampton	10,428	
	Essex	5,904	
	Haddam	6,769	
	Killingworth	4,814	
	Lyme	1,949	
	Marlborough	5,535	
	Portland	8,418	
	Westbrook	5,414	93,135
34	Cheshire	25,684	
	North Haven	22,247	
	Wallingford	40,822	88,753
35	Ashford	3,765	
	Brooklyn	6,681	
	Chaplin	2,048	
	Coventry (P)	4,525	
	Eastford	1,314	
	Ellington (P)	2,237	
	Hampton	1,578	
	Pomfret	3,102	
	Stafford	11,091	
	Tolland	11,001	
	Union	612	
	Vernon	29,841	
	Willington	5,979	
	Woodstock	6,008	89,782
36	Greenwich	58,441	
	New Canaan (P)	6,848	
	Stamford (P)	23,860	89,149

(P) - Part of a Town

State Map of Assembly Districts

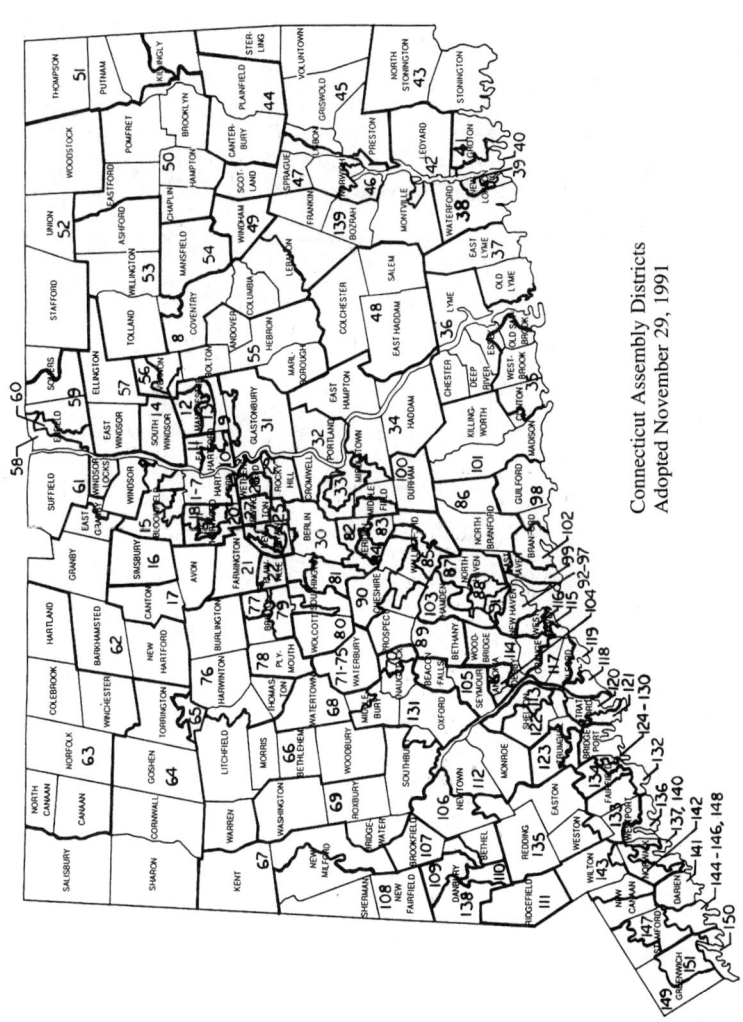

ASSEMBLY DISTRICTS
(Adopted November 29, 1991)

Assembly District No.	Towns	Town Population	District Population
1	Bloomfield (P)	6,613	
	Hartford (P)	14,151	20,764
2	Hartford (P)	20,894	20,894
3	Hartford (P)	21,014	21,014
4	Hartford (P)	20,781	20,781
5	Hartford (P)	20,728	20,728
6	Hartford (P)	21,674	21,674
7	Hartford (P)	12,554	
	Windsor (P)	8,372	20,926
8	Columbia	4,510	
	Coventry (P)	9,002	
	Lebanon (P)	2,443	
	Vernon (P)	4,510	21,798
9	East Hartford (P)	7,041	
	Glastonbury (P)	6,331	
	Manchester (P)	8,320	21,692
10	East Hartford (P)	22,022	22,022
11	East Hartford (P)	21,389	21,389
12	Manchester (P)	21,782	21,782
13	Manchester (P)	21,516	21,516
14	South Windsor	22,090	22,090
15	Bloomfield (P)	12,870	
	Windsor (P)	8,573	21,443
16	Simsbury	22,023	22,023
17	Avon	13,937	
	Canton	8,268	22,205
18	West Hartford (P)	21,668	21,668
19	West Hartford (P)	22,191	22,191
20	Hartford (P)	6,323	
	West Hartford (P)	16,251	22,574
21	Farmington	20,608	
	Plainville (P)	1,056	21,664

ASSEMBLY DISTRICTS
(Adopted November 29, 1991)

Assembly District No.	Towns	Town Population	District Population
22	Bristol (P)	5,920	
	Plainville (P)	16,336	22,256
23	Berlin (P)	1,250	
	New Britain (P)	20,005	21,255
24	New Britain (P)	21,096	21,096
25	New Britain (P)	13,359	
	Newington (P)	7,972	21,331
26	New Britain (P)	21,031	21,031
27	Newington (P)	21,236	21,236
28	Wethersfield (P)	21,916	21,916
29	Hartford (P)	1,620	
	Rocky Hill	16,554	
	Wethersfield (P)	3,735	21,909
30	Berlin (P)	15,537	
	Southington (P)	6,823	22,360
31	Glastonbury (P)	21,570	21,570
32	Cromwell	12,286	
	Middletown (P)	1,342	
	Portland	8,418	22,046
33	Middletown (P)	22,182	22,182
34	East Hampton	10,428	
	Haddam	6,769	
	Middletown (P)	5,306	22,503
35	Clinton (P)	11,747	
	Essex (P)	665	
	Old Saybrook (P)	3,327	
	Westbrook	5,414	21,153
36	Chester	3,417	
	Deep River	4,332	
	Essex (P)	5,239	
	Lyme	1,949	
	Old Saybrook (P)	6,225	21,162
37	East Lyme	15,340	
	Old Lyme	6,535	21,875
38	New London (P)	3,546	
	Waterford	17,930	21,476
39	New London (P)	21,224	21,224
40	Groton (P)	18,139	
	New London (P)	3,770	21,909
41	Groton (P)	21,968	21,968

ASSEMBLY DISTRICTS
(Adopted November 29, 1991)

Assembly District No.	Towns	Town Population	District Population
42	Groton (P)	5,037	
	Ledyard	14,913	
	Montville (P)	1,975	21,925
43	No. Stonington	4,884	
	Stonington	16,919	21,803
44	Canterbury	4,467	
	Killingly (P)	3,761	
	Plainfield	14,363	22,591
45	Griswold	10,384	
	Lisbon (P)	1,935	
	Preston	5,006	
	Sterling	2,357	
	Voluntown	2,113	21,795
46	Norwich (P)	21,798	21,798
47	Lisbon (P)	1,855	
	Norwich (P)	15,593	
	Scotland	1,215	
	Sprague	3,008	21,671
48	Colchester	10,980	
	East Haddam	6,676	
	Salem	3,310	20,966
49	Windham	22,039	22,039
50	Brooklyn	6,681	
	Chaplin	2,048	
	Eastford	1,314	
	Hampton	1,578	
	Killingly (P)	7,600	
	Pomfret	3,102	22,323
51	Killingly (P)	4,528	
	Putnam	9,031	
	Thompson	8,668	22,227
52	Somers (P)	3,514	
	Stafford	11,091	
	Union	612	
	Woodstock	6,008	21,225
53	Ashford	3,765	
	Coventry (P)	1,061	
	Tolland	11,001	
	Willington	5,979	21,806
54	Mansfield	21,103	21,103

ASSEMBLY DISTRICTS
(Adopted November 29, 1991)

Assembly District No.	Towns	Town Population	District Population
55	Andover	2,540	
	Bolton	4,575	
	Hebron	7,079	
	Marlborough	5,535	
	Vernon (P)	2,223	21,952
56	Vernon (P)	21,775	21,775
57	East Windsor	10,081	
	Ellington	11,197	21,278
58	Enfield (P)	21,021	21,021
59	Enfield (P)	15,419	
	Somers (P)	5,594	21,013
60	Enfield (P)	9,092	
	Windsor Locks	12,358	21,450
61	East Granby (P)	173	
	Suffield	11,427	
	Windsor (P)	10,872	22,472
62	Barkhamsted	3,369	
	East Granby (P)	4,129	
	Granby	9,369	
	New Hartford	5,769	22,636
63	Canaan	1,057	
	Colebrook	1,365	
	Hartland	1,866	
	Norfolk	2,060	
	North Canaan	3,284	
	Winchester	11,524	21,156
64	Cornwall	1,414	
	Goshen	2,329	
	Salisbury	4,090	
	Sharon	2,928	
	Torrington (P)	11,360	22,121
65	Torrington (P)	22,327	22,327
66	Bethlehem	3,071	
	Litchfield (P)	6,636	
	Morris	2,039	
	Warren	1,226	
	Woodbury	8,131	21,103

ASSEMBLY DISTRICTS
(Adopted November 29, 1991)

Assembly District No.	Towns	Town Population	District Population
67	Kent	2,918	
	New Milford (P)	18,202	21,120
68	Middlebury (P)	2,181	
	Watertown	20,456	22,637
69	Bridgewater	1,654	
	Roxbury	1,825	
	Southbury (P)	14,286	
	Washington	3,905	21,670
70	Naugatuck (P)	22,532	22,532
71	Waterbury (P)	22,298	22,298
72	Waterbury (P)	21,168	21,168
73	Waterbury (P)	21,823	21,823
74	Waterbury (P)	22,610	22,610
75	Waterbury (P)	21,062	21,062
76	Burlington	7,026	
	Harwinton	5,228	
	Litchfield (P)	1,729	
	Thomaston	6,947	20,930
77	Bristol (P)	22,304	22,304
78	Bristol (P)	10,767	
	Plymouth	11,822	22,589
79	Bristol (P)	21,649	
	Southington (P)	937	22,586
80	Southington (P)	8,400	
	Wolcott	13,700	22,100
81	Southington (P)	22,358	22,358
82	Meriden (P)	20,577	
	Middlefield (P)	1,803	22,380
83	Meriden (P)	16,586	
	Wallingford (P)	5,380	21,966
84	Meriden (P)	22,316	22,316
85	Wallingford (P)	21,477	21,477
86	East Haven (P)	5,211	
	Guilford (P)	2,774	
	North Branford	12,996	20,981
87	Hamden (P)	5,104	
	North Haven (P)	17,523	22,627

ASSEMBLY DISTRICTS
(Adopted November 29, 1991)

Assembly District No.	Towns	Town Population	District Population
88	Hamden (P)	13,279	
	New Haven (P)	3,334	
	North Haven (P)	4,724	21,337
89	Bethany	4,608	
	Cheshire (P)	8,679	
	Prospect	7,775	21,062
90	Cheshire (P)	12,836	
	Wallingford (P)	8,757	21,593
91	Hamden (P)	21,363	21,363
92	New Haven (P)	21,405	21,405
93	New Haven (P)	20,771	20,771
94	New Haven (P)	20,797	20,797
95	New Haven (P)	21,169	21,169
96	New Haven (P)	21,331	21,331
97	New Haven (P)	21,667	21,667
98	Branford (P)	4,151	
	Guilford (P)	17,074	21,225
99	Branford (P)	920	
	East Haven (P)	20,933	21,853
100	Durham	5,732	
	Middlefield (P)	2,122	
	Middletown (P)	13,932	21,786
101	Clinton (P)	1,020	
	Killingworth	4,814	
	Madison	15,485	21,319
102	Branford (P)	22,532	22,532
103	Cheshire (P)	4,169	
	Hamden (P)	12,688	
	Wallingford (P).	5,208	22,065
104	Ansonia (P)	15,505	
	Derby (P)	6,262	21,767
105	Ansonia (P)	2,898	
	Beacon Falls	5,083	
	Seymour	14,288	22,269
106	Bethel (P)	9,042	
	Newtown (P)	13,476	22,518
107	Bethel (P)	8,499	
	Brookfield	14,113	22,612

ASSEMBLY DISTRICTS
(Adopted November 29, 1991)

Assembly District No.	Towns	Town Population	District Population
108	New Fairfield	12,911	
	New Milford (P)	5,427	
	Sherman	2,809	21,147
109	Danbury (P)	21,756	21,756
110	Danbury (P)	21,702	21,702
111	Ridgefield	20,919	20,919
112	Monroe	16,896	
	Newtown (P)	5,340	22,236
113	Shelton (P)	22,613	22,613
114	Derby (P)	5,937	
	Orange (P)	7,466	
	Woodbridge	7,924	21,327
115	West Haven (P)	22,638	22,638
116	West Haven (P)	22,043	22,043
117	Milford (P)	7,476	
	Orange (P)	5,364	
	West Haven (P)	9,340	22,180
118	Milford (P)	21,320	21,320
119	Milford (P)	21,142	21,142
120	Stratford (P)	21,775	21,775
121	Stratford (P)	21,398	21,398
122	Shelton (P)	12,805	
	Stratford (P)	6,216	
	Trumbull (P)	3,545	22,566
123	Trumbull (P)	21,080	21,080
124	Bridgeport (P)	20,790	20,790
125	Bridgeport (P)	21,533	21,533
126	Bridgeport (P)	21,589	21,589
127	Bridgeport (P)	14,021	
	Fairfield (P)	8,326	22,347
128	Bridgeport (P)	20,868	20,868
129	Bridgeport (P)	22,019	22,019
130	Bridgeport (P)	20,866	20,866
131	Middlebury (P)	3,964	
	Naugatuck (P)	8,093	
	Oxford	8,685	
	Southbury (P)	1,532	22,274

ASSEMBLY DISTRICTS
(Adopted November 29, 1991)

Assembly District No.	Towns	Town Population	District Population
132	Fairfield (P)	22,265	22,265
133	Fairfield (P)	7,645	
	Weston (P)	2,821	
	Westport (P)	11,896	22,362
134	Fairfield (P)	15,182	
	Trumbull (P)	7,391	22,573
135	Easton	6,303	
	Newtown (P)	1,963	
	Redding	7,927	
	Weston (P)	5,827	20,020
136	Norwalk (P)	10,125	
	Westport (P)	12,514	22,639
137	Norwalk (P)	22,552	22,552
138	Danbury (P)	22,127	22,127
139	Bozrah	2,297	
	Franklin	1,810	
	Lebanon (P)	3,598	
	Montville (P)	14,698	22,403
140	Norwalk (P)	21,099	21,099
141	Darien	18,196	
	Norwalk (P)	4,436	22,632
142	Norwalk (P)	20,119	
	Wilton (P)	2,489	22,608
143	New Canaan (P)	9,076	
	Wilton (P)	13,500	22,576
144	Stamford (P)	21,947	21,947
145	Stamford (P)	20,807	20,807
146	Stamford (P)	21,227	21,227
147	New Canaan (P)	8,788	
	Stamford (P)	12,839	21,627
148	Stamford (P)	21,789	21,789
149	Greenwich (P)	13,184	
	Stamford (P)	9,447	22,631
150	Greenwich (P)	22,635	22,635
151	Greenwich (P)	22,622	22,622

(P) - Part of a Town

TOWNS AS DISTRICTED FOR ELECTION PURPOSES

(Congressional and Senatorial Districts adopted November 27, 1991.)
(House Assembly Districts adopted November 29, 1991.)

	Town	Congressional District No.	Senatorial District No.	House Assembly District No.	County
1	Andover	1	19	55	Tolland
2	Ansonia	5	17	104,105	New Haven
3	Ashford	2	35	53	Windham
4	Avon	6	8	17	Hartford
5	Barkhamsted	6	8	62	Litchfield
6	Beacon Falls	5	17	105	New Haven
7	Berlin	1	6	23,30	Hartford
8	Bethany	5	17	89	New Haven
9	Bethel	5	24	106,107	Fairfield
10	Bethlehem	6	32	66	Litchfield
11	Bloomfield	1	2,5	1,15	Hartford
12	Bolton	1,2	4	55	Tolland
13	Bozrah	2	19	139	New London
14	Branford	3	12	98,99,102	New Haven
15	Bridgeport	4	22,23	124-130	Fairfield
16	Bridgewater	6	32	69	Litchfield
17	Bristol	6	31	22,77-79	Hartford
18	Brookfield	5	32	107	Fairfield
19	Brooklyn	2	35	50	Windham
20	Burlington	6	5	76	Hartford
21	Canaan	6	30	63	Litchfield
22	Canterbury	2	29	44	Windham
23	Canton	6	8	17	Hartford
24	Chaplin	2	35	50	Windham
25	Cheshire	5	34	89,90,103	New Haven
26	Chester	2	33	36	Middlesex
27	Clinton	3	33	35,101	Middlesex
28	Colchester	2	33	48	New London
29	Colebrook	6	8	63	Litchfield
30	Columbia	2	19	8	Tolland
31	Cornwall	6	30	64	Litchfield
32	Coventry	2	19,35	8,53	Tolland
33	Cromwell	1	9	32	Middlesex
34	Danbury	5	24	109,110,138	Fairfield
35	Darien	4	25,27	141	Fairfield
36	Deep River	2	33	36	Middlesex
37	Derby	5	17	104,114	New Haven
38	Durham	3	33	100	Middlesex
39	Eastford	2	35	50	Windham
40	East Granby	6	8	61,62	Hartford
41	East Haddam	2	33	48	Middlesex
42	East Hampton	1	33	34	Middlesex
43	East Hartford	1	3	9-11	Hartford
44	East Haven	3	11,12	86,99	New Haven
45	East Lyme	2	20	37	New London
46	Easton	5	28	135	Fairfield
47	East Windsor	1	3	57	Hartford
48	Ellington	2	3,35	57	Tolland
49	Enfield	6	7	58-60	Hartford
50	Essex	2	33	35,36	Middlesex
51	Fairfield	4	28	127,132-134	Fairfield
52	Farmington	6	5	21	Hartford
53	Franklin	2	19	139	New London
54	Glastonbury	1	4	9,31	Hartford
55	Goshen	6	30	64	Litchfield
56	Granby	6	8	62	Hartford
57	Greenwich	4	36	149-151	Fairfield

TOWNS AS DISTRICTED FOR ELECTION PURPOSES

(Congressional and Senatorial Districts adopted November 27, 1991.)
(House Assembly Districts adopted November 29, 1991.)

Town	Congressional District No.	Senatorial District No.	House Assembly District No.	County
58 Griswold	2	18	45	New London
59 Groton	2	18	40-42	New London
60 Guilford	3	12	86,98	New Haven
61 Haddam	2	33	34	Middlesex
62 Hamden	3	11,17	87,88,91,103	New Haven
63 Hampton	2	35	50	Windham
64 Hartford	1	1,2	1-7,20,29	Hartford
65 Hartland	6	8	63	Hartford
66 Harwinton	6	8,30	76	Litchfield
67 Hebron	1	4	55	Tolland
68 Kent	6	30	67	Litchfield
69 Killingly	2	29	44,50,51	Windham
70 Killingworth	3	33	101	Middlesex
71 Lebanon	2	19	8,139	New London
72 Ledyard	2	20	42	New London
73 Lisbon	2	18	45,47	New London
74 Litchfield	6	30	66,76	Litchfield
75 Lyme	2	33	36	New London
76 Madison	3	12	101	New Haven
77 Manchester	1	4	9,12,13	Hartford
78 Mansfield	2	19,29	54	Tolland
79 Marlborough	1	33	55	Hartford
80 Meriden	5	13	82-84	New Haven
81 Middlebury	5	15	68,131	New Haven
82 Middlefield	3	13	82,100	Middlesex
83 Middletown	2	9,13	32-34,100	Middlesex
84 Milford	3	14	117-119	New Haven
85 Monroe	4,5	22,28	112	Fairfield
86 Montville	2	19	42,139	New London
87 Morris	6	30	66	Litchfield
88 Naugatuck	5	15,17	70,131	New Haven
89 New Britain	6	6	23-26	Hartford
90 New Canaan	4	26,36	143,147	Fairfield
91 New Fairfield	5	24	108	Fairfield
92 New Hartford	6	8	62	Litchfield
93 New Haven	3	10,11	88,92-97	New Haven
94 Newington	1	9	25,27	Hartford
95 New London	2	20	38-40	New London
96 New Milford	6	30,32	67,108	Litchfield
97 Newtown	5	28	106,112,135	Fairfield
98 Norfolk	6	8	63	Litchfield
99 North Branford	3	12	86	New Haven
100 North Canaan	6	30	63	Litchfield
101 North Haven	3	34	87,88	New Haven
102 North Stonington	2	18	43	New London
103 Norwalk	4	25	136,137,140-142	Fairfield
104 Norwich	2	19	46,47	New London
105 Old Lyme	2	20	37	New London
106 Old Saybrook	2	20	35,36	Middlesex
107 Orange	3	14	114,117	New Haven
108 Oxford	5	32	131	New Haven
109 Plainfield	2	29	44	Windham
110 Plainville	6	31	21,22	Hartford
111 Plymouth	6	8,31	78	Litchfield
112 Pomfret	2	35	50	Windham
113 Portland	1	33	32	Middlesex
114 Preston	2	18	45	New London

TOWNS AS DISTRICTED FOR ELECTION PURPOSES

(Congressional and Senatorial Districts adopted November 27, 1991.)
(House Assembly Districts adopted November 29, 1991.)

Town	Congressional District No.	Senatorial District No.	House Assembly District No.	County
115 Prospect	5	15	89	New Haven
116 Putnam	2	29	51	Windham
117 Redding	5	26	135	Fairfield
118 Ridgefield	5	26	111	Fairfield
119 Rocky Hill	1	9	29	Hartford
120 Roxbury	6	32	69	Litchfield
121 Salem	2	19	48	New London
122 Salisbury	6	30	64	Litchfield
123 Scotland	2	29	47	Windham
124 Seymour	5	17,21	105	New Haven
125 Sharon	6	30	64	Litchfield
126 Shelton	5	21	113,122	Fairfield
127 Sherman	6	30	108	Fairfield
128 Simsbury	6	8	16	Hartford
129 Somers	6	7	52,59	Tolland
130 Southbury	5,6	32	69,131	New Haven
131 Southington	6	16,31	30,79-81	Hartford
132 South Windsor	1	3	14	Hartford
133 Sprague	2	18	47	New London
134 Stafford	2	35	52	Tolland
135 Stamford	4	27,36	144-149	Fairfield
136 Sterling	2	29	45	Windham
137 Stonington	2	18	43	New London
138 Stratford	3	21	120-122	Fairfield
139 Suffield	6	7	61	Hartford
140 Thomaston	6	32	76	Litchfield
141 Thompson	2	29	51	Windham
142 Tolland	2	35	53	Tolland
143 Torrington	6	30	64,65	Litchfield
144 Trumbull	4	22	122,123,134	Fairfield
145 Union	2	35	52	Tolland
146 Vernon	2	35	8,55,56	Tolland
147 Voluntown	2	18	45	New London
148 Wallingford	3	34	83,85,90,103	New Haven
149 Warren	6	30	66	Litchfield
150 Washington	6	30	69	Litchfield
151 Waterbury	5	15,16	71-75	New Haven
152 Waterford	2	20	38	New London
153 Watertown	6	32	68	Litchfield
154 Westbrook	2	33	35	Middlesex
155 West Hartford	1	5	18-20	Hartford
156 West Haven	3	10,14	115-117	New Haven
157 Weston	5	26	133,135	Fairfield
158 Westport	4	26	133,136	Fairfield
159 Wethersfield	1	1,9	28,29	Hartford
160 Willington	2	35	53	Tolland
161 Wilton	5	26	142,143	Fairfield
162 Winchester	6	8	63	Litchfield
163 Windham	2	29	49	Windham
164 Windsor	1	2,7	7,15,61	Hartford
165 Windsor Locks	6	7	60	Hartford
166 Wolcott	5	16	80	New Haven
167 Woodbridge	3,5	17	114	New Haven
168 Woodbury	6	32	66	Litchfield
169 Woodstock	2	35	52	Windham

PARTY DESIGNATIONS

Major Parties

Republican	(R)
Democrat	(D)

Minor Parties
Party Designations used on Nominating Petitions

A Connecticut Party	(ACP)
Americans for Perot	(AFP)
Bristol Independent (BI)	(BI)
Connecticut Citizens	(CC)
Green	(G)
Independent	(I)
Libertarian	(L)
Natuaral Law	(NL)
New Alliance	(NA)
Petitioning Candidate	(PC)
Reform	(REF)
Tax The Rich	(TTR)
United Taxpayers	(UT)

ELECTORAL VOTES FOR PRESIDENT, 1964-1996

State	1964 R	1964 D	1968a R	1968a D	1972b R	1972b D	1976c R	1976c D	1980 R	1980 D	1984 R	1984 D	1988 R	1988 D	1992d R	1992d D	1996 R	1996 D
Alabama	10	...	...	...	9	...	9	...	9	...	9	...	9	...	9	...	9	...
Alaska	...	3	3	...	3	...	3	...	3	...	3	...	3	...	3	...	3	...
Arizona	5	...	...	5	...	6	...	6	...	6	...	7	...	7	...	8	...	8
Arkansas	...	6	...	...	6	...	...	6	6	...	6	...	6	...	...	6	...	6
California	...	40	40	...	45	...	45	...	45	...	47	...	47	...	...	54	...	54
Colorado	...	6	6	...	7	...	7	...	7	...	8	...	8	...	...	8	8	...
Connecticut	...	8	...	8	8	...	...	8	8	...	8	...	8	...	...	8	...	8
Delaware	...	3	3	...	3	...	...	3	3	...	3	...	3	...	...	3	...	3
D of Columbia	...	3	...	3	...	3	...	3	...	3	...	3	...	3	...	3	...	3
Florida	...	14	14	...	17	...	...	17	17	...	21	...	21	...	25	...	25	...
Georgia	12	...	...	...	12	...	...	12	...	12	12	...	12	...	...	13	13	...
Hawaii	...	4	4	...	4	...	...	4	...	4	4	...	...	4	...	4	...	4
Idaho	...	4	4	...	4	...	4	...	4	...	4	...	4	...	4	...	4	...
Illinois	...	26	26	...	26	...	26	...	26	...	24	...	24	...	...	22	...	22
Indiana	...	13	13	...	13	...	13	...	13	...	12	...	12	...	12	...	12	...
Iowa	...	9	9	...	8	...	8	...	8	...	8	...	...	8	...	7	...	7
Kansas	...	7	7	...	7	...	7	...	7	...	7	...	7	...	6	...	6	...
Kentucky	...	9	9	...	9	...	...	9	9	...	9	...	9	...	...	8	...	8
Louisiana	10	...	...	...	10	...	...	10	10	...	10	...	10	...	...	9	...	9
Maine	...	4	...	4	4	...	...	4	...	4	4	...	4	...	...	4	...	4
Maryland	...	10	...	10	10	...	...	10	...	10	10	...	10	...	...	10	...	10
Massachusetts	...	14	...	14	...	14	...	14	14	...	13	...	...	13	...	12	...	12
Michigan	...	21	21	...	21	...	...	21	21	...	20	...	20	...	...	18	...	18
Minnesota	...	10	...	10	10	...	...	10	...	10	...	10	...	10	...	10	...	10
Mississippi	7	...	...	...	7	...	...	7	7	...	7	...	7	...	7	...	7	...
Missouri	...	12	12	...	12	...	...	12	12	...	11	...	11	...	11	...	...	11
Montana	...	4	4	...	4	...	4	...	4	...	4	...	4	...	3	3	...	...
Nebraska	...	5	5	...	5	...	5	...	5	...	5	...	5	...	5	...	5	...
Nevada	...	3	3	...	3	...	3	...	3	...	4	...	4	...	4	...	...	4
New Hampshire	...	4	4	...	4	...	4	...	4	...	4	...	4	...	4	...	...	4
New Jersey	...	17	17	...	17	...	...	17	17	...	16	...	16	...	...	15	...	15
New Mexico	...	4	4	...	4	...	...	4	4	...	5	...	5	...	...	5	...	5
New York	...	43	...	43	41	...	...	41	41	...	36	...	...	36	...	33	...	33
North Carolina	...	13	12	...	13	...	...	13	13	...	13	...	13	...	14	...	14	...
North Dakota	...	4	4	...	3	...	3	...	3	...	3	...	3	...	3	...	3	...
Ohio	...	26	26	...	25	...	25	...	25	...	23	...	23	...	...	21	21	...
Oklahoma	...	8	8	...	8	...	8	...	8	...	8	...	8	...	8	...	8	...
Oregon	...	6	6	...	6	...	6	...	6	...	7	...	...	7	...	7	...	7
Pennsylvania	...	29	...	29	27	...	...	27	27	...	25	...	25	...	...	23	...	23
Rhode Island	...	4	...	4	...	4	...	4	4	...	...	4	...	4	...	4	...	4
South Carolina	8	...	...	8	8	...	...	8	8	...	8	...	8	...	8	...	8	...
South Dakota	...	4	4	...	4	...	...	4	4	...	3	...	3	...	3	...	3	...
Tennessee	...	11	11	...	10	...	...	10	10	...	11	...	11	...	...	11	...	11
Texas	...	25	...	25	26	...	...	26	26	...	29	...	29	...	32	...	32	...
Utah	...	4	4	...	4	...	4	...	4	...	5	...	5	...	5	...	5	...
Vermont	...	3	3	...	3	...	3	...	3	...	3	...	3	...	...	3	...	3
Virginia	...	12	12	...	11	...	12	...	12	...	12	...	12	...	13	...	13	...
Washington	...	9	...	9	9	...	9	...	9	...	10	...	...	10	...	11	...	11
West Virginia	...	7	...	7	6	...	...	6	6	...	6	...	...	6	...	5	...	5
Wisconsin	...	12	12	...	11	...	...	11	11	...	11	...	...	11	...	11	...	11
Wyoming	...	3	3	...	3	...	3	...	3	...	3	...	3	...	3	...	3	...
Totals	52	486	301	191	520	17	241	297	489	49	525	13	426	112	168	370	159	379
Plurality	...	434	64	...	503	...	...	56	440	...	512	...	314	...	...	202	...	...

[a]In 1968, a total of 46 electoral votes (Alabama 10; Arkansas 6; Georgia 12; Louisiana 10; Mississippi 7; and North Carolina 1 out of 13) were cast for American Independent Candidates.
[b]In 1972, 1 electoral vote (Virginia) was cast for John Hospers of the Libertarian Party.
[c]In 1976, 1 electoral vote (Washington) was cast for Ronald Reagan of California.
[d]In 1988, 1 Electoral vote (West Virginia) was cast for Lloyd Bentsen of Texas.

SUMMARY OF VOTE FOR PRESIDENT BY CONGRESSIONAL DISTRICT
NOVEMBER 5, 1996

CONGRESSIONAL DISTRICT	Presidential Electors for						
	Dole & Kemp (R)	Clinton & Gore (D)	Phillips & Zdonczyk (CC)	Nader & LaDuke (G)	Browne & Jorgensen (L)	Hagelin & Tompkins (NL)	Perot & Choate (REF)
1	68,483	136,775	374	3,953	648	229	20,862
2	73,863	123,595	407	5,413	826	345	29,790
3	71,009	129,756	383	4,304	575	269	22,916
4	88,181	113,411	233	2,719	2,083	320	14,825
5	92,570	110,596	569	3,006	890	229	24,265
6	89,003	121,607	459	4,926	766	311	26,865
Totals	483,109	735,740	2,425	24,321	5,788	1,703	139,523

SUMMARY OF VOTE FOR PRESIDENT BY COUNTY
NOVEMBER 5, 1996

COUNTY	Presidential Electors for						
	Dole & Kemp (R)	Clinton & Gore (D)	Phillips & Zdonczyk (CC)	Nader & LaDuke (G)	Browne & Jorgensen (L)	Hagelin & Tompkins (NL)	Perot & Choate (REF)
Fairfield	144,632	172,337	407	4,539	2,531	453	27,328
Hartford	111,566	203,549	622	6,098	958	363	33,685
Litchfield	31,645	37,375	155	2,100	344	133	9,646
Middlesex	22,960	37,695	104	1,540	258	93	9,136
New Haven	106,636	178,323	776	5,349	996	357	33,454
New London	33,039	54,377	173	2,066	361	163	12,916
Tolland	19,394	30,007	104	1,676	195	85	7,164
Windham	13,237	22,077	84	953	145	56	6,194
Totals	483,109	735,740	2,425	24,321	5,788	1,703	139,523

1996 CONNECTICUT NOMINEES FOR ELECTORS OF PRESIDENT AND VICE PRESIDENT OF THE UNITED STATES

REPUBLICAN

Pres.: Bob Dole, Russell, Kansas. *Vice Pres.*, Jack Kemp, Bethesda, Maryland.

Presidential Electors: John Miller, Wethersfield; Jo McKenzie, Madison; Ralph Marcarelli, New Haven; Edward Seder, Norwich; Scott Fossell, Greenwich; Fred Biebel, Stratford; Edward Krawiecki, Bristol; Ellie Klapatch, Bristol.

DEMOCRATIC

Pres.: Bill Clinton, Little Rock, Arkansas. *Vice Pres.*: Al Gore, Carthage, Tennessee.

Presidential Electors: Frank L. Aieta, Newington; Dominic F. Balletto, New Haven; Marjorie C. Bennett, Bethlehem; Leo Canty, Windsor; John Larson, East Hartford; Fleeta Hudson, Bridgeport; Hilda Santiago, Meriden; Kenneth Slapin, Norwalk.

CONCERNED CITIZENS

Pres.: Howard Phillips, Vienna, Virginia. *Vice Pres.*: Joseph A. Zdonczyk, Wolcott, Connecticut.

Presidential Electors: Henrietta R. Else, Cheshire; Katherine J. Celentano, Waterbury; Gary R. Garneau, Hartford; James E. Fitzpatrick, Simsbury; Edward R. Desplaines, Enfield; John F. Forry III, South Windsor; Virginia Vabalas, Manchester; John J. Hunt, Avon.

GREEN

Pres.: Ralph Nader, Winsted (Winchester), Connecticut. *Vice Pres.*: Winona LaDuke, Ponsford, Minnesota.

Presidential Electors: James M. Kowalyshyn, West Hartford; Anne M. Dettenborn, West Hartford; Harriet Lucinda Hannon, Simsbury; Edward E. Shatas, Meriden; John J. Reardon, Meriden; Paul F. Bassler, Norwalk; Sharon O'Neil Doyle, Durham; Michael F. Doyle, Durham.

LIBERTARIAN

Pres.: Harry Browne, Franklin, Tennesee. *Vice Pres.*: Jo Jorgensen, Greenville, South Carolina.

Presidential Electors: Richard A. Bucciarelli, Norwalk; George C. Eggert, Bethlehem; John M. Joy, Oxford; Richard W. Loomis, Enfield; Robert S. Loomis, East Granby; Jeffrey W. Nicholas, West Hartford; Carl E. Vassar, Trumbull; John H. Voorvaart, Simsbury.

NATURAL LAW

Pres.: John Hagelin, Fairfield, Iowa. *Vice Pres.*: Vinton D. Tompkins, Avon Lake, Ohio.

Presidential Electors: Gary D. Beane, Easton; Susan Smyth, Waterbury; David L. Smith, New London; Mary C. Grimes, New Haven; Maxine Gaudio, Greenwich; Elizabeth Dubs, Rowayton (Norwalk); Martha A. Calef, West Hartford; Thomas E. Hall, Coventry.

REFORM

Pres.: Ross Perot, Dallas, Texas. *Vice Pres.*: Pat Choate, Washington, D.C.

Presidential Electors: Robert B. Davidson, Cromwell; Donna Donovan, Glastonbury; Susan S. Brummett, Newington; Linda S. Cordero, Mystic; Barbara M. Foster, Waterford; Jonathan Hoyt, Westbrook; Loretta D. Farren, Monroe; Anna Schoenfeldt, Fairfield.

VOTE FOR PRESIDENT OF THE UNITED STATES
NOVEMBER 5, 1996

	Presidential Electors for						
TOWN	Dole & Kemp (R)	Clinton & Gore (D)	Phillips & Zdonczyk (CC)	Nader & LaDuke (G)	Browne & Jorgensen (L)	Hagelin & Tompkins (NL)	Perot & Choate (REF)
Andover	480	711	8	49	6	1	211
Ansonia	2,132	3,900	14	92	18	6	859
Ashford	559	977	4	85	9	6	294
Avon	4,014	3,606	8	138	21	8	510
Barkhamsted	677	735	1	69	7	4	204
Beacon Falls	868	1,055	3	41	11	3	346
Berlin	3,207	4,800	5	149	21	8	1,113
Bethany	1,047	1,246	4	66	13	5	314
Bethel	3,472	3,883	16	86	25	7	840
Bethlehem	867	711	1	65	12	6	258
Bloomfield	1,800	6,930	13	130	26	6	441
Bolton	964	1,210	2	55	8	2	302
Bozrah	398	574	1	16	6	3	215
Branford	4,356	7,077	15	281	35	20	1,353
Bridgeport	6,785	22,883	59	353	609	31	2,367
Bridgewater	461	439	1	23	7	3	99
Bristol	6,560	13,616	26	325	43	25	3,049
Brookfield	3,630	2,982	12	99	25	6	667
Brooklyn	965	1,363	5	40	7	0	415
Burlington	1,548	1,747	5	75	10	5	449
Canaan	180	302	0	35	2	0	75
Canterbury	799	917	2	39	7	1	417
Canton	1,795	2,109	9	153	19	7	479
Chaplin	276	418	3	60	7	1	154
Cheshire	5,536	6,227	20	205	53	11	1,161
Chester	536	1,089	3	65	7	4	210
Clinton	2,107	2,958	7	91	18	8	805
Colchester	1,774	3,094	8	112	7	3	1,006
Colebrook	275	345	2	30	5	2	80
Columbia	813	1,271	5	68	13	7	364
Cornwall	269	408	0	57	12	0	84
Coventry	1,564	2,591	11	163	18	17	760
Cromwell	2,007	3,389	9	90	14	7	737
Danbury	7,965	12,102	32	226	76	23	2,158
Darien	6,058	2,988	6	72	62	5	410
Deep River	696	1,160	3	52	13	5	309
Derby	1,477	2,636	6	50	14	6	590
Durham	1,209	1,504	4	80	7	5	451
Eastford	329	301	2	27	4	4	122
East Granby	952	1,093	7	44	10	5	323
East Hampton	1,768	2,429	4	100	22	8	770
East Hartford	4,525	11,904	38	269	36	15	2,156
East Haven	2,946	6,603	19	100	14	8	1,285
East Lyme	2,870	3,778	7	213	17	8	827
Easton	1,904	1,475	4	65	13	9	326

	Presidential Electors for						
TOWN	Dole & Kemp (R)	Clinton & Gore (D)	Phillips & Zdonczyk (CC)	Nader & LaDuke (G)	Browne & Jorgensen (L)	Hagelin & Tompkins (NL)	Perot & Choate (REF)
East Windsor	1,295	2,104	7	69	17	2	520
Ellington	2,152	2,643	12	126	24	6	569
Enfield	5,620	9,893	31	217	51	33	2,352
Essex	1,417	1,630	7	72	15	5	340
Fairfield	12,314	12,639	30	477	218	42	2,092
Farmington	4,739	5,415	12	226	35	11	966
Franklin	327	493	1	10	0	4	126
Glastonbury	6,754	7,811	16	275	45	17	1,510
Goshen	597	518	2	37	5	1	149
Granby	2,282	2,196	6	124	18	8	526
Greenwich	14,308	11,622	26	341	240	36	1,437
Griswold	1,064	2,116	11	54	16	4	611
Groton	4,364	6,570	19	281	42	20	1,413
Guilford	4,007	5,405	11	253	34	25	1,009
Haddam	1,328	1,756	2	94	14	4	676
Hamden	7,011	14,522	39	484	55	25	1,930
Hampton	279	393	0	43	7	0	131
Hartford	3,082	22,929	84	437	73	38	1,010
Hartland	496	317	4	26	3	1	134
Harwinton	1,095	1,086	6	68	7	4	400
Hebron	1,370	1,888	3	92	10	2	515
Kent	617	744	0	33	3	4	147
Killingly	1,698	2,915	11	83	15	2	878
Killingworth	1,016	1,342	1	73	14	3	478
Lebanon	1,101	1,378	7	92	12	3	517
Ledyard	2,546	2,805	18	106	31	6	709
Lisbon	524	974	4	24	4	0	283
Litchfield	1,682	1,762	5	117	25	7	393
Lyme	536	578	0	31	4	1	146
Madison	4,256	3,697	9	159	30	11	770
Manchester	7,490	13,003	35	456	62	29	2,833
Mansfield	1,473	4,005	10	446	21	15	558
Marlborough	1,027	1,379	3	68	11	3	367
Meriden	5,639	12,368	48	227	76	24	2,660
Middlebury	1,857	1,256	9	32	10	4	293
Middlefield	685	1,187	0	47	9	3	308
Middletown	4,436	11,243	39	488	66	20	1,823
Milford	8,159	11,191	32	385	59	31	3,040
Monroe	3,968	3,544	9	109	35	7	985
Montville	2,041	3,632	5	96	27	31	1,048
Morris	457	464	1	27	4	9	151
Naugatuck	4,030	5,400	40	157	55	9	1,623
New Britain	4,911	14,322	82	445	54	24	1,717
New Canaan	5,890	3,087	3	96	38	5	417
New Fairfield	3,107	2,500	8	92	31	6	650
New Hartford	1,202	1,377	4	104	9	7	342
New Haven	4,822	26,161	75	1,090	119	46	1,555
Newington	4,443	8,471	22	231	43	8	1,574
New London	1,726	5,177	19	154	34	15	542

	Presidential Electors for						
TOWN	Dole & Kemp (R)	Clinton & Gore (D)	Phillips & Zdonczyk (CC)	Nader & LaDuke (G)	Browne & Jorgensen (L)	Hagelin & Tompkins (NL)	Perot & Choate (REF)
New Milford	4,368	4,569	16	146	47	13	1,182
Newtown	4,904	4,454	10	181	39	12	1,030
Norfolk	310	409	1	44	5	1	98
North Branford	2,134	2,905	8	108	11	5	780
North Canaan	461	667	11	21	2	1	173
North Haven	4,422	5,952	20	153	19	5	1,149
North Stonington	846	1,071	5	47	13	6	338
Norwalk	10,800	17,354	29	406	331	102	2,237
Norwich	3,468	8,162	36	196	49	18	1,544
Old Lyme	1,690	1,848	1	80	11	5	464
Old Saybrook	2,147	2,496	2	83	16	5	563
Orange	3,245	3,318	8	103	14	8	660
Oxford	1,824	1,619	8	62	23	9	624
Plainfield	1,392	2,863	6	54	13	4	991
Plainville	2,072	4,379	17	99	12	5	915
Plymouth	1,422	2,294	11	68	23	5	751
Pomfret	693	770	3	52	3	1	235
Portland	1,407	2,387	10	80	19	8	587
Preston	697	1,032	3	48	7	5	344
Prospect	1,845	1,750	8	48	15	3	555
Putnam	1,084	1,920	5	46	17	4	559
Redding	2,113	1,850	2	78	16	1	305
Ridgefield	6,042	4,974	9	168	58	9	691
Rocky Hill	2,634	4,640	11	126	24	4	818
Roxbury	514	462	3	34	1	5	89
Salem	603	817	3	42	13	2	290
Salisbury	773	1,100	2	70	22	6	161
Scotland	240	337	0	23	3	2	125
Seymour	2,351	3,020	9	89	20	7	1,118
Sharon	551	638	1	57	5	7	123
Shelton	7,089	6,779	26	230	60	16	2,273
Sherman	710	696	1	44	5	0	179
Simsbury	5,781	5,553	20	246	44	8	894
Somers	1,799	1,627	10	72	6	6	477
Southbury	4,737	3,741	13	123	28	11	78
Southington	6,146	8,905	34	304	38	8	2,328
South Windsor	4,389	6,237	14	173	35	12	1,162
Sprague	375	742	4	25	0	0	222
Stafford	1,522	2,772	17	116	19	9	796
Stamford	14,696	25,005	54	407	368	40	2,595
Sterling	350	477	1	11	5	1	219
Stonington	2,738	4,303	11	213	25	14	974
Stratford	8,015	11,148	47	330	49	27	2,587
Suffield	2,459	2,506	9	100	16	5	583
Thomaston	1,293	1,409	8	53	6	5	483
Thompson	1,240	2,143	12	45	17	6	570
Tolland	2,205	3,006	7	136	20	5	781
Torrington	4,641	7,631	39	370	48	17	1,862
Trumbull	8,001	7,338	13	205	100	15	1,714

TOWN	Presidential Electors for						
	Dole & Kemp (R)	Clinton & Gore (D)	Phillips & Zdonczyk (CC)	Nader & LaDuke (G)	Browne & Jorgensen (L)	Hagelin & Tompkins (NL)	Perot & Choate (REF)
Union	135	162	2	18	1	0	64
Vernon	4,103	6,803	11	228	41	12	1,412
Voluntown	283	431	0	7	7	3	201
Wallingford	6,105	10,075	33	235	39	20	2,283
Warren	293	262	1	17	3	0	63
Washington	734	841	3	86	8	1	180
Waterbury	12,075	18,901	220	378	149	29	3,169
Waterford	3,068	4,802	10	219	36	12	1,096
Watertown	4,244	4,143	22	135	39	12	1,164
Westbrook	1,008	1,462	5	49	9	5	377
West Hartford	10,781	19,037	47	672	95	29	1,890
West Haven	5,021	12,755	53	253	36	17	2,230
Weston	2,217	2,252	3	83	22	11	235
Westport	5,785	7,331	4	269	82	37	697
Wethersfield	5,261	7,723	20	227	33	14	1,250
Willington	814	1,318	6	107	8	3	355
Wilton	4,859	3,451	4	122	29	6	436
Winchester	1,449	2,280	12	241	17	9	548
Windham	1,883	4,812	22	287	22	16	678
Windsor	3,844	7,864	23	212	48	17	1,117
Windsor Locks	1,659	3,060	14	82	15	8	699
Wolcott	2,866	3,099	49	83	28	6	1,000
Woodbridge	1,868	2,444	3	92	18	3	314
Woodbury	2,213	1,779	2	93	20	4	387
Woodstock	1,450	1,471	8	58	9	8	406
Totals	483,109	735,740	2,425	24,321	5,788	1,703	139,523

Plurality: 252,631

Votes for Registered Write-in-Candidate Johan Rust and Charles Fellon 1; James Harris and Laura Garza, 4

VOTE FOR REPRESENTATIVE IN CONGRESS, NOVEMBER 5, 1996
FIRST CONGRESSIONAL DISTRICT

TOWNS	Kent Sleath (R)	Barbara Bailey Kennelly (D)	Barbara Bailey Kennelly (ACP)	John F. Forry III (CC)	Daniel A. Wasielewski (NL)
Andover	419	817	92	19	8
Berlin	2,343	5,097	522	101	64
Bloomfield	1,439	6,809	518	65	27
Bolton, part of	759	1,285	121	23	15
Cromwell	1,595	3,682	268	72	36
East Hampton	1,500	2,819	300	67	39
East Hartford	3,676	12,239	1,243	224	116
East Windsor	1,124	2,240	277	66	23
Glastonbury	5,145	9,434	803	94	47
Hartford	2,368	21,084	1,897	202	144
Hebron	1,133	2,215	221	39	23
Manchester	6,192	13,997	1,483	276	134
Marlborough	861	1,626	147	29	23
Newington	3,490	9,073	907	159	84
Portland	1,157	2,644	273	44	30
Rocky Hill	2,033	4,976	479	92	52
South Windsor	3,200	7,174	642	136	75
West Hartford	8,206	21,225	1,372	151	90
Wethersfield	3,937	8,603	736	106	58
Windsor	3,089	8,130	752	134	61
Totals	53,666	145,169	13,053	2,099	1,149

Plurality: 104,556
Total votes cast for Barbara Bailey Kennelly (D) plus (ACP) equals: 158,222

VOTE FOR REPRESENTATIVE IN CONGRESSS, NOVEMBER 5, 1996
SECOND CONGRESSIONAL DISTRICT

TOWNS	Edward Munster (R)	Sam Gejdenson (D)	Sam Gejdenson (ACP)	Dianne G. Ondusko (I)	Thomas E. Hall (NL)
Ashford	762	973	62	54	24
Bolton, part of	55	70	8	3	1
Bozrah	517	543	55	52	8
Brooklyn	1,283	1,232	91	76	11
Canterbury	1,120	820	61	99	12
Chaplin	412	405	28	30	9
Chester	733	998	69	34	6
Colchester	2,686	2,651	205	206	33
Columbia	1,157	1,102	74	75	17
Coventry	2,097	2,350	236	115	82
Deep River	1,001	1,045	70	34	11
East Haddam	1,791	1,468	100	104	22
East Lyme	3,561	3,246	247	151	27
Eastford	415	290	30	23	2
Ellington	2,538	2,274	161	145	36
Essex	1,777	1,389	109	52	15
Franklin	471	400	30	34	4
Griswold	1,569	1,748	172	172	23

TOWNS	Edward Munster (R)	Sam Gejdenson (D)	Sam Gejdenson (ACP)	Dianne G. Ondusko (I)	Thomas E. Hall (NL)
Groton	5,787	5,600	495	342	62
Haddam	2,003	1,527	112	80	19
Hampton	374	392	27	27	7
Killingly	2,457	2,470	214	178	28
Lebanon	1,579	1,135	149	114	23
Ledyard	3,446	2,200	150	173	21
Lisbon	812	760	77	95	5
Lyme	700	468	47	16	16
Mansfield	1,856	3,946	287	143	38
Middletown	6,225	9,753	697	323	82
Montville	3,018	2,955	239	326	41
New London	2,298	4,200	398	220	42
North Stonington	1,315	748	77	57	9
Norwich	4,673	6,820	618	659	69
Old Lyme	2,090	1,661	121	67	14
Old Saybrook	2,601	2,224	149	84	19
Plainfield	2,223	2,431	189	190	28
Pomfret	861	731	46	42	5
Preston	1,153	744	55	81	12
Putnam	1,547	1,665	126	110	20
Salem	896	659	69	58	16
Scotland	340	290	20	28	5
Sprague	565	594	58	84	11
Stafford	2,052	2,501	301	128	28
Sterling	524	401	39	45	5
Stonington	3,696	3,537	300	207	31
Thompson	1,673	1,814	138	131	32
Tolland	2,722	2,793	230	126	31
Union	175	160	17	5	6
Vernon	5,294	6,008	437	259	62
Voluntown	399	387	35	61	6
Waterford	4,282	4,026	264	219	32
Westbrook	1,339	1,279	93	46	11
Willington	1,030	1,271	150	49	18
Windham	2,563	4,162	283	174	54
Woodstock	1,819	1,228	116	71	12
Totals	100,332	106,544	8,631	6,477	1,263

Plurality: 2
Total write-in votes for registered write-in candidate Howard E. Proper Lamchick: 2
Total votes cast for Sam Gejdenson (D) and (ACP) equals: 115,175.

VOTE FOR REPRESENTATIVE IN CONGRESS, NOVEMBER 5, 1996
THIRD CONGRESSIONAL DISTRICT

TOWNS	John Coppola (R)	Rosa L. DeLauro (D)	Rosa L. DeLauro (ACP)	Gail J. Dalby (NL)
Branford	3,621	7,928	705	98
Clinton	1,866	3,405	292	36
Durham	1,156	1,706	136	28
East Haven	2,465	7,008	571	50
Guilford	3,220	5,955	722	78
Hamden	5,767	15,028	1,389	126
Killingworth	982	1,496	180	21
Madison	3,553	4,369	477	50
Middlefield	666	1,299	74	18
Milford	6,554	12,755	1,456	106
New Haven	3,921	24,377	2,339	184
North Branford	1,853	3,190	383	47
North Haven	3,788	6,312	686	51
Orange	2,786	3,691	374	36
Stratford	6,303	12,574	1,407	73
Wallingford	5,278	11,028	1,000	104
West Haven	4,287	12,909	1,329	91
Woodbridge, part of	1,269	2,078	170	22
Totals	59,335	137,108	13,690	1,219

Plurality: 91,463
Total votes cast for Rosa DeLauro (D) plus (ACP) equals: 150,798

VOTE FOR REPRESENTATIVE IN CONGRESS, NOVEMBER 5, 1996
FOURTH CONGRESSIONAL DISTRICT

TOWNS	Christopher Shays (R)	Bill Finch (D)	Edward H. Tonkin (L)	Terry M. Nevas (NL)
Bridgeport	9,494	18,520	631	129
Darien	7,532	1,590	74	21
Fairfield	16,654	8,684	286	140
Greenwich	18,313	6,901	369	111
Monroe, part of	4,846	1,972	98	16
New Canaan	7,136	1,874	84	38
Norwalk	15,675	11,672	441	163
Stamford	22,950	15,364	510	193
Trumbull	10,805	4,768	207	51
Westport	8,544	4,557	115	184
Totals	121,949	75,902	2,815	1,046

Plurality: 46,047

VOTE FOR REPRESENTATIVE IN CONGRESS, NOVEMBER 5, 1996
FIFTH CONGRESSIONAL DISTRICT

TOWNS	Gary A. Franks (R)	James H. Maloney (D)	James H. Maloney (ACP)	Rosita Rodriguez (CC)	Walter F. Thiessen, Jr. (L)
Ansonia	2,567	3,585	228	108	37
Beacon Falls	946	1,017	84	36	27
Bethany	1,230	1,144	74	39	17
Bethel	3,391	3,821	314	105	59
Brookfield	3,675	2,896	189	85	40
Cheshire	6,061	5,869	225	126	61
Danbury	7,936	11,751	756	283	135
Derby	1,652	2,412	206	79	28
Easton	2,086	1,309	55	34	20
Meriden	6,347	11,719	764	342	128
Middlebury	1,839	1,233	92	18	20
Monroe, part of	451	362	16	12	4
Naugatuck	4,276	5,380	386	174	90
New Fairfield	3,128	2,459	209	82	58
Newtown	4,689	4,670	342	137	79
Oxford	2,095	1,545	101	31	37
Prospect	2,074	1,606	76	55	36
Redding	2,166	1,815	73	27	22
Ridgefield	6,076	4,854	257	76	71
Seymour	2,754	2,866	245	85	41
Shelton	7,689	6,618	473	196	76
Southbury, part of	945	584	33	15	12
Waterbury	13,663	17,177	1,004	646	203
Weston	2,403	2,035	82	25	22
Wilton	5,112	3,168	131	33	26
Wolcott	3,102	3,036	183	128	39
Woodbridge, part of	429	428	17	6	3
Totals	98,782	105,359	6,615	2,983	1,391

Plurality: 13,192
Total votes cast for James H. Maloney (D) plus (ACP) equals: 111,974

VOTE FOR REPRESENTATIVE IN CONGRESS, NOVEMBER 5, 1996
SIXTH CONGRESSIONAL DISTRICT

TOWNS	Nancy L. Johnson (R)	Charlotte Koskoff (D)	Charlotte Koskoff (ACP)	Timothy A. Knibbs (CC)
Avon	4,925	2,826	134	55
Barkhamsted	833	705	45	16
Bethlehem	1,002	639	63	48
Bridgewater	612	341	16	10
Bristol	7,942	13,097	1,151	338
Burlington	1,895	1,530	130	45
Canaan	261	241	21	5
Canton	2,323	1,786	123	45
Colebrook	333	324	32	8
Cornwall	378	358	34	6
East Granby	1,232	930	41	28
Enfield	7,377	8,417	571	331
Farmington	5,915	4,502	246	148
Goshen	728	431	42	16
Granby	2,876	1,797	125	52
Hartland	542	317	22	28
Harwinton	1,334	1,105	69	33
Kent	859	539	22	10
Litchfield	2,197	1,495	93	72
Morris	591	383	33	24
New Britain	6,937	11,856	744	227
New Hartford	1,472	1,285	82	33
New Milford	6,171	3,040	233	137
Norfolk	368	419	23	10
North Canaan	706	454	34	28
Plainville	2,490	4,219	312	94
Plymouth	1,736	2,301	182	85
Roxbury	673	359	16	12
Salisbury	1,115	839	49	19
Sharon	753	504	29	7
Sherman	948	545	30	13
Simsbury	7,508	4,120	266	139
Somers	2,048	1,458	126	77
Southbury, part of	4,646	2,402	137	62
Southington	7,802	8,185	560	253
Suffield	3,022	1,961	148	82
Thomaston	1,572	1,336	82	45
Torrington	5,992	6,834	456	228
Warren	376	203	17	12
Washington	953	726	43	15
Watertown	4,900	3,441	205	171
Winchester	1,907	2,039	155	78
Windsor Locks	2,192	2,488	181	108
Woodbury	2,578	1,448	85	50
Totals	113,020	104,225	7,208	3,303

Plurality: 1,587
Total votes cast for Charlotte Koskoff (D) plus (ACP) equals: 111,433

SUMMARY OF VOTE FOR GOVERNOR AND LIEUTENANT GOVERNOR
NOVEMBER 8, 1994

CONGRESSIONAL DISTRICTS	GOVERNOR AND LIEUTENANT GOVERNOR				
	Eunice Strong Groark and Audrey Rowe (ACP)	John G. Rowland and M. Jodi Rell (R)	Bill Curry and Joseph P. Ganim (D)	Joseph A. Zdonczyk and Robert B. Ratchford (CC)	Tom Scott and Glen R. O'Keefe (IND)
First................	48,404	44,513	72,671	1,529	32,264
Second.............	51,606	53,539	61,749	1,288	24,685
Third................	30,285	71,813	69,910	1,904	16,520
Fourth..............	22,731	80,661	53,561	1,433	4,955
Fifth	21,660	98,555	54,554	2,003	16,422
Sixth................	41,899	66,120	62,688	1,850	35,282
Totals............	216,585	415,201	375,133	10,007	130,128

Plurality: 40,068

Total write-in votes for registered write-in candidates: John Frank Demko and Albert Rich, 1; Robert S. Loomis and Carl E. Vassar, 29.

*Willington: O'Keefe—422.

SUMMARY OF VOTE FOR SECRETARY OF THE STATE AND TREASURER
NOVEMBER 8, 1994

CONGRESSIONAL DISTRICTS	SECRETARY OF STATE			TREASURER			
	Miles S. Rapoport (ACP)	Andrea Scott (R)	Miles S. Rapoport (D)	Joseph M. Suggs, Jr. (ACP)	Chris Burnham (R)	Joseph M. Suggs, Jr. (D)	Christopher C. Hebert (CC)
First	29,825	71,342	73,830	24,412	81,641	64,206	4,867
Second	26,839	77,275	64,057	23,214	84,182	57,074	5,332
Third.............	16,489	76,075	66,796	16,068	76,915	63,715	3,059
Fourth............	10,564	80,516	48,868	9,302	84,781	45,849	1,940
Fifth	16,603	95,427	52,670	14,747	100,513	47,935	3,573
Sixth..............	27,295	91,123	60,159	22,483	98,168	52,258	5,436
Totals	127,615	491,758	366,380	110,226	526,200	331,037	24,207

Total votes cast for Miles S. Rapoport (ACP) plus (D) equals: 493,995. Plurality: 2,237.
Total votes cast for Joseph M. Suggs, Jr. (ACP) plus (D) equals: 441,263. Plurality: 84,937.
Total write-in votes for registered write-in candidates for Secretary of the State:
Janice K. Loomis, 41; Abraham Ziskis, 13.

SUMMARY OF VOTE FOR COMPTROLLER AND ATTORNEY GENERAL
NOVEMBER 8, 1994

	COMPTROLLER			ATTORNEY GENERAL		
CONGRESSIONAL DISTRICTS	Nancy Wyman (ACP)	Gene Gavin (R)	Nancy Wyman (D)	Richard Blumenthal (ACP)	Richard E. Arnold (R)	Richard Blumenthal (D)
First	30,922	63,690	75,456	47,719	43,800	89,124
Second	34,927	63,637	69,599	46,514	51,402	76,847
Third............	19,558	66,284	69,235	32,134	54,146	79,371
Fourth...........	11,716	76,220	50,342	23,032	61,584	61,948
Fifth	19,175	89,313	54,738	33,877	72,024	65,339
Sixth............	30,778	80,329	63,263	49,603	61,671	73,805
Totals	147,076	439,473	382,633	232,879	344,627	446,434

Total votes cast for Nancy Wyman (ACP) plus (D) equals: 529,709: Plurality: 90,236.
Total votes cast for Richard Blumenthal (ACP) plus (D) equals: 679,313: Plurality: 334,686.
Total write-in votes for registered write-in candidate for Attorney General
Howard A. Grayson, Jr.: 36.

SUMMARY OF VOTE FOR UNITED STATES SENATOR
NOVEMBER 8, 1994

CONGRESSIONAL DISTRICTS	Joe Lieberman (ACP)	Jerry Labriola (R)	Joe Lieberman (D)	Gary R. Garneau (CC)
First................	48,630	50,154	84,528	4,387
Second	58,461	45,299	77,285	3,905
Third..............	44,699	48,394	80,556	2,892
Fourth.............	31,041	56,451	63,144	1,892
Fifth	41,965	70,417	66,535	3,296
Sixth...............	55,253	64,118	71,745	4,617
Totals............	280,049	334,833	443,793	20,989

Total votes cast for Joe Lieberman (ACP) plus (D) equals: 723,842.
Plurality: 389,009.
Total write-in votes for registered write-in candidates: Edward J. Arrowsmith, 11; Clarisse DiCandia, 6; Wildey J. Moore, 86.

VOTE FOR STATE SENATORS, NOVEMBER 5, 1996
SENATORIAL DISTRICTS

1st District	Penny Stanziale (R)	John W. Fonfara (D)
Hartford, part of	1,919	12,042
Wethersfield, part of	1,699	2,981
Totals	3,618	15,023
Plurality: 11,405		

2nd District	No Nomination (R)	Eric D. Coleman (D)
Bloomfield, part of		4,692
Hartford, part of		9,258
Windsor, part of		3,978
Totals		17,928
Plurality: 17,928		

3rd District	Kevin F. Rennie (R)	Gary D. LeBeau (D)
East Hartford	6,268	11,064
East Windsor	1,770	1,940
Ellington, part of	2,052	1,804
South Windsor	6,743	4,628
Totals	16,833	19,436
Plurality: 2,603		
Votes for Registered Write-in Candidate: 7 Abe Ziskis		

4th District	Paul Munns (R)	Mary Ann Handley (D)
Bolton	1,152	1,152
Glastonbury	8,835	6,638
Hebron	1,814	1,769
Manchester	9,953	12,287
Totals	21,754	21,846
Plurality: 92		

5th District	Geoffrey G. Fisher (R)	Kevin B. Sullivan (D)
Bloomfield, part of	948	1,961
Burlington	1,400	2,123
Farmington	4,362	6,101
West Hartford	10,668	19,724
Totals	17,378	29,909
Plurality: 12,531		

VOTE FOR STATE SENATORS, NOVEMBER 5, 1996
SENATORIAL DISTRICTS

6th District	No Nomination (R)	Thomas A. Bozek (D)	Louis J. Marietta (I)
Berlin		4,962	438
New Britain		13,651	1,056
Totals		18,613	1,494
Plurality: 17,119			

7th District	John A. Kissel (R)	John Bowles (D)
Enfield	9,951	6,474
Somers	2,089	1,608
Suffield	3,175	1,792
Windsor, part of	3,187	2,808
Windsor Locks	2,609	2,157
Totals	21,011	14,839
Plurality: 6,172		

8th District	James T. Fleming (R)	John R. Bement (D)
Avon	5,371	2,246
Barkhamsted	996	535
Canton	2,726	1,315
Colebrook	419	255
East Granby	1,421	724
Granby	3,414	1,313
Hartland	669	237
Harwinton, part of	597	257
New Hartford	1,753	1,043
Norfolk	442	332
Plymouth, part of	1,358	1,011
Simsbury	9,036	2,770
Winchester	2,285	1,728
Totals	30,487	13,766
Plurality: 16,721		

9th District	P. J. Hallisey (R)	Biagio "Billy" Ciotto (D)
Cromwell	2,585	3,151
Middletown, part of	2,380	3,510
Newington	5,625	7,820
Rocky Hill	3,567	4,094
Wethersfield, part of	4,303	4,362
Totals	18,460	22,937
Plurality: 4,477		

VOTE FOR STATE SENATORS, NOVEMBER 5, 1996
SENATORIAL DISTRICTS

10th *District*	Steven R. Mullins (R)	Toni N. Harp (D)
New Haven, part of	1,511	11,075
West Haven, part of	2,103	4,627
Totals	3,614	15,702
Plurality: 12,088		

11th *District*	No Nomination (R)	Martin M. Looney (D)
East Haven, part of		2,135
Hamden, part of		5,267
New Haven, part of		12,372
Totals		19,774
Plurality: 19,774		

12th *District*	William A. Aniskovich (R)	No Nomination (D)
Branford	6,670	
East Haven, part of	2,412	
Guilford	5,666	
Madison	5,493	
North Branford	3,117	
Totals	23,358	
Plurality: 23,358		

13th *District*	Len Suzio (R)	Thomas P. Gaffey (D)
Meriden	5,341	13,684
Middlefield	663	1,363
Middletown, part of	2,604	7,068
Totals	8,608	22,155
Plurality: 13,507		

14th *District*	Win Smith, Jr. (R)	Robert Saley (D)
Milford	11,628	9,319
Orange	4,183	2,411
West Haven, part of	4,201	6,409
Totals	20,012	18,139
Plurality: 1,873		

VOTE FOR STATE SENATORS, NOVEMBER 5, 1996
SENATORIAL DISTRICTS

15th District	Thomas F. Upson (R)	John W. Girouard (D)
Middlebury	2,268	816
Naugatuck, part of	4,878	2,574
Prospect	2,573	1,146
Waterbury, part of	8,930	7,126
Totals	18,649	11,662
Plurality: 6,987		

16th District	Stephen Somma (R)	Jim Lawlor (D)
Southington, part of	6,409	4,967
Waterbury, part of	6,933	7,766
Wolcott	3,665	2,836
Totals	17,007	15,569
Plurality: 1,438		

17th District	Erik Kuselias (R)	Joe Crisco (D)	Joe Crisco (ACP)
Ansonia	2,901	3,357	223
Beacon Falls	1,095	934	95
Bethany	1,220	1,202	99
Derby	1,925	2,247	165
Hamden, part of	6,737	7,493	428
Naugatuck, part of	1,107	1,002	97
Seymour, part of	877	947	92
Woodbridge	1,894	2,332	143
Totals	17,756	19,514	1,342
Plurality: 3,100			

Total votes cast for Joe Crisco (D) plus (ACP) equals: 20,856

18th District	Cathy Welles Cook (R)	Jeff Slate (D)	Cathy Welles Cook (ACP)
Griswold	1,391	1,740	312
Groton	6,085	4,790	921
Lisbon	713	731	157
North Stonington	1,228	804	123
Preston	830	1,018	137
Sprague	558	4545	125
Stonington	4,049	3,077	517
Voluntown	419	345	84
Totals	15,273	13,050	2,376
Plurality: 4,599			

Total votes cast for Cathy Welles Cook (R) plus (ACP) equals: 17,649

VOTE FOR STATE SENATORS, NOVEMBER 5, 1996
SENATORIAL DISTRICTS

19th District	Dave Bingham (R)	Edith Prague (D)	David Bingham (ACP)
Andover	479	807	61
Bozrah	372	645	79
Columbia	687	1,681	78
Coventry, part of	690	1,496	137
Franklin	275	608	42
Lebanon	1,012	1,746	158
Mansfield, part of	361	1,247	60
Montville	2,159	3,617	466
Norwich	3,688	7,812	771
Salem	919	584	189
Totals	10,642	20,243	2,041

Plurality: 7,560
Total votes cast for David Bingham (R) plus (ACP) equals: 12,683

20th District	Gregory P. Massad (R)	Melodie Peters (D)	Gregory P. Massad (ACP)
East Lyme	2,912	3,961	299
Ledyard	2,468	3,043	207
New London	2,015	4,400	511
Old Lyme	1,713	2,075	185
Old Saybrook	2,210	2,496	192
Waterford	3,367	4,878	401
Totals	14,685	20,853	1,795

Plurality: 4,373
Total votes cast for Gregory P. Massad (R) plus (ACP) equals: 16,480

21st District	George L. Gunther (R)	Anna M. Scala (D)
Seymour, part of	2,085	1,673
Shelton	9,606	4,982
Stratford	12,052	7,848
Totals	23,743	14,503

Plurality: 9,240

22nd District	Lee Scarpetti (R)	Frank E. Altieri (D)	Carl E. Vassar (L)
Bridgeport, part of	5,632	7,581	243
Monroe, part of	2,533	1,264	85
Trumbull	10,084	5,443	368
Totals	18,249	14,288	696

Plurality: 3,961

VOTE FOR STATE SENATORS, NOVEMBER 5, 1996
SENATORIAL DISTRICTS

23rd District	Antonio D. Diaz (R)	Alvin W. Penn (D)	
Bridgeport, part of	3,350	11,264	
Plurality: 7,914			

24th District	Mark Nielsen (R)	Thomas J. Arconti (D)	Mark Nielsen (I)
Bethel	3,906	3,511	292
Danbury	9,021	11,303	610
New Fairfield	3,399	2,408	215
Totals	16,326	17,222	1,117
Plurality: 221			
Total votes cast for Mark Nielson (R) plus (I) equals: 17,443			

25th District	Robert L. Genuario (R)	Chris Perone (D)	Richard A. Bucciarelli (L)
Darien, part of	4,280	1,137	52
Norwalk	14,705	11,991	653
Totals	18,985	13,128	705
Plurality: 5,857			

26th District	Judith G. Freedman (R)	Charles P. Jenney (D)	
New Canaan, part of	4,120	1,176	
Redding	2,699	1,257	
Ridgefield	8,015	2,876	
Weston	3,179	1,304	
Westport	8,611	4,368	
Wilton	6,080	2,083	
Totals	32,704	13,064	
Plurality: 19,640			

27th District	Vincent Mobilio (R)	George Jepsen (D)	
Darien, part of	1,941	1,391	
Stamford, part of	8,879	17,821	
Totals	10,820	19,212	
Plurality: 8,392			

VOTE FOR STATE SENATORS, NOVEMBER 5, 1996
SENATORIAL DISTRICTS

28th District	Fred H. Lovegrove, Jr. (R)	Thomas G. Ganim (D)
Easton	1,949	1,626
Fairfield	13,318	12,705
Monroe, part of	2,120	1,901
Newtown	5,393	4,284
Totals	22,780	20,516
Plurality: 2,264		

29th District	Virginia Raymond (R)	Donald E. Williams (D)	Stephen R. Myers (I)
Canterbury	1,061	897	40
Killingly	2,377	2,705	131
Mansfield, part of	1,740	2,530	78
Plainfield	2,345	2,327	117
Putnam	1,263	2,046	80
Scotland	357	279	14
Sterling	508	426	35
Thompson	1,376	2,284	115
Windham	2,850	3,816	143
Totals	13,877	17,310	753
Plurality: 3,433			

30th District	M. Adela Eads (R)	Harold Hansen (D)
Canaan	275	236
Cornwall	397	356
Goshen	802	367
Harwinton, part of	930	618
Kent	966	477
Litchfield	2,419	1,338
Morris	673	331
New Milford, part of	3,947	2,047
North Canaan	744	444
Salisbury	1,089	874
Sharon	762	513
Sherman	919	574
Torrington	6,806	5,843
Warren	413	185
Washington	1,035	652
Totals	22,177	14,855
Plurality: 7,322		

VOTE FOR STATE SENATORS, NOVEMBER 5, 1996
SENATORIAL DISTRICTS

31st District	Dick Clark (R)	Tom Colapietro (D)	Renee A. Ezbicki (CC)
Bristol	7,290	14,445	367
Plainville	2,499	3,918	133
Plymouth, part of	518	987	36
Southington, part of	1,754	2,549	90
Totals	12,061	21,899	626
Plurality: 9,838			

32nd District	Louis C. DeLuca (R)	Donald Pare (D)	Linda A. Moore (L)
Bethlehem	1,138	472	57
Bridgewater	566	342	15
Brookfield	4,350	1,932	110
New Milford, part of	1,964	1,033	84
Oxford	2,354	1,205	75
Roxbury	645	360	16
Southbury	5,706	2,750	111
Thomaston	1,715	1,050	55
Watertown	5,341	2,801	122
Woodbury	2,860	1,153	79
Totals	26,639	13,098	724
Plurality: 13,541			

33rd District	John A. Johns (R)	Eileen M. Daily (D)
Chester	543	1,190
Clinton	1,904	3,426
Colchester	1,739	3,555
Deep River	766	1,252
Durham	1,176	1,727
East Haddam	1,215	2,054
East Hampton	1,612	2,828
Essex	1,648	1,589
Haddam	1,283	2,076
Killingworth	1,026	1,509
Lyme	525	623
Marlborough	937	1,603
Portland	1,264	2,664
Westbrook	892	1,796
Totals	16,527	27,892
Plurality: 11,365		

VOTE FOR STATE SENATORS, NOVEMBER 5, 1996
SENATORIAL DISTRICTS

34th District	David C. Schrumm (R)	Brian McDermott (D)
Cheshire	6,397	5,977
North Haven	4,253	5,815
Wallingford	5,821	10,992
Totals	16,471	22,784
Plurality: 6,313		

35th District	Tony Guglielmo (R)	Linda Sumner (D)
Ashford	1,108	681
Brooklyn	1,439	1,091
Chaplin	466	347
Coventry, part of	1,352	1,014
Eastford	512	224
Ellington, part of	741	324
Hampton	443	337
Pomfret	1,060	572
Stafford	3,619	1,309
Tolland	4,035	1,622
Union	268	82
Vernon	7,357	4,047
Willington	1,647	770
Woodstock	1,981	1,081
Totals	26,028	13,501
Plurality: 12,527		

36th District	William H. Nickerson (R)	No Nomination (D)
Greenwich	18,223	
New Canaan, part of	2,947	
Stamford, part of	7,522	
Totals	28,692	
Plurality: 28,692		

VOTE FOR STATE REPRESENTATIVES, NOVEMBER 5, 1996
ASSEMBLY DISTRICTS

1st District	No Nomination (R)	Kenneth P. Green (D)	
Bloomfield, part of		2,163	
Hartford, part of		2,256	
Totals		4,419	
Plurality: 4,419			

2nd District	No Nomination (R)	Thomas D. Ritter (D)	
Hartford, part of		3,036	
Plurality: 3,036			

3rd District	Kevin R. Sheridan (R)	Minnie Gonzalez (D)	Harry Suarez (PC)
Hartford, part of	374	2,315	16
Plurality: 1,941			

4th District	No Nomination (R)	Edwin E. Garcia (D)	
Hartford, part of		2,061	
Plurality: 2,061			

5th District	No Nomination (R)	Marie Lopez Kirkley-Bey (D)	Cornell Lewis (PC)
Hartford, part of		2,394	290
Plurality: 2,104			

6th District	Art J. Feltman (R)	Art J. Feltman (D)	
Hartford, part of	653	3,401	
Plurality: 4,054			
Total votes cast for Art Feltman (R) plus (D) equals: 4,054			

7th District	No Nomination (R)	Annette W. Carter (D)	
Hartford, part of		2,468	
Windsor, part of		2,188	
Totals		4,656	
Plurality: 4,656			

VOTE FOR STATE REPRESENTATIVES, NOVEMBER 5, 1996
ASSEMBLY DISTRICTS

8th District	No Nomination (R)	Patrick J. Flaherty (D)	
Columbia		1,622	
Coventry, part of		2,798	
Lebanon, part of		694	
Vernon, part of		1,804	
Totals		6,918	
Plurality: 6,918			

9th District	Richard D. Veltri (R)	Allan T. Driscoll (D)	
East Hartford, part of	1,672	1,726	
Glastonbury, part of	1,588	1,561	
Manchester, part of	2,185	2,033	
Totals	5,445	5,320	
Plurality: 125			

10th District	Thomas D. Roy (R)	Melody A. Currey (D)	
East Hartford, part of	2,116	5,365	
Plurality: 3,249			

11th District	Todd M. Bossier (R)	Michael A. Christ (D)	Warren E. Avery (PC)
East Hartford, part of	1,389	4,473	99
Plurality: 3,084			

12th District	Joseph J. Noti (R)	James R. McCavanagh (D)	
Manchester, part of	2,328	6,661	
Plurality: 4,333			

13th District	James F. Skulski, Jr. (R)	John W. Thompson (D)	
Manchester, part of	2,618	5,435	
Plurality: 2,817			

14th District	John J. Mitchell (R)	Nancy E. Kerensky (D)	Anthony J. Pecoraro (PC)
South Windsor	5,150	6,246	72
Plurality: 1,096			

VOTE FOR STATE REPRESENTATIVES, NOVEMBER 5, 1996
ASSEMBLY DISTRICTS

15th *District*	No Nomination (R)	Mary U. Eberle (D)
Bloomfield, part of		4,608
Windsor, part of		2,652
Totals		7,260
Plurality: 7,260		

16th *District*	Thomas J. Herlihy (R)	Huguet P. C. Pameijer (D)
Simsbury	8,371	3,504
Plurality: 4,867		

17th *District*	Wade H. Horsey II (R)	Jessie Stratton (D)
Avon	3,987	3,962
Canton	1,865	2,397
Totals	5,852	6,359
Plurality: 507		

18th *District*	John W. Westcott III (R)	Andrew M. Fleischmann (D)
West Hartford, part of	3,381	7,450
Plurality: 4,069		

19th *District*	Robert Farr (R)	Julie Lewin (D)
West Hartford, part of	6,076	5,687
Plurality: 389		

20th *District*	Allen Hoffman (R)	John Ritter (D)
Hartford, part of	623	1,755
West Hartford, part of	3,515	4,632
Totals	4,138	6,387
Plurality: 2,249		

21st *District*	Beatrice C. Stockwell (R)	Demetrios Giannaros (D)
Farmington	4,364	6,546
Plainville, part of	129	286
Totals	4,493	6,832
Plurality: 2,339		

VOTE FOR STATE REPRESENTATIVES, NOVEMBER 5, 1996
ASSEMBLY DISTRICTS

22nd District	Helen B. Bergenty (R)	Elizabeth A. Boukus (D)	
Bristol, part of	682	1,333	
Plainville, part of	2,536	4,063	
Totals	3,218	5,396	
Plurality: 2,178			
23rd District	Arnold P. Schwartz (R)	Theresa B. Gerratana (D)	Stanley J. Wosczyna (CC)
Berlin, part of	159	469	21
New Britain, part of	1,197	4,403	290
Totals	1,356	4,872	311
Plurality: 3,516			
24th District	Peter A. Oshana, Sr. (R)	David Pudlin (D)	Patrick J. Cloutier (I)
New Britain, part of	920	2,967	209
Plurality: 2,047			
25th District	John J. Gubbins (R)	John C. Geragosian (D)	
New Britain, part of	768	2,353	
Newington, part of	1,208	2,099	
Totals	1,976	4,452	
Plurality: 2,476			
26th District	Anthony Tercyak (R)	Gary Pescosolido (D)	
New Britain, part of	3,315	2,511	
Plurality: 804			
27th District	Dom Mazzoccoli (R)	William J. Cariseo (D)	
Newington, part of	5,719	4,373	
Plurality: 1,346			
28th District	Nita Barrabee (R)	Paul R. Doyle (D)	
Wethersfield, part of	3,320	7,842	
Plurality: 4,522			

VOTE FOR STATE REPRESENTATIVES, NOVEMBER 5, 1996
ASSEMBLY DISTRICTS

29th District	No Nomination (R)	Richard D. Tulisano (D)
Hartford, part of		437
Rocky Hill		5,309
Wethersfield, part of		1,203
Totals		6,949
Plurality: 6,949		

30th District	Ann P. Dandrow (R)	Virginia W. Stelmack (D)
Berlin, part of	4,662	2,920
Southington, part of	1,936	1,021
Totals	6,598	3,941
Plurality: 2,657		

31st District	Sonya Googins (R)	No Nomination (D)
Glastonbury, part of	8,494	
Plurality: 8,494		

32nd District	Bernard Walsh (R)	Jim O'Rourke (D)
Cromwell	1,775	3,886
Middletown, part of	71	361
Portland	1,168	2,910
Totals	3,014	7,157
Plurality: 4,143		

33rd District	Salvatore A. Russo (R)	Joseph C. Serra (D)
Middletown, part of	1,979	5,474
Plurality: 3,495		

34th District	No Nomination (R)	Terry Concannon (D)
East Hampton		3,020
Haddam		2,523
Middletown, part of		1,665
Totals		7,208
Plurality: 7,208		

VOTE FOR STATE REPRESENTATIVES, NOVEMBER 5, 1996
ASSEMBLY DISTRICTS

35th District	Dan Gallagher (R)	Robert A. Landino (D)
Clinton, part of	2,284	2,759
Essex, part of	189	174
Old Saybrook, part of	659	947
Westbrook	1,171	1,510
Totals	4,303	5,390

Plurality: 1,087

36th District	Judy Ganswindt (R)	Claire Sauer (D)	Claire Sauer (ACP)
Chester	536	1,151	84
Deep River	720	1,241	86
Essex, part of	1,191	1,523	148
Lyme	435	718	85
Old Saybrook, part of	1,326	1,809	111
Totals	4,208	6,442	514

Plurality: 2,748
Total votes cast for Claire Sauer (D) plus (ACP) equals: 6,956

37th District	Richard A. Lickwar (R)	Gary J. Orefice (D)	Gary J. Orefice (ACP)
East Lyme	3,385	3,598	289
Old Lyme	2,007	1,681	88
Totals	5,392	5,279	377

Plurality: 264
Total votes cast for Gary J. Orefice (D) plus (ACP) equals: 5,656

38th District	No Nomination (R)	Andrea L. Stillman (D)	Andrea L. Stillman (ACP)
New London, part of		979	142
Waterford		5,478	635
Totals		6,457	777

Plurality: 7,234
Total votes cast for Andrea L. Stillman (D) plus (ACP) equals: 7,234

39th District	Thomas A. Perry, Jr. (R)	Wade A. Hyslop, Jr. (D)	Thomas A. Perry, Jr. (ACP)
New London, part of	1,144	2,885	356

Plurality: 1,385
Total votes cast for Thomas A. Perry, Jr. (R) plus (ACP) equals: 1,500

VOTE FOR STATE REPRESENTATIVES, NOVEMBER 5, 1996
ASSEMBLY DISTRICTS

40th District	Jerry S. Williams (D)	Nancy A. DeMarinis (D)	Jerry S. Williams (ACP)
Groton, part of	1,247	2,861	129
New London, part of	254	629	39
Totals	1,501	3,490	168
Plurality: 1,821			

Total votes cast for Jerry S. Williams (D) plus (ACP) equals: 1,669

41st District	Lenny T. Winkler (R)	No Nomination (D)	Lenny T. Winkler (ACP)
Groton, part of	4,848		1,007
Plurality: 5,855			

Total votes cast for Lenny T. Winkler (R) plus (ACP) equals: 5,855

42nd District	Christopher R. Ruest (R)	Mary K. McGrattan (D)
Groton, part of	15	5
Ledyard	2,730	3,223
Montville, part of	231	375
Totals	2,976	3,603
Plurality: 627		

43rd District	Robert R. Simmons (R)	John H. Mellow (D)
North Stonington	1,548	503
Stonington	5,160	2,199
Totals	6,708	2,702
Plurality: 4,096		

44th District	Michael A. Caron (R)	Thomas Rizer (D)
Canterbury	1,041	965
Killingly, part of	853	597
Plainfield	2,454	2,509
Totals	4,348	4,071
Plurality: 277		

VOTE FOR STATE REPRESENTATIVES, NOVEMBER 5, 1996
ASSEMBLY DISTRICTS

45th District	No Nomination (R)	Steven Mikutel (D)
Griswold		2,673
Lisbon, part of		614
Preston		1,312
Sterling		602
Voluntown		611
Totals		5,812
Plurality: 5,812		

46th District	Peter A. Nystrom (R)	Nancy A. DePietro (D)	Peter A. Nystrom (ACP)
Norwich, part of	3,337	3,240	646

Plurality: 743
Total votes cast for Peter A. Nystrom (R) plus (ACP) equals: 3,983

47th District	Barry Kolar (R)	Jack Malone (D)
Lisbon, part of	290	445
Norwich, part of	1,604	3,781
Scotland	324	327
Sprague	447	833
Totals	2,665	5,386
Plurality: 2,721		

48th District	Gale Balavender (R)	Linda A. Orange (D)
Colchester	2,231	3,306
East Haddam	1,394	1,882
Salem	821	773
Totals	4,446	5,961
Plurality: 1,515		

49th District	Richard Leydon (R)	John J. Lescoe (D)	Richard Leydon (I)
Windham	1,656	5,198	127

Plurality: 3,415
Total votes cast for Richard Leydon (R) plus (I) equals: 1,783

VOTE FOR STATE REPRESENTATIVES, NOVEMBER 5, 1996
ASSEMBLY DISTRICTS

50th District	John L. Bala (R)	Jefferson B. Davis (D)	
Brooklyn	925	1,673	
Chaplin	324	505	
Eastford	377	354	
Hampton	305	486	
Killingly, part of	708	1,452	
Pomfret	620	1,045	
Totals	3,259	5,515	
Plurality: 2,256			

51st District	Tasi Vriga (R)	Shawn T. Johnston (D)	William A. Warner (I)
Killingly, part of	306	1,162	40
Putnam	548	2,757	100
Thompson	688	2,783	227
Totals	1,542	6,702	367
Plurality: 5,160			

52nd District	Romeo A. Blackmar (R)	John D. Mordasky (D)	
Somers, part of	695	1,006	
Stafford	1,345	3,397	
Union	114	238	
Woodstock	1,404	1,655	
Totals	3,558	6,296	
Plurality: 2,738			

53rd District	Kathy W. Bach (R)	Michael J. Cardin (D)	
Ashford	748	1,087	
Coventry, part of	263	341	
Tolland	2,712	3,258	
Willington	1,057	1,442	
Totals	4,780	6,128	
Plurality: 1,348			

54th District	No Nomination (R)	Denise Merrill (D)	
Mansfield		4,748	
Plurality: 4,748			

VOTE FOR STATE REPRESENTATIVES, NOVEMBER 5, 1996
ASSEMBLY DISTRICTS

55th District	Pamela Z. Sawyer (R)	Anastasia Morianos (D)	
Andover	971	394	
Bolton	1,630	776	
Hebron	2,556	1,088	
Marlborough	1,795	809	
Vernon, part of	697	389	
Totals	7,649	3,456	
Plurality: 4,193			

56th District	Gary J. Merton (R)	Thomasina Clemons (D)	
Vernon, part of	2,459	4,984	
Plurality: 2,525			

57th District	Robert J. Clements (R)	Edward C. Graziani (D)	Robert J. Clements (I)
East Windsor	1,438	2,110	137
Ellington	2,095	2,792	157
Totals	3,533	4,902	294
Plurality: 1,075			
Total votes cast for Robert J. Clements (R) plus (I) equals: 3,827			

58th District	Patrick J. Danford (R)	Frederick A. Gelsi (D)	
Enfield, part of	2,227	4,764	
Plurality: 2,537			

59th District	No Nomination (R)	Stephen M. Jarmoc (D)	
Enfield, part of		4,114	
Somers, part of		1,163	
Totals		5,277	
Plurality: 5,277			

60th District	No Nomination (R)	Carl Schiessl (D)	Robert J. Petrelli (CC)	Richard W. Loomis (L)
Enfield, part of		2,201	179	170
Windsor Locks		3,664	240	189
Totals		5,865	419	359
Plurality: 5,446				

VOTE FOR STATE REPRESENTATIVES, NOVEMBER 5, 1996
ASSEMBLY DISTRICTS

61st *District*	Ruth C. Fahrbach (R)	No Nomination (D)	
East Granby, part of	36		
Suffield	3,515		
Windsor, part of	3,040		
Totals	6,591		
Plurality: 6,591			

62nd *District*	Richard F. Ferrari (R)	Carmella Lattizori (D)	
Barkhamsted	659	949	
East Granby, part of	1,351	762	
Granby	2,966	1,741	
New Hartford	1,425	1,410	
Totals	6,401	4,862	
Plurality: 1,539			

63rd *District*	F. Philip Prelli (R)	Carolyn B. Conway (D)	
Canaan	272	241	
Colebrook	384	310	
Hartland	621	271	
Norfolk	342	501	
North Canaan	782	416	
Winchester	2,494	1,719	
Totals	4,895	3,458	
Plurality: 1,437			

64th *District*	Andrew Roraback (R)	Mary Ann O'Sullivan (D)	Mary Ann O'Sullivan (ACP)
Cornwall	455	329	10
Goshen	942	291	27
Salisbury	1,240	766	42
Sharon	790	497	36
Torrington, part of	3,189	2,208	205
Totals	6,616	4,091	320
Plurality: 2,205			
Total votes cast for Mary Ann O'Sullivan (D) plus (ACP) equals: 4,411			

65th *District*	Brian E. Mattiello (R)	No Nomination (D)	
Torrington, part of	5,875		
Plurality: 5,875			
Votes cast for Registered Write-in Candidate Robert L. Reed 0			

VOTE FOR STATE REPRESENTATIVES, NOVEMBER 5, 1996
ASSEMBLY DISTRICTS

66th District	Robert A. Maddox, Jr. (R)	Eleanordawn R. Hughes (D)	Eleanordawn R. Hughes (ACP)	George C. Eggert (L)
Bethlehem	891	411	26	482
Litchfield, part of	1,701	907	52	410
Morris	576	300	22	115
Warren	362	183	10	41
Woodbury	2,494	1,248	50	284
Totals	6,024	3,049	160	1,332

Plurality: 2,815
Total votes cast for Eleanordawn R. Hughes (D) plus (ACP) equals: 3,209

67th District	Jeanne W. Garvey (R)	No Nomination (D)
Kent	979	
New Milford, part of	5,173	
Totals	6,152	

Plurality: 6,152

68th District	Brian J. Flaherty (R)	Frederick K. Fischer (D)
Middlebury, part of	860	276
Watertown	6,280	2,424
Totals	7,140	2,700

Plurality: 4,440

69th District	Arthur J. O'Neill (R)	Vin Perry (D)
Bridgewater	613	314
Roxbury	695	328
Southbury, part of	5,511	2,369
Washington	1,035	596
Totals	7,854	3,607

Plurality: 4,427

70th District	Kevin M. DelGobbo (R)	Kevin G. Knowles (D)
Naugatuck, part of	4,207	3,497

Plurality: 710

71st District	Anthony J. D'Amelio (R)	Ken Bouffard (D)
Waterbury, part of	4,224	2,701

Plurality: 1,523

VOTE FOR STATE REPRESENTATIVES, NOVEMBER 5, 1996
ASSEMBLY DISTRICTS

72nd District	Martin F. Spring (R)	Reginald G. Beamon (D)	
Waterbury, part of	1,033	3,230	
Plurality: 2,197			
73rd District	Michael J. Cofrancesco (R)	Joan V. Hartley (D)	
Waterbury, part of	2,675	5,621	
Plurality: 2,946			
74th District	Lisa E. Mason (R)	Michael J. Jarjura (D)	
Waterbury, part of	2,601	4,916	
Plurality: 2,315			
75th District	No Nomination (R)	Thomas F. Conway (D)	James Macary (PC)
Waterbury, part of		3,094	363
Plurality: 2,731			
76th District	John E. Piscopo (R)	No Nomination (D)	
Burlington	2,137		
Harwinton	1,699		
Litchfield, part of	526		
Thomaston	2,216		
Totals	6,578		
Plurality: 6,578			
77th District	Michael B. Rimcoski (R)	Roger B. Michele (D)	
Bristol, part of	3,326	5,602	
Plurality: 2,276			
78th District	William A. Hamzy (R)	Michael E. Ganem (D)	
Bristol, part of	1,693	2,042	
Plymouth	2,445	1,935	
Totals	4,138	3,977	
Plurality: 161			

VOTE FOR STATE REPRESENTATIVES, NOVEMBER 5, 1996
ASSEMBLY DISTRICTS

79th District	Richard F. Prindle (R)	Kosta Diamantis (D)	
Bristol, part of	2,457	4,699	
Southington, part of	216	169	
Totals	2,673	4,868	
Plurality: 2,195			

80th District	Dennis H. Cleary (R)	No Nomination (D)	John W. Obiden (CC)
Southington, part of	2,021		164
Wolcott	4,024		520
Totals	6,045		684
Plurality: 5,361			

81st District	Angelo M. Fusco (R)	Peter T. Dziedzic, Jr. (D)
Southington, part of	5,716	3,943
Plurality: 1,773		

82nd District	Philip T. Ashton (R)	Emil Altobello (D)
Meriden, part of	2,900	4,595
Middlefield, part of	376	555
Totals	3,276	5,150
Plurality: 1,874		

83rd District	Rick Kilham (R)	James W. Abrams (D)
Meriden, part of	2,029	4,298
Wallingford, part of	1,062	1,332
Totals	3,091	5,630
Plurality: 2,539		

84th District	Helen Macri (R)	Christopher G. Donovan (D)
Meriden, part of	1,246	3,877
Plurality: 2,631		

85th District	Barbara Chayer (R)	Mary M. Mushinsky (D)
Wallingford, part of	2,927	5,828
Plurality: 2,901		

VOTE FOR STATE REPRESENTATIVES, NOVEMBER 5, 1996
ASSEMBLY DISTRICTS

86th *District*	Robert M. Ward (R)	No Nomination (D)
East Haven, part of	761	
Guilford, part of	801	
North Branford	3,515	
Totals	5,077	
Plurality: 5,077		
87th *District*	Curtis D. Andrews, Jr. (R)	Steve Fontana (D)
Hamden, part of	1,008	1,565
North Haven, part of	3,830	4,410
Totals	4,838	5,975
Plurality: 1,137		
88th *District*	No Nomination (R)	Nancy Beals (D)
Hamden, part of		4,638
New Haven, part of		575
North Haven, part of		1,646
Totals		6,859
Plurality: 6,859		
89th *District*	Edwin M. Kania (R)	Vickie Orsini Nardello (D)
Bethany	1,001	1,439
Cheshire, part of	1,820	2,639
Prospect	1,481	2,399
Totals	4,302	6,477
Plurality: 2,175		
90th *District*	Michael J. Sittnick (R)	Mary G. Fritz (D)
Cheshire, part of	2,045	3,702
Wallingford, part of	1,024	2,570
Totals	3,069	6,272
Plurality: 3,203		
91st *District*	No Nomination (R)	Peter F. Villano (D)
Hamden, part of		5,710
Plurality: 5,710		

VOTE FOR STATE REPRESENTATIVES, NOVEMBER 5, 1996
ASSEMBLY DISTRICTS

92nd District	Henry C. Campbell (R)	Patricia Dillon (D)
New Haven, part of Plurality: 3,791	851	4,642
93rd District	No Nomination (R)	Howard C. Scipio (D)
New Haven, part of Plurality: 3,500		3,500
94th District	No Nomination (R)	William Dyson (D)
New Haven, part of Plurality: 3,801		3,801
95th District	Peter Gero (R)	John S. Martinez (D)
New Haven, part of Plurality: 2,840	338	3,178
96th District	Stanley M. Sanders (R)	Cameron C. Staples (D)
New Haven, part of Plurality: 3,251	640	3,891
97th District	Chris DePino (R)	No Nomination (D)
New Haven, part of Plurality: 3,171	3,171	
98th District	No Nomination (R)	Patricia Widlitz (D)
Branford, part of		1,170
Guilford, part of		5,435
Totals Plurality: 6,605		6,605
99th District	Richard J. Smith, Jr. (R)	Michael P. Lawlor (D)
Branford, part of	127	251
East Haven, part of	2,146	5,946
Totals Plurality: 3,924	2,273	6,197

VOTE FOR STATE REPRESENTATIVES, NOVEMBER 5, 1996
ASSEMBLY DISTRICTS

100th District	Joseph C. Gallo (R)	Susan Bysiewicz (D)
Durham	1,114	1,926
Middlefield, part of	359	773
Middletown, part of	1,928	3,935
Totals	3,401	6,634
Plurality: 3,233		

101st District	Peter A. Metz (R)	Todd R. Foust (D)
Clinton, part of	274	182
Killingworth	1,519	977
Madison	5,733	2,227
Totals	7,526	3,386
Plurality: 4,140		

102nd District	Richard K. Greenalch, Jr. (R)	Peter J. Panaroni, Jr. (D)
Branford, part of	3,900	5,942
Plurality: 2,042		

103rd District	Lucien A. DiMeo (R)	Craig Henrici (D)
Cheshire, part of	1,164	945
Hamden, part of	2,078	3,334
Wallingford, part of	1,178	1,137
Totals	4,420	5,416
Plurality: 996		

104th District	Randall W. Colette (R)	Vincent J. Tonucci (D)
Ansonia, part of	1,463	4,045
Derby, part of	479	1,339
Totals	1,942	5,384
Plurality: 3,442		

105th District	Paul H. Rosebrock (R)	John W. Betkoski III (D)
Ansonia, part of	209	514
Beacon Falls	567	1,579
Seymour	2,141	4,758
Totals	2,917	6,851
Plurality: 3,934		

VOTE FOR STATE REPRESENTATIVES, NOVEMBER 5, 1996
ASSEMBLY DISTRICTS

106th District	Julia B. Wasserman (R)	No Nomination (D)	Charles Noe (I)
Bethel, part of	2,384		338
Newtown, part of	4,478		434
Totals	6,862		772
Plurality: 6,090			

107th District	B. Scott Santa-Maria (R)	No Nomination (D)	Judy Bolt (I)
Bethel, part of	2,274		254
Brookfield	4,970		422
Totals	7,244		676
Plurality: 6,568			

108th District	Norma Gyle (R)	No Nomination (D)	Joseph Ribeiro (I)
New Fairfield	4,037		671
New Milford, part of	1,565		243
Sherman	996		94
Totals	6,598		1,008
Plurality: 5,590			

109th District	Donald W. Boughton (R)	Lew Wallace (D)	Donald W. Boughton (I)
Danbury, part of	3,246	3,883	231
Total votes cast for Donald W. Boughton (R) plus (I) equals: 3,477			
Plurality: 406			

110th District	Tyrone B. Humes (R)	Bob Godfrey (D)	Catherine V. DiBuono (I)
Danbury, part of	1,829	3,180	117
Plurality: 1,351			

111th District	Christopher R. Scalzo (R)	No Nomination (D)	
Ridgefield	8,644		
Plurality: 8,644			

112th District	William J. Varese (R)	No Nomination (D)	
Monroe	5,199		
Newtown, part of	1,556		
Totals	6,755		
Plurality: 6,755			

VOTE FOR STATE REPRESENTATIVES, NOVEMBER 5, 1996
ASSEMBLY DISTRICTS

113th District	Richard O. Belden (R)	No Nomination (D)	
Shelton, part of	6,586		
Plurality: 6,586			

114th District	Brendan E. Williams (R)	Ellen Scalettar (D)	Ellen Scalettar (ACP)
Derby, part of	864	1,542	135
Orange, part of	1,901	1,874	174
Woodbridge	1,654	2,617	188
Totals	4,419	6,033	497
Plurality: 1,098			
Total votes cast for Ellen Scalettar (D) plus (ACP) equals: 6,530			
Plurality: 2,111			

115th District	Paul M. Frosolone (R)	Stephen D. Dargan (D)	Anthony E. Basilicato (PC)
West Haven, part of	1,874	5,273	85
Plurality: 3,399			

116th District	John A. Samperi (R)	Louis P. Esposito, Jr. (D)
West Haven, part of	2,175	4,020
Plurality: 1,845		

117th District	Ray Collins (R)	H. Richard Borer (D)
Milford, part of	1,933	1,365
Orange, part of	1,586	1,189
West Haven, part of	1,894	2,607
Totals	5,413	5,161
Plurality: 252		

118th District	Mary Corriveau (R)	James A. Amann (D)
Milford, part of	3,248	5,066
Plurality: 1,818		

119th District	Barbara Genovese (R)	Richard F. Roy (D)
Milford, part of	3,973	5,068
Plurality: 1,095		

VOTE FOR STATE REPRESENTATIVES, NOVEMBER 5, 1996
ASSEMBLY DISTRICTS

120th District	John A. Harkins (R)	Joseph R. Cavallo (D)
Stratford, part of	5,439	3,898
Plurality: 1,541		

121st District	Gloria A. Davis (R)	Terrance E. Backer (D)
Stratford, part of	2,272	5,034
Plurality: 2,762		

122nd District	Lawrence G. Miller (R)	No Nomination (D)
Shelton, part of	3,796	
Stratford, part of	1,987	
Trumbull, part of	1,240	
Totals	7,023	
Plurality: 7,023		

123rd District	Elaine Hammers (R)	Bob Golger (D)
Trumbull, part of	6,041	4,394
Plurality: 1,647		

124th District	Hera Powell (R)	Ernest E. Newton II (D)
Bridgeport, part of	546	2,525
Plurality: 1,979		

125th District	Ralph Langlois (R)	Robert T. Keeley, Jr. (D)
Bridgeport, part of	1,091	4,011
Plurality: 2,920		

126th District	Peter Perillo, Jr. (R)	Christopher L. Caruso (D)
Bridgeport, part of	877	4,343
Plurality: 3,466		

127th District	Michael J. Horvath (R)	Jacqueline M. Cocco (D)
Bridgeport, part of	1,145	3,663
Fairfield, part of	1,267	2,031
Totals	2,412	5,694
Plurality: 3,282		

VOTE FOR STATE REPRESENTATIVES, NOVEMBER 5, 1996
ASSEMBLY DISTRICTS

128th District	Russell J. Tomatore (R)	Edna I. Garcia (D)	
Bridgeport, part of	372	1,974	
Plurality: 1,602			

129th District	George Oldroyd (R)	Lee Samowitz (D)	
Bridgeport, part of	1,738	3,628	
Plurality: 1,890			

130th District	Warren Johnson (R)	Hector A. Diaz (D)	Willie Matos (PC)
Bridgeport, part of	265	2,149	48
Plurality: 1,884			

131st District	Ronald S. San Angelo (R)	Scott P. Troemel (D)	
Middlebury, part of	1,383	567	
Naugatuck, part of	1,681	942	
Oxford	2,385	1,270	
Southbury, part of	485	242	
Totals	5,934	3,021	
Plurality: 2,913			

132nd District	Carl J. Dickman (R)	Judy Boos (D)	Carl J. Dickman (I)
Fairfield, part of	5,583	4,438	288
Plurality: 1,433			

133rd District	Paul M. Tymniak (R)	John C. Loeser (D)	Bernard A. Nevas (NL)
Fairfield, part of	2,804	1,418	36
Weston, part of	860	607	30
Westport, part of	3,220	2,984	171
Totals	6,884	5,009	237
Plurality: 1,875			

134th District	John E. Stone, Jr. (R)	Frederick E. Miller, Jr. (D)	
Fairfield, part of	4,135	2,996	
Trumbull, part of	2,055	1,285	
Totals	6,190	4,281	
Plurality: 1,909			

VOTE FOR STATE REPRESENTATIVES, NOVEMBER 5, 1996
ASSEMBLY DISTRICTS

135th District	John E. Stripp (R)	Tom Baptist (D)
Easton	2,196	1,210
Newtown, part of	637	400
Redding	2,246	1,759
Weston, part of	1,879	1,086
Totals	6,958	4,455
Plurality: 2,503		

136th District	G. Kenneth Bernhard (R)	Kevin L. Hoffkins (D)
Norwalk, part of	2,094	1,938
Westport, part of	4,036	2,484
Totals	6,130	4,422
Plurality: 1,708		
Votes for Registered Write-in Candidate: 0		

137th District	Richard J. Bonenfant (R)	Alex Knopp (D)
Norwalk, part of	2,720	4,417
Plurality: 1,697		

138th District	David Cappiello (R)	David J. Sessa (D)	David Cappiello (I)
Danbury, part of	4,869	2,978	290
Plurality: 2,181			
Total votes cast for David J. Cappiello (R) plus (I) equals: 5,159			

139th District	No Nomination (R)	Kevin Ryan (D)	Kevin Ryan (ACP)
Bozrah		647	132
Franklin		571	75
Lebanon, part of		909	184
Montville, part of		3,361	750
Totals		5,488	1,141
Plurality: 6,629			
Total votes cast for Kevin Ryan (D) plus (ACP) equals: 6,629			

140th District	Jon J. Velez (R)	Donnie R. Sellers, Sr. (D)
Norwalk, part of	1,964	3,396
Plurality: 1,432		

VOTE FOR STATE REPRESENTATIVES, NOVEMBER 5, 1996
ASSEMBLY DISTRICTS

141st District	John J. Ryan (R)	No Nomination (D)
Darien	6,964	
Norwalk, part of	1,365	
Totals	8,329	
Plurality: 8,329		

142nd District	Lawrence F. Cafero, Jr. (R)	Arnold Starr (D)
Norwalk, part of	5,684	3,193
Wilton, part of	841	334
Totals	6,525	3,527
Plurality: 2,998		

143rd District	Antonietta Boucher (R)	Stuart A. Smith (D)
New Canaan, part of	3,086	1,274
Wilton, part of	4,665	2,567
Totals	7,751	6,379
Plurality: 3,910		

144th District	No Nomination (R)	John Wayne Fox (D)
Stamford, part of		5,863
Plurality: 5,863		

145th District	No Nomination (R)	Christel H. Truglia (D)
Stamford, part of		3,372
Plurality: 3,372		

146th District	No Nomination (R)	Moira K. Lyons (D)
Stamford, part of		5,321
Plurality: 5,321		

147th District	Michael C. Fedele (R)	D. Matthew Lacerenza (D)
New Canaan, part of	3,488	976
Stamford, part of	3,676	2,457
Totals:	7,164	3,433
Plurality: 3,731		

VOTE FOR STATE REPRESENTATIVES, NOVEMBER 5, 1996
ASSEMBLY DISTRICTS

148th *District*	Philip M. Candito (R)	Anne B. McDonald (D)
Stamford, part of	1,996	4,667
Plurality: 2,671		

149th *District*	Janet K. Lockton (R)	Stephanie H.. Sanchez (D)
Greenwich, part of	3,537	2,182
Stamford, part of	2,416	2,183
Totals	5,953	4,365
Plurality: 1,588		

150th *District*	Marilyn A. Hess (R)	No Nomination (D)
Greenwich, part of	6,349	
Plurality: 6,349		

151st *District*	Claudia M. Powers (R)	Gwen M. Bylinsky (D)
Greenwich, part of	7,146	2,779
Plurality: 4,367		

SPECIAL ELECTION
VOTE FOR STATE REPRESENTATIVE, FEBRUARY 25, 1997
4TH ASSEMBLY DISTRICT

4th District	Hector L. Reyes (R)	Carmen Torres (D)	Juan A. Ortiz (PC)	Evelyn C. Mantilla (PC)	John N. Geraci (PC)	Charles E. Benton (PC)
Hartford, part of	52	348	88	618	61	20

Plurality: 270

SPECIAL ELECTION
VOTE FOR STATE REPRESENTATIVE, FEBRUARY 25, 1997
140TH ASSEMBLY DISTRICT

140th District	Jon J. Velez (R)	Joseph D. Clemmons, Sr. (D)
	920	1,063

Plurality: 143

SPECIAL ELECTION
VOTE FOR STATE REPRESENTATIVE, MARCH 4, 1997
105TH ASSEMBLY DISTRICT

105th District	Leonard C. Greene (R)	Lisa Betkoski (D)	Frank F. Stuban (PC)	Ronald A. Skurat (PC)
Ansonia	54	141	34	59
Beacon Falls	636	470	39	102
Seymour	926	557	308	779
Totals	1,619	1,168	381	940

Plurality: 451

SUMMARY OF VOTE FOR
PROPOSED CONSTITUTIONAL AMENDMENT
NOVEMBER 5, 1996

Summarized by Congressional District.

1. Shall the Constitution of the State be amended to provide certain rights to victims of crimes?

CONGRESSIONAL DISTRICT	YES	NO
First	120,790	37,665
Second	112,614	32,455
Third	94,113	22,672
Fourth	101,124	25,344
Fifth	111,832	27,883
Sixth	115,750	33,863
Totals	656,223	179,882

SUMMARY OF VOTE FOR
PROPOSED CONSTITUTIONAL AMENDMENT
NOVEMBER 5, 1996

Summarized by County.

1. Shall the Constitution of the State be amended to provide certain rights to victims of crimes?

COUNTY	YES	NO
Fairfield	167,540	40,654
Hartford	182,207	55,807
Litchfield	37,140	10,931
Middlesex	33,763	9,364
New Haven	137,354	34,987
New London	50,369	15,582
Tolland	29,008	8,327
Windham	18,842	4,230
Totals	656,223	179,882

VOTE FOR PROPOSED CONSTITUTIONAL AMENDMENT
NOVEMBER 5, 1996

1. Shall the Constitution of the State be amended
to provide certain rights to victims of crimes?

	YES	NO
Andover	598	157
Ansonia	2,746	896
Ashford	905	230
Avon	3,960	1,324
Barkhamsted	736	193
Beacon Falls	1,159	329
Berlin	4,904	1,031
Bethany	1,185	280
Bethel	3,822	949
Bethlehem	810	275
Bloomfield	3,501	1,326
Bolton	1,254	375
Bozrah	589	127
Branford	5,413	1,404
Bridgeport	11,750	2,526
Bridgewater	448	133
Bristol	10,667	2,731
Brookfield	3,711	921
Brooklyn	1,194	214
Burlington	2,195	522
Canaan	231	86
Canterbury	1,084	183
Canton	2,102	683
Chaplin	358	95
Cheshire	9,339	2,529
Chester	785	255
Clinton	2,529	571
Colchester	3,050	677
Colebrook	304	93
Columbia	1,622	334
Cornwall	351	107
Coventry	2,097	580
Cromwell	2,898	725
Danbury	11,060	2,922
Darien	4,122	1,103
Deep River	816	267
Derby	1,450	303
Durham	1,529	405
Eastford	414	88
East Granby	1,053	328
East Haddam	1,570	353
East Hampton	1,953	547
East Hartford	10,441	3,421
East Haven	4,190	770
East Lyme	3,540	1,260

VOTE FOR PROPOSED CONSTITUTIONAL AMENDMENT
NOVEMBER 5, 1996

1. Shall the Constitution of the State be amended
to provide certain rights to victims of crimes?

	YES	NO
Easton	2,078	361
East Windsor	2,006	509
Ellington	3,202	972
Enfield	10,405	2,979
Essex	1,294	448
Fairfield	13,704	2,639
Farmington	5,897	2,022
Franklin	411	100
Glastonbury	9,465	3,718
Goshen	77	9
Granby	2,932	893
Greenwich	11,507	3,741
Griswold	1,812	346
Groton	7,327	3,069
Guilford	5,659	1,294
Haddam	1,955	570
Hamden	8,648	2,022
Hampton	460	119
Hartford	10,531	3,097
Hartland	634	169
Harwinton	1,108	308
Hebron	2,155	559
Kent	720	203
Killingly	3,081	548
Killingworth	1,411	346
Lebanon	1,401	366
Ledyard	3,196	922
Lisbon	671	136
Litchfield	1,517	509
Lyme	527	198
Madison	4,649	1,089
Manchester	15,069	4,544
Mansfield	3,736	1,280
Marlborough	1,335	387
Meriden	8,709	1,809
Middlebury	1,460	508
Middlefield	1,008	237
Middletown	9,712	2,903
Milford	9,632	1,852
Monroe	5,425	876
Montville	3,391	843
Morris	446	144
Naugatuck	6,452	1,678
New Britain	7,628	2,060
New Canaan	5,024	1,188

VOTE FOR PROPOSED CONSTITUTIONAL AMENDMENT
NOVEMBER 5, 1996

1. Shall the Constitution of the State be amended
to provide certain rights to victims of crimes?

	YES	NO
New Fairfield	3,451	797
New Hartford	1,334	361
New Haven	11,333	3,831
Newington	8,538	2,279
New London	3,221	1,225
New Milford	4,991	1,269
Newtown	6,062	1,383
Norfolk	326	102
North Branford	3,062	571
North Canaan	538	195
North Haven	4,150	973
North Stonington	1,129	375
Norwalk	17,442	4,723
Norwich	7,950	2,101
Old Lyme	1,675	565
Old Saybrook	2,359	708
Orange	3,567	704
Oxford	1,948	470
Plainfield	2,406	457
Plainville	4,460	1,110
Plymouth	2,112	569
Pomfret	834	243
Portland	2,314	644
Preston	933	201
Prospect	2,124	644
Putnam	1,433	326
Redding	1,964	539
Ridgefield	6,404	1,319
Rocky Hill	4,148	1,217
Roxbury	479	149
Salem	862	183
Salisbury	1,008	363
Scotland	395	104
Seymour	3,116	684
Sharon	488	170
Shelton	8,360	1,532
Sherman	817	190
Simsbury	6,713	2,248
Somers	1,786	504
Southbury	4,307	1,355
Southington	8,366	2,161
South Windsor	8,411	2,232
Sprague	637	120
Stafford	1,666	431
Stamford	16,150	5,475

VOTE FOR PROPOSED CONSTITUTIONAL AMENDMENT
NOVEMBER 5, 1996

1. Shall the Constitution of the State be amended to provide certain rights to victims of crimes?

	YES	NO
Sterling	432	105
Stonington	3,729	1,382
Stratford	10,486	2,690
Suffield	3,328	1,218
Thomaston	1,227	350
Thompson	1,253	400
Tolland	3,253	976
Torrington	6,540	1,788
Trumbull	9,324	1,542
Union	124	29
Vernon	6,517	1,822
Voluntown	401	110
Wallingford	8,318	2,016
Warren	227	83
Washington	738	241
Waterbury	12,525	4,121
Waterford	3,917	1,276
Watertown	5,845	1,957
Westbrook	1,630	385
West Hartford	15,851	6,186
West Haven	6,826	1,396
Weston	2,570	569
Westport	7,409	1,605
Wethersfield	8,341	2,782
Willington	998	308
Wilton	4,898	1,064
Winchester	2,418	649
Windham	2,780	771
Windsor	7,144	1,951
Windsor Locks	2,182	679
Wolcott	3,192	850
Woodbridge	2,195	629
Woodbury	2,121	625
Woodstock	1,813	347
Totals	656,223	179,882

SUMMARY OF ELECTION DAY REGISTRATION, TURNOUT, AND ABSENTEE BALLOT STATISTICS, NOVEMBER 5, 1996

CONGRESSIONAL DISTRICTS	*Total number of names on official check list	*Total number checked as having voted	Percentage checked as having voted	Number of absentee ballots received from town clerk	Number of absentee ballots rejected	Number of absentee ballots voted
First	308,485	234,553	76.03%	14,300	173	14,127
Second	313,915	237,025	75.51%	13,941	199	13,742
Third	320,575	232,612	72.56%	13,118	209	12,909
Fourth	300,694	224,257	74.58%	16,803	238	16,565
Fifth	314,793	235,015	74.66%	14,376	165	14,211
Sixth	322,861	247,284	76.59%	15,403	193	15,210
Totals	1,881,323	1,410,746	74.99%	87,941	1,177	86,764

*Including "Overseas" voters.

SUMMARY OF ELECTION DAY REGISTRATION, TURNOUT, AND ABSENTEE BALLOT STATISTICS, NOVEMBER 5, 1996

COUNTY	*Total number of names on official check list	*Total number checked as having voted	Percentage checked as having voted	Number of absentee ballots received from town clerk	Number of absentee ballots rejected	Number of absentee ballots voted
Fairfield	468,921	355,997	75.92%	25,960	321	25,639
Hartford	475,690	362,086	76.12%	21,570	242	21,328
Litchfield	107,956	82,491	76.41%	5,666	95	5,571
Middlesex	93,972	72,427	77.07%	4,437	68	4,369
New Haven	460,896	330,838	71.78%	18,384	284	18,100
New London	139,958	104,249	74.49%	6,513	93	6,420
Tolland	75,071	59,345	79.05%	3,109	37	3,072
Windham	58,859	43,313	73.59%	2,302	37	2,265
Totals	1,881,323	1,410,746	74.99%	87,941	1,177	86,764

*Including "Overseas" voters.

ELECTION DAY REGISTRATION, TURNOUT, AND ABSENTEE BALLOT STATISTICS, NOVEMBER 5, 1996

TOWNS	*Total number of names on official check list	*Total number checked as having voted	Percentage checked as having voted	Number of absentee ballots received from town clerk	Number of absentee ballots rejected	Number of absentee ballots voted
Andover	1,810	1,477	81.6%	54	2	52
Ansonia	10,763	7,042	65.43%	254	2	252
Ashford	2,392	1,954	81.69%	81	3	78
Avon	9,965	8,421	84.51%	803	5	798
Barkhamsted	2,106	1,718	81.58%	75	1	74
Beacon Falls	3,049	2,353	77.17%	95	1	94
Berlin	11,461	9,434	82.31%	508	7	501
Bethany	3,440	2,726	79.24%	145	1	144
Bethel	10,609	8,407	79.24%	513	10	503
Bethlehem	2,396	1,943	81.09%	108	1	107
Bloomfield	12,407	9,497	76.55%	778	15	763
Bolton	3,074	2,561	77.13%	143	4	139
Bozrah	1,510	1,227	81.26%	77	1	76
Branford	17,964	13,432	74.77%	762	12	750
Bridgeport	55,898	33,983	60.79%	2,261	26	2,235
Bridgewater	1,300	1,040	80.0%	94	0	94
Bristol	31,762	23,869	75.15%	1,262	18	1,244
Brookfield	9,762	7,481	76.63%	468	8	460
Brooklyn	3,784	2,833	74.87%	183	0	183
Burlington	5,078	3,865	76.11%	207	1	206
Canaan	772	602	77.98%	55	2	53
Canterbury	2,867	2,204	76.87%	95	4	91
Canton	5,487	4,604	83.91%	290	0	290
Chaplin	1,234	927	75.12%	37	0	37
Cheshire	16,200	13,394	82.68%	1,011	5	1,006
Chester	2,554	1,934	75.72%	145	1	144
Clinton	7,945	6,023	75.81%	352	5	347
Colchester	7,849	5,717	72.84%	338	5	333
Colebrook	950	751	79.05%	55	0	55
Columbia	3,115	2,565	82.34%	137	0	137
Cornwall	991	835	84.26%	105	1	104
Coventry	6,584	5,192	78.86%	208	2	206
Cromwell	8,008	6,304	78.72%	382	8	374
Danbury	31,763	22,857	71.96%	1,427	18	1,409
Darien	11,729	9,679	82.52%	959	11	948
Deep River	2,942	2,278	77.43%	161	4	157
Derby	6,234	4,838	77.61%	202	1	201
Durham	4,019	3,286	81.76%	196	1	195
Eastford	963	799	82.97%	37	0	37
East Granby	2,939	2,389	81.29%	133	0	133
East Haddam	4,933	3,681	74.62%	194	5	189
East Hampton	6,788	5,139	75.71%	240	0	240

ELECTION STATISTICS

TOWNS	*Total number of names on official check list	*Total number checked as having voted	Percentage checked as having voted	Number of absentee ballots received from town clerk	Number of absentee ballots rejected	Number of absentee ballots voted
East Hartford	26,288	19,230	73.15%	780	11	769
East Haven	17,534	11,125	63.45%	544	6	538
East Lyme	10,457	7,873	75.29%	578	7	571
Easton	4,609	3,824	82.97%	347	7	340
East Windsor	5,676	4,091	72.08%	225	1	224
Ellington	7,162	5,596	78.13%	287	2	285
Enfield	25,350	18,451	72.79%	767	8	759
Essex	4,391	3,514	80.03%	229	2	227
Fairfield	36,177	27,999	77.39%	2,161	30	2,131
Farmington	14,490	11,547	79.69%	846	7	839
Franklin	1,191	976	81.95%	51	0	51
Glastonbury	19,817	16,560	83.56%	1,196	8	1,188
Goshen	1,662	1,321	79.48%	100	5	95
Granby	6,578	5,187	78.85%	298	0	298
Greenwich	35,749	28,150	78.74%	2,607	24	2,583
Griswold	5,673	3,923	69.15%	148	3	145
Groton	17,831	12,962	72.69%	982	10	972
Guilford	13,709	10,795	78.74%	753	9	744
Haddam	5,080	3,899	76.73%	223	2	221
Hamden	32,293	24,510	75.9%	1,512	46	1,466
Hampton	1,042	858	82.34%	43	2	41
Hartford	49,892	28,664	57.45%	1,493	35	1,458
Hartland	1,267	983	77.58%	32	0	32
Harwinton	3,327	2,691	80.88%	150	4	146
Hebron	4,845	3,905	80.6%	207	1	206
Kent	1,917	1,558	81.27%	213	1	212
Killingly	7,868	5,667	72.03%	248	5	243
Killingworth	3,740	2,945	78.74%	172	3	169
Lebanon	3,995	3,134	78.45%	143	3	140
Ledyard	8,512	6,266	73.61%	416	3	413
Lisbon	2,435	1,826	74.99%	76	0	76
Litchfield	5,618	4,150	73.87%	295	1	294
Lyme	1,593	1,308	82.11%	98	0	98
Madison	11,775	8,999	76.42%	644	6	638
Manchester	30,962	23,948	77.35%	1,242	12	1,230
Mansfield	8,903	6,606	74.2%	457	10	447
Marlborough	3,637	2,881	79.21%	201	6	195
Meriden	30,202	21,469	71.08%	1,226	15	1,211
Middlebury	4,161	3,495	83.99%	228	6	222
Middlefield	2,717	2,261	83.22%	109	3	106
Middletown	24,680	18,329	74.27%	1,108	19	1,089
Milford	30,551	23,138	75.74%	1,050	0	1,050
Monroe	11,336	8,713	78.74%	567	5	562
Montville	8,823	6,971	79.01%	351	8	343
Morris	1,422	1,119	78.69%	73	2	71

TOWNS	*Total number of names on official check list	*Total number checked as having voted	Percentage checked as having voted	Number of absentee ballots received from town clerk	Number of absentee ballots rejected	Number of absentee ballots voted
Naugatuck	16,198	11,497	70.98%	535	15	520
New Britain	30,488	22,209	72.85%	1,073	12	1,061
New Canaan	11,648	9,624	82.62%	1,028	14	1,014
New Fairfield	8,188	6,434	78.58%	417	2	415
New Hartford	3,778	3,153	83.46%	159	2	157
New Haven	55,584	34,782	62.58%	2,053	49	2,004
Newington	18,923	14,945	78.98%	841	8	833
New London	12,439	7,825	62.91%	484	19	465
New Milford	14,537	10,436	71.79%	675	11	664
Newtown	12,834	10,692	83.31%	666	3	663
Norfolk	1,148	882	76.83%	87	1	86
North Branford	8,433	6,028	71.48%	272	7	265
North Canaan	1,817	1,355	74.57%	97	1	96
North Haven	15,334	11,833	77.17%	595	3	592
North Stonington	3,168	2,343	73.96%	126	0	126
Norwalk	42,804	31,563	73.74%	1,591	30	1,561
Norwich	18,193	13,722	75.42%	761	13	748
Old Lyme	5,156	4,135	80.2%	319	4	315
Old Saybrook	6,557	5,359	81.73%	424	9	415
Orange	9,336	7,434	79.63%	472	14	458
Oxford	5,571	4,178	75.0%	174	3	171
Plainfield	7,668	5,409	70.54%	196	5	191
Plainville	9,604	7,624	79.38%	326	4	322
Plymouth	6,220	4,633	74.49%	169	3	166
Pomfret	2,133	1,764	82.7%	124	0	124
Portland	6,032	4,529	75.08%	314	6	308
Preston	2,846	2,161	75.93%	115	2	113
Prospect	5,395	4,261	78.98%	200	1	199
Putnam	5,252	3,702	70.49%	256	2	254
Redding	5,329	4,386	82.3%	389	4	385
Ridgefield	14,986	12,015	80.17%	1,066	6	1,060
Rocky Hill	10,756	8,331	77.45%	496	2	494
Roxbury	1,366	1,114	81.55%	125	3	122
Salem	2,190	1,792	81.83%	105	2	103
Salisbury	2,752	2,157	78.38%	311	4	307
Scotland	891	735	82.49%	40	0	40
Seymour	8,534	6,631	77.7%	254	9	245
Sharon	1,895	1,398	73.77%	164	3	161
Shelton	20,689	16,551	80.0%	779	1	778
Sherman	2,037	1,651	81.05%	162	4	158
Simsbury	15,857	12,710	80.15%	1,119	19	1,100
Somers	5,155	4,024	78.06%	254	3	251
South Windsor	14,437	12,139	84.08%	693	7	686
Southbury	12,254	9,438	77.08%	844	1	843
Southington	23,998	18,088	75.37%	858	9	849

ELECTION STATISTICS

TOWNS	*Total number of names on official check list	*Total number checked as having voted	Percentage checked as having voted	Number of absentee ballots received from town clerk	Number of absentee ballots rejected	Number of absentee ballots voted
Sprague	1,787	1,394	78.01%	100	2	98
Stafford	7,013	5,432	77.46%	245	6	239
Stamford	56,900	43,655	76.72%	2,814	76	2,738
Sterling	1,580	1,076	68.1%	28	1	27
Stonington	10,954	8,389	76.58%	596	7	589
Stratford	29,492	22,612	76.67%	1,220	7	1,213
Suffield	7,351	5,728	77.92%	354	4	350
Thomaston	4,354	3,294	75.65%	143	4	139
Thompson	5,360	4,091	76.32%	190	2	188
Tolland	7,766	6,217	80.05%	316	2	314
Torrington	19,388	14,794	76.3%	1,099	24	1,075
Trumbull	22,658	17,549	77.45%	1,257	5	1,252
Union	459	388	84.53%	24	0	24
Vernon	15,936	12,738	79.93%	678	0	678
Voluntown	1,236	943	76.29%	40	1	39
Wallingford	25,926	19,008	73.32%	1,103	15	1,088
Warren	763	645	84.53%	38	0	38
Washington	2,205	1,867	84.67%	185	1	184
Waterbury	55,757	35,828	64.26%	1,735	32	1,703
Waterford	12,120	9,362	77.24%	609	3	606
Watertown	13,018	9,867	75.8%	429	3	426
Westbrook	3,586	2,946	82.15%	188	0	188
West Hartford	39,995	32,649	81.63%	2,831	19	2,812
West Haven	29,662	20,606	69.47%	951	21	930
Weston	5,892	4,884	82.89%	626	8	618
Westport	16,999	14,290	84.06%	1,619	17	1,602
Wethersfield	17,477	14,755	84.43%	860	8	852
Willington	3,249	2,644	81.38%	99	5	94
Wilton	10,833	8,998	83.06%	1,016	5	1,011
Winchester	6,678	4,632	69.36%	375	15	360
Windham	11,626	7,850	67.52%	556	10	546
Windsor	16,388	13,389	81.7%	819	13	806
Windsor Locks	7,360	5,628	76.47%	239	3	236
Wolcott	9,310	7,236	77.72%	337	1	336
Woodbridge	5,727	4,762	82.93%	433	3	430
Woodbury	5,576	4,536	81.35%	287	2	285
Woodstock	4,199	3,444	82.02%	188	3	185
Totals	1,881,323	1,410,476	74.97%	87,941	1,177	86,764

*Includes "Overseas and "Presidential Ballot" voters.

SUMMARY OF REGISTRATION AND PARTY ENROLLMENT IN CONNECTICUT BY CONGRESSIONAL DISTRICT

October 22, 1996

(Based on figures submitted to the Secretary of the State by the Registrars of Voters.)

District	Rep.	Dem.	Minor	Unaffil.	Total
1	64,412	139,156	357	101,494	305,419
2	72,323	104,767	410	134,608	312,108
3	63,529	119,564	292	138,098	321,483
4	94,964	100,130	1,472	100,604	297,170
5	86,099	96,481	681	129,311	312,572
6	89,447	108,149	299	123,266	321,161
Totals	470,774	668,247	3,511	727,381	1,869,913

SUMMARY OF REGISTRATION AND PARTY ENROLLEMNT IN CONNECTICUT BY COUNTY

October 22, 1996

(Based on figures submitted to the Secretary of the State by the Registrars of Voters.)

County	Rep.	Dem.	Minor	Unaffil.	Total
Fairfield	149,023	141,654	2,065	171,853	464,595
Hartford	106,939	204,772	531	159,889	472,131
Litchfield	33,023	29,285	96	44,593	106,997
Middlesex	23,716	30,890	89	38,796	93,491
New Haven	95,278	172,101	355	192,676	460,410
New London	32,929	44,555	194	61,281	138,959
Tolland	16,874	24,028	128	33,849	74,879
Windham	12,992	20,962	53	24,444	58,451
Totals	470,774	668,247	3,511	727,381	1,869,913

REGISTRATION AND PARTY ENROLLMENT IN CONNECTICUT
October 22, 1996

(Based on figures submitted to the Secretary of the State by the Registrars of Voters.)

Town	Rep.	Dem.	Minor	Unaffil.	Total
Andover	512	633	1	658	1,804
Ansonia	1,659	4,091	21	3,937	9,708
Ashford	521	896	0	940	2,357
Avon	3,943	2,437	12	3,528	9,920
Barkhamsted	690	487	0	920	2,097
Beacon Falls	789	991	0	1,267	3,047
Berlin	3,118	5,204	7	3,138	11,467
Bethany	1,182	746	0	1,502	3,430
Bethel	3,131	2,400	80	4,985	10,596
Bethlehem	834	597	5	976	2,412
Bloomfield	2,114	6,415	17	3,664	12,210
Bolton	1,040	885	3	1,131	3,059
Bozrah	260	690	0	560	1,510
Branford	3,173	5,101	58	9,581	17,913
Bridgeport	7,774	30,647	160	16,802	55,353
Bridgewater	456	310	1	523	1,290
Bristol	6,047	13,670	0	11,863	31,580
Brookfield	3,960	2,079	6	3,668	9,713
Brooklyn	767	1,137	0	1,860	3,764
Burlington	1,445	1,483	0	1,993	4,921
Canaan	272	205	0	290	767
Canterbury	965	684	0	1,210	2,859
Canton	1,840	1,616	8	1,978	5,442
Chaplin	363	306	1	541	1,211
Cheshire	4,631	3,517	6	7,994	16,148
Chester	694	758	0	1,069	2,521
Clinton	2,510	2,166	8	3,227	7,911
Colchester	1,778	2,500	7	3,562	7,847
Colebrook	251	297	0	393	941
Columbia	774	1,130	1	1,202	3,107
Cornwall	312	307	6	364	989
Coventry	1,500	2,062	4	3,010	6,576
Cromwell	1,908	2,639	6	3,459	8,012
Danbury	7,330	9,723	240	14,384	31,677
Darien	7,220	1,854	4	2,628	11,706
Deep River	746	849	3	1,344	2,942
Derby	981	3,030	1	2,198	6,210
Durham	1,162	873	7	1,967	4,009
East Granby	1,005	750	3	1,194	2,952
East Haddam	1,149	1,535	6	2,240	4,930
East Hampton	1,554	2,100	6	2,995	6,655
East Hartford	3,893	14,033	15	8,222	26,163
East Haven	2,817	8,000	2	6,633	17,452
Eastford	414	255	2	293	964

REGISTRATION AND PARTY ENROLLMENT IN CONNECTICUT
October 22, 1996

Town	Rep.	Dem.	Minor	Unaffil.	Total
East Lyme	2,729	2,631	25	4,465	9,850
Easton	1,839	868	2	1,878	4,587
East Windsor	1,215	1,912	1	2,456	5,584
Ellington	1,663	1,740	6	3,742	7,151
Enfield	4,960	10,302	24	10,011	25,297
Essex	1,572	1,005	4	1,803	4,384
Fairfield	12,209	9,179	289	14,461	36,138
Farmington	4,576	4,232	27	5,656	14,491
Franklin	365	373	0	450	1,188
Glastonbury	6,412	6,092	15	7,243	19,762
Goshen	729	318	1	605	1,653
Granby	2,336	1,576	13	2,640	6,565
Greenwich	16,621	7,033	37	12,058	35,749
Griswold	1,609	2,592	0	1,982	6,183
Groton	4,362	4,818	23	8,588	17,791
Guilford	3,949	3,788	5	5,942	13,684
Haddam	1,269	1,499	6	2,299	5,073
Hamden	6,509	11,062	57	14,439	32,067
Hampton	337	338	0	377	1,052
Hartford	3,363	34,435	51	9,956	47,805
Hartland	587	303	2	369	1,261
Harwinton	1,116	847	5	1,369	3,337
Hebron	1,234	1,336	1	2,270	4,841
Kent	702	517	0	691	1,910
Killingly	1,493	2,514	4	3,853	7,864
Killingworth	1,020	774	7	1,933	3,734
Lebanon	1,151	1,073	9	1,753	3,986
Ledyard	2,601	1,937	11	3,992	8,541
Lisbon	501	926	2	1,002	2,431
Litchfield	2,027	1,452	19	2,097	5,595
Lyme	669	287	4	608	1,568
Madison	4,422	2,352	9	4,969	11,752
Manchester	7,765	11,748	17	11,317	30,847
Mansfield	1,598	3,500	8	3,800	8,906
Marlborough	943	1,017	0	1,681	3,641
Meriden	5,049	9,640	10	15,492	30,191
Middlebury	1,763	884	0	1,475	4,122
Middlefield	570	909	11	1,224	2,714
Middletown	4,329	11,376	14	8,852	24,571
Milford	7,184	8,071	6	14,942	30,203
Monroe	3,316	2,036	52	5,854	11,258
Montville	1,619	2,803	8	4,277	8,707
Morris	495	383	1	544	1,423
Naugatuck	2,915	5,719	10	7,542	16,186
New Britain	5,383	18,284	15	6,749	30,431
New Canaan	6,675	1,971	6	2,927	11,579
New Fairfield	3,180	1,535	65	3,382	8,162

REGISTRATION AND PARTY ENROLLMENT IN CONNECTICUT
October 22, 1996

Town	Rep.	Dem.	Minor	Unaffil.	Total
New Hartford	1,099	991	10	1,682	3,782
New Haven	3,617	38,750	64	14,869	57,300
Newington	4,211	8,263	15	6,427	18,916
New London	1,932	5,609	29	4,878	12,448
New Milford	4,647	2,927	12	6,171	13,757
Newtown	4,758	3,034	124	4,918	12,834
Norfolk	261	326	0	558	1,145
North Branford	1,784	1,751	0	4,807	8,342
North Canaan	541	365	3	902	1,811
North Haven	4,912	3,023	11	7,453	15,399
North Stonington ...	928	785	1	1,453	3,167
Norwalk	10,031	12,821	894	16,306	40,052
Norwich	3,099	7,215	25	7,482	17,821
Old Lyme	1,811	1,158	9	2,165	5,143
Old Saybrook	2,662	1,490	4	2,358	6,514
Orange	2,817	1,804	3	4,666	9,290
Oxford	1,715	992	4	3,026	5,737
Plainfield	1,286	2,922	4	3,292	7,504
Plainville	2,205	3,898	9	3,472	9,584
Plymouth	1,333	1,686	2	3,180	6,201
Pomfret	736	579	4	806	2,125
Portland	1,296	2,087	4	2,576	5,963
Preston	888	649	0	1,306	2,843
Prospect	1,808	1,178	0	2,421	5,407
Putnam	1,038	2,116	0	2,055	5,209
Redding	2,275	1,169	1	1,879	5,324
Ridgefield	6,984	3,570	59	4,348	14,961
Rocky Hill	2,394	4,382	9	3,844	10,629
Roxbury	475	360	0	541	1,376
Salem	567	656	7	953	2,183
Salisbury	956	699	10	1,049	2,714
Scotland	210	294	0	380	884
Seymour	2,059	1,948	0	4,475	8,482
Sharon	768	415	3	761	1,947
Shelton	5,764	4,174	0	10,096	20,034
Sherman	891	411	0	729	2,031
Simsbury	6,558	4,098	34	5,087	15,777
Somers	1,425	1,340	0	2,389	5,154
Southbury	4,928	2,197	10	5,095	12,230
Southington	5,427	7,747	34	10,757	23,965
South Windsor	3,676	5,248	9	5,517	14,450
Sprague	342	816	2	626	1,786
Stafford	974	3,581	2	2,443	7,000
Stamford	17,945	24,683	21	14,266	56,915
Sterling	410	358	0	808	1,576
Stonington	2,702	3,102	9	5,070	10,883
Stratford	5,972	8,436	0	15,279	29,687

REGISTRATION AND PARTY ENROLLMENT IN CONNECTICUT
October 22, 1996

Town	Rep.	Dem.	Minor	Unaffil.	Total
Suffield	2,348	1,951	4	3,023	7,326
Thomaston	1,167	1,238	0	1,933	4,338
Thompson	1,069	2,294	5	1,988	5,356
Tolland	1,829	2,049	7	3,844	7,729
Torrington	5,129	7,283	0	6,965	19,377
Trumbull	6,569	5,250	12	10,824	22,655
Union	189	118	0	149	456
Vernon	3,390	4,755	78	7,643	15,866
Voluntown	265	424	0	538	1,227
Wallingford	5,086	7,401	18	13,321	25,826
Warren	315	166	1	279	761
Washington	904	481	2	804	2,191
Waterbury	10,577	27,802	24	17,223	55,626
Waterford	2,751	3,511	23	5,571	11,856
Watertown	3,503	3,405	5	6,042	12,955
Westbrook	1,275	830	3	1,450	3,558
West Hartford	9,977	17,167	147	12,988	40,279
West Haven	4,718	14,133	16	10,795	29,662
Weston	2,469	1,542	4	1,843	5,858
Westport	6,977	4,907	4	5,065	16,953
Wethersfield	4,353	7,076	15	6,006	17,450
Willington	746	899	17	1,568	3,230
Wilton	5,163	2,332	5	3,273	10,773
Winchester	1,493	1,950	10	3,198	6,651
Windham	1,902	5,132	17	4,506	11,557
Windsor	3,477	6,558	18	6,013	16,066
Windsor Locks	1,368	2,875	10	3,097	7,350
Wolcott	2,587	2,657	10	4,048	9,302
Woodbridge	1,647	1,473	10	2,564	5,694
Woodbury	2,548	1,273	0	1,756	5,577
Woodstock	1,481	1,137	16	1,535	4,169
Totals	470,774	668,247	3,511	727,381	1,869,913

SECTION IX

UNITED STATES GOVERNMENT

U.S. Government—Executive and Judiciary

Members of 105th Congress, 1st Session

U.S. Courts Serving Connecticut

U.S. Departments and Agencies Serving Connecticut

U.S. and Territories

THE EXECUTIVE
(The White House Office, 1600 Pennsylvania Avenue,
Washington, D.C. 20500)

President, William J. Clinton of Arkansas

(The President receives a salary of $200,000 a year and an expense allowance not exceeding $50,000, nontaxable, to assist in defraying expenses relating to the discharge of his official duties, and not exceeding $100,000, nontaxable, a year for travel expenses; term of office, four years, January 20, 1993 to January 20, 1997.)

Vice President, Albert A. Gore of Tennessee

(The Vice President receives a salary of $171,500 a year and $10,000 for taxable expenses.)

The Cabinet
Salary of each member, $148,400)

Secretary of State, Madeleine Albright, Virginia.
Secretary of the Treasury, Robert E. Rubin, New York.
Secretary of Defense, William E. Cohen, Maine.
Attorney General, Janet Reno, Florida.
Secretary of the Interior, Bruce Babbit, Arizona.
Secretary of Agriculture, Dan Glickman, Kansas.
Secretary of Commerce, William A. Daley, Illinois.
Secretary of Labor, Alexis M. Herman, Alabama.
Secretary of Health and Human Services, Donna E. Shalala, Wisconsin.
Secretary of Housing and Urban Development, Andrew Cuomo, New York.
Secretary of Transportation, Rodney Slater, Arkansas.
Secretary of Energy, Frederico Peña, Colorado.
Secretary of Education, Richard W. Riley, South Carolina.
Secretary of Veterans Affairs, Jesse Brown, Illinois.

The Judiciary
The Supreme Court of the United States
Washington, D.C. 20543

Chief Justice, William H. Rehnquist, of Virginia, 1986 — Salary, $171,500
Associate Justices, with year of appointment — Salary of each, $164,100

John Paul Stevens, of Illinois	1975	David H. Souter, of New Hampshire	1990
Sandra Day O'Connor, of Arizona	1981	Clarence Thomas of Georgia	1991
Antonin Scalia, of Virginia	1986	Ruth Bader Ginsberg, of New York	1993
Anthony M. Kennedy, of California	1988	Stephen G. Breyer, of Massachusetts	1994

Clerk, William K. Suter
Marshal, Dale Bosley

Reporter of Decisions, Frank D. Wagmer
Librarian, Shelley L. Dowling
Public Information Officer, Toni House

THE ONE-HUNDRED FIFTH CONGRESS

1st SESSION, 1997

The Congress convenes annually on January 3, unless it has, by law, fixed a different date.

The Senate

The term of a Senator is six years; annual salary, $133,600.00.

The dates opposite the names of Senators indicate when they entered the Senate and when their present terms expire.
Democrats, 45; Republicans, 55;
total, 100.

President Pro Tempore, Strom Thurmond, South Carolina
Majority Leader, Trent Lott, Mississippi
Minority Leader, Thomas Daschle, South Dakota
Secretary of the Senate, Gary Sisco, Tennessee

Alabama		*Hawaii*	
Jeff Sessions, R	1997-2003	Daniel K. Inouye, D	1963-1999
Richard C. Shelby, R	1987-1999	Daniel K. Akaka, D	1990-2001
Alaska		*Idaho*	
Ted Stevens, R	1968-1997	Larry E. Craig, R	1991-1997
Frank H. Murkowski, R	1981-1999	Dirk Kempthorne, R	1993-1999
Arizona		*Illinois*	
Jon Kyl, R	1995-2001	Carol Moseley-Braun, D	1993-1999
John S. McCain, R	1987-1999	Richard J. Durbin, D	1997-2003
Arkansas		*Indiana*	
Dale Bumpers, D	1975-1999	Richard G. Lugar, R	1977-2001
Tim Hutchison, R	1997-2003	Dan Coats, R	1989-1999
California		*Iowa*	
Barbara Boxer, D	1993-1999	Charles E. Grassley, R	1981-1999
Dianne Feinstein, D	1992-2001	Tom Harkin, D	1985-1997
Colorado		*Kansas*	
Wayne Allard, R	1997-2003	Sam Brownback, R	1997-2003
Ben N. Campbell, R	1993-1999	Pat Roberts, R	1997-2003
Connecticut		*Kentucky*	
Christopher J. Dodd, D	1981-1999	Wendell H. Ford, D	1974-1999
Joseph I. Lieberman, D	1989-2001	Mitch McConnell, R	1985-1997
Delaware		*Louisiana*	
William V. Roth, Jr., R	1971-2001	Mary L. Landrieu, D	1997-2003
Joseph R. Biden, Jr., D	1973-1997	John B. Breaux, D	1987-1999
Florida		*Maine*	
Bob Graham, D	1987-1999	Susan Collins, R	1997-2003
Connie Mack, R	1989-2001	Olympia Snowe, R	1995-2001
Georgia		*Maryland*	
Max Cleland, D	1997-2003	Paul S. Sarbanes, D	1977-2001
Paul Coverdell, R	1993-1999	Barbara A. Mikulski, D	1987-1999

Massachusetts
Edward M. Kennedy, D	1962-2001
John F. Kerry, D	1985-1997

Michigan
Spencer Abraham, R	1995-2001
Carl M. Levin, D	1979-1997

Minnesota
Rod Grams, R	1995-2001
Paul D. Wellstone, D	1991-1997

Mississippi
Thad Cochran, R	1978-1997
Trent Lott, R	1989-2001

Missouri
John Ashcroft, R	1995-2001
Christopher S. Bond, R	1987-1999

Montana
Max Baucus, D	1978-1997
Conrad R. Burns, R	1989-2001

Nebraska
Chuck Hagel, R	1997-2003
J. Robert Kerrey, D	1989-2001

Nevada
Harry Reid, D	1987-1999
Richard H. Bryan, D	1989-2001

New Hampshire
Robert C. Smith, R	1990-1997
Judd Gregg, R	1993-1999

New Jersey
Robert G. Torricelli, D	1997-2003
Frank R. Lautenberg, D	1982-2001

New Mexico
Pete V. Domenici, R	1973-1997
Jeff Bingaman, D	1983-2001

New York
Daniel P. Moynihan, D	1977-2001
Alfonse M. D'Amato, R	1981-1999

North Carolina
Jesse Helms, R	1973-1997
Lauch Faircloth, R	1993-1999

North Dakota
Byron L. Dorgan, D	1992-1999
Kent Conrad, D	1987-2001

Ohio
John Glenn, D	1974-1999
Mike DeWine, R	1995-2001

Oklahoma
John Ashcroft, R	1995-2001
Don Nickles, R	1981-1999

Oregon
Gordon Smith, R	1997-2003
Ron Wyden, D	1996-1999

Pennsylvania
Rick Santorum, R	1995-2001
Arlen Specter, R	1981-1999

Rhode Island
Jack Reed, D	1997-2003
John H. Chafee, R	1976-2001

South Carolina
Strom Thurmond, R	1956-1997
Ernest F. Hollings, D	1966-1999

South Dakota
Tim Johnson, D	1997-2003
Thomas A. Daschle, D	1987-1999

Tennessee
Fred Thompson, R	1995-1999
Bill Frist, R	1995-2001

Texas
Kay B. Hutchinson, R	1993-2001
Phil Gramm, R	1985-1997

Utah
Robert F. Bennett, R	1993-1999
Orrin G. Hatch, R	1977-2001

Vermont
Patrick J. Leahy, D	1975-1999
James M. Jeffords, R	1989-2001

Virginia
John W. Warner, R	1979-1997
Charles S. Robb, D	1989-2001

Washington
Patty Murray, D	1993-1999
Slade Gorton, R	1989-2001

West Virginia
Robert C. Byrd, D	1959-2001
John D. Rockefeller IV, D	1985-1997

Wisconsin
Russell Feingold, D	1993-1999
Herb Kohl, D	1989-2001

Wyoming
Craig Thomas, R	1977-2001
Mike Enzi, R	1997-2003

THE ONE-HUNDRED FIFTH CONGRESS

1ST SESSION, 1997

The House of Representatives

The term of a Representative is two years; annual salary, $133,600.00.

The Speaker, Newt Gingrich, Georgia
Majority Leader, Richard K. Armey, Texas
Minority Leader, Richard A. Gephardt, Missouri
Clerk of the House of Representatives, Robin H. Carle, Virginia

Democrats, 205; Republicans, 227; Independents, 1; vacancies 2, 28th Texas; 3rd New Mexico.

ALABAMA. 1. Sonny Callahan, R; 2. Terry Everett, R; 3. Bob Riley, R; 4. Robert B. Aderholt, R; 5. Robert E. Cramer, Jr., D; 6. Spencer T. Bachus, R; 7. Earl F. Hilliard, D.

ALASKA. At large, Don Young, R.

ARIZONA. 1. Matt Salmon, R; 2. Ed Pastor, D; 3. Bob Stump, R; 4. John B. Shadegg, R; 5. Jim Kolbe, R; 6. J. D. Hayworth, R.

ARKANSAS. 1. Marion Berry, D; 2. Victor F. Snyder, D; 3. Asa Hutchinson, R; 4. Jay Dickey, R.

CALIFORNIA. 1. Frank Riggs, R; 2. Wally Herger, R; 3. Vic Fazio, D; 4. John T. Doolittle, R; 5. Robert T. Matsui, D; 6. Lynn C. Woolsey, D; 7. George Miller, D; 8. Nancy Pelosi, D; 9. Ronald V. Dellums, D; 10. Ellen Tauscher, D; 11. Richard W. Pombo, R; 12. Tom Lantos, D; 13. Fortney H. Stark, D; 14. Anna G. Eshoo, D; 15. Tom Campbell, R; 16. Zoe Lofgren, D; 17. Sam Farr, D; 18. Gary A. Condit, D; 19. George P. Radanovich, R; 20. Calvin M. Dooley, D; 21. William M. Thomas, R; 22. Walter H. Capps, D; 23. Elton Gallegly, R; 24. Brad Sherman, D; 25. Howard P. McKeon, R; 26. Howard L. Berman, D; 27. James E. Rogan, R; 28. David T. Dreier, R; 29. Henry A. Waxman, D; 30. Xavier Becerra, D; 31. Matthew G. Martinez, D; 32. Julian C. Dixon, D; 33. Lucille Roybal-Allard, D; 34. Esteban E. Torres, D; 35. Maxine Waters, D; 36. Jane Harman, D; 37. Juanita Millender-McDonald, D; 38. Stephen Horn, R; 39. Edward R. Royce, R; 40. Jerry Lewis, R; 41. Jay C. Kim, R; 42. George E. Brown, Jr., D; 43. Kenneth S. Calvert, R; 44. Sonny Bono, R; 45. Dana Rohrabacher, R; 46. Loretta Sanchez, D; 47. Christopher Cox, R; 48. Ron Packard, R; 49. Brian P. Bilbray, R; 50. Bob Filner, D; 51. Randy D. Cunningham, R; 52. Duncan Hunter, R.

COLORADO. 1. Diana L. DeGette, D; 2. David E. Skaggs, D; 3. Scott McInnis, R; 4. Robert Schaffer, R; 5. Joel Hefley, R; 6. Dan Schaefer, R.

CONNECTICUT. 1. Barbara B. Kennelly, D; 2. Sam Gejdenson, D; 3. Rosa L. DeLauro, D; 4. Christopher Shays, R; 5. James H. Maloney, D; 6. Nancy L. Johnson, R.

DELAWARE. At large, Michael N. Castle, R.

FLORIDA. 1. Joe Scarborough, R; 2. F. Allen Boyd, Jr., D; 3. Corrine Brown, D; 4. Tillie K. Fowler, R; 5. Karen L. Thurman, D; 6. Clifford B. Stearns, R; 7. John L. Mica, R; 8. Bill McCollum, R; 9. Michael Bilirakis, R; 10. C. W. Bill Young, R; 11. Jim Davis, D; 12. Charles T. Canady, R; 13. Dan Miller, R; 14. Porter J. Goss, R; 15. Dave Weldon, R; 16. Mark A. Foley, R; 17. Carrie P. Meek, D; 18. Ileana Ros-Lehtinen, R; 19. Robert I. Wexler, D; 20. Peter Deutsch, D; 21. Lincoln Diaz-Balart, R; 22. E. Clay Shaw, Jr., R; 23. Alcee L. Hastings, D.

GEORGIA. 1. Jack Kingston, R; 2. Sanford D. Bishop, Jr., D; 3. Michael Collins, R; 4. Cynthia Ann McKinney, D; 5. John Lewis, D; 6. Newt Gingrich, R; 7. Bob Barr, R; 8. Saxby Chambliss, R; 9. Nathan Deal, R; 10. Charles W. Norwood, Jr., R; 11. John Linder, R.

HAWAII. 1. Neil Abercrombie, D; 2. Patsy Takemoto Mink, D.

IDAHO. 1. Helen Chenoweth, R; 2. Michael D. Crapo, R.

ILLINOIS. 1. Bobby L. Rush, D; 2. Jesse Jackson, Jr., D; 3. William O. Lipinski, D; 4. Luis V. Gutierrez, D; 5. Rod R. Blagojevich, D; 6. Henry J. Hyde, R; 7. Danny Davis, D; 8. Philip M. Crane, R; 9. Sidney R. Yates, D; 10. John E. Porter, R; 11. Jerry C. Weller, R; 12. Jerry F. Costello, D; 13. Harris W. Fawell, R; 14. J. Dennis Hastert, R; 15. Thomas W. Ewing, R; 16. Donald A. Manzullo, R; 17. Lane Evans, D; 18. Ray LaHood, R; 19. Glenn Poshard, D; 20. John M. Shimkus, R.

INDIANA. 1. Peter J. Visclosky, D; 2. David M. McIntosh, R; 3. Tim Roemer, D; 4. Mark E. Souder, R; 5. Stephen E. Buyer, R; 6. Dan Burton, R; 7. Edward A. Pease, R; 8. John N. Hostettler, R; 9. Lee H. Hamilton, D; 10. Julia M. Carson, D.*

IOWA. 1. James A. Leach, R; 2. Jim Nussle, R; 3. Leonard Boswell, D; 4. Greg Ganske, R; 5. Tom Latham, R.

KANSAS. 1. Jerry Moran, R; 2. Jim Ryun, R; 3. Vincent K. Snowbarger, R; 4. Todd Tiahrt, R.

KENTUCKY. 1. Ed Whitfield, R; 2. Ron Lewis, R; 3. Anne M. Northup, R; 4. Jim Bunning, R; 5. Harold Rogers, R;* 6. Scotty Baesler, D.

LOUISIANA. 1. Bob Livingston, R; 2. William J. Jefferson, D; 3. W. J. Tauzin, R; 4. Jim McCrery, R; 5. John C. Cooksey, R; 6. Richard H. Baker, R; 7. Chris John, D.

MAINE. 1. Thomas H. Allen, D; 2. John E. Baldacci, D.

MARYLAND. 1. Wayne T. Gilchrest, R; 2. Robert L. Ehrlich, Jr., R; 3. Benjamin L. Cardin, D; 4. Albert R. Wynn, D; 5. Steny H. Hoyer, D; 6. Roscoe G. Bartlett, R;* 7. Elijah Cummings, D; 8. Constance A. Morella, R.

MASSACHUSETTS. 1. John W. Olver, D; 2. Richard E. Neal, D; 3. James P. McGovern, D; 4. Barney Frank, D; 5. Martin T. Meehan, D; 6. John F. Tierney, D; 7. Edward J. Markey, D; 8. Joseph P. Kennedy II, D; 9. John J. Moakley, D; 10. William Delahunt, D.

MICHIGAN. 1. Bart Stupak, D; 2. Peter Hoekstra, R; 3. Vernon J. Ehlers, R; 4. Dave Camp, R; 5. James A. Barcia, D; 6. Frederick S. Upton, R; 7. Nick Smith, R; 8. Debbie Stabenow, D; 9. Dale E. Kildee, D; 10. David E. Bonior, D; 11. Joe Knollenberg, R; 12. Sander M. Levin, D; 13. Lynn N. Rivers, D; 14. John Conyers, Jr., D; 15. Carolyn C. Kilpatrick, D; 16. John D. Dingell, D.

MINNESOTA. 1. Gil Gutknecht, R; 2. David Minge, D; 3. Jim Ramstad, R; 4. Bruce F. Vento, D; 5. Martin O. Sabo, D; 6. William P. Luther, D; 7. Collin C. Peterson, D; 8. James L. Oberstar, D.

MISSISSIPPI. 1. Roger F. Wicker, R; 2. Bennie G. Thompson, D; 3. Charles Pickering, Jr., R; 4. Mike Parker, R; 5. Gene Taylor, D.

MISSOURI. 1. William L. Clay, Sr., D; 2. James M. Talent, R; 3. Richard A. Gephardt, D; 4. Ike Skelton, D; 5. Karen McCarthy, D; 6. Patricia Danner, D; 7. Roy Blunt, R; 8. Jo Ann Emerson, R; 9. Kenny C. Hulshof, R.

MONTANA. At large, Rick A. Hill, R.

NEBRASKA. 1. Douglas K. Bereuter, R; 2. Jon Christensen, R; 3. Bill Barrett, R.

NEVADA. 1. John E. Ensign, R; 2. James A. Gibbons, R.

NEW HAMPSHIRE. 1. John E. Sununu, Jr., R; 2. Charles F. Bass, R.

NEW JERSEY. 1. Robert E. Andrews, D; 2. Frank A. LoBiondo R; 3. Jim Saxton, R; 4. Christopher H. Smith, R; 5. Marge Roukema, R; 6. Frank Pallone, Jr., D; 7. Bob Franks, R; 8. William J. Pascrell, D; 9. Steven R. Rothman, D; 10. Donald M. Payne, D; 11. Rodney P. Frelinghuysen, R; 12. Michael Pappas, R; 13. Robert Menendez, D.

NEW MEXICO. 1. Steven H. Schiff, R; 2. Joe Skeen, R; 3. Bill Richardson, D.

NEW YORK. 1. Michael P. Forbes, R; 2. Rick Lazio, R; 3. Peter T. King, R; 4. Carolyn McCarthy, D; 5. Gary L. Ackerman, D; 6. Floyd H. Flake, D; 7. Thomas J. Manton, D; 8. Jerrold Nadler, D; 9. Charles E. Schumer, D; 10. Edolphus Towns, D; 11. Major R. Owens, D; 12. Nydia M. Velazquez, D; 13. Susan Molinari, R; 14. Carolyn B. Maloney, D; 15. Charles B. Rangel, D; 16. Jose E. Serrano, D; 17. Eliot L. Engel, D; 18. Nita M. Lowey, D; 19. Sue W. Kelly, R; 20. Benjamin A. Gilman, R; 21. Michael R. McNulty, D; 22. Gerald B. H. Solomon, R; 23. Sherwood L. Boehlert, R; 24. John M. McHugh, R; 25. James T. Walsh, R; 26. Maurice D. Hinchey, D; 27. Bill Paxon, R; 28. Louise M. Slaughter, D; 29. John J. LaFalce, D; 30. Jack Quinn, R; 31. Amory Houghton, R.

NORTH CAROLINA. 1. Eva M. Clayton, D; 2. Bob Etheridge, D; 3. Walter B. Jones, Jr., R; 4. David E. Price, D; 5. Richard M. Burr, R; 6. Howard Coble, R; 7. Mike McIntyre, D; 8. W. G. Hefner, D; 9. Sue Myrick, R; 10. Cass Ballenger, R; 11. Charles H. Taylor, R; 12. Melvin L. Watt, D.

NORTH DAKOTA. At large, Earl Pomeroy, D.

OHIO. 1. Steve Chabot, R; 2. Rob Portman, R; 3. Tony P. Hall, D; 4. Michael G. Oxley, R; 5. Paul E. Gillmor, R; 6. Ted Strickland, D; 7. David L. Hobson, R; 8. John A. Boehner, R; 9. Marcy Kaptur, D; 10. Dennis J. Kucinich, D; 11. Louis Stokes, D; 12. John R. Kasich, R; 13. Sherrod Brown, D; 14. Thomas C. Sawyer, D; 15. Deborah Pryce, R; 16. Ralph Regula, R; 17. James A. Traficant, Jr., D; 18. Robert W. Ney, R; 19. Steven C. LaTourette, R.

OKLAHOMA. 1. Steve Largent, R; 2. Tom A. Coburn, R; 3. Wes W. Watkins, R; 4. J. C. Watts, Jr., R; 5. Ernest J. Istook, Jr., R; 6. Frank D. Lucas, R.

OREGON. 1. Elizabeth Furse, D; 2.Robert F. Smith, R; 3. Earl Blumenauer, D; 4. Peter A. DeFazio, D; 5. Darlene Hooley, D.

PENNSYLVANIA. 1. Thomas M. Foglietta, D; 2. Chaka Fattah, D; 3. Robert A. Borski, D; 4. Ron Klink, D; 5. John E. Peterson, R; 6. Tim Holden, D; 7. Curt Weldon, R; 8. James C. Greenwood, R; 9. Bud Shuster, R; 10. Joseph M. McDade, R; 11. Paul E. Kanjorski, D; 12. John P. Murtha, D; 13.Jon D. Fox, R; 14. William J. Coyne, D; 15. Paul McHale, D; 16. Joseph R. Pitts, R; 17. George W. Gekas, R; 18. Michael F. Doyle, D; 19. William F. Goodling, R; 20. Frank Mascara, D; 21. Philip English, R.

RHODE ISLAND. 1. Patrick J. Kennedy, D; 2. Robert A. Weygand, D.

SOUTH CAROLINA. 1. Marshall Sanford, R; 2. Floyd Spence, R; 3. Lindsey O. Graham, R; 4. Bob Inglis, R; 5. John M. Spratt, Jr., D; 6. James E. Clyburn, D.

SOUTH DAKOTA. At large, John R. Thune, R.

TENNESSEE. 1. William L. Jenkins, R; 2. John J. Duncan, Jr., R; 3. Zach Wamp, R; 4. W. Van Hilleary, R; 5. Bob Clement, D; 6. Bart Gordon, D; 7. Ed Bryant, R; 8. John S. Tanner, D; 9. Harold E. Ford, Jr., D.

TEXAS. 1. Max A. Sandlin, D; 2. Jim Turner, D; 3. Sam Johnson, R; 4. Ralph M. Hall, D; 5. Pete Sessions, R; 6. Joe Barton, R; 7. Bill Archer, R; 8. Kevin P. Brady, R; 9. Nicholas V. Lampson, D; 10. Lloyd Doggett, D; 11. Chet Edwards, D; 12. Kay Granger, R; 13. William M. Thornberry, R; 14. Ron E. Paul, R; 15. Reuben E. Hinojosa, D; 16. Sylvestre Reyes, D; 17. Charles W. Stenholm, D; 18. Sheila Jackson-Lee, D; 19. Larry Combest, R; 20. Henry B. Gonzalez, D; 21. Lamar S. Smith, R; 22. Tom D. DeLay, R; 23. Henry Bonilla, R; 24. Martin Frost, D; 25. Ken Bentsen, Jr., D; 26. Richard K. Armey, R; 27. Solomon P. Ortiz, D; 28. Frank Tejeda, D; 29. Gene Green, D; 30. Eddie Bernice Johnson, D.

UTAH. 1. James V. Hansen, R; 2. Merrill Cook, R; 3. Christopher Cannon, R.

VERMONT. At large, Bernard Sanders, I.

VIRGINIA. 1. Herbert H. Bateman, R; 2. Owen B. Pickett, D; 3. Robert C. Scott, D; 4. Norman Sisisky, D; 5. Virgil H. Goode, D; 6. Bob W. Goodlatte, R; 7. Thomas J. Bliley, Jr., R; 8. James P. Moran, Jr., D; 9. Frederick Boucher, D; 10. Frank R. Wolf, R; 11. Thomas M. Davis III, R.

WASHINGTON. 1. Richard White, R; 2. Jack Metcalf, R; 3. Linda Smith, R; 4. Richard Hastings, R; 5. George R. Nethercutt, Jr., R; 6. Norman D. Dicks, D; 7. Jim McDermott, D; 8. Jennifer B. Dunn, R; 9. Adam Smith, D.

WEST VIRGINIA. 1. Alan B. Mollohan, D; 2. Robert E. Wise, Jr., D; 3. Nick J. Rahall II, D.

WISCONSIN. 1. Mark W. Neumann, R; 2. Scott L. Klug, R; 3. Ronald J. Kind, D; 4. Gerald D. Kleczka, D; 5. Thomas M. Barrett, D; 6. Thomas E. Petri, R; 7. David R. Obey, D; 8. Jay W. Johnson, D; 9. F. James Sensenbrenner, Jr., R.

WYOMING. At large, Barbara Cubin, R.

PUERTO RICO. Resident Commissioner, Carlos A. Romero-Barcelo, D.

AMERICAN SAMOA. Delegate, Eni F. H. Faleomavaega, D.

DISTRICT OF COLUMBIA. Delegate, Eleanor H. Norton, D.

GUAM. Delegate, Robert A. Underwood, D.

VIRGIN ISLANDS. Delegate, Donna Green, D.

U.S. COURTS SERVING CONNECTICUT
(As of April 1, 1997)

U.S. COURT OF APPEALS. *Associate Justice of the Supreme Court for Second Circuit,* Ruth Bader Ginsburg.

Chief Judge, Ralph K. Winter, Hartford, CT; *Secys.,* Aneita Delgado, Jeanne Ostapkevich, CT.

Judges: Amalya L. Kearse, NY; *Secy.,* Anna Lombardi. Ralph K. Winter, New Haven, CT; *Secys.,* Maggie DebiellaGerri A. Malloy. vacancy, Albany, NY; *Secys.,* Shirley Hicks, Mary Ann Tangorre. vacancy, Uniondale, NY; *Secys.,* Marie Armato, Dolores Joy. vacancy, Milford, CT; *Secys.,* Pamela Monahan, Barbara L. Sbalbi. John M. Walker, Jr., NY; *Secy.,* Kathryn Bucich. Joseph M. McLaughlin, NY; *Secys.,* Betty Rapoli, Donna Raschella. Dennis G. Jacobs, NY; *Secy.* Patricia Chin-Allen. Pierre N. Leval, NY; *Secy.,* Phyllis Bath. Guido Calabresi, New Haven, CT; *Secys.,* Marjorie Greenblatt, Susan Luccibelli. Jose A. Cabranes, New Haven, CT; Secys., Janet Hansen, Lillian M. Olejarczyk. Fred I. Parker, Burlington, VT; *Secy.,* Brandy LaGrange.

Senior Judges: J. Edward Lumbard, NY; *Secy.,* Jean L. Morin. Wilfred Feinberg, New York, NY; *Secys.,* Lois K. Levine, Frances D. Wasserman. James L. Oakes, VT; *Secy.,* Fran Rooney. Ellsworth A. VanGraafeiland, Rochester, NY; *Secy.,* Del Engler. Thomas J. Meskill, New Britain, CT; *Secy.,* Ann Schnitzke. Richard J. Cardamone, Utica, NY; *Secys.,* Rose Ann LaCroix, Leigh Paquette. Roger J. Miner, Albany, NY. Frank X. Altimeri, Uniondale, NY.

Clerk, George Lange III, U.S. Courthouse, Foley Sq., New York, NY 10007.

U.S. DISTRICT COURT. *Judges: Sr. Judge,* Ellen B. Burns at New Haven; *Secy.,* Patricia A. Corbett. *Sr. Judge,* Gerard L. Goettel at Waterbury; *Secy.,* Kathleen Williams. *Sr. Judge,* Warren W. Eginton at Bridgeport; *Secy.,* Sharon Daniels. *Chief Judge,* Peter C. Dorsey at New Haven; *Secy.,* Karen Miller. *Judge,* Alan H. Nevas at Bridgeport; *Secy.,* vacancy. Robert N. Chatigny at Hartford; *Secy.,* Lucia Macare. Alfred V. Covello at Hartford; *Secy.,* Catherine Verillo. Dominic J. Squatrito at Hartford; Secy., Corrine Mischel. Alvin W. Thompson at Hartford; *Secy.,* Marion Bock.

Federal Public Defender: Chief Defenders, Thomas G. Dennis, 241 Main St., Hartford 06103; *Secy.,* Annette Wiggins, at Hartford. *Asst. Defenders,* Terence S. Ward, Gary D. Weinberger; *Adm. Officer,* Lauren E. McCary, at Hartford; *Asst. Defenders,* Sarah A. Chambers, Richard A. Reeve, Michael O. Sheehan; *Adm. Asst.,* Cheryl Laccone, at New Haven. *Investigators,* Darcey Beausouleil, at Hartford; Robert E. Porter, at New Haven; *Secy.,* Sabrina Rose, at New Haven.

Clerk, Kevin F. Rowe, 141 Church St., New Haven 06510; *Chief Deputy Clerk,* Victoria C. Minor; *Deputy Clerks at New Haven: Deputy-in-Charge,* Lori A. Inferera; Christine Carfora, Chrystine W. Cody, Tanya Everett, Jody Gruber, Verna Jefferson, Serge Lord, Leona Masters, Patricia Moore, John Morrisson, Timothy Newsom, Michelle Sherman, Betty Torday Rita Warner, Patricia Zielinski; *Deputies at Bridgeport: Deputy-in Charge,* Carol Cannady; Catherine Boroskey, Frank DePino, Rochelle Jaiman, Diane Kolesnikoff, Rosalie Krajcik, Joan N. Oliveau, Cassandra Warren, Dorothy Watts; *Deputies at Hartford: Deputy-in-Charge,* Robin Tabora; Jane Allen, Angela Blue, Erin M. Bourke, Maria Carpenter, Theresa Glynn-Palacios, Barbara Grady, Carol Ihnatenko, Devorah Johnson, Linda Kunofsky, Ann Montgomery, Sandra L. Smith, Barbara Sunbury, Mary Wiggins, Robert Wood; *Deputies at Waterbury: Deputy-in-*

Charge, vacancy; Chrystine W. Cody, *Librarian at Hartford,* Arline Jacques; *Library Aide,* Eleanor Hoar. *Pro Se Law Clerks at Bridgeport,* Cynthia Earle, Brian Roche, Donna Thomas; *Librarians at New Haven,* Sara Hull.

Headquarters Office (New Haven): Chief Probation Officer, Maria R. McBride; *Deputy Chief Probation Officers,* Lawrence P. Cowper, Paul M. Visokay; *Supvrs.,* Patrick F. DiDomizio, Michael E. Sheehan; *Sr. Probation Officers,* Carmelo Medina, Deborah S. Palmieri, Virginia C. Swisher; *Probation Officers,* Jacqueline Carroll, Katherine Curtin, Wilfredo Duran, Ray Lopez, C. Warren Maxwell, Mark D. Myers, Vicki M. Stackpole; *Adm. Analyst/Secy. to Chief,* Marlyn R. Pollard; *DQA Mgr.,* Joan M. Levine; *Supervisory Clerk,* Joyce Crowther; *Sr. Probation Clerks,* Catherine D. DeMatteo, June Elovitz, Rosanna Gonsiewski, Debra Gray, Danus Thomas; *Personnel Specialist,* Margaret J. Cullinan; *Systems Mgr.,* James L. Reichelt; *Asst. Systems Mgr.,* John D. Ditoto; *(Hartford): Supvr,* John T. Ryan, Jr.; *Sr. Probation Officer,* Steven J. Lambert; *Probations Officers,* Alcides Evora, Estela M. Hermosillo, Bunita Keyes, Maureen Rooks, Brian J. Topor; *Clerk-in-Charge,* Sharon Crane; *Sr. Probation Clerks,* Claire Bergin, Therese Nadeau, Sheila Tracy; *(Bridgeport): Supvr.,* George W. Minor; *Sr. Probation Officers,* Robert J. Hassen, James R. LeBlanc; *Probation Officers,* Manuel J. Alonso, Wendy L. Brazalovich, Kim Cerullo, Michael P. Guglielmo, David W. Pond; *Clerk-in-Charge,* Maria K. Mullins; *Sr. Probation Clerks,* Betty Brosius, Cheryl Deedon, Susan Fowler, Debbie Soderberg.

Bankruptcy Judges for the Dist. of Conn., Alan H. W. Shiff, Chief Judge, Bridgeport. Albert S. Dabrowski, New Haven; Robert L. Krechevsky, Hartford. *Clerk of Court,* Bernardine A. Gordon, Hartford. *Chief Deputy Clerk,* Michael F. McHugh. *Deputy-in-Charge,* Nancy Humlicek; *Budget Mgr.,* Teresa R. Bruscia; *Secy. to Clerk;* Regina Miltenberger, Secy. to Bankruptcy Judge, Martha Drown; *Supvr,* Dorothy Jacobs; *Deputy Clerks,* Barbara Bialaski, Mairead Colbath, Lisa Dulude, Peggy Johnston, Beverly Leible, Joneen Pesce, Roberta Rickert, Barbara Roseberry, Catherine Wailgum, Christine Wentworth, Frank Zemak. *Systems Mgr.,* vacancy; *Systems Admin.,* Deirdre Allegro; *Systems Programmer,* Peter Armstrong; *Personnel Mgr.,* Shannon Green; *Financial Admin.,* James Bagni; *Financial Specialist,* Deenah Levine, *Deputy-in-Charge,* Cheryl L. Alusik; *Secy. to Bankruptcy Judge, Bridgeport,* Cheryl Heltke; *Supvr.,* Margaret Zawadski; *Deputy Clerks,* Penninah Burton, Darlene Byrd, Eunice Caban, Susanne D'Andrea, Anna Forrest, Keith Fox, Sujata Rai, Carol Revak, Renee Senteio, Sandra Staton. *P. C. Admin.,* Michael Dietz; *Secy. to Bankruptcy Judge, New Haven,* Vervet Matthews, *Deputy in Charge, New Haven,* Myrna Atwater; *Supvr.,* Elaine Benczkowski; *Deputy Clerks, New Haven,* Lynn Boulton, Deanna Boyles, Mary Anne Dubuc, Genetha Green, Fran Lalley, Doria Moales, Yolanda Ortiz, Susan Panone, Dierdre Shaw, Arlene Skiba; *Data Quality Analysts, Hartford,* Barbara Germain, John Sykes.

U.S. Magistrates (Full Time), Donna F. Martinez; *Secy.,* Dinah O. Montague, New Haven. F. Owen Eagan; *Secy.,* Sally Pascus, Hartford. Thomas P. Smith; *Secy.,* Barbara Stokes, Hartford. Joan G. Margolis; *Secy.,* Mary Hill, New Haven; Holly B. Fitzsimmons; *Secy.,* Joyce Miller, Bridgeport.

Official Court Reporters: John C. Brandon, Hartford; Paul A. Collard, Thea Finkelstein, New Haven; Susan E. Catucci, Bridgeport; Martha Montelongo, Waterbury.

Naturalization Sessions of Court: The petitions of aliens to become citizens of the United States shall be heard from time to time at the various seats of Court, as the Chief Judge shall direct.

U.S. DEPARTMENT OF JUSTICE

Federal Bureau of Investigation: Special Agent-in-Charge, Merrill S. Parks, Jr., 150 Court St., New Haven 06510.

Immigration and Naturalization Service: Officer-in-Charge, John P. Weiss, 450 Main St., Hartford 06103-3060. Tel., (860) 240-3050.

Drug Enforcement Admin.: Resident Agent-in-Charge, Michael A. Priore, Rm. 628, 450 Main St., Hartford 06103. Tel., (860) 240-3233.

U.S. ATTORNEY. Christopher F. Droney, P.O. Box 1824, New Haven 06508; *Deputy U.S. Atty.,* John Durham. *Exec. Asst. U.S. Atty.,* John A. Danaher, III, Hartford. *Asst.-in-Charge, Bridgeport Office,* James I. Glasser. *Chief, Criminal Div.,* Leonard C. Boyle, New Haven; *Deputy Chief, Criminal Div.,* Barbara B. Jongbloed, New Haven. *Chief, Drug Task Force,* Peter D. Markle, New Haven. *Chief, Civil Div.,* John B. Hughes, New Haven. *Chief, Strike Force,* Peter S. Jongbloed. *Asst. U.S. Attys., New Haven Office,* Peter A. Clark, Mark G. Califano, Denise Derby, Gates Garrity-Rokous, H. Gordon Hall, Joseph C. Hutchison, Anthony E. Kaplan, Keith King, Lisa Kral, Calvin B. Kurimai, Jeffrey Meyer, Thomas J. Murphy, Lauren A. Nash, Karen Peck, Michael Runowicz, Christine Sciarrino, David Sheldon, Alan Soloway, David X. Sullivan, Michael Zuk. *Legal Enforcement Coordinator,* Delcie Thibault. *Asst. U.S. Attys., Bridgeport Office,* Robert Appleton, Alex Hernandez, Sharon Jaffe, Alina Marquez, Deirdre O. Martini, Joseph W. Martini, Kari Pedersen, Althea Seaborn. *Asst. U.S. Attys., Hartford Office,* Ronald Apter, William Collier, Thomas Daily, Nora Dannehy, James G. Genco, Stephen V. Manning, David Ring, Carl J. Schuman, Deborah Slater. *Victim Witness Coordinator,* Linda DeFonzo, New Haven. *Collections Paralegal,* Joyce Sheraphin, New Haven. *EAGLE Technician (Computers),* John Holland, New Haven. *Admin. Officer,* Mary Lapitino, New Haven. *Personnel Officer,* Eileen Lombardi, New Haven. *Personnel Asst.,* Ann Bianco, New Haven. *Support Services Specialist,* Valerie Ferreira, New Haven. *Budget Officer,* Michele M. Genden. *Systems Mgr.,* Barbara A. Bizor, New Haven. *Secy. To U.S. Atty.,* Judith A. D'Auria, New Haven. *Secretaries and Legal Clerks, New Haven,* Bonnie J. Davis, Lorraine F. D'Urso, Marilyn D'Urso, Charlotte Esposito, Julie A. Goggins, Elsie Hernandez, Kathy Libby, Mary Mangines, Kathy McGovern, Sandy Reynolds, Susan Scott, Jerri Thomas, Linda M. Wilson, Cheryl Winn; *Bridgeport,* Martine Brophy, Janet D'Eramo, Amy Diaz, Judy L. Jackowski, Angellina R. Meekins, Dawn Sorensen; *Hartford,* Afrena Hokans, Diane Light, Jacqueline Martin, Cheryl Sliva, Lois A. Zabel. *Receptionist,* Marilyn J. Luzietti; *Docket Technician,* vacancy, New Haven. *File Clerk,* Claire Adams, New Haven.

U.S. MARSHAL. John R. O'Connor, U.S. Courthouse, 141 Church St. Mezzanine, New Haven 06510; *Chief Deputy Marshal,* Alfred J. Miller, Jr., New Haven; *Super-*

visory Deputy Marshal, Gary L. Dorsey, New Haven; *Deputy Marshals,* Michael Bushman, John V. Canale, Thomas R. Galluci, Michael Payne, John F. Reilly, David Remington, Edward Tenero, New Haven; *Warrant Coordinators,* James M. Killoy, Michael Payne; *Adm. Officer,* Kathleen M. King; *Seizure and Forfeiture Specialist,* Cheryl K. Tucker; *Prisoner Support Specialist,* Karen F. Windsor; *Legal Technician,* Andrea L. Whitfield, New Haven; *Supervisory Deputy U.S. Marshal,* Russell Sinni, Hartford; *Deputy U.S. Marshals,* Thomas Hammon, Joel A. Kirch, Michael Novak,Thomas Porro, Daniel W. Spellacy, Jr., Andrew Tingley, Hartford; *Deputy-in-Charge,* Paul S. Winterhalder, Bridgeport; *Deputy U.S. Marshals,* Anthony Iaquinto, James Masterson, Vladimir Mihailoff, Bridgeport; *Deputy in Charge,* Paul S. Strielkauskas, Waterbury.

Federal Correctional Institution, Warden, Charles Stewart, Danbury 06810.

U.S. DEPARTMENTS AND AGENCIES SERVING CONNECTICUT
(As of January 1, 1997.)

AGRICULTURE, U.S. DEPT. OF. *Federal Milk Market Admin.,* Erik F. Rasmussen, New England Marketing Area, Order No. 1, 30 Winter St., P.O. Box 1478, Boston, MA 02205-1478.

Farm Service Agency: USDA-FSA, 88 Day Hill Rd., Windsor 06095; Tel., (860) 285-8483. *Chm.,* Harvey Polinsky; *State Exec. Dir.,* Vincent R. Majchier; *Program Specialist,* Mark J. Ruwet; *Dist. Dir.,* Manuel Marshall; *Adm. Officer,* Theresa M. Currier.

Cooperative Extension System and Storrs Agricultural Experiment Station: Univ. of Conn., Storrs 06269-4066. *Dean/Dir.,* Kirklyn M. Kerr; *Assoc. Dean for Outreach and Public Service/Assoc. Dir., UCONN Cooperative System,* Nancy Bull; *Assoc. Dean for Academic Programs,* Suman Singha..

U.S. Department of Rural Economic and Community Development: Community Development Mgr., Garry B. Carabeau, 147 Providence St., P.O. Box 551, Putnam 06260. Receives applications, makes loans in rural areas to finance homes and building sites, assists borrowers with construction planning, credit counseling, and receives payments. Serves towns of Ashford, Brooklyn, Canterbury, Chaplin, Eastford, Hampton, Killingly, Plainfield, Pomfret, Putnam, Scotland, Sterling, Thompson, Woodstock. *Community Development Mgrs.,* Jon L. Slate, 238 West Town St., Norwich 06360; Serves Middlesex, New London, Eastern New Haven County and part of Tolland and Windham Counties. Jon L. Slate, 1185 New Litchfield St., Torrington, CT 06790; Serves Fairfield, Litchfield, Western New Haven County and parts of Hartford County.

Food and Consumer Service: 900 Northrop Rd., Suite C, Wallingford 06492. *Officer-in-Charge,* David Babington; *Program Specialist,* Karen Townley.

Forest Service: 51 Mill Pond Rd., Hamden 06514. *Dir. Rep.,* Dr. Philip M. Wargo, Northeastern Forest Experiment Sta. Northeastern Center for Forest Health Research.

Natural Resources Conservation Service: State Conservationist, Margo Wallace, 16 Professional Park Rd., Storrs 06268-1299. *Project Coordinators,* Carol Donzella, Coastal Basin Area, (203) 787-0390; Vivian Felten, Connecticut River Basin Area,

(860) 688-7725; Kathleen Johnson, Housatonic River Basin Area, (860) 626-8258; Elizabeth Rogers, Thames River Basin Area, (860) 774-0224.

AIR FORCE, CONNECTICUT AIR NATIONAL GUARD. *Comdr.,* BG George A. Demers, CTANG, Bradley ANG Base, East Granby 06026-9309. *Air Comdr.,* Col. James Skiff, 103d FW, Bradley ANG Base, East Granby 06026-9309. Maj. David C. Clarke, 103d Air Cont. Sq., Orange ANG Sta., Orange 06477-0533.

Conn. Wing, Civil Air Patrol: Auxiliary of the U.S. Air Force, P.O. Box 1233, Middletown 06457. *Comdr.,* Col. Lloyd R. Sturges, 40 Olmstead Rd., West Redding 06896; *Vice Comdr.,* Maj. James E. Palmer, 68 Saw Mill Rd., Bristol 06010; *Dir. of Logistics,* Lt. Col. Stewart B. Fritts, 38 Shaw Dr., North Haven 06473; *Dir. of Finance,* Maj. Lois M. Mitchell, 22 Olmstead Rd., West Redding 06896.

ARMY, DEPT. OF. *Comdr., 1st U.S. Army,* LTG Guy LaBoa, USA, Fort Gillem, Atlanta, GA 30050-7000; *Comdr., 94th U.S. Regional Support Command,* MG Peter W. Clegg, 695 Sherman Ave., Fort Devens, MA 01433-4000; *Adj. Gen., State of Conn.,* Maj. Gen. David W. Gay, State Armory, 360 Broad St., Hartford 06105-3795; *Chief of Staff,* Roy Pinette, CTARNG, State Armory, Hartford 06105; *Sr. Army Advisor,* CTARNG, LTC. Michael L. Trubia, State Armory, 360 Broad St., Hartford, CT 06105-3795; *Comdr., U.S. Army Corps of Engineers, New England Div.,* Col. Michael S. Meuleners, 424 Trapelo Rd., Waltham, MA 02254-9149.

COMMERCE, DEPT. OF. *Bureau of the Census,* Regional Office, 2 Copley Pl., Suite 301, P.O. Box 9108, Boston, MA 02117-9108. *Regional Dir.,* Arthur G. Dukakis.

Conn. Dist. Export Center, U.S. Dept. of Commerce, International Trade Admin., U.S. and Foreign Commercial Service: Dir., Carl R. Jacobsen, Suite 903, 213 Court St., Middletown, CT 06457-3346. Tel., (860) 638-6950.

National Oceanic and Atmospheric Admin. and National Weather Service: Officer-in-Charge, Walter B. Kemp, Weather Service Office, Hartford, Bradley International Airport, Windsor Locks 06096; *Official-in-Charge,* David L. Foose, Weather Service Office (Bridgeport-New Haven), Sikorsky Airport, Stratford; *Hydrologist-in-Charge,* Ron Martin, Northeast River Forecast Ctr., 445 Myles Standish Blvd., Taunton, MA 02780-1041.

National Marine Fisheries Service: National Marine Fisheries Service, Northeast Fisheries Science Ctr., 212 Rogers Ave., Milford 06460-6499. *Lab. Dir.,* Dr. Anthony Calabrese.

Economic Development Admin.: The Curtis Center, Suite 140 South, Independence Sq. West, Philadelphia, PA 19106. Tel., (215) 597-0642. *State Contact,* Stephen P. Grady.

Regional Emergency Planning: Coord., Frank J. O'Connor, *Dist. Dir.,* ITA, US&FCS, Boston Dist. Office.U.S. Dept. of Commerce, World Trade Ctr. Commonwealth Pier, Suite 307, Boston, MA 02210.

CONNECTICUT HUMANITIES COUNCIL. 955 South Main St., Suite E, Middletown 06457; Tel., (860) 685-2260. The State Program of the National Endowment for the Humanities. *Exec. Dir.,* Bruce Fraser; *Assoc. Dir.,* Laurie MacCallum-Rayner; *Coordinator of Admin. Services,* Lise Comstock; *Chm.,* William J. Cibes, Jr.; *Vice*

Chm., Sharon W. Hupp; *Secy.,* Gloria Stewart; *Treas.,* William Breck; *Council Members,* John Allison, Mary Boatwright, William Breck, Richard Buel, Constance M. Clark, Nini Davis, Maxine Dean, Luis Figueroa, Josephine Fuchs, Nancy Grover, Barbara Guerra, Merle Harris, Helen Higgins, Sherry Hupp, William Kennedy, Jerome Lowengard, John Miller, Stuart Parnes, Judith Perkins, Dana M. Prinz, Peter D. Shapiro, John Stone, Brenda Williams, John Zinsser.

DEFENSE, DEPT. OF. 130 Darlin St., East Hartford 06108-3234. Defense Logistics Agency, Defense Contract Mgmt. Command, Hartford; *Comdr.,* Col. Darrell J. Badurek, USAF.

ENVIRONMENTAL PROTECTION AGENCY. J. F. Kennedy Federal Bldg., Boston, MA 02203; Tel., (617) 565-3400. *Regional Admin.,* John P. DeVillars; *Connecticut State Office of Ecosystems Protection, Mgr.,* John F. Hackler; Tel., (617) 565-3474.

FEDERAL COMMUNICATIONS COMMISSION. *Compliance and Info. Bureau:* 1 Battery March Park, Quincy, MA 02169-7495. *Engineer-in-Charge,* Vincent F. Kajunski.

FEDERAL DEPOSIT INSURANCE CORPORATION. Federal Deposit Insurance Corp., Westwood Executive Ctr., 200 Lowder Brook Dr., Westwood, MA 02090. *Regional Dir.,* Patrick J. Rohan.

FEDERAL EMERGENCY MANAGEMENT AGENCY. Federal Emergency Mgmt. Agency, J. W. McCormack POCH, Rm. 442, Boston, MA 02109. *Regional Dir.,* Louis A. Elisa II.

FEDERAL ENERGY REGULATORY COMMISSION. 19 West 34th St., Suite 400, New York, NY 10001; Tel., (212) 273-5900. *Regional Dir.,* Anton J. Sidoti.

FEDERAL HOME LOAN MORTGAGE CORPORATION. 1410 Springhill Rd., Suite 600, McLean, VA 22102; Tel., (703) 902-7700. *Vice Pres., Marketing and Sales,* F. Michael Salb.

FEDERAL MEDIATION AND CONCILIATION SERVICE. *Region 1 Dir., Northeast U.S., Puerto Rico, U.S. Virgin Islands,* Kenneth C. Kowalski; *Mediation Services Dir.,* John E. Sweeney, 1 Newark Towers, Newark, NJ 07102; Tel., (212) 399-5038; *Comrs.,* Thomas J. Carroll, Tel., (860) 528-3121, Lawrence A. Gloekler, Tel., (860) 528-3301, William M. Hannon, Tel., (860) 528-3166; 333 East River Dr., Suite 507, East Hartford 06108.

FEDERAL PUBLIC DEFENDER. Thomas G. Dennis, 241 Main St., 1st Fl.-S, Hartford, CT 06106-5325; *Asst. Public Defenders,* Terence S. Ward, Gary D. Weinberger, Hartford; *Asst. Public Defenders,* Sarah A. Chambers, Richard A. Reeve, Paul F. Thomas, 2 Whitney Ave., Suite 300, New Haven 06510. *Investigators,* Darcey M. Beausoleil, Hartford; Robert E. Porter, New Haven.

FEDERAL RESERVE SYSTEM. Federal Reserve Dist. No. 1, Federal Reserve Bank of Boston, 600 Atlantic Ave., Boston, MA 02106, for all of Conn, except Fairfield County. Fairfield County: Federal Reserve Dist. No. 2, Federal Reserve Bank of New York, 33 Liberty St., New York, NY 10045.

FEDERAL AND STATE SURPLUS PROPERTY CENTER. P.O. Box 290170, 60 State St. Rear, Wethersfield 06129-0170. *Federal Surplus Property Admin.,* Philip Schulman, Tel., (860) 566-7190; *State Surplus Property Admin./Surplus Property Programs Dir.,* Ken Stephenson; Tel., (860) 566-7018; *Bureau of Business Services, Surplus Property Ctr.,* Tel., (860) 566-7018.

FEDERAL TRADE COMMISSION. Federal Trade Comm., 101 Merrimac St., Rm. 810 Boston, MA 02114. *Boston Regional Dir.,* Phoebe D. Morse.

GENERAL SERVICES ADMINISTRATION. *Property Management Center South.* Maryann A. Orlowski, CSR., Abraham A. Ribicoff Federal Bldg., U.S. Courthouse, Suite 635, 450 Main St., Hartford 06103; Arthur R. Hopkins, CSR, Brien McMahon Federal Courthouse, Suite 305, 915 Lafayette Blvd., Bridgeport 06604; William R. Cotter Federal Bldg., 135 High St., Hartford 06103; SSA Office, 147 Litchfield St., Torrington 06790. James H. Nelson, CSR, U.S. Courthouse, 141 Church St., New Haven 06510; Robert N. Giaimo Federal Bldg., 150 Court St., New Haven 06510.

HEALTH AND HUMAN SERVICES, DEPT. OF. Regional Office: 2100 J. F. Kennedy Federal Bldg., Boston, MA 02203; Tel., (617) 565-1500. Servicing Conn. and other New England States. *Acting New England Dir.,* Maureen Osolnik.

Food and Drug Admin.: Resident-in-Charge, Stephen A. Souza; 135 High St., Rm. 371, Hartford 06103.

HOUSING AND URBAN DEVELOPMENT, U.S. DEPT. OF. *New England Office,* Secys. Rep., Mary Lou K. Crane, 10 Causeway St., Boston, MA 02222-1092; *Hartford Office: State Coord.,* Raymond A. Jordan, 330 Main St., Hartford 06106.

INTERIOR, DEPT. OF THE. *Geological Survey, Water Resources Div.:* 450 Main St., Rm. 525, Hartford 06103. *Chief, Conn. Dist.,* Virginia de Lima.

U.S. Fish and Wildlife Service: Law Enforcement Div., 450 Main St., Rm. 607, Hartford 06103; Tel., (860) 2140-3232. *Special Agent,* Richard A. Moulton.

JUSTICE, DEPT. OF. See U.S. Department of Justice.

LABOR, DEPT. OF. *Bureau of Apprenticeship and Training:* Conn. State Office, 135 High St., Rm. 367, Hartford 06103-1190. *State Dir.,* vacancy.

Employment Standards Admin., Wage and Hour Div.: Dist. Office, Wm. R. Cotter Federal Bldg., 135 High St., Rm. 310, Hartford 06103-1198; Tel., (860) 240-4160; *Dist. Dir.,* Dianne M. Miller. Location of area offices: 414 Chapel St., Rm. 201, New Haven 06511; Tel., (203) 773-2249; 380 Westminster Mall, Rm. 346, Providence, RI 02903; Tel., (401) 528-4431.

Office of Labor Mgmt. Standards: 2 Whitney Ave., Rm. 301, New Haven 06510; Tel., (203) 773-2130. *Dist. Dir.,* Mary Spradlin.

Occupational Safety and Health Admin.: Area Office, 450 Main St., Suite 613, Hartford 06103. *Area Dir.,* John J. Stanton, Jr.

Office of the Inspector General: U.S. Dept. of Labor, Office of the Inspector General, Office of Investigations, JFK Federal Bldg., Rm. 300, Boston, MA 02203; Tel., (617) 565-2036. *Sr. Special Agent,* Michael J. Ford.

Veterans' Employment and Training Service, U.S. Dept. of Labor, Field Offices: *Dir.of Veterans' Employment and Training Service,* Robert B. Inman, c/o Conn. Labor Dept. Bldg., 200 Folly Brook Blvd., Wethersfield 06109; *Asst. Dir. of Veterans' Employment and Training Service,* William C. Mason, c/o CT Job Service Office, 500 State St., Bridgeport 06604.

NATIONAL AERONAUTICS AND SPACE ADMINISTRATION. 300-E St., S.W., Washington, D.C. 20546-0001. *Admin.,* Daniel S. Goldin.

NATIONAL LABOR RELATIONS BOARD. *Region I Dir.,* Rosemary Pye, Thomas P. O'Neill, Jr. Federal Bldg., 10 Causeway St., Rm. 601, Boston, MA 02222-1072, Covering Maine, Massachusetts, New Hampshire, Rhode Island, Vermont. *Region 34, Dir.,* Peter B. Hoffman, One Commercial Plaza, 21st Fl., Hartford 06103, covering all of Connecticut.

NAVY, DEPT. OF THE. *Commanding Officer,* Capt. Robert N. Nestlerode, USN, Naval Submarine Base New London, 06349-5000; *Officer-in-Charge,* Comdr. Patricia Cerchio, USN, Naval Undersea Warfare Center Detachment, Newport, RI 02840.

PERSONNEL MANAGEMENT, OFFICE OF. Hartford Field Office: *Chief Test Coord.,* Robert C. Vasnus, A. A. Ribicoff Federal Bldg., Rm. 135, 450 Main St., Hartford 06103.

SECURITIES AND EXCHANGE COMMISSION. 73 Tremont St., Boston, MA 02108-3912; Tel., (617) 424-5934. *Dist. Admin.,* Juan M. Marcelino.

SMALL BUSINESS ADMINISTRATION. 330 Main St., Hartford 06106. *District Dir.,* Jo-Ann VanVechten; *Deputy Dist. Dir.,* Greta Johonsson; *Chief, Finance Div.,* William Murray; *Asst. Dist. Dir., Economic Development.,* Gary Besser; *Dist. Counsel,* Harold A. Pitt; *Admin. Officer,* Edie Moccia.

SOCIAL SECURITY ADMINISTRATION. Field Offices: *Field Office Mgrs.,* Henry J. Allsworth, 2 Shaws Cove, Rm. 203, New London 06320-4975; Salvatore T. Anello, 580 Burnside Ave., East Hartford 06108; Doreen R. Dougan, 307 Main St., Ansonia 06401; Paul Gilfillan, 131 West St., Danbury 06810-9710; Jose A. Gonzalez, 225 North Main St., Rm. 400, Bristol 06010; David L. Grant, Federal Bldg., Rm. 325A, 150 Court St., New Haven 06510; David E. Kullgren, 2 Landmark Sq., Suite 105, Stamford 06901; Ernestine P. Mazon, Comtech Business Ctr., 470 Murdock Ave., Meriden 06450; Joseph J. Mucciaro, Jr., 20 Church St., Hartford 06103; James R. Pashley, 147 Litchfield St., Torrington 06790; Anthony J. Renzoni, 3885 Main St., 3rd Fl., Bridgeport 06606; Edith Richardson, 24 Belden Ave., Norwalk 06850; Patricia Serafin, 100 Arch St., New Britain 06051; Steven Silberfein, 425 Main St., 3rd Fl., Middletown 06457; Geoffrey A. Sorrow, 54 North St., Willimantic 06226; David J. St. Martin, Thames Plaza, 101 Water St., Norwich 06360.Thomas J. Wing, 14 Cottage Pl., Waterbury 06702.

TRANSPORTATION, DEPT. OF. *U.S. Coast Guard, Atlantic Area: Comdr., Vice Adm.,* James M. Loy, Governors Island, NY 10004-5099. *Comdr., Maintenance and Logistics Command Atlantic, Rear Adm.,* Douglas H. Teeson, Governors Island, NY 10004-5099. *Supt., U.S. Coast Guard Academy,* Rear Adm., Paul E. Versaw, New London; *Comdr., U.S. Coast Guard Group Long Island Sound,* Capt. Thad Allen, 120

Woodward Ave., East Haven; *Commanding Officer, Sta. New London*, LT John O'Connor, Fort Trumbull, New London.

Federal Aviation Admin.: FAA Airway Facilities System Service Operations, 8342, Bldg. 85-214, 2nd Fl., Bradley International Airport, Windsor Locks 06096. *Operations Mgr.*, William D. Reno.

Federal Highway Admin.: 628-2 Hebron Ave., Suite 303, Glastonbury 06033. *Div. Admin.*, Dwight A. Horne.

Federal Railroad Admin.: 55 Broadway, Rm. 10-77, Cambridge, MA 02142; Tel., (617) 494-2243. *Regional Admin.*, Mark H. McKeon; *Deputy Regional Admins.*, Leslie L. Fiorenzo, Laurence H. Hasvold; *Admin. Officer*, Robert R. Novak.

National Highway Traffic Safety Admin.—Region I: Transportation Systems Center, *Regional Admin.*, George A. Luciano, Kendall Sq., Cambridge, MA 02142.

TREASURY, DEPT. OF THE. *Bureau of Alcohol, Tobacco and Firearms/Law Enforcement: Acting Resident Agent-in-Charge,* James Markowski, 450 Main St., Rm. 501, Hartford 06103; Tel., 240-3185; Allan J. MacDonald, 150 Court St., Rm. 211, New Haven 06510; Tel., (203) 773-2060; *Area Supvr., Bureau of Alcohol, Tobacco and Firearms/Compliance Operations,* Sandra Thompson, 450 Main St., Rm. 401, Hartford 06103; Tel., (860) 240-3400.

Internal Revenue Service: Dist. Dir. of Internal Revenue, Richard L. McCleary, 135 High St., Hartford 06103; *Chief, Criminal Investigation Div.,* Robert Ragone; *Acting Chief, Collection Div.,* Elisabeth McQueeny; *Chief, Examination Div.,* Jack G. Holstein; *Chief, Info. Systems,* Kathleen Logiodice; *Chief, Research Div.,* Elisabeth McQueeney; *Chief, Appeals Branch,* Christine Haveles; *Dist. Dir. U.S. Savings Bonds Div.,* John R. Fantry, 450 Main St., Rm. 617-A, Hartford.

Connecticut-Rhode Island District Counsel: Commerce Center One, 333 East River Dr., Suite 200, East Hartford 06108. *Dist. Counsel,* Gerald A. Thorpe; *Asst. Dist. Counsel,* Bradford A. Johnson; *Attys.,* Elise F. Alair, John Aletta, Stephen C. Best, Michael P. Breton, Andrew R. Ceccherini, Michael Goldbas, Joseph F. Long, Robert E. Marum, Carmino J. Santaniello, Meryl Silver.

U.S. Customs Service: 135 High St., Rm. 350, Hartford 06103. *Area Dir.*, Thomas F. Waterman; Tel., (860) 240-4306.

U.S. Secret Service: 265 Church St., Suite 1201, New Haven 06510. *Resident Agent-in-Charge,* Arnold A. Cole.

DEPT. OF VETERANS AFFAIRS. *Secy. of Veterans Affairs,* Central Office, 810 Vermont Ave., NW, Washington, DC 20420.

Regional Office: 450 Main St., Hartford 06103, Tel. 1-800-827-1000. *Dir.*, Jeffrey Alger; *Mgmt. Analyst,* Donald N. Schnur; *Adjudication Officer,* Carolyn F. Hunt; *Veterans Services Officer,* Edward C. O'Brien; *Vocational Rehabilitation/Counseling,* Rick Underwood; *Support Services,* Michael T. Kirner; *Human Resources Mgmt. Div.,* Clement R. Pachnieski, Jr.; *Asst. Regional Counsel,* Denise Ridge.

Dept. of Veterans Affairs Offices: V. A. Medical Center, 555 Willard Ave., Newington 06111. V. A. Medical Center, 950 Campbell Ave., West Haven 06516.

Itinerant locations throughout the state are located at: Richard R. Martin Ctr., 120 Broad St., New London; Chase Bldg., 236 Grand St., Waterbury; City Hall, 45 Lyon Ter., Bridgeport. For office hours, call the toll-free number listed under U.S. Government in the local phone book, (800) 827-1000.

VETERANS ADMINISTRATION CONNECTICUT HEALTH CARE SYSTEM. West Haven 06516; Tel., (203) 932-5711. *Dir.,* Vincet W. Ng; *Assoc. Dir.,* Gordon L. Carr, Ph.D.; *Assoc. Patient Care Dir.,* Margaret Veazey, R.N.; *Chief of Staff,* Colin E. Atterbury, M.D.; *Assoc. Chief of Staff for Ambulatory Care, West Haven,* Kenneth Cohen, M.D.; *Assoc. Chief of Staff for Ambulatory Care, Newington,* vacancy; *Assoc. Chief of Staff for Education,* Jeffrey Lustman, M.D.; Ass*oc. Chief of Staff for Research and Development,* Fred Wright, M.D.; Assoc. *Chief of Staff, Geriatrics and Extended Care,* Margaret Drickamer, M.D.; *Assoc. Chief of Staff/Operations, Newington,* Juliet Vilinskas, M.D.; *Asst. Chief of Staff/Clinical Operations and Special Programs,* Paul Mulinski, Ph.D.

Admin. Services: Chief, Acquisition and Material Mgmt. Service, vacancy; *Chief, Canteen Service,* Thomas Tarasiewicz; *Chief, Nutrition and Food Service,* vacancy; *Chief, Facilities Mgmt. Service,* Stephen Hogle; *Chief, Fiscal Service,* Carl Lister; *Chief, Info. Resource Mgmt. Service,* vacancy; *Chief, Medical Admin. Service,* John Werner; *Chief, Human Resource Mgmt. Service,* Neil Falkner; *Chief, Voluntary Service,* Gloria Jorel; *Chief Info. Officer,* Joseph Erdos, M.D.; *Chief, Prosthetics Service,* Barry Gray; *Chief, Library Service,* Joan McGinnis; *Chief, Police and Security,* James McCarthy.

Professional Services: Chief, Anesthesiology Service, Albert Perrino, M.D.; *Chief, Eastern Blind Rehabilitation Ctr.,* Mark Hieftje; *Chief, Chaplain Service,* Paul Neff; *Chief, Audiology and Speech Pathology,* vacancy; *Chief, Dental Service,* vacancy; *Chief, Dermatology Service,* Leonard Milstone, M.D.; *Chief, Pathology and Lab. Med. Service,* Gary E. Stack, M.D.; *Chief, Medical Service,* David Coleman, M.D.; *Chief, Neurology Service,* Lawrence Brass, M.D.; *Chief, Nuclear Medicine,* Holly Dey, M.D.; *Deputy Chief Nurse,* Jan Joseph, R.N.; *Chief, Pharmacy Service,* Lydia Borysiuk; *Chief, Psychiatry Service,* Thomas Kosten, M.D.; *Chief, Psychology Service,* Robert Kerns, Ph.D.; *Chief, Radiology Service,* Caroline Taylor, M.D.; *Chief, Rehabilitation Medicine Service,* vacancy; *Chief, Social Work Service,* Anthony Cinquanta, MSW; *Chief, Surgical Service,* Barbara Kinder, M.D.

UNITED STATES AND TERRITORIES

THE THIRTEEN ORIGINAL STATES

State	Ratified the Constitution	State	Ratified the Constitution
Delaware	Dec. 7, 1787	South Carolina	May 23, 1788
Pennsylvania	Dec. 12, 1787	New Hampshire	June 21, 1788
New Jersey	Dec. 18, 1787	Virginia	June 25, 1788
Georgia	Jan. 2, 1788	New York	July 26, 1788
Connecticut	Jan. 9, 1788	North Carolina	Nov. 21, 1789
Massachusetts	Feb. 6, 1788	Rhode Island	May 29, 1790
Maryland	April 28, 1788		

ORGANIZATION OF TERRITORIES AND ADMISSION OF STATES INTO THE UNION

State	Territory Organized	Admitted
Vermont	Out of New Hampshire and New York	Mar. 4, 1791
Kentucky	Out of Virginia	June 1, 1792
Tennessee	Out of North Carolina	June 1, 1796
Ohio	Ordinance, 1787	Mar. 1, 1803
Louisiana	March 3, 1805	April 30, 1812
Indiana	May 7, 1800	Dec. 11, 1816
Mississippi	April 7, 1798	Dec. 10, 1817
Illinois	February 3, 1809	Dec. 3, 1818
Alabama	March 3, 1817	Dec. 14, 1819
Maine	Out of Massachusetts	Mar. 15, 1820
Missouri	June 4, 1812	Aug. 10, 1821
Arkansas	March 2, 1819	June 15, 1836
Michigan	January 11, 1805	Jan. 26, 1837
Florida	March 30, 1822	Mar. 3, 1845
Texas	Annexed	Dec. 29, 1845
Iowa	June 12, 1838	Dec. 28, 1846
Wisconsin	April 20, 1836	May 29, 1848
California	From Mexico	Sept. 9, 1850
Minnesota	March 3, 1849	May 11, 1858
Oregon	August 14, 1848	Feb. 14, 1859
Kansas	May 30, 1854	Jan. 29, 1861
West Virginia	Out of Virginia	June 20, 1863
Nevada	March 2, 1861	Oct. 31, 1864
Nebraska	May 30, 1854	Mar. 1, 1867
Colorado	February 28, 1861	Aug. 1, 1876
North Dakota	March 2, 1861	Nov. 2, 1889
South Dakota	March 2, 1861	Nov. 2, 1889
Montana	May 26, 1864	Nov. 8, 1889

State	Territory Organized	State Admitted
Washington	March 2, 1853	Nov. 11, 1889
Idaho	March 3, 1863	July 3, 1890
Wyoming	July 25, 1868	July 10, 1890
Utah	September 9, 1850	Jan. 4, 1896
Oklahoma	May 2, 1890	Nov. 16, 1907
New Mexico	September 9, 1850	Jan. 6, 1912
Arizona	February 24, 1863	Feb. 14, 1912
Alaska	July 27, 1868	Jan. 3, 1959
Hawaii	June 14, 1900	Aug. 21, 1959

Territory—District of Columbia*—Organized July 16, 1790—March 3, 1791.
*Reduced from 100 to 70 square miles by recession of part of Virginia in 1846.

TERRITORIES AND OTHER AREAS UNDER UNITED STATES ADMINISTRATION
(Source: Department of the Interior)

AMERICAN SAMOA. Governor, A. P. Lutali, elected by popular vote. Capital, Pago Pago.

GUAM. Governor, Carl T. C. Gutierrez, elected by popular vote. Capital, Agana, P.O. Box 2950, 060100.

MICRONESIA, FEDERATED STATES OF. Includes Pohnpei, Chuuk, Yap and Kosrae states. c/o Office of the President, Bailey Olter; Kolonia, Pohnpei, FM 96941.

NORTHERN MARIANA ISLANDS, COMMONWEALTH OF. Office of the Governor, Froilan G. Tenorio. Caller Box 10007, Capitol Hill, Saipan, MP 96950.

PALAU, REPUBLIC OF. c/o Office of the President, Kuniwo Nakamura, P.O. Box 100, Koror, Palau PW, WCI 96940. Tel., (680-9) 488-2403, 2828, 2541, 2532.

VIRGIN ISLANDS. Governor, Roy L. Schneider, elected by popular vote. Government House, 21-22 Kongens Gade, Charlotte Amalie, St. Thomas, VI 00802. Tel., (800) 774-0001; FAX, (809) 774-1361.

COMMONWEALTH OF PUERTO RICO. Territory of the United States, ceded by Spain under the Treaty of Paris, December 10, 1898; population granted United States citizenship by Congress, March 2, 1917; internally self-governing since July 25, 1952, under constitution ratified by local electorate and Congress. Governor, Pedro Rossello, La Fortaleza, POB 82, 00901. Tel., (787) 721-7000; FAX, (787) 721-7483. Capital, San Juan.

SECTION X

MISCELLANEOUS

Historical Societies

Museums

Public Libraries

Press of Connecticut

Radio Stations and TV Stations

Selected Facts about Connecticut

Legal Holidays in Connecticut

Medal of Honor Recipients

Illustrations and Descriptions of
State Seal, State Flag and
other Emblems

Index

HISTORICAL SOCIETIES

THE ACORN CLUB. *Pres.,* Richard Buel, Jr.; *Secy.,/Treas.,* Ralph Elliot; *Editor,* J. Bard McNulty.

ANDOVER HISTORICAL SOCIETY. *Pres./Treas.,* Scott Yeomans; *Vice Pres.,* Marie Burbank; *Cor. Secy.,* Martha Hardisty, 3 Hebron Rd., 06232.

THE ARCHAEOLOGICAL SOCIETY OF CONN., INC. c/o 10 South Cove La., Essex 06426. *Pres.,* Dan Cruson; *Vice Pres.,* vacancy; *Secy.,* Shirley Paustian; *Treas.,* Donald Malcarne; *Editor,* Lucianne Lavin; *Productions Mgr.,* Roger Moeller; *Newsletter Editor,* Ernest Wiegrand II.

ASHFORD HISTORICAL SOCIETY. *Pres.,* Lorraine McConnell; *Vice Pres.,* P. Jules Girardet; *Treas.,* Barbara B. Metsack, 69 Laurel La., 06278.

AVON HISTORICAL SOCIETY. P.O. Box 448, 06001. *Pres.,* Margaret Carnduff; *Vice Pres.* Leonard Tolisano; *Recording Secy.,* William Stokesbury; *Treas.,* Dennis Dix, Jr.; *Exec. Dir.,* Terri Atkinson.

BANTAM HISTORICAL SOCIETY. Box 436, 06750. *Pres.,* Fletcher Cooper.

BARKHAMSTED HISTORICAL SOCIETY, INC. P.O. Box 94, Pleasant Valley 06063. *Pres./Treas.,* George Terwilliger, Pleasant Valley; *Vice Pres.,* Kathleen Fox, Pleasant Valley; *Secy.,* Sharon Lynes, Pleasant Valley; *Hitchcock Museum Dir.,* Jamie Heuschkel, Pleasant Valley; *Stone Museum Dir.,* Walt Landgraf, Pleasant Valley.

BERLIN HISTORICAL SOCIETY, INC. *Pres.,* Kate Kearns; *Vice Pres.,* Joan Teske; *Secy.,* Marilyn Griswold, 453 Savage Hill Rd., 06037; *Treas.,* Stephen Buckley.

BETHEL HISTORICAL SOCIETY. *Pres.,* Timothy Beeble; *Vice Pres. 1st,* Lillian H. Emmons , *2nd,* Patricia Rist; *Secy.,* Ruthann Esselman, 30 Mansfield St., 06801; *Treas.,* Jeffrey Pagelson.

(BETHLEHEM) OLD BETHLEM HISTORICAL SOCIETY, INC. P.O. Box 132, 06751. *Pres.,* Douglas B. Tolles; *Vice Pres.,* Carol A. Brown; *Secy.,* Helen Woodward; *Treas.,* Ron Hurlbut.

(BLOOMFIELD) WINTONBURY HISTORICAL SOCIETY. *Pres.,* Jerry Wagner, P. O. Box 7454, 06002; *Vice Pres./Cor. Secy.,* Fannie Gabriel; *Rec. Secy.,* John Pinney; *Treas.,* Thomas Ciccarillo; *Historian,* Eileen Phelps.

BOLTON HISTORICAL SOCIETY. *Coordinator,* Cinde Smith, 25 Hebron Rd., 06043.

BRANFORD HISTORICAL SOCIETY, INC. P.O. Box 504, 06405. *Pres.,* John W. Ifkovic; *Vice Pres.,* Mary Hitchcock; *Secy.,* Harriet White; *Treas.,* Michael E. Sykes; *Asst. Secy./Treas.,* Priscilla Oliver.

BRIDGEWATER HISTORICAL SOCIETY. *Pres.,* Mary Allen; *Vice Pres.,* Patricia Schramm; Secy., Dorothy Gustafson, 139 Keeler Rd., 06752; *Treas.,* Glenn Degener.

(BRISTOL) THE GREATER BRISTOL HISTORICAL SOCIETY, INC. *Pres.,* Jeanne B. DiPietro; *Vice Pres. 1st,* Beryl Josephson, *2nd,* Sharon Krawiecki; *Cor. Secy.,* Jean Bradley, 54 West Washington St., 06010; *Rec. Secy.,* Laurie LaRue; *Treas.,* Patrick Leach.

BROOKLYN HISTORICAL SOCIETY. P.O. Box 90, 06234-0090. *Pres.,* Elaine Knowlton; *Vice Pres.,* James Stuyniski; *Secy.,* Ronald Wood; *Cor. Secy.,* Marion Glidden; *Treas.,* J. Gloria Lee.

(CANAAN) FALLS VILLAGE-CANAAN HISTORICAL SOCIETY. P.O. Box 206, Falls Village 06031. *Pres.,* Peter Lawson and Grabriel Seymour; *Vice Pres.,* Joseph Baldessari; *Cor. Secy.,* Barbara Kelsey; *Rec. Secy.,* Mrs. Robin Cockerline; *Treas.,* Ron Weinress, Falls Village; *Curators,* Mrs. Hendrik DeVries, Canaan, Mrs. Donald Stock, Falls Village; *Asst. Curator,* Mrs. Daniel Longaven, Falls Village.

CANTON HISTORICAL MUSEUM. 11 Front St., Collinsville 06022. *Pres.,* Carl F. Svenson, Jr.; *Vice Pres.,* Susan Hunt; *Secy.,* Joann Jurgen; *Treas.,* Vincent Vernon, Avon.

THE CANTERBURY HISTORICAL SOCIETY, INC. P. O. Box 2, 06022. *Pres.,* Charles W. Fairbrother; *Vice Pres.,* Paul Santagata; *Secy.,* Carol Burgess; *Treas.,* William Kivic; *Curator/Archivist,* Liz Fairbrother.

THE CHESHIRE HISTORICAL SOCIETY, INC. P.O. Box 281, 06410. *Pres.,* Virginia Eckerson; *Vice Pres.,* Elizabeth Floyd; *Membership Secy.,* Joy Deegan; *Rec. Secy.,* Doris Black; *Treas.,* Lawrence Gode; *Curators,* Lillian Andrews, J.E.B. Johnson, Warren Van Almkerk.

CHESTER HISTORICAL SOCIETY, INC. *Pres.,* Dawn Burr; *Secy.,* Doreen Joslow, 46 West Main St., 06412; *Treas.,* Bruce Watrous.

COLEBROOK HISTORICAL SOCIETY, INC. P.O. Box 85, 06021. *Pres.,* Robert Grigg; *Vice Pres.,* Patricia Mulcahey; *Cor. Secy.,* Shirley Draper; *Treas.,* Edward Kochey; *Curator,* Ann Travaglin; *Asst. Curator,* Gladys Dunbar.

COLUMBIA HISTORICAL SOCIETY, INC. *Pres.,* F. Belle Robinson; *Secy.,* Alice Levesque, 138 Rte. 66, Columbia 06237; *Treas.,* Albert B. Gray.

CONN. AERONAUTICAL HISTORICAL ASSOC., INC. (New England Air Museum.) Bradley International Airport, Windsor Locks 06096. *Pres.,* Lincoln S. Young, New Hartford; *Vice Pres.,* William A. O'Neill, East Hampton; *Secy.,* Roy C. J. Normen, South Windsor; *Treas.,* Michael J. Morneau, East Longmeadow, MA; *Exec. Dir.,* Michael P. Speciale, Middletown.

CONN. ANCESTRY SOCIETY, INC. Formerly known as the Stamford Genealogical Society, Inc., founded 1954. Office: P.O. Box 249, Stamford 06904-0249. *Pres.,* Robert W. Green; *Vice. Pres./Publicity,* Mrs. Meriwether C. Schmid; *Vice. Pres.,* Robert A. Ferry; *Secy.,* Carol W. Wister; *Acting Treas.,* Robert W. Green; *Genealogist,* Mary Ann Stewart; *Historian,* Elizabeth Hubert; *Editor, Conn. Ancestry,* Robert A. Ferry.

THE CONN. FIREMEN'S HISTORICAL SOCIETY, INC. 230 Pine St., Manchester, 06040. *Pres.,* Richard Symonds, Jr., Tolland; *Vice Pres.,* Laurence Ford, Redding; *Cor. Secy.,* Carol Genovese, 53 Croft St., Manchester 06040-1619; *Rec. Secy.,* Frances C. Doherty, Cheshire; *Treas.,* Bruce Cropper, Tolland; *Museum Curator,* Arthur H. Selleck, Fairfield.

CONN. HISTORICAL SOCIETY. 1 Elizabeth St., Hartford 06105. *Pres.*, Mrs. N. William Wawro; *Vice Pres.*, Frederick C. Copeland, Hugh C. Macgill; *Secy.*, Daniel P. Brown, Jr.; *Treas.*, Peter Grant; *Exec. Dir.*, vacancy.

THE CONN. LEAGUE OF HISTORICAL SOCIETIES, INC. *Pres.*, Steven K. Young, c/o Fairfield Historical Society, 636 Old Post Rd., Fairfield 06430; *Vice Pres.*, Mark McEachern, Torrington, Lisa B. Quintana, Meriden, Laurie M. Rayner, Middletown; *Rec. Secy.*, Arlene Palmer, New Britain; *Treas.*, Harry W. Jones, Orange.

THE CONN. RAILROAD HISTORICAL ASSOC., INC. P.O. Box 255, Canaan 06018. *Pres./Curator*, George H. Meach; *Exec. Vice Pres.*, Ross Grannan; *Secy.*, Laureen Reeve; *Treas.*, A. Paul Ramunni.

CONN. SOCIETY OF GENEALOGISTS, INC. Office: 175 Maple St., East Hartford 06118. Mailing address: P. O. Box 435 Glastonbury, 06033-0435. *Pres.*, Stuart C. Brush; *Vice Pres.*, Helen S. Coty; *Secy.*, Mary Lou Rath; *Treas.*, Richard G. Tomlinson; *Asst. Treas.*, Ida M. Ragazzi.

CORNWALL HISTORICAL SOCIETY. 7 Pine St., Box 115, 06753. *Pres.*, Michael R. Gannett; *Vice Pres.*, Robert G. Stetson; *Secy.*, Paula Holmes; *Treas.*, Maureen Prentice.

COVENTRY HISTORICAL SOCIETY. Address: P.O. Box 534, 06238. *Pres.*, Donald D. Harte; *Vice Pres.*, Judith Murdock; *Cor. Secy.*, Jane Covell; *Rec. Secy.*, Beth Murphy; *Treas.*, Leigh Wajda.

CROMWELL HISTORICAL SOCIETY. *Pres.*, Lois Donohue; *Vice Pres.*, Madeline Lowry; *Cor. Secy.*, Barbara Nevedomsky, 63 Field Rd., 06416; *Rec. Secy.*, Gerald Seagrave; *Treas.*, Mary Ellen Babcock.

DANBURY SCOTT-FANTON MUSEUM AND HISTORICAL SOCIETY, INC. 43 Main St., 06810. *Pres.*, Jim Arconti; *Vice Pres. 1st,* Debbie Grover, *2nd,* Barry Moller; *Secy.*, Nancy Kinkade; *Cor. Secy.*, Elizabeth Scott; *Treas.*, Mike McLachlan; *Exec. Dir.*, Maryann Root.

DARIEN HISTORICAL SOCIETY, INC. 45 Old King's Hwy., North, 06820. *Pres.*, Judith Groppa; *Vice Pres.*, Dee Goodnow, C. Richard Jahn; *Secy.*, Cynthia Ryan; *Treas.*, Karen Tobin; *Exec. Dir.*, Madeline Hart.

THE DEEP RIVER HISTORICAL SOCIETY, INC. Stone House, Main St., 06417. *Pres.*, Jeffrey Hostetler; *Curator,* Edith DeForest; *Vice Pres.*, Sumner Ziegra; *Secy.*, Charlotte Lazor; *Treas.*, Barbara Reinsch; *Historian,* Jean F. Spallone.

DERBY HISTORICAL SOCIETY, INC. *Pres.*, Jeanette LaMacchia, Shelton; *Vice Pres.*, Jeremiah Vartelas, Stratford; *Rec. Secy.*, Lois Young, Ansonia; *Treas.*, Arthur Tidmarsh, Ansonia; *Exec. Dir.*, Robert J. Novak, Jr., 102 High St., Shelton 06484.

DURHAM HISTORICAL SOCIETY. P.O. Box 345, 06422. *Pres.*, Francis E. Korn; *Vice-Pres.*, Thomas Francis; *Secy.*, Roger Newton; *Treas.*, Francis Korn.

EAST GRANBY HISTORICAL SOCIETY. P.O. Box 188, 06026. *Pres.*, John McIsaac; *Vice Pres.*, Ann Cronan; *Secy.*, Nancy Moody; *Treas.*, William Westervelt.

THE EAST HADDAM HISTORICAL SOCIETY, INC. *Pres.,* David Warner; *Vice Pres.,* Mary Grieco; *Cor. Secy.,* Elizabeth S. Brownell, P.O. Box 254, 06423; *Rec. Secy.,* Molly Swartz; *Treas.,* Susan Flynn; *Archivist,* Hazel Williams.

THE HISTORICAL SOCIETY OF EAST HARTFORD, INC. *Pres.,* Marie Carlson, 59 Brentmoor Rd., 06118; *Vice Pres.,* Elizabeth Knose; *Cor. Secy.,* Mary Guminiak; *Rec. Secy.,* Cynthia DiNino; *Treas.,* Dina Oliver; *Historian/Antiquarian,* Scott MacDonough.

THE EAST HAVEN HISTORICAL SOCIETY, INC. 133 Main St., P.O. Box 120052, 06512. *Pres.,* John T. Brereton; *Vice Pres.,* William Jackson; *Cor. Secy.,* Marian Tansey; *Rec. Secy.,* Marie Sunderland; *Treas.,* Roberta Watts.

(EAST HAVEN) CONN. IRISH AMERICAN HISTORICAL SOCIETY. P.O. Box 120-020, 06512. *Pres.,* Patricia A. Heslin, Hamden; *Vice Pres.,* Jeanne R. Whalen, New Haven; *Secy.,* Maureen Delahunt, Cheshire; *Treas.,* Thomas Slater, Hamden; *Historian,* Neil Hogan, Wallingford.

(EASTON) HISTORICAL SOCIETY OF EASTON, INC. P.O. Box 121, Easton 06612. *Pres/Historian,* Jerry Gabert; *Vice Pres.,* Henley Smith; *Treas.,* David Morgans; *Cor./Rec. Secy.,* Janice Burroughs.

(EAST WINDSOR) THE CONN. ELECTRIC RAILWAY ASSOC., INC. P.O. Box 360, 06088-0360. *Chm.,* Alex P. Goff, Newington; *Pres.,* Nancy Pescos, Salem; *Treas.,* Stanley Duro, Enfield; *Secy.,* Patricia A. Tripodi, East Windsor.

EAST WINDSOR HISTORICAL SOCIETY, INC. *Pres.,* Arend-Jan Knuttel; *Vice Pres.,* Barbara Mazurek; *Secy.,* Flicka Thrall, 145 Chamberlain Rd., Broad Brook 06016; *Treas.,* Jean Lamenzo.

ELLINGTON HISTORICAL SOCIETY. P.O. Box 73, 06029. *Pres.,* James Stoughton; *Vice Pres.,* Miriam Winther; *Cor. Secy.,* Catherine Dziadul; *Rec. Secy.,* Santina Fiore; *Treas.,* Mildred A. Dimock.

THE ENFIELD HISTORICAL SOCIETY, INC. *Pres.,* Anthony S. Secondo; *Vice Pres.,* Esta Clarke; *Cor. Secy.,* Murlie Bromage, 49 St. James, 06082; *Rec. Secy.,* Susan A. Pelton; *Treas.,* Paul D. Batchelder.

THE ESSEX HISTORICAL SOCIETY, INC. P.O. Box 123, 06426. *Pres.,* Deborah Weinstein; *Vice Pres.,* Valerie Shickel; *Secy.,* Kathryn Katz; *Cor. Secy.,* Patricia Pape; *Treas.,* Gretchen Makowicki.

FAIRFIELD HISTORICAL SOCIETY. 636 Old Post Rd., 06430. *Pres.,* Patricia C. Spaght; *Vice Pres.,* Virginia Hayes; *Secy.,* Laura Wilbur; *Treas.* David B. Cook; *Asst. Treas.,* Peter Kunkel; *Exec. Dir.,* Steven K. Young; *Curator,* Ellen E. Endslow; *Librarian,* Barbara Austen; *Curator for Education,* Heather Alexander.

FARMINGTON HISTORICAL SOCIETY. P.O. Box 1645, 06034. *Pres.,* Charles N. Leach, Jr.; *Vice Pres.* Marguerite Yung; *Secy.,* David Holmes; *Membership Secy.,* Sandra Grouten; *Treas.,* Steven Zarmsky.

(GLASTONBURY) HISTORICAL SOCIETY OF GLASTONBURY. P.O. Box 46, 06033. *Pres.,* Joseph F. Greene, Jr.; *Vice Pres.,* Edward C. Swift; *Rec. Secy.,* vacancy; *Treas.*, Charles W. Deane, IV; *Exec. Dir.*, Nancy W. Berlet; *Dirs.*, Hilary Baskin, Patricia Flaherty, Anne P. O'Connor, Donald B. Reid.

GOSHEN HISTORICAL SOCIETY. 21 Old Middle St., 06756. *Pres.*, N. Terry Hall; *Treas.*, Walter Horvay; *Curators*, Hazel Wadhams, Sylvia Wadhams.

(GRANBY) SALMON BROOK HISTORICAL SOCIETY. *Pres.*, J. Holden Camp; *Vice Pres.*, Seth Holcombe; *Secy.*, Marion Wilson, 43 Spring Glen Dr., 06035; *Treas.*, Russell Covell; *Historian*, William Vibert; *Curator*, Carol Laun; *Curator Emeritus*, Eva Dewey.

(GREENWICH) THE HISTORICAL SOCIETY OF THE TOWN OF GREENWICH, INC. Bush-Holley House, 39 Strickland Rd., Cos Cob 06807. *Chm.*, Claire F. Vanderbilt; *Pres.*, William C. Crooks; *Secy.*, Rachel Lorenetzen; *Treas.*, Bruce Dixon; *Executive Dir.*, Debra Walker-Mecky.

(GROTON) NOANK HISTORICAL SOCIETY, INC. 17 Sylvan St., Box 9454, Noank 06340. *Pres.*, James Giblin; *Vice Pres.*, John Butler; *Cor./Rec. Secy.*, Betty Wallsten; *Treas.*, Steven A. Anderson; *Curator*, Kenneth Hodgson.

(GUILFORD) THE DOROTHY WHITFIELD HISTORIC SOCIETY, INC. P.O. Box 229, 06437. *Pres.*, Mary F. Phelan; *Vice Pres. 1st*, Colin MacKenzie, *2nd*, Janet Seifried; *Cor. Secy.*, Nancy Elderbaum; *Rec. Secy.*, Jacqueline Plant; *Treas.*, Ellen C. MacFarland.

(GUILFORD) GUILFORD KEEPING SOCIETY. Thomas Griswold House, Box 363, 06437. *Pres.*, Sandra Rux; *Vice Pres.*, Thomas Black; *Treas.*, Alan Haesche.

THE HADDAM HISTORICAL SOCIETY. P.O. Box 97, 06438. *Pres.*, Melissa Gibson; *Vice Pres. 1st*, Beryl Thorpe; *Cor. Secy.*, Carol Smith; *Rec. Secy.*, Terry Smith; *Treas.*, Paul Hoover.

THE HAMDEN HISTORICAL SOCIETY, INC. P.O. Box 5512, 06518. *Pres.*, Brian W. Poirier; *Vice Pres.*, Charlton Gilbert; *Rec. Secy.*, Lois Casey; *Treas.*, Ward S. Becker; *Historian*, Martha Becker.

HAMPTON ANTIQUARIAN AND HISTORICAL SOCIETY, INC. P.O. Box 12, 06247. *Pres.*, Leila Ostby; *Vice Pres.*, Lois Kelley; *Cor. Secy.*, Janice Trecker; *Rec. Secy.*, Robert Burgoyne; *Treas.*, Raymond Ostby; *Asst. Treas.*, Henry Moon.

(HARTFORD) THE ANTIQUARIAN AND LANDMARKS SOCIETY, INC. Office: 66 Forest St., 06105. *Pres.*, Astrid T. Hanzalek, Suffield; *Vice Pres.*, Kay Clarke, East Haddam; William K. Paynter, Chester; Hallas H. Ridgeway, Chaplin; *Secy.*, J. Bard McNulty, Glastonbury; *Treas.*, Fleet Bank, Institutional Bookkeeping Dept., 777 Main St.; *Exec. Dir.*, R. Angus Murdoch; *Admin. Asst.*, Trudy K. Jones; *Assoc. Dir.*, Karin Peterson.

(HARTFORD) HARRIET BEECHER STOWE CENTER. 77 Forest St., 06105. Harriet Beecher Stowe House, fully restored, open to the public Tues.-Sat., 9:30 A.M.-4 P.M.; Sun., 12 Noon-4 P.M. June thru Columbus Day, open every day, 9:30 A.M.-4 P.M., Sun., Noon-4 P.M. Admission charged. Stowe-Day Library has 160,000 manuscript items of Beechers, Gillettes, Hookers, Harriet Beecher Stowe and other Connecticut notables; 15,000 volumes on architecture, the decorative arts, history and literature, open Mon.-Fri., 9 A.M.-4:30 P.M. *Pres.,* Norman Beecher; *Vice Pres.,* Louise Galvin; *Secy.,* Thomas Mahar; *Treas.,* Greg Madar; *Dir.,* Jo Blatti; *Librarian,* Diana Royce; *Dir., Education Programs,* Catherine Bermon; *Curator,* Debra Fillos.

HARTLAND HISTORICAL SOCIETY. P.O. Box 221, East Hartland 06027. *Pres.,* Joan Stoltze; *Vice Pres.,* Dominic Bosco; *Secy.,* Roxanne Kane; *Treas.,* Anne Anderson; *Curator,* Karen McNulty; *Librarian,* vacancy.

HARWINTON HISTORICAL SOCIETY, INC. P.O. Box 84, 06791. *Pres.,* George Beck; *Vice Pres.,* Jane Golec; *Secy.,* Karen Fowler; *Treas.,* Tom Schoenemann; *Co-Curators,* Beverly Mosher, Marion Thierry; *Auditor,* John Thrall; *Counsel,* John Febbroriello; *Bd. of Dirs.,* Stuart Bronson, Wendell Gunn, Susan McGlen, Lloyd Shanley; *Historian,* Lloyd T. Shanley, Jr.

HEBRON HISTORICAL SOCIETY. P.O. Box 43, 06248. *Pres.,* Kathy Sarnoski; *Vice Pres.,* Annie C. Piggott; *Cor. Secy.,* Margaret Ely; *Rec Secy.,* Nathalie Horton; *Treas.,* David Morrison; *Historian,* Clifford Wright.

KILLINGLY HISTORICAL SOCIETY, INC. 196 Main St., Danielson 06239; Biographical & Genealogical Library, est. 1972, *Pres.,* Natalie Coolidge, South Killingly; *Vice Pres.,* Kenneth Patridge, Brooklyn; *Secy.,* Gloria Bergeron, Plainfield; *Treas.,* Joseph Chauvin, Danielson; *Exec. Dir.,* Edwin R. Ledogar, Dayville.

KILLINGWORTH HISTORICAL SOCIETY. *Pres.,* W. David Levasseur; *Vice Pres. 1st,* Lewis W. Scranton, *2nd,* Florence Broach; *Membership Chm.,* Carol Annino, 294 Route 148, 06419; *Rec. Secy.,* Linda Dudek; *Treas.,* Claudette Lagassee.

KOSCIUSZKO HISTORICAL SOCIETY OF ANSONIA. *Pres.,* Cecelia Rafalowski; *Vice Pres.,* Stanley Muzyk; *Secy.,* Helen Ptak, 12 East St., 06401; *Treas.,* Alma Roginel; *Curator,* Wanda Sedor; *Historian,* Joseph Wardzala; *Bd. Dirs.,* Henry Bondos, Stella Bondos, Florence Hoinski, Isabelle Klik, Anthony Roginel, Stanley Zaprzalka; *Auditors,* Eve Turaj, Helen Wlodek.

LEBANON HISTORICAL SOCIETY. P.O. Box 151, 06249. *Pres.,* Claire Krause; *Vice Pres. 1st,* James Donnelly, *2nd,* Mary Ann Walter; *Cor. Secy.,* Arlene McCaw; *Rec. Secy.,* Richard Ames; *Treas.,* Alicia Wayland.

LEDYARD HISTORICAL SOCIETY. *Pres.,* James F. Bowersett, 50 Whalehead Rd., Gales Ferry 06335; *Vice Pres.,* William Fossum; *Cor. Secy.,* Lauren Arpin; *Rec. Secy.,* Margaret E. Wilson; *Treas.,* Barbara Williams; *Curator,* Anne King; *Historian,* Jan Bell.

LISBON HISTORICAL SOCIETY, INC. *Pres.,* Albert Gosselin, 232 Mell Rd., 06351; *Vice Pres.,* Richard Herrmann; *Rec. Secy.,* Sharon Gabiga; *Treas.,* Nina Chudy.

LYME HISTORICAL SOCIETY, INC. Florence Griswold Museum, 96 Lyme St., Old Lyme 06371. *Pres.,* Anthony C. Thurston; *Vice Pres. 1st,* Mary Ann Besier; *2nd,* Jeffrey W. Cooley; *Secy.,* Judith A. Lefebvre; *Treas.,* Harold Obstler; *Asst. Treas.,* Marilyn Percy; *Dir.,* Jeffrey W. Andersen; *Curator,* Jack Becker.

MADISON HISTORICAL SOCIETY, INC. Allis-Bushnell House, 853 Post Rd., P.O. Box 17, 06443. Tel., (203) 245-4567. Hours: Summer, 1-4 P.M., Wed., Fri., Sat. Winter, by appointment only. *Pres.,* A. Marion Chard; *Vice Pres./Treas.,* Kay Aurin.

MANCHESTER HISTORICAL SOCIETY, INC. 106 Hartford Rd., 06040. *Pres.,* Milton K. Adams; *Vice Pres.,* David K. Smith; *Cor. Secy.,* Bernice Frattaroli; *Rec. Secy.,* Vilma Kopcha; *Treas.,* Gertrude Sweeney.

MANSFIELD HISTORICAL SOCIETY. P.O. Box 145, Storrs 06268. *Pres.,* Mrs. Jack H. Lamb, Storrs; *Vice Pres.,* Bruce Clouette, Storrs; *Secy.,* Rita Braswell, Mansfield Ctr.; *Treas.,* John Brand, Storrs; *Museum Dir.,* Ann Galonska, Tolland.

THE MARLBOROUGH HISTORICAL SOCIETY. P.O. Box 281, 06447. *Pres.,* Sandra Soucy; *Vice Pres.,* Mary Chojnicki; *Secy.,* Betty Keister; *Treas./Curator,* Douglas H. Secord.

MERIDEN HISTORICAL SOCIETY, INC. P.O. Box 2025, Station A, 06450. *Pres.,* Rita Picciafochi; *Vice Pres.,* Lois Scofield; *Secy.,* Louise Cowing; *Treas.,* Dorothy Daly; *Curator,* Allen Weathers.

MIDDLEBURY HISTORICAL SOCIETY, INC. P.O. Box 104, 06762. *Pres.,* C. Andrew Monagan; *Vice Pres.,* Bradford E. Smith; *Secy.,* David W. Pope; *Treas.,* Colleen West.

MIDDLESEX COUNTY HISTORICAL SOCIETY. General Mansfield House, 151 Main St., Middletown 06457. *Pres.,* Elizabeth Warner; *Vice Pres.,* Deborah Shapiro; *Treas.,* Scott Bishel; *Dir.,* Dione Longley.

THE MILFORD HISTORICAL SOCIETY, INC. P.O. Box 337, Eells-Stow House, 34 High St., 06460. *Pres.,* Meredith Stowe; *Vice Pres. 1st,* Jean Bonyai, *2nd,* Robin O'Grady; *Cor. Secy.,* Marianne Cameron; *Rec. Secy.,* Janet Gray; *Treas.,* Michael Elgee.

MONROE HISTORICAL SOCIETY, INC. *Pres.,* vacancy; *Cor. Secy.,* Peggy Ann Rose, 36 Johnson Pl. 06468; *Rec. Secy.,* Barbara Waite; *Treas.,* Tony Majewski.

MONTVILLE HISTORICAL SOCIETY. P.O. Box 51, 06353-0051. *Pres.,* John F. Geary, Uncasville; *Vice Pres.,* Phyllis Porter; *Rec. Secy.,* Luise Ernest; *Cor. Secy.,* Sharon Land; *Treas.,* Ellen Desjardins; *Custodian of Records,* Helen Aldrich.

MORRIS HISTORICAL SOCIETY. P.O. Box 234, 06763. *Pres.,* Marilyn W. Birkett, Bantam; *Vice Pres. 1st,* Cornelia Downes, Morris, *2nd,* David Paletsky, Morris; *Secy.,* Lee Cook, Morris; *Cor. Secy.,* William A. Nelson, Morris; *Treas.,* Len Rothman, Bantam; *Curator,* Sherrie Woodward, Lakeside; *Historian,* Walter D. France, Bantam.

MYSTIC RIVER HISTORICAL SOCIETY. *Pres.,* Helen Keith, P. O. Box 245, Mystic, 06355; *Vice Pres.,* Susan Lund; *Cor. Secy.,* Willa Schuster; *Rec. Secy.,* Merle Frier; *Treas.,* Judith DuFlocq.

MYSTIC SEAPORT. See Stonington, Mystic Seaport, Inc.

NAUGATUCK HISTORICAL SOCIETY. *Pres.,* Martha Ann Simons; *Vice Pres.,* Bridget Mariano; *Secy.,* Sandra Clark, 164 Johnson St., 06770; *Treas.,* James Simons; *Registrar,* Lucille Russell.

NEW CANAAN HISTORICAL SOCIETY. 13 Oenoke Ridge, 06840. *Pres.,* Raymond D. Lenoue; *Vice Pres.,* Joseph C. Sweet, Mrs. Lawrence F. Tomaselli; *Secy.,* Mrs. Walter Poor; *Treas.,* J. Michael Farrell; *Exec. Dir.,* Janet Lindstrom.

NEW FAIRFIELD HISTORICAL SOCIETY, INC. *Pres.*, Martha Fairchild; *Vice Pres.*, Samuel Penny; *Secy.*, Linda Decker, 15 Titicus Mountain Rd., 06812; *Treas.*, Raymond Williams.

NEW HARTFORD HISTORICAL SOCIETY, INC. P.O. Box 41, 06057. *Pres.*, Robert Tonkin; *Vice Pres.*, Newman A. Hall; *Secy.*, Lisa P. Crowley; *Treas.*, Barbara Goff.

NEW HAVEN COLONY HISTORICAL SOCIETY. 114 Whitney Ave., 06510. *Pres.*, Carleton F. Loucks; *Vice Pres. 1st*, David G. Carter; *2nd*, Gilbert Kenna; *Secy.*, Richard Mazan; *Asst. Secy.*, Nancy Cassella; *Treas.*, Richard Hegel; *Asst. Treas.*, Virginia Hepler; *Exec. Dir.*, Robert Egleston, *Asst.*, Deborah Sanguineti; *Librarian*, James Campbell; *Dir. of Ed.*, Jeff Nicholls; *Curator*, Amy Trout.

(NEW HAVEN) ETHNIC HISTORICAL ARCHIVES CENTER OF NEW HAVEN, INC. P. O. Box 120-294, East Haven 06512, Tel., (203) 468-0426. *Pres.*, Denise Botto; *Vice Pres.*, Barry Herman; *Secy.*, Maureen Delahunt; *Treas.*, Philip Paolella; *Historian*, Neil Hogan; *Exec. Dir.*, Jeanne R. Whalen; *Chm. of Bd.*, Joel Wasserman.

NEWINGTON HISTORICAL SOCIETY AND TRUST, INC. 679 Willard Ave., 06111. *Pres.*, Linda Woods; *Vice Pres.*, Laurel Scialabba; *Secy.*, Angela DiMaio; *Treas.*, Gail Kelly; *Asst. Treas.*, Gary Husmer; *Dir.*, Neil Hogan.

NEW LONDON COUNTY HISTORICAL SOCIETY. Shaw Mansion, 11 Blinman St., 06320. *Pres.*, Ann Peabody; *Secy.*, Virginia Kelly; *Director*, Alice Sheriff.

NEW MILFORD HISTORICAL SOCIETY. Office: P.O. Box 566, 6 Aspetuck Ave., 06776. *Pres.*, Joy Gaiser; *Vice Pres. 1st*, Charles Barlow, *2nd*, Samuel Knowles; *Secy.*, Susan Metcalf; *Treas.*, Mark Malkin; *Curator*, Delores Dunn..

NORFOLK HISTORICAL SOCIETY, INC. P.O. Box 288, 06058-0288. *Pres.*, Richard Byrne; *Vice Pres. 1st*, Eric Anderson; *Vice Pres. 2nd*, Alan Redford; *Secy.*, Mary Welz; *Treas.*, Susan Dyer.

THE NORTH HAVEN HISTORICAL SOCIETY. 27 Broadway, 06473. *Co-Pres.*, Sylvia Garfield, Sharman Tait; *Vice Pres.*, Mary Krinsky; *Secy.*, Arline Tolette; *Treas.*, Elliott Barske; *Membership*, Shirley Barske; *Curator*, Gloria Furnival; *Historian*, Fred Foerster; *Archivist*, Sylvia Garfield.

NORTH STONINGTON HISTORICAL SOCIETY, INC. 1 Wyassup Rd., P.O. Box 134, 06359, Tel: (860) 535-9448. *Pres.*, George A. Jackson; *Vice Pres.*, Lucile Rutty; *Secy.*, Dorothy S. Hazard; *Treas.*, Mary Bishop.

(NORWICH) SOCIETY OF THE FOUNDERS OF NORWICH, CONNECTICUT, INC. P.O. Box 13, 06360, Tel: (860) 889-9440. *Pres.*, Jacqueline J. Kimsey; *Vice Pres.*, Annetta Cannon; *Secy.*, Beryl Fishbone; *Treas.*, David A. Walter.

NORWALK HISTORICAL SOCIETY. P.O. Box 335, 06852. *Pres.*, Dorothy Volo; *Vice Pres.*, Matthew P. Smith; *Secy.*, Gail MacDonald; *Treas.*, Glenn Iannacone.

(NORWALK) ROWAYTON HISTORICAL SOCIETY, INC. *Pres.*, Erik Rambusch; *Vice Pres.*, Mrs. Ed Carlson; *Cor. Secy.*, Mrs. Peter Van Slyck, 3 Witch La.,

Rowayton 06853; *Rec. Secy.,* Mrs. Harold Hubbell; *Treas.,* Thomas Cohn; *Curator,* Mrs. Thomas Cohn; *Publicity,* John Bender.

OLD SAYBROOK HISTORICAL SOCIETY. P.O. Box 4, 06475. *Pres.,* Donald M. Swan; *Vice Pres.,* Ivy N. Butler; *Cor. Secy.,* Lois Platt; *Rec. Secy.,* Joann North; *Treas.,* Louis Stoskopf, Jr.; *Asst. Treas.,* Marge Anderson.

ORANGE HISTORICAL SOCIETY. 605 Orange Center Rd., P.O. Box 784, 06477. *Pres.,* Harry W. Jones; *Vice Pres.,* Gregory J. Mulherin; *Treas.,* Marvin A. Jamron; *Historian,* Charlotte C. Turner; *League Delegate,* Marvin A. Jamron.

PLAINFIELD HISTORICAL SOCIETY, INC. P.O. Box 104, Central Village 06332. *Pres.,* Carl D. Plassmann; *Vice Pres.,* Martha Ridgway; *Secy.,* John Waller; *Treas.,* David Meade.

THE PLAINVILLE HISTORICAL SOCIETY, INC. *Pres.,* Mrs. Robert Hummel; *Vice Pres.,* Mrs. Charles Adams; *Cor. Secy.,* Mrs. Sebastian T. Misenti, 34 Peace Court, 06062; *Rec. Secy.,* Mrs. Gregg Stanley; *Treas.,* Pauline Schwartz.

POMFRET HISTORICAL SOCIETY. P.O. Box 152, Pomfret Ctr., 06259. *Pres.,* Elizabeth L. Cartier; *Vice Pres.,* Susan C. Nowak; *Secy.,* Ann Hennen; *Treas.,* Mary G. Page.

PORTLAND HISTORICAL SOCIETY. Box 98, 06480. *Pres.,* Christine Sullivan; *Vice Pres.,* Charles Johnson; *Secy.,* Ruth Freeburg; *Treas.,* Charles Woltmann; *Dirs.,* Walter Dower, Regina Woltmann, Donald Kelsey.

PRESTON HISTORICAL SOCIETY. *Pres.,* Peter Leibert; *Vice Pres.,* Liv Goldkopf; *Secy.,* Gail Rodgers; *Treas.,* David Oat, 142 River Rd., 06365.

THE PROSPECT HISTORICAL SOCIETY, INC. *Pres.,* Jane Fowler; *Vice Pres.,* Florine Wheeler; *Secy./Curator,* Richard Caouette, 15 Cornwall Ave., 06712; *Treas.,* Hazel Caouette.

(PUTNAM) ASPINOCK HISTORICAL SOCIETY OF PUTNAM, INC. P.O. Box 465, 06260. *Pres.,* Robert Chicoine; *Vice Pres.,* Gerald St. Jean; *Secy.,* Joseph Peterson; *Treas.,* Aline Blanchette; *Archivist,* Fabiola Cutler; *Dirs.,* Ruth Flagg, Ethel Hayden, Pat Hedenberg, Joe Peterson.

REDDING HISTORICAL SOCIETY, INC. P.O. Box 1023, 06875. *Pres.,* Judy Wylie; *Vice Pres.1st,* Pamela Reese, *2nd,* Martha Johnson; *Secy.,* Anda Cummings; *Treas.,* Virginia Gilligan.

RIDGEFIELD LIBRARY AND HISTORICAL ASSOC., INC. 472 Main St., 06877. *Pres.,* Morton Bailey; *Vice Pres.1st,* Barbara Dobbin; *2nd,* Joyce Ligi; *Rec. Secy.,* Ann Huntoon; *Cor. Secy.,* Charles Spire; *Treas.,* Sabina Slavin.

ROCKY HILL HISTORICAL SOCIETY, INC. P.O. Box 185, 06067. *Pres.,* Robert O. Hodges; *Vice Pres.,* Sandra Brown; *Secy.,* Lois P. Hooper; *Treas.,* Henry Neff; *Curator,* Amita Watson.

ROXBURY HISTORICAL SOCIETY. P.O. Box 212, 06783. *Pres.,* Robert Hodges; *Secy.,* Lois P. Hodges; *Treas.,* Henry Neff.

SALEM HISTORICAL SOCIETY., INC. *Pres.,* Jon A. Jennings, 109 Music Vale Rd., 06420; *Vice Pres.,* Paul Beucler; *Secy./Treas.,* Rosemary Beucler; *Curator,* Deanna St. Jean.

SCOTLAND HISTORICAL SOCIETY. *Pres.,* Frank Bird, P.O. Box 4, 06264; *Vice Pres.,* Henry Bowers; *Secy.,* Leslie Newman; *Treas.,* Susan Leete; *Dirs.,* Mathew Buonomano, William Newman, Georgia Stauffer.

SEYMOUR HISTORICAL SOCIETY, INC. *Pres.,* David N. Kummer, 69 Church St., 06483; *Vice Pres.,* Raymond Johnson; *Cor. Secy.,* Joan Weed; *Rec. Secy.,* Harriette Martin; *Treas.,* Paul Filipowich.

SHARON HISTORICAL SOCIETY. Box 511, 06069. *Pres.,* Francoise A. Kelz; *Vice Pres.,* Jano B. Fairservis; *Secy.,* Judy Loucks; *Treas.,* Clarence L. Roberts, Jr.; *Exec. Dir.,* Elizabeth Shapiro.

SIMSBURY HISTORICAL SOCIETY. Massacoh Plantation, 800 Hopmeadow St., 06070. *Pres.,* Evan W. Woollacott; *Vice Pres. 1st,* Richard Ostop, *2nd,* Marilyn Shull; *Secy.,* Priscilla G. Bergethon; *Treas.,* Gail Stempien; *Managing Dir.,* Lois W. Calvert.

SOUTHBURY HISTORICAL SOCIETY. P.O. Box 124, 06488-0124. Tel., (203) 264-8825. *Pres.,* Kevin T. Bennett; *Vice Pres.,* Edmund Schade; *Cor. Secy.,* vacancy; *Rec. Secy.,* Dorothy Manville; *Treas.,* Brian M. Jones; *Curator,* Arlene Mitchell.

SOUTHINGTON HISTORICAL SOCIETY, INC. 239 Main St., 06489. *Pres.,* Joseph Faust; *Secy.,* Betty Sullivan; *Treas.,* Bob Niebling.

SOUTH WINDSOR HISTORICAL SOCIETY, INC. *Pres.,* Linda Sunderland; *Vice Pres.,* Patrick Jones; *Cor. Secy.,* Gloria Watson, Quarry Brook Rd., 06074; *Rec. Secy.,* Mary Ann Cole; *Treas.,* Floyd Baranello.

STAFFORD HISTORICAL SOCIETY. P.O. Box 56, 06075. Museum: Haymarket Sq., Stafford Springs 06076. *Pres.,* David Bartlett, Stafford Springs; *Vice Pres.,* Duane A. Beffa-Negrini, Staffordville; *Cor. Secy.,* Esther DaRos; *Rec. Secy.,* Barbara Nevins, Stafford Springs; *Treas.,* Edward Festi, Stafford Springs; *Asst. Treas.,* Lucy Hatch; *Curator,* Isabell Zabilansky, Stafford Springs; *Historian,* Selah Sanger, Staffordville.

THE STAMFORD HISTORICAL SOCIETY, INC. 1508 High Ridge Rd., 06903. *Pres.,* Stephen L. Bishop; *Vice Pres. 1st,* Lois Pont-Briant, *2nd,* Joseph R. Mygatt; *Cor. Secy.,* Josephine Fulcher-Anderson; *Rec. Secy.,* Leola Cheney-Rosati; *Treas.,* Robert A. Langenhan.

STONINGTON HISTORICAL SOCIETY. P.O. Box 103, 06378. Tel., (860) 535-1131. *Pres.,* Michael Davis; *Vice Pres.,* Mrs. David L. Motherway; *Secy.,* Mrs. William L. Breed; *Treas.,* John Hinshaw.

STONINGTON INDIAN AND COLONIAL RESEARCH CENTER, INC. Indian & Colonial Research Ctr., Inc., P.O. Box 525, Old Mystic 06372. *Pres.,* Mrs. Joan Cohn, Old Mystic; *Acting Vice Pres.,* Capt. Stephen B. Lee, Noank; *Cor. Secy.,* Mrs. George Jackson, North Stonington; *Rec. Secy.,* Carol Becker, Stonington; *Treas.,* Barbara Hood, Old Mystic.

(STONINGTON) MYSTIC SEAPORT MUSEUM, INC. Mystic Seaport, Greenmanville Ave., Rte. 27, Mystic 06355. *Chm. of Bd.,* William E. Cook; *Pres.,* J. Revell Carr; *Vice Chm.,* W. Frank Bohlen, William C. Ridgway III, Alexandra Thorne; *Secy.,* Joseph C. Hoopes, Jr.; *Asst. Secy.,* Maureen Hennessey; *Treas.,* Richard Vietor; *Asst. Treas.,* Jacqueline Zeppieri.

THE STRATFORD HISTORICAL SOCIETY. Office: The Captain David Judson House and the Catharine B. Mitchell Museum, 967 Academy Hill, P.O. Box 382, 06497. Tel.,(203) 378-0630. Open early May thru October, Wed., Sat., and Sun., 11 A.M.-4 P.M. (other days by appointment). Admission charged. *Pres.,* Louis Petriel; *Vice Pres. 1st,* John Calhoon, *2nd,* Lewis Knapp; *Secy.,* Katherine Moore; *Treas.,* Donald Calkins.

SUFFIELD HISTORICAL SOCIETY. King House Museum, 232 South Main St., 06078. Mailing Address: P.O. Box 893, 06078. *Pres.,* Donald N. Rollet; *Vice Pres.,* Edward Chase III; *Secy., Hazel Phillips; Curator,* Lester Smith; *Treas.,* David Johnson; *Historian,* Hawley Rising.

THOMASTON HISTORICAL SOCIETY, INC. *Pres.,* Myron Roman; *Vice Pres.,* Frederick L. Hellerich; *Secy.,* Caroline R. Osowiecki, 350 Walnut Hill Rd., 06787-1132; *Treas.,* Barbara Kane.

THOMPSON HISTORICAL SOCIETY, INC. *Pres.,* Jane Vercelli, Thompson; *Vice Pres.,* Susan Vincent, Thompson; *Secy.,* Mary Anthony, P. O. Box 47, 06277. *Treas.,* Jeffrey Barske, Thompson.

TOLLAND HISTORICAL SOCIETY. *Pres.,* Stewart R. Joslin, 38 Corinne Dr., 06084; *Vice Pres.,* Richard Bozzone; *Secy.,* Joan Kerkin; *Treas.,* Stanley Szemreylo.

THE TORRINGTON HISTORICAL SOCIETY, INC. Hotchkiss-Fyler House, 192 Main St., 06790. *Pres.,* Joseph E. Cravanzola; *Exec. Vice Pres.,* David Bennett; *Sr. Vice Pres.,* Walter G. Gisselbrecht; *Vice Pres.,* Thomas F. Wall; *Secy.,* Lucia T. Fritz; *Treas.,* Richard Kittredge; *Exec. Dir.,* Mark McEachern; *Curator,* Gail Kruppa.

THE TOTOKET HISTORICAL SOCIETY, INC. P.O. Box 563, 1605 Foxon Rd., North Branford 06471. *Pres.,* Mrs. Donald F. Marx, Northford; *Vice Pres.,* Eugene MacMullen, *Secy.,* Janet S. Gregan; *Treas.,* Donald Guyer.

THE TRUMBULL HISTORICAL SOCIETY. 1856 Huntington Tpke., 06611. Tel., (203) 377-6620. Pres., John Packer; *Secy.,* Christina L. Pereiro; *Treas.,* Nancy Seltenreich.

UNION HISTORICAL SOCIETY, INC. *Pres.,* Jeannine M. Upson; *Vice Pres.,* Carol A. Mancini; *Secy.,* Lee Ann Fitzgerald, 1163 Buckley Hwy., 06076; *Treas.,* Betty J. Bragdon.

VERNON HISTORICAL SOCIETY. Tel., (860) 875-4326. *Pres.,* Carolyn Blouin; *Vice Pres.,* Richard Steele; *Cor. Secy.,* Carol Nelson, P.O. Box 2055, 06066; *Rec. Secy.,* Tara Ashe; *Treas.,* James Ashe; *Museum Dir.,* S. Ardis Abbott.

THE VOLUNTOWN HISTORICAL SOCIETY, INC. P.O. Box 130, 06384. *Pres.,* John Hargraves; *Vice Pres.,* vacancy; *Secy.,* Patricia Thevenet; *Treas.,* Marge Jabs; *Library/Museum Curator,* Kathy Wesa.

THE WALLINGFORD HISTORICAL SOCIETY, INC. Samuel Parsons House, P.O. Box 73, 180 So. Main St., 06492. *Pres.,* Robert N. Beaumont; *Cor. Secy.,* Doris Hall; *Rec. Secy.,* Patricia A. Chappell; *Treas.,* Noma G. Beaumont.

(WASHINGTON) THE GUNN MEMORIAL MUSEUM. Washington 06793. *Pres.,* Gretchen Farmer; *Treas.,* Barbara Braverman; *Dir./Curator,* Sarah Griswold; *Asst. Curator,* Alison G. Picton.

(WATERBURY) THE MATTATUCK HISTORICAL SOCIETY. 144 West Main St., 06702. *Pres.,* Sharon Drubner; *Cor. Secy.,* Andrew J. Pape; *Treas.,* Paul A. Gimbel.

WATERFORD HISTORICAL SOCIETY, INC. Office: P.O. Box 117, 06385-0177; *Pres.,* Laura P. Fitch; *Vice Pres. 1st,* J. Morgan Miner, Jr., *2nd,* Dorothy M. Reed; *Cor. Secy.,* Anne S. Carpino; *Rec. Secy.,* Emily C. Schacht; *Treas.,* Lawrence H. Strickland; *Asst. Treas.,* Herbert T. Schacht.

WATERTOWN HISTORICAL SOCIETY. *Pres.,* Ruth K. Getsinger; *Vice Pres.,* Hobart Van Deusen; *Secy.,* Mary L. Messenger; *Treas.,* Jeffrey S. Grenier; *Curator,* Florence T. Crowell, 22 DeForest St., 06795.

WESTBROOK HISTORICAL SOCIETY, INC. P.O. Box 148, 06498. *Pres.,* Sally H. Correll; *Vice Pres.,* Jane Hall; *Cor. Secy.,* Cathy Olsen, 772 Horse Hill Rd., 06498; *Rec. Secy.,* Cynthia Lord; *Treas.,* Virginia Spencer; *Curator,* Sue Pratt; *Historian,* Michael Wells.

(WEST HARTFORD) NOAH WEBSTER HOUSE/MUSEUM OF WEST HARTFORD HISTORY. 227 So. Main St., 06107. *Pres.,* John Davison; *Vice Pres.,* John Lemega, Tracey Wilson; *Treas.,* David Pruyne; *Secy.,* John O. Morris. (Operates and maintains birthplace of Noah Webster; participatory early American life and culture programs; exhibit gallery with changing exhibits on historical themes; preservation and conservation of archival collections including records, documents, books, early Webster works, and artifacts, and West Hartford history.)

WEST HAVEN HISTORICAL SOCIETY, INC. *Pres./Curator,* Mrs. Edward North; *Vice Pres.,* William Barr; *Cor. Secy.,* Betty Roy, 682 Main St., 06516; *Rec. Secy.,* Mrs. Eugene Mayer; *Treas.,* Alice Butler, New Haven.

WESTON HISTORICAL SOCIETY, INC. P.O. Box 1092, 06883. *Pres.,* Roger Core; *Vice Pres.,* Joseph Spetly; *Secy.,* Louis Bregy; *Treas.,* David Bushley.

THE WESTPORT HISTORICAL SOCIETY, INC. 25 Avery Pl., 06880. *Pres.,* Pete Wolgast; *Co-Vice Pres.,* Roy Dickinson, John Fifield, Elliott Netherton, Ann Sheffer; *Secy.,* Katherine Huber; *Treas.,* William F. Balch; *Exec. Dir.,* Sheila C. O'Neill.

THE WETHERSFIELD HISTORICAL SOCIETY. 150 Main St., 06109. *Pres.* Patricia Allen; *Vice Pres.,* Richard Standish; *Secy.,* M. Peter Barry; *Treas.,* Frank Falvo; *Dir.,* Brenda Milkofsky.

WILLINGTON HISTORICAL SOCIETY. *Pres.,* Carl Dal Bon, 334 Village Hill Rd., 06279.

WILTON HISTORICAL SOCIETY, INC. Wilton Heritage Museum, 249 Danbury Rd., 06897. Museum Hours: 10 A.M.-4:30 P.M., Tues., Wed., Thurs.; Sun. (Special Events). Tel., (203) 762-7257. *Chm. of Bd./Pres.,* Peter K. Warren; *Treas.,* Therese Goodwin; *Dir.,* Marilyn C. Gould.

WINCHESTER HISTORICAL SOCIETY. 225 Prospect St., Winsted 06098. *Pres.,* William Weber; *Vice Pres.,* Pauline Francher; *Secy.,* Janice Roy; *Treas.,* Milly Hudak; *Curator,* June Senack.

WINDHAM HISTORICAL SOCIETY. P.O. Box 105, Willimantic 06226. *Pres.,* Gordon MacDonald; *Vice Pres.,* Gertrude Bancroft; *Rec. Secy.,* Paula Gladue; *Treas.,* Beverly Haddad.

WINDSOR HISTORICAL SOCIETY, INC. Office: 96 Palisado Ave., 06095. *Pres.,* Marillyn Loomis; *Secy.,* Connie Whigham; *Treas.,* Sterling Viets; *Dir.,* Robert T. Silliman.

WINDSOR LOCKS HISTORICAL SOCIETY, INC. Hdqrs.: Noden-Reed Park, 58 West St., 06096. Open May through October, Wed. and Sun., 1-5 P.M., also by appointment. Tel., (860) 627-9212 or (860) 623-4143. *Pres.,* Joseph Bonito; *Vice Pres.,* Edward Lanati; *Secy.,* Sally Pascale; *Membership Secy.,* Scott Kernberg; *Treas.,* Lewis Pultz; *Curator,* Mickey Danyluk; *Assoc. Curator,* Ruth Bonito.

(WOODBRIDGE) AMITY AND WOODBRIDGE HISTORICAL SOCIETY, INC. c/o Thomas Darling House, 1907 Litchfield Tpke., 06525. *Pres.,* Donald Menzies; *Vice Pres.,* Wilson Kimnach; *Cor. Secy.,* Eleanor Jones; *Rec. Secy.,* Elaine Allen; *Treas.,* Stuart M. Peck, Jr.

WOODSTOCK HISTORICAL SOCIETY.—P.O. Box 65, 06281. *Pres.,* Dawn Castiglia; *Vice Pres.,* Cristine Waldrond; *Cor. Secy.,* Lucy Davis; *Rec. Secy.,* Beverly Stehlik; *Treas.,* Nancy M. Gale.

MUSEUMS

BERLIN. *New Britain Youth Museum at Hungerford Park,* 191 Farmington Ave., Kensington 06037. Tel., (860) 827-9064. Farm and exotic animals, exhibits, hands-on tractor, wild flower walk, picnicking, trails, pond, xeriscaped gardens and changing exhibitions. Hours: 1-5 P.M., Tues.-Fri.; 10 A.M.-5 P.M, Sat. Summer Hours: 11 A.M.-5 P.M, Tues.-Fri.; 10 A.M.-5 P.M., Sat. Seasonal special events, free animal programs, 11 A.M., 1:30 P.M., 3 P.M., Sat.; 2 P.M. summer weekdays. Admission, $2 adults; $1.50 senior citizens; $1 students, children under 2 and members free.

BRIDGEPORT. *Housatonic Museum of Art,* Housatonic Community-Technical College, 900 Lafayette Blvd., 06604-4704. Founded in 1967, the diverse Permanent Collection, strong in contemporary art, is exhibited throughout the college. Significant growing areas include the work of Connecticut and Latin American artists. The Museum schedules 6 changing exhibitions per year, which may initiate from the Permanent Collection, show the work of established or emerging artists, or feature traveling exhibitions. An academic resource, the Museum and Galleries are open to the public without charge with free parking. Closed major holidays, and college vacations. Info. Tel., (203) 332-5205; FAX, (203) 332-5123. *Dir.,* Jeanne A. DuBois.

BRIDGEPORT. *The Discovery Museum,* 4450 Park Ave., 06604. (Art Galleries, Science Galleries, Planetarium Shows, Challenger Learning Center for Space Education, and over 100 permanent hands-on art and physical science exhibits for schools, other groups and the general public.) *Pres.,* Elena de Murias. Admission for all activities, $6 adults; $4 children, senior citizens, and students with ID cards; members free. Regular weekend activities include planetarium show, science show, Challenger minimissions. Full Challenger missions by reservation. Planetarium show presented 1 and 3:30 P.M., weekdays; 2 P.M., July, Aug.; 1 P.M., 3: P.M., weekends. Museum hours: 12 Noon-5 P.M., Sun.; 10 A.M.-5 P.M. Tues.-Sat. Tel., (203) 372-3521.

BRIDGEPORT. *The Barnum Museum,* 820 Main St., 06604. (Circus memorabilia; Mementoes of P. T. Barnum, Tom Thumb and Jenny Lind. Period rooms and collectibles interpret Bridgeport's architectural and industrial history. Lively changing exhibits.) Open year round 10 A.M.-4:30 P.M., Tues.-Sat.; Noon-4:30 P.M., Sun. Open Mondays, 11 A.M.-4:30 P.M., July and August. Admission, $5 adults; $4 senior citizens, and students; $3 children 4-18; Bridgeport senior citizens, children under 4 and members free. Group rates available with advance registration.

BRISTOL. *The American Clock and Watch Museum, Inc.,* 100 Maple St., 06010. *Pres.,* Snowden Taylor; *Treas.,* Carlos E. Mason; *Exec. Dir.,* Nancy D. Connelly.

CANTON. *Roaring Brook Nature Center* (An affiliate of the Science Center of Connecticut) 70 Gracey Rd., 06019. A unique interpretive building features exhibits, dioramas, live animals. Store with books and nature-related items. Over five miles of trails through adjoining 100 acre Werner's Woods. It contains woods, swamp, streams, ponds and fields for the observation of wildlife and of interrelationships within the natural community. Programming throughout the year for school groups, after-school classes for children and adults, evening and weekend activities and summer programs during July and Aug. Open 10 A.M.-5 P.M., Tues.-Sat.; 1-5 P.M., Sun.; 10 A.M.-5

P.M., Mon., July-Aug. Admission, $2 adults, $1 children under 12, and senior citizens; free admission and benefits for members. Membership info. Tel., (860) 693-0263.

COLCHESTER. *Thames Science Center,* c/o Dir., Public Programs, 184 Old Hebron Rd., Colchester. Science and Technology Museum, Newport, RI Public Programs in Connecticut focus on Thames River Basin. Temporary exhibits, school programs, curriculum development. Teacher training and children workshops. Activities encompass the biological, physical environmental and applied sciences, including navigation, robotics and computer science. Museum Science Store. *Dir., Public Programs,* Marjory O'Toole. Located at 77 Long Wharf, Newport, RI. Info Tel., 1-800-587-2872.

DANBURY. *Danbury Scott-Fanton Museum and Historical Society,* 43 Main St., 06810. (History Museum, Historic Buildings, Reference Library, Exhibition Hall.) Museum and Library open 2-5 P.M. Wed.-Sun.; closed Mondays and Federal holidays. Office hours: 10 A.M.—5 P.M., Tues.-Fri. The Charles Ives Birthplace, 5 Mountainville Ave., open by appointment. Tel., (203) 743-5200.

EAST GRANBY. *Old New-Gate Prison and Copper Mine,* Newgate Rd., 06026. State owned museum operated by the Connecticut Historical Commission. First American chartered copper mine opened in 1707, requisitioned by General Washington for Tory prisoners of war during the Revolutionary War, later used as a state prison until abandoned in 1827. A National Historic Landmark. Open from mid-May to Oct. 31, 10 A.M.-4:30 P.M., Wed.-Sun. Admission, $3 adults; $1.50 children, and senior citizens. For group rates, appointments and further info., Tel., (860) 566-3005, 653-3563.

EAST HAVEN. *Shoreline Trolley Museum,* 17 River St., 06512. Transportation Museum, Street Railway and Rapid Transit Cars in operation and on display, rides and guided tours, educational programs for children and adults, special events, artifact display at visitor's center, library and research materials available. The Museum is enrolled on the National Register of Historic Places by the United States Department of The Interior. Special features included, world's first electric freight locomotive, world's oldest rapid transit car, and a rare operational trolley parlour car. Open daily, Memorial Day-Labor Day; weekends, May, Sept., Oct. and 4 weekends after Thanksgiving; Sundays, April, Nov. All hours: 11 A.M.-5 P.M. Tel., (203) 467-6927; 467-7635 (group sales).

EAST WINDSOR. *Connecticut Trolley Museum,* P.O. Box 360, 58 North Rd., Rte. 140, I-91 Exit 45, 06088-0360. Transportation Museum. Visitors ride 3.5 miles round trip on antique trolley cars through scenic Conn. countryside. More than 50 trolley cars vintage 1894 to 1949. Carbarn tour. Special events held throughout the year. Group tour reservations welcome. Restrooms, snack bar, visitors center. For further info. and group tour rates, Tel., (860) 627-6540.

FARMINGTON. *Hill-Stead Museum,* 35 Mountain Rd., 06032. Designated a National Historic Landmark in 1991 and is an outstanding example of Colonial Revival domestic architecture set on 152 aces of fields and woodlands. The Museum houses outstanding works by Monet, Degas, Cassatt and Whistler, which are shown with the furnishings and decorative arts as they were when the Pope and Riddle families were in residence. The main house is complimented by a Sunken Garden with period plantings restored after the original Beatrix Farrand design. The Museum is open Tuesday through Sunday for house tours; 10 A.M.-5 P.M., May through Oct.; 11 A.M.-4 P.M., Nov. through April. For more information or a calendar of events, call (860) 677-4787.

FARMINGTON. *The Stanley-Whitman House,* 37 High St., 06032. Tel., (860) 677-9222. Early New England Framed house built by John Stanley in 1720, opened as a museum in 1935, and named a National Historic Landmark in 1961. Features period furnishings and guided tours to represent the lives of Farmington families in the 18th century. The grounds reflect the utilitarian uses of a colonial dooryard with its culinary, medicinal and herbal plantings. Open May-Oct., 12 Noon-4 P.M., Wed.-Sun.; Nov.-April, 12 Noon-4 P.M., Sundays and by appointment. Closed major holidays. Group tours by appointment. Admission charged.

GREENWICH. *National Audubon Society,* 613 Riversville Rd., 06831. Tel., (203) 869-5272. Nature Center, Interpretive Building, Environmental Bookshop, Sanctuary. 485 acres, including Audubon Fairchild Garden within one mile's distance from Center; open trails for guided or unguided walks. Open 9 A.M.-5 P.M., Tues.-Sun. Closed Mondays and holiday weekends. Admission, $3 adults; $1.50 children, and senior citizens; National Audubon Society members free.

GREENWICH. *The Bruce Museum,* 1 Museum Dr., 06830 (Exit 3 of I-95). Tel., (203) 869-0376. Fully renovated and expanded museum of fine and decorative arts, ethnology, and environmental history. Changing exhibits in the arts and natural science galleries offer related programs for all ages. Environmental History Galleries include minerals, formation of Long Island Sound, a woodland diorama, and a marine center that features animals of Long Island Sound. Educational programs at the Museum and extension programs into area schools. Hours: 10 A.M.-5 P.M., Tues.-Sat.; 1-5 P.M., Sun; closed Monday. Admission, $3.50 adults; $2.50 senior citizens and children 5-12, children under 5 free; free admission for all on Tuesdays; Museum members free at all times. Museum Shop open during museum hours. Free parking on grounds.

GUILFORD. *Henry Whitfield State Museum (Old Stone House),* 248 Old Whitfield St., P.O. Box 210, 06437. State owned museum operated by the Connecticut Historical Commission. The oldest house in Connecticut and the oldest existing stone dwelling in New England (1639), featuring rare 17th to 19th century antiques and exhibits. Open to the public year-round; 10 A.M.-4:30 P.M., Feb. 1st-Dec. 14th, Wed. to Sun.; Dec. 15th to Jan. 31st, by appointment. Admission, $3 adults; $1.50 senior citizens, and children 6-18. For group rates, appointments and further info., Tel./FAX, (203) 453-2457 or (860) 566-3005.

HARTFORD. *Austin Arts Center, J. L. Goodwin Theater, Garmany Hall, Widener Gallery,* Trinity College, 300 Summit St., 06106-3100. Performing and Visual Arts.

HARTFORD. *Connecticut Historical Society,* Library, Museum, and Publications, 1 Elizabeth St., 06105. Eight modern museum galleries feature permanent exhibitions highlighting Connecticut's heritage from the colonial era through the early nineteenth century and changing temporary displays that examine topics ranging from the legend of the Charter Oak to historic fashion to the immigrant experience. The library contains 100,000 volumes and three million manuscripts, including an outstanding collection on New England genealogy. A broad selection of programs, lectures, classes, workshops, and bus tours is offered. The Society publishes a variety of materials, including a scholarly *Bulletin,* a news letter, and occasional books. Book Shop. Special arrangements should be made for guided adult or school group tours of the museum and/or library by advance reservation. Library open: 9 A.M.-4:45 P.M., Tues.-Sat.; summer hours, 9 A.M.-4:45 P.M. Tues.-Fri. Museum open 12 Noon-4:45 P.M., Tues.-Sun.; summer hours, 12 Noon-4:45 P.M., Tues.-Fri., Sun. Admission to the museum and library is free to Conn. Historical Society members, children under 18, and students with I.D. A combined fee of $3 entitles non-members to a one-day admission to the Museum and/or Library. Admission to the museum is free to the public the first Sunday of each month. Library and Museum are closed on Mondays year-round except for tours scheduled in advance, and on major holidays. Tel., (860) 236-5621.

HARTFORD. *The Mark Twain House,* 351 Farmington Ave., 06105-4498. Open daily to the public year round: 9:30 A.M.-5 P.M., Mon., Wed.-Sat.; 12 Noon-5 P.M., Sun. Open daily, 9:30 A.M.-5 P.M., Memorial Day-Columbus Day and Dec.; closed major holidays. Tel., (860) 247-0998.

HARTFORD. *Museum of Connecticut History,* 231 Capitol Ave., 06106. (State owned museum operated by the Connecticut State Library.) Memorial Hall features the official collection of Connecticut governors portraits, the "Fundamental Orders" of 1638-9 (which made Connecticut the "Constitution State"), the Royal Charter of 1662, and the State Constitutions of 1818 and 1965. The exhibit "Liberties and Legends" highlights the enduring legacy of the Charter Oak. The world famous Colt Firearms Collection is on permanent display; other exhibits explore various aspects of Connecticut's long political, industrial and military heritage. Open to the public free of charge, 9:30 A.M.-4 P.M., Mon.-Fri.; closed weekends and state holidays. Tel., (860) 566-3056.

HARTFORD. *The Old State House,* 800 Main St., 06103. Registered as a National Historic Landmark, it is the oldest state house in the nation. On the site of Old State House Square, Thomas Hooker preached a sermon that resulted in The Fundamental Orders, the first constitution to form a government in the New World [thus the phrase "Constitution State" on our automobile licenses.] Here Washington first met Rochambeau, Commander-in-Chief of the French Armies in America. Built in 1796, and designed by Charles Bulfinch, the Old State House features restored historic chambers, special exhibitions, statewide visitors information center, museum shop and, in warm weather outdoor concerts, farm markets and festivals on the large lawn. Also offered is the daily Yankee Doodle Cannon Salute, fired by guards in Continental Uniform at 10 A.M., 4 P.M., Mon.-Fri.; 11 A.M, 4 P.M., Sat. Open to the public free of charge, year-round, 10 A.M.-4 P.M., Mon.-Fri.; 11 A.M.-5 P.M., Sat. Under the direction of the Old State House Association. Tel., (860) 522-6766.

HARTFORD. *Wadsworth Atheneum,* 600 Main St., 06103. America's oldest continuously operating public art museum with over 45,000 works of art including paintings, sculpture, furniture, porcelain, silver, costumes, textiles, temporary exhibitions, MATRIX Gallery of contemporary art, and Amistad Foundation Collection of African-American art. Open year round, 11 A.M.-5 P.M., Tues.-Sun. Office hours: *9 A.M.-5 P.M., Mon.-Fri. Museum open 11 A.M.-5 P.M., Tues.-Sun.; closed Mon. and most major holidays. Gallery Tours: Weds.-Fri., noon; Sat., Sun., 2:30 P.M. Special exhibition tours, Sat. & Sun., 1 P.M. No extra charge. Group tours by appointment. Lectures and other educational programs on collections and special exhibitions available. General admission, $6 adults; $4 students with ID, and senior citizens. $3 youths age 6-17. Free to members, children under 6. Free to individuals all day 11 A.M.-5 P.M., Thurs.; before 12 Noon, Sat. Museum Cafe: 11:30 A.M.-2:30 P.M., Tues.-Fri.; 12 Noon-3 P.M., Sat.; 11:30 A.M.-2:30 P.M., Sun. Museum Shop: 11 A.M.-4:30 P.M., Tues.-Sun. Tel., (860) 278-2670.

*Note: Museum is open Monday for office hours only.

KENT. *The Sloane Stanley Museum and Kent Furnace,* Rte. 7, 06757. State owned museum operated by the Conn. Historical Commission. A collection of Early American tools and implements; re-created studio of artist-writer Eric Sloane. Open: mid May-Oct., 10 A.M.-4 P.M., Wed.-Sun. Admission, $3 adults; $1.50 children, and senior citizens. Group rates available with reservations for ten or more people. For group appointments and further info., Tel., (860) 566-3005 or (860) 927-3849.

LITCHFIELD. *White Memorial Conservation Center,* P.O. Box 368, 80 Whitehall Rd., 06759; located on the grounds of the 4,000 acre White Memorial Foundation Wildlife Sanctuary. Natural history exhibits, gift shop, and educational activities. Trails for hiking, cross-country skiing, horseback riding, including a self-guiding nature trail and unique nature trail of the senses. Fishing, swimming, boating and camping also available. Grounds open all year everyday. Admission to grounds free. Museum membership open to public. For non-membership Museum entrance contribution, hours and program info. call (860) 567-0857.

MANCHESTER. *Lutz Children's Museum,* 247 So. Main St., 06040. Open to public 2-5 P.M., Tues., Wed.; 9:30 A.M.-5 P.M., Thurs.; 9:30 A.M.-5 P.M., Fri; 12 Noon-5 P.M., Sat., Sun.; closed Mondays and holidays. Live animals, participatory and traditional exhibits. Group Tours by appointment in A.M. Programs, classes, happenings and nearby 53 acre Oak Grove Nature Center. Tel., (860) 643-0949.

MIDDLETOWN. *Wesleyan University,* Davison Art Center, 301 High St., 06459. Open: Sept.-early June, 12 Noon-4 P.M., Tues.-Fri.; 2-5 P.M., Sat., Sun.; Closed holidays and during academic vacations.

MYSTIC. *Mystic Marinelife Aquarium,* 55 Coogan Blvd., 06355-1997, (Exit 90, off I-95.) Open 7 days year-round, except Thanksgiving, Christmas, New Year's Day and the last week of Jan. 35 living exhibits of dolphins, whales, seals, penguins, fishes, and invertebrates, including the Northeast's largest collection of marine mammals. Daily demonstrations of whale and dolphin behavior in a climate-controlled, 1,200-seat auditorium. Discounts for school and youth groups. Numerous educational programs available. General info., (860) 572-5955. Group reservations and Education Dept., (860) 572-5955, Ext. 215.

MYSTIC. *Mystic Seaport,* Greenmanville Ave., 06355. Maritime Museum, Planetarium, Ships and Boats, exhibits, courses and special programs emphasis on Stories of America and the Sea, Library, Henry B. duPont Preservation Shipyard. Operated by Mystic Seaport Museum, Inc.

NEW BRITAIN. *New Britain Youth Museum,* 30 High St., 06051. Exhibits of Americana, dolls, circus miniatures, Native American artifacts, and changing exhibits of cultural and historic interest. Some exhibits lend themselves to participation. Hours: 1-5 P.M., Tues.-Fri.; 10 A.M.-4 P.M, Sat.; Summer hours: Mon.-Fri., 1-5 P.M.; closed Sat., July and August. Donation requested. Tel., (860) 225-3020.

NEW BRITAIN. *New Britain Museum of American Art,* 56 Lexington St., 06052. Tel., (860) 229-0257; FAX, (860)-229-3445. Closed major holidays. Admission: Adults-$3; Senior citizens and students-$2; Museum members and children under 12 are free. Free admission on Saturdays, 10 A.M.-12 Noon. Handicapped accessible. Hours: 1-5 P.M., Tues.-Fri.; 10 A.M.-5 P.M., Sat.; Noon-5 P.M., Sun. *Dir.,* Laurene Buckley; *Dir. of Admin.,* Mel Ellis; *Collections Mgr.,* Renee T. Williams; *Development Coordinator,* Claudia Thesing; *Education Coordinator,* Bonnie C. Garmisa.

NEW CANAAN. *New Canaan Nature Center,* 144 Oenoke Ridge, 06840. Tel., (203) 966-9577. Natural Science and Horticulture Education. *Exec. Dir.,* Anne H. Harper; *Naturalist,* Frank Gallo; *Early Childhood Programs,* Eve Ameer; *School Programs/Summer Nature Camp,* Cristen Nichols; Nature trails, exhibits, solar greenhouse, education programs, gardens, arboretum, nursery school, summer camp, maple syrup and apple cider making in season. Hours: 9 A.M.-4 P.M., Tues.-Sat.; 12 Noon-4 P.M., Sun.

NEW HAVEN. *Peabody Museum of Natural History,* Yale University, P.O. Box 208118, 170 Whitney Ave., 06520-8118. Natural History Museum. Tel., (203) 432-5050. *Public Relations,* Marge Kuhlmann.

NEW HAVEN. *Yale University Art Gallery,* 1111 Chapel St., 06520. Open to the public year round, except Aug.: Free admission 10 A.M.-5 P.M., Tues.-Sat.; 2-5 P.M., Sun.; closed Mondays and major holidays. Information on exhibitions and programs, Tel., (203) 432-0600.

NEW LONDON. *Connecticut College Arboretum,* Williams St., Connecticut College, 06320. Privately owned and open to the public. 435 acres with extensive native tree and shrub collections, wildflower gardens, native azalea garden, naturalistic landscape demonstration areas, two large natural areas for ecological research. Trail system throughout. Open daily dawn to dusk, free to public. Herbarium of New England flora in Botany Dept., New London Hall. Tel. (860) 439-5020.

NEW LONDON. *Lyman Allyn Art Museum,* 625 Williams St., 06320. Permanent and changing exhibits of American, European, and Non-Western art. Hours: 10 A.M.-5 P.M., Tues., Thurs.- Sat., 10 A.M.-9 P.M., Wed., 1-5 P.M., Sun.; closed Mon. and major holidays. Admission, $3; $2 students and seniors; children under 12 free. Facilities for the handicapped available.

Deshon-Allyn House, 613 Williams St. Mailing address, c/o Lyman Allyn Art Museum. 1830 Period House is on the National Historic Register. Tel., (860) 443-2545. *Public Relations Officer,* Susan Hendricks.

NORWICH. *The Leffingwell House Historic Museum,* 348 Washington St., 06360. The House incorporates seventeenth and eighteenth centuries architechtures, developing from a seventeenth century farmhouse to a mid-eighteenth century townhouse.

It was moved in 1956 from its original site, the home lot of a founding father of Norwich, Stephen Backus, to its present location as it was in the path of a proposed super highway. George Washington visited Christopher Leffingwell at the House during the Revolutionary War, seeking provisions and supplies. Utensils, tools, furnishings, silver and china of the period are displayed. An on-going search for additional pieces and continuing restoration are the purposes of The Society of the Founders of Norwich. The House is open to the public from May through Oct., with an annual open house in Oct. Call (860) 889-9440 for hours, admission fees, or private tours.

NORWICH. *Slater Memorial Museum,* located in the Slater Building and the adjacent Converse Art Building on the campus of the Norwich Free Academy, 108 Crescent St., 06360. Open: Tues.-Fri., 9 A.M.-4 P.M.; Sat. and Sun., 1-4 P.M.; July 1-Sept. 1, Tues.-Sun., 1-4 P.M.; closed Mondays and holidays throughout the year.

ROCKY HILL. *Academy Hall Museum,* 785 Old Main St., 06067. *Pres.,* Rod Wilscam; Open: June-Oct., Tues., 10 A.M.-12 Noon, Sat., 2-4 P.M.; Sun., 3-5 P.M., or by appointment. Tel., 563-6704.

STAMFORD. *The Stamford Museum and Nature Center,* 39 Scofieldtown Rd., 06903. 118 Acres include small New England farm with animals and country store, nature trails, lake, picnic area, nature's playground. Five galleries offer changing exhibitions on topics such as natural history, Indian cultures, Americana and art. Planetarium programs, 3 P.M., Sun.; observatory visitor's night, 8-10 P.M. Fri. Open: 9 A.M.-5 P.M., Mon.-Sat. and holidays; 1-5 P.M, Sun; closed Thanksgiving, Christmas, New Year's Day. Country Store open April-Dec., 10 A.M.-4 P.M., Mon.-Sat. and holidays; 12 Noon-4 P.M., Sun.; Jan.-March, 10 A.M.-3:30 P.M., Sat.; 12 Noon-3:30 P.M., Sun. Entrance fee and special event info., Tel. (203) 322-1646.

STRATFORD. *Boothe Memorial Park and Museum,* Main St. Putney, No. Stratford, P.O. Box 902, 06497. Rte. 15, Exit 53. A 32 acre former homestead of the Boothe family 1663-1949, with picnic facilities, playgrounds, and museum buildings. A National Register of Historic Places site featuring carriage barn, an 1820 homestead, blacksmith shop, trolley station, Merritt Park Way Toll Booth Plaza, windmill, clocktower museum, and ice house. An award winning wedding rose garden and sunken garden are open year round. Park open daily 9 A.M.-5 P.M.; museum tours June 1-Nov. 1, 11 A.M.-1 P.M, Tues.-Fri; 1 P.M.-4 P.M., Sat. and Sun. Free, and accessible to handicapped. Tel. (203) 381-2046.

National Helicopter Museum, 2480 Main St., 06497. Location: Eastbound Railroad station in Stratford. Open: Memorial Day to the second week of Oct. 1-4 P.M., Wed.-Sun. Free admission. Tel. (203) 375-5766.

WASHINGTON. *The Institute for American Indian Studies,* P.O. Box 1260, 38 Curtis Rd., 06793-0260. Museum and Education Center. *Chm. of the Bd.,* George A. G. Darlow; *Head of Education/Native American Studies,* Mary L.Fletcher; *Asst. Dir. for Public Programs,* Trudie L. Richmond; *Asst. Dir. of Admin.,*Elizabeth McCormick; *Exec. Dir.,* Alberto C. Meloni; Open year round. 10 A.M.-5 P.M., Mon.-Sat.; 12 Noon-5 P.M., Sun.; closed Mon. and Tues., Jan.-Mar. Tel., (860) 868-0518. Admission, $4 adults; $2 children; $3.50 senior citizens.

WEST HARTFORD. *Science Center of Connecticut,* 950 Trout Brook Dr., 06119. Comprehensive Science/Nature/Technology Center. Includes a planetarium, mini-zoo, laser shows, IBM computer lab and various science-related hands-on exhibitions including traveling exhibits that change three to four times each year. A full-size walk-in concrete model of a Sperm Whale greets visitors.

The Gengras Planetarium, New England's second largest, offers a changing selection of original shows. The mini-zoo includes a variety of birds, reptiles, and small mammals. Hands-on touch tank for gently touching ocean animals. Live animal demonstrations are featured daily

Wide selection of classes for both students and teachers are offered. Science events are scheduled throughout the year.

The Explore Store offers fun and educational items for the science minded. Science Center hours: 10 A.M.-4 P.M., Tues., Wed., Fri.; 10 A.M.-8 P.M., Thurs.; 10 A.M.-5 P.M., Sat.; 12 Noon-5 P.M., Sun.; General Admission, $5 adults; $4 children 3-15, and senior citizens; children under 3, free. $2 Planetarium and Laser Shows. Tel., (860) 231-2824. Exit 43 off I-84.

WESTPORT. *The Nature Center for Environmental Activities, Inc.,* P.O. Box 165, 10 Woodside La., 06881. Natural Science Museum, Live Animal Shelter, "Hands-on Aquarium," 62 acre sanctuary with nature trails and gift shop. Open: 9 A.M.-5 P.M., Mon.-Sat.; 1-4 P.M., Sun. Donation, $1 adults; $.50 children.

THE WILLIAM BENTON MUSEUM OF ART. *Connecticut's State Art Museum.* The Univ. of Conn., U-140, 245 Glenbrook Rd., Storrs 06269. The William Benton Museum of Art, located at the center of the University of Connecticut's Storrs campus opened in November of 1966. In addition to displays of works from its Permanent Collection, the Museum regularly schedules original and traveling exhibits. Supplemented by scholarly publications documenting the research and the event, these exhibits are interpreted through lectures, handbooks, gallery talks, video and films. The museum brings fine art in various media and from diverse historic periods and ethnic sources to Storrs. Exhibitions are designed for the student, the scholar, and the general public. Museum hours (during exhibit periods): 10 A.M.-4:30 P.M., Tues.-Fri.; 1-4:30 P.M., Sat.-Sun. Tel., (860) 486-4520. No admission charge. *Dir.,* Thomas P. Bruhn.

WINDSOR LOCKS. *New England Air Museum,* (owned and operated by the Conn. Aeronautical Historical Assoc., Inc.) Bradley International Airport, Windsor Locks, 06096. Tel., (860) 623-3305. Two large exhibit hangars with more than 70 aircraft of all types from 1909 to present. Sikorsky: "Recollections of a Pioneer" exhibit open with others, both inside and out. Movies, tour guides and two-seat cockpit simulator available every day. Special events throughout the year. Gift Shop, free parking, facilities for handicapped, free brochure on request. Hours: 10 A.M-5 P.M., daily, year round; closed Christmas and Thanksgiving. Admission, $6.50 adults; $3 children 6-11; $5.50 senior citizens. Group tour programs available.

WINDSOR LOCKS. Noden-Reed House and Barn Museums. 58 West Street, 06096. Tel., (860) 627-9212. Operated by The Windsor Locks Historical Society, Inc. since 1976. Victorian farmhouse with period room displays and an 1826 brick barn containing a farmer's tool collection, located in a 22-acre town park with nature trails. Listed on National Register of Historical Places; considered site of CT's first Christmas Tree (1777) by Hessian soldier. Open Sundays, May-Oct., 1-5 P.M. Free admission.

PUBLIC LIBRARIES OF CONNECTICUT

Town	Name of Library and Address*	Librarian
Andover	Andover Public	Teresa Goulden
Ansonia	Ansonia Public	Janet Fitol, Acting Dir.
Ashford	Babcock	Denise Bachand
Avon	Avon Free Public	Virginia G. Vocelli
Beacon Falls	Beacon Falls Public	Concelia Christensen
Berlin	Berlin Free	Barbara Lewis
	East Berlin, East Berlin	Francine Sencio
	Berlin Peck Memorial, Kensington	Eugene Devlin
Bethany	Clark Memorial	Mary Relyea
Bethel	Bethel Public	Alice S. Knapp
Bethlehem	Bethlehem Free Public	Anne Small
Bloomfield	Prosser Public	Beverly Lambert
Bolton	Bentley Memorial	Elizabeth Thornton
Branford	James Blackstone Memorial	Marlene Palmquist
	Willoughby Wallace Memorial, Stony Creek	Susan Donovan
Bridgeport	Bridgeport Public	Nancy Johmann
Bridgewater	Burnham Library	Sandy Neary
Bristol	The Bristol Public Library	Francine Petosa
Brookfield	Brookfield Center	Robert Gallucci
Brooklyn	Brooklyn Town Library	Catherine A. Tucker
Burlington	Burlington Public	Anne Walluk
Canaan	David M. Hunt, Falls Village	June Kubarek
Canterbury	Canterbury Public	Carol Somers
Canton	Canton Public, Collinsville	Margaret Perry
Chaplin	William Ross Public	Geraldine Helmer
Cheshire	Cheshire Public	Ann Wrege
Chester	Chester Public	Gloria Eustis
Clinton	Henry Carter Hull	Gary Cummings
Colchester	Cragin Memorial	Debra Carrier-Perry
		Siobhan Grogan
Columbia	Saxton B. Little Free	Janice Benda
Cornwall	Cornwall Free	Virginia Potter
	Hughes Memorial, West Cornwall	Estelle Stetson
Coventry	Booth & Dimock Memorial	Sharon Pacholski
Cromwell	Belden Library	Eileen Branciforte
Danbury	Danbury Public	Elizabeth McDonough
		Martha Walker
Darien	Darien	Louise Berry
Deep River	Deep River Public	Karen Carreras-Hubbard
Derby	Derby Neck	Judith Augusta
	Derby Public	Karen Higginson
Durham	Durham Public	Valerie J. Harrod
Eastford	Eastford Public	Barbara Pakenham
East Granby	East Granby Public	Linda Veirs
East Haddam	East Haddam Free Public, Moodus	Judith Westcott
	Rathbun Free Memorial	Kathleen Marszycki

Town	Name of Library and Address*	Librarian
East Hampton	East Hampton Public	Ann Davis
	Middle Haddam Public, Middle Haddam	Lynn Biega
East Hartford	East Hartford Public	Patrick Jones
East Haven	Hagaman Memorial	William Basel
East Lyme	East Lyme Public	William Deakyne
Easton	Easton Public	Bernadette Baldino
East Windsor	Broad Brook Public, Broad Brook	Marilyn Rajala
	Warehouse Point Library Assoc., Warehouse Point	Vincent Bologna
Ellington	Hall Memorial	Susan P. Phillips
Enfield	Enfield Central	Suzanne Jones
Essex	Essex Library Assoc.defined.	Barbara C. Smith
	Ivoryton Library Assoc., Ivorytown	Robbi Storms
Fairfield	Fairfield Public	Peggy Wargo
	Pequot, Southport	Mary Freedman
Farmington	Farmington Library	Barbara Gibson
Glastonbury	East Glastonbury Public	Virginia McGill
	South Glastonbury Public, South Glastonbury	Nancy St. Clair
	Welles-Turner Memorial	Jay Johnston
Goshen	Goshen Public	Winifred Tingley
Granby	Granby Public	Joan Fox
Greenwich	Greenwich	Elizabeth Mainiero
	Perrot Memorial, Old Greenwich	Michael Hagan
Griswold	Coit, Jewett City	Kathleen Freidenfelds
	Slater, Jewett City	Frances Coughlin
Groton	Bill Memorial	Hali Keeler
	Groton Public	Alan Benkert
	Mystic and Noank, Mystic	Joanna Case
Guilford	Guilford Free	Sandra Ruoff
Haddam	Brainerd Memorial	Annie Donahue
Hamden	Hamden	Sherry Hupp
Hampton	Fletcher Memorial	Eunice Fuller
Hartford	Hartford Public	Louise Blalock
Hartland	Hartland Public	Penny Ziarnak
Harwinton	Harwinton Public	Stasia Motuzick
Hebron	Douglas Library of Hebron	Anne S. Burgan
Kent	Kent Library Assoc.	Deborah Custer
Killingly	Killingly Public, Danielson	Marie Chartier
Killingworth	Killingworth Library Assoc.	Virginia Chapman
Lebanon	Jonathan Trumbull	Linda Wallace
Ledyard	Ledyard Public Libraries	Gale Bradbury
Litchfield	Gilbert, Northfield	Jacquelyn Foy
	Oliver Wolcott	Karen Bohrer
Lyme	Lyme Public	Theresa Conley
Madison	E. C. Scranton Memorial	Sandra Long
Manchester	Manchester Public	Douglas McDonough
Mansfield	Mansfield Library, Mansfield Center	Louise Bailey

Town	Name of Library and Address*	Librarian
Marlborough	Richmond Memorial Library	Nancy Wood
Meriden	Meriden Public	Marica Trotta
Middlebury	Middlebury Public	Jane Gallagher
Middlefield	Levi E. Coe Library Assoc.	Karen T. Smith
Middletown	Russell	Stuart Porter
Milford	Milford Public	Salvatore L. Stingo
Monroe	Monroe Public	Lynn Rosato
Montville	Raymond, 832 Raymond Hill Rd., Oakdale	Clara Faraci
Morris	Morris Public	Lee S. Cook
Naugatuck	Howard Whittemore Memorial	Joan Lamb
New Britain	New Britain Public	Ann M. Smith
New Canaan	New Canaan	David S. Bryant
New Fairfield	New Fairfield Free	Linda Fox
New Hartford	Bakerville	Mary Auclair
	New Hartford	Nancy Crilly-Kirk
New Haven	New Haven Free Public	vacancy
Newington	Lucy Robbins Welles	Maxine Bleiweis
New London	New London Public Library	Edward Murray
New Milford	New Milford Public	Judith E. Horgen
Newtown	Cyrenius H. Booth	Janet Woycik
Norfolk	Norfolk	Louise Schimmel
North Branford	North Branford Library Dept.	Robert Hull
North Canaan	Douglas, Canaan	Polly Fitting
North Haven	North Haven Memorial	Lois Baldini
North Stonington	Wheeler	Amy Kennedy
Norwalk	East Norwalk Improvement Assoc.	Eunice Van Zilen
	Norwalk Public	Les Kozerowitz
	Rowayton Assoc. of the Free Library, Rowayton	Bonnie B. Flowers
Norwich	Otis	Elsie L. Jenkins
Old Lyme	Phoebe Griffin Noyes	Anne Calvert
Old Saybrook	Acton Public, Saybrook	Janet Crozier
Orange	Orange Public	Marilyn Beattie
Oxford	Oxford Public	Matthew Vella
Plainfield	Aldrich Free Public, Moosup	Kathleen Hart
	Central Village Public, Central Village	Shirley DeFosse
	Plainfield Public	Nancy Wilcox
Plainville	Plainville Public	Peter Chase
Plymouth	Plymouth Library Assoc.	Kathy Maxwell
	Terryville Public, Terryville	Sharon La Course
Pomfret	Pomfret Free	Marjorie Sirrine
	Abington Social	Karen Stevens
Portland	Portland Public	Laurel Goodgion
Preston	Preston Public	Kathleen J. Flaherty
Prospect	Prospect Public	Barbara Peterson
Putnam	Putnam Free Public	Mary Brumbaugh
Redding	Mark Twain Library	Helen Stauderman

Town	Name of Library and Address*	Librarian
Ridgefield	Ridgefield	Anita Daubenspeck
Rocky Hill	Cora J. Belden	Betsy Wilkens
Roxbury	Minor Memorial	Timothy Beard
Salem	Salem Free Public	Suzanne H. Palmieri
Salisbury	Scoville Memorial	Martha Darcy
Scotland	Scotland Public	Elizabeth Doucet
Seymour	Seymour Public	Wayne Gudzinskas
Sharon	Hotchkiss	Gail Mirabile
Shelton	Plumb Memorial	Doris Buchheit
Sherman	Sherman Library Assoc.	Melissa Coury
Simsbury	Simsbury Public	Susan Bulluck
Somers	Somers Public	Francine Aloisa
Southbury	Southbury Public	Shirley Thorson
Southington	Southington Public	Audrey Brown
South Windsor	South Windsor Public	Mary J. Etter
Sprague	Sprague Public	Ann Marie Jones
Stafford	Stafford Library Assoc., 5 Spring St., Stafford Springs	Cheryl R. Wakely, Acting Dir.
Stamford	Ferguson	Ernest A. DiMattia, Jr.
Sterling	Sterling Public, Oneco	Rachel Vincent
Stonington	Stonington Free	Ann Gray
Stratford	Stratford Library Assoc.	Edythe Landes
Suffield	Kent Memorial	Joseph Cadieux
Thomaston	Thomaston Public	Jane Kendrick
Thompson	Thompson	Helaine Dauphinais
Tolland	Tolland Public	Kay Mahoney
Torrington	Torrington Library	Karen Worrall
Trumbull	Trumbull Library	Grace M. Birch
Union	Union Free Public	Brigitte Botnick
Vernon	Rockville Public	Peter Ciparelli
Voluntown	Voluntown Public	Barbara Ayrton
Wallingford	Wallingford	Leslie Scherer
		Karen Roesler
Warren	Warren Public	Pamela Buckley
Washington	Gunn Memorial	Jean Chapin
Waterbury	Silas Bronson	Leo Flanagan
Waterford	Waterford Public	Vincent Juliano
Watertown	Watertown Library Assoc.	Joan Rintelman
Westbrook	Westbrook Public	Lewis Daniels
West Hartford	West Hartford Public	Denis Lorenz
West Haven	The Public Library	Concetta Sacco
Weston	Weston Public	Jane Atkinson
Westport	Westport Public	Sally H. Poundstone
Wethersfield	Wethersfield Public	Om P. Wadhwa
Willington	Mary D. Edwards Public Library	Roberta S. Passardi
Wilton	Wilton Library Assoc.	Karen Ronald
Winchester	Beardsley & Memorial, Winsted	Ruth Backhaus

Town	Name of Library and Address*	Librarian
Windham	Guilford Smith Memorial, South Windham	Julie Culp
	Willimantic Public, Willimantic	Theodore Perch
	Windham Free Library	Sally Sumner
Windsor	Windsor Public	Laura Kahkonen
Windsor Locks	Windsor Locks Public	Ronald Hubbs
Wolcott	Wolcott Public	Bradley Green
Woodbridge	Woodbridge Town	Janet V. Day
Woodbury	Woodbury Public	Elaine Wyden
Woodstock	May Memorial Library Assoc., East Woodstock	Judy Schumacher
	Howard Bracken Memorial	Walter Izbicki
	North Woodstock	Mary E. Kelly
	West Woodstock Library Assoc., 5 Bungay Hill Connector, Woodstock	Dorothy Porter

*When no address is given in this column, the town in the first column is to be used.

THE ASSOC. OF CONN. LIBRARY BOARDS, INC.—Office: P.O. Box 196, Pomfret Center 06259. *Pres.,* Phillip G. James, Pomfret; *Vice Pres.,* Dorothy S. Willett, Durham; *Secy.,* Suzanne Lee, Guilford; *Treas.,* Jennifer Latici, Woodstock.

THE PRESS OF CONNECTICUT

The Associated Press, 55 Farmington Ave., Suite 402, Hartford 06105, Mary Anne Rhyne, Chief of Bureau; New Haven Office, 40 Sargent Dr., New Haven 06511, Brigitte Greenberg, Correspondent; Stamford Office, 75 Tresser Blvd., Stamford 06901, Denise Lavoie, Correspondent; Capitol Office, Press Room, State Capitol, Hartford 06106, Evan Berland, Correspondent. **Connecticut State News Bureau,** 122 Cumberland St., Hartford 06106, Vincent M. Valvo, Exec. Editor; Capitol Office, Press Room, State Capitol, Hartford 06106.

DAILY NEWSPAPERS
Except Sunday

BRIDGEPORT. *Connecticut Post*† Address: 410 State St., 06604. Tel., (203) 333-0161. *Publisher,* Robert H. Laska; *Editor,* Rick Sayers.

BRISTOL. *The Bristol Press.** Address: 2 Main St., Middletown 06457. Tel., (860) 347-3331, (800) 688-3540. *Gen. Mgr.,* Gregory R. Barden; *Editor/Editorial Dir.,* Karen A. Avitabile.

DANBURY. *The News-Times.*† Address: 333 Main St., 06810. Tel., (203) 744-5100. *Publisher,* Wayne J. Shepperd; *Exec. Editor,* Edward W. Frede.

GREENWICH. *Greenwich Time.** Address: Southern Conn. Newspapers, 20 East Elm St., 06830. Tel., (203) 625-4444. *Publisher,* William Rowe; *Managing Editor,* Joseph F. Pisani.

HARTFORD. *The Hartford Courant.*† Address: 285 Broad St., 06115. Tel., (860) 241-6200. *Publisher,* Michael Waller; *Editor/Vice Pres.,* David Barrett; *Sr. Vice Pres./Gen. Mgr.,* Marty Petty; *Managing Editor,* Cliff Teutsch; *Editorial Page Editor,* John Zakarian.

MANCHESTER. *Journal Inquirer.** Address: 306 Progress Dr., Box 510, 06045-0510. Tel., (860) 646-0500. *Publisher,* Elizabeth S. Ellis; *Managing Editor,* Chris Powell.

MERIDEN. *Record-Journal.*† Address: 11 Crown St., 06450. Tel., (203) 235-1661. *Publisher/Editor,* Eliot C. White.

MIDDLETOWN. *The Middletown Press.** Address: 2 Main St., 06457. Tel., (860) 347-3331, (800) 688-3540. *Gen. Mgr.,* Gregory R. Barden; *Editor/Editorial Dir.,* Karen A. Avitabile.

NAUGATUCK. *Naugatuck Daily News.** Address: 71 Weid Dr., 06770. Tel., (203) 729-2228. *Publisher,* Ronald Waer; *Managing Editor,* Mary Ellen Goodin.

NEW BRITAIN. *The Herald.** Address: 1 Herald Sq., 06050. Tel., (860) 225-4601. *Publisher,* Gerald Barcia; *Exec. Editor,* William F. Millerick.

NEW HAVEN. *The New Haven Register.*† Address: 40 Sargent Dr., 06511. Tel., (203) 789-5200. *Publisher/Chief Exec. Officer,* William J. Rush; *Editor,* Jack Krammer.

Yale Daily News.† Address: Box 209007, Yale Station, 06520. Tel., (203) 432-2424, 2414. *Publishers,* Julia Kahr, Jessica Jewell.

NEW LONDON. *The Day.*† Address: 47 Eugene O'Neill Dr., P.O. Box 1231, 06320-1231. Tel., (860) 442-2200. *Editor/Publisher,* Reid MacCluggage.

NORWALK. *The Hour.** Address: 346 Main Ave., 06851. Tel., (2103) 846-3281. *Publisher,* B. J. Frazier; *Exec. Editor,* John P. Reilly; *Managing Editor,* Jackson Ferry.

NORWICH. *Norwich Bulletin.*† Address: 66 Franklin St., 06360. Tel., (860) 887-9211. *Publisher,* David A. Whitehead; *Exec. Editor,* Keith Fontaine.

STAMFORD. *The Advocate.** Address: P.O. Box 9307, 75 Tresser Blvd., 06904-9307. Tel., (203) 964-2200. *Publisher,* William J. Rowe; *Editor,* Deirdre S. Channing.

TORRINGTON/WINSTED/NORTHWEST CORNER. *The Register Citizen.*† Address: 190 Water St., P.O. Box 58, 06790. Tel., (860) 489-3121. *Publisher,* William T. Murray; *Editor,* Silvio Albino.

WATERBURY. *Waterbury Republican-American.*† Address: 389 Meadow St., 06722. Tel., (203) 574-3636. *Publisher,* William J. Pape, II; *Managing Editor,* Bob Veillette.

WILLIMANTIC. *The Chronicle.** Address: Chronicle Rd., 06226. Tel., (860) 423-8466. *Pres.,* Lucy Crosbie; *Publisher,* Kevin Crosbie; *Editor,* Ron Robillard.

---

*EVENING †MORNING

SUNDAY NEWSPAPERS

BRIDGEPORT. *Connecticut Post.* Address: 410 State St., 06604. Tel., (203) 333-0161. *Publisher,* Robert H. Laska; *Editor,* Rick Sayers.

DANBURY. *The News-Times.* Address: 333 Main St., 06810. Tel., (203) 744-5100. *Publisher,* Wayne J. Shepperd; *Exec. Editor,* Edward W. Frede.

GREENWICH. *Greenwich Time.* Address: Southern Conn. Newspapers, 20 East Elm St., 06830. Tel., (203) 625-4444. *Publisher,* William Rowe; *Managing Editor,* Joseph F. Pisani.

HARTFORD. *The Hartford Courant.* Address: 285 Broad St., 06115. Tel., (860) 241-6200. *Publisher,* Michael A. Waller; *Editor/Vice Pres.,* David S. Barrett; *Sr. Vice Pres/Gen. Mgr.,* Marty Petty; *Managing Editor,* Cliff Teutsch; *Deputy Managing Editor,* G. Claude Albert; *Editorial Page Editor,* John Zakarian.

MERIDEN. *Record-Journal.* Address: 11 Crown St., 06450. Tel., (203) 235-1661. *Publisher/Editor,* Eliot C. White.

MIDDLETOWN. The Herald Press. Address: 2 Main St., 06457. Tel., (860) 347-3331, (800) 688-3540. *Gen. Mgr.,* Gregory Barden; *Editor/Editorial Dir.,* Karen A. Avitabile.

NEW HAVEN. *The New Haven Register.* Address: 40 Sargent Dr., 06511. Tel., (203) 789-5200. *Publisher/Chief Exec. Officer,* William J. Rush; *Editor,* Jack Krammer.

NEW LONDON. *The Day.* Address: 47 Eugene O'Neill Dr., P.O. Box 1231, 06320-1231. Tel., (860) 442-2200. *Editor/Publisher*, Reid MacCluggage.

NORWICH. Sunday Bulletin. Address: 66 Franklin St., 06360. Tel., (860) 887-9211. *Publisher*, David A. Whitehead; *Exec. Editor*, Keith Fontaine.

STAMFORD. *The Sunday Advocate.* Address: P.O. Box 9307, 75 Tresser Blvd., 06904-9307. Tel., (203) 964-2200. *Publisher*, William J. Rowe; *Editor*, Deirdre S. Channing.

TORRINGTON/WINSTED/NORTHWEST CORNER. *The Register Citizen.* Address: 190 Water St., P.O. Box 58, 06790. Tel., (860) 489-3121. *Publisher*, William T. Murray; *Editor*, Silvio Albino.

WATERBURY. *The Sunday Republican.* Address: 389 Meadow St., 06722. Tel., (203) 574-3636. *Publisher*, William J. Pape, II; *Managing Editor*, Bob Veillette.

WEEKLY NEWSPAPERS

ANSONIA. *The Valley Gazette.* Address: Hometown Publishing, P.O. Box 332, Monroe 06468. Tel., (203) 926-2080; FAX, (203) 926-2091; E-Mail, HomePubleaol.com. Publisher, Regina Burkhart; Exec. Editor, Lorraine Bukowski; Editor, John Voket. News Deadline: Monday A.M.

AVON. *The Valley News.* Address: Imprint Newspapers, 99 Main St., Bristol 06010. Tel., (860) 236-3571. *Publisher*, Michael R. Vanacore; *Marketing/Editorial Dir.*, Doreen Madden. *News Deadline:* Thursday Noon.

BETHANY. *Amity Observer.* Address: Hometown Publications, P.O. Box 332, Monroe 06468. Tel., (203) 926-2080; FAX, (203) 926-2091; E-Mail, HomePubl@aol.com. *Publisher*, Regina Burkhart; *Exec. Editor*, Lorraine Bukowski; *Editor*, John Voket. *News Deadline:* Monday, 10 A.M.

BETHEL. *Bethel Beacon.* Address: 219 Greenwood Ave., P.O. Box 302, 06801. Tel., (203) 798-7450; FAX, (203) 798-7457. Pubblisher; Walter N. Tothschild III; Exec. Editor, Art Cummings; Editor, Thom Hunt. News Deadline, Tuesday, 5 P.M.

BLOOMFIELD. *Bloomfield Journal.* Address: Imprint Newspapers, 99 Main St., Bristol 06010. Tel., (860) 236-3571. *Publisher*, Michael R. Vanacore; *Editorial Dir.*, Doreen Madden. *News Deadline*: Friday, Noon.

BRANFORD. *Branford Review.** Address: 230 East Main St., P.O. Box 829, 06405. Tel., (203) 488-2535. *Publisher*, William J. Rush; *Managing Editor*, Kimberly P. Ryan. *News Deadline:* Friday, Noon.

BRIDGEPORT. *The Bridgeport Inquirer.* Address: 3281 Main St., P.O. Box 1260, Hartford 06143. Tel., (860) 522-1462; FAX, (860) 522-3014. *Publisher*, William R. Hales; *Managing Editor*, Monique Jarvis. *News Deadline:* Thursday.

Bridgeport Jewish Ledger. Address: 4200 Park Ave., 06604; 740 North Main St., Hartford 06117. Tel., (203) 372-6504, Bridgeport; 231-2424, Hartford. *Publishers*, NRG Connecticut Limited Partnership; *Editor*, Jonathan Tobin; *Bridgeport Editor*, Valerie Newman. *News Deadline:* Wednesday, Noon for the following Friday.

The Bridgeport News. Address: Hometown Publications, P.O. Box 332, Monroe, 06468. Tel., (203) 926-2080; FAX (203) 926-2091; E-Mail, HomePubl@aol.com. *Publisher,* Regina Burkhart; *Exec. Editor,* Lorraine Bukowski; *Editor,* Brad Durrell. *News Deadline:* Monday, 5 P.M.

BROOKFIELD. *The Brookfield Journal.* Address: Box 268, 06804. Tel., (203) 775-2533. *Publisher,* Walter N. Rothschild, III; *Exec. Editor,* Art Cummings. *News Deadline:* Tuesday, 5 P.M.

CANTON. *Foothills Trader.* Address: 85 River Rd., Collinsville 06022. Tel., (860) 693-2990. *Publisher,* Bill Murray; *Events Editor,* Linda Curtis. *News Deadline:* Wednesday, 5 P.M.

The Valley News. Address: Imprint Newspapers, 99 Main St., Bristol 06010. Tel., (860) 236-3571. *Publisher,* Michael R. Vanacore; *Marketing/Editorial Dir.,* Doreen Madden. *News Deadline:* Thursday Noon.

CHESHIRE. *The Cheshire Herald.* Address: The True Publishing Co., 125 Commerce Ct., Unit 11, 06410. Tel., (203) 272-5316. *Publisher,* Joseph Jakubisyn; *Editor,* Clarke W. Hammersley. *News Deadline:* Monday, 5 P.M.

CLINTON. *Clinton Recorder.** Address: 16-D West Main St., P.O. Box 914, 06413. Tel., (860) 669-5727. *Publisher,* Journal Register Co.; *Editor,* Michael Lemanski. *News Deadline:* Wednesday, 5 P.M.

COLCHESTER. *Regional Standard.* Address: P.O. Box 510, 06415. Tel., (860) 537-2341. *Publisher,* William J. Rush; *Managing Editor,* Kimberly P. Ryan. *News Deadline,* Wednesday, Noon.

DARIEN. *Darien News-Review.* Address: Brooks Community Newspapers, 6 Squab La., 06820. Tel., (203) 655-7476; E-Mail, bcnnews3@netaxis.com. *Publisher,* B. V. Brooks; *Editor,* Gary Larkin. *News Deadline*: Tuesday, Noon.

DERBY. *The Valley Gazette.* Address: Hometown Publications, P. O. Box 332, Monroe 06468. Tel., (203) 926-2080; FAX (203) 926-2091; E-Mail, HomePubl@aol.com.. *Publisher,* Regina Burkhart; *Exec. Editor,* Lorraine Bukowski; *Editor,* John Voket. *News Deadline:* Monday, 10 A.M.

EAST GRANBY. *The Valley News.* Address: Imprint Newspapers, 99 Main St., Bristol 06010. Tel., (860) 236-3571. *Publisher,* Michael R. Vanacore; *Marketing/Editorial Dir.,* Doreen Madden. *News Deadline:* Thursday Noon.

EAST HARTFORD. *The East Hartford Gazette.* Address: 1171 Main St., 06108. Tel., (860) 289-6468. *Publisher*, The Journal Register Co.; *Editor,* Bill Doak. *News Deadline:* Friday, 5 P.M.

EAST HAVEN. *The Advertiser.* Address: Elm City Newspapers, 349 New Haven Ave., Milford 06460. Tel., (203) 876-6800. *Publisher,* William Rush; *Editor,* Jon Root. *News Deadline:* Wednesday, Noon.

EASTON. *Easton Courier.* Address: Hometown Publications, P.O. Box 332, Monroe 06468. Tel., (203) 926-2080; FAX (203) 926-2091; E-Mail, HomePubl@aol.com.. *Publisher,* Regina Burkhart; *Exec. Editor,* Lorraine Bukowski; *Editor,* Beth Bresnahan. *News Deadline:* Tuesday, Noon.

ENFIELD. *Connecticut Law Journal.* Address: Commission on Official Legal Publications, 111 Phoenix Ave., 06082. Tel., (860) 741-3027; FAX, (860) 745-2178; BBS, (860) 741-5129. *Publisher,* Judicial Branch, State of Conn.; *Managing Editor,* Richard J. Hemenway. *Deadline:* Friday, Noon, 11 days prior to Tuesday publication.

FAIRFIELD. *The Connecticut Law Tribune.* Address: One Post Rd., Suite 100, 06430. Tel., (203) 256-3600; FAX, (203) 255-3319. *Editor/Publisher,* Ava Plakins; *Associate Publisher,* Tom Januszewski. *News Deadline:* Thursday, 2 P.M.

The Fairfield Citizen-News.* Address: 220 Carter Henry Dr., 06430. Tel., (203) 255-4561; FAX (203) 255-0456. *Publisher,* Brooks Community Newspapers; *Editor,* Patricia A. Hines. *News Deadline:* Wednesday, Friday.

Fairfield County Weekly. Address: 1 Dock St., Stamford 06902. Tel., (203) 406-2406. *Publisher,* Robert Lippman; *Editor in Chief,* Lorraine Gengo. *News Deadline:* Friday, Noon.

Fairfield Minuteman. Address: 1300 Post Rd., Fairfield 06430. Tel., (203) 255-8877. *Publisher,* Trip Rothschild; *Editor,* John Schwing. *New Deadline:* Monday, Noon.

FARMINGTON. *The Valley News.* Address: Imprint Newspapers, 99 Main St., Bristol 06010. Tel., (860) 236-3571. *Publisher,* Michael R. Vanacore; *Marketing/Editorial Dir.,* Doreen Madden. *News Deadline:* Thursday Noon.

GLASTONBURY. *The Glastonbury Citizen.* Address: Box 373, 87 Nutmeg La., 06033. Tel., (860) 633-4691, FAX, (860) 657-3258. *Publisher,* James Hallas; *Editor,* Kathleen Stack. *News Deadline:* Monday, Noon.

The Rivereast News Bulletin. Address: 87 Nutmeg La., 06033. Tel., (860) 633-4691. *Publisher/Editor,* James Hallas. *News Deadline:* Wednesday, Noon.

GRANBY. *The Valley News.* Address: Imprint Newspapers, 99 Main St., Bristol 06010. Tel., (860) 236-3571. *Publisher,* Michael R. Vanacore; *Marketing/Editorial Dir.,* Doreen Madden. *News Deadline:* Thursday Noon.

GUILFORD. *Shore Line Times.** Address: 705 Boston Post Rd., P.O. Box 349, 06437. Tel., (203) 453-2711. *Publisher,* William J. Rush; *Managing Editor*, Kimberly Potter Ryan. *News Deadline*: Thursday, 5 P.M.

HARTFORD. *The Catholic Transcript.* Address: 785 Asylum Ave., 06105-2886. Tel., (860) 527-1175. *Pres./Publisher,* Most Rev. Daniel A. Cronin; *Exec. Editor,* Rev. John P. Gatzak; *Acting Managing Editor,* Ann M. Monteiro; *Business Mgr.,* Scott K. Parmelee; *Asst. Editor*, Dana Drezek; Advertising Mgr., Roy J.Rowland; *News Deadline:* Friday, 3 P.M.

The Connecticut Jewish Ledger. Address: 740 No. Main St. West Hartford, 06117. Tel., (860) 231-2424. *Exec. Editor,* Jonathan Tobin. *News Deadline:* Friday, 4 P.M.

Hartford Advocate. Address: 100 Constitution Plaza, 06103. Tel., (860) 548-9300. *Publisher,* Francis J. Zankowski; *Editor,* Russ Hoyle. *News Deadline:* Friday.

Hartford Inquirer. Address: 3281 Main St., P.O. Box 1260, 06143. Tel., (860) 522-1462; FAX, (860) 522-3014. *Publisher*, William R. Hales; *Managing Editor*, Monique Jarvis. *News Deadline:* Thursday.

The Hartford News. Address: 191 Franklin Ave., 06114. Tel., (860) 296-6128. *Publishers,* Jon B. Harden, Lynne A. Lumsden; *General Mgr.,* Andy Hart. *News Deadline*: Friday, Noon.

The Trinity Tripod. Address: Trinity College, Box 702582, 06106. Tel., (860) 297-2583, FAX, (860) 297-5361. *Publisher,* Trinity College; *Editor,* Amy Shackelford; *Managing Editor,* Elizabeth Perry. *News Deadline:* Saturday, 5 P.M.

HUNTINGTON. Huntington Herald. Address: Hometown Publications, P.O. Box 332, Monroe 06468. Tel., (203) 926-2080; FAX (203) 926-2091; E-Mail, HomePubl@aol.com.. *Publisher,* Regina Burkhart; *Exec. Editor,* Lorraine Bukowski, *Editor,* Thomas Henry. *News Deadline*: Monday, 1 A.M.

KENT. *Kent Good Times Dispatch.* Address: Kent Publishing Co., Box 430, 06757. Tel., (860) 927-4621. *Publisher,* Walter N. Rothschild, III; *Managing Editor,* Lesly Ferris. *News Deadline:* Wednesday, Noon.

KILLINGLY. *The Journal/Transcript.* Address: Box 299, Danielson 06239. Tel., (860) 774-5563. *Pres./Publisher,* David A. Whitehead; *Editor,* Vito J. Leo. *News Deadline:* Thursday.

LITCHFIELD. *Litchfield Enquirer.* Address: 45 West St., P. O. Box 547, 06759. Housatonic Valley Publishing Co., P.O. Box 1139, New Milford 06776. Tel., (860) 567-8766. *Publisher,* Walter Rothschild; *Managing Editor,* John McKenna; *Exec. Editor,* Art Cummings. *News Deadline:* Monday, 5 P.M.

The Litchfield Monitor. Address: Pinchpenny Park, P.O. Box 10, 06759. Tel., (860) 567-1000. *Publisher/Editor/Editorial Dir.,* Paul M. Rosenberg.

MIDDLETOWN. *The Wesleyan Argus.** Address: Wesleyan Station, Box 2200, 06459. Tel., (860) 685-3325. *Publisher,* Wesleyan Student Body; *Editors,* Chris Gaither, Brent Spodek.

MILFORD. *The Milford Mirror.* Address: Hometown Publications, P.O. Box 332, Monroe 06468. Tel., (203) 926-2080; FAX (203) 926-2091; E-Mail, HomePubl@aol.com.. *Publisher,* Regina Burkhart; *Exec. Editor,* Lorraine Bukowski; *Editor,* Jill Dion. *News Deadline:* Monday, Noon.

MONROE. *Monroe Courier.* Address: Hometown Publications, P. O. Box 332, Monroe 06468. Tel., (203) 926-2080; FAX (203) 926-2091; E-Mail, HomePubl@aol.com.. *Publisher,* Regina Burkhart; *Exec. Editor,* Lorraine Bukowski; *Editor,* Nancy Donigen. *News Deadline:* Tuesday, 10 A.M.

NEW CANAAN. *The New Canaan Advertiser.* Address: P.O. Box 605, 42 Vitti St., 06840. Tel., (203) 966-9541. *Publisher,* Hersam Publishing Co.; *Editor,* Edmund J. Chrostowski. *News Deadline:* Monday, 5 P.M.

NEW HAVEN. New Haven Advocate. Address: 1 Long Wharf Dr., 06511. Tel., (203) 789-0010; FAX (203) 787-1418. *Publisher,* Gail Thompson; *Editor,* Josh Mamis; *Listings Editor,* Karen Unger. *News Deadline:* Friday.

New Haven Inquirer. Address: 3281 Main St., P.O. Box 1260, Hartford 06143. Tel., (860) 522-1462; FAX, (860) 522-3014. *Publisher,* William R. Hales; *Managing Editor,* Monique Jarvis. *News Deadline:* Thursday.

New Haven Jewish Ledger. Address: 740 No. Main St., West Hartford 06117. Tel., (203) 231-2424. *Publishers,* NRG Connecticut Limited Partnership; *Editor,* Jonathan Tobin. *News Deadline:* Friday, 4 P.M.

NEWINGTON. *Newington Town Crier.* Address: Imprint Newspapers, 99 Main St., Bristol 06010. Tel., (860) 236-3571. *Publisher,* Michael R. Vanacore; *Exec. Editor,* Doreen Madden. *News Deadline:* Friday, Noon.

NEW MILFORD. *The Litchfield County Times.* Address: The Litchfield County Times, 32 Main St., 06776. Tel., (860) 355-4121. *Publisher,* Arthur Carter; *Editor,* Kenneth Paul; *Managing Editor,* Douglas P. Clement. *News Deadline:* Wednesday.

New Milford Times. Address: 132 Danbury Rd., P.O. Box 1139, 06776. Tel., (860) 354-2261. *Publisher,* Walter N. Rothschild, III; *Exec. Editor,* Art Cummings. *News Deadline:* Tuesday, 5 P.M.

NEWTOWN. *Antiques and The Arts Weekly.* Address: The Bee Publishing Co., 5 Church Hill Rd., P.O. Box 5503, 06470. Tel., (203) 426-8036; FAX, (203) 426-5169. *Publisher,* The Bee Publishing Co.; *Editor,* R. Scudder Smith. *News Deadline:* Friday, Noon.

The Newtown Bee. Address: The Bee Publishing Co., 5 Church Hill Rd., P.O. Box 5503, 06470. Tel., (203) 426-3141; FAX (203) 426-5169. *Publisher,* The Bee Publishing Co.; *Editor,* R. Scudder Smith; *Managing Editor,* Curtiss Clark. *News Deadline:* Tuesday, Noon.

NORTH HAVEN. *The Post.* Address: 349 New Haven Ave., Milford 06460. Tel., (203) 876-6800. *Publisher,* William J. Rush; *Editor,* Brian Overton. *News Deadline:* Monday, Noon.

NORWALK. *Fairpress, Inc.* Address: P.O. Box 951, 51 Riverside Ave., Westport 06881. Tel., (203) 846-3451. *Publisher,* Gannett Co.; *Managing Editor,* Ina Chadwick. *News Deadline:* Monday, 5 P.M.

OLD SAYBROOK. *The Pictorial Gazette.** Address: 162 Main St., P.O. Drawer O, 06475. Tel., (860) 388-3441. *Publisher,* William Rush; *Editor,* Beth Damarjian. *News Deadline:* Tuesday, Thursday, Noon.

ORANGE. *Amity Observer.* Address: Hometown Publications, P.O. Box 298, Trumbull 06611. Tel., (203) 926-2080; FAX (203) 926-2091; E-Mail, HomePubl@aol.com.. *Publisher,* Regina Burkhart; *Exec. Editor,* Lorraine Bukowski; *Editor,* John Voket. *News Deadline:* Friday, 10 A.M.

OXFORD. *The Valley Gazette.* Address: Hometown Publications, P. O. Box 332, Monroe 06468. Tel., (203) 926-2080; FAX (203) 926-2091; E-Mail, HomePubl@aol.com.. *Publisher,* Regina Burkhart; *Exec. Editor,* Lorraine Bukowski; *Editor,* John Voket. *News Deadline:* Monday, 10 A.M.

REDDING. *The Redding Pilot.* Address: Box 389, Georgetown 06829. Tel., (203) 544-9519; FAX (203) 544-9513. *Publisher,* Acorn Press; *Editor,* Susan Wolf. *News Deadline:* Monday, 5 P.M.

RIDGEFIELD. *The Ridgefield Press.* Address: 16 Bailey Ave., 06877. Tel., (203) 438-6544. *Publisher,* Thomas Nash; *Editor,* Macklin K. Reid; *Exec. Editor,* Jack Sanders. *News Deadline*: Wednesday, Noon.

ROCKY HILL. *Rocky Hill Post.* Address: Imprint Newspapers, 99 Main St., Bristol 06010. Tel., (860) 236-3571. *Publisher,* Michael R. Vanacore; *Editorial Dir.,* Laura U. Manente. *News Deadline:* Friday, Noon.

SALISBURY. *The Lakeville Journal.* Address: 33 Bissell St., P.O. Box 1688, Lakeville 06039. Tel., (860) 435-9873; FAX (860) 435-4802. *Publisher,* A. Whitney Ellsworth; *Editor,* David N. Parker; *Managing Editor,* Kathryn Boughton. *News Deadline:* Tuesday, 5 P.M.

SEYMOUR. *The Valley Gazette.* Address: Hometown Publications, P. O. Box 332, Monroe 06468. Tel., (203) 926-2080; FAX (203) 926-20913639; E-Mail, HomePubl@aol.com.. *Publisher,* Regina Burkhart; *Exec. Editor,* Lorraine Bukowski; *Editor,* John Voket. *News Deadline:* Monday, 10 A.M.

SHELTON. *Huntington Herald.* Address: Hometown Publications, P.O. Box 332, Monroe 06468. Tel., (203) 926-2080; FAX (203) 926-2091; E-Mail, HomePubl@aol.com.. *Publisher,* Regina Burkhart; *Exec. Editor,* Lorraine Bukowski; *Editor,* Thomas Henry. *News Deadline:* Monday, 1 P.M.

Suburban News. Address: 190 Coram Ave., 06484. Tel., (203) 924-4696. *Publisher,* Citizen Publications; *Editor*, Alan Olenick. *News Deadline:* Friday, 5 P.M.

SIMSBURY. *The Valley News.* Address: Imprint Newspapers, 99 Main St., Bristol 06010. Tel., (860) 236-3571. *Publisher,* Michael R. Vanacore; *Marketing/Editorial Dir.,* Doreen Madden. *News Deadline:* Thursday Noon.

SOUTHBURY. *Voices Sunday-Weekly Star.* Address: P.O. Box 383, 06488. Tel., (203) 263-2116; FAX, (203) 266-0199. *Publisher,* Rudy Mazurosky; *News Editor,* Miriam Schlicht; *Copy/Make-up Editor,* Pattie Wesley. *News Deadline:* Voices, Friday; Voices Sunday-Weekly Star, Wednesday.

SOUTH WINDSOR. *The Commercial Record.* Address: 435 Buckland Rd., P.O. Box 902, 06074. Tel., (860) 644-3489. *Publisher,* Vincent M. Valvo; *Editor/Assoc. Publisher,* Walter Perry; *Managing Ed.,* Harlan J. Levy. *News Deadline:* Tuesday, 9 A.M.

STRATFORD. *The Stratford Bard.* Address: 349 New Haven Ave., Milford, 06460. Mailing Address: P. O. Box 5339, Milford 06460. Tel., (203) 876-6800. *Publisher,* William Rush; *Editor,* Dorothy Euerle. *News Deadline:* Friday, Noon.

Stratford Star. Address: Hometown Publications, P. O. Box 332, Monroe 06468. Tel., (203) 926-2080; FAX (203) 926-2091; E-Mail, HomePubl@aol.com.. *Publisher*, Regina Burkhart; *Exec. Editor,* Lorraine Bukowski; *Editor,* Jack P. Terceno. *News Deadline*: Tuesday, Noon.

THOMASTON. *The Thomaston Express.* Address: 44 Union St., P.O. Box 250, 06787. Tel., (860) 283-4355; FAX (860) 283-4356. *Publisher,* Michael Vanacore; *Editor,* Michael Chaiken. *News Deadline*: Monday, 3 P.M.

TRUMBULL. *The Trumbull Times.* Address: Hometown Publications, P.O. Box 332, Monroe 06468. Tel., (203) 926-2080; FAX (203) 926-2091; E-Mail, HomePubl@aol.com. *Publisher,* Regina Burkhart; *Exec. Editor,* Lorraine Bukowski; *Editor,* Jack Terceno. *News Deadline:* Tuesday, Noon.

VERNON. *Reminder Press, Inc.* Address: 130 Old Town Rd., Vernon 06066. Tel., (860) 875-3366. *Editor,* George Cunningham. *News Deadline:* Wednesday.

WATERBURY. *The Waterbury Inquirer.* Address: 3281 Main St., P.O. Box 1260, Hartford 06143. Tel., (860) 522-1462; FAX, (860) 522-3014. *Publisher,* William R. Hales; *Managing Editor,* Monique Jarvis. *News Deadline:* Thursday.

WATERTOWN. *Town Times.* Address: 469 Main St., P.O. Box 1, 06795. Tel., (860) 274-6721. *Publisher,* Rudy Mazurosky; *Editor,* Tommy Valuckas. *News Deadline:* Friday, 5 P.M.

WEST HARTFORD. *West Hartford News.* Address: Imprint Newspapers, 99 Main St., Bristol 06010. Tel., (860) 236-3571. *Publisher,* Michael R. Vanacore; *Marketing/Editorial Dir.,* Doreen Madden. *News Deadline:* Thursday, Noon.

WEST HAVEN. *West Haven News.* Address: 666 Savin Ave., 06516. Tel., (203) 933-1000. *Publisher,* ABC Capital Cities; *Editor,* William V. Riccio, Jr. *News Deadline:* Monday, 4 P.M.

WESTON. *The Weston Forum.* Address: P.O. Box 1185, 06883. Tel., (203) 544-9990, FAX, (203) 544-9153. *Publisher,* Thomas Nash; *Editor,* Sybil Blau. *News Deadline:* Monday, A.M.

WESTPORT. *Westport Minuteman.* Address: 877 Post Rd., East, P.O. Box 3119, 06880. Tel., (203) 226-8877. *Publisher,* Trip Rothschild; *Editor,* Lawrence Fellows. *News Deadline:* Tuesday, Noon.

Westport News.* Address: 136 Main St., 06880. Tel., (203) 226-6311; FAX (203) 454-2765. *Publisher,* Brooks Community Newspapers; *Editor,* Woody Klein. *News Deadline:* Monday, Wednesday, Noon.

WETHERSFIELD. *Wethersfield Post.* Address: Imprint Newspapers, 99 Main St., Bristol 06010. Tel., (860) 236-3571. *Publisher,* Michael R. Vanacore; *Editorial Dir.,* Doreen Madden. *News Deadline:* Friday, Noon.

WILTON. *The Wilton Bulletin.* Address: P.O. Box 367, 06897. Tel., (203) 762-3866; FAX (203) 762-3120. Acorn Press, Inc. *Publisher,* Thomas B. Nash; *Editor,* Gregory K. Bartlett.

WINDSOR. *Windsor Journal.* Address: Imprint Newspapers, 99 Main St., Bristol 06010. Tel., (860) 236-3571. *Publisher,* Michael R. Vanacore; *Editorial Dir.,* Doreen Madden. *News Deadline:* Friday, Noon.

WINDSOR LOCKS. *Windsor Locks Journal.* Address: Imprint Newspapers, 99 Main St., Bristol 06010. Tel., (860) 236-3571. *Publisher,* Michael Vanacore; *Exec. Editor,* Doreen Madden. *News Deadline:* Friday, Noon.

WOODBRIDGE. *Amity Observer.* Address: Hometown Publications, P.O. Box 332, Monroe 06468. Tel., (203) 926-2080; FAX (203) 926-2091; E-Mail, Home-

Publ@aol.com.. *Publisher,* Regina Burkhart; *Exec. Editor,* Lorraine Bukowski; *Editor,* John Voket. *News Deadline:* Monday, 10 A.M.

WOODBURY. *Voices Sunday-The Weekly Star.* Address: 90 Middle Quarter Mall, P.O. Box 383, Southbury 06488. Tel., (203) 263-2116; FAX, (203) 266-0199. *Publisher,* Prime Publishers, Inc.; *Editors,* Miriam Schlicht, Pattie Wesley. *News Deadline:* Voices, Friday; Voices Sunday-Weekly Star, Wednesday.

*Published semi-weekly.

MONTHLY NEWSPAPERS AND PERIODICALS

BERLIN. *The Unionist.*[6] Address: 1781 Wilbur Cross Pkwy., 06037. Tel., 828-1400. *Publisher,* Ct. State Federation of Teachers; *Editorial Dir.,* Leo Canty.

BETHANY/WOODBRIDGE. *Beth-Wood News.*[2] Address: P.O. Box 883, 378 Boston Post Rd., Orange 06477-0883. Tel., (203) 795-0666. *Publisher,* Michele G. Collins. *Copy Deadline:* Tuesday Noon, one week prior. Published 2nd & 4th Tuesday of each month.

BRIDGEPORT. *Connecticut Magazine.*[6] Address: 789 Reservoir Ave., 06606. Tel., (203) 374-3388. *Publisher,* Michael Mims; *Editor,* Charles A. Monagan; *Managing Editor,* Dale B. Salm.

GLASTONBURY. *Connecticut Granger.*[5] Address: 769 Hebron Ave., P.O. Box 6517, 06033. Tel., (860) 633-7550. *Publisher,* Conn. State Grange; *Editor,* Todd Gelineau.

HAMDEN. *Connecticut Traveler.*[6] Address: 2276 Whitney Ave., 06518. Tel., (203) 288-7441, Ext. 4700; FAX, (203) 230-0182. *Publisher,* Conn. Motor Club; *Editor,* Jodi Amatulli.

HAMPTON. *The Hampton Gazette.*[5] Address: P.O. Box 101, 06247. Tel., (860) 455-9613. *Publisher,* Hampton Gazette; *Editor,* Georgia Rondeau; *Editorial Dir.,* Robert McDermott.

HARTFORD. *CBIA News.*[3] Address: 370 Asylum St., 06103. Tel., (860) 244-1900. *Publisher,* CBIA Service Corp.; *Editor,* Diane F. Edwards.

CEA Advisor.[4] Address: Capitol Place, Suite 500, 21 Oak St., 06106. Tel., (860) 525-5641. *Publisher,* Conn. Education Assoc.; *Managing Editor,* Michael G. Lydick.

CSEA News.[6] Address: 760 Capitol Ave., 06106. Tel., (860) 951-6614, Toll Free (800) 894-9479. *Publisher,* Conn. State Employees Assoc.; *Editor,* Frances C. Messenger.

Connecticut Law Review.[1] Address: Univ. of Conn. School of Law, 65 Elizabeth St., 06105-2290. Tel., (860) 570-5381. *Publisher,* Conn. Law Review Assoc.; *Managing Editor,* Scott W. Foster, *Editorial Dir.,* Adam L. Schwartz.

Metroline.[2] Address: 495 Farmington Ave., 06105. Tel., (860) 236-7813. *Publisher,* Metro Publications, Inc.; *Editor-in-Chief,* William J. Mann; *Editor,* Surin A. Khan.

MIDDLETOWN. *The Middletown Bulletin.*[6] Address: 790 Ridge Rd., 06457. Tel., (860) 346-8183. *Publisher/Editorial Dir.,* Mary Corvo; *Editor,* William J. Corvo.

NEW HAVEN. *American Journal of Science.*[3] Address: 217 Kline Geology Laboratory, Yale University, P.O. Box 208109, 06520-8109. Tel., (203) 432-3131. *Publisher,* American Journal of Science; *Managing Editor,* Marie C. Casey.

American Scientist.[2] Address: 99 Alexander Dr., P.O. Box 13975, RTP, NC 27709. Tel., (919) 549-0097. *Publisher,* Sigma Xi, The Scientific Research Society; *Editor,* Rosalind Reid.

Columbia.[6] Address: One Columbus Plaza, 06510. Tel., (203) 772-2130, Ext. 398. *Publisher,* Knights of Columbus; *Editor, R*ichard McMunn.

The Connecticut Elder. Address: 150 Dwight St., P.O. Box 984, 06504. Tel., (203) 787-1812. *Publisher,* The Elder, Inc.; *Editor,* Chris Gray.

Yale Alumni Magazine.[4] Address: 149 York St., P.O. Box 1905, 06509-1905. Tel., (203) 432-0645. *Publisher,* Yale Alumni Publications, Inc.; *Editor,* Carter Wiseman.

The Yale Law Journal.[4] Address: 127 Wall Street, P. O. Box 208215 Yale Station, 06520-8215. Tel., (203) 432-1666. *Publisher,* The Yale Law Journal Co. Inc.; *Editor,* Oona A. Hathaway.

The Yale Literary Magazine. Address: 243-A Yale Station, 06520. Tel., (203) 436-1767, (203) 624-4215. *Publishers,* Magazine staff, Pierson College; *Editors-in-Chief,* Andrew Rossi, Carrie Iverson.

The Yale Review.[1] Address: Yale University, P.O. Box 208243, 06520-8243. Tel., (203) 432-0499. *Publisher,* Blackwell Publishers; *Editor,* J. D. McClatchy. Appears quarterly.

Yale Scientific Magazine.[1] Address: 209117 Yale Station, 06520. Tel., (203) 432-2374. *Publishe/Editor-in-Chief.,* Elizabeth Arias; *Managing Editor,* Ahmen Ismail.

NORWALK. *Norwalk Lifestyles.* Address: 542 Westport Ave., 06851. Tel., (203) 849-1600. *Publisher,* B. V. Brooks; *Editor,* Louise Lancaster-Keim.

ORANGE. *Our Town Newspaper.*[2] Address: P.O. Box 883, 378 Boston Post Rd., 06477-0883. Tel., (203) 795-0666. *Publisher,* Michele G. Collins. News deadline, one week prior. Published 2nd & 4th Tuesday of each month.

ROCKY HILL. *The Connecticut Bar Journal.*[2] Address: 101 Corporate Pl., 06067-1894. Tel., (860) 721-0025. *Publisher,* Conn. Bar Assoc.; *Editor-in-Chief,* Livia D. Barndollar; *Managing Editor,* Kenneth R. Plumb.

The Connecticut Lawyer.[7] Address: 101 Corporate Pl., 06067. Tel., (860) 721-0025. *Publisher,* Conn. Bar Assoc.; *Editor,* Megan FitzGerald.

The Unionist.[6] Address: 35 Marshall Rd., Rocky Hill 06067. Tel., (860) 257-9782. *Publisher,* Conn. State Federation of Teachers; *Editorial Dir.,* Leo Canty.

STONINGTON. *The League Bulletin.*[1] Address: 220 North Water St., 06378. Tel., (860) 535-1492. *Publisher,* The Conn. League of Historical Societies, Inc.; *Editor,* Louise D. Pittaway.

WEST HARTFORD. *The Hartford Automobiler.*[2] Address: 815 Farmington Ave., 06119. Tel., (860) 236-3261. *Publisher,* James H. Doran; *Editor,* Jennifer Giorgio.

[1]Published quarterly; [2]bi-monthly; [3]10 times per year; [4]8 times per year; [5]11 times per year; [6]12 times per year; [7]9 times per year; [8]once a month.

CONNECTICUT NEWSPAPER CORRESPONDENTS IN WASHINGTON, D.C.

Correspondent, Lolita C. Baldor. Address: 1331 Pennsylvania Ave., N.W., Suite 524, Washington, DC 20004. Representing *The Connecticut Post.*

Correspondent, Matthew Mello, Ottaway News Service, Washington Bureau. Address: 1025 Connecticut Ave., N.W., Suite 310, Washington, DC 20036. Representing *Danbury News-Times.*

Correspondents, David Lightman, Bureau Chief; Rene E. Brown, John MacDonald, Michael A. Remez. Address: 1730 Rhode Island Ave., N.W., Suite 300, Washington, DC 20036. Representing *The Hartford Courant.*

Correspondents, Eileen McGann, States News Service. Address: 1333 F St., N.W., Suite 400, Washington, DC 20004. Representing *The Waterbury-Republican, The New York Times, The Journal-Inquirer* (Manchester).

Correspondents, Tamara Lytle. Address: 1333 F St., N.W., Suite 400, Washington, DC 20004. Representing New *The Haven Register.*

CONNECTICUT ASSOCIATED PRESS MANAGING EDITORS.—*Pres.*, Jim Smith, *The Record-Journal*, Meriden; *Vice Pres.*, Deirdre Channing, Southern Connecticut Newspapers, Stamford; *Secy./Treas.*, Mary A. Rhyne, *Associated Press*, Hartford; *Immediate Past Pres.*, Judith W. Brown, *The Herald,* New Britain.

CONNECTICUT COUNCIL ON FREEDOM OF INFORMATION.—*Chm.*, John Reilly, *The Hour,* Norwalk; *Vice Chm.*, Bob Brown, *Bristol Press,* Bristol; James Sweeney, *Cablevision,* Norwalk; *Exec. Secy./Treas.*, Edward W. Frede, *The News-Times,* Danbury.

CONNECTICUT DAILY NEWSPAPERS ASSOCIATION.—*Pres.*, Mack Stewart, *Middletown Press,* Middletown; *Vice Pres., 1st,* William B. Pape, *Waterbury Republican-American,* Waterbury; *2nd,* Dick King, *The Hartford Courant,* Hartford; *Secy./Treas.*, Frank O. King, *The News-Times,* Danbury; *Treas.*, Vance C. Brown, *The Herald,* New Britain.

AM RADIO STATIONS

Connecticut Radio Network, Inc., One Circular Ave., Hamden 06514. *Pres.*, Barry Berman, Tel., (203) 288-2002. *Exec. Vice Pres.,* S. Richard Kalt, CRMC. *Gen. Mgr.*, Gary E. Zenobia; *Capitol Bureau Chief,* Steve Kotchko, Tel., (860) 527-1901.

ANSONIA. WADS. *Frequency (KHZ),* 690. *Power,* 1,000W.—Licensee, Address: P.O. Box 384, New Haven 06513. Tel., (203) 782-3564. *Mgr.*, Abraham Hernandez.

BRIDGEPORT. WDJZ. *Frequency (KHZ),* 1530. *Power,* 5,000W.—Licensee, Address: Estate of Francis F. D'Addario, 513 Boston Ave., 06610. Tel., (203) 335-2544. *Mgr.*, Russ Knight.

WICC. Frequency (KHZ), 600. *Power,* 1,000W (day); 500W (night).—Licensee, Address: WICC Associates, 2 Lafayette Sq., 06604-6000. Tel., (203) 366-6000. *Gen. Mgr.,* Vince Cremona.

BROOKFIELD. *WINE. Frequency (KHZ),* 940. *Power,* 1,000W.—Licensee, Address: Danbury Broadcasting Inc., P.O. Box 95, Danbury 06813. Tel., (203) 775-1212. *Gen. Mgr.,* Thomas Principi.

DANBURY. *WLAD. Frequency (KHZ),* 800. *Power,* 1,000W; 287W (night).—Licensee, Address: The Berkshire Broadcasting Corp., 198 Main St., 06810. Tel., (203) 744-4800; FAX, (203) 778-4655. *Mgr.,* Irving J. Goldstein.

FARMINGTON. *WNEZ. Frequency (KHZ),* 910. *Power,* 5,000W.—Licensee, Address: American Radio Systems, 10 Executive Dr., 06032. Tel., (860) 677-6700.

GREENWICH. *WGCH. Frequency (KHZ),* 1490. *Power,* 1,000W.—Licensee, Address: The Greenwich Broadcasting Corp., 1490 Dayton Ave., 06830. Tel., (203) 869-1490. *Gen. Mgr.,* William Hoover.

GROTON. *WSUB. Frequency (KHZ),* 980. *Power,* 1,000W.—Licensee, Address: H & D Wireless Limited Partnership, 100 Fort Hill Rd., 06340. Tel., (860) 446-1980. *Gen. Mgr.,* Gregory D. Delmonaco.

HARTFORD. *WCCC. Frequency (KHZ),* 1290. Power, 500W.—Licensee, Address: Greater Hartford Communications Corp., 243 So. Whitney St., 06105. Tel., (860) 233-4426; FAX, (860) 232-6511. *Mgr.,* Milt Aninger.

WDRC. Frequency (KHZ), 1360. *Power,* 5,000W.—Licensee, Address: Buckley Broadcasting of Connecticut, 869 Blue Hills Ave., Bloomfield 06002. Tel., (860) 243-1115. *Mgr.,* Wayne Mulligan.

WPOP. Frequency (KHZ), 1410. *Power,* 5,000W.—Licensee, Address: SFX Broadcasting Inc., 345 East Cedar St., Newington 06111. Tel., (860) 666-1411. *Gen. Mgr.,* Dennis Lamme.

WRDM. Frequency (KHZ), 1550.—Licensee Address: Ital-Net Broadcasting, Corp., 886 Maple Ave. 06114. Tel., (860) 956-1303; FAX, (860) 956-6834. *Pres.,* Lucio C. Ruzzier; *Program Dir.,* Walter Martinez.

WTIC. Frequency (KHZ), 1080. *Power,* 50,000W.—Licensee, Address: American Radio Systems, One Financial Plaza, 06103. Tel., (860) 522-1080. *Vice Pres./Gen. Mgr.,* Suzanne R. McDonald.

MERIDEN. *WMMW. Frequency (KHZ),* 1470. *Power,* 2,500W.—Licensee, Address: AM Radio Inc., 900 East Main St., Suite 423, 06450. Tel., (203) 634-1470. *Mgr.,* Anthony Pescatello.

MIDDLETOWN. *WCNX. Frequency (KHZ),* 1150. *Power,* 2,500W.—Licensee, Address: Jan Peek Communications, Inc., 777 River Rd., Box 359, 06457. Tel., (860) 347-2565. *Mgr.,* Edward J. Creem, Jr.

MILFORD. *WFIF. Frequency (KHZ),* 1500. *Power,* 5,000W.—Licensee, Address: K. W. Dolmar Broadcasting Co., Inc., 90 Kay Ave., 06460. Tel., (203) 878-5915. *Pres./Gen. Mgr.,* William A. Blount.

NEW BRITAIN. *WRYM. Frequency (KHZ),* 840. *Power,* 1,000W.—Licensee, Address: Hartford County Broadcasting Corp., 1056 Willard Ave., Newington 06111. Tel., (860) 666-5646. *Mgr.,* Barry A. Kursman.

NEW HAVEN. *WELI. Frequency (KHZ),* 960. *Power,* 5,000W.—Licensee, Address: Clear Channel Radio Licenses, Inc., P.O. Box 85, 06501. Tel., (203) 281-9600. *Vice Pres./Gen. Mgr.,* Faith Zila.

WNHC. Frequency (KHZ), 1340. *Power,* 1,000W.—Licensee, Address: Willis Communications, Inc., 300 Whalley Ave., New Haven 06510. Tel., (203) 752-1340. *Pres./Gen. Mgr.,* Edith Rozier.

WAVZ. Frequency (KHZ), 1300. *Power,* 1,000W.—Licensee, Address: Clear Channel Radio, Inc., 495 Benham St., Hamden 06514. Tel., (203) 248-8814. *Vice Pres./Gen. Mgr.,* Faith Zila.

NEW LONDON. *WNLC. Frequency (KHZ),* 1510. *Power,* 10,000W (day); 5,000W (night).—Licensee, Address: Hall Communications, Inc., P.O. Box 1031, 06320. Tel., (860) 442-5328. Gen. Mgr., Jim Reed; *Station Mgr.,* Andy Russell.

NORWALK. *WNLK. Frequency (KHZ),* 1350. *Power,* 1,000W.—Licensee, Address: CRB of Norwalk, Inc., 148 East Ave., 06851. Tel., (203) 838-5566. *Gen. Mgr.,* Scott J. Bacherman.

NORWICH. *WICH. Frequency (KHZ),* 1310. *Power,* 5,000W.—Licensee, Address: WICH, Inc., Cuprak Rd., 06360. Tel., (860) 887-3511. *Mgr.,* Richard P. Reed.

OLD SAYBROOK. *WLIS. Frequency (KHZ),* 1420. *Power,* 5,000W (day); 500W (night).—Licensee, Address: Crossroads Communications of Old Saybrook, 77 Springbrook Rd., P.O. Drawer W, 06475. Tel., (860) 388-3546. *Pres.,* Don DeCesare.

PUTNAM. *WINY. Frequency (KHZ),* 1350. *Power,* 5,000W.—Licensee, Address: Gerardi Broadcasting Corp., 45 Pomfret St., 06260. Tel., ((860) 928-1350. *Pres./Gen. Mgr.,* Michael J. Gerardi.

RIDGEFIELD. *WREF. Frequency (KHZ),* 850. *Power,* 2,500W.—Licensee, Address: The WREF, Inc., 165 Danbury Rd., P.O. Box 779, 06877-9085. Tel., (203) 438-1211; FAX, (203) 431-8473. *Mgr.,* Arthur Liu.

SOUTHINGTON. *WNTY. Frequency (KHZ),* 990. *Power,* 2,500W.—Licensee, Address: WNTY Associates, P.O. Box 459, 440 Old Turnpike Rd., 06489. Tel., (860) 628-0311. *Owner/Mgr.,* George W. Stevens.

STAMFORD. *WSTC. Frequency (KHZ),* 1400. *Power,* 1,000W.—Licensee, Address: Commodore Media, 100 Prospect St., 06901. Tel., (203) 327-1400. *Sta. Mgr.,* Peter Mutino.

TORRINGTON. *WSNG. Frequency (KHZ),* 610. *Power,* 1,000W (day); 500W (night).—Licensee, Address: Consumer Service Radio, Inc., 8 Church St., Box 657, 06790. Tel., (860) 489-4181; FAX, (860) 496-8262. *Mgr.,* Jay Sheldon.

WATERBURY. *WATR. Frequency (KHZ),* 1320. *Power,* 5,000W (day); 1,000W (night).—Licensee, Address: WATR, Inc., 1 Broadcast La., 06706. Tel., (203) 755-1121; *Mgr.,* Thomas Chute.

WQQW. Frequency (KHZ), 1590. *Power,* 5,000W.—Licensee, Address: Comko Ltd., c/o WQQW, Broadcast Center, 101 South Main St., 06706. Tel., (203) 753-2121. Gen. Mgr., Tom Coffey.

WWCO. Frequency (KHZ), 1240. Power, 1,000W.—Licensee, Address: Mattatuck Communications, Inc., P.O. Box 99, 06720-0099. Tel., (203) 755-9926; FAX, (203) 753-8729. *Vice. Pres./Gen. Mgr.,* Tom Coffey.

WESTPORT. *WMMM. Frequency (KHZ),* 1260. *Power,* 1,000W.—Licensee, Address: Minuteman Broadcasting, Inc., 1 Lois St., Norwalk 06851-4406. Tel., (203) 849-9955. *Exec. Vice Pres.,* Mark S. Graham; *Sales Mgr.,* Walter G. Broadhurst.

WILLIMANTIC. *WILI. Frequency (KHZ),* 1400. *Power,* 1,000W.—Licensee, Address: Nutmeg Broadcasting Co., 720 Main St., 06226-2604. Tel., (860) 456-1111. *Mgr.,* David M. Evan.

WINDSOR. *WKND. Frequency (KHZ),* 1480. *Power,* 500W.—Licensee, Address: Hartcom Inc., P.O. Box 1480, 06095. Tel., (860) 688-6221. *Mgr.,* Marion Thornton-Anderson.

FM RADIO STATIONS

BLOOMFIELD. *WJMJ. Frequency (MHZ),* 88.9 (Hartford), 93.1 (Hamden), 107.1 (New Haven). *Power,* 7,000W.—Licensee, Address: St. Thomas Seminary, 467 Bloomfield Ave., 06002. Tel., (860) 242-8800. *Gen. Mgr.,* John L. Ellinger.

BRIDGEPORT. *WEZN. Frequency (MHZ),* 99.9. *Power,* 27,500W.—Licensee, Address: New City Communications, Inc., 10 Middle St., 06604. Tel., (203) 366-9321. *Mgr.,* James T. Morley.

WPKN. Frequency (MHZ), 89.5. *Power,* 10,000W.—Licensee, Address: WPKN, Inc., 244 University Ave., 06604-5700. Tel., (203) 331-9756. *Mgr.,* Henry D. Minot.

BROOKFIELD. *WRKI. Frequency (MHZ),* 95.1. *Power,* 50,000W.—Licensee, Address: Commodore Media Inc., 1004 Federal Rd., 06804. Tel., (203) 775-1212. *Mgr.,* Wayne Leland.

DANBURY. *WDAQ. Frequency (MHZ),* 98.3. *Power,* 3,000W.—Licensee, Address: The Berkshire Broadcasting Corporation, 198 Main St., 06810. Tel., (203) 744-4800; FAX, (203) 778-4655. *Mgr.,* Irving J. Goldstein.

WXCI. Frequency (MHZ), 91.7. *Power,* 760W.—Licensee, Address: Campus Broadcast Assoc., 181 White St., 06810. Tel., (203) 792-8666. *Mgr.,* Chris Nolan.

FAIRFIELD. *WSHU. Frequency (MHZ),* 91.1. *Power,* 20,000W.—Licensee, Sacred Heart Univ. Address: 5151 Park Ave., 06432. Tel., (203) 371-7989. *Mgr.,* George Lombardi.

WVOF. Frequency (MHZ), 88.5. *Power,* 100W.—Licensee, Address: Fairfield University Board of Trustees, Dept. of Student Affairs, North Benson Rd., 06430. Tel., (203) 254-4000, Ext. 2371. *Mgr.,* Matthew Dinnan.

FARMINGTON. *WRCH-FM. Frequency (MHZ),* 100.5. *Power,* 50,000W.—Licensee, Address: American Radio Systems, Inc., 10 Executive Dr., 06032. Tel., (860) 677-6700. *Vice. Pres./Gen. Mgr.,* Suzanne McDonald.

WZMX. Frequency (MHZ), 93.7. *Power,* 50,000W.—Licensee, Address: America Radio Systems, Inc., Ten Executive Dr., 06032. Tel., (860) 677-6700. *Vice Pres./Gen. Mgr.,* Suzanne McDonald.

GROTON. *WQGN. Frequency (MHZ),* 105.5. *Power,* 3,000W.—Licensee, Address: H & D Wireless Limited Partnership, 100 Fort Hill Rd., 06340. Tel., (860) 446-1980. *Gen. Mgr.,* Gregory D. Delmonaco.

WVVE. Frequency (MHZ), 102.3. *Power,* 3,000W.—Licensee, Address: Shoreline Communications, Inc., P.O. Box 97, Mystic 06355. Tel., (860) 599-2214; FAX, (860) 599-3568. *Pres.,* David J. Quinn.

HAMDEN. *WKCI. Frequency (MHZ),* 101.3. *Power,* 50,000W.—Licensee, Address: Clear Channel Communications, P. O. Box 85, New Haven 06510. Tel., (203) 248-8814. *Vice. Pres./Gen. Mgr.,* Faith Zila.

HARTFORD. *WCCC-FM. Frequency (MHZ),* 106.9. *Power,* 23,500W.—Licensee, Address: Greater Hartford Communications Corp., 243 So. Whitney St., 06105. Tel., (860) 233-4426; FAX, (860) 232-6511. *Mgr.,* Milt Aninger.

WDRC. Frequency (MHZ), 102.9. *Power,* 19,500W.—Licensee, Address: Buckley Broadcasting Corp. of Conn., 869 Blue Hills Ave., Bloomfield 06002. Tel., (860) 243-1115. *Mgr.,* Wayne Mulligan.

WHCN. Frequency (MHZ), 105.9. *Power,* 50,000W.—Licensee, Address: WHCN, Inc., 1039 Asylum Ave., 06105. Tel., (860) 247-1060. *Station Mgr.,* Gordon Weingarth.

WRTC. Frequency (MHZ), 89.3. *Power,* 350W.—Licensee, Address: WRTC-FM, Trinity College, 06106. Tel., (860) 297-2450 (studio), (860) 297-2439 (business). *Mgr.,* Patrice Evans.

WTIC. Frequency (MHZ), 96.5. *Power,* 20,000W.—Licensee, Address: American Radio Systems, One Financial Plaza, 06103. Tel., (860) 522-1080. *Vice Pres./Gen. Mgr.,* Suzanne R. McDonald.

HARTFORD/MERIDEN. *WKSS. Frequency (MHZ),* 95.7. *Power,* 50,000W.—Licensee, Address: Precision Media Corp., Hartford Square North, Hartford 06106. Tel., (860) 249-9577. *Mgr.,* Timothy J. A. Montgomery.

WEDW. Frequency MHZ, 88.5. *Power,* 3,000W. Licensee, Address: CT Public Broadcasting, 307 Atlantic St., Stamford 06901. Tel., (203) 965-0440. *Mgr.,* Don Russell.

WPKT. Frequency (MHZ), 90.5. *Power,* 19,000W.—Licensee, Address: CT Public Broadcasting, 240 New Britain Ave., P.O. Box 260240, Hartford 06126. Tel., (860) 278-5310. *Mgr.,* John Berky.

LITCHFIELD. *WZBG. Frequency (MHZ),* 97.3. *Power,* 3,000W.—Licensee,Address: Local Boys and Girls Broadcasting, Corp., 49 Commons Drive, P.O. Box 1497, Litchfield 06759. Tel., (860) 567-3697. *Mgr.,* Jennifer Parsons.

MANSFIELD (Storrs). *WHUS. Frequency (MHZ),* 91.7. *Power,* 3,200W.—Licensee, Address: Board of Trustees, University of Connecticut, Box U8R, 2110 Hillside Rd., Storrs 06269. Tel., (860) 486-4007 (Office), 429-WHUS (Studio). *Gen. Mgr.*, John E. Murphy.

MIDDLETOWN. *WESU. Frequency (MHZ),* 88.1. *Power,* 1,500W.—Licensee, Address: The Wesleyan Student Assembly., Wesleyan Station, 06459. Tel., (860) 685-3668. *President,* Dahlia Schweitzer.

WIHS. Frequency (MHZ), 104.9. *Power,* 3,100W.—Licensee, Address: Connecticut Radio Fellowship, Inc., 1933 So. Main St., 06457. Tel., (860) 346-3846. *Mgr.,* G. J. Gerard.

MONROE. *WMNR. Frequency (MHZ),* 88.1. *Power,* 5,000W.—Licensee, Address: Board of Education, 1014 Monroe Tpke., 06468. Tel., (203) 268-9667. *Mgr.,* Kurt Anderson.

NEW BRITAIN. *WFCS. Frequency (MHZ),* 107.7. *Power,* 36W.—Licensee, Address: Board of Trustees/CCSU, 1615 Stanley St., 06050. Tel., (860) 832-1883. *Mgr.,* Chip McCabe.

NEW HAVEN. *WPLR. Frequency (MHZ),* 99.1. *Power,* 50,000W.—Licensee, Address: Michael Ferrel, General Broadcasting of Connecticut, Inc./General Communicorp Inc./Multi-Market Radio, Inc., WPLR, 1191 Dixwell Ave., Hamden 06514. Tel., (203) 287-9070. *Mgr.,* Robert L. Williams.

WYBC. Frequency (MHZ), 94.3. *Power,* 1,700W.—Licensee, Address: The Yale Broadcasting Co., Inc., 165 Elm St., Box 209050, Yale Station 06520. Tel., (203) 432-4118. *Station Mgr.,* Kuba Stolarski; *Gen. Mgr.*, Mike Corwin; *Program Dir.,* Matt Spanjers; *Training Dir.,* Natasha John; *Comptroller,* John McGann.

NEW LONDON. *WTYD. Frequency (MHZ),* 100.9. *Power,* 3,000W.—Licensee, Address: Hall Communications, Inc., 90 Foster Rd., Waterford 06385. Tel., (860) 442-5328. *Station Mgr.,* Andy Russell; *Gen. Mgr.,* Jim Reed.

NORWALK. *WEFX. Frequency (MHZ),* 95.9. *Power,* 3,000W.—Licensee, Address: CRB of Norwalk, Inc., 148 East Ave., 06851. Tel., (203) 838-5566. *Gen. Mgr.,* Scott J. Bacherman.

NORWICH. *WCTY. Frequency (MHZ),* 97.7. *Power,* 1,900W.—Licensee, Address: WICH, Inc., Cuprak Rd., 06360. Tel., (860) 887-3511. *Mgr.,* James J. Reed.

WNPR. Frequency (MHZ), 89.1. *Power,* 5,100W.—Licensee, Address: CT Public Broadcasting, 240 New Britain Ave., P.O. Box 260240, Hartford 06126-0240. Tel., (860) 278-5310. *Mgr.,* John Berky.

SHARON. *WQQQ. Frequency (MHZ),* 103.3. *Power (ERP),* 3,700 .—Address: P.O. Box 446, 7 Ethan Allen St., Lakeville 06039. Tel., (860) 435-3333; FAX, (860) 435-3334; E-mail-9103-fmeli.com. *Mgr.,* Marshall Miles.

STAMFORD. *WKHL. Frequency (MHZ),* 96.7. *Power,* 3,000W.—Licensee, Address: Commodore Media Inc., 100 Prospect St., 06901. Tel., (203) 327-1400. *Sta. Mgr.*, Greg Martin.

WATERBURY. *WMRQ. Frequency (MHZ),* 104.1. *Power,* 50,000W.—Licensee, Address: SFX Broadcasting Group, Inc., P.O. Box 31-1410, Newington Branch, Hartford 06131. Tel., (860) 666-1411. *Gen. Mgr.,* Dennis Lamme.

WWYZ. Frequency (MHZ), 92.5. *Power,* 17 KW ERP.—Licensee, Address: WWYZ, One Broadcast La., 06706. Tel., (203) 755-3111. *Mgr.,* Steve Gilmore.

WEST HARTFORD. *WWUH. Frequency (MHZ),* 91.3. *Power,* 1,000W.—Licensee, Address: University of Hartford, 200 Bloomfield Ave., 06117. Tel., (860) 768-4703. *Gen. Mgr.,* John N. Ramsey.

WILLIMANTIC. *WILI. Frequency (MHZ),* 98.3. *Power,* 3,000W.—Licensee, Address: Nutmeg Broadcasting Company, 720 Main St., 06226-2604. Tel., (860) 456-1111. *Mgr.,* David M. Evan.

TELEVISION STATIONS IN CONNECTICUT

BRIDGEPORT. *WEDW. Channel Number,* 49.—Licensee, Address: Conn. Public Broadcasting Inc., 240 New Britain Ave., P. O. Box 260240, Hartford 06126-0240. Tel., (860) 278-5310. *Pres./CEO,* Jerry Franklin.

HARTFORD. *WEDH. Channel Number,* 24.—Licensee, Address: Conn. Public Broadcasting Inc., 240 New Britain Ave., P. O. Box 260240, 06126-0240. Tel., (860) 278-5310. *Pres./CEO,* Jerry Franklin.

WFSB. Channel Number, 3.—Licensee, Address: Post-Newsweek Stations, Conn., Inc., 3 Constitution Plaza, 06103-1892. Tel., (860) 728-3333. *Vice Pres./Gen. Mgr.,* Christopher J. Rohrs.

WTIC. Channel Number, 61.—Licensee, Address: Hartford Television Inc., 1 Corporate Center, 06103. Tel., (860) 527-6161. *Vice Pres./Gen. Mgr.,* Robert Gluck.

WRDM-TV13. Channel Number, 13.—Licensee, Address: Channel 13 Television Inc., 886 Maple Ave., 06114. Tel., (860) 956-1303; FAX, (860) 956-6834. Pres., Lucio C. Ruzzier; *Gen. Mgr.,* Gaetano Leone.

NEW BRITAIN/HARTFORD/NEW HAVEN/WATERBURY. *WVIT. Channel Number,* 30.—Licensee, Address: WVIT, Inc., 1422 New Britain Ave., West Hartford 06110. Tel., (860) 521-3030. *Vice Pres./Gen. Mgr.,* Alfred T. Bova.

NEW HAVEN. *WTNH. Channel Number,* 8.—Licensee, Address: Lin Television, 8 Elm St., 06510. Tel., (203) 784-8888. *Mgr.,* Hank Yaggi.

WEDY. Channel Number, 65.—Licensee, Address: Conn. Public Broadcasting Inc., 240 New Britain Ave., P. O. Box 260240, Hartford 06126-0240. Tel., (860) 278-5310. *Pres./CEO,* Jerry Franklin.

NEW LONDON. *WTWS. Channel Number,* 26.—Licensee, Address: Paxon Communications, 3 Shaws Cove, Suite 226, 06320. Tel., (860) 444-2626. *Mgr.,* Bruce Fox.

NORWICH. *WEDN. Channel Number,* 53.—Licensee, Address: Conn. Public Broadcasting Inc., 240 New Britain Ave., P. O. Box 260240, Hartford 06126-0240. Tel., (860) 278-5310. *Pres./CEO,* Jerry Franklin.

WATERBURY. *WTXX-UPN 20 .*—Licensee, Address: Counterpoint Communications, Inc., 15 Peach Orchard Rd., Prospect 06712-1052. Tel., (203) 758-3900. *Gen. Mgr.,* David L. Brewer, Jr.

TRANSLATOR TELEVISION STATIONS

WATERBURY. *W12BH. Channel Number,* Translator 12.—Licensee, Address: Connecticut Public Broadcasting, Inc., 240 New Britain Ave., P. O. Box 260240, Hartford 06126-0240. Tel., (860) 278-5310. *Pres./CEO,* Jerry Franklin.

BROADCASTERS' ASSOCIATIONS

CONN. ASSOCIATED PRESS BROADCASTERS ASSOC.—*Chm./Bd. of Dirs.,* Steve Coates, WPOP, Hartford; *Bureau Chief,* MaryAnne Rhyne, AP, Hartford; *Secy.-Treas.,* CAPBA.

CONN. BROADCASTERS ASSOC.—*Chm.,* Andy Russell, WTYD/WNLC, New London; *1st Vice Chm.,* Chris Rohrs, WFSB-TV, Hartford; *2nd Vice Chm.,* Suzanne McDonald, WTIC Radio, Hartford; *Secy.,* Mike Rice, WILI-AM, Willimantic; *Treas.,* Tom Principi, CRN, Brookfield; *Pres.,* Paul K. Taff, P.O. Box 678, Glastonbury 06033.

Dirs., Al Bova, WVIT-TV, West Hartford; Suzanne McDonald, WZMX/WRCH, Farmington; Bruce Fox, WTWS-TV, New London; Hank Yaggi, WTNH-TV, New Haven; Robert Gluck, WTIC-TV, Hartford; Jennifer Parsons, WZBG-FM, Litchfield; Vince Cremona, WICC/WEBE, Bridgeport; Mike Rice, WILI-AM/FM, Willimantic; Chris Rohrs, WFSB-TV, Hartford; Andy Russell, WNLC/WTYD, New London; John Ryan, WEZN-FM, Bridgeport; Edith Rozier, WNHC-AM, North Haven; Jim Simonetti, WKCI/WELI, New Haven.

SOME FACTS ABOUT CONNECTICUT

Name of State .... Connecticut

Official Designation: "The Constitution State" was adopted by Act of the Legislature, 1959.
Indian Name (Beside the Long Tidal River) .... Quinnehtukqut
State Motto: *Qui Transtulit Sustinet*—He Who Transplanted Still Sustains.
The emblems of the State are the Seal, the Armorial Bearings, the Flag, the Flower, the Bird, the Tree, the Animal, the Insect, the Mineral, the Song, the Ship, the Hero, the Shellfish, the Composer, the Fossil.
  The State Seal was provided for in the Constitution, 1818.
  The State Flag was adopted by Act of the Legislature, 1897.
  The State Flower, the Mountain Laurel, was adopted by Act of the Legislature, 1907.
  The State Bird, the Robin, was adopted by Act of the Legislature, 1943.
  The State Tree, the White Oak, was adopted by Act of the Legislature, 1947.
  The State Animal, the Sperm Whale, *Physeter Catodon,* was adopted by Act of the Legislature, 1975.
  The State Insect, the Praying Mantis, *Mantis Religiosa,* was adopted by Act of the Legislature, 1977.
  The State Mineral, the Garnet, was adopted by Act of the Legislature, 1977.
  The State Song, "Yankee Doodle," was adopted by Act of the Legislature, 1978.
  The State Ship, USS Nautilus, was adopted by Act of the Legislature, 1983.
  The State Hero, Nathan Hale, was adopted by Act of the Legislature, 1985.
  The State Shellfish, the Eastern Oyster, was adopted by Act of the Legislature, 1989.
  The State Composer, Charles Edward Ives was adopted by Act of the Legislature, 1991.
  The State Fossil, *Eurbrontes Giganteus,* was adopted by Act of the Legislature, 1991.
  The State Heroine, Prudence Crandall, was adopted by Act of the Legislature, 1995.
  The State Tartan was adopted by Act of the Legislature, 1995.
Hartford has been the sole Capital City since 1875
Population, 1990, U.S. Official Census 3,287,116
Cities with largest population (1990):   1. Bridgeport, 141,686
2. Hartford, 139,739   3. New Haven, 130,474
4. Waterbury, 108,961   5. Stamford, 108,056
Counties 8   Towns 169   Cities 21   Boroughs 9
Grand List of Taxable Property (1994) .... est. $175,045,501,735
Average rate of taxation (1994) .... est. 26.02 mills
Number of dwelling houses (1994) 867,755
  Average assessment (1994) $70,781
Number of condominiums (1994) 138,274
  Average assessment (1994) $65,059
Total of dwelling houses and condominiums (1994) 1,006,029
  Average assessment (1994) $69,995
Birth Rate (1994—per 1,000 pop.) 14.0
Death Rate (1994—per 1,000 pop.) 8.9
Area of State .... 5,009 square miles; 3,205,760 acres
Length of Boundary .... 371 miles
Length of Shoreline .... 253 miles
Highest Altitude .... Mt. Frissell in Salisbury, 2,380 feet above sea level
Total mileage of Rivers and Streams .... approx. 8,400

Total number of Lakes and Ponds .... approx. 6,000
State Parks .... 91 .... 31,729 acres
State Forests .... 30 .... 144,768 acres
State Monuments .... 8 .... 14 acres
Miles on State Highway System (as of Dec. 31, 1996) 4,094.28
    State Maintained Access Roads and Ramps 362.17
    State Maintained Routes 3,732.11
Miles of Divided Lane Highways in System 720.46
Receipts of State Government for the fiscal year 1995 to
    June 30, 1996, including sales of State bonds, notes and commercial paper .. $17,360,000,000
Disbursements of State Government for the fiscal year July 1, 1995
    to June 30, 1996, including retirement of bonds, redemption
    of notes and payment of commercial paper $16,532,000,000

GOVERNMENT STATISTICS

Elective State Officers 6
    Governor, Lieutenant Governor, Secretary of the State, Treasurer,
    Comptroller and Attorney General.
United States Senators from Connecticut 2
United States Representatives 6
State Senators in the General Assembly 36
Representatives in the General Assembly 151

STATE EMPLOYEES IN EXECUTIVE BRANCH
(January 31, 1996)

Number of full-time state positions 52,490
Number of part-time state positions (working less than 35 hours per
    week) 8,695

JUDICIAL STATISTICS

Justices of Supreme Court 7	Judges of Superior Court 176
Sr. Justice of Supreme Court 1	(includes Supreme Court Justices,
Judges of Appellate Court 9	Appellate Court Justices)
Sr. Judge of Appellate Court 1	Probate Courts 132

LAW ENFORCEMENT

Dept. of Public Safety Headquarters 1
State Police Troops 12
Community Correctional Centers 3
    Number of Inmates, Oct. 1, 1996 2,610
Correctional Institutions 19
    Number of Inmates, Oct. 1, 1996 12,549

HOSPITALS AND INSTITUTIONS

University of Connecticut's John N. Dempsey Hospital (State, General)	1
Number of in-patient beds	204
Bassinets	28
State Inpatient Facilities for Mental Health and Addiction Services	4
Number of patients on books, Oct. 1, 1996	631
State Training Schools for the Mentally Retarded	1
Regions	5
Number of clients in residential settings, July 1, 1996	5,917

EDUCATIONAL STATISTICS
(1995)

	Number	Full-Time Faculty	Students
University of Connecticut (Including the UConn Health Center)	1	1,557	22,973
State Universities	4	1,085	33,540
Community-Technical Colleges	12	729	42,828
Charter Oak State College[3]	1	60	1,998
Independent Four-Year Colleges and Universities	18	4,308	55,549
Independent Two-Year Colleges	6	87	1,766
U.S. Coast Guard Academy	1	42	862

	Number	Full-Time Equivalent Professional Staff	1995 Students
Local Public Schools	995	40,147.1	499,815
Academies	3	251.1	3,119
State Vocational-Technical Schools	17	1,117.1	10,322
State or State-Aided Schools[1]	26	314.3	3,755
Regional Educational Service Centers	6	471.5	2,047
Nonpublic Schools[2]	338	7,501.0	74,943

[1] Includes 4 institutions run by the Department of Children and Families, and 22 by the Department of Correction.
[2] Includes 48 state approved nonpublic special education facilities.
[3] External degree program; students and faculty included in above counts.

AGRICULTURAL STATISTICS
(1995)

Number of Farms	3,800
Agricultural Land Resources (acres)	
Farmland	400,000
Commercially viable forest land	1,777,000
Shellfish grounds	51,923
Total Agricultural Acreage	2,228,923
Total Agricultural Employment	13,148

Value of Agricultural Products produced	$841,285,000
Nursery/Greenhouse	$381,150,000
Eggs/Poultry	$100,851,000
Dairy	$72,208,000
Livestock	$21,507,000
Shellfish	$61,881,000
Tobacco	$34,294,000
Fruits and Vegetables	$39,537,000
Field Crops (Hay & Silage)	$29,057,000
Forestry	$45,000,000
Mushrooms	$44,000,000
Christmas Trees	$8,000,000
Other	$3,800,000
Numbers of Farmers Markets	52
Total Number of WIC and Senior Farmers' Market Participants	57,331

MISCELLANEOUS STATISTICS

Connecticut Corporations (March 31, 1997)	approx. 109,978
Foreign Corporations (March 31, 1997)	approx. 20,804
Corporation Business Tax July 1, 1995 to June 30, 1996	$504,494,391.48
Fees received by Office of Secretary of the State from July 1, 1995 to June 30, 1996	$15,788,340

(1996)

Notaries Public .... approx. 51,995

Water Companies - Investor owned	45	Domestic Telephone Companies providing service in Conn.	3
" " - municipal	52		
Water and Sewer Investor Companies	1	Number of access lines	2,500,000
Sewer Companies	0	Community Antenna Television Companies (CATV)	26
Electric Companies - Investor	2		
" " - Municipal	7	Route miles of active trackage	570
Gas Companies - Investor owned	3	Track miles of active trackage	822
Gas and Electric Co. - municipal	1	(includes multi-track commuter mainline & Amtrack lines; excludes yard tracks)	
Number of Railroads	14		

Number of Bus Companies .... 33 Interstate, 11 urban, 4 rural Transit Districts operating own systems, plus Conn. Transit and 3 private contractors operating 8 state-owned urban systems.

Number of Taxi Companies	97
Banks and Thrifts	100

National Banks	11	Federal Savings and Loan Associations	4
State Banks and Trust Companies	31	State Credit Unions	70
Savings Banks	46	Federal Credit Unions	159
Federal Savings Banks	3	Check Cashiers	27
Savings and Loan Associations	5	Small Loan Licensees	40
Sales Finance Licensees			201

Sales Finance Licensees (Limited)	26
Consumer Collection Agencies	382

Secondary Mortgage Loan Licensees:
- Affiliated with Small Loan Licensees ... 38
- Non-affiliated Lenders ... 389
- Brokers only ... 199

Debt Adjusters ... 5

First Mortgage Licensees:
- Lenders ... 688
- Affiliated with Small Loan Licensees ... 33
- Brokers only ... 146

Insurance Companies with Home Office Headquarters in Connecticut
  As of June 30, 1996 ... 110
Motor Vehicle Registrations issued, all classes, July 1, 1995 to June 30, 1996 ... 1,531,223
Motor Vehicle Licenses issued, July 1, 1995 to June 30, 1996 ... 745,772
Motor Vehicle Fees, July 1, 1995 to June 30, 1996 ... $219,094,292
Gasoline Tax and Special Motor Fuel Tax Receipts, including Motor
  Carrier Road Tax, July 1, 1995 to June 30, 1996 ... $746,182,337.46
Newspapers published in State (daily, Sunday, weekly and monthly) ... approx. 148
Broadcasting Stations (AM) ... 36   (FM) ... 39
Television Stations in State ... 11

SOME OCCUPATIONAL STATISTICS
(1996)

Securities Broker/Dealers	2,071	Barbers	2,159
Securities Agents	79,887	Natureopaths	89
Agents of Issuer	313	Podiatrists	334
Investment Advisers	1,163	Physical Therapists	3,220
Investment Adviser Agents	10,708	Hypertrichologists	246
Physicians and Surgeons	12,100	Registered Nurses	48,322
Dentists	2,936	Licensed Practical Nurses	11,465
Dental Hygienists	2,963	Advanced Practice Reg. Nurses	1,155
Speech Pathologists	1,637	Optometrists	629
Nurse Midwives	119	Opticians	574
Osteopaths	189	Homeopaths	23
Chiropractors	845	Veterinarians	856
Audiologists	192	Occupational Therapists	1,033
Hair Dressers	22,860	Psychologists	1,328

AVIATION & PORTS
(1996)

State-owned Airports: Bradley International Airport, Windsor Locks; Groton-New London Airport, Groton; Hartford-Brainard Airport, Hartford; Danielson Airport, Killingly; Waterbury-Oxford Airport, Oxford; Windham Airport, Windham.

Commercial Airports 26*	Private Seaplane Bases 5
Commercial Heliports 8	Commercial Seaplane Bases 2
Private Heliports .... 52†	Private Airports 29**

*Includes state-owned and municipally owned.
**Includes 2 restricted military airports.
†Includes state heliport.

Major seaports: Bridgeport, New Haven, New London (State piers).

CONNECTICUT INDIANS

Number of Indian Reservations in Connecticut 5
  Golden Hill Paugussett Reservation, Trumbull (1/4 acre):
    Number of residents 4
  Golden Hill Paugussett Reservation, Colchester (106 acres):
    Number of residents 4
  Paucatuck Eastern Pequot Reservation, North Stonington (225 acres):
    Number of residents 10
  Mashantucket Pequot Reservation, Ledyard (1,500 acres federal trust land):
    Number of residents 115
  Schaghticoke Reservation, Kent (300 acres):
    Number of residents 15

LEGAL HOLIDAYS IN THE STATE

January 1	New Year's Day
First Monday on or after January 15	Martin Luther King, Jr. Day
February 12	Lincoln Day
Third Monday in February	Washington's Birthday
Last Monday in May	Memorial Day
July 4	Independence Day
The First Monday in September	Labor Day
The Second Monday in October	Columbus Day
November 11	Veterans' Day
December 25	Christmas

Whenever any of such days occurs upon a Sunday, the Monday next following such day shall be a legal holiday and whenever any of such days occurs upon a Saturday, the Friday immediately preceding such day shall be a legal holiday. (Sec. 1-4 CT. Gen. Stat.)

*The Friday before Easter Sunday	Good Friday
*The Fourth Thursday in November	Thanksgiving Day

*These days are designated by the Governor.

MEDAL OF HONOR RECIPIENTS
STATE OF CONNECTICUT

CIVIL WAR

NAME	RANK	UNIT	DATE OF ACTION	TOWN	BORN/RES.
Babcock, William J.	SERGEANT	Co E, 2d RI Infantry	2 Apr 1865	Griswold	B
Bacon, Elijah W.	PRIVATE	Co F, 14th CT Infantry	3 Jul 1863	Burlington	B
Beckwith, Wallace A.	PRIVATE	Co F, 21st CT Infantry	13 Dec 1862	New London	B
Beebe, William S.	1ST LIEUTENANT	Ordinance Dept., US Army	23 Apr 1864	Thompson	R
Briggs, Elijah A.	CORPORAL	Co B, 2d CT Heavy Artillery	3 Apr 1865	Salisbury	B
Buck, F. Clarence	CORPORAL	Co A, 21st CT Infantry	29 Sep 1864	Hartford	B
Burke, Daniel W.	1ST SERGEANT	Co B, 2d US Infantry	20 Sep 1862	New Haven	B
Corliss, George W.	CAPTAIN	Co C, 5th CT Infantry	9 Aug 1862	New Haven	R
Crocker, Henry H.	CAPTAIN	Co F, 2d MA Cavalry	19 Oct 1864	Colchester	B
Curtis, John C.	SERGEANT MAJOR	9th CT Infantry	5 Aug 1862	Bridgeport	B
Denning, Lorenzo	LANDSMAN	US Pickett Boat #1	27 Oct 1864	Connecticut	B
Ennis, Charles D.	PRIVATE	Co G, 1st RI Light Artillery	2 Apr 1865	Stonington	B
Flynn, Christopher	CORPORAL	Co K, 14th CT Infantry	3 Jul 1863	Sprague	R
Fox, Nicholas	PRIVATE	Co H, 28th CT Infantry	14 Jun 1863	Greenwich	R
Gibbs, Wesley	SERGEANT	Co B, 2d CT Heavy Artillery	2 Apr 1865	Sharon	B
Gray, Robert A.	SERGEANT	Co C, 21st CT Infantry	16 May 1864	Groton	R
Harding, Thomas	CPT OF FORECASTLE	US Navy, USS Dacotah	9 Jun 1864	Middletown	B
Hickok, Nathan E.	CORPORAL	Co A, 8th CT Infantry	29 Sep 1864	Danbury	B
Hincks, William B.	SERGEANT MAJOR	14th CT Infantry	3 Jul 1863	Bridgeport	R
Hooper, William B.	CORPORAL	Co L, 1st NJ Cavalry	31 Mar 1865	Willimantic	B
Horne, Samuel B.	CAPTAIN	Co H, 11th CT Infantry	29 Sep 1864	Winsted	R
Hubbell, William S.	CAPTAIN	Co A, 21st CT Infantry	30 Sep 1864	Wolcott	B
Jackson, Frederick R.	1ST SERGEANT	Co F, 7th CT Infantry	16 Jun 1862	New Haven	B
Jones, John	LANDSMAN	USS Rhode Island	30 Dec 1862	Bridgeport	B
Lanfare, Aaron S.	1ST LIEUTENANT	Co B, 1st CT Cavalry	6 Apr 1865	Branford	B
Marsh, Charles H.	PRIVATE	Co D, 1st CT Cavalry	31 Jul 1864	Milford	B
Murphy, James T.	PRIVATE	Co L, 1st CT Artillery	25 Mar 1865	New Haven	R
Neville, Edwin M.	CAPTAIN	Co C, 1st CT Cavalry	6 Apr 1865	Waterbury	R
Norton, Elliott M.	2ND LIEUTENANT	Co H, 6th MI Cavalry	6 Apr 1865	Connecticut	B

MEDAL OF HONOR RECIPIENTS

NAME	RANK	UNIT	DATE OF ACTION	TOWN	BORN/RES.
Palmer, John G.	CORPORAL	Co F, 21st CT Infantry	13 Dec 1862	Montville	B
Peck, Oscar E.	2ND CLASS BOY	USS Varuna	24 Apr 1862	Bridgeport	B
Shaler, Alexander	COLONEL	65th NY Infantry	3 May 1863	Haddam	B
Simonds, William Edgar	SERGEANT MAJOR	25th CT Infantry	14 Apr 1863	Canton	R
Swift, Frederic W.	LIEUTENANT COLONEL	17th MI Infantry	16 Nov 1863	Mansfield Ctr.	B
Tinkham, Eugene M.	CORPORAL	Co H, 148th NY Infantry	3 Jun 1864	Sprague	B
Tracy, Charles H.	SERGEANT	Co A, 37th MA Infantry	12 May 1864	Jewett City	B
Tucker, Allen	SERGEANT	Co F, 10th CT Infantry	2 Apr 1865	Lyme	B
Weeks, John H.	PRIVATE	Co H, 152d NY Infantry	12 May 1864	Hampton	B
Whitaker, Edward W.	CAPTAIN	Co E, 1st CT Cavalry	29 Jun 1864	Killingly	B
Wilson, Christopher W.	PRIVATE	Co E, 73d NY Infantry	12 May 1864	West Meriden	R
Wright, Robert	PRIVATE	Co G, 14th US Infantry	1 Oct 1864	Woodstock	R

INDIAN CAMPAIGNS

NAME	RANK	UNIT	DATE OF ACTION	TOWN	BORN/RES.
Babcock, John B.	1ST LIEUTENANT	5th US Cavalry	16 May 1869	Stonington	R
Baird, George W.	1ST LIEUTENANT	5th US Infantry	30 Sep 1877	Connecticut	B
Canfield, Heth	PRIVATE	Co C, 2d US Cavalry	15 May 1870	New Milford	B
Forsyth, Thomas H.	1ST SERGEANT	Co M, 4th US Cavalry	25 Nov 1876	Hartford	B
O'Neill, William	CORPORAL	Co I, 4th US Cavalry	29 Sep 1872	Tariffville	B
Sheppard, Charles	PRIVATE	Co. A, 5th US Infantry	21 Oct 1876-8 Jan 1877	Rocky Hill	B

INTERIM 1871-1898

NAME	RANK	UNIT	DATE OF ACTION	TOWN	BORN/RES.
Manning, Henry J.	QUARTERMASTER	US Navy, USS New Hampshire	4 Jan 1882	New Haven	B
Ryan, Richard	ORDINARY SEAMAN	US NAVY, USS Hartford	4 Mar 1876	Connecticut	B

WAR WITH SPAIN

NAME	RANK	UNIT	DATE OF ACTION	TOWN	BORN/RES.
Hill, Frank	PRIVATE	USMC, Aboard USS Nashville	11 May 1898	Hartford	B

PHILIPPINE INSURRECTION

NAME	RANK	UNIT	DATE OF ACTION	TOWN	BORN/RES.
Downs, Willis H.	PRIVATE	Co H, 1st ND Volunteer Infantry	13 May 1899	Mt. Carmel	B

MEDAL OF HONOR RECIPIENTS

CHINA RELIEF-BOXER REBELLION

Name	Rank	Unit	Date	City	
Rose, George	SEAMAN	US Navy, USS Newark	13-22 Jun 1900	Stamford	B

PHILIPPINES 1911

Henrechon, George F.	MACHINIST'S MATE, 2ND CLASS	US Navy, USS Pampang	24 Sep 1911	Hartford	B

WORLD WAR I

Cann, Tedford H.	SEAMAN	US Navy, USS May	5 Nov 1917	Bridgeport	B
MacKenzie, John	CHIEF BOATSWAIN'S MATE	US Navy, USS Remlik	17 Dec 1917	Bridgeport	B
*Talbot, Ralph	2ND LIEUTENANT	Sqd C, 1st Marine Aviation Force	8-14 Oct 1918	Connecticut	R

INTERIM 1920 to 1940

Breault, Henry	TORPEDOMAN, 2ND CLASS	US Navy, US Submarine O-5	28 Oct 1923	Putnam	B
Crandall, Orson L.	CHIEF BOATSWAIN'S MATE	US Navy (Rescue and Salvage Operations USS Squalus)	13 May 1939	Connecticut	R

WORLD WAR II

Daly, Michael J.	CAPTAIN	US Army, Co A, 15th Inf, 3d Inf Div	18 Apr 1945	Southport	R
*Fournier, William G.	SERGEANT	US Army, Co M, 35 Inf, 25th Inf Div	10 Jan 1943	Norwich	B
Johnston, William J.	PRIVATE FIRST CLASS	US Army, Co G, 180th Inf, 45th Inf Div	17-19 Feb 1944	Colchester	R
*Magrath, John D.	PRIVATE FIRST CLASS	US Army, Co G, 85th Inf, 10th Mt Div	14 Apr 1945	East Norwalk	B
Nett, Robert P.	CAPTAIN	US Army, Co E, 305th Inf, 77th Inf Div	14 Dec 1944	New Haven	B
*Reeves, Thomas James	WARRANT OFFICER	US Navy, (Pearl Harbor), USS California	7 Dec 1941	Thomaston	B
Soderman, William A.	PRIVATE FIRST CLASS	US Army, Co K, 9th Inf, 2d Inf Div	17 Dec 1944	West Haven	B
*Witek, Frank Peter	PRIVATE FIRST CLASS	USMC, 1st Bn, 9th Mar, 3d Mar Div	3 Aug 1944	Derby	B

KOREAN CONFLICT

*Hartell, Lee R.	1ST LIEUTENANT	US Army, Bat A, 15th Field Artillery Bn, 2d Inf Div	27 Aug 1952	Danbury		R
*Libby, George D.	SERGEANT	US Army, Co C, 3d Engr Cbt Bn, 24 Inf Div	20 Jul 1950	Waterbury		R
*Skinner, Sherrod E., Jr.	2ND LIEUTENANT	USMC (Res.), Btry F, 2d Bn, 11th Mar, 1st Mar Div	26 Oct 1952	Hartford		B

VIETNAM ERA

Barnum, Harvey C., Jr.	CAPTAIN	USMC, Co H, 2d Bn, 9th Mar, 3d Mar Div	18 Dec 1965	Cheshire		B
*Fratellenico, Frank F.	CORPORAL	US Army, Co B, 2d Bn, 502d Inf, 1st Brigade, 101st Airborne Div	19 Aug 1970	Sharon		B
Kellogg, Allan J., Jr.	STAFF SERGEANT	USMC, Co G, 2d Bn, 5th Mar, 1st Mar Div	11 Mar 1970	Bethel		B
Levitow, John L.	SERGEANT	US Air Force, 3d Special Operations Sqd	24 Feb 1969	Hartford		B
*Shea, Daniel J.	PRIVATE FIRST CLASS	US Army, 3d Bn, 21st Inf, 196 Inf Brigade	14 May 1969	Norwalk		B

*Killed in action.

RECAPITULATION:

PERIOD	TOTAL AWARDS	USA	USN	USMC	USAF
CIVIL WAR	41	37	4	—	—
INDIAN CAMPAIGNS	6	6	—	—	—
WAR WITH SPAIN	1	—	1	—	—
CHINA RELIEF-BOXER REBELLION	1	—	1	—	—
WORLD WAR I	3	—	2	1	—
WORLD WAR II	8	6	1	1	—
KOREAN CONFLICT	3	2	—	1	—
VIETNAM ERA	5	2	—	2	1
OTHER	6	1	5	—	—
TOTALS:	74	54	13	6	1

STATE OF CONNECTICUT

Sites • Seals • Symbols

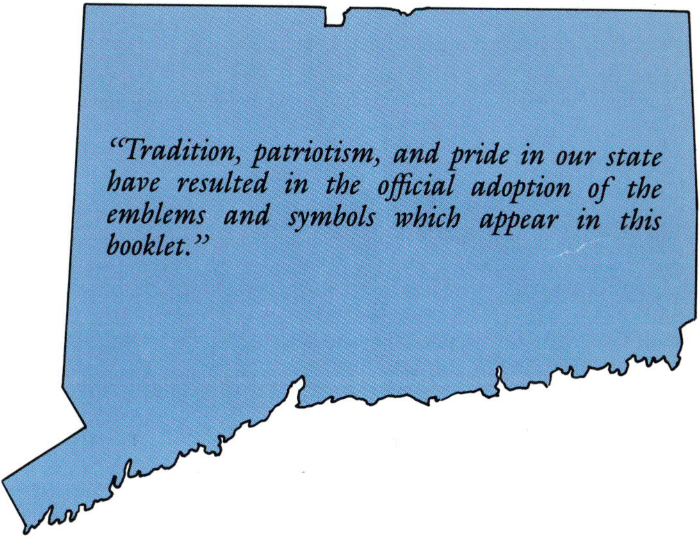

"Tradition, patriotism, and pride in our state have resulted in the official adoption of the emblems and symbols which appear in this booklet."

Secretary of the State

The American Flag

Out of the profusion of designs and symbols inspired by the fervent patriotism and pride of our infant days as a nation, came the flag which is the basis of our present national flag. By 1776 there were many flags for individual military companies and sections of the country and the Continental Congress instructed a committee composed of George Washington, Robert Morris and Colonel George Ross to devise and produce a flag for the United States.

Tradition has it that Betsy Ross, as early as June 1776, made a Stars and Stripes flag from a pencil sketch supplied by Washington. The flag with 13 stripes and 13 stars was officially adopted on June 14, 1777. This was altered to 15 stripes and 15 stars with the admission of Vermont and Kentucky to the Union in 1795.

On April 4, 1818, the final form of our flag was adopted by Congress to allow for the admission of new states. As of July 4, 1960, the flag contains fifty stars with each star symbolizing a state.

The State Flag

Inspired by a memorial from the Anna Warner Bailey Chapter of the Daughters of the American Revolution, Governor O. Vincent Coffin, on May 29, 1895, introduced to the General Assembly the first proposal for the adoption of a State Flag. On that same day the Assembly passed a resolution appointing a special committee to prepare a designation of the flag already generally accepted as the official flag of the state.

The General Assembly of 1897 provided an official description of the flag setting the dimensions at five feet, six inches in length and four feet, four inches in width, of azure blue silk, with the armorial bearings in argent white silk with the design in natural colors and bordure of the shield embroidered in gold and silver. Below the shield there is a white streamer, cleft at each end, bordered in gold and browns, the streamer bearing in dark blue the motto "Qui Transtulit Sustinet."

The Armorial Bearings

On March 24, 1931, the General Assembly adopted a design for the official Arms of the State, which it ordered drawn and filed with the Secretary of the State. The official description of the Arms called for: A shield of rococo design of white field, having in the center three grape vines, supported and bearing fruit. Below the shield shall be a white streamer, cleft at each end, bordered with two fine lines, and upon the streamer shall be in solid letters of medium bold Gothic the motto

"QUI TRANSTULIT SUSTINET."
(He Who Transplanted Still Sustains)

The official arms and seal of the State of Connecticut, whether as a reproduction, imprint or facsimile, shall be made and used only under the direction and with the approval of the Secretary of the State.

The Original Seal

Connecticut's first seal was brought from England by Colonel George Fenwick in 1639. It was the seal of the Saybrook Colony and was turned over to the Connecticut Colony at about the time that it purchased the land and fort at Saybrook Point from Colonel Fenwick in 1644. The seal was used by the General Court (General Assembly) from that time forward, but there is no clear record of who had custody of the seal. On October 9, 1662, the same day that the new Royal Charter was read aloud at Hartford, the assembly formally declared that the seal would be kept by the Secretary of the Colony and used as the Seal of the Colony on necessary occasions. It remained the colony's seal until October 1687, when Sir Edmund Andros took control of the colony's government and the seal disappeared. It is presumed to have been destroyed.

Self-government returned to Connecticut in 1689, but for a number of years only a poorly fashioned substitute seal was used. On October 25, 1711, a meeting of the Governor and Council (the upper house of the assembly) resolved, "that a new stamp shall be made and cut of the seal of this Colony, suitable for sealing upon wafers, and that a press be provided with the necessary appurtenances, for that purpose, as soon as may be, at the cost and charge of this Colony, to be kept in the secretary's office."

The new, less elaborately decorated seal was larger in size and more oval shaped than the original. The words of the motto remained the same, but the number of grape vines was reduced to three and the legend SIGILLUM COLONIAE CONNECTICENSIS (Seal of the Connecticut Colony) is added to the edge of the seal. The three vines may have been intended to represent the three colonies, New Haven, Saybrook, and Connecticut (Hartford), which, by 1665, had merged to form the Connecticut of that time.

The Colonial Seal

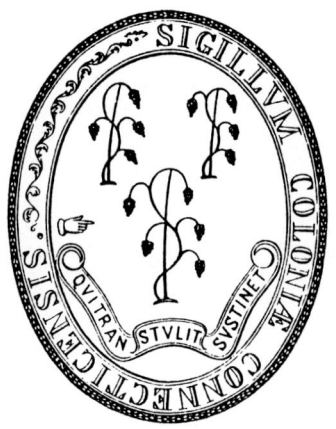

The Great Seal

After the conclusion of the Revolutionary War, the inscription on the colonial seal was no longer appropriate. Therefore, in May of 1784 the General Assembly directed the Secretary to alter the inscription to read "SIGILL. REIP. CONNECTICUTENSIS." However, when a new version of the seal was prepared, the inscription contained the words spelled out — SIGILLUM REIPUBLICAE CONNECTICUTENSIS (Seal of the State of Connecticut). There has been no subsequent alteration to the official state seal. In 1931, the General Assembly required that all representations of the state seal conform to the description in Chapter 54 of the Public Acts of that year. This legislation also prohibited reproduction of the seal except by or under the direction of the Secretary of the State.

The State Motto

The motto "Qui Transtulit Sustinet," (He Who Transplanted Still Sustains), has been associated with the various versions of the seal from the creation of the Saybrook Colony Seal. While the origin of the motto is uncertain, the late Charles J. Hoadly, a former State Librarian, suggested in an article entitled "The Public Seal of Connecticut," which appeared in the 1889 edition of the *Connecticut State Register and Manual*, that we look to the 80th Psalm as a possible source. "Thou hast brought a vine out of Egypt: thou hast cast out the heathen, and planted it."

Secretary of the State's Seal

The office of the Secretary of the State was created under the Fundamental Orders of 1638/39 and is, therefore, one of the original offices of government in Connecticut. From its inception, the duties of the office of secretary included overseeing elections and the keeping of public records. In 1662 the secretary also became the keeper of the colonial seal. The responsibilities of the office have grown tremendously since that time, but the secretary is still the constitutional and stautory keeper of the public records and the state seal. The motto on the secretary's seal, REIP. CONN. SECRET. ET SIGILL. CUSTOS (Secretary of the State of Connecticut and Keeper of the Seal), is a reflection of the history of the office.

Connecticut—The Constitution State

Connecticut was designated the *Constitution State* by the General Assembly in 1959. As early as the 19th Century, John Fiske, a popular historian from Connecticut, made the claim that the Fundamental Orders of 1638/39 were the first written constitution in history. Some contemporary historians dispute Fiske's analysis. However, Simeon E. Baldwin, a former Chief Justice of the Connecticut Supreme Court, defended Fiske's view of the Fundamental Orders in Osborn's *History of Connecticut in Monographic Form* by stating that "never had a company of men deliberately met to frame a social compact for immediate use, constituting a new and independent commonwealth, with definite officers, executive and legislative, and prescribed rules and modes of government, until the first planters of Connecticut came together for their great work on January 14th, 1638-9." The text of the Fundamental Orders is reproduced in Section I of this volume and the original is on permanent display at the Museum of Connecticut History at the State Library.

Connecticut has also been known as the *Nutmeg State*, the *Provisions State*, and the *Land of Steady Habits*.

"The Charter Oak - *Charles D. Brownell*" (Collection, Wadsworth Atheneum, Hartford.)

State Tree
The Charter Oak
(White Oak Quercus Alba)

Deep-rooted in the historic tradition of Connecticut, the Charter Oak is one of the most colorful and significant symbols of the spiritual strength and love of freedom which inspired our Colonial forebears in their militant resistance to tyranny. This venerable giant of the forest, hundreds of years old when it hid the treasured Charter in 1687, finally fell during a great storm on August 21, 1856.

Two English kings, a royal agent, a colonial hero and a candle-lit room are the figures and backdrop in one of the most thrilling chapters of America's legend of liberty. The refusal of our early Connecticut leaders to give up the Charter, despite royal order and the threat of arms, marked one of the greatest episodes of determined courage in our history.

On October 9, 1662, the General Court of Connecticut formally received the Charter won from King Charles II by the suave diplomacy of Governor John Winthrop, Jr., who had crossed the ocean for the purpose.

Twenty-five years later, with the succession of James II to the throne, Connecticut's troubles began in earnest. Sir Edmund Andros, His Majesty's agent, followed up failure of various strategies by arriving in Hartford with an armed force to seize the Charter.

After hours of debate, with the Charter on the table between the opposing parties, the candle-lit room went suddenly dark. Moments later when the candles were re-lighted, the Charter was gone. Captain Joseph Wadsworth is credited with having removed and secreted the Charter in the majestic oak on the Wyllys estate.

State Bird
The American Robin

(Turdus Migratorius)

The American Robin was adopted as the official State Bird by the General Assembly in 1943. The name Robin is applied to a number of familiar birds, but in North America it is the migratory thrush. (Turdus Migratorius.)

Our Robin, a true thrush, is a migratory bird with a reddish-brown or tawny breast and a loud cheery song. It was first called the Robin by the early colonists, in remembrance of the beloved English bird. Despite the protests of some naturalists, we still retain that traditional name.

Familiar, in the summer, throughout North America, the American Robin is seen from Alaska to Virginia. Most people do not know that many Robins spend the entire winter in New England. They roost among the evergreens in the swamps where they feed on winter berries.

State Flower
The Mountain Laurel

(Kalmia Latifolia)

Designated as the State Flower by the General Assembly in 1907, the Mountain Laurel is perhaps the most beautiful of native American Shrubs. Its fragrance and the massed richness of its white and pink blossoms so vividly contrast with the darker colors of the forests and the fields that they have continually attracted the attention of travelers since the earliest days of our colonization. First mentioned in John Smith's "General History" in 1624 specimens were sent to Linnaeus, the famous botanist by Peter Kalm, the Swedish explorer in 1750.

Linnaeus gave it the name of Kalmia Latifolia, honoring the name of his correspondent and at the same time describing the "wide-leaved" characteristic of the plant. In addition to being called "Mountain Laurel," the plant has also been spoken of as "Calico Bush" and "Spoonwood."

State Insect
European Mantis

(Mantis Religiosa)

The European "praying" mantis (family, Mantidae, order, Orthoptera) officially became the State Insect on October 1, 1977. The name "mantis," derived from the Greek, originally meant prophet or diviner, and, appropriately, described the mantids' distinctive habit of standing motionless on four hind legs, with the two highly specialized forelegs raised in an attitude of meditation.

The European mantis is not native to Connecticut. Its origin is Northern Africa, Southern Europe, and temperate Asia. These mantids can be found, however, throughout the state from early May or June until the cold weather sets in, when they die rapidly.

Harmless to humans, and averaging 2-2½ inches in length, this small green or brown insect feeds on aphids, flies, grasshoppers, small caterpillars and moths. Although probably not a significant factor in biological control, mantids are beneficial insects, friends to the farmer, and are, therefore, symbolic reminders of the importance of the natural environment to human and biological survival.

State Animal
Sperm Whale

(Physeter Macrocephalus)

The Sperm Whale was designated as the state animal by the General Assembly in 1975. Its selection was made both because of its special contribution to the state's history and because of its present-day plight as an endangered species.

The Sperm Whale is the largest of the toothed whales, growing up to 60 feet in length and capable of diving over 3,000 feet in search of the squid and cuttlefish on which it feeds. The sperm whale's brain is the largest of any creature ever existing on earth. "Moby Dick" was a sperm whale.

During the 1800s Connecticut ranked second only to Massachusetts as a whale hunting state. The sperm whale was the species most sought after by Connecticut whalers circling the globe on ships out of New London, Mystic and other Connecticut ports to bring back needed oil for lamps and other products.

State Mineral
The Garnet

(Almandine Garnet)

$Fe_3Al_2Si_3O_{12}$

Connecticut is one of the finest sources in the world of the almandine garnet, named the State Mineral by the 1977 General Assembly. An ancient gem, it was named "garnata" in the 13th century by Albertus Magnus, and was known as the "Carbuncle," likening it to a small, red hot coal.

The garnets are actually a group of similar minerals, complex silicates of the same atomic structure, but differing in chemical composition. They vary in color from pale to dark tints, including the deep violet-red of the almandine garnet.

This mineral's significant hardness, 7 on the Mohs scale, has made the garnet, as an abrasive, important industrially throughout Connecticut's history. It contributed to this development by providing the base for grinding wheels, saws, and the better cutting quality of garnet paper, a variety of sandpaper.

State Shellfish
Eastern Oyster

(Crassostrea Virginica)

The Eastern oyster was designated as the State Shellfish by the General Assembly in 1989. The oyster, which is a bivalve mollusk, occurs naturally in Connecticut's tidal rivers and coastal embayments and is cultivated by the oyster industry in the waters of Long Island Sound.

Oysters were consumed in great quantities by Connecticut's native American inhabitants, and early European settlers found oysters to be a staple and reliable food source. The first colonial laws regulating the taking of oysters in Connecticut appeared in the early 1700s.

Oyster farming developed into a major industry in the State by the late 19th century. During the 1890s, Connecticut held the distinction of having the largest fleet of oyster steamers in the world.

Today, Connecticut's oyster industry continues to thrive. Annually, thousands of bushels of these delicious Connecticut grown mollusks are marketed throughout the country. Of all the shellfish species associated with the Connecticut shoreline, the oyster is by far the best known for its colorful history, continued economic importance and esteemed reputation for quality.

State Ship
USS Nautilus (SSN-571)

Built by Connecticut craftsmen, USS Nautilus was the world's first nuclear powered submarine and logged more than 500,000 nautical miles during her distinguished 25 year career. The USS Nautilus, named Connecticut's State Ship by the 1983 General Assembly, has been designated a National Historic Landmark and is permanently berthed next to the Submarine Force Library and Museum at Goss Cove in Groton.

State Fossil
Eubrontes Giganteus

The Connecticut Valley is the world's foremost dinosaur track locality. Many different types of fossil track impressions have been found in the Valley's sandstones of the early Jurassic Period (200 million years ago). *Eubrontes* a large three-toed track, was designated the State Fossil in 1991. Although no skeletal remains of the specific trackmaking dinosaur have been found, the shape, size, and stride of *Eubrontes* indicate that the animal was a carnivorous dinosaur approximately eighteen feet in length, and was closely related to the western genus *Dilophosaurus*. Two thousand *Eubrontes* tracks were discovered on a single layer of rock in Rocky Hill, in 1966, and subsequently Dinosaur State Park was created for their preservation and interpretation. This Registered Natural Landmark site receives visitors from throughout the world.

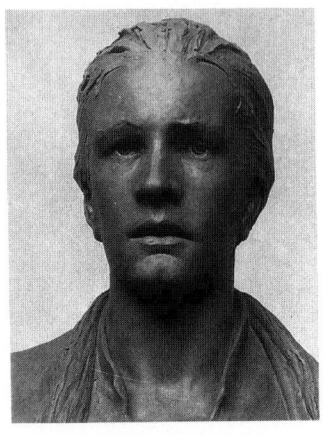

State Hero
Nathan Hale 1755 - 1776

On October 1, 1985, by an act of the General Assembly and the efforts of the Nathan Hale Chapter of the Sons of the American Revolution, Nathan Hale officially became Connecticut's State Hero.

Born in Coventry, and educated at Yale University, Hale served as a school master until commissioned as a Captain in the Continental Army, in 1775. In September of 1776, at General George Washington's request for a volunteer, Nathan Hale crossed enemy lines to gather information as to the strength and plans of the British. Caught while returning, he was hanged as a spy on September 22, 1776, without benefit of a trial.

The Patriot's dedication to our country is enshrined in the immortal words "I only regret that I have but one life to lose for my country." By every action of his short life, Hale exemplified the ideals of patriotism.

The Hale Homestead, located at 2299 South Street in Coventry, is maintained as a museum by the Antiquarian and Landmarks Society, Inc.

State Heroine
Prudence Crandall 1803 - 1890

On October 1, 1995, by an act of the General Assembly, Prudence Crandall became Connecticut's State Heroine.

In 1833, Prudence Crandall established the first academy for African-American women in New England. During its 18 months of operation, Crandall and her students faced hardships and violence. She was placed on trial twice for breaking a law specifically designed to prevent the school from operating. In the fall of 1834, although the charges against her were dismissed, the school was closed.

Prudence Crandall demonstrated great courage and moral strength by taking a stand against prejudice. In 1886 the legislature honored her with an annual pension of $400.00.

The Prudence Crandall House is a National Historic Landmark located at the intersection of 14 and 169 in Canterbury. It is operated by the Connecticut Historical Commission.

State Song

"Yankee Doodle"

Words

> Yankee Doodle went to town,
> Riding on a pony,
> Stuck a feather in his hat,
> And called it macaroni.

Chorus

> Yankee Doodle keep it up,
> Yankee Doodle dandy,
> Mind the music and the step,
> And with the folks be handy.

State Poet Laureate

Leo Connellan of Hanover has been appointed the Poet Laureate of the State of Connecticut by the Commission of the Arts.

State Troubadour

Sally Rogers, Pomfret, has been named the State Troubadour of Connecticut by the Commission on the Arts.

State Composer

Charles Edward Ives (1874-1954) was designated the State Composer by the General Assembly in 1991.

The Executive Residence

Georgian Colonial in design, the Executive Residence is located on six beautifully landscaped acres, at 990 Prospect Avenue, overlooking the city of Hartford. The furniture and decorations of the nineteen-room governor's residence are 18th Century originals and reproductions.

The residence was built in 1909 by Dr. George C. F. Williams, who occupied it until 1933. The original cost of the development of the property was $300,000. It was purchased by the State in 1943 for $38,928, after inspection of 38 different pieces of property by the Legislative Committee on the Executive Residence.

Governor Raymond E. Baldwin and his family first occupied the residence on September 14, 1945. The formal public opening ceremonies were held on October 18, 1945.

The First State House

The first State House in Hartford served from 1720 until 1796, when the adjacent and recently completed Old State House opened. Earlier buildings occupied the site, but this was the first structure built as a state house. The square was laid out in 1636 with the founding of Connecticut and city of Hartford. The Fundamental Orders of 1638/39 were ratified on this site. In 1687, the Charter of 1662 was stolen from this site and hidden in the Charter Oak Tree. Here General Washington first met Rochambeau and the French armies in America, and planned the Yorktown strategy. And, it is here that Connecticut delegates gathered to consider ratification of the U.S. Constitution. In 1783, a watchman dropped a lighted candle and the building partially burned. As a consequence of the damage caused by the fire, the present Old State House was built.

The "Old" State House

Designed by Charles Bulfinch and built in 1796, the Old State House is the oldest state house in the nation.

The building opened in May of 1796. Oliver Wolcott, signer of the Declaration of Independence was the first Governor to serve here. The building was the seat of state government until 1878, when the present Capitol was opened.

Major state and national events have, and continue to occur at the Old State House. Lafayette was made a citizen here, many American presidents, including Jackson, Monroe, Johnson, Ford and Bush have visited. President Carter gave the U.S.S. Nautilus to Connecticut in a ceremony at the Old State House in 1981. The trials of Cinque and the Amistad opened here in 1839. P.T. Barnum served in the legislature here, and notables such as Mark Twain, Charles Dickens, Samuel Colt and Harriet Beecher Stowe visited the building.

The Old State House is a registered National Landmark and open to the public year-round, free of charge. The restored historic chambers, and grounds are now the site of events such as exhibitions, concerts, cannon firings, tours and a full museum store. It is run as a non-profit by the Old State House Association, Inc.

The State Capitol

Overlooking Hartford's 41 acre Bushnell Memorial Park, the Connecticut State Capitol first opened for the General Assembly in January, 1879.

Initial work on the project had begun eight years before in 1871 when the legislature established a special commission and appropriated funds for construction of a new statehouse. The site was contributed by the city of Hartford, and the commission retained James G. Batterson to build the Capitol from plans designed by noted architect Richard M. Upjohn.

Constructed of New England marble and granite and crowned by a gold leaf dome, the Capitol was built at a cost of $2,532,524.43 and has an estimated replacement value of more than $200,000,000.

In addition to housing the State Senate Chamber, Hall of the State House of Representatives and offices of the Governor, Lieutenant Governor, and Secretary of the State, the statehouse and surrounding grounds abound with memories and mementos of Connecticut's early years.

The Connecticut State Capitol was declared a national historical landmark by the United States Department of Interior in 1972.

INDEX

A

Absentee Ballot Statistics, Election Day Registration, Turnout, 1996 *736-739*
Absentee Ballot Statistics, Election Day Registration, Turnout and, Summary of 1996 *735*
Academic Awards, State Board for *253*
Accountancy, State Board of *206*
Addiction Services, Commissioner of Mental Health and *258*
Addiction Services, Department of Mental Health and *258-261*
Adjutant General *205, 277-278*
Administrative Services, Commissioner of *214*
Administrative Services, Department of *214-218*
Admission to the Bar *320*
Admission to the Bar, Standing Committees on Recommendations for *320-321*
Admission of States to Union *764-765*
Adoption Review Board *223*
Adoption Subsidy Review Board *222*
Adult Probation *310*
Advocacy for Persons with Disabilities, Office and Board of Protection and *226*
Aeronautics and Space Administration, National *761*
Agencies, Boards, Commissions, Departments, State *214-298*
Agencies, Boards and Federal Departments Serving Connecticut *757-763*
Aging, Area Agencies on *284*
Aging, Commission on *283*
Aging, Municipal Commissions on *354-595*
Agricultural Development, Governor's Council for *219*
Agricultural Experiment Station Board of Control, Connecticut *267-268*
Agricultural Statistics *817-818*
Agriculture, Commissioner of *218*
Agriculture, State Department of *218-220*
Agriculture, United States Department of *757*
Air Force, United States Department of *758*
Air National Guard, Connecticut *278*
Air Pollution Control Compact, Mid-Atlantic States *244*
Airport Commission, Bradley International *291*
Airports, State *287*
Alcohol, Tobacco and Firearms, Bureau of Treasury Department, United States *762*
Aldermen *354-595*
American Flag and Description of *826-827*
American and Francophone Cultural Affairs, Advisory Commission on *292*
American Robin, State Bird *832*
Animal, State *833*

(841)

Appeals Court, United States *754*
Appellate Court Judges *150-154, 301*
Appraisal Commission, Connecticut Real Estate *225-226*
Apprenticeship and Training, United States Bureau of *760*
Apprenticeship Council, Connecticut State *256*
Aquaculture Division, Department of Agriculture *218*
Arbitration, Connecticut Board of Mediation and *255*
Arbitration Panel, State Department of Education *236*
Archaeology, Office of *248*
Architects, Connecticut State Board of Landscape *224*
Architectural Licensing Board *224*
Archivist, State *238*
Area Cooperative Educational Services *598-599*
Areas, Towns and Cities *354-595*
Armorial Bearings of the State *826-827*
Armories, State *278*
Army, Department of *758*
Art, State Museum of *248*
Arts, State Commission on the *237*
Asnuntuck Community-Technical College *251*
Assembly Districts, Connecticut *669-677*
Assessment Appeals, Board of, Towns and Cities *354-595*
Assessors, Towns, Cities and Boroughs *354-595*
Associate Justice of Supreme Court for Second Circuit, United States *754*
Associate Justices, Supreme Court, Connecticut *146-148, 301*
Associated Press *796*
Associated Press Managing Editors, Connecticut *807*
Atlantic States Marine Fisheries Commission *244*
Attorney General, State *116-117, 208-210*
Attorney, United States District *756*
Attorneys General of Connecticut, Since 1899 *94*
Attorneys, Prosecuting, Geographical Areas *314-317*
Attorneys, State's *210-211*
Attorneys, Town *354-595*
Auditors of Public Accounts, State *157*
Aviation Administration, Federal *762*
Aviation Facilities, Military Department *278*
Aviation and Ports, Bureau of, Department of Transportation *286*
Aviation Statistics *819-820*

B

Bail Commissioners, Geographical Areas *314-317*
Banking Commissioner *220*
Banking, Department of *220*
Bankruptcy, Judges for District of Connecticut *755*
Bar, Admission to *320*
Bar, Examining Committee, State *320*
Barbers, Hairdressers and Cosmeticians, Connecticut Examining Board for *269*

Barracks, Location and Officers, State Police *274-275*
Berdon, Robert I. *146, 147, 301*
Bill of Rights, United States Constitution *18-19*
Biographies and Photographs, Appellate Court Judges *150-154*
Biographies and Photographs, Leaders of the 1997-98 General Assembly *134-145*
Biographies and Photographs, State Officers *110-117*
Biographies and Photographs, Supreme Court Justices *146-149*
Biographies and Photographs, United States Senators and Representatives *118-133*
Biography and Photograph, President of the United States *104-105*
Bird, State *832*
Blind, Board of Education and Services for the *285*
Blumenthal, Richard *116-117, 208*
Boards, Commissions and Departments, State *321-334*
Bond Commission, State *266*
Bond Committee, Expressway *266*
Borden, David M. *146, 147, 301*
Borough Clerks *354-595*
Borough Elections, Dates of *346*
Borough Incorporation Dates *346*
Borough Officers *354-595*
Boroughs, Town and City Statistics *354-595*
Boundary Marks, State *290*
Bradley International Airport Commission *291*
Bridgeport, Connecticut Mental Health System *261*
Bridgeport Correctional Center *227*
Bridgeport Regional Planning Agency, Greater *602*
Bridgeport Transit District, Greater *607*
Broadcasters Association, Connecticut *814*
Broadcasters Association, Connecticut Associated Press *814*
Broadcasting Stations in Connecticut *807-814*
Brooklyn Correctional Institution *229*
Budget and Financial Management, Office of Policy and Management *265, 266*
Building Inspector, State *276*
Building Inspectors, Municipal *354-595*
Building Services, Division of Fire, Emergency and *276*
Bureau of Engineering and Highway Operations *287*
Burgesses, Borough *354-595*
Burnham, Christopher B. *112-114, 206-207*
Business Services, Bureau of *215*

C

Cabinet, Governor's *205-206*
Cabinet, United States *747*
Callahan, Robert J. *146, 147, 301*
Camping Areas, State *239-241*
Capital Community-Technical College *251*
Capitol Preservation and Restoration, State Commission on *160*

INDEX

Capitol Region Council of Governments *597*

Capitol Region Council of Governments, Regional Planning Commission *602*

Capitol Region Education Council *599*

Capitol Region Library Council *601*

Capitol Region Mental Health Center, Hartford *260*

Capitol, State *840*

Career Mobility Committee *215*

Carl Robinson Correctional Institution *230*

Cedarcrest Regional Hospital, Newington *260*

Census Bureau, United States *758*

Census, Connecticut, 1800-1990 *610-612*

Census, Connecticut, 1995 estimated *354-595*

Central Committees, State *643-646*

Central Connecticut Regional Planning Agency *602*

Central Connecticut State University *251*

Central Naugatuck Valley Council of Governments *597*

Charter of the Colony of Connecticut, 1662 *60-66*

Charter Oak *831*

Charter Oak College *253*

Chemists, State *292*

Cheshire, Connecticut Correctional Institution *228*

Cheshire Office for Mentally Retarded *262*

Chief Clerks, Superior Court *311-314*

Chief Court Administrator *307*

Chief Deputy Sheriffs, County *337-341*

Chief Justice, Supreme Court, Connecticut *146, 147*

Chief Justice, Supreme Court, United States *747*

Chief Justices of Connecticut, Since 1711 *95-96*

Chief Public Defender *319*

Chief State's Attorney *210*

Chiefs of Fire Departments, Towns, Cities and Boroughs *354-595*

Chiefs of Police, Towns, Cities and Boroughs *354-595*

Child Day Care Council *285-286*

Child Treatment Home, High Meadows *222*

Children, Commission on *159-160*

Children and Families, Commissioner of *220*

Children and Families, Department of *220-223*

Children's Trust Fund, Council to Administer *223*

Chiropractic Examiners, State Board of *269*

Citizens Advisory Council for Housing Matters *294*

City Clerks *354-595*

City Elections, Dates of *345*

City Incorporation Dates *346*

City Managers *354-595*

City Mayors *354-595*

City Officers *354-595*

City, Town and Borough Statistics *354-595*

Civil Defense and Disaster Compact, Interstate *277*

INDEX 845

Civil Preparedness Directors, Towns, Cities and Boroughs *354-595*

Claims Commissioner, Office of *208*

Clerks, Senate and House *158-159*

Clerks, Superior Court *311-314*

Clerks, Town *354-595*

Clerks, United States District Court *754-755*

Clinton, William J. *104-105, 747*

Coast Guard, United States *761-762*

Codes Standard Committee, State *276-277*

Collection Services, DAS Bureau of *214*

Colleges of Connecticut, Board of Trustees for Community-Technical *251*

Colleges of Connecticut, Board of Trustees for Connecticut State University *250-251*

Colleges of Connecticut, Board of Trustees, University of Connecticut *248*

Colleges, Community-Technical *251-252*

Colonial Seal *828*

Commerce, United States Department of *758*

Commerce, Regional Office, *758*

Commissioners for New Haven Harbor *289*

Commissions, Agencies and Boards, State *214-298*

Committees, 1997 General Assembly *181-187*

Committees, State Central *643-646*

Community Correctional Centers *227-228*

Community-Technical Colleges of Connecticut, Board of Trustees for *251*

Community-Technical Colleges, State *251-252*

Commuter Council, Metro North New Haven Rail *296*

Compensation Commission for Elected State Officials and Judges *160*

Compensation Commission, Workers' *257*

Comptroller, State *114-115, 207-208*

Comptrollers of Connecticut, Since 1786 *92-93*

Congress, United States, One-Hundred Fifth *748-753*

Congressional Districts, Connecticut *657-662*

Congressmen from Connecticut *118-133, 748, 750*

Congressmen from Connecticut Since 1789 *72-79*

Congressmen from Connecticut, Vote for, 1996 *689-693*

Congressmen from United States (50 States) *750-753*

Connecticut Advisory Commission on Intergovernmental Relations *267*

Connecticut Agricultural Experiment Station, Board of Control *267-268*

Connecticut Association of Zoning Enforcement Officials *596*

Connecticut Attorney General *116-117, 208-210*

Connecticut Attorneys General, Since 1899 *94*

Connecticut Charter of the Colony of, 1662 *60-66*

Connecticut Chief Justices, Since 1711 *95-96*

Connecticut Comptroller *114-115, 207-208*
Connecticut Comptrollers Since 1786 *92-93*
Connecticut Congressmen, United States *118-133*
Connecticut Congressmen Since 1789 *72-79*
Connecticut Constitution of 1965 *26-54*
Connecticut Daily Newspapers Assoc. *807*
Connecticut, Date of Admission to Union *764*
Connecticut Development Authority *231*
Connecticut Electric Railway Association, Incorporated *772*
Connecticut Emergency Response Commission *243*
Connecticut Equestrian Center Authority *219*
Connecticut, Facts About *815-820*
Connecticut, First Constitution of *55-59*
Connecticut 4-H Development Fund Incorporated *249*
Connecticut General Assembly *162-180*
Connecticut Governor *106-107, 205*
Connecticut Governors, Since 1639 *80-83*
Connecticut Historical Commission *237*
Connecticut History, Important Dates In *67-69*
Connecticut House of Representatives *165-176, 178-180*
Connecticut House Speakers, Since 1819 *99-100*
Connecticut Housing Finance Authority *232*

Connecticut Indian Affairs Council *246*
Connecticut Indians *820*
Connecticut Innovations, Incorporated *233*
Connecticut Law Library System *309*
Connecticut Law Revision Commission *158*
Connecticut Legislature *162-180*
Connecticut Legislature, Length of Sessions *188-191*
Connecticut Legislature, Political Division of *192-195*
Connecticut Lieutenant Governor *108-109, 206*
Connecticut Lieutenant Governors, Since 1639 *84-86*
Connecticut Osteopathic Examining Board *271*
Connecticut Partnership for Long Term Care *268*
Connecticut Poison Center *249*
Connecticut Population by Counties, 1995 est. *609*
Connecticut Population by Towns *354-595*
Connecticut Post Offices *613-616*
Connecticut Presidents Pro Tempore of the State Senate Since 1845 *97-98*
Connecticut, Press of *796-806*
Connecticut Probate Assembly *321-322*
Connecticut Public Libraries *791-795*
Connecticut Public Transportation Commission *288*
Connecticut Radio Network *807*
Connecticut Real Estate Commission *225*
Connecticut Real Estate Appraisal Commission *225-226*

INDEX

Connecticut Resources Recovery Authority *246*
Connecticut River Estuary Regional Planning Agency *602*
Connecticut River Gateway Commission *245*
Connecticut River Valley Flood Control Commission *245*
Connecticut Sea Grant College *248*
Connecticut Secretaries of the State, Since 1639 *87-89*
Connecticut Secretary of the State *110-111, 206*
Connecticut Senate *162-164, 177*
Connecticut Siting Council *279-280*
Connecticut Speakers of the House of Representatives Since 1819 *99-101*
Connecticut State Apprenticeship Council *256*
Connecticut State Board of Labor Relations *254*
Connecticut State Employees, Number of *816*
Connecticut State Employees Retirement Commission *207*
Connecticut State Government, Executive *205-213*
Connecticut State News Bureau *796*
Connecticut State Office of Information and Technology *267*
Connecticut State Officers, Biographies and Photographs *106-117*
Connecticut State Secretaries of, Since 1639 *87-89*
Connecticut State Tree Protection Examining Board *226*
Connecticut State University Board of Trustees *250-251*

Connecticut Student Loan Foundation *253*
Connecticut Supreme Court *146-149*
Connecticut Television Stations *813-814*
Connecticut Towns in the Order of their Establishment *631-639*
Connecticut Transportation Commission, Public *288*
Connecticut Treasurer *112-113, 206-207*
Connecticut Treasurers, Since 1639 *90-91*
Connecticut, University of *247*
Connecticut Valley Hospital, Middletown *259-260*
Connecticut Veterans Home and Hospital, Rocky Hill *291-292*
Connecticut's Washington Office *205*
Conservation Commissions, Town *354-595*
Conservation, Connecticut Council on Soil and Water *243-244*
Constables, Towns and Cities *354-595*
Constitution of Connecticut *26-54*
Constitution of Connecticut, First *55-59*
Constitution State, Designation *830*
Constitution of the United States of America *8-25*
Consumer Counsel, Office of *280*
Consumer Protection, Commissioner of *223*
Consumer Protection, Department of *223-227*
Cooperative Educational Services *599*
Cooperative Extension System, University of Connecticut *249*
Cooperative Extension System and Storrs Agricultural Experiment Station *757*

Correction, Commissioner of *227*
Correction, State Department of *227-231*
Correctional Centers, Community *227-228*
Corrections Compact, New England Board of, Interstate *231*
Corrigan, Connecticut Correctional Institution *229*
Cosmeticians, Hairdressers and Barbers, Connecticut Examining Board for *269*
Council to Administer the Children's Trust Fund *223*
Counties in Connecticut *342*
Counties, Dates Constituted *322-334*
Counties, Population of *609*
County Extension Service Officers *249-250*
County Sheriffs and Deputy Sheriffs *337-341*
Court Administrator, Chief *307*
Court, Appellate *150-154, 301*
Court, Juvenile Matters *318*
Court Reporter, Supreme *302*
Court, Superior *302-306*
Court, Superior, Sentence Review Division *311*
Court, Supreme, Connecticut *146-149, 301*
Court, United States District *754*
Court, United States Supreme *747*
Courts, Probate *321-334*
Courts, State *301-302*
Crandall, Prudence *836*
Crane Operators Examining Board *276*
Crime Control Task Force Policy Board, Statewide Narcotics *275-276*

Criminal Justice Commission *210*
Customs Service, United States *762*
Cybulski Correctional Institution *231*

D

Danbury Office for Mentally Retarded *263*
Dates of Borough, Town and City Elections *345-346*
Dates in Connecticut History, Selected Important *67-69*
Dates Counties Constituted *337-341*
Dates of Incorporation, Boroughs *346*
Dates of Incorporation, Cities *346*
Dates of Incorporation, Towns *354-595*
Deaf and Hearing Impaired, State Commission on the *285*
Declaration of Independence *3-7*
Defense, Department of *759*
DeLauro, Rosa *126-127, 750*
Democratic State Central Committee *643-644*
Democratic Town Chairpersons and Vice Chairpersons *647-651*
Dempsey Hospital, John *248*
Dempsey Center for Mentally Retarded, John *263*
Dental Commission, State *269*
Departments, State *214-298*
Deputy or Lieutenant Governors of Connecticut Since 1639 *84-86*
Descriptions and Photographs, Flags, State Emblems and State Capitol *825-840*
Development Authority, Connecticut *231*

Development and Industrial Commissions, Municipal *354-595*
Developmental Disabilities, State Planning Council on *262*
Disabilities, Governor's Committee on Employment of People with *257-258*
Disabilities, Office and Board of Protection and Advocacy for Persons with *226*
Disabilities, State Plainning Council on Developmental *262*
Displaced Homemakers, Advisory Council on *257*
Distances, Connecticut River, Hartford to *630*
Distances to Towns from Hartford *630*
District Attorney, United States Dept. of Justice *756*
District Clerks, Juvenile Matters *318*
District Court Marshal, United States *756-757*
District Court Naturalization Sessions *756*
District Court, United States *754-755*
District Judges, United States *754-755*
Districts, Assembly *669-677*
Districts, Congressional, Connecticut *657-662*
Districts, Senatorial *663-668*
Districts, Voting, Towns and Cities, Number of *354-595*
Dodd, Christopher J. *118-119, 748*
Drug Control Division, Consumer Protection Department *223*
Drug Enforcement Administration, United States *756*
Dupont, Antoinette L. *151, 301*

E

Eads, M. Adela *138-139*
Eastern Connecticut Libraries *601*
Eastern Connecticut State University *251*
Eastern Connecticut Regional Educational Service Center *599-600*
Eastern Oyster, State Shellfish *834*
Economic and Community Development, Commissioner of *231*
Economic and Community Development, Department of *231-234*
Economic Development Administration, United States *758*
Education, Advisory Council on Special *236*
Education Arbitration Panel, State Department *236*
Education Boards, Towns and Cities *354-595*
Education Commission of the States *247*
Education, Commissioner of *234*
Education, Commissioner of Higher *234*
Education, Connecticut Board of Governors for Higher *246*
Education, Connecticut Department of *234-238*
Education Connection *600-601*
Education Council, Capitol Region *599*
Education, Department and Board of Governors for *246-253*
Education and Services for the Blind, Board of *285*
Education, State Board of *234*

Educational Facilities Authority, State of Connecticut Health and *252*
Educational Statistics *817*
Elderly Commissions, and Agents, Municipal *354-595*
Elderly Services Division Regional Ombudsmen *354-595*
Election Statistics *658-693*
Elections, Dates of Town, City and Borough *345-346*
Election Day Registration, Turnout and Absentee Ballot Statistics, 1996, Summary of, *735*
Election Day Registration, Turnout and Absentee Ballot Statistics, 1996, *736-739*
Elections Division, Secretary of the State *206*
Elections Enforcement Commission, State *678-680*
Elections, Special *729*
Elections, Towns as Districted for *678-680*
Electoral Votes for President, 1964-1996 (50 States) *682*
Electrical Work, State Examining Board for *224*
Elevator Repair Work, State Examining Board for *224*
Ella T. Grasso Center *263*
Embalmers and Funeral Directors, Connecticut Board of Examiners for *270*
Emergency and Building Services, Division of Fire *276*
Emergency Management Agency, Federal *758*
Emergency Management, Office and State Director of *277*
Emergency 911 Commission, Statewide *277*
Emergency Response Commission, Connecticut *243*
Emergency Telecommunications, Office of Statewide *276*
Employees' Review Board *215*
Employment Security, Board of Review and Referee Section *256*
Employment Standards Administration, Wage, and Hour Division, United States *760*
Employment and Training Commission, Connecticut *255*
Enactment of Bills *199-202*
Energy Advisory Board, Connecticut *266-267*
Energy Regulatory Commission, Federal *759*
Enfield, Connecticut Correctional Institution *230*
Engineering and Highway Operations, Bureau of *287*
Engineers and Land Surveyors, State Board for Professional *225*
Environmental Protection Agency, Federal *759*
Environmental Protection, Bureau of Administration *239*
Environmental Protection, Commissioner of *238-239*
Environmental Protection, Department of *238-246*
Environmental Quality, Council on *243*
Equestrian Center Authority, Connecticut *219*
Establishment of Towns, Order of, and Origin of Their Names *631-639*

Ethics Commission, State *212*
Eubrontes Giganteus, State Fossil *835*
European Mantis, State Insect *833*
Executive Government, Federal *747*
Executive Government, State *205-213*
Executive Residence *838*
Expressway Bond Committee *266*
Extension Service Councils and Foundations, Cooperative, University of Connecticut *249-250*
Extension System, University of Connecticut Cooperative *249*

F

Facts About Connecticut *815-820*
Fairfield County Agricultural Extension Council, Incorporated *249*
Family Relations Supervisors, Superior Court *311-317*
Family Services Supervisors, State *311-314*
Farm Land Preservation *218*
Farm Service Agency, United States *757*
Federal Aviation Administration *762*
Federal Bureau of Investigation *756*
Federal Communications Commission *759*
Federal Correctional Institution *757*
Federal Departments and Agencies Serving Connecticut *757-763*
Federal Deposit Insurance Corporation *759*
Federal Emergency Management Agency *759*
Federal Energy Regulatory Commission *759*
Federal General Services Administration *760*
Federal Highway Administration *762*
Federal Home Loan Mortgage Corporation *759*
Federal Mediation and Conciliation Service *759*
Federal Public Defender *759*
Federal Reserve System *759*
Federal Surplus Property Center *760*
Federal Trade Commission *760*
Film, Video and Media Commission, State *233-234*
Finance Advisory Commission, Municipal *266*
Finance Advisory Committee, State *161*
Finance Boards, Towns and Cities *354-595*
Fire Academy, Connecticut State *293*
Fire Administration, Office of State *292*
Fire, Emergency and Building Services, Division of *276*
Fire Marshal, State *276*
Fire Marshals, Towns and Cities *354-595*
Firearms Permit Examiners, Board of *277*
Fire Prevention and Control, Commission on *292-293*
Fire Protection Sprinkler Systems Board *234*
Fiscal Analysis, Office of *158*
Fish Hatcheries *242*
Fish and Wildlife Service, United States *760*
Fitness, Governor's Committee on Physical *297*

Five Mile River Commission *245*
Flags *826-827*
Flood Commission, Greater Hartford *293*
Flood Control Commission, Connecticut River Valley *245*
Flood Control Commission, Thames River Valley *245*
Food Division, State *223*
Food and Drug Administration, United States *760*
Food and Consumer Service, United States *757*
Foot Guard, Commandants of Governor's *205*
Foot Guard Facilities *279*
Forest Fire Protection Commission, Northeastern *245*
Forest Service, United States *757*
Forests, State *241-242*
Foti, Paul M. *150-151, 301*
Freedman, Frederick A. *150, 153-154*
Freedom of Information Commission *213*
Freight Service, Towns and Cities *354-595*
Fundamental Orders, The, 1638-1639 *55-59*
Funeral Directors and Embalmers, Connecticut Board of Examiners *270*

G

Gaming Policy Board *282*
Garner Correctional Institution *227*
Garnet, State Mineral *834*
Gates, Connecticut Correctional Institution *228*
Gateway Community-Technical College *251*
Gejdenson, Sam *124-125, 750*
General Assembly Committees, 1997 *181-187*
General Assembly, Leaders of, 1997-98 *134-145*
General Assembly, Length of Sessions *188-191*
General Assembly, Members of, 1997-98 *162-180*
General Assembly, Political Division Since 1887 *192-195*
General Services Administration, United States *760*
Geographical Areas, Superior Court *314-317*
Geological Survey, United States *760*
Government Statistics *816*
Government, Towns and Cities, Form of *354-595*
Governments, Regional Councils of *597-598*
Governor of Connecticut *106-107, 205*
Governor of, Summary of Vote for, 1994 *694*
Governor's Bridgeport Office *205*
Governor's Cabinet *205-206*
Governor's Committee, Employment of People with Disabilities *257-258*
Governor's Committee on Physical Fitness *297*
Governor's Connecticut Office, Washington, D.C. *205*
Governor's Eastern Connecticut Office *205*

INDEX 853

Governor's Guard Facilities *278-279*
Governor's Military Staff *205*
Governor's Office *205*
Governor's Residence *838*
Governors, Board of, for Higher Education *246-247*
Governors of Connecticut, Since 1639 *80-83*
Governors, Deputy or Lieutenant, Connecticut, Since 1639 *84-86*
Governors for Higher Education, Department and Board for *246-253*
Grand Lists, Municipal, Tax Rates *347-353*
Grasso, Ella T. Center *263*
Great Seal of Connecticut *829*
Greater Bridgeport Regional Planning Agency *602*
Greater Bridgeport Transit District *607*
Greater Hartford Flood Commission *293*
Greater Hartford Transit District *606-607*
Greater New Haven Transit District *607*
Grievance Committee, Statewide *321*
Guard Facilities, Governor's *278-279*

H

Hairdressers, Cosmeticians and Barbers, Connecticut Examining Board for *269*
Hale, Nathan *836*
Harbor Commissioners, New Haven Harbor *289*
Harbor Masters, and Deputies *289-290*
Harbors *289-290*
HART, Housatonic Area Regional Transit *607*

Hartford, Capital Region Mental Health Center *260*
Hartford Cooperative Extension Council, Incorporated *249*
Hartford Correctional Center *230*
Hartford County Commissioners of the Metropolitan District *296*
Hartford, Old State House *839*
Hazardous Waste Management Service, Connecticut *293*
Health Care Access, Office of *271*
Health Care System Connecticut, Veterans Admin., West Haven *763*
Health Center, University of Connecticut *248*
Health Directors, Towns and Cities *354-595*
Health and Educational Facilities Authority, State *252*
Health and Human Services, Department of (United States) *760*
Health Protection, New England Compact on Radiological *244*
Hearing Impaired, State Commission on the Deaf and *285*
Heating, Piping and Cooling Work Examining Board *225*
Heiman, Maxwell *150, 152, 301*
Hennessy, Francis X. *150, 153, 301*
Hero, State *836*
Heroine, State *836*
High Meadows *222*
Higher Education, Advisory Committee to Board *247*
Higher Education, Commissioner of *246*
Higher Education, Board of Governors for *246-247*

Higher Education, Department and Board of Governors for 246-253

Higher Education, New England Board of 247

Higher Education Supplemental Loan Authority, Connecticut 293-294

Highway Operations, Bureau of Engineering and 287

Highway Superintendents, Municipal 354-595

Highways, District Offices 287-288

Historian, State 248

Historic Assets in Connecticut, Committee for Restoration of 233

Historic District Commissions, Towns 354-595

Historic Preservation, The Connecticut Trust for 237-238

Historical Commission, Connecticut 237

Historical Records Advisory Board, State 294

Historical Societies 769-781

History, Connecticut Museum of Natural 248

History, Selected Important Dates in Connecticut 67-69

Holidays, Legal 820

Home Loan Mortgage Corporation, Federal 759

Homemakers, Advisory Council on Displaced 257

Homeopathic Medical Examining Board, Connecticut 270

Horse Guard, Governor's Commandants of 205

Horse Guard Facilities 278-279

Hospital, Connecticut Valley, Middletown 259-260

Hospital, Riverview for Children 222

Hospital, Veterans Home and, State of Connecticut, Rocky Hill 292

Hospitals and Institutions (Statistics) 817

Housatonic Area Regional Transit 607

Housatonic Community-Technical College 252

Housatonic Resources Recovery Authority 604

Housatonic Valley Council of Elected Officials 602-603

House Clerk, State 159

House of Representatives, Connecticut 165-176, 178-181

House of Representatives, United States 750-753

House Speakers, Connecticut, Since 1819 99-101

Housing Authorities, Municipal 354-595

Housing Finance Authority, Connecticut 232

Housing Matters, Citizens Advisory Council for 294

Housing Sessions 317-318

Housing and Urban Development, United States Department of 760

Human Relations Committees, Municipal 354-595

Human Resources, Bureau of 215

Human Rights and Opportunities, Commission on 216

Human Rights and Opportunities, Hearing Officers 216

Human Services, United States Department of Health and 760

Humanities Council, Connecticut 758-759

Hypertrichologists, Board of Examiners of *270*

I

Illustrations, State Seal, State Flag and Emblems *825-840*
Immigration and Naturalization Service, United States *756*
Incorporation Dates, Cities and Boroughs *354-595*
Incorporation Dates, Towns *354-595*
Independence, Declaration of *3-7*
Indian Affairs Council, Connecticut *246*
Indians, Connecticut *820*
Industrial and Development Commissions, Municipal *354-595*
Information and Technology, Connecticut State Office of *267*
Information, Summary of *815-820*
Inland Wetlands Commissions, Municipal *354-595*
Innovations, Connecticut, Incorporated *233*
Institutions, State Correctional *228-231*
Insurance Commissioner *253*
Insurance, Department of *253*
Insurance Purchasing Board, State *217*
Intergovernmental Policy, Office of Policy and Management *266-267*
Intergovernmental Relations, Connecticut Advisory Commission on *267*
Interior, United States Department of the *760*
Internal Revenue Service, United States *762*
Interstate Civil Defense and Disaster Compact *277*
Interstate Compact on Juveniles *222*
Interstate Compact on Mental Health *259*
Interstate Compact on Mental Health (for Children and Youth) *222*
Interstate Compact for Parole and Probation Supervision *231*
Interstate Compact on Placement of Children *222*
Interstate Corrections Compact, New England Board of *231*
Interstate Sanitation Commission *244*
Interstate Water Pollution Control Commission, New England *244-245*
Investment Advisory Council *207*
Irish American Historical Society, Connecticut *772*

J

Jepsen, George C. *136-137*
Job Centers *255-256*
John N. Dempsey Center for Mentally Retarded *263*
John N. Dempsey Hospital, University of Connecticut Health Center *248*
John R. Manson Youth Institution, Cheshire *228*
Johnson, Nancy L. *132-133, 750*
Judges, Appellate Court *150-154, 301*
Judges, Probate Court *321-334*
Judges, Superior Court *302-305*
Judges, Supreme Court *146-149*
Judges, United States District Court *754-755*

Judicial Decisions, Reporter of *302*
Judicial Departments, Connecticut Law Library System *309*
Judicial Department, Director *310*
Judicial Districts *311-314*
Judicial Review Council *294-295*
Judicial Section, State *301-321*
Judicial Selection Commission *295*
Judicial Statistics *816*
Judiciary, United States Supreme Court *747*
Jury Administration, Superior Court *308*
Justice, Chief, Connecticut *146, 147, 301*
Justice Commission, Criminal *210*
Justice Department, United States *756*
Justices of Connecticut, Chief (Past) *95-96*
Justices of the Peace *354-595*
Justices, Supreme Court, Connecticut *146-149, 301*
Juvenile Detention Centers *310, 319*
Juvenile District Clerks *311-314*
Juvenile Justice Advisory Committee *268*
Juvenile Matters *318*
Juvenile Probation Officers *318*
Juveniles, Interstate Compact on *222*

K

Katz, Joette *146, 148, 301*
Kennelly, Barbara B. *122-123, 750*

L

Labor Commissioner *254*
Labor Department, Connecticut *254-258*
Labor Department, United States *760*
Labor Management Standards *760*
Labor Relations Board, National *761*
Labor Relations, Connecticut State Board of *254*
Landscape Architects, Connecticut State Board of *224*
Land Surveyors and Professional Engineers, State Board of Examiners for *225*
Landau, Sidney S. *150, 152, 301*
Latino and Puerto Rican Affairs Commission *161*
Lavery, William J. *150, 151-152, 301*
Law Enforcement Statistics *816*
Law Library System, Connecticut Judicial Departments *309*
Law, Practice of *320*
Law Revision Commission, Connecticut *158*
Leaders of the 1997-98 General Assembly, Photographs and Biographies of *134-145*
Legal Holidays in Connecticut *820*
Legal Publications, Commission on Official *307*
Legislative Branch of State Government *157-191*
Legislative Commissioner's Office *157*
Legislative Committees, 1997 *181-187*
Legislative Fiscal Analysis, Office of *158*
Legislative Management, Joint Committee on *157*
Legislative Program Review and Investigations Committee *158*

Legislative Reporters *176*
Legislative Research, Office of *157*
Legislatures, Connecticut *162-180*
Legislatures, Connecticut, Length of Sessions *188-191*
Librarian, State *238*
Libraries, Connecticut Law Library System *309*
Libraries, Connecticut Public *791-795*
Library Board, State *238*
Library Boards, Incorporated, The Association of Connecticut *795*
Library Council, Capitol Region *601*
Library Directors, Municipal *354-595*
Library, State *238*
Library System, Law *309*
Licensing, Registration and Examination, State Boards of *224-226*
Lieberman, Joseph I. *120-121, 748*
Lieutenant Governor *108-109, 206*
Lieutenant Governors of Connecticut, Since 1639 *84-86*
Liquor Control Commission *224*
Litchfield County Cooperative Extension Association, Incorporated *249*
Litchfield Hills Council of Elected Officials *603*
Long Lane School, Middletown *222*
Long Range Educational Assistance for Regional Needs *600*
Long Term Care, Connecticut Partnership for *268*
Low Level Radioactive Waste Advisory Committee *295*
Lower Fairfield County Center for Mentally Retarded *264*
Lyons, Moira K. *142-143*

M

MacDougall Correctional Institution *229*
Magazines and Periodicals, Monthly *805-806*
Magistrates, District Court, United States *755*
Maloney, James H. *130-131, 750*
Management Advisory Council *217-218*
Management and Performance, Office of Policy and Management *266*
Managers, Cities and Towns *354-595*
Manchester Community-Technical College *252*
Manson, John R., Youth Institution, Cheshire *228*
Map, Connecticut Assembly Districts *669*
Map, Connecticut Congressional Districts *657*
Map, Connecticut Senatorial Districts *663*
Marine Fisheries Commission, Atlantic States *244*
Marine Fisheries Service, National *758*
Marketing Authority, Connecticut *219-220*
Marshal, United States District Court *756-757*
Martin Luther King Jr. Commission *295-296*
Mayors of Cities and Towns *354-595*
McDonald, Francis M., Jr. *146, 148, 301*
Medal of Honor Recipients *821-824*
Media Commission, Connecticut Film, Video and *233-234*

Mediation and Arbitration, Board of *255*
Medical Examiner, Office of the Chief *272*
Medical Examiners, Assistant *272-273*
Medical Examining Board, Connecticut *270*
Medical Examining Board for State Employe Disability Retirement *208*
Medicolegal Investigations, Commission on *272*
Ment, Aaron *307*
Mental Health Center, Capital Region *260*
Mental Health Center New Haven, Connecticut *260*
Mental Health and Addiction Services, Board of *259*
Mental Health and Addiction Services, Commissioner of *258*
Mental Health and Addiction Services, Department of *258-261*
Mental Health Authorities *260-261*
Mental Health Facilities *259-260*
Mental Health, Interstate Compact on *259*
Mental Health, Interstate Compact on (for Children and Youth) *222*
Mental Retardation, Commissioner of *261*
Mental Retardation, Council on *262*
Mental Retardation, Department of *261-264*
Mental Retardation, State Planning Council on Developmental Disabilities *262*
Mentally Retarded, Regional Offices *262-264*
Meriden Transit District *607*
Metro North New Haven Rail Commuter Council *296*
Metropolitan District, Commissioners of, Hartford County *296*
Mid-Atlantic States Air Pollution Control Compact *244*
Middlesex Community-Technical College *252*
Middlesex County Extension Council, Incorporated *250*
Middletown, Connecticut Valley Hospital *259-260*
Middletown, Long Lane School *222*
Middletown Transit District *607*
Midstate Regional Planning Agency *603*
Midstate Regional Resource Recovery Authority *604*
Mileage from Hartford to Towns *629-630*
Miles, Square, By Counties *609*
Milford Transit District *607-608*
Military Department *277-278*
Military Staff, Governor's *205*
Milk Regulation Board, State *218*
Miscellaneous Facts About Connecticut *815-820*
Mobile and Manufactured Home Advisory Council *227*
Monuments, State *242*
Motor Vehicles, Commissioner of *264*
Motor Vehicles, Department of *264-265*
Motor Vehicles, Local Branch Offices *264-265*
Motto, State *829-830*
Mountain Laurel, State Flower *832*
Municipal Finance Advisory Commission *266*

Municipal, Grand Lists, Tax Rates 347-353
Municipal Officers 354-595
Municipalities, Connecticut Conference of 596
Museum of Art, State 248
Museum of Natural History, Connecticut 248
Museums, General 782-790

N

Narcotics Task Force Policy Board, Statewide 275
National Aeronautics and Space Administration 761
National Highway Traffic Safety Administration 762
National Labor Relations Board 761
National Marine Fisheries Service 758
National Oceanic and Atmospheric Administration 758
National Weather Service 758
Natural History, Connecticut Museum of 248
Naturalization Service, United States 756
Natureopathic Examiners, State Board of 270
Naugatuck Valley Community Technical College 252
Naugatuck Valley Loan Fund Advisory Committee 232-233
Nautilus, USS, State Ship 835
Navy, United States Department of 761
Navy, United States Naval Underwater Systems, New London 761
Navy, United States Submarine Base 761
New Britain, Central Connecticut State University 251
New England Board of Higher Education 247
New England Board of Interstate Corrections Compact 231
New England Compact on Radiological Health Protection 244
New England Interstate Water Pollution Control Commission 244-245
New England State Police Administrators' Compact 275
New Haven, Connecticut Mental Health Center 260
New Haven Correctional Center 228
New Haven County Cooperative Extension Resource Council, Incorporated 250
New Haven Harbor, State Commissioners of 289
New Haven, Southern Connecticut State University 251
Newington, Cedarcrest Regional Hospital 260
Newington Office for Mentally Retarded 263
New London County Agricultural Extension Council, Incorporated 250
News Bureau, Connecticut State 796
Newspaper Correspondents in Washington, D.C., Connecticut 807
Newspapers, List of Connecticut 796-806
Niantic, Conncticut Correctional Institution 228

Norcott, Flemming L., Jr. *146, 148, 301*
Northeast, Connecticut Correctional Institution *229*
Northeastern Connecticut Council of Governments *597*
Northeastern Connecticut Regional Resource Recovery Authority *604*
Northeastern Forest Fire Protection Commission *245*
Northern, Connecticut Correctional Institution *230*
Northwestern Connecticut Community-Technical College *252*
Northwestern Connecticut Council of Governments *597-598*
Northwestern Connecticut Transit District *608*
Norwalk Community-Technical College *252*
Norwalk Transit District *608*
Nursing, Connecticut State Board of Examiners for *270*

O

Occupational Information Coordinating Committee, State *258*
Occupational Licensing, State Boards for *224-227*
Occupational Safety and Health Administration, United States *760*
Occupational Safety and Health, Division of *254*
Occupational Safety and Health Review Commission *254*
Occupational Statistics *819*
Oceanic and Atmospheric Administration, National *758*
O'Connell, Edward Y. *150, 151, 301*
Office Hours and Locations, Judges of Probate *322-334*
Office Hours and Locations, Town, City and Borough Clerks *354-595*
Office Hours, State Buildings *214*
Office Locations, County Sheriffs *337-341*
Office Locations, State Boards and Commissions *214-298*
Office of Policy and Management *265-268*
Office of Policy and Management, Secretary of *265*
Officials and Their Duties *196-199*
Opticians, Connecticut Board of Examiners for *270*
Optometrists, Connecticut Board of Examiners for *271*
Orders, The Fundamental, 1638-1639 *55-59*
Organization of States and Dates of Admission *764*
Origin of Names of Connecticut Towns in Order of Their Establishment *631-639*
Original Seal *828*
Original States, Thirteen *764*
Osborn Correctional Institution *230*
Osteopathic Examining Board, Connecticut *271*

P

Palmer, Richard N. *146, 148, 301*
Pardons, Board of *297*

INDEX

Park and Recreation Commissions, Municipal *354-595*
Parks, State *239-241*
Parole, Board of *297*
Parole and Probation Supervision, Interstate Compact for *231*
Party Designations *681*
Periodicals and Magazines *805-806*
Permanent Commission on the Status of Women *159*
Personnel Management, United States Office of *761*
Peters, Ellen A. *149*
Pharmacy, Commission of *225*
Photograph and Biography, President of the United States *104-105*
Photographs and Biographies, Appellate Court Judges *150-154*
Photographs and Biographies, Leaders of the 1997-98 General Assembly *134-145*
Photographs and Biographies, State Officers *106-117*
Photographs and Biographies, Supreme Court Justices *146-149*
Photographs and Biographies, United States Senators and Representatives *118-133*
Photographs and Descriptions of Flags, State Emblems and State Capitol *825-840*
Physical Fitness, Governor's Committee on *297*
Physical Therapists, Connecticut State Board of Examiners for *271*
Planning Agencies, Regional *602-604*
Planning, Bureau of Policy and, Department of Transportation *288*
Planning, Emergency, United States Regional *758*
Planning, Emergency Commissions, Municipal *354-595*
Planning, Policy Development and, Office of Policy and Management *266, 267*
Plumbing and Piping Work, State Examining Board for *225*
Podiatry, Connecticut Board of Examiners in *271*
Poet Laureate, State *237, 837*
Poison Center, State *249*
Police Administrators Compact, New England State *275*
Police Barracks, State *274-275*
Police Chiefs, Towns and Cities *354-595*
Police Commissioners, Municipal *354-595*
Police Officers, Standards and Training Council *275*
Police, State Division of *273*
Policy and Management, Secretary of the Office of *266*
Political Division of the Connecticut General Assembly Since 1887 *192-193*
Political Parties, State Central Committees *643-646*
Population of Counties, 1990, 1995, estimated, *609*
Population of Towns, 1800-1990, *610-612*
Population of Towns, 1995 estimated *354-595*
Post Office Addresses of Town Officers *354-595*

Post Offices in Connecticut *613-616*
Practice of Law *320*
Praying Mantis, State Insect *833*
President, Electoral Votes for,
 1964-1996 (50 States) *682*
President of the United States *104-105, 747*
President, Summary of Vote for, 1996, *683*
President, Vote for *685-688*
Presidents of the United States, Since 1789, *70*
Presidents Pro Tempore of the Connecticut State Senate Since 1845 *97-98*
Press of Connecticut *796-806*
Press, Connecticut Correspondents in Washington, D.C. *807*
Prison and Jail Overcrowding, Commission on *268*
Probate Assembly, Connecticut *321-322*
Probate Court Administrator *321*
Probate Courts and Probate Judges *321-334*
Probate, Judicial Conduct, Council on *322*
Probation, Office of Adult *310*
Probation Officers, District Court, United States *755*
Professional Engineers and Land Surveyors, State Board of Examiners for *225*
Program Review and Investigations Committee, Legislative *158*
Properties Review Board, State *218*
Psychiatric Security Review Board *261*
Psychologists, Board of Examiners of *271*

Public Accounts, Auditors of *157*
Public Defender, Federal *754*
Public Defender, Office of Chief *319*
Public Defender Services Commission *319*
Public Health, Dept., Commissioner of *268-269*
Public Health, Department of *268-273*
Public Libraries, Connecticut *791-795*
Public Records Administration *238*
Public Safety, Commissioner of *273*
Public Safety, Department of *273-279*
Public Transportation, Bureau of *288*
Public Transportation Commission, Connecticut *288*
Public Utilities Control Authority *279*
Public Utility Control, Department of *279-280*
Public Works, Commissioner of *280*
Public Works, Department of *280*
Public Works Directors, Municipal *354-595*
Puerto Rican Affairs Commission, Latino and *161*

Q

Quinebaug Valley Community-Technical College *252*

R

Radgowski, Connecticut Correctional Institution *229*
Radio Network, Connecticut *807*
Radio Stations AM and FM *807-813*

Radio and Television Service Examiners, State Board of *226*
Radiological Health Protection, New England Compact on *244*
Railroad Administration, Federal *762*
Rapoport, Miles S. *110-111, 206*
Real Estate Appraisal Commission, Connecticut *225-226*
Real Estate Commission, Connecticut *225*
Real Estate, Professional Trades Division, State *224*
Real Estate and Urban Economics Studies Center, University of Connecticut *250*
Recommendations for Admission to the Bar, Standing Committees on *320-321*
Redevelopment Agencies, Towns and Cities *354-595*
Referee Section, Employment Security Board of Review and *256*
Referees, State, Circuit and Juvenile Courts *302*
Referees, State Supreme, Superior, and Appellate Court *301-302*
Region Education Council, Capitol *599*
Regional Councils of Governments *597-598*
Regional Education Councils *598-601*
Regional Library Councils *601*
Regional and Municipal Transit Districts *606-608*
Regional Offices for Mentally Retarded *262-264*
Regional Planning Agencies *602-604*
Regional Resource Recovery Authorities *604-605*
Regional School Districts *605-606*
Regional Vocational-Technical Schools *235*
Regional Water Authorities *608*
Registrars of Vital Statistics, Towns and Cities *354-595*
Registrars of Voters, Towns and Cities *354-595*
Registrars of Voters, Association of Connecticut *596*
Registration and Examination, State Boards of *224-226*
Registration and Party Enrollment, 1996 *740-744*
Rehabilitation Services, Bureau of *284*
Rell, M. Jodi *108-109, 206*
Reporter of Judicial Decisions, Supreme Court *302*
Reporters, Legislative *176*
Representatives in Congress from Connecticut *118-133, 750*
Representatives in Congress from Connecticut Since 1789 *74-79*
Representatives in Congress from Connecticut, Vote for, 1996 *689-693*
Representatives in Congress, U.S. (50 States) *750-753*
Representatives, State *165-176, 178-180*
Representatives, State, Special Elections *729*
Representatives, State, Vote for, 1996 *705-729*
Republican State Central Committee *645-646*
Republican Town Chairpersons and Vice Chairpersons *652-656*
Resources Recovery Authorities, Regional *604-605*

Resources Recovery Authority, Connecticut *246*
Retirement Board, Teachers' *298*
Retirement Commission, Connecticut State Employees *207*
Retirement, Medical Examining Board for State Employees Disability *208*
Revenue, Division of Special *282*
Revenue Services, Commissioner of *280*
Revenue Services, Department of *280-282*
Rights of Way Screening Committee *289*
Ritter, Thomas D. *140-141*
River Gateway Commission, Connecticut *245*
River Valley Services, Middletown *260-261*
Riverview Hospital *222*
Robin, American, State Bird *832*
Robinson, Carl Correctional Institution *230*
Rocky Hill, Veterans Home and Hospital, State of Connecticut *292*
Rowland, John G. *106-107, 205*

S

Salaries, County Sheriffs *337-341*
Salaries, State Agencies and Departments, Heads of *214-298*
Salaries, United States President *747*
Salaries, United States Senators and Representatives *748, 751*
Sanitarians, Municipal *354-595*
Sanitation Commission, Interstate *244*
Savings Bonds, U.S. *762*

Schaller, Barry R. *150, 152-153, 301*
School Districts, Regional *605-606*
Schools, Superintendents of *354-595*
Sea Grant College Program, Connecticut *248*
Seal, State *829*
Seals *828-830*
Secret Service, United States *762*
Secretaries of the State of Connecticut, Since 1639 *87-89*
Secretary of the State *110-111, 206*
Secretary of the State's Seal *830*
Securities and Exchange Commission (United States) *761*
Selected Important Dates in Connecticut History *67-69*
Selectmen, Town *354-595*
Senate Clerk, State *158-159*
Senate, State *162-164, 177*
Senate, United States *748-749*
Senatorial Districts, Connecticut *664-668*
Senators, State *162-164, 177*
Senators, State, Vote for, 1996 *696-704*
Senators, United States, from Connecticut *118-121, 748*
Senators, United States, from Connecticut Since 1789 *72-73*
Senators, United States, (50 States) *748-749*
Senators, United States Summary of Vote for *695*
Senior Executive Service Board *215-216*
Sentence Review Division *311*
Sessions, Length of (Connecticut Legislature) *188-191*
Sewer Commissions, Municipal *354-595*

Shays, Christopher *128-129, 750*
Sheriffs, County and Deputies *337-341*
Ship, State, USS Nautilus *835*
Siting Council, Connecticut *279*
Small Business Administration, United States *761*
Small Towns, Connecticut Council of *596*
Social Security Administration, Federal *761*
Social Services, Commissioner of *282*
Social Services, Department of *282-286*
Societies, Historical *769-781*
Soil and Water Conservation, Connecticut Council on *243-244*
Soldiers', Sailors' and Marines' Fund *297-298*
Somers, Osborn Correctional Institution *230*
Southbury Training School *264*
South Central Connecticut Regional Water Authority *608*
South Central Regional Council of Governmentrs *598*
South Central Regional Council of Governments/Planning Commission *603*
Southeast Area Transit (SEAT) *608*
Southeastern Connecticut Council of Governments *598*
Southeastern Connecticut Regional Resources Recovery Authority *605*
Southeastern Connecticut Water Authority *608*
Southeastern Mental Health Authority, Norwich *261*
Southern Connecticut Library Council *601*
Southern Connecticut State University *251*
Southwest Connecticut Mental Health System, Bridgeport *261*
Southwestern Regional Planning Agency *604*
Speakers of the House of Representatives of Connecticut Since 1819 *99-101*
Spear, E. Eugene *150, 153, 301*
Special Education, Advisory Council on *236*
Special Elections, *729*
Special Revenue, Division of *282*
Sperm Whale, State Animal *833*
Standardization Committee *216*
Standards Committee, State Codes and *276-277*
Standing Committees on Recommendations for Admission to the Bar *320-321*
State Animal, Sperm Whale *833*
State Armorial Bearings *826*
State Bird, American Robin *832*
State Boards, Commissions and Departments, Office Locations *214-298*
State Boards for Occupational Licensing *224-226*
State Boards of Registration, Examination and Licensing *224-226*
State Boundary Marks *290*
State Building Inspector *276*
State Capitol *840*
State Central Committees *643-646*
State Composer *837*
State Composer Laureate *837*
State Courts *301*

State Departments *214-298*
State Employees, Number of *816*
State Employees Retirement Commission *207*
State Fire Marshal *276*
State Flag *826*
State Flower, Mountain Laurel *832*
State Fossil, Eubrontes Giganteus *835*
State Hero, Nathan Hale *836*
State Heroine, Prudence Crandall *836*
State Historian *248*
State House of Representatives *165-176, 178-180*
State House, The First *839*
State House, The "Old" *839*
State Insect, Praying Mantis *833*
State Institutions, Correctional *227-231*
State Mineral, Garnet *834*
State Motto *829*
State Officers, Biographies and Photographs of *106-117*
State Officers, Summary of Vote for, 1994 *694-695*
State Poet Laureate, *837*
State Receiving Home *222*
State Representatives *165-176, 178-180*
State Representatives, Vote for, 1996, *705-729*
State Seals *828-830*
State Senate *162-164, 177*
State Senators, Vote for, 1996, *696-704*
State Shellfish, Eastern Oyster *734*
State Ship, USS Nautilus *735*
State Song, Yankee Doodle *837*
State Tree, Charter Oak *831*
State Troubadour, *837*
State's Attorney, Chief *210*
State's Attorneys *210-211*
States, Admission to the Union *764*
States, Education Commission of the *247*
Statewide Cooperative Crime Control Task Force Policy Board *275*
Statewide Emergency Telecommunications, Office of *276*
Statewide Emergency 911 Commission *277*
Statewide Grievance Committee *321*
Statewide Narcotics Task Force Policy Board *275*
Statistics, Election *664-680*
Statistics, Miscellaneous *815-820*
Student Loan Foundation, Connecticut *253*
Sullivan, Kevin B. *134-135*
Summary of Information *815-820*
Sunday Newspapers *797-798*
Superior Court *302-307*
Superior Court Judges *302-306*
Superior Court Officers *311-314*
Superior Court Reporters *311-314*
Superior Court, Sentence Review Division *311*
Support, Bureaus of, Judicial Districts *311-314*
Supreme Court, Connecticut *146-149, 301*
Supreme Court, United States *747*
Surplus Property Center, Federal and State *760*

T

Tax Collectors, Towns, Cities and Boroughs *354-595*

Taxpayers Service, Internal Revenue
762
Tax Rates, Municipal Grand Lists
347-353
Teachers' Retirement Board *298*
Technical Services, Bureau of *214-215*
Technology, Connecticut State Office of Information and *267*
Telecommunications, Office of Statewide Emergency *276*
Telephone Numbers, State Agencies, Commissions and Departments *214-298*
Telephone Numbers, Town, City and Borough Clerks *354-595*
Television and Radio Service Examiners, State Board of *226*
Television Stations in Connecticut *813-814*
Territories, United States *765*
Thames River Campus *249*
Thames River Valley Flood Control Commission *245*
Three Rivers Community-Technical College *252*
Thirteen Original States *764*
Tolland County Extension Council, Incorporated *250*
Torrington Officies for Mentally Retarded *263*
Tourism Council, Connecticut *232*
Town Chairpersons and Vice Chairpersons, Democratic *647-651*
Town Chairpersons and Vice Chairpersons, Republican *652-656*
Town, City and Borough Statistics *354-595*

Town Clerks *354-595*
Town Clerks Association, Incorporated, Connecticut *595-596*
Town Clerks, Office Hours and Locations *354-595*
Town Elections, Dates of *345*
Town Managers, Mayors and Officers *354-595*
Town Principal Industries *354-595*
Town Registrars of Vital Statistics *354-595*
Town Registrars of Voters *354-595*
Towns as Districted for Election Purposes *678-680*
Towns, Forms of Government *354-595*
Towns In Order of Their Establishment and Origin of Names *631-639*
Towns, Population, 1800-1990 *610-612*
Towns, 1995 estimasted Population *354-595*
Towns, Villages and Districts With No Post Office of Same Name *617-628*
Towns, Villages and Districts With Post Office of Same Name *613-616*
Traffic Commission, State *290*
Transit Districts, Regional and Municipal *606-608*
Translator Television Stations *814*
Transportation, Bureau of Engineering and Highway Operations *287-288*
Transportation, Bureau of Finance and Administration *288*
Transportation, Bureau of Policy and Planning *288*
Transportation, Bureau of Public *288*
Transportation Commission, Connecticut Public *288*

Transportation, Commissioner of *286*
Transportation, Connecticut Department of *286-291*
Transportation, Towns and Cities *354-595*
Transportation, United States Department of *761-762*
Treasurer, State *112-113, 206*
Treasurers of Connecticut, Since 1639 *90-91*
Treasurers of Towns, Cities and Boroughs *354-595*
Treasury, United States Department of *762*
Tree Protection Examining Board, State *226*
Tree Wardens, Towns and Cities *354-595*
Troubadour, State *837*
Tunxis Community-Technical College *252*

U

Underground Storage Tank Petroleum Clean Up Review Board, Connecticut *244*
Undertakers (See Connecticut Board of Examiners of Embalmers and Funeral Directors) *270*
Uniform Legislation, Commission on *160-161*
United States Agencies Serving Connecticut *757-763*
United States Agriculture Department *757*
United States Air Force, Department of *758*
United States Army, Department of *758*
United States Assistant District Attorneys *756*
United States Bankruptcy Judges for Connecticut *755*
United States Cabinet *747*
United States Census Bureau, SESA *758*
United States Circuit Judges *754*
United States Coast Guard *761*
United States Commerce Department *758*
United States Congress *748-753*
United States Congressmen, Connecticut *118-133, 748, 750*
United States, Constitution of the *8-25*
United States Court of Appeals *754*
United States Courts Serving Connecticut *754*
United States Declaration of Independence *3-7*
United States Defense Department *759*
United States Department of Transportation *761-762*
United States Deputy Marshals *756-757*
United States District Attorney *756*
United States District Counsel's Office, IRS *762*
United States District Court and Judges *754-755*
United States Drug Enforcement Administration *756*
United States Economic Development Administration *758*
United States Emergency Management Agency *759*

INDEX

United States Environmental Protection Agency 759

United States Fish and Wildlife Service 760

United States Forest Service 757

United States General Services Administration 760

United States Government 747-753

United States Health and Human Services Department 760

United States House of Representatives 750-753

United States Housing and Urban Development Department 760

United States Interior Department 760

United States Internal Revenue Service 762

United States Justice Department 756-757

United States Labor Department 760

United States Magistrates 755

United States Marshal, District Court 756-757

United States Naval Underwater Systems Center, New London 761

United States Navy Department 761

United States Navy Submarine Base 761

United States Occupational Safety and Health Administration 760

United States Personnel Management, Office of 761

United States Post Offices in Connecticut 613-616

United States, President of the *104-105,* 747

United States Presidents of, Since 1789 70

United States Probation Officers 755

United States Railroad Administration 762

United States Representatives, Connecticut, Biographies and Photographs *122-133*

United States Representatives from Connecticut, Since 1789 74-79

United States Representatives from Connecticut, Vote for, 1996, *689-693*

United States Savings Bonds, State Director 762

United States Secret Service 762

United States Senate 748-749

United States Senators, Connecticut, Biographies and Photographs *118-121*

United States Senators from Connecticut, Since 1789 72-73

United States Senators, Summary of Vote for, 1994, *695*

United States Small Business Administration 761

United States Supreme Court 747

United States Surplus Property Center 760

United States Territories and Other Areas 765

United States Transportation Department 761-762

United States Treasury Department 762

United States Veterans Affairs, Department of 762

United States Veterans Affairs Medical Center, West Haven 762

United States Vice Presidents of, Since 1789 71

United States Weather Service 758

INDEX

University of Connecticut *247-250*

University of Connecticut Board of Trustees *248*

University of Connecticut Cooperative Extension System *249*

University of Connecticut Health Center, John Dempsey Hospital *248*

University of Connecticut Real Estate and Urban Economic Studies Center *250*

University, The Connecticut State, Board of Trustees *250-251*

V

Valley Council of Governments *598*

Valley Regional Planning Agency *604*

Valley Transit District *608*

Veterans Administration Medical Center, West Haven *762*

Veterans Administration, Connecticut Health Care System *763*

Veterans Affairs, Commissioner *291*

Veterans Affairs, Department of *291-292*

Veterans Affairs, Department of, United States *762*

Veterans Employment and Training Service *761*

Veterans Home and Hospital, State of Connecticut Rocky Hill *292*

Veterinarian, State *218*

Veterinary Medicine, Connecticut Board of *271*

Vice President of the United States *747*

Vice Presidents of the United States, Since 1789 *71*

Victim Services, Office of *311*

Video, Connecticut Film, Media Commission *233*

Villages and Districts Containing Post Office of Same Name *613-616*

Villages and Districts With No Post Office of Same Name *617-628*

Vocational Technical School System *234-236*

Vocational Technical Schools, Regional *234-236*

Vote for President of United States, *685-688*

Vote for President of United States Electoral (50 States), 1964-1996, *682*

Vote for President of United States Summary of, 1996, *683*

Vote for Proposed Constitutional Amendment, 1996 *731-734*

Vote for Proposed Constitutional Amendment, Summary of, 1996 *730*

Vote for State Officers, Summary of, 1996 *694-695*

Vote for State Representatives, 1996 *705-729*

Vote for State Senators, 1996 *696-704*

Vote for United States Representatives in Congress from Connecticut, 1996 *689-693*

Vote for United States Senators, Summary of, 1994 *695*

Voting Districts, Towns and Cities, Number of *354-595*

W

Wage and Hour Division, United States Labor Department *760*

Wage and Workpace Standards *254*
Walker Reception and Special Management Center *229*
Ward, Robert M. *144-145*
Warden, Federal Correctional Institution *757*
Wardens of Boroughs *354-597*
Wardens, Connecticut Correctional Institutions *227-231*
Water Authorities, Regional *608*
Water Pollution Control Commission, New England Interstate *244-245*
Weather Service, National *758*
Webster Correctional Institution *228*
Weights and Measures Division, State *224*
Western Connecticut Library Council *601-602*
Western Connecticut Mental Health Network *261*
Western Connecticut State University *251*
West Haven Veterans Medical Center, United States *762-763*
Westport Transit District *608*
Whale, Sperm, State Animal *833*
Wilderness School *222*
Willard Correctional Institution *230*
Windham County Agricultural Extension Council, Incorporated *250*
Windham Region Transit District *608*
Windham Regional Planning Agency *604*
Women, Permanent Commission on the Status of *159*
Workers' Compensation Commission *257*
Wyman, Nancy S. *114-115, 207*

Y

Yankee Doodle, State Song *837*
York/Niantic, Connecticut Correctional Institution *228*
Youth Institution, Cheshire, John R. Manson *228*

Z

Zip Codes, Connecticut Post Offices *613-616*
Zoning Boards, Towns and Cities *354-595*
Zoning Boards of Appeal, Towns and Cities *354-595*
Zoning Enforcement Officials, The Connecticut Association of *596*